FOR REFERENCE

Do Not Take From This Room

Conservation and Environmentalism

Conservation and Environmentalism
An Encyclopedia

Editor
Robert Paehlke

FITZROY DEARBORN PUBLISHERS
London & Chicago
1995

Published in 1995 by Fitzroy Dearborn Publishers. This edition published by
arrangement with Garland Publishing, Inc.

For further information, contact:
Fitzroy Dearborn Publishers
11 Rathbone Place
London W1P 1DE
England

or

Fitzroy Dearborn Publishers
70 East Walton Street
Chicago, Illinois 60611
U.S.A.

British Library Cataloguing-in-Publication Data

Conservation and Environmentalism, an encyclopedia
I. Paehlke, Robert C.
337.3

ISBN 1-884964-14-1

Cover design by Lawrence Wolfson, NY
Cover photograph research by Marjorie Trenk
Cover photograph © by Wolfgang Kaehler

Printed on acid-free, 250-year-life, recycled paper
Manufactured in the United States of America

Contents

Introduction

Concern with conservation and environmental protection can be traced almost throughout human history. But the elevation of this concern to an important and comprehensive place within the world of human ideas and actions probably dates from only the nineteenth century. In a short time, then, conservation and environmentalism have altered the way in which humans think about the Earth. These perspectives have also begun to change the ways in which governments, corporations, organizations, and individuals throughout the world behave on a daily basis. This volume is an attempt to bring together in a succinct way the many dimensions of this transformation in the worlds of ideas and practice.

The overarching classification scheme for the alphabetically arranged entries is a division of conservation and environmental concerns and actions under three headings: ecology, pollution, and sustainability or "beauty, health, and permanence" in the words of environmental historian Samuel P. Hays. Ecology is taken here to include the protection of animal and plant species and communities, the preservation of habitats and wilderness, and the conservation of places of special beauty and significance. Pollution is a comprehensive catchword for the many ways in which human activities—largely economic, and especially industrial—chemically and physically alter the air, water, and/or land of our planet in ways detrimental to health, especially human health. Sustainability includes those concerns and issues associated with the long-term quality functioning of human economies and societies within our planet's physical and biological limits.

The roughly 500 individual entries in *Conservation and Environmentalism: An Encyclopedia* fit into twelve classifications. An understanding of these classifications will help readers locate information quickly. Additionally, we have used a three-part cross-referencing scheme, described briefly below. The twelve entry classifications, with examples and, in some cases, explanations, are:

• *Concepts, Issues, and Methods*—These include deep ecology, urban form, environmental justice, climate warming, landscape ecology, biodiversity, biodepletion, habitat fragmentation, ecosystem, trace analysis, environmental impact assessment, sustainable development, regulation, and soft energy path.

• *Place and Linkage Surveys*—For some distant locations survey articles provide comprehensive inquiries as for the former Soviet Union, Eastern Europe, and Africa; other survey articles center on the connections between environmental concerns and other subjects as in religion and environmental protection or labor and the environment.

• *Conservation and Environmental Organizations*—There is a strong emphasis on organizations originating in or based in the United States and Canada, such as the Sierra Club, Natural Resources Defense Council, Wilderness Society, Environmental Action, or Pollution Probe, and there is also an attempt to cover major international organizations, such as International Union for the Conservation of Nature and Natural Resources (IUCN), the Nature Conservancies, and the World Wildlife Fund as well as a few Australian organizations and even some other locations via survey articles.

• *Academic Disciplines and Subdisciplines*—Conservation and environmentalism have greatly affected the way humans study the world and organize knowledge. Thus, we have included entries on environmental ethics, environmental history, conservation biology, environmental education, green economics, epidemiology, toxicology, and other types of—and approaches to—environmental inquiry.

• *Governmental Organizations and Agencies*—Here again is an emphasis on the United States and Canada with the (U.S.) Army Corps of Engineers, the (U.S.) Bureau of Land Management, or Environment Canada. Also covered are international agencies such as International Joint Commission (IJC) and the United Nations Environment Programme (UNEP).

• *Legislation and Case Law*—Legislation drafted in the European Community, Great Britain, Australia, Canada, and the United States and under the heading Environmental Case Law or a few variants are included. There are also entries on a large number of individual statutes, especially, but not exclusively, in the United States and coverage of international law under both treaties (Montreal Protocol) and broader headings (environmental diplomacy, toxic wastes in international trade).

• *Individuals*—There are short biographies of many important individuals, mostly from the United States, mostly historical, some contemporary. Entries for individuals include Bob Marshall, Farrington Daniels, and Jacques-Yves Cousteau among others.

• *Species or Classes of Species*—Conservation concerns, studies, and initiatives are often classed by species or groups of species. Some animals will be treated several times: polar bears, for example, do not have their own entry, but are covered as bears, as marine mammals and as top predators. To some extent species were chosen by the level of conservation concern generally expressed, such as the peregrine falcon, rhinos, dolphins and porpoises, tigers and the bald eagle. Balance was achieved, however, with less "attractive" species, such as amphibians, bats and butterflies.

• *Special Habitats and Places*—Examples include coral reefs, tropical rainforests, old growth forests, the St. Lawrence River, Lake Pedder (in Australia), the Arctic, the Everglades, and Yellowstone National Park.

• *Pollutants and Classes of Pollutants*—Heavy metals are treated separately. Other pollutants can be found under a variety of more comprehensive categories: e.g., air pollution, volatile organic chemicals, pesticides, (the) pulp and paper industry, and various types of mining and smelting. Pollution events—Chernobyl, Bhopal, and Donora, Pennsylvania—and places with pollution problems—the Great Lakes and the Rhine River, for example—are also included.

• *Dimensions of Sustainability*—Sustainability concerns focus primarily on resources and on waste and waste disposal, with some emphasis on energy, agriculture, and forestry. Individual entries include hydroelectricity (and the Aswan and several other individual dams), nuclear power and energy conservation, nonrenewable resources, forest regeneration, new forestry, sustainable agriculture, erosion, packaging, recycling, and municipal solid waste (MSW) landfill.

• *Publications*—Selected magazines and journals and other periodical publications are mentioned within the entries for environmental organizations, academic subdisciplines, and animal species. A very small number of seminal books have been included as entries themselves. Almost every entry provides a short list of further readings at the end of the article for further research.

The system of cross-referencing used throughout the *Encyclopedia* includes three categories: "*See also*," "*See*," and an index. "*See also*" references appear at the end of each entry designed to lead the reader to related articles and, in some cases, into directions he might not have anticipated. The "*See*" entries will redirect the reader to actual entries (incineration, for example, is listed under MSW [municipal solid waste] incineration; Convention on International Trade in Endangered Species is listed under CITES). Futhermore, there is also an extensive index at the back of the book, which includes individuals discussed within entries about concepts, agencies, or organizations or particular pollutants discussed within larger categories, and so forth.

The editorial goal throughout the long process of producing this volume—from selecting the topics and authors through producing guidelines and suggestions to editing—was guided by a desire to make the book comprehensive, to offer a balanced point of view, and to make it both comprehensible to non-experts and accessible to those new to a particular subject.

Comprehensiveness is indicated in part by the discussion above and in the fact that the contributors to *Conservation and Environmentalism: An Encyclopedia* write from the perspectives of literally dozens of different disciplines, subdisciplines, and professions from physics to art history and from medicine and law to landscape architecture, including a wide variety of perspectives from the biological and social sciences and the humanities, especially history and philosophy. Comprehensiveness as a goal also involved a considerable tension in topic and author selection between the recognitions that the audience would be almost exclusively based in English-speaking countries and that the problems are truly global. In the end the authors and topics are predominantly from and emphasize concerns in North America, Great Britain, Australia, and New Zealand. Yet, the 500 original articles were written in some 20 different countries and reflect even broader field research experiences.

The concern with balance centered most often on perspective as conditioned by place of employment. Much of the "action" in conservation and environmental matters is based in environmental organizations and agencies. More than half of the entries were written by persons in academic and research institutions, and a good proportion come out of governmental agencies and from those working full time in environmental advocacy organizations. Readers should be aware of this because a difference in perspective can produce some difference in tone in the article, though there will be no consistent pattern to that difference.

This sort of concern, of course, holds true for authors within the most prestigious of academic and research settings—a forester may see a forest differently than an ecologist or conservation biologist. By all means, readers should note the background and experiences of the individual authors, but also be confident that every effort was made by both authors and editors to present authoritative, fair, and accurate coverage. We raise this matter here because conservation and environmental issues are fraught with disagreements—many of the issues treated here are in their public manifestations defined by scientific disagreements. That is why they are so politically significant, interesting, yet troublesome. The best defense against biases and perspective-rooted distortions in the end is the presentation of diverse perspectives, the selection of experienced and responsible analysts and authors, and, most important, the awareness of intelligent readers.

Finally, every effort was made to present these diverse viewpoints and subjects in a style that is intelligible to those with little or no background in the discipline of the author. In the end this was a very great challenge for all concerned. But it can be argued that conservation and environmental protection cannot be effected in the real world unless we can bring together our understanding of the problems in a comprehensive way and develop a body of appropriate knowledge that is more integrated—a more interdisciplinary perspective. Effective democratic action on these vital problems also requires that even larger numbers of individual citizens appreciate the many dimensions of these problems and act responsibly to address them.

Robert Paehlke
Editor

Acknowledgments

This book would not have been possible without the help and advice of many people. I have always hesitated to provide this sort of recognition in the past for fear of leaving someone out. However, in the case of this project, the help I have received is too overwhelming to allow that concern to stand in the way. To begin, I'd like to acknowledge some of the people who advised me regarding the selection of appropriate topics and authors (and many other matters) very early on in the project. Thanks are owed to several colleagues at Trent University, including Tom Whillans, John Wadland, John Marsh, Magda Havas, and Tom Hutchinson. Many others also contributed their ideas and insights in the early stages of the project, including Donald Worster, Mary E. Clark, Sheila Jasanoff, Norman Myers, Timothy O'Riordan, Robyn Eckersley, Gene Hargrove, Raymond F. Dasmann, and Max Oelschlaeger—whose works I have long admired. I cannot thank them enough for taking time from their busy lives to help.

Most important to the completion of this project are the more than 240 people who have written one or more articles. An editor's job is made easier with the right contributors, and I am confident that that is the case here. Not only were the submitted materials consistently intelligent, creative, and interesting, but many authors came through with organizational ideas, with the names of colleagues who could fill in on a subject not covered, and with suggestions regarding important subjects that neither I nor anyone else had thought about to that point. Particularly helpful were Robert Bartlett, David Brooks, Baird Callicott, Anne Peyton Curlee, Kenneth Dahlberg, David Ehrenfeld, Val Geist, Michael Kraft, David Orr, Barry Rabe, Chris Risley, Peter Victor, Norman Vig, Pamela Welbourn, and Arthur Westing among others.

Among the many people from whom I received constant, if not daily, help for the three years of putting this book together were: Sharon Pelton, Vivian Hall, Ray Dart, Ben Wolfe, Birgitte Berkowitz, and Luba Eleen. I would also thank my sons Jesse, Matthew, and Nicholas for reducing my level of computer illiteracy on an ongoing basis. Wayne Trusty and Jamie Meil, colleagues with whom I worked on another project over the past two years, were unceasingly supportive and flexible. David Morrison, until recently dean of arts and science at Trent University and a friend for now nearly 25 years, helped in several ways that allowed this project to come together in a timely fashion. Finally, I acknowledge the initial suggestion for the project from Gary Kuris of Garland Publishing. I must admit that there have been moments over the past few years during which I was not entirely sure I wanted to thank him for the idea—but I do now.

Contributors

Craig W. Allin teaches in the Department of Political Science at Cornell College in Mt. Vernon, Iowa. He has published extensively on the U.S. conservation movement, including authoring the widely cited book *The Politics of Wilderness Preservation* (1982).

James Allum is completing a Ph.D. in history at Queen's University in Kingston, Ontario. He has a broad interest in environmental history and is particularly focused on the Trail (British Columbia) Smelter controversy between the Canadian, U.S., and state and provincial governments.

Leslie R. Alm is an assistant professor in political science and public affairs at Boise State University in Boise, Idaho. His most recent work has been published in *Policy Studies Journal*, *Environmental Management*, and *The Environmental Professional*. He contributed the chapter on the policymaking process in editor Zachary A. Smith's *Environmental Politics and Policy in the West* (1993).

Douglas J. Amy teaches in the Department of Politics at Mount Holyoke College in South Hadley, Massachusetts. He is the author of several publications on environmental dispute resolution, including *The Politics of Environmental Mediation* (1987).

Roger Anderson is an associate professor in the Department of Political Science at Bowling Green State University in Bowling Green, Ohio, where his research emphasis is on U.S. and comparative environmental politics and policy. He is the author of several articles and papers on the environmental consequences of nuclear weapons production facilities including "Environmental, Safety and Health Issues at Nuclear Weapons Production Facilities, 1946–1988," published in *Environmental Review* in 1989.

Richard N.L. Andrews is director of the Environmental Management and Policy Program, Department of Environmental Sciences and Engineering, at the University of North Carolina in Chapel Hill. He is the author of *Environmental Policy and Administrative Change* (1976) and numerous articles and chapters on environmental policy, impact and risk assessments, and benefit-cost analysis.

B. Theresa Aniskowicz is program director for Wildlife and Conservation Habitat for the Canadian Nature Federation. She has extensive experience with the protection of bison habitat. The Canadian Nature Federation is a not-for-profit conservation organization located at 453 Sussex Drive, Ottawa, Ontario K1N 6Z4.

Jim Baird teaches in the Department of English at the University of North Texas in Denton, Texas. He has a long interest in literature and art as they relate to the environment and conservation.

Dale E. Bandy is a Ph.D. crop scientist trained at Cornell University and is the recipient of the Order of Agricultural Merit from the government of Peru. He is currently the coordinator of the Global Initiative on Alternatives to Slash and Burn and is based in Nairobi, Kenya.

Robert V. Bartlett is a professor of political science at Purdue University in West Lafayette, Indiana. His publications include *The Reserve*

Mining Controversy: Science, Technology, and Environmental Quality (1980), *Policy Through Impact Assessment: Institutionalized Analysis as a Policy Strategy* (1989), and a forthcoming book on environmental policy in New Zealand.

Fikret Berkes is a professor and the director of the Natural Resources Institute at the University of Manitoba in Winnipeg, Manitoba, Canada. His many publications on environmental and resource policy issues include the book *Common Property Resources: Ecology and Community-Based Sustainable Development* (1989).

R.J. Berry is professor of genetics in the Department of Biology at University College London, England. He is the author of numerous works, including *Inheritance and Natural History* (1977).

Rosalie Bertell, a Ph.D. in biometry, is president of the International Institute of Concern for Public Health based in Toronto, Ontario and editor of *International Perspectives in Public Health*. She is the author of *No Immediate Danger* (1985), *Handbook for Estimating the Health Effects of Exposure to Ionizing Radiation* (1986), and over eighty other publications on nuclear power, radiation, and environmental health.

Keith L. Bildstein is director of research at the Hawk Mountain Sanctuary in Kempton, Pennsylvania. He is coauthor of the North American species account for Northern Harriers and is overseeing the analysis of the Hawk Mountain Sanctuary's fifty-five-year data set which includes extensive data on many raptor species.

Patricia W. Birnie lectured in public international law at Edinburgh University and the London School of Economics between 1968 and 1989. She became the first director of the International Maritime Organization's International Maritime Law Institute in Malta, returning to Britain in 1992 where she continues to specialize in law of the sea and internal environmental law. She is the coauthor of *International Law and the Environment* (1993).

Sonja A. Boehmer-Christiansen is a research fellow at the Science Policy Research Unit at the University of Sussex in Brighton, England. She has published extensively on subjects related to energy use and the environmental impacts thereof and such related subjects as transportation policy.

Gary R. Bortolotti teaches in the biology department at the University of Saskatchewan in Saskatoon, Saskatchewan. His Ph.D. thesis was on the bald eagle, and he has since published extensively on the biology and conservation of this important species, including a coauthored book, *The Bald Eagle: Haunts and Habits of a Wilderness Monarch* (1988).

Christopher J. Bosso is an associate professor of political science at Northeastern University in Boston, Massachusetts. His many publications include *Pesticides and Politics: The Life Cycle of a Public Issue* (1987), which won the 1988 Policy Studies Organization award for the best book in policy studies.

Susan P. Bratton teaches in the Department of Philosophy and Religion Studies at the University of North Texas in Denton, Texas. She holds degrees in both biology and theology and is the author of *Six Million and More: Christian Ethics and Human Population Regulation* (1992) and *The Original Desert Solitaire: Wilderness and Christianity* (1993).

David B. Brooks is an environmentalist and resource economist working in the international arena at the International Development Research Centre (IDRC) in Ottawa, Ontario. He is also a member of the board of directors of Ontario Hydro Corporation and a contributing editor for *Alternatives: Perspectives on Society, Technology, and Environment*. He is the author of *Conservation of Mineral and Environmental Resources*, *Economic Impact of Low Energy Growth in Canada: An Initial Analysis* (1978), *Zero Energy Growth for Canada* (1981), and coauthor of *Life After Oil: A Renewable Resource Policy for Canada* (1983) and *The Economic, Ecological, and Geopolitical Dimensions of Water in Israel* (1993).

Jake Brooks is executive director of the Independent Power Producers' Association of Ontario (IPPAO), based in Toronto, Ontario. IPPAO is a nonprofit corporation for the promotion of independent electrical power in Ontario and Canada, essentially an association of non-utility generators; it publishes the magazine *Ippso Facto* six times per year.

Conrad G. Brunk is an associate professor at Conrad Grebel College, University of Waterloo (Waterloo, Ontario, Canada), and is an associate in the Risk Research Institute. He is the coauthor of *Value Assumptions in Risk Assessment: A Case Study of the Alachlor Controversy* (1991).

Gary C. Bryner is a political scientist at Brigham Young University in Provo, Utah. He is the author of *Bureaucratic Discretion: Law and Policy in Federal Regulatory Agencies* (1987) and *Blue Skies, Green Politics: The Clean Air Act of 1990* (1992), and editor of *Global Warming and the Challenge of International Cooperation: An Interdisciplinary Assessment* (1992) and *Science, Technology, and Politics: Policy Analysis in Congress* (1992).

Robert D. Bullard, a sociologist, is presently with the Center for Afro-American Studies at the University of California in Los Angeles (UCLA). He is the leading North American researcher on the subject of environmental justice and his recent publications include *Dumping in Dixie: Race, Class and Environmental Quality* (1990), *Confronting Environmental Racism: Voices from the Grassroots* (1993), and *Unequal Protection: Environmental Justice and Communities of Color* (1994).

Lynton K. Caldwell is the Arthur F. Bentley Professor of Political Science Emeritus and professor of public and environmental affairs at Indiana University in Bloomington, Indiana. He is the author of 200 articles and monographs and twelve books (translated into nineteen languages); his books include *Science and the National Environmental Policy Act* (1982), *International Environmental Policy* (2nd ed., 1990), and *Environment as a Focus for Environmental Policy* (1994). He is perhaps particularly noted as a principal architect of the U.S. National Environmental Policy Act of 1969 and the "inventor" of the environmental impact statement.

J. Baird Callicott is a professor of philosophy and natural resources at the University of Wisconsin at Stevens Point. He is the author of numerous articles and chapters on environmental ethics as well as *In Defense of the Land Ethic* (1989); he is also editor of *Companion to a Sand County Almanac* (1987), and coeditor (with Roger T. Ames) of *Nature in Asian Traditions of Thought* (1989).

Monica Campbell is an environmental health specialist for the City of North York Public Health Department; she also teaches environmental policy and science courses at Innis College, University of Toronto. She holds a Ph.D. in toxicology and was for some years a member of the staff of Pollution Probe, a major environmental organization based in Toronto, Ontario.

John E. Carroll, a political scientist, teaches at the University of New Hampshire in Durham, New Hampshire. He is the author of numerous works on environmental diplomacy and Canadian-American relations including *Acid Rain: An Issue in Canadian-American Relations* (1982), *Environmental Diplomacy: An Examination and a Prospective of Canadian-U.S. Transboundary Environmental Relations* (1986), and *International Environmental Diplomacy: The Management and Resolution of Transfrontier Environmental Problems* (1990).

Cyril Carter has recently retired from full-time teaching in the mathematics department and the Environmental and Resource Studies Program at Trent University, Peterborough, Ontario, Canada. He is a past chairman of the Environmental and Resource Studies Program (at Trent) and the Peterborough Utilities Commission, and coauthor (with J. DeVilliers) of *Passive Solar Building Design* (1987).

J.E. Cebek has recently completed a Ph.D. in biology at York University in Toronto, Ontario, and is presently teaching in the biology department at Trent University in Peterborough, Ontario. His research and teaching have focused on many aspects of conservation biology and ecology, including an emphasis on the biology and conservation of amphibians and bats.

Peter Christoff was until recently assistant to the Commissioner for the Office of the Environment in the state government of Victoria, Australia. He is currently working as an environmental consultant and completing a Ph.D. in politics at the University of Melbourne.

Jennifer Clapp is currently a research fellow in the Global Security Programme in the Faculty of Social and Political Sciences at the University of Cambridge in Cambridge, United Kingdom, working on the international trade in toxic waste and its impact on Africa. She has also published several articles on structural adjustment in Africa.

Mary E. Clark, a biologist by training, is Cumbie Professor of Conflict Resolution at George Mason University in Fairfax, Virginia. She is the author of numerous works including *Ariadne's Thread: The Search for New Modes of Thinking* (1989). She served as a member of the initial advisory group on topics and authors for this volume.

Ray E. Clement is a senior research scientist in the laboratory services branch of the Ontario Ministry of Environment and Energy. He has written more than 100 articles and other publications on trace analysis and environmental and analytical chemistry, especially regarding dioxins and furans.

Bruce E. Coblentz teaches in the Department of Fisheries and Wildlife at Oregon State University in Corvallis, Oregon. His research and teaching emphasize exotic and feral species in a variety of settings, and his publications include many articles on the environmental impacts associated with feral sheep and feral pigs on Catalina Island.

Michael P. Cohen is the author of *The Pathless Way: John Muir and American Wilderness* (1984) and *The History of the Sierra Club: 1892–1970* (1988). He lives in Cedar City, Utah.

William Conway is president of the Wildlife Conservation Society based in Bronx, New York. He has played a major role in the development of wildlife parks and refuges in Patagonia and East Africa and the American Zoo and Aquarium Association's Species Survival Plan.

Dan A. Cothran is a professor in the Department of Political Science at Northern Arizona University in Flagstaff, Arizona. His diverse teaching and research interests include the study of politics and policy in Latin America and his publication *Political Stability and Democracy in Mexico* (1994).

Irena Creed is a Ph.D. candidate in physical geography at the University of Toronto. Her principal research interest is in the biogeochemistry of forested ecosystems.

Anne Peyton Curlee is executive director of the Northern Rockies Conservation Cooperative (NRCC) in Jackson, Wyoming, and was a founding member of the editorial staff of *Earth Island Journal*. She holds an M.S. in wildlife ecology and conservation biology from the Yale University School of Forestry and Environmental Studies and is presently (with Tim Clark) completing a book titled *Conserving the Greater Yellowstone Ecosystem: Understanding and Improving Natural Resource Management*.

Kenneth A. Dahlberg is a professor of political science at Western Michigan University in Kalamazoo, Michigan. He is the author of *Beyond the Green Revolution* (1979), coauthor of *Environment and the Global Arena* (1985), coeditor of *Natural Resources and People* (1986), and editor of *New Directions for Agriculture and Agricultural Research* (1986).

Raymond F. Dasmann is Professor Emeritus at the University of California, Santa Cruz, and is one of the leading figures in the development of conservation research and environmental studies. He is the author of the standard text *Environmental Conservation* (5th ed. 1984), and has published such other works as *Ecological Principles for Economic Development* (1973), and *Wildlife Biology* (2nd ed., 1981). He served as a member of the initial advisory group on topics and authors for this volume.

Bruce W. Davis is deputy director of the Institute for Antarctic and Southern Ocean Studies at the University of Tasmania in Hobart, Tasmania, Australia. He has been associated with the Australian Heritage Commission and his major research focus is on federal/state environmental conflict and environmental policy in Tasmania.

Peter Duinker is an associate professor and chair of forest management and policy in the School of Forestry at Lakehead University in Thunder Bay, Ontario. His research interests include environmental assessment, forest planning for non-timber values, and conflict resolution.

Linda F. Duncan is the assistant deputy minister of resource management for the Government of the Yukon in Whitehorse, Yukon. Previously she served as a consultant on environmental regulation and enforcement to the governments of Indonesia and Jamaica, and served as chief of enforcement compliance at Environment Canada, and as the founding executive director of the Environmental Law Centre in Edmonton, Alberta.

Riley E. Dunlap, a professor of sociology and rural sociology at Washington State University in Pullman, Washington, has studied environmental attitudes and behaviors for nearly two decades. He recently directed a twenty-four-nation survey of public perceptions and opinions regarding environmental issues for the George H. Gallup International Institute, where he was appointed Gallup Fellow in Environment.

Robert F. Durant is a professor and the Schaeffer Research Chair in Public Policy at the University of Baltimore in Baltimore, Maryland. He is the author of many works including *When Government Regulates Itself: EPA, TVA, and Pollution Control in the 1970s* (1985) and *The Administrative Presidency Revisited: Public Lands, the BLM, and the Reagan Revolution* (1992).

Robyn Eckersley lectures on environmental politics in the politics department and is program director for environment and development at the Institute of Ethics and Public Policy, Graduate School of Government, Monash University in Melbourne, Australia. She is the coeditor of *Environmental Politics in Australia and New Zealand* (1989) and author of *Environmentalism and Political Theory: Toward an Ecocentric Approach* (1992). She served as a member of the initial advisory group on topics and authors for this volume.

David Ehrenfeld teaches biology in the Department of Natural Resources at Rutgers University in New Brunswick, New Jersey, and is the founding editor of the journal *Conservation Biology.* He is also the author of many works including *The Arrogance of Humanism* (1978) and *Beginning Again: People and Nature in the New Millennium* (1993).

Paul Ekins is a research fellow in the Department of Economics, Birkbeck College, University of London (England) and cofounder of The Other Economic Summit (TOES). He has recently published several books on environmental economics including *The Living Economy:*

A New Economics in the Making (1968) and *The Gaia Atlas of Green Economics* (1992).

D. Paul Emond, one of Canada's leading environmental lawyers, teaches law at the Osgoode Hall Law School at York University in Toronto, Ontario. Among his many activities are duties at Emond Montgomery Publications Limited, Canadian Law Publishers, also located in Toronto.

Neil Evernden is a professor in the Faculty of Environmental Studies at York University in Toronto, Ontario. His publications include *The Social Creation of Nature* (1992) and *The Natural Alien: Humankind and the Environment* (2nd ed., 1993).

Timothy J. Fahey teaches forestry and forest ecosystems in the Department of Natural Resources at Cornell University in Ithaca, New York. His research focuses primarily on forested ecosystems in the Northeastern United States and in Latin America.

Janine Ferretti is executive director of Pollution Probe, a major Canadian environmental organization based in Toronto, Ontario. She has ten years experience with this organization including some years with Pollution Probe International. She holds a degree in environmental studies from the University of California, Santa Cruz, and is presently completing a Master's degree in environmental studies emphasizing international environmental policy at York University (Toronto).

Douglas E. Fisher teaches in the Faculty of Law at Queensland University of Technology in Brisbane, Australia. He is the author of *Natural Resources Law* (1987) and *Environmental Law: Text and Materials* (1993).

A. Lee Foote, Ph.D., works at the U.S. Fish and Wildlife Service's National Wetlands Research Center in Lafayette, Louisiana. He has extensive experience with the protection of coastal marsh wetland habitat.

Pamela Foster is the ozone campaigner for Friends of the Earth (FOE) Canada in Ottawa, Ontario, and has represented FOE International at the Montreal Protocol meetings. In addition, she prepares educational materials on depletion and impacts and does extensive policy analysis on this issue. She is completing a Master's degree at the Norman Paterson School of International Affairs at Carleton University in Ottawa.

Michael G. Fox teaches in the Environmental and Resource Studies Program at Trent University in Peterborough, Ontario. A biologist, he has extensive and diverse scientific consulting experience. His research and teaching focus on resource management, fisheries management, and aquaculture.

Warwick Fox is an Australian Research Fellow at the Centre for Environmental Studies at the University of Tasmania in Hobart, Tasmania. He is the author of numerous papers on ecophilosophy and ecopsychology as well as *Toward a Transpersonal Ecology: Developing New Foundations for Environmentalism* (1990).

Charles A. Francis is professor of agronomy, extension crop specialist, and director of the Center for Sustainable Agricultural Systems at the University of Nebraska in Lincoln, Nebraska. His research and over 400 publications focus primarily on plant breeding, agronomy, and cropping systems, and he now dedicates most of his energy to the process of designing a resource-efficient, equitable, future agriculture.

George Francis is a professor in the Department of Environment and Resources at the University of Waterloo in Waterloo, Ontario, Canada. His research and teaching interests cover many aspects of environmental policy with a focus on ecosystem management, groundwater, land use planning, and the Great Lakes bioregion.

Nat B. Frazer, Ph.D., is associate director of the Savannah River Ecology Laboratory in Aiken, South Carolina. He is a member of the Executive Committee of the World Conservation Union's (IUCN) Marine Turtle Specialist Group and is the former editor of the *Marine Turtle Newsletter*.

John C. Freemuth teaches in the political science department at Boise State University in Boise, Idaho. He is the author of numerous articles and chapters, as well as *Islands Under Siege: National Parks and the Politics of External Threats* (1991) and *The Politics of Ecosystem Management: Lessons from Greater Yellowstone* (1995).

Odelia Funke is chief of the Information Access Branch, Office of Pollution Prevention and Toxics at the U.S. Environmental Protection Agency. She holds a Ph.D. in political science from the University of Virginia, has taught at George Washington University, American University, and the University of Missouri, and has written widely on environmental politics and policy.

Yaakov J. Garb is a MacArthur Fellow for humanities studies of the environment at the Massachusetts Institute of Technology in Cambridge, Massachusetts. He has published several articles and chapters on imagery of nature in environmentalist, ecofeminist, and other forms of discourse.

Michel Gareau has extensive experience in environmental organizations and is presently climate change and energy campaigner for Friends of the Earth (FOE) Canada in Ottawa, Ontario. His responsibilities include preparing educational materials for Canadians on climate change, monitoring international agreements, and analyzing and critiquing domestic policies both at a federal and regional level.

Dennis P. Garrity, Ph.D., is a systems agronomist conducting research on the development of conservation-oriented agroforestry systems to rehabilitate degraded uplands in Southeast Asia for the International Centre for Research in Agroforestry. He lives in Indonesia.

Valerius Geist is professor and program director for environmental science in the Faculty of Environmental Design at the University of Calgary in Calgary, Alberta. His research focuses on conservation policy, environmental health, and the biology of ungulate mammals.

Robert B. Gibson, a political scientist, is an associate professor in the Department of Environment and Resources at the University of Waterloo, in Waterloo, Ontario. He is also the editor of the journal *Alternatives: Perspectives on Society, Technology, and Environment* and has published extensively on the subject of environmental assessment.

John Martin Gillroy holds a Ph. D. in political science, and is both a researcher at the Northeast Center for Comparative Risk in

South Royalton, Vermont and a graduate student at the Vermont Law School. His primary research interest is in the relationship between political thought and public policy choices. His numerous publications include recent articles in such journals as *Environmental Ethics* and a book: *Environmental Risk, Environmental Values, and Political Choices* (1993).

James M. Glover, a historian, teaches in the recreation department at Southern Illinois University in Carbondale, Illinois. He is the author of *A Wilderness Original: The Life of Bob Marshall* (1986) and is completing a biography of American conservationist Olaus Murie.

J. Bernard Gollop recently retired as a shorebird researcher at the Prairie and Northern Wildlife Research Centre of the Canadian Wildlife Service in Saskatoon, Saskatchewan. He wrote the endangered species account on the Eskimo Curlew for the Committee on the Status of Endangered Wildlife in Canada (COSEWIC), as well as *Eskimo Curlew: A Vanishing Species?* (1986).

Laurie J. Goodrich is the conservation ecologist at the Hawk Mountain Sanctuary in Kempton, Pennsylvania. She is the coauthor of the North American species accounts for the broad-winged hawk and the sharp-shinned hawk.

Andrew S. Goudie is professor and chairman of the Department of Geography at Oxford University and the author of numerous standard texts on environmental geography including *The Human Impact on the Natural Environment* (4th ed., 1993), *The Nature of the Environment* (3rd ed., 1993), and *Environmental Change* (3rd ed., 1992).

Cheri L. Gratto-Trevor, a Ph.D. biologist, is an Arctic shorebird researcher at the Prairie and Northern Wildlife Research Centre of the Canadian Fish and Wildlife Service in Saskatoon, Saskatchewan. Her research has focused primarily on shorebird mating systems and habitat conservation.

Robert E. Grese studied landscape architecture at the University of Georgia in Athens and at the University of Wisconsin in Madison. He has taught at the University of Virginia in Charlottesville and at the University of Michi-

gan in Ann Arbor where he is currently an associate professor of landscape architecture. He is the author of *Jens Jensen: Maker of Natural Parks and Gardens* (1992).

Pete A.Y. Gunter teaches in the Department of Philosophy and Religion Studies at the University of North Texas in Denton, Texas. He has been a conservation activist for many years and is the author of *The Big Thicket: A Challenge for Conservation* (1973) and *The Big Thicket: An Ecological Reevaluation* (1993).

Peter M. Haas teaches in the Department of Political Science at the University of Massachusetts in Amherst, Massachusetts. He is the author of numerous publications including the widely cited *Saving the Mediterranean* (1990) and coeditor of *Institutions for the Earth* (1993).

Susan G. Hadden is a political scientist working at the LBJ School of Public Administration at the University of Texas in Austin. She is the author or coauthor of numerous books, articles, and monographs on environmental policy including *Siting of Hazardous Waste Treatment Facilities in Texas* (1982), *Environmental Protection and Economic Development in India* (1984), and *A Citizen's Right to Know: Risk Communication and Public Policy* (1989).

Ellen Hagerman has worked on agroforestry development in rural Ghana and presently is program coordinator for Global ReLeaf, a national community reforestation program of Friends of the Earth (FOE) Canada in Ottawa, Ontario. Her responsibilities include providing financial and technical assistance to communities applying to plant trees, doing research and education relating to urban and community forestry, and serving on a number of major committees such as the Advisory Committee on urban forestry for the Eastern Ontario Model Forests Program.

Susan M. Haig is an associate professor with the South Carolina Cooperative Fish and Wildlife Unit at Clemson University in South Carolina. She has authored numerous reports and articles on the habitat and conservation of the piping plover.

Derek Hall is a graduate student in the Department of Political Science at York University in

Toronto, Ontario. His interests focus on international ecological politics.

June D. Hall is a research associate at the Henson College of Public Affairs and Continuing Education at Dalhousie University in Halifax, Nova Scotia, where she studies Canada's role in global environmental change. She is the coauthor of *A New Kind of Sharing* (1993).

Eugene C. Hargrove is a professor and chair of the Department of Philosophy and Religion Studies at the University of North Texas in Denton, Texas. He is also the founding (and present) editor of the journal *Environmental Ethics*, editor of several books including *Religion and Environmental Crisis* (1986) and *The Animal Rights/Environmental Ethics Debate: The Environmental Perspective* (1992), and author of *Foundations of Environmental Ethics* (1989). He served as a member of the initial advisory group on topics and authors for this volume.

Peter Harnik is the Director of Rails-to-Trails Conservancy based in Washington, D.C., a not-for-profit organization dedicated to the preservation and use of abandoned railroad lines as hiking and cycling trails. He is a long-time environmental activist serving on the staff of Environmental Action in its earliest days following Earth Day 1970.

Kathryn Harrison is an assistant professor in the Department of Political Science at the University of British Columbia in Vancouver, British Columbia. She is the author of many articles and chapters on environmental policy institutions and issues in Canada and the United States.

Magda Havas is an associate professor in the environmental and resource studies and science education programs at Trent University in Peterborough, Ontario. She has a Ph.D. from the University of Toronto and has done postdoctoral research at Cornell University in Ithaca, New York. An aquatic toxicologist, her research focuses on acid precipitation, heavy metals, drinking water quality, and the recovery of acidic aquatic environments.

Peter R. Hay is lecturer in the Centre for Environmental Studies at the University of Tasma-

nia in Hobart, Tasmania, Australia. From 1989 through 1991 he was seconded to the Office of the Minister for Environment and Planning of Tasmania. He has written extensively on green politics and environmental policy issues and is coeditor of *Environmental Politics in Australia and New Zealand* (1989).

Stephen Herrero teaches in the Faculty of Environmental Design at the University of Calgary, Alberta. He is one of Canada's leading experts on bears and their conservation and his many publications include *Bear Attacks: Their Causes and Avoidance* (1988).

Karl Hess is senior associate in environmental studies at the Foundation for Research on Economics and the Environment in Seattle, Washington and author of several books and numerous articles on rangelands ecosystems and management. He has a Ph.D. in range ecology from Colorado State University and has served in the roles of consulting plant ecologist for the U.S. Forest Service and the National Park Service and instructor and assistant professor, respectively, at New Mexico State University and Oregon State University.

M.B.C. Hickey completed his Ph.D. in biology at York University in Toronto, Ontario, in 1993. His research in the biology of bats includes a Ph.D. thesis on thermoregulatory behavior of hoary bats, and has resulted in several articles in such journals as *Canadian Journal of Zoology* and *Journal of Mammology*.

Christoph Hohenemser is a professor of physics and founder of the Program on Environment, Technology and Society at Clark University in Worcester, Massachusetts. He is a fellow of the American Physical Society and the Society for Risk Analysis and author of three books and more than 140 articles and chapters on nuclear solid state physics, environmental hazard management, and nuclear risk assessment.

Randee Holmes is a researcher based in North York (Toronto), Ontario. She has recently completed a book titled *Additive Alert: A Consumer's Handbook* (1994) published through Pollution Probe, a major Canadian environmental protection organization based in Toronto.

Robert Hornung is presently working with the Organisation for Economic Co-operation and

Development (OECD) in Paris, France, on a project related to reporting under the Climate Change Convention. In recent years he has worked on environmental policy issues, especially the policy implications of climate warming, for the Lasalle Academy of the Atmospheric Environment Service of Environment Canada and for Friends of the Earth (FOE) Canada in Ottawa, Ontario.

Peter Horsley teaches in the Department of Geography at Massey University in North Palmerston, New Zealand. He has done extensive research on resource conflicts, the environment, and the Maori peoples in New Zealand.

Michael Hough is a partner with the landscape architecture firm of Hough, Stansbury, and Woodland in Toronto, Ontario, and is an adjunct professor in the Faculty of Environmental Studies at York University. He is the author of City Form and Natural Process (1984) and Out of Place: Restoring Identity to the Natural Landscape (1990) and is a past president of the Canadian Society of Landscape Architects.

Ken W.F. Howard is director of the Groundwater Research Group based at the Scarborough Campus of the University of Toronto (Ontario). His research and many publications focus on the development and protection of groundwater resources in Canada, Europe, and East Africa.

Thomas A. Huff has had long experience with the conservation of reptile species and is former executive director of the Reptile Breeding Foundation. He is presently manager of the Little Cataraqui Creek Conservation Area in Picton, Ontario, and a consulting herpetoculturist.

J. Donald Hughes, a leading environmental historian, teaches in the history department at the University of Denver in Colorado. He has authored many books on diverse subjects including In the House of Stone and Light: A Human History of the Grand Canyon (1978), American Indian Ecology (1983), and Ecology in Ancient Civilizations (1975).

Thomas C. Hutchinson was, until recently, chairman of the environmental and resource studies program at Trent University in Peterborough, Ontario. He has published more than 150 scientific articles, many dealing with

ecosystem responses to air pollution and in 1980 and 1985 edited for NATO Advanced Research Institutes the effects of acid rain on terrestrial ecosystems, on forests, and on agriculture.

John Jackson has worked with citizens' groups on waste management issues for the past fifteen years. He is the author of Resources—Not Garbage (1993), and coauthor of Chemical Nightmare: The Unnecessary Legacy of Toxic Wastes (1982). He is the coordinator of both the Citizens' Network on Waste Management and the Ontario Toxic Waste Research Coalition. He lives in Kitchener, Ontario.

Barbara Jancar-Webster is a professor of political science at the State University of New York in Brockport, New York. She is the author of many works, including the award-winning volume Environmental Management in the Soviet Union and Yugoslavia (1989).

Sheila Jasanoff is a political scientist teaching and chairing in the Department of Science and Technology Studies at Cornell University in Ithaca, New York. She is the author of Risk Management and Political Culture (1986) and The Fifth Branch: Science Advisers as Policymakers (1990). She served as a member of the initial advisory group on topics and authors for this volume.

Edward A. Johnson teaches in the Department of Biological Science at the University of Calgary, Alberta. His research and teaching interests include a focus on the ecological effects of fires in forested settings.

William R. Jordan III is director of the historic University of Wisconsin Arboretum in Madison, Wisconsin. He is the editor of the journal Restoration Ecology and also recently edited a book titled Restoration Ecology: A Synthetic Approach to Ecological Restoration (1990).

Mohammed Kassas teaches in the Faculty of Science at the University of Cairo, Egypt, and has served in many national and international posts related to aspects of environmental policy, especially desertification. He has published extensively on desertification through the United Nations Environment Programme and is coeditor of The World Environment, 1972–1982 (1982).

Lloyd F. Kiff has been the director of the Western Foundation of Vertebrate Zoology in Camarillo, California, since 1968. He is currently president of the Cooper Ornithological Society and was leader of the California Condor Recovery Team from 1986 to 1993.

Hamish Kimmins is a professor of forest ecology in the Department of Forest Sciences at the University of British Columbia in Vancouver and author of *Forest Ecology* (1987) and *Balancing Act: Environmental Issues in Forestry* (1992). He has served as the chairman of the British Columbia Ecological Reserves Committee and the (Canadian) National Forest Round Table.

R. Andreas Kraemer is a senior fellow with the Institute for European Environmental Policy in Berlin and Bonn, Germany, and teaches environmental policy with the Berlin Programme of Duke University (Durham, North Carolina). As a policy analyst his main focus has been on "chemical policy" and water pollution policy initiatives at the national and European Community level.

Michael E. Kraft is Herbert Fisk Johnson Professor of Environmental Studies at the University of Wisconsin-Green Bay. He is coeditor and contributing author of *Population Policy Analysis* (1978), *Environmental Policy in the 1980s: Reagan's New Agenda* (1984), *Technology and Politics* (1988), *Public Reactions to Nuclear Waste* (1993), and *Environmental Policy in the 1990s: Toward a New Agenda* (2nd ed., 1994).

Anita Krajnc is a Ph.D. student in the Department of Political Science at the University of Toronto. She has prior experience in environmental policy matters as an aide to Charles Caccia, M.P., a former minister of the environment for Canada. Her research focus is on Canadian forest policy.

Frank N. Laird teaches in the Department of Political Science at the University of Denver in Colorado. He is presently completing a book on the history of solar energy policy in the United States.

W. Henry Lambright teaches in the Department of Political Science at the Maxwell School at Syracuse University in New York. He is the author of numerous publications on science and technology policy including *Presidential Management of Science and Technology: The Johnson Presidency* (1985).

Mark B. Lapping is the founding dean and professor in the Bloustein School of Planning and Public Policy at Rutgers University in New Brunswick, New Jersey. His broad professional career includes extensive editing experience and the publication of some 200 articles, chapters, and monographs focusing on rural planning, land use, environmental protection, and economic development. Presently, he is provost and vice president for Academic Affairs and professor of Public Policy at the University of Southern Maine, Portland.

Linda J. Lear teaches in the Department of History at the University of Maryland. She is the author of *The Aggressive Progressive: The Early Career of Harold L. Ickes, 1874–1952* (1981) and is currently completing a biography of Rachel Carson.

Philippe Le Prestre teaches in the political science department at Université de Québec a Montréal (UQAM). He is the author of *The World Bank and the Environmental Challenge* (1989).

James P. Lester is a professor of political science at Colorado State University in Fort Collins, Colorado. He edited and contributed to *Environmental Politics and Policy: Theories and Evidence* (1989), is coauthor of *Implementation Theory and Practice: Toward a Third Generation* (1990), and author of numerous articles and chapters on hazardous waste politics, environmental policy, and public policy implementation.

Hok-Lin Leung is a professor in the School of Urban and Regional Planning at Queen's University in Kingston, Ontario. His many publications include *Urbanization of Canada, 1890–1990* (1992) and *City Images: An Internal View* (1992).

Chris H. Lewis, Ph.D., is an instructor in the Program in American Studies at the University of Colorado at Boulder. His recently completed manuscript, *Science and the End of the Modern World*, examines the ways in which scientific activists have helped shape the modern environmental movement by popularizing modern science's increasing loss of faith in progress.

Ronald H. Limbaugh is the director of the John Muir Center for Regional Studies, executive director of the Conference of California Historical Societies, and Rockwell Hunt Professor of California Studies at the University of the Pacific at Stockton, California. He is the author of three books on aspects of Western American history and is currently completing a fourth on the origins and writing of John Muir's *Stickeen*.

Richard D. Lindgren is counsel with the Canadian Environmental Law Association (CELA) based in Toronto, Ontario, where, among other duties, he represents CELA on the Ontario Attorney General's Advisory Committee on Class Action Reform. He also teaches environmental law in the Environmental and Resource Studies Program at Trent University in Peterborough, Ontario.

John A. Livingston has recently retired from full-time teaching in the Faculty of Environmental Studies at York University in Toronto, Ontario. He is the author of *Birds of the Northern Forest* (1966), *Birds of the Eastern Forest* (1968), *One Cosmic Instant: A Natural History of Human Arrogance* (1973), *Arctic Oil* (1981), and *The Fallacy of Wildlife Conservation* (1981), and coauthor of *Darwin and the Galapagos* (1966).

Ralph H. Lutts is director of the outreach division at the Virginia Museum of Natural History in Martinsville, Virginia. He is the author of many articles, reviews, and chapters on the history of nature study, conservation, and environmental protection including the book *The Nature Fakers: Wildlife, Science and Sentiment* (1990).

Doug Macdonald is a past executive director of the Canadian Environmental Law Research Foundation and author of *The Politics of Pollution* (1991). He is currently a consultant and Ph.D. student in the Faculty of Environmental Studies at York University in Toronto.

Donald Mackay is a professor in the Department of Chemical Engineering at the University of Toronto. He is an international authority on the environmental impacts of oil spills and author of numerous publications including the two-volume *Illustrated Handbook of Environmental Fate for Organic Chemicals* (1991).

Richard Macrory is Denton Hall professor of environmental law at the Centre for Environmental Technology of the Imperial College of Science, Technology and Medicine in London, England. His recent publications include studies of hazardous waste law, the privatization and regulation of the water industry, and many other aspects of British and European Community environmental law.

Sheila Malcolmson is a research associate with the Borealis Energy Research Association, and manager of regulatory interventions for the Energy Probe Research Foundation, a charitable environmental and policy research group based in Toronto, Ontario.

Raymond E. March, a fellow of the Canadian Institute of Chemists, is a professor in the Department of Chemistry at Trent University in Peterborough, Ontario. He directs the Gas Phase Ion Chemistry Laboratory at that same location and is widely recognized as a leading authority on mass spectrometry and the trace analysis of pollutants.

John Marsh is a professor in the geography department and Director of the Leslie Frost Centre graduate program at Trent University in Peterborough, Ontario. He has published extensively in the field of recreational geography and parks management and is a past president of the Canadian Parks and Wilderness Society.

Roderic B. Mast is vice president of Conservation International (CI), an international not-for-profit conservation organization with biodiversity protection projects located throughout Asia, Africa, and Latin America. A marine biologist and conservationist with fifteen years experience in Latin America, Madagascar, and Africa, he has authored numerous articles and chapters on biodiversity conservation and currently edits *Lemur News*, the newsletter of the Madagascar subsection of the International Union for the Conservation of Nature and Natural Resources (IUCN)/Species Survival Commission's Primate Specialist Group. CI is located at 1015 18th Street NW, Washington, D.C., 20036; telephone (202) 429-5660, fax (202) 887-0192.

Doug McEachern is the professor of politics at the University of Adelaide South Australia. He has published a study of the politics of the

Hawke Labor Government which includes a lengthy discussion on environmental conflict, articles on a number of questions of Australian environmental politics, and is currently completing a book on resource company responses to environmental challenges.

Jack McGinnis is a widely recognized pioneer in recycling in North America, and has worked in the three "r's" (reduction, reuse, and recycling) field since 1974. He was the founder of many key organizations and programs, including the recycling council of Ontario (1978) and the first multi-material, curbside recycling program (1974).

William McGucken is a professor of history at the University of Akron in Ohio. He is the author of *Nineteenth Century Spectroscopy: Development of the Understanding of Spectra, 1802–1897* (1970), *Scientists, Society and State: The Social Relations of Science Movement in Great Britain, 1931–1947* (1984), and *Biodegradable: Detergents and the Environment* (1991).

Kevin McNamee is the director of the Wildlands Program for the Canadian Nature Federation in Ottawa. For the past eleven years he has advocated the creation and ecological management of national parks and protected areas. He recently taught courses on wilderness resources at Trent University in Peterborough, Ontario.

Lettie McSpadden teaches public law and public policy in the Department of Political Science at Northern Illinois University in DeKalb, Illinois. She is the author of numerous articles and chapters on pollution, conservation, and environmental policy as well as *One Environment Under Law* (1976), *The Environmental Decade in Court* (1982), and *U.S. Energy and Environmental Groups* (1990).

Curt Meine, a Ph.D. environmental historian, presently works at the International Crane Foundation in Baraboo, Wisconsin. Previously he was with the National Academy of Science in Washington, D.C. His many publications include *Aldo Leopold: His Life and Work* (1988).

Martin V. Melosi is director of the Christine Womack Institute for Public History at the University of Houston in Houston, Texas. He is the author of numerous works on environmental history including *Pollution and Reform in America's Cities, 1870–1930* (1980), *Refuse, Reform, and the Environment, 1880–1980* (1983), and *Coping with Abundance: Energy and Environment in Industrial America* (1985).

David Mercer is a senior lecturer in the Department of Geography and Environmental Science at Monash University in Melbourne, Victoria, Australia. His major area of research interest focuses on resource conflicts in Australia.

Gray Merriam is a professor in the Department of Biology at Carleton University in Ottawa, Ontario, Canada. He has conducted research and published extensively on the ecological effects of habitat fragmentation in several contexts.

Chris D. Metcalfe is an associate professor in the Environmental and Resource Studies Program and the biology department and was until recently chair of the Watershed Ecosystems Graduate Program at Trent University in Peterborough, Ontario. He has published more than 40 scientific articles in environmental toxicology focusing primarily on environmental fate and the toxic effects of organic compounds.

Lisa Mighetto holds a Ph.D. in environmental history from the University of Washington. She works for Historical Research Associates, where she recently completed a book-length study of the use of salmon and steelhead in the Columbia River Basin. Her books include *Muir Among the Animals: The Wildlife Writings of John Muir* (1986) and *Wild Animals and American Environmental Ethics* (1991), and her articles have appeared in *Harper's, Sierra, Pacific Historical Review*, and *The Alaska Journal*.

Lester W. Milbrath has recently retired from full-time teaching in the Department of Political Science at the State University of New York at Buffalo. He has written extensively on environmental politics and policy, with an emphasis on environmental education and sustainability. His books include *Environmentalists: Vanguard for a New Society* (1984) and *Envisioning a Sustainable Society: Learning Our Way Out* (1989).

L. Scott Mills teaches in the Department of Fisheries and Wildlife at the University of Idaho in

Moscow, Idaho. His research includes studies of the role and the importance of the conservation of keystone species.

Russell A. Mittermeier is chairman of the Primate Specialist Group of the International Union for the Conservation of Nature and Natural Resources (IUCN) Species Survival Commission and president of Conservation International (CI). A global authority on biodiversity conservation, Dr. Mittermeier's field work spans twenty countries over the past twenty-five years. CI blends environmental protection with culturally sensitive, economically and scientifically sound solutions and is located at 1015 18th Street NW, Washington, D.C., 20036; telephone (202) 429-5660, fax (202) 887-0192.

Dominic Moran is a research fellow with the Centre for Social and Economic Research on the Global Environment (CSERGE) at University College London in London, England. His research focuses on several aspects of ecological and natural resource economics.

M. Granger Morgan is a professor and head of the Department of Engineering and Public Policy at Carnegie Mellon University in Pittsburgh, Pennsylvania. He is the coauthor of a major report on the biological effects of power transmission lines for the U.S. Office of Technology Assessment.

Stephen P. Mumme teaches in the political science department at Colorado State University in Ft. Collins, Colorado. His primary research interest is in environmental policy in Mexico and in Mexico-U.S. relationships. His publications on the subject include *Apportioning Groundwater Beneath the U.S.-Mexico Border: Obstacles and Alternatives* (1988).

Joan Murray is the director of The Robert McLauglin Gallery in Oshawa, Ontario. She has had a long-standing research interest in Canadian art and her very many publications include *The Best of Tom Thomson* (1986), *The Last Buffalo: The Story of Frederick Arthur Verner* (1984), and *The Best of the Group of Seven* (1984).

Norman Myers is an independent research scientist living in Oxford, England, and is the winner of numerous international awards including the 1992 Volvo Environmental Prize. He is the author of *Ultimate Security: The Environmental Basis of Political Stability* (1993), as well as *The Long African Day* (1972), *The Sinking Ark* (1979), *The Primary Source* (1992), and numerous other works. He served as a member of the initial advisory group on topics and authors for this volume.

Robert T. Nakamura is a political scientist at the Rockefeller College of Public Affairs and Policy at the State University of New York in Albany. He is the coauthor of *The Politics of Policy Implementation* (1980) and *Cleaning up the Mess: Implementation Strategies in the Superfund Program* (1993).

Susan Rhoades Neel is currently a postdoctoral research fellow in the Department of History at the University of California, Los Angeles (UCLA). The controversy surrounding the Echo Park dam was the subject of her Ph.D. dissertation.

David N. Nettleship, Ph.D., is a senior research scientist with the Canadian Wildlife Service, Environment Canada, Bedford Institute of Oceanography, Dartmouth, Nova Scotia, Canada, and heads a long-term research program on the reproductive and pelagic ecology of seabird populations in eastern Canada that he began in 1971. His publications include seven books on marine birds and over 100 papers in scientific journals.

Charles Noble teaches in the Department of Political Science at California State University in Long Beach, California. He is the author of *Liberalism at Work: The Rise and Fall of OSHA* (1986).

Reed F. Noss, one of the leaders in the development of the field of conservation biology, is a member of the faculty at the Department of Fisheries and Wildlife at Oregon State University in Corvallis, Oregon. He is currently the editor of the journal *Conservation Biology*.

Max Oelschlaeger teaches the philosophy of ecology in the Department of Philosophy and Religion Studies at the University of North Texas in Denton, Texas. He has authored and edited many works on the environment and conservation including *The Environmental*

Imperative: A Socioeconomic Perspective (1977), *The Idea of Wilderness: From Prehistory to the Age of Ecology* (1991), *The Wilderness Condition: Essays on Environment and Civilization* (1991), and *After Earth Day: Continuing the Conservation Effort* (1992). He served as a member of the initial advisory group on topics and authors for this volume.

Larry Olmsted is a writer and journalist living in Wilder, Vermont. He is the grandson of Frederick Law Olmsted, whose entry is included in this encyclopedia.

Kevin H. Olson is a Ph.D. student in the political science department at the University of Pittsburgh in Pittsburgh, Pennsylvania. He is broadly interested in conservation and environmental policy and his primary research focus is on the use of economic incentives for environmental initiatives, especially within the European Union.

Ronald Orenstein holds a Ph.D. in zoology and an LL.B. and is project director for the International Wildlife Coalition based in Toronto, Ontario. He has a broad experience in the protection of wildlife and habitat and has recently edited the book *Elephants: The Deciding Decade* (1991).

Timothy O'Riordan teaches in the School of Environmental Sciences at the University of East Anglia in Norwich, England, where he has also for many years been an editor of *Environment* magazine. He is the author, editor, or coeditor of many works including the four-volume *Progress in Resource Management and Environmental Planning* (1979), as well as such books as *Environmentalism* (2nd ed., 1981), and *Project Appraisal and Policy Review* (1981). He served as a member of the initial advisory group on topics and authors for this volume.

David W. Orr, a political scientist, teaches in the environmental studies program at Oberlin College in Oberlin, Ohio. His studies focus on environmental education; he is a contributing editor of *Conservation Biology* on that subject and author of *Ecological Literacy* (1992).

Joseph Michael Pace is a doctoral student and teaching assistant in the Department of Political Science at Northern Arizona University in Flagstaff, Arizona. His areas of study include public policy, public administration, and American government and history.

Jesse Paehlke has recently graduated from McGill University in Montreal, Quebec, with a degree in art history.

Robert Paehlke is a professor in the Political Studies Department and the environmental and resource studies program at Trent University, Peterborough, Ontario. He is the founding editor (1971) of the journal *Alternatives: Perspectives on Society, Technology, and Environment*, author of *Environmentalism and the Future of Progressive Politics* (1989), and coeditor of *Managing Leviathan: Environmental Politics and the Administrative State* (1990).

Albert L. Page teaches in the Department of Soil and Environmental Science at the University of California in Riverside, California. He is the coeditor of the two-volume work *Methods of Soil Analysis* (1982), as well as *Land Application of Sludge* (1987).

Robert J.D. Page, a historian, is dean of the School of Environmental Design at the University of Calgary, Alberta, Canada, and served, until recently, as chair of the Canadian Environmental Advisory Council in Ottawa. He has authored many publications including *Northern Development: The Canadian Dilemma* (1986).

Sara Parkin is formerly cosecretary of the European Greens and former spokesperson of the British Greens. She is the author of *Green Parties: An International Guide* (1989) and *The Life and Death of Petra Kelly* (1994).

Barry Peers is a project leader in the Public Education Division of the Canadian Museum of Nature in Ottawa, Ontario, Canada. He recently completed a major exhibit on the conservation of the monarch butterfly and its migration.

V. Setty Pendakur is a professor in the School of Community and Regional Planning at the University of British Columbia in Vancouver. He is very active in research initiatives in Thailand, Singapore, and elsewhere in Asia where he recently completed a term as visiting professor at the Asian Institute of Technology in Pathumthani, Thailand. His research, writing, and teaching focus on the role of the automobile in urban planning and in the quality of urban life.

John H. Perkins teaches biology and the history of environment and technology at Evergreen State College in Olympia, Washington. He is the author of numerous articles, chapters, and reviews on a wide variety of agricultural policy and environmental protection issues, including the book *Insects, Experts, and the Insecticide Crisis: The Quest for New Pest Management Strategies* (1982).

Patricia E. Perkins is an assistant professor on the Faculty of Environmental Studies at York University in Toronto, Ontario. She was formerly a policy coordinator for the Ontario government on trade and environment issues; her current research focuses on sustainability and trade.

David A. Perry is a professor of ecosystem studies in the Department of Forest Science at Oregon State University in Corvallis, Oregon. He has written extensively on forest policies and practices, especially as regards the Pacific Northwest, and his publications include *Maintaining the Long-term Productivity of Pacific Northwest Ecosystems* (1989).

Sherry L. Pettigrew actively promotes large carnivore conservation through awareness and conservation programs. She is the coauthor of *Wild Hunters: Predators in Peril* (1991) and can be reached through Second Wind Services, R.R. # 3, Cookstown, Ontario.

Cassandra Phillips is Antarctic and Cetacean Officer for the World Wide Fund (WWF) for Nature (United Kingdom). She has much experience in conservation matters and regularly attends meetings of the International Whaling Commission on behalf of WWF.

John C. Pierce teaches in the Department of Political Science at Washington State University in Pullman, Washington. He has published several articles on postmaterialism as a trend in public opinion and is coauthor of *Political Knowledge and Environmental Politics in Japan and the United States* (1989).

David N. Pimentel teaches in the Department of Entomology in the College of Agriculture and Life Sciences at Cornell University in Ithaca, New York. A leading researcher on pesticides, agriculture, and the environment, his recent publications include *Food and Natural Resources* (1989) and the three-volume *Handbook of Pest Management in Agriculture* (2nd ed., 1990).

Nicholas Polunin, a botanist and graduate of Oxford, Yale, and Harvard universities, is the founding editor of several major publications including the journal *Environmental Conservation*, published in Geneva, Switzerland. As author and editor of some thirteen books on environmental subjects with some emphasis on Arctic settings, and as one of the leading environmentalists in the world, he has received awards and recognitions from the United Nations Secretary-General, UNEP, and from governments and organizations in many countries including India, the United States, China, the former Soviet Union, and the Netherlands.

William O. Pruitt, Jr. is a professor in the zoology department at the University of Manitoba in Winnipeg, Manitoba. He has a broad expertise in conservation biology with a research emphasis on northern forested and tundra habitats and species, especially the woodland caribou.

Christine Pryde is a policy analyst with the Non-Smokers' Rights Association (NSRA), a pioneering Canadian environmental health organization based in Toronto, Ontario. NSRA has developed an international reputation for its successful advocacy of legislative approaches to tobacco control including high taxation policies, precedent-setting warnings on tobacco packages, and the banning of tobacco advertising through the *Tobacco Products Control Act*. NSRA is located at 344 Bloor Street West, Toronto, Ontario, M5S 3A7.

Philip R. Pryde teaches in the geography department at California State University in San Diego, California. His central research interest is in environmental policy in the former Soviet Union, and he is the author of *Environmental Management in the Soviet Union* (1991); he is also the coeditor of *San Diego: An Introduction to the Region* (1984).

Robert Michael Pyle is a leading expert on the conservation of butterflies and in 1971 founded the Xerces Society, an organization dedicated to the study and protection of butterflies and butterfly habitat. He is the author of numerous works on the subject, including *Handbook for Butterfly Watchers* (1992) and was earlier coauthor of *Audubon Society Field Guide to North American Butterflies* (1981).

Barry G. Rabe is a political scientist teaching in the Department of Public Health Policy and Administration in the School of Public Health at the University of Michigan in Ann Arbor. He is a former research fellow with the Conservation Foundation in Washington, D.C. He has written on many aspects of pollution, environmental, and public health policy and is the author of *Fragmentation and Integration in State Environmental Management* (1986) and *When Federalism Works* (1986).

Henry A. Regier is a professor in the Department of Zoology and director of the Institute for Environmental Studies at the University of Toronto. He has published widely on a wide variety of issues of environmental concern and is one of Canada's leading authorities on the Great Lakes.

Donald G. Reid is a Ph.D. candidate in the Department of Zoology at the University of British Columbia in Vancouver, British Columbia, Canada. His research includes the study of Giant Panda habitat and conservation.

Neville Reid, Ph.D., is the acting manager of atmospheric studies in the Science and Technology Branch of the Ministry of Environment and Energy of the province of Ontario. He is an atmospheric chemist with fourteen years experience in this field.

Chris Risley is a biologist, avid birder, and conservation activist living in Peterborough, Ontario. He works as an environmental consultant on biodiversity and bird habitat issues.

Thomas R. Roach is a writer and environmentalist living in Nairobi, Kenya and is associated with the International Development Research Centre, the International Centre for Research in Agroforestry, and the Leslie Frost Centre for Environmental Studies. He was editor of the journal *Agroforestry Today* (1993) and is the coauthor of *Lost Initiatives: Canada's Forest Industries, Forest Policy, and Forest Conservation* (1986).

David B. Robertson is an associate professor in the political science department at the University of Missouri in St. Louis, Missouri. His primary research focus is on various aspects of labor policy, including the relationship between labor issues and environmental issues.

John B. Robinson is the director of the Sustainable Development Research Institute at the University of British Columbia. He published extensively on energy policy, computer simulation, resource conservation, and soft energy paths and is coauthor of *Life After Oil: A Renewable Resource Policy for Canada* (1983).

Steven C. Rockefeller teaches in the Department of Religious Studies at Middlebury College in Middlebury, Vermont. He is coeditor of *Spirit and Nature: Why the Environment Is a Religious Issue* (1992).

Daniel J. Rohlf teaches law at Northwestern School of Law and is associated with the Natural Resources Law Institute at Lewis and Clark College in Portland, Oregon. His research and writing focuses on several aspects of environmental and resources law, and he is the author of *The Endangered Species Act: A Guide to Its Protections and Implementation* (1989).

Walter A. Rosenbaum, a professor of political science at the University of Florida in Gainesville, Florida, was in 1991–1992 special assistant to the assistant administrator for policy, planning, and evaluation of the U.S. Environmental Protection Agency. He is the author of *Energy, Politics, and Public Policy* (1987), *Environmental Politics and Policy* (2nd ed., 1991), and numerous articles and chapters on related subjects.

William D. Rowley teaches in the Department of History at the University of Nevada at Reno. He is the author, coauthor, or editor of numerous works including *M.L. Wilson and the Campaign for the Domestic Allotment* (1970), *The American West* (1980), *U.S. Forest Service Grazing and Rangelands: A History* (1985), and *History of Nevada* (1987).

Wolfgang Rüdig is senior lecturer in the Department of Government at the University of Strathclyde in Glasgow, Scotland. He is author and editor of numerous works including *Green Politics III* (1994) and *Anti-Nuclear Move-*

ments: *A World Survey of Protest against Nuclear Energy* (1990).

Mikko Saikku, licentiate of philosophy, is a junior fellow for the National Council for the Humanities at the Academy of Finland. He is currently working on a doctoral dissertation for the Department of History at the University of Helsinki, Finland.

Liora Salter teaches at Osgoode Hall Law School at York University in Toronto, Ontario. Her research focuses on a variety of issues in environmental and science policy and her many publications include the book *Mandated Science* (1988).

Beth Savan teaches in the environmental studies program at Innis College, University of Toronto. Her broad research and public education experience includes a recent radio-broadcast course on environmental science (over CJRT in Toronto). She is also the author of *Science under Siege* (1988).

Hans G. Schabel teaches in forestry at the University of Wisconsin in Stevens Point, Wisconsin. He has broad experience with forestry research and practices in both Europe and North America.

Denise Scheberle is an assistant professor in the Department of Public and Environmental Affairs at the University of Wisconsin at Green Bay. She has written several articles on intergovernmental environmental policy implementation for *Policy Studies Journal* and a chapter on surface mining policy.

Edgar A. Schmidt, M.Sc., P.Eng., has been a project manager with the Ontario Waste Management Corporation (OWMC) since 1981. OWMC is a public corporation charged with the siting and development of a hazardous waste treatment facility. Dr. Schmidt's responsibilities focus on the technologies associated with the management and treatment of hazardous wastes.

Yrjö Sepänmaa teaches at the University of Joensuu and is associated with the Department of Comparative Literature, Theatre Research, and Aesthetics at the University of Helsinki, Finland. He is the author of many works including *The Beauty of Environment: A General Model for Environmental Aesthetics*. 2nd ed. (1993).

George Sessions teaches in the Department of Philosophy at Sierra College in Rocklin, California. He is a green politics activist, author of many publications, and coauthor of the widely read volume *Deep Ecology: Living as if Nature Mattered* (1985).

Peter D. Shemitz is an environmental analyst and activist working on a Ph.D. in environmental history at the University of Kansas in Lawrence, Kansas.

James E. Sherow is an associate professor in the History Department at Kansas State University in Manhattan, Kansas, where he teaches environmental history. He is the author of *Watering the Valley: The Development along the High Plains Kansas River, 1870–1950* (1990) and many articles on environmental history.

Joseph V. Siry is an environmental historian who teaches in the Department of Environmental Studies at Rollins College in Winter Park, Florida. His many publications include the book *Marshes of the Ocean Shore* (1984).

Duane A. Smith is a professor of history and southwest studies at Fort Lewis College in Durango, Colorado. He is the author of many books, including *Mining America: The Industry and the Environment, 1800–1980* (1993).

Lesbia F. Smith, M.D., is Senior Medical Consultant in the Environmental Health and Toxicology Unit of the Ontario Ministry of Health in Toronto, Ontario. She has extensive responsibilities for a variety of environmental health emergencies within the province of Ontario.

Kenneth E. Smith is a senior engineer at the science and technology branch of the Ministry of Environment and Energy of the Province of Ontario. His work includes responsibilities for source testing, continuous monitoring, and air pollution regulations and control technologies.

Kirk R. Smith works in the Program on Environment at the East-West Center in Honolulu, Hawaii. His many publications include *Global Greenhouse Regime: Who Pays?* (1993) and an important article on the health implications of indoor air published in *Environment* magazine.

Zachary A. Smith teaches environmental and natural resource policy in the Ph.D. program in the Department of Political Science at Northern Arizona University in Flagstaff, Arizona. He is author and editor of six books on environmental and policy topics, including *The Environmental Policy Paradox* (1992).

Bent Sørensen is professor of physics at the Institute of Mathematics and Physics at Roskilde University Center in Roskilde, Denmark. His research focuses on renewable energy technologies and other environmentally relevant subjects and his many publications in several languages include *Renewable Energy* (1979) and *Life-Cycle Assessment of Energy Systems* (1991).

Marvin S. Soroos is professor and head of the Department of Political Science and Public Administration at North Carolina State University in Raleigh, North Carolina. He coedited *Global Predicament: Ecological Perspectives on World Order* (1979), coauthored *The Environment in the Global Arena: Actors, Values, Politics, and Futures* (1985), and is the author of *Beyond Sovereignty: The Challenge of Global Sovereignty* (1986).

Harold K. Steen is the executive director of the Forest History Society located in Durham, North Carolina. He is the author of *The U.S. Forest Service: A History* (1992), editor of *History of Sustained-Yield Forestry* (1984), and editor or author of many other works.

Peter Steer is the air toxics coordinator in the Science and Technology Branch of the Ministry of Environment and Energy of the province of Ontario. He has nine years experience in the field of air pollution monitoring.

Robert F. Stone is a research economist specializing in environmental policy at the Center for Technology, Policy and Industrial Development at the Massachusetts Institute of Technology in Cambridge, Massachusetts. His published research in the area of package recycling include *The Art of the Possible: The Feasibility of Recycling Standards for Packaging* (1991), *Package Deal: The Economic Impacts of Recycling Standards for Packaging in Massachusetts* (1991), and "Recycling the Plastic Package," in *Technology Review* (July 1992).

Colette T. Stushnoff has a B.S.A. from the University of Saskatchewan and is a research officer with the Saskatchewan Soil Survey, concentrating on soil and land-use classification.

Richard D. Stushnoff has a B.S.A. from the University of Saskatchewan and is a research officer with the Saskatchewan Soil Survey, concentrating on soil, land use, and irrigation suitability classification.

M.S. Swaminathan is chairman of the Centre for Sustainable Agricultural and Rural Development in Madras, India, and has recently served as president of the (Indian) National Academy of Agricultural Sciences, president of the Worldwide Fund for Nature-India, and chairman of the Editorial Advisory Board of the World Resources Institute (Washington, D.C.). His many publications include the edited book *Wheat Revolution: A Dialogue* (1993).

Susan Tanner holds a Master's degree in environmental studies and is presently executive director of Friends of the Earth (FOE) Canada, a major environmental organization based in Ottawa, Ontario. She has extensive environmental and policy experience as a consultant to the Law Reform Commission of Canada, as a member of the Ontario Environmental Assessment Board, as a member of the Board of the Canadian Environmental Law Research Foundation, and as founding chair of the Women's Legal Education and Action Fund.

Nigel J. Tapper, Ph.D., is senior lecturer and leader of the Environmental Climatology Group within the Department of Geography and Environmental Science at Monash University in Melbourne, Australia. He has wide ranging teaching and research interests in the general area of environmental climatology.

Bron R. Taylor is an associate professor of religious studies and social ethics at the University of Wisconsin at Oshkosh, Wisconsin. He is the author of many articles and chapters on religion, politics, and environmental movements and is completing a book on radical environmental movements around the world.

Philip S. Taylor is a wildlife habitat biologist with the Canadian Wildlife Service, Environment Canada in Saskatoon, Saskatchewan. He has worked widely across Canada and is now responsible for the management of federally protected wildlife lands in the province of Saskatchewan including migratory bird sanctuaries and national wildlife areas.

Robert Tessier, Ph.D., is a researcher for GRIEGE (*Groupe de recherche interdisciplinaire en gestion de l'environnement*), at Université du Québec à Montréal. His research is in the field of sociology of values about global change (acid rain, greenhouse effect, and other environmental controversies).

John B. Theberge teaches in the Department of Urban and Regional Planning at the University of Waterloo in Waterloo, Ontario, Canada. His many publications in natural history and related subjects include *Grouse* (1985) and *Legacy: The Natural History of Ontario* (1989).

Paul L. Tidwell teaches in the Department of American Studies at the University of New Mexico in Albuquerque, New Mexico. His research interests include Ralph Waldo Emerson, Native American literature, and the emerging field of ecocriticism.

James A. Tober, a political scientist, is presently dean of arts and science at Marlboro College in Marlboro, Vermont. He is the author of *Who Owns the Wildlife?* (1981) and *Wildlife and the Public Interest: Nonprofit Organizations and Federal Wildlife Policy* (1989).

Glen Toner, a native of Western Canada, is an associate professor of public administration and political science at Carleton University in Ottawa, Ontario. He is the author of numerous publications on environment and energy policy, and from July 1989 to July 1991 was senior policy advisor to the deputy minister of Environment Canada.

Jean-Guy Vaillancourt is chair of the Department of Sociology at the University of Montreal; his research focuses on the sociology of religion and the sociology of social movements. He has also, for many years, been involved in environmental protection initiatives in the province of Quebec and his many relevant publications include

Movement paix, énergie et environnement: essais d'ecosociologie (1982), *Environnement et développement: questions éthiques et probléme socio-politique* (1991), and *Roots of Peace: The Movement against Militarism in Canada* (1986).

Peter A. Victor, a Ph.D. economist, is an assistant deputy minister in the Department of Energy and Environment for the Province of Ontario and is formerly a partner in the environmental consulting firm Victor, Burrell. He is the author or coauthor of numerous monographs, books, and articles on environmental economics including *Economics of Pollution* (1972), *Alternative Policies for Pollution Abatement: Ontario Pulp and Paper Industry*, 3 vols. (1976), *Solar Heating and Employment in Canada* (1979), and *Economic, Ecological and Decision Theories* (1991).

Norman J. Vig is a professor of political science and codirector of the technology and policy studies program at Carleton College in Northfield, Minnesota. He was a member of the staff of U.S. senator Paul Wellstone (D.-Minn.) in 1991. He is the author of *Science and Technology in British Politics* (1968), and contributing coeditor of *Politics in Advanced Nations* (1974), *Environmental Policy in the 1980s: Reagan's New Agenda* (1984), *Political Economy in Western Democracies* (1985), *Technology and Politics* (1988), and *Environmental Policy in the 1990s* (2nd ed., 1994).

John Henry Wadland teaches bioregionalism and other environmentally-oriented courses in the Canadian studies program at Trent University in Peterborough, Ontario, Canada. He is the winner of university- and provincial-level teaching awards, a past editor of *The Journal of Canadian Studies* and author of *Ernest Thompson Seton: Man in Nature and the Progressive Era* (1978).

Rhodri H. Walters holds M.A. and D.Phil. degrees from Oxford University. He is a chief clerk in the Parliamentary Office and former clerk to the select committee on science and technology in London, England. He has a special interest in the U.S. Congress' Office of Technology Assessment and its possible applicability in a British context.

Karen J. Warren teaches in the philosophy department at Macalester College in St. Paul,

Minnesota. She is one of the most widely read and cited authors in the now well-established area of inquiry of ecological feminism and is most recently the coauthor of the book *Ecological Feminism* (1994).

Robert B. Weeden lives on an island in Ganges, British Columbia. He is the author of *Messages from Earth: Nature and the Human Prospect in Alaska* (1992).

Pamela Welbourn recently retired as a professor of botany and environmental science at the University of Toronto and is currently conjunct professor in the environmental and resource studies program at Trent University in Peterborough, Ontario. She also works as a consultant in environmental science, specializing in environmental assessment and environmental toxicology.

Geoff Wescott is an associate professor in environmental management in the School of Aquatic Science and Natural Resource Management at Deakin University in Clayton, Victoria, Australia. His major research emphasis centers on Australia's national parks and their protection.

Arthur H. Westing, a resident of Putney, Vermont, is the leading authority on the relationship between war and environmental protection. He is affiliated with the International Peace Research Institute in Oslo, Norway, and is the author of numerous books including *Environmental Warfare: A Technical, Legal, and Policy Appraisal* (1984), *Explosive Remnants of War: Mitigating the Environmental Effects* (1985), *Cultural Norms, War, and the Environment* (1988), and *Environmental Hazards of War: Releasing Dangerous Forces in an Industrialized World* (1990). His helpful suggestions greatly improved this volume.

Thomas H. Whillans is an associate professor in the environmental and resource studies program at Trent University in Peterborough, Ontario. His research and teaching focus on bioregionalism, wetlands management, the Great Lakes, and fisheries conservation and development in a Latin American context.

Gilbert F. White has recently served as interim director of the Natural Hazards Research and Applications Information Center at the University of Colorado in Boulder and has for many years been an editor of *Environment* magazine. He has conducted research on a many subjects including the environmental impacts associated with the Aswan Dam, and his many publications include *Water, Health and Society: Selected Papers, Drawers of Water: Domestic Water Use in East Africa* (1972), and *Assessment of Research on Natural Hazards* (1975).

Jeremy Wilson teaches in the Department of Political Science at the University of Victoria in Victoria, British Columbia. One of his major areas of research and publication is wilderness and forest policy in British Columbia and the Pacific Northwest.

Mark S. Winfield, a Ph.D. political scientist, is director of research for the Canadian Institute for Environmental Law and Policy in Toronto, Ontario. He also teaches courses in environmental policy at Innis College, University of Toronto.

Donald Worster is Hall Distinguished Professor in the Department of History, Hall Center for the Humanities, University of Kansas in Lawrence, Kansas. A leading environmental historian, he is a former president of the American Society for Environmental History. His books include *Nature's Economy: The Roots of Ecology* (1977), *Rivers of Empire: Water, Aridity, and the Growth of the American West* (1985), and *The Ends of the Earth: Perspectives on Modern Environmental History* (1988). He served as a member of the initial advisory group on topics and authors for this volume.

David A. Wright is an associate professor at the Center for Environmental and Estuarine Studies at the University of Maryland Chesapeake Biological Laboratory in Solomons, Maryland. His principal areas of research interest are comparative physiology, the effects of inorganic pollutants on marine and estuarine organisms, and biotoxicity assays.

Stephen Wright is an associate professor in the Department of Political Science at the Northern Arizona University in Flagstaff, Arizona. His research and teaching interests include both voting studies and African policy and politics and his publications in this latter area include the book *West African Regional Cooperation and Development*.

Bernd Würsig works in the Marine Mammal Research Program of Texas A & M University based in Galveston, Texas. He has numerous major publications regarding the protection of marine mammals, dolphins, porpoises, and whales in such publications as *Scientific American*. He has recently conducted new field research out of New Zealand.

Richard L. Wyman, a Ph.D. biologist, is executive director and research biologist at the Edmund Niles Huyck Preserve and Biological Research Station in Rensselaerville, New York. He is also the editor of *Global Climate Change and Life on Earth* (1991).

Lisa K. Younger was until recently the coordinator of the International Coastal Cleanup volunteer initiative throughout the United States and in other countries. She is also the coauthor of *Cleaning North America's Beaches: 1990 Beach Cleanup Results* (1991) and *1991 International Coastal Cleanup Results* (1992) published by the Center for Marine Conservation in Washington, D.C.

Sue Zielinski works in promotion and coordination of bicycle transportation for Planning and Development Department of the City of Toronto. She has a broad interest in transportation technologies and in "automobile culture" and has recently coauthored a book titled *Beyond the Car* (1994).

Anthony R. Zito is a doctoral candidate in the political science department and a program associate of the West European studies program at the University of Pittsburgh. He has completed extensive field work in Europe and is currently completing a Ph.D. thesis entitled "The Role of Technical Expertise and Institutional Innovation in EC Environmental Policy."

Abbey, Edward

Edward Abbey (1927–1989) is a novelist, essayist, polemicist, and activist whose contribution to the environmental movement is greater than most writers because of his status as a cult figure. Born in Pennsylvania, Abbey fell in love with the desert southwest while on a hitchhiking trip. From 1956 to 1971 he worked as a park ranger for the National Park Service while writing on the side. During the 1950s he worked at the largely undeveloped Arches National Monument in Utah. His experiences there as he watched both the unspoiled desert and the efforts of those trying to make it more "accessible" (i.e., in Abbey's view, more like the city and less like the desert), are described in his most famous nonfiction work, *Desert Solitaire* (1968). In addition to describing the beauty and mystery of the desert he sees as he sits on the step of the trailer he calls his home, Abbey also presents its roughness and sheer terror; he describes waiting for hours to fill his canteen at a spring in the mountains that gives only one drop at a time, while fighting off a swarm of gnats.

To Abbey, such painful experiences are important and valuable because they reflect a reality absent from the automated, mechanized, "labor-saving" (Abbey would say "life-destroying") unchallenging ways of the city. His writing is unflinching in its recognition of the harshness of nature when seen from a human perspective and of the inevitability of failure and death. For example, the resourceful hero of his novel *The Brave Cowboy* (1956), which was made into the film *Lonely Are the Brave* (1962), is run down with his own horse by a truck loaded with toilets. Nonetheless, it is precisely Abbey's insistence on fighting for a cause that may already be lost—the preservation of the wilderness—which endears him to his readers.

Jim Baird

Further Readings
Abbey, Edward. *Desert Solitaire*. 1968.
———. *The Monkey Wrench Gang*. 1975.
———. *Abbey's Road*. 1979.

See also EARTH FIRST!; KRUTCH, JOSEPH WOOD; RADICAL ENVIRONMENTALISM

Acid Precipitation: Aquatic Impacts

The term "acid rain" was first coined in 1872 by R.A. Smith, a chemist in England who identified effects such as corrosion of metal and health effects suffered by vegetation which he suggested had been caused by factory smoke. During the course of the twentieth century other scientists identified the phenomenon of acidified waters which had been affected by airborne pollutants. Effects of acidity on fish populations in Ontario were identified by Dr. Harold Harvey in 1966. The term is used today to refer to the deposition of two primary substances of concern—sulfur dioxide and nitrogen oxides. Acid precipitation includes both all forms of wet precipitation (rain, snow, and fog) and dry precipitation in the form of dust. The brief discussion which follows is limited to a description of these pollutants and their effects on ecological health of aquatic ecosystems.

"Acidity" is a measure of the hydrogen ion concentration in a solution. It is measured on a "pH" scale which increases logarithmically in ten-fold increases from 1, the most acidic, to 14, the most alkaline. The neutral balance point is 7. There are a number of natural factors, however, which influence the acidity of unpolluted precipitation and receiving waters, which means they are seldom found at precisely 7. "Pure" natural water has a pH in the order of 5.6, since atmospheric carbon dioxide enters the water and disassociates to carbonate and hydrogen. On a global basis, precipitation is usually slightly acidic, with a pH of 5.6 to 5. Waters are considered to be acidified if the pH is 5 or less. Central Ontario, an area which suffers from acid rain damage, has an average precipitation pH of 4.2.

Historically, the aquatic impacts of acid rain have been concentrated in the industrialized regions of Europe and North America. More recently, however, acidification levels in parts of China have approached those found in the United States and acid rain damage has been detected in Brazil, Venezuela, South Africa, and Australia.

Over 90 percent of annual sulfur and nitrogen emissions have anthropogenic sources, primarily the smelting and refining of metals which contain sulfur and the combustion of fossil fuels as an energy source. Sulfur emissions, associated primarily with the burning of oil or coal to generate electricity, tend to be clustered in a limited number of locations, while nitrogen emissions, a significant portion of which are associated with motor vehicles, tend to be more widely dispersed. These pollutants are then carried by air currents, in some cases for hundreds of miles. This long-range transport has historically hampered policy development, since effects felt in one country, such as Sweden, may have been caused by sources beyond the authority of that country's courts, for instance in England or Germany.

As noted, some waters may be slightly acidic in their natural state. By the same token, some waters, due to the presence of natural buffers in the soil and rock of the lake or riverbed, will be better able to withstand the effects of acid rain than others. Aquatic impacts, therefore, are influenced by factors associated with both the incoming pollution and the state of the receiving water. Such impacts may be permanent or transitory. Acidification may gradually increase over time, and may also take the form of episodic events, such as sudden increases caused by spring run-off of acidic snow. When waters first begin to be acidified the effects are neutralized by the bicarbonate present in vegetation, soils, and sediments. When that available bicarbonate has been exhausted, pH begins to drop below 5.

At low levels of acidity, effects are often first experienced by crustaceans, insects, algae, and zooplankton species. In many cases, such effects are then transmitted through the food chain. Effects on fish are first experienced as reproductive failures, leading to an aging of the fish stock. Reproduction of amphibians will also be affected. As pH drops below 5 in a given body of water, entire fish species may be killed. Birds are affected both by loss of fish and other organisms on which they rely as food and by release of toxic metals from sediments into the food chain. Humans may be exposed to indirect health threats from toxic metals, such as mercury, which have been released into drinking water as a result of acidification.

During the past twenty years a number of jurisdictions have experimented with methods of neutralizing acidified waters by artificially adding lime. This approach is problematic, since lime, which is not highly soluble, diffuses slowly and is therefore not able to quickly neutralize acidic waters. Repeated additions are needed if precipitation remains acidic. Liming also has adverse effects on the health of some plankton and aquatic plants and in any case runs counter to the generally accepted policy maxim of "anticipate and prevent."

Regulatory action to reduce acid rain emissions has to some extent mitigated the problem in North America and Europe. In those areas, accordingly, annual emissions will likely remain stable over the next half century and aquatic effects, while not eliminated, are not likely to significantly increase. In other parts of the world, however, such as newly industrializing regions of China and some nations of southeast Asia, regulatory action is still in its early stages and aquatic effects are likely to increase significantly in the years ahead.

Doug Macdonald and Irena Creed

Further Readings

Environment Canada. *The State of Canada's Environment.* 1991.

Paces, Tomas. "Sources of Acidification in Central Europe Estimated from Elemental Budgets in Small Basins." *Nature* 315 (May 2, 1985): 31–36.

Woodin, Sarah, and Ute Skiba. "Liming Fails the Acid Test." *New Scientist* (March 10, 1990): 50–54.

See also ACID PRECIPITATION: EUROPEAN EXPERIENCES; ACID PRECIPITATION: LEGISLATIVE INITIATIVES; ACID PRECIPITATION: TER-

Acid Precipitation: European Experiences

History of Understanding

Europeans today emit about 70 million tonnes of SO_2 and 45 million tonnes of NO_x into the atmosphere every year, about 40 percent of the global anthropogenic emissions. This number has, however, begun to decline significantly for the oxides of sulfur; those of nitrogen remain a major problem.

The scientific understanding of the effect of these gases began in the early nineteenth century. Scottish scientists noted changes in the pH value of rain water and observed damage to plants. Some time later the Norwegian poet Ibsen complained about black smoke drifting from the British Isles over to Norway.

Technological change, fuel substitution in several countries and industries, two major wars, and the political weakness of those most affected by air pollution in cities, meant that "acid rain" received little attention until the late 1960s. In Britain and France the air was becoming cleaner. The Italians and Southern Europeans cared little about pollution in general. Only in Germany was there a growing demand for purer and healthier air by both government and the public. Industry was less keen, fearing losses in competitive advantage, if too heavily regulated.

All this began to change when a Swedish scientist named Oden made serious allegations based on carefully kept records to the effect that acid gases from power stations and vehicles were damaging the Swedish environment. While these sources were by that time regulated in most countries on human health grounds, regulations were not established for the protection of lakes, forests, or natural ecosystems. The way of diminishing the local effects of emissions from stationary sources had been to increase the height of chimney stacks. This resulted, according to Oden, in acid gases as transboundary air pollution, thereby harming Swedish lakes and possibly trees. The polluters were most likely to be found to the south and west of Sweden. This accusation was made at the Stockholm Conference in 1972 and immediately taken up by European researchers paid to either prove or dis-

prove it. Research first emphasized the modeling and measurement of transboundary movements and deposition, then atmospheric chemistry and the understanding of specific damage effects.

Politically, the most important scientific input to the story, however, did not come until the late 1970s when the German scientist Ulrich claimed that acid rain was causing the approaching death of the German forest. Twenty years of research and atmospheric modeling followed and largely substantiated the Swedish allegation of transboundary pollution—the oxides of sulfur and nitrogen are precipitated far from their sources and tend to accumulate in soil. The resulting damage, however, is less readily proven, and is more varied and complex than had been assumed. Acid precipitation is a contributory factor to the stressed state of many European forests. The acidification of fresh waters harms plant and animal life.

Policy Responses

With the help of the OECD and later the UN Economic Commission for Europe, monitoring networks feeding into transport and deposition models were set up and now underpin intergovernmental regulatory efforts. These are based on the "critical load" approach, which combines national and international emissions and aims to control precipitation with reference to the most sensitive receiving ecosystems by calculation of emission reductions.

Policy responses reflect political power, energy policies, administrative capacities, and perceptions of the problem, all important variables in Europe that explain the long bargaining process begun in the late 1980s. Energy, environmental, forestry, and industrial interests engage in protracted negotiations and alliance formation, each having different perceptions of the problem, diverging interests, and unequal access to the resources of power, including "scientific evidence" and state protection.

The "victims" (Scandinavia) initiated these negotiations by demanding changes in Britain, Germany, Eastern Europe, and the former USSR. The responses by Germany, the former USSR, and Britain are particularly revealing and demonstrate the "systemic" nature of environmental policy—in the end there is no such policy, only a national policy mix which either favors emission abatement or further depletes natural resources.

The Soviets promised to reduce only transboundary fluxes, and for SO_2 complied by shifting coal-fired power stations to the east, leaving nuclear plants, including Chernobyl, in the west. In Germany senior bureaucrats had already decided that investing in the environment meant economic development through technological progress. They prepared precautionary legislation that would enable government to "force" investment in technological change by environmental standard setting, provided sufficient political support was available.

Germany was ready to change sides in the SO_2 debate in 1982, when successive Bonn governments (Social democrat and Conservative) felt sure enough of public and party political support to demand huge counter cyclical investment from its unwilling but wealthy polluters, the largely private and wealthy power generators, and a car industry that was already exporting catalytic cars to the United States. Germany did so with the help of Waldsterben, the alarmist perception of which it thoroughly supported until about 1985 (when it was replaced by the climate threat), as well as considerable subsidies to the car industry through side payments to the buyers of clean cars and unleaded petrol.

Germany has more than implemented its international obligations by adopting fluegas desulfurization and the catalytic reduction of NO_x for all its power stations, as well as the voluntary, but subsidized, introduction of autocatalysts since the mid-1980s. These obligations, it should be noted, represent no more than national preferences diluted in negotiations by others who were unable to follow its high cost/investment approach.

The nuclear French had few problems with power-station emissions, but became deeply involved during the 1980s in resisting (together with the British and the Italians) German demands to adopt autocatalysts and unleaded petrol for cars of all sizes, in order, it was claimed, to reduce NO_x emissions. But by the early 1990s Bonn had won this battle as well. In fact, over time the Germans won all "environmental" battles devoted to industrial emission control by already available state-of-art technologies. These were thereby disseminated throughout Europe with the help of the European Commission and Parliament.

The main loser was Britain, which resisted both sets of legislation until outvoted or outargued. It had to comply against its wishes and understanding of the issues, because of the more highly valued membership of the European Community (EC). To people in the British Isles, acid rain was a foreign problem with foreign solutions imposed on them. The technology-centered approach to pollution control was not only alien, but was also seen as a deliberate German attempt to further weaken the industrial base of Britain (which it probably did).

British scientists also failed to see that there was a serious problem. Lakes in Norway could be protected much more cheaply by liming. Catalytic cars were not only more expensive but also less energy efficient. Germans were imposing a big car solution just when British engineers were about to produce a small, clean "leanburn" engine. Hence the government in resisting international pressure acted in line with societal demands. In the end it opted for, and is still in the process of implementing, lower cost solutions for stationary sources, such as fuel switching to natural gas and the installation of low NO_x burners. It is, however, complying with EC regulations on vehicle emissions, albeit slowly and against its better judgment. In 1984, about 10% of the cars checked were equipped with autocatalysts. The ultimate goal remains unchanged: to comply to the extent that no additional costs to the state are involved. That state, like many others, is in a very precarious situation financially. International solutions do not always serve the weaker members of the community of states.

The main remaining "acid rain" generators in Europe are Spain, Poland, the former CSSR, and eastern Germany. The latter is now a German problem with deindustrialization and (West) German regulation already making "sulfurous" air a memory of the Communist past. Vehicles, most secondhand and pretty dirty, are another matter.

All these largely national battles were coordinated and influenced by two international sets of mechanisms:

1. The UN–ECE LRTAP (Long Range Transport of Atmospheric Pollutants) Convention of 1979 (in force since 1983) and its four protocols: two controlling SO_2 emissions (one in force since 1987; the second to be implemented into the next century); one controlling NO_x emissions (in force since 1988); and one controlling volatile organic compound (vol) emissions (in the process of implementation).

2. Numerous directives issued by the EC, especially the Large Combustion Direc-

tive of 1986 and the 1991 Consolidated Directive on vehicle emissions limits. Controls on small combustion plants and heavy-duty vehicles (trucks) are in the pipeline.

Each of these mechanisms is iterative and subject to revision. The SO_2 protocol is currently being renegotiated and requires all European governments to come to terms with the "scientific" approach adopted under the Geneva Convention. The ability of governments to adopt the "critical loads" approach is being tested and responses so far are mixed: the Dutch (who suffer from ammonia precipitation as well) like it and are tailoring their national policies towards it; the British government is divided, with energy interests strongly opposed because of contradictions with the "market-based" approach recently adopted; the Germans dislike it because it does not necessarily bring out the adoption of the best technology everywhere. The debate continues with transport increasing and presenting an enormous problem, not only for environmental reasons.

Sonja A. Boehmer-Christiansen

Further Readings

Johnston, Stanley, and Guy Corcelle. *The Enviromental Policy of the European Communities.* 1989.

See also ACID PRECIPITATION: AQUATIC IMPACTS; ACID PRECIPITATION: LEGISLATIVE INITIATIVES; ACID PRECIPITATION: TERRESTRIAL IMPACTS; LEGISLATION: EUROPEAN COMMUNITY; LONG RANGE TRANSPORT; WESTERN EUROPE: POLLUTION

Acid Precipitation: Legislative Initiatives

The U.S. Clean Air Act Amendments of 1977, the dominant U.S. legislation governing air quality in the United States for most of the period of bilateral, acid rain debate in North America (in force from 1977 to 1990), did not address, or even recognize, the existence of the acid rain phenomenon. More than that the Act exacerbated the acid rain problem. It was the last piece of major legislation in the United States to promulgate the false notion that the solution to pollution is dilution. The statute did this with its much discussed "tall stacks policy," namely a policy to encourage the construction of tall smokestacks so as to reduce the intensity of local sulfur dioxide and other pollutant emis-

sions. This protected local air near the ground from high levels of pollution, but simultaneously permitted the emission of large quantities of pollution at a higher altitude for dispersal far and wide, but particularly downwind. Downwind can be any direction at any point in time, but is predominantly in temperate North America to the east, northeast, or southeast.

Basic U.S. federal air quality policy, in practice the basic governance at state and local levels as well, was thus worsened and did not in any sense alleviate acid rain (or any other form of long-range transport of air pollutants). In Canada such matters are governed by legislative action at the provincial level and, given the nature of Canada's legal philosophy, involve the maintenance of objectives related to ambient air quality overall, rather than the U.S. system of emission standards at the source. One finds little relevant Canadian legislation in this period.

The bilateral U.S.-Canada Acid Rain Agreement of 1980 was one of the last actions of the Carter administration, but was not supported in spirit by either the Reagan or Bush administrations (albeit observed in the letter of the agreement through the holding of fruitless negotiating sessions in Ottawa and Washington). Although it is better known than any other legislation, it is not itself legislation and does not, therefore, fall under this heading.

During the 1980s there was legislation in both the United States and Canada governing acid rain research which became the basis of a joint bilateral acid rain research agreement (erroneously reported in some areas of the press as broader than it was, and thus a bilateral resolution of the problem, which it was not). Being limited to research, this legislation was consistent with the position of the U.S. administration that there was no certainty of acid rain's existence as a problem, but that more research was needed. Also in this period a number of state legislatures in the United States passed nonbinding state resolutions of a bilateral (i.e., state-provincial) nature. During this period Canada became, with a number of European nations, a member of the "30 Percent Club," a group of downwind complainant nations pledging to reduce their SO_2 emissions (SO_2 being a prime precursor of acid rain) by 30 percent by 1993 (based on 1980 emission levels).

Most of the acid rain legislation has focused almost exclusively on control of sulfur dioxide (SO_2) emissions, only one of the two principal precursors of acid rain. There is a practical political reason: SO_2 involves a small number of very large sources of pollutants, namely coal and oil-fired power plants, metal smelters, and a very few others, whereas the other principal precursor, oxides of nitrogen (NO_x), involves the opposite circumstance—a very large number of very small sources, namely motor vehicles and virtually every industrial process involving high temperature combustion. Hence, SO_2 control, which provides opportunities to name a culprit, has been called a "regulator's dream," while NO_x control, which threatens politically unacceptable changes in lifestyle and points an accusing finger at most of the population vis-à-vis its lifestyle, has been called a "regulator's nightmare." Lawmakers who are also politicians invariably see opportunity in SO_2 control and only political danger in any effort toward NO_x control.

There were numerous attempts in the U.S. Congress starting about 1981 to pass new clean air legislation which would address acid rain, among other things. All such efforts failed throughout the 1980s. It was not until the Clean Air Act of 1990 became law that acid rain was finally formally addressed and the first emission limits and reductions came into legal being, albeit not to take effect until later into the 1990s. The levels of emission reductions set in this statute are just barely within consistent Canadian demands for such reduction in transborder pollution fluxes, leaving no extra leeway. The significance of this legislation is probably more symbolic than real, in its recognition for the first time in the United States that a problem exists and that emissions reduction is in fact justified. It is also the first federal clean air act in thirteen years, with many failed attempts. It remains to be seen, however, especially in light of a declining U.S. economy, if the reductions are actually made or if the legislation is amended before that time to avoid reductions (or increase them, as the case may be).

It is now likely that the time for much specific acid rain legislation has now passed, for with the passing of the 1980s public attention began to rapidly change to matters of climate warming, holes in the ozone layer, and the ability of the human species to upset the balance of the earth. In brief, attention turned to matters of global change, of which acid rain and long-range transport of air pollutants are only a part. Given that primary causes of both acid rain and global change are involved in fossil fuel burning, energy use in a high energy society, and in questions on the future of the planetary ecosys-

tem, it is likely that future legislative efforts to address acid rain in any of the industrial emitting countries, individually or collectively, will likely be subsumed in these broader generic debates on energy, society, atmospheric chemistry, and the limits of the planetary ecosystem. Acid rain is not any longer as likely to stand apart from such broader questions.

John E. Carroll

Further Readings

Carroll, John E. *Acid Rain: An Issue in Canadian-American Relations*. 1982.

——. "Transboundary Air Quality Relations: The Canada-United States Experience." In *University of Maine Policy Papers on U.S.-Canadian Relations*. Orono, ME: University of Maine. 1990.

——. *International Environmental Diplomacy: The Management and Resolution of Transfrontier Environmental Problems*. 1990.

See also ACID PRECIPITATION: AQUATIC IMPACTS; ACID PRECIPITATION: TERRESTRIAL IMPACTS; AIR POLLUTION: REGULATION (U.S.); REAGAN, RONALD

Acid Precipitation: Terrestrial Impacts

While the damaging effects of acidic deposition on sensitive lakes systems appears to be widespread and not in dispute, the effects on terrestrial systems are less clear cut. This may be partly because in the areas of highly acidic deposition many of the soils are already acidic and support a relatively acid tolerant flora. These soils, derived from the Precambrian Shield in North America and the equivalent granitic rocks in Scandinavia, have been formed since the last glaciation 10,000–12,000 years ago. These soils are shallow podzols with low nutrient status. They are covered by predominantly boreal evergreen forest dominated by spruce, pine, and fir. The climate is cold and decomposition processes are slow. The coniferous needles yield an acidic humus, the pHs of the soils vary from 3.5 to 5.0, and the soils are low in calcium.

When such forests and soils are subject to acidic deposition the downward leaching of nutrients is accelerated, with further reductions in calcium and magnesium. The surface layers may show increased concentrations of the phytotoxic element aluminum. Even quite small decreases in pH below 4.5 can cause substantial increases in aluminum concentration. In a large number of experiments, aluminum toxicity to root systems has been shown to be a major consequence of surface soil acidification. In Swedish and German studies where soils had been chemically analyzed in the past and where it was possible to locate the exact sites from which the soils were obtained, comparisons showed a striking increase in acidity over the past 25 to 35 years, coinciding with the major spread of regional acidic deposition. The depth to which soils had acidified in southern Sweden was greater than one meter.

The chemistry of the rainwater is altered upon contact with leaf surfaces and bark. Acidic rain accelerates the leaching from the leaves of such essential nutrients as calcium, magnesium, and potassium, and it may also remove some nitrogen. The waterproof waxy cuticle of a number of plant species has been shown to be eroded by acid rain. This leaching and cuticular erosion causes depletion of nutrients especially in the upper canopy. Trees need to take up more of these elements from the soils to maintain their nutrient status. The erosion of the cuticle can cause excessive water loss. Both of these factors could lead to deterioration in the health of the forest.

It has been found that the runoff from the trunks of European beech trees in some German forests subjected to acidic deposition is as low as pH 2.8. The major determining factor in this is both wet and dry sulfate deposition together with nitrate. In forests near Freiburg it has been shown that over the past twenty years an acid-tolerant ground flora has developed around the trunks of these beech trees. In simulated acid rain experiments in Norway where acid rain was sprayed onto the forest floor over a number of years, substantial changes in the ground flora occurred. Similarly in experiments in the Canadian boreal forest it was shown that simulated acid rain of pH 3.5 or less caused damaging effects to the dominant feathermosses and lichens of the ground flora. It was also shown that the damaging effects were greatest when sulfate was the predominant acidic radical whereas nitrate inputs often enhanced growth due to a fertilizer effect.

Forest Decline

Throughout the 1980s forests in central Europe and in parts of eastern North America in areas where acidic deposition was occurring were found to be increasingly unhealthy. The general phenomenon was called forest decline. It oc-

curred particularly on shallow, nutritionally poor soils and began with reports of one or two species showing thinning of the crown due to loss of leaves, and dieback from the top of the tree downward. Norway spruce and European beech were particularly affected in Europe, while in North America red spruce and sugar maple showed the greatest damage. Maximum damage was noted at higher elevations where acidic fogs occurred in the mountains. These areas were not only subject to acidic deposition but often also to elevated levels of photochemical oxidants. The areas of damage spread rapidly from 1983 to 1989. Many people ascribed it to acid rain but it has been a subject of much scientific debate. Extreme climatic events and such local but severe stresses as major insect attacks are also believed to be factors in this decline. Some have argued that a series of hot summers with some severe droughts were triggers in initiating the decline phenomenon. Others have suggested that mild winters combined with thin snow cover in the forests have allowed root systems to be damaged by the occasional severe frost penetrating into the ground. Interestingly there are signs that the situation is improving both in Europe and in North America. The reduction in sulfur emissions in the regional air masses over the past few years correlates with the recovery.

Agriculture

The effects of acid rain on crops through changes in soil chemistry have generally been regarded as insignificant. This is because the farmer maintains the soils within a pH range suitable for good crop growth. When surface soils are acidified either by acid deposition or by super phosphate fertilizer additions then the farmer responds by liming the soil. It was therefore assumed by many that there would be no effects on crops by acidic deposition. However, detailed studies on crops in the United States have shown that a number of crops are adversely affected by the ambient acidic rain falling in the 1980s due to direct effects on foliage. Estimated damage of many millions of dollars for soy bean, white bean, and salad crops was suggested. It was also shown that acidic deposition can interfere with pollination and fertilization thereby affecting seed yield.

Bird Populations

In a number of recent studies the deleterious effect on the breeding success of insect-eating birds has been demonstrated in forests affected by acidic deposition. The most dramatic examples are reported from the Netherlands where substantial reductions over a five- to ten-year period were reported for some resident species. This was accompanied by egg shell thinning which was attributed to interference with calcium metabolism. It was suggested that acidic deposition, especially driven by very high nitrogen inputs in the Netherlands, had caused a depletion of soil calcium causing a reduced calcium together with increased aluminum content in the foliage. This change in foliar nutritional quality was believed to cause a change in the nutritional status of the insects on which the birds fed. A recent study in Canada has shown a food chain effect in areas of sugar maple decline but without the reduction in nesting success of the insect eating birds. This seemed to be partly because the birds changed their position of feeding in the foliage concentrating more in the lower canopy at the decline site.

We do know that there has been a substantial decline in migrant song bird populations in North America and in Europe. While many causes are being examined, it remains a possibility that regional acidic deposition is a factor.

Thomas C. Hutchinson

Further Readings

Lynch-Stewart, P., E.B. Wilken, and G. Ironside. *Acid Deposition on Prime Resource Lands in Eastern Canada.* Environment Canada, Lands Directorate, 1987.

Krause, G.H.M., et al. "Forest Decline in Europe: Development and Possible Causes." *Water, Air, and Soil Pollution* 31 (1986): 647–68.

Environment Canada. *The State of Canada's Environment.* 1991.

See also ACID PRECIPITATION: AQUATIC IMPACTS; ACID PRECIPITATION: EUROPEAN EXPERIENCES; ACID PRECIPITATION: LEGISLATIVE INITIATIVES; ALUMINUM; BLACK FOREST; LEACHING

Adams, Ansel

Ansel Adams (1902–1984) is one of a small number of photographers whose name, work, and reputation are known to the general public. Although Adams originally trained to become a musician, a visit to the Yosemite Valley and his dissatisfaction with the pictures he took of that landscape prompted him to redirect his efforts toward photography. Soon he found that he was not only interested in developing his own skills, but advancing theories of photography itself and working toward that field's acceptance as an art. With several others he formed "f 64," a group named after the smallest camera aperture, which gives the most clarity of image and depth of field of focus. Adams and his friends attempted to move photography away from imitation of the effects of painting toward the appreciation of the photographic image itself as artistically valuable. Among his other contributions is the widely used zone system of exposure.

Adams was born in San Francisco and lived most of his life in California in either Yosemite or on the coast at Carmel. His favorite subjects include Yosemite Valley, Point Lobos and the Big Sur coast, Lone Pine peak in the eastern Sierras, and the deserts of the Southwest. Although Adams did work in color, his greatest achievements are his black-and-white images, which are so detailed, textured, and rich in gradation from stark white to deepest black that one remembers them as if they were color photographs.

Although Adams did much to advance the cause of conservation, including membership on the board of directors of the Sierra Club from 1934 to 1971, his most outstanding contribution to environmental awareness remains the stunning photographs through which he made others aware of the beauty, power, and richness he found in nature.

Jim Baird

Further Readings

Adams, Ansel (with Nancy Newhall). *This is the American Earth.* 1960.

———. *Ansel Adams: Images 1923–1974.* 1974.

———. *Yosemite and the Range of Light.* 1980.

See also SIERRA CLUB

Africa: Environmental Problems

Africa's environmental problems have often been perceived quite differently by Western and African observers, but are now being widely recognized as extremely serious. Difficulty in producing policies to ameliorate the situation is compounded by (1) the chronic economic weakness of the continent, (2) the attempt to promote "development" often with little regard for the environment, and (3) by disinterest within the developed world for Africa's plight. Desertification, deforestation, pollution, and wildlife depletion are among the serious problems facing African policy-makers, with rapid population growth and increasing urbanization being factors that exacerbate the problems just mentioned.

Africa is not densely populated, but it has the fastest growing population of any continent. Population growth is presently 3.1 percent a year, and the World Bank predicts that the population of Sub-Saharan Africa alone will double from 672 million in the year 2000 to 1.3 billion in 2025. Kenya's population is expected to quadruple between 1980–2025, whereas Nigeria's population will triple during the same period.

Compounding this problem of rapid growth is the upward trend in urbanization. Africa is the least urbanized continent, with 34 percent of the population currently living in cities. However, this figure is double that of 1965, and by 2025 it is anticipated that 54 percent of the population will live in cities. The strain on resources is further exacerbated by the trend of population living in just one or two cities within any given country. For example, the population in Botswana's capital, Gaborone, has increased by 124 percent during the last decade. This rapid urbanization across Africa has placed tremendous strain upon infrastructure, has led to the mushrooming of shanty towns without adequate sanitation and thereby water pollution, and has contributed as well to average levels of unemployment or underemployment in African cities of 40 percent.

Additional features of the population crisis are the average fertility rate across the continent of six children per female; the youthful character of the population itself, with 45 percent under the age of fifteen years; half of the world's reported AIDS cases; and the lowest average life expectancy rates of forty-nine years (male) and fifty-two years (female) anywhere in the world. Attempts in the past to control population growth have been largely unsuccessful, hampered by cultural and political resistance and by the widespread contrary belief that the continent was underpopulated. To date, only one-third of African states have officially adopted population policies. As Africa comprises almost one-quarter of the world's land-mass and yet has only 12 percent of its population, there are some grounds to support this argument. However, economic conditions se-

verely limit the carrying capacity of the continent as regards humans, at least at this time.

A combination of factors, including localized population density pressure, the migration of many able rural workers to the cities, overcultivation, overgrazing, and often basic mismanagement, has led to increased desertification, explained here in terms of the conversion of productive land into wasteland. It is estimated that some 36,000 square kilometers are lost to desert every year in Africa. The relatively poor quality of the soil and the paucity of effective fertilizers and irrigation compound difficulties, forcing people increasingly to farm marginal lands.

During colonization earlier this century, the best arable land was converted to cash crop production, an economic sector on which many countries remain highly dependent for export earnings. Consequently, cash crops command high priority from both governments and foreign donors, whereas subsistence farming has been neglected and relegated to marginal areas. The contrast is marked. During the severe Sahelian drought of 1974–1975, which displaced 10 million farmers, record harvests of the cash crops cotton and groundnuts were produced. Similarly, during the Ethiopian famine of 1985, record coffee exports were recorded.

According to the United Nations (UN), food production per person has been falling at the rate of 1 percent annually since the early 1970s, brought about by both declining agricultural yields and rapidly rising population. Pressures to move onto more marginal farming land and to overcultivate existing poor land without allowing adequate fallow periods will increase the pace of desertification. The United Nations Environment Programme (UNEP), headquartered in Nairobi, currently believes that an area twice the size of India is under threat of desertification in Africa.

The pattern of shifting and expanding agriculture has had a devastating impact on Africa's forests, accounting for 70 percent of total deforestation according to UNEP figures. Some countries, such as Gabon and Zaire, have important timber export industries, which partially account for deforestation, but more significant than timber is deforestation caused by the demand for fuel. Wood provides 90 percent of Africa's energy requirements, and deforestation as a result of tree-cutting for fuel is a serious problem, especially around urban areas.

The UN estimates that a very high percentage of total forest has been lost in most states.

Some examples include Côte d'Ivoire with 78 percent of its forest lost, Ethiopia with 86 percent, the Gambia 91 percent, Liberia 87 percent, and Uganda 79 percent. In fact, two-thirds of total forest area has been lost in at least twenty-three African states. It is estimated that Africa is losing 2.7 million hectares of forest every year. Replanting of trees, though beneficial where carried out, is only at about 10 percent the rate at which the forest is being cleared. During the 1980s alone, 7 percent of Africa's total forest was lost.

Other environmental issues interrelated with desertification and deforestation are overgrazing, drought, and soil erosion. Marginal land has suffered under the impact of overgrazing by cattle, as since 1950 the number of livestock in Africa has estimated to have doubled to 590 million head. Drought by itself is not an insuperable problem, but in the absence of correct land management and effective irrigation it has from time to time caused severe emergencies in virtually all parts of the continent. Approximately 65 percent of Africa is desert or dryland, so naturally prone to dry spells. But over the last thirty years rainfall in the Sahelian region has been down 25 percent from the previous thirty-year period, a trend common in other parts of the continent. Drought has also forced lifestyle changes on many nomadic populations, often converting them into (unsuccessful) sedentary farmers.

Access to safe water supplies, influenced by both drought and infrastructural problems, is also a serious environmental problem. More than one-third of Africa's population receives water supplies below that needed for life support. Access to safe water is available to less than 20 percent of the population in the Central African Republic, Côte d'Ivoire, Ethiopia, and Uganda, and to less than half of the population in another nineteen countries.

When rainfall does occur, it often is in the form of violent storms that wash away valuable topsoil laid bare by the clearing of forest or overcultivation of land. The UN Food and Agriculture Organization (FAO) calculated that soil erosion alone could reduce agricultural production in Africa by 25 percent in the period 1975–2000. Ethiopia, already devastated by severe environmental difficulties, is estimated to lose 1 billion tons of topsoil every year.

Population pressures and poverty have also had a significant impact upon the continent's wildlife and habitat. Expanding population has decreased original wildlife habitat by 65 percent across the continent. Poaching, particularly of elephant and rhinoceros, has decimated herds. In Kenya, for example, the elephant population dropped from 165,000 to 16,000 between 1970 and 1990. No African country to date has developed comprehensive environmental legislation, and sometimes only grudgingly are environmental concerns taken into account for fear of hindering economic development. Conventional wisdom in separating wildlife from populations has proved disastrous, and now fresh attempts are being made to provide local farmers with incentives to protect wildlife. Attempts to link debt equity owed to the West with environmental conservation are just beginning in the continent, but hold out some promise for the future protection of wildlife and biodiverse habitats.

The relative weakness of African states vis-à-vis Western multinational corporations has served to diminish protection against pollution. Documentation is meager, but, where available, such as in Nigeria's oil fields, indicates that scant regard is given to the environment. Toxic dumping by Western corporations without adequate safeguards was widespread in many African countries during the 1980s, but the Bamako Declaration of 1991 attempts to prevent such dumping, even though its level of success is uncertain.

Other political and economic factors limit the likelihood of improving the protection of the African environment in the near future. The combined debt for the continent stands at over $250 billion, with debt repayments averaging more than one-third of export earnings across the continent, and in some countries much higher. This total debt figure pales in comparison with that of Latin America, but that reality does not diminish the fact that debt forms a high percentage of individual African countries' and the continent's GNP. Lack of financial resources severely hampers greater environmental protection, and structural adjustment programs (SAPs) imposed by the International Monetary Fund (IMF) on more than thirty African states have done little to lessen these environmental problems and, some would argue, have possibly exacerbated them. Faulty aid programs, combined with the common inability of donors to tailor programs to suit local conditions, have also detracted from protection of the environment.

Political conditions of minimal democracy and widespread kleptocratic rule gravitate against protection for the environment. As well, the prevalence of civil war in a number of countries, especially in the Horn of Africa, provides a distortion of economic life, driving farmers from their land and so endangering further the fragile agricultural situation. Food production in Somalia and southern Sudan, for example, has been cut dramatically because of the ongoing internal wars. The UN High Commission for Refugees estimates that there are 5 million refugees in Africa, often fleeing both war and hostile environmental conditions. Differing perceptions held by African and Western policymakers on what to do with these environmental refugees, combined with critical shortages of funding, make this another tragic story in Africa.

Initiatives toward solving Africa's environmental crises are plentiful and often contradictory, but doubts remain about the ability and willingness of African leaders to pursue them. The key concept emerging in the 1990s is "sustainable development," with its premise that economic growth is to be pursued only in a manner that is socially, economically, and environmentally viable in the long term. This approach was also promoted extensively at the 1992 UN Conference on Environment and Development (UNCED) in Rio de Janeiro.

Besides the widely held view that crude economic growth is not synonymous with development, there has been little definitive explanation of how sustainable development can be achieved. Differences of opinion (and some resistance) exist among international agencies such as the UN, the World Bank, and the IMF, as well as among individual African governments. Self-reliance has been touted as a worthwhile strategy to undertake, thereby diminishing Western involvement in Africa, but such a program is also considered difficult to implement. Nevertheless, given the fact that financial flows into Africa fell by 14 percent in 1991 and by 43 percent in 1992, increasing self-reliance may become unavoidable.

A serious debate on Africa's economic and environmental future is now underway, but the obstacles hindering solutions should not be underestimated. Besides those listed already, other specific strategies are being discussed. These include a greater participatory role for farmers, with improved pricing and market structures; extending land rights and title to farmers, especially to women farmers, in order to encourage better conservation of the land; improved biotechnical research, paying attention to specific needs and conditions in individual countries; greater governmental efforts to lure people away from overcrowded cities and back into the rural areas; stronger regional cooperation, such as through the Economic Community of West African States (ECOWAS) and the Southern African Development Community (SADC), in promoting economic prosperity and cooperative environmental protection; and the impetus to improve prospects for local democracy and accountability.

The increasing poverty of Africa's rapidly expanding population, the political instability found in many of its states, and the marginalization of the continent in global political and economic affairs, all mean that Africa's environmental problems are likely to worsen in the short-term before they improve.

Stephen Wright

Further Readings

James, Valentine Udoh. *Africa's Ecology: Sustaining the Biological and Environmental Diversity of a Continent.* 1993.

Timberlake, Lloyd. *Africa in Crisis: The Causes, the Cures of Environmental Bankruptcy.* 1986.

See also Aswan High Dam; Debt-for-Nature Swaps; Desertification; Elephants: Conservation and Habitat; Environmental Movement: Less-Affluent Nations; Environmental Protection in Wartime; Environmental Refugees; Forestry, History of; Hydroelectricity; Rhinoceros: Conservation and Habitat; Rio Conference (1992); Sustainable Development; Toxic Wastes in International Trade, United Nations Environment Programme; World Bank

Agenda 21

See Rio Conference (1992)

Agent Orange

See Herbicides

Agricultural Land Protection

Agricultural land protection or the retaining of land for agricultural use is not universally perceived to be an environmental problem. Indeed, in many developing nations, other lands—usually forest and wildlands—are actually being converted for use as agricultural land, often at great environmental and social cost. Throughout much of the world the demand for land reform, widespread hunger and malnutrition, and the need to raise rural incomes have led to policies and programs that increase the amount of land devoted to range and cultivation. This is often accomplished through the conversion of rainforests, the drainage of wetlands and savannahs, the destruction of significant wildlife habitats, the loss of home territories of indigenous peoples, and the movement of marginal lands into farming uses. The loss of agricultural land due mainly to urbanization, the erosion of agriculture's economic viability, and similar pressures, tends to be a significant problem primarily in developed and "mature" market economies.

The actual dimensions and significance of agricultural land loss are matters of substantial debate. In the United States, for example, estimates of the decline in the amount of farmlands made by the National Agricultural Lands Study in 1980 have been the subject of intense controversy. The upper hand in the debate now belongs to those who think that the diminution of the farmland base nationally is not a substantial problem. Likewise in Canada, where there has been much discussion of the problem, there is little pressure at the national level to seek a halt in the process of farmland loss. This lack of pressure and concern may be due, in no small part, to the fact that in both nations land-use policy tends to be a local responsibility such that the individual states and provinces have particular obligations to define, monitor, evaluate, and develop land policy. Another justification that is just as likely, though, in these and other nations is the tendency to agglomerate statistics and provide a national overview of the issue, which masks genuinely serious regional and local problems and concerns.

Though largely unintentional, such national statistical assessments often treat pieces of land as largely interchangeable production factors. The loss of acreage in one place can be offset by gains in other areas. Such an approach fails to consider idiosyncratic land characteristics—such as soil quality, microclimatic conditions, and hydrology—and still other social and economic factors—such as available agribusiness support services—which may contribute to production versatility or uniqueness. Further, proponents of free trade argue that self-sufficiency in food production is becoming increasingly irrelevant thus making it less and less important to view agricultural land as a strategic resource worthy of protection. Then, too, there has been the assumption that further advances in agricultural technology, which have played a major role in the fantastic increases in productivity over the past half century or so, will continue to be routine. Technological innovation has made it possible to produce even more from a smaller land base. But such assumptions are coming under closer scrutiny as structural and other uncertainties in the agricultural system have begun to emerge. Still, declines in farm incomes and the on-farm population, and huge commodity surpluses, have led a number of countries to implement land set-aside policies—such as the Cropland Reserve Program in the United States and the European Community's 1988 Regulation No. 1094—to actually reduce the amount of land in active production.

An array of programs and techniques have evolved to address the problems of farmland loss. Some of these are land-focused approaches, while others tend to reflect a strong economic orientation. Perhaps the single most popular retention program, at least in the United States, is tax policy manipulation. Various forms of differential or preferential taxation schemes have been developed to lessen the overall impact of property taxation on farmers. Here the emphasis lies in reducing tax burdens with the assumption that the savings will help farmers stay in active production. Property tax burdens in the United States are especially serious because funding for most local and county services, including schooling, is derived from land taxes. Also under the principle of "highest and best use," farmlands are frequently valuated for taxation purposes not on their actual "use value" in agriculture, but rather for a "market value," which reflects what the land could yield in the way of taxes if it were used for a more intensive and urban land use. Further, agricultural yields seldom bear any relationship to tax liability and, especially in those areas and regions under development pressure from urbanization and suburbanization, rarely generate enough income to offset increasing taxation rates.

Tax programs for farmland retention seek to treat farmland as a preferred land use by requiring valuation on the basis of "use value." In return for such treatment states and localities seek to receive from farmers contracts or agreements to keep their lands in active agricultural use for a set period of time. Rollbacks of tax liabilities and penalties may be applied to farmers if they break the agreement within the specific contract period. Considerable empirical evidence suggests that in the urban/rural fringe—among the most contested lands in mature market economies—such programs rarely offset the immense profits farmers can derive from land transfer and conversion, even when penalties are levied. This has much to do with the dynamics of active land markets relative to farming incomes. Conversely, in those areas where farming is strong and is a major factor in the regional economy, these programs tend to deflect tax burdens onto nonfarming members of the community, even though tax rates for farmers may be relatively low and are not perceived as a threat to land retention. Other programs, such as the State of Vermont's Capital Gains Taxation Program, have emerged to take much of the profit out of land speculation brought about by the rapid turnover of property.

In terms of land policy many jurisdictions have used agricultural zoning to preserve lands in farming uses. But because local planning and zoning programs are impermanent and susceptible to easy amendment and change, this approach has rarely been effective, except in those areas where the local political will is overwhelmingly in favor of preservation and more or less permanent zoning is possible.

The situation in the United States is further complicated by the "taking clause" of the U.S. Constitution, which requires compensation to owners when land is regulated in such a way as to diminish its value for development purposes. The "taking clause" principle is still evolving and, over the years, political jurisdictions have gained greater flexibility in implementing planning strategies which, on the one hand, protect the public's interest in land and environmental protection while limiting, on the other hand, the notion of compensation. Still, this legal principle has imposed significant limitations on the U.S. planning system, at least relative to those in other nations. As a consequence farmland retention programs have changed direction: new programs seek to remove the right to develop land from all other landholder rights by either purchasing or transferring "development rights" from landowners. By so doing society gains the permanent protection of agricultural assets while property owners receive their necessary compensation and still are able to remain in agriculture. Further, although farmland owners retain the right to sell their farms to other would-be farmers, they may not sell for the

purpose of developing since the development potential of the land has been retired.

Many states have created funding mechanisms that endow programs to annually purchase farmland development rights and then "retire" those rights from the market. But the sheer cost to the public treasury of the purchase of development rights has militated against the widespread implementation of this method of land conservation. A smaller number of jurisdictions, such as New Jersey and Maryland, have experimented with the "transfer of development rights" technique, wherein farmers who lose the right to develop land in one place gain rights in other areas through an increase in building density allowances. Because this is a far more complicated process, one which is dependent upon a certain scale of development pressure to provide the element of compensation to owners, its potential to be an effective tool is still largely unrealized.

Finally, the vast majority of states, and an increasing number of Canadian provinces, have implemented "right-to-farm" programs that attempt to protect farm operations in those areas undergoing rapid and intense land-use change. These programs seek to establish a "first in time, first in right" principle that protects farmers from lawsuits and local ordinances, which would seek to enjoin them from farming or utilizing management practices that might be opposed by nonfarming majorities within the local community. Efforts to nullify such programs through court cases have proven to be unsuccessful, thus upholding the constitutionality and legitimacy of right-to-farm laws.

As central as land-use controls may be to any effort to preserve farmland, these interventions will likely fail in the long run unless agriculture continues to be an economically viable activity. Put simply, farmland without farmers makes little sense. A growing number of local and national governments, then, are seeking ways to enhance the inherent viability of farming. Leadership in this area has been provided by the Canadian government through its supply management system which keeps prices that farmers receive relatively high by limiting production, and the European Community's various structural programs, such as the Community Support Frameworks and the overall Common Agricultural Policy. While critics have charged that such policy interventions have had undesirable consequences—high food prices for consumers, the maintenance of inherently uneconomical farming units, strict barriers to imported foodstuffs, and very high deficits—the goals of such programs have been to keep people in rural areas and farms in production.

In the United States, government has failed to meld land-use policy with agricultural policy in such ways that farmers, especially family farmers, can make an adequate living without having to further capitalize their land assets and put farmlands at risk of conversion. But here, too, numerous jurisdictions are beginning to seek ways to make agriculture more entrepreneurial and competitive. Iowa, North Dakota, Wisconsin, and several other states are leading the way in this important effort.

Some of the most innovative programs to preserve farmlands have focused less on the agricultural side of the equation and more on the urban side. The impetus of these programs is to limit the spread of urbanization into rural areas in ways that maintain the integrity of agriculture, enough "critical mass" of farms to preserve vital agribusiness services, and the appropriate rural-scale land markets. Within the United States Oregon has led the way with land-use controls that seek to define and then limit its urban boundaries, while in Canada the provinces of British Columbia and Quebec have pioneered in attempting to limit urbanization pressures. Denmark has successfully limited urban sprawl through its Agricultural Holdings Act, as has Italy through its limitations on the ability of regions to convert lands into urban uses. France's national urban policy and rural settlement program, which include the "SAFERS" (Societes pour l'amenagement foncier et l'establissement rural), have also been effective in reducing urbanization pressures, as have been the rules adopted in the Netherlands, which are binding upon all land owners and all levels of government.

While numerous laws and programs have been established to retain and protect farmlands, and more have yet to be promulgated, the loss of agricultural land remains a substantial problem. The unevenness of program implementation and the very nature of the issues involved are themselves at fault. Agricultural land conversion tends to be highly incremental, with one farm going out of production here and then another there. As a consequence, the cumulative impact of agricultural land loss is too rarely appreciated until much has already been lost. Further, political pressure for stricter laws and more innovative programs to secure a strong farming sector have yet to materialize in ways

that would bring about truly effective policy initiatives, at least in the North American context. Perhaps this will remain the case so long as the public fails to see the direct and intimate linkages among agricultural land loss, the deterioration in overall environmental quality, and rural community stability.

Mark B. Lapping

Further Readings

Flora, C., et al. *Rural Communities: Legacy and Change*. 1992.

Lapping, Mark B., and I. Szedlmayer. "On the Threshold of the 90s: Issues in U.S. Rural Planning and Development." In *Progress in Rural Policy & Planning*. Ed. A. Gilg. 1991.

———, T. Daniels, and J. Keller. *Rural Planning and Development*. 1989.

See also AGRICULTURE: ENVIRONMENTAL IMPACTS; LAND USE PLANNING

Agriculture: Environmental Impacts

Agriculture has had a profound impact on the natural environment. Invented approximately 9,000 to 10,000 years ago, agriculture can be defined as a complex set of methods for directing the growth of plants and animals toward human purposes. In ecological terms, agriculture is the prime method by which people capture the products of photosynthesis as food, fiber, medicines, building materials, animal feed, fuels, and many industrial inputs. Agriculture's impacts are both direct and indirect.

Agriculture, including arable and pasture land, occupies about 4.8 billion hectares (37 percent) of the total 13.1 billion hectares of land on the earth. Destruction of wildlife habitat is, therefore, the most direct impact of agriculture. Farms and ranches destroy natural ecosystems in favor of the plants and animals desired by people. Forests have been cleared, grasslands plowed under, and wetlands drained or filled for agriculture. For example, losses of the American bison and the passenger pigeon from North America during the nineteenth century were partly the result of the spread of agriculture.

Soil degradation is another direct impact. Crop production, grazing, and deforestation since 1945 degraded about 17 percent of the earth's vegetated land. Over 1.2 billion hectares—an area about equivalent to India and China together—suffer from moderate to extreme degradation. Soil erosion threatens the future viability of agriculture. It also damages rivers, reservoirs, and wetlands as soil is moved and deposited elsewhere by wind and water.

Much agriculture is in arid and semiarid environments. In order to prosper, people divert large amounts of water from rivers, lakes, and underground aquifers. Many rivers have been changed into a series of lakes by dams designed partially to provide irrigation for agriculture. India, for example, has 1,137 dams in excess of fifteen meters high, while the United States has 5,459 and China has 18,820. A total of 8 percent of the world's annual renewable freshwater supply is used by people each year, and 69 percent of this is for agriculture.

Farmers use many inputs, and these materials often cause serious environmental impacts. Fertilizers—mostly nitrogen, phosphorus, and potassium—are used at an average global rate of ninety-seven kilograms per hectare of cropland (1987–1989). These chemicals, while not highly toxic, can cause eutrophication when they run off or leach from soils. Nitrate nitrogen, when present in drinking water, can cause blood diseases, including methaemoglobinaemia, and some are concerned that it may be associated with cancer. Pesticides, poisons deliberately used in agriculture, can cause extensive problems for human health and wildlife. Pesticides are covered elsewhere in this volume in more detail.

Agriculture also produces serious waste products. Manure is a byproduct of animal husbandry. A farm of forty hectares with fifty cows and a pig population based on fifty sows can produce manure equivalent to a town of 1,000 people. Ammonia, hydrogen sulfide, and other gases are given off, and plant nutrients, especially nitrogen, can cause eutrophication of surface waters. Silage, an anaerobic fermentation product of grasses and grain crops, produces gasses (e.g., nitrogen dioxide) dangerous to farm operators and an acid effluent that can damage surface water and agricultural land.

Direct impacts of agriculture are usually easy to identify and correct. More subtle impacts of agriculture on the environment may be difficult to understand and manage. Perhaps the most important such effect is the linkage between agriculture and the human population size. Hunter-gatherer societies may typically have been limited by food supply to about one person per square mile (259 hectares). Currently, the earth's human population is supported at a density of about 1.1 persons per

hectare of crop and pasture land, over 200 times as dense as hunter-gatherers. Put bluntly, agriculture, despite its negative impacts, is necessary for human survival at the current population size. It is unlikely, therefore, that agriculture's effects on the environment will end in the foreseeable future.

Agriculture also is a dynamic activity, so its impacts on the environment change over time. Some of these changes involve alterations of the inputs farmers use. For example, synthetic pesticides and fertilizers were not used on a large scale before 1940. Hence a whole class of toxic hazards to people and wildlife have been known only for about fifty years. Similarly, mechanization has had large environmental impacts. In the United States, for example, the number of mules on farms peaked at about 5.9 million in the mid-1920s, but by 1950 they had dropped to about 2.2 million as tractors replaced them. Land formerly used to feed work animals was switched to producing human food. In addition, the U.S. farm population fell from 42 percent in 1900 to 5 percent in 1970, because fewer people were needed in agriculture.

Uses of farm outputs also have changed over time and thus affected the environmental impacts of agriculture. For example, the botanical dye indigo was commonly used before the nineteenth century. Invention of synthetic chemical dyes led to the demise of the indigo industry. Other crops increased due to changing uses. For example, soybean was grown largely as a fodder crop in North America until after the 1920s. Since then the soybean has changed almost entirely to seed production for use as livestock feed, human food, and a variety of industrial uses. Efforts to promote the use of maize for ethanol for a motor vehicle fuel have waxed and waned since the 1930s. To date only Brazil makes extensive use of ethanol as a transport fuel, but if the practice spreads, the environmental impacts of agriculture will also change.

Finally, agriculture is linked to the security of nation states. Countries must provide food to their people, either from domestic production or from imports. Countries heavily dependent upon food imports, such as Great Britain and Japan, were disadvantaged by the breakdown of their import systems during World War II. Since that time, India has from time to time been critically dependent upon imported foodgrains, generally to the detriment of her economy and national autonomy. After 1989 the food import system of Cuba, based on trade

A

with Eastern Europe and the former USSR, collapsed, leaving the Cubans without easy access to food, despite its large agricultural output of sugar and tobacco. Countries faced with serious threats to their autonomy due to dependency on imported food typically make massive investments in their agriculture.

John H. Perkins

Further Readings

Cohen, Mark Nathan. *Health and the Rise of Civilization.* 1989.

Conway, Gordon R., and Jules N. Pretty. *Unwelcome Harvest: Agriculture and Pollution.* 1991.

Wright, David E. "Alcohol Wrecks a Marriage: The Farm Chemurgic Movement and the USDA in the Alcohol Fuels Campaign in the Spring of 1933." *Agricultural History* 67 (1993): 36–66.

See also BIODIVERSITY: PLANTS; BISON: CONSERVATION AND HABITAT; EUTROPHICATION; PASSENGER PIGEON; PESTICIDES; SOIL CONSERVATION; SUSTAINABLE AGRICULTURE

Agroforestry

Agroforestry is an approach to land use based on the deliberate integration of trees and shrubs in crop and livestock production systems. It has the potential to provide rural households with food, fodder, fuelwood, and other tree products. At the same time, agroforestry can help ensure the sustained productivity of the natural resource base by enhancing soil fertility, controlling erosion, and improving the microclimate of cropping and grazing land.

For many generations farmers have developed farming systems that combined trees with crops. The term "agroforestry" only came into scientific use in 1977 when a conference was convened by the International Development Research Centre of Canada. The objective of the conference was to set priorities for forestry research in the tropics up to the end of the twentieth century. The conference concluded, however, that priority had to be given to systems integrating forestry and agriculture so as to improve land use in the tropics. These recommendations led to the founding of the International Centre for Research in Agroforestry (ICRAF) and agroforestry as a science was born.

All agroforestry systems are considered to belong to one of the following categories:

agrosilviculture, in which woody plant species and seasonal crops are grown together; silvopastoralism, where woody perennial plants are grown and animals grazed on the same area; and agrosilvopastoralism, where plants with wood-forming stems, annual plants, and animals are associated together. These three main categories are divided into five groups according to the relationship between the trees and the crops.

The first group includes agroforestry practices where crops are grown under a tree cover either in a mixed or scattered arrangement. This includes fruit-bearing trees growing in a forest.

Dense, mixed, multilayered agroforestry techniques make up the second group. These are sometimes called "agroforests" and are best illustrated by Indonesian, rural forest-gardens. When it is examined closely, the structure of this type of agroforestry technique closely resembles that of a typical forest. In contrast, the other classifications more resemble agricultural systems familiar to North Americans and Europeans.

The third group is made up of agroforestry techniques where trees are grown in rows with the crops between the rows. The patterns include wind breaks, trees planted to mark boundaries, hedges designed to act as fences, hedges planted along the contours of a slope, and hedges planted in parallel rows with two or more meters open between each row in which crops are planted.

Sequential agroforestry techniques are placed in the fourth group. In this case trees and crops are not planted together by the farmer but follow each other, as in an improved fallow. This method involves growing a crop on a field, harvesting it, and then planting fast-growing trees. The tree species chosen are usually capable of fixing atmospheric nitrogen as well as providing fuelwood or fodder.

The last group is composed of minor agroforestry techniques. Aquaforestry refers to the rearing of aquatic animals in association with trees. Fish-farming tree fodder or shrimp and oyster breeding in mangroves are examples of this type of relationship. Entomoforestry refers to insect rearing in association with trees, such as sericulture (silkworm breeding), lac production (a secretion produced by hemipteran living on the branches of specific trees), or sometimes apiculture (bee-keeping).

Current research has confirmed the initial impression that the agroforestry approach to land use is a viable option for solving rural development problems in tropical countries. The foremost constraint to the application of agroforestry techniques is, however, ecological, and concerns competition between trees and crops for the available space (above and below ground), for water (particularly soil water), and for light. A major agroforestry research objective is to analyze competition or synergy phenomena between trees and crops and to understand why there are good and bad associations.

A second constraint is that agroforestry is labor intensive. Planting trees can be time consuming and other agricultural activities may be negatively affected. Unless the farmer carries out planting operations correctly, a large proportion of the newly planted trees are likely to die. Once planted, the trees have to be managed properly in order to maintain the best relationship with the crops.

A third problem is the requirement that the tree species selected provide the best possible support to the crops. This means that new species have to be carefully introduced into agroforestry systems. A farmer cannot just go out and choose any tree; there are many species about which little is known and the use of that tree, or its introduction into a new area, might be disastrous.

The scientific consensus is that agroforestry is a system with great potential, but one that is not yet well understood or utilized. For those engaged in research most effort is placed upon the identification of situations where certain tree species are compatible with a variety of crops and agricultural activities. The term "tree-crop interface" is an important one in agroforestry, and if the interface is positive then the association between tree and crop is considered sound. In cases where the association is not positive, current policy is not to use that species of tree with the crop concerned, rather than to investigate the cause. This is so because there are many more opportunities for positive associations than there are known negative ones.

Thomas R. Roach

Further Readings

Agroforestry Today. Published by the International Centre for Research in Agroforestry (ICRAF), Nairobi, Kenya.

See also AGRICULTURE: ENVIRONMENTAL IMPACTS; CROPPING SYSTEMS: ENVIRONMENTAL IMPLICATIONS; FORESTRY, HISTORY OF; HABITAT FRAGMENTATION, PATCHES, AND CORRIDORS; SOIL CONSERVATION

Air Pollution Abatement

See COAL: ENVIRONMENTAL IMPACTS; HAZARDOUS WASTE TREATMENT TECHNOLOGIES; MUNICIPAL SOLID WASTE: INCINERATION

Air Pollution: Impacts

The heart of air pollution regulation in the United States has been the requirement that the Environmental Protection Agency (EPA) establish National Ambient Air Quality Standards for major pollutants: ozone, carbon monoxide, particulates, sulfur dioxide, nitrogen dioxide, and lead. These pollutants differ considerably in terms of their sources, health impacts, levels, and control measures developed to reduce their concentration in the air. Ozone has been the most pervasive and difficult to regulate of these pollutants; levels of carbon monoxide and particulate matter also exceed national standards in most urban areas.

The second kind of regulatory program provides for the regulation of toxic or hazardous air pollutants. Air toxics vary significantly in the threats they pose to human health. Many of them are carcinogens; others cause neurological damage or destroy organ tissue. There is little information available concerning the health effects of most chemicals and little understanding of the relationship between exposure and contraction of disease. There are significant differences in sensitivity to chemicals and pollutants among different groups in the population, and little is known about the synergistic or interactive effect of exposure to a variety of potentially harmful substances. The variety of substances involved, the large number and diversity of sources, and the cost of regulatory controls has made regulation particularly challenging. Instead of establishing standards for the ambient air, hazardous air pollutants have been regulated through emission standards imposed on major sources.

Two global air pollution issues emerged in the late 1970s and 1980s that also pose health risks: acid rain and depletion of the stratospheric ozone layer. Acid rain threatens the health of trees and other plant and aquatic life, and also poses a serious threat to human health. Similarly, destruction of the ozone layer threatens aquatic life and may trigger skin cancer and cataracts in humans.

Although there have been some major acute air pollution disasters, chronic, long-term exposure to pollutants has had a much greater impact on human health and ecological systems. Air pollution-related disorders include asphyxiation, pulmonary irritation, systemic toxicity, and cancer. Individuals with chronic respiratory problems such as emphysema, asthma, and bronchitis suffer increased damage to lung tissue that is already extremely sensitive. Some pollutants are absorbed into the bloodstream and are carried to sensitive organs, where they do their damage. Two of the most general consequences of air pollutants for body tissues are formation of scar tissue and the accumulation of fluid, particularly in the lungs. Air pollution can harm individuals who might otherwise be healthy, but who are adversely affected by high levels of pollutants that weaken their immune system and make them more susceptible to colds, infections, and other diseases that are seemingly unrelated to air pollution. Some of the health effects of the major pollutants, except ozone and acid rain, which are discussed elsewhere, are briefly outlined below.

Particulate matter is a broad category of pollutants that includes a variety of chemicals and particles. Primary particulates are composed of dust, dirt, soot, smoke, and liquid droplets, which are directly emitted into the air by factories, power plants, wood-burning stoves, and naturally occurring windblown dust. Secondary particulates are formed when gases such as sulfur dioxide and volatile organic compounds are transformed in the atmosphere into tiny particles. Until 1987 the ambient air standard for particulates regulated levels of total suspended particulates (TSP); during that year the EPA issued a national air quality standard for particulate matter that has an aerodynamic diameter of ten micrometers or less (PM10).

These fine particulates pose a much greater risk to human health than larger particulates. Larger particulates are usually filtered out by the body's defense mechanism in the nasal-pharynx region; fine particulates, in contrast, are much more difficult for the body to filter out. They bypass the defense mechanisms and travel deep into the lungs. Some may remain in the lungs at the deepest or alveoli level for life. Particulates of heavy metals, such as chromium and nickel, arsenic, asbestos, sulfates, hydrocarbons, radioactive particles, diesel particles, wood and coal smoke, and other chemicals, are particularly dangerous when they are inhaled

and become imbedded in lung tissue. They are a major cause of or contributor to respiratory diseases and many are known carcinogens. Deep penetration into the lungs is especially dangerous if high concentrations of other pollutants (especially sulfur and nitrogen oxides) are also inhaled. High levels of particulates have been associated with increased hospitalization of children for respiratory problems, increased school absenteeism, reduced lung function among healthy as well as sick children, and increased mortality.

High levels of carbon monoxide (CO), a colorless, odorless, and highly poisonous gas produced by transportation vehicles and other sources, have been associated with reduced attention, problem-solving ability, sensory activity, and visual acuity. These effects are usually reversible after a few hours and generally cause no lasting effects. CO has been implicated, however, in accidents that result from the loss of attention and sensory abilities. There is some evidence that it causes or contributes to the severity of respiratory diseases such as asthma, bronchitis, and reduced respiratory function. The most serious health threat from exposure to CO in urban areas is its ability to reduce the capacity of blood to deliver oxygen throughout the body. It can cause asphyxiation, heart and brain damage, and impaired perception under acute high doses. Chronic exposure to CO can cause an increased density of red blood cells in the blood, contributing to cardiovascular disease.

Sulfur dioxide (SO_2) is not generally the most harmful of sulfur compounds in the atmosphere, even though it is the form that is most often monitored. SO_2 can thicken tracheal mucous layers, inhibit clearance of particles that are inhaled, cause bronchial constriction, and, in very high concentrations, can damage the lining of the trachea. SO_2 may be rapidly transformed into sulfates and sulfuric acid that in turn pose more serious problems. Acute high exposure to sulfur oxides can cause accumulation of fluid in tissue or edema, bronchial spasms, shortness of breath, irritation of the respiratory tract, impaired pulmonary function, impaired lung clearance, increased susceptibility to disease, and, at very high levels, death.

Nitrogen oxides can impair the sense of smell, damage tissue, and aggravate respiratory diseases such as asthma, bronchitis, and emphysema. In high concentrations, nitrogen dioxide (NO_2) causes pulmonary edema and death.

Relatively little is known about the long-term effects of NO_2 at current ambient air levels.

Lead poses a major health risk at high levels. It decreases red cell production, affects the central nervous system and causes loss of sensation, and has reduced the mental development of young children. The level of lead is still a problem in a few areas, primarily where lead smelters are located.

Most of the information concerning environmental and health hazards posed by toxic air pollutants comes from laboratory tests with animals that produce only tentative knowledge, since it is not clear to what extent results can be extrapolated from animals to humans and from high experimental doses to low actual exposure levels. Epidemiological data on which regulatory action might be based is often incomplete or inconclusive, because of conditions in the environment in which the exposure occurs. According to one estimate, there is only partial or minimal toxicity information available for about 15 percent of the 13,000 chemicals that are produced in large quantities in the United States.

These toxic air pollutants pose serious health hazards, especially in high concentrations. Most of them can irritate the nose, throat, mouth, eyes, and lungs. Asbestos, for example, is implicated in a variety of lung diseases. Toluene can also cause dizziness and headaches; damage bone marrow, liver, and kidneys; and damage the developing fetus. Ammonia and chlorine can burn skin and eyes, causing permanent damage, and can cause pulmonary edema (buildup of fluid in the lungs). Acetone is flammable; it can irritate the eyes, nose, and throat and burn the skin. Benzene is believed to cause leukemia; vinyl chloride to cause lung and liver cancer. Mercury damages brain and kidney tissue, arsenic is a carcinogen, as are radionuclides.

Gary C. Bryner

Further Readings

Godish, Thad. *Air Quality*. 1991.
Pope, C.A., III, et al. "Respiratory Health and PM10 Pollution: A Daily Time Series Analysis." *American Review of Respiratory Disease* 144 (1991): 668–74.

See also ACID PRECIPITATION: AQUATIC IMPACTS; ACID PRECIPITATION: TERRESTRIAL IMPACTS; AIR POLLUTION: REGULATION (U.S.); AUTOMOBILES: IMPACTS AND POLICIES; CARBON MONOXIDE; EASTERN EUROPE: ENVIRONMENTAL PROBLEMS; LEAD; SMOG; VOLATILE ORGANIC COMPOUNDS

Air Pollution: Regulation (U.S.)

The first clean air laws in the United States were enacted by cities. Chicago and Cincinnati passed ordinances in the 1880s to limit smoke emissions. In 1962 Oregon became the first state to establish a comprehensive air pollution program. The federal government's involvement in air quality began in 1955, when the Public Health Service was authorized to conduct research on air pollution. The Clean Air Act of 1963 increased funds for research and established a legal process by which states and the federal government could take regulatory action against sources of pollution. Much of the attention was focused on carbon monoxide, hydrocarbon, and nitrogen oxide emissions from motor vehicles, blamed for 60 percent of all air pollution. Stationary sources were responsible for the balance of these pollutants, as well as for sulfur oxides and particulates.

Between 1955 and 1970 the federal government became increasingly involved in helping to fund state air pollution regulatory efforts, but Congress was very reluctant to give any real regulatory power to federal officials. In 1965, Congress authorized the Secretary of the Department of Health, Education, and Welfare (HEW) to establish standards for hydrocarbons and carbon monoxide emissions from new motor vehicles. The regulations were issued in 1966 and took effect in the 1968 model year.

A major expansion of regulatory authority occurred under the Air Quality Act of 1967. The federal government was ordered to establish air quality regions throughout the United States. States were authorized to develop air quality standards and plans to achieve them. If they failed to do so HEW was authorized to issue and enforce federal standards. Nevertheless, by 1970 no state had put in place a complete set of standards for any pollutant and the federal government had designated less than one-third of the metropolitan air quality regions that had been projected.

A wave of public concern over the environment in 1970 led to the first Earth Day in April, the creation of the Environmental Protection Agency (EPA) by a presidential reorganization plan, and widespread demands for increased protection of air quality that culminated in the passage of the Clean Air Act in December. The 1970 Act provided the basic structure of federal air pollution policy that continues today. It promised to clean up the nation's air within five years by establishing national air quality standards and giving states responsibility for developing and enforcing implementation plans to realize the federal standards. The Act made federal funds available to states for the development of air quality plans and increased funding on the health effects of airborne pollutants. The EPA was to ensure that the plans included emission limitations and monitoring requirements for stationary sources, a program to regulate new sources of pollution, inspection and testing of motor vehicle emissions, and adequate resources to implement and enforce the plan. If acceptable plans were not submitted by states, the EPA was authorized to amend them or formulate a federal plan to achieve air quality standards.

The Clean Air Act of 1970 was amended in 1971, 1973, 1974, and 1976, primarily to provide waivers for achievement of the motor vehicle emission standards. A number of developments pressured Congress to take action in 1976 to amend the Clean Air Act. The 1975 deadline for achieving national air quality standards and implementing state cleanup plans passed with thousands of sources not in compliance. The deadlines for meeting auto tailpipe standards were extended three times, twice by the EPA and once by Congress, as auto industry representatives argued that they needed an additional five years to find ways of meeting the emission standards, particularly that for nitrogen oxide, without adversely affecting fuel economy. Major amendments were enacted in 1977 that provided for the nondeterioration of air quality in relatively clean air areas and extended the deadlines for compliance with air quality standards. Civil penalties of up to $25,000/day for violations of the Act were authorized; criminal sanctions were to be imposed for knowing violations. In a key compromise, standards for new fossil fuel-burning power plants required the use of control technologies; even if companies used low sulfur coal, additional controls were still required, thus removing much of the incentive to replace high sulfur coal with its low sulfur counterpart and protecting the high sulfur coal industry.

Some progress in cleaning the air was achieved during the 1970s, particularly in reducing levels of particulates, sulfur dioxide, and carbon monoxide. But ozone and nitrogen dioxide levels remained high. Authorization for the Clean Air Act expired in 1981, and Congress funded implementation of the law throughout the 1980s through appropriations resolutions. Political maneuvers began in earnest and lasted for a decade. Several factors came together in 1989 to alter fundamentally the politics of clean air in Congress, break the decade-long deadlock, and produce the Clean Air Act of 1990. The summer of 1988 was the hottest on record, fueling fears of global warming and broader concerns that we were not giving sufficient attention to protecting our environment. The fact that many urban areas continued to fail to meet cleanup goals gave renewed impetus to demands for Congress to update the law, even though the EPA had decided not to impose sanctions so long as Congress was considering clean air legislation.

The debate over the Clean Air Act brought together two powerful forces—a broad alliance of environmental groups and a coalition of most of the major industries in the United States—in a classic test of political power. Industry and environmental groups were able to evoke powerful images of job loss and economic devastation on the one hand, and ecological damage and human health risks on the other. Just as divisive as industry-environmentalist debates were regional conflicts. Air pollution from the Midwest was blamed by Northeasterners for damage to their forests and lakes. Midwestern coal miners competed with Westerners for provisions that would favor the use of their resources. Heavily polluted communities like Los Angeles demanded the most stringent controls possible, while other areas resisted the cost of controls that they might not need.

Clean air legislation has been heavily dependent on personalities. One of the singular events in the evolution of the clean air bills was the replacement in 1988 of Senate majority leader Robert Byrd, champion of West Virginia high sulfur coal-miners, with Senator George Mitchell of Maine, whose state was threatened by acid rain. Byrd had blocked clean air bills from reaching the Senate floor for several years, and Mitchell's leadership was indispensable in finally bringing a bill to a vote. In the House, John Dingell's position as chair of the Energy and Commerce Committee put him in a powerful position to protect his constituents in Detroit from new regulatory requirements. Representative Henry Waxman, who chaired the Health and the Environment Subcommittee that had initial jurisdiction over the bill, represented Los Angeles, home of the most serious air pollution problem in the United States. Waxman served throughout the 1980s as the focal point of efforts to protect the Clean Air Act against efforts to weaken it during the Reagan years.

The importance of congressional apprehension over the direction the EPA was taking under direction of the Reagan White House was also a major factor in the clean air debate. EPA officials were defiant in their criticisms of existing laws. Much of Congress's attention was diverted from legislation and to oversight. The legislation that was eventually enacted was highly detailed and prescriptive as Congress expressed its frustration with the unwillingness of the EPA and Reagan administration to implement the law in a way demanded by congressional Democrats.

The 1990 amendments to the Clean Air Act made major additions to the old Act, while maintaining its basic structure. The most difficult air quality standard to meet has been that for ground-level ozone, a main ingredient of urban smog. The new law established six categories of ozone nonattainment areas, from marginal to extreme, and sets deadlines of from three to twenty years for attaining standards. It included three major initiatives aimed at reducing pollution caused by motor vehicles: tightening the standards for emissions from new motor vehicles; requiring the production of new, cleaner burning vehicles; and mandating the use of alternative, less polluting fuels. The amendments made a major departure from the existing law, by requiring that technology-based emission limits be established for all major sources of hazardous air pollutants to be followed by a second round of risk-based standards. The 1990 amendments added two major new provisions to the Clean Air Act: acid rain, featuring an innovative scheme of trading pollution permits; and stratospheric ozone protection. A worker compensation program for those who would lose their jobs as a result of the Act's requirements was also included for the first time in an environmental statute.

Gary C. Bryner

Further Readings

Ackerman, Bruce, and William T. Hassler. *Clean Coal/Dirty Air: How the Clean Air Act Became a Multibillion Dollar Bail-Out for High-Sulfur Fuel Producers.* 1981.

Jones, Charles O. *Clean Air: The Policies and Politics of Pollution Control.* 1975.

Vanderver, Timothy A. *Clean Air Law and Regulation.* 1992.

See also AUTOMOBILES: IMPACTS AND POLICIES; CARBON MONOXIDE; LEGISLATION:

UNITED STATES; OZONE POLLUTION; SMOG; VOLATILE ORGANIC COMPOUNDS

A

Alachlor Controversy

On February 5, 1985, the Canadian Minister of Agriculture canceled the registration of the herbicide alachlor. Registered by Monsanto Canada, Inc., under the Pest Control Products Act in 1969, alachlor had been used by Canadian corn and soy bean farmers for nearly sixteen years.

The 1969 registration had been authorized through toxicological studies of the chemical done by United States-based Industrial Bio-Test Laboratories (IBT). However, investigations of fraudulent research at IBT in the late 1970s led to official suspicion of their alachlor studies. In addition, studies had come to the attention of the Environmental Protection Agency (EPA) and Health and Welfare Canada indicating alarmingly high levels of alachlor in well water tested in certain farming areas, including southwestern Ontario. At the government's request Monsanto submitted replacement studies for alachlor in 1982. These studies created new concerns about cancer risks from alachlor, since levels of exposure within the range of possible human exposures produced significant carcinogenic responses in the laboratory animals.

As provided by the Pest Control Products Act, Monsanto appealed the government's cancellation decision to the Alachlor Review Board, a board of five scientists appointed by the Minister of Agriculture. The Review Board heard expert testimony from the company, the government, farm organizations, and other interest groups. Monsanto scientists argued that government scientists had: 1) grossly overestimated the risks of alachlor, especially the likely levels of exposure to the chemical; 2) underestimated the risks of its chief registered competitor, metolachlor; and 3) failed to articulate an appropriate safety standard and apply it fairly to alachlor.

With respect to the estimation of alachlor's cancer risks, the issue was primarily whether farmers would be exposed to levels of the chemical approximating the levels associated with cancer in lab animals. Government exposure estimates exceeded this threshold, whereas the manufacturer's estimates were as much as six orders of magnitude below it. This wide discrepancy in the exposure estimates of the two groups of scientists was largely the result of the different assumptions they made about nonscientific matters such as:

1. Whether careless as well as careful farm practices should be considered a part of the exposure scenario for determining the risk of alachlor.
2. Whether to handle uncertainties in the data with a view toward erring on the side of health safety or on the side of the benefits to be gained from the risk-taking.
3. Whether the burden of scientific proof should lie with the manufacturer to prove that the risks were below acceptable levels or with the government to prove that the risks were above acceptable levels.

The Alachlor Review Board itself decided the issue by identifying a "range" of possible risks, based upon a choice of assumptions midway between the government and the industry. Since the upper end of this risk range (their "reasonable worst case") fell well below the threshold level for cancer appearance in rats, the Review Board concluded that this was a "reasonable margin of safety" and recommended that the government reinstate the registration of alachlor in Canada. The government did not, however, reverse its cancellation decision.

The alachlor case is an instructive example of the way regulatory science depends as much upon extrascientific value assumptions as upon the empirical science itself.

Conrad G. Brunk

Further Readings
Alachlor Review Board. *Report of the Alachlor Review Board*. 1987.
Brunk, Conrad, Lawrence Haworth, and Brenda Lee. *Value Assumptions in Risk Assessment: A Case Study of the Alachlor Controversy*. 1991.

See also INDUSTRIAL BIO-TEST LABORATORIES; PESTICIDES; RISK ANALYSIS; STANDARD SETTING

Alaska: Park, Wilderness, and Resource Issues
Alaska is the eastern keystone of the arching Pacific Rim, site of prehistoric migrations of humans, animals, and plants from Asia to the Americas and latitudinal zone of transition from cool temperate to arctic. Marine environments range from the north temperate Gulf of Alaska to the Chukchi and Beaufort seas, ice-locked except for summer leads near shore. Three terrestrial regions (coniferous rainforest, boreal forest, and arctic and alpine tundras) encompass a spectrum of biological communities. Historical movements and isolations have created biota with circumpolar, circumboreal, Beringean, alpine, and north temperate affinities.

About 75,000 Native Americans—Inuit, Aleut, Athabasca, Haida, and Tlingit—lived in Alaska when the first European ship arrived in 1741. Nearly all were coastal people. Russian commercial interests controlled trade (fur exports) in the first two-thirds of the nineteenth century. Full-scale domination of land and resources was ushered in by the 1867 sale of Alaska to the United States. Between 1880 and 1960 overlapping pulses of immigration by fishery workers, gold miners, military and civilian federal employees, and pulp mill and woods workers produced today's pattern of settlement and urbanization. About 85 percent of Alaska's 550,000 people in the early 1990s are nonnatives.

Alaska looked like an untouched wilderness to early Euro-Americans. In the political morality of the times, Alaska was freely available for resource exploitation. Under early U.S. rule, however, Congress was reluctant to transfer land wholesale to private individuals. Only 0.2 percent of Alaska's 375 million acres were privately owned when Alaska became a state in 1958. The rest was federal land. However, the Alaska Statehood Act authorized the new state to select and gain title to 104 million acres of public domain. That process is now nearly complete. In 1971, in partial settlement of native land claims, Congress authorized native village and regional corporations to choose 44 million acres in small- to medium-sized parcels throughout the state.

Concerned that areas of outstanding national conservation value were being transferred to native corporations and the state, Alaskan and national environmentalists urged immediate dedication of new federal conservation areas. President Carter in 1980 signed a law establishing protective management on the largest area of land that had or ever would be so designated in a single piece of legislation in the United States. The law established 44 million acres of national parks and preserves, 54 million acres of national wildlife refuges, and 5 million acres in other federal conservation reserves. Over half of the 103 million acres were designated as units of the National Wilderness Preservation System. Alaska now contains 74 percent of all National Park Service lands and 89 percent of all lands in the National Wildlife Refuge System.

These events set the permanent pattern of ownership of Alaskan lands. However, owner objectives are neither fixed nor easily predicted. All major Alaska landholders are political entities subject to gradual or rapid changes in land-use policies as their perceived needs and those of the rest of society change. State or federal designations of parks and refuges establish the overall objectives of management. However, by no means do they eliminate managerial discretion, or prevent amendment to legislative direction should the original balance of interests shift.

For example, in 1980 Congress instructed agencies to allow rural Alaskans to hunt within refuges, national forests, and national park preserves except in cases when overriding reasons (such as endangerment of local wildlife populations) dictated that this practice should be restricted or prohibited. Hunting (for subsistence only) is allowed on national preserves. On all other federal lands subsistence hunting has legal priority over recreational hunting when game is scarce. Because most rural hunters are native and most urban (i.e, sport) hunters are nonnative, this policy rekindled longstanding urban/rural and native/nonnative frictions. By also permitting snowmobile use by subsistence hunters, Congress aroused concern among conservationists hoping to keep motorized vehicles out of park and wilderness areas.

The advent of large-scale, export-based logging in lands rimming the Gulf of Alaska in the 1950s created a divisive resource issue still far from resolution. Part of the issue is an allocative one: on public (mainly federal) lands, where should logging be allowed and where should it be prohibited? After a series of piecemeal actions by Congress establishing Glacier National Park, Admiralty Island, and Misty Fiords as national forest monuments, as well as other national forest wilderness areas—and after agency actions zoning certain forest lands against logging—the allocative question is mostly answered except for smaller but strategic areas of ancient forests near shore whose accessibility makes them valuable to wilderness proponents and loggers alike.

The other half of the issue involves management protocol regarding where timber will be harvested. For forty years the managers' and industry's choice of silvicultural systems has been to cut all trees in a multi-acre block in a few days or weeks, then wait 100 years for another harvest—meanwhile logging other blocks. Under that system, however, environments such as those of the original, precutting forest are never reestablished. Because the region's wildlife evolved in environments of extensive ancient forest, management organized around clearcutting obviously affects wildlife dramatically. Agencies and interest groups have barely begun to think about alternative harvest systems.

Surface access via roads or railroads has been a pivotal and contentious issue throughout Alaska's frontier period. Assuming that more roads will bring more resource extraction activity, Alaska's urban interests involved in construction, mining, and associated businesses have promoted expansion of the state's slim road and railroad network. They also favor state jurisdiction over little-used rights-of-way across federal land. Rural people, who have the resource access they need without roads and who fear an influx of townspeople, oppose both ideas. So do environmentalists, who want a lessening, not an intensification, of hinterland use. In practical terms major expansion of surface networks is limited somewhat by the position of parks and wilderness areas, more by the lack of justification to build particular routes, and even more by the present inability of either state or federal governments to afford the costs.

Much of Alaska's mystique derives from its wildlife, especially caribou, moose, mountain sheep, wolves, and black and brown (grizzly) bears. Long-term survival of this interlocked community of species is becoming more questionable as more people crowd the state and access technology (aircraft, airboats, snowmobiles, etc.) improves. Hunters can—and even under increasingly strict regulation, occasionally do—overharvest any of Alaska's big ungulate populations. Critical parts of the extensive ranges essential to these mobile species are under threat from logging (southeast Alaska) or petroleum mining (arctic coastal plain). State, federal, and native corporate landowners have found it hard to agree on practical, enforceable, cooperative land management plans with priority on wildlife habitat protection. And sport as well as subsistence hunters, seeing bears and wolves as competitors for a beleaguered and fluctuating ungulate resource, continually call for reduction of predator numbers.

A

Marine environments also harbor contentious resource issues. Ineffective regulation of salmon, halibut, and herring fisheries by the 1950s and 1960s resulted in sharp declines in most stocks bordering the Gulf of Alaska. Some have recovered. At the same time, factory ships from foreign fleets netted huge tonnages of pollock, ocean perch, sablefish, halibut, salmon, and other fish offshore, severely depleting many stocks. Sketchy evidence suggests that these depletions disrupted seabird and marine mammal populations and the composition of the finfish fauna itself. The Gulf of Alaska and southern Bering Sea are now so changed by modern fishing and earlier whaling that no one can ever know its pristine functioning.

Offshore petroleum activities could, but have not yet, affected Alaska's marine environments substantially. The 1989 spill from the *Exxon Valdez*, carrying crude oil from arctic coastal plain fields, made this concern very real. Potentially oil-bearing formations occur widely offshore around Alaska's 30,000-mile coastline. To date no commercial deposits have been discovered and produced except in Cook Inlet, northern Gulf of Alaska.

Until the 1980s the history of Alaska could be seen as a frontier play on a cold northern stage. The balance of power among chief protagonists (indigenous people, resource exploiters, and resource preservers) was quite different in post-statehood Alaska than in the Old American West, but the basic plot of colonialization was there. "The frontier" is now as relevant as stale popcorn. Today's play in Alaska is also on marquees all over the world: a deep struggle for a new justice among people and a new relation with nature, on whose final act hangs the survival of life and life's processes on earth.

Robert B. Weeden

Further Readings

Morehouse, Thomas A., ed. *Alaskan Resources Development: Issues of the 1980s.* 1984.

Weeden, Robert B. *Messages from Earth: Nature and the Human Prospect in Alaska.* 1992.

See also BEARS: CONSERVATION AND HABITAT; CLEARCUT; FISHERIES CONSERVATION; OIL SPILLS; TOP PREDATORS IN CANADA: AN OVERVIEW; UNGULATES; WILDERNESS; WOLF: A CONSERVATION CHALLENGE

Albright, Horace

See NATIONAL PARKS: UNITED STATES

Algonquin Provincial Park

Located on the southern edge of the Canadian Shield between Georgian Bay and the Ottawa River, Algonquin Provincial Park is Canada's first and oldest provincial park. The park protects a diversity of habitats and wildlife within its 7,600 square kilometer area. Each year, hundreds of thousands of people visit this park which celebrated its centennial year in 1993.

Algonquin contains a transition zone between southern broadleaf forests and northern coniferous forests. Its vast interior includes maple hills, rocky ridges, spruce bogs, and thousands of lakes, ponds and streams. Over 1,500 kilometers of canoe routes wind their way through southern Ontario's largest protected wilderness. Over 250 bird species have been seen in the park, along with such mammals as moose, white-tailed deer, wolves, black bears, beaver, otter, marten, muskrat, and mink.

The idea of creating Algonquin Provincial Park originated with Robert W. Phipps, Ontario's clerk of forestry. In 1884 he recommended protection of the watersheds south of Lake Nippissing because of the growing threat of settlement to the region's wildlife, waters and forests. Alexander Kirkwood, chief clerk in the Department of Crown Lands, wrote to the Commissioner of Crown Lands in 1885, promoting the idea of a large reserve in the highlands of southern Ontario. Premier Oliver Mowat created a Royal Commission in 1892 to review Kirkwood's idea. A year later, the Commission recommended a 3,800 square kilometer reserve to protect the headwaters of seven rivers originating in the region. On May 27, 1893, the Ontario Legislature established Algonquin Provincial Park.

Algonquin Provincial Park has a long, varied, and rich history. One of Canada's oldest camps for girls, Northway, was set in the park in 1908. Along with a number of other camps, it continues to introduce children to nature. Tom Thomson, landscape painter, first visited Algonquin in 1912 to capture its rugged landscape using brilliant colors, and later persuaded the Group of Seven to visit. Thomson died in the park in July 1917 under mysterious circumstances.

The most controversial aspect of Algonquin's history is the continued logging of its forests. The 1893 act creating the park did not prohibit logging. Rather, the government's intent was to plan lumbering to ensure long-term productivity of the forests. At the time, valuable timber was being wasted by fire, irresponsible logging practices, and misguided settlement.

In 1968 a group of citizens concerned over the mismanagement of Algonquin formed the Algonquin Wildlands League to advocate stronger protection of the park's conservation values. The League focused its efforts on: 1) reducing the impact of logging; 2) decreasing water pollution and noise; 3) restricting or prohibiting the use of powerboats on wilderness lakes; and 4) combating the growing pressure to allow automobiles into the park's interior. Over the next twenty-five years, the League continued its efforts in becoming a powerful force for wilderness protection across the province.

During the park's centennial year, the League called on the Ontario government to end any further logging of Algonquin's forests. At that time over 70 percent of the park was zoned for exploitation, raising concern over its long-term ecological viability. In December 1993 the government announced the creation of a large wilderness zone in the eastern part of the park.

Kevin McNamee

Further Readings

Lundell, Liz. *Algonquin: The Park and its People.* 1993.

See also FORESTRY, HISTORY OF; GROUP OF SEVEN; WILDERNESS

Alligators

See REPTILES: CONSERVATION AND HABITAT

Alternative Dispute Resolution

Alternative dispute resolution (ADR) is the technique of using informal, face-to-face negotiations and consensus building to resolve disputes over environmental issues. Typically, an impartial mediator brings together representatives from all the groups involved in a dispute including environmentalists, government officials, and business(es). All parties attempt to arrive at a solution that is mutually satisfactory. Mediators facilitate communication, suggest new alternatives, and help draft a final agree-ment. The process is usually a voluntary one in which no agreement can be forced upon any of the parties.

ADR now takes place commonly in the United States, Canada, and Japan; and it has been used to address a wide variety of environmental controversies, including fishing rights, wetlands protection, mining, logging, sewage treatment, air quality, water quality, toxic waste, and landfills. When ADR first began in the 1970s, it was usually employed in an ad hoc fashion to address local environmental issues. Today the process has become more institution-alized, particularly in the United States. Several states now require the use of negotiation in issues such as the siting of hazardous waste disposal facilities. Some U.S. environmental agencies also now use negotiation in the initial phases of rule development, a process known as "reg-neg" or regulatory negotiation.

ADR is usually seen as an alternative to the courts, and proponents of this process believe it has a number of advantages over litigation. First, it is thought to be cheaper and faster than litigation. A second advantage of dispute resolution is that it allows the involved parties to focus on the real issues in the dispute. In litigation, the focus more often than not is on narrow legal or procedural issues rather than the real substance of the disagreement. For example, to challenge development projects in the courts, environmentalists often must attack a developer on procedural grounds, such as failure to complete an adequate environmental impact statement. Side-stepping the real concerns of environmentalists—usually the substantive environmental impacts of a project—litigation can only be brought on procedural issues. ADR has no such limitation and allows disputants to identify the real basis of their disagreement, which is the first step toward actually resolving a dispute.

The informal structure of negotiations also allows disputants to explore a wider variety of possible remedies, thus maximizing the chance of finding "win-win" solutions (i.e., solutions in which all parties receive some of what they want). Court decisions are typically of the "win-lose" variety in which only one party is the victor. These decisions may resolve a dispute temporarily; however, the loser, being unsatisfied, may seek other ways to continue the conflict. A negotiated agreement that satisfies all parties can actually end a dispute. Mediators stress that "win-win" solutions are often possible because, although the disputants may have different interests, these interests may not be incompatible. For instance, creative tradeoffs may allow for both development and environmental protection. A developer that is filling in wetlands for one project may agree to buy and preserve other wetland areas in order to satisfy the interests of environmentalists.

Alternative dispute resolution can also provide unique opportunities for citizen groups, whose lack of power and resources often keep them out of traditional decision-making processes. ADR offers these individuals a seat at the table, helping them to develop new skills in communication and negotiation. Through this process, citizen groups can also establish ongoing relationships with policy-makers and business leaders that could be useful in the future.

Despite its potential for equitable solutions and its empowering nature, alternative dispute resolution is not without drawbacks. Critics of the process question some of the alleged advantages of the process and point to a number of potential problems. They note, for example, that there is little evidence that ADR is cheaper or faster than litigation. Also, while mediation is portrayed as an open, participatory process, sometimes less-powerful or less-organized groups—typically local citizen and environmental groups—have been left out of the negotiations. In addition, while face-to-face negotiations give the impression of a balance of power between the participants, significant imbalances often exist that give one side a substantial advantage in this process. Business groups, for instance, can usually afford well-paid, experienced negotiators, who often produce a large number of technical reports and scientific studies to support their position. In contrast, environmental groups are usually understaffed and have fewer analytic resources available to make their case. These groups sometimes complain that they are "outgunned" at the negotiation table.

Another complaint about ADR is that it distorts the true nature of environmental conflicts. Mediators often portray these conflicts as mere matters of miscommunication or misunderstanding; at worst, they are seen as clashes of equally valid interests. Environmentalists on the whole believe that environmental issues take precedence over the interests of business and thus they would see a negotiated agreement allowing mining in a wilderness area, even with environmental safeguards, not as a reasonable compromise but as one that dangerously undermines the principle of wilderness preservation. When conflicts involve such basic principles, compromise may amount to capitulation.

Many of the potential drawbacks of alternative dispute resolution can be minimized if it is used only in the appropriate circumstances. ADR tends to produce the best results for disputes in which: 1) the number of disputants is small; 2) a relative balance of power exists between the disputants; 3) there are no legal precedents at stake; and 4) there are no basic disagreements on values and principles. Many, perhaps most, environmental disputes do not meet these criteria. But clearly, enough do so that alternative dispute resolution is likely to continue to play a small but important role in the resolution of environmental controversies.

Douglas J. Amy

Further Readings

Amy, Douglas. *The Politics of Environmental Mediation*. 1987.

Bingham, Gail. *Resolving Environmental Disputes: A Decade of Experience*. 1986.

Crowfoot, James E., and Julia M. Wondolleck. *Environmental Disputes: Community Involvement in Conflict Resolution*. 1990.

See also CLASS ACTIONS; ENVIRONMENTAL CASE LAW: EUROPEAN COMMUNITY; ENVIRONMENTAL CASE LAW: UNITED STATES; ENVIRONMENTAL ETHICS; REGULATION; STANDARD SETTING

Alternatives

Alternatives: Perspectives on Society, Technology, and Environment is Canada's oldest and largest interdisciplinary journal on environmental issues. An independent quarterly publication including news articles and reviews as well as formally-refereed feature articles and review essays, *Alternatives* is a somewhat unconventional learned journal that is dedicated to accessibility and serves a diverse range of environmental scholars, professionals, and activists.

The journal emphasizes analysis of prevailing environmental policy and behavior along with examination of proposals for reform or more radical change. While generally critical of conventional thinking and practice, the journal has not favored any one ideological position. The journal's original statement of purpose, drafted by founding editor Robert Paehlke, still applies:

The environmental crisis, if it is to be resolved by other than biological disaster, requires more than mere technical improvements. We must confront the implications it has for our economic structures, our political process and institutions, our living habits, and the moral basis of our philosophy and culture. We must pose and confront the necessary questions, and offer imaginative and serious alternatives (*Alternatives* 1:1 (1971), p. 2).

Most issues of *Alternatives* are devoted to a particular theme. Recent theme issues have addressed ecosystem theory and application, citizen activism, international environmental agreements, waste reduction, and approaches to managing common property resources. In addition to peer-reviewed feature articles, each issue includes shorter reports and notes, commentaries, book reviews, a "podium" essay, and a humor column.

The journal covers topics or international interests and has subscribers in twenty-six countries. Its main focus, however, is on Canadian concerns and initiatives. Its mandate is:

- To provide critical and informed analysis of environmental problems, related social issues and technological developments;
- To foster alternative responses to these challenges for Canada and the world;
- To present sound research to a broad audience in an attractive and popular manner; and
- To create a publishing opportunity for Canadian scholars and professionals.

Alternatives is published by Alternatives, Inc., a nonprofit charitable corporation founded in 1971 by a collective of academics centered at Trent University in Peterborough, Ontario. Since 1984, the journal has been based in the Faculty of Environmental Studies at the University of Waterloo. Editorial and subscription information can be obtained from *Alternatives*, c/o Faculty of Environmental Studies, University of Waterloo, Canada, N2L 3G1; phone (519) 888-4567 ext. 6783; or Email alternat@watserv1.uwaterloo.ca.

Robert B. Gibson

Aluminum

Aluminum (chemical symbol Al) is the most abundant metal in the lithosphere and com-

prises approximately 8 percent by weight of the earth's crust. It does not occur as a free metal in nature but instead can be found in bauxite, the primary ores for the production of aluminum metal. The bauxite is purified and hydrolyzed to produce alumina (aluminum oxide, Al_2O_3) which is then electrolytically reduced to aluminum metal. This purification process is energy intensive, requiring considerably more energy than producing aluminum by recycling aluminum containers.

Aluminum has low density, high electrical and thermal conductivity, high reflectivity, and is corrosion resistant. The pure metal is soft and weak and is typically combined with other metals to provide light, strong, and readily workable metal alloys. Its light weight and corrosion resistance are particularly important in transportation, construction, electrical equipment, containers and packaging, consumer durables, and mechanical equipment.

Aluminum is found in igneous rocks (feldspars), hydrothermal deposits (zeolite, cryolite), and sedimentary rock (clays such as kaolinite). Concentrations of aluminum in rocks ranges from 9,000 µg/g (0.9 percent) in limestone, to 88,000 µg/g (8.8 percent) in shale. Concentrations of aluminum in soils average 70,000 µg/g (7 percent) and range from 10,000 to 300,000 µg/g (1 to 30 percent). Aluminum is tightly bound to soil and rocks and weathers slowly, hence concentrations in soil water, groundwater, and surface water are generally low. However, weathering and leaching of aluminum can be increased by acid rain or the natural production of organic and mineral acids.

Aluminum in Water and Air

The concentration of aluminum in natural water depends on pH and on the presence of complexing agents. In circumneutral waters (pH 6 to 8), aluminum concentrations are generally below 20 µg/L. However, as the pH decreases (more acidic conditions) aluminum concentrations increase exponentially to values above concentrations considered to be toxic to freshwater fishes, and the forms of aluminum change from $Al(OH)_3$, to $Al(OH)_2^+$, to $Al(OH)^{2+}$, to Al^{3+}, which is the common form below pH 4.0. In alkaline water (above pH 7) the predominant dissolved form of aluminum is the anion $Al(OH)_4^-$.

Although pH is one of the most important factors affecting the solubility and speciation of aluminum, organic ligands, fluoride, sulfate, phosphate, silicates, and suspended solids can all bind with aluminum and thus change its chemical form, solubility, bioavailability, and toxicity. Because aluminum binds strongly with phosphate, it is added to nutrient rich drinking water to remove the phosphorus. Tentative guidelines set by the Environmental Protection Agency (EPA) for aluminum state that concentrations should not exceed 100 µg/L in waters with a pH greater than 6.5 and should not exceed 5 µg/L in waters with a pH equal to or below 6.5.

Aluminum occurs in a particulate form in the atmosphere, being derived from wind-blown soil and particulate emissions from smelters and coal-fired power plants. Concentrations of aluminum deposited from the atmosphere (wet and dry fallout) vary considerably, but are generally less than 0.16 mg/L.

Aluminum in Terrestrial Biota
Aluminum concentrations in biota tend to be highly variable. Values may be as low as 0.1 µg/g in some herbaceous plants and as high as 6,000 µg/g in others (certain lichens and bryophytes). There are a few aluminum accumulators, such as tea, which may have foliar aluminum concentrations as high as 30,000 µg/g (3 percent by weight). Aluminum does not appear to be an essential nutrient in either plants or animals. However, a few plants that normally grow on soils high in bioavailable aluminum have been shown to be more productive in the presence of small quantities of aluminum in controlled culture solutions.

Early studies of plants growing on acidic soils were concerned with yield of agricultural crops. Poor growth of these plants was attributed to high concentrations of available aluminum, although availability of other potentially toxic metals was also high. We now know that aluminum does become more bioavailable and more toxic in acidic soils and interferes with root growth and with the uptake of phosphate, an essential nutrient. Liming and fertilizing with phosphorus can reduce aluminum toxicity in agricultural crops.

Recent reports of forest decline, especially in Germany, suggest that aluminum may be one of several factors responsible for the death of trees. Conditions are triggered by the first rainfall following periods of drought. These conditions favor the oxidation of sulfur and ammonium and increase the acidity of the soils and the leaching of aluminum. High concentrations of aluminum found in soil solution and in roots resemble classical symptoms of aluminum tox-icity (inhibition of root elongation, dwarfing, browning of root tip, and lack of fine root branching). Above-ground symptoms include stunting, reduced yield, small dark green foliage, delayed maturity, purple-tingeing of various tissues, and yellowing or browning of leaf tips.

Aluminum in Aquatic Biota
Concentrations of aluminum as low as 50 µg/L can be acutely toxic to fish and planktonic crustaceans, especially in soft water (low calcium). Aluminum interferes with respiration, salt regulation, and calcium uptake in some species. Fish kills in Scandinavia and the failure of some restocking programs in the United States have been attributed to high concentrations of aluminum in the water. Maximum aluminum toxicity to fish occurs at pH 5.5; the presence of organic ligands, fluoride, and calcium can reduce the toxicity of aluminum to aquatic biota. Brook trout, rainbow trout, and brown trout are moderately sensitive to aluminum as are some species of zooplankton. Insects in contrast are less sensitive to aluminum. High concentrations of aluminum in insects emerging from acidic, aluminum-contaminated lakes may contribute to reproductive impairment in pied flycatchers in Sweden.

Liming, used successfully to alleviate aluminum toxicity in agricultural crops, has had devastating effects on indigenous fish populations in acidic, aluminum-enriched lakes. The lime increases the pH and converts most of the aluminum to the $Al(OH)_3$ form, which is a particulate and clogs fish gills. Fish develop respiratory problems, osmoregulatory problems, and, if the stress is sufficiently severe, death can result within a few hours to a few days.

Aluminum Uptake by Humans
Nonoccupational sources of aluminum include air, drinking water, food, and pharmaceuticals. North Americans ingest an average of thirty-six milligrams of aluminum per day, although individual intake varies greatly depending on the type of food and aluminum-containing medication consumed. Processed cheese and pickled vegetables contain high concentrations of aluminum, as do some common drugs such as buffered aspirin, some antacids, and antidiarrheals. Uptake of aluminum from antacid tablets increases if these are taken with orange juice instead of water. Tea has high concentrations of aluminum, typically two to six mg/L, but most of this appears to be in a

nonbioavailable form. Cooking salty or acidic food in aluminum cookware and storing food in aluminum foil can increase the aluminum content of food.

Drinking water may have elevated concentrations of aluminum due to natural sources or the purification process which may involve alum additions. Based on the Ontario Drinking Water Surveillance Program for 1984–1992, the average total aluminum concentration in drinking water was 105 µg/L with a range of 0.5 to 6,200 µg/L. A mean intake of aluminum from drinking water is 160 µg per day for Ontario residents. Epidemiological evidence indicates that aluminum concentrations in drinking water may be associated with dementia.

Although ingestion is the major route of aluminum uptake, it is reassuring to know that very little aluminum is absorbed through the gut. In healthy humans, fecal and urinary excretion approximately equals intake. Under average conditions of exposure, the skin, lungs, and gastrointestinal tract are effective barriers to aluminum.

Aluminum Toxicity to Humans

High concentrations of aluminum in humans have been associated with several illnesses. Lung disease, such as pulmonary fibrosis and emphysema, have been reported among workers exposed to high levels of finely powered aluminum metal. There is little evidence to support carcinogenicity related to aluminum exposure in the workplace, although some studies have reported a slight increase in bladder cancer among workers, especially smokers, exposed to aluminum emissions. Fatal encephalopathy was reported for patients on dialysis for chronic renal failure. Two types of bone disease are associated with aluminum: hypophosphatemic osteomalacia, which is an indirect effect of systemic aluminum exposure and is unrelated to dialysis encephalopathy syndrome (DES); and osteomalacic renal osteodystrophy, which appears to be a direct manifestation of aluminum toxicity and is an important consideration in all cases of renal failure. Severe anemia has been reported in patients with extremely high (550 µg/L) serum aluminum concentrations. Aluminum appears to interfere with hemoglobin synthesis, gastrointestinal disturbances, including anorexia, vomiting, and weight loss. Perhaps one of the most feared diseases associated with aluminum is Alzheimer's disease, which accounts for approximately 60 to 70 percent of senile dementia cases and is a major social and

medical health problem throughout the world. Elevated concentrations of aluminum have been found in brain tissue of some Alzheimer's patients although the exact role it plays in this disease is not known.

Magda Havas

Further Readings

Burrows, W.D. "Aquatic Aluminum: Chemistry, Toxicology, and Environmental Prevalence." *CRC Crit. Rev. Environ. Control* 7 (1977): 167–216.

Havas, M., and J.F. Jaworski, eds. *Aluminum in the Canadian Environment.* National Research Council of Canada, Publication No. NRCC 24759, 1986.

Nieboer, E., and G.L. Gibson. *Health Effects of Aluminum: A Critical Review with Emphasis on Aluminum in Drinking Water.* Ontario Ministry of Health, 1993.

See also ACID PRECIPITATION: AQUATIC IMPACTS; ACID PRECIPITATION: TERRESTRIAL IMPACTS; BIOACCUMULATION; CADMIUM; LEAD; LEAD IN SOILS; MERCURY; RECYCLING; WATER POLLUTION ABATEMENT TECHNOLOGIES

American Conference of Governmental Industrial Hygienists

The American Conference of Governmental Industrial Hygienists (ACGIH) is an independent, American, nonprofit organization that originates standards for industrial airborne contaminants and other workplace hazards. More than 800 ACGIH standards are used throughout the world as reference documents. They are often also adapted, or sometimes adopted without modification, and used by governments as guidelines or formal regulations for workers' compensation and workplace safety. ACGIH standards are used as the basis for extrapolation in the development of some environmental standards, for example, standards concerning airborne lead.

ACGIH was formed in 1938 and today attracts its members and voluntary participants or consultants in its standard setting committees from among government regulators, industry or privately employed industrial hygienists, the military and the insurance industry, and from universities. Meetings are open to the public, and a public record is kept of the proceedings of the annual general meeting where ACGIH standards or revisions to standards are approved. ACGIH carries on its standard setting activities mainly through its many technical/scientific committees, which are staffed by volunteers. ACGIH is not a consensus organization, relying upon experts rather than representations from producer, user, labor, and government groups for its committee membership.

ACGIH derives its income from the sale of its publications, primarily its annual list of standards for airborne contaminants. ACGIH offers these standards only as guidelines for good practices, and takes no role or responsibility for their later possible adoption by governmental bodies.

As a voluntary organization, ACGIH does not hold hearings or submit its deliberations to an adversarial process. Historically, ACGIH has been criticized for being industry-dominated (industry members do not vote on standards, although they submit the data and participate in committee deliberations), insufficiently responsive to public debate, and inattentive to the new scientific data. In the early days, ACGIH did rely upon whatever scientific information was available, but set its standards primarily on the basis of the practical experience of its industrial hygienist and government regulator members and, consequently, upon the informed guesswork of its contributors. ACGIH argued that it was more important to develop a standard for immediate use than to wait until adequate scientific information was available. Today, these criticisms of ACGIH still exist, but ACGIH has made considerable efforts to enhance the quality of its scientific assessments. Its record of revising standards in light of new scientific information, while not always adequate to deflect criticism, is often as good as or better than many government regulatory agencies which subject their standards to extensive scientific and public debates.

ACGIH standards reflect threshold limit values (TLVs), designating levels of contamination below which it can be assumed that little harm to human health will occur. Although much debate now exists about the validity of using a threshold, in light of recent data concerning the negative health effects of low dosages of contaminants, alternative approaches to standard setting have proven equally controversial. ACGIH retains its commitment to the TLVs, as do most government departments and agencies that adopt the TLVs as their own regulatory standards.

Liora Salter

Further Readings

Epstein, Samuel S. *The Politics of Cancer.* 1978.

Mintz, Benjamin W. *OSHA: History, Law, and Policy.* 1984.

See also EPIDEMIOLOGY; OSHACT AND OSHA; STANDARD SETTING; TOXICOLOGY

Amicus Journal
See NATURAL RESOURCES DEFENSE COUNCIL

Amphibians: Conservation and Habitat

Amphibians are abundant, relatively small aquatic and terrestrial vertebrate organisms that occur on all continents except Antarctica. There are about 4,000 amphibian species of which about 87 percent are frogs and toads, and the remainder are salamanders (10 percent) and the legless caecilians (3 percent), the latter found only in the moist tropics. Amphibians possess remarkable adaptations which allow them to occupy diverse habitats.

Declines

At the First World Congress of Herpetology, held in Canterbury, United Kingdom, in August 1989, many herpetologists reported on the evidently unconnected yet simultaneous and global disappearance of amphibian populations and species. Examples of declining and disappearing amphibian species include the gastric brooding frog (*Rheobatrachus silus*) of Australia; golden toad (*Bufo periglenes*) and yellow and black harlequin frog (*Atelopus varius*) of Costa Rica; Cascade frog (*Rana cascadae*), western toad (*Bufo boreas*), and Yosemite toad (*Bufo canorus*) of western United States; Pine Barrens tree frog (*Hyla andersonii*) and several species of mole salamanders (*Ambystoma tigrinum, Ambystoma laterale, Ambystoma jeffersonianum*) of the eastern United States; the leopard frog (*Rana pipiens*) of Canada and of the United States, and natterjack toad (*Bufo calamita*) of Great Britain. These are only a few of the reported cases.

One of the herpetologists in attendance at the meeting was David Wake of Berkeley. Upon his return from Canterbury, Wake organized a small meeting of leading herpetologists in Irvine, California. This group recommended that a scientific society host a meeting to further investigate whether or not the decline in amphibians was a general problem and to determine the cause(s). In addition the group created the Declining Amphibian Population Task Force (DAPTF) as a part of the Species Survival Commission of the International Union for the Conservation of Nature. Subsequently John Wright of the Los Angeles Museum organized a symposium on declining amphibian populations. The symposium was part of a joint meeting of the Herpetologists' League and the Society for the Study of Amphibians and Reptiles held at Tulane University in August 1990.

At that meeting, herpetologists presented information on declines in eastern and western Canada, the far western United States, Rocky Mountains, southeastern and northeastern United States, nuclear Central America, Costa Rica, Guatemala, the lowland Amazon Basin, cloud forests of the Andes, and Australia. These reports suggested that while populations of amphibians were declining, the degree of decline varied from area to area and within and among species. Declines appeared to be more extensive in the Northwest United States than in the Northeast. In the Northeast 26 of 43 (61 percent) amphibian species in the region were at some level of risk (i.e., 65 percent of the salamanders [15 of 23] and 55 percent of the frogs and toads [11 of 20] were listed by one or more states as either endangered, threatened, or species of special concern). Amphibians in the Southeast United States appeared to be faring somewhat better. In Central and South America, many species were disappearing or declining particularly in high elevation forests. In Australia species were declining throughout the continent.

The DAPTF was organized and opened its office for business in July 1991 at the Center for Analysis of Environmental Change in Corvallis, Oregon. The first coordinator was James Vial, formerly from the University of Oklahoma. The DAPTF in 1993 consisted of nearly 100 working groups in forty regions throughout the world.

In December 1993 the DAPTF published its first report authored by James Vial and Loralei Taylor entitled *Declining Amphibian Population Task Force Working Document No. 1, The Status of Amphibian Populations: A Compilation and Analysis*. This document presents a listing of species reported by DAPTF working groups around the globe to be in some degree of risk. There are over 720 status reports listed, although all reports do not suggest declines, the vast majority do. This is somewhat alarming because as recently as 1990 the Red

Book, the IUCN (International Union of the Conservation of Nature and Natural Resources) official list of threatened and endangered species, listed only sixty-three species of amphibians as being in some degree of risk. Clearly either the status of many populations has changed dramatically in a few years or the Red Data Book dramatically underestimated amphibians at risk.

Reasons for Decline

One factor that makes the reduction in numbers and/or disappearance of amphibian species distressing is that for many of the declines we cannot pinpoint the cause. The potential causal factors include acidic deposition and other forms of landscape-scale pollution, changing climatic conditions such as more frequent and intense droughts, increased intensity or changed frequency of ultraviolet light reaching the earth's surface, habitat destruction and fragmentation, and alterations in species interaction (i.e., predation, competition, disease) precipitated by one or more of the preceding factors. Scientists around the globe are conducting research in an attempt to determine which of these factors is most significant in influencing amphibian populations. Because these factors may interact synergistically to eliminate amphibian populations, the experimental elucidation of cause and effect will be extremely complex.

In the overwhelming majority of cases reported by Vial and Taylor the decline in amphibians appears to be due to habitat destruction, disturbance, and fragmentation. This was reported to be the case in Canada, throughout the United States, Central and South America, and the Commonwealth of Independent States. The detrimental effects of environmental pollutants have been documented in Africa, Asia, Australia, Canada, Commonwealth of Independent States, Europe, United States, and Zambia.

Research has shown a causal role for acidic deposition in eastern United States, Europe, and the United Kingdom and recent data suggests that increased ultraviolet radiation associated with ozone depletion may also play a significant role in some cases at least. Changes in hydrology combined with deforestation may be responsible for Costa Rican losses. The introduction of nonnative fish, frogs, and mammals has been implicated in declines in the western United States and Australia. Negative indirect effects of alien species have also been documented.

Weather is also known to influence amphibian populations. Drought has been implicated in declines in western United States, Australia, and Europe while flooding is thought to be responsible for a decline in the U.S. Pacific Northwest. Norman Scott, Jr., described a "postmetamorphic death syndrome" (PDS), in which the death of all postmetamorphic individuals in one area over a short period is followed by an outward ripple effect wherein surrounding populations suffer the same fate. This appears to be similar to disease epizootics familiar in humans (e.g., influenza) and other vertebrates (e.g., rabies). More research is called for regarding the hypothesis that increased levels of UV-B radiation, perhaps in conjunction with severe weather, weakens the immune system of amphibians resulting in disease outbreaks.

In Australia the cause of decline in amphibian populations seems to be habitat destruction and pollution associated with gold prospecting and mining. At the Canterbury congress, habitat destruction, pollution, and acidic deposition were identified as primary causes of declines in Europe and Africa.

Characteristics of Amphibians

Amphibians possess a suite of characteristics which make them sensitive to possible anthropogenic changes in their natural ecosystems. For example many species have complex life cycles which expose them to environmental changes in both terrestrial and aquatic phases; some species therefore face adverse conditions in two habitat types. Also some species are completely terrestrial while others are completely aquatic allowing for the differentiation between factors influencing only terrestrial or aquatic species. Young of many species have high growth rates, especially during the aquatic stages of the life cycle, that predispose them to perturbation effects because they require large amounts of energy for growth in a short time. Developing organisms are usually more sensitive to toxic conditions than are adults. The adult stage is relatively long lived, often greater than ten years. Thus adults may persist during conditions that kill embryos and larvae. Renewal of successful reproduction would give strong evidence of subsequent mitigation of anthropogenic and natural stress factors. Intra- and interspecific competition for resources, especially in the larval phase, amplifies stress effects and reflects differences in tolerance to stress among species.

Other characteristics that increase amphibian species' susceptibility to toxic conditions are their permeable eggs, gills, and/or skin, which are in constant contact with water or soils. Amphibians are ecothermic, a condition that makes them more vulnerable to extreme temperature fluctuations than endotherms. Aestivation and hibernation in soil and mud exposes these animals to potential toxins during a time when they can not actively respond either physiologically or behaviorally.

Amphibian species show a range of tolerance to stressful conditions with some species being very sensitive and others less sensitive to toxins. In fact different populations of some species differ in their response to acidic conditions suggesting that local adaptation has occurred.

Unlike most birds, amphibians do not leave the region during winter and thus analyses of factors causing population changes are unlikely to be confounded by perturbations taking place elsewhere. Unlike most large mammals, amphibians do not possess the ability to leave a landscape when stressful conditions appear.

Importance of Amphibians

Amphibians play a very significant role as predators in detritus and grazing food webs of aquatic and terrestrial habitats. In many habitats they appear to be the most abundant terrestrial vertebrates. For instance, the biomass of the population of red-backed salamanders (*Plethodon cinereus*) in Hubbard Brook, New Hampshire, is greater than that of breeding birds or small mammals occupying the same habitat. In the Northeast United States amphibians often average a density of one individual per two square meters (5,000 per hectare or 2,100 per acre) and their densities have been shown to be much higher in more southern latitudes. They influence cycling of calcium and sodium in forests of northeastern United States. They are also a high protein content prey for larger carnivores including the raccoon, fox, screech owl, brown thrasher, garter snake, and others.

They may also influence the structure and function of the detritus food web because they prey heavily on consumers of that food web. They eat springtails, mites, worms, millipedes, centipedes, spiders, and the larvae and adult of many kinds of insects. A single individual salamander in a northeastern U.S. forest may consume, depending on size of prey and of amphibian, 30 to 100 food items a day. They are active perhaps for 200 or more days per year and there may be 5,000 per hectare. This means the amphibian community in a single hectare of forest may consume 30 to 100 million prey items per year.

A recently completed experiment on the Huyck Preserve in east-central New York demonstrated that the red-backed salamander affected the species composition and abundance of invertebrates of the forest floor. Experimental enclosures with salamanders contained significantly fewer enchytraeid worms, millipedes, insect larvae, and spiders than enclosures without salamanders. In addition the presence of salamanders slowed decomposition of leaf litter probably because the salamanders consumed leaf litter fragmenters (larvae, enchytraeids, and millipedes). The reduced abundance of leaf fragmenters meant a reduced rate of litter fragmentation with a concomitant reduction in the rate of colonization of litter by fungi and bacteria and a reduced rate of decomposition. These results suggest that predation in terrestrial habitats may influence a basic ecosystem function, the dynamics of carbon cycling.

Conclusion

Amphibian numbers are declining—that fact by itself is reason for concern—but they are not alone. Thousands of species of plants, invertebrates, insects, fish, reptiles, birds, and mammals have been listed as threatened or endangered. The Red Data Book lists just under 5,000 species of animals as being in some state of decline. Thousands wait for listing, and reports of declining populations of various life forms occur daily in the scientific literature. Human beings are animals dependent on all those basic ecological processes upon which all life is dependent. Large scale, quasi-mysterious, changes in life on Earth may represent significant threats to human beings.

Richard L. Wyman

Further Readings

Duellman, W.E., and L. Trueb. *Biology of Amphibians*. 1986.

Heyer, W.R., M.A. Donnelly, R.W. McDiarmid, L.C. Hayek, and M.S. Foster, eds. *Measuring and Monitoring Biological Diversity: Standard Methods for Amphibians*. 1994.

Wyman, R.L. "Multiple Threats to Wildlife: Climate Change, Acid Precipitation, and Habitat Fragmentation." In *Global Cli-*

mate Change and Life on Earth. Ed. R.L. Wyman. 1991.

See also CLIMATE WARMING; EXOTIC SPECIES; FOOD CHAINS; HABITAT FRAGMENTATION, PATCHES, AND CORRIDORS; IUCN; OZONE DEPLETION; REPTILES: CONSERVATION AND HABITAT; WEB OF LIFE

Anarchism and the Environment
See ECOANARCHISM

Ancient Forests
See OLD GROWTH FORESTS

Animal Rights

The focus of the animal rights movement has historically been the elimination of unnecessary suffering, with sentience replacing rationality as the justification for rights attributions. The philosophical basis for this position was first developed by the utilitarian philosopher Jeremy Bentham in *Introduction to the Principles of Morals and Legislation* (1780), which contains the now famous passage: "The question is not, Can they *reason?* not, Can they *talk?* but, Can they *suffer?*" In the nineteenth century the central issues were the mistreatment of domestic animals and the abuse of wild animals for sport. Today, the issues center on the use of animals for research and abusive practices on factory farms. These concerns are historically distinct from scientific concerns about the "wanton destruction" of wild animals, in which the focus is on the extinction of species rather than the suffering of individual animals.

Although the rights of women, minorities, and children were established in principle by the early twentieth century, the rights of animals have remained more controversial. According to John Passmore, in *Man's Responsibility for Nature: Ecological Problems and Western Traditions* (1974), the change in moral behavior toward animals in the nineteenth century was not a recognition of their rights, but rather a restriction of the rights of humans to mistreat animals. The idea that animals have rights was revived by Peter Singer in his influential book, *Animal Liberation: A New Ethics for Our Treatment of Animals* (1975). Using sentience as his starting point, Singer calls for equal consideration, but not equal treatment, permitting more elaborate treatment of self-aware beings to take into account their additional capacities for suffering. He is concerned, nevertheless, about "speciesism," which on analogy with racism, is discrimination against animals. He avoids it by holding that healthy, self-aware animals should be treated as well as mentally dysfunctional humans. In terms of their sentience, he separates animals from plants "somewhere between a shrimp and an oyster." Although his book was originally considered a defense of animal rights, Singer announced in "The Fable of the Fox and the Unliberated Animals," *Ethics* (1978), that rights were not "essential" to his position. Since then his views have gradually been reinterpreted as a straightforward utilitarian position.

After the publication of Tom Regan's *The Case for Animal Rights* (1983), the term "animal rights" commonly began to refer to his view that to have rights animals must possess "inherent value." Based on this view, determinations about rights are based on the application of Regan's "subject-of-a-life" criterion, which in practice limits the animals clearly possessing rights to "mentally normal mammals of a year or more" (even though Regan leaves open the possibility that other arguments may someday be devised to include other animals). Although Regan argues that the extension of moral concern to species and ecosystems is "environmental fascism," his position is, nevertheless, in some respects similar to positions in environmental ethics based on the "good of its own" of an organism, which do not advocate rights for nonhumans: Paul Taylor defends "inherent worth" in *Respect for Nature* (1986), a biocentric egalitarianism that gives plants and animals equal status, and Holmes Rolston, III defends "intrinsic value" in *Environmental Ethics: Duties to and Values in the Natural World* (1988), which includes a hierarchy of value and extends it beyond animals and plants to species and ecosystems. The idea that rights can be based on sentience continues to be defended by S.F. Sapontzis in *Morals, Reason, and Animals* (1987).

Related rights positions for nature also exist in legal and environmental ethics literature. Joel Feinberg's "The Rights of Animals and Unborn Generations," in William Blackstone's *Philosophy and Environmental Crisis* (1974), applies rights only to entities capable of having interests, which are based on desires and aims arising out of some kind of belief or cognitive awareness. Christopher D. Stone, in *Should Trees Have Standing? Toward Legal Rights for Natural Objects* (1974), argues

for legal rights for nature generally analogous to those of mentally dysfunctional humans and corporations as legal persons. Most calls for rights for nature can be traced to two references to rights in Aldo Leopold's essay, "The Land Ethic," in *A Sand County Almanac* (1949): the right to continued existence and the biotic rights of songbirds. J. Baird Callicott, "Animal Liberation: A Triangular Affair," *Environmental Ethics* (1980), has held that a Leopoldian rights position can in principle be developed but has so far declined to do so. The development of a rights theory for nature is inhibited by the fact that, traditionally, rights are protections of the interests of individuals. Although the extension of rights to individual nonhuman organisms is plausible, environmentalists usually want a theory for species and ecosystems, which are not individuals and do not have interests in any straightforward sense. R.G. Frey, in *Interests and Rights: The Case against Animals* (1980), has argued that animals cannot have rights because they cannot make claims about their interests. Although his position has ideologically been ignored, Richard A. Watson in "Self-Consciousness and the Rights of Nonhuman Animals and Nature," *Environmental Ethics* (1979), has successfully defended primary and secondary rights for animals on traditional grounds. Problems with rights theory in environmental ethics have led to the development of alternative theories of intrinsic value.

A debate about the relationship of environmental ethics and animal rights was begun with Callicott's "Animal Liberation," in which he argues that they are incompatible. Mary Anne Warren, "The Rights of the Nonhuman World," in Robert Elliot and Arran Gare's *Environmental Philosophy* (1983), has responded that the two positions are complementary. Callicott, in "Animal Liberation and Environmental Ethics: Back Together Again," *Between the Species* (1988), has revised his position, adopting the "mixed community" position of Mary Midgley in *Animals and Why They Matter* (1983) and arguing that a single theoretical umbrella covering both positions is possible.

Eugene C. Hargrove

Further Readings

Hargrove, Eugene C., ed. *The Animal Rights/ Environmental Ethics Debate: The Environmental Perspective.* 1992.
Regan, Tom, and Peter Singer, eds. *Animal Rights and Human Obligations.* 2nd ed. 1989.

See also ENVIRONMENTAL ETHICS; INTRINSIC VALUE; LEOPOLD, ALDO

Anthropocentrism

Anthropocentrism—a fundamental and powerful concept in ecophilosophical thinking—is often employed vaguely, misunderstood, and/or misinterpreted. The dictionary definition of the term "anthropocentric" refers to any view that regards humans as the most important and central factor in the universe (from *anthropo-*, a combining form indicating "man" or, in its most inclusive and nonsexist formulation, "human"; and -*centric*, a suffix forming adjectives meaning "having a center as specified").

Historically, the assumption of human importance in and centrality to the larger scheme of things has arguably been the single deepest, most pervasive, and most persistent assumption of (at least) the Western mind. This applies to both secular and religious views, since even avowedly theocentric views—which might, in any case, be viewed simply as anthropocentric projections upon the cosmos—have, for all earthly purposes, been employed to legitimate the importance and centrality of humans to the cosmic drama. Moreover, as Fox (1989) has argued, the depth, pervasiveness, and persistence of this culturally dominant assumption is such that it also has issued in a multitude of consequential "higher-order" versions over and above its most general formulation. That is to say, certain classes of humans (e.g., Christians, "civilized" people/Europeans, whites, men, the wealthy) have typically adjudged themselves to be more human than others—to partake more in what they have taken to be the essence of humanness, such as closeness to God or rationality—in order to legitimate their domination over these others.

Like the terms "sexism" and "racism," anthropocentrism is typically used in reference to an unwarranted view or a prejudice. If there were ample evidence that humans were the most important and central factor in the universe then, having discriminated between views that are more anthropocentric and less anthropocentric, one would be justified in judging the former to be more correct and more valuable than the latter. In other words one could use the term "anthropocentric" in a discriminating way such that it would carry a positive connotation.

However, the facts increasingly appear to line up in the other direction. Powerful arguments can be made against anthropocentric views on: 1) scientific, 2) pragmatic, 3) logical, 4) moral, and 5) experiential grounds. The briefest overview of these classes of arguments runs as follows:

1. Humans do not dwell at the center of the physical universe, nor can they be said to represent the end point or apex of biological evolution in terms of any cosmic agenda that can be ascertained independently of human presumptions about such an agenda (instead, evolution appears to be a highly contingent—as opposed to directed—affair whose course resembles that of a luxuriously branching bush as distinct from a linear scale of increasing developmental perfection).
2. Anthropocentric assumptions have been serving to legitimate and encourage the ecological destruction of the earth.
3. It is not possible to specify a single, clearly discernible, morally relevant characteristic that includes all humans but excludes all members of the nonhuman world.
4. When contemporary philosophers have made a deliberate attempt to examine the question of moral consideration from first principles, as opposed to assuming an anthropocentric framework of reference from the outset, they have almost always concluded that the serious candidates for a criterion of moral consideration are ones whose beneficiaries extend well beyond the limits of humanity (e.g., sentience, life, and the capacity for self-renewal).
5. Many people feel that genuinely opening themselves to, say, the intricate lifeworlds of other forms of existence or the vastness of mountains, oceans, and deserts—let alone the universe itself, as when lying out under the stars—makes it very difficult to seriously believe in the overwhelming importance and centrality of humans to the larger scheme of things.

Thus this range of scientific, pragmatic, logical, moral, and experiential arguments against the validity of anthropocentric views means that the term "anthropocentric" typically carries a distinctly negative connotation.

The consequences of taking the developing critique of anthropocentric views seriously are potentially enormous. This critique, currently spearheaded by ecophilosophers, has the potential to alter the Western tradition and the conduct of human affairs globally and ineradicably.

Warwick Fox

Further Reading

Fox, Warwick. "The Deep Ecology-Ecofeminism Debate and its Parallels." *Environmental Ethics* 11 (1989): 5–25.
———. *Toward a Transpersonal Ecology: Developing New Foundations for Environmentalism.* 1990.

See also ANIMAL RIGHTS; DEEP ECOLOGY: EMERGENCE; DEEP ECOLOGY: MEANINGS; ECOPHILOSOPHY AND ECOPSYCHOLOGY; ENVIRONMENTAL ETHICS; INTRINSIC VALUE; RELIGION AND ENVIRONMENTAL PROTECTION

Appropriate Technology

"Appropriate technology" (AT) studies presuppose that technology is never neutral, since the consequences of any technique go beyond "useful work" to affect the quality of life, ecosystem integrity, political freedom, and other aspects of culture. Since judgments of AT are value laden, they are frequently contentious, reflecting differing economic and anthropological theories, or even philosophies of life. Proponents of AT are not antitechnology; they rather seek to incorporate variables beyond engineering and economic considerations into technological design and implementation.

Appropriate technologies vary across cultures and ecosystems; AT advocates characteristically attempt to minimize use of nonrenewable resources, pollution, and disruption of natural ecosystemic process, while optimizing use of renewable resources in ways that are culturally viable, economically feasible, and temporally plausible. AT in Third World countries is generally labor intensive, provides products for local consumption, avoids reliance on imported raw materials and machinery, minimizes capital investment, and utilizes local knowledge and expertise. In developed countries AT attempts to be ecologically and socially sensitive; accordingly, a mix of evaluative criteria, including political, health, and ecosystem variables, are included in AT studies.

While no one method dominates, AT studies suspend the presupposition that so-called high technology, which is capital and energy intensive, is superior to intermediate technology. A variety of issues are thus opened to inquiry, many of which challenge the so-called Western economic development model. Questions asked include: are capital intensive, high technology projects, like hydroelectric dams, more appropriate for developing countries than low cost, intermediate technology projects such as systematic drilling of village wells? Is no-till, organic agriculture based on the cultivation of perennials an appropriate technological alternative to the present energy and chemical intensive system of agricultural technology? Is nuclear power politically and ecologically benign or does it entail onerous political and ecological consequences?

AT studies are essential if we are truly to face up to these and other important value-laden questions and if technology is ever to be more our servant than our master.

Max Oelschlaeger

Further Readings

Heidegger, Martin. *The Question Concerning Technology.* 1977.
Schumacher, E.F. *Small Is Beautiful: Economics as if People Mattered.* 1973.

See also BICYCLE TRANSPORTATION; INTEGRATED PEST MANAGEMENT; NUCLEAR ELECTRIC POWER; RECYCLING; SCHUMACHER, E.F.; SOFT ENERGY PATHS; SUSTAINABLE AGRICULTURE

Aquaculture

Aquaculture, the farming and husbandry of aquatic organisms, has been practiced by the Chinese and other early civilizations for thousands of years. Technology in this field has developed rapidly in the past 200 years, concurrent with the worldwide growth of aquaculture as a source of food, a means of economic diversification, and a tool in fisheries management. Technological improvements in genetic enhancement, nutrition, disease control, and culture systems have made it possible to greatly intensify and expand aquacultural operations on a broad scale; these improvements have also made it feasible for aquaculture to surpass yields of capture fisheries of some species in the near future. Other technological improvements related to the rearing of game fish species have resulted in large-scale, government-operated stocking programs to enhance or rehabilitate dwindling stocks (e.g., the Salmonid Enhancement Program in British Columbia).

The technology used in aquacultural systems varies with the species raised, the environment in which the organisms are reared, and the intensity and scale of operation. Intensive culture systems, such as the type used to rear salmon and trout in Western countries, require large amounts of artificial feed, and either large amounts of water or recirculation systems to maintain high dissolved oxygen levels and remove nitrogenous waste products. Intensive operations may be carried out indoors in artificial troughs or circular tanks, outdoors in flow-through raceways, or in net cages placed in lake embayments or coastal waters. In extensive culture systems, the cultured animal or plant is reared in natural or artificial ponds with or without the addition of fertilizer to increase yields. These systems operate at a lower level of technology, using animals such as carp, tilapia, or crayfish that are more tolerant of warm water and low dissolved oxygen conditions. This lower level of technology makes extensive culture systems more widely adopted worldwide, particularly in third world countries.

The predominant aquaculture systems in Canada are cage culture of Atlantic, chinook and coho salmon in inshore areas along the East and West Coasts, and hatchery rearing of juvenile and yearling game fishes for stocking into natural waterbodies. A major concern with both of these systems is the effects of cultured fish on native fish populations, whether through purposeful stocking or accidental escape from cages. Cultured fish usually have different genetic and behavioral characteristics than native stocks, and since they are capable of interbreeding and cohabiting within the same environment, problems with gene pool alteration, competition, and disease transmission are a concern. In the case of Atlantic salmon, the North Atlantic Salmon Conservation Organization, an international body sponsored by participating North American and European countries, has developed recommendations to guide introductions and transfers of salmon stocks.

Another set of environmental concerns related to cage culture is eutrophication, oxygen depletion, and organic pollution of local waters where the culture operation is located. These effects are the result of the high density of fish reared in cages, the waste products of these fish, and the large quantity of feed required for high production. Much of this feed is uneaten by the fish and falls to the bottom of the ocean or lake where decomposition occurs. Some of this waste can be controlled by the use of high-energy diets that increase digestibility (thus decreasing feces production) and minimize the quantity of feed required. Another means of minimizing the negative effects of cage culture on the local aquatic environment is to restrict cage culture operations to areas with high water flushing rates from tides and currents. For example, British Columbia's Aquaculture and Commercial Fisheries Branch has developed criteria for the siting of cage culture operations and uses data on proposed operations and local environmental conditions to model the potential impact of effluents before operations are licensed.

A more global perspective on the sustainability of aquacultural production is taken by Carl Folke and Nils Kautsky. In their article "Ecological Economic Principles for Aquaculture Development," in *Nutritional Strategies and Aquaculture Waste* (1991), these authors examined typical aquacultural systems from the perspective of fossil fuel energy input per protein energy output, with the rationale that aquaculture is connected to the overall environment by the throughput of energy and matter from all ecosystem sources. Folke and Kautsky found that cage culture of salmon and salmonid enhancement through hatchery release of smolts (juveniles) are both very inefficient means of producing animal protein. The authors argue that aquaculture systems should not only have minimal impact on the local site, but also should be environmentally sustainable on a broader scale. In the case of salmonid cage culture, they recommend that it be practiced as a polyculture with mussels to reduce marine pollution and increase efficiency of energy use.

Michael G. Fox

Further Readings

Cowey, C.B., and C.Y. Cho, eds. *Nutritional Strategies and Aquaculture Waste: Proceedings of the First International Symposium on Nutritional Strategies in Management of Aquaculture Waste.* 1991.

Folke, Carl, and Nils Kautsky. "The Role of Ecosystems for a Sustainable Development of Aquaculture." *Ambio* 18 (1989): 234–43.

Mäkinen, Timo, ed. *Marine Aquaculture and Environment.* 1991.

Pillay, T.V.R. *Aquaculture and the Environment.* 1992.

See also EUTROPHICATION; FISHERIES CONSERVATION

Arctic

Present and potential problems of the arctic are related to the intrinsic vulnerability of its biological communities to extrinsic anthropogenic factors. This is not to say that the arctic is "fragile" in any sense; its communities have developed remarkable tolerance to even quite violent short-term natural oscillations in weather conditions, for example. But over the longer term, adaptive processes are slow by comparison with those in lower latitudes; persistent fundamental change may have profound effects on both macro- and micro-environments.

For plant communities, slow adaptive process is a function of very slow vegetative growth rates on scattered, thin, poorly drained soils. Low in temperature, limited in precipitation, evaporation, solar energy supply, and species diversity, the terrestrial arctic does not offer a safety net of ecological options or alternative opportunities of the sort enjoyed by species and communities in more "benign" biomes.

The short and constrained growing season available to plants slows genetic change. "Pincushion" growth patterns, "layering," and other forms of vegetative (asexual) replication are common. In many short summers sexual reproduction may not be possible, and it follows that adaptive genetic response to environmental perturbation will be limited accordingly. But successive, unusually severe years on any individual site are exceptional, and under undisturbed natural conditions plant communities are able to thrive over the long term.

Animals as well are remarkably able to endure the "boom-and-bust" nature both of weather patterns and population cycles such as those of lemmings and hares. Mammalian predators are usually able to turn to other food sources; numbers of hawks, owls, and jaegers may move farther south than usual in the hardest winters. But a breeding nucleus of the prey species always remains and stocks normally recover quickly.

Population cycles and weather anomalies are not pan-arctic; they tend to be localized. Adapted though they are to oscillations in both weather and food supply, terrestrial arctic communities become especially vulnerable when on the downswing. At such times any foreign stress—which is to say a stress with which the communities have not evolved to naturally cope—could have dire consequences. Arctic communities are by and large stretched almost to the limit of their tolerance in the best of times; to overload them is all too easy.

Marine arctic communities are probably less limited than terrestrial ones in some ways, but are dependent on regular seasonal ebbs and flows in the relative distribution of open water and ice cover. This is of critical importance to whales, seals, polar bears, and sundry seabirds, among others. Invertebrates and microorganisms as a whole are influenced by the availability of sunlight, and those especially abundant communities close inshore (upon which so many fishes, birds, and mammals are dependent) must have regular and uninterrupted seasonal supplies of fresh water from river mouths. The tuning of food webs thus sustained is exquisitely fine, and the potential ecological ramifications of their disturbance or obstruction are incalculable.

Environmental problems in the arctic are not new. For years it has been known, for example, that caribou "mosses" (lichens) store radioactivity, and that polar bear livers may contain large quantities of the toxic residues of certain chemical biocides. These are of course "global" contaminants that are in no sense unique to the arctic, but their presence in the thinly spread and relatively sparse biosystems of high latitudes may have more import there than in more resilient southern communities.

No doubt the arctic may be expected to be affected by the postulated increases in ultraviolet (UV) radiation as the result of a depleted ozone layer, and by some measure of global warming as currently foretold. One might reasonably anticipate measurable changes in vegetative communities—although in what direction it is impossible to predict. Warmer growing seasons could promote a deeper annual thawing of the permafrost and enrich the sparse plant cover that presently prevails over much of the arctic. This could accelerate soil buildup from a faster turnover of increased seasonal plant litter. Botanical immigrants from the south might find higher latitudes no longer quite so difficult, and native species could be replaced by more flexible and more fecund southern forms. New and more varied plant communities could conceivably emerge, and no doubt animal species of the boreal regions could extend their ranges proportionately. New mutations no doubt could be predicted on the basis of increased UV radiation. Such changes in the terrestrial environment might or might not be seen as beneficent, depending upon one's point of view.

There is no doubt, however, that a significant warming trend would have a profound influence on the marine ice regime. The first animals to be adversely affected would be the polar bears, which depend on ice cover for travel and hunting, and the species of seals which haul themselves out onto the ice surface. On the positive side, seasonal movements of such species as bowhead, beluga, narwhal, eider ducks, and murres might be greatly facilitated. Effects on marine food chains, given changes in light intensity and water temperature, can only be guessed at.

More susceptible to examination at the present time are the environmental problems presented by the penetration of the arctic by industry (notably, fossil fuel exploration and extraction, mining, and to a lesser but growing extent, tourism). All require at least semipermanent bases and other support facilities; all require supply and transport; all create waste; all disturb plant and animal communities both terrestrial and marine.

Critically attuned as they are to environmental conditions that allow little if any margin for error and limited ecological flexibility (in the sense of alternative pathways, processes, and participating constituents), arctic communities are intensely vulnerable to all manner of disturbances. Leaving aside the obvious on-site physical damage and attendant polluting effluent caused by construction and "development" generally, there are many subtler but potentially even more problematic and more widecast industrial impacts.

Life is not evenly dispersed across the arctic. Much biological activity, both marine and terrestrial, tends to be concentrated in pockets or "oases"—places where optimum conditions of natual productivity allow the greatest seasonal opportunities for large numbers of many species. Estuaries, polynias, sedge meadows, brackish lagoons, and ocean upwelling sites are typical examples, but they are few in number and often widely separated. Ironically enough, such places have long been known and used by the native people as well as the wildlife, and have thus tended to attract the attention of white southerners as well.

Arctic animals are remarkably different in their responses to human activities. Most larger species will avoid campsites, equipment-staging areas, and so forth, although the occasional wolf or bear, to its eventual cost, may become too interested in garbage. Ravens, jaegers, and gulls commonly forage in human refuse as do foxes from time to time. This is not a problem usually, but it can create unhealthy and potentially dangerous dependence.

Such installations become a major concern when they happen to be set in place in an area critical to the seasonal movements of wildlife. The polar bears of the Churchill area are a prime example. It is less well known that most species of arctic waterfowl have a number of different and particular places that are essential to their yearly cycles: for migration stop-overs in spring, for nesting, for moulting, for feeding, and premigratory staging in the autumn. None of these is required any more or less than any of the others. Each must be available at the correct juncture through the season. The same is true of beluga calving grounds and the migratory routes of the caribou herds. The arctic, vast and homogeneous though it may appear to be, is a mosaic of discrete, particular traditional places for individual wildlife species and populations at critical times of the year. There are no alternative sites for them.

Much disturbance of wildlife arises from boats and aircraft. Species vary in the nature and degree of their responses, which may differ through the several stages of the season. Also, most observers will agree that sporadic and/or unexpected disturbance may be more damaging, at least to some species, than a permanent site to which at least some individuals, perhaps prone to scavenging, may become "habituated" or even attracted.

Since both surface and air transport, and their supporting infrastructures, are prerequisite to the advancement of the several industries now penetrating the arctic, this form of disturbance must be placed in the first rank of present and potential environmental impacts. Quite sufficient is our knowledge from bitter experience of the biological significance of oil spills to make another recital of that danger unnecessary here. One would merely remind the reader that fossil fuel exploration proceeds apace in the arctic, that wells do blow out, that accidents during oil transport are all too familiar, and that the peculiar nature of arctic marine and terrestrial communities, and their inshore and coastal integration, renders them probably the most vulnerable of the world's ecosystems to destruction by this particular and virtually inevitable side effect of industrial penetration.

John A. Livingston

Further Readings

Livingston, John A. *Arctic Oil: The Destruction of the North?* 1981.
Page, Robert. *Northern Development: The Canadian Dilemma.* 1986.

See also ALASKA: PARK, WILDERNESS, AND
RESOURCE ISSUES; BEAUFORT SEA; BERGER
INQUIRY; CLIMATE WARMING; LONG RANGE
TRANSPORT; OIL SPILLS; PERMAFROST

Arctic National Wildlife Refuge

At the heart of the Arctic National Wildlife
Refuge is the coastal plain. Stretching from the
Mackenzie Delta in the Northwest Territories
to Prudhoe Bay in Alaska, it is the vibrant core
of a larger international arctic ecosystem defined by the annual migration of the Porcupine
caribou herd. Each year, the 180,000-head caribou herd migrates north from central Alaska,
the Yukon, and the Northwest Territories,
through mountain ranges to the coastal plain.
The coastal plain has also been at the heart of
a longstanding battle to exploit its potential oil
and gas reserves. At risk is one of the world's
great undisturbed ecosystems, and a subsistence
culture of 7,000 aboriginal people who live in
isolated villages such as Old Crow, Yukon, and
Arctic Village, Alaska.

In 1960 U.S. President Dwight D.
Eisenhower established an 8.9 million-acre
Arctic National Wildlife Refuge in northeast
Alaska to conserve the area's significant wildlife values and unparalleled recreational opportunities. The U.S. government was urged to
protect this arctic wilderness by such American conservation leaders as Olaus Murie and
Bob Marshall.

In 1980 Congress more than doubled the
size of the Arctic National Wildlife Refuge to 19
million acres when it passed the landmark
Alaska National Interest Lands Conservation
Act (ANILCA). The purpose of this enlarged
refuge is to conserve fish and wildlife populations including caribou, polar and grizzly bears,
muskoxen, wolves, and migratory birds and
their habitats. It also fulfills international treaty
obligations and ensures continued subsistence
use by local native populations.

All of the original refuge, except for the 1.5
million-acre coastal plain, was legally designated as wilderness under ANILCA. Congress
refused to designate it as wilderness because of
the area's potential oil and gas reserves. It called
for a study of the coastal plain's wildlife and
wilderness values and its potential for oil and
gas reserves. In April 1987 the Reagan administration completed the study and recommended Congress approve full leasing of the
coastal plain to industry for oil and gas development.

An international coalition of environmental and aboriginal organizations have to date
successfully persuaded Congress to forego development of the coastal plain. While the
coastal plain is only 1 percent of Porcupine caribou herd's range, it constitutes 90 percent of the
caribou's calving range. Each spring, over
80,000 pregnant cows gather on the coastal
plain where their calves are born. By July, most
of the females and calves have migrated to the
Alaskan portion of the coastal plain, gathering
into spectacular concentrations of caribou. Scientists fear that oil development in the nursery
of the herd would result in its decimation.

Canada's federal government is also opposed to development of the coastal plain. To
protect its portion of the coastal plain and the
herd's calving grounds, Canada established
Ivvavik National Park in 1984 through a comprehensive land claims agreement with the
Inuvialuit. And in 1987 Canada and the United
States signed the International Agreement for
the Conservation of the Porcupine Caribou
Herd to conserve both the animal and its habitat.

The ultimate goal of environmental and
aboriginal groups is to have Congress legally
designate the coastal plain as wilderness. In his
1992 presidential election platform, Bill Clinton
promised to act on this goal, but Congress has
yet to pass the appropriate legislation. Thus, the
coastal plain and its wildlife, along with aboriginal people in the area, remain at risk.

Kevin McNamee

Further Readings
McNamee, Kevin. "Wilderness or Oil
      Fields?" *Probe Post* 12(1): 6–11.
Alaska Coalition. *Arctic National Wildlife
      Refuge: Treasure of the North*. Washing-
      ton, D.C., January 1988.

See also ALASKA: PARK, WILDERNESS, AND
RESOURCE ISSUES; ARCTIC; BEAUFORT SEA;
BERGER INQUIRY; MARSHALL, BOB; UNGU-
LATES; WILDERNESS; WILDERNESS ACT

Army Corps of Engineers (U.S.)

The U.S. Army Corps of Engineers established
its first district in 1779. During the nineteenth
century Congress authorized the Corps of Engineers to take a major part in internal defense
projects, designing and building transportation
routes, including roads and navigation channels. It also began to regulate bridge construc-

tion and other potential obstructions to navigation. At the same time, a dual role for the Corps began to emerge. Congress expanded Corps activities well beyond military needs to encompass public works (e.g., surveys and the design and construction of buildings and parks). From the mid-nineteenth century through World War I, the Corps grew dramatically. In 1941 the Corps took responsibility for all army military and industrial construction, involving more than 27,000 projects and costing $15.3 billion.

Since World War II, the Corps has increasingly undertaken large civil works projects. Water resource projects included flood control, navigation, irrigation, water storage, hydroelectric power and recreation; disaster assistance and fish and wildlife management also came under the Corps' authority. It manages more than 2,500 recreation areas in forty-three states. By the early 1990s, the Corps' work in environmental restoration alone cost close to 1 billion dollars per year.

Today the Corps is one of the Army's seven major commands. With about 350 engineer officers and 39,000 civilians, it provides engineering, mobilization and construction support for the army, including plans, policies, and research and development at its four labs. It also manages the Army's considerable real estate holdings. The Corps has a broad range of customers and clients, including numerous federal agencies, state and local governments, and over eighty foreign countries. The UN, NATO and the World Bank sponsor its projects. The Corps has worked to establish a strong political base in its thirty-six districts, which have come to rely on its projects. Thus, the Corps has sources of power independent of the Army. The Corps has its own public affairs operation, with a reputation for sophisticated products.

The Corps has promoted itself as the Army's central environmental element. As the Corps has taken on more and larger projects, it has become embroiled in numerous battles with citizen groups. Projects to build dams and flood areas for lakes, and a preference for expensive, high-tech engineering have engendered strong opposition. Critics assert that the Corps fails to give sufficient weight to environmental protection compared to promoting commerce and growth, resulting in damage to or loss of precious habitats and ecosystems. Throughout the 1980s, the EPA opposed numerous Corps projects as detrimental to wetlands protection. In 1990, Congress directed the Army to include environmental protection as a primary mission of the Corps. In late 1993, a comprehensive federal policy was crafted to end the interagency battles over wetlands policy.

For over 100 years, the Corps has worked on flood control. In 1936 it gained responsibility for most federal flood control projects. It operates more than 500 dams and thousands of miles of levees, walls, and channels to control floods—costing about $23 billion over the past fifty years. Opponents argue that flood waters "controlled" in one area will produce greater destruction in other segments of the river. Another controversial consequence is that floodplains become habitable. With catastrophic flooding—which is inevitable, though less frequent with flood control—toxic chemicals stored on the floodplain are swept into the ecosystem and dispersed. Reestablishing flood controls came under debate during the 1993 Midwest floods. Some called for "bigger and better" controls; others suggested planning land use around flood plains. The Army Corps of Engineers decided to rebuild its levees before significant public debate took place. Federal government policies generally endorse rebuilding.

As with any large and successful organization, Corps policies have not changed quickly. After years of pressure, the Corps has moved toward greater environmental awareness in evaluating projects, and its control of environmental issues within the army has been challenged. For many years, the army's civilian officials responsible for environmental matters were often overruled or outmaneuvered by Corps leadership. In the early 1990s, the Army reorganized its environmental elements; coincidentally, leadership of the Army Corps changed. These changes, and Department of Defense restructuring initiated in 1993, have resulted in greater influence over environmental policy by other Army elements.

Odelia Funke

Further Readings

Mazmanian, Daniel A. *Can Organizations Change: Environmental Protection, Citizen Participation, and the Army Corps of Engineers.* 1979.
Morgan, Arthur E. *Dams and Other Disasters.* 1971.

See also CHANNELIZATION; HYDROELECTRICITY; WATER ALLOCATIONS AND SHORTAGES; FRESHWATER WETLANDS

Arsenic

The element arsenic (chemical symbol, As) is a metalloid which can take many chemical forms, and may behave as a cation (As^{+3}, As^{+5}) or as an anion (AsO_3^-, AsO_5^-). Different chemical forms of arsenic can have widely differing effects on living organisms. Conversion of one form into another can have dramatic effects. For example, arsenic used in wallpaper pigments can be converted to volatile forms of arsenic (arsines) by molds which develop on the walls of damp dwellings. Inhabitants of these dwellings can inhale the gas and will suffer toxic effects.

Of all poisons, arsenic is arguably the most well known, because of its reputation with professional poisoners and through the writings of mystery stories such as *Arsenic and Old Lace*. Its availability as a rat poison has added to its poor public image, but in fact arsenicals make relatively crude poisons. There have been suggestions that Napoleon Bonaparte was poisoned by arsenic, and certainly rather large amounts of arsenic were detected in samples of his hair (for many elements including arsenic hair or fur retains a record of the body burden of an individual; this property has been used in forensic science). Others argue that arsenic was so widely used in Napoleon's time, that the arsenic in his hair did not indicate unusual exposure.

Known since 2000 B.C. the element has been used in various forms for many purposes: industrial, agricultural, and medical. It also occurs as an environmental pollutant, entering the environment through deliberate application as a pesticide or as a byproduct of fossil-fuel burning and smelting of metal ores.

Concern for arsenic in the environment and the workplace is based upon its known toxic and carcinogenic properties. In humans, arsenicals cause slow, painful death, and doses too low to be toxic have been known since 1820 to be associated with various forms of cancer, particularly of the skin and nasal septum. Occupational exposure originally provided a link between arsenic and human cancer, but environmental contamination of water and food from the mining and smelting of gold (e.g., Yellowknife, Northwest Territories of Canada) has also resulted in arsenic-related cancer in humans.

Arsenic's biocidal properties were the basis of many of its applications: in human medicine (to treat ulcers, 460 B.C.; against trypanosomes, A.D. 1905) and as a pesticide (Paris Green, copper acetoarsenite was one of the earliest insecticides, A.D. 1867; arsenic trioxide was used as a rodenticide until quite recently; arsenic acid, a defoliant, used in modern times). Interestingly, the simple arsenic acids, while being very toxic to plants, are relatively nontoxic to humans and other animals. Arsenic has also been used in pigments, although arsenical pigments are no longer in wide use.

The therapeutic application of arsenic in medicine is now under strict control and during the latter half of the twentieth century most of the early uses of arsenic have been eliminated. Environmental exposure of plants, humans, and other animals to arsenic, which still occurs in some specific locations, is the major remaining source of concern regarding this element in developed countries.

Pamela Welbourn

Further Readings

Frost, D.V. "Arsenicals in Biology." *Fed. Amer. Soc. for Exper. Biol. Fed. Proc. 26* (1967): 194–208.

National Research Council of Canada. *The Effects of Arsenic in the Canadian Environment.* 1978.

See also MINING AND SMELTING: HISTORIC IMPACTS; PESTICIDES

Asbestos

Asbestos is nearly indestructible—it resists fire, heat, and most chemicals—and that is why it has been both widely used and deadly to humans for more than two millennia. Asbestos is a grave threat to human health because its tiny fibers are lodged in the lungs bypassing the human body's usual defense mechanisms—the protective hairs and mucus of the nose and throat. They are trapped in the lungs and scar tissue forms around them. Repeated or heavy exposures can result in excessive scar tissue, reduced lung capacity, and persistent shortness of breath. That condition has been given the name of asbestosis. Asbestosis in turn is associated with a variety of even more serious health problems including heart problems, resulting from the stress of continuously forcing oxygen into the damaged lungs, and a variety of cancers: lung, throat, chest cavity, stomach, colon, rectum, and larynx.

Asbestos was used in manufacturing as early as Roman times and even then it was known that it posed a threat to the health of those who worked with it. The specific disease asbestosis was reported by a London physician in 1900 and enough was known by 1918 that some insurance companies were refusing coverage to asbestos workers. Deaths and single-case links between asbestosis and lung cancer were increasingly reported in England and the United States by the 1920s. Thereafter the science of epidemiology and the evidence against asbestos had a parallel development. In 1935, for example, a study of the health of 126 randomly chosen asbestos workers in Canada and the United States found that fully half had asbestosis. Little was done to protect the health of workers and during World War II very large numbers of people were working with the substance in the shipbuilding industry, for example.

There is usually a time lag between exposure to asbestos and the onset of lung cancer. It was not conclusively proven that there was a connection until the publication in the 1960s of the epidemiological studies of Dr. Irving Selikoff and others using evidence regarding the health of 632 randomly chosen workers in the wartime shipbuilding industry. Death certificates were painstakingly located and the assembled data revealed that lung cancer incidence was six times higher than it was within the general population. Nonetheless, even after these studies were published, many buildings were constructed with asbestos in walls, ceilings, and even heating ducts.

Study upon study of those who worked with, or were exposed to, asbestos showed linkages. Even random autopsies of the general population in large cities found asbestos-related lung damage in a high proportion of people, most of whom had never worked with asbestos. This later finding was believed to have been the result in most cases of exposures related to the wide use of asbestos fibers in the brake linings of automobiles and trucks. The grinding of millions of brakes put the fibers into the ambient air. Class action lawsuits on behalf of asbestos mine and mill workers forced the Johns-Manville Corporation, the leading producer, into bankruptcy.

In the 1970s, and since, the number and variety of asbestos uses has declined sharply. But the mineral is still mined in considerable quantities in, for example, Quebec. Miners are exposed and, although exposure levels are much lower than they once were, it is likely that there are still negative health effects, both there and within the workplaces where it is still used (mostly in the manufacture of asbestos-cement sewer pipe). Asbestos removal became and remains an industry of considerable size; this too,

however, is an occupation that is not without risks to human health. The history of asbestos illustrates—perhaps better than that of any toxic substance—the arbitrariness of separating in regulatory treatment outdoor air, indoor air, and the safety of consumer products. It also demonstrates the importance of responding with a prudence that considers the long-term risks to human health as more important than short-term challenges to economic output.

Robert Paehlke

Further Readings

Dupré, J.S., et al. *Report of the Royal Commission on Matters of Health and Safety Arising from the Use of Asbestos in Ontario.* 3 vols. Government of Ontario, 1984.

Selikoff, I.J. "Asbestos Air Pollution." *Archives of Environmental Health* 25 (1972): 1–13.

Stellman, Jeanne, and Susan Daum. *Work Is Dangerous to Your Health.* 1973.

See also EPIDEMIOLOGY; INDOOR AIR POLLUTION; LABOR AND THE ENVIRONMENT; OSHACT AND OSHA; STANDARD SETTING; TOXICOLOGY

ASEAN Haze

Visibility impairment due to aerosol haze is now a common phenomenon throughout the ASEAN region, as it is in continental North America and Europe. Transboundary pollution of haze is seen by regional governments as an issue of major environmental concern. ASEAN is an acronym for the Association of South East Asian Nations, comprising the nation states of Brunei, Indonesia, Malaysia, The Philippines, and Thailand. It is an industrializing tropical region with rapidly expanding national economies.

During the dry season (April to October through much of the region) there is a ubiquitous background regional haze which is thought to arise from a number of urban and rural sources. These include the photochemical production of aerosol from anthropogenic emissions of gaseous precursors such as SO_2, NO_X, and reactive hydrocarbons; primary aerosol emissions from transport, industry, and agriculture; and primary aerosol emissions from domestic, refuse, and agricultural (nonforest) burning. In addition, the haze problem can become particularly acute during times of drought, when large forest fires in the heavily forested areas of Sumatra and Kalimantan can become established, providing heavy aerosol loadings to the regional atmosphere. Such severe haze events occurred during August 1990 and during September and October 1991. During the latter event daytime horizontal visibility in parts of Peninsular Malaysia dropped below 1 kilometer for periods, closing airports and affecting shipping movements. Reduced sunshine hours and levels of solar radiation in Malaysia during October 1991 are also thought to have affected plant growth and consequently crop yields. It is also believed that radiative cooling above the regional polluted layer created stable conditions that were favorable for trapping pollutants emitted locally.

For a number of reasons there is developing regional and international interest in gaining a better understanding of ASEAN haze. First, there is widespread concern over the reduction in visual amenity associated with dense urban/regional haze. Second, there is a growing recognition that respirable atmospheric particles pose a significant local and regional health risk. Third, the processes of air pollution formation and destruction are not as well understood in the humid tropics as they are in the mid-latitude, industrial nations. Finally, it is now recognized that perturbations to the regional atmospheric aerosol load, when summed globally, may affect global climate. Therefore it is clear that assessments of aerosol loadings, properties, sources, and dynamics are required for all parts of the globe, especially in the rapidly developing tropical Asian region where aerosol haze is now endemic.

Nigel J. Tapper

Further Readings

Goldammer, J.G., ed. *Fire in the Tropical Biota: Ecosystem Processes and Global Challenges.* 1990.

Levine, J., ed. *Global Biomass Burning: Atmospheric, Climatic and Biospheric Implications.* 1991.

See also AIR POLLUTION: IMPACTS; SMOG

Asian Environmental Thought

Asian intellectual traditions differ from one another no less than from European thought. The various traditions discussed here include Hinduism, Jainism, Buddhism, Confucianism, and Taoism.

Hinduism

Fundamental to Hindu belief is the idea that a single, universal Being, *Brahman*, resides at the core of all phenomenal beings. A sense of identity with other beings leads to sympathy and compassion.

Arne Naess adopted the concepts of "identification" and "Self-realization" from Hindu thought and made them the central doctrines of Deep Ecology. If we can identify with the beings in the world around us we may treat them less callously. When we realize that we are not disconnected from the natural environment—that the environment is the "wider Self"—we may come to see biocide as tantamount to suicide.

The unity of phenomena posited in Hindu thought has been compared to the unity of terrestrial nature posited by ecology. There is, however, a signal difference. In ecology animals and plants remain separate and distinct beings. They are united into hierarchically ordered ecosystems by their functional relationships. In Hindu thought, however, things only appear to be many; they are not represented as systemically unified, but instead are alleged instead to be essentially one.

Jainism

In contrast to the core monistic philosophy of Hinduism, Jainism is dualistic. Individual immortal souls inhabit material bodies of every kind. Embedded in gross physical matter, a soul's perceptions are distorted and its consciousness dimmed. Carnal desires attach souls more firmly to the material world and determine the form of life into which each will be reborn. The purpose of Jain religious practice is to purify the soul and thus liberate it from the necessity of physical rebirth. The most direct path to such liberation is the practice of asceticism and *ahimsa*, or not harming any living being.

Even though Jainism is an otherworldly religion, Jains are bidding for global leadership in environmental ethics. Their asceticism leads them to live a life of very low material consumption. And their *ahimsa* ethic is analogous to the reverence-for-life and respect-for-life environmental ethics developed in the West by Albert Schweitzer and Paul Taylor, respectively.

Buddhism

The main problem in life with which the Buddha sought to deal was suffering (*dukkha*). His enlightened solution to it was overcoming desire. One may then live in the world in a state of disinterested wonder and joy. When our perceptions are not distorted by desire and aversion, we accept the world as it is and do not try to make it over.

As Buddhism took root and flowered in China and Japan it took on characteristics of the thought indigenous to those countries. In China, Taoism's attunement to natural rhythms and processes, and in Japan, the Shinto nature-gods, or *kami*, variously gave East Asian Buddhism a less anthropocentric focus. The Buddha was a compassionate teacher full of a boundless loving kindness. Buddhism's overarching concern with *dukkha* eventually led Far Eastern Buddhists to a universal extension of beneficence and to feel a sense of solidarity with all other suffering beings. All living beings came to be regarded as endowed with a Buddha-nature. All creatures thus are fellow-seekers, walking the path to enlightenment together—each in its own way.

Confucianism

In the West Confucianism connotes blind adherence to custom and hollow social forms, maudlin filial piety, and knuckling under to a hierarchical bureaucratic regime. Looking beneath the surface, however, Confucianism, much more than Hinduism, provides the classical Asian analog of the contemporary "ecological self" for which the Deep Ecologists are groping.

In the West the essential self has been associated with the God-given soul that temporarily inhabits a physical body. Thus the "individual" is conceived to be independent and autonomous. In Confucian thought the self is no less unique, but each person is socially constituted—defined by his or her social relationships—and thus far from independent and autonomous.

This Confucian concept of the self may be generalized and, so to speak, ecologized. Human beings are environmentally constituted. The human brain is big and the mind powerful because the world in which Homo sapiens evolved is biologically diverse and ecologically complex. Thus the loss of biodiversity and the simplification and homogenization of ecosystems cannot be conceived, as it often is in the West, as an unfortunate but necessary sacrifice of the natural "other" to human values. It is rather a diminishment of human nature.

Taoism

Taoism is vaguely anti-urban, anti-humanistic, and anti-bureaucratic, tending toward bioregional anarchy. Thinking of nature through the concept of the *tao*, or "way," evokes a world of processes rather than things, and change rather than stasis, similar to the evolutionary, ecological worldview.

To live in accord with the *tao*—the practical goal of Taoists—is to live in harmony with nature. Contemporary environmentalists have found a prescription for "appropriate technologies" in the Taoist concept of *wu wei* or "not-doing." Not-doing does not mean inaction. Instead it means allying oneself with—rather than opposing—the forces of nature to accomplish one's purposes. Boiling water to generate electricity by nuclear fission is *yu wei*, doing. Generating electricity with wind mills is *wu wei*.

J. Baird Callicott

Further Readings

Callicott, J. Baird. *Earth's Insights: A Multicultural Survey of Ecological Ethics*. 1994.

———, and Roger T. Ames, eds. *Nature in Asian Traditions of Thought: Essays in Environmental Philosophy*. 1989.

See also APPROPRIATE TECHNOLOGY; DEEP ECOLOGY: EMERGENCE; ECO-SPIRITUALITY; ENVIRONMENTAL ETHICS; NAESS, ARNE; RELIGION AND ENVIRONMENTAL PROTECTION

Aswan High Dam

The High Dam on the Nile River at Aswan attracted world attention because of the magnitude of its alteration of a great river basin and because of the controversy it provoked as to its economic and environmental effects. It was constructed during 1960–1969 to serve three major purposes, and in so doing changed the physical, biological, and social character of the lower Nile drainage in major ways.

The High Dam, known in Arabic as Sadd el-Ali, is located in the vicinity of the lowest cataract of the Nile where a low dam had been constructed for irrigation purposes in three stages between 1902 and 1933. It is about 111 meters high and causes the inundation of over 3,000 to 6,000 square kilometers of riverside and desert land depending upon the volume of water stored at any one time. After intricate international discussions it was undertaken by Egypt and the Soviet Union in 1957 to: 1) control all floods of the Nile by detention in the reservoir; 2) store water from annual floods so that specified releases for irrigation and other purposes could be assured throughout the year and over a period of at least 100 years regardless of upstream flows; and 3) generate hydroelectric power. The regulated flows of water and electricity were viewed as powerful aids to the development of irrigated agriculture, industrial production, and associated commerce.

The direct physical effects were massive. In the space permitted here it is impossible to give detailed figures on their dimensions, and they can be described only in general terms. Pastoralists were deprived of grazing from the lands flooded by the reservoir. More than 100,000 Nubians were relocated from inundated villages in Egypt and the Sudan. Large numbers of archeological monuments were flooded, removed to other sites (as with Abu Simbel temple), or protected (as with the island of Philae).

The new reservoir in the desert resulted in the evaporation of some water that otherwise would flow downstream, the seepage of some water into underlying aquifers, and the deposition of silt that would also have moved downstream. Due to storage and mixing, the quality of water in the new reservoir and downstream changed. The new water body provided an environment for plankton and fish populations and for varying lengths of shorelines and seasonally inundated shores.

Below the dam, flows were regulated to prevent either great floods or low flows in all but a few years. Channel degradation by the clearer waters increased. Navigation benefited from decreased surface fluctuations and from the use of the lake for transport. Power production and transmission expanded to the plant's capacity. The quality of water in the river changed by a decrease in turbidity and increases in dissolved solids, salt burden, and phytoplankton density. The annual load of silt and renewal of brick-making materials was terminated, and large areas of farmland were lost by excavation to groundwater tables.

For several reasons there was a small net decline in formerly irrigated land. With new multiple cropping, cropped area increased substantially, crop production nearly doubled, and crop combinations changed. Progress was made in extending drainage. While fish catches and the number of species of fish along the river declined, the fishing landings in the eastern part of the Mediterranean declined substantially.

Those losses were offset by landings of freshwater fish from the reservoir behind the dam. As a result of silt deprivation, coast land was lost by erosion in a few sectors.

Thirty years later, the basic aims of controlling river flow for curbing flood overflow, enlarging irrigation production, and boosting power generation had been achieved. Many of the side effects noted above had been anticipated in the planning, but at least three had been missed: the full effects of changes in water quality and of available nutrients in cultivated fields; the need to provide for a supplemental emergency flood outlet upstream of the dam in the event of a very great flood; and the consequences of cutting off materials for brick making.

It has been popular in some circles to assert that the negative effects of the dam outweigh the benefits. This is difficult to test; on the one hand the full social and economic benefits to the Egyptian people have not been calculated with care; on the other hand the value of the environmental losses has also been estimated only roughly. A comprehensive appraisal is lacking. The building of Aswan High Dam illustrates how easy it is to undertake a huge, complex project without persistently assessing its full consequences for natural systems and people.

Gilbert F. White

Further Readings

Abu-Zeid, Mohmoud. "Environmental Impact Assessment for the Aswan High Dam." In *Environmental Impact Assessment for Developing Countries*. A.K. Biswas and Q. Geping. 1987.

Goldsmith, Edward, and Nicholas Hildyard. *The Social and Environmental Effects of Large Dams*. 1984.

White, Gilbert F. "The Environmental Effects of the High Dam at Aswan." *Environment* 30 (1988): 4–11, 34–40.

See also Colorado River; Columbia River Basin; Echo Park Dam; Hydroelectricity; James Bay; Rhine River; St. Lawrence River; Water Allocations and Shortages (U.S. West)

Audubon, John James

John James Audubon (1785–1851), famous artist and ornithologist, was born in Aux Cayes, Santo Domingo (now Haiti). He was the illegitimate son of Jean Audubon, a French seaman and planter. His mother, who died several months after John's birth, was apparently a creole servant named Mademoiselle Rabine. There has been uncertainty regarding her race, though Audubon biographer Alice Ford has identified her as Jeanne Rabine, a French chambermaid. Rabine's child, Jean Rabine, was adopted by Audubon and his wife in 1794 and was baptized Jean Jacques-Fougère Audubon in 1800. He later began using the English translation of his name, John James. Audubon was evasive about his origins and even encouraged the belief that he was the lost dauphin of France. This was just one of his many autobiographical embellishments.

Audubon grew up in France and the United States and developed an early interest in art and birds. He married Lucy Bakewell in 1808 and was granted United States citizenship in 1812. He tried a number of unsuccessful business ventures, including work as a merchant in Kentucky. Throughout this period, Audubon studied and drew birds. A visit by Alexander Wilson to his store in 1810 fired Audubon's ambition to surpass Wilson as an artist and naturalist. Following bankruptcy in 1819, he gave up hopes of being a businessman and supported his family by working as a portraitist and teacher. His wife, also a teacher, helped to support the family while he sketched birds and pursued his ornithological studies on sometimes arduous journeys into the wilderness.

In 1824 Audubon went to Philadelphia in the hope of having his birds published. Thomas Sully gave him his first instruction in painting with oil while he was there. His publishing ambitions, though, were thwarted by George Ord, who was completing the posthumous ninth volume of Wilson's *American Ornithology*. Audubon then turned to Europe. In 1826 he traveled to England where he exhibited his bird paintings and found support for his project. Producing *Birds of America*, which was sold to subscribers in groups of five plates ($1,000 for the set in the United States), was a massive undertaking that spanned 1827–1838. The 435 plates, which included every North American bird then known, measured 27 by 40 inches each, a format chosen to allow the birds to be presented in full size. Between 175 and 200 complete sets were produced. The illustrations, which presented the birds in lifelike poses amidst appropriate vegetation, were praised for their detail, accuracy, and artistry.

He traveled extensively in America gathering specimens, information, and illustrations as the plates were produced. Audubon's five-volume *Ornithological Biography* appeared in 1831–1839. It provided detailed accounts of the species set in the same order as the *Birds of America* plates. Less expensive editions of his work made Audubon's accomplishments more accessible to the public. In his last years Audubon produced a study of American mammals, *Viviparous Quadrupeds of North America*.

Today, Audubon's name is best known for the National Audubon Society and the independent state societies that are named for him. The first Audubon Society was created by George Bird Grinnell, who was tutored in his youth by Audubon's widow.

Ralph H. Lutts

Further Readings
Ford, Alice. *John James Audubon: A Biography.* 1988.
Herrick, Francis Hobart. *Audubon the Naturalist: A History of His Life and Time.* 1938.

See also BIRDING; ENVIRONMENTAL AESTHETICS; NATIONAL AUDUBON SOCIETY

Audubon Society
See NATIONAL AUDUBON SOCIETY

Australia: Resource Use Conflicts

With an area of 768 million hectares, Australia is several times larger than Western Europe yet it has a population of only 17 million. The country is enormously rich in mineral and energy resources and these, together with wheat, wool, and woodchips, make up around 80 percent of Australia's exports by value, an increasing proportion of which is aimed at the Asian market. The economy, then, is heavily dependent upon commodity exports and there is often enormous controversy if specific new mining or similar ventures are opposed on environmentalist or native land rights' grounds. In June 1992, for example, the Full Bench of the High Court handed down its judgment in the long-awaited case of *Mabo v. Queensland and the Commonwealth*. The dispute centered on the question of native title and whether or not this had been extinguished by European conquest. Dramatically overturning previous High

Court rulings on the *terra nullius* issue, the judges decided that native title had not been extinguished. It is no exaggeration to say that this was a revolutionary judgment without precedent in Australian history and the subsequent consternation on the part of the mining and pastoral sectors has been without parallel. The full ramifications of the judgment are as yet unclear but historically it comes only a year after a major Resource Assessment Commission Inquiry concluded that a proposed large new mining venture should not be allowed to proceed at Coronation Hill in the Northern Territory, largely because of the adverse impacts this would have on aboriginal lands.

While still relatively small, the present population of Australia is around forty times higher than in pre-European times and each Australian, on average, now uses 100 to 150 times more energy than the country's earliest inhabitants. Of the total population, 75 percent live within 50 kilometers of the coast and 35 percent are in just two cities: Melbourne and Sydney. However, by far the most rapidly growing part of the country in terms of population is Australia's "Sunbelt" in southeastern Queensland, especially between Brisbane and the Gold Coast. With a current growth rate of 2.5 percent—well in excess of the national average—the Moreton metropolis in southeastern Queensland is expected to have 500,000 more people by the year 2000, and a population of 3.1 million by 2005. With 13 percent of Brisbane's sewage currently passing, untreated, into Moreton Bay, all the signs indicate that population growth is fast outstripping infrastructure provision.

Declining near-shore water quality is becoming a serious problem in many areas and is now starting to impact on the fishing and tourism industries. In addition, there was considerable public outrage in 1993 when a government inquiry released its *Ships of Shame* report. This document highlighted the poorly maintained state of many of the bulk oil and ore carriers plying Australian waters and warned of a catastrophe just waiting to happen in globally significant areas like the Great Barrier Reef.

Urban residential densities are extremely low by world standards. Brisbane, for example, with a population of 800,000, covers the same area as Greater London, with some 8 million. Such low densities are both caused by, and also encourage, one of the highest levels of per capita car ownership in the world. Only 10 percent of Australian households do not have access to a

motor vehicle and all but 95 percent of total land travel is by car. In addition, ready access to some of the most bountiful coal reserves in the world means that coal-fired—and often highly inefficient—electricity generation is the norm in most states. Increasingly, power generation—like water supply—is being privatized, though not without strong public opposition. As a consequence, with 0.3 percent of the world's population, Australia produces 1.6 percent of the annual carbon dioxide output, or around 124 million tonnes. A continuation of present trends will see a 35 percent increase in carbon dioxide emissions over 1988 levels by the year 2000. The Australian government has made a commitment to reduce greenhouse gas emissions by 20 percent on 1988 levels by the year 2005 (an annual cut of around 14.2 million tonnes). A recent assessment (in May 1993) was that the government was at least 12 months behind schedule in implementing these reforms.

The initial data give a hint of one of the most fundamental ideological conflicts in contemporary Australia—that between the dominant (combined corporate and state) power interests favoring minimal government controls (over such things as private enterprise mining or pastoral developments and car ownership) and those urging much stricter state regulation of such activities and a renewed emphasis on environmental preservation and very much lower resource consumption levels. As in Canada and the United States, the regulatory framework is complicated by a federal system of administration which, under the Constitution of 1901, sees six States and two Territories having major control over natural resources' decision-making. These States often have governments in power of quite different political persuasions. There are also almost 1,000 separate local government entities and, in addition, in some circumstances, the Commonwealth government can use one of its several constitutional powers to override the States on environmental issues. Whether or not this happens depends largely on the political philosophy of the ruling administration in Canberra. Thus, under the Hawke, Labor government, the State of Tasmania was overruled in 1983 in its bid to build a new hydro-dam on the Lower Gordon River in the World Heritage wilderness in the west of the State. However, for political reasons, a year later the same federal government also chose not to use its reserve powers to overrule the State of Queensland to prevent the construction of a highly controversial tourist road in the north of the State through the pristine Daintree rainforest, adjacent to the Great Barrier Reef.

Principally because most of the interior is so arid, the population is strongly concentrated along the eastern and southern seaboards. This alone contributes directly to a range of significant environmental problems because it means that much of the country's best agricultural lands and scenic resources are under constant pressure from urban development. The combination of population concentration and aridity also means that there is worsening ocean and beach pollution, caused in part by aging or non-existent sewer systems, and a strongly localized demand for water for the rapidly expanding urban population. The water supply difficulties for Perth and Adelaide are especially serious. There is also the added problem of burgeoning urban and industrial wastes and the difficulty of finding suitable landfill sites. Logging interests are currently pushing to gain access to the tall hardwood trees in the formerly closed catchment forests near Melbourne. However, recent controversial research findings point to a strong correlation between logging and decreased water yields in these valuable water supply catchments.

The population question is inextricably linked with natural resource issues and for most of the twentieth century there has been an ongoing—and often heated—debate as to how many people the world's driest populated continent can support. As a rule, conservative governments have always tended to encourage high immigration levels on the grounds that continental Australia has the potential for a very large population, perhaps as high as 150 million. Reformist governments, and many environmental groups, on the other hand, have frequently argued for much lower population targets. Organizations such as Australians for an Ecologically Sustainable Population (AESP) emphasize the country's generally poor soils and El Nino, Southern Oscillation-dominated climate as major constraints to population growth which, in their opinion, should be stabilized at between 6 and 12 million. At its current rate of growth Australia appears to be heading for a population of around 30 million by the year 2031, a figure that many environmentalists regard as totally unjustifiable.

On top of this, Australia plays host to over 2 million overseas tourists annually, a figure that is rising rapidly each year and is expected to reach 5 million by the turn of the century. The country is a favored destination for the burgeoning Asian market, but this trend is not without its vocal critics. In recent years Japanese business interests, for example, have been busily buying up local real estate for a network of large integrated golf course and resort complexes, notably in Queensland and Western Australia. Not only do such resorts have extensive space requirements but they also place enormous demands on limited water resources. One major golf course requires over 3,000 cubic meters of water per day and the most recent estimates are that, by the turn of the century, water demand will have outstripped available supply in all but one of Australia's eleven water demand regions.

There is no doubt that the Australian environment has been dramatically transformed in the brief 200-year period since initial European settlement. Land degradation is by far the nation's most serious environmental problem, and has been for many decades, but this of course has as much to do with the depredations of introduced rabbits, sheep and cattle as it has with simple population numbers. Land clearance has been especially damaging. At the time of European settlement 10 percent of Australia was forested and woodlands covered an additional 23 percent of the land. Since then, around 50 percent of the forests (but 75 percent of the rainforests) and 35 percent of the woodlands, have been either totally cleared or severely modified. The impact on indigenous plants and animals has been catastrophic. Of the 188 mammals that were endemic to the continent, 10 percent are now extinct, a destruction rate that is five times the global average. Ninety-seven vascular plant species have also been made extinct and an estimated 2,000 plant species and forty mammal species are currently classified as endangered. Plans for comprehensive Endangered Species Legislation were systematically attacked by developmentalist interests in 1992 with the result that only a very weak act was eventually passed by federal parliament. For the same reason Australia has no national wilderness legislation.

Since the 1970s forestry issues have always been among the most contentious of environmental disputes. Over the years Australia's unique native forests have been decimated for sawlogs, woodchips and pulp. In recent times the timber industry has become much more interested in large-scale, high-volume, woodchip and pulpmill operations than in sawmilling. In the face of strong opposition the commonwealth government continues to grant export woodchip licenses to a small number of companies. In 1992 some of these companies attempted to have Resource Security Legislation put in place to guarantee long-term timber supply but the move was blocked by the conservation movement. Similarly, in recent times, a coalition of farmers and residents' groups successfully stopped the construction of a large kraft pulp mill in northern Tasmania.

Environmental disputes have often been so heated and have received so much media attention in Australia in recent years that the federal government has taken action to depoliticize environmental issues. This has been attempted in two main ways. First, a Resource Assessment Commission (RAC) was established in 1989 to provide impartial policy advice on contentious issues. So far the RAC has investigated the proposed Coronation Hill mining project, national forestry issues, and the management of the coastal zone. Second, throughout 1990 and 1991 the government established a number of working groups to give advice as to how different industry sectors could change their practices in line with what the groups deemed as "ecologically sustainable development." These reports were published in late 1991, but thus far the government has shown little enthusiasm for the implementation of the numerous recommendations.

David Mercer

Further Readings
Mercer, David. "*A Question of Balance.*" *Natural Resources Conflict Issues in Australia*. The Federation Press, 1995, Second Edition.
Papadakis, Elim. *Politics and the Environment. The Australian Experience*. 1993.

See also AUTOMOBILES: IMPACTS AND POLICIES; CARRYING CAPACITY; LEGISLATION: AUSTRALIA; URBAN FORM; WATER ALLOCATIONS AND SHORTAGES (U.S. WEST)

Australian Conservation Foundation
The Australian Conservation Foundation (ACF) was established in 1965, as a national organization of somewhat moderate orientation, dealing with the new agenda of environmental concerns then being dimly perceived. ACF subsequently became a much larger, more complex but nonetheless mainstream environmental organization, following a rapid change in leadership led by more activist members in 1973.

Given the geographic scale and diversity of the Australian continent, the ACF has had to deal with an enormous range of issues, as well as the competing demands of its spectrum of members. Its large national council has tended to undergo internal tensions, yet many significant conservation victories have been achieved and the organization has gained representation on a number of government advisory bodies and international delegations.

In recent years the ACF has sometimes forged alliances with former opponents (e.g., it has cooperated with the primary industry sector in promoting landcare programs). Although the Foundation has never sought to be regarded as the principal voluntary organization in Australia it virtually fulfills that role and is likely to remain an ongoing contributor to nature conservation and environmental management for many years to come.

Bruce Davis

Further Readings
Hay, Peter, Robyn Eckersley, and Geoff Holloway, eds. *Environmental Politics in Australia and New Zealand*. 1989.

See also AUSTRALIA: RESOURCE USE CONFLICTS; FRANKLIN DAM; GREEN PARTIES-AUSTRALIA; LAKE PEDDER; LEGISLATION-AUSTRALIA; TASMANIAN WILDERNESS SOCIETY

Automobiles: Impacts and Policies
World population has increased from 2.5 billion in 1950 to 5.3 billion in 1990 and is expected to reach 6.5 billion by the year 2000. By 1990, 45 percent of this population was urban and this is expected to increase to 50 percent by 2020. The growth in urbanization will be most pronounced in Africa, Asia, and Latin America. The degree of urbanization is strongly influenced by economic activity, while motorization is linked to economic activity and urbanization. Of the estimated 630 million motor vehicles in 1990 globally, 460 million were private passenger vehicles, 140 million buses and trucks, and 30 million two- and three-wheelers. In 1990, 80 percent of the world's automobiles were in North America and Europe. Asia had 11 percent of these automobiles, with Japan accounting for 70 percent of Asia's total. The developing countries as a group had 10 percent of the world's automobiles (see table 1).

The world automobile fleet has been increasing faster than population during 1950 to

TABLE 1

Global Distribution of Motor Vehicles 1990

Region	Automobiles (%)	Trucks & Buses (%)
North America	40	41
Europe	40	21
Asia	11	28
South America	5	4
Oceania	2	4
Africa	2	4

Source: Based on Motor Vehicles Manufacturer's Association, 1991.

1990, at a rate of 5.9 percent. It is concentrated in the high-income countries. In 1990 the OECD countries alone accounted for 80 percent of the world's cars, 70 percent of the trucks and buses, and over 50 percent of the two- and three-wheelers (see table 2). Since 1950 the global vehicle fleet has grown tenfold and is expected to double from the present total of 630 million within twenty to thirty years.

TABLE 2

Growth of Passenger Cars (in millions) 1970 to 1990

Year	Soviet Union & Eastern Europe	Developing Countries	Industrial Countries	World
1970	6	13	175	194
1975	12	21	227	260
1980	20	31	270	321
1985	27	41	307	375
1990	32	57	401	490

Source: Based on Motor Vehicles Manufacturer's Association, 1991 and various years.

Increasing incomes, combined with an increasing propensity for personal mobility, are likely to result in pronounced increases in automobile ownership in Asia, Eastern Europe, and parts of Africa. As motor vehicle ownership rates approach saturation levels in North America, Western Europe, and Japan, much of the future growth will be concentrated in the developing countries. During 1985 to 1990, the annual growth rate in the motor vehicle fleet in the Republic of Korea was 30 percent, in Kenya 28 percent, China 20 percent, Brazil 12 percent, Pakistan 9 percent, and Thailand 40 percent, compared to 2 percent in the United Kingdom and 4 percent in Canada. As household incomes increase, individuals' investment choice sways toward greater mobility. Even though at present only a small number of households in developing countries can afford to own a motor vehicle, this situation will change as incomes increase. Private vehicle fleets in the megacities of developing countries are expected to increase by 30 to 100 percent in twenty years, depending upon income increases in different regions.

Impacts of Automobiles

Perhaps more than any other invention, the automobile embodies Jacques Ellul's observation of all technologies: "It makes a good servant but a bad master." Yet obeying the demands of the private car has become a passive routine for most of the world's cities. Automobile use has dictated the very nature of urban life, most obviously in the design of the modern city.

Transport Energy Consumption

The estimated global energy consumption by transport in 1985 was 56 quads, which amounts to about one-third of the world's total energy consumption. There are large regional variations in energy consumed by the transport sector. The United States, by far the largest consumer, uses over 35 percent of the world's transport energy (see table 3). A large share of energy consumption by the transport sector is characteristic of many developing countries, especially because of increasing vehicle population (see table 4).

There is a direct relationship between transport energy consumption and pollutant emissions from transport sources. The greater the concentration of population and motor vehicles, the more severe the air pollution, as air sheds have a finite capacity to absorb emissions with inacceptable air quality limits.

Air Pollution

The combustion of fossil fuels in motor vehicles is a major contributor to pollutant emissions and ambient pollution. However, the proportion of pollutants from transport and industry will vary from country to country. Most common air pollutants are sulfur dioxide (SO_2), nitrogen oxides (NO and NO_2, collectively termed as NOx), carbon monoxide (CO), ozone (O_3), suspended particulate matter (SPM), and lead (Pb). Combustion of fossil fuels leads to the production of SO_2, NOx, and SPM (primary particulates in the form of fly ash and soot, and secondary particulates such as sulfates and nitrate aerosols). Gasoline-fueled motor vehicles are the principle source of NOx, CO, and Pb, whereas diesel-fueled engines emit significant quantities of SMP, SO_2, and NO_2.

TABLE 3

Global Transport Energy Consumption 1985

Region	Transport Energy in Quads	Regional Share(%)
United States	20.0	35.4
Canada and Western Europe	13.0	23.0
Eastern Europe (including USSR)	8.4	14.9
Japan, Australia, and New Zealand	4.4	7.8
Latin America and Caribbean	4.1	7.3
South and East Asia	2.5	4.4
Africa	2.0	3.5
Middle East	1.0	1.8
China	0.9	1.6
Global Total	56.3	100.0
Industrialized countries	44.6	79.6
Developing countries	11.4	20.4

Source: Faiz, Asif, et al., 1990, p. 29.

Ozone is a petrochemical oxidant and the main constituent of petrochemical smog. It is not emitted directly from combustion, but is formed in the lower atmosphere in the presence of sunlight from NO_x and volatile organic compounds (VOCs). The VOCs may be emitted from a variety of man-made sources, including road traffic and the transport and use of crude oil. Cities in warmer sunny locations with high traffic densities tend to be especially prone to the net formation of O_3 and petrochemical oxidants.

Health Impacts
Air pollutant emissions from different motor vehicles are summarized in table 5 and health impacts of pollutants are detailed in table 6. These pollutants directly affect the human respiratory and cardiovascular systems. Increased mortality, morbidity, and impaired pulmonary function have been associated with elevated lev-

els of SO_2 and SPM. NO_2 and O_3 also affect the respiratory system. Acute exposure can cause inflammatory and permeability responses, lung function decrements, and increases in airway reactivity. Ozone is also known to irritate the eyes, nose, and throat and to cause headaches. CO has a high affinity for hemoglobin and is able to displace oxygen in the blood, which in turn can lead to cardiovascular and neuro-behavioral effects. Lead inhibits hemoglobin synthesis in red blood cells in bone marrow, impairs liver and kidney function, and causes neurological damage.

The direct human health effects of air pollution vary according to both the intensity and the duration of exposure, and also with the health status of the population exposed. Some groups may be at greater risk, for example, street vendors, the young and the elderly, those already suffering from respiratory and cardiopulmonary diseases, and hyper-responders.

Other Impacts
The SO_2 and NO_x are the principle precursors of acidic deposition. Long-range transport of SO_2 and NO_x, and their corresponding acidic transformation products, has been linked to soil and fresh water acidification with consequent adverse impacts on aquatic and terrestrial ecosystems. SO_2, NO_2, and O_3 are phytotoxic. O_3 in particular has been implicated in crop losses and forest damage.

Air pollution levels in selected cities are shown in table 7 and impacts attributed to ambient air pollution are shown in table 8. Furthermore, the economic losses because of lost working days and school closures are enormous. For example, when the ozone levels are very high in Mexico City the schools are closed and all outdoor activities are suspended. All industries are subjected to a 30 percent power cut and many employees are forced to take days off without pay. In 1991 residents of Mexico City were exposed to 1,400 hours of high ozone levels, while the World Health Organization recommends that such exposure should not exceed one hour per year.

Policies

Alternative Fuels and Technology
Some argue that the solution might be to adopt new fuels and more efficient engines. Alternative fuels range from hydrogen, methanol, ethanol, and compressed natural gas (CNG), to electricity. The introduction of additives to

TABLE 4

Motor Vehicles in Selected Countries 1985 to 1990 (in millions).

Region	Year	Cars	Buses	Vans	Two-wheelers	Goods Vehicles
United States	1987	135.3	0.6	—	4.9	41.2
Japan	1988	30.8	0.2	—	11.5	21.4
United Kingdom	1988	18.4	0.1	0.6	0.9	—
Canada	1988	12.6	0.07	0.2	0.5	3.6
China	1987	0.8	0.4	—	8.0	2.8
India	1986	1.2	0.2	—	5.0	0.8
Indonesia	1986	1.1	0.3	—	5.1	0.9
Thailand	1988	15.0	0.2	—	1.7	1.4
Mexico	1987	5.3	—	—	—	2.2

Source: Faiz, Asif, et al., 1990, p. 37.

petroleum products can in some cases improve their efficiency. Several alternatives proposed are cleaner fuels (electricity, CNG, and hydrogen). However, as long as fossil fuels are cheap, the status quo will remain the norm. A recent study indicates that CNG may be competitive at twenty to thirty U.S. dollars (crude oil price per barrel) in 1988 prices. Electric and hydrogen-fueled vehicles are still very much in the prototype stage and much more research and development efforts are needed to bring them into mass production.

Rethinking the Car Culture

Automobile dependency plagues the world's major cities with traffic congestion and air pollution problems so severe that simply further tinkering with car technology will not solve these problems. To fully confront traffic congestion, pollution, oil dependence, and unlivable cities, governments will need to end the reign of the automobile. In the megacities of the world automobile dependency is causing economic, social, and health problems (see especially Newman and Kenworthy, 1989; and Lowe, 1990). What is needed is a rethinking of the

TABLE 5

Emissions from Different Transport Modes (per vehicle-km for road vehicles)

Mode Fuel Type or Fuel Source (for electrical energy) and Emission in Grams

		CO	HC	NO_x	So_x	Aldehydes	SPM
Motorcycle	Gasoline						
2-stroke Engine		17.00	9.9	0.075	0.024	0.068	0.21
4-stroke Engine		20.00	2.39	0.150	0.14	0.029	0.029
Passenger Car	Gasoline						
Low speed: 30Km/hr		33.66	2.63	1.05	0.21	—	0.33
High speed: 60Km/hr		18.75	1.11	0.75	0.11	—	—
Van/Light-Duty Truck	Gasoline						
Low speed		84.18	7.61	1.88	0.26	—	—
High speed		40.15	3.41	5.87	0.22	—	—
Small Bus	Diesel						
Low speed		47.18	5.81	1.88	0.26	—	—
High speed		12.53	0.82	1.61	0.12	—	—
Large Bus	Diesel						
Low speed		7.66	5.50	12.37	15.27	—	0.75
High speed		6.77	4.76	11.61	11.55	—	—
Heavy duty vehicle	Diesel						
		12.70	2.10	21.00	1.50	0.2	0.75

Source: Faiz, Asif, et al., 1990, p. 42.

automobile's role, with an aim toward truly sustainable cities. This rethinking will require a new planning strategy for our cities, with an emphasis on efficient ways to move about within them. It is necessary to match appropriate modes for appropriate times of the day and for appropriate purpose of travel. Freedom to move does not automatically bestow the right to cause air pollution and uneconomic conditions. More emphasis will need to be placed on walking, cycling, mass transit, and an environment-friendly design of the urban habitat.

Servant or Master: Taming the Private Car
The private car has provided us with privacy and mobility unparalleled in recent history. Megacities of the world are now reaching those population and density levels, where in many cities, livability is decreased because of traffic congestion, and noise, air and ground pollution

TABLE 6

Health Impacts of Pollutants

Pollutant	Health Effects
Carbon Monoxide	Interferes with absorption of oxygen by hemoglobin (red blood cells); impairs thinking, slows reflexes, causes drowsiness, brings on angina, and can cause unconsciousness and death; affects fetal growth in pregnant women and tissue development of young children; acts synergistically with other pollutants to promote morbidity in people with respiratory or circulatory problems; associated with less worker productivity and general discomfort.
Nitrogen Oxides	Can increase susceptibility to viral infections such as influenza; irritates the lungs and cause edema, bronchitis and pneumonia; can result in increased sensitivity to dust and pollen in asthmatics. Most serious health effects are in combination with other air pollutants.
Hydrocarbons and other Volatile Organic Compounds	Low-molecular weight compounds cause unpleasant effects such as eye irritation, coughing and sneezing, drowsiness, and symptoms akin to drunkenness; heavy-molecular weight compounds may have carcinogenic or mutagenic effects. Some hydrocarbons have a close affinity for diesel particulates and may contribute to lung disease.
Ozone	Irritates mucous membranes of respiratory system causing coughing, choking, and impaired lung function; causes headaches and physical discomfort; reduces resistance to colds and pneumonia; can aggravate chronic heart disease, asthma, bronchitis and emphysema.
Lead	Affects circulatory, reproductive, nervous and kidney systems; suspected of causing hyperactivity and lowered learning ability in children; hazardous even after exposure ends.
Sulfur Dioxide	Exacerbates asthma, bronchitis, and emphysema; causes coughing and impaired lung functions.
Particulate Matter	Irritates mucous membranes and may initiate a variety of respiratory diseases; fine particles may cause cancer and exacerbate morbidity and mortality from respiratory dysfunctions. A strong correlation exists between suspended particulates and infant mortality in urban areas. Suspended particulates have the ability to adhere to carcinogens emitted by motor vehicles.
Toxic Substances	Suspected of causing cancer, reproductive problems, and birth defects. Benzene and asbestos are known carcinogens; aldehydes and ketones irritate the eyes, cause short-term respiratory and skin irritation and may be carcinogenic.

Source: Faiz, Asif, et al., 1990, p. xi.

Table 7

Air Pollution in Selected Cities

Sulfur Dioxide: Number of days over 150µg/cubic meter
Particulate Matter: Number of days over 230µg/cubic meter

Country	City	Years	Min	Avg	Max	Years	Min	Avg	Max
Canada	Toronto	9	0	1	3	14	0	1	7
	Vancouver	5	0	1	3	14	0	1	7
United States	Chicago	4	0	1	2	7	0	6	14
	New York	12	1	8	22	12	0	0	0
China	Beijing	8	0	68	157	8	145	272	338
	Guangzhou	12	0	30	74	10	7	123	283
	Shanghai	10	0	16	32	10	19	133	277
	Xian	7	4	71	114	10	189	273	327
Hong Kong	Hong Kong	10	0	15	74	—	—	—	—
India	Bombay	13	0	3	32	12	23	100	207
	Calcutta	8	0	25	85	8	189	268	330
	Delhi	12	0	6	49	12	212	294	338
Indonesia	Jakarta	—	—	—	—	7	4	173	268
Iran	Tehran	15	6	104	163	15	8	174	347
Israel	Tel Aviv	9	0	3	24	—	—	—	—
Japan	Osaka	20	0	0	0	20	0	0	2
	Tokyo	15	0	0	0	15	0	2	4
Malaysia	Kuala Lumpur	1	0	0	0	5	10	37	59
Philippines	Manila	4	3	24	60	7	0	14	225
Korea	Seoul	6	5	87	121	—	—	—	—
Thailand	Bangkok	3	0	0	0	12	5	97	209
Australia	Melbourne	13	0	0	0	4	0	0	0
	Sydney	12	0	2	11	10	0	3	19
New Zealand	Auckland	12	0	0	2	—	—	—	—

Source: United Nations, 1993, pp. 5–17.

resulting from high intensity peak-hour automobile use. Taming the automobile frenzy requires the provision of efficient alternatives in walking, cycling and mass transport. This means placing high priority on collective transport rather than on private transport during peak and highly congested times.

Cars are heavily subsidized all over the world. If the total cost of (building and maintaining) related highway and street infrastructure is taken into account, in the United States this subsidy is about $2,800 per car per year. If the costs of air pollution are included, these subsidies are much higher. If taming the use of private cars as a goal is to be reached, then private car users should pay the total cost of that use and, at the same time, governments should provide efficient alternative public transport.

Singapore is the only country with very strict controls on growth, ownership, and peak-hour use of private cars. Private cars with less than three occupants require a special license and pay a fee to enter the city center during the peak hours. This Area Licensing Scheme (ALS) has been operating successfully since 1975. Travel by car during peak hours has decreased from 48 percent of total trips in 1974, to 27 percent in 1975, to 17 percent in 1980 and to 14 percent in 1990. During this period, Singapore authorities have increased the buses in service and built an efficient rapid transit system. By 1995 they are planning to have Electronic Road Pricing (ERP), a system wherein car users pay according to how much they use and when. The Singapore systems demonstrate that it is possible to reduce car use during the highly congested hours, increase air quality, and reduce accidents provided the governments are willing and persistent.

The private car—as an important technological tool of mobility, comfort, convenience, and privacy—may be useful to retain, but not necessarily in its present incarnation. Policy instruments, chosen by governments, must be capable of reducing traffic congestion by more rigorous and sustainable traffic demand man-

TABLE 8

Impacts Attributed to Ambient Air Pollution

City	Pollutants	Impact
Bangkok	Particulates	51 million restricted activity days (including 29 million work loss days) and 1,400 excess mortalities in 1989.
	Carbon Monoxide	20,000 to 50,000 people at risk of increased angina pain per day; 900,000–2,300,000 per day at risk of minor effects such as headaches.
	Lead (all sources)*	200,000 to 500,000 cases of hypertension per year; 300 to 900 heart attacks and strokes per year; 200 to 400 deaths per year; 400,000 to 700,000 IQ points per year lost in children.
	Air toxic *mobile sources*	90 to 100 cancer cases per year.**
	Air toxic *at city dumpsite*	Less than one cancer case per year. 900,000 cases of respiratory illness.
Beijing		Lung cancer rates increased 145 percent from 1949 to 1979.
Bombay		Tuberculosis and respiratory diseases are the major killers in the city.
Calcutta		60 percent of residents suffer from respiratory diseases.
Chinese cities		Lung cancer mortality is four to seven times higher in cities than in the nation as a whole.
Chinese cities		High rates of chronic bronchitis and chronic respiratory infections in the cities as opposed to the rural areas.
Delhi		30 percent of the population suffers from respiratory disease, twelve times the national average. 30 percent decrease in crop yield and poor quality of grains; millions of rupees lost in engineering materials, textiles, building materials, and leather goods.
Manila		471,100 cases of upper respiratory tract infection and 79,400 cases of bronchitis reported in 1988.

* Airborne lead may account for about 40 percent of the lead intake of adults and 70 percent of that for children.

** Recalculated with the authors' adjusted unit risk (Vol. 2, p. A19).

Source: United Nations, 1993, pp. 5–18.

agement techniques, which at the same time provide efficient alternatives for mobility. To achieve these goals, governments can adopt a variety of economic and noneconomic policy instruments to require car users to pay full direct and indirect (pollution) costs of car ownership and use. Finally, the chosen policy instruments must aim toward sustainable and healthy cities, in which transportation methods include walking, cycling, and riding in automobiles or larger vehicles with higher vehicle occupancies. Success of these policies depends on governments' desire and ability to understand clearly the full cost of using the automobile.

V. Setty Pendakur

Further Readings

Faiz, Asif, K. Sinha, M. Walsh, and A. Varma. *Automobile Air Pollution.* 1990.

Lowe, Marcia D. *Alternatives to the Automobile: Transport for Livable Cities.* Worldwatch Institute, 1990.

Moreno, R., Jr., and D.G.F. Bailey. *Alternative Transport Fuels from Natural Gas.* 1989.

Motor Vehicles Manufacturer's Association. *Facts and Figures.* 1991 and annually.

Newman, Peter, and Jeffrey Kenworthy. *Cities and Automobile Dependence: An International Source Book.* 1989.

Pendakur, V. Setty. "Congestion Management and Air Quality: Lessons from Bangkok and Mexico City." *Asian Journal of Environmental Management* 1 (1993).

United Nations. *State of Urbanisation in Asia and the Pacific 1993.* 1993.

United Nations. *The Prospects for World Urbanisation 1990.* 1990.

World Health Organisation. *Urban Air Pollution in Megacities of the World 1992.* 1992.

See also ACID PRECIPITATION: LEGISLATIVE INITIATIVES; AIR POLLUTION: IMPACTS; CARBON MONOXIDE; ENERGY EFFICIENCY; LAND USE PLANNING; LEAD; OZONE POLLUTION; SMOG; URBAN DESIGN

A

B

Bacillus thuringiensis

Bacillus thuringiensis (*B.t.*) is a spore-forming bacteria that can kill certain types of insects. In 1961 it was first made into a commercial insecticide. By the 1990s these bacterial insecticides were receiving wide use in agriculture, forestry, and mosquito control.

B.t.'s toxicity to insects derives from its production of a crystalline protein that, when eaten by sensitive insects, becomes soluble and activated in the insect gut. Considerable debate has focused on how the toxin kills the insect. Some researchers now believe that the bacterial protein forms complexes in the cell membranes of the cells lining the insect gut. These complexes create pores, which cause the insect gut either to disintegrate or to be nonfunctional for feeding.

A number of different strains of *B.t.* have been identified. These different varieties are toxic to lepidopterans (moths and butterflies), dipterans (flies), and coleopterans (beetles), respectively.

Use of *B.t.* has increased since the 1970s. New strains of the bacterium, better formulations, and new modes of delivering the toxin to the target pest have all made *B.t.* much more versatile and easy to use. Organic farmers appreciate that its residues are not toxic to people and most wildlife. Public agencies have chosen the safety of *B.t.* for programs to control pests like gypsy moths in urban areas. Recombinant DNA techniques have enabled researchers to place the bacterial genes coding for the protein toxins into crop plants, thus making the plants both the manufacturer and carrier of their own protective insecticides.

Despite its many successes and attractive features, *B.t.* has attracted some recent concern. Proponents of its use fear that its increased popularity will result in the emergence of insect populations resistant to it. Opponents of urban spraying have raised questions about the safety of *B.t.* or other chemicals in its formulated products. Even amid these controversies, the development of *B.t.* as an insecticide remains an important environmental improvement over its chemical competitors.

John H. Perkins

Further Readings

DeBach, Paul, and David Rosen. *Biological Control by Natural Enemies*. 2nd ed., 1991.
Gill, Sarjeet S., Elizabeth A. Cowles, and Patricia V. Pietrantonio. "The Mode of Action of *Bacillus thuringiensis* Endotoxins." *Annual Review of Entomology* 37 (1992).

See also BUTTERFLIES: CONSERVATION AND HABITAT; INTEGRATED PEST MANAGEMENT; PESTICIDES; SUSTAINABLE AGRICULTURE

Backcasting

Backcasting is a method of analyzing alternative futures, often energy futures. Its major distinguishing characteristic is a concern with how desirable futures can be attained. It is thus explicitly normative and involves working backward from a desired future end point or set of goals to the present to determine the physical feasibility of that particular future and the policy measures that would be required to reach that end point. In order to permit time for futures significantly different than the present to come about, end points are usually chosen for a time twenty-five to fifty years into the future.

Unlike predictive forecasts, backcasts are not intended to reveal what the future will likely be, but to indicate the relative feasibility and implications of different policy goals. While the value and quality of a predictive forecast depend upon the degree to which it accurately suggests what is likely to happen under specified conditions, backcasting is intended to suggest the implications of different futures, chosen not on the basis of their likelihood but on the basis of other criteria defined externally to the analysis (e.g., criteria of social or environmental desirability). No estimate of likelihood is possible since such likelihood would depend upon whether the policy proposals resulting from the backcast were implemented. Thus, while the emphasis in forecasts is upon discovering the underlying structural features of the world that would cause the future to come about, the emphasis in backcasts is upon determining the freedom of action, in a policy sense, with respect to possible futures.

In order to undertake a backcasting analysis, future goals and objectives are defined, and then used to develop a future scenario. The scenario is specified by analyzing the technological and physical characteristics of a path that would lead toward the specified goals. The scenario is then evaluated in terms of its physical, technological, and socioeconomic feasibility and policy implications. Iteration of the scenario is usually required to resolve physical inconsistencies and to mitigate adverse economic, social, and environmental impacts that are revealed in the course of the analysis.

Since backcasting approaches explicitly introduce the question of policy choice, they serve to refocus the use of analysis away from responding to inevitable futures and toward exploring the nature and feasibility of alternative directions of policy. This helps to put the onus for choosing back where it belongs: in the policy arena.

John B. Robinson

Further Readings

Robinson, John B. "Energy Backcasting: A Proposed Method of Policy Analysis." *Energy Policy* 10 (1982): 337–45.

———. "Of Maps and Territories: The Use and Abuse of Socio-Economic Modelling in Support of Decision-Making." *Technological Forecasting and Social Change* 42 (1992): 147–64.

———. "Unlearning and Backcasting: Rethinking Some of the Questions We Ask About the Future." *Technological Forecasting and Social Change* 33 (1988): 325–38.

See also BENEFIT-COST ANALYSIS; DEMAND-SIDE MANAGEMENT; ENVIRONMENTAL IMPACT ASSESSMENT; LEAST-COST UTILITY PLANNING; LIFE-CYCLE ANALYSIS; RISK ANALYSIS; SOFT ENERGY PATHS

Bailey, Liberty Hyde

Liberty Hyde Bailey (1858–1954), was a botanist, horticulturalist, educator, and author. Born in South Haven, Michigan, he received his B.S. (1882) and his M.S. (1886) at the Michigan Agricultural College (which became Michigan State University). Before completing his M.S. he worked for two years as an assistant to Asa Gray at Harvard.

He was professor of horticulture at Michigan State College (1885–1888) and Cornell University (1888–1903). He then became the first dean of the New York State College of Agriculture at Cornell, remaining in that position until he retired from teaching in 1913. In the course of his prolific career Bailey played a prominent role in establishing horticulture as a biologically based applied science. He was founder and first president of American Society of Horticultural Science (1903–1907). Bailey wrote over fifty books, edited over 100 others, and published about 700 articles.

Bailey had a broad and somewhat romantic perspective on agriculture and rural life. He promoted rural education and was a philosopher of the country life movement. Theodore Roosevelt appointed him to chair the Commission on Country Life (1908), which recommended establishing a national extension service and other programs to improve the quality of life in rural areas. He was a proponent of nature study, which he believed was an important part of agricultural education. His book *The Nature-Study Idea* (1903) influenced this movement. He was president of the American Nature Study Society (1914–1915).

He founded and directed the Bailey Hortorium (1935–1952), the first herbarium devoted to the study of cultivated plants, and developed a very important botanical collection. Widely respected as a botanist, Bailey was an authority on the classification of a number of genera. He received numerous honors for his work and served as president of both the American Association for the Advancement of

Science and the Botanical Society of America in 1926.

Ralph H. Lutts

Further Readings

Dorf, Philip. *Liberty Hyde Bailey: An Informal Biography.* 1956.

Rodgers, Andrew Denny, III. *Liberty Hyde Bailey: A Story of American Plant Sciences.* 1949.

Bald Eagle

Few species have commanded as much public attention, legislative protection, and research as the bald eagle. It has been an important biomonitor of environmental health and a model for conservation action, but its popular image as an endangered species must be qualified as being on a local scale. Although the bald eagle was extirpated from much of its range in the conterminous United States, it was never at serious risk of extinction.

Bald eagles were common inhabitants of pre-European North America, but pristine populations are now largely limited to remote areas in Canada and Alaska. Initial population declines can be attributed largely to persecution and habitat degradation. Many eagles were shot, trapped, or poisoned to protect livestock or to reduce depredations on game and fish. These actions were largely unwarranted as eagles have little economic impact. Bald eagles are primarily piscivorous, but will eat virtually any animal matter. Carrion typically predominates in winter. The number of shooting deaths has declined, but other anthropogenic sources of mortality such as electrocution, collisions, and secondary poisoning continue to be significant.

Another serious population decline followed World War II with the widespread application of DDT and other pesticides. One of the first indications of the hazards of DDT to any wildlife was the precipitous decline in bald eagle reproduction documented by Charles Broley. In 1946 Broley banded 150 eaglets in 105 nests on the Gulf Coast of Florida. By 1952 there were only fifteen eagles in eleven nests in the same area. As DDT use ended (by 1972), the contamination of eagles subsequently declined and reproduction improved.

Eagles are exposed to several other harmful contaminants. Many, like organochlorine pesticides, mercury, and PCBs biomagnify in the environment: concentrations increase with each trophic level until dangerous accumulations occur in eagles at the top of the food chain. Reduced reproductive success is the usual consequence. The bald eagle's scavenging habits also result in lethal secondary poisoning (e.g., by strychnine [predator control], organophosphate insecticides [on livestock], and lead [shot in waterfowl]). Protection of the bald eagle was a major impetus for banning lead shot in the United States.

Habitat loss has always been a significant problem. Shorelines are important for nesting and foraging perches. Development of the land and recreational activities on water bodies has removed habitat in the breeding and non-breeding seasons. In addition, such activities create excessive human disturbance which may lead to reproductive failures, or even mortality if birds are prevented from finding sufficient food. Legislation, particularly in the United States, restricts land use that may impinge on eagle habitats.

One of the most important aspects of habitat is the prey base. Nesting densities and concentrations outside the breeding season are known to correlate well with fish abundance. Overexploitation of fish stocks and removal of rough fish to improve sport fisheries have had negative consequences. This species' sensitivity to human alterations of ecosystems is exemplified by migratory eagles at Glacier National Park, Montana. Eagles first used the Flathead Lake area in 1937 after the introduction of kokanee salmon. Dramatic increases in both predators and prey occurred over the next four decades to the point where this was the densest concentration of eagles south of Canada. However, stocking of the opossum shrimp resulted in the total collapse of kokanee and hence eagle populations within a few years.

Bald eagle populations are increasing in most areas where declines occurred, by natural means and through reintroduction programs that have released young birds. Many areas have reported increases of 100 to 400 percent in the last decade, while pristine populations are probably stable. However, habitat loss and contaminants continue to pose a significant threat to many local populations.

Gary R. Bortolotti

Further Readings

Gerrard, Jon M., and Bortolotti, Gary R. *The Bald Eagle: Haunts and Habits of a Wilderness Monarch.* 1988.

Stalmaster, Mark. *The Bald Eagle.* 1987.

See also BIOACCUMULATION; FOOD CHAINS; FOREST FRAGMENTATION AND BIRD HABITATS; HAWK SHOOTING; PEREGRINE FALCON; PESTICIDES

Baleen Whales

Baleen whales belong to the taxonomic order Cetacea, which includes the whales, dolphins, and porpoises. There are two suborders: the Odontoceti, comprising about sixty-five species, includes all the toothed whales, from the large sperm whale to the small dolphins and porpoises; and the Mysticeti, comprising eleven distinct species, includes non-toothed whales from the up-to-thirty-meter-long blue whale, the largest creature on earth, to the only six-meter-long pygmy right whale (all sizes given are adult maximums). Baleen whales belong to the mysticeti suborder and, although they have teeth as fetuses, these teeth are resorbed by the body before birth, and keratinous baleen plates (analogous to the ectodermal structure of fingernails and hair) grow from the upper lip. These plates fringe on their inner edges, and form a dense sieve-like structure used to net food and to separate prey from water. Because larger "nets" are more efficient at taking clouds of invertebrate and small vertebrate (fish) prey, baleen whales have evolved toward gigantism. Large size also allows for large fat reserves, which are necessary since the larger baleen whales fast for about six months of the year, generally while they breed in lower latitudes, and feed in colder more productive waters during the other half of the year. They undergo lengthy migrations between breeding and feeding sites. The best-known and perhaps longest migration is that of the north Pacific gray whale, with a yearly 16,000- to 20,000-kilometer round-trip between Mexican calving lagoons and the northern Bering Sea.

Cetaceans evolved from a now-extinct stock of carnivorous ungulates, the mesonychid condylarths, over 60 million years ago. These ancient cetaceans we now call the suborder Archaeoceti. About 30 million years ago, archaeocetes gave rise to both the odontocetes (differentiated from their ancestors by homodont or "all same" teeth and by skull modifications), and the mysticetes with their baleen. All three suborders coexisted for at least 10 million years, but the archaeocetes then went extinct, probably outcompeted by the more specialized odontocetes, which evolved efficient echolocation for finding food and avoiding predators, and the batch or bulk-feeding mysticetes.

There are now three extant taxonomic families of mysticetes, each family with strikingly different morphology and feeding modes. Representatives of each family have also been decimated by intensive hunting in the past several centuries, right up to modern times. Conservation progress and needs will be addressed with the following descriptions of families and species.

The smallest family, the Eschrichtiidae, includes only one species, the gray whale. The gray whale is intermediate in size of the mysticetes, at about thirteen meters. It has a relatively small mouth and short bristly baleen used for sucking in copious quantities of mud, water, and bottom dwelling prey, consisting mainly of ampeliscid amphipods from the productive shallow undersea flats of the northern Bering Sea. The gray whale now exists only off the western coast of North America; a north Atlantic stock (the scrag whale) was exterminated by whaling in the seventeenth or eighteenth century, and a Korean or western Pacific stock was almost or totally exterminated in the twentieth century. Gray whales are coastal shallow water dwellers, and this trait made them easy targets for intensive whaling in the nineteenth and early part of the twentieth centuries. They were hunted on their feeding grounds in the Bering Sea in summer and on their mating/calving grounds in and near the lagoons of Baja California, Mexico, in winter. Numbers dwindled from an estimated 20,000 pre-exploitation, and by the time they were afforded protection by international agreement in the 1930s, there were probably no more than 1,000 animals, and they were economically but not quite biologically extinct.

Gray whales of the eastern Pacific or Californian stock represent one of the few success stories in cetacean conservation. Numbers rapidly increased after hunting ceased, with adult females generally producing one young every two years, and at times even in subsequent years. Other baleen whales tend to give birth at intervals greater than two years. At the present time, there are an estimated 20,000 to 22,000 gray whales in the eastern Pacific stock, at and possibly above pre-exploitation levels; they appear to be extending their ranges to the Beaufort Sea in the north and the central Pacific coastline of Mexico in the south. Nevertheless, their well-being may still be labeled fragile, because of their very coastal habits wherever they travel. One ill-fated ecological disaster, such as a major oil spill, off a mating, calving, or migration area could seriously impact a huge proportion of the entire species. About 160 gray whales have been taken per year by whaling vessels supplying meat to far Asian (Russian or Siberian) Eskimos; this practice is likely to continue at some level.

The second taxonomic family is that of the right whales, or Balaenidae. There are four species: the northern and southern hemisphere right whales (which look very much alike), the bowhead whale (termed the Greenland right whale by seventeenth-to-nineteenth-century whalers), and a small southern hemisphere species, the pygmy right whale. This latter species appears to have characteristics of both Balaenidae and the rorquals (see descriptions below), and its taxonomic status is not totally secure. While pygmy right whales have not been hunted commercially, the other three larger species (up to seventeen meters long) were hunted intensively in the past 300 years. They tend to float and have a round fat (oil-rich) body, making them obvious hunting choices before the advent of modern mechanized whaling. As was the case for gray whales, right whales became economically extinct by the early twentieth century, and were afforded international protection in the 1930s.

Right whales have a strongly curved upper jaw which holds the longest and most thin-stranded baleen plate of any group. Right whales open their mouths wide and swim through clouds of invertebrate prey, from two-centimeter crustaceans (termed krill) to the several-millimeter-long copepods. They skim food, often near the surface, as they strain water through their mouths. This kind of feeding can go on for hours, even days, without pause as the whales zig-zag through productive areas of generally high-latitude waters. One of the most productive of these areas for bowhead whales is the Beaufort Sea above Alaska and in the high Canadian Arctic.

Bowhead and both hemisphere right whales have made only slow and, in some areas, tenuous progress as populations and species coming back from the brink of extinction. Bowheads have nearly died out from the north Atlantic, and only the north Pacific, or Bering-Chukchi-Beaufort Sea stock is apparently healthy, at a present 8,000 to 10,000 animals and increasing. A small indigenous Eskimo hunt on the north slope of Alaska is responsible for about forty-five bowhead deaths per year. Right whales in the north Atlantic and north Pacific, once very abundant, are now rare. Right whales in the southern oceans appear to be doing a bit better, especially in the south Atlantic where intensive research has documented an apparent increase from several hundred to well over 1,000 animals in the past twenty years. Many of these whales congregate on the Argentine coast for mating and calving, and are only as secure as the protection afforded them by Argentina and the International Whaling Commission (IWC). It would unfortunately be rather easy for private whaling ships to decimate these whales as they head to or from the coastal calving grounds.

The final taxonomic family, of Balaenopteridae (or "rorquals," a Norwegian term that refers to the whales' throat grooves) includes six species. These range from the nine-to ten-meter long minke whale; to the intermediate-sized Bryde's (thirteen meters), humpback (fifteen meters), and sei (seventeen meters) whales; and to the very large fin (twenty-five meters) and blue (thirty meters) whales. The smaller rorqual whales tend to feed on fishes and squid, while the fin and blue whales specialize on krill. All are lunge feeders, rapidly surging ahead into their food with wide open mouths. Their throat pleats expand with the forward pressure, allowing tons (in the larger species) of food and water to enter the mouth and expanded throat. They then almost close the mouth, to expose only their racks of intermediate-length baleen (compared to the short baleen plates of the gray whales and the very long baleen plates of the right whales) between the upper and lower jaw. Muscular action contracts the throat grooves, and water is expelled through the baleen after each lunge, while food is swallowed. These whales are energetic swimmers and lungers, and their thin long bodies betray their active lifestyle. Two to three whales often lunge side-by-side, as they use each others' bodies as walls through which the prey cannot escape. Humpback whales have developed especially varied prey-concentrating techniques: they "net" their prey with bubble trails emitted from mouth or blowhole; they "flick" prey towards their mouths with long pectoral flippers or large tail; and they coordinate lunges with up to twenty other humpbacks to attack prey *en masse* and from all sides.

Rorqual whales are swift and generally open-ocean animals, and were therefore not hunted until the advent of modern mechanized whaling technology. First to be taken, and decimated, were the large blue and fin whales, especially in the southern hemisphere. These were followed by humpback whales in all oceans, and large numbers of sei and minke whales as well. Only the more sparsely-distributed tropical Bryde's whale escaped widespread decimation by early- to mid-twentieth-century whaling.

It is presently not clear how well any of the larger rorquals are doing. Fin whales appear to be on the increase in the north Atlantic, as are blue whales in the northeastern Pacific, and humpback whales perhaps in all oceans. Minke whales are undoubtedly the most abundant, with several hundred thousand animals in the southern hemisphere. There has been an almost total IWC-mandated "moratorium" on whaling since the late 1980s, but there is now pressure by Norway and Japan especially to escalate whaling—at least on the more abundant minke whales—for meat for human consumption by these two nations. It is undoubtedly the case that minke whale populations can withstand a limited hunt of several thousand whales yearly; however, conservation associations worry that resumption and increase of commercial harvesting of minke whales (and some fin whales in Norwegian waters) will more easily lead to larger scale and increased-species resumption of commercial harvesting. The issue of whaling has become perhaps more of an animal rights issue than one of conservation of populations and species. A large segment of Western society believes that whales (and dolphins) are special creatures (perhaps because of their large brains, sophisticated and largely unknown societal structures, and other more "mysterious" features of human endearment), and need to be afforded special and uncompromising protection. Whales may thus be thought of as representatives of ocean problems—to protect the oceans we must protect the whales. It is also true, however, that in an increasingly protein-poor world, pressures on whaling will likely continue and may very well escalate in future.

Bernd Würsig

Further Readings

Klinowska, M. *Dolphins, Porpoises, and Whales: The IUCN Red Data Book.* 1991.

Thorne-Miller, Boyce, and John Catena. *The Living Ocean: Understanding and Preserving Marine Biodiversity.* 1991.

See also BEAUFORT SEA; DOLPHINS AND PORPOISES; INTERNATIONAL WHALING COMMISSION; MARINE MAMMALS

Bamaka Convention
See TOXIC WASTES IN INTERNATIONAL TRADE

Bambi
Walt Disney's 1942 animated film *Bambi* has strongly influenced public attitudes toward wildlife. It was based on Austrian novelist Siegmund Saltzmann's 1926 book published under his pseudonym, Felix Salten. Whittaker Chamber's fluent English translation appeared in 1929. The novel tells of a deer's growth to maturity while learning the lessons of survival and of his and the other animals' efforts to understand the god-like creature called "He," the hunter. It is a powerful statement against hunting, set within an ecological context of natural predation and death that the forest creatures accept with little complaint. Salten wrote a sequel, *Bambi's Children* (1939).

The film, which set a new standard for naturalistic animation, is one of Disney's finest works of art. However, in the process of converting the novel into a film he simplified Salton's story. It became a love story bounded by Bambi's birth and that of his children. Salten's philosophical perspective was lost and nature became an earthly Eden with little conflict and no predation. Humans (the god-like "Man") are the sole source of evil, death, and destruction in nature. The film is also an emotionally powerful anti-hunting statement and the death of Bambi's mother is one of the cinema's most remembered moments.

The quality of the film, Disney's massive marketing efforts, and over a half century of repeated releases made *Bambi* one of the most successful films in history. Only two other films released before 1969 earned more rental income from theaters as of 1989: *Gone With the Wind* (1939) and *The Sound of Music* (1965). A continual stream of commercial spin-offs, including books, toys, records and tapes, and educational products, also help make Bambi a part of everyone's childhood. The term "Bambi" is now virtually synonymous with "deer" and the film's idyllic vision of nature shapes public responses to wildlife policy. People who object to this sentimental vision of nature call the film's influence the "Bambi syndrome."

Ralph H. Lutts

Further Readings

Cartmill, Matt. *A View to a Death in the Morning: Hunting and Nature through Time.* 1993.

Johnson, Ollie, and Frank Thomas. *Walt Disney's Bambi: The Story and the Film.* 1990.

Lutts, Ralph H. "The Trouble with Bambi: Walt Disney's *Bambi* and the American Vision of Nature." *Forest & Conservation History* 36 (1992): 160–171.

Basal Convention

See TOXIC WASTES IN INTERNATIONAL TRADE

Bats: Conservation and Habitat

Bats include about 900 living species and represent the second largest mammalian order, the Chiroptera. They occur in virtually all terrestrial habitats, from deserts to rainforests. While most species are insectivorous the diets of some bats can include fruit, nectar, pollen, frogs, fish, and mammals. Their natural history, behavior, and ecology are diverse, as are the roles they play in natural ecosystems.

The number of bat species is highest in the tropics and the destruction of tropical rainforests is one of the most serious threats to bat species diversity. Preliminary data from the Yucatan Peninsula, Mexico, suggests that deforestation dramatically alters the composition of bat communities and reduces the number of species present. Reduced diversity can in turn hamper the reestablishment of tropical forests because bats are pollinators and seed dispersers. Bats disperse many of the first plants to recolonize deforested areas. In Ivory Coast, West Africa, bats can contribute to more than 80 percent of the "seed rain." Some trees such as the cape fig (*Ficus capensis*) are almost entirely dependent on bats for seed dispersal.

In North America most of the native old-growth forests have been logged and replaced with cities or agricultural land. Studies of old-growth forests in the United States have shown a positive link between old growth and bat abundance and diversity. The presence of large hollow trees that bats use as roosts is a critical factor linking them to old growth. The two most common bat species in Canada and much of the United States, the big brown bat (*Eptesicus fuscus*) and the little brown bat (*Myotis lucifugus*), have responded to the loss of natural roosting cavities by moving into attics, barns, bridges and other human-built structures. Other species, such as small-footed bats (*Myotis leibii*) and northern long-eared bats (*Myotis septentrionalis*), seldom roost in buildings and are rare in urban or rural settings.

In Micronesia, many species of flying foxes (*Pteropodidae*) are threatened by unregulated hunting and habitat destruction. For the Chamorro people of Guam and the Commonwealth of the Northern Marianas, flying foxes are a delicacy eaten on special occasions. As flying fox populations on Guam have declined from the pressure of unregulated hunting, residents have begun importing bats from nearby islands. At the 1989 Convention on International Trade in Endangered Species of Wild Fauna and Flora (CITES), seven species of flying foxes (*Pteropus mariannus, Pteropus pilosus, Pteropus insularis, Pteropus molossinus, Pteropus phaeocephalus, Pteropus tonganus* and *Pteropus samoensis*) were placed on CITES Appendix I, prohibiting trade except under special circumstances. The remaining species in the genus *Pteropus* and five species of *Acerodon* were placed on Appendix II.

Bats frequently form large colonies, ranging from hundreds to several millions of individuals, in caves or abandoned mines. In Canada and the northern United States, these sites are used as winter hibernacula. During hibernation bats are vulnerable to disturbance because they have limited fat reserves which must sustain them until insects are available in the spring. Arousal from hibernation resulting from disturbance by cavers or vandals is a major cause of the declines observed at many hibernation sites.

Some North American species inhabit caves year-round. Summer colonies of the endangered gray bat (*Myotis grisescens*) surveyed in Alabama and Tennessee showed a 54 percent overall decline in numbers from 1968 to 1976. There was a strong correlation with the rate of decline at specific caves and the frequency of human disturbance.

In other areas, bats use caves only during the summer when pregnant females form large colonies. In Bracken Cave, Texas, more than 20 million Mexican free-tailed bats gather each summer and give birth to their young. The tendency for some bats to gather in such large colonies increases their vulnerability as the loss of even a single colony can have a major impact on their population size.

Several steps have been taken recently to protect bat populations, but progress has been

B

slow because of the negative impressions most people have about these mammals. In Britain, bats are protected under the Wildlife and Countryside Act (1981) and home owners must obtain permission from the Nature Conservancy Council before evicting bats from their attics. Worldwide, several species have been placed on endangered species lists and have gained legal protection. Some biologists have cautioned, however, that this may give legislators the false sense that those species that do not appear on these lists are not in danger. Bats are difficult to census and, in reality, many species are not on these lists because critical information about their populations is lacking, rather than because their populations are secure.

In the United States, several caves with large bat colonies are now protected. In some circumstances, entrances to caves and abandoned mines with bat colonies have been physically modified to prevent human disturbance. However, not all modifications may be beneficial to the bats. A masonry wall built at the entrance to Wyandotte Cave in Indiana, appears to have altered the winter temperature regime of the cave enough to make it largely unsuitable for the endangered Indiana bats (*Myotis sodalis*) that the wall was intended to protect. Steel gates may more effectively allow bats to use caves and mines while preventing human disturbance.

In several countries including Canada and the United States, attempts have been made to attract bats to artificial roosts (bat houses) but success rates have been low. No large-scale systematic studies have been conducted to determine whether bat houses could provide a suitable alternative to natural roosts or the attics from which bats are often evicted. A few anecdotal accounts of success, however, suggest that properly designed and placed bat houses might provide appropriate roosting sites for some species.

M.B.C. Hickey and J.E. Cebek

Further Readings
Fenton, M. Brock. *Bats*. 1992.
Kunz, Thomas H. *Ecological and Behavioral Methods for the Study of Bats*. 1988.

See also CITES; NATURE CONSERVANCIES; OLD GROWTH FORESTS; TROPICAL DEFORESTATION; TROPICAL RAINFORESTS

Bears: Conservation and Habitat
Bears are large-bodied members of the mammalian order Carnivora, family Ursidae. They evolved from smaller, tree-dwelling, predatory ancestors (Miacids) about 25 million years ago. A primarily carnivorous diet gave way to an omnivorous one—a characteristic still maintained by all living bear species, although the polar bear is primarily carnivorous, and the giant panda is almost exclusively herbivorous. Bears that live in seasonal climates enter a prolonged period of winter dormancy usually inside of a den they have built. Dormancy may last for up to seven months without a bear eating, drinking, urinating, defecating, or losing bone mass.

Bears have prominent noses and an acute sense of smell, small ears (relatively larger when young), small eyes, and a mere stub of a tail. They walk like human beings on the surface of their feet. Normally they walk placing all four feet on the ground, although they can walk for short distances using only their two hind feet.

Bears occupy a special place in human culture. Many people see bears as having humanlike characteristics, such as walking on their hind legs. They have few young and look after them with focused care reminiscent of human mothers. Bears are curious, and extremely playful when young. Above all, bears are seen by people throughout the world as having power. Power—meaning physical strength combined with spiritual influence—is coveted by the numerous human cultures around the world that symbolically or physically try to incorporate the power of bears into their people. This power transfer is brought about by worshipping bears, eating various parts of bears, wearing their claws or skins as ornaments, being able to tame or display bears, taking their picture, and even by doing research on them. The bear image also has unique power to evoke love and warmth through the hundreds of thousands of teddy bears sold each year.

Species and Their Distribution
Most taxonomists recognize eight species of bears in the world, although the giant panda's classification (*Ailuropoda melanoleuca*) is subject to debate as to whether the panda is a bear, a raccoon, or in a family of its own. Here it is classified as a bear. Today bears are found on all continents except Australia and Africa. There are many more bears in the northern hemisphere than in the southern. The spectacled bear (*Tremarctos ornatus*) of South America is the only bear found exclusively in the southern hemisphere. There are three species of bears in North America: the American black bear (*Ursus*

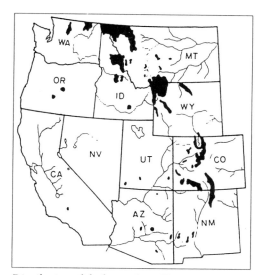

Distribution of the brown bear (Ursus arctos) in the western United States in 1922. State Codes: WA = Washington; MT = Montana; WY= Wyoming; ID = Idaho; OR = Oregon; CA = California; NV = Nevada; UT = Utah; CO = Colorado; AZ = Arizona; NM = New Mexico. From Merriam (1922).

americanus), the brown or grizzly bear (*Ursus arctos*), and the polar bear (*Ursus maritimus*). Europe and Asia, including India, have six bear species: brown bear, polar bear, Asiatic black bear (*Ursus thibetanus*), sloth bear (*Melursus ursinus*), sun bear (*Helarctos malayanus*), and the giant panda.

Conservation

According to the 1993 proposed revision to the International Union for the Conservation of Nature and Natural Resources (IUCN) Red Book list, most of the world's eight species of bears are threatened by the activities of human-kind. Servheen (1990) estimates that bears have been eliminated from 50 to 75 percent of their worldwide historic range. In the contiguous United States the grizzly bear occupies only 2 percent of its former range, and it is classified as a threatened species.

Bears are found from the high Arctic (po-lar bears) to lowland tropical forest (sun-honey bear). Because of their wide geographical and habitat coverage, bears are an umbrella species. By protecting the habitat of bears, the habitat and home ranges of many other species are also maintained.

The most seriously threatened of the world's bear species is the giant panda. Only about 1,000 exist in the wild. The sun bear is

either endangered or threatened by tropical deforestation and poaching, however we don't know enough about the species to properly clas-sify its status. Every country in the world that has bears has some populations at risk. Only the American black bear of North America is com-pletely secure as a species.

Bear populations and even species are of-ten among the first taxa to decline as people develop a landscape. This is because most bear species share biological traits that make them vulnerable when interacting with human popu-lations. As a rule bears have low reproductive rates. Females first reproduce when they are three to eight years old. Then they have on av-erage two offspring (often called cubs) every two to four years. Because of low reproductive rates bears recover slowly from population de-clines induced by people, and throughout the world most bears die because they are killed by people.

Another general bear characteristic is that they require much space to survive. In interior portions of North America grizzly bear males typically have home ranges exceeding 1,000 square kilometers. Adult males usually occupy home ranges two to four times as large as those of adult females, and home ranges overlap, so overall population densities may be one bear

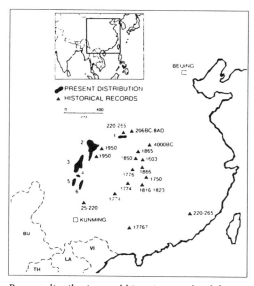

Present distribution and historic records of the giant panda (Ailuropada melanoleuca) in China. Present populations occur in the following moun-tain ranges: (1) Quinling; (2) Min; (3) Quianglai; (4) Daxiangling; (5) Xiaoxiangling; (6) Liang. Country Codes: BU = Burma; TH = Thailand; LA = Laos; VI = Vietnam. From Shaller et al. (1985).

per 100 square kilometers. Large home range size means that typically bears compete with people for space. While techniques are still evolving to determine how many bears and how much space is needed to form viable populations, current estimates for grizzly bear populations in Canada's Rocky Mountains suggest that a population of 300 grizzly bears would require 30,000 square kilometers. This size of population is believed to be large enough to prevent inbreeding and to have a high probability of persistence over 100 years. But in the Rocky Mountains there are no national parks, or even groups of contiguous national parks of this areal extent.

This situation highlights a major, general conservation problem for bears. Because they range over large areas it is seldom possible to strictly protect enough habitat for a viable population. Because of this bears require complex management arrangements. They do not recognize jurisdictional boundaries. For example, the typical grizzly bear in the Yellowstone Ecosystem enters an average of 4.2 different management jurisdictions each year. Management policies must be supportive of grizzly bear maintenance in each jurisdiction for grizzlies to survive in the region.

A related conservation challenge that the world's bear species face is habitat fragmentation. This is illustrated by examining the historical and current distributions of grizzly bears in the contiguous United States, and of the giant panda in China. The recent loss of small, isolated, populations of both species, shows the importance of population size for persistence. For smaller populations to persist without augmentation they must be connected to larger populations. Establishing connections among small, fragmented bear populations of the same species, is a central conservation challenge regarding bears. Road construction, resource development, cottage and housing construction—these are a few of the many human activities that need to be carefully planned and sometimes canceled to avoid further fragmenting and impacting bear populations.

Even when biological data is available conservation of bears requires broad societal support because humankind often must forgo land uses that impact bears. Ultimately bear conservation requires organized government policy and practice, and support of local people. Public education and support remains one of the main challenges of bear conservation.

The conservation of bears in Asia is especially challenging. In most parts of Asia all bears are seriously threatened because they are killed both legally and illegally in large numbers for their gallbladders which are used in traditional Asian medicine. Dried bear gall can exceed the price of gold and approach the price of heroin in select markets such as Japan and Korea. In China thousands of bears are kept in cages so that their gallbladders can be "milked" by implanted catheters. Traditional Asian cultural values and medicinal uses contrast strongly with western conservation ethics and understanding. There will be few places that bears survive in Asia unless situations change. The threat to all bears posed by the Asian demand for bear gall and other bear parts has been recognized by the Convention on International Trade in Endangered Species of Wild Fauna and Flora (CITES). All of the world's eight bear species are listed on either Appendix 1 or 2 of CITES. This underlines the threat posed by trade.

Future for Bears

The giant panda, the sun bear, grizzly bears in the contiguous United States, and many other bear populations are threatened or endangered by the activities of humankind. If bear populations and species are to survive people will need to carefully regulate their impacts on the land base—the habitat that bears need for survival.

Bears can be regarded as an environmental litmus paper. Where bears survive, wild nature survives, providing potential recreation, inspiration, and other resources to people. When bears are taken from a landscape people lose a species that fires our imagination as few others do. If we can learn to live with bears then perhaps we can also learn to live on our planet without destroying it.

Stephen Herrero

Further Readings

Servheen, Chris. *The Status and Conservation of the Bears of the World.* International Conference on Bear Research and Management Monograph Series. 1990.

Mills, Judy A., and Chris Servheen. *The Asian Trade in Bears and Bear Parts.* Traffic USA, World Wildlife Fund, Washington, D.C. 1991.

See also CITES; GIANT PANDA; HABITAT LOSS IN NORTH AMERICA; TOP PREDATORS IN CANADA: AN OVERVIEW

Beaufort Sea

The Beaufort Sea is that portion of the Arctic Ocean lying to the north of Alaska and west of the Canadian high Arctic islands. The dominant characteristic of the Beaufort is floating pan ice interspersed with a few large ice islands which are former chunks of glaciers. Driven by the winds and currents, this pack ice migrates slowly in a clockwise direction through Canadian, American, Russian, and back to Canadian waters (the Beaufort gyre). During the summer months open water develops along the coast but the retreating sun and colder temperatures of the fall bring the moving pack ice south to grind along the shore fast ice reaching out from the land. Large columns of fresh water enter the Beaufort via the extensive shallow flats of the Mackenzie Delta which is critical habitat for many species of ducks and geese as well as marine mammals.

The area came into environmental prominence in 1968 with the Prudhoe Bay oil discoveries on the north slope of Alaska and the extension of the geological structures out under the Beaufort Sea. In the early 1970s, Canada was the first country in the world to allow offshore drilling in such ice-prone areas and the arrival of the Dome Petroleum drillships sparked domestic and international protests. It was argued that with the winds and the currents any major oilspill or blowout would foul not only the Canadian but the Alaskan north slope as well. While major Canadian oil and natural gas reserves were discovered out under the Beaufort Sea, the decline in world oil prices and the enormous capital costs of production facilities delayed indefinitely development of the fields. The geotechnical design challenges were great. The physical risk of ice scour required unique floating or submarine production facilities costing billions.

Today, a number of environmental, geophysical, and geotechnical problems remain but there is little interest or concern. It would require a major increase in world prices to beyond $30 per barrel to revive interest. In 1993, offshore oil drilling in the Canadian Beaufort Sea had ceased. In the last two decades the area has aroused other environmental concerns because of the test flights of Cruise Missiles but no accidents occurred. In the scientific discussions of global climate change there have been predictions that long term warming of the Beaufort could progressively melt the Arctic ice pack and erode the stable "Arctic high" weather system over the pole with serious implications for weather patterns elsewhere in the northern hemisphere. Thus the Beaufort Sea demonstrates the interdependency of the circumpolar areas as well as their importance for the areas to the South.

Robert J.D. Page

Further Readings

Livingston, John A. *Arctic Oil: The Destruction of the North?* 1981.
Page, Robert J.D. *Northern Development: The Canadian Dilemma.* 1986.
Vanderzwaag, David, and Linda Duncan. "Canada and Environmental Protection." In *Canadian Environmental Policy: Ecosystems, Politics, and Process.* Ed. Robert Boardman. 1992.

See also ALASKA: PARK, WILDERNESS, AND RESOURCE ISSUES; ARCTIC; BERGER INQUIRY; OIL SPILLS; WATERFOWL: CONSERVATION AND HABITAT

Benefit-Cost Analysis

Benefit-cost analysis—a method for evaluating the economic efficiency of public policy proposals—has been widely applied both to public investments in natural resource development (such as water resource projects) and more recently to environmental and health regulatory proposals ("regulatory impact assessments"). Its use in simple form can be traced at least to the mid-nineteenth century, in calls by then-Senator Abraham Lincoln and others for more explicit accounting of the benefits and costs of proposals for public financing of river navigation projects by the Army Corps of Engineers. It was established as a formal requirement for water projects by the Flood Control Act of 1936, elaborated in guidelines by the Bureau of the Budget from the late 1940s through the 1960s, and required for major environmental regulatory proposals since a presidential executive order (Executive Order 12,291) was signed in 1981.

Benefit-cost analysis is derived from the subfield of welfare economics, which holds that government actions should be taken only if their overall benefits in economic terms exceed their costs, and that such benefits should be measured by the sum of individuals' willingness to pay for them. The analysis therefore requires identifying what types of economic benefits and costs are expected to result from the action, identifying monetary indicators or surrogates for each, and estimating their magnitudes; discounting the values of future benefits and costs so that they are economically comparable to present ones; and aggregating the results into one of three possible decision criteria: a net present value (benefits minus costs), an internal rate of return (benefits per unit of costs), or a ratio (benefits divided by costs).

Benefit-cost analysis was instituted as a public policy reform proposal to force reasoned evaluation of policy proposals on their economic merits in place of perennial political temptations to seek projects (or regulations) that were locally beneficial or politically popular regardless of their general costs. However, it has itself been subject to serious debate and criticism, in both principle and practice. One set of issues concerns the selection of what economic effects "count" as benefits and costs, how to represent effects that are simultaneously benefits to some individuals and costs to others, and which of these can realistically be attributed to a particular proposed action. Costs, for example, have often been limited to direct capital, operating, and maintenance costs, ignoring harder-to-measure social and environmental costs; and both benefits and costs have often included only those for which individuals today are estimated to be willing to pay, ignoring potentially larger costs such as the replacement cost of the natural services provided by wetlands or other ecological processes that would be destroyed.

A second problem is selection of an appropriate discount rate: a low rate implies a high public valuation of future benefits, but in practice also makes it easier to justify expenditures for more speculative projects. Third, applications to regulatory problems have special problems in that costs are incurred by regulated parties who have strategic incentives to overestimate rather than minimize them, and are difficult to verify independently.

Finally, benefit-cost analysis has been criticized as an inappropriately narrow basis for public policy decisions in principle, since it pays no attention either to the equity of the resulting redistribution of economic gains and losses (unlike economic impact assessment, for instance, which is a more richly descriptive but less normative method) or to noneconomic moral, aesthetic or ethical principles for valuation of nature. Economists have argued that it at least raises the minimum estimated values of such considerations, which otherwise would be implicitly accorded no value in economic calcula-

tions. Some environmental advocates have sought therefore to use it and extend its methods themselves to justify environmental protection actions or attack natural resource development proposals. Others, however, have condemned this strategy as a two-edged sword, which may be effective in some cases but counter-productive in others, and perhaps even a "Faustian bargain" which distorts and undermines more fundamental principles by which they believe such decisions should be made. At its best benefit-cost analysis is therefore a useful tool, but not by itself an adequate basis for making decisions.

Richard N.L. Andrews

Further Readings
Bentkover, J.D., V.T. Covello, and J. Mumpower. *Benefits Assessment: The State of the Art.* 1986.

Kneese, A.V. *Measuring the Benefits of Clean Air and Water.* 1984.

Swartzman, D., R.A. Liroff, and K. Croke, eds. *Cost-Benefit Analysis and Environmental Regulations: Politics, Ethics and Methods.* 1982.

Smith, V. Kerry. *Environmental Policy Under Reagan's Executive Order: The Role of Benefit-Cost Analysis.* 1984.

See also DISCOUNTING THE FUTURE; ENVIRONMENTAL IMPACT ASSESSMENT; GNP AND THE ENVIRONMENT; GREEN ECONOMICS; RISK ANALYSIS; SUSTAINABLE DEVELOPMENT

Berger Inquiry
Canadian governments have frequently employed the public inquiry process to investigate complex and controversial public issues. While the results have varied, the process does allow serious consideration of new ideas and policies without the constraints of partisan politics. One such success was the Mackenzie Valley Pipeline Inquiry (1974–1978) headed by the Honorable Thomas Berger of the British Columbia Supreme Court. In the early 1970s the federal government of Canada was having difficulty addressing the new challenges of the environment, native land claims, and Arctic energy megaprojects. These issues were brought to a political focus by the application of a huge consortium to build a massive 2,600-mile natural gas pipeline from Prudhoe Bay, Alaska, across Canada to California and Chicago. The emerging environmental movement in Canada linked

up with native rights groups, energy conservationists, consumer activists, and nationalists to build a broad coalition of groups committed to fighting the project. The Mackenzie Valley Pipeline project became a symbol to many of what was wrong with our fossil fuel driven "Growth Economy." They feared it would destroy the pristine Arctic environment and native societies merely for access to a few trillion cubic feet of natural gas.

In an exhaustive two-year public inquiry, Berger presided over public hearings from the Alberta border to the Arctic Ocean. Every night the images and commentary went out in the television news packages. Environmental and native leaders articulated their concerns, deeply influencing southern middle class attitudes. The inquiry set new standards for public participation by minority groups including the use of aboriginal languages. Berger funded interventions by a coalition of non-governmental organizations (NGOs) and other public parties. He hired his own independent consultants to advise his staff and prepare cross-examination of the expert witnesses. It was these advisors who found the scientific errors in the Arctic Gas design for controlling frost heave in discontinuous permafrost which had not been caught by the Federal Power Commission (Washington) or the National Energy Board (Ottawa).

The Berger Report created an immediate sensation when it was released in May 1977. It was eloquently written accompanied with large color photographs of native people on the land and the Arctic wildlife. The two main conclusions were clear and unequivocal. Pipelines should be permanently prohibited from crossing the environmentally fragile North Slope of the Yukon and any pipeline in the Mackenzie Valley should be delayed for ten years to allow for the negotiation and implementation of native lands of the Dene, the Metis, and the Inuit. The Report was a moving and powerful statement achieving a new and compelling legitimacy for environmental and aboriginal values. While the report received wide public and media acclaim, it was viewed as a revolutionary and subversive document in some corporate and a few government offices. The report became an instant best seller in Canada and part of the international literature on the environment, aboriginal peoples, and development. Within a few years, his arguments became part of the accepted wisdom of Canadian bipartisan politics and a major contributing force to the progress on native land claims. In turn, Berger

went on to conduct a similar inquiry, the Alaskan Native Review Commission (Village Journey) and co-chaired an independent inquiry into the Sardar Sarovar dam in India. While the specifics of the Mackenzie Valley Pipeline have retreated into history, the values articulated in the Berger Report remain fresh and compelling.

Robert J.D. Page

Further Readings

Berger, Thomas. *Northern Frontier, Northern Homeland.* 1977.
Livingston, John A. *Arctic Oil: The Destruction of the North?* 1981.
Page, Robert J.D. *Northern Development: The Canadian Dilemma.* 1986.

See also ALASKA: PARK, WILDERNESS, AND RESOURCE ISSUES; ARCTIC; ENVIRONMENTAL IMPACT ASSESSMENT; PERMAFROST

Bhopal

This once obscure city of about 800,000 people in the central Indian state of Madhya Pradesh entered the annals of environmental history on the night of December 3, 1984, as the site of the deadliest accident of the industrial era. The disaster occurred at a pesticide plant operated since the early 1970s by Union Carbide of India Limited (UCIL), a subsidiary of the giant American multinational, Union Carbide Corporation. A runaway chemical reaction, caused by water flowing into a tank containing the highly toxic compound methyl isocyanate (MIC), unleashed its devastating effects on areas south and east of the plant which were densely settled by some of the poorest inhabitants of Bhopal. Though estimates vary, more than 3,500 people died and more than 150,000 were injured by the toxic cloud; perhaps as many as 25,000 were permanently disabled with conditions ranging from lung ailments to severe nervous disorders and psychological impairments.

The means by which water entered the MIC storage area may never be ascertained with complete accuracy. Most Indian analysts hotly contested Union Carbide's unsupported assertion that a disgruntled employee was to blame for an intentional act of sabotage. No one, however, denied the bleak record of risk management at the Bhopal facility. Although designed with numerous backup safety systems, the plant had been constructed in India with no special sensitivity to local conditions and constraints. It had been plagued for years by a history of poor maintenance, technological failures, human error, and deteriorating standards of operator training. In the absence of adequate siting and land-use policies, a mini-population explosion had taken place in the plant's immediate vicinity, increasing the probability of a catastrophic accident. The decision to store large volumes of MIC on the premises was made in 1978 without any evaluation of the associated risks. Neither municipal officials nor neighboring communities possessed reliable knowledge about the chemical's hazards or how to respond in the face of disaster.

The tragedy prompted worldwide reevaluation of chemical safety policies by both public and private sector organizations. The scope, complexity, and confusion of the relief effort in Bhopal focused attention on unresolved problems of information flow and emergency preparedness around hazardous chemical facilities. Public pressure for more openness led to a strengthening of national and international right-to-know policies. In the United States, home of Union Carbide, the 1986 amendments to the federal Superfund law (q.v.) imposed a duty on companies to report unplanned releases of "extremely hazardous substances" listed by the Environmental Protection Agency (EPA). Taking another cue from Bhopal, the law mandated the formation of "local emergency planning committees," with representatives from local government, industries, and communities, to formulate emergency responses to potential chemical accidents.

In India, as well, the Bhopal disaster substantially heightened the level of environmental awareness. Citizen groups active in the tragedy's aftermath built lasting networks, as organizations with widely distributed interests in urban development, poverty, women's issues, and public health discovered a common focus in controlling environmental hazards. People's science groups, which made important contributions to the medical diagnosis, treatment, and monitoring of Bhopal victims, went on to prepare technical support for the legal challenges against Union Carbide and Indian authorities. Human rights lawyers from universities and private practice also came to the victims' aid, adding issues of environmental protection to their traditional agenda of combating state repression.

The Government of India responded to the tragedy with a number of concrete legislative measures. Most notable was the umbrella Environment Protection Act of 1986, which materially expanded the central government's powers to enter, inspect, and close down facilities that had formerly operated under inadequate state supervision. The Factories (Amendment) Act of 1987 sought to control the siting process, increase worker participation in safety management, and make management formally accountable for emergency-response plans. Modeled on comparable provisions in more industrialized countries, the Hazardous Wastes (Management and Handling) Rules of 1989 imposed responsibilities for the proper handling of these materials on owners and operators of waste disposal facilities. The innovative Public Liability Insurance Act of 1991 required factory owners to insure against potential personal injury and property damage in surrounding communities. Sadly, preliminary experiences indicated that implementation would lag substantially behind the formal enactment of this impressive edifice of laws and regulations.

The victims' prolonged legal battle to win compensation from Union Carbide, and the resulting changes in Indian liability law, may well be remembered as the most lasting legacy of Bhopal. In a widely criticized move, partly motivated by the unexpected descent of entrepreneurial American lawyers on Bhopal, the Indian government first decided to seek compensation on behalf of all the Bhopal victims in the U.S. court system, which was known to be uniquely sympathetic to the claims of tort plaintiffs. A U.S. federal court, however, rejected India's contention that justice could not be obtained surely or speedily enough under Indian law. Remanded to India, the litigation dragged on for several more years in the state courts of Madhya Pradesh and eventually reached the Supreme Court of India. There, on February 14, 1989, the parties finally agreed to a politically controversial $470 million settlement, an amount far below the level originally demanded by the Indian government or expected by activist victims' groups. An effort to reopen the controversy in late 1991 failed when the Supreme Court upheld the basic terms of the settlement but acknowledged, in a largely symbolic act, that criminal proceedings could be reinstated against Union Carbide.

The years of litigation introduced some striking innovations into Indian tort law: the precedent-setting assumption of legal responsibility for tort victims by the state, based on the *parens patriae* principle; a standard of absolute liability, admitting no defenses, for hazardous industrial facilities; and the idea of interim payments to claimants pending the ultimate settlement of mass tort actions. The reach of these novel doctrines even within India remains to be tested, and they may never be generalized beyond the immediate context of Bhopal. Nonetheless, they represent an extraordinary case of legal adaptability and will stand as one of the more hopeful memorials to that city's tragic encounter with the dangers of industrialization.

Sheila Jasanoff

Further Readings

Baxi, Upendra, and Amita Dhanda, eds. *Valiant Victims and Lethal Litigation: The Bhopal Case.* 1990.

Jasanoff, Sheila, ed. *Learning from Disaster: Risk Management After Bhopal.* 1994.

Shrivastava, Paul. *Bhopal: Anatomy of a Crisis*, 2nd ed. 1992.

See also ENVIRONMENTAL MOVEMENTS: LESS-AFFLUENT NATIONS; PESTICIDES; RISK ANALYSIS; SEVESO; SUPERFUND

Bicycle Transportation

Pleasure is one of the greatest and most often overlooked environmental advantages of riding a bicycle. The sheer delight of independent, self-propelled movement causes millions worldwide to indulge in this ecological, economical, and equitable form of transportation repeatedly, whenever and wherever they can. Unfortunately, "wherever they can" is shrinking rapidly. The space gobbled up by the private automobile and its expanding infrastructure is squeezing out not only the safety and enjoyment of human powered transportation, but the very possibility of it. Projections of future car encroachment are even more foreboding. As such, the greatest challenge for the future of the bicycle is dealing with the future of the car.

When cities are built for cars the problems facing bicycle advocates are not only environmental, they are also spatial, economic, and cultural. In North America alone, over $5 billion are spent annually on car ads aimed at convincing people of the freedom, independence, convenience, safety—and of course status—that the car can bring to their lives. On the tiniest fraction of the car's advertising budget, the entire cycling movement is left to contend with making a dent in one of our society's most entrenched and most highly funded cultural icons.

But against such odds, a striking number of North Americans still say they would choose to bicycle if there were more bike lanes, if shower facilities were provided at work, and if secure bike parking were provided near the home, the school, the workplace, and the local shopping area. A 1991 Louis Harris poll found that 21 percent of all adult Americans said they would sometimes commute by bicycle if there were better bike facilities, and 21 percent said they would sometimes commute by bicycle if incentives were offered by their employers.

Unfortunately, these facts seldom filter through to the decision makers. In a Europe-wide public opinion poll, 75 percent of the public and 85 percent of the politicians said they support giving priority to cyclists, pedestrians, and transit at the expense of other traffic. But the same poll found that the politicians believed public support for these measures to be no more than 35 percent.

By contrast, in cities where politicians and other decision makers *do* provide facilities and support (at a very low cost relative to car infrastructure), bicycle use has snowballed.

In Copenhagen, for example, where extensive cycling facilities have been provided since the 1920s, and where the climate is similar to that of many northern U.S. and even some Canadian cities, about 25 percent of all everyday trips (including work trips) are made by bicycle year-round. As well, this number continues to grow with the addition of even more cycle facilities and political support. In Amsterdam, where substantial support for bicycle transportation policy and infrastructure began only in the early 1970s, there has been an exponential rise in bicycle use.

It seems that the cities which have been most successful at "bicyclization" have chosen to balance cultural, infrastructural, and political approaches to shifting away from the private automobile and toward the bicycle. This balance has included the process of removing the barriers to bicycle use—such as fear, fashion, and facilities—while at the same time actively building the alternative physical and cultural infrastructure.

Changing attitudes about the role of the bicycle is usually the first step to gaining broad-based support for bicycle transportation. Some cities have helped to push this attitude change through efforts to create an overall "bicycle culture." Examples of building bicycle culture include:

* Community and corporate outreach programs to relate and integrate bicycles with all aspects of life and work;

- High-profile bicycle events, such as focused "bike weeks" and mass commuter bicycle rides through cities and towns;
- Educational courses in safety and bicycle mechanics;
- Local economic development efforts emphasizing bicycles (including working with retailers, linking bikes and urban tourism, bike fashion design and manufacture); and
- Use of the arts in relation to bikes, for example bicycle ballet, bicycle art, and choirs on bikes.

Efforts to provide a more extensive bicycle infrastructure include:

- Lobbying government for bike lanes and better bike parking, and asking employers and building managers to provide adequate showers and bike parking at the workplace and at home;
- Hiring bicycle planners within municipal and regional planning and public works departments (it is no coincidence that the cities that have hired bicycle coordinators and bicycle planners are the cities with higher bicycle use);
- Building a network of bicycle recycling and repair centers, usually out of community centers, churches, or schools, to provide recycled bicycles at low cost to more people in the community, and to provide a focus for dialogue about bicycles;
- Supporting the design, manufacture, and use of work bikes and delivery bikes and trailers at local places of business so that grocery and other small deliveries are not dependent on motorized transportation; and
- Building links with other transportation modes so that long trips can combine cycling with transit or with car pooling (this is called "mixed mode" transportation).

The political aspect of bicyclization involves democratizing the process of change. Ways to accomplish this include: forming and supporting a municipal bicycle advisory committee to give cyclists a direct voice in local government; forming a Bicycle User Group (BUG) in the workplace or place of residence, as a concerted effort to meet specific work-related or community bicycle needs; coalition building with other transportation groups and with other community groups that are affected by transportation decisions; and directing concerted lobbying efforts toward affecting transportation policy.

To summarize, current directions of the bicycle transportation movement include:

- Cultural change to diminish the status of the automobile, while integrating the bicycle into all aspects of the life of the community;
- Finding and working with allies in all sectors of society, moving bicycles out of the fringe and into the mainstream;
- Economic development in the area of bike-related and auto-reduced infrastructure and services; and
- Efforts to change land-use policy and practice; taking space away from cars and conferring it to pedestrians, cyclists, and transit users; including measures such as bike lanes, widened sidewalks, traffic calming, mixed use zoning and intensification; improving transit service and mixed mode possibilities; auto speed reduction; countering road and highway expansion; and converting parking and road space into public spaces, green spaces, and food production spaces.

Sue Zielinski

Further Readings

Laird, Gordon, and Sue Zielinski. *Beyond the Car.* 1994.
Lowe, Marcia. *The Bicycle: Vehicle for a Small Planet.* 1989.
Smith, Robert A. *A Social History of the Bicycle.* 1972.
Wilson, David Gordon, and Frank Whitt. *Bicycling Science.* 1974.

See also AIR POLLUTION: REGULATION (U.S.); AUTOMOBILES: IMPACTS AND POLICIES; CLIMATE WARMING; ENERGY EFFICIENCY; LAND USE PLANNING; URBAN DESIGN

Bierstadt, Albert
See HUDSON RIVER SCHOOL

Big Thicket
Once roughly the size of Connecticut, the Big Thicket of Southeast Texas is now reduced to around 300,000 acres. Termed the Biological

Crossroads of North America, its semitropical climate, over fifty-inch annual rainfall, and proximity to western, southeastern, and temperate vegetation combine with a wide variety of soil types to produce a profound wealth of animal and plant life. Its uplands, winding streams, and flatlands support over 1,000 varieties of flowering plants: 100 species of overstory trees, 200 species of small trees and bushes, over thirty species of orchids, four of North America's five species of insectivores. Over 350 bird species are found there. Some animal and plant species there are rare, scarce, or endangered.

A former sanctuary for Indians, outlaws, backwoodsmen, and escaped slaves, the Big Thicket has been as much a place of legend as a biological entity. During the Civil War deserters hid there, evading Confederate troops. As late as World War I and World War II descendants of these original holdouts concealed themselves in the Thicket to avoid the draft. Through the 1950s and 1960s some settlers still lived there in log cabins without electricity or running water. Few live in such circumstances now, though the area remains a rich source of folklore.

Though many forces—dams, oilfields, highways, growing urban settlement—have lead to the reduction of the once vast wilderness, the greatest destructive force has clearly been lumbering. From the 1870s through the 1930s lumber barons removed the original timber from all but a few remote areas. Original timbering methods, though destructive, did allow the original forest ecology to regrow. With the emergence of clearcutting in the 1950s this was no longer true. The new "even-aged forest management," euphemistically so-called, leveled vast areas, replacing them with endless rows of pine (monoculture). Attempts to save the remaining wilderness became a race with the power saw and the bulldozer.

Efforts to conserve the region began in 1927 with the founding of the Big Thicket Association of East Texas. Through its actions a bill was proposed to create a Big Thicket National Park of 400,000 acres. The bill failed to pass Congress, however, and by 1950 the first attempt at protection had faded. In 1964 conservationists began again, founding the Big Thicket Association. A second campaign, waged against the determined opposition of lumber interests, resulted in 1974 in the creation of the Big Thicket National Biological Preserve of 84,550 acres. The first biological preserve in the history of the National Park Service, it consists of specimens of each of the region's eight major forest types, partially connected by stream corridors. In 1981 the preserve was named a United Nations Man and the Biosphere Reserve. In 1993 it was enlarged through the addition of the upper Neches Canyonlands Unit and the Big Sandy-Village Creek Corridor.

Environmentalists assert both that the Big Thicket Preserve, with its system of connecting corridors and units, provides a model for regional biological conservation, and that many unprotected areas in the region remain to be added to the preserve.

Pete A.Y. Gunter

Further Readings

McLeod, Claude A. *The Big Thicket of East Texas.* 1967.
Gunter, Pete A.Y. *The Big Thicket: An Ecological Reevaluation.* 1993.

See also BIOSPHERE RESERVES; CLEARCUT; CONSERVATION MOVEMENT; HABITAT FRAGMENTATION, PATCHES, AND CORRIDORS; NATIONAL PARKS: UNITED STATES; SUSTAINED YIELD FORESTRY

Bioaccumulation

Toxic chemicals in the environment, such as pesticides and heavy metals, may become concentrated in organisms in the ecosystem by two mechanisms. The first is by predacious organisms feeding on prey which contain the toxicant, and the second is by the chemical itself having an affinity for organisms that come into contact with it in water, soil, and/or air. An important aspect of bioaccumulation of chemicals in organisms is the type of chemical. The chemicals that easily bioaccumulate are those that persist in the environment and have a high lipid/water coefficient. The latter indicates that the chemical is "lipophilic," that is, it does not dissolve well in water but does in lipids (fats and oils). Most organisms contain lipids (fats) and, hence, are likely to take up lipophilic chemicals (such as many organochlorine insecticides) from their soil and water environments.

Obviously, the longer a chemical, such as a pesticide, remains in the environment, the greater is the possibility that it will spread or be transported from the one location, i.e., a treated crop, to another. If the life of the chemical exceeds the frequency of application to the environment, the chemical is likely to accumulate in the environment. Classic examples of chemicals that persist for many years are mercury and organochlorine pesticides such as DDT and dieldrin.

Bioaccumulation in the Food Chain

Several different pesticides concentrate in various organisms in the food chain with the highest concentrations present in those organisms that feed highest in the food chain. For example, DDT residues were found to reach a level of more than 15 kilograms per hectare in a Long Island saltmarsh. In a sampling of both the marsh and organisms present in the saltmarsh, DDT in the water was estimated at 0.05 ppb (parts per billion) and in plankton the DDT level was 40 ppb. The highest concentrations were detected in the scavenging and carnivorous fish and birds. The birds that were feeding on the fish were found to have ten to 100 times more DDT than the fish species.

The mechanism of accumulation in food chains is simple. In contrast to chemical energy, losses of DDT and other lipophilic toxicants along the food chain are small compared to the amounts that are transferred upward through the chain because these chemicals tend to be neither degraded nor eliminated from the organisms. Consequently, the concentration of DDT increases with each step in the food chain. Concentrations in organisms at the top of the food chain, such as birds, may be hundreds of times greater than in organisms further down the chain.

In Lake Michigan, for example, DDT and its metabolites averaged 0.014 ppm (parts per million) in the sediments on a wet weight basis. From the same habitat an amphipod averaged 0.41 ppm for DDT and its related metabolites. This is about thirty times the level found in the mud. A sampling of alewives removed from the lake had residues of 3.35 ppm and whitefish had residues of 5.60 ppm, or about ten times the level in the amphipod. The DDT level found in gulls' breast muscle averaged twenty-seven times the level of DDT found in the alewives.

Also, in a DDT-sprayed elm environment, DDT was found to average 9.9 ppm in the soil. The pesticide was found to accumulate to a level of 141 ppm in earthworms and to a level of 444 ppm in robin brains that were feeding on the earthworms. This level of DDT in the robin brains was reported to be highly toxic to the robin population.

Direct Bioaccumulation from the Environment

In some situations, bioaccumulation of chemicals directly from the environment can be more important than bioaccumulation in the food chain. Although organisms higher in the trophic levels of the food chains tend to have higher pesticide concentrations, the concept of the gradual concentration of residues through the food chain is based mainly on field evidence. In some cases, the evidence may be oversimplified. This concept has been demonstrated using three aquatic species: a fish (*Poecelia reticulata*), which fed on a crustacean (*Daphnia magna*), which in turn fed mainly on an alga (*Scenedesmus obliquus*). When these organisms were exposed separately to water containing dieldrin, the alga concentrated the chemical 1,300 times, the crustacean 14,000 times, and the fish 49,000 times. Contaminated crustaceans fed to fish in clean water led to residues in the fish only one-tenth as large. In terrestrial ecosystems as well, there are ways by which predators high in the trophic levels can acquire large concentrations of pesticide other than by simple concentration through the food chain. For example, there may be differential rates of uptake and excretion in the predator.

The chemical attributes of DDT make it susceptible to bioaccumulation in algal living systems. For example, four species of algae concentrated DDT about 220-fold when exposed to a concentration of DDT at 1 ppm in water for seven days. *Daphania*, a zooplanktonic organism, concentrated DDT 100,000 fold during a fourteen-day exposure to water containing 0.5 ppb of DDT.

Eastern oysters exposed in flowing seawater for ten days to dieldrin at 0.001 ppm concentrated the toxicant 1,000 times (1 ppm). Also, trout concentrated the level of dieldrin by 3,300-fold in their bodies when the water contained 0.0023 ppm of dieldrin.

Bioaccumulation also takes place in terrestrial environments. For example, earthworms and slugs in cotton fields were reported to bioaccumulate DDT from the soil. DDT in the soil was found to be 2.9 ppm, but the earthworms were reported to contain 32 ppm and slugs 53 ppm of DDT. Therefore, the earthworms and slugs had eleven to eighteen times the concentration of DDT in their bodies.

In summary, bioaccumulation of toxic chemicals by bioconcentrating either in the food chain or by obtaining the chemicals directly from the environment through contact with the toxic chemicals in water, soil, and probably air have proven to be a major risk to organisms in nature.

David Pimentel

Further Readings

Raven, P.H., L.R. Berg, and G.B. Johnson. *Environment.* 1993.

Tardiff, R.G., ed. *Methods to Assess Adverse Effects of Pesticides on Non-target Organisms.* 1992.

See also FOOD CHAINS; HERBICIDES; INTEGRATED PEST MANAGEMENT; PESTICIDES; SUSTAINABLE AGRICULTURE; WEB OF LIFE

Biodepletion

The term biodepletion is generally taken to refer to the mass extinction of species underway. Unlike all other environmental problems, species extinction is irreversible. Evolution may eventually come up with replacement species offering numbers and variety to match today's array. But so far as we can discern from episodes of mass extinction and their "bounce back" periods in the prehistoric past, the time required will be at least 5 million years, possibly several times longer. If we allow the present mass extinction to proceed unchecked, we shall impoverish the biosphere for a period equivalent to at least 200,000 human generations, or twenty times longer than the period since humankind itself emerged as a species. This means that the present generation is making a decision to the effect that our descendants can certainly do without large numbers of species, perhaps as many as half of all species—and the number of descendants on whose unconsulted behalf we are making this decision will likely total 500 trillion persons, making it far and away the biggest decision ever made by one human community with respect to future communities.

Species Extinction Rate

That we are into the opening phase of a mass extinction episode is beyond scientific doubt. Earth's stock of species is widely estimated to total at least 10 million. Some scientists believe the true total could well be 30 million, possibly 50 million and conceivably 100 million. Since most of the additional species are considered to exist in tropical moist forests, the real total is not a matter of mere speculation. It is precisely in these forests where habitats are being lost fastest and where the great bulk of species ex-

tinctions is occurring. So if the real total is 30 million species, the extinction rate will be between two and three times higher than the rate postulated for a planetary total of only 10 million species. But for the sake of being cautious and conservative, let us accept a total of 10 million species; and that at least half of these species live in tropical forests, even though remaining forests cover only 6 percent of the earth's land surface.

The forests are being destroyed at a rate of at least 150,000 square kilometers per year. In addition, an expanse equally as large is being grossly disrupted through over-heavy logging and slash-and-burn cultivation, with much degradation and impoverishment of ecosystems and their species' life-support systems. But in the interest of being cautious and conservative again, let us consider only the first form of habitat loss, namely outright destruction of forests. The current loss of 150,000 square kilometers per year represents 2 percent of remaining forests. The annual loss increased by 80 to 90 percent during the 1980s, and if present patterns and trends of forest destruction persist with still more acceleration in the annual rate, the current amount of 2 percent will increase much more again during the 1990s.

According to analyses by a number of leading biologists, there is an annual loss of at least 27,000 species in tropical forests alone. Widespread habitat destruction is overtaking a number of other species-rich biomes as well, notably Mediterranean-type zones, coral reefs, wetlands, montane environments, and many islands. So the overall total can be safely reckoned to be at least 30,000 species per year, or an average of eighty-two per day. A less cautious and more realistic estimate could put the total at well over 50,000 species per year, for an average of 150 per day. An annual extinction rate of 30,000 species is 120,000 times greater than the "natural" rate of extinction before the advent of the human era, considered to be roughly one species every four years.

This calculation is generalized, viewing tropical forests and other ecological zones as undifferentiated expanses (i.e., with regular or constant species distributions from end to end). So let us consider an alternative approach, this one being a "hot spots" analysis relating to areas that: 1) feature exceptional concentrations of species with exceptional levels of endemism; and 2) face exceptional threat of imminent habitat destruction. This approach reveals that fourteen hot spots in tropical forests and four hot spots in Mediterranean-type zones contain 50,000 endemic plant species or a full 20 percent of all the earth's plant species, facing severe threat of habitat destruction in just 0.5 percent of the earth's land surface. These hot spots contain a still higher though unquantified proportion of the earth's animal species.

So much for current extinctions. How about the future? The same biologist experts calculate that we face the prospect of losing 20 percent of all species within thirty years and 50 percent or more thereafter. If we are indeed on track toward a biotic holocaust that will eliminate half of the earth's species within the foreseeable future, this will be a unique event in life's history since it will be due to the activities of a single species. Fortunately humankind has the unique power not only to eliminate other species but to save other species as well—and right now we have the chance to save them in their millions. We still have time to convert a profound problem into a glorious opportunity.

Yet as we continue to eliminate unique manifestations of life with even greater energy and ingenuity, we also continue to expand the limits of our knowledge of biodiversity, albeit at a snail's pace. We are gaining a preliminary grasp of the abundance and variety of species, including the lesser known categories. It seems there could be 1.8 million micro-organisms, including 1.5 million fungi as opposed to a total of 69,000 fungi documented. The other 300,000 micro-organisms comprise bacteria and viruses, though we have named only 14,000 bacteria. There could also be one million each of nematodes and mites, though only 12,000 nematodes and 30,000 mites are known to us. Could it be that God's inordinate fondness was not for beetles but for creatures generally smaller than the smallest beetle (which is about the size of a full stop)? One acre of English pasture has been found to contain an estimated 71 million beetle individuals, 249 million springtails and 666 million mites, plus 135 million assorted aphids, bristletails, and miscellaneous other arthropods (creatures with jointed appendages).

In addition, it turns out that there are spectacular assemblies of species on the deep-sea floor—a world with no light, near-freezing temperatures and many atmospheres of pressure. The marine realm has traditionally been viewed as biotically depauperate in comparison with the terrestrial realm, with an estimated 1 million species or so. But recent research by Dr.

Fred Grassle of Rutgers University in the United States suggests the true total in just the ocean benthos could be as high as 10 million, mostly made up of molluscs, crustaceans, and polychaete worms. In an area 2.5 miles down and no bigger than two tennis courts, Grassle has found 90,677 small invertebrates living on or in the sediments, many of them no larger than half a millimeter. They comprised 798 species, of which 460 were new to science. More important still, they represented 171 families and fourteen phyla—a higher-taxon diversity that could not remotely be matched on land. Whereas terrestrial habitats feature eleven of the super-categories known as phyla (only one of which is limited to land), the seas are home to twenty-eight phyla, thirteen of them found nowhere else.

The seas have even revealed a new species of whale. Discovered off Peru's coast in 1976, *Mesoplodon peruvianus* is the smallest of thirteen known species in its genus, reaching a length of no more than four meters and with a remarkably diminutive cranium. The same year also produced the largest shark species, the megamouth, so distinctive that it warrants a family all to itself.

Regrettably the seas are being degraded by human activities. Coral reefs are often richer in species per unit area than are tropical forests, and they are undergoing widespread depletion. They cover around 600,000 square kilometers, or only 0.2 percent of the oceans' surface (tropical moist forests, 7.5 million square kilometers or 6 percent of land surface), yet in this limited expanse they may well contain one third of the oceans' fish species. As many as 93 percent of coral reefs have already been damaged and possibly 5 to 10 percent destroyed by human activity, and at the present depletion rate a full 60 percent could be lost within twenty to forty years.

Similarly, freshwater ecosystems feature exceptional concentrations of certain taxa of species. For example, the three main East African Rift Valley lakes harbor almost 1,000 cichlid fish species, virtually all of them endemic; Lake Victoria has already lost at least 200 of its 300 cichlids, making this the largest vertebrate mass extinction of the modern era. Many North American freshwater fish species are endangered or have already been made extinct; and many are at extreme risk due to their ultra-restricted distribution—the Desert Hole pupfish has a global habitat totaling a few cubic meters.

As we have seen, invertebrates dominate biodiversity, making up perhaps 9 million out of the minimum global total of 10 million species. Bugs are not going to inherit the earth; they own it already. (Bacteria too are more important than we might think: they make up one tenth of our body weight.) If current trends continue and we lose around half of all mammal species within the foreseeable future—primates, carnivores, and the like—that will not be a fraction so drastic as if we lose half of all invertebrates. Dr. David Pimentel and his student colleagues at Cornell University have calculated that more than forty U.S. crops are absolutely dependent upon insects for pollination, with a farm-gate value of $30 billion per year. About one third of the human diet is made up of insect-pollinated fruits, vegetables, and legumes. We could get by materially without the panda or the blue whale, but the demise of the honeybee would cause us ecological and economic hiccups aplenty.

The Economics of Extinction

In hundreds of ways, species and their genetic resources contribute to our material welfare. In the public health field, one in two medicines, drugs, and pharmaceuticals owes its origin to germ plasm materials or other key products of plant species. These products include antibiotics, analgesics, diuretics, tranquilizers, and a host of similar items. The contraceptive pill stems from a plant of West Africa's forests. Three promising responses to AIDS are based on plant materials. A child suffering from leukemia in 1960 faced only one chance in five of remission, but today a child enjoys four chances in five thanks to two potent drugs derived from alkaloids of Madagascar's rosy periwinkle. These drugs, also used against Hodgkin's disease and a number of other cancers, generate commercial sales totaling more than $200 million per year in the United States alone, while the economic benefits to American society, in terms of worker-productivity saved, among other things, are estimated at $400 million a year. The 1985 commercial value of all plant-based pharmaceuticals in developed countries reached $45 billion, and the societal benefits (e.g., deaths avoided) several times greater. Anticipated plant extinctions in the United States during the last 15 years of this century will cost Americans more than $3 billion per year in plant-based drugs foregone.

As we have seen, similar benefits accrue in the fields of agriculture and industry, with commercial values alone reckoned in the tens of billions of dollars per year. Yet we enjoy all these diverse products after scientists have conducted intensive investigation of only one in 100 of the earth's 250,000 plant species, and a far smaller proportion of animal species—even though it is among the latter that we may eventually find most economic applications to support our material welfare.

We Can Still Save Biodiversity

What can we do to save biodiversity? Consider four broad-front actions:

1. We need to establish many more parks and reserves, especially in those areas where there is most at stake, the tropical developing world. Scientists estimate we need three to five times more protected areas forthwith.

2. Recognize that the best safeguarded parks, even with walls around them 100 meters tall, will still not protect their ecosystems from acid rain, ultraviolet radiation and global warming—nor, in many instances, from fast-growing multitudes of impoverished peasants. Increasingly it is the case that we can save biodiversity only by saving the biosphere (just as we can ultimately save the earth only by saving the world—and vice versa). Fortunately, we should be saving the biosphere for all manner of other cogent reasons anyway. A plausible prospect is that within another few decades we shall have no more parks and reserves, either because they will have been destroyed by land-hungry throngs and atmospheric pollution, or because we shall have learned to manage all our landscapes in such a way that the needs of biodiversity will have been taken care of along the way.

3. Rejoice that more is being done than formerly. The Global Environmental Facility under the World Bank has assigned around half a billion dollars over three years to support biodiversity. But it should be several times more. If it were $500 million every year, and insofar as the funds would come mainly from the pockets of rich-world taxpayers, it would amount to the equivalent cost of half a beer a year.

4. Keep reminding ourselves, above all, that we can still turn an appalling problem

into a magnificent opportunity. Charles Darwin once said he would have assigned years of his professional life to saving the dodo. What would he have given to be alive today with the chance to save species in their millions? To paraphrase another Charles, this time Dickens: we live in the worst of times and the best of times.

Norman Myers

Further Readings

Ehrlich, Paul R., and Edward O. Wilson. "Biodiversity Studies: Science and Policy." *Science* 253 (1991): 758–62.

Myers, Norman. *A Wealth of Wild Species.* 1983.

———. "The Biodiversity Challenge: Expanded Hot-Spots Analysis." *The Environmentalist* 10 (1990): 243–56.

Oldfield, Margaret L. *The Value of Conserving Genetic Resources.* 1989.

Raven, Peter R. "The Politics of Preserving Biodiversity." *BioScience* 40 (1990): 769–74.

Wilson, Edward O. *The Diversity of Life.* 1992.

See also BIODIVERSITY; BIODIVERSITY: PLANTS; CAROLINA PARAKEET; CONSERVATION BIOLOGY; CORAL REEFS; ENVIRONMENTALISM; FLORIDA PANTHER; PASSENGER PIGEON; TROPICAL DEFORESTATION; TROPICAL RAINFORESTS

Biodiversity

Biodiversity, synonymous with "biological diversity," is one of the most complex, misunderstood, yet central topics in conservation. Although sometimes considered equivalent to species richness (the number of species in an area), biodiversity is much more. Biodiversity has become nothing less than a shorthand expression for the full variety of life on earth and a powerful symbol for those interested in preserving this variety.

Biological diversity first entered scientific literature about 1980 and the term biodiversity was used as the title for a symposium sponsored in Washington D.C. in 1986. The papers from that symposium were published in a landmark book, *Biodiversity*, edited by Edward O. Wilson. At about that time, as people became more aware of the extinction crisis, biodiversity emerged as a significant issue in North American and international environmental policy. However, biodiversity did not become a familiar term to the general public until the United Nations Conference on the Environment and Development (UNCED) in 1992, when the refusal of U.S. president George Bush to sign the popular Biodiversity Convention was widely reported by the press and the term biodiversity appeared on the front pages of newspapers worldwide.

Components of Biodiversity

Biodiversity is the variety of life and its processes. It includes the variety of living things in an area, the genetic differences among them, the communities and ecosystems in which they occur, and the ecological and evolutionary processes that keep them functioning. Most definitions of biodiversity recognize variety at several levels of biological organization. Four levels commonly considered are: genetic, species, community or ecosystem, and landscape or regional. Each of these levels can be further divided into compositional, structural, and functional components. Composition includes the genetic makeup of populations and the kinds of species, habitats, and communities in an area. Structure includes the physical features of a habitat, such as pools and riffles in a stream or logs in a forest. At a broader spatial scale, structure includes the horizontal patchiness of vegetation across a landscape. Function includes the climatic, geological, hydrological, ecological, and evolutionary processes that generate and maintain biodiversity.

Biodiversity at the genetic level can be measured within or among populations of species. Genetic diversity within a population generally increases with population size. As population size declines or as social factors restrict breeding to fewer individuals, inbreeding can occur and can lead to reduced fitness or survival. The among-population component of genetic diversity is related to the geographic range of a species and the extent to which local populations have diverged genetically due to adaptation to local conditions or to random factors. Genetic diversity provides the raw material for adaptation to changing environments and for the evolution of new life forms.

Biodiversity is most commonly measured at the species level. Yet, the vast majority of species in the world are unknown. Scientists have classified only about 1.8 million of an estimated 10 to 100 million species on earth. Known species are largely insects, half of them beetles. Many invertebrates, bacteria, and other organisms remain to be discovered, even in the highly settled temperate zone. The goal of maintaining maximal species richness has proven problematic because areas disturbed by human activity are often quite diverse in opportunistic species at little risk of extinction. Thus, the species richness goal is best applied at a global scale; at any smaller scale, quality is more important than quantity. Conservationists today usually emphasize maintaining the native species composition of an area and devote most attention to species sensitive to human disturbance.

Biodiversity at the community or ecosystem level has been less studied, but the concept is simple enough. An area with several kinds of forest, grassland, lakes, and stream communities is more diverse than an area with only one or two communities. In many cases, conservation is most efficient when focused directly on the community or ecosystem, rather than on species individually. Many kinds of ecosystems—for example, tallgrass prairie and longleaf pine forests in the United States—have become highly endangered, just like many species. But as with species richness, the goal of maintaining a maximal variety of communities in an area is potentially dangerous if it entails manipulation of habitats to create variety. For example, clearcutting has been justified on the grounds that it increases habitat diversity. However, studies have shown that logging and other habitat manipulation often favor weedy species over others at greater risk of extinction. Conservation of biodiversity at the ecosystem level demands representation of all types of ecosystems in protected areas, and attention to habitat structure and processes such as disturbance regimes and nutrient cycles that allow ecosystems to function sustainably.

Finally, biodiversity at a landscape or regional level involves more than just the kinds of communities and species—it depends on the spatial arrangement of habitats across a large area and on the fluxes of energy, nutrients, disturbances, and organisms across this area. Many animals need a variety of habitats to meet their life history needs and may furthermore require that these habitats be physically connected to allow safe movement from one to another. Thus, patterns and processes at a landscape scale can affect biodiversity at many levels of organization.

Conserving Biodiversity

Conserving biodiversity requires that the forces threatening it be reduced or reversed. The most important ultimate threats are the growth of the human population and the increasing per capita consumption of resources. These pressures lead to habitat destruction—the greatest proximal threat to biodiversity. Direct killing or collection of organisms by people was historically a leading cause of extinction and remains a problem for certain species (e.g., large carnivores, primates, sharks, parrots, rare cacti) in some regions. Climate change and other atmospheric alterations such as ozone depletion may soon become dominant threats worldwide.

Habitat degradation can occur in many ways. Outright conversion of natural habitats to agricultural fields, pastures, or cities is the most visible form of destruction and the consequences are predictable: any species or community type that occurred only in that area will be eliminated and overall population sizes or extent of other species or communities will be reduced. Fragmenting habitats into smaller and more isolated pieces will compound the effects of habitat destruction. Many small populations surviving on fragments will be vulnerable to extinction from stochastic and deterministic factors.

Other kinds of habitat degradation are more subtle. They include, for example, suppression of native grasses by livestock grazing followed by invasion of alien grasses, changes in aquatic communities caused by dams or by introduction of game fishes, and conversion of diverse natural forests to simplified tree farms. The conservation of biodiversity requires that destructive human activities be stopped and that steps be taken to restore habitats already damaged.

Reed F. Noss

Further Readings

Noss, Reed F. "Indicators for Monitoring Biodiversity: A Hierarchical Approach." *Conservation Biology* 4 (1990): 355–64.

Noss, Reed F., and Allen Y. Cooperrider. *Saving Nature's Legacy: Protecting and Restoring Biodiversity*. 1994.

Wilson, Edward O., ed. *Biodiversity*. 1988.

———. *The Diversity of Life*. 1992.

See also BIODEPLETION; BIODIVERSITY: PLANTS; CLEARCUT; CONSERVATION BIOLOGY; ECOLOGICAL RESTORATION; FOREST FRAGMENTATION AND BIRD HABITATS; HABITAT FRAGMENTATION, PATCHES, AND CORRIDORS; LANDSCAPE ECOLOGY; RIO CONFERENCE (1992)

Biodiversity: Farmscapes

Biodiversity is a term generally used to describe the total genetic diversity found in natural ecosystems. In contrast to undisturbed areas, agricultural systems represent a relatively homogeneous planting of one or a few plant species for commercial harvest and sale. What diversity exists is usually in weed species, and those are controlled if possible. Today's conventional monoculture cropping systems are designed to dominate the natural environment and ignore the biological potentials of a carefully designed and biodiverse agricultural farmscape.

Traditional farming systems were highly diverse, including a number of crop species and animals that consumed crop residues, waste products, and forages that were not useful for humans. This diversity provided a certain degree of buffering against unfavorable or unpredictable weather conditions, since the individual crops would mature at different times of the year and could provide food through all seasons if stored properly. Animals were there to provide a continuous source of food as well as a bank account of sorts that could be cashed in for food or income at any time. Such diverse systems provided both a food supply and economic resilience in uncertain climates.

Modern monoculture farming that depends entirely on a single species (e.g., irrigated corn in Central Nebraska or rainfed wheat in the Palouse Region of Washington) provides none of this resilience. Although the farmer may operate on a large scale with the newest and most efficient equipment, there is a single harvest each year and complete dependence on the costs of inputs and prices received for that crop. Farmers who have not been able to compete in today's specialized and complex production and marketing environment, including that fostered by federal price supports and other programs, have not been able to continue.

Biodiversity can be introduced into modern farming systems in several ways. Diversity over time is achieved by rotation of different crops, with most success coming from alternating patterns of crops that are most unlike: cereals with legumes, annuals with perennials, summer with winter crops. Such rotations help to control unwanted weeds, insects, pathogens, and nematodes by interrupting the reproductive cycles of these pests. Different crops make use of different resources, and often contribute to greater accumulation of organic matter in the soil and improved soil fertility. Crop rotations generally increase the yield of each component by about 10 percent.

Spatial diversity in a cropping environment can be designed through use of alternating strips of different species, often planted on the contour to reduce soil erosion. Strips of annual crops alternating with perennial strips of alfalfa or other grass or legume hay can substantially reduce the loss of soil from a hilly field. Another way to introduce diversity is to plant a legume or grass or mixed cover crop into the major field crop before or shortly after harvest. This will provide some vegetative growth late in the season, help take up and hold nutrients that would otherwise erode with surface drainage or leach through the soil profile, and supply some additional organic matter to the soil. Another innovative way to maintain growing crop cover through more of the year is to relay plant one crop into another before the first crop is mature. Soybeans can be planted into winter wheat in mid-May in the maize growing regions of North America; wheat is harvested at the normal time, and the soybeans mature in early fall. These types of farmscape diversity provide a practical departure from conventional monoculture, and can promote efficient resource use and diversify sources of food and income from tomorrow's farming systems.

Charles A. Francis

Further Readings

Edwards, C.A., et al. *Sustainable Agricultural Systems*. Ankeny, IA: Soil & Water Conservation Society, 1990.

Francis, Charles A., et al. *Sustainable Agriculture in Temperate Zones*. 1990.

See also AGRICULTURE: ENVIRONMENTAL IMPACTS; AGROFORESTRY; BIODIVERSITY: PLANTS; HERBICIDES; SOIL CONSERVATION

Biodiversity: Plants

Plant biodiversity is comprised of the genetic richness of plant species, populations, and habitats. Species are evaluated in terms of their numbers, their range and distribution, and how useful they are. Populations are evaluated in terms of population dynamics, genetic diversity and variation, and how localized (or endemic) they are. Habitats are evaluated in terms of their richness and extent. All three are evaluated in terms of how endangered or threatened they are.

In addition to their basic existence value, plants and their biodiversity have been crucial in both natural and human evolution. The domestication of plants and animals represents one of the major transition points in human evolution. Many religions ascribe sacred origins to crop seeds. Most share the biblical understanding that "all flesh is grass." Besides humankind's food, plants have provided much of its shelter and medicines as well as much aesthetic pleasure.

The lower plants include bryophytes, lichens, and algae. The higher plants consist of three groups: the pteridophytes (ferns and fern allies) with some 12,000 species, the gymnosperms (non-flowering trees—mainly conifers and cycads) with some 600 species, and angiosperms (flowering plants) with some 250,000 species.

The major natural habitat types include forests, grasslands, wetlands, and mangroves. Each has many subcategories that largely reflect adaptations to climatic and soil variations. Wetlands and mangroves are often centers of marine diversity and reproduction. The most prominent human-shaped habitats are agricultural and grazing lands. Indigenous and peasant agricultural systems are much more species diverse than the monocultures of modern industrial agriculture and forestry.

In addition to expanding monocultures, plant genetic diversity is threatened by a range of other industrial processes and impacts, including urbanization, deforestation, various types of pollution, and climate change. Burgeoning human and livestock populations have also greatly increased pressures on forests and grasslands.

General efforts to protect and maintain plant biodiversity emphasize conserving species and habitats in their natural setting (in situ). In temperate zones (which are generally less species rich), the focus of national and international efforts has been on endangered or threatened species—which, once identified and listed, receive some type of protection. In the tropics, the richness of species, especially in tropical moist forests, has led to a focus on habitat protection. The IUCN (International Union for the Conservation of Nature and Natural Resources) has a Plant Conservation Program to identify and describe some 250 particularly rich "Centers of Plant Diversity." While many national parks and protected areas have been established, including a number which are designated as UNESCO "biosphere reserves," the real challenge has been to try to establish effective incentives for local people to respect these areas and maintain their diversity.

Protection and maintenance of crop germplasm has focused on *ex situ* approaches, in which seeds and genetic samples are held in national and international seed banks around the world. Equivalent efforts are needed to preserve crop and livestock diversity in the fields of peasants and farmers. Currently, much of the world's potato diversity is maintained by different Andean tribes each cultivating a number of different varieties at different elevations—an example that shows the important links between preserving cultural diversity and biodiversity.

The conservation of crop and medicinal plant biodiversity has been complicated by development of plant "patenting"—turning what for millennia had been a common property resource into a proprietary commodity. One of the most contentious issues at the 1992 United Nations (UN) Earth Summit was the Biodiversity Convention (treaty) and its provisions on who would receive the benefits from genetically-engineered crops and plant-derived medicines.

Maintenance of the biodiversity of the world's forests, grasslands, and wetlands, as well as its heritage of crop and medicinal plants, must be understood to be a central component of humankind's search for a sustainable future.

Kenneth A. Dahlberg

Further Reading

Groombridge, Brian, ed. *Global Biodiversity: Status of the Earth's Living Resources.* 1992.

See also BIODEPLETION; BIODIVERSITY; GENETIC DIVERSITY; IUCN; RIO CONFERENCE (1992)

Bioregion

The term bioregion is a contraction of biological or biotic region. In this sense it refers to an area that differs ecologically from other areas in terms of topography, microclimates, vegetation cover, or species composition. Thus, it may be considered the equivalent of ecoregion or ecological region. However, the biological meaning of the term has been overlaid by consideration of human use or human perception of ecologically distinct areas, and in this sense becomes the equivalent of eco-cultural region. It is difficult to arrive at a precise definition of the term since it is used in many different senses in both the scientific and popular literature.

There have been many attempts to describe and map the ecological regions of the earth. One of the earliest and best known is the system devised by Alfred Russell Wallace, who had noted marked differences in animal species from one area of the world to another. In 1876 he described six major "biographic realms": Palaearctic (Europe and northern Asia), Nearctic (North America), Neotropic (Tropical Central and South America), Ethiopian (Africa), Oriental (Southern Asia), and Australian. In each of these realms animal species have evolved separately during the millions of years that the land areas have been separated.

At another level, Lee R. Dice has described and mapped the "biotic provinces" of North America, using differences in vegetation and fauna as a basis for distinguishing the separate provinces. His terminology was later used by Raymond F. Dasmann in mapping the biotic provinces of the world. Dasmann's work was completed by Miklos D.F. Udvardy in a map distributed through Unesco, using the term "biogeographic provinces" in place of biotic provinces.

Udvardy has described twenty-two ecologically different provinces in Nearctic North America, including such categories as Rocky Mountain province, Grassland province, and Eastern Forest province. Those who seek a more human-centered definition of bioregion find Udvardy's categories too all-inclusive and prefer to recognize smaller, ecologically distinguishable areas considered to be "home territories" by their human inhabitants. These work well enough where human populations have been relatively sedentary over long periods of time, but become less useful when applied to highly mobile urban populations. Still others prefer to use watershed units or drainage basins as a basis for defining a bioregion, even where watersheds include many ecologically distinct communities. It is open to question whether any general agreement can be reached on the meaning of the word, or even if one is needed.

The value of the bioregional concept is primarily educational. If people can become familiar with the conditions for life and the other living species in the area in which they live, presumably they will be equipped to exercise greater care in the use they make of their bioregion, and may take a greater interest in protecting its natural diversity. A knowledge of the ecological constraints imposed by climate, topography, rock structure, soil types, hydrology, and vegetation could prevent the kind of misuse of land, water, and resources which has caused serious ecological damage in many parts of the world and has made some areas virtually uninhabitable.

A knowledge of the animal and plant species that occur naturally in one's bioregion, as well as those introduced by human agency can lead to an early recognition of changes that are taking place in one's home area. Such changes may result from the normal operation of ecological processes, such as climatic cycles or the successional changes that occur on land previously disturbed. Such changes in species abundance may serve as warning signals of serious environmental degradation. Thus the disappearance of spotted owls does not just imply that the habitat has become less suited to owls, but the loss of a unique ecological community of which the owls form only a small, but important, ecological link.

A bioregional approach has value also in the management of natural resources. Within a single bioregion, all government and private agencies are working with similar biotic communities. Awareness of this fact may facilitate cooperation and coordination of activities aimed at conservation and sustainable use of living resources, as well as the sharing of information among separate jurisdictions. For example, all who live and work in desert bioregions encounter many of the same problems and constraints, which are not shared by those who work in bioregions characterized by humid forests. Exchange of information among scientists and managers in the deserts of Southwest Asia, the Sahara of Africa, or the Mojave and Sonoran deserts of North America can, and has benefited all concerned and may lead to better agricultural and pastoral management, as well as conservation of natural environments.

Since most states and counties in the United States have been delineated somewhat arbitrarily, with little or no recognition of natural features, some would recommend a bioregional approach to redefining these political units. There would be obvious advantages to bringing a unified political control over the management of a single ecosystem, such as the Pacific Coastal Forest ecosystem, or the watershed of the Shenandoah River. However, the political difficulties involved in redefining longstanding county or state boundaries are sufficiently formidable to discourage even strong believers in a bioregional approach. In the latter part of the twentieth century it appears more feasible to seek close cooperation among the agencies involved in the management of a bioregion than to attempt the redrawing of political maps. Such cooperation shows promise in such areas as the Greater Yellowstone Ecosystem, the Pinelands Biosphere Reserve of New Jersey, the Lake Tahoe Basin of Nevada and California, and the Adirondacks ecosystem of New York. These and other examples suggest that bioregional approaches to management and conservation may become more the rule than the exception in the future.

Raymond F. Dasmann

Further Readings

Dasmann, Raymond F. *The Biotic Provinces of the World.* (IUCN Occasional Paper No. 9). 1973.

Dice, Lee R. *The Biotic Provinces of North America.* 1943.

Udvardy, Miklos D.F. *A Classification of the Biogeographical Provinces of the World.* (IUCN Occasional Paper No. 18). 1975.

Wallace, Alfred Russell. *The Geographic Distribution of Animals.* 2 vols. 1876.

See also BIOSPHERE RESERVES; ECOSYSTEMS; LANDSCAPE ECOLOGY; RADICAL ENVIRONMENTALISM

Biosphere Day

Being the peripheral sphere of the planet earth and its atmosphere in which any form of life exists naturally, The Biosphere is Humankind's and Nature's sole habitat and life-support apart from the energy received from the sun. Yet, probably because it is intangible, and invisible as a whole, The Biosphere is little understood by the vast majority of people. In an attempt towards remedying this ignorance, which is dangerous because of the manner in which The Biosphere is increasingly threatened by human numbers and profligacy, the Foundation for Environmental Conservation, through its Journal *Environmental Conservation*, instituted some years ago an annual Biosphere Day, choosing September 21—heralding in the Autumn Equinox in the Northern Hemisphere and the Spring Equinox in the Southern Hemisphere—as the day on which to remind humanity of its dependence on The Biosphere and the quintessential necessity of safeguarding that sole habitat and source of life in every possible way.

April brings a yearly Earth Day, and early June, Environment Day, so it seemed fitting that September would be a suitable month to provide such a vital reminder regularly each year and as widely as possible. Proposed elements of Biosphere Day include the announcement of the winners of a major "Biosphere Prize" and satellite prizes for significant improvements in the areas of: earth, air, freshwater, marine and/or coastal, biomass supply, and global integration. Prize allocations should come from a major "Biosphere Fund" as soon as sufficient endowment can be found. The Foundation also proposes a system of autonomous but integrated "Biosphere Clubs" which might well span the world in the manner of Rotary and Lions Clubs, especially in view of their very real and solid basis and objective.

Nicholas Polunin

Further Readings

Polunin, Nicholas, in *Environmental Conservation 18* (1990): 199; *19* (1992): 194; *20* (1993): 3; *21* (1994): 97.

See also EARTH DAY

Biosphere Reserves

The concept of a "biosphere reserve" originated within the UNESCO "Man and the Biosphere" Programme (MAB), an international program of cooperation which has been underway since November 1971. The broad purpose of MAB is to promote ecological and environmental research and monitoring, with related education and training activities, oriented toward policy and management issues concerning conservation and resource management. The ideal MAB research project involves interdisciplinary research teams composed of both natural and social scientists who work closely with resource managers and resource user groups or beneficiaries on issues mutually identified and agreed upon. Some 120 countries now participate in MAB.

Protected areas, such as national parks, ecological reserves, wildlife refuges, or equivalent reserves, provide important reference sites for research on the cumulative consequences of particular resource management or use patterns in nearby areas, as well as for studies on the conservation role of protected areas within a larger regional landscape. MAB soon realized the importance of giving recognition to areas where the kinds of activities promoted by MAB were being put into practice. The concept of a "biosphere reserve" was created in 1974, as a designation of recognition for this purpose. The term "biosphere" associates a designated area with MAB, and the term "reserve" acknowledges its association with some protected area(s).

The concept of a biosphere reserve can be depicted in a schematic diagram which shows a spatial configuration of three kinds of zonation, which collectively serve three main functions. The three zones are: a "core" area of minimally disturbed and strictly protected ecosystems characteristic of a terrestrial or coastal region; a protective "buffer zone" around the core that allows certain kinds of resource use providing these don't impact on the core; and a "transition area" or "zone of cooperation" extending outward from the core in all directions, but with no fixed boundary, within which the full range of human use of resources occurs. The three main functions of biosphere reserves are: conservation of ecosystems (which was initially the most emphasized); a "development" function exemplified by demonstrations of ecologically sustainable resource management and use, including the rehabilitation of degraded areas; and a "logistical" function (i.e., using biosphere reserves as sites for research, monitoring, education and training directed toward local or regional issues of conservation and resource use). The main challenge for biosphere reserves is to adapt these general specifications to the particular ecological and societal conditions found in any given place.

Two variants of the concept have been developed. One is a multiple-site "cluster biosphere reserve" set in some larger bioregion; if the sites collectively serve the functions of biosphere reserves and there is sufficient coordination among the administrative authorities for each site in the cluster, then the concept of a biosphere reserve can be realized in practice on a more expanded scale. The biosphere reserve concept has also been reviewed for adaptation to the needs of marine conservation.

A UNESCO designation of recognition does not, and cannot, interfere with legal mandates, private property rights, aboriginal rights, and management policies that are already in place. The designation signifies only that the arrangements in place appear sufficient for developing the functions of biosphere reserves.

By January 1995, there were some 324 biosphere reserves in 82 countries. Most serve a conservation function, often because of their association with some established protected area which serves as their "core" area. Some have developed effective local level cooperation for carrying out the logistical and demonstration functions. However, many have yet to develop all three main functions which biosphere reserves are meant to serve, and the networking among them has yet to be developed on a regular basis.

How successful are biosphere reserves? On a global level it is difficult to know. Presentations on biosphere reserves prepared for international meetings by participating countries are generally restricted to descriptions of the landscapes, formal administrative structures, and program activities within the biosphere reserves. There has been little or no analysis of implementation problems, and how they were overcome.

UNESCO has urged MAB national committees to cooperate more closely on a regional basis to foster the development of biosphere reserves and networks of exchange. "EuroMAB," representing twenty-four national committees in the European region (including North America), initiated a "Biosphere Reserves Integrated Monitoring Program" in 1991 to examine possible protocols for inventories of biota, environmental monitoring, and information exchange among 166 biosphere reserves in this region.

The ideals of MAB remain as valid and as urgent as ever. It has become increasingly evident that goals for the conservation of biodiversity, the maintenance of ecosystem health or integrity, and the achievement of ecologically sustainable resource use, have to be considered in the context of "meso-scale" regional landscapes. Biosphere reserves provide some guidelines and experience for the partnerships that have to be forged and the kinds of regional planning to conduct.

George Francis

Further Readings

Batisse, M. "Developing and Focusing the Biosphere Reserve Concept." *Nature and Resources* 22 (1986): 1–10.

UNESCO 1984. "Action Plan for Biosphere Reserves." *Nature and Resources* 20 (1984): 1–12.

UNESCO 1993. Biosphere Reserves: The Theory and the Practice. *Nature and Resources* 29, Nos 1–4: 1–46. Batisse, M. 1993. The Silver Jubilee of MAB and Its Revival. *Environmental Conservation*, 20(2): 107–112.

UNESCO/MAB. *Man Belongs to Earth: In-*

ternational Co-operation in Environmental Research. 1988.

See also BIOREGION; LANDSCAPE ECOLOGY; NATIONAL PARKS: UNITED STATES; RESOURCE MANAGEMENT

Birding

Birding (or birdwatching) is a recreational hobby enjoyed by millions around the world. It can involve simply watching birds out the window at a feeder or actively traveling to remote areas to see and identify rare species. Recent estimates of the numbers of birders indicate that there are 60 to 76 million birders in the United States alone.

The modern era of birding started in the 1930s when improvements in binoculars and field guides made identification of birds in the wild easier. The first popular guide created especially for field identification of North American birds was written by Roger Tory Peterson in 1934. This bestseller, now in its fourth edition, features accurate color profile drawings of all species likely to be encountered and characteristics for separating them from other similar species. There are now guides for all regions of the world following the format started by Peterson.

People become birders for many reasons. Birding can give pleasure on many levels: aesthetic appreciation of wild birds, competitive challenge of finding new species, observations of bird behavior, and simply the personal satisfaction of seeing and identifying birds. Many birders start watching birds attracted to feeders and gradually become interested in seeing more species. Species are identified by observing combinations of field marks such as bill, feet, habitat, behavior, size, and plumage color. Field trips to new habitats and other places give the opportunity to observe new species. The most popular spots to bird are often locations where one can see the spectacle of migration, when many species of birds and many individuals congregate or pass by. Migrating songbirds are especially concentrated at coastal peninsulas; migrating hawks on mountain ridges; flocking species such as gulls, waterfowl, and shorebirds at beaches or open habitats, where they may migrate during the day or night. Some birders, known as listers, enjoy seeing as many species in an area as possible during the course of a day or a year. One team of four birders observed 231 bird species in twenty-four hours in Cali-

fornia, on April 29, 1978. The world record for a single day is 331 species in Peru in 1982. Phoebe Shetsinger of Missouri has a world list of 7,212 species, about three quarters of all known species. While birders generally rely on their own integrity to authenticate their sightings some organizations have rarity committees to review birder's reports and can accept or reject observations.

Watching birds can contribute to a greater awareness of environmental issues. Observations by birders have been used to monitor populations of breeding or wintering birds, to document range expansions of birds, or to learn of bird-window collisions. There are many opportunities for amateurs to aid in ornithological research. These include Christmas Bird Counts (National Audubon Society), Project FeederWatch (Cornell Laboratory of Ornithology and Long Point Bird Observatory) and Breeding Bird Surveys (U.S. Fish and Wildlife Service).

The popularity of birding is increasing. Surveys show it to be a rapidly increasing recreational pastime in North America. Birding can be pursued inexpensively using just binoculars and field guides but as interest and skill increase birders may be compelled to purchase spotting scopes and tripods for better views. Purchases of equipment and travel expenditures of active birders are estimated at more than $2,000 per year per birder. One in five North Americans feeds birds at least once a winter. In areas visited frequently by birders such as Point Pelee (Ontario, Canada), High Island (Texas) or Cape May (New Jersey), millions of dollars are brought into the local economy by visiting birders.

Although considered a solitary hobby, many associations allow birders to share their interests. Some groups like the National Audubon Society and the Royal Society for the Preservation of Birds have local chapters offering bird walks and lectures. The American Birding Association is devoted to the interests of listers and competitive birders. Other institutions such as bird observatories, British Trust for Ornithology, or the Cornell Laboratory of Ornithology concern themselves with research on birds as well as conservation and education issues. Journals aimed at birders include: *American Birds, Birding, Birders World, Birders Digest, British Birds*, and numerous state and provincial publications. Telephone hot lines provide recorded messages on rare birds in areas. The fastest growing travel market segment (ecotourism) caters to birders who wish to travel to new countries for organized birding trips. Some of the best spots to bird are hard to get to locations such as Attu Island (Alaska), Shetland Islands, Antarctica, countries with high numbers of endemic species like Madagascar, and regions with high species numbers (northern South America, central Africa, Southeast Asia, and Australia).

Chris Risley

Further Readings

Ehrlich, Paul R., D.D. Dobkin, and D. Wheye. *The Birder's Handbook: A Field Guide to the Natural History of North American Birds.* 1988.

Kress, S.W. *Audubon Society Handbook for Birders.* 1981.

Webster, R.E. "Building a Birder's Library." *Birding* 25 (1993): 10–45.

See also ECOTOURISM; NATIONAL AUDUBON SOCIETY

Bison: Conservation and Habitat

Bison—hoofed mammals of the cattle family (*Bovidae*)—are represented by two living species, the European bison or wisent (*Bison bonasus*), and the American bison (*Bison bison*), also called the buffalo. The latter has been subdivided into two subspecies, the plains bison (*B. b. bison*) which inhabited the vast open plains of the southern Prairie Provinces (Canada) and the United States, and the wood bison (*B. b. athabascae*) which frequented forested areas to the north of the prairies. Because the wood bison was first named and described based on a secondhand account, and because the two subspecies interbreed freely without any loss of reproductive capability, the validity of this classification has been questioned.

Both subspecies are large, cattle-like animals. The bison has a massive, shaggy head with curved horns and a beard, a distinct shoulder hump, a woolly cape covering the head, neck, and shoulders and extending down to the forelegs, short hair on the rest of the body, and a relatively short tail tipped with a tassel. Wood bison are larger than their plains counterparts, with darker, shorter hair and a higher shoulder hump. Bulls reach adulthood at six to eight years of age, but do not mate until they can successfully defend cows, which mature at about four years of age.

Fifty to sixty million plains bison once darkened the prairies. By 1855, they were exterminated from the wild by white settlers who hunted them for food, hides, and sport. A few captured individuals gave rise to private herds which multiplied prolifically. The Canadian government bought one of these herds and shipped it to Buffalo National Park near Wainwright, Alberta, where the animals grazed among cattle, contracting bovine tuberculosis and brucellosis.

Wood bison were never very numerous. Because their numbers were dwindling, the Canadian government provided wood bison with Royal Canadian Mounted Police (RCMP) protection in the 1890s and established Wood Buffalo National Park (WBNP) in 1922. Contrary to the advice of biologists, 6,673 plains bison from Wainwright were shipped to WBNP in 1924–1926. The bison hybridized and disease spread.

In 1957, a small isolated herd of what were believed to be pure wood bison was found in the northern part of the park. Animals were removed from that herd, but some were found to be infected with the two bovine diseases, indicating that genetic exchange between the two subspecies had occurred. After extensive procedures to eliminate disease, sixteen animals were used to start a herd in Elk Island National Park near Edmonton, Alberta, and another twenty-one were shipped to the Mackenzie Bison Sanctuary (MBS) near Great Slave Lake in the Northwest Territories. From these thirty-seven individuals come all of the animals that are most similar to the original wood bison. The two herds number about 300 and 2,000 animals, respectively.

Currently, all plains bison in Canada are in captive herds in several national parks, zoos, and private collections, except for a feral herd in the Pink Mountain area in British Columbia. They are treated as domestic livestock under the law. The WBNP animals, as hybrids, have no protection outside park boundaries. Only the so-called pure wood bison, listed as a nationally threatened species, are fully protected.

In 1989, Agriculture Canada proposed that all the bison in and around WBNP be slaughtered to prevent possible spread of brucellosis and tuberculosis to cattle, humans, and the healthy bison of the MBS. Following an environmental assessment, where some vigorously opposed the elimination of the largest, most diverse bison gene pool in existence, the Northern Bison Management Board was formed to find an acceptable and ecologically sound solution. The matter has not yet been resolved.

However, the controversy has resulted in accelerated research into many relevant but unanswered questions. It appears that the presence of brucellosis among the park animals is no longer of concern. Within two years after infection, most bison develop resistance to the disease and can function normally.

Recent genetic studies of the plains and wood bison from Elk Island National Park suggest that the populations diverged only recently and that the magnitude of this divergence is too slight to justify subspecies designation but is similar to that observed in geographically isolated races of other species. Given the very narrow genetic bottlenecks through which both populations in the park have come, differences may have been enhanced by genetic drift.

The results of the genetic research are consistent with Dr. Valerius Geist's conclusion that the physical differences between plains and wood bison are caused by ecological factors. Consequently all current American bison should be classified as *B. bison*.

B. Theresa Aniskowicz

Further Readings

Aniskowicz, B. Theresa. "Life or Death?" *Nature Canada* 19 (1990): 35–38.
———. "Staring Death in the Face: Wood Buffalo National Park." *Earthkeeper* (1991): 26–29.
Foster, John, Dick Harrison, and I.S. MacLaren, eds. *Buffalo*. 1992.
Geist, Valerius. "Phantom Subspecies: The Wood Bison *Bison bison 'athabascae'* (Rhoads 1897) Is Not a Valid Taxon, but an Ecotype." *Arctic* 44 (1991): 283–300.

See also UNGULATES; WOOD BUFFALO NATIONAL PARK

Black Forest

The Black Forest, an ancient, largely crystalline mountain range, occupies 6,000 square kilometers in the southwestern German state of Baden-Württemberg. Its maximum width is 60 kilometers, and it extends north to south for about 160 kilometers, paralleling the Vosges Mountains, across the Rhine Valley in neighboring France.

The interior Black Forest remained a wilderness until the tenth century, when the establishment of several monasteries (St. Blasien A.D. 948) started a first wave of forest clearings. The rise of mercantilism in the sixteenth and seventeenth centuries ushered in another significant era of land clearing. The highly lucrative business of rafting long timbers as far north as the Dutch shipyards boomed, and so did naval store operations. Charcoal and various other forest products made possible the development of iron, salt, and silver mining, as well as glass manufacturing. The result of industrial exploitation, together with settlement and concurrent practices such as forest grazing, litter removal, and hunting was the serious depletion of beech and fir, the degradation of soils, and the elimination of bear, wolf, lynx, otter, beaver, and black cock from the region. The 1787 appointment of the world's first academic forester, Professor Trunk of the University of Freiburg, coincided with the peak of resource destruction in the neighboring Black Forest and heralded a growing concern for the introduction of sustainable yield practices.

Importance as Recreational Space

The Black Forest is now one of Central Europe's most fabled recreation landscapes, luring droves of vacationers and weekend visitors alike throughout the year. The attraction of this area is largely due to its natural charms, but includes cultural and infrastructural factors as well. It is the state's most heavily forested (61 percent) landscape. The terrain includes gentle as well as rugged topography, accentuated by wild gorges and rivers, waterfalls, lakes, and bogs. Within a short distance the very mild oak and vineyard climate of the foothills changes to, in the words of Mark Twain, the "rich cathedral gloom" of the upper reaches, where cool summers can be enjoyed, and where winter reliably brings snow.

Excellent access via autobahns and other roads, such as the scenic Schwarzwald-höhenstrasse, puts practically every spot in the Black Forest within one hour's reach of one of the state's major cities. A 21,000-kilometer trail system, maintained by the Black Forest Club (Schwarzwald Verein), Germany's first hiking club established in 1864, affords pedestrian access throughout. Although hiking is still a major pastime, other recreational pursuits continue to gain popularity, including berry picking, skiing, rock climbing, mountain biking, and jogging. Visits to the many cultural-historical sites, cozy villages, culinary establishments, and world-famous spas such as Baden-Baden, Badenweiler, Bad Liebenzell, and Wildbad typically are integrated with physical activities as well as nature-appreciation pursuits in diversified leisure packages.

Current Problems

At certain scenic sites, such as the range's highest peak, the Feldberg (1,493 meters), the impact of more than 2 million visitors per year has forced periodic road closures and other measures necessary for the protection of the delicate subalpine-subarctic flora and eroding slopes. In addition to correcting such local management problems, there are presently more comprehensive attempts to correct former silvicultural mistakes, and to cope with serious air pollution effects throughout the Black Forest.

According to economic dictates prevailing during the nineteenth and early twentieth centuries, two reforestation waves on degraded sites in the Black Forest relied to a great extent on reforestation with fast-growing conifers such as Norway spruce and Scotch pine. While generally growing well, these monotypes on certain sites tended to contribute to soil acidification, and the shallow-rooted spruce proved unstable during the major storms of 1967, 1986, and 1990. For several decades, spruce and pine on these sites have been replaced by the formerly prevailing silver fir-beech communities. The resulting uneven-aged, mixed forest is considered better for soil fertility, more stable against pests, wind and snow, and more pleasing aesthetically. To accelerate this transition to a biologically more diverse forest, browsing ungulates such as roe deer are currently being curtailed, and red deer are limited to two special management units. Endangered species such as the turkey-sized capercaillie grouse are assisted through breeding programs and habitat management.

Unfortunately, just as this site-sensitive forest was taking shape, an ominous setback occurred. As early as the 1960s, silver fir started showing signs of poor health and unusual mortality. By the early 1980s, most other species partook in what by then had become a disastrous decline ("Waldsterben"). Based on intense research, it is now believed that this "novel" forest disease results from a complex and presumably synergistic interaction of climatic, biotic, and anthropogenic factors. Among the latter, automobile exhausts such as nitrous oxides (NO_x) appear to be the key factor. As gases and acids, these are believed to affect tree crowns; in the form of acid rain they affect soil and tree roots. The effects include disruption of normal assimilation, water absorption and transpiration, the leaching of important nutrients, effects on soil biota including mycorrhizae, and the release of phytotoxic heavy metals. Ironically, this Waldsterben, more than any other environmental malaise, has accounted for the rise of the Green Party, which succeeded in forcing emission controls in a nation torn between its fascination with cars and its legendary forests.

Hans G. Schabel

Further Readings

Greenberg, D.S. "Fast Cars and Sick Trees." *International Wildlife* 15 (1985): 22–24.
Kiester, E. "A Deathly Spell Is Hovering above The Black Forest." *Smithsonian* 16 (1985): 211–.
Lo Bello, N. "The Fabled Black Forest." *Harper's Bazaar* 116 (1983): 8–.

See also Acid Precipitation: European Experiences; Automobiles: Impacts and Policies; Forestry, History of; New Forestry; Sustained Yield Forestry; Top Predators in Canada: An Overview; Western Europe: Pollution

Bookchin, Murray

See Echoanarchism; Radical Environmentalism

Breeder Reactors: Environmental Problems

Like other nuclear power plants, breeder reactors (also called fast or liquid metal reactors) generate electricity by splitting atoms to release heat, boil water, and drive a steam generator. But unlike other nuclear plants, which use a moderator like water or graphite to slow down the neutrons that carry the chain reaction, the breeder reactor typically has no moderator. Its chain reaction—like that of an atomic bomb—is maintained by "fast" neutrons. Breeders can be operated to produce or "breed" more fissionable material than they consume, typically by bombarding a blanket of depleted uranium with neutrons, transforming some of it into fissionable plutonium. Motivated by expectation of dwindling uranium supply, breeder reactors were designed to provide a near-infinite source of atomic fuel.

However, markets for uranium have not grown as expected. Alternatives to nuclear power are presently making further nuclear development both unnecessary and unlikely. Beset by technological problems and cost over-runs, breeder technology remains economically unfeasible. Far from the Atomic Energy Commission's 1974 prediction that 400 breeder reactors would be in operation by the year 2000, none operates commercially today.

Britain and Germany have halted their breeder research programs and ordered the permanent closure of experimental breeders at Dounreay and Kalkar. Japan operates one experimental breeder and is building a second, but doesn't expect commercial viability for another forty years. France's Superphenix has operated at full power for less than six months in eight years and has been closed for repairs since 1990. Its construction costs were three times higher than for a standard light water reactor, and it is now threatened with permanent closure. India and the former USSR each has an experimental breeder with a poor operating record. In the United States, Detroit's Fermi-1 breeder reactor operated at full capacity for 378 hours in nine years, produced no saleable plutonium, and was permanently closed after a partial meltdown in 1966. Nevertheless, U.S. breeder spending has continued, most recently on the advanced liquid metal reactor.

At every stage of the breeder reactor cycle, serious environmental problems arise. First, the plutonium fuel is manufactured by reprocessing radioactive wastes, which generates huge volumes of liquid radioactive waste.

The liquid metal coolant, usually sodium, can catch fire on contact with air and explode if it touches water. When a breeder reactor suffers a loss-of-coolant accident, fissioning increases and an explosion could occur, distributing plutonium downwind. If inhaled or swallowed, plutonium can deposit in lungs, bones, lymph nodes, and the liver: a minute particle can cause cancer, and stays dangerously radioactive for millennia.

Plutonium is also the explosive element in most atomic bombs. Whereas a 1,000-megawatt conventional reactor typically produces enough plutonium in a year to make about twenty bombs, a breeder reactor of the same size would produce enough to make as many as 100. With tons of commercial plutonium in circulation, it might well be easier to obtain the few pounds needed to make a bomb.

Given the absence of economic justification for the breeder as a power generation technology, proponents are now advancing a waste-management mission for the breeder. A design modification would burn plutonium without breeding: the exact opposite role to that originally planned. However, the radioactive byproducts created by the plutonium burn-up would be more radioactive, greater in volume, and would contain elements even longer-lived than the plutonium itself.

Sheila Malcolmson

Further Readings

Safe Energy Communication Council. *Economic Implications of DOE's Advanced Reactor Program*. Washington, D.C., 1993.

Sene, Monique. "Superphenix: The Reality Behind the Myth." *The Ecologist* 16, No. 4/5 (1986).

See also CHERNOBYL; IONIZING RADIATION; NUCLEAR ELECTRIC POWER; NUCLEAR WASTE; NUCLEAR WINTER; URANIUM MINING: OCCUPATIONAL HEALTH

Brower, David

David Brower was born in Berkeley, California, on July 1, 1912, a second generation native Californian. He attended college briefly in 1929–1930 and worked as a publicity manager for the Yosemite Park and Curry Company, 1935–1938. He joined the Sierra Club in 1933 and was appointed to the editorial board of the *Sierra Club Bulletin* in 1935. Brower was a pioneer of technical rock climbing in Yosemite and the Sierra Nevada in the 1930s, making a historic first ascent of Shiprock, New Mexico, in 1938. He was first elected to the Sierra Club board of directors in 1941 and was appointed the Sierra Club's first executive director, 1952–1969. He founded Friends of the Earth (FOE) in 1969 and formed Earth Island Institute in 1982.

Designated the "Archdruid" in John McPhee's influential book, Brower has been the most visible and influential environmentalist in the post World War II era. A member of a group of young men who led Sierra Club outings, Brower followed the traditional path of Club leadership: as an elected member of the Sierra Club's board of directors, he helped transform the Sierra Club from the outings organization of the 1930s into a militant political force. Brower, Ansel Adams, Richard Leonard, and other "young Turks" altered the Club's conservation policy, by revising the Club's stated purposes in 1951, from "explore, enjoy, and render accessible the mountain regions of the Pacific Coast," to "explore, enjoy and preserve the Sierra Nevada and other scenic resources of the United States."

As the first professional administrator of the Club he enlarged the conservation agenda of the organization to include national issues outside California, directing campaigns opposing dams in Dinosaur National Park and the Grand Canyon, criticizing the National Forest Service policy of multiple-use and lobbying for the Wilderness Act. His outspoken no-compromise style returned the Club to the sermonizing rhetoric of John Muir. Believing in "boldness" of strategy and "purist" positions on wilderness matters, his voice became that of the Sierra Club in the 1960s, and led to its reputation as "the gangbusters of the conservation movement." He also fostered the meteoric growth of Sierra Club membership through innovative methods of publishing and publicity.

Under his editorship, the *Sierra Club Bulletin* became a crusading magazine. He organized the influential early Sierra Club biennial Wilderness Conferences and edited the published proceedings. He directed a major publishing venture by the Club, the nineteen Exhibit Format Books published in the 1960s, beginning with the black and white *This Is the American Earth* (1960) by Ansel Adams and Nancy Newhall, and epitomized by the dramatic color prints of *The Place No One Knew: Glen Canyon on the Colorado* (1963) by Eliot Porter. These large format "coffee-table" books publicized campaigns for Grand Canyon National Park, Redwoods National Park, and North Cascades National Park, as well as bringing issues of wilderness preservation and conservation philosophy to the public in a sophisticated aesthetic form.

Brower developed powerful mass-media techniques, making films for the Club's conservation campaigns, and running full-page advertisements in the national newspapers, including the *New York Times*. The most famous read: "Should we also flood the Sistine Chapel so the tourists can get nearer the ceiling?" As a result of these highly visible publicity techniques, the Sierra Club was catapulted into national prominence, but lost its tax-exempt status in 1967.

Brower's authoritarian and single-minded attitudes toward Sierra Club policies, his confrontational political stance toward federal agencies, and his financial risk-taking in publishing led to the "Brower Controversy" of the late 1960s. He was forced to resign from his position in the Club in 1969, and immediately organized a new group, Friends of the Earth. Similar problems later occurred in that organization. However, his influence has been and continues to be pervasive in these and other institutions, shaping the publicity methods, rhetoric, and political strategies of citizen-based environmentalism in the late twentieth century.

Michael P. Cohen

Further Readings
Brower, David. *Work in Progress*. 1992.
Cohen, Michael. *The History of the Sierra Club*. 1988.
McPhee, John. *Encounters with the Archdruid*. 1971.

See also ADAMS, ANSEL; EARTH FIRST!; ECHO PARK DAM; ENVIRONMENTALISM; FRIENDS OF THE EARTH; GRAND CANYON; MUIR, JOHN; REDWOODS; *Sierra*; SIERRA CLUB; WILDERNESS ACT

Brown, Bob
See FRANKLIN DAM

Brown, Lester
See WORLDWATCH INSTITUTE

Brundtland, Gro Harlem
Gro Harlem Brundtland was chairman of the World Commission on Environment and Development. She was born on April 20, 1939. Her father was a passionate social democrat, holding several portfolios in the Norwegian government; her mother was a worker with the party. After graduating in 1963 from Oslo University Medical School and receiving a Master's degree in public health from Harvard in 1965, Brundtland worked as a public health official in Norway. Her education and early career were combined with active party politics, marriage, and the birth of four children.

Brundtland rose to prominence in Norway in the early 1970s when she led a press campaign to reform the country's abortion law. Although not elected to Parliament until 1977, she was invited in 1974 to become minister of the environment, a post she held until 1979. She became deputy leader of the Norwegian Labour Party in 1975 and has been party leader since 1981. She has served three terms as prime minister of Norway (February–October 1981,

1986–1989, and 1990–1993). She is the first woman and youngest person to hold that office. In September 1993 she was elected to a fourth term.

An ardent social democrat, Brundtland has been a determined campaigner for equal rights, especially in the Norwegian political process. In her commitment to international cooperation she is regarded as an heir to Olaf Palme, with whom she worked closely as a member of the Independent Commission on Disarmament and Security in the early 1980s. She is vice president of the Socialist International.

As the only person in the world who had served as both prime minister and environment minister, Brundtland was a logical choice to head the United Nations-sponsored World Commission on Environment and Development. Charged with the task of drafting a global agenda for change, the twenty-three-member Commission spent three years touring the world, receiving advice from thousands of individuals, institutions and organizations. The final report, *Our Common Future* (1987), pointed to poverty and inequity as the underlying reasons for environmental decline, and promoted the concept of "sustainable development."

Since 1987, Brundtland has engaged in an exhausting round of public appearances and diplomatic shuttling in a crusade to persuade the world community to adopt the agenda of *Our Common Future*. A moral, humanitarian politician, she is recognized on the world stage as a tireless champion of environmental quality and human rights, both at home and abroad.

Brundtland has won many international prizes and awards, including the 1988 Third World Peace Prize. She has written numerous articles on political, environmental, and development issues. In 1993 she became a controversial figure because of her support of limited Norwegian whaling.

June D. Hall

Further Readings
World Commission on Environment and Development. *Our Common Future.* 1987.

See also Our Common Future; SUSTAINABLE DEVELOPMENT

Buffalo
See BISON: CONSERVATION AND HABITAT

Bureau of Land Management
The General Land Office was created by Congress in 1812 to " . . . superintend, execute, and perform all such acts and things touching or respecting the public lands of the United States." Located within the Treasury Department it was transferred to the newly created Department of the Interior in 1849. During most of the 1800s the General Land Office surveyed and disposed of public lands—ensuring clear title. The General Land Office was also responsible for administering numerous laws providing for special disposition of the public lands including homesteading, using lands for grants (for canals, railroads, and land grant colleges), and satisfying competing demands for lands (mining, timber, grazing, recreation).

The Grazing Service was established under the 1934 Taylor Grazing Act. The Taylor Grazing Act permitted the secretary of the interior to create grazing districts out of up to 80 million acres of land—valuable chiefly for grazing and forage crops. Lands within the grazing districts were then leased to landowners or homesteaders adjacent to the grazing lands. During the early 1940s the Grazing Service sought on several occasions to raise its grazing fees (which at the time were one sixth the rate being charged by the Forest Service for grazing). Western senators fought any fee increase while the House of Representatives Appropriations Committee supported the fee increase. When the Grazing Service decided to drop the plan the House Appropriations Committee reacted by severely cutting the service's budget allocation, thus forcing the Service to cut its staff from 250 to eighty-six and forcing the closure of eleven of sixty grazing offices. The difficulties the Grazing Service was having with Congress prompted Harold Ickes, secretary of the interior, to recommend, in January 1946, that the General Land Office and the Grazing Service be consolidated. While the Grazing Service dealt primarily with grazing policy within grazing districts, the General Land Office handled land sales, exchanges, and mineral rights within the grazing districts, as well as grazing on other public lands.

President Harry S. Truman forwarded the merger recommendation to Congress in May 1946. To prevent its taking effect, the recommendation would have had to be denied by concurrent resolution of both the House and Senate. The House voted to prevent the merger but the Senate did not and on July 16, 1946, the General Land Office and the Grazing Service joined to become the Bureau of Land Management (BLM).

The Bureau of Land Management presides over 27 million acres of public lands primarily in the far West and Alaska, as well as 300 million acres where mineral rights are owned by the federal government. After farmers had taken those federal lands that they wanted for farming, prime forests were reserved in the U.S. Forest System, and the most spectacular or unique lands were preserved in the National Park Service. What was left—those lands that no one wanted—became the responsibility of the General Land Office or the Grazing Service and, ultimately, the Bureau of Land Management. Ironically, those "unwanted" lands are now the focus of much controversy in federal land management.

For three decades the Bureau of Land Management operated without an "organic act" (a specific statutory authority outlining the agency's mission). The Bureau, under director Marion Clawson, did develop a "multiple-use" management philosophy in the early 1950s. But for most of the Bureau's history, the agency has been criticized for serving the interests of the ranchers that depend on bureau grazing permits to the exclusion of other interests. It became a standard joke that BLM actually stood for "Bureau of Livestock and Mining." In 1976, passage of the Federal Land Policy and Land Management Act (or FLPMA) led to a formal change in BLM land management practices. FLPMA required that the BLM adopt the management principles of multiple use and sustain yield that were the mandate of the Forest Service. FLPMA also directed the BLM to examine its holdings to determine which were suitable for wilderness designation. The BLM, with the FLPMA mandate, has been attempting to expand its political base by reaching out to interests beyond the traditional ranching and grazing interests of the past.

Zachary A. Smith

Further Readings

Boss, Phillip O., ed. *Federal Lands Policy.* 1987.

Clarke, J.N., and D. McCool. *Staking Out the Terrain.* 1985.

Culhane, Paul J. *Public Lands Politics.* 1981.

See also ALASKA: PARK, WILDERNESS, AND RESOURCE ISSUES; DEPARTMENT OF THE INTERIOR (U.S.); ICKES, HAROLD; MINING AND SMELTING: HISTORIC IMPACTS; NATIONAL PARKS SERVICE (U.S.); RANGELANDS (U.S.); WILDERNESS

Burford, Anne McGill

Born on April 21, 1942, Anne Burford received her B.A. and L.L.B. from the University of Colorado in 1961 and 1964 respectively. Burford is best known as president Ronald Reagan's first Environmental Protection Agency (EPA) administrator, a post she held from 1981 to 1983. Throughout the 1970s, the EPA enjoyed bi-partisan support and a reputation for strong enforcement of environmental statutes. The Reagan administration brought a new approach to the management of the EPA. As Reagan's first EPA administrator, Burford sought to ease the enforcement of environmental laws and place more emphasis on voluntary compliance.

Uncharacteristic of typical agency behavior, Burford sought smaller, not larger appropriations for her agency and, atypically for EPA administrators, a top priority during her tenure was relief for regulated industries. During the first two years of the Reagan administration, the EPA's enforcement budget was cut by 45 percent. The number of cases referred by the EPA to the Department of Justice for prosecution, which had hovered at about 200 per year prior to the Reagan administration, dropped to fifty during Burford's first year as EPA administrator. Burford also eliminated the enforcement division of the EPA by reassigning enforcement lawyers to other divisions. Under Burford the agency promoted voluntary compliance by industry and sought to limit the role of the federal government in enforcement activities. Accusations of a politicized environmental enforcement leveled against Burford, and the EPA generally, led to a great deal of turmoil within the agency early in 1983 and subsequently forced Burford's resignation.

Prior to becoming the EPA administrator Burford held positions as assistant district attorney for Jefferson County (1968–1971); deputy district attorney for the city of Denver (1971–1973); hearing officer for various Colorado state boards (1974–1975); corporate counsel for Mountain Bell Telephone (1975–1981); and member of the Colorado House of Representatives (1977–1981).

Zachary A. Smith

Further Readings

Eads, George C., and Michael Fix. *Relief or Reform.* 1984.

Lash, Jonathan, Katherine Gillman, and David Sheridan. *A Season of Spoils.* 1984.

See also ENVIRONMENTAL PROTECTION AGENCY; REAGAN, RONALD; SAGEBRUSH REBELLION; WATT, JAMES G.

Burroughs, John

One of the best known and best loved literary naturalists of his time, John Burroughs (1837–1921) grew up on a farm in the Catskill hills of New York. In 1863, having worked as a teacher, he moved to Washington, D.C., and secured a job with the U.S. Treasury Department. He became a close friend and lifelong advocate of Walt Whitman. His *Notes on Walt Whitman as Poet and Person* (1867) was the first book published about the poet.

Burroughs' first volume of nature essays, *Wake Robin* (1871), was praised for its vivid images of birds. His second volume, *Winter Sunshine*, appeared in 1875 and a steady stream of books followed—over two dozen in his lifetime. His nature essays were accessible to readers and introduced them to wildlife and wildflowers close to their homes. Though traditionally associated with birds in the public's mind, Burroughs wrote about many aspects of farm and forest life, geology, literary criticism, animal behavior, travel, and philosophy.

In 1873, he returned to New York, built a home beside the Hudson River, and supported himself as a bank examiner, farmer, and author. By the turn-of-the-century, Burroughs was revered as a nature writer and apostle of the simple life. Classroom editions of his essays became required reading in schools through the nation. Many schools sponsored John Burroughs Society nature clubs. He was idolized by many prominent people, including Theodore Roosevelt and Henry Ford, who grew up reading his books.

Burroughs gave the nature essay its definitive form for his time. He believed that literary naturalists must be faithful to both science and the emotional experience of nature. In 1903, he accused several prominent nature writers of relying more on fancy than facts. This launched the nature fakers controversy, which helped set standards for the field.

Ralph H. Lutts

Further Readings

Barrus, Clara. *The Life and Letters of John Burroughs.* 1925.

Lutts, Ralph H. *The Nature Fakers: Wildlife, Science and Sentiment.* 1990.

Westbrook, Perry D. *John Burroughs.* 1974.

See also NATURE FAKERS

B

Bush, George

George Bush, forty-first president of the United States (1989–1993), followed an inconsistent course on the environment. During the 1988 campaign he broke with the Reagan administration's negative approach to environmental regulation by pledging to enact a new Clean Air Act, to tighten enforcement of toxic waste laws, to end the net loss of wetlands, and to address global warming and other international environmental issues. He pledged to appoint an environmentalist to head the Environmental Protection Agency (EPA).

Bush's appointments were a mixed lot. Environmentalists were pleased by the selection of William Reilly, president of the Conservation Foundation and World Wildlife Fund, as EPA administrator. Bush also revived the moribund Council on Environmental Quality under chairman Michael Deland. But he delegated much of the responsibility for environmental and energy policy to his chief of staff, John Sununu. Sununu, along with Office of Management and Budget (OMB) director Richard Darman and chief economic adviser Michael Boskin, frequently opposed environmental initiatives by Reilly, Deland, and others, leading to an increasingly divided administration.

Bush's greatest achievement was passage of the Clean Air Act of 1990, which ended a decade-long stalemate over control of acid rain, toxic air emissions, and urban smog. The bill, which was introduced by the president and guided through Congress by White House aides, broke new ground in providing for control of sulfur dioxide emissions through a market-oriented tradeable allowance system. The law also tightens tailpipe emission standards for cars and light trucks and requires that a percentage of automobiles sold in California after 1998 be "zero emission" vehicles (electric cars).

Bush's record on other environmental issues was mixed at best. He opposed strengthening several major statutes up for reauthorization, including the Clean Water Act, Resource Conservation and Recovery Act, and Endangered Species Act. His new "national energy strategy" emphasized production of conventional fossil fuels and nuclear power and called for opening the Arctic National Wildlife Refuge in Alaska to oil and gas development. Although the latter provision was rejected by the Senate, the Energy Policy Act of 1992 provided only modest support for energy conservation and development of renewable energy sources. The president did, however, initiate voluntary programs in industry to install efficient lighting and encourage pollution prevention.

Bush's record on natural resource issues was particularly weak. His secretary of the interior, Manuel Lujan Jr., and other appointments to the public lands agencies continued many of the consumptive policies of the Reagan administration. After a federal judge halted timber sales in much of the old-growth forest area of the Pacific Northwest to protect the threatened northern spotted owl, Bush vowed to rewrite the Endangered Species Act to give primacy to economic interests. He vigorously supported the loggers during his 1992 reelection campaign.

Bush may be remembered best for his opposition to international treaties on climate change and on biodiversity during preparations for the United Nations Conference on Environment and Development (the Earth Summit) in June 1992. Bush refused to accept specific targets and timetables for reduction of CO_2 emissions in the climate treaty and did not sign the biodiversity treaty, resulting in virtual diplomatic isolation of the United States at the conference.

On the other hand, Bush supported acceleration of the timetable for phaseout of chlorofluorocarbons (CFCs) under the Montreal Treaty for protection of the ozone layer. He also substantially increased funding for global climate research ($1.1 billion in 1992) and for toxic waste cleanup at military bases and weapons production facilities in the United States.

Vice president Dan Quayle played an increasingly active and controversial role in environmental policy during the second half of the term as chairman of the Council on Competitiveness, a White House body charged with regulatory oversight. The council revised or delayed dozens of environmental regulations that were opposed by business. Its efforts to rewrite a new manual for delineation of wetlands would have removed up to half of all wetland areas from federal protection, and caused a storm of protest. The council also took the lead in blocking the international biodiversity treaty. Other controversial actions weakened implementation of various provisions of the new Clean Air Act, eased restrictions on incineration of mixed hazardous wastes, and reduced opportunities for citizen appeals of timber harvesting and other public lands decisions. Congressional critics charged that the Quayle council violated administrative procedures and laws by providing secret access by favored interests to the regulatory process.

Norman J. Vig

Further Readings
Council on Environmental Quality. *Environmental Quality*. Annual Reports.
Shanley, Robert A. *Presidential Influence and Environmental Policy*. 1992.
Vig, Norman J., and Michael E. Kraft, eds. *Environmental Policy in the 1990s*, 2nd ed., 1994.

See also COUNCIL ON ENVIRONMENTAL QUALITY; ENVIRONMENTAL PROTECTION AGENCY; MONTREAL PROTOCOL; REAGAN, RONALD; RESOURCE CONSERVATION AND RECOVERY ACT; RIO CONFERENCE (1992); TRADEABLE EMISSION PERMITS

Butterflies: Conservation and Habitat

Butterflies comprise part of one suborder of the order Lepidoptera, scaly-winged insects, most of which are moths. Some 17,000 species are recognized worldwide, with the centers of diversity concentrated in the tropics. Butterflies occupy almost every terrestrial habitat with the exception of polar icecaps. Because of their widespread appeal, they have been among the most studied, collected, and observed insects. As their abundance and richness began to decline with human impact, butterflies received early conservation attention that continues to exceed the level of activity on behalf of most other invertebrates.

Like other profoundly metamorphosing insects, butterflies live two lifestyles—as a wormlike, herbivorous caterpillar (larva) and as a flying, sucking adult (imago), with the egg and pupal stages in between. This dual identity makes for specific ecological needs, including particular larval host plants and more general adult nectar sources. When these resources become scarce because of habitat alteration, butterfly numbers decline, sometimes to the point of local or total extinction. Additional habitat characteristics such as topography, exposure, cover, soils, predators and parasitoids, moisture, and temperature further affect the ability of a butterfly population to survive. Both conspicuous and sensitive to change, butterflies are considered excellent indicators of environmental degradation.

Since butterflies occur almost everywhere on land, they are sensitive to all kinds of development. In particular, human activities that remove or alter vegetation tend to limit the number and kinds of butterflies that can occupy a given area. These changes are not always negative. Several species have certainly thrived in North America under rural and suburban land use, such as the alfalfa-feeding orange sulphur and certain swallowtails common in cities. British biologists consider the entire butterfly fauna of Great Britain to have developed since glaciation in concert with humans, and that most of the endangered species have suffered from the abandonment of traditional forms of agriculture.

However, most changes to butterfly populations since the industrial revolution have been negative. The factors involved in reducing the butterfly fauna include plowing, fertilizing, and grazing native grasslands; logging natural woodlands, especially tropical rainforests where most species occur; draining of wetlands and mining of peatlands, especially in northern Europe; intensification of agriculture; proliferation of toxic chemicals, especially insecticides and herbicides, not only in fields but in neighborhoods and through roadside spraying; and the direct development of all kinds of habitat, primary and secondary, by paving and building. In short, many of the effects of an expanding human population are contrary to butterfly abundance and diversity, which have declined dramatically in many areas.

Butterfly collecting plays a very minor part in depleting populations. Like other insects, butterflies are effective reproducers, difficult to deplete directly. While endangered or ecologically stressed species should not be taken, overcollecting is very seldom a threat to wild populations. In fact, butterfly collectors have laid the groundwork for effective conservation action by establishing surveys of distribution. Without the records of occurrence provided by professional and amateur lepidopterists, we would not know where the uncommon species occur or how their status has changed over the years. Laws banning collecting outright, as in Germany, retard this important work and divert attention from more serious habitat issues.

Ranching butterflies for collectors and museums has become an innovative conservation tool. In Papua New Guinea and elsewhere, this activity has provided economic benefits to local people while furnishing them with an incentive to protect the source of wild females in forests adjacent to their villages.

Most of the efforts to conserve butterflies are directed at protecting and managing critical habitats. This has a long history, in relative terms. The loss of the English large copper when the fens of East Anglia were drained caused wide concern among entomologists of Darwin's time. Following the large copper's extinction in the 1860s, the first British butterfly reserves were established by the Rothschilds on private property. Concern was voiced over the impending demise of several San Francisco butterflies as early as 1875. This concern was justified in 1943 with the extinction of the Xerces blue and the subsequent listing of several species of California coastal blues and others as endangered.

The listing of endangered butterfly species became possible through the U.S. Endangered Species Act of 1973. By 1993, sixteen butterflies from the United States and elsewhere were listed as threatened or endangered under the Act. This strong legislation is designed to protect habitat and prevent taking. Dealers trafficking in listed endangered species have been indicted under the Act. An amendment, however, does permit incidental taking of listed species in the course of development, once a Habitat Conservation Plan has been agreed upon. This far-reaching amendment was intended to prevent tedious and expensive conflicts, though some conservationists are skeptical of the ability of planners to mitigate losses. The amendment came about in response to a major development conflict over the mission blue butterfly on San Francisco's San Bruno Mountain—not far from where the Xerces blue last flew.

Several organizations have arisen to address butterfly conservation. In Britain, the British Butterfly Conservation Society (now Butterfly Conservation) directs its members toward the protection and hands-on management of habitats vital to colonies of uncommon species. The Xerces Society, detailed further on in this entry, began as a North American equivalent. The international Lepidopterists' Society, originally created to advance the study of butterflies and moths, has become increasingly concerned with habitat conservation as members find their favorite places changing. The Society also publishes a Code of Conduct for its collecting members. The North American Butterfly Association promotes butterfly watching and hopes to bring about conservation through a greater understanding and awareness of butterflies and their needs in nature. The Society of European Lepidopterists, the Mexican Lepidopterists Society, and other groups have held international symposia on this topic. Many general environmental groups, such as The Nature Conservancy and Worldwide Fund for Wildlife, have adopted butterfly-oriented projects. The World Conservation Union (IUCN) maintains a Lepidoptera Specialist Group that stimulates butterfly and moth conservation projects worldwide.

The most important actions to be taken on behalf of endangered and threatened butterflies fall into four categories: survey, protection, research, and management. First, it is essential to determine present habitats and numbers of certain species. The Biological Records Centre at Monks Wood Experimental Station in the United Kingdom developed a sophisticated Butterfly Recording Scheme and produced a detailed Atlas. This approach, emulated in many countries and states, makes it possible to locate key habitats or, if the former range has contracted, to ascertain why. The next step is to protect the habitats from development or major change, usually through easements, landowner agreements or purchases. Several butterflies have become celebrated causes for local communities. Successful management depends upon an understanding of the species' life history and needs. As needs are often unknown, many projects fail to get past this step. A vigorous program of basic research on the natural history of butterflies is vital to their conservation. Sound information on behavior, flight period, food plants, physiology, mortality, and interactions can all affect management. This was proven by dramatic recoveries of the black hairstreak and heath fritillary in England based on research application.

Successful management programs have been carried out for the endangered Lange's metalmark and other California lycaenid species by modifying damaged dunes to accommodate lost host plants. The threatened Oregon silverspot has required an intensive program of mowing to free violet host plants from overgrown thatch on scarce coastal meadows. Tallgrass prairie butterflies in the American Midwest need grassland maintenance through some agency such as light grazing or haying, but the controlled burns widely used for tallgrass reserve management can be destructive to rare prairie butterflies if too frequent or intense.

Reintroduction is a radical management measure that is doomed to failure unless the habitat has been prepared to receive the butterflies. In England, where ecological studies on rare butterflies for management purposes were pioneered at Monks Wood, reintroductions have been used with some success. The English large copper, extinct in the previous century, was replaced early in this century with Dutch livestock of a related subspecies. Although the colony thus established at Woodwalton Fen National Nature Reserve continues to require intensive management, the descendants of the founders still exist and might one day fly independent of the managers' care. The British large blue, despite attempts to protect it for decades, became extinct in the 1970s. Once scientists understood how to manage its coastal heathland habitat, they were able to introduce the Swedish subspecies, and this seems to be a successful transplant.

Butterfly gardening is becoming a popular activity among those who admire both plants and butterflies. By manipulating the available resources in their own home environments, such gardeners are able to enhance the variety and abundance of butterflies around them. This has little to do with endangered species, but it helps to keep common species abundant and to encourage people to appreciate the needs of butterflies. Any activity that builds public awareness and enjoyment of the beneficial insect resource contributes to butterfly conservation. Gardening and reintroductions can augment but not substitute for the protection of natural habitats. Therefore those who wish to preserve a rich assemblage of butterflies concentrate much of their effort on significant land conservation projects.

Future topics in butterfly conservation will include monitoring the effects of acid rain, considered significant for its impacts in Europe; surveying faunal change due to global warming; and arresting the effects of new toxins. For example, *Bacillus thuringiensis (B.t.)*, a bacterium, is frequently used to control gypsy moths, spruce budworms, cabbage butterflies, and other injurious lepidopterans. The spray is widely considered nontoxic, yet it is deadly to all species of butterflies and moths. Just as DDT eliminated giant silkworm moths and butterflies from large areas of the American East in the 1950s, *B.t.* is now causing high butterfly and moth mortality in western forestlands.

Two of the great challenges of butterfly conservation will be: 1) saving Queen

Alexandra's birdwing, the largest butterfly in the world, endangered by oil palm plantations and logging in Papua New Guinea; and 2) saving the North American migratory monarch, whose massive overwintering colonies are at risk from development in California and logging in Mexico.

Conservation of monarchs has been one of the major goals of the Xerces Society and its subsidiary, the Monarch Project. The Xerces Society was founded on December 9, 1971, by R.M. Pyle. Inspired by the British experience in butterfly conservation, Xerces took its name from the extinct Xerces blue—a butterfly endemic to the San Francisco Peninsula whose last colony was lost at the Presidio in 1943. The Society was launched to prevent such extinctions. Its objectives include raising positive public awareness of butterflies and other beneficial insects, and using all available means to conserve disappearing habitats.

Based at Yale University in its early years, the Society worked on many local issues around North America and encouraged the extension of the Endangered Species Act to list truly rare species of butterflies. Later, the emphasis was broadened to cover terrestrial arthropods, and later still, all invertebrates. Xerces published the scientific journal *Atala*, now discontinued, and the newsletter *Wings*, which has become a color magazine subtitled "Essays in Invertebrate Conservation." The major activity involving members directly is the Xerces Society Fourth of July Butterfly Count (4JBC), an annual census of butterflies carried out in more than 100 locations around North America and beyond.

Modeled on the National Audubon Society's Christmas Bird Counts, the 4JBC has become a meaningful source of information for monitoring the well-being of butterflies in representative localities within different kinds of habitats and land-use policies. In 1992, the North American Butterfly Association assumed leadership of the 4JBC, which retains the Xerces name.

Headquartered in Portland, Oregon, since 1985, the Xerces Society currently concentrates its energies on the invertebrate fauna of the Northwest old-growth forests, saving the biodiversity of Madagascar and Jamaica through applied butterfly science, promoting butterfly farming as a sustainable resource in Costa Rica and elsewhere, and compiling a directory of invertebrate specialists. The Society's mission could be summarized as understanding and advertising the overwhelming role invertebrates play in biodiversity everywhere, and conserving their systems. In 1994, organizational membership stood at 5,400.

Robert Michael Pyle

Further Readings

Pyle, Robert M. *Handbook for Butterfly Watchers*. 1992. Houghton Mifflin, Boston. 280pp.

New, T. R. *Butterfly Conservation*. 1991. Oxford University Press, New York and Oxford. 224pp.

See also Bacillus thuringiensis; Endangered Species Act (U.S.); Gypsy Moths; IUCN; Monarch Butterfly Migration; Old Growth Forests; Tropical Rainforests

B

C

Cadmium

Cadmium (chemical symbol: Cd) is a non-ferrous metal which has no known physiological function (i.e., it is not required by living organisms). In this it is similar to the metals lead and mercury, but differs from metals such as copper and zinc. Cadmium is known to have highly toxic effects on living organisms in the natural environment as well as on humans in the workplace.

Electroplating accounts for about 34 percent of cadmium production. Other uses include the manufacture of nickel cadmium batteries (15 percent) and as a polyvinyl chloride (PVC) stabilizer (15 percent). Major anthropogenic sources of cadmium to the environment include the smelting and refining of non-ferrous metals including copper, nickel, and zinc; fossil fuel burning; and industrial and domestic boilers. The use of sewage sludge as a fertilizer to agricultural land is now monitored for concentrations of cadmium in most advanced jurisdictions. Natural emissions result from weathering of rocks and soils, natural combustion, and volcanic activity. The ratio of anthropogenic to natural emission rates is about 7 to 1. The annual global emission of cadmium to the atmosphere is 7,500 tonnes which is assumed to be partitioned 70 percent to land and 30 percent to water.

Elemental cadmium and its oxide (CdO) are the principal chemical forms of the element released to the atmosphere. In the workplace, dusts containing elemental cadmium and cadmium oxide constitute the main pathways to humans through inhalation. In water and soil solution inorganic salts of cadmium are the principle forms in which the element is available to living organisms. Cadmium can be ingested through water or food, and a limited amount of absorption through skin is known to occur.

The toxicity of inhaled cadmium to vertebrates is exerted through penetration of the alveoli by fumes containing cadmium oxide dust; this can lead to edema, pneumonitis, and proliferation of type I pneumocytes of the alveolar lining. Cadmium is listed by the International Agency on Cancer as a carcinogen, with primary relationship to cancer of the prostate. Cadmium is also a nephrotoxin. Whether inhaled or ingested, cadmium can cause injury to the excretory system, through damage to kidney tubules, manifested by abnormal urinary excretion of protein, amino acids, and glucose. Acute cadmium poisoning is known as *itai itai* (ouch ouch) disease, and one of the earliest records of this disease came from Japan, where a community's water supply was contaminated with cadmium from a nearby industrial operation; members of the community suffered from a syndrome which included proteinurea, pain in limbs, and, in some instances, death. Environmental exposure rarely results in such dramatic effects; the major concern is still for occupational exposure.

Cadmium is also toxic in plants and lower animal organisms, exerting its effects in a number of ways including replacing calcium and other required elements in bone and exoskeletons. Cadmium is considered to be a serious contaminant in aquatic systems, and is regulated at low concentrations: 200 ng/L in fresh water is the present guideline for Canada.

Most living organisms have a built-in mechanism to detoxify cadmium and certain other metals. In response to exposure to cadmium, living organisms produce a small protein, called metallothionein, which binds with cadmium and renders it harmless. When this mechanism is overwhelmed, cadmium exerts its toxic effects. Since the metallothionein in vertebrates is produced in the excretory or storage organs, cadmium tends to accumulate preferentially in liver and kidney. For this reason, the consumption of organ meats, which are excellent nutritionally, may have to be restricted if the animals from which they come have been environmentally exposed to cadmium.

Pamela Welbourn

Further Readings

National Research Council of Canada. *The Effects of Cadmium in the Environment.* NRCC 16743, 1979.

Nriagu, J., and J. Sprague, eds. *Cadmium in the Aquatic Environment.* 1987.

See also LABOR AND THE ENVIRONMENT; LEAD; MERCURY; MUNICIPAL SOLID WASTE: INCINERATION; OSHACT AND OSHA; STANDARD SETTING

California Condor

The California condor is a large New World vulture (Cathartidae), weighing over twenty pounds and with a wingspread of nine and a half feet. It eats only carrion, never preying on living animals; in fact, the condor family may be more closely related to the storks than to typical birds of prey. Condors lay only a single greenish-white egg per nesting attempt, which is placed in a natural cavity in rocky cliffs or (rarely) in giant sequoia trees. Some, perhaps most, pairs of condors may breed successfully only every two years under natural conditions, but this slow reproductive rate is offset by the species' apparent great longevity.

Throughout its 200-year recorded history, the California condor has been known as one of the rarest birds in the world. It was one of several widespread large scavenging bird species in North America in the late Pleistocene Epoch, occurring from the Pacific coast across the southern United States and northern Mexico east to Florida and north to the boreal forests of upstate New York. Coinciding with the disappearance of the North American megafauna from the southwestern United States about 10,000 years ago, the condor's range declined greatly. By the time the species was encountered by American explorers Meriwether Lewis and William Clark in 1806 at the mouth of the Columbia River (where the birds were feeding on beached salmon), its range had been reduced to a narrow strip along the Pacific coast between British Columbia and the northern Baja California peninsula in Mexico.

The nineteenth century saw a further drastic decline of the condor's range and numbers due entirely to human-induced factors, mostly indiscriminate shooting, but also from ingesting lead bullet fragments, strychnine, and other range poisons placed in carcasses for predator control. Other mortality factors included hobbyist egg collecting and the capture of birds as pets and for display. By 1890, California naturalist James G. Cooper wrote: "There can be little doubt that unless protected our great vulture is doomed to rapid extinction."

Early in the twentieth century, the killing of condors was prohibited, but occasional losses from shooting and egg collecting still occurred. By the late 1930s, there was growing realization that surprisingly little was known about this unusual species. In 1939, University of California graduate student Carl Koford initiated a detailed field study of the California condor which lasted almost a decade, and his findings led to the creation of the 53,000-acre Sespe Condor Sanctuary, a remote portion of the Los Padres National Forest in Ventura County, California, which contained most of the condors' known nesting sites. A smaller refuge, the 2,700-acre Sisquoc Condor Sanctuary in Santa Barbara County, had been set aside by the U.S. Forest Service in 1937.

Koford estimated that there were only sixty condors left by 1950, although later researchers have concluded from additional evidence that there were probably still as many as 100 still in existence at that time. Despite modest efforts to protect it, the species continued to decline over the next thirty years, and less than thirty birds survived by the late 1970s. Following the recommendations of an American Ornithologists' Union-National Audubon Society panel, which convened in 1978, the Condor Research Center, a joint effort with the U.S. Fish and Wildlife Service, was established in 1980 to undertake last-ditch measures to save the species. During the next five years researchers studied condor behavior intensively, using radiotelemetry to follow movements of the wild birds to identify critical habitats and to determine causes of mortality. In addition, beginning in 1982, the nucleus of a captive breeding flock was established at the San Diego Wild Animal Park and Los Angeles Zoo through the capture of several wild adults and juveniles and by the removal of first eggs laid by wild pairs of condors. Condors usually replace eggs that are lost early in the incubation cycle, and researchers took advantage of this natural behavior to increase the normal low rate of reproduction. Following an all-time population low of twenty-two to twenty-three condors in 1982, the species as a whole began to gradually increase in numbers for the first time in its known history.

Nevertheless, despite stringent protection measures, the wild population continued to decline. A particularly precipitous drop from fifteen to nine individuals occurred in the winter of 1984–1985, prompting officials to recommend the capture of the few remaining wild birds. It was hoped that the birds could be induced to reproduce in more secure captive conditions at a rate three to six times higher than in the wild. If all went as planned, some captive-produced offspring could eventually be released into the wild, and a new wild population could be established. The last wild condor, an individual code-named "AC-9" (Adult Condor-9), was taken into captivity on Easter Sunday, 1987.

Between 1988 and 1991, several Andean condors, a closely related South American species, were released in the Sespe Condor Sanctuary as surrogates in a project designed to perfect condor release techniques and to see how captive-produced condors would react to wild conditions. The young Andean condors, all females, were followed closely by field technicians using radiotelemetry, and the birds were provided only with artificial food, stillborn dairy calves. Over the three years of this novel experiment, only one of the thirteen condors released was lost—it collided with a powerline. The survivors were later recaptured and successfully "re-released" to the wild in Colombia and Venezuela, where the native Andean condor populations had been seriously depleted.

The first successful captive breeding of California condors occurred at the San Diego Wild Animal Park in 1988, when a single chick, "Molloko," was produced. Between 1989 and 1993, more than fifty additional condor offspring were produced by the captive birds. As sufficient genetic representation of successfully breeding pairs was achieved, releases of condors back to the wild were initiated. Beginning in January 1992, when two California condors, Chocuyens ("Valley of the Moon") and Xewe ("To Cast a Shadow"), were released in the Sespe region with two young Andean condors.

Four more condors were released in December 1992. Several of these birds were eventually lost, including one from the unlikely factor of drinking antifreeze and three others from collisions with powerlines. The surviving four condors were moved with five additional young of that year to a new release site in a remote portion of Santa Barbara County in December 1993.

By the end of 1993 there were seventy-five living California condors, including the nine birds in the wild in a remote region in Santa Barbara County, and sixty-six in captivity. Twelve of the latter birds reside at a new captive condor facility at the World Center for Birds of Prey in Boise, Idaho, where they were moved in September 1993. The Condor Recovery Team has recommended that birds eventually be released at additional sites disjunct from the historic California range, including possible locations in Arizona, New Mexico, and northern Baja California, Mexico, in order to enhance the species' chance of survival.

Lloyd F. Kiff

Further Readings

Phillips, David, and Hugh Nash, eds. *The Condor Question: Captive or Forever Free?* Friends of the Earth, 1981.
Tober, James A. *Wildlife and the Public Interest*. 1989.
U.S. Fish and Wildlife Service. *California Condor Recovery Plan*. 1995.

See also CAROLINA PARAKEET; NATIONAL AUDUBON SOCIETY; FOREST SERVICE (U.S.); ZOOS: INSTITUTIONS IN TRANSITION

Calvert Cliffs

Calvert Cliffs near Lusby, Maryland, on the west shore of the Chesapeake Bay, is the location of both an extensive fossil bed of Miocene Epoch marine creatures and a nuclear-powered electrical generating plant. The dispute over the siting of this facility on America's largest estuary had implications for national attitudes with respect to technology, law, coastal preservation, and grass roots citizen participation in the political decision-making process.

Between 1957 and 1969 through the actions of industry, the Congress, and the courts, nuclear-fueled electrical power moved from the prototype stage to mass production. In 1957 Congress limited the liability of private owners of nuclear plants with the passage of the Price

Anderson Act. In 1957 the first nuclear-powered, utility-owned, generating plant was built near Pittsburgh, in rural Pennsylvania. In 1961, the Supreme Court gave the Atomic Energy Commission (AEC) broad powers to regulate, license, and inspect nuclear power plants. In this climate of technological optimism the Calvert Cliffs proposal by a Maryland utility was part of a larger national effort to use boiling water reactors to generate steam to produce electricity. From 1965 to 1967 over fifty nuclear facilities were ordered by private utilities to meet the growing demands for energy and particularly to keep pace with consumer demand at peak times of the day (early morning and early evening).

The Chesapeake Bay, the largest estuary in the United States, was at the time of the Calvert Cliffs controversy (1965–1971), the most productive oyster and coastal fishery in the country. Since colonial settlement the waters of the bay draining the Susquehanna, Patuxent, Potomac, and James Rivers' watersheds sustained sport and commercial fisheries, ports, naval bases, and extensive urban settlements. In order to supply sufficient electrical power to the burgeoning Washington and Baltimore metropolitan areas a proposal was made to construct a nuclear plant on the south shore of the Patuxent River where it enters the west side of the Chesapeake Bay in southern Maryland.

Local opposition to the siting of this plant was led by the Calvert Cliffs Coordinating Committee, which was made up of professionals, scientists, local citizens, and concerned fishermen. The committee was able to garner support against the siting because the plant was expected to dump heated water into the bay, leak small amounts of wastes from the decay of tritium, cesium, and strontium into the sediments and marine life of the bay, and disturb some of the finest marine fossil beds in the country. After losing an attempt to stop the licensing of the plant by the Atomic Energy Commission (AEC) the Coordinating Committee filed suit in the courts.

The Washington D.C. Federal Court of Appeals, in a decision in July 1971, handed down by judge Skelly Wright, determined that Congress' intent in the then-recently passed National Environmental Policy Act (NEPA) bound the AEC to demand an Environmental Impact Statement (EIS) on the proposal before granting any permits to build or operate the facility. In doing so the court set an important precedent that interpreted and expanded the rather vague act of Congress. The court decision held that the act ordering a detailed study of the ecological costs and economic benefits applied to all federally authorized projects, not just those projects paid for by the federal government. Although the EIS process slowed down the construction and operation of the plant thereby increasing its cost to investors, the plant was later permitted by the AEC's Atomic Safety and Licensing Board. The fossil beds were protected as a State park. The decision did, however, diminish the promotional role of the AEC after 1971, when the Chairman of the AEC, James Schlesinger, agreed to comply with the court decision and consider citizen issues of safety and ecological damage in the licensing and operation of future nuclear power plants.

The clash of views between the grassroots opposition to nuclear power and the industrial, governmental axis of interests promoting boiling water reactors represents a social and intellectual watershed in the political history of technology and the environment in the United States. As part of a larger international citizen's movement against the allegedly "peaceful" applications of nuclear energy to meet electrical needs, the Calvert Cliffs decision slowed the growth rate of nuclear power in the United States and marks the beginning of an interim phase between the rapid promotion and the demise of the nuclear power industry.

Joseph V. Siry

Further Readings

Hays, Samuel P. *Beauty, Health & Permanence, Environmental Politics in the United States, 1955–1985.* 1987.

Melosi, Martin. *Coping with Abundance.* 1985.

Rosenbaum, Walter. *Energy, Politics & Public Policy.* 1987.

Siry, Joseph V. *Marshes of the Ocean Shore.* 1984.

See also CHESAPEAKE BAY: POLLUTION AND FISHERIES; ENVIRONMENTAL IMPACT ASSESSMENT; NATIONAL ENVIRONMENTAL POLICY ACT (U.S.); NUCLEAR ELECTRIC POWER

Canadian Environmental Assessment Act
See ENVIRONMENTAL ASSESSMENT (CANADA)

Canadian Environmental Protection Act
In June 1988 the Canadian Environmental Protection Act (CEPA) became law, creating the

potential for a broader, more assertive federal role in environmental protection. The preamble to CEPA declares that the protection of the environment is essential to the well-being of Canada and proclaims the presence of toxic substances in the environment to be a matter of national concern necessitating national leadership to protect the Canadian environment and to fulfill international obligations in this regard.

To meet these far reaching objectives CEPA provides a legal framework for the "cradle to grave" regulation of toxic substances. Subject to a few exceptions CEPA represents a consolidation of federal laws controlling toxic substances, fuels, nutrient levels in water, ocean dumping, and international air pollution. Significant federal laws not yet consolidated include those regulating pesticides and herbicides, the pollution of fisheries, and the transportation of hazardous goods.

CEPA expanded federal regulatory powers to enable intervention in the control of the full life cycle of any toxic substance with the exception of general controls over air pollution which are now limited to transboundary pollution. The Act establishes a comprehensive scheme for the implementation of national standards for the import, export, manufacture, use and research, distribution, and ultimate disposal or release of any toxic substance. Controls may be exercised through guidelines, codes of conduct, permits, regulations, orders, or enforcement action. CEPA also gives the federal government the power to regulate environmental impacts associated with any federal works, undertakings, and activities on federal lands.

The Act was among the first in Canada to introduce stringent penalties for environmental offenses including multi-million dollar fines, jail terms, and innovative court orders for remedial or preventative action. Simultaneous to creating CEPA the government also released an Enforcement and Compliance Policy which prescribes the available responses to any violation of the Act or regulations.

The Act requires the assessment of toxicity of new substances prior to import or manufacture in Canada. When an assessment indicates actual or potential harm to the environment, the substance may be added to the Toxic Substances List. Once listed the substance may be regulated regarding its use, storage, distribution, manufacture, import or export, and disposal. Examples of regulations in force include controls on the use, import and export of PCBs, release of vinyl chloride, import of ozone-depleting substances, and toxic emissions from pulp and paper mills including dioxins and furans.

To assist the government in determining which of the hundreds of potentially toxic substances should be assessed and ultimately regulated, CEPA requires the preparation of a Priority Substances List. This list was prepared in consultation with provincial governments, industry, labor, and environmental organizations and published in February 1989. If no action is taken within prescribed time periods to either assess toxicity or to institute controls, the public has the right to require a board of review.

Additional environmental rights provided under the Act include the right to compel the investigation of any reported violation of the Act and limited statutory right of access to the courts to seek damages or an injunction as a result of personal injury suffered from a violation of the Act.

Since its inception, CEPA has attracted considerable debate as to its constitutionality and national ambit. Among those provisions drawing the most criticism are the equivalency provisions which enable provinces to replace federal standards with similar provincial laws. CEPA has also been called weak as a preventive measure as it applies only to substances listed under the Act, currently less than twenty. The Parliamentary review of CEPA required by 1994 will provide new opportunities for changing the ambit of the federal role in regulating toxic substances and, more broadly, in achieving protection of the Canadian environment.

Linda F. Duncan

Further Readings

Lucas, Alastair. "Jurisdictional Disputes: Is 'Equivalency' a Workable Solution?" In *Into the Future: Environmental Law and Policy for the 1990s*. Ed. Donna Tingley. 1989.

Northey, Rodney. "Federalism and Comprehensive Environmental Reform: Seeing Beyond the Murky Medium." *Osgoode Hall Law Journal* 29 (1989): 128–81.

Vanderzwaag, David, and Linda F. Duncan. "Canada and Environmental Protection: Confident Political Faces, Uncertain Legal Hands." In *Canadian Environmental Policy: Ecosystems, Politics, and Process*. Ed. Robert Boardman. 1992.

See also DIOXINS AND FURANS; ENVIRONMENTAL CASE LAW (CANADA): COMMON LAW

CAUSES OF ACTION; FEDERALISM AND ENVIRONMENTAL PROTECTION: CANADA; LEGISLATION: CANADA; PULP AND PAPER MILLS; TOXIC SUBSTANCES CONTROL ACT; TOXICOLOGY

Canadian Nature Federation

The Canadian Nature Federation (CNF) is one of the oldest national conservation organizations in Canada, and is the national voice for naturalists. Its mandate is to protect the Canadian landscape, to maintain the integrity of natural ecosystems, and to encourage understanding and enjoyment of nature through its publication *Nature Canada*.

The CNF traces its roots to the 1930s with a dedicated naturalist named Mabel Frances Whittemore. When Whittemore died in 1939, her husband launched a magazine, *Canadian Nature*, in her memory. In 1948, the Audubon Society of Canada was formed, and purchased *Canadian Nature* with the support of its parent body, the (U.S.) National Audubon Society.

The magazine was re-named *Canadian Audubon* in 1958 and its editorial policy broadened to include topical, urgent conservation problems facing Canada. In 1961, the Audubon Society of Canada became independent of its American parent and incorporated as the Canadian Audubon Society. With its small membership, it worked on a wide range of national conservation issues.

The Canadian Audubon Society was re-born as the Canadian Nature Federation in May 1970. Leaders of provincial naturalists' federations, concerned individuals, and directors of the Society confirmed the need for a national federation to represent the conservation concerns of a broad spectrum of the Canadian public. The founding meeting of the CNF was held in Ottawa in September 1971.

The CNF has worked to protect creatures great and small. It helped prevent the slaughter and loss of the genetic diversity of the bison in Wood Buffalo National Park. The CNF helped to identify and develop recovery plans to protect endangered species including the piping plover and the beluga whale. It helped save the last remaining pieces of Oak Savannah, habitat of the Karner Blue butterfly.

The CNF has successfully advocated the protection of a number of wilderness areas including the Tatshenshini River, Aulavik National Park, Gwaii Haanas National Park Reserve, and Grasslands National Park. The CNF works with World Wildlife Fund Canada on its Endangered Spaces program with a focus on completing the national park system by the year 2000.

The CNF currently has three major conservation programs: habitat and wildlife conservation, parks and protected areas, and bird conservation. Its national office is located in Ottawa, and it currently has 25,000 members and supporters and almost 150 affiliate organizations.

Kevin McNamee

Further Readings

Warecki, George. "The Way We Were in the Beginning . . ." *Nature Canada* 18 (1989): 44–47.

See also BALEEN WHALES; BISON: CONSERVATION AND HABITAT; BUTTERFLIES: CONSERVATION AND HABITAT; NATIONAL AUDUBON SOCIETY; PIPING PLOVER; WOOD BUFFALO NATIONAL PARK; WORLD WILDLIFE FUND

Carbon Monoxide

Carbon monoxide (chemical formula CO) is a colorless odorless gas which is produced when materials containing carbon (C) are burned at oxygen levels too low to result in complete combustion. Typically CO occurs in automobile exhaust, in fumes from furnaces where there is inadequate oxygen supply and in cigarette smoke.

If large amounts of CO are inhaled, the gas combines with hemoglobin, the red pigment which normally carries oxygen in blood. Acute carbon monoxide poisoning, which is reversible in its early stages, causes death from lack of oxygen.

Carbon monoxide is one of the gases of concern in the context of air pollution; it originates from various combustion processes, notably from automobiles. There is general agreement that polluted air affects humans and animals and may be the primary cause of certain diseases, especially those of the respiratory system. Studied health conditions include bronchitis, emphysema, pneumonia, tuberculosis, asthma, lung cancer, cardio-vascular disease, as well as total or non-specific morbidity or mortality.

In polluted air CO is not present in sufficiently high concentrations to cause the acute effects of suffocation. The specific effect(s) of this gas on human health or on components of the natural environment are difficult to separate from the effects of other components of polluted air such as oxides of sulfur, oxides of nitrogen, carbon dioxide, trace volatile organics and particulates.

Epidemiological studies have not as yet demonstrated unequivocally that CO concentrations in polluted air are statistically related to studied diseases. In contrast, using the same methods, epidemiologists do sometimes see disease or mortality relationships for suspended particulates and sulfur dioxide.

The fact remains that CO is present in polluted air and is a toxic gas. There is sufficient concern for its health effect(s) that most developed countries have criteria or standards for this gas in air or industrial emissions. Modern automobiles in North America are required to be fitted with devices that reduce the emission of CO as well as other gases.

Carbon monoxide is not one of the so-called "greenhouse gases," but it can influence the formation of methane, which *is* important in the greenhouse effect.

Pamela Welbourn

Further Readings

Environment Canada. *The State of Canada's Environment*. Ottawa: Minister of Supply and Services, 1991.

Lave, L.B., and E.P. Seskin. *Air Pollution and Human Health*. 1977.

See also AIR POLLUTION: IMPACTS; ASEAN HAZE; AUTOMOBILES: IMPACTS AND POLICIES; SMOG

Carbon Tax

To combat global warming a carbon tax has been proposed which would discourage fossil-fuel use and so reduce carbon dioxide (CO_2) emissions. Carbon taxes—normally based on the carbon content of oil, coal and gas—have already been introduced in several European countries and are widely recognized as the most cost-effective policy option to curb emissions.

Although there are other ways to reduce CO_2 emissions, they can be less economically efficient than carbon taxes. A tax just on petrol, for example, would reduce the use of oil, but much of the reduction would be negated as energy users switch over to coal and natural gas, which also emit CO_2. It also would not affect the use of heating oil and other petroleum products. As for energy efficiency standards and other regulatory alternatives, because they would not raise the price of emitting carbon, they would neither discourage energy use nor provide electricity generators with incentives to move away from carbon-intensive fuels. A carbon tax, on the other hand, would give all users of fossil fuels the same incentive to reduce carbon emissions.

While such a tax might seem awkward to apply, estimates of each fuel's carbon content could easily be used to translate the carbon tax into separate taxes on coal, oil, and natural gas. Since fossil fuels are already taxed in most countries, this would make the carbon tax easy to administer. Unfortunately, many of the national carbon tax programs already in existence are not well designed. Some countries allow exemptions for the electricity industry or lower charges for other industrial producers. Such exemptions have the effect of raising the country's overall cost of abating any given level of CO_2 emissions.

The effect that a tax has on emissions depends on how energy users and suppliers respond to it. Economists have made a range of estimates for the effects different carbon taxes would have. The firmest conclusion that emerges from their work is that the tax would have to be high—some $100 per ton of carbon—for it to reduce emissions substantially in the long run. A $100 per-ton tax would raise a crude oil price of $20 per barrel by about two thirds. The tax would have to be this high in part because economic growth will, in the absence of abatement policy, increase emissions over time. Hence, the tax would have to be raised every now and then to keep emissions levels stable. On the other hand, future technological innovations may reduce the cost of abatement in the very long run, allowing carbon taxes to be reduced.

Faced with a carbon tax of $100 per ton of carbon, individuals and firms would seek to avoid the penalty by spending up to—but not more than—$100 to abate a ton of carbon emissions. Quantitative emissions limits, on the other hand, would guarantee how much CO_2 is emitted, but not the price for achieving that level. Therefore, a quantitative limit on emissions could turn out to be too costly (higher, for example, than the damage avoided) or not costly enough. In many industrialized countries, CO_2 emissions are no higher today than they were in 1973 due to real increases in the price of energy. If energy prices, always volatile and unpredictable, increase in the future, a given quantitative ceiling on emissions might be attainable without devoting any additional resources to abatement; if prices fall, the costs of achieving a given quantitative target could turn out to be much higher than expected. A key virtue of the carbon tax is that it fixes the incentive to abate emissions independently of energy price fluctuations (that is, a $100 tax provides a $100 incentive). In addition, the tax could be adjusted up or down if new scientific information becomes available about the damages caused by particular emissions levels.

A high carbon tax would raise substantial sums of money which would allow either other taxes to be reduced or budgets to be balanced. A carbon tax may therefore be a revenue neutral policy (keeping the total tax burden unchanged). While taxes on income and savings distort economic decision making by individuals and firms, a carbon tax actually reduces distortions in the economy. Factoring in the contribution to economic performance will help calculate the true cost of an abatement policy based on a carbon tax.

Because poor households tend to spend a greater percentage of their total income on energy than do rich ones a carbon tax is likely to be regressive. But this effect can be neutralized by indexing transfer payments to inflation (as is already done in many countries) and/or by increasing the personal deductions households can take on their income taxes. At the same time, it should be recognized that other policies for abating net greenhouse gas emissions would also impact the distribution of income, even if less transparently than would a carbon tax. For example, energy efficiency standards would hit the poor hardest because the poor tend to buy cheaper, less-energy-efficient appliances than do richer households.

The most cost-efficient carbon tax would be one that is comprehensive and internationally coordinated. A one-ton reduction in carbon emissions has the same benefit as a one-ton increase in the amount of carbon absorbed by trees or other "sinks." The most efficient policy, then, would be to offer a subsidy for sink enhancement that is equivalent to the tax on CO_2 emissions. In addition, taxes should also be imposed on other greenhouse gases: such taxes would be calculated according to the global warming potential of each particular gas. If such taxes were set at the same level in every country, the total cost of reducing greenhouse gas emissions would be lowered. There then would be no need for an international tax to be imposed by an international agency, an arrangement many countries would not accept in any case. Instead, as exemplified by the current proposal by the European Community, a standard carbon tax could be coordinated internationally but administered nationally.

Dominic Moran

Further Readings

Pearce, David. "The Role of Carbon Taxes in Adjusting to Global Warming." *The Economic Journal* 101 (1991): 938–48.

Poterba, J.M. "Tax Policy to Combat Global Warming: On Designing a Carbon Tax." In *Global Warming: Economic Policy Responses.* Ed. R. Dornbusch and J.M. Poterba. 1991.

See also AIR POLLUTION: IMPACTS; DEMAND-SIDE MANAGEMENT; ENERGY EFFICIENCY; OIL SPILLS; TRADABLE EMISSION PERMITS

Caribou

See ARCTIC NATIONAL WILDLIFE REFUGE; HABITAT LOSS IN NORTH AMERICA; UNGULATES

Carmanah Valley

A 6,700-hectare valley adjoining Pacific Rim National Park on the southwest coast of Vancouver Island, the Carmanah was the object of a fierce logging versus old-growth preservation struggle in the late 1980s. This contest pitted groups such as the Sierra Club of Western Canada and the Western Canada Wilderness Committee against MacMillan Bloedel, which held cutting rights to the area under the terms of its Tree Farm License 44. The preservation groups were galvanized into action in 1988 after it appeared that MacMillan Bloedel was preparing to begin logging some of the valley's stands of giant Sitka spruce. Arguing that this was one of the last unlogged watersheds on Vancouver Island, the groups used an array of approaches to build public support for preservation. They constructed hiking trails and a research station, arranged visits for hundreds of visitors, distributed posters and newsletters, and published a book (*Carmanah: Artistic Visions of an Ancient Rainforest*) containing artistic renderings of the valley's natural splendors by Robert Bateman, Jack Shadbolt, and many others.

In response to news that a ninety-five-meter tall Sitka spruce (the "Carmanah Giant")

had been discovered, MacMillan Bloedel proposed that two small protective reserves be established. This and a subsequent company proposal to expand the protected zone were rejected by the environmental groups. The stalemate continued until spring 1990 when the British Columbia government introduced legislation to preserve the lower portion of the valley by creating a new 3,600-hectare Class A provincial park (Carmanah Pacific Park). In an announcement laced with references to "balance," the government indicated that the upper valley would remain in the Tree Farm License but that logging would be governed by a special planning and monitoring regime under the guidance of a newly created Carmanah Valley Forest Advisory Committee. Arguing that logging in the upper valley would cause ecological damage downstream, environmental groups refused to sit on this committee and continued to lobby for preservation of the entire valley. Most of these groups have also been involved in a less successful campaign to protect the nearby Walbran Valley.

Jeremy Wilson

Further Readings

Western Canada Wilderness Committee. *Carmanah: Artistic Visions of an Ancient Rainforest.* 1989.

See also CLAYOQUOT SOUND; OLD GROWTH FORESTS; SIERRA CLUB; WESTERN CANADA WILDERNESS COMMITTEE

Carolina Parakeet

The single endemic North American parrot, the now-extinct Carolina parakeet (*Conuropsis carolinensis*), was medium-sized (about thirty centimeters in length) with long, pointed wings and tail. The adults' general plumage was green with orange-yellow head feathers. The Carolina parakeet, divided into two geographical races (the eastern *carolinensis* and the western *ludovicianus*), originally inhabited most of the eastern half of the United States, being unusual among parrots living at northerly latitudes. Over their wide range the birds were usually found in mature bottomland forests and cypress swamps. The parakeets were often seen in large flocks that ranged widely in search for food. According to most accounts the birds also nested socially, laying two to five eggs in tree cavities.

The Carolina parakeet's food originally consisted of various native seeds, fruits, and nuts, but after the European colonization of North America the species became a serious pest in the settlers' fields, orchards, and gardens. The parakeets were deliberately shot on every occasion, a task made easy by their behavioral patterns. In the beginning of the nineteenth century the Carolina parakeet was still common over its whole wide range, but soon its numbers began to dwindle, and the last unquestionable sighting of the species in the wild was made in Florida in 1904. No concentrated efforts for captive breeding were attempted, and the last known individual died in February 1918 at the Cincinnati Zoo.

Dates of the Carolina parakeet's extirpation coincide well with the growth of human populations, increase of farming area, and destruction of forests in the United States. It is conceivable that the killing of the parakeets for agricultural reasons, connected with the vast destruction of their habitat, started the species' decline. Along with such later causes as the millinery and cage bird trade and specimen collecting, these forces resulted in the extinction of the Carolina parakeet.

Mikko Saikku

Further Readings

McKinley, Daniel. "The Balance of Decimating Factors and Recruitment in Extinction of the Carolina Parakeet." *Indiana Audubon Quarterly* 58 (1980): 8–18, 50–61, 103–14.

See also HAWK SHOOTING; NATIONAL AUDUBON SOCIETY; PASSENGER PIGEON

Carr, Emily

Emily Carr (1871–1945) remains Canada's best-known woman artist. She spent most of her life in Victoria, British Columbia, but received some artistic training in California and Europe. Her name is immediately associated with paintings of west coast forests and the symbols of aboriginal peoples. She left autobiographical writings which tell of her solitary excursions into the British Columbia wilderness to record her favorite subjects. Her published works include *Klee Wyck* (1941), winner of the Governor General's award —Canada's highest literary distinction—as well as *Book of Small* (1942) and *House of All Sorts* (1944).

She studied and taught at a variety of art schools from a young age. After a period of sporadic painting, she became encouraged again in 1927 both by increased recognition and by her contact with the Group of Seven, Canada's innovative landscape painters.

Reviewing the first exhibition Carr took part in, a critic for a local newspaper already recognized in 1909 what remains—though now understates—the public's opinion of her work, that it shows "much sympathetic appreciation of the woodland side of British Columbia's scenery." While her paintings are based on observations from her excursions, they are quite expressionistic in style, emphasizing her own emotional state and giving her forests a dark brooding quality. As well, she would often juxtapose tiny human settlements against a looming, rather threatening backdrop of natural surroundings. At the same time her painting has greatly affected our sense of awe regarding the forests of the Pacific Northwest, now so highly contested. Her work is found in most major Canadian museums, especially on the west coast in Vancouver and Victoria, British Columbia.

Jesse Paehlke

Further Readings

Buchanan, Donald W. "Emily Carr—Painter of the West Coast." *Canadian Geographic Journal* 33 (1946): 186–87.

Carr, Emily. "An Address by Emily Carr." Oxford University Press, 1955.

Shadbolt, Doris. *Emily Carr.* Vancouver: Vancouver Art Gallery, 1975.

Tippett, Maria. "A Paste Solitaire in a Steel Claw Setting: Emily Carr and Her Public." *BC Studies* 20 (1973–1974): 3–14.

See also CARMANAH VALLEY; CLAYOQUOT SOUND; GROUP OF SEVEN; HUDSON RIVER SCHOOL; OLD GROWTH FORESTS; STEIN VALLEY

Carrying Capacity

Carrying capacity is a term used widely by those concerned with the growth of populations, both human and nonhuman. The meaning of the term, however, has been often obscured in common usage. The concept can be traced at least as far back as the work of Justus Liebig (1840) who determined that the growth of a plant is dependent on the amount of an essential nutrient available to the plant in relation to its needs. This concept, known as Liebig's Law of the Minimum, has been expanded by later scientists. Eugene Odum (1953) developed his "combined concept of limiting factors" in which a limiting factor is defined as one which approaches or exceeds the limits of tolerance of an organism or group of organisms.

The idea that any population is limited in size ultimately by shortages of food or water, or excesses of other factors such as toxic substances, temperature, or water has been widely known by humans since they first sought to support themselves on the resources of limited environments. The recognition that you cannot support an unlimited number of sheep on a small pasture has been obvious since the beginnings of animal domestication and pastoralism. Yet, as people have become urbanized and lose touch with rural environments or the natural world, they may also lose touch with an understanding of limits.

The term carrying capacity is used in ecology in relation to the study of population dynamics. It describes the upper limit of growth in a population introduced into an environment in which resources are initially abundant. Such a population will grow rapidly (exponentially) at a rate determined by its reproductive capacity. However, as individuals become more crowded and resources more limited, the rate of growth will decline. The population will begin to level off and eventually cease to grow or even suffer from a severe decline. The upper limit, beyond which the scarcity of resources or the prevalence of unfavorable conditions will not permit further growth is said to be the carrying capacity.

Carrying capacity, however, has been used in senses other than the upper limit of possible growth, determined by shortages of necessary resources or an excess of unfavorable conditions. Populations often tend to level off before an absolute limit to growth is reached. Four different population density levels for which the term carrying capacity has been applied have been described by R.F. Dasmann (1981). These are subsistence density, optimum density, security density, and tolerance density.

Subsistence density is the upper limit to growth described earlier, a level at which populations are in a state of deprivation or suffer from an excess of unfavorable factors.

Optimum density, a term used in range management, means a level at which food supplies and other environmental conditions are adequate to support well-fed and healthy animals. Population growth does not cease at such a level, but populations may be held at this level by removal of surplus individuals, or restrictions on breeding. In the absence of such removal or restrictions growth would continue toward subsistence density.

Security density is used in wildlife management such that a population's growth is restricted by predation or hunting. It is determined by conditions of the habitat that permit animals to evade predators or hunters. It may coincide with an optimum density level, but can be either higher or lower.

Tolerance density is determined by the behavior of the animal species. It is most marked in territorial species such as many songbirds and carnivorous mammals which do not tolerate the presence of strange individuals within an area which they have defined as their territory. Tolerated territorial inhabitants may be breeding pairs and their young offspring, or in some species such as wolves, a hunting pack. Tolerance density ideally should approach optimum density, but with some species, particularly those that are less strongly territorial, it may be at a level closer to subsistence density.

All of these levels of carrying capacity fluctuate from year to year. A population previously maintained at an optimum density may be pushed to subsistence density levels by prolonged drought. Furthermore, individuals that are normally strongly territorial, such as grizzly bears, may increase their tolerance of strangers when food supplies are abundant, as during a salmon run or at a garbage dump.

It is often difficult to apply the carrying capacity concept to human populations. Where people still maintain a self-sufficient way of life within a limited territory, as in many surviving tribal cultures, limits to growth are set by the available resources. However, many such groups tend to level off their own populations at densities closer to an optimum level. With humans, carrying capacity will fluctuate with changes in technology. New crops or methods of cultivation can bring marked changes in the carrying capacity of an area.

With human populations which are largely dependent on trade and commerce for provision of necessities, determining the subsistence carrying capacity of the area in which they live may be meaningless, since their food and other needs come from other places. Furthermore, the degree of human tolerance to crowding obviously differs widely both with individuals and cultural conditions. Judging from the prevalence of malnutrition, starvation, and disease, many human populations exist close to a maximum

subsistence density, or are frequently pushed to such a level by unfavorable environmental changes. Whether or not humans can agree to limit their populations to achieve more nearly optimum conditions remains an open question.

Carrying capacity remains a useful concept for examining the state of human populations. However, it should always be related to the limiting factors under consideration—food, water, or accumulation of wastes or toxins—and to the technological and cultural conditions of the society being considered.

Raymond F. Dasmann

Further Readings

Dasmann, Raymond F. *Wildlife Biology*. 2nd ed. 1981.

Krebs, Charles J. *Ecology*. 1972.

Odum, Eugene P. *Fundamentals of Ecology*. 2nd ed. 1959.

See also BIODEPLETION; ODUM, EUGENE; POPULATION CONTROL; WEB OF LIFE

Carson, Rachel

Rachel Carson's personal witness to the interconnectedness of the living environment and her skill as a scientist and writer in communicating these relationships helped launch the environmental movement of the 1960s. Carson never intended to be a reformer or to challenge the post-war scientific establishment and industrial power structure. Yet her career as a government biologist and editor, and her commitment to the natural world suggest that, once confronted with evidence of what humans had done to the environment, Carson was compelled to speak out.

Rachel Carson was born in Springdale, Pennsylvania, on May 27, 1907—the youngest of three children. Her mother, Maria Frazier McLean, loved nature and books and recognized her daughter's intelligence and literary talent. She was her daughter's most important role model. They remained close until Mrs. Carson died in 1958. Carson loved writing as a child and was rewarded for her efforts with several prizes in children's literary magazines. The Carsons lived very modestly and Mr. Carson was unsuccessful at business so it was a great sacrifice to send Rachel to Pennsylvania College for Women (now Chatham College) in 1925 so that she might become a writer.

A solitary but self-confident student, Carson excelled academically. In her sophomore year Carson met a gifted young biology professor, Mary Scott Skinker, who became her mentor and encouraged her to change her major from English to biology. Although there were few careers in science open to women at this time, Carson took the challenge, graduating *magna cum laude* in 1929. Her academic achievements earned her a place as beginning investigator at the Woods Hole Biological Laboratory that summer where she saw the ocean for the first time and started her lifelong study of marine life. She earned a Master's degree in zoology at Johns Hopkins University in 1932, teaching part-time there and at the University of Maryland. Although Carson planned to pursue a doctorate, the depression and the need to support her extended family after her father's death in 1935 made further graduate education impossible. After a successful part-time job writing radio scripts for the Bureau of Fisheries, she won a permanent appointment as junior biologist in 1936. In 1937 she published the essay "Undersea" in the *Atlantic Monthly*. Carson expanded the essay, which received critical notice, into the book *Under the Sea-Wind* (1941), perhaps her best natural history, although it was unnoticed when it first appeared. Carson completed the sea's biography with the internationally acclaimed *The Sea Around Us* in 1951 and *The Edge of the Sea* in 1955. These works won Carson awards in science and literature and remained best sellers for record periods of time.

As a biologist writing about marine life for the general public Carson's task was to synthesize an enormous amount of scientific research and, by her extraordinary literary style, make it understandable as well as scientifically accurate. Fascinated by the ocean and its mysteries as well as the shoreline of life, Carson introduced millions of readers to the myriad intricate relationships which were basic to the ecology of this environment. Embedded in all her natural histories was the recognition that humans had interfered with the processes of the natural world and a sense of foreboding about the unintended consequences of those actions.

Carson remained a writer and editor at the U.S. Fish and Wildlife Service until 1952 when she retired to write full time. In 1949 she became editor-in-chief of all Service publications and enjoyed particular success with a series of pamphlets on wildlife refuges called "Conservation in Action," four of which she wrote herself. Carson's editorial work gave her scientific breadth and kept her apprised of the latest wildlife research. As early as 1945 Carson had misgivings about the safety and wisdom of the increasing use of synthetic hydrocarbon pesticides in agriculture and in government insect eradication programs.

In late 1957 Carson began an inquiry into the impact of pesticides at the request of a friend. She concluded that their broadcast use, like the effects of atomic radiation, endangered the whole fabric of life. Determined to bring her conclusions to the public and to expose what she believed was the potential destruction of the living world by the unimpeded use of "biocides," she worked under great physical and emotional constraints. Four years later *Silent Spring* (1962) was published and had such public impact that the federal government was compelled to investigate the subject of pesticide pollution.

Literally a book which changed the course of history, *Silent Spring* attacked the scientific establishment, the agrichemical industry, and the government for acting irresponsibly. Carson was denounced by industry and government as an alarmist and a poor scientist but she had illustrated as no one else had before that humankind was part of the earth's ecosystem and that, by destroying a part of nature, all of life was placed at risk.

She was acclaimed by the public and many in the world of science and letters, but lost her battle to cancer, April 14, 1964, at the age of fifty-six. She lived long enough to see that once informed the public would demand the right to know the effects of the technologies it was obliged to endure. Her crusade inspired a younger generation of environmental activists and made the word "ecology" commonplace. She was awarded the Presidential Medal of Freedom posthumously in 1980. Carson's vision has been widely accepted around the world, but her warnings about the dangers of pesticides often remain unheeded.

Linda J. Lear

Further Readings

Brooks, Paul. *The House of Life: Rachel Carson at Work*. 1972.
Graham, Frank, Jr. *Since Silent Spring*. 1970.
Lear, Linda J. "Rachel Carson's *Silent Spring*." *Environmental History Review* 17 (1993): 23–48.
McCay, Mary. *Rachel Carson*. 1993.

See also ECOFEMINISM; ENVIRONMENTALISM; PESTICIDES

Carter, Jimmy

The thirty-ninth president of the United States, Jimmy Carter held office from 1977 through 1981. As governor of Georgia he studied and rejected a major proposed water project of the U.S. Army Corps of Engineers as well as channelization projects of the Soil Conservation Service of U.S. Department of Agriculture. He ran his campaign for nomination by the Democratic Party as presidential candidate in 1976 on an environmental platform, but his subsequent campaign for president against Gerald Ford was not based on environmental issues. However, once elected he appointed many environmental activists to offices in his administration, such as Douglas Costle as Environmental Protection Agency administrator, Rupert Cutler as an assistant secretary of agriculture, and Joe Browder as an official in the Department of Interior. So many environmentalists joined the administration that Earth First! accused the environmental establishment of allowing itself to be coopted by the Carter administration.

President Carter delivered a special environmental message on May 23, 1977, in which he expressed concern for preservation of wilderness, wildlife, and other parts of America's heritage. Responding to the oil crisis of the mid-1970s, he lifted price controls on oil, but signed the windfall profits tax on oil in 1980 to recapture some of the deregulated price on domestic oil. Some of the funds raised were used by the Department of Energy to fund weatherization of low-income homes and solar energy research. Because of the severe shortages of oil on the world market during the Organization of Petroleum Exporting Countries (OPEC) oil embargo, however, President Carter advocated increased domestic production, which turned some environmental groups against his energy program. He also disapproved of the profligate use of energy in the United States and declared a war on waste, symbolized by his address from the White House in which he wore a sweater to urge Americans to turn down their thermostats in winter and reduce air conditioning use in summer.

Carter's Water Policy Task Force redefined water conservation to mean more than storage of runoff for use in the later summer; rather it was to include demand management, metering water use, conserving water used for agriculture, and increasing the share of costs paid by beneficiaries of water projects. He issued two executive orders (E.O.'s) on May 24, 1977, that were advocated by water conservationists and adopted by the Water Resources Council. The first, E.O. 11988, ordered all federal agencies to avoid encouraging development in floodplains and to restore and preserve the beneficial uses of them specifically to store flood waters rather than to seek structural solutions to flooding problems. The second, E.O. 11990, ordered federal agencies to protect wetlands by minimizing the destruction, loss or degradation of them through federal projects and policies. He also prohibited the use of off-road vehicles in fragile ecological areas. President Carter and his advisors compiled a hit list of water projects to terminate, which they felt were economically not justified and environmentally destructive. However, many of these were saved through traditional pork barrel politics in Congress.

During the Carter administration a number of environmental initiatives passed Congress and were signed by the president. Foremost among them was the Alaska National Interest Lands Conservation Act of 1980, which preserved large areas of public land in Alaska. In addition, the Marine Sanctuaries, Fish and Wildlife Conservation, Surface Mining Control and Reclamation, Nuclear Waste Storage, and the Comprehensive Environmental Response, Compensation, and Liability Acts (Superfund) were all supported and signed by President Carter.

Jimmy Carter believed that environmental protection for workers' health and the general public's benefit was consistent with a sound economy and urged a concern for the global environment. U.S. problems of energy supply and rampant inflation, induced by the oil embargo of the 1970s, forced him to retreat from some of his environmental initiatives, which reduced his credibility with environmentalists. At the end of 1980 the administration released *Global 2000 Report to the President*, a study that argued that drastic changes were needed to support global population control and resource management in order to avoid major catastrophes in the twenty-first century. However, it was ignored after Carter was defeated in his bid for a second term.

Lettie McSpadden

Further Readings
Lester, James P., ed. *Environmental Politics and Policy*. 1989.
Vig, Norman J., and Michael E. Kraft, eds. *Environmental Policy in the 1990s*, 2nd ed. 1994.

See also ARMY CORPS OF ENGINEERS (U.S.); DEPARTMENT OF ENERGY (U.S.); ENVIRONMENTAL PROTECTION AGENCY; LEGISLATION: UNITED STATES; SOLAR ENERGY; SUPERFUND

Case Law

See ENVIRONMENTAL CASE LAW (CANADA): COMMON LAW CAUSES OF ACTION; ENVIRONMENTAL CASE LAW: EUROPEAN COMMUNITY; ENVIRONMENTAL CASE LAW: GREAT BRITAIN; ENVIRONMENTAL CASE LAW: NEW ZEALAND; ENVIRONMENTAL CASE LAW: UNITED STATES

Channelization

Channelization (see table 1) is a direct and deliberate means of river manipulation. It involves the construction of embankments, dikes, levees, and floodwalls to confine floodwaters; and the straightening, widening, deepening, or smoothing of channels to improve their ability to transmit floods or to provide navigation.

Some of the world's greatest rivers are now lined by extensive embankment systems, which, while fulfilling their purpose, also create some environmental problems and have some disadvantages. For instance, they may reduce natural storage for floodwaters, both by preventing water from spilling over much of the floodplain and by stopping bank storage in cases where impermeable floodwalls are used. They can also constrain the flow of water down tributaries (which may be ponded back) and sometimes they may exacerbate the flood problem they were designed to reduce by preventing floodwater downstream of a breach from draining back into the channel once flow has subsided.

Some of the greatest criticism, however, has been leveled against channel "improvements" designed to improve the flow of water and to facilitate navigation. Thus, the more rapid movement of water along such modified channel sections can serve to aggravate flood peaks further downstream and cause accelerated erosion, while also changing groundwater levels. Most importantly of all, however, channelization can have adverse effects on riverine fauna through the increased flow velocities, reduction in the extent of shelter in the channel bed, and reduction in nutrient inputs due to the destruction of overhanging bank vegetation. The latter process can also remove shade, causing thermal pollution. Channelization of rivers through swampland can wipe out large areas of important wetland habitat. For these reasons, proposals to channelize the Nile through the Sudd, or the Okavango through the Okavango Swamps of Botswana have been strenuously opposed by some ecologists.

TABLE 1

Terminologies for Channelization

American Term	British Equivalent	Procedure
Widening	Resectioning	Manipulating width and/or depth variable to increase the channel capacity
Deepening	Resectioning	
Straightening	Realigning	Steepening the gradient to increase the flow velocity
Levee construction	Embanking	Confining floodwaters by raising the height of the channel banks
Bank stabilization	Bank protection	Use of structures such as gabions and steel piles to control bank erosion
Clearing and snagging	Pioneer tree clearance Weed Control Dredging of silt Clearing trash from urban areas	Decreasing the hydraulic resistance and increasing the flow velocity by removing obstructions

Source: Brookes, 1988, table 1.

There is also an aesthetic argument against many channelization schemes. At worst concrete-lined channels are boringly repetitive and unnatural in appearance.

Andrew S. Goudie

Further Readings

Brookes, Andrew. "River Channelization: Traditional Engineering Methods, Physical Consequences, and Alternative Practices." *Progress in Physical Geography* 9 (1985): 47–73.

———. *Channelized Rivers*. 1988.

Keller, E.A. "Channelization: Environmental, Geomorphic and Engineering Aspects." In *Geomorphology and Engineering*. Ed. D.R. Coates. 1976, 115–40.

See also ARMY CORPS OF ENGINEERS (U.S.)

Chavis, Benjamin F., Jr.

See ENVIRONMENTAL JUSTICE MOVEMENT

Chemiepolitik (Germany)

Chemiepolitik or chemical policy, as developed most prominently in Germany, can be defined as an ecologically motivated, sectoral industrial policy. It is aimed at restructuring the chemical industry to reduce the environmental harm caused by its procurement of raw materials, by its emissions, processes, and products, including the risk of environmental damage emanating from them. Its purpose as a public policy is to create a chemical industry based on material flows fully compatible with the metabolisms of natural ecosystems. It builds on risk assessments of substances, processes, and products based on human toxicology and ecotoxicology and on assessments of the benefits of chemical products. The aim is to minimize material flows within industry and the economy in general. Chemical policy is thus much broader than chemicals policy, or chemical control policy.

The term *Chemiepolitik* was coined in 1984 by an environmental organization, the *Bund für Umwelt und Naturschutz Deutschland* (BUND) (the German Federation for the Environment and the Protection of Nature), in response to a lack of public discussion about the risks of environmental degradation and damage presented by the chemical industry. The chemical industry was identified as a key industry in the conversion of materials and the shaping of material flow patterns in industrial societies. The associated risks are connected to the volume of material throughput as well as the properties of the substances generated. The main partners in discussion were the BUND, the chemical industry and its trade union, with evangelical church academies providing a forum. Industrial accidents, notably in Union Carbide's Indian Bhopal plant and Sandoz's Schweizerhalle fire which led to significant peak pollution of the Rhine river, resulted in an early polarization which has yet to be overcome.

From the beginning, the discussion addressed toxic substances and dangerous processes, and focused on chlorine chemistry, the manufacture and use of chloro-organic substances, and, in particular, the role of polyvinyl chloride (PVC). In some respects, the positions adopted by environmental organizations on one side and industry on the other mirrored those of the debate about nuclear power. The link between the debate about chemical policy and nuclear energy was provided by the electricity consumption of chlorine production by electrolysis.

Three operational aims are pursued through chemical policy: 1) to minimize the consumption of all substances, dangerous or not; 2) to close material loops, to use substances in closed or well controlled systems, and to provide for recycling; and 3) to stimulate the development, wherever closed systems are impractical, of substances and products which can be incorporated into natural biochemical cycles without harm. At the same time, the quantitative mentality prevalent in the chemical industry is supposed to give way to attention to the service needs of customers while still considering environmental protection requirements.

Chemical policy has been provided with a prominent but temporary institutional anchor through the establishment by the German *Bundestag* of an Enquête Commission on "Protection of Humanity and the Environment," which has one group on chlorine chemistry and another on substances and material flows. Two further groups focus on the textile industry and the issue of mobility. In its first report in 1993, the Commission discusses ways and means to develop practicable policy approaches toward a sustainable management of substances and material flows. It thus attempts to broaden the scope of chemical policy by switching to a sectoral approach, which includes producers and users of chemical substances, and to overcome the polarization caused by the previous focus on chlorine chemistry.

R. Andreas Kraemer

Further Readings

Amato, Ivan. "The Slow Birth of Green Chemistry." *Science* 259 (1993): 1538–41.

Enquête Kommission. *Verantwortung für die Zukunft—Wege zum nachhaltigen Umgang mit Stoff- und Materialströmen.* Ed. *"Schutz des Menschen und der Umwelt" des Deutschen Bundestages.* 1993.

Held, Martin. *Leitbilder der Chemiepolitik— Stoffökologische Perspektiven der Industriegesellschaft.* Frankfurt am Main, Campus, 1991.

See also BHOPAL; LEGISLATION: EUROPEAN COMMUNITY; PESTICIDES; POLLUTION PREVENTION; RISK ANALYSIS; RHINE RIVER; TOXICOLOGY; WESTERN EUROPE: POLLUTION

Chernobyl

At 1:23:44 A.M. local time on April 26, 1986, Unit 4 of the Chernobyl nuclear plant, eighty kilometers north of Kiev in the Ukraine, suffered two explosions three seconds apart. Unit 4 was a graphite moderated, 1,000 MWe (megawatts electric) pressure tube reactor of the RMBK[1] type, of which there are fourteen in the former Soviet Union. The events leading to the explosions are rooted in design errors common to all fourteen RMBKs. The single most important feature in this regard is that steam generation in the fuel channels increases reactivity in an unstable manner. This condition is known as a "positive void coefficient."

The specific events of April 26 involved a dramatic sequence of faulty and arrogant operator judgments, including operating in a reactivity region recognized as unstable, and knowingly disabling substantial portions of the safety system. The result was an uncontrolled critical excursion in which reactor power went from 6 percent to over 3,000 percent of rated capacity in two seconds. The resulting explosion sheared off the top of all 1,661 pressure tubes, lifted the 1,000-ton cover off the core, ruptured existing containment, dislodged the refueling crane, discharged hot molten and pulverized fuel to an altitude of at least seven and a half kilometers, and started as many as thirty fires.

The Radiological Fallout

The radiological release at Chernobyl Unit 4 was the largest ever recorded in a technological accident and was greater than the largest contemplated in the Western reactor risk assessment literature. The release lasted ten days and was believed to have been quenched by air drops of boron carbide, clay, lead, and sand on the glowing core. From the fallout monitored in Europe, it soon became clear that the release included not only volatile fission products such as cesium and iodine, but substantial fragments of the core itself with a full complement of non-volatile and trans-uranic elements. This was a scenario that had not been deemed possible in the extensive Western literature on reactor accidents, which envisioned core melting inside a containment structure.

The fallout from the explosion was discovered initially in Sweden before the Soviet Union officially announced the accident. Eventually fallout reached most parts of western USSR, Europe, Japan, and even the United States. In all cases fallout was intensified by rainfall and unfavorable wind direction. For example, parts of southern Germany, 1,500 kilometers from the accident, received fallout comparable to Kiev only eighty kilometers from the accident.

Worldwide Emergency Response

Most European countries instituted ad hoc emergency responses to the fallout, and in many cases these responses involved a plethora of inconsistent instructions to the public which created as much fear as effective health protection. The problem that affected most of these responses was lack of information about the distribution of the fallout. The timeliness of emergency response was particularly inadequate in the Soviet Union where evacuation took as long as two years in some cases. The fundamental problem in all locations was that no one was prepared for a radiological disaster with the transnational dimensions of Chernobyl.

Local Emergency Response

Initial local emergency efforts focused on extinguishing the fires in the damaged reactor building and evacuating 116,000 people from the emergency zone. It took ten days to fully accomplish both tasks. Extinguishing the fires, fueled by heat from the core and the carbon moderator, led to acute radiation exposure for some 200 firefighters, and resulted in thirty-one prompt deaths. Mortality did not end with the immediate acute radiation deaths. According to V.M. Chernousenko (1991), sixty-five of the original staff of the Chernobyl plant had died by 1991, and as a group they have experienced mortality rates 100 times higher than expected.

The years 1986 and 1987 saw intense efforts to rectify the condition at the Chernobyl nuclear power station. This involved extensive cleanup efforts and encasing the ruins of Chernobyl Unit 4 in a "sarcophagus" to prevent the dispersal of further radioactive material. The work involved radiation fields as high as 4,000 rads/hr (500 rads constitutes a lethal dose).

Attempts to use German and Japanese robots were abandoned because these could not operate in the high radiation fields. Eventually human "volunteers," many of them soldiers, described facetiously as "bio-robots," accomplished the work. Assigned tasks typically involved a maximum planned individual doses of twenty rads, and five minutes in the high radiation environment. Given the uncertainty of dosimetry, it may be safely assumed that many workers received higher doses.

As of 1987, according to Chernousenko (1991), a total of 650,000 temporary workers, or "rectifiers" had been used in sarcophagus construction and other cleanup tasks. This expanded the concept of "temporary nuclear workers" far beyond anything ever encountered or even imagined in the West. Initially these cleanup workers were seen as "heroes." Later, they were forgotten, as they have not been followed medically, nor have they received any special benefits. Their story is a major human tragedy whose magnitude has been unrecognized in the West. Many have complained in anger about unidentified maladies. Their fate has become doubly tragic with the disintegration of the Soviet Union and the loss of central responsibility in 1991.

Beyond construction of the sarcophagus, volunteer scientists engaged in an exploration of the inner core of the reactor shell in what has been termed as a "trip to the jaws of hell." The purpose was to determine whether remains of core material might produce further critical events (i.e., explosions). Large volumes of material, apparently consisting of molten core mixed with molten sand, were found. The risk of further critical events remains unsettled. As in the construction of the sarcophagus, the work of exploring the inner core was performed without the use of robots. This work has been documented in a film provided by Soviet scientists and shown on U.S. Public Television.

In 1994, a MIT Ph.D. dissertation provided the first detailed description by an independent Western scientist of the accident sequence. Based on an eighteen-month on-site study and collaboration with Russian and Ukrainian scientists, Alexander Sich concluded that: 1) the air drops of boron carbide, clay, lead, and sand missed the damaged core, and were ineffective in quenching the core melt; 2) essentially all of the core melted, and the molten material, in the form of "hot lava," made its way to the lower levels of the reactor building, where it spread out and froze in place after ten days; 3) the core melt and ten-day release explains the earlier observation in worldwide fallout of higher than expected fractions of non-volatile fission products; 4) the core-melt scenario, combined with ineffective covering of the material by the sarcophagus leads to a conjectured total release of radioactive material three to five times larger than earlier Soviet and American estimates; and 5) the instability and leakage of the sarcophagus poses a continuing risk to the air and water environment in the local region.

Land Contamination beyond the Emergency Zone

Land contamination greater than 5.5 kBq/m^2 of ^{137}Cs occurred over approximately 100,000 square kilometers north and west of Chernobyl. By any standard, this contaminated area was far too large to evacuate, but should have prompted caution in agricultural use and efforts of informing the public about ways of avoiding unnecessary exposure. Instead, Soviet authorities withheld the details of contamination from the public and countered widespread fear by rewarding farmers for increased agricultural production.

According to Chernousenko, the birth of deformed animals soon panicked farmers in the Ukraine and Byelorussia. Distinct evidence of human illness could be read from informal census records as early as 1989. Morbidity and mortality from leukemia, lung disease, skin disease, tonsillitis, abdominal disease, each more than doubled in certain regions of the Ukraine and Byelorussia.

Since radiation sensitivity is known to be substantially higher in children than adults, children are expected to be the most vulnerable victims in the contaminated land. This expectation is confirmed by medically observed childhood illness at rates four times larger than in the pre-accident period (Chernousenko, 1991). Motivated by these discoveries, local citizens of the Ukraine and Byelorussia have made special appeals to the United States to help with further cleanup, and thus to "save the children."

C

Human Health Consequences Worldwide

Studies by the U.S. Department of Energy (USDOE) and a host of other agencies, including the International Atomic Energy Agency (IAEA), led to exposure estimates of 1.2 million person Grays (i.e., 120 million person rems) worldwide. Using the most recent analysis of the biological effects of ionizing radiation, the impact on humans is estimated at 50,000 to 100,000 cancer fatalities over the next fifty years (Hohenemser, 1988). This analysis assumes that the dose is received from radiation sources *external* to the body.

Such an analysis does not deal with the special conditions associated with beta emitting particles of the pulverized core, known as "hot particles," which resulted from the accident. The size of these particles range from 0.1 to 100 microns (10^{-6}m). Hot particles 1 to 2 microns in diameter were found in aerosols thousands of kilometers from the accident, including southern Germany. Some hot particles consisted of pure radionuclides, such as pure ^{103}Ru. In the range of 1 to 2 microns, the particles are respirable, and may become a permanent part of the lung burden. It is not clear to what extent such particles may increase or decrease the expected worldwide cancer burden based on external exposure (IAEA, 1991).

Christoph Hohenemser

Note

1. RMBK are Russian language initials for a graphite-moderated, water-cooled reactor.

Further Readings

Chernousenko, V.M. *Chernobyl*. 1991.

Hohenemser, Christoph. In *Annual Review of Energy* 13 (1988): 383–428.

International Atomic Energy Agency. *Working Material the Radiobiological Impact of Hot Beta-Particles from the Chernobyl Fallout: Risk Assessment*. 1991.

Sich, Alexander. *Nuclear Safety*. Unpublished Ph.D. Thesis, Massachusetts Institute of Technology. 1994.

See also EASTERN EUROPE: ENVIRONMENTAL PROBLEMS; FORMER SOVIET UNION; IONIZING RADIATION; NUCLEAR ELECTRIC POWER

Chesapeake Bay: Pollution and Fisheries

Derived from the flooded Susquehanna River Valley the Chesapeake Bay is the largest and most productive estuary in the United States. It is approximately 340 kilometers in length from the Susquehanna flats in the north to Cape Charles in the south and has a surface area of 7,740 square kilometers. It has a shoreline of over 11,000 kilometers with numerous wetlands and protected creeks but is relatively shallow with an average depth of 8.1 meters. Over 150 rivers contribute to the drainage basin of the Bay, although only fifty are considered major. Of these fifty, six contribute 90 percent of the freshwater within the main stem of the Bay. These are the Susquehanna, Potomac, Patuxent, Rappahannock, York, and James. The Susquehanna is by far the largest river in the basin, supplying about half the freshwater entering the main stem of the Bay. This is reflected in the salinity profile, which varies from freshwater at the head of the Bay to almost full strength sea water at Cape Charles. The 166,000 square kilometer watershed encompasses most of Maryland, Virginia, Pennsylvania and portions of New York, Delaware, and West Virginia. Currently, the port of Baltimore on the Patapsco River and the Hampton Roads/Norfolk complex surrounding the James and Elizabeth rivers are among the five largest North Atlantic ports in the United States. By the year 2000 it is estimated that these ports will export over 100 million tons of coal (approximately 65 percent of the total U.S. coal exports). In both of these industrial complexes are found large-scale paint industries, plastic and resin manufacturers, leather tanning, and steel making and shipbuilding industries.

However, a major commercial and cultural factor in the two states surrounding the Bay, Maryland and Virginia, is the seafood industry now approaching 400 years old. The average annual dockside value of commercial Chesapeake Bay fish species landed in Maryland and Virginia over the last ten years is between $50 to 60 million with a slightly lower income from offshore fisheries. The value of the sport fishery has been estimated at approximately $300 million annually and this approaches $1 billion when secondary income related to sport fishing is taken into account. In addition, there is invisible income derived from the aesthetic aspect of living close to this estuary. Waterfront property commands high prices. Yet, with the population of the Baltimore/Washington complex climbing to 3 million and a projection of 14.6 million living within the Chesapeake drainage basin by the year 2000, the demand for property adjacent to the Bay continues to rise dramatically. Currently the contribution which the Chesapeake Bay makes to the regional economy is conservatively estimated at $2 billion. Fears about suburban sprawl go back at least to the 1950s. In 1959 the Harvard political scientist, V.O. Key, predicted that Maryland's growth pattern in the latter part of the twentieth century would make the westward migration of the previous century seem like "a trickle."

Dramatic signs that this population avalanche was taking its toll on the Bay began to appear in the 1960s and 1970s with the disappearance of large areas of submerged aquatic vegetation and the decline in key Chesapeake Bay fisheries such as oysters (*Crassostrea virginica*) and striped bass (*Morone saxatilis*). Following the 1977–1983 Environmental Protection Agency (EPA) Chesapeake Bay Program (CBP), attention initially focused on the eutrophication of the system; particularly, which of the major nutrients (nitrogen or phosphorus) limits phytoplankton production and how these nutrients are recycled within the system. Significant advances in this regard have included the banning of phosphate detergents in Maryland and Virginia since 1988. Projected improvements in sewage treatment have included the relatively expensive removal of nitrogen in some areas, and measures have been designed to meet a 1987 target of a 40 percent reduction in nutrient input from tributaries by the year 2000. The Toxics Reduction Strategy used the requirements of the 1987 Clean Water Act as a basis for action and was signed in 1988. This strategy sponsored by the states of Maryland, Pennsylvania, Virginia, and the District of Columbia was stated as follows: "By the year 2000 the input of toxic substances from all controllable sources to the Chesapeake Bay will be reduced to levels that result in no toxic or bioaccumulative impacts on the living resources that inhabit the Bay or on human health."

There has been considerable effort over the past several years to define the bounds of water quality and habitat conditions within which commercially and ecologically important species can survive and multiply in the Bay. There are dozens of Bay-dependent species, hundreds of toxic substances delivered to the Bay from a variety of sources, and thousands of square kilometers of the estuary and its watershed. Usually, no single chemical or group of chemicals can be identified as the causative agent of toxic problems in the Bay. Similarly, no single species can be utilized as the sentinel for gauging toxic contamination in the Bay. Indeed, those species which are of direct interest to man are fre-

quently the most poorly investigated species in relation to effects of toxicants. Regulatory water quality limits and monitoring requirements are based upon the toxicity of chemicals or effluents to standard test species. In some cases, these species are not even resident species in the Bay (e.g., fathead minnows).

Before the goals of the Toxics Reduction Strategy can be achieved it will be necessary, despite the problems articulated earlier, to develop some form of risk assessment which will provide an estimate of the ecological "cost" of toxic chemical pollution in the Bay ecosystem. A risk assessment typically has two basic components: an exposure assessment and a hazard assessment. An "exposure" assessment quantifies the amount of chemical reaching a species of concern. Components include loading, chemical transformation, and environmental partitioning which may affect bioavailability; a "hazard" assessment defines the degree of toxicity which might be expected from such an exposure. In working toward such an assessment, the U.S. EPA CBP produced, in 1992, an initial "toxics of concern" list—a compilation of substances (see table 1) that represent an immediate or potential threat to the Bay system. The selection of such a list of chemicals essentially reflects a "bottom-up" or "source-driven" approach in which individual chemicals or specific effluents are evaluated for fate, transport, and toxicity. The CBP also issued a "species of concern" list (see table 2) which implies a more effects-driven initiative wherein biota at different levels of cellular organization or trophic level are evaluated in the ambient environment for damage/deterioration.

Historically, toxic chemical research in the Chesapeake Bay has been dominated by a source-driven strategy, usually triggered by a single chemical threat or pollution event. Typical examples of such cases, with some chronology of their genesis and resolution, are listed in table 3. Investigation of the effect of PAH re-

TABLE 1

Chesapeake Bay "Toxics of Concern."

Atrazine	Copper
Benzo [a] anthracene	Fluoranthene
Benzo [a] pyrene	Lead
Cadmium	Mercury
Chlordane	Naphthalene
Chrysene	PCBs
Chromium	Tributyltin

TABLE 2

Chesapeake Bay "Species of Concern."

Alosa sapidissima	Perca flavescens
Brevoortia tyrannus	Callinectes sapidus
Leiostomus xanthurus	Mercenaria mercenaria
Morone saxatilis	Mya arenaria
Morone americana	Crassostrea virginica

leases from wood treatment (creosote) plants on the fauna of the Elizabeth River, Virginia, might also be included in this table. However, this work is probably more appropriately categorized as one of the more recent generation of studies in which ambient toxicity is being tested without specific focus on a particular industry or effluent. Although hydrocarbons clearly dominate this area, the multiplicity of industries in this tributary makes this essentially an effects-driven study involving a variety of toxic components. Four broad categories of tests are currently being used to characterize ambient toxicity in the Bay:

1. Collectively, a broad suite of biochemical and suborganismal indicators of toxic stress, given the name biomarkers.
2. Histopathological examinations and etiology of lesions and tumors in aquatic organisms (mainly fish).

TABLE 3

Selected pollution events/situations in the Chesapeake Bay and resultant management actions.

Type of Environmental Containment	Discovery of Problem/ Initiation of Toxicological Investigation	Type of Evidence Used for Management Decision	Date(s) of Management Action/ Remediation
Cu Contamination of Patuxent River from power plant condenser tubing.	Greening of oysters adjacent to power plant. Discovered in 1966.	Chemical/biological monitoring (oysters) of copper in Patuxent River. Broad literature on aquatic toxicology of copper.	Replacement of Cu:Ni tubing by Ti 1985-1988.
CL/CL-produced oxident (cpo) toxication through disinfection of sewage/ power plant antifouling.	1973/74 fish kills in James River coincident with excess Cl water treatment plant.	Intense research effort into Cl chemistry and toxicity bioassays. Concerns over CPO toxicity and low-level formation of chlorinated organics.	Rationalization of chlorination time-tables: dechlorination procedures with respect to spawning season begun in 1982.
Chlordecone (Kepone) contamination of James River from manufacturing plant.	July 1975. Neuromotor symptoms in manufacturing, plant workers and identification of unknown peak in chromatographic traces from James River biota as Kepone.	Clinical data (see left); bioaccumulation data indicated high BFs. Aquatic bioassays showed low EC50/LC5-s in some species.	USFDA action level for Kepone in food set for PCBs. Immediate closure of manufacturing plant and James River fisheries. Seed oyster export allowed following depuration Fall, 1975.
Tri(n)butylin in formulations of anti-fouling plant: threat to non-target organisms.	Mainly European work on effects of TBT on bivalve growth/larval development 1979/80.	Bioassays on local species confirmed high toxicity (see sections on stress protein, macrophage chemilumescent response; whole animal bioassays). Later work on abnormal sexual development in gastropods.	VA and MD adopt restriction on use of TBT-based paints in coastal waters similar to French and British legislation in 1988.

3. Whole animal indicators ranging from acute and chronic lethality tests to feeding and reproductive activity and measurement of energy budgets.
4. Field observations of population and community dynamics through several generations (mainly benthic community studies).

The current strategy adopts a regional approach and involves the division of the Bay into a number (perhaps thirty to forty) "areas of concern," and the construction of a comparative toxicity index using information from the tests outlined earlier. Results from biomarkers and histopathological studies have already given clear indications of toxic stress in heavily industrialized regions such as the Elizabeth River, Virginia, although data from less obviously polluted tributaries is more equivocal. Since 1984 *in situ* and on-site toxicological data have consistently shown larval striped bass mortality in important spawning areas, some of them far removed from industrial activity. However, the connection between the data and estimates of recruitment as determined by collections of juveniles appears uncertain. Two large areas of uncertainty remain. First, we do not yet have appropriate models to differentiate between early life stage mortality caused by toxic pollution and that resulting from extraneous biological influences such as predation and climate. Second, even where chemical toxicity is unequivocal, we are still unable to differentiate source with any degree of uncertainty. Sometimes this may be a bigger problem in less industrialized areas where non-point source run-off and/or atmospheric fall-out may make substantial contributions to the toxic chemical loading. Pollutants derived from atmospheric fallout may not be controllable by any strategy adopted by jurisdictions immediately adjacent to the Bay.

In more heavily industrialized areas, the most effective regulatory mechanism is likely to be strict enforcement of the National Pollutant Discharge Elimination System (NPDES). To their credit, Maryland and Virginia have incorporated a bioassay screening procedure into the process of issuing discharge permits and have substantially tightened their regulation. In marginally contaminated, less-developed areas, there is a broad range of management options available, including integrated pesticide management and other farming practices, land-use restrictions (e.g., the Chesapeake Bay Critical Areas Act of 1984) as well as specific chemical and discharge

regulation. An October 1994 adoption statement deleted the year 2000 deadline from the Toxics Reduction Strategy statement and set a more modest but more detailed list of objectives. Many of these relate to a 75 percent reduction of toxic discharges from point sources by the year 2000, and the elimination of acute and chronic toxic impacts of waste water discharge by 2005. As a model for other complex systems, the current Chesapeake Bay Program is under close national and international scrutiny, and the next five years will be critical in evaluating its success or failure.

David A. Wright

Further Readings

D'Elia, C.F. "Too Much of a Good Thing: Nutrient Enrichment of the Chesapeake Bay." *Environment* 29 (1987): 7.

Huggett, R.J., M.E. Bender, and M.A. Unger. "Polynuclear Aromatic Hydrocarbons in the Elizabeth River, Virginia." *Fate and Effects of Sediment-Bound Chemicals in Aquatic Ecosystems*. Ed. K.L. Dickson, A.W. Maki, and W.A. Brungs. 1987, 327–41.

See also COASTAL MARSHES, CONSERVATION OF; FISHERIES CONSERVATION; FRESHWATER WETLANDS; HOPEWELL, VIRGINIA (KEPONE) SPILL; PERSISTENT ORGANOCHLORINE COMPOUNDS; TOXICOLOGY

Chimpanzees

See PRIMATES: CONSERVATION AND HABITAT

Chipko Movement

The Chipko movement is one of the pioneering peasant movements in free India, aimed at preserving the environment. The word Chipko, which means "to hug," put environment on the development agenda of the nation for the first time.

The movement is usually traced back to April 24, 1973, when villagers of the Dasholi Gram Swarjya Mandal (DGSM) in Chamolli District, led by Chandi Prasad Bhatt, prevented the agents of the Allahabad-based sporting goods company Symmonds from felling fourteen ash trees. Concern of the hill people for their environment goes back as far as the early part of the twentieth century when the people of Kumaon opposed British officials' opening up of forests to commercial exploitation, which, the people felt, deprived them of their traditional rights to forest produce.

In May 1930, a massive *satyagraha* was held at Tilari in Garhwal to protest against the forestry policies of the then Tehri Garhwal State. Despite opposition, the forests were opened to forest officials and contractors after 1962, resulting in overexploitation leading to landslides, soil erosion, and irreversible damage to watersheds.

The DGSM was formed in 1964 at Gopeshwar by Bhatt with the blessings of the Sarvodaya movement. It worked to promote Vinoba Bhave's concept of a nonviolent, self-reliant village society based on rural industries. The DGSM became involved in anti-liquor campaigns and in the 1970s, it got the people together on the issue of environment. In December 1973 the villagers repeated the act of preventing the Symmonds agents from felling the Phata-Rampur forests about sixty kilometers from Gopeshwar.

Women too began to participate actively in the movement. On March 24, 1974, the women of Reni (a village in Joshimath Block) drove away the laborers employed by a Rishikesh contractor to fell the trees. This was a turning point in the movement as it marked the first time initiative was taken by women.

This incident prompted the state government to set up a nine-member committee headed by professor Virendra Kumar of Delhi University and consisting of government officials and politicians, apart from Bhatt and the block leader. The committee's report, submitted two years later, led to a ten-year ban on commercial forestry in Reni. The report also led to the formation of a state-owned forest corporation in 1975 to take over all forms of forest exploitation from private contractors with the belief that the government would not be as ruthless and corrupt as private contractors in exploiting forest resources.

Meanwhile, the movement spread to the Uttarakhand region. The struggle launched on July 25, 1974, reached a peak in October when villagers from the Vyali forest area near Uttarkashi sought to halt tree felling.

The movement made its debut in Kumaon at the Nainadevi fair in Nainital in 1974 when activists proceeded to block a forest auction at several places including Nainital, Ramnagar, and Kotdwar. Student activists joined the movement in 1977 when they successfully blocked the auction at Shailley hall in Nainital.

In Tehri Garhwal the activists led by Sunderlal Bahuguna opposed the felling of trees in the Henwal valley in May 1977. They resorted to direct action in December 1977 to protect the Advani and Salet forests, during which twenty-three volunteers including women were arrested for opposing a forest auction at Narendranagar.

The movement resumed in Chamoli during 1977–1978 with women from Pulna stopping the felling of forests in Bhyunderr valley and Dongri-Paintoli and in Bacher during the 1980s.

The Impact

The movement was interpreted differently by different groups of people. Ecologists saw Chipko as a cultural response of the people's love for their environment, while feminists looked at the movement as manifestation of the link that women share with nature. Whatever the interpretation, one fact that cannot be denied is that the movement brought to the forefront the need to empower local communities to manage their resources.

The transformation of Chipko from a struggle to control local resource use to a national movement was influenced heavily by the media.

Within the movement itself, three streams can be identified. One, led by Bahuguna, blames materialism for ecological degradation and wants strict conservation. Another, led by Bhatt, works at environmental regeneration with people at the center. The third, called the *Uttarakhand Sanghursh Vahini (USV)*, seeks to move Chipko away from being publicly identified with Bahuguna and Bhatt and which insists that the human-nature relationship must be viewed in the context of relationship between humans. Hence, for this group, social and economic redistribution are more important than ecological harmony. The *USV* does not associate itself with state-sponsored development programs and has on occasion engaged in sharp confrontation with the administration of Kumaon.

The Situation Today

Most people today feel quite pessimistic about the movement. The general feeling is that the movement has not helped them to achieve the original goal of restoring harmony between humankind and nature. Even their traditional right to forest produce has been taken away from them. Far from eliminating the problem, the government has taken over the role of the private contractors. In addition, the entire area has been declared to be under the Nanda Devi Biosphere Reserve—further denying people the right to derive benefits like fodder and herbs out of the forest produce.

Though leaders like Bhatt and Bahunguna say that their respective agitation against the extension of the Vishnu Prayag hydroelectric project and the Tehri dam are nothing but an extension of the Chipko movement, the villagers who joined the movement to further their struggle for basic subsistence rights that had been denied to them by state institutions, are dissatisfied with what they got.

The local population would like the principles of equity and employment linked with those of ecology and economics. The major lesson of Chipko is that, unless steps to promote ecological security strengthen the livelihood security of the local population, the poor will suffer more from state-sponsored environmentalism.

M.S. Swaminathan

Further Readings

Bahuguna, Sunderlal. "Women and Non-Violent Power in the Chipko Movement." In *In Search of Answers: Indian Women's Voices from Manushi*. Ed. M. Kishwar. 1984.

Dankelman, Irene, and Joan Davidson. *Women and Environment in the Third World*. 1988.

Kunwar, Shishupal Singh, ed. *Hugging the Himalaya: The Chipko Experience*. 1982.

See also BIOSPHERE RESERVES; ECOFEMINISM; ENVIRONMENTAL MOVEMENTS: LESS-AFFLUENT NATIONS; FORESTRY, HISTORY OF; SUSTAINABLE DEVELOPMENT

Chlorine
See PULP AND PAPER MILLS

CITES

The Convention on International Trade in Endangered Species of Wild Fauna and Flora (CITES) is one of the principal international agreements aimed at protecting vulnerable species of plants and animals. Under its auspices, the majority of the world's nations strictly control trade in endangered and threatened species

in order to prevent their extinction due to overexploitation by humans.

Every year, a vast number of animals and plants are taken from the wild for their fur, horns, or other physical attributes; for use as pets, for food, or for a myriad of other purposes. Much of the commerce in these species occurs in international markets. In the 1990s, the value of world trade in wild species exceeds $5 billion annually. The populations of many wild species have declined severely as a result of such commerce. For example, rhino populations in Africa and many species of parrots throughout the world now face extinction as a result of excessive commercial exploitation.

The first call for international regulation of trade involving endangered species came in the form of a resolution by the International Union for the Conservation of Nature and Natural Resources (IUCN) in 1963. Later, at the 1972 United Nations Conference on the Human Environment in Stockholm, the international community approved a recommendation calling for a convention dealing with international commerce in wild species. This goal was realized a year later when twenty-one countries signed CITES. Like other international conventions, only countries may sign on as parties to CITES. The Convention became effective in 1975 after ten countries had ratified the agreement. As of 1993, participation in CITES had grown to include 118 countries.

As with the U.S. Endangered Species Act, CITES applies to a species only if it appears on one of the Convention's protected lists. There are three lists under CITES, known as Appendices I through III, with Appendix I species facing the greatest degree of risk, the highest danger of extinction. The countries which are parties to the Convention must vote to add species to Appendices I and II, but a country may unilaterally add a species within its borders to Appendix III. As of 1993, there were several hundred species and families of species listed in the CITES appendices.

The Convention establishes detailed requirements for international trade in listed species which are designed to ensure their protection. It prohibits trade in Appendix I species for commercial purposes. While trade in these species is allowed for scientific, conservation, or even display purposes, both the exporting country and importing country must issue a permit before such a transaction may take place. To issue these permits, the countries must be satisfied that the individual animals or plants to be

C

traded were not taken from the wild in violation of the exporting nation's species protection laws, and must find that the transaction will not be detrimental to the survival of the species as a whole. Species listed in Appendices II and III may be traded for commercial purposes, but the exporting country must first issue a permit after, in the case of Appendix II species, making findings similar to those described above. Each country participating in CITES must designate a Scientific Authority and Management Authority to carry out the tasks of making these findings and issuing permits. Countries usually add these duties to the job of an existing agency. In the United States, for example, the U.S. Fish and Wildlife Service serves as both Scientific Authority and Management Authority.

The Convention contains other important provisions in addition to its basic scheme for regulating trade in listed species. A country which is a party to CITES may declare a "reservation" for a particular species listed in Appendix I or Appendix II. This can have the effect of allowing that country to engage in trade in that species as if it were not protected. The Convention also allows parties to CITES to engage in trade of protected species with non-parties, provided that non-party countries provide "comparable" documentation to that required under CITES. Finally, CITES establishes a "Conference of Parties." This body, to which all countries participating in the Convention belong, oversees implementation of CITES and issues resolutions which set forth additional rules and procedures governing trade in protected species. The Conference of Parties meets once every two years, though a bit less frequently since 1989. During such meetings, the parties discuss important issues and vote on additions to, removals from, and transfers between the protected lists. A permanent body called the Secretariat helps the parties coordinate on a day-to-day basis.

While CITES has been instrumental in conserving many endangered species, a number of factors have hampered its effectiveness. The sheer volume of trade in wild species strains the regulatory and enforcement capabilities of many countries beyond the breaking point. Many parties to CITES simply lack the resources and trained personnel to both implement their obligations under the Convention and prevent illegal shipments of protected species. Unfortunately, the prospect of large profits continues to fuel a huge international black market in wildlife. Even relatively wealthy nations such as the United States have been unable to halt illicit trade. Additionally, since CITES does not establish a central authority to regulate international trade in wildlife, each party establishes its own agencies and procedures to carry out its obligations under the Convention. The resulting lack of uniformity among the many parties sometimes makes both administration of the Convention and legal trade in protected species confusing and difficult.

Additionally factors inhibit CITES' effectiveness. Record-keeping under the Convention has been notoriously poor. A study by the World Wildlife Fund found that half or more of transactions involving listed species go unreported, despite requirements to the contrary. This has made it difficult for the parties to keep track of the amount of trade in listed species and evaluate CITES' effectiveness in controlling that trade. Finally, CITES itself does not precisely define some key terms. For example, the Convention defines protected species to include "recognizable specimens" of protected plants and animals, but does not elaborate on this term. It was left unclear whether items such as pills or drugs made from protected species constitute recognizable specimens and thus were controlled under CITES.

Efforts to protect elephants have presented parties to CITES with one of their biggest challenges. Until 1989, elephants were listed as an Appendix II species, a status which permitted regulated trade in ivory. Despite this listing status, Africa's elephant populations declined dramatically as poachers took a heavy toll. In 1989, CITES parties voted to list elephants as an Appendix I species, thus instituting an international ban on commercial trade in ivory. While this action has showed promise for reducing poaching, several countries in southern Africa with relatively healthy elephant populations have criticized the trade ban and threatened to withdraw from CITES. They argue that limited commercial trade in ivory, with proceeds going to wildlife conservation efforts and local communities, will better protect elephants in the long run by providing a sustainable source of funding for species protection efforts and providing local people with incentive to protect elephants. The controversy over how to best protect elephants raises some fundamental questions: should species conservation efforts focus on sustainable exploitation of imperiled species or a hands-off, preservation-oriented approach? And, can legal protections be effectively enforced if trade is permitted by some states and not by others?

CITES has played a key role in conserving endangered species through regulation of international trade. While parties to the Convention face many challenges in increasing the effectiveness of their efforts, CITES provides a tested framework for global action to prevent extinctions.

Daniel J. Rohlf

Further Readings
Hill, Kevin. "The Convention on International Trade in Endangered Species: Fifteen Years Later." *Loyola International and Comparative Law Journal* 13 (1990): 231–78.
Lyster, Simon. *International Wildlife Law: An Analysis of International Treaties Concerned with Conservation of Wildlife.* 1985.

See also ELEPHANTS: CONSERVATION AND HABITAT; ENDANGERED SPECIES ACT (U.S.); ENVIRONMENTAL DIPLOMACY; IUCN; RHINOCEROS: CONSERVATION AND HABITAT; STOCKHOLM CONFERENCE; TIGERS: CONSERVATION AND HABITAT; WILD BIRD TRADE; WORLD WILDLIFE FUND

Citizens' Clearinghouse for Hazardous Waste

Founded by Lois Marie Gibbs in 1981, the Citizens' Clearinghouse for Hazardous Waste (CCHW) is an environmental organization that is self-consciously oriented to the needs and interests of working people, minorities, and the poor. Gibbs' home was one of over 500 that, some fifteen years ago, were found to be located over the notorious toxic waste dump at Love Canal in northern New York State. Organizing support to focus attention on the problem and to gain a remedy for herself and her neighbors, Gibbs has since stayed directed toward preventing exposure to toxic waste. The organization which she now leads has a nationwide focus with perhaps some emphasis on the South, an area which had previously been less organized regarding environmental concerns than had the West Coast or New England, for example.

The decision to locate in the South was a deliberate one. The principal objective of CCHW is to reach those people who are not usually reached by major environmental organizations, to provide them with essential services with regard to toxic exposures and potential or actual environmental catastrophes. CCHW is at the heart of the environmental justice movement. It connects everyday citizens—especially those lacking middle-class professional skills—with scientific and legal help regarding environmental problems that they are facing head-on. The people whose neighborhoods are more likely to be chosen for Municipal Solid Waste (MSW) incinerators or landfills, or other undesirable or high-risk facilities are more likely to be minorities, poor, or at least unrich. More than that, such citizens may well find that the only places they can afford to live already face such problems.

CCHW has assisted more than 7,000 grassroots citizen groups with one-on-one advice and information. It helps them to understand the risks they face and to make the necessary legal, scientific, and bureaucratic connections. CCHW publishes *Everyone's Backyard*—a publication whose name conveys the view that all of us face environmental problems and must work toward resolving them, rather than imposing them on more vulnerable backyards and neighborhoods. CCHW can be contacted at P.O. Box 6806, Fall's Church, Virginia (703) 237-2249.

Robert Paehlke

Further Readings
Bullard, Robert. *Dumping in Dixie: Race, Class and Environmental Quality.* 1990.
Hofrichter, Richard. *Toxic Struggles: The Theory and Practice of Environmental Justice.* 1993.

See also ENVIRONMENTAL JUSTICE MOVEMENT; HAZARDOUS WASTE TREATMENT TECHNOLOGIES; LOVE CANAL; MUNICIPAL SOLID WASTE: INCINERATION; RIGHT-TO-KNOW: COMMUNITY (U.S.); RIGHT-TO-KNOW: WORKPLACE (U.S.)

Class Actions

Sometimes referred to as a "representative action" or "class proceeding," a class action is a lawsuit brought by a named individual on behalf of himself and a number of other persons who have a common claim against another party. In most North American jurisdictions, class actions may be brought by plaintiffs or defendants.

Class actions originated in the English Court of Chancery in the seventeenth century as a procedural device to facilitate efficient multi-party litigation of common questions of law or fact. However, despite this common English origin, class actions have evolved differently in the United States than in Commonwealth countries such as Canada.

In the United States, Rule 23 of the Federal Rules of Civil Procedure permits class actions to be undertaken in the federal courts. To bring a federal class action, the proposed class representative must be able to satisfy the four prerequisites contained in Rule 23(a): first, that the members of the class are so numerous that it is impracticable to join individual claims; second, that there are questions of law or fact common to class members; third, that the claim of the class representative is typical of those of other class members; and fourth, that the class representative will fairly and adequately protect the interest of the class.

In addition, the proposed class representative must demonstrate that the claim falls into one of three categories of class actions recognized by Rule 23(b): actions where a common disposition of claims is desirable to prevent inconsistent individual judgments or potential prejudice to nonparticipants; actions where injunctive or declaratory relief is claimed against a defendant which has acted or refused to act on grounds generally applicable to the class; or actions for damages where common questions of law or fact predominate the questions peculiar to individual class members, and where a class action is the best method to ensure the fair and efficient adjudication of the claim. If a claim for damages is certified by the court as a class action, the class representative is required to provide notice to all members of the class, who will be bound by the ultimate judgment in the case unless they "opt out" of the litigation.

Most American states have incorporated the Rule 23 model or variations thereof into their state court procedures in order to facilitate class actions at the state level. Although class actions are often complex, expensive, and time-consuming, a number of environmental class actions have been brought within the United States, including claims regarding: groundwater contamination from toxic waste dumps, the release of radioactive substances, the release of coal dust, pesticide spraying, funding for sewage treatment facilities, wetlands protection, and marine and freshwater pollution. Class actions have also been used in the United States to pursue claims respecting product liability and occupational health, which may incidentally involve environmental aspects. Environmental class actions have enjoyed mixed success in the United States; nevertheless, class actions will continue to be used in the environmental context, particularly where environmental damage has affected large numbers of people.

In Canada, however, environmental class actions have been seldom used due to various restrictions placed by the courts upon the availability of class actions. The Federal Court Rules and most provincial rules of procedure specifically permit class actions to be undertaken where class members share a common or identical interest in the litigation. However, Canadian courts have generally required class representatives to demonstrate that: the class has been properly defined; class members have a common interest; the wrong is common to class members; damage is identical except as to amount; relief is beneficial to all class members; and no class members have interests which are antagonistic to other class members. As a result of these restrictive common law criteria, few environmental class actions have been brought in Canada to date.

Unlike most provinces, Quebec and Ontario have undertaken legislative reform of class action procedures. Both Quebec's Code of Civil Procedure and Ontario's Class Proceedings Act contain comprehensive class action procedures designed to facilitate the conduct of class actions. Both provincial schemes include a judicial certification procedure to determine whether a proposed class action satisfies the applicable statutory criteria, which are similar to the Rule 23(a) criteria described above. In addition, both provinces require that notice of the class action be given to class members, who have the right to opt out of the litigation. Similarly, the courts have been given broad powers regarding the granting and distribution of monetary relief, and both provinces have established a special class action fund to encourage the use of class actions in appropriate circumstances. In light of these statutory reforms, it is likely that an increasing number of environmental class actions will be brought in Quebec and Ontario rather than in other Canadian provinces or at the federal level.

Richard D. Lindgren

Further Readings

Elrod, James W. "The Use of Federal Class Actions in Mass Toxic Pollution Torts." *Ten-*

nessee Law Review 56 (1988): 243–89.
Ministry of the Attorney General (Ontario). *Report of the Attorney General's Advisory Committee on Class Action Reform.* 1990.

See also ENVIRONMENTAL CASE LAW (CANADA): COMMON LAW CAUSES OF ACTION; ENVIRONMENTAL CASE LAW: UNITED STATES

Clayoquot Sound

Clayoquot Sound (pronounced "Klak-wat") is a coastal temperate rain forest ecosystem on the central west coast of Vancouver Island in British Columbia, Canada. It consists of 3,500 square kilometers of ancient rain forest, mountainous watersheds, alpine meadows, tidal mud-flats, river estuaries, beaches, and coastal islands. Clayoquot Sound has one of the largest areas of intact, old-growth, temperate rain forest remaining in the world, and three of the six last unlogged watersheds over fifty square kilometers on Vancouver Island (the Moyeha, Megin, and Sydney Rivers). The major tree species are western hemlock and western redcedar, many as old as 1,500 years. This type of forest ecosystem contains the highest biomass (weight of organic matter per land area) of any forest type.

The Clayoquot Biosphere Project, a community-based research and education organization set up in Tofino in 1991, estimates that a minimum of 4,500 known plant and animal species reside in Clayoquot Sound, in addition to potentially thousands of insects and microorganisms yet to be discovered and named. A number of the species appear on the Canadian Endangered Species list, including the sea otter, humpback whale, Keen's long-eared bat, wolverine (Western population), and marbled murrelet. The threatened marbled murrelet, a diving seabird, nests in large old-growth trees and, along with many other species, depends on the coastal temperate rain forest habitat for its survival.

A History of Conflict

The Nuu-chah-nulth (meaning "all along the mountains") native community has lived in the area for 8,000 to 9,000 years without degrading the coastal temperate rain forest. In the past couple of decades, clearcut logging has threatened the region with massive soil erosion, the destruction of salmon spawning streams, and species extinction. In 1984, an open confrontation emerged when the local native and nonnative communities joined forces to oppose logging on Meares Island, setting up the first blockade that gained Clayoquot Sound international attention. A moratorium on logging has since been in place while the status of Meares Island is the subject of litigation before the Supreme Court of British Columbia.

A second blockade was set up by environmentalists in June 1988 at Sulphur Pass. The conflict culminated in April 1993 when the government of British Columbia announced the Clayoquot Sound Land Use Decision after fourteen years of "talk and log" planning processes. It allows logging in two thirds of the land base, while protecting one third. In response, the Friends of Clayoquot Sound, a local environmental group, organized a blockade on a logging road in July 1993. By the end of the year, more than 850 protesters had been arrested, making it the largest civil disobedience movement in Canadian history. Environmental groups, such as the Western Canada Wilderness Committee, Greenpeace, and the Sierra Club have launched a series of local, national, and international campaigns, including the construction of a twenty-kilometer Clayoquot Valley Witness Trail, slide show presentations, and the international boycott of MacMillan Bloedel and International Forest Products.

Anita Krajnc

Further Reading

Breen-Needham, Howard, et al., eds. *Witness to Wilderness: The Clayoquot Sound Anthology.* 1994.

See also BATS: CONSERVATION AND HABITAT; CARMANAH VALLEY; GREENPEACE; MARINE MAMMALS; OLD GROWTH FORESTS; SEABIRDS; SIERRA CLUB; STEIN VALLEY; TOP PREDATORS IN CANADA: AN OVERVIEW; WESTERN CANADA WILDERNESS COMMITTEE; WILDERNESS

Clean Air Act

See AIR POLLUTION: REGULATION (U.S.); LEGISLATION: UNITED STATES

Clean Water Act

See LEGISLATION: UNITED STATES

Clearcut

A clearcut is a forest area from which almost all merchantable trees have been removed in one cut. The clearcut is distinguished from other forms of timber harvest such as shelterwood, seed-tree harvests, and thinning that leave substantial numbers of standing live merchantable trees. Small canopy openings created by timber harvest often are not considered clearcuts because the canopy of surrounding forest influences the climate and soil of the entire cut area. Clearcuts usually are at least one or two hectares in size. Smaller cleared areas are often called block cuts, patch cuts, or strip cuts. There are no maximum sizes used in defining clearcuts.

Clearcutting is an even-aged silvicultural system. It is a common method both for removing all merchantable timber from a site and for starting the forest regeneration process. While clearcutting is used to regenerate tree species across a wide range of competition tolerance, it is especially applicable for competition-intolerant species that need full light on the forest floor to regenerate successfully.

There is great variation within the general operation known as clearcutting. Clearcuts are created in a broad range of sizes and shapes. In Canada, clearcuts are commonly tens to hundreds of hectares in extent, although some have been as large as several thousand hectares. They may be circular or square, or of very irregular boundary and shape. They may be spaced far apart, with long periods before adjacent areas are cut, or they may be located close to one another, with narrow uncut strips between. They may be created by cut-and-skid crews or mechanical harvesters. Slash (branches and tops) may be left at the site or taken to landings and roadsides. Clearcuts may be undertaken with care to protect soil, advance regeneration, snags, and woody debris, or they may be undertaken without regard for these factors. They may be full of haul roads, or haul roads may be few and far between.

There is also much variability in the silvicultural treatments that follow clearcutting. Often, unassisted natural regeneration will suffice to secure adequate stocking of the site to the desired tree species. Treatments may range from light scarification and seeding, to heavy scarification, planting, and weed control.

Clearcutting is by far the predominant method of timber harvest in Canada, accounting for about 90 percent of the area annually harvested. It is usually the only harvest entry into a forest stand, but in many other parts of the world, particularly Europe, it represents the final harvest following a series of stand thinnings. Most European forests used for timber production are ultimately clearcut and regenerated as new, even-aged stands.

Clearcutting is often compared to fire as a disturbance and renewal mechanism. Some experts point to the similarities; others to the differences. Both can kill the forest overstory over large areas, and both can leave unaltered patches in a matrix of killed or removed overstory. They can affect areas of similar shapes and sizes, but historically, in the boreal forest at least, the distributions of number and areas of different sizes of fires and of clearcuts have been substantially different. Severe forest fires can result in substantial nutrient losses from sites, as can some clearcutting operations. However, fire often leaves large numbers of snags, contrary to most clearcutting operations. Snags are an important form of habitat and food for many species of insects, birds, and small mammals.

Clearcutting is a controversial operation in forest management. It has many advantages. It is generally the cheapest method of timber harvest, and operationally the simplest to design and implement. It is relatively safe for timber harvesters, since removal of the entire forest canopy eliminates overhead danger from broken, dying, or dead trees. It is a rapid approach to stand improvement, since it creates the possibility to regenerate a new stand by planting or seeding genetically superior stock. Clearcutting favors many wild species, especially species such as deer that thrive near forest edges and in new openings and young even-aged stands.

However, clearcutting receives much criticism. It may create undesirable water-table changes at the site and lead to increased streamflow. Nutrients are lost from the site in harvested material, especially when slash is removed, and also into groundwater through increased leaching. Regeneration may be expensive, particularly if planting and weed control are required. Clearcuts are invariably deemed visually unattractive. Clearcutting is disadvantageous to many wild species that require mature forest cover.

Indiscriminate clearcutting, with only timber objectives in mind, has occurred frequently throughout the world, and has damaged many forest ecosystems. Advocates of clearcutting maintain that the practice can be carried out in an acceptable way so long as it is made more sensitive to ecological and social values. Making clearcutting more and more like a natural disturbance such as fire is desirable. In uneven-aged stands and stands on sensitive sites, clearcutting is giving way to alternative methods of timber harvest. At the site level, clearcutting is increasingly being done in a way that protects soil, nutrient pools, advance regeneration, and habitat structures such as snags and woody debris. At the landscape level, clearcuts are increasingly being designed to be less visually disruptive and to serve explicit functions in overall forest biodiversity.

Yet public demands for less clearcutting continue. Many want clearcutting banned altogether, while others are asking for less area to be clearcut, for smaller cuts of more varied shapes, and for strict rules to protect various ecosystem components. The likely consequences of such trends will be higher harvest and access costs for timber producers, more aesthetically pleasing woodland, more of some wild forest species and less of others, and possibly a reduced need for chemical herbicides and pesticides.

Clearcutting is at times an inappropriate timber harvest method, and at times appropriate. Whether it is right for a particular stand or site must be determined on the basis of many ecological, economic, and social factors. Clearcutting may be an appropriate tool for forest managers in some circumstances, but its use must be very carefully designed and executed.

Peter Duinker

Further Readings

Freedman, Bill. *Environmental Ecology: The Impacts of Pollution and Other Stresses on Ecosystem Structure and Function.* Second Edition, 1994.

Kimmins, Hamish. *Balancing Act: Environmental Issues in Forestry.* 1992.

Matthews, John. *Silvicultural Systems.* 1989.

See also FOREST FRAGMENTATION AND BIRD HABITATS; FORESTRY, HISTORY OF; HABITAT FRAGMENTATION, PATCHES, AND CORRIDORS; NEW FORESTRY; OLD GROWTH FORESTS; SUSTAINED YIELD FORESTRY

Clements, Frederick E.
See CLIMAX THEORY

Climate Warming

Climate warming will result from continued human-induced increases in the atmospheric concentration of greenhouse gases. It has potentially serious implications for the well-being of existing ecosystems and economies and has led to international action to limit greenhouse gas emissions.

The Greenhouse Effect

An important function of the atmosphere is to maintain temperatures over the earth's surface within the narrow range to which living things have adapted. The atmosphere warms the earth because it contains greenhouse gases such as water vapor, carbon dioxide (CO_2), methane, and nitrous oxide (N_2O). These gases allow solar energy to pass through the earth's atmosphere to the surface, where it is absorbed and reemitted as infrared radiation (heat). Some of this infrared radiation is then absorbed by the greenhouse gases and prevented from escaping into space. This heat-trapping ability enables greenhouse gases to warm the earth's surface and lower atmosphere.

Known as the greenhouse effect, this process has allowed the development and maintenance of life on earth. Greenhouse gases currently keep the earth's average temperature at about 15 degrees Celsius. Without these gases, the earth's average temperature would be 33 degrees colder and the planet would be lifeless. This does not mean that the earth's average temperature has not varied over time. During the ice ages, the earth's average temperature was only about 10 degrees Celsius. Such temperature changes are related to variations in the tilt of the earth's axis and its orbit around the sun.

Studies of air bubbles in Antarctic ice core samples, however, have shown that there has also been a direct correlation between fluctuations in the earth's average temperature and changes in the atmospheric concentration of greenhouse gases over the past 160,000 years. For example, it has been determined that the atmospheric concentration of CO_2 was 280 parts per million (ppm) during the industrial revolution, but only 190 ppm at the peak of the ice ages.

While it is likely that greenhouse gases have reinforced and amplified the earth's natural temperature variability, it is only recently that scientists have expressed concern about the possible impacts of human activity that significantly increases the atmospheric concentration of these gases.

Greenhouse Gases and Human Activity

Natural processes exchange carbon between the earth's biomass, atmosphere, oceans, and crust in a closely balanced system known as the carbon cycle. Human activity is upsetting this natural balance by putting CO_2 into the atmosphere more quickly than it can be naturally removed.

CO_2 emissions are a direct product of modern economic activity. Fossil fuels such as coal, oil, and natural gas are the primary energy source in industrialized societies: fueling automobiles, heating homes, and powering industries. Burning these fuels releases CO_2 into the atmosphere. It is estimated that global fossil fuel combustion adds nearly 22 billion tonnes of CO_2 to the atmosphere every year. Coal is the most carbon intensive fossil fuel. Oil contains 17 percent less carbon per unit of energy than coal; natural gas contains 43 percent less.

Land-use decisions also impact CO_2 emissions because forests and soils are natural carbon sinks that take in CO_2 from the atmosphere. Human activities such as forest cutting can reduce or eliminate these natural sinks. Even if new trees replace those lost, the net change in the atmospheric concentration of CO_2 may increase for a time. If the trees are not replaced the effect will be more serious in both the short and the long term. Overall, it is estimated that deforestation adds an additional 5.3–8.9 billion tons of CO_2 to the atmosphere annually.

While human activity produces much smaller quantities of other greenhouse gases, these gases are often more effective heat-trappers than CO_2 on a per molecule basis. For example, over a 100-year time span, methane is thought to be at least eleven times more effective than CO_2 and N_2O 270 times more effective. Anthropogenic methane emissions are produced through the anaerobic decomposition of organic materials in landfills, digestive processes in cattle and sheep, and the production of rice. N_2O emissions are produced through fossil fuel combustion and the use of agricultural fertilizers.

Other important human-produced greenhouse gases are ground level ozone (smog), chlorofluorocarbons (CFCs) and chemically similar substitutes, and polyfluorocarbons (PFCs). Many of these greenhouse gases have long atmospheric lifetimes. This means that emissions resulting from human activity have the potential to influence global climate for hundreds of years.

The majority of anthropogenic greenhouse gas emissions have historically been produced within industrialized countries and this continues to be the case. Nonetheless, economic development and high rates of population growth in developing countries will result in these countries being responsible for most of the world's anthropogenic greenhouse gas emissions before the middle of the twenty-first century.

Is Climate Warming Occurring?

The first scientist to express concern about the impact of human-induced greenhouse gas emissions on global temperatures was a Swedish chemist named Svante Arrehenius. He argued in 1896 that the coal burning that was fueling the Industrial Revolution could increase the atmospheric concentration of CO_2 and warm the planet.

Arrehenius's concern did not become a major focus for the scientific community until the 1950s and 1960s when measurements indicated that the atmospheric concentration of CO_2 was steadily increasing. It is now known that the atmospheric concentration of CO_2 in 1990 was 356 ppm, significantly higher than the 315 ppm measured in 1958. Indeed, ice core samples indicate that the atmospheric concentration of CO_2 has not reached 350 ppm at any other time in the past 160,000 years.

Other greenhouse gases have exhibited similar trends. The atmospheric concentration of methane is more than double preindustrial levels. Synthetic greenhouse gases, such as CFCs, did not even exist before the Industrial Revolution. The evidence of increasing atmospheric concentrations of greenhouse gases was supplemented in the 1980s by data on global temperatures that indicated that the earth's average temperature had increased by 0.3 to 0.6 degrees Celsius over the previous 100 years. It is now known that the warmest years on the global temperature record since measurements first began in the mid-nineteenth century were 1991 and 1990, with the next five warmest years in the 1980s.

In an effort to begin formulating an international scientific consensus on the climate warming issue, more than sixty nations agreed in November 1988 to bring the world's leading climatologists and biologists together on an Intergovernmental Panel on Climate Change (IPCC) under the auspices of the United Nations Environment Program and the World Meteorological Organization.

A consensus report was released by the IPCC in 1990 and updated in 1992. This report stated that it is impossible to determine if climate warming is already underway. While the observed increase in the earth's average temperature over the past 100 years is within the range of natural climatic variability, it is also possible that the presence of other pollutants in the atmosphere, such as sulfur dioxide, may have helped to offset any temperature increase that might have been produced by increasing atmospheric concentrations of greenhouse gases.

The IPCC concluded that it will take at least an additional decade to determine if the temperature changes seen over the past 100 years are linked to human-induced increases in greenhouse gas concentrations.

Climate Warming

Despite its contention that an additional decade will be required to determine human-induced effects on temperature changes, the IPCC also concluded that if no action is taken to reduce the emission of greenhouse gases from human activity, climate warming will occur in the future. Drawing on the results of computer models of the world's climate, the IPCC concluded that an equivalent doubling of the atmospheric concentration of CO_2 from preindustrial levels would increase the earth's average temperature by 1.5 to 4.5 degrees Celsius. Depending on the assumptions made about international efforts to reduce greenhouse gas emissions, this would occur between 2025 and late in the twenty-first century.

Such warming would not be uniform across the planet. Some regions, such as the Canadian Arctic, could see temperatures increase by up to 10 degrees Celsius. More importantly, the rate of temperature change would be 0.2 to 0.5 degrees Celsius per decade, more rapid than at any time in the past 10,000 years.

Climate warming, however, means much more than warmer temperatures. Changes in temperature directly affect other elements of climate such as precipitation, wind patterns, and ocean circulation.

The IPCC concluded that the rapid increases in the earth's average temperature projected by computer models could lead to climatic changes that would threaten natural ecosystems, human communities, and economies. For example, the IPCC projected:

- A sea-level rise of three to ten centimeters per decade (as a result of thermal expansion of the oceans) that could pose a threat to low-lying areas and challenge the existence of some small island states,
- An increased frequency and severity of extreme climatic events such as hurricanes and droughts, as normal weather patterns are disrupted, and
- Rapid shifts in the geographic location of climate zones that would have an impact on economic activity (e.g., some areas may no longer be suitable for agriculture) and also threaten many plant and animal species that are unable to easily or quickly migrate.

Efforts have been made to be more specific about the possible impacts of climate warming, but the IPCC concluded that any such assessments must be treated with caution. The atmosphere is a complex system and the computer models used to generate projections of the future are still incomplete. Many uncertainties remain with respect to projections of the timing, magnitude and regional patterns of climate change.

The Political Response

While the possibility of climate warming has been discussed within the scientific community for many years, it has only recently become a focus for political discussion. Media coverage of three events in the summer of 1988 drew public, and subsequently political, attention to the climate warming issue for the first time. The first was a series of extreme climate anomalies, including a severe drought in the midwestern United States and harsh monsoons in India and Bangladesh. The second was a statement by American scientist James Hansen to a U.S. Senate Committee that an enhanced greenhouse effect was already changing global climate. The third event was the gathering of scientists, government officials, and representatives of nongovernment organizations in Toronto, Canada, at an international conference on the changing atmosphere. The conference's final statement described climate warming as "an unintended, uncontrolled, globally pervasive experiment whose ultimate consequences could be second only to a global nuclear war." It called for a 20 percent reduction in global CO_2 emissions from 1988 levels by the year 2005.

The public concern generated by these events, and a growing consensus on climate warming science, led several governments to make national commitments to limit their country's greenhouse gas emissions over the next ten to fifteen years. These commitments ranged from stabilization of future emissions at current levels to reductions of up to 25 percent in future emissions from current levels.

In November 1990, delegations from over ninety countries gathered at the Second World Climate Conference to receive the report of the IPCC. Despite the scientific uncertainties surrounding climate change, it was agreed that the scientific consensus on the possible threat of climate change was strong enough to warrant precautionary action. Accordingly, governments agreed to begin negotiations on an international agreement to address climate change. Negotiations began in February 1991 and were successfully completed in May 1992. More than 150 countries signed the United Nations Framework Convention on Climate Change at the June 1992 Earth Summit in Rio de Janeiro.

The ultimate objective of the Convention is ". . . stabilization of greenhouse gas concentrations in the atmosphere at a level that would prevent dangerous anthropogenic interference with the climate system." Such a level should be achieved within a time frame sufficient to allow ecosystems to adapt naturally to climate change, to ensure that food production is not threatened, and to enable economic development to proceed in a sustainable manner.

The agreement reached at the 1992 Earth Summit is the first step in international efforts to meet this objective. It contains no legally binding targets and schedules to limit greenhouse gas emissions but it does state that industrialized countries should aim to reduce their greenhouse gas emissions to 1990 levels by the end of the decade. Developing countries are not required to adhere to targets and schedules for emissions controls.

The Convention directs countries to: facilitate adequate adaptation to climate change, increase public awareness about climate change, reduce the scientific uncertainties surrounding climate change, and include climate change considerations in decision making. Industrialized countries have an additional commitment to provide new and additional financial and technological assistance to developing countries to help them meet their commitments under the Convention.

All countries are also required to provide greenhouse gas emission inventories and report on their actions to address climate change. This reporting commitment is an important component of the Convention because it ensures that

countries can be held publicly accountable for their progress in meeting their Convention obligations.

The Convention is designed to be an evolving document. Its commitments will be reviewed and updated regularly on the basis of evaluations of the Convention's effectiveness and new scientific and technical information. Some of the first issues to be addressed after the Convention enters into force include: the content and format of reports to the Convention, modalities for the transfer of financial and technical resources to developing countries, criteria for joint efforts to reduce greenhouse gas emissions, and the adequacy of existing commitments under the Convention.

The Policy Response

While responding to climate warming requires that actions be taken to address all sources and sinks of greenhouse gases, it is clear that a critical component of any strategy to fight climate warming must be to limit greenhouse gas emissions produced through fossil fuel combustion. Such emissions can be reduced in the short-term by improving the efficiency with which equipment, buildings, and automobiles use energy produced by fossil fuels. In the long-term, emission reductions will require the substitution of low- or non-greenhouse gas emitting energy sources (e.g., small scale hydro, biomass, wind, solar) for non-renewable carbon based fossil fuels. Other possible actions to limit greenhouse gas emissions include reducing the amount of waste heading to landfills, decreasing the use of nitrogen-based fertilizers, and enhancing the capacity of forests and soils to serve as sinks for CO_2.

There is general agreement within industrialized countries that there are first step measures to limit emissions that offer economic benefits or meet other policy objectives. The economic costs associated with moving beyond first steps, however, are under extensive debate. Opinions range from the view that further action will cripple economies to a belief that it will provide a net economic benefit. The debate is complicated by the fact that measures offering a net benefit to society can often impose significant costs on specific regions or sectors.

Most industrialized countries are in the process of developing climate warming action plans. In light of the economic uncertainty surrounding emission limitation actions, many of them are relying heavily on voluntary action by stakeholders to meet their initial climate warming mitigation commitments. Some regulatory action is also being taken, particularly with regard to improving the energy efficiency of equipment, buildings, and automobiles. An increasing number of countries also are exploring the use of economic instruments like taxes and emissions permits.

Robert Hornung

Further Readings
Intergovernmental Panel on Climate Change. *Climate Change: The IPCC 1990 and 1992 Assessments.* 1992.
United Nations Framework Convention on Climate Change. 1992

See also ARCTIC; AUTOMOBILES: IMPACTS AND POLICIES; CARBON TAX; ENERGY EFFICIENCY; RIO CONFERENCE (1992); SOLAR ENERGY; WIND ENERGY

Climax Theory

Climax theory in ecology is attributed to the work of Frederick E. Clements (1916) who had studied changes in plant communities over time, particularly where fire or other disturbance destroyed existing vegetation and permitted other species to take its place. Clements proposed that in any given climatic region vegetation would develop through a successional series (seres or seral stages) to a final, steady-state condition known as the climax vegetation of the area or the climax formation.

Succession could begin on bare rock or other arid substrate (xerosere), or in ponds, streams, or lake edges (hydrosere); in either case, vegetation would develop toward the same climax formation, determined by the regional climate. Succession could be primary—taking place on sites which had not previously supported vegetation—or secondary—taking place on developed soil from which vegetation had been removed or destroyed. However, in any climatic region, all succession would lead to the same climax. Thus, in a broadleaf deciduous forest such as the oak-hickory or maple-basswood forests of the eastern United States, every successional change would develop over time toward the same forest type. In the grassland climate of the American Middle West succession would proceed toward a perennial grass community.

Clements divided climax formations into climax associations made up of different species groups determined by local climatic differences but all belonging to the same prevailing formation type. Clements went further to propose an elaborate classification and a complex terminology to describe North American vegetation.

The Clementsian theory is termed a monoclimax theory. Other ecologists have proposed polyclimax theories in which it is recognized that in any region other factors than climate, such as soil or rock, topography, the prevalence of fires, or the invasion of exotic species, could lead to vegetation differences other than those predictable from the regional climate. Furthermore, climatic changes and the frequency of major disturbances such as landslides, floods, fires, volcanic eruptions, or hurricanes produce landscape mosaics that bear little resemblance to the vegetation predictable from a Clementsian system. Thus, Clements postulated a more stable, orderly sequence of events than other ecologists found to be existing in nature. Nevertheless, he focused attention on the more likely or frequent course of events that can still be observed in cutover forests, heavily grazed grasslands, or other disturbed plant communities in North America.

Clements worked with Victor E. Shelford (1939) to produce the biome system of classification, based on Clements's plant formations. A biome is simply a climax formation with its associated animal life. As a descriptive tool, the biome system is still in widespread use although its theoretical basis is usually ignored. Major biomes of the world include tundras, taigas or boreal forests, grasslands, deserts, tropical rainforests, tropical dry forests, and savannas.

Raymond F. Dasmann

Further Readings
Clements, Frederick E. *Plant Succession.* Carnegie Institute of Washington, Pub. No. 242. 1916.
Clements, Frederick E., and Victor E. Shelford. *Bio-Ecology.* 1939.

See also BIOREGION; BIOSPHERE RESERVES; ECOSYSTEMS; EXOTIC SPECIES; FOREST FIRES AND CONSERVATION; LANDSCAPE ECOLOGY

Club of Rome
See Limits to Growth

Coal: Environmental Impacts
Although it is common to talk about "scarce" natural resources, this term is not easily applied

to U.S. coal. Coal is America's most abundant fossil fuel, with demonstrated reserves of over 400 billion tons. The United States currently gets more than 55 percent of its electricity from coal, consuming over 894 million short tons of coal in 1992. America's reliance on coal as an energy source is not expected to diminish in this century. Coal use, however, can be environmentally disruptive. Potential environmental effects of coal include pollutants released in the air during coal combustion, and a variety of damages to land and water that result from coal mining.

Environmental Effects of Coal Combustion

Environmental effects of coal combustion include acid deposition, urban smog, and global warming. Air pollutants released in large quantities by coal-fired power plants, industrial boilers, and other combustion units include the oxides of sulfur, nitrogen, and carbon, as well as particles of ash. Smaller quantities of trace inorganic elements, radionuclides, and hydrocarbons are also emitted, usually absorbed on the surface of the ash particles.

Sulfur dioxide (SO_2) receives more attention than any other emission from the combustion of coal, primarily because it is a major precursor to acidic deposition (acid rain). SO_2 and oxides of nitrogen are converted to acids when they combine with water in the atmosphere, and return to earth as acidic precipitation. Acid rain has long been suspected of damaging lakes, streams, forests and soils by lowering the pH content of rain and, thus, surface water and soils. Coal fired power plants are the major source of SO_2, accounting for 66 percent of total U.S. emissions in 1991.

The amount of SO_2 released during combustion depends on the amount of sulfur in coal and the effectiveness of control technologies used by coal-burning electric utilities and other industries. The sulfur content of coal mined in the West and in parts of southern Appalachia is typically low; coal mined in northern Appalachia and in the midwestern states usually contains much higher sulfur concentrations. The most common method of reducing SO_2 emissions is flue-gas scrubbing.

Oxides of nitrogen also contribute to acid rain as well as ground-level, or tropospheric, ozone (smog). Smog is a product of sunlight, acting on nitrogen oxides, carbon monoxide and volatile organic compounds. About 30 percent of nitrogen oxides released into the atmosphere by man-made causes derives from the combustion of coal.

Particulates are also a product of coal combustion, either by direct emission of primary particles (fly ash) or by release of gases that are precursors to the formation of secondary particles. Secondary particulates include sulfates, nitrates, and particulate hydrocarbon.

Environmental Effects of Coal Mining

The major concern associated with mining is effective reclamation of post-mined lands. U.S. coal mining has a history of "rape and run" mining practices, in which coal companies would mine the land and then move to another location. Prior to the passage of the Surface Mining Control and Reclamation Act (SMCRA, 1977), more than one million acres of disturbed land, primarily within the Appalachian coal region, were unreclaimed. Soil erosion, loss of vegetative productivity and wildlife habitat are among the major surface effects of coal mining when reclamation is not successful. Besides unreclaimed land, coal mining imposes other social and environmental costs such as water pollution, erosion, slope failures, loss of fish and wildlife resources, and property damage. The nature of environmental damage varies by region, type of coal, and mining technique.

In eastern coal fields, mining spoil pushed downslope of mining conducted in mountainous areas may cause landslides, sedimentation of streams, and flooding. Unstable highwalls may crumble, ruining drainage patterns and polluting water resources. In the arid and semiarid western coal fields, reestablishing native vegetation is difficult because of poorly developed soils and low rainfall. Revegetation problems also contribute to erosion of sparse topsoil supplies.

A major environmental effect of underground mining is subsidence of overlying or adjacent land. Subsidence due to mining using conventional "room and pillar" excavation techniques (which extracts coal and leaves unexcavated coal pillars to support the underground mined area) is an unintentional occurrence. Pillars collapse and the overlying surface area subsides into the mined area. High extraction techniques such as longwall mining, on the other hand, allow subsidence to occur as part of the mining process. However, environmental consequences of "planned" subsidence can be equally as severe as unplanned subsidence.

Coal mining, both surface and underground, results in impacts to water resources. Surface water impacts include an increase in total solids dissolved (TSD), salinity, and acid mine drainage. Increased TSD, such as sulfate, in local watersheds results from runoff and erosion of mining waste piles or unstabilized spoil banks. Erosion is greatest from surface mines in areas with rugged terrain and rainy climates, such as southern Appalachia.

Acid mine drainage is a particularly severe byproduct of mining in the Appalachia region and parts of the interior mining regions, including Indiana, Illinois, and Kentucky. In these areas, coal seams are rich in pyrite (iron disulfide). The mining process exposes pyrites to water and air, causing a reaction that forms sulfuric acid and iron. The acidic water increases the solubility of toxic heavy metals, such as arsenic, lead, and mercury, and renders the water toxic to aquatic life and unfit for consumption.

Mining can also have significant effects on ground water. Coal mining operations can contaminate ground water as surface water seeps through mining wastes or spoil banks and enters underground aquifers. Direct interception of aquifers by large surface mining operations in the western United States or longwall mining in the eastern United States may physically dislocate groundwater supplies. This is especially problematic in the arid western region, where aquifers may not recharge for decades.

Denise Scheberle

Further Readings

McElfish, James M., and Ann E. Beier. *Environmental Regulation of Coal Mining: SMCRA's Second Decade.* 1990.

U.S. Department of Energy, Energy Information Administration. *Coal Data: A Reference.* 1989.

U.S. Office of Technology Assessment. *The Direct Use of Coal: Prospects and Problems of Production and Combustion.* 1979.

See also ACID PRECIPITATION: AQUATIC IMPACTS; AIR POLLUTION: IMPACTS; ECOLOGICAL RESTORATION; MINING AND SMELTING: HISTORIC IMPACTS

Coastal Debris and Cleanup

At one time or another, everyone has visited the beach; some are even fortunate enough to live within walking distance of the seashore. The character of the world's beaches may vary greatly from one area to another, but there is one constant: trash. No matter what the geographic area, no matter the time of year, the one thing coastal visitors are certain to encounter is garbage.

There is no argument that garbage despoils the view, but of even greater concern is the hazard this trash, particularly plastic trash, poses to wildlife. Thousands of marine mammals, sea turtles, seabirds, and fish die each year from entanglement in debris such as rope, six-pack rings, or monofilament fishing line, or from ingesting items such as plastic bags and sheeting. Marine debris can also jeopardize vessel navigation by tangling propellers, causing damage, and endangering human safety.

The sources of this trash are as varied as the trash itself, making it difficult to identify any specific group or individual as the dominant source. But the Center for Marine Conservation (CMC) has developed a program that not only gets the trash off the beach, but also identifies the sources responsible for putting it there. Follow-up efforts can then begin to stop the problem at the source.

The first CMC-coordinated beach cleanup took place in 1986 as a statewide effort on the beaches of Texas. Organizers wisely realized that unless an effort was made to find out exactly what types of debris were out there and begin to pinpoint sources of this debris, volunteers would be doing beach cleanups for the rest of their lives, as well as the lives of their children. This foresight prompted the 2,800 volunteers who turned out to participate in the cleanup not only to collect trash but also to record information on the types and amounts of trash they found. Using Beach Cleanup Data Cards designed by CMC that listed forty-one different debris items, volunteers also recorded other details, such as entangled wildlife they found, or debris with identifying markings.

Volunteers at that first Texas cleanup recorded 171,496 individual debris items. This information was entered into the first Marine Debris Database, analyzed, and compiled into the first beach cleanup report, giving a profile of the debris littering Texas beaches. This report showed that a significant portion of Texas beach debris was generated by shipping and cargo vessels, and provided the first of many directions for CMC to move to get to the sources of marine debris.

But the report did more than just provide information about Texas' marine debris problem; it gave a very sobering report of the extent of the marine debris problem throughout the United States. The report was used in Congressional testimony to support U.S. ratification of Annex V of the MARPOL Treaty, which put a halt to the dumping of plastic trash from ships at sea. The 1986 cleanup report was also used to support passage of the Marine Plastic Pollution Research and Control Act of 1987, which implemented Annex V in U.S. waters.

In 1988, CMC expanded beach cleanups to include all the coastal states in the nation. The resulting National Beach Cleanup was the largest single-day cleanup ever, encompassing twenty-five U.S. states and territories. Approximately 47,000 volunteers collected 1,954,800 pounds of trash from 3,518 miles of beach. Analysis of the data paralleled findings from the previous cleanups in Texas. About 65 percent of the trash collected was plastic, supporting earlier findings that plastics are the major component of our nation's marine debris.

Participation at beach cleanups continues to grow at an amazing rate, from 65,000 volunteers in 1989 to 108,000 in 1990 to 130,000 in 1991 to an incredible 150,000 in 1992. As it became more and more evident that the marine debris problem is global in scope, and that the United States alone could not solve it, the cleanup began to reach beyond U.S. borders. In 1989, Canada and Mexico joined the United States in the first North American coastal cleanup. The results of the Canada and Mexico cleanups again pointed to plastics as the number one problem in the marine environment.

What makes this event so attractive to so many people around the world? After all, picking up trash is not an activity that most would choose voluntarily. Comments from volunteers indicate that the most compelling reason for participating in the cleanup year after year is knowing that the information they collect is useful. The data collected by this army of volunteers has provided, for the first time, an accurate snapshot of the specifics of the marine debris problem. It has been determined that plastics make up the largest percentage of trash on the world's beaches, and that, while plastics are consistently abundant on all beaches worldwide, the sources of debris may vary greatly from one geographic area to another. For example, a significant portion of beach debris in the Gulf of Mexico can be attributed to ocean-based sources, such as commercial fishing vessels and offshore activities, while Japan seems to have its biggest problem with land-based garbage carried to coastal areas through storm drains or left on the shore by beachgoers.

Because beach cleanup data points so clearly to the specific sources of trash, many organizations are using the information to halt the flow of marine debris. For example, North Carolina State University uses the cleanup data as baseline information to determine the economic impacts of marine debris. A steering committee in California used that state's cleanup data to develop the California Marine Debris Action Plan, which has been accepted by the California legislature for implementation. But perhaps the most important point that cleanup information makes is that legislation designed to solve the marine debris problem is having little or no effect. Are people ignoring the law? Do they even know about the law? Or do they realize that this may be an unenforceable regulation, given the enforcement manpower and resources available? Or is there just so much trash in our oceans that we are still collecting debris from years ago? These questions and many more are currently being explored by CMC and other organizations, including federal lawmakers, to determine what must still be done to solve this enormous problem.

Lisa K. Younger

Further Readings

Debenham, Patty, and Lisa K. Younger. *Cleaning North America's Beaches: 1990 Beach Cleanup Results.* 1991.
Younger, Lisa K., and Karen Hodge. *1991 International Coastal Cleanup Results.* 1992.

See also COASTAL MARSHES, CONSERVATION OF; PACKAGING; SHOREBIRDS

Coastal Marshes, Conservation of

Coastal marshes occur where the margins of the continents gradually slope to meet oceans, bays, and river deltas. Marshes dominate the lowlands at the mouths of large rivers, such as the Ganges in Bangladesh, the Mississippi in North America, or the Yangtze in China. Thousands of square kilometers of deltaic coastal marshes range from uniform stands of salt marsh vegetation to diverse freshwater marshes. Most coastal salt marshes and many brackish marshes experience some tidal and saltwater influence directly from the ocean. Freshwater coastal marshes, on the other hand, experience tidal effects as a result of oceanic tides backing fresh river flows over the wetlands. The coastal wetlands of the tropics and some subtropics of the world are dominated by mangrove forests that, although not technically marshes, share many of the same functions and values of marshes. Moreover, some large inland water bodies, such as Lake Baikal in the former Soviet Union and the Laurentian Great Lakes between the United States and Canada, may be considered inland seas. These huge lakes develop distinctive freshwater coastal marshes as a result of wind movement of water that is similar to the lunar gravitational tides of the sea coasts.

Threats to Coastal Wetlands

In the past, coastal marshes have not been valued highly or protected across most of their distribution because their functions have been misunderstood. Because of the difficulties of farming, traversing, building upon, or living within coastal marshes, they were viewed as having little economic or social value. Since the rapid development of technology following World War II, drainage, agricultural, and construction techniques have been developed to convert coastal marshes to other land uses that can produce more direct forms of income for those who sponsor the land-use transitions. Natural loss of coastal wetlands also occurs through slight rises in sea level, which drown even wetland-adapted plants. Small changes in the balance of factors such as wave erosion and sediment deposition may cause the line separating sea and marsh to recede landward or seaward. Marsh losses through geologic subsidence of ancient river deltas, which are continually sinking into the sea floor, tend to be offset by marsh increases from land building at the mouths of rivers.

Wetlands along the world's coasts are threatened by the effects of population growth and urban development. Over 50 percent of the U.S. population lives and works in coastal areas with a land area comprising less than 10 percent of the entire country. Farmers drain the fertile soils found in coastal marshes by building levees to isolate them from their normal flooding regime and make them drier to permit crop production or livestock grazing. To convert coastal marshes to housing or commercial development areas, these wetlands are filled with soil from nearby areas or surrounded by levees to isolate them from tides. Water is pumped out whenever precipitation or floods raise the water level behind the levees. In addition, water pollution is a serious threat to plants, animals, and humans in coastal wetlands. Rivers collect urban runoff, industrial waste, and farm chemicals before spreading these polluted waters throughout the coastal wetlands that form where rivers meet the sea. For example, 40 percent of the historic river inflow into San Francisco Bay in the western United States has been diverted for municipal use; of the remaining freshwater inflow, 24 percent is agricultural runoff or domestic and industrial wastewater. Loss of freshwater and the addition of pollutants has affected both the hydrology and water quality of the coastal marshes.

Conservation activities usually develop concurrent with an understanding of the benefits of coastal wetlands remaining in their original conditions. Moreover, increased public appreciation for the aesthetic values of natural ecosystems tends to mount pressure to conserve wetlands.

Values of Coastal Marshes

Perceptions of value and appreciation of coastal marshes vary by region. With few exceptions though, the accumulation of benefits such as natural flood control, improved water quality, fish-rearing habitat, waterfowl habitat, biological diversity, groundwater or aquifer recharge, recreation, and erosion control, are valued by all peoples regardless of nationality. Wetland values, though generally acknowledged, are not as easily converted to dollars or other units of measure, unlike the profits or losses from most development projects. Land-use conflicts arise when individuals or subsets of the public act to generate income from real estate, agriculture, or mineral and industrial uses in a way that causes losses or degradation of coastal marsh and the concomitant loss of public values associated with them. Conservation efforts are often complicated by a lack of understanding of wetland functions and values on the part of developer, public, and policy makers. For example, by converting coastal marshes to uses such as resorts or intensive agriculture, the former wetland may produce income for individuals or small groups of investors, and this income is easily measured. In contrast, the suite of benefits that coastal marshes provide to the public by remaining in their natural state is nearly impossible to compare in similar terms. Furthermore, the people benefiting from existing wetlands are difficult to identify because they often

C

do not realize that coastal wetlands reduce their flooding risk, protect their drinking water, and provide many other intangible benefits—that is, until the wetlands are altered or lost.

Conservation

Conservation activities in coastal marshes can be grouped into three broad categories: 1) governmental influence through incentives such as tax credits or subsidies, or through codified restriction or regulation of activities known to be harmful to wetlands; 2) protection through purchase by national, state, or private conservation groups; and 3) participation of users in ecologically sound management activities that promote marsh sustainability.

Public and political involvement influences all three of these categories. Citizen involvement has become an especially important factor in the United States where local and national decisions are greatly affected by public opinion.

Thus far, the most complete and successful method of conserving wetlands is to protect the integrity and continuity of the original wetland through designation of sanctuaries, parks, refuges, and reserves. In cases where no other options exist and wetlands become threatened, attempts to enhance, add to, or create a replacement wetland to offset losses may be made through restoration and mitigation. Human efforts, however earnest, may not be capable of reproducing the complexity of forces—such as tides, sediments, and the succession of plant and animal assemblages—that operate over the long time periods usually required to create a sustainable unit of coastal wetland. Therefore, human-created coastal marshes may not be of equal value to a natural marsh of the same size. The field of restoration ecology was begun during the 1980s in response to these problems.

Engineered alternatives designed to help conserve coastal wetlands are often used in developed countries. Engineered approaches are of two types: 1) installing hard structures such as weirs, culverts, jetties, locks, diversions, levees, and breakwaters, all of which are designed to influence water levels, movement and salt content; and 2) carrying out engineered plans to influence natural processes, such as channel training, sand management on beaches, sediment and water diversions, marsh vegetation plantings, prescribed burning, grazing management, and techniques to affect fertilization and sedimentation.

A. Lee Foote

Further Readings

Mitsch, William J., and James G. Gosselink. *Wetlands*. 1986.

Watzin, Mary C., and James G. Gosselink. *The Fragile Fringe: Coastal Wetlands of the United States.* U.S. Fish and Wildlife Service, 1992.

See also COASTAL DEBRIS AND CLEANUP; FRESHWATER WETLANDS; SHOREBIRDS

Coastal Zone Management

Coastal zone management refers to a body of laws passed and amended by the U.S. Congress to assist comprehensive land-use planning in counties adjacent to the sea. The law affects all of those states bordering the Great Lakes, Atlantic, Gulf, and Pacific waters in the implementation and enforcement of comprehensive regional planning. The attempt to balance conservation with development in the densely populated counties was necessary to forestall existing and potential resource conflicts. The legislation established broad guidelines under which planning agencies were to implement comprehensive land-use plans to minimize antagonism among competing users of beaches, marshes, wetlands, or estuarine waters. Seventy-five percent of the nation's largest cities are in these coastal zones.

Conflicts among landowners and resource users along the coast arise from transportation improvements, electrical power plant siting, wildlife protection, sufficient and accessible recreation areas, limited fresh water, and diminished salt-water quality. Governments have a financial burden to insure coastal and barrier island property from the risk of flooding due to storms. State and county governments have constructed and maintained breakwaters, jetties, bridges, causeways, or dikes to provide access or assist in the protection and evacuation of coastal residents.

Coastal zones differ in size and may extend inland from the tidal shoreline from one to several kilometers. Coast is derived from the Spanish word *costa* meaning the side of, or beside, referring to the edge of the sea. Coastal areas are characterized by a variety of types: sandy beaches, silt-laden marshes (mangroves in the tropics), rocky shores, and submerged lands beneath rivers, bays, sounds, or lagoons. The engineering required to make economically productive use of wetlands, islands, harbors, or marinas enormously benefits developers, the local tax base, and investors in seaside property.

Federal regulation of these activities has always been important due to the interstate character of coastal waters and the commerce clause of the Constitution. State governments have both a sovereign interest in the submerged lands and in the development of coastal resources for fisheries, ports, transportation development, and the promotion of recreation or tourism. Local governments have bonding, zoning, and taxing authority in coastal counties.

Since colonial times the coast has been the most heavily settled area of North America. Currently over two-thirds of the U.S. population lives within fifty miles of the coasts. Over 60 percent of the national fisheries catch, by weight, is dependent on near shore, inshore, or estuarine waters. This includes crab, clams, oysters, salmon, and/or shrimp. Migratory and native shorebirds, waterfowl, and wading birds all depend upon the extensive marshes and mud flats of the Atlantic, Pacific, Gulf, and Great Lakes shorelines for nesting or feeding.

Migratory birds and their coastal habitats are protected under an international treaty among the United States, Canada, and Mexico. Marine mammals frequenting the coastal areas are also protected by federal law including the breeding habitats of seals, sea lions, manatees, porpoises, or whales. In Florida four varieties of sea turtles nest annually on beaches while tropical mangrove forests dominate the quiet bay waters. In California elephant seals and sea lions nest on shore. Sea grass beds from Alaska to the Gulf and up to Maine are the nurseries of the small fish that sustain commercial and sport fisheries.

Land in those areas immediately adjacent to the ebb and flood of the tide were treated differently by the law due to English legal precedents. In all states the land lying between the high and the low tide lines is considered "sovereign land." This means that regardless of private property titles, or actions of legislative bodies, the land between the tides can never be fully owned in fee simple absolute as is other real estate in the United States.

Tidelands are "encumbered" with restrictions referred to as a "public trust" that legally protects these lands for the common good. This protection furthers two competing benefits, the promotion of commerce and citizen access to hunting and fishing. Private property rights in tidal land is severely limited by this public trust held by the states.

Coastal zone management seeks to balance natural and cultural amenities peculiar to seaside regions because of mounting ecological problems. These problems arise from the pressure of increased population density, continuing consumption of electricity from polluting energy facilities, the siting of landfills for garbage disposal, dumping of industrial chemical and municipal wastes, and second-home development. The intensity of these competing uses almost destroyed the ecological basis of marine productivity in all but the most remote locations. Serious declines in wildlife due to the destruction of coastal habitats represents a serious threat to biodiversity, ocean fisheries, and climate.

Joseph V. Siry

Further Readings

Healy, Robert G., ed. *Protecting the Golden Shore*. 1974.
Myers, Jenning C. *America's Coasts in the 1980s: Policies and Issues*. 1981.
Siry, Joseph V. *Marshes of the Ocean Shore*. 1984.

See also COASTAL MARSHES, CONSERVATION OF; DOLPHINS AND PORPOISES; FISHERIES CONSERVATION; GREAT LAKES; MARINE MAMMALS; SEA TURTLES; SHOREBIRDS; WATERFOWL: CONSERVATION AND HABITAT

Cogeneration

Cogeneration is a highly efficient means of simultaneously generating heat and electric power. Displacing fossil fuel combustion with heat that would normally be wasted in the process of power generation, it reaches efficiencies that triple, or even quadruple, those of conventional power generation. Although cogeneration has been in use for nearly a century, in the mid-1980s relatively low natural gas prices made it a widely attractive alternative for new power generation. In fact, cogeneration is largely responsible for the dramatic decline of nuclear and hydraulic power plant construction that occurred in the 1980s. Cogeneration accounts for well over half of all new power plant capacity built in North America in the last decade.

The environmental implications of cogeneration stem not just from its inherent efficiency, but also from its decentralized character. Because it is impractical to transport heat over any distance, cogeneration equipment must be located physically close to its heat user. A number of environmentally positive consequences flow from the fact that cogenerated power tends to be generated close to the power consumer, significantly reducing transmission losses, stray current, and the need for distribution equipment. Cogeneration plants tend to be built smaller, and owned and operated by smaller and more localized companies. As a general rule, they are also built closer to populated areas—a fact that causes them to be held to higher environmental standards. In northern Europe, and increasingly in North America, cogeneration is at the heart of district heating and cooling systems. District heating combined with cogeneration has the potential to reduce human greenhouse gas emissions by more than any other technology except public transit.

To understand cogeneration, it is necessary to know that most conventional power generation is based on burning a fuel to produce steam. It is the steam pressure which actually turns the turbines and generates power in an inherently inefficient process. Because of a basic principle of physics no more than one third of the energy of the original fuel can be converted to the steam pressure which in turn generates electricity. Cogeneration, in contrast, makes use of the excess heat, usually in the form of relatively low-temperature steam exhausted from the power generation turbines. Such steam is suitable for a wide range of heating applications, and effectively displaces the combustion of carbon-based fuels, with all of the environmental effects inherent in that burning.

In addition to cogeneration, there are a number of related technologies which make use of exhaust steam at successively lower temperatures and pressures. These are collectively known as "combined cycle" systems. They are more efficient than conventional power generation, but not as efficient as cogeneration, which produces about 30 percent power and 70 percent heat. Combined cycle technologies can be financially attractive despite their lower efficiencies, because they can produce proportionately more power and less heat. Environmentally, combined cycle systems are controversial, because they make low-cost power available, reducing the incentive for efficient consumption, and also because they are not as efficient as true cogeneration.

Jake Brooks

Further Readings
Ottinger, Richard L., et al. *Environmental Costs of Electricity*. 1991.

See also DEMAND-SIDE MANAGEMENT; ENERGY EFFICIENCY; SOFT ENERGY PATHS

Cole, Thomas
See HUDSON RIVER SCHOOL

Colorado River
The Colorado is one of the most dramatic rivers in the world, and its recent history is a revealing case study in the modern use of water. The river drains a basin covering 244,000 square miles, or one-twelfth of the conterminous United States and a portion of Mexico. Geologically, the headwaters lie in Wyoming's Wind River Mountains, but the upper river was declared by Colorado politicians in 1921 to be the portion flowing down from Rocky Mountain National Park, and so it became on the maps. The river, which is 1,440 miles long, has an average annual flow of 14 million acre-feet, or about one-fourth that of the Nile—a river to which it is often compared since both pass through vast arid landscapes. The Colorado watershed includes some of the highest mountains and lowest deserts in the world. Its most famous scenic feature is the Grand Canyon, an immense declivity that even today seems untouched by civilization. Little of the rest of the river, however, can make that claim. The Colorado has become the most fought over, politicized, and engineered river on the North American continent.

Except for its lower portion, the river was unexplored by Americans until 1869, when John Wesley Powell led a navigation party through its whitewater canyons. Sixty years later the river was still wild and the country around it still one of the most sparsely settled areas in the Western Hemisphere. Then in 1922 the river was divided politically into two basins, upper and lower; much of the water in the lower basin was claimed by California for irrigation and urban development. The largest dam ever attempted, named after President Herbert Hoover, was constructed near Las Vegas, Nevada, and dedicated in 1935. The dam mainly benefited agribusinessmen in California's Imperial Valley and real estate interests in Los Angeles. Besides storing water, the dam generated enormous amounts of electricity. After World War II other dams appeared in both the upper and lower basins.

By 1970 the population living within the Colorado watershed was over 2 million, and some of the fastest growing cities in the country were there. Phoenix, for example, exploded from a mere village to a megalopolis. Although cities were the most visible consumers of the river, farmers used by far the largest portion of its water to irrigate alfalfa, cotton, fruit, and vegetables. More water was diverted out of the Colorado River basin than any other American river, going to eastern Colorado, to northern New Mexico, to Salt Lake City, and above all to California.

Over the past half century the Colorado River has been the focus of many heated conservation battles. In 1956 conservationists succeeded in stopping a dam in Dinosaur National Monument, but at the cost of allowing Glen Canyon Dam, completed in 1963, drowning some of the basin's most spectacular canyons. Today, the river is heavily encased in concrete and is so depleted it seldom reaches the sea.

Donald Worster

Further Reading

Fradkin, Philip. *A River No More: The Colorado River and the West*. 1981.

Hundley, Norris, Jr. *Water and the West: The Colorado River Compact and the Politics of Water in the American West*. 1975.

Reisner, Marc. *Cadillac Desert: The American West and Its Disappearing Water*. 1986.

Worster, Donald. *Rivers of Empire: Water, Aridity, and the Growth of the American West*. 1985.

See also ECHO PARK DAM; GRAND CANYON; POWELL, JOHN WESLEY; WATER ALLOCATIONS AND SHORTAGES (U.S. WEST)

Columbia River Basin

Environmental historians often point to New England as a microcosm of environmental change but the Columbia River Basin is equally worthy of such a distinction. The basin encloses a river of colossal length and enormous breadth; the mighty Columbia wends a torturous route through British Columbia and Washington. The Columbia River Basin has been the site of at least five—natural, native, commercial, industrial, and hydraulic—ecological formations over the thousands of years of its evolution. The first of these, rooted in nature's economy, had its origins over 9,000 years ago when glacial retreat, topography, and climate combined to produce a series of vegetational zones characterized by heavily forested regions in the more mountainous terrain to the north and more open grasslands along the plateaus of the south. This distinctive ecological matrix came to serve as the traditional homeland of a heterogeneous and complex collection of native bands associated with the Interior Salish and the Columbia Indians.

For a millennia, the interaction between native culture and the natural environment produced a highly durable, if constantly evolving, ecological formation in which the plants, trees, waters, and wildlife of the river basin provided the original inhabitants with both material and spiritual sustenance. European penetration of the Columbia and the consequent expansion of the fur trade into the coastal interior marked the emergence of a third ecological formation in which the natural environment of the river basin became the nexus of a commercial capitalist economy whose existence largely depended on the extraction of a single component of a complex biosphere. More than just beginning the process of commodifying nature, the fur trade was also significant for introducing a variety of European plants, animals, and diseases which effectively marginalized the animistic quality the landscape once held for the natives while at the same time demonstrating the potential for more intensive colonization in pockets of the river basin.

Eventually, the fur trade was eclipsed by the advance of the mining frontier which by stimulating permanent settlement, railway construction, and a local market for agricultural and timber products produced a fourth—industrial capitalist—ecological formation. The result was the full-scale incorporation of nature in which the natural environment no longer served as the basis of a symbiotic relationship between nature and culture, but as natural resources to be utilized in the service of economic growth and industrial development.

Indeed, the harnessing of the Columbia River for massive hydroelectric and irrigation projects throughout the twentieth century facilitated the development of a fifth—hydraulic capitalist—ecological formation which culminated in the signing of the Columbia River Treaty between Canada and the United States in 1964. Though somewhat consistent with the environmental history of the region where change and adaptation have been the norm, this last stage represents an unparalleled transformation of the lands and waters of the Columbia River Basin. Yet throughout it all, the basin has remained a unified ecological complex which even an ideology rooted in domination and exploitation could not entirely obliterate.

James Allum

Further Readings

Holbrook, Stewart. *The Columbia.* 1956.

Turner, Nancy J., et al. *Ethnobotany of the Okanagan-Colville Indians of British Columbia and Washington.* 1980.

Wilson, J.W. *People in the Way: The Human Aspects of the Columbia River Project.* 1973.

See also ASWAN HIGH DAM; COLORADO RIVER; ECHO PARK DAM; HYDROELECTRICITY; RHINE RIVER; ST. LAWRENCE RIVER

Commission of Conservation

Few Canadian governmental organizations have been as highly regarded as the Commission of Conservation. Established in 1909 as an independent agency of the Canadian government to promote the economic and efficient utilization of natural resources, the Commission has been acclaimed for its work in the areas of forest conservation, water development, town planning, public health, and wildlife protection. Yet the Commission's enduring reputation as a "proto-environmental" organization has obscured many of the tangible weaknesses in its internal operation. This has led in turn to an overestimation of its overall impact. Historians, for example, have long been impressed with the Commission's astutely constructed committee system whose membership, led by Sir Clifford Sifton, included prominent academics, industrialists, and politicians. But, as Sifton himself recognized, the Commission's formal structures and prestigious membership largely served as a front for the work of the permanent and temporary staff who, under the direction of the secretary James White, were responsible for the vast majority of the Commission's publications and recommendations on conservation issues. Despite its apparent prestige, the Commission largely consisted of a small group of technical experts who operated out of a dingy Ottawa office with few of the resources necessary to perform the tasks for which it was designed.

These weaknesses in the Commission's internal operations had three important consequences. Chief among these was that the Com-

mission had, at best, a marginal impact on public policy. Though the progressive era may well have marked the ascendancy of scientific management and social engineering, political considerations, especially those related to jurisdictional questions, dominated the public policy process on matters relating to natural resource management. Consequently, the governing elite in Ottawa demonstrated a strong disinclination to accept policy initiatives from an independent body dominated by apolitical scientific experts.

A second consequence, designed to disguise the structural deficiencies within the organization, was that the Commission engaged in an aggressive publicity campaign which, while placing the conservationist discourse at the centre of the debate over natural resource management strategies, nevertheless antagonized both the government and the bureaucracy. Indeed, the Commission's smartly bound reports, the eclectic nature of its interests, and its appeal to both lay and expert audiences had the effect of entrenching its reputation as a vital and valuable organization.

Alarmed by the threat which the "gospel of efficiency" posed to the traditional political treatment of natural resource matters and deeply envious of the Commission's public image, the government engaged in a campaign of its own to undermine the Commission's reputation. By reducing its annual budget, stripping the Commission of prominent personnel, and creating the National Research Council, the government was able to cast the Commission as a costly and duplicating organization whose original mandate had largely been subsumed by the federal bureaucracy. The third consequence of the Commission's weak internal structure, therefore, was that in 1921 the Commission of Conservation was abolished—the victim, ironically, of its own propaganda.

James Allum

Further Readings

Foster, Janet. *Working for Wildlife: The Beginning of Preservation in Canada.* 1978.

Hall, D.J. *Clifford Sifton: A Lonely Eminence, 1901–1929.* 1985.

Gillis, R. Peter, and Thomas Roach. *Lost Initiatives: Canada's Forest Industries, Forest Policy and Forest Conservation.* 1986.

See also CONSERVATION MOVEMENT; FORESTRY, HISTORY OF; RESOURCE MANAGEMENT

Common Law and the Environment

See ENVIRONMENTAL CASE LAW (CANADA): COMMON LAW CAUSES OF ACTION

Common Property Resource Management

In 1968 *Science* magazine published a paper called "The Tragedy of the Commons," written by ecologist Garrett Hardin. In that paper Hardin argued that the environment could be protected only if it was privately owned, since open access would mean that each person would maximally use the "commons" to his or her own personal advantage, with the cumulative effect being the collective overuse and destruction of the resource. Whatever Hardin may have intended, this argument has been used to support the idea that resources must be owned and used by discrete individuals, that any other socioeconomic arrangement is not sustainable.

Recently, this capitalistic argument for private property has been challenged by a growing group of social scientists and anthropologists who have discovered a great number of economic systems in which private property, far from being the norm, is either eschewed or is totally unknown. What is more, these systems have often proved sustainable through many generations, and indeed seem more sustainable than most "modern" economies, based as they are on individual, private ownership embedded in competitive market exchange systems.

"Common property" comes in several forms: 1) open-access property, where anyone (local or stranger) has free access to its usufruct; 2) state-owned property where access and use are legally limited (user fees, rents); and 3) communal property, where the local inhabitants own and collectively obtain benefit from a given resource (pasture, field, forest, water). It is the last of these that is here regarded as "managed common property."

In these latter instances (as distinct from the others), economic activity is intimately intertwined with the rest of social life. Resources and work are closely linked with personal relations, with religious ideas, and with cultural norms and expectations. Tradition often regulates not only social behavior, but resource use.

In general, common property resource management systems have three distinctive characteristics: 1) they have physical (territorial) boundaries; 2) they have a discrete membership that has access to the resource; and 3) there are shared rules for "use" and for distribution of the usufruct of the resource. These criteria are met in a wide variety of ways, depending on the nature of the resource being shared (a fishery, an irrigation system, a forest, or a whole island), and the traditions and values of the people involved.

Benefits from common property systems are often remarkable. First, they guarantee food security to all; no one starves. Further, the system is felt to be equitable by its members, which greatly reduces communal conflict and increases social stability. Often, different sets of "work teams" form to accomplish particular tasks, so each person becomes an integral member of the whole community, not of just a subset of it. Significantly, such systems are conservative in their approach to the environment, aiming at self-sufficiency rather than exploitation, which results in long-term ecological sustainability.

Common property systems are as ancient as those of the Inuit and the Japanese coastal fishing villages, and as recent as the "harbor gangs" of the Maine lobster fishermen; they are as broad in scope as an entire South Pacific island, with its surrounding lagoon and reef, and as narrow as a small irrigation system in an upland valley in Nepal, Mexico, or the Philippines.

Lessons are clearly to be learned from these common property systems relative to a sustainable future planet. One important observation is that common lands do not suffer ecological destruction so long as they remain a commons—even when they have admitted technological and economic development. For scientists, economists and development planners, trained as they are to regard common-property systems as a "hindrance" to economic progress, this is a difficult reality to accept. Yet the repeated failure, in practice, of conventional development theories suggests major new approaches are needed.

Aside from total dismantlement through external forces, common property systems can come under threat from both uncontrolled population growth (as in Fiji) or from excessive state interference (in many places). The latter comes in many forms. An obvious one is when a group of local systems is forcefully replaced by a larger, centrally managed institution, often introducing massive new technologies. Another is when governments impose regulations on individuals, such as limits on catches of fish, trees felled, or water used per hectare, which effectively displace the local, traditional rules.

Not only are such regulations often clumsy and inflexible, but they have the effect of destroying old social surveillance patterns, leading to poaching and the need for costly, often ineffective policing of the resource. With cultural breakdown comes increasing misuse of the resource, a fact governments, so far, have been slow to realize.

As stated by Fikrit Berkes and M. Taghi Farvar: "An ecosystem view of people-nature relations is a richer, more informative and ultimately more sustainable approach than a disembodied study of the resources or social institutions themselves."

Mary E. Clark

Further Readings
Berkes, Fikrit, ed. *Common Property Resources: Ecology and Community-Based Sustainable Development.* 1989.
Bromley, Daniel W., ed. *Making the Commons Work: Theory, Practice, and Policy.* 1992.
McCay, Bonnie J., and James M. Acheson, eds. *The Question of the Commons: The Culture and Ecology of Communal Resources.* 1987.

See also HARDIN, GARRETT; GREEN ECONOMICS; TRAGEDY OF THE COMMONS

Commoner, Barry

While still a graduate student at Harvard, ecologist Barry Commoner (1919–) began his career as a scientific activist, committed to the belief that scientists must advise the public and undertake research with social needs in mind. From the late 1940s to the mid-1960s, he focused his scientific and environmental activism on the danger of nuclear war and fallout. In the mid-1960s, he shifted his interest to the health of the global environment. Reflecting on the successful effort to stop above-ground nuclear testing in 1963, he called on scientists, citizens, and government administrators to help preserve the earth. By the late 1960s, he had become one of the most visible ecologists and made a career out of being an environmental crusader.

Responding to the success of ecologist Paul Ehrlich's *The Population Bomb* (1968), Commoner challenged Ehrlich's approach to political and scientific crusading, not so much on scientific grounds as on ideological and political grounds. In *The Closing Circle* (1971), Commoner argued that the environmental cri-

sis cannot be traced to biological causes such as population growth but to economic, social, and political forces. In the so-called Commoner-Ehrlich debate that followed, Commoner claimed environmentalism for the progressive left.

From the 1970s to the present in his speeches and writings Commoner continued to speak out about the economic and political crises that were the real causes of the environmental crisis. Trying to bring his scientific activism into mainstream politics, he ran for president of the United States as the Citizen's Party candidate in 1980. In his 1990 book, *Making Peace with the Planet*, Commoner reveals again his major differences with Ehrlich's philosophy. He argues that the global environmental crisis is not an ecological but a social and political problem and that socialism is the only solution. Committed to scientific and political activism, Commoner found it difficult to be pessimistic about the human future after witnessing the growth of the environmental movement in the 1960s and 1970s. His work as a scientific activist and environmentalist after World War II renewed Commoner's faith in the future of modern industrial civilization.

Chris H. Lewis

Further Readings
Commoner, Barry. *Science and Survival.* 1967.
———. *The Closing Circle.* 1971.
———. *Making Peace with the Planet.* 1990.

See also ECOSOCIALISM; ENVIRONMENTALISM; NUCLEAR WEAPONS PRODUCTION

Community Right-to-Know
See RIGHT-TO-KNOW: COMMUNITY (U.S.)

Comparative Risk

The comparative risk process is an attempt not only to assess, analyze, and understand the risks posed by the broad range of environmental problems, but also to compare and rank risks for the purposes of policy action. Comparative risk goes beyond risk analysis in five ways: 1) it is an attempt to make comprehensive judgments on all the critical risks facing a community; 2) its function is to compare and rank the risks, applying the same criteria across the board; 3) it assumes that it is as critical to recognize and analyze risks to ecosystems and to the general quality of human life as it is to focus on human health risk; 4) the process asserts that the normative values of the participants are as important to the analysis and ranking of the risks as the science and other empirical "facts" related to the perceived environmental problems; and 5) its purpose is to accomplish the risk ranking so that environmental policy can be improved with the replacement of "crisis management, inertia and conventional wisdom" with "informed judgment" (Minard 1991).

Historically, the U.S. Environmental Protection Agency (EPA) developed the comparative risk methodology in 1986; it published the first comprehensive analysis of the nation's risk entitled *Unfinished Business* in 1987. In 1990 the EPA's Science Advisory Board reviewed this analysis in their document *Reducing Risk*. Meanwhile, in 1989, three of the EPA's ten regional offices published comparative risk studies and the results of these studies encouraged the EPA to use the methodology as a tool to shift policy focus and spending from low ranked to more highly ranked risks.

The EPA also encouraged states to undertake comparative risk studies. Two of the pilot comparative risk projects were undertaken by the State of Washington, which published *The State of the Environment Report* in 1989, and the State of Vermont which published the results of its project in the 1991 document *Environment 1991: Risks to Vermont and Vermonters*. Other states soon followed the example set by Washington and Vermont. Colorado, Pennsylvania, and Louisiana were among the first states to undertake comparative risk projects. As of December 1993 twenty-two states were either planning, implementing, or conducting comparative risk projects. In addition, the cities of Seattle, Washington, Jackson, Mississippi, Houston, Texas, and Columbus, Ohio, and tribal organizations from both Wisconsin and the West, as well as Guam have experience with the comparative risk process.

A comparative risk project can be undertaken at any level of political jurisdiction (e.g., city/state/tribe/territory/nation) and usually involves a two-stage process. The first stage is the *comparative risk analysis*, which requires that assessment and ranking criteria be created for comparison of risks in three areas: 1) human health, which includes concern for both increased cancers and other health affects; 2) quality of life, which might include recreation, aesthetics, economic impact on jobs and standard of living as well as concern for future gen-

erations; and 3) health or functioning of ecosystems, which entails analysis of risk impact on exposed ecosystems, the size of area affected and length of effect as well as estimates of recovery time. The end result of this phase of the process is a final integrated ranking over all the risks perceived to be of concern by the participants.

Step two is the movement from comparative risk analysis to *comparative risk management* or the transformation of the risk ranking into a policy agenda for future action. Comparative risk management assumes that all government entities have limited funds and time to apply to the prevention, regulation or mitigation of environmental risk; the purpose of the ranking, therefore, is to help set political and budget priorities by providing normative and empirical data about environmental risks.

Although the structures set up by individual comparative risk projects are different (some have appointed directors and oversight committees to supervise the process), all have created two critical levels of organization that are the foundation of the comparative risk process: a set of technical working groups and a public advisory committee. These two entities exist to combine technical expertise and public participation at all stages of the project.

The most important component of any comparative risk project is the public advisory committee. The public advisory committee is usually given the job of generating questions about the risks affecting them and defining those environmental risks which will become part of the project ranking. They are involved in all phases of the comparative risk project and are charged with determining the final risk rankings for each subsection (health, ecosystem, and quality of life) as well as an integrated risk list that combines the three subsections into a single ranking.

Because the job of the public advisory committee is to coordinate the input of ideas into the project and to communicate the findings of the project to the public at large, it is important that the public advisory committee be as independent as possible and very open to comments and suggestions of all kinds, so that the widest possible range of views are introduced into the comparative risk process. To accomplish their task the members of the public advisory committee must study the issues in enough depth to understand and make a persuasive argument about the components of the ranking and the assigned place of any particular risk.

In addition to the public advisory committee, projects normally organize a set of technical working groups to correspond to the concerns for risk to human health, ecosystems, and quality of life. These three technical working groups are created to provide data, analysis, and information to the public advisory committee about the risks that are being considered for potential ranking. They are charged with working through the preliminary rankings of the public advisory committee and providing analysis to that committee as to how each risk affects human health, ecosystem persistence, and/or the collective quality of life. Each group is responsible to first define and rank the risks in their sector of concern, as taken from the deliberations of the public advisory committee, and then to cooperate in the compilation of a preliminary master list, ranked across categories, which is then transferred back to the public advisory committee for final action. In the end the public advisory committee will compile and communicate the final risk ranking, taking the data, analysis, and recommendations of the technical working groups as a point of departure.

The now widespread undertaking of comparative risk studies has shown that risk ranking is a valuable exercise at any level of government. Not all jurisdictions have set the same ranking or priorities, nor have they worked with identical lists of environmental risks. The completion of comparative risk projects at various levels of political jurisdiction allows policymakers to get a wide view of what risks exist and what risks are perceived, by both public and technical experts, as those most needing a policy response. Although there are guidelines and common characteristics of comparative risk studies, the final decisions on which risks count, how they will be measured, and by whom are the concerns that each individual state or community must answer for themselves. This allows the process to be comprehensive and dynamic while remaining sensitive to the distinct geographic and demographic circumstances of each project team. In all cases however, the comprehensive nature of the undertaking, as well as its focus on policy, remains a common thread.

A second phenomenon made clear in comparative risk projects is that bringing a diverse group of people together with a variety of experiences and backgrounds and making them debate and rank risks comprehensively helps to construct a coalition that can be utilized to move to the management phase and apply political action to risk priorities. In addition, by making scientists and non-scientists, technical and non-technical, and environmental professionals and citizens sit down with one another in a common effort, one produces an environment in which a variety of viewpoints and values find common principles and methods to attack public problems. The exercise of coming to terms with the normative as well as the empirical dimensions of risk, as a collective and comparative exercise, has the potential to replace decision making in isolation with integrated and comprehensive public policy argument.

Overall, the critical concern of the comparative risk process is to bring comprehensive normative and empirical analysis to the process of setting an environmental risk policy agenda. The primary purpose of the process is to provide information on environmental risk to decision makers so that policy can be formulated to deal with it.

The EPA has two regional risk centers that are available to anyone in North America for further information about risk projects and the comparative risk process:

1) The Northeast Center for Comparative Risk, c/o Vermont Law School, P.O. Box 96, Chelsea Street, South Royalton, VT 05068. Phone: (802) 763-8303, FAX: (802) 763-2920.
2) The Western Center for Comparative Risk, P.O. Box 7576, Boulder, CO 80306. Phone: (303) 494-6393, FAX: (303) 499-8340.

John Martin Gillroy

Further Readings

Minard, Richard A. *Hard Choices: States Use Risk to Refine Environmental Priorities.* South Royalton, VT: Northeast Center for Comparative Risk, 1991.

———, and Kenneth Jones. *State Comparative Risk Projects: A Force for Change.* South Royalton, VT: Northeast Center for Comparative Risk, 1993.

United States Environmental Protection Agency. *A Guidebook to Comparing Risks and Setting Priorities.* Washington, D.C.: Office of Policy, Planning and Evaluation, 1993.

United States Environmental Protection Agency. *Reducing Risk: Setting Priorities* and *Strategies for Environmental Protection*. Washington, D.C.: Science Advisory Board, 1987.

See also BENEFIT-COST ANALYSIS; ENVIRONMENTAL IMPACT ASSESSMENT; LEAST-COST UTILITY PLANNING; RISK ANALYSIS

Composting

Composting is the bacterial decomposition of biological material under aerobic conditions (i.e., ventilation with air). The bacteria should comprise acid producers usually found in manure but presumably a large number of bacteria and processes are involved. If such bacteria are absent (e.g., due to antibiotics treatment), composting does not take place. The process of composting produces heat, mostly from decomposition of carbon hydrates (the process opposite to photosynthesis).

A composting device should allow air infiltration, either by frequent re-stacking (heaps of dry biomass) or by blowing air through the biomass reservoir (e.g., in case of wet manure). Ideally, the temperature in the composting unit may reach 30 to 40 degrees centigrade above ambient temperature. This heat may be utilized by installing a heat exchanger with forced circulation but, in most cases, the ventilation and extraction of heat require as much primary energy as that contained in the heat extracted. The value of composting is thus not the energy gain but the fact that the composted product usually has much better qualities as a fertilizer than the original biomass refuse.

Bent Sørensen

Further Readings
Sørensen, Bent. *Renewable Energy*. 1979.

See also MUNICIPAL SOLID WASTE: INCINERATION; MUNICIPAL SOLID WASTE: LANDFILL

Condor

See CALIFORNIA CONDOR

Conservation Biology

Conservation biology emerged as a recognized discipline in the 1980s, given impetus and focus by two conferences with that name. Perhaps the critical moment in the formation of the discipline occurred at the Second Conference on Conservation Biology, when participants decided to form a Society for Conservation Biology to guide the development of the new field. The conference, organized by biologist Michael Soulé (who also organized the first conference), took place in Ann Arbor, Michigan, in May 1985.

In addition to Soulé, the key figures in the early organization of the society were biologists Peter Brussard, Jared Diamond, Robert May, and Katherine Ralls, political scientist David Hales, and zoo directors William Conway and George Rabb. By 1986 the society had contracted to publish a new journal, *Conservation Biology*, and had selected as its founding editor biologist David Ehrenfeld. The first issue of *Conservation Biology* appeared in June 1987; it soon was established as the central force in defining the still formative discipline and in airing and mediating its various conflicts. The society and journal grew unusually quickly—by 1993 there were 5,000 members and institutional subscribers. This evidence of vitality was confirmed by the subsequent appearance of new journals with similar themes, including Australia's *Pacific Conservation Biology* and the U.S. journal *Restoration Ecology*, by the proliferation of numerous programs in conservation biology at North American universities, and by the decision of the U.S. National Science Foundation to begin to award research grants in conservation biology.

Despite all of this enthusiasm and momentum, there is nothing entirely new in conservation biology, nor is it easily defined. The British journal *Biological Conservation* antedated the Ann Arbor meeting by more than a decade and scientists working in fields such as forestry, wildlife biology, and ecosystems ecology have been studying and writing about conservation for years. Nevertheless, conservation biology does have a recognizable identity. What distinguishes it from older conservation fields is its multidisciplinary scope and its admitted character as a mission-oriented crisis discipline.

A single study in conservation biology can move from theory to practice and can sweep all the way from molecules to landscapes. For example, a paper entitled "Population Structure of Loggerhead Turtles (*Caretta caretta*) in the Northwestern Atlantic Ocean and Mediterranean Sea," published in the December 1993 issue of *Conservation Biology*, had six authors from four institutions, ranging from a university genetics department to the Sea Turtle Protection Society of Greece. Using molecular biological techniques and other methods to determine the amount of gene flow between geographically separated nesting populations of loggerhead sea turtles, the authors concluded that there is hardly any dispersal of nesting females from one population to another. If the turtles at one nesting beach are wiped out, there is little chance that they will be replaced by nesters from other populations. Consequently, conservationists must manage and protect each nesting population as a separate unit.

Because of the highly mathematical parts of some studies in conservation biology and the frequent use of population modeling, the field has sometimes seemed overly theoretical to critics; however, a review of papers shows that most studies are rich in field data and in practical conservation recommendations. Indeed, the use of biological theory and data to shape conservation policy is a hallmark of conservation biology.

The subdisciplines most strongly represented in conservation biology are population genetics and population biology, which measure the change in genetic composition and abundance of wild and confined populations of plants and animals, and landscape ecology, which describes the changing relationship among species, natural communities, and landscapes. The latter subdiscipline makes use of the computer-based Geographic Information System and other techniques to answer questions about conservation-related landscape issues such as the consequences of habitat fragmentation on survival of various species and the advantages and disadvantages of corridors connecting nearby patches of protected habitat. Other subjects included within the boundaries of conservation biology range from philosophy and ethics to law to development to economics, yet all are tied together by and dependent upon the limiting biological factors that ultimately control the fates of all species.

During the first few years of *Conservation Biology*'s publication the majority of papers, reflecting the state of the field, concerned vertebrate species, especially endangered mammals and birds. This horizon has now broadened to include invertebrates, plants, marine ecosystems, global climatic change, paleoecology, and other subjects. Areas of future growth will probably include rapid taxonomic assessment and the biodiversity and conservation of soils and below-ground ecosystems.

Unlike other fields in biology that may contain some conservation, conservation biology is openly crisis-driven: its mission is to preserve sustainable assemblages of as much of the earth's biodiversity as it is possible to save. The metaphor of health is often invoked—Soulé has referred to conservation biologists as "physicians to nature." Because it does not claim to be value-free, conservation biology is different from ecology or geography; it more closely resembles medicine. As medicine has the goal of preserving human health and is empowered by crises of personal sickness, so conservation biology has the goal of preserving the health of the biosphere and is empowered by the looming crises of global habitat alteration and mass extinction.

David Ehrenfeld

Further Readings

Norton, Bryan G. "What is a Conservation Biologist?" *Conservation Biology* 2 (1988): 237–38.

Soulé, Michael Ellman. "Conservation Biology and the Real World." In *Conservation Biology: The Science of Scarcity and Diversity*. Ed. Michael E. Soulé. 1986, 1–12.

———. "History of the Society for Conservation Biology: How and Why We Got Here." *Conservation Biology* 1 (1987): 4–5.

See also BIODEPLETION; BIODIVERSITY; ECOLOGICAL RESTORATION; *Environmental Conservation*; HABITAT FRAGMENTATION, PATCHES, AND CORRIDORS; LANDSCAPE ECOLOGY; SEA TURTLES

Conservation Foundation

In 1947, with the support of the New York Zoological Society, Fairfield Osborn helped to found and became president of the Conservation Foundation, an organization committed to ending the destruction of the global environment and to reestablishing a balance between humanity and the natural world. Prominent scientists and conservationists such as Aldo Leopold, Paul Sears, Charles Elton, G. Evelyn Hutchinson, and Carl Sauer served on the Conservation Foundation's advisory council. As president of the Foundation, Osborn was determined to reconcile free enterprise and capitalism with ecology and conservation.

In the late 1940s and 1950s, the Conservation Foundation provided research support and a public forum for some of America's leading scientists, who wanted to make science socially responsible. In the mid-1950s, it helped fund the work of scientists such as John George, Roger Hale, Robert Rudd, and George Woodwell, who were concerned about the environmental impact of massive aerial pesticide spraying. Rachel Carson used much of this work in *Silent Spring*, her 1962 indictment of science, government, and the chemical industry. In the 1950s and 1960s, the Conservation Foundation became a major funder of environmental and conservation research. It was its refusal to engage in "political action" that allowed the Conservation Foundation to flourish under Osborn and later presidents. Its scientific research and conservation education in the 1950s and 1960s helped create public support for the creation of the Environmental Protection Agency and the Council on Environmental Quality. Drawing on the support of the Conservation Foundation, the Federation of American Scientists, the Scientists Institute for Public Information, and the Union of Concerned Scientists, scientific activists such as Carson, Woodwell, Sears, Paul Ehrlich, and Barry Commoner have worked to educate Americans about their interdependence with the natural world and the danger of uncontrolled population and economic growth.

Chris H. Lewis

Further Readings

Conservation Foundation. *A Report for the Thirtieth Year.* 1978.

Meine, Curt. *Aldo Leopold: His Life and Work.* 1988.

See also CARSON, RACHEL; COMMONER, BARRY; COUNCIL ON ENVIRONMENTAL QUALITY; EHRLICH, PAUL; ELTON, CHARLES; ENVIRONMENTAL PROTECTION AGENCY; LEOPOLD, ALDO; OSBORN, FAIRFIELD; SEARS, PAUL; UNION OF CONCERNED SCIENTISTS

Conservation Movement

The conservation movement embraces a diverse set of individuals and organizations sharing a belief that the earth's natural resources ought to be used wisely and with a view to the impact of that use on future generations.

The earliest practice of conservation is lost in antiquity. From time immemorial, aboriginal cultures around the world developed taboos that served conservation purposes, and wildlife reserves are known to have been established more than a thousand years ago. The modern conservation movement, however, was a reaction to the global spread of European technology in the nineteenth century and the massive environmental destruction that resulted. In North America forests were felled with abandon, and buffalo, which once roamed the Great Plains by the tens of millions, were nearly exterminated. These excesses attracted the attention of thoughtful Americans. In 1832 George Catlin wrote of "the probable extinction of buffaloes and Indians," and advocated a large national park where both might be preserved. Henry David Thoreau echoed Catlin's concerns in 1858, calling for "national preserves . . . in which the bear and the panther, and even some of the hunter race, may still exist, and not be 'civilized off the face of the earth.'" In 1864 George Perkins Marsh published *Man and Nature,* the earliest important text with an ecological perspective. That same year the U.S. Congress ceded the Yosemite Valley and Mariposa Big Tree Grove to the State of California "for public use, resort and recreation . . . for all time." Yellowstone National Park was created eight years later, and the first U.S. forest reserves in 1891. The American Forestry Association was begun in 1875 and the Sierra Club in 1892. Toward the end of the nineteenth century these disparate threads were woven into a fabric called the conservation movement.

Gifford Pinchot, first Chief of the U.S. Forest Service, has written that the terms "conservation" and "conservation movement" originated in 1907 among President Theodore Roosevelt's top natural resource advisors, and were coined to label their realization that all the natural resource problems were really one problem: "the use of the earth for the permanent good of man."

The intellectual and organizational unity of what came to be called the conservation movement did not survive the nineteenth century in which it was born. Conservation advocated a somewhat contradictory agenda, preaching both preservation and use. Nowhere was this division better revealed than in the persons of John Muir and Gifford Pinchot. Muir was the intellectual heir of Thoreau and Catlin. A perceptive scientist, popular author, and cofounder of the Sierra Club, Muir devoted his life to the exploration, enjoyment, and preservation of natural ecosystems around the world. Pinchot had studied scientific forestry at its source in Europe. A gifted politician, his passion was not for preservation but for wise use. In contradistinction to the more aesthetic and spiritual view of resources espoused by Muir, Pinchot's commitment to "the greatest good for the greatest number in the long run" was utilitarian and largely economic.

In 1896 Muir and Pinchot were friends and fellow travelers, but they disagreed profoundly on how the new national forests ought to be managed. By 1897 their friendship was at an end. Muir devoted the rest of his career to preservation epitomized by national parks. Pinchot devoted himself to the multiple-use and sustained-yield management of the national forests.

Although overly simplistic, many historians emphasize three eras of American conservation corresponding roughly to the presidencies of Theodore Roosevelt (1901–1909) and Franklin D. Roosevelt (1933–1945) and to the so-called environmental decade of the 1970s. Some scholars suggest that we are in the early stages of a fourth era characterized by the globalization of environmental issues.

In fact, the first era extends at least from establishment of Yellowstone National Park (1872), through creation of the first national forests, national wildlife refuges, and national monuments, to the establishment of U.S. Forest Service (1905) and the National Park Service (1916). The principal accomplishments of this era involved the reservation of public lands for public purposes and the creation of governmental agencies to protect and manage them.

The second conservation era is closely associated with Franklin Roosevelt's New Deal. Thousands were employed in the Civilian Conservation Corps. Conservation management was introduced to public grazing lands, and programs aimed at soil conservation were undertaken on private lands.

In the third era new attention was focused on the interconnectedness of environmental problems. For Americans the beginnings of this ecological awakening are often associated with the publication of *Silent Spring* (1962), Rachel Carson's study of the effects of the pesticide DDT. The most significant political manifestation of the new environmental awareness was the unprecedented public participation in celebrating the first Earth Day (1970).

The public's embrace of environmentalism produced dramatic results. The economic impact of environmental regulation grew at an unprecedented rate. Organizations in the preservation wing of the conservation movement adapted more easily than their wise-use counterparts to the new environmentalism. Some, like the Sierra Club, dramatically broadened

their political agendas. Almost all entered increasingly into broad policy coalitions to promote equally broad environmental goals. In a period of about twenty years beginning in the mid-1960s, the United States enacted legislation requiring environmental impact studies of proposed governmental actions, established the President's Council on Environmental Quality and the Environmental Protection Agency, and passed laws protecting wilderness, undammed rivers, marine environments, and endangered species. Unprecedented acreages in Alaska were designated national parks, wildlife refuges, and wilderness areas. Congress acted to regulate municipal sewage; solid, hazardous, and nuclear wastes; pesticides and toxic chemicals; national forests and BLM lands; surface mining; and the pollution of air and water.

After the environmental frenzy of the 1970s, the 1980s was a decade of consolidation. Presidents Ronald Reagan (1981–1989) and George Bush (1989–1993) regarded environmentalism primarily as a threat to economic prosperity. The undisguised hostility toward environmental regulation characteristic of the early Reagan years stimulated unprecedented growth in the memberships of major conservation organizations.

Despite its divisions and contradictions, the modern conservation movement has prospered almost everywhere. In the United States Pinchot's legacy of wise-use is alive and well in the utilitarian management principles of the Forest Service and the Bureau of Land Management and in membership groups such as the Society of American Foresters, the International Society of Fish and Wildlife Managers, the National Rifle Association, and the Soil Conservation Society of America. Preservation has been institutionalized in the National Park Service and in membership organizations such as the National Audubon Society, the Nature Conservancy, the Sierra Club, and the Wilderness Society.

Today the conservation movement has become a part of the political establishment in most industrialized nations and has an increasing presence in the international arena. Important international organizations include the United Nations Environmental Programme, the International Union for the Conservation of Nature and Natural Resources (IUCN), and the World Wildlife Fund, which have together authored a *World Conservation Strategy* (1980) emphasizing environmentally sustainable economic development. The success of international conservation efforts can be gauged by the rapidly expanding list of treaties and international agreements dealing with topics as diverse as biosphere reserves, marine mammals, seabed mining, endangered species, acid rain, and global climate stabilization.

Craig W. Allin

Further Readings

Allin, Craig W. *The Politics of Wilderness Preservation*. 1982.

Clepper, Henry. *Origins of American Conservation*. 1966.

Hays, Samuel P. *Conservation and the Gospel of Efficiency: The Progressive Conservation Movement, 1890–1920*. 1959.

Nash, Roderick. *Wilderness and the American Mind*. 1982.

See also BUREAU OF LAND MANAGEMENT; ENVIRONMENTALISM; FOREST SERVICE (U.S.); IUCN; MARSH, GEORGE PERKINS; MUIR, JOHN; NATIONAL AUDUBON SOCIETY; NATIONAL FORESTS (U.S.); NATURE CONSERVANCIES; PINCHOT, GIFFORD; SIERRA CLUB; WILDERNESS SOCIETY; YELLOWSTONE NATIONAL PARK

Conserver Society

The term "conserver society" entered the political dialogue of environmental protection in the 1970s. It was an extension of the concept of "conservation," which had emerged during the latter part of the nineteenth century, as newly created professions in such fields as agriculture, forestry, and urban planning worked to increase the efficiency of natural resource extraction and processing. The ideal of a conserver society can be understood by contrast with its opposite—the post-war "consumer societies"—whose expanding economies were based on mass production of goods, for which demand was maintained by the high wages made possible by steadily increasing productivity. Prior to the rise of modern environmentalism, critiques of consumerism were advanced in such forms as Thorstein Veblen's *The Theory of the Leisure Class* (1899) and Vance Packard's *The Waste Makers* (1963).

The concept of a conserver society includes the conservationist focus on resource-use efficiency, but also encompasses the latter stages of the extraction-manufacture-disposal process, when products reach the end of their useful life and are discarded as waste. These related themes were presented in the widely read 1977 Science Council of Canada report titled *Canada as a Conserver Society*. This report called for an interconnected series of policy initiatives in such areas as land-use, transportation, and waste management. The report called for more efficient energy use, greater recycling and re-use of products, and changes in product design to increase durability and product life. The report also drew attention to the role of advertising in stimulating consumer demand. The ideal envisaged by the Science Council may have fallen somewhat short of a true steady-state economy but was undoubtedly closer to that utopian state than to the then-current realities of the industrialized nations.

During the latter part of the 1970s and first half of the 1980s the energy and material conservation themes inherent in the "conserver society" phrase were eclipsed by pollution concerns such as acid rain, hazardous waste, and depletion of the stratospheric ozone layer. In the latter part of the 1980s, however, resource conservation and waste minimization re-emerged on the policy agenda, driven both by enhanced environmental awareness and by pending shortages of disposal capacity, which in turn were caused by the difficulties of gaining land-use and environmental approvals for disposal facilities. Thus, a 1991 speech by the Ontario Minister of the Environment stated that: "Waste reduction is the key to success in changing a consumer society into one that conserves. There are principles which, we believe, are essential to the conserver society." Those principles include: 1) conservation, defined as minimal use of materials and energy; 2) product durability; 3) true cost accounting for waste disposal; 4) accountability of the waste generator; and 5) product stewardship responsibility of the product manufacturer. The conserver society is a durable notion, one which has led the way to more contemporary conceptions such as sustainability and sustainable development.

Doug Macdonald

Further Readings

Canada as a Conserver Society, Report No. 27 of the Science Council of Canada, 1977.

Durning, Alan. *How Much Is Enough? The Consumer Society and the Future of the Earth*. 1992.

Rees, Judith. *Natural Resources: Allocation, Economics and Policy*. 2nd ed., 1990.

See also CONSERVATION MOVEMENT; NONRE-
NEWABLE RESOURCES; RECYCLING; SUSTAIN-
ABLE DEVELOPMENT; THROWAWAY MENTAL-
ITY/SOCIETY

Contingent Valuation

The Contingent Valuation (CV) method for assessing an individual's willingness to pay (WTP) for preservation or willingness to accept (WTA) loss of an environmental good has become increasingly popular in recent times. Now broadly accepted as a reliable starting point for a judicial or administrative determination of environmental damage, the technique is essentially a direct attempt to elicit environmental preferences by questionnaire. Questionnaires take the form of structured conversations which provide respondents with critical information concerning the nature of the hypothetical market in which they are participating. Depending then on the preferred survey format the inquirer poses questions such as: "What are you willing to pay for X or to prevent Y" and/or "What are you willing to accept to forego Z or to tolerate A." This open-ended format allows respondents to set their own prices. Alternative methods include dichotomous choice responses (yes or no to a presented sum), which can lead to an iterative bidding process in which the inquirer systematically raises or lowers the original offer depending on the first response. Payment cards have also been used to elicit responses from a choice of sums, however, this method is employed less commonly. Resulting survey results from all formats need econometric analysis to derive mean values of WTP bids which then may be aggregated over a relevant population.

Literature on studies carried out to date tends to suggest that most sensible results come from cases in which respondents are familiar with the asset being "valued." Further aspects of procedural validity identified in the literature concern various forms of potential bias in responses. Mitchell and Carson have identified nine types of questionnaire bias plus seventeen scenario misspecification problems. "Strategic bias" arises if respondents make bids that do not reflect their "true" values, which they may do if they think there is a "free rider" situation. Hypothetical bias arises because respondents are not making "real" transactions. Expense usually limits the number of experiments involving real money (criterion validity), but some studies exist.

A further test of validity—convergent validity—can be checked by comparing the CV method with benefit estimates derived from alternative economic methods of environmental valuation (travel cost or hedonic prices). Construct validity (verifying that the technique is consistent with the underlying economic theory of preference measurement) is debated, especially the marked divergence in many studies between WTP and WTA. Discussion of the causes of this divergence is ongoing, although it has been suggested that people essentially reply to WTA questions not in terms of prices but in terms of quantities of substitutes. If a good in question has few substitutes—the case for some wild species or, say, the respondent's own life—the amount a respondent would be willing to pay might at the limit equal his entire (finite) wealth; the amount he or she would accept as compensation could well be infinite.

The potential bias in survey results has underscored much of the debate concerning the validity of CV. Highly publicized contingent valuation exercises such as the Exxon oil spill in Alaska and the Kakadu National Park in Australia have raised the profile of hypothetical techniques. Hypothetical techniques are widely applicable since they can be used to derive values for almost any environmental change. More importantly survey techniques are the only suitable method for eliciting non-use values.

Dominic Moran

Further Readings

Hanneman, W. "Willingness to Pay and Willingness to Accept: How Much Can They Differ?" *American Economic Review* 81 (1991): 633–47.
Mitchell, R.C., and R.T. Carson. *Using Surveys to Value Public Goods: The Contingent Valuation Method.* 1989.
"A Price on the Priceless." *The Economist* (August 17, 1991).

See also BENEFIT-COST ANALYSIS; GREEN ECONOMICS; PUBLIC OPINION AND THE ENVIRONMENT

Convention on International Trade in Endangered Species of Wild Fauna and Flora

See CITES

Coral Reefs

Coral reefs are located throughout the tropical seas within the waters of 109 nations. They have existed as an ecosystem variety for perhaps 450 million years. As an ecosystem they are unbelievably complex and provide home to an amazing variety of creatures—the level of biodiversity is exceeded only within the collective tropical rainforests of the world. Coral reefs create coral islands and contribute to the creation of sand beaches. As well, they serve as protective barriers for many land areas, coastal marshes, and mangrove swamps. But most important they are incredibly productive of life in a myriad of forms, both beautiful and beautifully grotesque.

Corals themselves are tiny animals dependent on even tinier algae called zooxanthellae. Charles Darwin was among the first to realize that corals were not in themselves a type of plant life. There are thousands of coral species, some reef building, some not. There are a seemingly endless variety of coral forms and structures—platelike forms, fans, whips, staghorns, "brains"—some reaching to thousands of years in age. Coral reefs grow only in warm, shallow waters often near to the maximum temperatures and minimum oxygen levels that they can tolerate. Many types are vulnerable to warming (or cooling) and to turbidity or sedimentation. Some varieties, however, can withstand temperature ranges from 13 degrees Celsius to 38 degrees Celsius.

There has been increasing concern in recent decades for the health of the biological communities living within coral reefs and for the reefs themselves. Coral reefs and the ecosystems that they support are vulnerable to a variety of changes within the natural world. Particularly notable is the damage that can take place during severe tropical storms. This type of damage is not the major concern, however, since coral reef ecosystems have evolved the means to recover from these and other severe natural events. There is some evidence, for example, that coral can spread by attaching themselves to floating materials from volcanic eruptions. A more serious threat to the coral reefs and their inhabitants involves the variety of direct and indirect human assaults taking place in many locations. There are still other of our interventions that may be damaging but to what extent we do not fully understand because we do not know very well either the natural history of coral reefs or their biodynamics.

Five kinds of human threat or potential threat can be identified, some painfully obvious, others more subtle and uncertain. The five are: 1) direct assaults such as mining, dredging, and turbidity and sedimentation from land-based forestry and agricultural activities; 2) overfishing and poor fisheries practices; 3) the introduction of sewage and/or toxic chemicals; 4) ecologically harmful removals of animal species from coral ecosystems; and 5) the possible effects of climate warming. The first two of these are the least subtle and most easily demonstrable of negative human interventions. They are all too frequent occurrences.

Turbidity in the water can result from land-based practices such as mining, agriculture, deforestation, or road-building, or sea-based activities such as dredging or extraction of limestone or aggregates from the coral reef itself. The latter of these practices may seem particularly rapacious, but it does sometimes happen when roads, tourist facilities, or other structures are built on small islands where there are few land-based sites available. Another occurrence on small islands is that roads frequently are built along the coast, resulting in siltation of nearby waters. Turbidity reduces photosynthesis and thereby the food supply for the coral animals themselves. Siltation interferes with coral larvae when they attempt to attach themselves and thus impedes the formation of new colonies. Elkhorn coral is particularly vulnerable to siltation.

Recreational overfishing has been a problem in some locations, particularly the hunting of large, slow-moving species with spear guns. Commercial fishing is more problematic generally and this includes the catching of fish for the aquarium trade (though freshwater fish are in greater demand for this purpose). Perhaps the most threatened of harvested coral reef species is, however, the giant clam removed primarily for decorative purposes and the tourist trade. The greatest threat to the reef itself associated with fishing is the practice of dynamite fishing, taking place most prominently in Tanzania and the Philippines. This practice is one of desperation or stupidity or both. It routes fish from their hiding places, but it soon undermines the fishery itself and the ecosystem that sustains it.

There are a variety of ways that humans introduce harmful chemicals to the coral reef environment. The most common assault is via sewage—billions of liters of sewage are emitted into the ocean environment daily. In addition excess nutrients are also introduced via agricultural runoff. Coral reefs are vulnerable to excessive nutrients which result in too thick algae and thick growth of seaweed. Another common source of chemical assault is via oilspills. Little is known, however, about the effects of the release of industrial chemicals within coral reef environments. This suggests perhaps that these latter problems at least are not rampant thus far.

Other human disturbances of the coral reef sometimes involve the removal of predator species with resultant explosions in the population of sea urchins or crown-of-thorns starfish (*Acanthaster planci*). The latter species feed directly on coral and it has been argued by some researchers that the prior removal of large numbers of giant tritons for their shells contributed to population explosions of the coral-eating starfish. It has not been widely accepted by researchers that this particular threat has been either widespread or permanent. However, ecological disruptions are from time to time likely given the numbers of humans and the range of desires that are met by human extractions of living creatures from the reefs around the world. This assault is one often oblivious to the complex interactions of the undersea world. Indeed, there is a very great deal about the ecology of the coral reefs that is simply not understood. We do not know if the coral reef diebacks and recoveries that now occur are within the range of long-term historic norms. It is plausible that they are not. We do know, for example, that the removal of predators of sea urchins through overfishing has been highly problematic for coral reef ecology in several locations.

Finally, it is known that some coral reefs are vulnerable to temperature increases, especially increases in summer maximum temperatures. Coral reef bleaching incidents were associated with 1-degree Celsius increases in French Polynesia in 1991 and with 2-degree Celsius increases off Thailand. Thus it is suggested that some coral reefs are or will be vulnerable to climate warming. Recently it has been asserted by several scientists that warmer temperatures are indeed the cause of recent increases in coral bleaching and diebacks in the Caribbean and elsewhere. These coral formations are claimed as the first casualties of climate warming. One cannot be certain at this point, particularly because sea temperature records have not been kept for very long periods in most locations. Nonetheless this and the total array of human-source impacts on coral reef ecology are enough to warrant more effective international protections.

Robert Paehlke

Further Readings

Brower, Kenneth. "State of the Reef." In *1990 Audubon Nature Yearbook*. Ed. Les Line. 1989.

Wells, Sue, and Nick Hanna. *The Greenpeace Book of Coral Reefs*. 1992.

See also CLIMATE WARMING; ECOSYSTEMS; EUTROPHICATION; FISHERIES CONSERVATION; FOOD CHAINS; OIL SPILLS; SEDIMENTATION; WEB OF LIFE

Corridors (Wildlife)

See HABITAT FRAGMENTATION, PATCHES, AND CORRIDORS

Cost-Benefit Analysis

See BENEFIT-COST ANALYSIS

Costle, Douglas

See ENVIRONMENTAL PROTECTION AGENCY

Cougars: Conservation and Habitat

The Eastern cougar or Eastern panther, the Florida panther, and the Costa Rican panther are all endangered cougar subspecies listed in the Convention on International Trade in Endangered Species of Wild Fauna and Flora (CITES) Appendix I since 1975 as well as under the protection of the U.S. Endangered Species Act. Two other subspecies (the Yuma puma and the Wisconsin puma) are also rare but most of the subspecies of Western North America seem to have retained viable population levels despite human assaults on many varieties. Cougars once inhabited the entire range of the United States and the southern portions of Canada from coast to coast. Their wild habitat is now limited to Alberta, British Columbia, and all the states west of (and including) Montana, western South Dakota, Wyoming, Colorado, New Mexico, and Texas. There is a small pocket of threatened Florida panthers in southern Florida and there have been a few recent sitings in the eastern Canadian provinces of New Brunswick and Nova Scotia.

Cougars are lone predators and require a large range, from 25 to 500 square miles for males and from 8 to 400 square miles for females. The great variation is dependent essentially on how plentiful are the prey of the cougar. Cougars will eat almost any animal species—from insects to moose, rabbits and squirrels to bobcats, bears, and other cougars, mice and turkeys to dogs, cattle, sheep, and horses. Their inability or disinclination to respect what humans deem as their animal "property" has been a key basis for hunting, threatening the well-being and the very existence of cougars. The last wild cougar in the state of Vermont was killed in 1881; the last cougar in Pennsylvania was killed in 1891.

Cougars throughout the remaining portions of North America have been subjected to bounties, poisoning attempts, systematic slaughter by employees of the U.S. government, and the open loathing (for a considerable time) of America's conservationist president, Teddy Roosevelt. In Arizona, for example 2,400 cougars were slain as "undesirable predators" between 1918 and 1947. Thereafter a $50 to $100 bounty was added and 5,400 were killed by 1969. In California the bounty kill took out 12,452 cougars between 1907 and 1963. Poisoned baits were favored in the 1930s and 1940s and killed all kinds of animals including eagles, but, ironically, bypassed most cougars who prefer to kill their own fresh meals. U.S. government employees, as part of an animal damage control policy, killed 7,255 cougars between 1937 and 1970. (They also killed 477,104 bobcats and millions of coyotes.) President Reagan permitted the restoration of poisonings for anything which might threaten domestic animals even occasionally.

But generally since the 1960s cougars have gained at least some favor from some state and provincial governments. They were reclassified from injurious predators to game animals in Washington, Utah, California, Alberta, and British Columbia and later other states. This afforded cougars the protection of a need for a permit, the imposition of a limited hunting season, and a bag limit (usually one cougar per person per year). In 1990 though, by referendum, the state of California voted to disallow all sport hunting of cougars. Other states and provinces have not followed suit. Indeed most still permit or do not even enforce rules against "will-call" hunting of cougars, whereby professional guides (with dogs) chase a cougar up a tree and then phone the "hunter" (at the office or elsewhere). The dogs keep the cougar up the tree until the hunter arrives (via offroad vehicle or helicopter or whatever) and shoots the cougar still sitting in a tree. This may in some cases pose a challenge to his or her abilities as a marksperson.

Despite the protections being implemented several thousand cougars are still shot in the wild each year. But the game laws and the removals of the bounties may have helped to stabilize their numbers in some Western states and provinces. Their survival is uncertain; they have survived thus far only because they are elusive creatures, disinclined to human detection. Even so, cougars do from time to time attack humans. Ten fatal attacks and forty-three injuries were recorded between 1890 and 1990, half of them in British Columbia. In contrast in 1989 alone deer were involved in 130 human fatalities, mostly in automobile accidents. Cougars are protected through the Mountain Lion Foundation and other conservation organizations.

Robert Paehlke

Further Readings

Hansen, Kevin. *Cougar: The American Lion.* 1992.

Smith, R.H., ed. *Proceedings of the Third Mountain Lion Workshop.* 1989.

See also CITES; ENDANGERED SPECIES ACT (U.S.); FLORIDA PANTHER; HABITAT FRAGMENTATION, PATCHES, AND CORRIDORS; TOP PREDATORS IN CANADA: AN OVERVIEW; WILDLIFE PROTECTION: HISTORY

Council on Environmental Quality

The Council on Environmental Quality (CEQ) is a small agency of the U.S. federal government located in the executive office of the president. It was created by the National Environmental Policy Act (NEPA), which was signed by President Nixon on January 1, 1970. CEQ has had a crucial role in U.S. environmental policy development and coordination since 1970 but continues to lead a precarious existence. Because of its size and mission it has developed few powerful friends and protectors in the Congress or among the administrative agencies. It has been neither understood nor appreciated by new presidents and has several times been the target of presidential reorganization proposals.

By law the CEQ is to be composed of three members appointed by the president and subject to confirmation by the Senate, although it has frequently functioned with fewer than three members. The statutory duties and functions of CEQ, as specified in NEPA, are to prepare an annual environmental quality report, to gather information and conduct studies, to review and appraise programs and activities of the federal government, and to offer environmental policy advice and recommendations to the president. Part of the research mission of CEQ was transferred to the new Environmental Protection Agency (EPA) during the Nixon administration.

Another responsibility of CEQ, which was not clearly specified in NEPA and which has evolved under several presidents, is oversight of the implementation of NEPA, particularly with respect to requirements for doing environmental impact assessment. In 1970–1973, CEQ issued guidelines to federal agencies for the preparation of environmental impact statements. By executive order under President Carter, CEQ was vested with authority to issue binding regulations governing implementation of NEPA. Those regulations became effective in 1979 and a major role of CEQ since has been to provide interpretation and guidance for the federal agencies. CEQ has ongoing responsibility for monitoring and evaluating the effectiveness of the regulations. CEQ also is responsible for resolving disputes among agencies involving environmental impact assessment.

President Nixon, whose administration in 1969 had opposed the legislative creation of CEQ, nevertheless appointed a distinguished first Council, with competence in law, science, and public information (Russell Train, chair, Gordon McDonald, and Robert Cahn). CEQ was established almost a year earlier and was deeply involved in the creation of the EPA. Especially in the period from 1970 to 1973, CEQ played a major role in the development of the federal government's environmental policies and programs ranging from legislative initiatives to executive actions to international negotiations.

In terms of public profile and in many areas of policy influence, CEQ was gradually eclipsed by the much larger EPA. Nevertheless, the position of CEQ in the executive office of the president, its statutory foundation, and its independent oversight and advisory role have permitted it to continue to be effective in ways unavailable to line departments or agencies such as EPA.

Succeeding Train as chair in the 1970s were Russell Peterson, then Charles Warren, and later Gus Speth. Other council members under presidents Nixon, Ford, and Carter tended to be less eminent than the initial appointments.

At the beginning of President Carter's term his reorganization advisors recommended that CEQ and all its staff be transferred to the Department of the Interior. Carter opted instead to retain CEQ and assign it additional responsibilities. In addition to the NEPA regulations, for example, Carter designated CEQ and the State Department to be the lead agencies for the pioneering *Global 2000 Report*, issued in July 1980. By the end of Carter's presidency CEQ's professional staff had grown to more than fifty persons.

In 1981 the Reagan administration considered abolishing CEQ entirely but instead fired the entire professional staff and reduced its budget by nearly three-fourths. Nevertheless, CEQ was still able to exert some limited policy influence behind the scenes in the Reagan administration, particularly after the scandals that led to new appointments to head the EPA and Interior Department in 1983. A 1981 review of CEQ by the General Accounting Office found that it was effective and that its "role is unique and is best filled by the current arrangements."

In the 1980s, under presidents Reagan and Bush, CEQ appointees tended not to be "exceptionally well qualified" by training, experience, and attainments (qualifications specified by NEPA). Under President Bush, the staff of CEQ again grew modestly, to approximately thirty persons.

In 1993 the CEQ was again threatened by the reorganization zeal of a new administration, as President Clinton proposed to replace CEQ with a White House Office on Environmental Policy and to shift some of its responsibilities to the EPA. Because CEQ was established by statute, its formal abolition required amending NEPA. Legislation to replace CEQ with an Office of NEPA Compliance and to elevate the EPA to a cabinet department was considered by Congress as a modification of the original administration plan.

Robert V. Bartlett

Further Readings

Caldwell, Lynton K. *Science and the National Environmental Policy Act: Redirecting Policy Through Procedural Reform.* 1982.

Liroff, Richard A. *A National Policy for the Environment: NEPA and Its Aftermath.* 1976.

Train, Russell E. "Foreword." *Environmental Quality: Twentieth Annual Report.* Council on Environmental Quality, 1990.

Courts and the Environment

See ENVIRONMENTAL CASE LAW (CANADA):
COMMON LAW CAUSES OF ACTION; ENVIRON-
MENTAL CASE LAW: UNITED STATES

Cousteau, Jacques-Yves

Commandant Cousteau is a famous naval officer, oceanographer, and marine environment
conservationist who has spent most of his life
exploring, filming, and defending the undersea
world. He has undertaken more than 150 marine exploring missions and is now president of
the Cousteau Society/Équipe Cousteau. Born on
June 11, 1910, in Saint-André de Cubzac
(Gironde), he joined the French Navy in 1930,
and had navigated around the world by the time
he was twenty-two. In 1943, he co-invented the
Cousteau-Gagnan Aqualung, a self-contained
breathing apparatus which gives underwater
explorers a large degree of autonomy. After
World War II, he founded the French Navy's
Undersea Research Group in Toulon and, in
1950, acquired his legendary ship, the Calypso.
In this ship he has explored numerous marine
environments, starting with the Red Sea, the
Mediterranean, the Persian Gulf, the Black Sea,
and the Atlantic. Since 1985, he has also used
a more modern wind-powered ship, the Alcy-
one, for some of his expeditions. A new ship,
called Calypso II, will replace the old Calypso,
which will be scuttled at sea rather than transformed into a marine museum.

Cousteau's documentary on his sea adven-
tures, *The Silent World*, won both a top prize
at the Cannes Film Festival in 1956, and an
Oscar in 1957 for best documentary—a feat he
repeated a few years later with *The Golden
Fish*. He also won a third Oscar in 1965 for
World Without Sun. In 1957, he left the French
Navy to become director of the Oceanographic
Museum of Monaco, a post he held until 1988.
From 1966 to 1988 he was also secretary general of the International Commission for the
Scientific Exploration of the Mediterranean. In
the course of his activities, he helped develop
many original marine life observation techniques, including the bathyscaphe, the
turbosail, diving saucers, undersea dwellings
and underwater cameras, as well as a one-per-
son jet-propelled submarine.

His first television documentary, *The
Sharks* (1967), which aired in January 1968 as
part of the television series *The Undersea World
of Jacques-Yves Cousteau*, was a huge success
in the United States, as were other documenta-
ries such as *Desert Whales* (1969) and *The
Tragedy of the Red Salmon* (1970). In 1968
Cousteau was made a member of the American
Academy of Sciences and, in 1970, he obtained
honorary doctorates from Berkeley and from
Brandeis.

In 1974 following some financial difficulties in France resulting from the failed construction of an ultra-modern submarine called
Argyronète, Cousteau moved to the United
States. There he founded the Cousteau Society
in order to be able to finance his Calypso expeditions and to distribute his television films on
the marine environment and the need to protect
it from the degradation perpetrated on it by
humans. Other Cousteau enterprises have not
been financially successful, from his plan to
transform the *Queen Mary* into a marine museum in California to his efforts to create
Cousteau Oceanic parks in Norfork, Virginia,
and in Les Halles in Paris. His television docu-
mentaries, however, continue to be immensely
popular, including his recent *The Mirage of the
Sea*, which was first shown at the Rio Summit
in June 1992. Cousteau was acclaimed as a hero
at the NGO Global Forum in Rio's Flamengo
Park.

Cousteau explored coastal waters of
Newfoundland, the St. Lawrence and the
Saguenay rivers, and the Great Lakes in 1980,
and produced two films on Canada in 1982,
Les pièges de la mer and *Du grand large aux
Grands Lacs*. In 1988, he produced another
one called *Au pays des totems vivants*, and the
Canadian government issued a $100 com-
memorative gold coin in honor of his work for
the exploration and protection of the marine
world. That same year he was elected to the
prestigious French Academy. More recently
Cousteau has started a new venture called
New Orientations for Ecotechnology (NOE),
an educational project linking economics, ecology, social sciences, and technology in an effort to improve the earth's habitability for future generations.

Cousteau has written more than forty
books (including a twenty-volume encyclopedia
on oceans in 1974 and the Cousteau Almanac
of the Environment in 1981). Over the years, he
has produced (and starred in) over 100 movies
on nature, and published many articles in *Na-*

tional *Geographic Magazine* and in his magazine *Calypso Log*, which appears both in French and in English. His numerous campaigns for the protection of whales, of sharks and of forests, for the preservation of Antarctica, the Danube, and many other bodies of water and land, and more recently for the rights of future generations of humans to live in a cleaner environment have attracted wide attention and sympathy. His petition on this last issue has collected more than 3 million signatures in France alone. His aim is to present it to the United Nations in order to get the General Assembly to vote a Declaration of the Rights of Future Generations similar to the Declaration of Human Rights.

Cousteau's struggle against overpopulation and for the need to stabilize the earth's population at a level of about 2 billion people has recently attracted some criticism from people who see him as more preoccupied with animals, trees, and future human beings than with existing human beings. In a November 1991 article in the *UNESCO Courrier* he is quoted as saying: "It is a terrible thing to say. The world's population must be stabilized and, for that, it would be necessary to eliminate 350,000 people a day." Few contemporary environmentalists take such a conservative and anti-humanist neomalthusian position. On the other hand, Cousteau is not as conservative as his critics picture him. At a recent preparatory conference leading to the 1994 Cairo Conference on Population and Development, Cousteau is quoted as saying that necessary funds for population programs could be mobilized from existing military budgets.

Jean-Guy Vaillancourt

Further Readings
Cousteau, Jacques-Yves. *Le monde du silence: le voyage de la Calypso.* 1957.
Jacquier, Henri. *Le troisième fluide ou l'aventure financière du commandant Cousteau.* 1993.
Violet, Bernard. *Cousteau, une biographie.* 1993.

See also COASTAL DEBRIS AND CLEANUP; DOLPHINS AND PORPOISES; FISHERIES CONSERVATION; MARINE MAMMALS

Crocodilians
See EVERGLADES OF SOUTH FLORIDA; REPTILES: CONSERVATION AND HABITAT

Cropping Systems: Environmental Implications
Design of a cropping system involves the deliberate manipulation of a natural environment and landscape to provide food, feed, fiber, or raw materials for human or domestic animal use. Choice of crops and planting systems has focused on maximizing the output of crops and income per unit of land, labor, or other scarce resource. Until recently the major emphasis has been on short-term productivity and profits, increasing food for a growing global population, and improving technology for predominant monoculture cropping systems. Today there is growing awareness of the finite supply of non-renewable resources, the unintended off-farm effects of farming, and the long-term implications of increasing human population and its potential impact on the environment. Increased concern about the future of high fossil fuel inputs in agriculture and other sectors of the global economy has led to interest in agroecology and sustainable development. Because of the central role of food for human survival, there is now a shift in focus toward a sustainable agriculture.

Environmental implications of cropping systems begin with the division of agricultural regions with political and property lines that rarely correspond to natural features in the landscape. Section lines each mile in the United States do not respect natural land forms, and the rectangular fields we design within those sections are primarily to accommodate large mechanized equipment. These political divisions and human-designed boundaries have led to labor- and machine-efficient cultivation techniques that go up and down slope, across low areas and natural waterways, and parallel to field boundaries, with little respect for the landscape. More environmentally conscious design of systems includes contour cropping to prevent soil erosion, diversification of crops within a farm and field to provide habitat for beneficial insects, and crop rotations to enhance soil fertility and reduce use of pesticides. Seeding of waterways, planting shrubs and trees as filter strips along streams, and connection of non-cultivated areas from one farm to the next to provide wildlife corridors are some methods used to lessen the environmental impact that is encouraged by ecologically arbitrary human divisions of the landscape.

Soil management for cropping systems includes land preparation, planting and crop cultivation, and providing sufficient nutrients for adequate crop production. Over the past 200 years a sophisticated process has evolved to include primary land preparation through plowing and disking, weed management with herbicides and cultivation, planting crops in rows with mechanized equipment, and application of large quantities of chemical fertilizers to provide nutrients. Environmental impacts of this approach have included massive erosion of topsoil due to action of wind and rainfall, loss of some pesticides and nutrients with water runoff from heavy rainfall events, and leaching of some soluble nutrients, pesticides, and breakdown products through the soil profile and vadose zone into the groundwater. These are unintended effects of current cropping systems and they reduce profits by increasing input costs as well as causing large-scale environmental degradation that will eventually be paid by society. Reduced tillage and increased residue from crops left on the soil surface can drastically reduce runoff, thus loss of soil, nutrients, and water. Band application of herbicides rather than complete coverage with a broadcast application, coupled with timely cultivation can reduce the environmental costs of weed management. Careful soil testing and setting realistic yield goals can lead to reduced nutrient application rates and less potential for contamination of the groundwater, especially by nitrate. Such changes are being implemented by farmers for economic as well as environmental reasons.

Monoculture systems have led to some environmental problems. Continuous cropping of favored cereals (i.e., rice in lowland Asia, maize in Central North America, wheat in Northern Africa) has required increasing applications of fertilizers and pesticides to maintain productivity. These monoculture crop systems have received the majority of attention by agricultural researchers and by companies that provide fertilizers and pesticides. The Green Revolution that resulted in substantial increases in cereal grain production (i.e., wheat, rice, maize, grain sorghum) has reduced cost of food in some countries and helped to alleviate hunger in parts of the developing world. However, monoculture systems could be called a short-term solution that allows farmers to dominate the natural environment for immediate production gains with a large investment of fossil fuel based production inputs. Too often this domination leads to ignoring the biological cycling and efficiencies of resource use that occur in natural ecosystems. Crop rotations and mul-

tiple cropping systems provide benefits in soil fertility and pest protection that are not available in monocultures. Use of green manure crops and animal manure or compost obviates the need for large importation of chemical fertilizers. Often these external resources such as fertilizers have a high energy cost for production, transportation, and application to fields. Learning from dominant ecosystems in each place can provide clues in the design of more complex cropping systems that make more efficient use of production resources.

Control of weeds, insects, plant pathogens (causing diseases), and nematodes (parasites) in monoculture systems is complicated by the selection of pest species that are resistant to known chemical products. While only a few dozen pest species resistant to pesticides had been identified up to about three decades ago, there are now reports of close to 1,000 known pests that are resistant to the available arsenal of pesticides. There is no doubt about the efficacy of chemical pesticides applied at the right time if they can target an undesirable pest, yet farmers and industry are caught in a vicious circle that requires continuous search for new products to control an accelerating array of undesirable species that limit production. The alternative is to carefully scout fields and identify specific problems that need treatment, and to design an integrated pest management program that will combine the potentials of genetic resistance in crops, rotation of crop species, multiple cropping to provide diversity and homes for favorable predators, choice of planting dates and methods, and judicious use of minimal application of chemical or biological pesticide where absolutely needed. This will reduce costs to the producer as well as environmental impact of products arriving where they are not wanted. It will also slow the evolution of pest species to biotypes or strains that are resistant to known products.

Integration of crop and animal production systems provides another type of biological efficiency that cannot be realized in monoculture cropping. Use of crop residues for livestock grazing during winter months in the higher latitudes, and primary reliance on forages and grazing provide low-cost feed sources as well as leaner meat than that produced on only grain. Livestock can harvest some fields and areas that are not easily farmed, and can take advantage of some feedstuffs such as low-quality hay or roughage that has little other value on the farm. Manure from grazing animals enhances the organic matter and fertility of the soil. Animal manure, which is considered a burdensome waste product in areas where animals are confined and concentrated, should instead be considered a valuable resource. The combination of crops and livestock provides a wider range of products for sale, thus buffering the variations in weather and prices that cause financial difficulties for farmers in most countries. These efficiencies of cropping system design can not only contribute to profitability, but also to a reduction in the negative environmental impact of many of today's prevalent cropping practices.

Charles A. Francis

Further Readings

Edwards, C.A., et al. *Agriculture and the Environment.* 1993.

Hatfield, J.L., and D.L. Karlen. *Sustainable Agriculture Systems.* 1994.

See also AGRICULTURE: ENVIRONMENTAL IMPACTS; AGROFORESTRY; BIOACCUMULATION; ENERGY EFFICIENCY IN AGRICULTURE; HERBICIDES; NO-TILL AGRICULTURE; PESTICIDES; SOIL CONSERVATION; SUSTAINABLE AGRICULTURE

D

Daniels, Farrington

Farrington Daniels (1889–1972), a physical chemist, was a major advocate of solar energy from the late 1940s through the 1950s and 1960s, conducting research and writing technical and popular articles and books for wide audiences. He stressed particularly that less developed countries could use solar energy to raise their living standards, especially in rural areas.

Born in Minneapolis, Daniels earned his Ph.D. from Harvard University and after some teaching and government research moved to the University of Wisconsin at Madison in 1920, retiring in 1959. A distinguished chemist, he served in the 1950s as the president of the American Chemical Society.

Late in World War II, Daniels worked at the Metallurgical Laboratory in Chicago, part of the Manhattan Project to build the first nuclear weapon, and stayed on for a year after the war as the director of the new Argonne National Laboratory. He designed the Daniels pile, a prototype civilian nuclear power reactor, but resigned from the lab in part due to frustration that the government was more interested at the time in the military uses of nuclear power and unwilling to invest heavily in civilian power plants. Upon his return to Madison in 1947 he took up solar energy as one of his research tasks.

Daniels established a solar energy research lab at the university and actively promoted solar outside of academia. He helped found the Association for Applied Solar Energy, later the International Solar Energy Society, serving as president. His 1964 book, *Direct Use of the Sun's Energy*, became a popular work, both explaining how various solar technologies worked and arguing for more attention to them.

He lectured widely on solar energy, and traveled to less developed countries to lecture and consult with scientists and engineers on problems in utilizing solar energy.

Frank N. Laird

Further Readings
Daniels, Farrington. *Direct Use of the Sun's Energy.* 1964. Reprinted by Ballentine Press, 1974.

See also SOFT ENERGY PATHS; SOLAR ENERGY

Danube River

See EASTERN EUROPE: ENVIRONMENTAL PROBLEMS

Darling, Jay Norwood "Ding"

In the course of a fifty-year journalism career that began in 1900, Jay Norwood Darling became the most widely known and respected political cartoonist of his day. He achieved equal fame, however, for his important contributions to conservation as an illustrator, administrator, and advocate.

Born in Michigan in 1876, Darling grew up in Iowa, where he developed the strong love of duck hunting that became the basis for his lifelong commitment to conservation. Darling had intended to pursue a career in medicine but after completing college found himself employed as a reporter. Sidetracked into cartooning, he soon cultivated a unique style and editorial perspective that gained a wide public following. Known to his readers by the contracted nickname "Ding," Darling reached a national audience from his base at the Des

Moines *Register* and eventually received two Pulitzer Prizes for his work.

Through his daily cartoons Darling often delivered strong conservation messages. In particular he brought attention to the plight of declining waterfowl populations in the late 1920s and helped to stimulate national-level reforms. In 1934 Darling was appointed (along with publisher Thomas Beck and Aldo Leopold) to Franklin Roosevelt's Committee on Wild Life Restoration. Their report outlined ways of integrating wildlife conservation with other New Deal initiatives.

Darling's work on the committee led to an invitation from Roosevelt to become director of the U.S. Bureau of Biological Survey (BBS), forerunner of the Fish and Wildlife Service. Despite reservations—Darling was active nationally in Republican Party politics—he agreed to serve, and became head of the BBS in 1934. Although his tenure at the BBS lasted less than two years it was an important turning point in the administration of wildlife conservation programs in the United States. Darling succeeded in reinvigorating the Bureau, securing increased funds for its programs, enlarging the wildlife refuge system, and promoting scientific research and education on conservation problems.

Darling's most active years as a conservation leader came during the last three decades of his life. From the mid-1930s until his death in 1962 he remained deeply involved in conservation policy debates, devoting himself especially to improving education on conservation issues, and to efforts to unite conservation organizations for more effective representation. In 1965 the National Wildlife Federation, which he was instrumental in founding, chose him as one of the first initiates in its Conservation Hall of Fame.

Curt Meine

Further Readings
Lendt, David L. *Ding: The Life of Jay Norwood Darling*. 1984.

See also CONSERVATION MOVEMENT; DEPARTMENT OF THE INTERIOR (U.S.); LEOPOLD, ALDO; NATIONAL WILDLIFE FEDERATION; WATERFOWL: CONSERVATION AND HABITAT; WILDLIFE PROTECTION: HISTORY

Darwin, Charles
Modern ecological thinking has its roots in the scientific theories of Charles Darwin (1809–

1882), the greatest naturalist of the nineteenth century. Before Darwin observers of nature regarded the flora and fauna as stable, fixed parts of an ideal design. In Christian Europe and America the designer was most commonly seen as a benevolent God. That view assumed humans could do little to upset the order of nature; all their disturbances were merely rearrangements of the parts, not threats to the design. Each species, it was believed, worked for the good of others as much as for itself, and all worked for the good of humankind. But Darwin shook that assumption to its core. After him the order of life on the planet came to be seen as the result of struggle, competition, adaptation, and opportunism. What Darwin called "the web of life" showed no design or conscious plan, only the individualistic strivings of independent species.

Darwin's new perception of nature was influenced by the rapid economic changes going on in his native England and by his travels to South America and the Pacific Islands, particularly the Galápagos archipelago, where he found strange creatures living in an alien landscape. He searched for natural explanations of their forms and interactions. A student of the Reverend Robert Thomas Malthus, he was impressed with the imbalance between the power of the earth to produce food and the power of species to reproduce themselves; those whose offspring survive the competition for resources are the "fittest." In 1859 he published his revolutionary work, *On the Origin of Species*, followed in 1871 by *The Descent of Man*. Together, they provided a naturalistic mechanism for understanding how new species come into being, why some species become extinct, how and why they are distributed geographically as they are, and how the interdependencies in nature evolve. Darwin called his theory "evolution through natural selection." Following its appearance, the science of ecology also emerged to study the interactions of plants and animals with each other and with the inorganic environment over time.

Darwin, who lived before the conservation movement began, saw this designless process as benign and progressive. Like other Victorians he applauded the march of civilization, the triumph of technology over wild and savage continents. Nowhere did he call for any restraint on man's economic behavior. However, he also found an impressive kind of order in nature— an order commanding respect—though it was completely the result of species pursuing their own ends. And he did see that his theory of evolution implied a sense of kinship linking humans and other species, "our fellow brethren." Moreover, he was a man of passionate enthusiasm for natural beauty. Darwin's tangled legacy, therefore, was that, in removing the sense of permanence and sacredness from "the Creation," he made it possible for humans either to take ruthlessly whatever they wanted for their own aggrandizement or to create a new secular ethic to restrain their impact on a vulnerable earth.

Donald Worster

Further Readings

Bowles, Peter. *Charles Darwin: The Man and His Influence.* 1990.

Worster, Donald. *Nature's Economy: A History of Ecological Ideas.* 1977.

Young, Robert M. *Darwin's Metaphor: Nature's Place in Victorian Culture.* 1985.

See also EVOLUTION; MALTHUS, ROBERT THOMAS; WEB OF LIFE

DDT

See BIOACCUMULATION; PESTICIDES

Debt-for-Nature Swaps

Emerging in the 1980s, debt-for-nature swaps were a response to two coinciding trends: the huge foreign debt of less-developed nations and international concern for environmental degradation in those same countries, especially the destruction of large forests. The exchanges convert the unpaid debt of developing countries into conservation activities in those countries. In the swap a bank holding a country's debt sells it at a deep discount (or contributes it) to a conservation organization and writes it off at face value for tax purposes. The indebted country's central bank in turn acquires the debt from the conservation organization in return for a promise to issue bonds in the local currency. The interest on those bonds is then used to finance environmental protection projects.

An early formulation of the idea appeared in an op-ed piece in the *New York Times* in October 1984 by Thomas Lovejoy, vice-president for science at the World Wildlife Fund. Congressional legislation and Internal Revenue Service rulings were necessary to encourage U.S. banks to participate, and the first swap came in

1987 between Bolivia and Conservation International in which that organization purchased $650,000 of Bolivian commercial bank debt for $100,000. In return for the cancellation of the debt the Bolivian government agreed to establish an endowment fund of $250,000 in local currency to pay the operating costs of a "biosphere reserve" and buffer zone in the Beni River region of the Bolivian Amazon. Other countries that have participated in such exchanges include Costa Rica, Belize, Ecuador, Madagascar, Zambia, the Dominican Republic, the Philippines, and Brazil. From 1987 to mid-1993, about $100 million of developing country debt had been purchased for $16 million. To mid-1993, Costa Rica was the most active participant in the swaps, accounting for 80 percent of the total. The swaps involve mainly conservation organizations, governments of developing countries, and commercial banks. However, two of the largest governmental lenders, the World Bank and the International Monetary Fund, are prevented by their charters from making such arrangements.

So far, at least four problems with the concept have surfaced. First, the debt of the developing countries has not been greatly reduced by the exchanges. Second, except perhaps in Costa Rica, the creation or expansion of national parks has not preserved a large portion of the threatened natural resources against the pressures of economic forces. Third, some people see such agreements as a violation of the sovereignty of the developing countries. Even though such swaps are voluntary, some argue that the developing country is enticed to do what it would not otherwise do in response to its intense need to reduce its foreign debt. Some, especially in Latin America, see this as "environmental imperialism." A fourth problem, a sin in any environmental action, is the alleged ill-effects on the economic well-being of people affected by the preservation. In Latin America, these often involve indigenous populations and peasants whose use of the land may be limited by the exchange.

There has been especially strong opposition to swaps in Brazil, the country with the largest rainforest in the world. Brazil did not approve its first exchange until 1992, a swap which provided operating funds to manage a 200,000-acre savannah park in central Brazil. The Nature Conservancy in the United States purchased $2 million in face value debt at about 35 cents on the dollar. (In 1992, Brazil had a total foreign debt of $121 billion.)

Supporters, on the other hand, point out the advantages of such swaps. The developing countries receive at least some debt relief, even if it is not a large portion of the total. Moreover, they achieve it by using their local currency, not scarce dollars, and the interest payments are kept in the country, rather than sent abroad. In addition, important natural resources are protected at least to some extent. So far as national sovereignty is concerned some argue that the rainforests and certain other natural resources should not be seen merely as the preserve of a particular country but as a global resource and that such swaps are a way for the developed countries to contribute to their preservation without infringing on the national sovereignty of the recipient countries. Moreover, the problem of displacement of indigenous or peasant peoples can be reduced by either guaranteeing their right to continue on the land or giving them employment. For example, the World Wildlife Fund has created a department to integrate the welfare of farmers and squatters into the programs by teaching them how to use the lands in a sustainable way or by providing employment opportunities in the newly established or expanded parks.

For the environmental organization, the swap can magnify the impact of its conservation dollars several times since one dollar of acquired debt costs the organization only a fraction of a dollar. The banks receive some payment or tax relief on debts which otherwise might be uncollectible. They also receive positive publicity for their participation. Finally, proponents argue that environmental protection in general can be consistent with economic development. One way in which the environment and the economy can be harmonized is through ecotourism in which preservation of natural areas attracts tourists from other countries who bring in much-needed foreign exchange while presumably not doing great damage to the fragile ecosystem.

Even the strongest supporters of debt-for-nature swaps do not see them as a solution to the problems of debt and resource depletion. The total debt is much too large and the ability of conservation groups to broker exchanges is much too limited for this particular mechanism to have a major effect on either problem. However, the swaps may focus greater attention on both debt and conservation problems and the alleged links between them.

Dan A. Cothran

Further Readings

Hultkrans, Andrew. "Greenbacks for Scenery." *Sierra* (November/December 1988): 43–45.

The Nature Conservancy. "Swapping Debt for Nature." (July 1993).

Rosebrock, J., and H. Sondhof. "Debt-for-Nature Swaps: A Review of the First Experiences." *Intereconomics* (March/April 1991): 82–87.

See also AFRICA: ENVIRONMENTAL PROBLEMS; BIODEPLETION; TROPICAL DEFORESTATION; TROPICAL RAINFORESTS; WORLD WILDLIFE FUND

Decentralization
See ECHOANARCHISM

Deep Ecology: Emergence

The term deep ecology was coined by the Norwegian philosopher Arne Naess (1912–) and was first advanced to a general audience in his short paper "The Shallow and the Deep, Long-Range Ecology Movement: A Summary" published in *Inquiry* in 1973. (*Inquiry* is a respected interdisciplinary journal of philosophy and the social sciences, which Naess founded in 1958 and continued to edit until 1975.) Notwithstanding its place of publication, however, Naess's shallow/deep ecology distinction remained completely dormant in the literature until the late 1970s when it was jointly taken up, elaborated, and popularized by Bill Devall, a California-based sociologist, and George Sessions, a California-based philosopher.

Although Naess is indisputably the father figure of deep ecology and the primary source of its central ideas, it is difficult to underestimate the influence of Devall and Sessions in elaborating Naess's distinction, bringing it to a wider audience, and pointing others to Naess's then relatively little-known ecophilosophical work. Without Devall and Sessions's concerted efforts, Naess's distinction would in all likelihood have remained buried in the literature for at least two reasons. First, beyond his initial announcement, Naess did not continue to advance this distinction in the literature during the 1970s. Second, a number of similar distinctions—similar at least to the popular anthropocentric/ecocentric understanding of the shallow/deep ecology distinction—had also been advanced by other writers by the end of the 1970s (some even prior to 1973). It is plausible that any one of these alternatives could have been taken up to occupy the theoretical niche that the shallow/deep ecology distinction has come to occupy.

Devall and Sessions's collaboration culminated in their popular 1985 book *Deep Ecology*. Since then they have continued to work on deep ecology independently. During the 1980s other philosophers also joined in the elaboration and analysis of deep ecological ideas, most notably Alan Drengson (British Columbia), Warwick Fox (Tasmania), Andrew McLaughlin (New York), and Michael Zimmerman (Louisiana).

Warwick Fox

Further Readings

Fox, Warwick. *Toward a Transpersonal Ecology: Developing New Foundations for Environmentalism*. 1990.

See also ANTHROPOCENTRISM; DEEP ECOLOGY: MEANINGS; ENVIRONMENTAL ETHICS; INTRINSIC VALUE; RADICAL ENVIRONMENTALISM

Deep Ecology: Meanings

The shallow/deep ecology distinction is *popularly* associated with the distinction between adopting an anthropocentric (i.e., human-centered) approach in our relations with the non-human world as opposed to an ecocentric (i.e., ecology-centered) approach. Beyond that, however, many people find the ideas of deep ecology somewhat nebulous. This is due in part to the fact that any individual presentation of deep ecology tends to emphasize any or all of up to three rather different, albeit theoretically interrelated, meanings. Depending on which of these meanings is or are emphasized, deep ecology may be presented as any or all of the following: 1) a sociological description cum political platform (it is this meaning that most corresponds to the popular "ecocentric" understanding of deep ecology); 2) a method; and 3) a particular ecophilosophical approach. These will be considered in turn.

The Norwegian philosopher Arne Naess originally advanced the term deep ecology in the context of characterizing the central ideas and values subscribed to by the so-called deep ecology movement, which Naess held to consist of a minority (or at least a less influential membership) of the global ecology movement. He de-

scribed these ideas and values by way of a loosely formulated list of seven points. Naess admitted at the time (1973) that these points represented "rather vague generalizations"; did not repeat this list in other English language publications; admitted in response to subsequent criticism (1984) that the most contentiously worded of his original seven points—"biospherical egalitarianism—in principle"—did "perhaps more harm than good"; and, together with George Sessions, drew up in 1984 a rather differently formulated eight-point list characterizing the values espoused by the deep ecology movement.

This list has been republished many times and has gained wide currency. It is generally referred to as "the deep ecology platform" and runs along the following lines: non-human entities—including ecological systems in general—are intrinsically valuable (i.e., valuable in and of themselves, not simply because of their use value to humans); in living their own lives humans therefore also have an obligation to do as much as possible to preserve the richness and diversity of the non-human world; this means working toward substantial decreases in human population, material consumption, and ecologically inappropriate forms of technology; and this, in turn, means working toward fundamental changes in our economic, technological, and ideological structures as well as in the sources of our psychological satisfactions.

While Naess has claimed that he has been merely articulating the values subscribed to by a particular social movement—albeit one that he has christened—it is also clear that he and his colleagues have been helping to bring the deep ecology movement into being not only by naming it but also by articulating its ideological content and championing that content. The deep ecology platform thus carries the dual burden of operating as both a sociological description and a political platform.

The deep ecology platform is limited in several respects. First, there is nothing particularly distinctive about it. Many Green thinkers and organizations have expressed broadly similar ideas under a variety of other labels. Second, the platform is limited in terms of political scope. Of the widely known "four pillars" of Green politics—ecology, social justice, grassroots democracy, and nonviolence (principles that originally emerged in the context of discussions of the German Greens in the early 1980s)—the deep ecology platform essentially picks up on just one: ecology (and its direct implications). The platforms of almost all Green political organizations are broader than the deep ecology platform, even if they are not always as attuned to the implications of the "ecology" pillar. Third, the deep ecology platform is limited in philosophical terms precisely because it *is* just a platform. One necessarily has to dig deeper in order to locate the arguments upon which the platform is founded.

Naess was aware of this last problem when he coined the term deep ecology. What he actually intended by the term was an approach to the relationship between humans and the non-human world that was derived from the process of "asking deeper questions." Thus, the term "deep ecology" was effectively a shorthand for a "deep questioning approach to ecology." Naess believed that people should ask progressively deeper questions of their socially conditioned, taken-for-granted views until the point where they struck philosophical bedrock, which is to say their most fundamental assumptions. He realized that there would inevitably be a tremendous variety in the assumptions thus revealed; for example, different people's fundamental assumptions might be religious or secular in orientation, Eastern or Western, mythic or philosophical, intuitive or scientific, and so on. However, Naess claimed that if people then worked backward and carefully derived their own views from their most fundamental assumptions they would necessarily reach views that were broadly compatible with the deep ecology platform. Thus, for Naess, the essential difference between anthropocentric, "shallow" ecology views and ecocentric, "deep" ecology views was not that one set of views was "better" in some sense—for example, more defensible on moral grounds, more desirable on practical grounds, or more "fitting" in terms of some general cosmological understanding—but rather simply that one set of views was derived from "deeper" premises than the other. On this understanding, then, the shallow/deep ecology distinction is essentially a methodological one.

Although this idea is certainly distinctive, at least in the context of ecophilosophical discussion, and has a certain face appeal (especially for those who want to believe that ecocentric views are somehow "deeper" than anthropocentric views), critical scrutiny shows that it is simply untenable. As Fox (1990) has shown, there is ample evidence to suggest that people can, have, do, and no doubt will continue to derive not only ecocentric views but even the most aggressively anthropocentric views from

their most fundamental assumptions. It is perhaps not surprising, then, that active elaboration (as distinct from mere repetition) of this conception of deep ecology has been wholly confined to Naess's work—notwithstanding the fact that the name deep ecology actually derives from this idea!

What has been of great interest however to those philosophers who have been writing specifically under the banner of deep ecology is the central idea associated with the particular fundamental assumption from which Naess has derived his own ecocentric views. It is this assumption that constitutes the central philosophical idea of deep ecology. Naess refers to his most fundamental assumption as "Self-realization!," which means the active (hence the exclamation point) realization of as wide and deep a sense of self as possible (hence "Self" with a capital "s"). However, "self" language is notoriously vague and slippery, so the real interest lies in how Naess has explicated this term: for Naess, one realizes a wider and deeper sense of self through the psychological capacity for identification.

The other main philosophical writers on deep ecology have followed Naess in stressing the importance of the psychological capacity for identification in response to our relationship with the non-human world in general and the ecological crisis in particular. For them, this represents a more fundamental and significant level of analysis and response than that of arguing for the objectively existing intrinsic value of the non-human world, and the human obligations that are therefore entailed *irrespective of how people might actually feel about the world around them.*

This third emphasis in deep ecology theorizing represents an approach to ecophilosophy—albeit one that pulls it in the direction of ecopsychology—that is both distinctive and tenable. The shortcomings of this approach, however, consist primarily in its lack of elaboration. Its original proponents have not developed this emphasis into a coherent theory that addresses the obvious, more detailed questions that must necessarily follow from a focus on the psychological capacity for identification: How precisely can the concept and experience of identification be delineated?; Are there various basic forms of identification and, if so, what are they?; Can these forms of identification be actively developed and, if so, how?; and What are the relative advantages and disadvantages of these forms of identification? Fox (1990) has initiated the task of addressing this group of questions but has done so under the rubric of *transpersonal ecology*. This approach sets aside the nondistinctive and untenable aspects of deep ecology, zooms in on the identification approach, and elaborates that approach substantially beyond that previously found in the deep ecological literature. This degree of departure from the general cluster of ideas that has been associated with what might be thought of as "orthodox" deep ecology, along with the fact that this orthodoxy shows some signs of becoming more rather than less entrenched, suggests that transpersonal ecology might best be regarded as a post deep ecological development.

The extent to which transpersonal ecology or any other theoretical developments of central deep ecological ideas will make significant ecophilosophical inroads remains to be seen. At present deep ecology itself looks more likely to be known primarily as a label for a general ecocentric orientation (popularly set forth in the deep ecology platform) than as a detailed and coherently developed approach to ecophilosophy.

Warwick Fox

Further Readings

Devall, Bill, and George Sessions. *Deep Ecology: Living as if Nature Mattered*. 1985.

Fox, Warwick. *Toward a Transpersonal Ecology: Developing New Foundations for Environmentalism*. 1990.

McLaughlin, Andrew. *Regarding Nature: Industrialism and Deep Ecology*. 1993.

Naess, Arne. *Ecology, Community and Lifestyle: Outline of an Ecosophy*. 1989.

See also ANTHROPOCENTRISM; DEEP ECOLOGY: EMERGENCE; EARTH FIRST!; ECOPHILOSOPHY AND ECOPSYCHOLOGY; ENVIRONMENTAL ETHICS; GREEN PARTIES; INTRINSIC VALUE; NAESS, ARNE; RADICAL ENVIRONMENTALISM

Deep-Well Injection

Deep-well injection is a method of waste disposal that involves the pressurized injection of liquid and semi-liquid waste into deep subsurface formations. Typical depths range from over 4,000 meters to as little as 200 meters below ground level. The method was first used by the petroleum industry in the early 1930s to dispose of large quantities of brine co-produced with crude oil. It is estimated that as many as 40,000 such wells exist in the United States today. The method was later adopted by the chemical and pharmaceutical industry for the disposal of acids, heavy metal solutions, organic solvents, and other liquid wastes. During the 1970s deep-well injection was seen as a viable and cost-effective method of hazardous waste disposal. It was not until the 1980s that deep-well disposal became a controversial issue. Some countries introduced strict legislation; others banned its use entirely.

Proponents of deep-well injection argue that the technique is appropriate for waste disposal providing that the wells are properly sited, constructed, operated, and maintained (LaMoreaux and Vrba, 1990). It is particularly well suited for oil field brines which can be reinjected into underground formations without special treatment, salt bearing solutions, processed brines, and brines from industrial solution mining (Suess and Huismans, 1983). Used acids can also be included in this category, provided that the host rock has sufficient neutralizing capacity.

The approach may also be used for the disposal of more hazardous materials. The risks are minimal only if the host rock of the subsurface reservoir: 1) provides adequate storage; 2) contains no commercial petroleum or mineral deposits; 3) is hydrogeologically isolated by confining beds that retard upward and downward movement of water and native wastes; and 4) lacks natural discontinuities such as geological faults and open fractures, unplugged wells, or high hydraulic gradients that could cause unacceptably rapid migration of contaminants. It is also important to maintain chemical compatibility between the various waste streams and the mineral and fluid components of the host reservoir. Chemical reactions can produce precipitates that may plug the pore spaces and seal the well; reactions can also create solution openings providing unexpected contamination pathways. In many cases it may be necessary to treat waste prior to disposal.

Opponents of the deep-well injection technique question whether permanent, out-of-sight entombment of hazardous wastes represents an appropriate and environmentally responsible approach to hazardous waste management. Furthermore, they argue from a practical standpoint that it is impossible to characterize a potential disposal zone with sufficient hydrogeological detail to ensure indefinite long-term environmental protection. Numerous problems have been documented ranging from aquifer contamination to surface eruption of

D

wastes and increased earthquake activity. In some cases, injected wastes have all but disappeared. In south-western Ontario, for example, 10 million cubic meters of industrial waste was injected into Devonian limestones during the 1960s and 1970s. Despite a good knowledge of the local geology based on numerous oil exploration wells, the fate of the waste is currently unknown. While it can be argued that most documented cases of detrimental impact are associated with older injection wells that were constructed prior to the enactment of enforcing legislation, there is still concern that the technology for managing hazardous waste through deep-well disposal remains well behind the technology for generating it.

Ken W.F. Howard

Further Readings

LaMoreaux, P.E., and J. Vrba. "Hydrogeology and Management of Hazardous Waste by Deep-Well Disposal." *International Contributions to Hydrogeology* 12. 1990.

Suess, M.J., and J.W. Huismans. *Management of Hazardous Waste: Policy Guidelines and Code of Practice.* World Health Organization. 1983.

See also GROUNDWATER POLLUTION; HAZARDOUS WASTE TREATMENT TECHNOLOGIES

Defenders of Wildlife

Defenders of Wildlife traces its origins to the Anti-Steel-Trap League (1925), which grew into Defenders of Furbearers (1947) before assuming its present name in 1959. Defenders has retained its primary focus on wildlife, especially mammals and predators, but has broadened from its early animal welfare emphasis to become a major Washington player in the domestic and, increasingly, the international wildlife policy arenas.

Defenders has pursued litigation, advocacy, education, and research. Notable recent efforts have addressed the reauthorization and strengthening of the Endangered Species Act; protection and reintroduction of predators, particularly the wolf; the enforcement and enhancement of the Convention on International Trade in Endangered Species of Wild Fauna and Flora (CITES); education and action on marine debris, especially driftnets and plastics; the protection of wildlife refuges; the development of strategies to conserve biological diversity; pro-

motion of non-lethal methods of livestock predator management; and the regulation of commerce in wild-caught birds for the pet trade.

An innovative program compensates ranchers who lose livestock to wolves near designated wolf recovery areas in the Northern Rockies. Another initiative, "Watchable Wildlife," coordinates federal, state, and private efforts in creating statewide networks of wildlife viewing sites, for which twelve guidebooks have so far been issued. Defenders often works in concert with other conservation organizations as well. Its staff members chair the Dolphin Coalition and the Entanglement Network Coalition, and they play a leadership role in Endangered Species Act Reauthorization Coalition.

Defenders derives support from 80,000 members and supporters, 10,000 of whom constitute an activist network. This reflects membership stability in recent years but a six-fold increase since 1970. This growth was materially aided by a very large bequest received over a period of years in the 1970s. The accompanying growth in influence paralleled an evolution in organizational mission and staff composition that brought Defenders nearer to the policy mainstream. Whereas the 1977 *Annual Report* saw the main work of the organization as combating domestic practices that were "needlessly cruel to wild creatures and wasteful of our precious wildlife," the 1983 report spoke to the need "to preserve and protect the natural abundance and diversity of wildlife."

Annual total revenues (1991) of $5.2 million are derived largely from contributions (39 percent), memberships (24 percent), and bequests (26 percent). Expenditures are directed to programs (56 percent), public information combined with fund-raising (21 percent), fund-raising (13 percent), and management (10 percent).

Members receive the quarterly magazine, *Defenders*, alternating with the new quarterly newspaper, *Wildlife Advocate*. Occasional publications include annual reports on the status of the Endangered Species Act, the proceedings of a symposium on "Biodiversity and Landscape Linkages: A Strategy for Survival," and "Putting Wildlife First," the report of Defenders' Commission on New Directions for the National Wildlife Refuge System.

James A. Tober

Further Readings

Defenders of Wildlife. *Annual Reports.* 1977–1991.

Tober, James A. *Wildlife and the Public Interest: Nonprofit Organizations and Federal Wildlife Policy.* 1989.

See also CITES; COASTAL DEBRIS AND CLEANUP; WATER POLLUTION ABATEMENT TECHNOLOGIES; WOLF: A CONSERVATION CHALLENGE

Deforestation
See FORESTRY, HISTORY OF; TROPICAL DEFORESTATION

Delaney Clause
Adopted in haste and almost without deliberation by the U.S. Congress in 1958, this short amendment to the Federal Food, Drug, and Cosmetic Act (FDC Act) of 1954 exerted an impact on American environmental law far beyond its framers' intentions. Named for its principal proponent, Congressman John Delaney of New York, the clause added a seemingly harmless proviso to the FDC Act's "general safety clause," stipulating that no food additive should be approved for use if it had been found to induce cancer when ingested by humans or animals; similar provisos were later incorporated for color additives and new animal drugs. The clause remained essentially inactive during the 1960s, but its zero-risk mandate gradually assumed greater legal and commercial significance as both testing procedures and detection methods for carcinogens became more sophisticated. By the early 1990s, both the Food and Drug Administration (FDA) and the Environmental Protection Agency (EPA) had tried and failed to reinterpret the Delaney Clause consistently with contemporary scientific and technological reality.

For the FDA, the chief anomaly was that the clause appeared to prohibit the use of substances presenting only trivial risks to human health. The FDA sought to avoid these irrational regulatory outcomes by exempting from the Delaney ban additives that fell below a certain *de minimis* threshold of risk. In *Public Citizen v. Young* (1987), a federal appeals court rejected this strategy for color additives, holding that substances definitively shown to cause cancer in animals could not be exempted from the prohibition merely on the ground that they posed minimal risks to people.

For the EPA, the primary difficulty lay in the interaction between the Delaney Clause and the legal provisions regulating pesticide residues in food. Although potentially carcinogenic pesticides could be used on raw agricultural commodities if they met applicable safety requirements, such pesticides had to be treated as food additives, and therefore be subjected to the Delaney Clause, if they became more concentrated during food processing. The EPA's effort to secure consistency by applying a *de minimis* exception to this class of pesticide residues was rejected by an appeals court in *Les v. Reilly* (1992).

Judicial opposition to the attempted administrative reinterpretations of the clause returned the Delaney problem to the political realm, where many felt it was long overdue for resolution. It fell to the environmentally friendly but politically weak Clinton administration to revise the law in the 1990s without arousing the antagonism of the perennially skeptical U.S. environmentalist community.

Sheila Jasanoff

Further Readings
National Research Council. *Regulating Pesticides in Food: The Delaney Paradox.* 1987.

See also ENVIRONMENTAL PROTECTION AGENCY; EPIDEMIOLOGY; FOOD ADDITIVES; HERBICIDES; PESTICIDES; TOXICOLOGY

Demand-Side Management
Using energy more efficiently is vital to restoring environmental quality. The most pressing environmental problems of our time—radioactive contamination and waste disposal, acid rain and global warming, widespread flooding and mercury contamination of rivers and lakes—are all linked directly to the way we develop and use energy. Enormous environmental and economic savings would result from improved efficiency—on this there is little disagreement. But how to achieve those efficiency improvements is another question.

Demand-side management (DSM) attempts to meet increased energy demands by altering consumption levels, as an alternative to the traditional approach of examining supply-side construction options alone. DSM has been embraced especially by North American electric utilities, but some experience has been gained by natural gas utilities as well.

Conservation could be achieved by pricing energy at its full cost, including environmental costs, so consumers get some price feedback as to the real cost of energy options. Specific actions could include a carbon tax on fossil fuels and/or the removal of some or all subsidies to nuclear power, resulting in higher prices for these polluting energy sources. Consumers would then have increased incentive to invest in conservation technology—insulation, energy efficient lighting, and more efficient appliances, for example—and cleaner, renewable power sources would have a chance at proving themselves able to meet society's power needs.

Adopting sophisticated metering technology would also give consumers better price signals and incentives for conservation. Eliminating "promotional rate structures" or arbitrary "declining block rates," whereby customers are charged lower rates for each succeeding block of power consumed, and eliminating uncontrolled flat-rate water heaters and bulk metering of new electrically heated apartment buildings, whereby consumers pay a flat rate for power and have no incentive to conserve, would also be excellent conservation tools.

As an alternative, in combination with changes in pricing structures, utilities can also sell unsubsidized demand management services, providing conservation technology and installation assistance in competition with other energy service companies. However, instead of instituting such fundamental reforms, many utilities have approached DSM in the traditional utility megaproject fashion, spending millions of dollars subsidizing conservation at ratepayers' expense, and not always getting good results.

For example, Ontario Hydro, North America's largest electric utility, spent $7 million to distribute 52-watt light bulbs to almost 4 million households in Ontario, yet saved just $4 million worth of electricity. The utility also subsidized heat pumps (which can build, rather than reduce, demand for power due to the new cooling load that many of these units create) with incentives of $500 to $2,500 which half of the participants said they might have done without. Now, some energy service companies are threatening to sue Hydro, both for cutting back subsidies upon which they were reliant, and for ruining the market for conservation: consumers, having been spoilt by cut-rate prices, are now unwilling to pay the full price of energy-efficient products.

Such programs can cause perverse effects. Conservation planners routinely overestimate savings by ignoring the incentives such programs give consumers to increase their consumption: after a program to insulate homes, for example, homeowners may not keep their thermostats as low because their heating cost has dropped. DSM programs often delay and punish responsible investments by consumers: when conservation subsidies are announced, consumers have an incentive to postpone their purchases until they can qualify, and those who invest in conservation before subsidies are available feel cheated when their neighbors benefit from subsidies borne by all consumers. And conservation programs attempt to solve environmental problems by reducing power production without discriminating between power from relatively clean sources on one hand and dirty, dangerous sources on the other. For improved environmental quality, spending money on better pollution controls would be cheaper and more effective than traditional DSM programs.

Utility regulators and executives should be very cautious about using utility monopoly power to cross-subsidize either supply-side or demand-side measures that cannot otherwise compete in the market. Demand management subsidies may remain necessary where market barriers to conservation truly exist—in rental accommodation, for example—but requiring consumers to pay for what they get remains the best way to ensure efficiency in the provision and use of energy services. Many, many energy conservation initiatives are indeed now cost effective, especially as regards electricity. Demand management services should be as available to consumers as supply services.

Sheila Malcolmson

Further Readings

Adams, Thomas. *Seven Problems with Subsidized, Utility-Driven Conservation Programs.* Reprint of Hearing Brief, Energy Probe (Toronto, Ontario), 1991.

Flavin, Christopher, and Nicholas Lenssen. "Reshaping the Power Industry." In *State of the World.* Ed. Lester R. Brown, et al., 1994.

See also ENERGY EFFICIENCY; LEAST-COST UTILITY PLANNING; LOVINS, AMORY B.; SOFT ENERGY PATHS

Department of Energy (U.S.)

The U.S. Department of Energy (DOE) was created as a cabinet department by executive order in October 1977. Constituted from a multitude of energy agencies previously scattered throughout the federal government, the DOE was intended to centralize and coordinate national energy planning and program administration at a time when the United States was experiencing severe political and economic shocks created by Arab oil embargoes and the Iranian Revolution. Numerous new and existing regulatory programs were transferred to the DOE, including the regulation of domestic petroleum prices, federal electric power production, interstate natural gas and wholesale electricity prices, interstate oil pipelines, and federal electric power production. Other important inherited programs included research, development, and promotion of fossil fuel and civilian energy technologies, the acquisition and publication of energy information, and the management and regulation of military nuclear weapons production facilities.

The DOE's creation has improved national energy management in limited but important ways. Energy research and development programs are now coordinated; energy information is more efficiently gathered and disseminated; and coordination among energy programs has sometimes improved. But DOE has not become a national energy planning and management agency. Burdened from its inception by many difficult and unpopular regulatory programs, the DOE has lacked a strong political constituency and dependable congressional support. Congress and the White House have seldom looked to the DOE or its national energy plans for initiatives in energy policy making. The many disparate programs absorbed by the DOE are inconsistent and sometimes contradictory, impeding program coordination.

Over time, the DOE's program priorities have altered. Its energy regulatory mission has diminished with the fading of the energy crisis after 1980. However, the DOE does possess significant authority to regulate energy supply, prices, and conservation during a national energy emergency. Its research and development budget continues to influence significantly the evolution of national energy technologies. Between 1980 and 1992, the Reagan and Bush administrations shifted the DOE's budget and priorities heavily toward promotion of fossil fuels and nuclear power and sharply away from energy conservation or regulatory programs. The Clinton administration shifted the DOE's program priorities again toward research and development of energy conservation technolo-gies, the encouragement of energy conservation, and energy regulation, and away from promotion of increased fossil energy production and nuclear energy technologies.

The DOE has also been compelled to make a major, unexpected shift in its program and budget priorities since 1987 when it had to undertake the enormous task of cleaning up widespread, dangerous nuclear wastes at its thirty-seven military weapons production sites, an inheritance of massive incompetence and negligence in site administration since the early 1940s. The cleanup effort, estimated to cost more than $300 billion, is expected to absorb much of the DOE's budget and staff for several decades. The controversy engendered by mismanagement of the military weapons program has impeded the DOE's efforts to improve its administrative and political reputation. The DOE, despite its failures as a national energy planner and the chronic contention it evokes, continues to be an important participant in the nation's energy policy making, a role certain to increase in importance if the nation again faces a major energy crisis.

Walter A. Rosenbaum

Further Readings
Rosenbaum, Walter A. *Energy, Politics, and Public Policy.* 1987.

See also ENERGY CRISIS; NUCLEAR ELECTRIC POWER; NUCLEAR WASTE; NUCLEAR WEAPONS PRODUCTION; OIL SHALE

Department of the Interior (U.S.)

The Department of the Interior (DOI) is a cabinet-level administrative division in the executive branch of the U.S. government. Needing to address the duties respecting the internal affairs of the United States, Congress created the DOI on March 3, 1849. Previously, such duties were overseen by the Department of State. Since the 1950s, the DOI has gained a sharper focus, functioning now as the nation's principle conservation agency. It is charged with conserving, developing, and utilizing mineral, water, fish, and wildlife resources; coordinating federal and state recreation programs; preserving and administering federal scenic and historical areas; undertaking land reclamation projects; and reclaiming strip-mined coal lands. The DOI also administers programs that provide services to American Indians and to the indigenous populations of Alaska, and is concerned with the economic and social development of U.S. Territories.

Historical Development

Created as a "Home Department," the DOI's origins were not without controversy. John C. Calhoun declared, "Everything on the face of God's earth will go into the Home Department." The original functions of the DOI seemed to confirm the fear of "everything." Forming the original jurisdiction of the DOI were the General Land Office, the Patent Office, Indian Affairs, and the Pension Office. Each of these were spun off from other departments (e.g., War, Treasury), thus helping to clarify the missions of these departments. The result, however, was a lack of a unifying purpose in the DOI, but this absence allowed Congress to take a more expansive interest in the internal needs of a developing nation.

Several of the DOI's operations have given it a predominately Western focus. The General Land Office and the Bureau of Indian Affairs operated mainly in the West. The Bureau of Reclamation develops water resources for the Western states. The DOI's park operations were centered in the West—the first national parks east of the Mississippi River were not created until 1926. The need to explore, map, and catalogue the West also contributed to this focus. As a result, the DOI has found itself enmeshed in controversy when Western interests seem detrimental to the nation as a whole. One recurring example is the setting of grazing fees on federal lands.

The DOI has also administered programs which transferred public lands in the West to private control. Notable are the Public Land Sales Act (1820), and the 1862 trio of the Morrill Act, the Pacific Railroad Act, and the Homestead Act. Under the latter two, more than 380 million acres were transferred to private concerns. The Mining Control Act (1872) allowed prospectors to protect their interests by "staking their claim." Since there was no requirement to demonstrate mineral production, thousands of acres, providing no public or private benefit, became encumbered with claims. Present generations may lament the loss of the lands and processes by which these transfers occurred.

Throughout its history, the DOI has had a variety of operations, many of which became independent agencies. The agricultural division became the Department of Agriculture (1862). The Bureau of Labor, along with some commercial concerns, became the Department of Commerce and Labor (1903). The Patent Office moved to the Department of Commerce (1925). The Bureau of Pensions evolved into Veteran's Affairs (1930). Finally, several operations helped form the Department of Energy (1977).

As the twentieth century has progressed, the DOI has obtained a sharper focus on natural resources. Its original mission, to dispose of natural resources to private enterprise, reflected the predominant belief of nineteenth-century America: natural resources were inexhaustible and government regulation of their exploitation was undemocratic. Due to the efforts of individuals such as Ferdenand V. Hayden and Major John Wesley Powell, a conservation ethic began to permeate the DOI by the early 1900s. This ethic is not one which attempts to end the exploitation of resources, but emphasizes their rational and orderly use, guided by science and regulated by the government for the benefit of society. Later, a preservationist ethic, emphasizing the intrinsic value of natural resources, would be overlaid. Consequently, there is a conflict within the DOI due to these different orientations, which are institutionalized in different programs. The Bureau of Land Management, for example, is often seen as a promoter of the conservation approach, while the National Park Service embodies a more preservationist perspective.

The conservation approach has tended to dominate within the DOI and on several occasions the Department has attempted to change its name to reflect this orientation. It also has attempted to bring within its purview other government agencies (such as the U.S. Forest Service) whose functions are to manage the nation's natural resources. In 1935, Secretary Ickes pushed to rename the DOI "The Department of Conservation." In 1949, the Hoover Commission recommended the DOI become the "Department of Natural Resources." In 1973, Secretary Morton proposed a "Department of Energy and Natural Resources." In each case, various interests mobilized to prevent these actions.

Administrative Divisions

The Secretary of the Interior is assisted by six assistant secretaries: Policy, Management, and Budget; Fish and Wildlife and Parks; Indian Affairs; Land and Minerals Management; Territorial and International Affairs; and Water and Science.

The Assistant Secretary of Policy, Management, and Budget oversees the Office of Hearings and Appeals. The office, with administrative judges and three formal boards of appeal, renders decisions in cases pertaining to contract disputes, Indian probate and administrative appeals, and public and acquired lands and their resources. Board decisions are final for the DOI.

The Assistant Secretary for Fish and Wildlife and Parks oversees three divisions: the National Park Service, the U.S. Fish and Wildlife Service, and the National Biological Survey. The first, the National Park Service (NPS; 1916) governs more than 360 parks and monuments of natural and scientific value. It also manages recreation areas and reservoirs. In 1933, the NPS was given management of historic battlefields and forts, broadening its reach to both natural and historic preservation.

The U.S. Fish and Wildlife Service (1939) conserves, protects, and enhances fish and wildlife and their habitats for the public good. It is responsible for migratory birds, endangered species, inland sport fisheries, and research activities to support its mission. In 1987, it operated 434 national wildlife refuges and 150 waterfowl production areas. Within the DOI, it manages a total acreage second only to the Bureau of Land Management. By 1987 the "duck stamp," mandated by the Migratory Bird Hunting Stamp Act (1939), which requires all waterfowl hunters over the age of fifteen to purchase an annual stamp, had generated more than $313 million, and was used to acquire and preserve more than 3.7 million acres of wetlands. The Service allows recreational and commercial enterprises to operate simultaneously on many of its refuges. Thus, hunting, fishing, logging, farming, and oil and gas extraction all coexist. The Service encourages a stewardship ethic based on ecological principles and scientific knowledge.

The National Biological Survey (1993) is the newest division in the DOI. Formed to catalogue the diversity of plants and animals in the United States, the Survey selected its staff from other divisions in the DOI. Its primary role is to provide scientific information to the DOI focusing on three areas: ecosystems, species biology, and population dynamics. Its key function is to coordinate ongoing biological inventory and monitoring efforts, with a goal of providing an adequate scientific basis to protect natural resources.

The Bureau of Indian Affairs (1824), under the assistant secretary for Indian affairs, works with Indian and native Alaskan peoples. It assists in the full development of their human and natural resource potential. The Bureau acts as a trustee for the lands and monies held in trust by the United States.

The assistant secretary for land and minerals management oversees three divisions: the Bureau of Land Management (BLM), the Minerals Management Service, and the Office of Surface Mining Reclamation and Enforcement. The BLM (1946) administers more than 270 million acres of public lands, located primarily in the West and Alaska. The BLM is also responsible for the subsurface resource management for an additional 300 million acres where the mineral rights are held by the federal government. It has the broadest range of management functions in the DOI, extending from timber and hard rock minerals to oil and gas. The BLM is a merger of the General Land Office (1812, acquired from treasury at DOI's creation) and the Grazing Service. The latter was created by the Taylor Grazing Act (1934), which attempted to control overgrazing by restricting the disposition of public land. After the Act, land use was contingent on the secretary's judgment that the lands in question were more suitable for uses other than grazing. Land-use plans, backed by the principles of multiple use and sustained yield, are developed with public involvement to provide orderly use and development while maintaining and enhancing the quality of the environment. The BLM also manages watersheds to protect soils and to enhance water quality.

The Minerals Management Service (1982) assesses the nature, extent, recoverability, and value of leasable minerals on the Outer Continental Shelf. The revenues generated by minerals leasing are one of the largest non-tax sources of income to the federal government.

The Office of Surface Mining Reclamation and Enforcement (1982) ensures that surface coal mining is done without permanent damage to land and water resources. Since states now have primary responsibility for mining regulation, the Office assists states with meeting the objectives of the Surface Mining Control and Reclamation Act (1977). It also regulates mining and reclamation activities in those states choosing not to assume primary responsibility.

The assistant secretary for water and science also oversees three divisions: the Bureau of Mines, the U.S. Geological Survey (USGS), and the Bureau of Reclamation. After a series of coal mine disasters in the early 1900s, Congress created the Bureau of Mines (1910) to promote minerals technology and mine safety. Since 1977, when fossil fuels went to the Department of Energy and mine health and safety went to the Department of Labor, the Bureau of Mines has become primarily a fact-finding agency, with a goal of ensuring that the United States has adequate supplies of non-fuel materials. The Bureau conducts research to provide the technology for the extraction, processing, use, and recycling of resources at a reasonable cost without harm to the environment or the workers involved.

The USGS (1879) provides for the classification of public lands and the examination of geological structure, mineral resources, and products of the national domain. Provisions were later added for gauging streams and determining the water supply of the United States. The USGS functions as the principle source of information about the nation's land, and its mineral and water resources.

The Reclamation Act of 1902, which created the Bureau of Reclamation, directed the DOI to secure a year-round water supply for irrigation in the seventeen contiguous Western States. Through the development of a water storage and delivery system, this Bureau has helped settle and develop the West. Since the infrastructure is largely in place, the Bureau now focuses more on resource management and protection than on development.

The Department of the Interior is a diverse operation, charged with environmental protection, natural resource development, royalty collections, and assisting native Alaskan and Indian populations. Though it incorporates ethics and programs which are often contradictory, the DOI provides invaluable scientific information and management guidance to a variety of operations within the United States.

Kevin H. Olson

Appendix I

AGENCIES IN THE U.S. DEPARTMENT OF THE INTERIOR

Agency	Established
Bureau of Indian Affairs	1849*
U.S. Geological Survey	1879
Bureau of Reclamation	1902
Bureau of Mines	1910
National Park Service	1916

Agency	Established
U.S. Fish and Wildlife Service	1940†
Bureau of Land Management	1946‡
Office of Surface Mining Reclamation and Enforcement	1977
Minerals Management Service	1982
National Biological Survey	1993

* Originally in War Department, formed in 1824.
† Combined from the Bureau of Fisheries (1871) and the Bureau of Biological Survey (1885).
‡ Combined from General Land Office (1812; originally in Treasury Department) and the Grazing Service (1934).

Appendix II

LIST OF SECRETARIES (TWENTIETH CENTURY)

Name	From
Ethan A. Hitchcock	1898
James R. Garfield	1907
Richard A. Ballinger	1909
Walter L. Fisher	1911
Franklin K. Lane	1913
John B. Payne	1920
Albert B. Fall	1921
Hubert Work	1923
Roy O. West	1928
Ray Lyman Wilbur	1929
Harold L. Ickes	1933
J.A. Krug	1946
Oscar L. Chapman	1949
Douglas McKay	1953
Fred A. Seaton	1956
Stewart L. Udall	1961
Walter J. Hickel	1969
Rogers C.B. Morton	1971
Stanley K. Hathaway	1975
Thomas S. Kleppe	1975
Cecil D. Andrus	1977
James G. Watt	1981
William P. Clark	1983
Donald P. Hodel	1985
Manuel Lujan, Jr.	1989
Bruce Babbitt	1993

Further Readings

Foss, Philip O., ed. *Federal Lands Policy.* 1987.
Smith, Zachary A. *The Environmental Policy Paradox.* 1992.

See also BUREAU OF LAND MANAGEMENT; CONSERVATION MOVEMENT; ICKES, HAROLD L.; NATIONAL PARK SERVICE (U.S.); POWELL, JOHN WESLEY; UDALL, STUART L.; WATT, JAMES G.

Desertification

Terms like "encroachment of the Sahara" (Bovill, 1921) and "creeping desert" (Stebbing, 1953) suggest that a desert may extend its area beyond its natural (climatic) limits and engulf adjoining territories. This perception may have been animated by the case of sand bodies that move from their desert sites and overwhelm productive land and settlements in oases or in territories outskirting the desert. Desertification is perceived not as a threat of invasion of the productive lands from outside, but as degradation of these lands initiated through land-use practices that overstep the inherent carrying capacity of the resource ecosystem. It is defined (UNEP, 1992) as "land degradation in arid, semiarid and dry subhumid areas resulting mainly from adverse human impact." This definition integrates: 1) the fragility of productive land ecosystems in world drylands; and 2) excessive pressures of exploitation.

Fragility of dryland ecosystems relate to a number of ecological attributes including: 1) surface water resources that are limited (low rainfall); 2) rainfall that is seasonal (long rainless season); 3) rainfall that is variable and non-dependable (recurrent incidence of drought); 4) plant cover that is thin and does not afford effective protection against soil erosion; 5) bioproductivity that is low (carrying capacity limited); and 6) biogeochemical processes that retain nutrients within the aboveground biomass (removal of plant growth leaves the soil poor in nutrients).

Excessive pressures of use relate to practices driven by increase of human population and escalation of their consumption, or by change of national economic policies from subsistence resource use to production for national and international markets. The world drylands (6.1 billion hectares) include about 1 billion hectares of hyper-arid deserts that are not included in our present consideration and about 5.1 billion hectares of productive lands (arid, semi-arid, and dry subhumid territories) that are home and source of livelihood for one quarter of the human race. Three principal agricultural land-use systems prevail: irrigated farmlands, rainfed croplands, and rangelands. Collection of biomass for fuel and other uses is a widespread practice.

Table 1 gives data on the global status of desertification in continental drylands. Desertification in irrigated farmlands is usually due to an imbalance between irrigation (excessive) and drainage (inefficient). This results in water-logging, salinization, and alkalinization—all forms of soil deterioration. It is estimated that about 43 million hectares (30 percent of the world total) are at least moderately degraded. The share of Asia is largest (about 31.8 million hectares) followed by North America (about 5.8 million hectares). Overcultivation in rainfed farmlands relate to practices that: 1) shorten periods of fallow in shift cultivation rotations; or 2) extend ploughing and farming into territories that are usually zoned for grazing. The

TABLE 1.

Global status of desertification/land degradation in agriculturally used drylands (areas in millions of hectares).

Continent	Irrigated Lands			Rainfed Cropland			Rangeland			Total agriculturally used drylands		
	Total	Degraded		Total	Degraded		Total	Degraded		Total	Degraded	
	m.ha	m.ha	%	m.ha	m.ha	%	m.ha	m.ha	%	m.ha	m.ha	%
Africa	10.42	1.90	18	79.82	48.86	61	1342.35	995.08	74	1432.59	1045.84	73.0
Asia	92.02	31.81	35	218.17	122.28	56	1571.24	1187.61	76	1881.43	1311.70	69.7
Australia	1.87	0.25	13	42.12	14.32	35	657.22	361.35	55	701.21	375.92	53.6
Europe	11.90	1.91	16	22.11	11.85	54	111.57	80.52	72	145.58	94.28	64.8
N. America	20.87	5.86	28	74.17	11.61	16	483.14	411.15	85	578.18	428.62	74.1
S. America	8.42	1.42	17	21.35	6.64	31	390.90	297.75	76	420.67	305.81	72.7
Total	145.80	43.15	30	457.74	215.56	47	4556.42	3333.46	73	5159.66	3562.17	69.0

Source: Dregne et al. (1991).

latter practice is often tempted by years of above-average rainfall. It is estimated that about 215 million hectares of rainfed croplands within the world drylands are at least moderately degraded. The largest areas of desertified croplands are in Asia (about 122.3 million hectares) and Africa (about 48.8 million hectares). Degraded rangelands are most extensive: the worldwide total is 3.3 billion hectares. Overgrazing seems rampant (numbers of livestock animals increase without the management of rangelands that makes grazing sustainable).

Other aspects of excessive use include overcutting of woody biomass for fuel and other domestic use and transformation of agricultural land to non-agricultural use (i.e., urban sprawl, etc.). The Gulf War of 1991 demonstrated the devastating impacts of military activities on drylands.

Global impacts of desertification relate to its effects on world food-producing capacity, world biodiversity, and world climate. The destruction of vegetation entails diminution of many plant and animal populations and loss of species. Many crops (i.e., wheat, barley, sorghums, millets, etc.) and fodder species (i.e., medicagos, trifoliums, etc.), that form the backbone of world agriculture and pasture husbandry have their origins in arid and semi-arid regions. Hundreds of wild plant species native to drylands are sources of valuable medicinal materials. Loss of those plant populations and their wild relatives represents loss of valuable and irreplaceable genetic materials. The impact of desertification on loss of germplasm resources may be, from the economic perspective, no less severe than the impact of deforestation.

Impacts of desertification on climate relate to several processes. First, deserts and desertified territories are sources of atmospheric dust that may modify the scattering and absorption of solar radiation in the atmosphere. Its effect on temperature depends on altitude to which it is borne. Climatic impacts of suspended particulate substances in the atmosphere may be no less than that of other pollutants including greenhouse gases. Second, impoverishment of plant cover would have impacts on surface energy budget and on temperature of near-surface air. Two processes are involved: increased surface albedo and reduced removal of soil moisture by evapotranspiration. Third, the extensive area of non-productive drylands plays little part in the global sinks of carbon dioxide. They represent space available for programs of afforestation and other forms of revegetation. The greening of these areas would expand the global sinks for greenhouse gases.

Mohammed Kassas

Further Readings

Bovill, E. "The Encroachment of the Sahara on the Sudan." *Journal of the African Society*, 20 (1921): 175–85, 259–69.
Dregne, H.E., M. Kassas, and B. Rozanov. "A New Assessment of the World Status of Desertification." *UNEP Desertification Control Bulletin* 20 (1991): 6–18.
Stebbing, E.P. *The Creeping Desert in the Sudan and Elsewhere in Africa.* McCorquodale, Khartoum, The Sudan. 1953.
UNEP. *World Atlas of Desertification.* 1992.

See also AFRICA: ENVIRONMENTAL PROBLEMS

Dinosaur National Monument

See ECHO PARK DAM

Dioxins and Furans

Dioxin is an abbreviated name for a series of organic compounds called the chlorinated dibenzo-p-dioxins. From one to eight chlorine atoms may be positioned on the basic dioxin ring structure to give a total of seventy-five different compounds in the dioxin group. The general chemical formula for dioxins is $C_{12}H_xO_2Cl_y$, where x+y = 8. The different members of the group are distinguished from each other by the number and position of the chlorine atoms on the ring. The most toxic member of this group is 2,3,7,8-tetrachlorodibenzo-p-dioxin (also called 2,3,7,8-TCDD or just TCDD), which has been shown to cause a number of adverse effects in laboratory animal studies. The name 2,3,7,8-TCDD shows that there are four chlorine atoms attached to the basic ring, at the 2,3,7 and 8-positions of the structure. Of the entire group of seventy-five dioxins, only those that have chlorines on the 2,3,7 and 8-positions (there are seven of them) of the structure are considered to be hazardous to animals and humans. The furans, or more correctly, the chlorinated dibenzofurans, are a group of 135 compounds that are structurally very similar to the dioxins (formula = $C_{12}H_xO_1Cl_y$, where x+y = 8), and which cause similar effects. Only those furans with chlorines at the 2,3,7 and 8-positions (there are ten of them) on the basic furan structure are considered toxic. Therefore, there are 210 possible dioxins and furans, of which seventeen have chlorines at the 2,3,7 and 8-positions of the basic structures and are considered to be toxic.

Dioxins came to the attention of the public through several widely publicized pollution episodes, including Seveso (Italy), Times Beach (Missouri), Love Canal (New York), and herbicide (Agent Orange) spraying during the Vietnam War. The dioxins and furans were trace byproducts from the manufacture of certain chemicals used to formulate some pesticides and herbicides. There was no intent to make dioxins and furans and there is no use for these chemicals. Other reports of dioxin and furan contamination have appeared from many different countries. Initial efforts in these incidents were focused on human exposure to only 2,3,7,8-TCDD, but as more research was performed it was determined that all of the 2,3,7,8-substituted dioxins and furans had to be monitored. Other sources of dioxins and furans were discovered over many years of monitoring, including municipal waste incinerators, automobile tailpipe emissions, leaking chemical waste sites, polychlorinated biphenyl (PCB) fires, chlorine bleaching during the manufacture of paper products, wood burning (wood stoves and forest fires), and almost any combustion process that is not carefully controlled to inhibit formation.

The effects of dioxins and furans on humans are still not well understood. After incidents such as those that occurred at Seveso and elsewhere, the health of exposed humans was followed over many years and compared to the health of humans from the same area who were not exposed. In Seveso human exposure was so great that many people developed a serious skin rash condition known as chloracne; however, so far no human deaths can be attributed with any certainty to dioxin exposure. Although the exposure at Seveso occurred in 1976 the health of those exposed is still being monitored to determine whether there are serious long-term effects from the dioxin exposures. The possible effects on humans from long-term exposure to trace concentrations of dioxins and furans are not known. This is important because most people are exposed to traces of dioxins and furans through food, air, soil, and, to a lesser extent, water.

Measurements of human tissue from around the world have shown that most people can expect parts-per-trillion (1 part in 1,000,000,000,000) concentrations of dioxins and furans to be in their fatty tissues. Dioxins and furans accumulate in the fat and are practically insoluble in water. Therefore for many people food is the major route of exposure—especially from eating fish caught from polluted waterways. There are many different guidelines for how much total dioxin and furan concentration is safe for human exposure. In Canada it is estimated that a total dioxin and furan intake of 10 picograms (per kilogram of a person's body weight) per day, over a lifetime will not result in any adverse health effects. To determine human exposure, only the concentrations of the seventeen 2,3,7,8-substituted dioxins and furans are used.

Government regulations, improved manufacturing processes, and modern pollution abatement equipment (i.e., to prevent incinerator emissions) have resulted in much lower dioxin and furan emissions from industrial sources. For example, switching from leaded to unleaded gasoline has reduced automobile emissions by about a factor of 100; pulp and paper bleaching processes have been improved to greatly reduce the amount of chlorine used, which has significantly lowered dioxin and furan formation; and, modern incinerators equipped with state-of-the-art pollution control devices and operating within specifications can reduce dioxin and furan emissions by better than 99 percent.

Because any uncontrolled combustion (e.g., forest fires) can be expected to produce some dioxins and furans—although at very trace concentrations—it is impossible to completely eliminate these compounds from the environment. However, the controls and improvements already implemented have reduced the amount of the more toxic 2,3,7,8-substituted dioxins and furans, which are generally more prevalent in emissions from industrial sources. Because they are very resistant to degradation the dioxins and furans already in the environment will be around for many years. Therefore, human exposure to trace levels of dioxins and furans, principally from the food chain, will continue for the forseeable future. Studies to date have not yet shown that this long-term, low concentration exposure is hazardous to human health. Research is underway to investigate possible long-term effects, but it may be many years before this difficult problem is resolved.

Ray E. Clement

Further Readings

Kamrin, M.A., and P.W. Rodgers, eds. *Diox-ins in the Environment*. 1985.

Young, A.L., and G.M. Reggiani, eds. *Agent Orange and its Associated Dioxin: Assessment of a Controversy*. 1988.

See also BIOACCUMULATION; EPIDEMIOLOGY; HAZARDOUS WASTE TREATMENT TECHNOLOGIES; HERBICIDES; LOVE CANAL; MUNICIPAL SOLID WASTE: INCINERATION; PULP AND PAPER MILLS; SEVESO

Discounting the Future

Many environmental problems—nuclear waste storage or global warming damage—are likely to have their major impacts well into the future. The costs are therefore likely to be borne by people alive in fifty years time and after that. Conventional benefit-cost approaches for deciding such investments would regard $1 of future damage as being less important than $1 of damage now because of the phenomenon of discounting. The underlying value judgments of benefit-cost analysis are that people's preferences count and that preferences are justifiably weighted according to the existing distribution of incomes. If the sovereignty of preferences is to be applied consistently, then the bias of the preferences of the current generation toward present as opposed to future benefits, and against present as opposed to future costs, needs to be reflected in decision-making aids. This is the essential rationale for discounting. Typically, any benefit (or cost) accruing in T years time is recorded as having a present value of:

$$PV(B) = B_T (1 + r)^T$$

where r is the rate at which future benefits are discounted, the discount rate.

The problem that arises with discounting is that it discriminates against future generations. In one sense this discrimination is deliberate—the discount rate is meant to discriminate in this way: this is its purpose. But such a discrimination presupposes an agreed objective to the effect that meeting the current generation's wants is more important than meeting future generations' wants. Discounting is consistent with imposing a major cost on the future for the sake of a relatively small gain now. The usual justification for this is that future generations will be better off anyway—their incomes will be higher because of economic growth. They will therefore attach less value to an extra $1 of income than a current generation (the diminishing marginal utility of income argument) and will perhaps be better placed to counteract any ill effects of current generation activities that spill over to them. To see the kind of implied shifting of burdens, a cost accruing in 100 years time and amounting to $100 billion would, at a 10 percent discount rate, have a present value of :

$$\$100 \text{ billion } (1.1)^{100}$$

which comes to $7.25 million. That is, any benefit-cost study of a project imposing such a future cost would record the damage done at only $7.25 million even though the actual damage done is nearly 14,000 times greater than this.

If there is concern with intergenerational equity, then, discount rates of the order of 10 percent—which are typically applied to investments in the developing world—would be inconsistent with that concern. Intergenerational concerns would therefore seem to call for some fairly fundamental revision in the way project and policy appraisal is carried out. Two broad categories of modification have been suggested, although it is important to note that all the arguments are the subject of extended controversy. The first set of modifications requires what might be called a "two-tier" approach. Allocations of resources over time are treated differently to allocations within a period of time. Some kind of "sustainability rule" is applied to the intergenerational allocation, and fairly conventional rules, such as maximizing the net present value of benefits, are applied within a time-frame. The second set of modifications are made directly to the discount rate itself (i.e., the framework of maximizing net present values is left intact, but the actual rate of discount is changed to reflect intergenerational concerns).

Some authors argue that simply changing the discount rate—usually by lowering it—is a mistaken procedure because it is an attempt to modify a procedure based on efficiency gains and losses rather than accepting a major redefinition of the underlying objective—namely, intergenerational fairness. On this argument, it should not be surprising to find that an issue of fairness cannot be handled by modifying efficiency criteria. Added to this, an appraisal procedure that evolved from concerns with mainly localized and certainly marginal changes to the state of the economy is being called upon to apply to issues that are global in a non-marginal sense (i.e., significant changes in well-being are involved). A tool for fine-tuning decisions is being applied to contexts where fine-tuning is not the issue.

More fundamentally, transfers between generations should not be treated in the same way as decisions about how to use resources available to the current generation. Equity issues within a generation can be treated by making resource transfers between individuals. Equity issues between generations need to be treated the same way: pursuing efficiency within a generation does not guarantee a fair distribution of resources through time.

Environmentalists have traditionally been more concerned to see actual discount rates lowered. Four approaches to modifying discount rates may be considered in the literature. These are: 1) setting the discount rate equal to zero; 2) computing a consumer discount rate; 3) computing a producer discount rate; and 4) computing some weighted average of consumer and producer rates.

Dominic Moran

Further Readings

Broome, J. *Counting the Cost of Global Warming.* 1992.

Lind, R.C. "A Primer on the Major Issues Relating to the Discount Rate for Evaluating National Energy Policy." In *Discounting for Time and Risk in Energy Policy.* Ed. Robert C. Lind, et al. 1982.

See also BENEFIT-COST ANALYSIS; CLIMATE WARMING; CONTINGENT VALUATION; ENVIRONMENTAL ETHICS; GREEN ECONOMICS; NUCLEAR WASTE

Dolphins and Porpoises

Dolphins and porpoises are the smaller (less than about four meters long) members of the whales or cetacean order. Cetaceans include baleen whales (eleven species, described elsewhere in the *Conservation and Environmentalism: An Encyclopedia*) and toothed whales (about seventy species). Some of the larger toothed whales, such as killer whales, pilot whales, and melon-headed whales, belong to the taxonomic family delphinidae along with their smaller dolphin cousins; they are termed "whale" simply because of their large size. Three families include dolphin-like animals: the delphinidae (true dolphins, thirty-five species), the platanistidae (river dolphins, five species), and the phocoenidae (porpoises, six species). While there are numerous skull morphology differences between dolphins and porpoises, three basic differences are easy to see: dolphins tend toward snouts with beaks while porpoise snouts are blunt; dolphins usually have distinct and curved (falcate) dorsal fins while porpoises have triangular-shaped dorsal fins; and dolphin teeth are pointed, or conical, while porpoise teeth are spade-shaped. Dolphins and porpoises are found in almost all oceanic habitats, from shallow bay to deep ocean; several species and populations of species occur in fresh water as well.

Dolphins and porpoises are all highly social animals, traveling in groups of a few in nearshore environments to several thousand in deep waters offshore. A lone dolphin is unlikely to be a healthy animal. Most dolphins and porpoises tend toward a fission-fusion society, where animals aggregate in different-size groups—and thereby associate with different individuals—on a periodic, often daily, basis. For example, dusky dolphins of the southern hemisphere travel in groups of six to twelve animals while resting and looking for food, but aggregate into groups of about 300 while feeding and for after-feeding social and sexual activity. Dusky dolphins, as apparently most species, cooperate during hunting of schooling fish; they show temporary restraint in feeding while corralling prey into tight balls, often using the water surface as a wall against which to push the trapped fish. Only when the prey are secured does feeding take place. Dolphins and porpoises also feed on non-schooling fishes, as well as on squid, jellyfish, shrimp, and other invertebrates. Most are quite catholic feeders, although a few deepwater species appear to specialize on squid.

Most odontocete cetaceans produce two basic sorts of sounds, consisting of whistles for communication between conspecifics and of clicks, termed click trains. While many types of clicks also serve to communicate, high frequency (ultrasonic, above 20 KH_z) clicks are mainly structured for echolocation. Clicks are sent out from the head, bounce off objects, and the returning echoes give information on size, shape, distance, speed, and density of the objects. Dolphins and porpoises can "see" with sound even in darkness, apparently to quite fine resolution, very similar to the echolocation abilities of some insectivorous bats. Several species of dolphins have very large brains, with highly convoluted foldings of the neocortex. The rough-toothed dolphin has a larger brain to body (weight and size) ratio than that of humans. These large brains have given rise to persistent speculations of extremely high intelligence of dolphins, including the possibility of complex as yet undiscovered languages. Dolphins are undeniably bright, capable of learning human-taught tricks much more rapidly than most animals. The intelligence question is still unanswered, however. Their large brains may simply have to do with their very social nature, remembering associations and alliances of many conspecifics, for example; and with their highly complex vocal/auditory capabilities. Most dolphins appear to be perpetually smiling, with an upturned mouth frozen into position by nature. This smile and their seeming friendliness (translated into a general lack of fear) toward humans has made them beguiling creatures for most human societies. They have generally not been hunted as a result.

Many populations of dolphins and porpoises, and some entire species, are in danger due to human contact, despite the fact that humans in general have not considered dolphins and porpoises as important prey. Dolphins and porpoises are having problems for several, often related, reasons:

1. Accidental net and line entanglement is killing animals worldwide. As mammals, dolphins and porpoises need to travel to the surface every few minutes to breathe, and when prevented from doing so, they suffocate.
2. Purposeful killing for food occurs in protein-poor parts of the world, for food as a substitute for whale meat, and because of perceived competition with human fisheries.
3. Accidental reproductive failure, reduced immunity responses, and mass die-offs occur apparently due to human habitat degradation, including toxin input from industries and agricultural runoff. Dolphins and porpoises are especially vulnerable to poisoned food, for they often feed high on the trophic level, on prey which have already bioaccumulated toxins. They also live long, and can themselves bioaccumulate heavy metals and organochlorine compounds which can be involved in metabolism during periods of starvation or illness.

In all cases of decimation, results are long-lasting and difficult to reverse because dolphins and porpoises are K-selected, long-lived, slowly reproducing species, with only one young every two to four years. As well, destruction of part of the society likely has profound effects on the efficient workings of the cooperative society as a whole. While the effects of disrupting K-selected mammals are well known, the potential effects due to sociality are not properly studied.

Accidental entanglement in fishing gear is high worldwide but exact numbers are not known. Especially destructive are the large monofilament gill drift nets of open seas. Although these have recently been outlawed or curtailed by legislative action of many countries, drift netting is profitable enough to assure fishing piracy for the foreseeable future. Drift nets for salmon and squid in the north Pacific killed an estimated 10,000 Dall's porpoises annually in the 1980s; also affected by the netting are harbor porpoises, Pacific white-sided dolphins, and northern right whale dolphins. The kill is now reduced, in part due to reduced fishing in the area, reduced target prey, and probably reduced porpoise and dolphin stocks as well. Drift nets kill unknown numbers of dolphins in the Mediterranean Sea, Indian Ocean, north and south Atlantic Ocean, and, indeed, worldwide. Nearshore set nets are responsible for decimating harbor porpoises in the north Atlantic, Hector's dolphins off New Zealand, Indopacific humpback dolphins in most of their range between west Africa and Malaysia, around the rim of the Indian Ocean, and all species of nearshore dolphins off Sri Lanka, the Philippines, and India. Net and line entanglements have been largely responsible for reducing the populations of Chinese river dolphins (or baiji) and Gulf of California harbor porpoises (or vaquita) to near-extinction. Overfishing by drift and set nets has probably contributed greatly to dolphin and porpoise population declines, for these upper-trophic level feeders rely in part on the same prey type as do humans.

One accidental netting technique has received much attention. This is the practice of setting nets around dolphins in the Eastern Tropical Pacific (ETP) to capture the yellowfin tuna which associate with dolphins. In the process, dolphins often get trapped in billowing or canopying netting and suffocate. In the 1970s and 1980s, up to one-half million dolphins died annually. The kill is now strongly reduced, with only about 20,000 to 40,000 dolphins killed per year, but stocks of spotted, spinner, and common dolphins of the ETP have been reduced to fractions of their former numbers.

Purposeful killing of dolphins is on the rise in many areas of the world. Off Chile and Peru, Sri Lanka, and the Philippines, a total of well over 100,000 dolphins and porpoises are netted, gaffed, and harpooned per year, for meat to serve as bait and human consumption. Dolphins and porpoises are seen as a relatively reliable food source, because many species approach boats in order to ride on or near the bow wave. As fish and squid stocks are being reduced, odontocete cetaceans are increasingly seen as adverse competitors with humans (and, typically, humans blame the dolphins, not themselves, for the decline in food stocks). Japan has been in the forefront of culling dolphins and other toothed whales off Japanese shores, by drive fisheries which can kill several thousand animals (often an entire oceanic herd) in one day. Sometimes but not always, the meat of the animals so killed is sold for human consumption. Since Japan and other countries have agreed to curtail most large species whaling, drive and harpoon fisheries have increased in popularity, not only to reduce fishing competition but also as a substitute for whale meat. There is a rapidly increasing awareness of ecosystem problems especially among young Japanese, and drive and harpoon fisheries are not likely to last too many more years. Whether this change in attitude is more rapid than present decimation and potential extinction of the toothed whale populations of the western north Pacific is not known.

Finally, there is an alarming increase in mass die-offs of dolphins and porpoises. In the late 1980s and again in 1992, 1993, and 1994, many hundreds of coastal bottlenose dolphins died in the western north Atlantic and Gulf of Mexico. Harbor porpoises died in the North Sea of Europe, and several thousand striped dolphins died in the western Mediterranean Sea. In the latter case, a morbillivirus was implicated in many deaths, and dolphins with morbillivirus had evidence of very high levels of PCBs in their blubber tissues. It is very possible but remains unproved that high levels of toxins, found sporadically in many stranded dolphins and porpoises, can weaken the immune system to a point where massive infections and subsequent die-offs can spread throughout a population.

In aggregate, dolphins and porpoises the world-over are being decimated by overfishing and habitat degradation. Two species, the Yangtze River dolphin and the Gulf of California harbor porpoise, are at the brink of extinction. Another at least thirty populations of species themselves not endangered are also at critically low level. As present trends are likely to continue, especially coastal and riverine species are projected to decrease to critical levels.

Bernd Würsig

Further Readings

Brownell, R.L., Jr., K. Ralls, and W.F. Perrin. "The Plight of the Forgotten Whales: It's Mainly Smaller Cetaceans That Are Now In Peril." *Oceanus* 32 (1989): 5–11.
Donoghue, M., and A. Wheeler. *Save the Dolphins*. 1990.
Klinowska, M. *Dolphins, Porpoises, and Whales of the World: The IUCN Red Data Book*. 1991.

See also BALEEN WHALES; BIOACCUMULATION; INTERNATIONAL WHALING COMMISSION; MARINE MAMMALS

Donora, Pennsylvania

Donora, Pennsylvania, was the scene of one of North America's worst air pollution disasters. A small industrial city on the Monongahela River twenty miles southeast of Pittsburgh, Donora's economy at the time of the tragedy (1948) was based on blast furnaces, steel mills, zinc smelters, sulphuric acid plants, and slag-processing mills. Controls on these were limited, often minimal.

Because of its industries and its location in a valley 500 feet below the surrounding countryside, Donora often experienced thick, smoky fogs. But from October 25 through October 30, 1948, the fog did not, as it usually did, lift at noon. A region-wide high pressure system had created a temperature inversion: a cap of warm air effectively sealing in pollutants. Gradually the acrid smell of sulphur dioxide filled the valley. Fog moved in, further darkening the skies. Virtually the entire population experienced respiratory distress. Thousands became ill. Twenty died.

Donora's experience proved to be a watershed. Not only did events there influence renewed efforts to create effective clean air legislation and enforcement: they produced an essential reformulation of the concept of air pollution. Prior to October 1948 smoke was widely believed to constitute air pollution's major component. Donora's painful experience (the most intensively studied event of its kind) demonstrated the falsity of this assumption.

Research showed that sulphur dioxide, hydrogen sulphide, nitrogen oxide, particulate metals, as well as "pea soup" fog, all played major roles in the disaster. So did the interaction of these factors. Smoke played a relatively minor role. Never again was air pollution to be viewed as single, or even simple.

Pete A.Y. Gunter

Further Readings

Schrenk, H.H., ed. *Air Pollution in Donora, Pennsylvania.* Federal Security Agency Public Health Bulletin 306, 1949.

See also AIR POLLUTION: IMPACTS; LONDON SMOG; SMOG

Douglas, Marjory Stoneman

Marjory Stoneman Douglas (1890–) is one of the most important twentieth century conservationists in the United States. She has been involved with a wide variety of issues in her native state of Florida, in particular the protection of the Everglades. Douglas is the author of *The Everglades: River of Grass*, a volume first published in 1947 and still selling in significant numbers to this day. This volume, originally commissioned by Rinehart and Company, was four years in the writing, but an immediate success. The book altered the public consciousness regarding the Everglades, changing its conception from that of "swamp" to that of broad, shallow river. Her book was published at about the time that the Everglades were declared a National Park by President Truman, after the conception of Ernest Coe and the efforts of Douglas and numerous others. The designation of the park has not been sufficient to the protection of the fragile and rich flora and fauna of South Florida, the ecology of which is threatened yet today, primarily by alterations in fresh water availability.

Marjory Stoneman Douglas was in her fifties when she approached the task of writing about the Everglades. Prior to that time she had been a journalist and a writer of fiction. Following that time, for more than another fifty years thus far, she has been an author of books primarily on Florida and conservation subjects, and a tireless campaigner in the defense of nature. She has worked in the defense of the Florida panther, at odds at times with scientists in her opposition to the use of radio collars on the animals. She opposed dikes in the Everglades and continues to fight for a variety of measures to increase the water flows to the South. Interventions to this flow along the way is doing grievous harm to the fragile ecology of the park and the state.

Marjory Douglas was instrumental in the creation of Friends of the Everglades, an organization with a very wide membership in Florida and throughout the United States. As she put it: "My book on the Everglades was 20 years old and I was 78 before I got absorbed in the great effort to save them." She has continued that effort for the balance of her long life. In early 1994 she traveled to Washington, D.C., to receive the Presidential Medal of Freedom from President Clinton.

Robert Paehlke

Further Readings

Douglas, Marjory Stoneman. *The Everglades: River of Grass.* 1947.
———. *Florida: The Long Frontier.* 1967.
———. (with John Rothchild). *Voice of the River.* 1987.

See also EVERGLADES OF SOUTH FLORIDA; FLORIDA PANTHER; FRESHWATER WETLANDS; REPTILES: CONSERVATION AND HABITAT; SHOREBIRDS

Douglas, William O.

William O. Douglas (1898–1980) served on the U.S. Supreme Court from 1939 to 1975, during which time he became perhaps the foremost conservation advocate in public life. Imbued with a passion for the outdoors and a devotion to conservation that dated from his boyhood in the state of Washington, Douglas brought to the bench an unusually well informed understanding of resource issues. Increasingly influenced by the writings of John Muir, Aldo Leopold, and other American conservationists, as well as his reading of non-Western philosophy, Douglas became a leading voice for stronger legal protections for natural objects and places. In a famous dissent in the case of *Sierra Club v. Morton* (1972), Douglas cited "contemporary public concern for protecting nature's ecological equilibrium" and suggested the need for "a federal rule that allowed environmental issues to be litigated . . . in the name of the inanimate object about to be despoiled, defaced, or invaded." His opinion became an important starting point for further developments in environmental law, ethics, and philosophy.

Douglas's involvement was not confined to his judicial activities. Even in the midst of his demanding schedule, Douglas maintained an active outdoor life and participated in numerous local conservation battles. His advocacy led to the protection of the C & O Canal, a 190-mile long semi-natural corridor that stretched from Washington, D.C., into the adjacent countryside. An indefatigable hiker, Douglas continued to hike the entire length of the canal trail every year into his seventies. Douglas died in 1980. His thirty-six years on the Supreme Court was the longest term of service in the history of the court up to that time.

Curt Meine

Further Readings

Douglas, William O. *Go East, Young Man.* 1974.

Stone, Christopher. *Should Trees Have Standing: Toward Legal Rights for Natural Objects.* 1974.

Wild, Peter. *Pioneer Conservationists of Western America.* 1979.

See also CONSERVATION MOVEMENT; ENVIRONMENTAL CASE LAW: UNITED STATES; LEOPOLD, ALDO; MINERAL KING CANYON; MUIR, JOHN; WILDERNESS

Drift Nets

See DOLPHINS AND PORPOISES; FISHERIES CONSERVATION

Ducks Unlimited

The Ducks Unlimited Program began in the United States, growing out of the More Game Birds in America Foundation, which was formed in the 1930s because of a long time concern that North American populations of migratory game birds—waterfowl—were diminishing. A 1935 census confirmed that the vast majority (almost 75 percent) of almost 43 million ducks were bred in Canada, that populations were declining due to habitat detoriation, and that the most valuable conservation initiatives lay in preserving breeding grounds located in Canada.

A conservation program called Ducks Unlimited was first suggested in 1935 by the Foundation. On January 29, 1937, Ducks Unlimited

Inc. of the United States was incorporated with the goal of raising the funds necessary to preserve northern breeding grounds and to restore more southerly ones. On March 10 of the same year, Ducks Unlimited Canada was incorporated to put funds to work in Canada that were raised from U.S. sportsmen.

Ducks Unlimited Canada is a private, non-profit, internationally supported conservation organization whose goal is to preserve, restore, enhance, and manage waterfowl habitats in Canada. Formed in 1937, the Canadian organization is part of an international network which includes organizations in the United States, Mexico, Australia, and New Zealand. By the beginning of the 1990s, Ducks Unlimited Canada had developed more than 2.4 million acres of habitat, securing about 150,000 acres each year.

Ducks Unlimited Canada traditionally concentrated on wetland development projects in prairie Canada. Now operational in all provinces and territories, Ducks Unlimited's habitat conservation programs focus on landowner stewardship. Under the auspices of the North American Waterfowl Management Plan, a multi-million-dollar international program designed to return waterfowl populations to the levels of the 1970s, 99 percent of new habitat programs focus on conserving massive acreages of breeding, staging, and wintering habitats continentwide. Through a range of partnership agreements with governments and private landowners, Ducks Unlimited has assisted in the protection of almost 18 million acres of wildlife habitat.

The Prairie CARE program (Conservation of Agriculture Resources and Environment) provides incentives to farmers to encourage conservation farming and habitat protection. Ducks Unlimited promotes sustainable agriculture on good quality land and revegetation of cropped marginal lands to enhance soil and water quality, waterfowl habitat, and biodiversity values.

Kevin McNamee

Further Readings

Anon. "Year One." *Conservator* 9 (1988): 4–7.

See also FRESHWATER WETLANDS; WATERFOWL: CONSERVATION AND HABITAT

D

E

Eagle

See BALD EAGLE

Earth Day

Earth Day, first celebrated on April 22, 1970, is a day that witnessed the active and visible participation of millions of North Americans in a plea to protect the environment. The day marked the culmination of a transformation and expansion of environmental concern from the traditional concerns of the conservation movement (including habitat, parks, and wilderness recreation) to a much broader agenda—one that emphasized the need to combat pollution, resource depletion (even before, and certainly after the 1973 energy crisis), the perils of technology (i.e., nuclear power), and overpopulation.

The idea for the event originated with U.S. Senator Gaylord Nelson (Democrat, Wisconsin) who, reading about the anti-war teach-ins, concluded that this technique could be applied to the then-rising wave of environmental concern in the United States. The date was chosen as one when schools and universities were still in session, but not yet into exams. Right-wing organizations promptly suggested that this was an ill-disguised attempt to secretly celebrate Lenin's birthday. Nelson replied that it was also the birth date of the original environmentalist, St. Francis of Assisi. More appropriately perhaps it is the day after John Muir's birthday, but that was by most accounts not taken into consideration. In any case, Senator Nelson generated enough money from speaking fees and other sources to hire three Harvard students to organize the event, with Denis Hayes serving as national coordinator.

The level of response took many by surprise: from the Nixon administration and others in government and industry to the traditional conservation organizations (despite the fact that most had seen their membership levels rise sharply in the late 1960s) and the organizers of the event themselves. There were major rallies in New York, Washington, and San Francisco and events on most U.S. campuses. The organizers suggested that there was participation on or from 1,500 universities and colleges and some 10,000 schools; *Time* estimated that 20 million people took part. Environmentalism had clearly achieved mass movement status and the legislative agenda was altered for some years to come.

More important, perhaps, was the fact that Earth Day moved existing conservation and environmental organizations to further increases in membership and activity levels, and served as the impetus to the creation of new organizations and emphases. The Washington-based Environmental Action arose directly out of the Earth Day event and the Natural Resources Defense Council was created in the same year. Many other organizations such as the Union of Concerned Scientists, and the anti-nuclear movement generally gained considerable momentum. The primary focus of environmental concern had become pollution and health, rather than the protection of the diminishing space of threatened flora and fauna.

By the reprise of Earth Day as a major event on April 22, 1990, emphases had changed yet again. Also considerably different were organizational styles and techniques. Environmentalism was again at the crest of a wave of popular concern, but the underlying movement had in the meantime grown in both organizational strength and general respectability (and those who would have doubted the desirability of such changes had largely changed their minds or grown quiet). Earth Day 1990 was again organized by Denis Hayes, but this time with a foundation and corporate-based budget of some $3 million. There were television specials and media stars. There was saturation coverage and some 100 million people participated in 140 countries worldwide. It was an event that was difficult to miss, but some have suggested that the organizational and political results were less significant than were those associated with Earth Day 1970.

Nonetheless, Earth Day 1990 provided an opportunity to observe the evolution of the environmental movement from protest to acceptability with both the advantages and disadvantages of that shift on public display. There could be no doubt that there still was widespread public concern regarding matters environmental. Moreover, clearly there had been a reintegration of the environmental (pollution, health, and resource sustainability) and conservation (wilderness and habitat protection) agendas. That reintegration was achieved in part by virtue of a globalization of all environmental concerns. The new focus was on biodiversity, climate warming, ozone depletion, tropical deforestation and the destruction of old growth forests, and both the unsafe disposal and the long-range transport of everything from municipal solid wastes to toxic chemicals. The movement had evolved in terms of social, political, and media sophistication, but also in terms of a well-integrated set of overall objectives.

Robert Paehlke

Further Readings
Sale, Kirkpatrick. *The Green Revolution: The American Environmental Movement, 1962–1992.* 1993.
Shabecoff, Philip. *A Fierce Green Flame: The American Environmental Movement.* 1993.

See also AIR POLLUTION: IMPACTS; CONSERVATION MOVEMENT; ENERGY CRISIS; ENVIRONMENTAL ACTION; ENVIRONMENTALISM; MUIR, JOHN; NATURAL RESOURCES DEFENSE COUNCIL; NELSON, GAYLORD A.; UNION OF CONCERNED SCIENTISTS

Earth First!
An account of the radical environmental activist organization Earth First! now appears in a number of places (e.g., Manes, 1990; Scarce,

1990; Zakin, 1993). Earth First! arose in the early 1980s as a reaction to the anthropocentric and pragmatic politics of the mainline environmental organizations, especially the political compromises made during the RARE II classification of public lands as legally protected wilderness. Some of the founders of Earth First! (Dave Foreman, Bart Koehler, Howie Wolke, and others) had been staff members of the Wilderness Society and other reform organizations and were themselves professionally involved in these politics; they were shocked and disillusioned by the political compromises being made over America's last wild places.

As the newest branch of ecology—conservation biology—arose in the 1980s, Earth First! leader's worst fears were confirmed. Michael Soulé and other conservation biologists were demonstrating that existing legally protected wilderness and wildlife preserves around the world were too small and isolated. The result of this newly-understood reality is that the natural flow of evolutionary processes for many species on earth has been severely disrupted.

Influenced by Edward Abbey's ecocentric novels, which dramatized monkey-wrenching, Foreman and the others saw the need for a revival of a no-compromise radical ecocentric environmentalism of the Muir-Brower type ("no compromise in defense of Mother Earth"). Many in Earth First! saw their organization as an activist wing of the ecocentric Deep Ecology movement. Earth First! was highly successful throughout the 1980s in its direct action forest and other wilderness campaigns (blockading logging roads, spiking trees, and tree-sitting until courts could issue injunctions, and protective legislation was passed) and in publicizing its ecocentric philosophy. Earth First! attracted a great deal of media attention and a large following. In retrospect, Foreman claims that Earth First! deserves credit for making the protection of ancient (old-growth) forests a major public issue, and for revitalizing a demoralized environmental movement during the Reagan era.

In the late 1980s, many of the newcomers to the Earth First! movement (from the ranks of urban anarchists, the Rainbow Coalition, and labor organizers) began to demand that Earth First! expand its concerns to cover more anthropocentrically oriented "social justice" issues. More dissension arose in 1987 when Murray Bookchin and his Social Ecology group attacked the Deep Ecology movement and apparently misanthropic statements made by

Foreman and others in Earth First! (Sale, 1988; Sessions, 1992). Earth First! was thrown into even further disarray by the FBI arrest of Foreman and others who were charged with destroying power lines.

But it was primarily the leftist social/political agenda and tactics, and the dilution of the original ecological mission of Earth First! which caused Foreman and others to leave the organization in 1990. In 1991 Foreman, along with John Davis (the editor of *Earth First! Journal*) initiated a new journal, *Wild Earth*, together with the Wildlands Project. These undertakings are devoted specifically to ecocentrism, conservation biology, and the establishment of greatly expanded wilderness areas with interconnecting corridors. Their goal is to protect and restore biodiversity and wild evolutionary processes in the United States and elsewhere throughout the world.

George Sessions

Further Readings

Davis, John, and Dave Foreman, eds. *Wild Earth*. (P.O. Box 455, Richmond, VT 05477).
Devall, Bill. "Maybe the Movement Is Leaving Me." *Earth First! Journal* 10 (1990): 6.
Foreman, Dave. *Confessions of an Ecowarrior*. 1991a.
———. "The New Conservation Movement." *Wild Earth* 1 (1991b): 6–12.
Manes, Christopher. *Green Rage: Radical Environmentalism and the Unmaking of Civilization*. 1990.
Sale, Kirkpatrick. "Deep Ecology and Its Critics." *The Nation* 22 (May 14, 1988): 54, 127.
Scarce, Rik. *Ecowarriors: Understanding the Radical Environmental Movement*. 1990.
Sessions, George. "Radical Environmentalism in the 90s" and "Postscript: March 1992." *Wild Earth* 2 (1992): 64–70.
Taylor, Bron. "The Religion and Politics of Earth First!" *The Ecologist* 21 (November/December, 1991).
Zakin, Susan. *Coyotes and Town Dogs: Earth First! and the Environmental Movement*. 1993.

See also ABBEY, EDWARD; ANTHROPOCENTRISM; BIODEPLETION; BIODIVERSITY; DEEP ECOLOGY: EMERGENCE; DEEP ECOLOGY: MEANINGS; OLD GROWTH FORESTS; RADICAL ENVIRONMENTALISM; WILDERNESS; WILDERNESS SOCIETY; WILDLANDS PROJECT

Earth Summit

See RIO CONFERENCE (1992)

Eastern Europe: Environmental Problems

Environmental problems in Eastern Europe are among the most serious and most intractable in the world. Eastern Europe or East Central Europe as it has been called since the fall of the communist regimes in 1990–1991 is an area whose northern boundary is the Baltic Sea; its southern boundary the Adriatic; its western boundary the eastern borders of Germany, Austria, and Italy; and its eastern boundary the western frontiers of the newly independent republics of Belorus and Ukraine. The countries of the region going from north to south are Estonia, Latvia, Lithuania, Poland, the Czech Republic, Slovakia, Hungary, Slovenia, Croatia, Romania, Yugoslavia, Bosnia, Macedonia, and Albania. Of the fourteen, ten are entirely new states, created as a result of the ethnic conflict spawned by the collapse of communism. Five of the new states came into being without conflict, Estonia, Latvia, Lithuania, known as the Baltic republics, and the Czech and Slovak Republics. In the former Yugoslavia, all the states with the exception of Slovenia are objects of actual or potential conflict. As of this writing the permanent boundaries of Croatia have yet to be fixed with war likely to determine the borders. Bosnia is in the process of being divided into three separate autonomous entities, with its continued existence as an independent state in doubt. The future of Macedonia also hangs in the balance.

Eastern Europe is divided by mountain ranges and rivers into small regions whose security and identity have been defined by geographic features. In the north Poland and the Baltic republics are part of the North European plain that stretches from the Netherlands to the Ural Mountains in Russia. Historically the region has been the scene of bloody conflicts between Poles, Germans, Swedes, Lithuanians, and Russians as each group sought to define a permanent border. Today's borders are only as old as World War II. The plain ends in the foothills of the Carpathian mountain ranges, which help form the borders of the Czech and Slovak Republics, and snake down through Romania. The Balkan peninsula is criss-crossed by mountains, with plateaus like the Bosnia plateau between them. The history of the South Slav populations is dominated by their struggle to maintain their existence in the river valleys and plains in the face of what was perceived as hostile intruders from East and West: Germans, Hungarians, and Turks. The absence of geographic unity contributed to the isolation of the Slav groups and promoted the development of strong feelings of national identity.

Natural resources are unevenly distributed in the region. Poland, Hungary, Slovakia, Romania, and Yugoslavia have rich agricultural land. The mountains on the borders of Poland and the Czech Republic contain large deposits of coal—the principal energy source for the two countries—while Romania is known for its petroleum and natural gas deposits. Hungary also has petroleum reserves in the Lipse field north of the Drava River that forms the border between Croatia and Hungary. There are natural gas reserves to the east of the Tisza River. Aside from coal, the Czech Republic has significant deposits of uranium ore in Western Bohemia. The region also contains a variety of mineral and metal reserves. Hungary and Albania are important producers of bauxite; Yugoslavia has one of Europe's largest copper fields, while the Czech Republic and Slovakia are particularly rich in metallic ores.

Before World War II, Czechoslovakia was the most highly developed of all the countries in the region. In 1939 it possessed an advanced electro-engineering industry and enjoyed the highest standard of living of any European state. The other countries were in the early stages of industrialization. After World War II, Stalin tried to force a Soviet-style economic system upon states whose economies had been ruined by war. In Czechoslovakia Stalinism meant deindustrialization as its advanced technology was forcibly replaced by smokestack first-generation industrial production. In the Baltic republics—Poland and Hungary—a centrally planned economy and one-party political system were the instruments of increasing the industrial tempo and collapsing the time between the first two stages of the industrial revolution. In Romania and Bulgaria, Stalinism effectively launched industrialization. The decision in favor of economic autarky in the 1950s meant that each country had to produce its own iron, steel, and aluminum. The key to Romanian growth was its refusal to follow a Comecon plan for agricultural development and its channeling of investment into metal-

lurgy, machine building, energy, and petro-chemical production.

Today regional pollution levels in every environmental category have the distinction of being among the highest in the world. East Central Europe produces one-third of Europe's GNP and two-thirds of its sulfur dioxide. After the former East Germany, Czechoslovakia ranks second in the world in sulfur dioxide emissions with an increase from 900,000 tons in 1950 to 3,150,000 tons in 1985. The major source of severe air pollution is the regional reliance on brown coal for energy. Destruction of forests by acid precipitation has reached catastrophic proportions. Significant damage has been sustained in 71 percent of the forests in the former Czechoslovakia, 48 percent in Poland, 44 percent in the former East Germany, and 43 percent in Bulgaria. In some areas of former East Germany and eastern Bohemia, the entire forest stand is dead.

The health costs of air pollution are still being assessed but they are high by any measure. The Hungarians estimate that the annual health costs of air pollution in loss of work, death, and sick leave for 1990 was 13.3 percent of all health and social welfare expenditures. Czechoslovakia has the highest density of sulfur dioxide deposits in Europe (228 pounds per acre per year) and the highest death rate due to cancer of all 150 member states of the United Nations. In 1989 life expectancy in the Most coal district of eastern Bohemia was three years less for men and two years less for women than the national averages, and eleven and three years less than for Europe as a whole. Czech officials have found a significant correlation between deterioration of a locality's air quality, higher infant mortality rates, and increased incidence in the number of allergies, pulmonary diseases, and breathing difficulties, especially among children. Children from polluted regions are regularly sent to "green classes" in the mountains for several weeks a year during the school terms and to less polluted areas for vacation in the summer.

In Estonia the "gray snow" from the Kunda cement factory on the Estonian coast hardens like mortar on roofs and is the cause of numerous medical problems. In Bulgaria the ecological movement began in the Danubian port of Ruse where prevailing winds blow toxic chemicals across the river from a chemical plant on the Romanian side. According to Romanian health officials 80 percent of the draftees from Ruse have lung damage. In former East Germany life expectancy in the Halle-Leipzig metropolitan area was five years less and the incidence of heart and respiratory disease fifteen times higher than elsewhere in the former Communist country. Air pollution affects some 10 percent of Romanian territory and 20 percent of the population (or 4.5 million people). Of these roughly a third are suffering from the effects of pollution on a permanent basis. The grimy metallurgical and mining towns in the mountainous regions of Transylvania are plagued with severe health problems. A 1985 study showed that 95 percent of a sample of 200,000 Romanian women showed signs of diseased uteri. In the former Yugoslavia ambient air quality across the area as a whole is not a significant problem. However, in the large urban centers, pollution regularly exceeds the permissible legal levels for the major pollutants. In the mid-1980s, air pollution in the Macedonian capital of Skopje was reportedly so bad that it impeded normal breathing. In 1990 Belgrade had the highest concentration of sulfur dioxide and nitrous oxides per cubic meter of air of any capital in the world. Comprehensive data is so far not available for Albania, but reports indicate that pollution is high in those cities where the smoke-stack industries (i.e., cement, tanning, chemicals, and metallurgy) and coal-fired power plants are located.

Water pollution has also reached crisis proportions. The "Blue Danube" is gray brown with industrial wastes. As much as 70 percent of all water in Poland may be undrinkable. Over the past three decades there has been a steady deterioration in water quality in Hungary's five major rivers. In the Czech Republic and Slovakia 57 percent of the drinking water in 1990 failed to meet established water quality criteria. By the early 1960s nearly all Bulgarian rivers were polluted. Although the government undertook several remedial measures, including the installation of 150 water purification plants, 60 million tons of waste products still enter Bulgaria's rivers annually. In Yugoslavia, the Sava River was called "dead" by the mid-1980s. In Croatia, not one single river in 1990 could be listed in category I, the category of highest water quality, and most of the urban and industrial agglomerations reported no waste treatment or sewage plants. Information on Albania is not systematic. However, reports of substantial spillages in the oilfields, run-off of pesticides, and leaching of manure indicate that there are localized water problems. Large quantities of regional water

pollutants are carried into the Baltic and Adriatic seas. Both are now severely polluted, forcing the closing of popular coastal summer beaches.

Soil pollution has kept pace with air and water degradation. Plans during the 1980s to enlarge the phosphate strip-mine along the Estonian coast were thwarted only through sustained popular protest. The unrestrained use of fertilizers and pesticides, particularly the continued use of DDT, has contaminated water supplies and soils in every country of the region. Lead contamination in Poland's apples and lettuce exceeds the United Nations' health standards by ten times. Many of Hungary's soils suffer from severe nitrate pollution. In Bulgaria many areas suffer from industrialization. Heavy metals pollute large sections of arable land with concentrations measured in places at 1,300 milligrams per kilogram (mg/kg) of lead, 3,000 mg/kg of zinc, 650 mg/kg arsenic, 22 mg/kg of cadmium, and 3,950 mg/kg copper. Uranium production has affected soils in Pervomai and Simitli. The zinc and lead plant near Plovdiv has been poisoning crops and killing livestock for years, while in the central part of the country around Srednogorie, the dumping of industrial wastes has contaminated some 13,000 hectares of cropland. In Romania almost one-third of the land is subject to some kind of pollution. Over 900,000 hectares are chemically polluted, of which 200,000 hectares can no longer be utilized. In Yugoslavia the dumping of tailings from the Bor copper mine over a forty-year period has destroyed the river bottom land and experts estimate it will take from eighty to 100 years to make it arable again.

Erosion is another serious problem. In the former Yugoslavia the rapid pace of urbanization and the abandonment of small farms meant that, by 1978, 54 percent of that country's total agricultural area was designated moderately to severely eroded. In Northwestern Bohemia the visitor travels through veritable moonscapes of crater-filled land to reach the historic city of Most, of which all that remains is a small chapel teetering on the brink of an abandoned brown coal pit. The consolidation of collective farmland further contributed to erosion in valuable agricultural lands as traditional hedgerows were eliminated and fields joined to accommodate the huge Soviet tractors and cultivators. Since the large machines could not be used in hilly areas many hectares of cropland were taken out of production. In Romania it is estimated that 16.3 tons of material are lost from each hectare

E

of land every year, with particularly high losses reported on the slopes of the sub-Carpathians. Salt accumulation is also a problem. The 1980s saw serious efforts in Poland to reclaim wasteland. However, according to official statistics, in 1991 there were still over 93,500,000 hectares of devastated land and only 2,264,000 hectares had been returned to cultivation. In Hungary, research by the Research Institute for Soil Science and Agricultural Chemistry in Budapest found that 30 percent of the country's land was endangered by wind and soil erosion. Over 10 percent of the land suffered from salinity and/or alkalinity.

Of all the countries Poland suffered the most from the radioactive fallout from the nuclear accident at Chernobyl. Between April 27 and April 29, 1986, virtually the whole of Poland was covered by fall-out. The long-term effects of the disaster are unknown. An immediate consequence that year was that Poland lost over $6 million US in vanished tourism and another $24 to $27 million as a result of the European Community (EC) ban on agricultural produce.

Causes of Pollution

The seriousness of East Central Europe's environmental problems is compounded by two sets of factors: those determined by regional geopolitics and those specific to the former socialist states in process of transition. In the first set the first factor is the small size and multiple borders of all the countries. The Czech Republic, Slovakia, and Hungary are landlocked. As a consequence, not only are the Czech Republic, Slovakia, Poland, and former East Germany among the largest producers of sulfur dioxide in Europe, they are also the largest importers and exporters of emissions. Poland imports 46 percent of its depositions; the Czech Republic, 47 percent; and former East Germany 22 percent. The dieback of the forests in Krkonose National Park in the frontier triangle where Poland, the Czech Republic, and Germany meet is silent testimony to the problems faced by small countries in their attempt to handle transboundary airborne pollution.

Few waterways lie wholly within one East European country. The Elbe River rises in Czechoslovakia and empties into the North Sea at Hamburg, Germany. The Danube rises in Germany and flows through seven European countries before it empties into the Black Sea in Romania. Despite international agreements, such as that for the Danube and the Elbe, con-

flicting national demands have increased rather than abated pollution. Examples are the water pollution problems in southern Poland caused in large part by Czech plants on the other side of the border and disagreements between Slovakia and Hungary over the completion of the Gabcikovo-Nagymoros Dam on the Danube River.

The most sinister kind of cross-boundary vulnerability is radioactivity. One long-term effect of Chernobyl was that soil pollution by trace particles became a transboundary phenomenon. Contamination by trace minerals in those countries in the path of the radioactive cloud—particularly Poland and Hungary—has aggravated the already serious problem of cross-boundary soil pollution caused by seepage of chemical and agricultural waste.

The cost of technology associated with pollution abatement is a second general factor. Before 1989 most East European countries could not afford to import environmental technology developed in the West. In countries such as Yugoslavia, where trade with the West was permitted, investors in the country consistently found it cheaper to import old polluting machinery rather than to spend money on new pollution-abating equipment. Czechoslovakia, East Germany, and Bulgaria traded with the West only within very limited parameters. We are only now discovering how much machinery in the region is outdated, relics of the 1950s. Today all the countries suffer from a hard currency deficit, and have preferred imports vital for economic restructuring over pollution controls. Moreover, while Yugoslavia, Hungary, and Poland benefited from scientific exchanges with the West, the rest of the region was cut off from the mainstream of environmental research for forty years. Many new technologies are still untried and the risks involved in experimentation over tested products, coupled with the cost, are too high to encourage struggling economies to invest in them.

The third problem is energy structure. In East Central Europe every country but Poland is a net energy importer with Russia being the major energy supplier. Any change in domestic energy use is linked directly to developments in Russia and the availability of hard currency to purchase oil on the international market. Unsettled conditions in Russia discourage reliance on its oil and gas reserves, yet there is no viable alternative. Coal thus continues to figure prominently in long-term energy calculations in those countries with large deposits. The prospects for alternative energy sources, including the capacity for further generation of hydropower, with the possible exception of Albania, are small. Solar power is unfeasible at this point. Hence, governments have reverted to the pursuit of nuclear power development to the widespread anxiety of the East European populations.

The second set of factors relates to the unique characteristics of the former Communist systems. First among these was their wasteful use of raw materials. In 1987 it took Poland 88,829 kilojoules to produce $1.00 of GNP; Hungary, 48,542; and Yugoslavia, 22,084. The figure for the United States, among the most wasteful energy users in the Organisation for Economic Co-operation and Development (OECD), was 20,645. Between 1970 and 1988 U.S. energy consumption per unit of GDP dropped by 27 percent, while Yugoslavia's increased by 15 percent.

The second characteristic of Communist systems was the leadership's total hold over all aspects of society legitimated through the institution of central planning. This control was sufficiently absolute that the economy and civil society ceased to exist as autonomous entities. The chief function of the economy thus became not so much production as the perpetuation of the ruling group in power. As an extension of the state, the economy shared in the political patronage game, promoting the loyal, disregarding competence, and permitting the emergence of no organization which could acquire sufficient independent means to challenge the ruling hierarchy. During the 1980s, national economic plans increasingly included environmental parameters. However, the bottom line for management to receive its bonus was fulfillment of the production quotas. Environmental quotas, like production quotas, tended to be based on quantity rather than quality, while overlapping rival jurisdictions in the implementation of environmental policy made everyone's responsibility no one's responsibility. Censorship kept the populations ignorant of the overall scope of environmental problems. Poland was the first country to start down the path of easing censorship with the advent of the Solidarity movement in 1980. After Chernobyl Eastern Europe only partially responded to Gorbachev's policy of *glasnost*. Albania, Bulgaria, Romania, Czechoslovakia, and East Germany did not experience any substantial lifting of censorship until the collapse of communism in 1989.

Finally, the Communist leaders themselves lacked the political will to tackle the mounting environmental problems. The policy of rapid economic development focused on heavy industry was dictated by Moscow. Every reform program had to receive Moscow's imprimatur or, as in Hungary in 1956 and Czechoslovakia in 1968, be forcibly destroyed by Soviet tanks. The population was told that pollution was the price of progress, and older people with vivid memories of World War II tended to accept the situation. With few exceptions environmental activists came from the younger generation of East Europeans.

As the 1980s came to an end environmental movements had proliferated over the entire region and were particularly active in bringing down the Lithuanian, Estonian, Czechoslovak, and Hungarian regimes. However, in the first democratic elections, environmentalists were not able to translate their initial activism into public support for environmental remediation. The new governments' primary concern has been the reform of the economy with minimum social cost.

Problems of Environmental Remediation

Comprehensive environmental remediation is not something any of the countries can do on their own or the region as a whole can achieve. Environmental stress is "built-in" to regional relations because of each country's unequal access to natural resources and the inability to control trans-border pollution through the domestic policy process. Nevertheless, steps have been taken in intra-regional cooperation. These include the 1990 agreement to develop an action plan by the members of the Baltic Marine Environmental Protection Committee, the formation of the Elbe River Commission by the riverine states to clean up that waterway, the Alps-Adria Project, and the establishment of a Carpathian bioregion.

To facilitate environmental information gathering and exchange, the U.S. government provided $12 million of seed money for the establishment in Budapest in September 1990 of the Regional Environmental Center for Central and Eastern Europe. In 1992 the EC funded two projects relating to Elbe water quality in the Czech Republic to reduce pollution of the main river and decrease sedimentation at the German port of Hamburg. Sweden has allocated $40 million to Poland for sewage treatment on the Vistula and Oder Rivers. Four international banks have agreed to fund the Baltic Sea Action Plan. Hungary and Slovakia have agreed to EC arbitration of their differences in the

E

Gabcikovo-Nagymoros dispute. Finally, the new governments' elaboration of comprehensive environmental legal frameworks is going forward with the aid of economic, technical, and political assistance from the EC, the international lending institutions, and the United States.

Barbara Jancar-Webster

Further Readings

Carter, F.W., and Turnock, D. *Environmental Problems in Eastern Europe*. 1993.

DeBardeleben, Joan, ed. *To Breathe Free: Eastern Europe's Environmental Crisis*. 1991.

Jancar-Webster, Barbara, ed. *Environmental Action in Eastern Europe: Responses to Crises*. 1993.

See also ACID PRECIPITATION: EUROPEAN EXPERIENCES; AIR POLLUTION: IMPACTS; CHERNOBYL; COAL: ENVIRONMENTAL IMPACTS; FORMER SOVIET UNION; PESTICIDES; SOIL CONSERVATION

Echo Park Dam

Along the northern border of Colorado and Utah, the Green and Yampa rivers cut through the Eastern Uinta Uplift producing a series of spectacular canyons and parks. These form the principal scenic features of Dinosaur National Monument, a 200,000-acre wilderness reserve managed by the U.S. National Park Service. Echo Park lays roughly in the center of the monument, near the confluence of the two rivers. In the early 1950s, a proposal by the U.S. Bureau of Reclamation to construct several dams in Dinosaur National Monument, including one near Echo Park, provoked intense public controversy. In a political battle that served as crucible for the emerging post-World War II environmental movement in the United States, a coalition of preservationist groups defeated the proposal.

Created in 1915 to protect the site of a fossil quarry, Dinosaur National Monument remained a small (80 acres) and obscure reserve until the mid-1930s. As part of a New Deal program to expand the national park system in the upper Colorado River basin, in 1938 the Franklin D. Roosevelt administration added the scenic canyons of the Green and Yampa rivers to Dinosaur National Monument (Executive Order No. 2290). Aware that reclamationists looked upon these canyons as critical to future utilization of the basin's water resources, the administration included legal provisions in the 1938 enabling proclamation making Dinosaur subject to reclamation and hydroelectric development. Anticipating the likelihood of such development, in 1941 the National Park Service signed a memorandum of understanding with the Bureau of Reclamation calling for the eventual conversion of Dinosaur into a multiple-use national recreation area.

With the ratification in 1949 of the Upper Colorado River Basin Compact, which resolved long-standing disputes over interstate water rights, the Bureau of Reclamation was ready to proceed with a comprehensive, basin-wide development project. The Colorado River Storage Project (CRSP) included plans for a series of large storage and power-generating dams, including two (Echo Park and Split Mountain) in Dinosaur National Monument. By 1949, however, the National Park Service had come to regret its earlier acquiescence to dam construction in Dinosaur, partly because of a growing appreciation among the service's personnel for the region's distinctive wilderness aesthetics, and partly out of concern over the scope of the Bureau of Reclamation's ambitions in the Colorado River basin.

Commissioner of Reclamation Michael Straus and National Park Service Director Newton B. Drury submitted the matter to Secretary of the Interior Oscar L. Chapman for resolution. Straus appealed to reclamation supporters in the upper Basin states to exert pressure on the Secretary; Drury responded in kind, alerting the service's allies in the Sierra Club and other preservationist groups to the controversy. After a brief public hearing in April 1950, Chapman gave the Bureau of Reclamation permission to circulate a detailed plan for the CRSP, including Echo Park dam, for comment by state and federal officials, but he postponed submitting the plan to Congress for authorization. The CRSP hung in bureaucratic limbo for two years until the Eisenhower administration came into office. In 1953 the new Secretary of the Interior, Douglas McKay, ordered the Bureau of Reclamation to draft authorizing legislation for submission to the U.S. Congress. CRSP bills were considered by the 83rd and 84th Congresses, with public hearings in 1954 and 1955.

With the Eisenhower administration's decision to support the CRSP, the National Park Service could not openly oppose Echo Park dam and the defense of Dinosaur fell to a coalition of preservationist organizations. An aggressive and politically astute cadre of young activists, most notably David Brower of the Sierra Club and Howard Zahniser of the Wilderness Society, provided leadership. Bolstered by the financial and political support of powerful allies, including the Congress of Industrial Organizations and California reclamationists opposed to upper basin development, the preservationist coalition undertook a well-orchestrated and highly effective lobbying and publicity campaign. The campaign found a receptive audience in the increasingly affluent, well-educated, and mobile post-war middle-class who by the mid-1950s were spending more of their leisure time on new forms of recreational activity such as wilderness backpacking and commercial river running.

As the opposition campaign gained force, preservationists began to challenge the entire CRSP, not just the Echo Park unit, exposing technical errors in the Bureau of Reclamation's engineering and economic calculations. In particular, some preservationists began to object to the Glen Canyon unit of the CRSP, arguing that the wilderness values of the area warranted preservation. Fearing that continued controversy over Echo Park threatened the future of all reclamation in the region, supporters of the CRSP negotiated a compromise with the preservationists in November 1955. The Echo Park and Split Mountain units were eliminated from the project. Preservationists agreed to withdraw their objections to the CRSP, including Glen Canyon dam, in exchange for provisos in the authorizing legislation guaranteeing the sanctity of national parklands in the upper basin (these provisions were later struck down in federal court). On March 28, 1956, the Senate and the House adopted the amended bill and a few weeks later President Eisenhower signed it into law (U.S. *Statutes at Large*, LXX: 106–108).

Susan Rhoades Neel

Further Readings

Richardson, Elmo P. *Dams, Parks & Politics: Resource Development and Preservation in the Truman–Eisenhower Era.* 1973.

Stegner, Wallace, ed. *This is Dinosaur.* 1955.

Stratton, Owen, and Phillip Sirotkin. *The Echo Park Controversy.* 1959.

See also BROWER, DAVID; COLORADO RIVER; HYDROELECTRICITY; SIERRA CLUB; WILDERNESS SOCIETY; ZAHNISER, HOWARD

Ecoanarchism

Ecoanarchism is a broad, generic term that may be applied to any ecologically oriented political theory that defends the local community, commune, or municipality, *rather than* the State, as the primary locus of economic, political and environmental decision making. The contemporary ecoanarchist tradition covers an extraordinarily wide range of different theories and visions, including the social ecology of Murray Bookchin, bioregionalism, the liberated zones of Rudolf Bahro, ecologically oriented monasteries or "ecosteries," and a variety of defences of ecocommunal living. Despite this diversity, it is possible to identify a number of common threads in ecoanarchist theory.

First, ecoanarchists share a tendency to appeal to "nature" as a regulative ideal, providing a source of philosophical and ethical inspiration and guidance in matters ranging from education, civic participation, spirituality, and community organization. In locating the human community in a broader web of life, ecoanarchists reject industrial society's anthropocentric and instrumental posture toward nature. Instead, ecoanarchists seek to restore and cultivate a sense of continuity and harmony between humans and the biophysical world. Perhaps the most ecologically attuned expression of ecoanarchism is bioregionalism, which seeks the integration of the local human community with the local ecosystem, employing metaphors, practices, and forms of civic consciousness that are drawn from, and structured in relation to, the particular characteristics of the local ecosystem.

Second, ecoanarchists seek an integrated solution to the ecological crisis at the level of the local community, whether urban or rural. Self-managed local communities, communes, or municipalities, rather than centralized and hierarchical institutions such as the nation state, are seen to maximize the opportunity for individuals to participate in democratic decisions that affect their own lives. Self-management is seen as more likely to deliver decisions that fulfill the needs of local communities and protect the environment. The desire for an integrated solution to a complex range of human and ecological problems also extends to a desire to find a balance between thought and labor, factory and field, mind and body, and culture and nature (ideas that may be traced to the Russian anarchist Peter Kropotkin and to utopian socialists such as William Morris).

Finally, ecoanarchists seek consistency between ends and means. Engagement with hierarchical political organizations such as political parties, or centralized institutions such as the state, is seen as likely to subvert central ecoanarchist goals such as participatory democracy. It is generally believed that lasting change is more likely to be achieved by building an alternative culture and society within the shell of the old, rather than by engaging in conventional forms of political participation. This kind of fundamentalist argument has been influential in some of the ideological and strategic debates within green parties, creating a tension between those who wish to take the conventional electoral route to attain political power and those who would prefer to build a new society through exemplary action within local communities.

Many ecoanarchist arguments have attracted considerable criticism (particularly from ecosocialists) for being voluntarist, simplistic, and blind toward certain recalcitrant aspects of human nature in believing that humans will cooperate once distorting centralized power structures are removed. The argument that the local community is the best locus of economic, political, and environmental decision making is typically criticized for failing to address problems of parochialism, regional resource disparities, and the need for regional and international cooperation. Finally, some ecoanarchists are criticized for adopting an inaccurate and self-serving model of nature as something that is "balanced," kindly and cooperative or as a source of "objective" authority.

Robyn Eckersley

Further Readings

Eckersley, Robyn. *Environmentalism and Political Theory: Toward an Ecocentric Approach*. 1992.

See also BIOREGION; ECOSOCIALISM; ENVIRONMENTALISM

Ecofeminism

Ecofeminism is one of the newest and most interesting concepts in environmental conservation. A term coined by Françoise d'Eaubonne in 1974 to bring attention to women's potential to bring about an ecological revolution, ecofeminism has since come to serve as an umbrella term for a variety of different positions on so-called "women-nature connections."

Most frequently, ecofeminism refers to a grassroots, women-initiated, local or indigenous political, activist movement which has as its twofold goal heightening awareness of and resolving those environmental problems that touch the lives of women directly, daily, and disproportionately. For example, environmental problems that disproportionately affect women include: contaminated water, deforestation and biomass fuel shortages, desertification, soil erosion, toxic household products, and the location of uncontrolled hazardous waste sites and garbage incinerators. Why? Because in the Southern hemisphere ("the South") women (especially poor women and children) have gendered role responsibilities for water collection and distribution, food production, forest management, and maintenance of "domestic economies" which make them more susceptible to tree shortages, unpotable water, and toxins than men—even local men.

For other women, such as the infamous Chipko ("tree-hugging") women of India, First World development policies that are aimed at replacing indigenous forests with monoculture species forests (e.g., teak or eucalyptus) are resisted by nonviolent protest actions because these women appreciate that the value of trees is not simply timber or resin but "*soil, water, and oxygen.*" In the United States, various studies of uncontrolled hazardous waste sites, lead poisoning, and the effects of uranium tailings on Native American reservations reveal that race is a primary factor in the location of these environmental hazards. In these communities of color, it is women (especially pregnant and older women) and children who disproportionately suffer the ill effects of these contaminants. Community organizing around these issues often is initiated by women because it is about what women know best—the effects in their daily lives of environmental pollutants on their ability to maintain a healthy household. For such women, ecofeminist conservation and environmentalism refers not to a conception of nature as abstract wilderness, but as a concrete, felt, material reality in their lives which deserves immediate attention.

Ecofeminism is also associated with earth-based spiritualities that affirm women's closeness to the earth, or the importance of Mother Earth as a living organism with which all life is intimately and inextricably connected, or that call for regenerative, nurturing, women-centered practices and theologies (i.e., Wicca, neo-paganism, Goddess worship, and Native American world views). These spiritual orientations toward conservation and environmental protection often draw on rich historical, allegedly non-patriarchal, sources for inspiration on alternative ways of conceiving both what it is to be human and the nature of the relationship of humans to the nonhuman natural world. These "spiritual ecofeminists" often address the historically and socially constructed myths, lore, rituals, language, and symbol systems which have been fostered by or about women, people of color, and nature. They ask whether these are hopelessly androcentric (male-biased) or helpfully salvageable in the creation of a new, ecofeminist-inspired earth-respectful spirituality or theology. Whether any of these spiritual positions is ecofeminist or ecofeminine is one of the many issues of debate among ecofeminists.

Also a part of ecofeminism are feminists in a variety of non-academic professional fields (i.e., forestry, agriculture, wildlife biology and protection, water and waste management) who are active in wedding their feminist concerns with their environmental conservation concerns in a mutually reinforcing way. Initially, this inclusion typically takes the "add women and stir" approach; that is, these women attempt to add to historically male-dominated fields a more gender inclusive perspective and approach. For example, they seek to hire and retain more competent women, to recognize women as potentially effective role models in fields traditionally dominated by men, and to promote women to high status decision-making positions. Given the well-researched feminist scholarship on the limitations of the "add women and stir" approach for bringing about fundamental (rather than merely reformist) change in any practice or field of study, including conservation and preservation, many of these feminists find themselves engaged in reformist and revisioning projects—ones that attempt to rethink what counts as nature or conservation or protection and how one might reconceive conservation strategies that self-consciously include the voices of traditionally omitted groups (e.g., local persons, indigenous populations, and women).

All of the above concerns have been explored by both disciplinary academic feminists (i.e., those in art, literature, history, philosophy, psychology, sociology, and theology) and interdisciplinary academic feminists (i.e., those in women's studies, ethnic studies, environmental studies, international studies, and development studies) who see important connections between the treatment of women, people of color, poor people, and children and the treatment of the earth. The feminist perspective constitutes a glorious range of media, approaches, and topics that reflects the rainbow of diverse academic ecofeminist positions.

Among the academic ecofeminists is a group of ecofeminists whose positions are distinctively philosophical. Ecofeminist philosophers and ethicists are interested in developing distinctive environmental ethics, policies, and theories which critique androcentric accounts of humans, nonhumans, and human-nonhuman relationships and replace them with accounts that are not androcentric. The theoretical work of ecofeminist philosophers does two things. It challenges basic, traditional mainstream assumptions about what is meant by "nature," what it is to be human, what counts as knowledge of the nonhuman world, and what constitutes a healthy relationship between humans and their nonhuman habitats. It also offers suggestions for an adequate conservation program and environmental philosophy that includes ecofeminist insights about women-nature connections.

Typically, ecofeminist philosophers argue that if ecofeminist insights into women-nature connections were taken seriously, conservation and environmentalism would need to change its epistemological claims about what nature is (e.g., nature as active subject, as a living organism, and/or as the biotic community to which humans belong), about what women know (for instance, by advocating women's "indigenous technical knowledge" in forestry, agriculture, and weeding), about the tenability of one correct, impartial, objective, universalizable ecological position on conservation and environmentalism, and about the future direction of environmental ethics. In this respect, ecofeminist philosophy often involves critiques of other environmental ethics (for example, Deep Ecology, Leopoldian Land Ethics, Kantian Rights-Based Animal Liberationism)—those that are feminist, antifeminist, and nonfeminist—for their failure to see that the history of anthropocentrism (human-centeredness) has largely been one of androcentrism and that both anthropocentrism and androcentrism must be changed to frame an acceptable environmental position from an ecofeminist point of view.

Despite this variety in ecofeminisms and differences among ecofeminist positions, what these different "ecofeminisms" have in common is a commitment to the position that there are important connections ("women-nature connections")—historical, symbolic, political, conceptual—between the domination of women and the domination of nature, such that an understanding of the nature of these connections is crucial to any adequate environmentalism, conservationism, or environmental ethic. Each offers a different starting point and perspective on what the connections are, which are most important, ways to make them visible, and strategies for developing conservation and environmental practices and policies that dismantle the twin dominations of women and nature. Whether or not these different starting points and perspectives are mutually compatible is an open debate among ecofeminists and others interested in developing workable conservation and environmentalism programs at local and global levels.

The significance of ecofeminist perspectives was never more clearly evidenced than in conjunction with the global Earth Summit in Rio de Janeiro in June 1992. From the various local meetings to the Miami conference of 3,000 women in November 1991 to the various nongovernmental agencies (NGO's) conferences (for example, the International Seminar on Ecofeminism, held as part of "Rio Ciencia," a conference sponsored by the major scientific societies of Brazil on issues of environmentally safe biotechnology and sustainable development, and the Women's Forum, with an estimated attendance of 50,000 at some of its Earth Summit related events), ecofeminist themes and issues were alive among the non-official delegate/participants in the Earth Summit activities. The sheer presence of women addressing *en masse* the need for the input and expertise of women cross-culturally is testimony to the rising interest in and popularity of ecofeminism globally. This rising ecofeminist concern emphasizes 1) the disproportionate suffering of women where there is environmental deterioration, particularly in the South, 2) environmental conservation and protection that doesn't address energy overconsumption by the North (Northern hemisphere), 3) North-imposed models of development on the South (whether or not those models fit the local to intermediate technology needs and resources of local communities of the South), and 4) the virtual absence of women as official delegates to the Earth Summit. Whether or not any particular ecofeminist position ultimately accomplishes its own goals, ecofeminism clearly is more than

"the new kid on the block." It is a powerful grassroots initiated political movement with impressive scholarly support for the position that one cannot seriously discuss conservation and preservation of the natural environment without also talking about women. Any conservation practice, policy, or ethic which attempts to do so is doomed to failure.

Karen J. Warren

Further Readings

Adams, Carol, ed. *Ecofeminism and the Sacred.* 1993.
Caldecott, Helen, and Stephanie Leland, eds. *Reclaim the Earth: Women Speak Out for Life on Earth.* 1983.
d'Eaubonne, Françoise. *Le Feminisme ou la Mort.* 1974.
Davion, Victoria. "Is Ecofeminism Feminist?" *Ecofeminism: Multidisciplinary Perspectives.* Ed. Karen J. Warren. 1994.
Plant, Judith, ed. *Healing Our Wounds: The Power of Ecological Feminism.* 1989.
Warren, Karen J. "Re-Writing the Future: The Feminist Challenge to the Malestream Curriculum." *Feminist Teacher* 4 (1989): 46–52.
———. "The Power and the Promise of Ecological Feminism." *Environmental Ethics* 12 (2) (1990): 125–46.
———, ed. *Hypatia: A Journal of Feminist Philosophy, Special Issue on Ecological Feminism.* 6 (1) (1991).

See also ANTHROPOCENTRISM; DEEP ECOLOGY: MEANINGS; ECO-SPIRITUALITY; ENVIRONMENTAL ETHICS; ENVIRONMENTAL JUSTICE MOVEMENT; RADICAL ENVIRONMENTALISM; RELIGION AND ENVIRONMENTAL PROTECTION; RIO CONFERENCE (1992)

Ecological Economics
See GREEN ECONOMICS

Ecological Feminism
See ECOFEMINISM

Ecological Niche
An ecological niche is the unique place or role each species occupies in an ecosystem or an ecological community. Joseph Grinnell first applied the term in 1917 to the way a bird—the California thrasher—differentiated its foraging

and habitat utilization from other similar bird species. Charles Elton, in *Animal Ecology* (1927), applied the term to a wide variety of organisms and pointed out that similar niches (such as the earthworm's "job" or function within the ecosystem of breaking down organic materials in soil) may be filled by different species, known as ecological equivalents, in different parts of the world. A niche may be defined either in terms of the species' total capabilities for survival or in terms of the environment to which it is best adapted. Ecologist G.E. Hutchinson distinguished the "fundamental niche," the total range of conditions under which a species can survive and reproduce without competition from other species, as larger than the "realized niche," that portion of available resources utilized by a species when there are competitors present. For Hutchinson the niche was a multi-dimensional hypervolume of resource axes. A desert plant might be found in sandy soils where there is very bright sunlight, low wind, an average of 25 centimeters of rain a year, and moderate grazing disturbance.

According to the competitive exclusion principle, first experimentally demonstrated by G.F. Gause, no two species can occupy the same niche within the same community without one being out-competed and eventually becoming extinct. Coexisting tropical bird species, all foraging on fruits, may have bills of different sizes or shapes, so that one species uses smaller fruits than another, thus direct competition is avoided. Species that live in the same habitat and utilize a common resource, such as fruit, are termed a "guild," and such species usually display some degree of "niche-overlap." A species with a small bill will, on the average, harvest smaller fruits, but may occasionally eat the larger ones preferred by a larger-billed species. According to evolutionary theory, continued competition should lead to further "character displacement," such as further differentiation in bill size or foraging behavior, and increased specialization among competing species.

Habitats with very complex structure provide more potential niches. Communities with very high species diversity often have greater "niche-packing"—several similar species have partitioned resources via subtle differences in behavior or physical adaptations. According to John Terborgh in *Diversity in the Tropical Rainforest*, there are more bird species in the tropical rainforest than in any other type of ecosystem because the multi-storied vegetation offers high habitat complexity; the variety of plant species—and therefore, fruit, seed, and flower varieties—is very large. There are more large insects as well as insects, such as army ants, that provide specialized niches; the less seasonal environment produces a large number of potential guilds, and the guilds are very closely packed. Niche availability is critical in limiting both the size of individual species populations, and the total biodiversity of an ecological community, thus the concept of the niche, and the study of niche diversification through evolutionary time, is critical to contemporary investigations of the worldwide decline of biodiversity.

Susan P. Bratton

Further Readings
Whittaker, R.H., and S.A. Levin. *Niche: Theory and Application*. 1975.

See also BIODIVERSITY; CARRYING CAPACITY; ELTON, CHARLES; ECOSYSTEMS; KEYSTONE SPECIES; TROPICAL RAINFORESTS; WEB OF LIFE

Ecological Reserves
See BIOSPHERE RESERVES; NATIONAL PARKS: UNITED STATES

Ecological Restoration
Restoration means bringing something back to an earlier or "original" condition. Ecological restoration is defined as doing just that to an ecological system, whether conceived as a population, a community, an ecosystem, or a landscape. Alternatively, it may be defined as any attempt to compensate for novel influences on an ecological system in such a way that the system can continue to behave as if those influences were not present.

Restoration is one of a cluster of closely related forms of land management—rehabilitation, reclamation, revegetation, creation, and so forth—all of which involve attempts to ameliorate or reverse what are considered destructive or otherwise undesirable changes to natural or historic ecosystems. What distinguishes restoration from these related activities is that the objectives of restoration projects are defined by specific, historic, or natural systems and typically take into account the entire system rather than just a few favored elements. An example would be an attempt to return a segment of prairie in the Midwestern United States or

Canada to its condition prior to the arrival of European settlers by removing exotic species, reintroducing species that had been lost, and reinstating processes such as periodic burning that had been interrupted as a result of settlement. In cases involving more extreme forms of disturbance, restoration might entail wholesale replanting of vegetation and even attempts to rehabilitate soil on a site where the historic vegetation had been eliminated by activities such as plowing or grazing.

History

The practice of ecological restoration has a long history and has roots in game management practices, reforestation efforts, and attempts to rehabilitate land disturbed by activities such as mining, and also in the romantic and "natural landscape" traditions of landscape architecture. Some of the work of late nineteenth- and early twentieth-century landscape designers such as Frederick Law Olmsted and Jens Jensen included representations of natural vegetation which, though often stylized and designed for appearance rather than ecological authenticity, were clearly a step toward restoration in the modern sense.

The first modern restoration project was initiated in 1934 at the University of Wisconsin Arboretum in Madison. Distinguishing this effort from earlier projects was the fact that it was guided from the beginning by ecological rather than primarily esthetic considerations, and that it was carried out systematically over an extended period of time for explicitly scientific purposes. A major feature of this project was restoration of a tallgrass prairie—now known as Curtis Prairie—and, in the years since, work on the tallgrass prairies of the Midwest has played a leading role in the development of restoration and is now widely regarded as a paradigm for restoration in its "purest" form, uncompromised by economic or other considerations.

For many years following the early work at Wisconsin, restoration underwent little development and was not taken seriously as a strategy for the conservation of natural landscapes. Beginning in the 1980s, however, it began to receive more attention. There were at least two reasons for this and, taken together, they clearly illustrate the reasons for the ambiguity environmentalists have tended to feel toward the promise of restoration.

One of the reasons for renewed attention was the obvious fact that restoration provides techniques for reversing environmental damage, and even for expanding and upgrading natural areas. Environmentalists have generally welcomed restoration for these purposes, though typically remaining skeptical about the costs involved and the quality of the resulting ecosystems.

In certain areas, however, a major impetus for the development of restoration techniques and its emergence as a discipline and a profession has been new laws that allow for restoration as a way of compensating for—or "mitigating"—environmental damage, in effect justifying it *before* it occurs. In practice this has often meant that the promise of restoration is used to undermine arguments for the preservation of existing natural areas, or that high-quality natural areas are traded away for an artificial replacement of uncertain quality.

Environmentalists have expressed deep concern about such laws and their interpretation of restoration, especially in the area of wetland conservation. One result of this concern has been a growing emphasis on finding ways to define the objectives of restoration projects and to monitor the results to ensure a high level of ecological authenticity.

Application and Value

Because restoration has yet to be fully defined in practical terms, the question of the value of restoration as a conservation technique continues to be an important issue within the environmental community. In the past most discussion of this topic has concentrated on the quality, size, and ecological value of restored ecosystems as a way of increasing habitat for rare species, contributing to ecosystem processes such as water-cycling, carbon dioxide sequestering, and so forth. In recent years, however, there has been increasing interest in the value of the process of restoration itself as a way of learning about natural ecosystems, and also in the experience of restoration as a way of achieving an intimate, constructive relationship with a natural landscape.

This interest in restoration as a process, an intellectual challenge, and an experience has led to several new ideas about the value of restoration. An example is the idea of *restoration ecology*, or the restoration of ecosystems specifically as a technique for basic research—a way of raising questions and testing basic ideas about the ecosystems being restored. Examples of the heuristic value of restorative and other attempts to reassemble or partly reassemble ecosystems are abundant both in the literature of ecology and of restoration, suggesting a fertile meeting-ground for theoretical and more practically-oriented ecological research in this area.

More broadly, the experience of restorationists has led to a growing awareness of the value of restoration as a way for people simply to learn about nature, to explore their relationship with it, and to achieve a positive, constructive relationship with it. This has led to increasing use of restoration as a basis for environmental education, and to the idea of restoration as a performing art, a way of defining and celebrating the relationship between a human community and the landscape it inhabits.

Those interested in further information about restoration should keep in mind that this is a new and immature discipline, and that much of the best information in this area is not in print, but exists only in the minds of practitioners and is conveyed informally at meetings and in conversation. For this reason, though there is a growing literature in this area, especially in the form of conference proceedings and special reports, it is often best to make direct contact with practitioners working in the appropriate area.

Further Information

A primary source for contacts and for publications and other information about restoration is the Society for Ecological Restoration (SER). SER publishes the quarterly journal *Restoration Ecology*, the only peer-reviewed journal devoted specifically to restoration, and is also served by the more informal, twice-yearly journal *Restoration & Management Notes*, published by the University of Wisconsin Madison Arboretum. SER's address is 1207 Seminole Highway, Madison, WI 53711, phone/fax: (608) 262-9547.

William R. Jordan III

Further Readings

Jordan, William R., III, et al., eds. *Restoration Ecology: A Synthetic Approach to Ecological Restoration*. 1990.
Society for Ecological Restoration. *Restoration Ecology.*

See also EXOTIC SPECIES; FRESHWATER WETLANDS; JENSEN, JENS; OLMSTED, FREDERICK LAW

Ecologist

The *Ecologist* is the longest running environmental magazine in the United Kingdom. Noted for its hard-hitting critiques of conventional economics, politics, and environmental management, the *Ecologist* contains well-referenced articles by reputable authors on topics that cover both developed and developing country themes. It is remembered for its 1972 article "Blueprint for Survival" that predated the 1972 United Nations (UN) Conference on Environment and Development in Stockholm, and for its 1992 follow-up "Whose Common Future," timed to coincide with the UN Conference on Environment and Development at Rio. The *Ecologist* has campaigned for a shift in the scientific method to take into account the cooperative and communicative theories now emerging in physics and biology. Its editor, Edward Goldsmith, consistently supports the Gaia hypothesis proposed by James Lovelock, and has successfully fought to make the World Bank and the Food and Agriculture Organization more environmentally and socially accountable. The *Ecologist*'s editorial offices are located at Agriculture House, Bath Road, Sturminster, Newton, Dorset, DT10 1DN, England, UK.

Timothy O'Riordan

Further Readings

Goldsmith, Edward, ed. "Blueprint for Survival." *Ecologist* 2 (1972).
Goldsmith, Edward, and Nicholas Hildyard, eds. *The Earth Report: The Essential Guide to Global Ecological Issues.* 1988.

See also GAIA HYPOTHESIS; RIO CONFERENCE (1992); STOCKHOLM CONFERENCE; WORLD BANK

Economic Growth and the Environment

There is perhaps no more perplexing issue facing environmentalists and society at large than the complex relationship between economic activity and environmental protection. Just as there is no easy and definitive statement that can be put forward regarding this matter, of equal certainty is the fact that there is no avoiding the issue. The economy and the environment are inextricably intertwined in innumerable ways. Virtually all economic activities affect the environment in some way, just as all routes to environmental protection carry some economic implication.

The history of this relationship permeates as well the history of the conservation and environmental movements. The distinction between the wise-use conservation of Gifford Pinchot and the preservationism of John Muir can be read as a difference between those who would seek to compromise environmental protection in some circumstances for increments of economic opportunity and those who would make no such compromise. The modern day equivalent is the parallel clash between advocates of sustainable development and advocates of deep ecology (or perhaps of steady state economics).

But then, as now, the underlying economic realities are more complex than they might appear on the surface. Lands preserved from mining or other forms of economic exploitation, especially when preserved within national parks, generate considerable economic activity in other (often more benign) forms, especially over the long term. Moreover, resources that are expended, even when extracted with care, are perhaps less economically productive than they might have been had the same lands been used at some later date or in some other way. It also must be observed that, historically, resource extraction less often has been carried out wisely than it has been seen through in environmentally destructive ways. That is, all things considered, there is often an economic upside to environmental protection, especially in the long term.

Is the wide acceptance of this last observation regarding the economic benefits of environmentalism, whether in terms of immediate or potential benefits, becoming a defining difference between the environmentalism of the 1990s and the environmentalism of the 1970s? Perhaps. But the more important question might be one that focuses on whether or not that change is, on balance, a positive or a negative development in the history of the movement.

The environmentalism of the 1970s was sometimes naive in its willingness to reject prosperity as the source of all environmental evils, forgetting that the dislocations associated with declines in prosperity were not likely to be distributed in socially benign ways. That is, the relative economic security of the early 1970s was an illusion, especially for the young, the poor, and those whose adaptability is limited in some way. The 1990s perspective which seeks win-win solutions, promotes "green" products, and favors sustainable development is in many ways an improvement on that earlier perspective. But this more current view is also prone to overstatement, to say the least.

True, there is an economic upside to many environmental protection initiatives, especially when they are not foreclosed out-of-hand. True, as well, there are many forms of economic activity and economic growth that are relatively benign. But equally there are and will continue to be issues and situations that call for economically negative governmental interventions on behalf of wilderness, habitat, human health, and long-term environmental and economic sustainability. There are tough decisions even in a world whose central guiding policy objective is sustainable development and even when that concept is understood in ways that genuinely and fairly balance economic and environmental values.

Perhaps the central policy challenge of the coming decades is finding ways which allow global GNP to grow at a moderate rate while wilderness protection, pollution prevention, and ecological and resource sustainability are simultaneously enhanced on a global basis. This may or may not be possible; there is no way to be sure in advance. But we can be sure of some things. There cannot be indefinite growth in the human population. We cannot continue to cut old-growth forests in the tropics or anywhere else at historic or present rates and preserve global biodiversity. Increasing use of automobiles—ever more vehicles, ever more miles traveled—cannot continue. Even present global levels of total energy consumption will probably be a challenge to maintain over the next century. Many types of ecologically productive lands and waters cannot be utilized as they have in the past. Newly developing industrial processes must strive to be ever less polluting than the old processes. All of these environmental needs will have real, especially short-term economic costs which must be borne.

Economic activity and growth, whether measured as GNP or in some more sophisticated way, may well be a positive societal objective, even in wealthier countries. But if environmentalism means anything it means that environmentalists will advance objectives which sometimes require society and government to make difficult economy-environment trade-offs. A successful environmental movement is one that can make environmental protection more often than not the highest priority when such choices must be made.

Robert Paehlke

Further Readings
Sagoff, Mark. *The Economy of the Earth.* 1988.

See also CONSERVATION MOVEMENT; EARTH DAY; ENVIRONMENTALISM; GREEN ECONOMICS; GREEN PRODUCTS; MUIR, JOHN;

Ecophilosophy and Ecopsychology

Ecophilosophy at the most general level could be described as being concerned with the time-honored philosophical question of humanity's place in the larger scheme of things. Yet every age stamps its own mark upon this ancient, perplexing, and insistent question, and ours is no exception. The emergence of ecophilosophy has been impelled by the growing recognition in the latter part of the twentieth century that we are in the midst of a deepening, global ecological crisis that is *directly attributable to human activity*. Ecophilosophy's focus on the general question of humanity's place in the larger scheme of things is therefore directed toward the human-nonhuman axis and specifically toward the question of the appropriate relationship between humans and the nonhuman world. Expressing this question in its most essential and most active form, the central question of ecophilosophy is simply: Why care about the world around us? Upon elaboration, this condensed form of the question immediately splits into two related but analytically distinct questions: Why *should* we care about the world around us? and Why might we be *inclined* to care about the world around us? The first question is concerned with how we ought to behave—with duties and obligations, rights and wrongs—and, hence, with ethics; the second question is concerned with how we are naturally drawn or spontaneously desire to behave—with human motivation—and, hence, with psychology.

Both questions are vital. The most meticulous ethical argument as to why people ought to behave in a given way is of little practical consequence if it ignores significant contrary aspects of human motivation. On the other hand, even if one deliberately works with the grain of human motivations to articulate a view that is attractive to people in terms of the ways in which they are actively seeking to develop their potentials, those who encounter this view still remain intellectually entitled and morally bound to ask whether or not people *ought* to be encouraged to develop in this way.

Although ethics is thought of as being part of philosophy while psychology is these days thought of as a separate discipline, both disciplines can formally be thought of as philosophical in the sense that both grow out of the sorts of foundational questions that characterize philosophical thinking. (Historically, of course, the sciences in general, including psychology, have grown out of such philosophical questioning.) These considerations mean that, theoretically, ecophilosophical questioning should lead in the direction of two primary areas of study: on the one hand, ecological ethics, or, as it is usually referred to, environmental ethics, and, on the other, ecopsychology. (Ideally, an ecopolitics would then be developed on the basis of these approaches.) In practice, however, the present specialization of disciplines—and other factors—has meant that ecophilosophers have, with some significant exceptions, tended to focus upon the development of an environmental ethics and to ignore the development of an ecopsychology. (Regrettably, psychologists have also ignored the development of an ecopsychology. There are glimmerings that this might be beginning to change however.)

Discussion of environmental ethics is typically couched in terms of value theory, more formally referred to as "axiology" (from the Greek *axios*, worthy). The central distinction made here is between those approaches that stress the "use value" or "resource" value of the nonhuman world to humans and those approaches that stress the value that the nonhuman world (or certain kinds of entities within the nonhuman world) may be said to have in and of itself. Ecophilosophers refer to these two kinds of values as "instrumental value" (from the Latin *instrumentum*, tool, equipment) and "intrinsic value" (from the Late Latin *intrinsecus*, inwardly) respectively. This axiological distinction also maps directly onto the general distinction that ecophilosophers make between anthropocentric and non-anthropocentric approaches: approaches that stress the instrumental value of the nonhuman world are clearly anthropocentric while those that stress the intrinsic value of the nonhuman world are, in varying degrees, nonanthropocentric.

There are many approaches that argue for the exploitation, conservation, or preservation of the nonhuman world on the basis of its instrumental value to humans, and these approaches, in turn, articulate a range of instrumental values. The "unrestrained exploitation and expansionism" approach and the "resource conservation and development" approach both emphasize the physical transformation value of the nonhuman world, that is, the value—typically the economic value—that can be realized by physically transforming the nonhuman world in some way, such as damming, farming, logging, mining, and slaughtering. Where these approaches differ is primarily in the extent to which they recognize the fact that there are limits to material growth and, consequently, in their sense of obligation to future generations of humans and their corresponding modes of planning.

In contrast to these approaches, the "resource preservation" approach seeks to preserve the nonhuman world (or at least certain aspects of it) rather than physically transform it, but still to do so on the basis of the nonhuman world's instrumental value. This approach is represented by a range of arguments that stress the nonhuman world's physical nourishment value, informational value, experiential value, symbolic or instructional value, and psychological nourishment value.

Ecophilosophers have generally been concerned to move beyond these dominant, anthropocentric, instrumentally-based approaches to the nonhuman world and to argue instead for the intrinsic value of the nonhuman world (or certain aspects of it). The main approaches they have advanced have focused on the moral relevance of sentience (i.e., the capacity to feel and, hence, to suffer); life; holistic integrity or, more technically and precisely, autopoiesis (i.e., the capacity for self-renewal, a criterion which includes not only individual biological forms but also other kinds of highly-integrated, self-renewing collectivities, such as ecosystems and the ecosphere); and coherence with some postulated form of cosmic purpose (whether of a secular evolutionary kind or a religious kind). The approaches corresponding to these criteria could loosely be referred to as zoocentric, biocentric, ecocentric, and teleological respectively.

The most notable exception to the mainstream ecophilosophical focus upon intrinsic value theory (and, hence, environmental ethics) has come from a small but influential group of writers generally referred to as deep ecologists. Rather than arguing for the intrinsic value of certain entities and the moral implications that follow from this, deep ecologists have preferred to address the central question of ecophilosophy—Why care about the world around us?—by focusing upon the importance of the psychological capacity for identification. For the most part, however, this ecopsychological emphasis has been just that—an emphasis—rather than having been worked into a coherently developed theory that addresses the obvious, more detailed questions that must

necessarily follow on from a focus on the psychological capacity for identification. Thus, it may be that deep ecology will come to be viewed as a precursor to a systematic ecopsychology rather than as constituting the very foundations of such a psychology, as might have been the case.

In contrast, mainstream ecophilosophy (i.e., environmental ethics or intrinsic value theorizing) has shown more obvious signs of detailed elaboration and development, although this is perhaps not surprising given that many more thinkers have been concentrating on intrinsic value theorizing than on deep ecology. Vigorous debates continue within environmental ethics as to the defensibility and implications of the various competing criteria of intrinsic value, but the degree of elaboration of basic issues that has occurred within a relatively short time (the central journal in the area, *Environmental Ethics*, dates only from 1979) is undeniably impressive. Of course, this area still represents a minefield of fundamental and extremely difficult questions, but it would be unfair or naive, at this still early stage at least, to expect anything else. The fact of the matter is that, in attempting to redress the anthropocentric assumptions that have for so long dominated Western thought and action, ecophilosophers have taken on an enormous task— one of genuinely revolutionary theoretical and practical consequence.

Warwick Fox

Further Readings

Fox, Warwick. *Toward a Transpersonal Ecology: Developing New Foundations for Environmentalism.* 1990.

Johnson, Lawrence. *A Morally Deep World: An Essay on Moral Significance and Environmental Ethics.* 1991.

Zimmerman, Michael, ed. *Environmental Philosophy: From Animal Rights to Radical Ecology.* 1993.

See also DEEP ECOLOGY: EMERGENCE; DEEP ECOLOGY: MEANINGS; ENVIRONMENTAL ETHICS; *Environmental Ethics*; INSTRUMENTAL VALUE; INTRINSIC VALUE; RELIGION AND ENVIRONMENTAL PROTECTION; RESOURCISM

Ecosocialism

Ecosocialism represents a theoretical convergence of the socialist and ecological critiques of capitalism, providing a revival and further development of democratic socialist thought in a new ecological context. Although there are many varieties of ecosocialist thought, its essential analysis is that the present ecological crisis is largely the product of the capitalist mode of production. Accordingly, attempts by the state to "manage" capitalism or to "green" capitalism are seen to provide only a temporary solution to the crisis because the state remains fiscally dependent on private capital accumulation and unable to carry out far-reaching reforms. Ecosocialists therefore argue that the capitalist mode of production must be replaced with a democratized economy, entailing common ownership of the means of production and genuine producer democracies that are able to give priority to the satisfaction of human needs.

There are many significant resonances between ecosocialism and ecoanarchism, most notably their ecological and social critique of capitalism and their emphasis on the virtues of democratic self-management at the level of the local community, factory, municipality, or commune. However, ecosocialism differs from ecoanarchism in one crucial respect. Whereas ecoanarchists eschew engagement with state institutions, ecosocialists insist that genuine political and economic democracy would not be possible or viable without citizen involvement in, and action by, state institutions. Indeed, the state is seen as playing an essential and primary role in facilitating the shift toward an ecosocialist society by guaranteeing civil rights and democratic participation, ensuring an egalitarian coordination of production and distribution between regions, protecting the environment, and engaging in international diplomacy. In particular, ecosocialists envisage the state playing a key role in extensive environmental planning in such areas as energy and resource use, pollution and waste treatment, transport, and ecosystem protection. In this respect, ecosocialists seek to transform both the capitalist relations of production (via common ownership of the means of production) *and* the capitalist forces of production (by introducing appropriate environmental and nonalienating technologies). Ecosocialists maintain that the opportunity for bureaucratic domination stemming from an expanded state would be offset by parallel moves that extend the opportunity for democratic participation in all tiers of government and in the organization and management of production.

Ecosocialists reject the indiscriminate economic growth consensus upon which both capitalism and communism have rested. Although many ecosocialists are critical of the idea of absolute "limits to growth," they nonetheless concede that there are different ecological thresholds corresponding to different modes of production. Instead of redressing the indignities of poverty by stimulating economic growth and expanding production, ecosocialists seek a more equitable distribution of existing resources on both a national and international scale. The standard of living of the average American or European is not considered a desirable international yardstick. A cornerstone of this new internationalism is a redefinition of human needs that is designed to bring overall resource consumption down to a level that is compatible with global justice and global ecological integrity.

Ecosocialists differ over whether the working class should still be regarded as the leading agent of social and political change. Some ecosocialist theorists, such as André Gorz, look to an alliance between new social movements and the "nonclass" or "post-industrial neo-proletariat" (the growing number of unemployed or marginally employed as distinct from the shrinking number of full-time skilled wage earners). Others, such as David Pepper, seek to cultivate the "green potential" of the labor movement, building on historical examples of trade union action in defence of the environment (such as "green bans"). A third approach (represented by the late Raymond Williams) is to seek a broader alliance of new social movements working with the labor movement. Ecosocialists also divide over whether these new political alliances should be pursued through established social democratic or labor parties, through the green movement and green parties, or through an alternative leftist "rainbow" movement and party. Despite these differences, most ecosocialists have been critical of the environment movement for neglecting the class dimensions of ecological degradation and/or for failing to incorporate the concerns of the labor movement into their political struggle. The environment movement is seen not as an end in itself but merely as a stage in a larger and broader struggle to overcome capitalism.

Ecosocialists tend to be urban-based in their environmentalism (rather than focussing on wilderness or nature preservation). Although there are some versions of "biocentric socialism," most ecosocialists generally prefer to de-

E

fend a humanist ecological ethic against an ecocentric or biocentric ethic. "Nature" and "natural values" are understood as socially constructed; an excessive preoccupation with ecological principles or notions of intrinsic value in "Nature" is seen to be at odds with this social constructionism while also deflecting attention away from the social origins of ecological degradation and from questions concerning the ownership and control of resources.

Robyn Eckersley

Further Reading

Eckersley, Robyn. *Environmentalism and Political Theory: Toward an Ecocentric Approach*. 1992.

Pepper, David. *Eco-Socialism: From Deep Ecology to Social Justice*. 1993.

Ryle, Martin. *Ecology and Socialism*. 1988.

See also ECOANARCHISM; ENVIRONMENTALISM

Eco-Spirituality

Since Lynn White's 1967 essay "The historical roots of our ecologic crisis" blaming Western religion for fostering environmentally destructive attitudes, environmentalists have debated as to which spiritualities are congruent with nature conservation. As a remedy White urged Christians to appropriate Saint Francis of Assisi's reverence for life as a basis for an ecological Christianity. Some Christian theologians responded; see especially Thomas Berry's *The Dream of the Earth* (1988), John Cobb Jr.'s *The Liberation of Life: from Cell to Community* (1981), and Jay McDaniel's *Earth, Sky, Gods and Mortals: Developing an Ecological Spirituality* (1990).

Others affirmed religions originating in the Far East, especially Buddhism and Taoism, believing them to be more beneficent toward nature; two important examples linking Buddhism to ecology are Charlene Spretnak's *States of Grace* (1991) and Joanna Macy's *World as Lover, World as Self* (1991). Such works have been influenced and buttressed by "systems theory" and "new physics" emphasizing the metaphysical interrelationship of the universe, popularized by Fritjof Capra's *The Turning Point* (1982), among other works.

Still others have been drawn to pagan spiritualities which they linked to the worldviews of primal peoples or the earth's remnant indigenous peoples. Gary Snyder, for example, blends such spiritualities with Buddhism in *The Practice of the Wild* (1990), while Dolores LaChapelle believes primal spiritualities have great affinity with Taoism in *Sacred Land, Sacred Sex—Rapture of the Deep* (1988).

The public proliferation of eco-spirituality was made possible by the increasing openness to non-Western spiritualities that accompanied 1960s social upheavals. Although eco-spiritualities are plural and continually unfolding it is possible to discern several trends.

Eco-spiritualities generally agree that all reality is metaphysically interdependent and interrelated. Species are related as kin because they all evolved through the same process from a common ancestor. Ecological spiritualities generally either express an affirmation of nature as having sacramental value for humans (i.e., it mediates or symbolizes in some way the grace of God and/or the Goddess) or involve the perception that nature itself is sacred. In either case nature preservation is a spiritual obligation. It should also be noted that, although Deep Ecology includes the idea that natural systems are intrinsically valuable, it is not always spiritually based. Yet many if not most deep ecologists find their way to such a perspective through some form of nature-based spirituality.

It is not unusual for pagan spirituality, whether originating in pantheistic perceptions of the sacrality of land or in experiences of inter-species communication, to underlie the moral passions of conservationists. See Stephen Fox's *The American Conservation Movement* (1981) and Michael Cohen's *The Pathless Way* (1984). What is novel about contemporary eco-spirituality is that: 1) sciences explicating the sub-atomic relatedness of matter buttress these spiritualities against secularized skepticism; 2) partly because science can now be employed to defend spiritual worldviews, conservationists have less fear that expressing spirituality is politically counterproductive; 3) some environmentalists are, therefore, weaving the Arts—especially poetry, prose, music, dance, and theater—into rituals designed to foster human spiritual connections to nature; and 4) "Transpersonal Ecology" and "Ecopsychology" are accompanying these developments, tracing neurosis to the human alienation from nature, prescribing ritual and diverse therapies as a means to mystically reunite the human spirit with the natural world. See Warwick Fox's *Toward a Transpersonal Ecology* (1990), Theodore Roszak's *The Voice of the Earth* (1992), Roger Walsh and Francis Vaughan's *Paths beyond Ego* (1993), and the Journals

Talking Leaves: A Bioregional Journal of Deep Ecology and Spiritual Activism and *Revision: A Journal of Consciousness and Transformation.*

Most eco-religions share the view that Western culture is spiritually adrift and that ecological sanity requires both a backward glance, appropriating spiritual insights from primal peoples, and a look forward, borrowing insights from those sciences that illuminate the path to ecological harmony. Eco-spirituality expresses the hope that humans can heal both personal and ecological wounds—those which have resulted from dualistic Western religions that have desacralized nature and separated humans from it—and that this can only occur by resacralizing the natural world and acknowledging that humans are embedded within it.

Bron R. Taylor

Further Readings

Taylor, Bron R. "Resacralizing Earth: Pagan Environmentalism and the Restoration of Turtle Island." In *American Sacred Space.* Ed. E.T. Linenthal and D. Chidester. Indiana University Press, 1995.

———. *Once and Future Primitive: The Spiritual Politics of Deep Ecology.* Forthcoming 1996.

White, Lynn. "The Historical Roots of our Ecological Crisis." *Science* 155 (1967): 1203–07.

See also ANTHROPOCENTRISM; DEEP ECOLOGY: EMERGENCE; DEEP ECOLOGY: MEANINGS; ENVIRONMENTAL ETHICS; INTRINSIC VALUE; RELIGION AND ENVIRONMENTAL PROTECTION

Ecosystems

Of the many descriptive terms that are widely used in ecology and environmental science, "ecosystem" is probably the most familiar, at least to practitioners of either of those widely overlapping sciences. Introduced by A.G. Tansley in 1935, the term "ecosystem" is chiefly, if not entirely of value only when used in its "classical" sense as an ecological unit of relatively uniform dominance by a particular life form of plants on land—as, for example, the Northern Coniferous Forest for so far as it extends (though, in such a macro-instance, the ecosystem commonly encloses other, more limited ecosystems, such as tracts of alpine or other tundra. Even the latter will normally enclose

still more limited micro-ecosystems such as, for example, those of cryptogam (chiefly lichen and/or moss) dominance on exposed rocks).

As thus embracing the inorganic, inert soil, or aquatic, as well as organic-decaying components together with its dependent plant and animal "superstructure," the ecosystem is a fundamental unit of the earth's surface as well as a scientific concept and necessary term of both descriptive and analytical ecology. Its problem is that, to students of other sciences or of nothing in particular, it sounds so attractive and seemingly learned that it gets used indiscriminately in a much wider sense than was originally intended. This misuse and, indeed, overuse renders the term meaningless to scholars as a scientific term. But as the term ecosystem is needed for what it was introduced and long employed to signify, far-too-wide usages such as "the world ecosystem" and "the marine ecosystem" should be avoided as not only devoid of any precise meaning but, far worse, ruining the valuable "classical" one.

Toward remedying this objection, the term "ecocomplex" was introduced by Nicholas Polunin & E. Barton Worthington in 1990. Noting that ecosystem "is *not* a mere smart-sounding catchword for any kind of system or quasi-system that, involving both living biota and inert components, may seem desirable to a would-be user needing a term that sounds learned or technical, [but] certainly should not be so-employed," Polunin and Worthington affirmed that "some such or other term is . . . needed to imply the holistic but less-integrated nature of particular and usually major entities that are held together in some way by an ecological factor or consideration while embracing more-or-less numerous ecosystems." For such an agglomerate they proposed the term "ecocomplex," examples being an "island ecocomplex," a "lake ecocomplex," a "river ecocomplex," or even "the global ecocomplex."—though that would seem to constitute the ultimate "superecocomplex."

Deploring in a similar manner, if less forcibly, the much-widened use of the term "ecology"—ranging from the classical "study of living organisms in relation to their environment" to seemingly anything connected with environment or the merest unscientific interest in any human habitat or component thereof—R.A. Lewin & Nicholas Polunin proposed the term "ecostasis" to be used in reference to "conservation business" or in cases when some connection with environment, however loose, is stated or even at least implied. But whereas "ecocomplex" has caught on fairly widely in the literature as a useful and indeed necessary concept and term, "ecostasis" has not, at least as yet.

Nicholas Polunin

Further Reading

Polunin, Nicholas, ed. *Ecosystem Theory and Application.* 1986.

See also BIOREGION; ECOLOGICAL NICHE; WHOLE EARTH IMAGE

Ecotourism

Ecotourism can be defined as travel to natural attractions that contributes to their conservation, respects the integrity of local communities, and enhances the tourist's understanding of the natural attraction, its conservation, and the local community. It should have a minimum impact on soil, water, air, flora, fauna, and biophysical processes; use little energy; cause little pollution; educate the tourist; and contribute to the welfare of local and indigenous populations.

Ecotourism can be beneficial. It can help to justify nature protection, enable public enjoyment and understanding, and provide income and employment contributing to development. Ecotourism can also become problematic if it involves activities, transport, facilities, or levels of visitation that have major environmental impacts, or if it occurs in areas that are environmentally fragile, or with vulnerable communities. Accordingly, while there are reasons to encourage ecotourism, it must be controlled so that it is ecologically and socially sustainable. There must be controls on tour operators, tourist behavior, and tourism development in natural areas, as well as enforcement of regulations, and monitoring of impacts.

While ecotourism has been around since the nineteenth century, it has grown considerably in popularity and commercial significance in just the past ten years in response to interest in the environment and exotic and adventure holidays, increases in leisure time and personal incomes, the improved accessibility of many natural attractions, promotion by selected countries and businesses for economic benefits, and a belief that ecotourism will build support for conservation.

Ecotourism has been developed particularly in East Africa, Central America, North America,

Antarctica, the Himalayas, New Zealand, Australia, and parts of Europe. Costa Rica's national parks now receive over 300,000 visitor-days of use per year; over 40,000 tourists now visit the Galapagos Islands each year, and even Antarctica attracts over 5,000 tourists annually. Ecotourism is a major source of foreign exchange for countries such as Kenya and Costa Rica. The estimated gross value of tourism on the Galapagos Islands in 1991 was $33 million. It should be noted, however, that there must be a considerable initial and continuing investment in nature protection, facilities, services, promotion, and training to earn such revenues.

To ensure that ecotourism is environmentally and culturally sustainable, standards for tour operators and guidelines for tourist behavior are being developed, while managers of protected areas are studying the impacts and introducing measures, such as permits, quotas, guiding, and interpretation. There have been numerous conferences, training courses, and publications dealing with ecotourism, and the Ecotourism Society has been established in the United States. Located in North Bennington, Vermont, the Ecotourism Society recently provided a special library collection on the subject to George Washington University (Washington, D.C.). The Society is " . . . dedicated to finding the resources and building the expertise to make tourism a viable tool for conservation and sustainable development."

John Marsh

Further Readings

Boo, E. *Ecotourism: The Potentials and Pitfalls.* World Wildlife Fund, 1990.
Nelson, J.G., R. Butler, and G. Wall. *Tourism and Sustainable Development: Monitoring, Planning, Managing.* 1993.
Scarce, R.C., E. Grifone, and R. Usher. *Ecotourism in Canada.* Ministry of Supply and Services, Ottawa, 1992.

See also ENVIRONMENTAL EDUCATION; NATIONAL PARKS: UNITED STATES; REPTILES: CONSERVATION AND HABITAT

Ecotoxicology

See TOXICOLOGY

Edge, Rosalie

See HAWK SHOOTING; NATIONAL AUDUBON SOCIETY

Ehrlich, Paul

Ecologist Paul Ehrlich (1932–) became interested in ecology after reading William Vogt's *Road to Survival* (1948) while still in high school. In 1954 he married Anne Howland, a biological research assistant, with whom he collaborates on most of his research and writing projects. Inspired by the heated public debate over Rachel Carson's *Silent Spring* (1962) in the early 1960s, Ehrlich, Barry Commoner, and other ecologists began to speak out against the "plundering of the planet." In the mid-1960s, the Ehrlichs began to write and speak out about the threats to the human future caused by biological ignorance of the natural world.

Ehrlich's book, *The Population Bomb* (1968), became an immediate bestseller, and Ehrlich became a leading spokesman for the environmental movement. Surpassing the sales of *Silent Spring*, it became the most widely read ecology book of the 1960s. In *The Population Bomb*, Ehrlich argues that population control is the only solution to the global environmental crisis. Unlike ecologist Barry Commoner who blamed modern science and technology, Ehrlich believed that overpopulation and uncontrolled economic growth were the primary causes of the environmental crisis. For the Ehrlichs, modern science and technology had become a new religion—one that justified and supported modern industrial civilization's addiction to economic growth and progress.

In the 1960s and 1970s, the Ehrlichs' scientific activism helped fuse ecology, conservationism, and politics into a powerful environmental movement. From the 1960s to the 1990s, the Ehrlichs have been leading scientific activists, environmentalists, and writers, demanding nothing less than the economic and political transformation of the modern industrial world. Ecologists such as the Ehrlichs, Commoner, and E.O. Wilson have helped make ecology both a science and politics of human survival. In the early 1990s the Ehrlichs have argued that humanity can "heal the planet" only if it transforms its understanding and use of the environment.

Chris H. Lewis

Further Readings

Ehrlich, Paul. *The Population Bomb*. 1968.
———, and Anne Ehrlich. *Earth*. 1987.
———, and Anne Ehrlich. *Healing the Planet*. 1991.

See also CARSON, RACHEL; COMMONER, BARRY; ENVIRONMENTALISM; POPULATION CONTROL

Elephants: Conservation and Habitat

The evolutionary lineage of elephants traces back some 55 million years. Ancestors gave rise to various branches as well as to the direct line leading to living elephants. Early proboscideans originated in Africa and southwest Asia and migrated via land bridges to every continent except Antarctica and Australia.

There are at least ten variants of elephant in the evolutionary history of proboscidians:

1. Remains of Moeritherium dated from 50 million years BP, were found in North Africa. This hog-size creature had two small tusks in each jaw.
2. Deinotherium, a quite distinct evolutionary line, apparently originated in Africa during the late Eocene. Lacking upper tusks, its lower jawbone curved backward to reveal tusk-like front teeth used for digging.
3. Four tusks also appeared in Palaeomastodon from North Africa at the end of the Eocene. Palaeomastodon began the main line to today's elephants.
4. By the time Mammut developed in Africa during the early Oligocene, proboscideans had prominent tusks and trunks that allowed them to eat leaves from treetops.
5. By the late Oligocene epoch Gomphotherium roamed Eurasia and Africa.
6. Stegodon, once deemed the progenitor of modern elephants, lived near African and Asian lakes and rivers.
7. The last four-tusker, Primelephas, was the immediate ancestor of the extinct Mammuthus.
8. Mammuthus lived in Africa, Eurasia, and North America during the Pliocene and Pleistocene eras.
9. About 10,000 years ago or longer today's Elephas (Asian elephant) and
10. Loxodonta (African elephant) brought the 55-million-year evolutionary history into modern times.

Changes in climate and food supply—and perhaps overhunting in the Pleistocene—caused widespread extinctions, leaving modern elephants as the only survivors.

Elephants, like people, need land, food, and water, thus a competition has arisen between humans and elephants for scarce resources—but hardly a sporting one. Armed with chainsaws, tractors, bulldozers, and guns, humans have developed the land thus forcing earth's largest terrestrial mammal onto smaller and smaller tracts of savanna and forest, right to the brink of extinction in the case of Elephas. Shrinking habitat and poaching are the most dire threats to the modern elephant's existence. For instance, the Asian elephant, Elephas maximus, once spanned Asia from Syria to northern China. Now it inhabits only small parts of India, Sri Lanka, and Southeast Asia. It has an arched back, an enormous domed head with relatively small ears, and a single protuberance, or "finger," at the tip of its trunk. Only males carry tusks, the specialized upper incisors whose lustrous white dentin, or ivory, has spurred trade since the earliest empires arose.

The African elephant, Loxodonta africana, once ranged throughout most of Africa, even to the shores of the Mediterranean. Today it is found only south of the Sahara Desert. It has a swayed back, a tapering head with large ears, and two trunk "fingers." Both sexes carry the ivory that changed millions of human lives as the practice of using forced labor to transport countless tusks to the coast was closely linked to the development of the slave trade. Larger than the Asian giants, bulls can reach seven to eight tons and females about three. The greatest among them stand thirteen feet tall at the shoulder, bearing tusks that can each weigh as much as an average adult human and measure twice as long. But now such titans are rare indeed.

At the beginning of the twentieth century Asian elephants numbered perhaps 200,000. Today there may be no more than 35,000 to 54,000 left in the wild. Many, if not most, are in isolated pockets of habitat too small to sustain them over the long run. Human settlement prevents elephants from migrating freely and consequently impedes them from seeking fresh sources of food in times of stress. In a word, the fundamental problem is that elephants need expansive areas of land to live, and humans have become their direct competitors for it. Even the African elephants, which numbered nearly 600,000 in 1989 (down from 1.3 million in 1979) were, in late 1989, placed on Convention on International Trade in Endangered Species of Wild Fauna and Flora (CITES) Appendix 1 along with the Asian elephants.

In recent decades poaching has proved to be the primary cause of the decline of the African elephant population. For instance, after poachers decimated many of Africa's largest tuskers, they turned their guns on others of the species. For each ton of ivory poachers shot nearly twice as many elephants in 1988 as in 1979. Throughout the 1980s the tusk size entering the ivory market dropped severely.

To help stop the carnage that reduced the African elephant populations by 50 percent during the 1980s, most parties to CITES have agreed to ban all trade for commercial purposes. South Africa, Zimbabwe, Botswana, Malawi, China, the United Kingdom (on behalf of Hong Kong), and Zambia "took reservations" under the terms of the treaty. Namibia joined this group, but the United Kingdom, China, and Zambia have since withdrawn. To some extent some of the nations with healthy elephant herds dispute an approach which attempts to ban all trade.

Tough conservation programs in some of these countries have protected a valuable natural resource, but an ivory trade ban, some argue, could undermine that success. Some countries allow villagers to cull herds as a motivation for providing protection for the elephants. But in most nations the ban has had its intended effect, causing ivory prices, hence poaching, to plummet. Ultimately, though, the human population—more than poachers—and growth—not guns—pose the most serious long-term threat to the elephant's survival. With Africa's human population projected to double in twenty-four years and Asia's in perhaps fifty, elephants cling to a habitat under siege.

In an ironic sense while humans are the central cause of the elephant's decline increased human activity in the form of tourism can, as in Kenya, also provide an incentive for stopping poaching. Poachers can contribute to a restraint on the growth of tourism. It is not certain, however, that tourism will be an adequate long-term incentive for a viable conservation formula. In crude terms it may well be the case that if elephants are worth more alive than dead then they are less likely to be killed. Kenya, for example, is profiting from showing off its elephants to tourists. This simple, yet effective, conservation strategy demonstrates that the task in conserving the elephant is not necessarily simply another economic burden to a struggling continent. More important, of course, it is also an opportunity for us all to continue living in a world with great and intelligent beings.

Joseph Michael Pace

Further Readings

Chadwick, Douglas H. "Out of Time, Out of Space: Elephant." *National Geographic* 179 (May 1991): 2–49.

Douglas-Hamilton, Oria, and Iain Douglas-Hamilton. *Battle for the Elephants.* 1992.

Orenstein, Ron, ed. *Elephants: The Deciding Decade.* 1991.

Pagel, Mark, and Ruth Mace. "Keeping the Ivory Trade Banned." *Nature* 351 (May 23, 1991): 265–66.

See also AFRICA: ENVIRONMENTAL PROBLEMS; CITES; CONSERVATION MOVEMENT; IUCN; RHINOCEROS: CONSERVATION AND HABITAT; WORLD WILDLIFE FUND

Elton, Charles

Oxford ecologist Charles Elton (1900–1991) was one of the founders of modern ecology. His book, *Animal Ecology* (1927), helped lay the foundation for modern ecosystem ecology. It introduced many of the concepts—trophic layers, food chains, food webs, and the pyramid of numbers—that now dominate ecology. Concerned with population and ecological communities, he helped establish ecology as the quantitative and experimental study of living organisms in relation to their environment.

A product of the great British natural history tradition, Elton described ecology as "scientific" natural history. Unlike contemporary conservationists and environmentalists, he was opposed to the concept of the balance of nature, arguing that nature was, in fact, dynamic and in constant flux. Recognized as a leader in the new field of ecology, conservationists such as Aldo Leopold, William Vogt, Rachel Carson, Fairfield Osborn, and others used Elton's work to help them describe the relationship between humankind and biological communities.

After meeting Aldo Leopold in 1931 at the Matamek Conference on Biological Cycles, Elton began to write and talk about the need for a "conservation ethic." After meeting Elton, Leopold became a convert to the ecological view of nature. Indeed, Leopold popularized Elton's ecology in his bestselling book, *A Sand County Almanac* (1949), which has introduced ecology to generations of conservationists and environmentalists.

Like Leopold, G. Evelyn Hutchinson, Paul Sears, and George Woodwell, Elton worked to bring the findings of ecology to the lay public. Drawing on ecology, Elton argued that for moral as well as economic reasons, humanity needs to live more carefully on the earth. His efforts to combine his interests in science and ecology with conservationism influenced ecologists such as Woodwell, E.O. Wilson, Paul Ehrlich, and Barry Commoner to become scientific activists. Like other concerned ecologists, Elton believed that ecology should educate humanity about the threats to its future created by the accelerating deterioration of the global environment.

Chris H. Lewis

Further Readings

Elton, Charles. *Animal Ecology.* 1927.

———. *Voles, Mice, and Lemmings.* 1942.

———. *The Pattern of Animal Communities.* 1966.

See also BIOACCUMULATION; CARRYING CAPACITY; ECOLOGICAL NICHE; ECOSYSTEMS; LEOPOLD, ALDO; ODUM, EUGENE; WEB OF LIFE

Emerson, Ralph Waldo

Ralph Waldo Emerson (1803–1882), essayist, philosopher, and poet, was the son of a Unitarian minister with ties to traditional New England puritanism. His work serves as a bridge between Calvinist and modernist views of nature. He attended Harvard and was approved to the Unitarian ministry in 1826. Central to his Unitarian belief was the truth that Christianity is grounded in the proposition that "God is one" and the belief in the existence of God is conditional on the belief that grace must be accessible to everyone at every moment. In addition, Emerson found reason to judge scriptural value according to how fully it was met by nature's observable truths—a test in which the human takes part in the divine.

In 1832 his opposition to orthodoxy within the Unitarian religion led him to resign his ministry and travel to England. There he met Carlyle, Wordsworth, and Coleridge and was introduced to transcendental thought. Everything that the Puritan associated with the sovereignty of God and everything that the Enlightenment saw as rational "truth" existed for

Emerson in the act of our apprehension of "it." Emerson located knowledge in the "local precincts" of our experience—with people, with sensuality, and with the world of nature.

Emerson's first book, *Nature*, was published in 1836 as an attempt to correct both materialist and idealist epistemological conceptions in a radical new vision that casts off an outmoded model in order to conceptualize new truths. In *Nature* Emerson locates knowledge in facts and in things, in which mind and matter both participate. At times in *Nature* the rhetoric becomes so immediate and close-to-the-bone that Emerson's language is stressed to the breaking point as he tries to convey that which in nature can only be intuited. By fusing Cartesian subject-object dualism, Emerson found transcendent unity in an Oversoul that defines the essential divinity of the self within the divinity of nature. This unity is situated in those poetic moments when words unite with things in the one *Logos*. In becoming "one with nature," the true poet intuitively chooses symbolic forms that represent the fusion of mind and world which reveals nature in such a way that the ordinary is made extraordinary.

Emerson worked out the metaphysics of transcendentalism for a large community of writers and philosophers in and around Concord. It was this contribution that earned him recognition as the father of American transcendentalism. His call for a strong poet of nature was realized in the work of his protégé Henry David Thoreau. Emerson also had a very strong influence on John Muir. His face-to-face meeting with Muir in Yosemite is beautifully described by Roderick Nash in *Wilderness and the American Mind* which also notes: "When the high country trails opened again, a tattered volume of Emerson's essays, heavily glossed in Muir's hand, went along in his pack."

As a seminal American environmental thinker, Emerson contributed a wide variety of themes present today in both American letters and American environmental thought, including the importance of direct description of natural scenes. Also, the belief, still resonant with much American nature writing, that close personal observation of the natural world—the fusion of individual and natural—can provide salient insights into proper relations. For Emerson, all questions have answers so long as the artist or scientist is willing to challenge orthodox belief against the test of personal, original experience. Finally, and most powerfully,

the essential beauty and sublimity of the material world (the "not me") when reconciled with experience, provides a power that unifies understanding. Stated differently, it is the personal experience of nature that makes an understanding of the essential divinity of humankind possible. Thus, for Emerson, any extension of human knowledge confirms man's dependence on nature and vice versa.

Paul L. Tidwell

Further Readings

Nash, Roderick. *Wilderness and the American Mind*. 1967.

Oelschlaeger, Max. *The Idea of Wilderness: From Prehistory to the Age of Ecology*. 1991.

See also ECOPHILOSOPHY AND ECOPSYCHOLOGY; ECO-SPIRITUALITY; RELIGION AND ENVIRONMENTAL PROTECTION; THOREAU, HENRY DAVID; WILDERNESS

Employment and Environmental Protection

See JOBS AND THE ENVIRONMENT; LABOR AND THE ENVIRONMENT

Endangered Species Act (U.S.)

The U.S. Supreme Court has called the United States' Endangered Species Act (ESA) "the most comprehensive legislation for the preservation of endangered species ever enacted by any nation." The ESA directs U.S. government agencies to carry out rigorous assessment procedures to identify how proposed agency actions are likely to affect imperiled species, and forbids these agencies from pushing species closer to the brink of extinction. The law also sets forth additional protections applicable to private as well as government conduct. Countries around the world have looked to the ESA as a model for legal protection of biodiversity.

The U.S. Congress passed the ESA in 1973, replacing weaker federal species protection laws. The ESA's first section contains a congressional finding which declares that fish, wildlife, and plants "are of aesthetic, ecological, educational, historical, recreational, and scientific value to the Nation and its people." In addition to protecting species, Congress declared that an additional purpose of the statute is the conservation of ecosystems upon which endangered species depend. While lawmakers have amended the statute several times, they have refused to significantly weaken it.

Two federal agencies bear responsibility for implementing the ESA, the U.S. Fish and Wildlife Service (FWS) (for terrestrial species) and National Marine Fisheries Service (NMFS) (for marine species). A species receives protection under the ESA only if FWS or NMFS has placed it on the list of endangered species or the list of threatened species. While legal protections for species on the endangered list do not differ significantly from protections for threatened species, the former list includes those species most in danger of becoming extinct. FWS and NMFS must base their listing decisions solely on biological information; the agencies cannot consider economics in making determinations of threatened and endangered species. The ESA broadly defines "species" to include subspecies and populations, thus allowing protection of a segment of the entire biological species. At the time a species is listed, FWS/NMFS must also designate "critical habitat" of the species (i.e., habitat necessary for recovery of the species). As of 1994 over 1,200 species were listed as threatened or endangered, including many species found outside the United States.

One of the ESA's most important provisions applies only to U.S. government agencies. These agencies cannot take or grant permission for an action that "jeopardizes the continued existence" of listed species or which destroys critical habitat. To assist federal agencies in complying with this requirement, the ESA sets forth a process for agencies to consult with FWS or NMFS for advice on how a proposed agency action is likely to affect listed species. The "biological opinion" issued by FWS/NMFS at the conclusion of this consultation process influences substantially the decision whether to proceed with an action, modify the action, or abandon it altogether. Since the U.S. government owns a great deal of land, as well as issues permits for a broad array of private activities, this consultation process applies to many proposed actions.

If a federal agency's proposed action presents an unresolvable conflict with the interests of a listed species, the agency may attempt to secure an exemption from the ESA to permit the action to go forward. The Endangered Species Committee, composed of high-level government officials and nicknamed the "God Squad," has authority to exempt actions from the ESA if it finds that the benefits of doing so outweigh the

harm to a protected species. This exemption process has very rarely been used.

The ESA sets forth several additional prohibitions which apply to all persons subject to U.S. jurisdiction. Import, export, and commerce in listed species is prohibited. The statute also forbids federal, state, and private entities from "taking" listed species. The Act broadly defines takings to include not only killing, injuring, or capturing a protected species, but also destruction of habitat resulting in injury or death to listed species. This effectively extends federal species protections to activities on private land. A federal agency or private party may, nevertheless, obtain permission to "incidentally" take endangered or threatened species, provided that such takings are not the purpose of the action and a plan is in place to assure that such takings will not harm the overall population's chances for survival. The ESA also provides for stiff criminal and civil penalties to punish violators.

An important feature of the ESA is its many opportunities for the public to participate in efforts to protect endangered and threatened species. The statute permits any interested person to petition FWS or NMFS to add a species to the protected lists. Many listed species have been added through this process. The law also requires FWS and NMFS to seek public comments on these agencies' plans for recovery of listed species. Finally, the ESA allows any interested person to file a law suit to enforce protections for endangered and threatened species, and allows for awards of attorneys fees to successful litigants.

The ESA's ultimate goal is to see species replenished in numbers so that they are no longer considered endangered. Thus far few listed species have sufficiently increased in number to warrant removal from the protected lists. However, the ESA has played a key role in stemming the decline of many endangered and threatened species, and in preventing significant erosion of many important habitats.

The ESA also has played an increasing role in land management issues in the United States. The statute's prominent influence in halting or restricting some economic activities has made it the focus of a great deal of controversy. For example, ESA protections for northern spotted owls—which depend on old-growth forests—have curtailed timber harvest in the Northwest United States, thereby spurring an argument over lumber rights in those areas. This and similar controversies have prompted some to call for amending the law to allow for more consideration of economic factors. On the other hand, other people have advocated dramatically increasing the number of species on the endangered and threatened lists and strengthening the statute's habitat protections.

The ESA has long been regarded as one of the United States' most powerful environmental laws. Its detailed procedural and substantive requirements have integrated protections for endangered and threatened species into virtually all federal activities and many private actions in the United States.

Daniel J. Rohlf

Further Readings

Houck, Oliver. "The Endangered Species Act and its Implementation by the U.S. Departments of Interior and Commerce." *Colorado Law Review* 64 (1993): 277–370.

Rohlf, Daniel J. *The Endangered Species Act: A Guide to Its Protections and Implementation.* 1989.

See also BIODEPLETION; BIODIVERSITY; CITES; OLD GROWTH FORESTS

Energy Crisis

The link between national and international energy issues was never clearer than in the 1970s. The Arab oil embargo in 1973 and the Iran crisis in 1979 raised serious questions about the vulnerability of the United States, Canada, Western Europe, and Japan in the acquisition and control of petroleum resources.

The outbreak of the Arab-Israeli war in 1973 provided a catalyst for the emergence of the Organization of Petroleum Exporting Countries (OPEC) as the world leader in crude oil pricing and production. Coming on the heels of global price inflation, rising nationalism in the Third World, and the shift in oil exploitation from the Western Hemisphere to the Middle East and North Africa, the war offered the Arab members of OPEC a chance to influence diplomatic relations with the West. The Saudis had blocked strong sanctions against the United States in the early days of the war, but they felt compelled to threaten an oil embargo if further aid was extended to Israel. After President Nixon authorized a weapons airlift to Israel, the Saudis supported an Arab boycott of oil against supporters of Israel.

The embargo produced results for OPEC. As oil prices rose, imports to the United States dropped, and Japan and European nations yielded to demands to move away from their pro-Israeli positions. Although the embargo lasted only six months, a new order was developing in international oil, and diplomatic leverage was tipping toward the Middle East.

"Energy crisis" was on everyone's lips in 1973. The United States was never more dependent on oil and natural gas than in the 1970s. Practically all the increases in American energy consumption after 1970 came from oil imports, as domestic production steadily declined. For the Nixon administration, energy policy was ensnared in a conflict between anti-inflation measures and energy scarcity, in Middle East diplomacy, and in the cancer of Watergate.

The quadrupling of oil prices and the lack of adequate preparation for a transition to a period of relative scarcity left the United States facing a critical juncture. On November 27, 1973, Nixon signed the Emergency Petroleum Allocation Act which established a new allocation plan, provided authority for gas rationing, maintained price controls, and established Project Independence—a proposal to free the country from foreign oil by 1980. In June 1974 the Federal Energy Administration was created to centralize executive control over energy policy. But the impact of the oil embargo on the American people was as much emotional as practical. By November 1974 gas stations were shutting down because of shortages, lines of automobiles stretched for several blocks in car-dominated California, and debate over mass transit, car pooling, and Detroit gas-guzzlers was widespread. In the eyes of most Americans it was the oil companies, the federal government, and the Arabs who were to blame.

Despite the initial trauma of the embargo, the world oil market remained relatively orderly between 1974 and 1978. Demand for OPEC oil temporarily dipped because of slow economic growth throughout the world, increased production from the North Sea and Alaska, and conservation practices. The Ford administration shared its predecessor's aim to decontrol oil prices, but faced similar economic constraints and Congressional resistance. Congress continued price controls and mandatory allocation of domestic oil for an additional three years. The Ford administration also failed to gain much ground in clarifying the federal role in developing new energy sources. The only significant organizational changes were the establishment of the Energy Research and Development Administration and the Nuclear Regulatory Commission, which replaced the Atomic Energy Commission, and the forming of the Energy Resources Council, meant to coordinate the formulation and implementation of national energy policy.

The Carter administration hoped to move the nation in a new direction in the energy arena after the 1976 election. However, Carter was more successful in changing the tone of the debate over energy than the substance of national policy. On April 18, 1977, the President announced his National Energy Plan (NEP), describing the energy situation as "the moral equivalent of war." The goal was to ease into a transition from the petroleum-based economy of the past to a system based on energy conservation and alternative fuels by reducing annual energy growth and gasoline consumption, increasing the use of coal, and establishing strategic petroleum reserves. At the heart of NEP was the Crude Oil Equalization Tax (COET) to raise oil prices, to reduce demand, and to provide revenue for various energy programs. Despite its controversial provisions, the NEP was pushed through Congress in 1978. However, the COET was killed in committee and the legislation had no provisions for oil pricing. In addition to the NEP, the Carter administration raised the energy issue to cabinet-level status with the creation of the Department of Energy, which replaced or codified several government energy programs.

However, the dual track of new legislation and new organizational activity was too much, too soon. No sooner had the new legislation and new department come into existence than the administration faced its own energy emergency. The stability of the world oil market was broken in 1978 when the Shah of Iran—a major American ally—was forced into exile, and replaced by Ayatollah Khomeini, the leader of the Islamic Revolution. The Shah's flight from oil-rich Iran coupled with the Soviet invasion of Afghanistan in December 1979, turned uncertainty into pessimism along the Persian Gulf.

The Iran crisis produced renewed disruptions in the world energy market and new shock waves in the United States. Double-digit inflation reappeared, and oil prices were again on the rise. Like Ford and Nixon, Carter was forced to battle interlacing economic and energy woes.

At home, the impact of the 1979 crisis was as visible and dramatic as the embargo had been a few years earlier. Weekend and even weekday closing of gas stations hit the big cities, and by the summer shortages struck many populous states. Several states tried odd-even gas rationing systems, but problems continued. By April 1979 gasoline nudged toward $1 a gallon—an unheard-of price in the United States at the time.

Carter appealed to Americans to drive less and pay more attention to thermostat settings; he also tried to use the crisis to recoup losses in his original energy proposals, especially COET, by calling for phased decontrol of oil accompanied by a windfall profits tax. The tax would be used to subsidize mass transit, develop synfuels, and give energy assistance to the poor. The timing of the new legislation ensured its passage. However, Carter had to shoulder the onus of higher prices due to decontrol, and the new Windfall Profits Tax of 1980 was predictably unpopular with many in the business world. The renewed energy crisis, coupled with the taking of American hostages in Iran, increased Carter's political vulnerability in the upcoming presidential election.

Aside from the political and economic repercussions of the energy crisis, events of the 1970s also resulted in a vigorous environmental debate and soul-searching about "alternative energy futures." What made the energy crisis more confounding was its confluence with the burgeoning environmental movement. Concern over energy scarcity clashed with concern over ecological or environmental scarcity. It is not surprising that so much of the environmental protest of the 1970s was a response to energy issues: nuclear power, the Alaskan pipeline, oil spills, and air pollution. Environmentalists warned about "ecodisasters," but also questioned the economic, political, and social structures that produced these problems. Such inquiry came at a time when fuel scarcity, faltering productivity, inflation, and other anxieties were intensified by the energy crisis. As a counterweight to environmental protests, business leaders, government officials and economists warned about energy shortfalls, threats to national security, and the deterioration of the standard of living. Nuclear power sometimes became a focal point of these debates as proponents argued that further development of reactors could provide at least a mid-term solution to oil scarcity. On another level, a search for alternative energy futures led to an investi-

E

gation of new or little-used energy sources to replace those perceived as scarce. Several untapped sources of fossil fuels were available, including conversion of coal into gas or liquid, the liquefaction of shale, and extraction of oil from tar sands. Various forms of solar energy attracted attention and some began to demonstrate commercial viability: solar thermal conversion, photovoltaic cells, wind power, tidal power, ocean thermal conversion, and biomass. But even with federal involvement in several projects, these efforts were too diffuse, uncoordinated, and underfunded to have much national impact.

The debate over energy futures and alternative fuels inevitably broadened to engulf a more general concern over the ends of economic growth. A Resources for the Future study stated that "Energy has become a testing ground for conflict over broader social choices." Proponents of continued energy growth stressed past benefits—comfort, material well-being, and high employment. They maintained a faith in the market mechanism to adjust to scarce resources, to produce technical fixes in exploiting available energy sources, and to create or discover new sources. Opponents of unlimited growth questioned the equity in distribution of wealth due to past economic practices. They viewed growth as leading to more material goods, rather than better service or an improved quality of life. Those holding the most extreme position were apprehensive about continued industrialization, fearing that it would lead to the exhaustion of resources and future ecological disasters. Those with more moderate views did not fear total exhaustion of resources or the reaching of absolute environmental limits but were concerned about scarcities and increased costs, which would put goods and services beyond the reach of many Americans.

As quickly as the debate over energy futures reached intensity, events in the early 1980s marked an end to the energy crisis of the 1970s. The newly elected Reagan administration represented an approach to government that was built on traditional faith in the productive capacity of the United States, not on a fear of future energy shortages. Within the next few years, oil prices stabilized and even declined in the wake of an international oil glut based in both new sources of supply and a significant reduction in demand. The lower demand was attributable in turn to both economic recession and energy conservation.

Somewhat prematurely, OPEC's imminent demise was proclaimed in newspapers and magazines—a sign of a rapidly changing national mood. However, as the American economy began to climb out of recession, it seemed that the crisis of the 1970s was overstated. The National Energy Policy Plan, issued in October 1983, formally abandoned the goal of energy independence. The Reagan administration tapped the historic American commitment to progress through economic growth by focusing on energy production rather than consumption through, as one historian noted, "the elixir of 'supply-side economics' mixed with a strong draught of military spending."

The crisis of the 1970s may have been too easily dismissed in the 1980s, however. Long-term energy shortages may have been exaggerated, but the political, economic, and environmental circumstances which produced the crisis have appeared in the past and could well be revisited in the future.

Martin V. Melosi

Further Readings

Clark, John G. *The Political Economy of World Energy.* 1990.

Melosi, Martin V. *Coping with Abundance: Energy and Environment in Industrial America.* 1985.

Yergin, Daniel. *The Prize: The Epic Quest for Oil, Money and Power.* 1991.

See also CARTER, JIMMY; ENERGY EFFICIENCY; NONRENEWABLE RESOURCES; REAGAN, RONALD; SOFT ENERGY PATHS; SOLAR ENERGY; SUSTAINABILITY

Energy Efficiency

Energy is the base upon which our current highly industrialized, technological society stands. This base, however, is not as sturdy as we might think. Eating away at the base are two factors: society's failure to diversify its energy future and to its wasteful use of energy. Energy efficiency, the cornerstone of sustainable development, is one tool at our disposal that will allow us to secure our energy future. Environmentally, economically, and ethically, energy efficiency is the right path to follow.

All forms of energy production produce waste or cause degradation. Although alternative and renewable forms of energy have a lesser impact, all energy production has some effect on the environment. Burning fossil fuels emits greenhouse gases and air pollution particles; excessive fuel harvesting often results in deforestation and desertification; nuclear electric power use yields high levels of radioactive waste and proliferation of weapons of mass destruction; and large-scale hydroelectric projects are often accompanied by flooded lands and ecosystem destruction. Reducing our energy needs will slow the deterioration of our environment in many, many ways.

Perhaps the most significant long-term environmental concern related to energy use is global climate change. Greenhouse gas emissions are increasing at a rate never before seen. Current average Celsius temperatures are 6 degrees higher than they were a century ago. Scientific consensus suggests that this global warming will continue at a considerably faster pace in the future. The effects of climate change are expected to be severe, including not only global warming, but also a rise in sea level, changes in precipitation patterns and soil moisture, and loss of productivity from the land and sea. The longer the delay in taking action, the more costly the social and economic impacts are likely to be. Investing in energy efficiency is taking out an insurance policy against climate change. We take out insurance policies on the premise that catastrophes much less likely than climate change will occur.

The best answer to these environmental concerns is to make much more efficient use of our available energy. Significant increases in energy efficiency, coupled with a shift from resource-based to renewable energy production, will enable us to meet our energy needs, sustainably, well into the next century.

Another benefit associated with increased energy efficiency is the positive economic feedback it would produce. Energy efficiency in almost every case is more labor intensive than is the development of new energy supplies, especially from non-renewable sources. That is, money invested in energy efficiency produces more jobs than the same amount of money invested in energy production. Improving energy efficiency spurs the development of a wide variety of new or improved technologies—technologies associated with every process, product, or device that uses energy. These new technologies become commodities which can be produced, marketed, sold, and exported.

Energy efficiency is based on a simple concept: do more with less. Many no-regrets opportunities for enhancing energy efficiency are available today with incentives for both the economy and the environment. Each involves taking a given amount of energy and accomplishing a greater amount of "work" with it. The concept is exceedingly simple, logical, and obviously recognizable as a positive step. However, it is an idea that is only now being given its due and many barriers remain to the full implementation of the opportunities which already exist in technical terms.

Improving residential, and especially commercial electricity use affords perhaps the greatest opportunities at this time. Motors, appliances, lighting, heating, air conditioning—all are areas for which technology exists to significantly, even radically improve efficiency. Particularly promising are new technologies for lighting—a field that accounts for about 25 percent of existing electricity use in the United States. Some utilities have recently begun to invest directly in efficiency (i.e., by providing customers with incentives to use less and rebates for buying energy efficient products). This supplies the utilities with more electricity to sell, thereby removing the need to invest large amounts of capital in increased production capacity.

Renovating existing buildings to save energy is also economically prudent. Some U.S. utilities have participated in and monitored such initiatives since the mid-1970s. In the residential sector 40,000 retrofits were monitored and saw a 25 percent average reduction in energy use and an average annual return on investment of 23 percent. Savings on the redesign of new buildings are even higher, especially in commercial and office buildings. New buildings can be made airtight whereas old buildings generally cannot. The energy savings are considerable and indoor air pollution problems can be handled through the use of ventilation systems with built-in air-to-air heat exchangers. New windows are twice as efficient as old windows and these can be retrofitted.

Transportation is another area in which major gains in efficiency can be made; this is critical because the United States, for example, burns 63 percent of its oil in transportation uses. Fuel efficiency in North American vehicles doubled between 1975–1985, due in part to the oil shortage. Many believe that by using available technologies, such as multi-valve fuel injection and better transmissions, this level of advance could be accomplished again through the 1990s. Some argue motor vehicle efficiency could be improved exponentially by employing more revolutionary approaches. Perhaps even more important, modal shifts within the transportation system can definitely result in sharp improvements in overall transportation efficiency. People can be induced to switch from private automobiles to public transportation or, as an even better alternative, to walking and cycling. The latter, which amounts to only a few persons in Los Angeles, makes up 25 percent or more of trips in a typical European city. Those levels will not be obtained, however, without a gradual shift in urban form; short of that many initiatives are possible, especially perhaps in Eastern North American and medium-sized cities.

Industry and manufacturing can and do also benefit significantly from enhanced efficiency. Pumps, motors, lighting, refrigeration, and production processes all can be improved to use less energy. Cogeneration—the use of waste steam to produce electricity or district heating—improves overall efficiency significantly and is one of the most promising of opportunities. Improvements in efficiency have the added benefit of improving competitiveness, since per-unit production costs decrease. As a result, between 1973 and 1986 energy use in U.S. industry fell by 17 percent while output rose by an equal amount. Roughly half of this change can be attributed to more efficient equipment and processes; the other half to a shift within the economy from heavy industries to services. Both trends can and should be accelerated through, for example, shifting the proportion of taxes collected from employment, income, and payrolls to energy use.

Energy efficiency is not the total solution to our energy and pollution problems. To have a truly sustainable energy future we need to gradually, but comprehensively localize and diversify our "soft path" energy production, change the structure of our economy and society, and fundamentally change our perception of energy use. Energy efficiency is, however, an important first step whose first stages can be accomplished quickly, cheaply, and at a net benefit to both the environment and the economy.

Michel Gareau

Further Readings

Vine, Edward, and Drury Crawley. *State of the Art of Energy Efficiency: Future Directions*. 1991.

Johansson, Thomas B. *Electricity: Efficient End-Use and New Generation Technologies, and Their Planning Implications*.

Lund (Sweden) University Press, 1990.

See also AUTOMOBILES: IMPACTS AND POLICIES; CLIMATE WARMING; COGENERATION; DEMAND-SIDE MANAGEMENT; ENERGY EFFICIENCY IN AGRICULTURE; LEAST-COST UTILITY PLANNING; LOVINS, AMORY B.; SOFT ENERGY PATHS; URBAN FORM

Energy Efficiency in Agriculture

As non-renewable fossil fuels become more scarce for the support of human activities, competition increases for this resource among regions, countries, and sectors of society. In the industrialized or highly developed regions, there is a relatively small amount of energy used for food, fiber, and raw material production. Yet, energy efficiency in all sectors is an important goal for the future.

The most energy efficient food systems in recorded history are the extensive, modified planting and gathering systems still found in remote areas of Southeast Asia. They return about 20 Kilocalories (Kcal) of energy for each Kcal invested, primarily the input from human labor. Such systems obviously support a low level of human population density. Especially over the past two centuries, the introduction of animal-drawn or tractor-powered equipment has helped to increase production per unit of human labor, but energy use efficiency has been reduced from 20 to 1 to about 4 to 1 in modern agriculture. This ratio has not changed, though introduction of fertilizers and pesticides has increased return to labor and productivity per unit land area and reduced the return to capital and to energy investment.

Remarkable gains in labor and land-use efficiency can be illustrated by maize production in the United States. Over the past sixty years, yields have increased from about forty to more than 120 bushels per acre (2.5 to 7.5 tons per hectare). This has been accomplished through the use of new hybrids, substitution of chemical fertilizer for legumes and animal manure, and chemical pesticides to reduce crop losses and minimize mechanical cultivation. Such systems depend on larger tractors and implements, both requiring greater capital and energy investment. Although the large tractor is a highly visible symbol of energy use, in irrigated agriculture there is a much greater investment in energy for pumping water and producing nutrients than for all mechanical operations combined. In fact, larger equipment has only increased labor efficiency, but has not changed overall energy efficiency in agriculture.

Because of current cost and potential future energy security, researchers and farmers are searching for ways to reduce energy use and increase efficiency in farming. To reduce energy costs for irrigation, farmers can improve irrigation scheduling, use lower rates early in the season, and choose crops that are efficient in water use. Rainfall can be used more efficiently when tillage is reduced and a residue cover is maintained on the soil through the entire year. Nutrients can be used more efficiently when cropping systems are designed to prevent soil erosion, increase soil organic matter, accommodate more legumes, and use animal manure. When pests are managed through integrated methods including resistant varieties, crop rotations, and limited chemical application, less energy is used than in conventional chemical-based agriculture. When renewable, locally available resources can be used in place of non-renewable, imported, fossil-fuel based resources, increased energy efficiency can often result.

Energy use by society must be viewed in a broad perspective. About 15 percent of energy use in developed countries is dedicated to food systems. Of that energy, less than one-fourth is used in actual production of crops and animals in the field. Increased energy use efficiency in production agriculture may help the farmer increase profits, but it will do little to reduce total energy use in industrialized societies.

Charles A. Francis

Further Readings

Goldemberg, José, et al. *Energy for Development*. World Resources Institute, 1987.
Pimentel, David. *Handbook of Energy Utilization in Agriculture*. 1980.

See also ENERGY EFFICIENCY; IRRIGATION IMPACTS; SUSTAINABLE AGRICULTURE

Energy Probe

Energy Probe is a Toronto-based Canadian nongovernmental organization that focuses on the economic, environmental, and social impacts of energy production and use. Energy Probe originated as a part of Pollution Probe in 1973. In 1980 the two organizations decided to separate, and Energy Probe continued as one of several projects within the newly created Energy Probe Research Foundation.

Energy Probe tries to educate the public and decision makers by: 1) producing research reports and books; 2) intervening in public hearings and court cases; and 3) responding to media requests. In its early years, the focus of activities was roughly equally divided between provincial concerns (mainly electrical utilities and natural gas distribution) and federal concerns (mainly oil and gas production and pipelines). In recent years, the former has become the focus of its activities except for a continuing interest in the Nuclear Liability Act and other forms of federal support for the nuclear industry.

Energy Probe is uncommon among Canadian ENGOs (Environmental Non-governmental Organizations) in basing its approach primarily on neoclassical economics. It favors the extension of market processes with only a limited role for government. Thus it has based its objections to nuclear power largely on excessive costs plus concerns about safety and it argues for a breakup of Ontario Hydro with only transmission lines remaining under direct provincial control. Except for the most toxic pollutants Energy Probe prefers that pollution effects be monetized and included in prices so that those responsible for emissions pay for damages.

In the early 1990s Energy Probe had an annual budget of some $600,000 and a staff of seven. Its income is derived from donations (50 percent), from intervenor funding (30 percent), and from sale of reports and consulting services (20 percent). Some 10,000 people donate annually to Energy Probe.

David B. Brooks

Further Reading

Marmorek, Jan. *Over a Barrel: A Guide to the Canadian Energy Crisis*. 1981.

See also BREEDER REACTORS: ENVIRONMENTAL PROBLEMS; DEMAND-SIDE MANAGEMENT; NUCLEAR ELECTRIC POWER; NUCLEAR WASTE; POLLUTION PROBE

Environment

In its most general sense the word environment refers to the area that surrounds or circumscribes human or nonhuman beings. It has not always had such a univocal meaning for both social and natural scientists. There was a time when sociologists, anthropologists and psychologists called environment the social milieu that surrounds and has an impact on human activity; while natural scientists, biologists for example, used the word environment to signify natural ecosystems independent of humans and surrounding a living being or an animal or plant population. Today, there seems to be a consensus to define environment in a more global and unified manner. The environment thus is now considered to be an organized, dynamic, and evolving system of natural (i.e., physical, chemical, biological) and human (i.e., economic, political, social, and cultural) factors in which living organisms operate or human activities take place, and which has a direct or indirect, immediate or long-term effect or influence on these living beings or on human actions at a given time and in a circumscribed area. For example, the environment is often seen as having an impact on individual and collective behavior and attitudes, on motivation, intelligence, technology development, forms of social organization and disorganization, demographic processes, and on the way human beings feed, clothe, and house themselves.

Environments exist in terms of the organisms or of the human beings that inhabit them. Environments can thus be infinitely overlapping. They can be natural or built, rural or urban, biotic or cultural. In this sense, environment is often used as a synonym for the words nature, or milieu, or ecosphere inasmuch as they are influenced or threatened by human activity or have some impact on that activity. Environment has often replaced these terms, starting in the 1960s, when problems of pollution and of resource scarcity began to appear.

Environmental problems are considered to be the social aspects of natural problems, and the natural aspects of social problems. The word environment then, entails both natural and social dimensions. It can also be conceived as the total sum, or aggregate of juxtaposed, fragmented elements, or of an organic unified totality or ecosystem where the parts are intimately and organically interrelated. It is often used today in the expressions "quality of the environment" and "protection or conservation of the environment." It has inspired the use of the word environmentalism to refer for some analysts to a moderate middle-of-the-road tendency in the green movement, halfway between conservationism and ecologism. Many college and university courses now focus on the economics, the politics, the sociology, or the history of the environment. The International Sociological Association now has a research committee called "Environment and Society." An important magazine called *Environment* was established in 1959 by the Committee for Environmental Information, a nonprofit St. Louis, Missouri corporation. It is currently published in Washington, D.C. by the Helen Dwight Reid Foundation (Heldref Publication).

Jean-Guy Vaillancourt

Further Readings

Koller, A.H. *The Theory of the Environment.* 1918.

Nicholson, M. *The Environmental Revolution.* 1972.

Schnaiberg, Allan. *The Environment: From Surplus to Scarcity.* 1980.

Watt, K.E.F. *Understanding the Environment.* 1982.

See also ENVIRONMENT: EUROPEAN USAGE; ENVIRONMENTALISM

Environment Canada

Environment Canada, also known as the Department of the Environment (DOE), was founded in June 1971. It was created by combining several existing units from other departments and by forming a new environmental protection service. Generally speaking DOE has been a junior department—having had no less than sixteen largely ineffectual ministers over the past twenty-two years. The exception was the period 1990–1993 when the DOE led the government-wide Green Plan initiative and was headed by strong ministers. The department's history has been characterized as "the rise" 1971–1975, "the fall" 1975–1985, and "the rise" 1986–1993 reflecting the relative political attention, support and resources the DOE experienced in these various periods. The department experienced another "fall" in June 1993 when its resources and support from the center were once again weakened. Between 1971 and 1993 DOE retained a staff of around 10,000, but in June 1993 suffered a 40 percent reduction in staff and budget when the Canadian Parks Service was removed.

Historically, DOE has been a poorly integrated department composed of several autonomous units, each with its own organizational culture and goals. These units have been combined and recombined in numerous reorganizations. At various times, DOE has had responsibility for fisheries, forestry, and parks. All of these are now in other departments, leaving atmospheric environmental services, environmental protection, pollution prevention, conservation and wildlife, environmental policy, and state of the environment reporting, as DOE's chief responsibilities. A core internal struggle for DOE historically had to do with the relationship between its resource management functions and its conservation and protection functions. It might be argued that this friction was largely solved with the removal of Fisheries and Forestry services, and the Canadian Parks Service.

DOE has a strong scientific research and technical assessment capacity to support its regulatory and policy functions. For most of its history, science (research, development, and related scientific activities) has accounted for about half of DOE's budget. Roughly 40 percent of DOE employees have a university degree or a diploma in a technical subject, a figure which exceeds every other major department in Ottawa. DOE's statutory base includes the Fisheries Act (Sections 36–42), the Canadian Environmental Protection Act, the Migratory Birds Convention Act, the Canada Water Act, the International Rivers Improvement Act, the Canada Wildlife Act, and the Canadian Environmental Assessment Act. DOE was long criticized for lacking sophisticated economic analysis skills but in the 1990s took steps to upgrade its economic analysis and social science capabilities.

Despite a lack of support from other departments and the political center, DOE has always prided itself on the skills and dedication of its staff and it has led several successful initiatives. The 1972 Stockholm Conference, the acid rain campaign of the 1980s, the creation of the Canadian Environmental Protection Act in 1987, the Montreal Protocol, the Green Plan, the 1992 Rio Conference and its Climate Change and Biodiversity Conventions, and breakthroughs in ultraviolet (UV) monitoring are all initiatives for which the DOE deserves credit.

Glen Toner

Further Readings

Doern, G. Bruce, and Thomas Conway. *The Greening of Canada*. 1994.

Brown, M. Paul. "Organizational Design as Policy Instrument: Environment Canada in the Canadian Bureaucracy." In *Canadian Environmental Policy*. Ed. Robert Boardman. 1992.

See also FEDERALISM AND ENVIRONMENTAL PROTECTION: CANADA; FISHERIES ACT (CANADA); GREEN PLAN (CANADA); MONTREAL PROTOCOL; POLLUTION PREVENTION; RIO CONFERENCE (1992); STOCKHOLM CONFERENCE

Environment and Development

See SUSTAINABLE DEVELOPMENT; WORLD BANK

Environment: European Usage

Dictionaries do not give precise meanings for the word environment, referring to surrounding, milieu, relationships, and setting. Meaning is defined by usage and context; it will change over time and varies between languages. In general, the term "environment" has come to draw attention to a world view which asserts that change, and hence government policies, are needed for the sake of our planet and, more importantly, for the sake of the many societies inhabiting it. Concepts which tend to exclude the environment are technology, capital, culture, and art—yet all make use of or have effects upon it. Distinctions become blurred as we strive for more environmentally benign technologies, more environment friendly attitudes, green investments, and ecologically sound behavior.

Different uses and interpretations reflect different philosophical and intellectual traditions. For example, ecologists and geographers have long used the word to describe the importance of the interrelationships between parts of objects within one system, between an object and its wider surroundings, and between people and nature. The environment may be seen as the life-support system of communities—their ultimate source of the energy and materials required for life and the growth of culture. For economists, the environment means natural resources and land, "factors" that need costing and pricing to prevent deterioration and exhaustion. The number of books written on environmental ethics is increasing as societies realize that costs and prices change as values change. The rarer and more desired a thing becomes, the more its value increases. The vagueness and flexibility of the concept reflects major philosophical debates about the reality and usefulness of "dualism," attitudes and policies which are based on the sharp distinction between culture and nature, or society and environment.

In Britain the word environment was rarely used before the nineteenth century; in the 1950s it was incorporated into pollution control legislation requiring the national electricity utility "to take into account" the nuisance impacts of its activities not only on people inside the plant perimeter, but beyond as well. The environment became those aspects of the local and, at the most, regional surroundings of industrial sites that invited protection from pollution. However, no British regulator at that time had to take note of any impacts outside the national sphere; the natural world was believed to be too large and forgiving to be harmed so long as sufficient dilution was achieved. In English it is also possible to talk of an intellectual environment, the built environment, or to make the distinction between a natural and a social environment.

In contrast, the equivalent term in German, *Umwelt*, came into use only in the 1970s. It was introduced from the English to more clearly define the needs of *Natur* and *Land* as these were burdened by society's impacts. *Umwelt* literally means "surrounding world" and includes the materials and objects which make up the surface of the earth. Its protection (*Umweltschutz*) was added to "nature protection" (*Naturschutz*), usually translated as conservation. In the German language and hence perception, therefore, the "environment" is not only global but also requires conservation by definition. In German, there cannot be a national environment because the physical systems of water, air, and even land are interconnected.

As the environment became an issue and subject of policy, all types of expertise have absorbed the concept and added their own interpretations. The French prefer to talk about ecology and ecologists, while words derived from environment have remained more popular in English-speaking countries and the Germans use both concepts, distinguishing between them.

By the early 1990s the term has lost any precise meaning it may have had for specific disciplines and systems of thought. Everybody, from business manager to school teacher and politician, has discovered the environment, often asking for government subsidies for activities which the market would not reward. Economists and accountants are trying to "correct market failures" because the market (making, selling, and buying) tends to ignore the environment.

Environmental costs and benefits should be measured and brought into balance. Engineers are trying to design processes and products that use fewer environmental resources and generate less waste and pollution. Schools are trying to teach children to be more aware of natural objects and to value them more highly. For politicians the term has become a mixed blessing. While environmental regulation enhances their competence and attracts voters, raising taxes to spend money on the environment or passing prohibitions and regulations are not usually popular.

The environment has become a major political issue behind which many competing interests are maneuvering for advantage. The use and meaning of the word needs careful analysis.

Sonja A. Boehmer-Christiansen

See also ENVIRONMENT; ENVIRONMENTALISM

Environmental Action

Environmental Action (EA) is a non-tax exempt environmental lobby of around 20,000 members founded in 1970 by the student organizers of the original Earth Day. With its roots as a student collective EA generally is regarded as on the "left wing" of the "mainstream" environmental community, though its pragmatism generally separates it from such "anti-establishment" groups as Earth First!

EA has evolved from a general environmental organization to one focused most on toxic substances and waste disposal. With respect to the former, EA works most to promote citizens' right to know about substances being used and disposed by industries within their communities. On solid waste disposal, EA has worked to promote bottle deposit and recycling measures. EA has also been active in the fight against nuclear power, particularly after it merged with the Energy Conservation Coalition in 1986.

Although early on it identified with the kinds of "direct action" made famous by Greenpeace, EA's primary tactics revolve around lobbying and public education. It also tries to influence election campaigns by disseminating the environmental records of candidates and through direct contributions made by its affiliated Environmental Action Political Action Campaign (EnAct/PAC). EA perhaps is most widely known for its annual "Dirty Dozen," a list of the twelve members of the U.S. House and Senate who had the most "anti-environmental" voting record in the previous congressional session.

EA is based in Washington, D.C., and has a staff of about twenty. Decision making traditionally is based on consensus, though this model was modified as the organization struggled with budgetary problems in the late 1980s. It has an annual operating budget of around $1 million, most of which comes from member dues and contributions. Additional non-lobbying oriented funding comes through the Environmental Action Foundation, EA's tax-exempt research arm. EA publishes a bimonthly magazine, *Environmental Action*, through which it urges write directly to their Congressional representatives.

Christopher J. Bosso

Further Reading

Dunlap, Riley E., and Angela G. Mertig, eds. *American Environmentalism: The U.S. Environmental Movement, 1970–1990.* 1992.

Wenner, Lettie M. *U.S. Energy and Environmental Interest Groups.* 1990.

See also EARTH DAY; EARTH FIRST!; ENVIRONMENTALISM; GREENPEACE; RIGHT-TO-KNOW: COMMUNITY (U.S.); RIGHT-TO-KNOW: WORKPLACE (U.S.)

Environmental Aesthetics

Environmental aesthetics is a sub-area of aesthetics, the objects of which are the physical world examined from the point of beauty and the opinions presented about it in criticism. It is a part of environmental philosophy, as is environmental ethics, and is supported by specific environmental sciences and cultural studies.

The environment can be divided into the natural environment and the cultural or built environment. In each there are units (animals and plants, buildings and implements) and entireties (spaces and landscapes, villages and towns) formed by them. The natural environment is outside of direct human influence. Signs of human activity can be seen in the cultural environment; culture produces things that nature cannot, and thus increases the diversity of forms of life in the environment. A cultural expert can ask what the meaning and significance of an act is, and also how well the work has been done when examined from a certain point of view, such as the aesthetic. In the natural environment there is no responsible maker in the same literal sense. Nature exists only as given, formed by geological and biological processes. The experts of nature are its depicters and researchers.

Following this division it is possible to distinguish between "positive" and "critical" aesthetics (see Carlson 1984). The goal of the former is to create and find grounds for the understanding and approval of the object in an aesthetic sense; the goal of the latter is critical appreciation and evaluation. Positive aesthetics concentrates on the environment in a natural state; critical aesthetics on human activity and its marks in the environment.

The Art World and the Environment World

Art and environment only occasionally meet on the surface level but, on a deeper level, they have a close similarity. The fundamental cultural similarity lies in the fact that in both, production, transmission, and reception are regulated by special institutions, so basically, they have a common structure. In art the institutional practice is governed by the art world (artist training, the transmission and recording of works, art criticism and research—all with their institutions); in environment it is governed by the environment world (with its corresponding personnel and institutions). Together these two aesthetic practices belong to one aesthetic culture.

The aesthetic process is formed by a chain from the maker to the work and from the work to the receiver. The more natural the environment, the more the role of the receiver is emphasized. By means of his or her choices and emphases, the receiver molds objects in accordance with the models provided by his or her own culture, while renewing these models at the same time. Thus even the natural environment becomes culturized.

The environment has been described and interpreted and its quality evaluated. Equipment and vocabulary have been developed for talking about environmental objects: criticism, travel and nature writing, design discussion, and, for instance, architectural discourse can be seen as paradigmatic cases. These activities have established their traditions in nature writing and speaking of cultural objects—produced by, for example, design and architecture—as well as in the fields of environmental sciences, such as geography. The language of environmental criticism, including such tools as photography and video, is the research material of

E

metacritical environmental aesthetics, as are behavior, shopper's choices and other activities in which evaluations appear, such as tourism and rambling in nature.

The environment itself can be compared to language. In the case of the environment transformed by human hands, individuals and groups have "written" it in signs and symbols; in the case of the natural environment we have a ready "book of nature" to read. The language of environment is responded to in the language of criticism. The critic and the researcher are a kind of communal pre-reader and authorial understander. On the basis of their public positions, they have a power to direct the common reactions; their selections, for example, raise objects to the status of natural and cultural sights: national landscapes, historical landmarks, and related entities and symbols.

The environment is molded with many different goals in mind but, nevertheless, without any need to ask the intentions of the maker, the aesthetic form of examination may always be selected. Because the question is one of the real environment treatment of it cannot be totally free, as is possible in those fictional arts constructing imaginary personal worlds (i.e., literature, music, and cinema). Forms of art dealing with the physical environment, such as architecture, landscape planning and environmental art, become parts of our common reality and, therefore, cannot be independent of other human causes. Solutions involving the environment, whether made within the sphere of art or outside of it, must be made within a framework determined by ethical and other life values.

In the same way as the institutional theory of art has met its challenge in anti-art, the institutional theory of environment will meet its challenge in anti-environment (e.g., artificial nature and avant-garde landscape architecture). In handling these challenges the two worlds differ: the art institution can freely and easily accept novelty and shocking innovation, even to its self-destruction; but the environmental institution, because it is dealing with our common reality, must follow ecological guidelines. Thus ecology sets limits on the possibilities of ethically sound development of the environment and, for that reason, the environment institution might outlive its parallel, the art institution.

The Ecosystem as a Point of Departure

The examiner is in immediate contact with the environment, part of the same reality (see, for example, Berleant). An environmental observation is the result of the joint activity of all the senses; this is regulated by knowledge, attitudes, and associations. The environmental object—unlike the work of art—is actively selected, delimited, and articulated; that which comes to the "aesthetic object," and with what emphasis, is in the final resort to be decided by the examiner.

The demands set by the ecosystem should, however, regulate even cultural practices related to the environment (of ecological aesthetics, see Meeker). The natural environment is a series of ecosystems and, correspondingly, it is possible to speak of "cultural ecosystems," of which, too, we can demand sustainability. In a cultural ecosystem, the needs of people are adjusted to one another to form a totality; human benefit is maximized while minimizing injury to the rest of nature. The aesthetic understanding of these systems presupposes their scientific mastery.

Accordance and compatibility with an ecosystem can be regarded as being a norm. In a well-grounded system of taste the ideal is an undisturbed totality regulated by life values; the goal should be the preservation and development of the richnesses and variety of the environment. Economic, ethical, and intellectual values, as well as those affecting health, security, and comfort, must be adjusted to one another in an overall social planning (see, for example, Eaton).

Four demands can be set for competent appreciation: 1) the material freedom of the observer from the necessities of nature—it makes the required distance possible; 2) a move from a mythical worldview to a scientifically-based one—this means the adoption and mastery of contemporary relevant information; 3) knowledge and understanding of natural and cultural processes and their history—it is possible to see the beauty of a system only once its underlying laws and principles are understood and articulated; and 4) the ability to locate the object in its correct class and category—the goal should not be the maximization of aesthetic value by any means possible, but rather seeing it in harmony with other areas of value.

Applied Environmental Aesthetics

The field of environmental aesthetics has a passive and an active aspect. The passive side is the theoretical investigation of the field: ontologically, what kind of aesthetic object is the environment? and metacritically, what is the nature of the claims presented of it? The active side means influencing what will be done to and how one should relate to the environment. In this activism, both hard and soft methods are used: legislation and supervision on the one hand; and public discussion, aesthetic education, and appeal to our sense of responsibility on the other.

Yrjö Sepänmaa

Further Readings

Berleant, Arnold. *The Aesthetics of Environment.* 1992.

Bourassa, Steven C. *The Aesthetics of Landscape.* 1991.

Carlson, Allen. "Appreciation and the Natural Environment." *The Journal of Aesthetics and Art Criticism* 37 (1979): 267–75.

———. "Nature and Positive Aesthetics." *Environmental Ethics* 6 (1984): 5–34.

Eaton, Marcia Muelder. *Aesthetics and the Good Life.* 1989.

Hargrove, Eugene C. *Foundations of Environmental Ethics.* 1989.

Kemal, Salim, and Ivan Gaskell, ed. *Landscape, Natural Beauty, and the Arts.* 1993.

Meeker, Joseph W. *The Comedy of Survival.* 1974.

Naser, Jack L., ed. *Environmental Aesthetics: Theory, Research, and Applications.* 1988.

Sadler, Barry, and Allen Carlson, eds. *Environmental Aesthetics: Essays in Interpretation.* 1982.

Sepänmaa, Yrjö. *The Beauty of Environment: A General Model for Environmental Aesthetics.* 2nd ed. 1993. (1st ed.: Academia Scientiarum Fennica, Helsinki 1986.)

Tuan, Yi-Fu. *Topophilia.* 1974.

See also POSTMODERNISM AND THE ENVIRONMENT

Environmental Assessment (Canada)

Over the past twenty-five years most Canadian jurisdictions have imposed environmental assessment requirements on those seeking approval for new capital projects and certain other undertakings that may have significant negative effects. The specifics of these requirements vary widely but their common intent is to anticipate and avoid or at least reduce environmental damage by demanding better initial planning and decision making. When they are effective, environmental assessment obligations force decision makers to take into account environmental factors along with conventional technical, financial, and political considerations in the selection, design, approval, and implementation of environmentally significant activities.

Like the expansion of environmental protection regulations that occurred over the same period, environmental assessment requirements came as government responses to public concerns—in particular, concerns about the negative effects of public and private sector undertakings that had gone ahead without serious regard for potential biophysical and socioeconomic impacts. Because of this root in public concern, environmental assessment processes in Canada are usually seen as means of improving the openness as well as environmental responsibility of decision making.

Generally, proponents subject to environmental assessment requirements are required to carry out specific research on the existing environment and on how it could be affected by proposed undertakings. To ensure that the research findings are valid and are used properly in the choice and detailed design of proposals, proponents are required to seek approval through a formal review and decision-making process. Public involvement and consultation with relevant government agencies, if not mandatory, are encouraged in most processes. Usually there are formal mechanisms for incorporating assessment review conclusions in binding decisions.

Although they emerge from some of the same pressures as regulatory initiatives, environmental assessment requirements represent a more ambitious attempt to reform decision making. Environmental regulations have required identification of certain kinds of environmental impacts but have typically focused on activities of individual sectors (e.g., projects of the nuclear industry) or particular receptors (e.g., damage to fish habitat or pollution of air) and have attempted to ensure compliance with specified standards. While useful these initiatives have tended to be too reactive, too narrowly focused, and too tolerant of reduced but continuing degradation. In general environmental assessment requirements apply earlier and more broadly, encouraging proponents and decision makers to address environmental concerns from the outset of planning that may lead to an undertaking with potentially significant negative effects. As well environmental assess-

E

ment provides for comprehensive and integrated consideration of bio-physical and (at least some) socioeconomic effects.

In Canada, the federal government, most of the provincial and territorial governments, some municipalities, and several aboriginal governments that have reached land claim settlements in the past two decades have established environmental assessment processes. The details of these environmental assessment laws and administrative requirements vary widely. "Undertakings" subject to assessment may be defined narrowly to include only certain large capital projects, or broadly to cover policies, programs, plans, and projects of government as well as a range of private sector initiatives. Mandatory consideration of "environmental effects" may be limited to biophysical matters or approached more comprehensively to recognize biophysical, social, economic, and cultural matters and their interrelations. Some processes focus simply on proposed projects and merely require evidence that the impacts will be "acceptable." More demanding processes force proponents to evaluate the "need" or purpose to be served and to justify the selection of the proposed undertaking through a comparison of its environmental implications with those of other reasonable alternatives. Provisions for public information and involvement range from restricted opportunities late in decision making to mandatory early openings and financial assistance. Finally, while some processes lead to recommendations which may be incorporated in final decisions under other laws, others incorporate a formal environmental assessment approval that may be subject to specified terms and conditions and is directly enforceable.

Following the original lead of the 1969 U.S. National Environmental Policy Act, environmental assessment requirements were first introduced in Canada by the federal government in 1973. This first Canadian step was much more tentative than the approach used in the United States. The federal Environmental Assessment and Review Process was only vaguely defined and based in policy only. Its implementation was left largely in the hands of proponent departments of government. No legal obligations were imposed and compliance with the policy was voluntary. The federal process was strengthened in 1984 with the issuing of a formal Environmental Assessment and Review Process Guidelines Order which was meant to signal stronger government commitment to environmental assessment (an "order")

while retaining flexibility of application ("guidelines"). The ambiguity was short-lived, however. In 1989 the courts, in a series of decisions concerning the Rafferty-Alameda dams in Saskatchewan and the Oldman dam in Alberta, ruled that the noun prevailed over the adjective and the "order" imposed legally enforceable obligations. These rulings finally moved the federal government to introduce an intentionally-legislated process.

The Canadian Environmental Assessment Act, which was given royal assent in June 1992, requires environmental screening or more demanding "comprehensive" assessment of specified categories of projects proposed or funded by federal authorities, using federal lands or requiring certain federal regulatory approvals. Mandatory assessment work centers on prediction and evaluation of biophysical and related socioeconomic effects, and identification of appropriate mitigation measures. The law provides for public involvement, especially in comprehensive study cases, and establishes mediation and public review mechanisms for cases of major conflict or controversy. Assessment findings are treated as recommendations for inclusion in approval decisions. The federal government has also introduced a non-legislated process for assessment of government policies and programs.

Different and, in some cases, much more demanding requirements have been imposed by provincial governments. The first and in most ways still the most ambitious environmental assessment law in Canada was passed by the province of Ontario in 1975. It applies automatically to undertakings (including plans as well as projects) of the provincial and municipal governments. As well it can be but rarely is applied to private sector undertakings. "Environment" is broadly defined to include biophysical, social, economic, and cultural factors and their interrelations, and proponents are required to justify their purposes, and carry out a comparative evaluation of alternatives to establish that the proposed activity is environmentally preferable to other reasonable options. Submitted assessments are subject to public as well as government reviews which may be followed by formal quasi-judicial hearings before a decision-making board. In every case, a decision is rendered under the environmental assessment law and approvals are typically subject to enforceable terms and conditions. Ontario also uses a more streamlined "class environmental assessment process" for certain categories of moderately significant, repetitive undertakings.

Like other environmental initiatives of government, environmental assessment requirements have been criticized by some for adding to regulatory burdens and administrative complexity and by others for inadequacy in face of deepening environmental worries. These pressures have led many Canadian jurisdictions to review their approaches, usually with an aim to improve efficiency while extending or strengthening application. Some efforts are also underway to encourage "harmonization" of assessment processes across Canada.

The resulting changes are expected to continue the gradual evolution of environmental assessment processes toward more effective empowerment of public participants, broader application, more comprehensive consideration of effects (including the cumulative effects of neighboring or otherwise related undertakings), higher standards of approval (seeking best options rather than merely adequate mitigation), and better monitoring of results and enforcement of obligations. At the same time, financial constraints and efficiency concerns are encouraging initiatives to integrate environmental assessment requirements into a more streamlined overall package wherein environmental assessment would no longer be one piece in a puzzle of disjointed environmental requirements but rather part of a linked set of processes for policy development, regional and sectoral planning, and project specific review, approval, and permitting.

Environmental impact assessment methodologies have also evolved in Canada, moving from a concentration on developing inventories of environmental features and identifying specific individual impacts to a more explicitly value-laden and systemic approach emphasizing ecological realities, concern for valued ecosystem components, and links between biophysical and social, economic and cultural effects.

New methodological challenges are arising from efforts to focus assessment work more effectively at the higher decision levels of planning and policy where overall guidance is given to many individual undertakings and where attention can be given to larger cumulative effects and sustainability considerations.

Robert B. Gibson

Further Readings
Boardman, Robert, ed. *Canadian Environmental Policy: Ecosystems, Politics, and*

Process. 1992.
Estrin, David, and John Swaigen. *Environment on Trial.* 1993.
Gibson, Robert B. "Environmental Assessment Design: Lessons from the Canadian Experience." *Environmental Professional* 15 (1993): 12–24.

See also BENEFIT-COST ANALYSIS; COMPARATIVE RISK; ENVIRONMENTAL CASE LAW (CANADA): COMMON LAW CAUSES OF ACTION; ENVIRONMENTAL IMPACT ASSESSMENT; NATIONAL ENVIRONMENTAL POLICY ACT; OLDMAN RIVER; RAFFERTY-ALAMEDA DAMS; RISK ANALYSIS

Environmental Case Law: Australia
See AUSTRALIA: RESOURCE USE CONFLICTS; FRANKLIN DAM

Environmental Case Law (Canada): Common Law Causes of Action
Faced with an environmental problem, Canadians have a number of legal options. One that is often proposed although seldom pursued is the civil suit or common law action. While some statutes, most notably the Ontario Environmental Bill of Rights, permit a person to sue (i.e., commence an action), most environmental law suits are based on the historical actions of nuisance, negligence, trespass, riparian rights, the doctrine in *Rylands v. Fletcher* (1866), and the relatively new doctrine of statutory breach. Before examining the substance of these actions, a brief word about actions is in order.

Actions are legal proceedings brought by a person or persons (plaintiffs) who have suffered some injury (or who may suffer some injury) as a result of another person's (the defendant's) behavior or proposed behavior. Not every injury will support or justify an action. Generally speaking, for an action to commence three conditions must be present: 1) the injury or loss must be substantial (trivial inconveniences are of little concern to the law); 2) the person or his or her property must be adversely affected; and 3) there must be a direct link (causal connection) between the offending behavior and the injury. If a person can satisfy the preconditions then he or she may, as the plaintiff, commence an action in a court that has the power to hear the case (a county or superior court, depending on the nature and size of the claim). If a number of people are similarly affected by the behavior(s) of the defendant, they may qualify as a class and join their actions together as a class action (see, for example, the Ontario Class Proceedings Act).

By itself, the fact that someone has suffered some financial, proprietary, or personal loss as a result of a defendant's behavior does not necessarily enable one to sue. The plaintiff must also allege that the defendant's actions and the plaintiff's loss fit within one of the prescribed causes of actions that have been recognized by the courts. The question then remains: What fact situations have the courts recognized as legal causes of actions? While one can never answer that question with complete certainty (the courts are always able to create new causes of actions—although they do so with considerable reluctance), the principal causes of actions can be described under the six broad headings already noted.

Private Nuisance

Private nuisance is probably the most likely basis upon which an environmental plaintiff will sue a polluting defendant. The typical fact situation will involve a defendant whose pollution is adversely affecting the plaintiff's land (spoiled crops or even physical damage to buildings) or the plaintiff's use and enjoyment of land. Injury to the physical or psychological well-being of the plaintiff is only relevant to the extent that it impairs the plaintiff's use and enjoyment of his or her land (or land in which the plaintiff has some legal interest, such as through a lease). The essence of the action is the defendant's indirect interference with the plaintiff's use and enjoyment of land. The source of the pollution is irrelevant, although it will in most cases originate from the defendant's land.

Public Nuisance

Although also labeled a nuisance, public nuisance has very little in common with private nuisance or indeed any of the other common law causes of action. It is more in the nature of a criminal action, initiated by a person who has suffered a loss as a result of a public nuisance. The typical public nuisance fact situation will involve a defendant's interference with some public right, such as the right to fish, or the right of passage on a public road. Previously, for the plaintiff to sue successfully, he or she must have been able to show some unique or special loss, quite distinct from that suffered by other members of the public whose public right has also been adversely affected. Recent legislative amendments, however (most notably the Ontario Environmental Bill of Rights Act), have dispensed with the need for the plaintiff to show damages that are unique or "different in kind" rather than merely degree as a precondition to suing.

Trespass

If private nuisance describes the indirect interference to a plaintiff's property, trespass speaks to direct interferences. Thus a passing car whose loud noise and air emissions foul the air and hence the enjoyment of adjacent property is a nuisance, while the car that drives onto the property or deposits emissions on the property without permission commits a trespass. Trespass demands some direct and physical interference with property. As measuring devices become more and more sophisticated it becomes easier to demonstrate the relationship between adverse effects and direct incursions onto the property. A distinguishing feature of trespass is that even the slightest interference is actionable. One need not show that a trespass has produced some substantial or even measurable loss.

Negligence

A third basis upon which an environmental plaintiff may sue an alleged polluter is negligence. This is the same action that a pedestrian might bring against a driver who negligently hit him or her in a pedestrian crosswalk. The elements of the action are deceptively simple. It requires the law to recognize that one person owes another a duty of care, that one has breached that duty, and that, as a result of that breach, the plaintiff has suffered some damages. In other words, negligence is designed to establish a standard of civil conduct between members of society. Like nuisance it is unconcerned with the trifling and insignificant clashes between individuals that have become typical of modern society. It is infused with such concepts as reasonableness (what would a reasonably prudent person do in these circumstances?), remoteness (is the defendant's action too distant, too far removed from the accident that led to the loss?), and causal connection (is there a clear link between the actions of the defendant and the loss of the plaintiff?). Its relevance to pollution control is clear. Much pollution is a result of the carelessness or sloppiness of defendants. As a result, it will often be possible to establish that a defendant failed to take reasonable care to avoid a discharge or emission, that the discharge adversely affected the plaintiff (or some legally protected right of the plaintiff, such as property), and that the defendant knew or should have known that the adverse effect was a likely result of the discharge. If a defendant was advised of the impact or the likely impact of its carelessness on the plaintiff, then there will be very few situations in which the continued actions of the defendant would not be negligent. Knowledge of the causal connection between pollution and damage make it very difficult for a defendant to argue that its actions were reasonable or that it did not know the consequences of its actions.

Rylands v. Fletcher

The common law causes of actions are fashioned out of cases that courts have decided after hearing similar fact situations. Periodically, the case that gives rise to a new action or an important variation on an old action will give its name to the new action. That is precisely what happened with *Rylands v. Fletcher*. The facts of the case had little to do with environmental matters (it concerned a dam that burst on the defendant's property and flooded the plaintiff's adjoining land), but the principles that have been extracted from the case do. The elements of this action are as follows: any person who brings a non-natural substance (sometimes described as an ultra-hazardous substance) onto his/her property, and the substance subsequently escapes resulting in injury to another or to another's property, is strictly liable for the loss or injury. This action has been used frequently against defendants whose toxic pesticides have escaped onto adjoining land, against municipal defendants whose sewers have backed up and escaped into plaintiffs' basements (although some municipal statutes exempt municipalities from liability for such events) and against polluters whose toxic emissions and discharges damage a plaintiff's real or personal property.

Although closely related to nuisance, *Rylands v. Fletcher* is different in two important respects. First, it is concerned with problems (escapes) that emanate from the defendant's property. Nuisance, on the other hand, is not concerned with the source of the pollution, but rather with the impact (an interference with property). Second, liability for *Rylands v. Fletcher* is strict. The fact that the defendant took all reasonable care to avoid an escape and the resulting damage is irrelevant. Many nuisances, on the other hand, especially those leading to personal inconvenience (described as

"personal" sensible discomfort), do involve a balancing of interests: did the plaintiff come to the nuisance?, is the plaintiff extraordinarily sensitive?, and so on, and thus make success a good deal more problematic. Whatever advantages the plaintiff enjoys under the doctrine in *Rylands v. Fletcher* are somewhat offset by the courts' often restrictive interpretation of what qualifies as "non-natural" and as an "escape."

Riparian Rights

The riparian rights action is concerned with protecting water rights for riparian owners (i.e., those who own the bank of a river or lake to the water's edge). The doctrine is comprised of two parts: positive rights that a riparian owner may exercise over the water without incurring liability, and negative rights that a riparian owner may exercise against another riparian owners' use of the water.

On the positive side, a riparian owner may take as much water as is necessary for domestic purposes. There is no obligation to return the water in its original state. If domestic uses impair the quality of the water or diminish the flow of water in the water body, then so be it. A riparian owner may also take as much water as is necessary for uses connected with the land (ordinary or reasonable uses), provided the waterway is undiminished in both flow (quantity) and in quality. The negative right is the reverse of this last point. A riparian owner may enjoin (seek a court order prohibiting some activity) another riparian owner from taking (or impairing) any water unconnected with the land, and may enjoin any taking connected with the land (other than for domestic purposes) that either reduces the quantity or impairs the quality of the water. While the doctrine has been used to achieve significant environmental protection (for example, banning a power boat regatta on a lake used for the City of Sudbury's domestic water supply), much of the action has been supplanted by legislation and regulation controlling water use.

The doctrine is equally applicable to surface and ground water, provided the water flows in defined channels. It does not, however, apply to percolating ground water, or to surface run off. Water flowing through artificial or machine-made canals will, after a passage of sufficient time, also be subject to riparian rights.

Breach of Statutory Standard

A new civil action of breach of statutory standard has received some recent recognition from

Canadian courts. The essence of this action is as follows: many environmental protection statutes impose obligations on persons to do certain things (such as reporting a spill) or refrain from doing certain things (such as discharging a contaminant into the natural environment). Failure to comply with these obligations constitutes an offense under the statute. As such, it may be prosecuted by officials of the regulatory department, by the Attorney General, or by an individual (private prosecution). If the prosecution is successful the defendant may be fined, required to carry out the terms of a court order, and/or in the case of officers and directors, imprisoned.

But what if the defendant's breach adversely affects some private right, such as the land of some nearby property owner? May that person sue and recover damages or win an injunction to prevent future breaches? If the defendant's actions fall within any of the enumerated causes of actions described above, the answer is "yes." But what if they do not? Or what if the answer is "yes," but the time and expense of proving the elements of a nuisance or negligence action are so high and the outcome so fraught with uncertainty that there is little prospect of success? Under these circumstances the aggrieved plaintiff may simply sue and allege that the defendant's breach of the statute lead to his or her loss and that the defendant, therefore, should be made to pay an appropriate remedy. This type of action, however, is tricky at best and should only be taken in some circumstances. While the courts are reluctant to expand the categories of actions available to the plaintiff, there is no doubt that statutes designed to protect the rights of private persons (as well as the public) may be used by those persons to seek redress.

Remedies and Defenses

A number of defenses are available to defendants. To some extent they vary from one cause of action to another. For that reason it is difficult to generalize about defenses. There are few defenses to the plaintiff's proof that a trespass was committed, that a non-natural substance escaped from the defendant's land and caused damage, or that riparian water was impaired through some unreasonable or extraordinary use of water. One can always dispute the proof but that is not, strictly speaking, a defense. One can also attempt to show that the act was done with the permission (express or implied) of the plaintiff—known as "prescription" or "acquiescence" or of the legislature—known as "statutory authority." Occasionally a new statutory defense is created by a statute, such as the Farm Practices Protection Act that enables a defendant to defend a common law action by proving that he or she is or was engaged in certain statutorily protected activities, such as "normal farm practices."

If a plaintiff successfully establishes the necessary elements of a cause of action and if the defendant's defenses fail, then the plaintiff is entitled to a remedy. Civil remedies (as contrasted with criminal and quasi criminal sentences) fall into two main categories: monetary damages and injunctions. Of the two, injunctive relief is almost always the environmental plaintiff's preferred remedy. Damages or a cash award may compensate the plaintiff for the injury suffered (to land or person), but it does nothing to restore or remediate the damaged environment. An injunction, on the other hand, prohibits further discharges or in some cases mandates the defendant to carry out a court prescribed remediation or clean-up program. While courts are fond of saying that plaintiffs are entitled to an injunction "as of right," the fact of the matter is that courts are reluctant to enjoin a defendant's activity if damages will "make the plaintiff whole again." It is then at the discretion of the plaintiff whether damages will be spent on restoring the environment.

D. Paul Emond

Further Readings

Estrin, David, and John Swaigen. *Environment on Trial: A Guide to Ontario Environmental Law and Policy.* 1993.

Canadian Bar Association. *Sustainable Development in Canada: Options for Law Reform.* 1990.

Duncan, Linda F. *Enforcing Environmental Law: A Guide to Private Prosecution.* Edmonton, Alberta: Environmental Law Centre, 1990.

See also CLASS ACTIONS; ENVIRONMENTAL CASE LAW: EUROPEAN COMMUNITY; ENVIRONMENTAL CASE LAW: GREAT BRITAIN; ENVIRONMENTAL CASE LAW: NEW ZEALAND; ENVIRONMENTAL CASE LAW: UNITED STATES; FEDERALISM AND ENVIRONMENTAL PROTECTION: CANADA; LEGISLATION: CANADA; OLDMAN RIVER; RAFFERTY-ALAMEDA DAMS

Environmental Case Law: European Community

The European Court of Justice is one of the key institutions of the European Community (EC). Over the years the Court has played a vital and dynamic role in creating a distinctive Community legal order, and has not been dissuaded from developing bold principles aimed at ensuring the supremacy of Community law within member states. Member states that fail to comply with obligations under Community legislation may be brought before the Court by the European Commission, and national courts within member states are obliged to apply the principles of the Court, even if this implies ignoring conflicting national legislation. Courts at any level, when a point of Community law is in issue, may refer the matter directly to the European Court for authoritative guidance; the result is that Community law penetrates into national legal orders to a far deeper extent than conventional international obligations.

Only fairly recently has the European Court begun making a substantive input to the interpretation of Community environmental law. This is hardly surprising given that the development of explicit environmental legislation at the Community level commenced only in earnest in the late 1970s, and there is an inevitable time-lag before substantial issues reach the Court. But already a body of case law is emerging, which suggests that the Court is by and large environmentally sensitive and will play an increasingly important role in this field.

The European Commission, based in Brussels, is responsible for the development of Community policies and the preparation of draft legislation but also has a duty to ensure that member states fulfill their obligations to implement laws once agreed. Article 169 of the Treaty of Rome provides it with special legal procedures to take action against defaulting member states; these actions can ultimately lead to proceedings before the European Court.

Most Community environmental legislation in the environmental sector has taken the form of directives which oblige a member state to achieve the policy objectives contained in each directive but give each state discretion as to the necessary national legal and administrative measures needed to secure those ends. Directives require member states to communicate to the Commission the text of any such national measures within a time-limit specified in each directive, normally two or three years from the date of its agreement, and a critical function of the Article 169 enforcement procedures is to ensure that such formal implementation does in fact take place. In its case law on the subject, the European Court has developed a rigorous approach which provides member states with little in the way of justification for any failure to meet the time limits specified or objectives contained in a directive. Internal constitutional difficulties, such as a change of national government or problems associated with regional administrations, have been held to provide no defense. In *Commission v. Belgium* (1990), the Court went further and held that the financial costs or technical difficulties encountered by the member state in meeting standards contained in a directive were no excuse for non-implementation.

Although directives give member states considerable discretion as to the means that they may adopt within their national system for achieving the goals specified in directives, the Court of Justice has developed principles which reject over-reliance on informal guidelines and administrative circulars. Thus in *Commission v. Netherlands* (1982), the Court held that "mere administrative practices which by their nature may be altered at the whim of the administration" were an insufficient means for transposing a directive, and certainly where public rights or liabilities are involved, the Court has been insisting upon binding, transparent measures. In the environmental sector, countries such as the United Kingdom frequently relied in the past upon such administrative devices to communicate government policy aims, but where EC directives are involved this practice is becoming increasingly difficult to sustain in the light of the rulings of the European Court, and many more environmental standards and similar requirements are now having to be given expression in national legislation or regulations.

Disputes over the legal basis of Community environmental legislation has been the subject of recent case law before the European Court, and is likely to prove a continuing source of litigation. Community legislation must derive its legal basis from one or more articles of the Treaty of Rome, and the Court has consistently held that the choice of legal basis is not a matter of discretion for the Community institutions but must be based on objective grounds capable of justiciable review. In *Council v. Commission* (1991) the Commission disputed the decision of the Council of Ministers (the final legislative body of the Community composed of representatives of the governments of member states) to adopt Article 130S of the Treaty as the legal

E

basis of the directive prescribing environmental standards for the titanium dioxide industry. Article 130S relates expressly to environmental measures but the Commission argued that Article 100A, which concerns harmonizing measures concerning the establishment of the internal market, was the correct basis. The choice of legal basis critically affects the procedures to be followed for the adoption of the relevant measures, with Article 130S requiring unanimous voting at Council level and giving little more than a consultative role to the European Parliament. In contrast, measures based on Article 100A need only qualified majority voting (a weighted voting system which requires roughly three-quarters of the member states to approve), and gives the European Parliament a far greater opportunity to influence the outcome of the decision. In the event the European Court sided with the Commission, holding that since such environmental protection measures entailed increased costs for industry, competition would be distorted in the absence of harmonization. But in a case involving a similar legal dispute, this time concerning a proposed general framework directive for waste (*Commission v. Council,* 1993), the Court agreed with the Council that this was primarily an environmental measure and that Article 130S was the correct legal basis. In truth it is difficult to reconcile the two judgments, and given the different procedural requirements that will continue to apply after the Maastricht amendments to the Treaty (for measures based on Article 100A the European Parliament will have far greater powers under the new "co-decision" procedures, effectively giving it the right to veto) the Court is likely to be faced with further cases on this issue in the future.

One of the most troublesome legal areas of dispute is the extent to which member states have the freedom to introduce national environmental measures even where this might restrict the basic principle of the freedom of movement of goods under Article 30 of the Treaty. In the so-called Danish bottles case, *Commission v. Denmark* (1988) the European Court gave a landmark decision in holding that the needs of environmental protection could justify such national measures, in that case a national scheme concerning returnable bottles. More recently in *Commission v. Belgium* (1992) the European Court upheld a regional measure prohibiting the import and disposal of waste from other regions or countries on the grounds that this was consistent with one of the general en-

vironmental principles contained in Article 130R of the Treaty that environmental damage should as a priority be rectified at the source. These general principles are applicable in the absence of specific community legislation on the subject, but even where such legislation has been agreed, both Articles 100A and 130T expressly permit member states to introduce stricter environmental standards. But the extent to which member states have complete freedom to do so, even under these provisions, is likely to be another issue for the Court before too long.

Despite the European Court's undoubted influence on the direction of Community environmental law, at present it possesses no power other than its moral authority to require member states to comply with its judgments. Under the Maastricht amendments to the Treaty, however, it will be given new powers to impose financial penalties on member states that fail to obey a ruling from the Court. This is a significant change which will give the European Court a heightened new status among supra-national tribunals.

Richard Macrory

Further Readings

Axelrod, Regina S. "Environmental Policy and Management in the European Community." In *Environmental Policy in the 1990s.* Ed. Norman Vig and Michael Kraft. 1994.

Johnson, Stanley P., and Guy Corcelle. *The Environmental Policy of the European Community.* 1989.

Sbragia, Alberta. "Environmental Policy in the European Community: The Problem of Implementation in Comparative Perspective." in *Towards a Transatlantic Environmental Policy.* 1991.

See also ENVIRONMENTAL CASE LAW: GREAT BRITAIN; LEGISLATION: EUROPEAN COMMUNITY; LEGISLATION: GREAT BRITAIN

Environmental Case Law: Great Britain

Environmental law in Great Britain follows from both common law and statute law. Common law is the law derived by the courts over centuries of judicial decisions. The principle issues are nuisance, negligence, riparian ownership rights, and strict liability. The principal remedies are awards of damage, injunctions, or legally binding agreements. The cost of the court action is normally borne by the losing party, as there is no equivalent of the contingency fee principle common in the United States. Common law is dependent on precedent, some of which attaches to rulings made in a distant social and economic age, let alone environmental and scientific awareness. In general class action, or litigation adopted by groups who feel commonly aggrieved, is uncommon compared to that position in the United States. This is because the right to appear before the court (locus standi) is constrained by ownership of property, special damage, and burden of proof on the plaintiff. In addition, many environmental impairment issues, such as air pollution or noise, are subject to regulations that are controlled by ministerial discretion sanctioned by Parliament. Even though, in principle, common law nuisance overrides statutory obligation, what the courts tend to define as a nuisance is strongly influenced by discretionary regulation.

Statute law is determined by Parliament but, in practice, the bills emanate from the Whitehall policy machinery. Normally the draft legislation is based on consultation documents which benefit from the comments of specialized interests. The British approach to consultation is to restrict the scope so that participants can be aware of what others are saying, and to confine reaction to the secrecy of administrative departments. This does not allow for mediation, though vested interests can lobby members of Parliament as the bill passes through both Houses of Parliament (the Commons and the Lords). Statute law is usually couched in discretionary terms, allowing ministers freedom for maneuver. Technical legislation on pollution control or environmental impact assessment, for example, is usually supplemented by regulations that are not debated in Parliament.

In recent years the courts have been used for judicial review of the legality of ministerial or departmental action seen to be at odds with the intent of the legislation. As in the common law case, judicial review proceedings are usually paid for by a losing party. So environmental intervenors are cautious about seeking remedy for apparently high-handed administrative action. Duties of environmental care do not exist to bind ministers to good environmental practice or formal policy integration. Nor is there usually any means whereby ministers are tied to specific environmental protection targets. Regulatory legislation normally includes phrases such as "best practicable means" (air pollution); "as low as reasonably achievable" (health and safety, including risk); "best available techniques not involving excessive costs" (for integrated pollution control); or "best practicable environmental option" (for specified mega-projects). These concepts are subject to rules of thumb which take time and experience to develop. In general ministers are shielded from claims so long as they can show that their agents have followed the rules. A certain amount of case law is spent on defining these rules.

A growing amount of UK legislation is designed to implement European Community (EC) environmental directives. The EC does not pass binding legislation on its member states; rather it expects the states to devise their own ways of meeting the particular needs of a directive. In the fields of hazardous chemical control, pollution control, environmental assessment, and waste management, European law dominates the scene. UK state law is influenced by EC law, as it is also by the rulings of the European Court of Justice in Luxembourg. This Court determines the legality of EC rights under the various treaties and acts of European Union. It is the nearest thing to a common written constitution, though only a small number of cases actually appear before the Court.

In general British courts interpret environmental legislation conservatively. The major breakthroughs are beginning to appear in the areas of strict liability over the disposal of waste, fettered ministerial discretion under judicial review, and the steady rise in criminal penalties against directors for failing to comply with regulatory procedures in the running of their businesses. Still to come are more formal duties of environmental care, citizens' environmental rights, and guarantees of access to environmental information. In all probability these developments will emanate from Brussels rather than from London.

Timothy O'Riordan

Further Readings
Hughes, David. *Environmental Law.* 1992.
Vogel, David. *National Styles of Regulation: Environmental Policy in Great Britain and the United States.* 1986.

See also ENVIRONMENTAL IMPACT ASSESSMENT; ENVIRONMENTAL CASE LAW: EUROPEAN COMMUNITY; LEGISLATION: EUROPEAN COMMUNITY; LEGISLATION: GREAT BRITAIN; STANDARD SETTING

E

Environmental Case Law: New Zealand

Environmental law in New Zealand must be seen in the context of the Treaty of Waitangi, an agreement concluded in 1840 between the Crown of the United Kingdom and a group of Maori Chiefs. Kawanatanga, a form of limited sovereignty, was ceded to the Crown but subject to the retention by the Maori community of full authority over their lands, homes, and things prized. The Court of Appeal has indicated that "the compact between the Crown and the Maori through which the peaceful settlement of New Zealand was contemplated called for the protection by the Crown of both Maori interests and British interests and rested on the premise that each party would act reasonably and in good faith towards the other within their respective spheres": *New Zealand Maori Council v. Attorney General* (1987). The Treaty is not only part of the constitutional framework of New Zealand; it has been incorporated in various ways in legislation.

Until 1991 the environmental legal system in New Zealand was fragmented. There was legislation providing for access to the resources of the environment, legislation controlling pollution, and legislation providing for the management of areas of Crown land for conservation purposes. Planning legislation provided the opportunity for integrated land-use management but the courts restricted its application to site specific land-use control. A balancing approach was adopted so that no particular value, environmental or otherwise, was given priority. During the late 1980s the Court of Appeal recognized the priorities enacted in specific statutes. The Resource Management Act mandated a new approach in 1991.

The movement toward the recognition of statutory priorities may be seen through an examination of four judicial decisions. The first two decisions concerned the Water and Soil Conservation Act 1967. *Keam v. Minister of Works and Development* (1982) involved an application for a right to take geothermal water from an underground reservoir. The Planning Tribunal had rejected the application because the benefit that might accrue was not sufficient to justify the detriment which might be caused to the scenic and natural features of the thermal area. The Court of Appeal confirmed that the right approach was to balance the resulting advantages and disadvantages. A balancing approach would be inappropriate only if there were no apparent disadvantages.

In *Auckland Acclimatisation Society Inc. v. Sutton Holdings Ltd.* (1985) two farmers applied for a water right to enable them to drain parts of their farms within an important terrestrial wetland. The issue was "whether the economic benefit obtainable from converting the 172 hectares to land available for grazing throughout the year outweighs the desirability of preserving that area as part of a wetland." The approach that land drainage was more important than the conservation of wildlife habitats was rejected by the Court of Appeal. There was no priority in favor of the farming interest over the conservation interest or otherwise. In the case of a conflict, each interest had to be weighed against the others "without any general presumption." There was nothing in the legislation to displace this approach.

Section 3(1) of the Town and Country Planning Act 1977 declared that a number of specified matters were of national importance, including environmental values. In *Environmental Defence Society Inc. v. Mangonui County Council* (1989) the Court of Appeal indicated that matters of national importance carried greater weight than other matters. The specific issue was a rezoning proposal to enable the construction of a large scale destination tourist resort. This was governed by section 4, matters of regional and district significance. However, section 4 was stated to be subject to section 3. In the event, the provisions of section 3 were not given "absolute primacy." Nevertheless the matters referred to in section 3(1), including Maori cultural values, environmental issues and the wise use and management of New Zealand's resources were given greater weight because of their status as matters of national importance.

This approach was taken further in *Ashburton Acclimatisation Society v. Federated Farmers Inc.* (1988). The issue was the status of a section containing "the object of this Act": to recognize and sustain the amenity afforded by waters in their natural state. The Court of Appeal placed considerable weight upon conservation as the object of the Act. It was not given overriding effect because of other provisions in the legislation. "Although certainly not to be pursued at all costs, it has been laid down as the primary goal." Although the section created priority it was a matter of relative rather than absolute priority.

Douglas E. Fisher

Further Readings

Fisher, Douglas E. "Environmentalism, Policy Factors and the Courts in New Zealand." *Environmental and Planning Law Journal* 6 (1989): 316–31.

Waitangi Tribunal. *Report on the Orakei Claim.* 1987.

Williams, David. *Environmental Law.* 1980.

See also ENVIRONMENTAL CASE LAW (CANADA): COMMON LAW CAUSES OF ACTION; ENVIRONMENTAL CASE LAW: EUROPEAN COMMUNITY; ENVIRONMENTAL CASE LAW: GREAT BRITAIN; ENVIRONMENTAL CASE LAW: UNITED STATES; RESOURCE MANAGEMENT ACT (NEW ZEALAND): TREATY OF WAITANGI (NEW ZEALAND)

Environmental Case Law: United States

Environmental litigation is the development and enforcement of environmental policy through the use of the judicial branch of government. There are three typical kinds of court cases involving environmental laws. In the first kind of case the state or federal government sues industry for not complying with the law (e.g., the U.S. Environmental Protection Agency (EPA) can prosecute industrial plants for violating the terms of their permits to discharge pollutants into streams and lakes). The remedy in such cases can be either administrative or criminal fines and, in extraordinary cases, criminal prison terms. In these cases the government assumes an environmentally protective posture in court. Industry's defense is usually based on the economic well-being of the community, especially the need for employment. Corporate attorneys argue that industry cannot afford the pollution control technology or that such technology is not worth the achievable benefits in reduced public health risks.

The second modal type of environmental law case occurs when industry sues the government, arguing that the enforcement agency has exceeded its authority in making regulations to enforce environmental laws. For example, the timber industry may sue the Forest Service for refusing to permit it to cut as many trees in a national forest as it wishes. Many of the regulations that the EPA and other agencies set are directly appealable to the federal courts of appeals rather than to the district trial courts. Therefore, many cases initiated by industry begin at the appellate level because of the manner in which the law is written. In these cases the government agency argues the case for environmental protection.

The third type of case occurs when an environmental interest group sues a government agency because the group believes that the government is not taking its responsibility to enforce the laws seriously or is itself doing something that is against one or more of the laws designed to protect the environment or conserve natural resources. For example the Sierra Club may sue the Department of the Interior for planning to build a dam that will destroy the habitat of an endangered species. In such cases the government agency represents the economic interest in making developmental arguments against the public interest group that argues in favor of conservation or environmental protection. During the 1970s this kind of case was the most common as environmental groups tried to maximize the impact of the environmental legislation they had been instrumental in developing or changing.

In addition to these three modal types of environmental law cases it is possible for environmental organizations to sue directly an industry that is flouting a pollution control law. For example, the Natural Resources Defense Council may sue a meat packing plant for not complying with its pollutant discharge permit because the Clean Water Act provides for citizen action groups to sue industry as private attorneys general when the appropriate government agency fails to act. These cases became common during the 1980s in the United States when various environmental groups came to believe that the federal government was not interested in actively enforcing many of the pollution control laws.

There are also examples of intergovernmental environmental cases. The U.S. EPA has prosecuted municipal governments for not conforming to the requirements of their sewage discharge permits. Reversing roles, states have sued federal agencies such as the U.S. army for polluting the water or air in the state's jurisdiction from its military bases. There have even been some incidents of two agencies in the federal government becoming involved in litigation with each other, as when the U.S. EPA sued the Tennessee Valley Authority for polluting the air with its numerous coal-fired electric generating plants.

Before major federal pollution control legislation was passed in the 1960s and 1970s common law remedies were sometimes used by people injured by pollution, mostly to little avail. Because of long latency periods and multiple contributory causes it was difficult for victims to prove the liability of the defendant. Parties injured by polluted air, water, or toxic wastes may still ask courts for compensation after the fact but the existence of public laws regulating pollution now adds to the difficulties of proving their cases. Industry can and does now argue that meeting regulatory standards and having a valid permit immunizes it from common law suits for personal injury. In *Illinois v. Milwaukee II* (1972) the U.S. Supreme Court effectively eliminated federal common law in water pollution cases; however, it is still possible to sue under some state laws.

During the early 1970s the most common kind of environmental law suit was that in which an environmental group sued the federal government under the National Environmental Policy Act (NEPA) arguing that a federal agency should write an environmental impact statement (EIS) before building an environmentally destructive project. Several federal courts, especially the D.C. Circuit Court, agreed with environmental groups and ordered federal agencies to consider more environmental factors in their statements. However, after the U.S. Supreme Court chastised the D.C. Circuit Court in *Vermont Yankee v. NRDC* (1978) for second guessing the Nuclear Regulatory Commission's decision to issue nuclear reactor permits, lower federal courts became more cautious in criticizing agencies. Some experts argued that the EIS-writing process had become essentially a paper exercise. Others believe that the act of writing an EIS and the threat of outside criticism influences the government to propose fewer environmentally damaging projects.

Absolute numbers of NEPA cases subsequently fell, and water and air pollution cases came to dominate the federal environmental docket. Some of these established major precedents that changed environmental policy substantially. Environmental groups challenged EPA's administrative interpretation of the Clean Air Act to allow industry to use tall stacks to disperse air pollutants more broadly rather than to reduce the pollutants coming from those stacks. It also challenged EPA's decision to focus all efforts on dirty metropolitan areas—a decision some felt would force all new industrial development into pristine unpolluted areas. Federal courts agreed with environmental groups in both these cases, and ultimately the concepts of continuous treatment of air pollutants and no significant deterioration of air quality were added to the Clean Air Act itself. The groups that raised these issues before the courts were also instrumental in getting the EPA to rewrite its regulations and Congress to amend the law, but the court was the first forum to accept these arguments.

In the 1980s new laws focused the federal courts' attention on interpreting the issue of hazardous waste disposal. Court interpretation of Superfund centered around who among multiple contributors was responsible for cleaning up numerous abandoned leaking hazardous waste dumps. The courts faced a new kind of environmental case in which one industry or property owner sued another and/or both their insurance companies to determine liability for multi-million dollar cleanups.

During the latter part of the 1970s major corporations increased their legal expertise in environmental law, and the number of cases business initiated against federal and state government regulations escalated. In addition cases started by environmental groups that argued that EPA or a state government's regulations were too lenient were often joined by industry to argue that the same regulation was too severe. By 1990 no regulation issued by the EPA could hope to escape court challenge even after it had been commented on in detail during the lengthy regulation writing process.

During the 1980s the property rights movement gained considerable credibility in conservative law schools and journals. Developers and other landowners instituted numerous lawsuits arguing that any land use regulation by local, state, or federal authorities "took" their property by limiting development of it. Several courts, especially the U.S. Court of Claims and the Supreme Court including *Lucas v. S. Carolina* (1992) and *Dolan v. Tigard* (1994), made several rulings favorable to such property rights arguments. Hence, as a new environmentally oriented administration took over in the early 1990s, it seemed likely that developers would turn increasingly to the federal courts to protect themselves from the impact of such laws as the Endangered Species Act and state protection of ecologically sensitive areas such as coastal zones and wetlands.

During the twenty-five years that environmental law cases have been common, government agencies, whether acting as plaintiff or defendant, have been the most likely victor in any particular case. This generalization can be made about all kinds of cases, as courts in general tend to favor government litigants. Environmental groups, despite their reliance on public subscription and lack of financial resources, proved to be slightly more successful than business litigants in getting courts to uphold their point of view. In some areas, such as the Northeastern part of the United States and the West Coast states, they have been especially successful in challenging government actions. Judges in other locations, such as the Southeast and Southwest and the Supreme Court, have proved singularly unimpressed with environmental arguments and tend to favor business litigants.

Many environmental issues are international in scope, as pollution knows no boundaries, and the degradation of natural resources in one area of the world often has substantial impacts elsewhere. There are few precedents thus far in settling such international disputes by courts. Normally sovereign nations turn to bilateral negotiation agreed to by both sides to the dispute.

One example of such a dispute occurred in the 1920s when the United States complained about sulfurous fumes coming from a Canadian copper smelter in Trail, British Columbia. In 1933 Canada and the United States agreed to form an arbitral tribunal in 1935, consisting of one member each from Canada and the United States, and one from Belgium. In 1937 the tribunal found that indeed the Trail Smelter was liable for damage to the United States in the form of reduced crop and timber yields. By the terms of the settlement Canada agreed to impose a smoke abatement system on the smelter, but it fell short of eliminating the pollution because neither country wished to establish a precedent that would impose excessive costs on industry on either side of the international border. Because there were no international precedents to use, this decision was based almost entirely on precedents from the U.S. Supreme Court concerning disputes between states within the United States about air pollution.

There has been only one case of an environmental problem taken to the International Court of Justice (ICJ) at The Hague, created after World War II for adjudication of international disputes, and its outcome was at best indecisive. In the 1960s a partial nuclear test ban treaty was negotiated among the nuclear powers to ban tests above ground, but both France and China refused to sign. In 1974 Australia and New Zealand sued to halt France's planned tests of nuclear weapons on French Polynesia in the Pacific Ocean, claiming that they would receive harmful radioactive fallout. Using the Trail Smelter case as precedent the members of the ICJ voted 8 to 6 to protect Australia and New Zealand against such tests. Although France refused to recognize ICJ authority in the case, in 1974 it announced that it would conduct all future tests underground, as other nuclear powers were then doing. Subsequently, the ICJ decided that the case had become moot and dropped it from its agenda (*Australia v. France*, 1974). In so doing the ICJ did little to increase its own authority, prestige, and potential for influence in future cases.

Lettie McSpadden

Further Readings

Findley, Roger W., and Daniel A. Farber. *Environmental Law.* 3rd ed. 1992.

Firestone, David B., and Frank C. Reed. *Environmental Law for Non-Lawyers.* 1983.

Liroff, Richard A. *A National Policy for the Environment: NEPA and Its Aftermath.* 1976.

Sax, Joseph L. *Defending the Environment: A Strategy for Citizen Action.* 1970.

Wenner, Lettie M. *The Environmental Decade in Court.* 1982.

See also CLASS ACTIONS; ENVIRONMENTAL CASE LAW (CANADA): COMMON LAW CAUSES OF ACTION; ENVIRONMENTAL CASE LAW: EUROPEAN COMMUNITY; ENVIRONMENTAL CASE LAW: GREAT BRITAIN; ENVIRONMENTAL CASE LAW: NEW ZEALAND; ENVIRONMENTAL PROTECTION AGENCY; MINERAL KING CANYON; NATIONAL ENVIRONMENTAL POLICY ACT (U.S.); NATURAL RESOURCES DEFENSE COUNCIL; SIERRA CLUB; TRAIL SMELTER INVESTIGATION

Environmental Conservation

The now widely familiar phrase *Environmental Conservation* is at once the theme of conservation or lasting preservation of the environment or total surroundings of Mankind and Nature, and the title of a pioneering journal in that most important field of endeavor. Of the former use little needs to be said to enlightened readers short of stressing that, without a reasonably stable environment, scarcely any hope would remain for the long-continuation of reasonably equable human existence on the planet earth (the only known source and natural habitat of life in the entire universe). It therefore behooves our species, as the only one possessed of conscious intelligence and the capability of safeguarding life on earth, to do all it possibly can in that direction now that we have detailed knowledge of the threats to our environment and of how they could be averted.

The quarterly journal *Environmental Conservation*, now in its twenty-second year and volume, followed the pioneering *Biological Conservation* when its founder, Nicholas Polunin, after editing the latter journal from 1967 to 1974, felt the need to change to a more environmental basis. Commenced at the urging of the late Sir Hugh Elliott, then Secretary-General of the International Union for Conservation of Nature and Natural Resources (IUCN, now the World Conservation Union), *Biological Conservation* began publishing in London in 1968 and has continued under multiple editorship, now reaching its twenty-seventh year and seventy-first volume. *Environmental Conservation*, distributed by Elsevier Sequoia SA, P.O. Box 564, 1001 Lausanne, Switzerland, has remained to this day under the sole editorship of Polunin. Throughout its existence, *Environmental Conservation* has carried on its cover of various shades of green and marine-blue the statement of its objective: "The international Journal devoted to maintaining global viability through exposing and countering environmental deterioration resulting from human population-pressure and unwise technology."

Environmental Conservation accordingly "advocates timely action for the protection and amelioration of the environment of Mankind and Nature throughout the world. Topics range from pertinent case-histories of the past and present to rational use of resources, foreseeing ecological consequences, enlightened environmental policy, anti-pollution measures, low-impact development, environmental education and law, and ecologically sound management of all land and fresh water, sea and air, for the lasting future of Earth's fragile Biosphere."

In addition to the usual seven or eight main papers, each ranging commonly from four to twelve pages in length, every issue contains, in its ninety-six-page format, five regular sections as follows: 1) an *Editorial, Guest Editorial,* and/ or *Guest Comment(s), Open Letter, Editorial Notes* or *Notice(s)* or a combination thereof; 2) *Short Communications & Reports,* each normally not exceeding three pages of the Journal; 3) *Notes, News, & Comments,* short information pieces filling preferably one page or less of

the Journal; 4) Conferences & Meetings, summary reports or important prospects; and 5) *Reviews & Notices* of, for example, new books. Each issue thus contains some 40 to 50 original contributions of which a substantial proportion are illustrated.

A recent, independent body's unanimous comment on this Journal was to the effect that it "publishes papers of an exceptionally high standard and accomplishes the stated objectives with admirable success. Indeed with its additional 5 regular sections *Environmental Conservation* seems to us clearly the leading journal in its wide and vital alliance of fields."

The Journal is owned and printed by the Foundation for Environmental Conservation (FEC), a small Swiss-based international non-governmental concern which holds the copyright and, through the annual general meetings of its governing board, approves the Journal's policy and financing which is practically self-supporting. Each year there is a Best Paper Prize, winners of which are chosen by the FEC's confidential awards committee.

The fact that the annual Prize is usually divided three or four ways is said to testify to the quality of the papers in the Journal or chapters in the books published by or on behalf of the Foundation.

Nicholas Polunin

See also CONSERVATION BIOLOGY; IUCN

Environmental Defense Fund

The Environmental Defense Fund (EDF) is a private, nonprofit organization that engages in research, political, and legal action involving a variety of environmental issues in the United States and internationally. Founded in 1967 by Arthur Cooley, Dennis Puleston, Robert Smolker, and Charles Wurster, largely in reaction to DDT pollution in Long Island, New York, the EDF has grown from a relatively small organization with a small staff primarily involved in litigation with a budget of $100,000 in 1970 to an organization with a $25 million budget and a staff of more than sixty—including twenty-five lawyers, twenty-five scientists, ten economists, and five engineers—in 1993. Like many environmental organizations the EDF has enjoyed significant membership growth since 1970. Membership stood at 10,000 in 1970; that number grew to 40,000 in 1980 and 200,000 in 1990. Thus far in the

1990s membership has fluctuated between 200,000 and 250,000.

The EDF strives to link science, law, and economics to find scientifically and economically viable solutions to environmental problems. The EDF pursues its goals by lobbying, publishing research findings, issuing a newsletter and press releases, providing testimony at legislative and other public hearings and through litigation. Major issues with which the EDF has been involved include: air pollution (ozone depletion, acid rain, global warming), water management (preserving wetlands and water pollution), land management (tropical rainforests and wildlife habitats), and waste disposal (toxic waste management and recycling). Examples of EDF policy activities include developing a waste reduction plan with McDonalds Corporation which will lead to an 80 percent reduction of the solid waste generated by McDonalds restaurants and their involvement (by invitation of the Bush administration) in the development of the acid rain reduction components of the 1990 Clean Air Act amendments.

Headquartered in New York City, the EDF has five regional offices located in Washington D.C.; Oakland, California; Boulder, Colorado; Raleigh, North Carolina; and Austin, Texas. The local offices are primarily involved in those issues that are most important to each region. The bulk of EDF funding comes from membership dues and foundation grants (more than 90 percent) with most of the balance from awards won in court cases.

Zachary A. Smith

Further Readings

Pierce, John C., et al. *Political Communication and Interest Groups: Environmental Organizations in Canada and the United States.* 1992.

Lowe, Philip, and Jane Goyder. *Environmental Groups in Politics.* 1983.

See also ENVIRONMENTAL MOVEMENT: LESS-AFFLUENT NATIONS; ENVIRONMENTAL CASE LAW: UNITED STATES; PACKAGING; PESTICIDES

Environmental Diplomacy

A transboundary environmental problem arises when the benefits of a polluting activity accrue to one nation, while the costs of that activity accrue to the nation across the border. It is the existence of the border and the imbalances in costs and benefits that result between two (or more) nations, which defines the existence of a transboundary environmental problem, and not necessarily the actual environmental impact of the activity in question. In the context of policy and diplomacy, perception most often equals reality, and thus, if people of a nation believe that damage is being done to them, a transboundary environmental problem exists, regardless of whether there is "real" (i.e., scientifically verifiable) environmental damage or cost. The reverse also holds, namely, if real damage occurs but is not sufficiently perceived by those who are affected or by others with power who might raise an issue, then there is no problem so far as diplomacy is concerned. The conduct of international environmental diplomacy represents diplomatic practice(s) by a government in an attempt to resolve such transboundary and transnational environmental problems to the satisfaction of the governments concerned. Once such governments are satisfied, there is no further transboundary environmental issue even if scientifically verifiable environmental or ecological damage continues.

The existence of transboundary environmental problems is related to the geography of upstream-downstream relationships in water and upwind-downwind relationships in air. However, to a certain degree these formerly important relationships are becoming superfluous as international environmental diplomacy expands its range from small, local, site-specific situations and circumstances to geographically broader transnational, transhemispheric, or even transglobal circumstances in which ultimately everyone is both upstream and downstream, both upwind and downwind, of one another, both in ecological reality and, increasingly, in human perception.

It is also the case that nations can be (or can be perceived to be) the environmental "sinners" at one period of time and the hapless environmental "victims" at another. For example in the 1970s the United States, with its quickening pace of environmental regulations and court injunctions, felt itself the victim of much pressure of environmental damage coming from energy development and other forms of resource use and exploitation on the Canadian side of the border. Canada's primary "development corridor," where most of its people live and work and from which much of its energy and other resource needs must be met, is immediately adjacent to the United States and extends not much more than 100 miles from the

U.S. border. Canadian impacts on the U.S. environment, quantitative and qualitative, are thus inevitable. The reverse is not as likely, since much of the U.S. northern border is lightly populated, relatively wild, and, in some cases, viewed as pristine wilderness and treasured accordingly. This is a circumstance ripe for bilateral difficulty, and a circumstance especially supportive of accusations against Canada for environmental pressure which spills across the border and damages U.S. ecosystems. The dominant view from Washington by the late 1970s was clearly one of a Canadian threat—through that nation's drive for mega-scale energy and other resource extractive economic development—to environments which many Americans, including large environmental organizations, state governments, and members of Congress were interested in protecting. The dominant view from Ottawa was one of a U.S. threat to Canada's chances for economic development much desired by all major political parties, private business interests, and particularly provincial governments, regardless of the party in power in the province in question.

At the end of the decade and through much of the 1980s, however, the tables turned with the emergence of the acid rain issue. All agreed that Canada, the recipient of over 50 percent of its acid pollution from U.S. sources, albeit with its own acid emissions acknowledged, was a legitimate complainant against uncontrolled and unregulated U.S. acid emissions, particularly from the U.S. Midwest. Canada's complainant status was strongly based on grassroots concern which affected the position of all national political parties and most provincial governments. However, the Canadian government came up against an increasingly recalcitrant and stubborn U.S. administration which chose to question the existence of the problem and to hide behind demands for ever more scientific research on the question. Thus, the tables can turn. By the late 1980s, the situation fundamentally altered with another turning of a different kind, as a Canadian government, committed to the negotiation of a "free trade" agreement with the United States, came to believe, probably correctly, that it could not simultaneously attack the United States on acid rain and still expect a successful bilateral trade agreement. It opted for the latter, and accepted the 1990 changes to the U.S. Clean Air Act as sufficient recompense. Acid rain was pushed aside as developing global environmental concerns (e.g., climate warming and a depleting ozone layer)

largely supplanted acid rain as both a bilateral and (in Europe) a multi-lateral issue.

The conduct of environmental diplomacy exists from the mid-nineteenth century in Europe and the end of that century along the Canada–United States border. Early disputes were restricted to bilateral matters between nations sharing a border, and focused largely on water quantity issues, namely diversions—damming and flooding—with the needs of one nation (generally upstream) being fulfilled by harm (usually inadvertent) to another nation. It should be noted that an upstream nation could occasionally be the complainant if the matter involved dam construction and resultant land inundation which backed up into the upstream nation. Diversions generally mean a downstream complainant, either one deprived of water (i.e., diversion out of the watershed) or, less frequently, one receiving too much water and thus experiencing flood damage (i.e., diversion into the watershed). The Chicago Diversion out of the North American Great Lakes, with both positive and negative impacts in the United States and negative impacts in Canada, is an early example, as are a number of local bilateral issues along European borders. Early bilateral water quality issues are few in number and very local, as are a very few early air quality issues.

With the emergence of Great Lakes water quality concerns in the 1960s, quality issues took on much greater importance and began to displace quantity issues. The events leading up to the first Great Lakes Water Quality Agreement in 1972 marked a new phase in international environmental diplomacy, from local transboundary to regional/continental in scope, albeit still on a bilateral level. The economies, regional and national, and the local and state/provincial governments affected by these negotiations was much greater than had been seen before, and signaled the emergence of environment as a force to be reckoned with on the foreign policy agenda. Similarly, and simultaneously, the emergence of acid rain as a multi-lateral European question raised such diplomacy to a more prominent position than heretofore.

The Great Lakes, and later the North American as well as European acid rain experience, established the place of significant qualitative controversies (with acid rain, multi-lateral as well as bilateral and, to add further complexity, bilateral non-adjacent situations) on the permanent agenda of international diplomacy. (Also at this time transboundary air pollution problems, bilateral and multi-lateral, came into their own.) Acid rain caused serious regional disputes within nations (particularly the Northeast-Midwest dispute in the United States) requiring serious domestic political diplomacy, as well as transnational and intercontinental and even trans-hemispheric disputes, all presaging global concerns to come. Broad questions of economic development and political power became so inherent that acid rain signaled the emergence not only of a wholly new era in transboundary and international environmental relations but the beginning of involvement in inscrutable and intractable problems for which real remedy could not be found in conventional politics and diplomacy—a more fundamental change in values began to appear to be necessary.

As acid rain and other long-range air pollutant transport issues raged through the 1980s (side-by-side with similarly complicated and intractable marine pollution problems) a further evolution occurred with the emergence of concern over the twin challenges of climate change (which, with its likely multiple ecological effects, is now referred to as global change) and the discovery of holes in the planet's atmospheric ozone layer, holes known to be both multiplying and growing. One now hears little about acid rain and attendant problems of a similar order of magnitude, and much about problems perceived as global, including forest destruction, desertification, soil erosion, and the death of aquatic environments. Much more attention is focused on the interconnectedness (and seeming interdependency) of these questions with social concerns (violence, hunger, starvation, war, crime, economic collapse) not conventionally thought of as environmental issues. Thus, evidence is now emerging that environmental concern, including the conventional parameters of international environmental diplomacy, will now converge under broader umbrellas and become part of deeper questions of ethics, values, lifestyles, and fundamental philosophical beliefs about the definition, meaning, and direction of life, however broadly defined. Without question, however, international environmental diplomacy has come to be prominent on the agenda of most nation-states, large and small, from necessity rather than from choice. Its parameters are blurring more and more with most other significant issues on those agendas. Its future, or lack thereof, lies partly in a continuation of this blur-

ring of parameters, and partly in the very future of the nation-state itself, a future not at all certain.

John E. Carroll

Further Readings

Carroll, John E. *Environmental Diplomacy: An Examination and a Prospective of Canadian-U.S. Transboundary Environmental Relations.* 1986.
———, ed. *International Environmental Diplomacy: The Management and Resolution of Transfrontier Environmental Problems.* 1990.

See also ACID PRECIPITATION: AQUATIC IMPACTS; ACID PRECIPITATION: EUROPEAN EXPERIENCES; ACID PRECIPITATION: LEGISLATIVE INITIATIVES; ACID PRECIPITATION: TERRESTRIAL IMPACTS; CLIMATE WARMING; INTERNATIONAL JOINT COMMISSION; MONTREAL PROTOCOL; RIO CONFERENCE (1992); STOCKHOLM CONFERENCE (1972); UNITED NATIONS ENVIRONMENT PROGRAMME

Environmental Economics

See GREEN ECONOMICS

Environmental Education

It is clear beyond any reasonable doubt that ecological, climate, resource, and demographic trends represent a substantial and growing threat to human tenure on the earth. Each, in turn, compounds virtually every other issue on the human agenda. If these trends are to be reversed short of catastrophe the present generation of students will have to initiate substantial conservation measures, namely:

1. Stabilize the world's population;
2. Stabilize the world's climate by reducing the emission of all greenhouse gases;
3. Protect biological diversity;
4. Reverse the destruction of rainforests now being lost at the rate of 116 square miles per day;
5. Conserve soils being eroded at the rate of 72 million tons per day;
6. Learn how to use energy and materials efficiently;
7. Learn how to run civilization on sunlight;
8. Rebuild economies in order to eliminate waste and pollution;

9. Learn how to use all resources sustainably; and
10. Repair, as much as possible, the damage done to the earth in the past 200 years.

And they must do all of this while reducing egregious inequities. No generation has ever faced a more daunting agenda.

For the most part, however, we are still educating the young as if there were no planetary emergency. It is widely assumed that environmental problems will be solved by one technology or another. Better technology can certainly help but the crisis is not primarily one of technology. Rather, it is one of mind, hence one within the minds that develop and use technology. The disordering of ecological systems and of the great biogeochemical cycles of the earth reflects a prior disorder in the thought, perception, imagination, intellectual priorities, and loyalties inherent in the industrial mind. The ecological crisis, then, is a challenge to those institutions purporting to shape and refine the capacity of minds to think clearly. It is a crisis *of* education not a crisis *in* education. Resolution of the great ecological quandaries of the next century, then, will require us to reconsider the substance, process, and purposes of education at all levels.

The most compelling reason for environmental education is grounded in the obligation that educators have to equip students to meet the challenges of their age knowledgeably and with practical competence, intellectual clarity, and moral energy. To do so students must be able to think broadly, beyond the boundaries of conventional disciplines. They must understand systems and the patterns that connect disparate phenomena. They must think in terms of decades, centuries, and even millennia. They must be bold enough to ask large and vexing questions. And they must understand the biophysical foundations of human life and well-being and how these are connected to their own individual prospects.

Yale historian Yaroslav Pelikan, however, questions the willingness of educators "to address the underlying intellectual issues and moral imperatives of having responsibility for the earth, and to do so with an intensity and ingenuity matching that shown by previous generations in obeying the command to have dominion over the planet." What would it mean for educators and educational institutions to respond with "intensity and ingenuity" to the environmental challenge? There are at least three elements of such a response.

The first has to do with the "fundamental principles" of environmental learning, beginning with the recognition that all education is environmental education. By what is included or excluded, emphasized or ignored, students learn that they are a part of or apart from the natural world. As well, environmental issues are complex and cannot be understood through any single discipline. Further, the experience of the natural world is an essential part of environmental education and is an antidote to indoor and more abstract kinds of learning. A great deal of environmental education at all levels must be done outdoors. The process of education is as important for environmental learning as its content. Students taught environmental awareness in a manner that does not alter their relationship to the environment, learn that it is sufficient to intellectualize, emote, or posture about such things without having to live differently. Environmental education, in other words, ought to change the way people live, not just how they talk. Finally, environmental education ought to increase students' practical ecological competence by giving them opportunities to solve real environmental problems. Doing so both sharpens the intellect and engages students in the long-term task of moving the world toward sustainability.

A second element of an "intense and ingenious" response has to do with curriculum and the content of education. What should students know and how should they learn it? Students need to acquire the analytic abilities, ecological wisdom, and practical wherewithal essential to making things that fit harmoniously on a planet with a biosphere. This can be called "ecological design intelligence," or the ability to get beyond the boxes we call disciplines in order to see things in their ecological context. Design applies to the making of nearly everything that directly or indirectly requires energy and materials or governs their use including farms, houses, communities, neighborhoods, cities, transportation systems, technologies, economies, and energy policies.

Ecological design is the careful meshing of human purposes with the larger patterns and flows of the natural world and the study of those patterns and flows to inform human purposes. Ecological design intelligence is the ability to incorporate intelligence about how nature works into the way we think, design, build, and live. And it requires the wisdom to know the difference between what can be done and what should be done. An ecological design focus in education directs attention to issues of scale, resilience, redundancy, durability, the fit between means and ends, efficiency, and simplicity. It requires a liberal education that integrates first-hand experience and practical competence with theoretical knowledge. The beginnings of a curriculum in ecological design are becoming apparent in the emergence of new fields of ecological restoration, ecological engineering, ecological economics, sustainable agriculture, sustainable forestry, pollution prevention, ecological architecture, solar design, and environmental ethics. And it is evident in the development of new analytical techniques of systems analysis, least-cost/end use analysis, and full-cost pricing.

A third element of an intense and ingenious response has to do with the institutional setting in which education occurs. Schools, colleges, and universities teach by what they do as well as by what they say. Accordingly, institutions purporting to induct the young into responsible citizenship on a planet with a biosphere ought to be examples of good environmental citizenship. The reasons are twofold: 1) an institution that presumes to induct students into responsible adulthood ought to act responsibly; and 2) doing so has proven to be financially rewarding. On many campuses improvements in energy efficiency, for example, have had payback times of .5 to 3 years. A comprehensive institutional response would require policies to promote:

1. The efficient use of energy, paper, water, and other materials
2. The elimination of toxic wastes on campus
3. Ecological landscaping
4. The use of recycled paper and materials
5. Campus-wide composting of organic wastes
6. Standards for new construction and renovation that include energy efficiency and use of nontoxic/recycled materials.

Moreover, schools, colleges, and universities should use their buying and investment power to promote local energy efficiency and the development of sustainable regional economies.

Finally, any education that imparts only facts, theories, models, and technical skill without also developing moral stamina will prove to be inadequate for the challenges ahead—challenges that will not be solved quickly or painlessly. The task of environmental educators is to foster a long-term shift in human consciousness, an ecological enlightenment that establishes in the mind of students that they are citizens of the biotic community. And, in Aldo Leopold's words, "if education does not teach us these things, then what is education for?"

David W. Orr

Further Readings

Berry, Wendell. "The Loss of the University." In *Home Economics*. Ed. Wendell Berry. 1987.

Bowers, C.A. *Education, Cultural Myths, and the Ecological Crisis*. 1993.

Gray, J. Glenn. *Re-Thinking American Education*. 1984.

Midgley, Mary. "Why Smartness Is Not Enough." In *Rethinking the Curriculum*. Ed. Mary Clark and Sandra Wawrytko. 1990.

Miller, Ron, ed. *The Renewal of Meaning in Education*. 1993.

Orr, David W. *Ecological Literacy*. 1992.

Pelikan, Yaroslav. *The Idea of the University: A Reexamination*. 1992.

See also CONSERVATION BIOLOGY; ENVIRONMENTAL ETHICS; ENVIRONMENTAL HISTORY; INTERDISCIPLINARITY; LEOPOLD, ALDO

Environmental Ethics

Environmental ethics, a branch of applied philosophy, deals with ethical issues related to the natural environment. It includes several movements—deep ecology, based on the philosophy of the Norwegian philosopher Arne Naess; ecofeminism, a form of feminist philosophy applied to environmental issues, in which there is no single leading figure; and social ecology, based on the anarchist writings of Murray Bookchin—and a mainstream literature, not associated with particular movements, that has evolved thematically over the last two decades but is best characterized by the writings of a number of major figures: in particular, Holmes Rolston, III, J. Baird Callicott, Eugene C. Hargrove, John B. Cobb, Jr., Paul W. Taylor, Kristin Shrader-Frechette, Bryan G. Norton, and Mark Sagoff.

Environmental ethics theory is aimed primarily at extending ethical concern beyond traditional limits—human life, health, and welfare—to include a large number of entities and collections of entities—for example, species and ecosystems—that haven't been given previous moral consideration. As a result, environmental ethicists generally take traditional ethics as a given and discuss it only to the degree that it conflicts with new theory. In practice, environmental ethics theory is expected to complement and correct traditional ethics, not entirely replace it. It differs from most other forms of applied ethics, in particular, medical ethics, in that it is more concerned with justifying environmental positions than with solving tough cases. This emphasis reflects the needs of environmentalists and environmental professionals, who frequently find standard methods of justification—most often, cost-benefit analysis—to be counterintuitive.

Environmental ethics is broadly based on a set of culturally evolved intuitions that have arisen in the modern period out of the interaction of the natural history sciences—geology, biology, botany, and finally ecology—with landscape gardening, landscape painting and photography, and nature poetry and prose. These intuitions are most often accessed today through the writings of Henry David Thoreau, John Muir, and Aldo Leopold. Leopold's seminal essay, "The Land Ethic," from his book *A Sand County Almanac* (1949), provides the general framework within which nearly all research in environmental ethics has been undertaken.

As a professional field within philosophy, environmental ethics is a product of Earth Day in 1970, when environmentalists first began encouraging philosophers to create the field. Most writing in the 1970s was focused on preliminary matters: whether it was possible to establish such a field and how it would be related to other areas in applied ethics. The first conference on environmental ethics was organized by William T. Blackstone and held at the University of Georgia in 1971. A copy of the proceedings of this meeting, edited by Blackstone, *Philosophy and Environmental Crisis* (1974), includes a still influential paper by Joel Feinberg, "The Rights of Animals and Unborn Generations."

The first full-length environmental ethics book by a philosopher was Cobb's *Is It Too Late? A Theology of Ecology* (1972). Although it focuses on religion and theology and was intended for classes in adult Christian education, it includes a discussion of environmental ethics in terms of Whitehead's process philosophy. In 1973 Richard Routley (now Sylvan) called international attention to the need for environmental ethics research by presenting "Is There a New, an Environmental, Ethic?" at the Fifteenth World Congress of Philosophy in Bulgaria. The deep ecology movement was begun with the publication of Arne Naess's "The Shallow and Deep, Long-Range Ecology Movement" (*Inquiry,* 1973), which was followed by an influential series of newsletters throughout the rest of the decade by George Sessions, part bibliography and part commentary. Much of the discussion and debate throughout the 1970s involved the Lynn White debate, a reaction to Lynn White, Jr.'s "The Historical Roots of Our Ecologic Crisis" (*Science,* 1967), in which he blamed Christianity for the environmental crisis. Another theme involved reaction to Peter Singer's *Animal Liberation: A New Ethics for Our Treatment of Animals* (1975) and Christopher Stone's *Should Trees Have Standing? Toward Legal Rights for Natural Objects* (1974), which introduced comparative discussion of the role of rights in animal welfare and legal contexts respectively.

Research on future generations culminated with Ernest Partridge's anthology, *Responsibilities to Future Generations* (1981). Environmental ethics began to take shape as a distinct literature with the publication of John Passmore's *Man's Responsibility for Nature: Ecological Problems and Western Traditions* (1974), in which he argued that environmental ethics and animal welfare ethics are dangerously inconsistent with Western traditions. The book, which remained the only single-authored book specifically on professional environmental ethics for nearly a decade, was the chief target of most environmental ethicists until positive book-length theories began to appear in the 1980s, beginning with Charles Birch and Cobb's *The Liberation of Life: From the Cell to the Community* (1981), Robin Attfield's *The Ethics of Environmental Concern* (1983), and Mary Midgley, *Animals and Why They Matter* (1983). The field first achieved respectability in mainstream professional philosophy with the publication of Rolston's "Is There an Ecological Ethic?" *Ethics* (1975). In 1979, Hargrove founded *Environmental Ethics,* which provided a regular outlet for environmental ethics research and permitted a forum for sustained debate.

Although Roderick Nash (*The Rights of Nature: A History of Environmental Ethics,* 1989), characterizes environmental ethics as an extension of rights to nature, mainstream environmental ethics largely rejected rights theory in the early 1980s. Environmental ethics and animal rights were definitively split into separate fields with the publication of Callicott's "Animal Liberation: A Triangular Affair" (*Environmental Ethics,* 1980). Arguing that pain is "primarily information" and drawing out the implications of holism for Leopold's land ethic, Callicott concluded that environmental ethics and animal liberation are incompatible positions. Norton, in "Environmental Ethics and Nonhuman Rights" (*Environmental Ethics,* 1982), argued that rights are conceptually intended as protections of the interests of individuals and have no clear application at the level of such environmental collectives as species and ecosystems. Today environmentalist claims that nature has or ought to have rights are usually considered to be rhetorical or emotivist claims.

With the abandonment of rights theory much research has focused on nonanthropocentric value theories as an alternative. Taylor's *Respect for Nature* (1986) develops a biocentric egalitarian theory of "inherent worth" based on the "good of its own" of the individual organism that provides equal consideration for plants and animals. Rolston's conception of "intrinsic value" in *Environmental Ethics: Duties to and Values in the Natural World* (1988) also focuses on the "good of its own" of individual organisms, but adds the "good of its kind" of an organism and systemic value for species and ecosystems. Unlike Taylor, Rolston's position includes a value hierarchy in which more complex organisms generally receive more consideration than less complex ones, although less complex organisms, for example, plants, take precedence when they are endangered. The positions of Taylor and Rolston are similar to Tom Regan's conception of "inherent value" in *The Case for Animal Rights* (1983), although Regan's "subject-of-a-life" criterion limits moral considerability to healthy mammals more than one year old, and he argues that moral consideration for plants, species, and ecosystems is "environmental fascism."

In opposition to such objectivist nonanthropocentric theories, Callicott has developed a subjectivist nonanthropocentric theory of intrinsic value in a series of papers now collected in *In Defense of the Land Ethic* (1989). This position, a "truncated" theory that permits the human valuing of nature "for itself" but not "in itself" is based on Hume's sentiments, Darwinian evolution, and Leopold's land ethic. In addition Callicott has developed a self-realization position based on quantum physics with similarities to the deep ecology position.

Norton in "Environmental Ethics and Weak Anthropocentrism" (*Environmental Ethics,* 1984) and *Why Preserve Natural Variety?* (1988), has argued against nonanthropocentric intrinsic value theories on the grounds that weak anthropocentrism in terms of considered (versus felt) preferences produces the same practical consequences while avoiding the metaphysical and epistemological difficulties involved in intrinsic value attributions. In *Toward Unity among Environmentalists* (1991) Norton has taken a pragmatic approach that abandons the distinction between instrumental and intrinsic value altogether. Hargrove in *Foundations of Environmental Ethics* (1989) has argued for a weak anthropocentric intrinsic value theory in which intrinsic value depends upon human judgment in the context of socially evolved ideals. This position is similar to Callicott's subjectivist nonanthropocentric theory and complementary to Sagoff's position in *The Economy of the Earth: Philosophy, Law, and the Environment* (1988), in which he distinguishes between consumer and citizen preferences in terms of evolved social ideals that define national character.

Bill Devall and Sessions's *Deep Ecology: Living as if Nature Mattered* (1985) was the primary book-length account of deep ecology in the 1980s. It was more fully and technically explained in Arne Naess's *Ecology, Community and Lifestyle: Outline of an Ecosophy* (1989). It has been criticized from within by Warwick Fox (*Toward a Transpersonal Ecology,* 1990) and from without from ecofeminist, Third World, and postmodern perspectives: for example, Ariel Salleh, "The Ecofeminism/Deep Ecology Debate" (*Environmental Ethics,* 1992), Ramachandra Guha, "Radical American Environmentalism and Wilderness Preservation: A Third World Critique" (*Environmental Ethics,* 1989), and Jim Cheney, "The Neo-Stoicism of Radical Environmentalism" and "Postmodern Environmental Ethics: Ethics as Bioregionalism" (*Environmental Ethics,* 1989).

Despite the central focus on value theory the field continues to be quite eclectic. Stone has created a new controversy over the nature of environmental ethics with *Earth and Other*

Ethics: The Case for Moral Monism (1987). In response Callicott ("The Case against Moral Monism," *Environmental Ethics,* 1990), has argued that environmental ethics should be monistic and, in this context, he has attempted to develop a general framework to reunite animal welfare ethics and environmental ethics. Max Oelschlaeger's *The Idea of Wilderness from Prehistory to the Age of Ecology* (1991) is the first full-scale philosophy of wilderness. Wilderness philosophy has been challenged by Thomas H. Birch, "The Incarceration of Wildness," *Environmental Ethics* (1990). Yrjö Sepänmaa in *The Beauty of Environment* (1986) has developed a model for the aesthetic foundations of environmental ethics with environmental policy implications. Hargrove in his edited anthology *Beyond Spaceship Earth* (1986) has applied environmental ethics to the solar system and the space program. Callicott and Roger T. Ames's edited anthology, *Nature in Asian Traditions of Thought* (1989), has revived comparative environmental ethics, which fell victim to the Lynn White debate in the 1970s. Susan Power Bratton has revealed an environmental tradition within Christianity in *Christianity, Wildlife, and Wilderness: The Original Desert Solitaire* (1992) and examined Christian attitudes toward population control in *Six Billion and More: Human Population Regulation and Christian Ethics* (1992). Criticism of cost-benefit and risk-benefit analysis include Sagoff's *Economy of the Earth* (1988), Shrader-Frechette, *Risk Analysis and Scientific Method* (1985), and Herman E. Daly and Cobb, *For the Common Good* (1989).

Eugene C. Hargrove

Further Readings

Armstrong, Susan J., and Richard G. Botzler, eds. *Environmental Ethics: Divergence and Convergence.* 1993.

Hargrove, Eugene C. *Foundations of Environmental Ethics.* 1989.

See also ANTHROPOCENTRISM; DEEP ECOLOGY: EMERGENCE; DEEP ECOLOGY: MEANINGS; EARTH DAY; ECOPHILOSOPHY AND ECOPSYCHOLOGY; ECO-SPIRITUALITY; INTRINSIC VALUE; LEOPOLD, ALDO; MUIR, JOHN; RELIGION AND ENVIRONMENTAL PROTECTION; THOREAU, HENRY DAVID

Environmental Ethics

Environmental Ethics: An Interdisciplinary Journal Dedicated to the Philosophical Aspects of Environmental Problems, the major journal in the field, began publication at the University of New Mexico in spring 1979. Its founding editor, Eugene C. Hargrove, moved the journal to the University of Georgia in 1981 and the University of North Texas in 1990. Subjects include, but are not restricted to, animal liberation and animal rights, land ethics, intrinsic value theory, deep ecology, ecofeminism, comparative philosophy, process philosophy, ecological restoration, environmental aesthetics, and environmental economics. The journal is refereed and draws from an international readership. Since 1980 the journal has been owned by a nonprofit corporation, Environmental Philosophy, Inc., created specifically to advance research and education in the field of environmental ethics.

Through its Center for Environmental Philosophy, the corporation regularly offers workshops for college and university professors, nature interpreters, and religious professionals and, on an occasional basis, refereed research conferences. In cooperation with the University of North Texas Department of Philosophy and Religion Studies and the Faculty of Environmental Ethics, it provides scholars with opportunities to undertake research in the field in an interdisciplinary context. It is associated with the university's graduate program in environmental ethics: the Master of Arts in Philosophy with a Concentration in Environmental Ethics and the Master of Science in Interdisciplinary Studies. In 1990 the center created Environmental Ethics Books to reprint important books in the field. Publications currently include Charles Birch and John B. Cobb, Jr., *The Liberation of Life: From the Cell to the Community* (1990); Eugene C. Hargrove, ed., *Beyond Spaceship Earth: Environmental Ethics and the Solar System* (1993); Yrjö Sepänmaa, *The Beauty of Environment: A General Model for Environmental Aesthetics,* 2nd ed. (1993); and John B. Cobb, Jr., *Is It Too Late? A Theology of Ecology,* rev. ed. (1995).

Eugene C. Hargrove

See also ANIMAL RIGHTS; DEEP ECOLOGY: EMERGENCE; DEEP ECOLOGY: MEANINGS; ECOFEMINISM; ECOLOGICAL RESTORATION; ENVIRONMENTAL AESTHETICS; ENVIRONMENTAL ETHICS; GREEN ECONOMICS

Environmental Groups: Western Europe

Environmental groups are firmly established players in the political process throughout

Western Europe. Within the twelve countries of the European Union (EU, formerly European Community), more than 10 million citizens are members or supporters of environmental groups.

The history of European environmental groups goes back to the second half of the nineteenth century. A broad range of environmental groups campaigning primarily on nature conservation but also on air and water pollution emerged in the late nineteenth and early twentieth centuries. One of the earliest environmental groups still in existence is the Commons, Open Spaces and Footpaths Preservation Society, which was formed in England in 1865. In most Northern European countries traditional conservation groups were thus well established at the time of the rise of new environmentalism in the 1960s. During the following two decades increased awareness and concern for the environment not only provided the impetus for rising membership and increased support for established environmental organizations, but also spurred the emergence of a whole range of new groups addressing the new environmental issues coming to the fore. These new groups introduced new campaigning techniques and, at least initially, displayed a new radicalism in terms of both political action and environmental aims.

The first wave of new groups emerged in response to the establishment of the environment as a new policy area in Europe in the late 1960s and early 1970s and the emergence of a new environmental radicalism questioning the future of industrial society based on economic growth. Books such as *The Blueprint for Survival* (1972) and *The Limits of Growth* (1972) were widely translated and read in Western Europe and stimulated a wide-ranging political debate. They formed the basis of a more fundamental critique of industrialism going beyond the moderate and pragmatic approaches focusing on individual issues that had been followed by the established groups. New groups often formed as a direct result of a seemingly inadequate response to the new issues by established groups. While the established conservation groups often relied on informal contacts with decision makers and discouraged publicity, the new groups sought to mobilize public opinion and challenge state authority more directly. The new, mainly young environmental campaigners were often influenced by the experience of the peace and student movements of the 1960s, and demonstrations and direct action techniques were often used to highlight the new issues.

While the predictions of world environmental doom typical of the early 1970s were an important development point for the new groups, the most important campaigning topic emerged only during the 1970s: nuclear energy. Opposition to the civil use of nuclear power intensified in the mid- to late 1970s, often involving local opposition groups as well as the New Left protest potential which had been created by the student movement of the 1960s. The protest movement against nuclear energy produced many new local and national organizations but it also involved most new and many old environmental groups and generally had a radicalizing effect on these groups. The 1980s saw other issues come to the fore which had a more international focus. First, acid rain was a major campaigning issue in the early 1980s. Second, after another major anti-nuclear interlude stimulated by the 1986 Chernobyl accident, new global environmental issues—destruction of the rain forest, desertification, the ozone layer, and global warming—provided the major impetus for environmental group activity.

With the relative decline of the nuclear energy issue environmental groups have experienced a number of changes. The direct political mobilization of environmental activists for demonstrations and other actions has decreased substantially. Most environmental groups have either gone through an institutionalization process or have disappeared altogether. In all West European countries we thus have a number of highly professional environmental organizations which are essentially run by relatively small groups of activists. Ordinary members or supporters mainly play a passive role, with financial contributions to the group constituting their main input. Groups that have succeeded in building up a mass membership often concentrate their efforts in mobilizing expert opinion, and their range of activity matches that of other established interest groups. In many cases, these groups started with very radical approaches and placed themselves deliberately outside establishment politics. Those radical groups that resisted "institutionalization" and "professionalization" usually found that the mobilization potential was disappearing fast. With the decline of the "new social movements," the traditional environmental interest groups often adapted very well to the new environmental climate, and have benefited most from the substantial increase in the salience of environmental issues that has occurred over the

E

past thirty years. The current focus on global environmental issues and the opportunities for environmental groups to partake in international decision-making processes as "nongovernmental organizations" has accelerated this "institutionalization" process.

The internationalization of environmental policy also highlights the transnational dimension of the organization of the environmental movement. One of the most visible international environmental networks is Friends of the Earth International (FOEI). The formation of Friends of the Earth in the United States in 1969 had been followed by other Friends of the Earth groups being set up in some European countries and, later, some major independently formed environment groups affiliated to FOEI. Other key groups operating throughout Western Europe (and the rest of the world) are Greenpeace and the Worldwide Fund for Nature (WWF). There are many other transnational networks concerned with specific issues, for example pesticides and climate change. With the increasing role of European environmental policymaking, a wide range of environmental groups from all EU countries formed the European Environment Bureau (EEB) in 1974 to represent environmental interests at EU level.

While the main features of the development of environmental groups described earlier can be found throughout the region, there are important differences between European countries in the intensity of environmental conflict, the importance of individual issues, the mobilization of the movement, and the action repertoire adopted by groups.

Environmental groups generally have received the most public support in Northern Europe. Until the mid-1970s, the development of environmental groups was inhibited by authoritarian regimes in Portugal, Spain, and Greece. But more generally, lower economic living standards represent an important obstacle in some Southern European countries, as well as Ireland, while environmental groups have benefited in many Northern countries from a greater cultural predisposition to belonging to voluntary groups and/or political mass organizations.

Looking more closely at the nature of environmental groups in a number of individual countries, some more specific differences become apparent. (All membership figures are for 1991; source: Hey, et al., 1992.) In Denmark, the Danish Society for the Conservation of Nature (formed in 1911) with 263,000 members is the largest environmental group, followed at some distance by Greenpeace and World Wildlife Fund (WWF) with 30,000 members each. Arguably the most important activist environmental group, however, known by the acronym NOAH, was formed by student activists in 1969 that brought many of the new environmental issues into the political debate. With just 300 members, NOAH is clearly not a mass organization. In Germany the new environmental movement emerged in force with the anti-nuclear movement in 1975. An umbrella group representing local environmental protest groups formed in 1972, the Bundesverband Bürgerinitiativen Umweltschutz (BBU) (Federal Association of Citizen Initiatives for the Protection of the Environment) played a leading role in the anti-nuclear campaign based mainly on direct action, but has since lost much of its previous importance. The Bund für Umwelt und Naturschutz Deutschland (BUND) (the German Federation for the Environment and the Protection of Nature), formed in 1975 as a more traditional lobbying organization, has emerged in the 1980s as perhaps the leading national environmental pressure group. In terms of members, the BUND with 200,000 members was overtaken by Greenpeace whose membership rose rapidly in the late 1980s to reach more than half a million in 1991. The German environmental movement is clearly more decentralized than, say, the British movement, with a wide range of local groups.

Environmental groups have reached the highest membership figures—proportional to the national population—in the Netherlands, where up to one in five citizens claims to be a member of an environmental group. Greenpeace has 830,000 members, the main nature conservation group 580,000, and the WWF 328,000. There is a wide range of activist groups that do not match the former groups in terms of membership but often are closely involved in decision-making processes. In Belgium, mass mobilization for environmental groups has not reached the levels of its Northern neighbor, although continually high support for ecology parties is indicative of a high level of environmental concern. Greenpeace Belgium manages "only" 65,000 members. The United Kingdom has a range of quite old conservation groups that are very active and have made special efforts to increase their membership base: the National Trust (2,152,072 members) and the Royal Society for the Protection of Birds (850,000) are the most successful ones in that respect. Greenpeace (380,000) and Friends of the Earth (200,000) also increased their membership dramatically in the 1980s. British groups are often more moderate and pragmatic than their continental counterparts, aiming to lobby vigorously for individual environmental concerns while remaining strictly non-political.

In Southern Europe France has seen a wide variety of national and local environmental groups springing into action in the early 1970s. After playing a forerunner role within Europe French environmentalists found their highly centralized political system extremely difficult to penetrate. While the main national conservation organization claims 850,000 members, the new groups have found it extremely difficult to build up a mass membership in a political culture where Anglo-American-type public interest groups have little role to play and syndicalist traditions with preference for spontaneous action and, if necessary, violent confrontation of state authority are still important. Friends of the Earth has 6,000 members, Greenpeace 35,000, and the WWF 30,000. In Italy the WWF played a front-runner role since the formation of its branch in 1966, and the WWF thus benefited by becoming the country's largest environmental organization with 300,000 members. Other Italian groups have considerably fewer members, with the League for the Environment at the top of the new groups with 90,000. Spain, Portugal, and Greece have no large environmental groups to match, with the top membership groups in these countries having no more than 6,000 (Portugal) to 26,400 (Spain) members.

Overall these membership figures give an indication of the relative strength of environmental concern in different countries. They also demonstrate the important transformation of environmental groups, with the increasing importance of elite groups supported by a mass membership that provides ample funds for political campaigning but usually is not otherwise involved in the decision-making process. Many environmental groups have, in fact, become fairly large bureaucracies run by professional staff, with the relationship between staff/activists and supporters being managed as a "marketing" exercise. While the internal structure of some of these groups, in particular Greenpeace, has been the subject of some criticism by other environmentalists, there is at present little sign in Europe for a return to the movement-style, activist campaigning that was typical of the 1970s.

Earth First! (EF!)-type actions have remained rare, and the EF! groups set up in Europe in the early 1990s have remained marginal. More radical ecologists have often found their way into green parties, but here also a process of professionalization and a turn toward greater pragmatism has taken place. There is certainly a danger that the large new environmental groups may become detached from grass-roots environmental concerns. The globalization of environmental action, with the increased participation of environmental groups at the international level, has arguably further removed these groups from the environmental concerns of ordinary people. But just as these groups themselves were formed in response to the unwillingness of the then established environmental groups to address new environmental issues adequately, it is only through the emergence of a new generation of distinctive environmental issues that one could expect renewed, grass-roots-based environmental activism.

Wolfgang Rüdig

Further Readings

Dalton, Russell J. *The Green Rainbow: Environmental Groups in Western Europe.* 1994.

Hey, Christian, Frank C. Lasch, and Juan Gärtner. *Directory of Environmental Organisations in the EC.* Freiburg, Germany: EURES, 1992.

Jamison, Andrew, Ron Eyerman, and Jacqueline Cramer. *The Making of the New Environmental Consciousness: A Comparative Study of the Environmental Movements in Sweden, Denmark and the Netherlands.* 1990.

McCormick, J. *Reclaiming Paradise: The Global Environmental Movement.* 1989.

Rüdig, Wolfgang. *Anti-Nuclear Movements: A World Survey of Protest against Nuclear Energy.* 1990.

See also ACID PRECIPITATION: AQUATIC IMPACTS; ACID PRECIPITATION: EUROPEAN EXPERIENCES; CHERNOBYL; EARTH FIRST!; *Ecologist*; ENVIRONMENTAL MOVEMENTS: LESS-AFFLUENT NATIONS; ENVIRONMENTALISM; FRIENDS OF THE EARTH; GREENPEACE; *Limits to Growth*; NUCLEAR ELECTRIC POWER; RADICAL ENVIRONMENTALISM; WORLD WILDLIFE FUND

E

Environmental History

Nearly every academic discipline has been altered in some way, often urged to innovative research subjects and insights, by the emergence of environmentalism. Each of these altered disciplines has participated in turn in the growth and development of environmentalism as an evolving view of the world. But perhaps no discipline or sub-discipline has offered so great a burst of creative energy to contemporary intellectual life as has environmental history. The sub-discipline of environmental history is itself multifaceted. Environmental history assesses the history of the conservation and environmental movements, the emergence and history of the environmental sciences, the history of human valuation and appreciation of nature, the history of environmental policy formation, and the history of nature itself—especially as non-human nature has been altered by human actions as in agricultural and settlement practices, energy and resource extraction and use, introduction of exotic species, hunting, polluting, and imposing upon the habitat of other species.

It is impossible to identify all the central figures in the development of environmental history in so short an article but we can mention some—most particularly Clarence J. Glacken, Samuel P. Hays, Roderick Nash, and Donald Worster. Other important scholars in the field (within a North American context) include: Michael P. Cohen, Alfred W. Crosby, Thomas R. Dunlap, J. Donald Hughes, Martin Melosi, Carolyn Merchant, Alfred Runte, and Susan Schrepfer.

Needless to say any such list leaves out many, including some others who have contributed to this volume. Perhaps the best way to get a solid sense of the more recent evolution of this emerging subject of study is to review the issues of the journal *Environmental History Review*. This excellent journal is published by the American Society for Environmental History. It began in 1976 as *Environmental Review*, incorporated the *Environmental History Newsletter* in 1983, and made the change to its present name in 1989. It has been self-characterized as: an international journal that seeks understanding of the human experience of the environment with emphasis placed on the perspectives of history and the liberal arts and sciences.

The overall objectives of environmental history were nicely captured in 1987 by Donald Worster in the then-titled *Environmental Review* (11 [Winter 1987]: 251): "Some years back the main struggle in environmental history was to establish the grand idea that our primary subject is the interaction of whole societies with the entirety of their natural surroundings. We are not concerned merely with the history of literary reactions to nature or of conservation policies, as important as those are. We are, in the largest sense, interested in all the ways people organize themselves into patterns of power, production, and ideology in the presence of what we conventionally call nature—the nonhuman world. Our goal is to discover, through the study of the past, some general ideas about how to make those patterns work better in the future for both ourselves and the rest of the world."

Robert Paehlke

Further Readings

Glacken, Clarence J. *Traces on the Rhodian Shore: Nature and Culture in Western Thought from Ancient Times to the End of the Eighteenth Century.* 1967.

Hays, Samuel P. *Conservation and the Gospel of Efficiency: The Progressive Conservation Movement, 1890–1920.* 1959.

Nash, Roderick. *Wilderness and the American Mind.* 1967.

Worster, Donald. *Nature's Economy: The Roots of Ecology.* 1977.

See also CONSERVATION BIOLOGY; ENVIRONMENTAL ETHICS; EPIDEMIOLOGY; INTERDISCIPLINARITY; TOXICOLOGY

Environmental Impact Assessment

"Environmental assessment" and "environmental appraisal" are common synonyms for environmental impact assessment (EIA), a widely prescribed set of information gathering, analysis, and synthesis activities that originated with the "action forcing" provisions of the U.S. National Environmental Policy Act of 1969 (NEPA). Formal environmental impact assessment is clearly one of the major innovations in policy and decision making in the twentieth century.

Since 1970 environmental impact assessment systems have been adopted independently by both industrialized and less developed nations worldwide, by numerous provincial and local governments, and by multilateral international organizations such as the World Bank and the European Union. EIA has now begun to be incorporated into international law, for example in the Convention on Environmental

Impact Assessment in a Transboundary Context and in an annex to the Antarctica Protocol. EIA is also becoming a routine business practice in some sectors, for example, commercial lending.

The idea of trying to determine and evaluate possible effects before committing to final design or action is an idea older and broader than EIA, of course. Numerous environmental assessment techniques and methodologies predate NEPA. For instance, the U.S. Army Corps of Engineers developed impact assessment techniques as early as 1870. Inspired by EIA, other impact assessment approaches have also been developed, of which social impact assessment (SIA) and risk assessment are the best known and most widely institutionalized. Proposals for new impact assessment systems are now commonplace. But modern EIA as established by NEPA is distinguishable from these other and earlier activities in several respects: (1) by linking assessment with substantive policy goals; (2) by emphasizing the modern concept of "environment"; (3) by conditioning action on the prior completion of EIA; and (4) by formally requiring systematic compilation of assessment results (in a formal document often called an environmental impact statement, or EIS).

EIA systems vary widely in their effectiveness; many produce only symbolic or perfunctory assessment. Despite the considerable potential of EIA to force the transformation of policy institutions and processes so as to make policy more integrative, more comprehensive, more interdisciplinary, more science-based, and more directed toward the cultivation of environmental values and the institutionalization of ecological rationality, this potential has seldom if ever been fully realized. In the United States, the policy effectiveness of EIA under NEPA has always been greatly constrained by limited executive guidance and by slow progress in integrating it with government policy, planning, and decision processes. Few other governments or organizations establishing EIA systems in the 1970s and 1980s were willing to impose requirements as demanding as those of NEPA. Experience with EIA expanded rapidly but unequally in the 1970s and early 1980s, such that the United States dominated both EIA policy innovation and the generation of detailed analyses of procedural and political issues. But in recent years the experiences of other countries such as Canada and the Netherlands have had a greater impact on thinking about EIA. In the 1990s new, comprehensive, and potentially far reaching systems have been adopted in several

nations, notably Canada and New Zealand, and have been established by international organizations, for example the Organisation for Economic Co-operation and Development (OECD), the United Nations Environment Programme (UNEP), and the Antarctic Treaty Consultative Parties.

Much of the early EIA literature focused on methodological and legal issues. Many conceptual innovations in EIA methodology were made in the 1970s and were reflected in the regulations for implementing NEPA issued by the U.S. Council on Environmental Quality in 1978. In the 1970s EISs were the subject of much litigation in the United States as opponents of proposed agency actions contested the adequacy of impact statements. In the 1980s litigation over EISs greatly declined in frequency and methodological work became more specialized and shifted away from the production of new handbooks, checklists, and matrices. Attention in the United States and elsewhere has focused increasingly on the effectiveness of EIA in the policy system.

Nevertheless EIA as a policy strategy remains poorly understood and understudied. Most analyses of EIA have characterized it as entailing a fairly simple set of mechanisms with narrow objectives, only one or two modes of policy influence, and a limited number of policy effects. EIA is most often interpreted in terms of a rational information model, a view of decision and policy making that makes EIA information gathering and processing an activity antecedent to actual decisions. In this view the purpose of EIA is merely to provide more and better information on possible impacts. The effect of this provision of information on policy is assumed to be automatic and entirely beneficial.

EIA can also be understood as aimed at influencing policy by affecting the ways that political forces external to an organization can influence that organization (e.g., interagency coordination, public participation, or judicial review). Or EIA can be interpreted in terms of its effects on relationships internal to an organization (e.g., procedures, hiring practices, training, formal structures, or informal networks). Finally, EIA can be understood in terms of the potential it has for affecting policy through the development of values, the construction and elaboration of meaning, forced learning, political discourse, and the evolution of social norms—in short, the institutionalization of ecological rationality. Thus, any meaningful evaluation of a given EIA system must be a conceptually rich one that relies on multiple perspectives and criteria.

Recent studies have begun to identify several principles for effective EIA systems: (1) there must be a formal, legal, enforceable mandate for EIA; (2) there must be clear and automatic application of all requirements; (3) EIA must be linked with strong policies, goals, responsibilities, or rights; (4) there must be more than one type of mechanism to hold authorities to account for using EIA in decision making; (5) the process must be participative and open to external review; and (6) provisions must exist for monitoring and compliance enforcement.

Robert V. Bartlett

Further Readings

Bartlett, Robert V., ed. *Policy Through Impact Assessment: Institutionalized Analysis as a Policy Strategy.* 1989.

————, and Charles R. Malone, eds. "Guidance for Environmental Impact Assessment" (Special Issue) *The Environmental Professional* 15 (1) (1993).

Wathern, Peter, ed. *Environmental Impact Assessment: Theory and Practice.* 1988.

See also ENVIRONMENTAL ASSESSMENT (CANADA); NATIONAL ENVIRONMENTAL POLICY ACT (U.S.); RISK ANALYSIS; ARMY CORPS OF ENGINEERS (U.S.)

Environment Impact Assessment (Canada)

See ENVIRONMENTAL ASSESSMENT (CANADA)

Environmental Justice Movement

Numerous studies dating back to the early 1970s document that lower-income persons, working-class individuals, and people of color are exposed to elevated health risks in their homes, in their communities, and on their jobs. People of color have borne greater health and environmental risk burdens than the society at large. This is the case even when income is held constant. For example, race has been found to be independent of class in the distribution of air pollution, contaminated fish consumption, location of municipal landfills and incinerators, abandoned toxic waste dumps, cleanup of Superfund sites, and lead poisoning in children.

Governments have been slow to address environmental justice and equity questions of who gets what, why, and how much, who can afford help and who cannot, why some communities are poisoned and others escape, and why some populations are studied while others get left off the research agenda. Today, disenfranchised communities are calling for greater input into shaping environmental priorities that were in the past left to a small homogeneous group of scientists, health professionals, government bureaucrats, and environmentalists.

Environmental Justice Comes of Age

The impetus for getting environmental justice concerns on the national agenda has *not* come from regulatory agencies or the national environmental groups. The impetus has come from the environmental justice movement. This movement is comprised of a loose alliance of grass-roots and national environmental activists, civil rights and social justice leaders, and academicians who question the foundation of the current environmental protection paradigm.

Several important events in the early 1990s brought environmental justice concerns into the national public policy debate. They include:

- The dialogue initiated in 1990 among social scientists, social justice leaders, national environmental groups, the federal EPA, and Agency for Toxic Substances and Disease Registry (ATSDR) around disparate impact and environmental equity;
- The January 1990 letters from Gulf Coast Tenants Organization, Southwest Organizing Project, Commission for Racial Justice, Southern Organizing Committee for Economic and Social Justice, and several dozen other grass-roots environmental justice groups to the "Big Ten" environmental groups challenging them to end their racism and elitism, whether intended or unintended;
- Letters from the "Michigan Coalition" in 1991 prompting the federal EPA to form a Work Group on Environmental Equity. The agency later created an Office of Environmental Equity, an Environmental Equity Cluster (coordinated by an assistant administrator for enforcement), issued an *Environmental Equity* report in 1992, and agreed to meet with environmental justice leaders on a quarterly basis;

- ATSDR's establishment of a minority health initiative (after some prodding from environmental, health, and social justice advocates). ATSDR also held a Minority Environmental Health Conference in 1991 and initiated a health study of communities of color found near National Priority List (NPL) hazardous waste sites;
- The 1991 First National People of Color Environmental Leadership Summit held in Washington, D.C. The Summit was attended by over 650 delegates from all fifty states (including Alaska and Hawaii), Puerto Rico, Mexico, Canada, and as far away as the Marshall Islands. This Summit galvanized grass-roots and national support for strategies to combat environmental racism;
- The 1992 EPA/ATSDR/NIEHS (National Institute for Environmental Health Sciences) jointly-sponsored "Equity in Environmental Health: Research Issues and Needs" Workshop in Research Triangle, North Carolina;
- The "Environmental Justice Act of 1992" introduced into Congress by Congressman John Lewis (D-Georgia) and Senator Albert Gore (D-Tennessee). The Act was redrafted and reintroduced in 1993 by Congressman John Lewis (D-Georgia) and Senator Max Baucus (D-Montana); and
- Appointment of the long-time environmental justice leader Dr. Benjamin F. Chavis, Jr. to head the NAACP, the nation's oldest civil rights organization.

Environmental justice concerns have even permeated the White House. In June 1993, for example, the EPA began drafting a presidential "Executive Order on Environmental Justice" for implementing Title VI of the 1964 Civil Rights Act—a provision that outlaws discrimination in the use of federal funds. The draft Executive Order on Environmental Justice calls for an Interagency Task Force to set guidance for social and economic impact reports under the National Environmental Policy Act (NEPA) and Clean Air Act (CAA), equal protection and enforcement under Title VI of the Civil Rights Act, and data collection and analysis on disparate risks and health effects.

Environmental justice concerns also are being voiced and actions initiated at the state level. States have begun to recognize the prob-

lem and enact legislation to address unequal protection. Arkansas and Louisiana were the first two states to pass environmental justice/equity laws. Virginia passed a legislative resolution on environmental justice. Several other states—including California, Georgia, New York, North Carolina, and South Carolina—have pending legislation to address environmental injustices. Texas set up a statewide task force to study environmental racism and disparate impact of its regulations on low-income and people of color communities.

Environmental justice leaders are now challenging those policies and practices that force individuals, workers, and community residents to accept risks others can avoid by "voting with their feet." In 1992 the Southern Organizing Committee for Economic and Social Justice held a labor/environment conference in New Orleans that was attended by over 2,500 grass-roots activists. Participants at this conference demanded that the problems of pesticides and farm workers, workers in sweat shops (mostly women and immigrants in the garment industry, computer assembly operations, poultry and catfish processing plants, and other dangerous occupations), and lead poisoning of inner-city children be elevated to the national environmental action agenda.

There are other signs that a "new" environmental movement is alive and well in the United States. Grass-roots groups are making their voices heard in Congress, the state houses, and city hall. They are speaking and doing for themselves. Some grass-roots groups (i.e., Southwest Organizing Project, Gulf Coast Tenants Organization, Mothers of East Los Angeles, West Harlem Environmental Action, Concerned Citizens of South Central Los Angeles, People for Community Recovery, etc.) have begun to form working relationships with national environmental groups (i.e., Citizens Clearinghouse for Hazardous Waste, Greenpeace, Natural Resources Defense Council, Sierra Club, Environmental Defense Fund, National Wildlife Federation, National Audubon Society, etc.), and civil rights and civil libertarian organizations (i.e., National Association for the Advancement of Colored People (NAACP), NAACP Legal Defense and Education Fund, Lawyers' Committee for Civil Rights Under Law, American Civil Liberties Union (ACLU), Center for Constitutional Rights, etc.).

In 1991 a coalition of environmental, social justice, and civil libertarian groups joined forces to address a childhood lead-screening

E

problem. The Natural Resources Defense Council (NRDC), NAACP Legal Defense and Education Fund, ACLU, and Legal Aid of Alameda County filed a lawsuit against the State of California for not living up to the federally mandated testing for lead of some 557,000 poor children who receive Medicaid. The coalition won an out-of-court settlement in the *Matthews v. Coye* lawsuit worth an estimated $15–20 million for a blood-lead testing program.

A groundswell of grass-roots organizing is taking place on a host of issues. Environmental justice has become a major organizing theme for mobilizing grass-roots support. More than 200 environmental justice groups were profiled in the *People of Color Environmental Groups Directory* (1992). The groups came from thirty-five states, the District of Columbia, Puerto Rico, and Quebec. These and other grass-roots environmental justice groups represent the fastest growing segment of the environmental movement. There can be no doubt that environmental activism is not the sole domain of white middle-class communities.

Environmental justice activists have not limited their attention just to toxics. The same principles of environmental justice—as adopted at the First National People of Color Environmental Leadership Summit—that challenge ecological destruction and health threats in Love Canal, Three Mile Island, and Times Beach also apply in Triana (Alabama), West Dallas and Texarkana (Texas), in Appalachia, on Native American reservations, and in our urban ghettos and barrios. Environmental justice does not stop at the U.S. borders. Because of the ethical, economic, and environmental dilemmas posed by the North American Free Trade Agreement (NAFTA), many grass-roots environmental justice leaders actively opposed this agreement.

Grass-roots groups are demanding an end to unequal protection and environmental injustices. Many of the grass-roots environmental justice groups may not have environment in their name, but they have redefined environmentalism. Whether they are the Cree in James Bay, the Sioux on the Rosebud, Latinos in the Central Valley of California, African Americans in West Harlem and the Southside of Chicago, or Asian American garment workers in Los Angeles—all are calling for a new environmental protection paradigm—one that has prevention as the overarching goal.

The current environmental protection paradigm manages, regulates, and distributes risks. In combination with systemic racism, and a general class bias, the current system: 1) institutionalizes unequal enforcement; 2) trades human health for profit; 3) places the burden of proof on the "victims" and not the polluting industry; 4) legitimates human exposure to harmful chemicals, pesticides, and hazardous substances; 5) promotes "risky" technologies; 6) exploits the vulnerability of economically and politically disenfranchised communities; 7) subsidizes ecological destruction; 8) creates an industry around risk assessment; 9) delays cleanup actions; and 10) fails to develop pollution prevention as the dominant strategy.

Environmental Racism and Radioactive Colonialism

Many of the nation's environmental, energy, and military policies distribute costs in a regressive pattern while providing disproportionate benefits for whites and individuals who fall at the upper end of the education and income scale. People of color and the poor have a vested interest in seeing that this nation's environmental and energy policies are just and fair.

Environmental racism is real. It is just as real as the racism found in the housing industry, educational institutions, employment arena, and judicial system. The term of "environmental racism" refers to any policy, practice, or directive that differentially affects or disadvantages (whether intentionally or unintentionally) individuals, groups, or communities based on race or color. Environmental racism is reinforced by government, legal, economic, political, and military institutions. Environmental racism combines with public policies and industry practices to provide benefits for whites while shifting costs to people of color.

Few people would dispute the fact that gasoline taxes are regressive and fall heaviest on the poor. People of color are disproportionately over-represented among the poor. The need for a just and fair energy policy was recently played out in Desert Storm. This "war for oil" fell heaviest on the poor, working class, and people of color who make up a disproportionately large share of America's all-volunteer armed forces. The costs and benefits of defending regressive energy and destructive policies are not equally distributed throughout society.

Similarly the practice of "radioactive colonialism" raises some special ethical and justice questions. Native American reservations are quasi-sovereign nations. Native lands are not subject to federal or state environmental regulations. As a result, more than three dozen reservations have been targeted for landfills, incinerators, and other waste disposal facilities. The vast majority of these proposals have been defeated by grass-roots groups on the reservations.

Of the twenty-one applicants for the U.S. Department of Energy (DOE) Monitored Retrievable Storage (MRS) grants, sixteen were Indian tribes. Sixteen tribes lined up for the $100,000 grants from DOE to study the prospect of "temporarily" storing nuclear waste for a half century under its MRS program.

Delegates at the Third Annual Indigenous Environmental Council Networking Gathering (held in Oregon on June 6, 1992) adopted a resolution of "No nuclear waste on Indian Lands." Northwest tribes living along the Columbia River—downstream from DOE's Hanford Nuclear Reservation—have experienced the negative side-effects of nuclear waste that have caused mutations in the salmon they depend on spiritually, culturally, and economically.

A Model Environmental Justice Framework

The question of environmental justice is not anchored in a debate about whether or not decision makers should tinker with risk management. The environmental justice framework rests on an ethical analysis of strategies to eliminate unfair, unjust, and inequitable conditions and decisions. The framework seeks to prevent environmental threats before they occur.

The environmental justice framework attempts to uncover the underlying assumptions that may contribute to and produce unequal protection. This framework brings to the surface the ethical and political questions of "who gets what, why, and how much." The framework includes the following five general characteristics:

1. The environmental justice framework incorporates the principle of the "right" of all individuals to be protected from environmental degradation.
2. The environmental justice framework adopts a public health model of prevention (elimination of the threat before harm occurs) as the preferred strategy.
3. The environmental justice framework shifts the burden of proof to polluters/dischargers who do harm, discriminate, or who do not give equal protection to

racial and ethnic minorities and other "protected" classes.
4. The environmental justice framework would allow disparate impact and statistical weight, as opposed to "intent," to infer discrimination.
5. The environmental justice framework redresses disproportionate impact through "targeted" action and resources.

Conclusion

The solution to unequal protection and unjust policies lies in the realm of environmental justice for all. No community, rich or poor, urban, suburban, or rural, black or white should be allowed to become a "sacrifice zone." The lessons from the American civil rights struggles around housing, employment, education, and public accommodations over the past four decades suggest that environmental justice will need to have a legislative foundation. It is not enough to demonstrate the existence of unjust and unfair conditions; the practices that caused the conditions must be made illegal—and ultimately eliminated.

How can environmental justice be incorporated into decision making? First, the environmental justice framework demands that the current laws be enforced in a nondiscriminatory way. Second, a legislative initiative is needed. Unequal protection needs to be attacked via federal legislation that moves protection from a "privilege" to a "right." Third, legislative initiatives will also need to come from states. Since many of the decisions and problems lie with state actions, states will need to model their legislative initiatives (or develop stronger initiatives) after the federal legislation.

Robert D. Bullard

Further Readings

Bryant, Bunyan, and Paul Mohai. *Race and the Incidence of Environmental Hazards.* 1992.

Bullard, Robert D. *Dumping in Dixie: Race, Class and Environmental Quality.* 1990.

———. *Confronting Environmental Racism: Voices from the Grassroots.* 1993.

———. *Unequal Protection: Environmental Justice and Communities of Color.* 1994.

Hofrichter, Richard. *Toxic Struggles: The Theory and Practice of Environmental Justice.* 1993.

See also BERGER INQUIRY; HAZARDOUS WASTE TREATMENT FACILITY SITING; JOBS

AND THE ENVIRONMENT; LABOR AND THE
ENVIRONMENT; RIGHT-TO-KNOW: COMMU-
NITY (U.S.); RIGHT-TO-KNOW: WORKPLACE
(U.S.); SUPERFUND

Environmental Mediation
See ALTERNATIVE DISPUTE RESOLUTION

Environmental Movements:
Less-Affluent Nations

The emergence and proliferation of grass-
roots environmental movements in less-affluent countries has been a striking feature of the
late twentieth century. It is now possible to
begin to identify commonalities in the social
contexts producing these movements, similar
characteristics in these movements themselves, and patterns to the resulting social
conflicts these movements engender. (The following generalizations, of course, do not apply in all cases.)

Few environmental movements in less-affluent countries have their primary origins in
ecological concerns or focus exclusively on environmental issues. Most commonly such
groups have their genesis in the survival efforts
of persons and communities living at the margins of existence, especially peasants and indigenous peoples in rural areas. Grass-roots environmental movements often begin with efforts
promoting community development, literacy,
and political empowerment. Such goals often
lead to battles over who owns and/or controls
the use of land.

These battles take one of two forms, involving either struggles to overturn current
ownership patterns and to reform current land
uses, or efforts to preserve traditional land
ownership and use patterns against the encroachment of the industrialized world. The
crucial issue is land reform or land defense.
Struggles over land shape popular movements
into environmental movements because, generally speaking, the land-use plans of poor people
living in the specific sites of their activism are
more ecologically sustainable than the more
centralized ownership and mechanized land-use
patterns they are trying to overturn or prevent.

Much commercial enterprise in rural areas
displaces long-term inhabitants, or threatens to
do so. Another form of displacement is the division of families when fathers and sons leave
to seek employment elsewhere after their traditional livelihoods are destroyed by changing

land-use patterns. The fear of displacement is a
crucial wellspring of environmental resistance.

Displacement fears aside, commercial development threatens traditional ways of life and
means of subsistence. The process usually begins with road building, followed by logging,
mining, and industrialized agriculture (ranching
and farming). Accompanying this process is the
increasingly centralized ownership of land by
outsiders (often preceded by the enclosure and
seizure of land previously held and managed as
a commons). Such threats contribute to the proliferation of grass-roots movements stressing
self-reliance, resistance to outside commercial
interests, and the pursuit of ecologically sustainable practices.

Grass-roots environmental groups in less-
affluent nations are, generally speaking, radical
in their genesis, or tend toward radicalism
through the experience of social struggle. First,
these movements often threaten private ownership of property, seeking to prevent private
ownership of commonly used lands or to overturn current private land ownership patterns.
Many are self-consciously socialist in orientation. Second, these movements increasingly critique industrial development and mechanized
agriculture, thereby placing themselves in opposition to elites who usually hope to emulate the
more technologically "advanced" societies.
Movements influenced by such a critique seek
to prevent or overturn industrial models of development. Third, radicalism is also found in
the increasingly militant tactics that many of
these groups employ, including illegal actions,
from civil disobedience to sabotage. Such resistance has even, although rarely, included homi-
cide justified as self-defense.

Not surprisingly, such radicalism is often
met by violence, sometimes governmental, often private, and seldom prosecuted. (See, for
example, Human Rights Watch and the Natural Resources Defense Council.) Such reactionary violence far outpaces in scope and brutality the more occasional, poorly armed, and
usually defensive violence of those involved in
grass-roots environmental movements. The efforts of such environmental groups to institute
land reform (or to retain possession of ancestral
lands) helps explain the brutality of the violent
response.

Obviously the above patterns suggest that
these environmental movements operate under
difficult circumstances. It is important to note
therefore two key forces driving and buttress-
ing these movements. First, women play impor-

tant and often decisive roles. This is remarkable given the traditional subjugation of women in most of these countries. Second, movement participants increasingly justify their activism with moral rationales other than self-interest. Such rationales are often based on religious sentiments, but this is often overlooked. Moreover, these movements usually rely exclusively on nonviolent tactics, for either pragmatic and/or moral and spiritual reasons.

The survival of movement participants and the prospects for their campaigns are enhanced through coalition building. Often, previously antagonistic local groups are brought together in a common cause against the perceived "outside" interests. Increasingly important is the solidarity sought from international environmental groups that apply political pressure on national governments and organize boycotts against corporations that extract resources in ways which threaten people and their environments. Such alliances are fragile, however. Activists from affluent countries are often perceived to be arrogant and uninterested in the perspectives of those on the front-lines of these struggles.

Grass-roots environmental movements have had successes, usually small-scale, but sometimes shaking the corridors of power in the international business, finance, and political sectors. For example, grass-roots efforts have secured changes in the lending practices of some international lending agencies, and have derailed or forced the downsizing of several large-scale "development" projects. Some groups have become famous—such as India's Chipko movement, the Kenyan Green Belt movement, Sahabat Alam Malaysia, and Brazil's rubber tappers—celebrated for their courage and sometimes their successes by the international environmental community. The number of grass-roots environmental groups is growing so rapidly that it is impossible to keep track of them all. The Rainforest Action Network's *Southeast Asia Rainforests: A Resource Guide and Directory* (1993), for example, catalogues over 125 such groups in nine Southeast Asian countries alone.

Despite the proliferation of such groups and some notable successes, the ecological and social context that gave rise to them remains so grave, the economic interests so intransigent, and the need for a comprehensive restructuring of political, social, economic and ecological relations so fundamental, that it appears naive to anticipate enduring successes, or even to

hope for the long-term survival of the peoples and the places at stake in these struggles.

Bron R. Taylor

Further Readings

Human Rights Watch and the Natural Resources Defense Council. *Defending the Earth: Abuses of Human Rights and the Environment.* 1992.

Pearce, Fred. *Green Warriors: The People and Politics behind the Environmental Revolution.* 1991.

Taylor, Bron R., ed. *Ecological Resistance Movements: The Global Emergence of Radical and Popular Environmentalism.* 1995.

See also CHIPKO MOVEMENT; SUSTAINABLE DEVELOPMENT; TROPICAL DEFORESTATION

Environmental Policy Institute

The Environmental Policy Institute (EPI) dates to 1972 when several Washington staff members for Friends of the Earth (FOE) split away to form the Environmental Policy Center as an environmental lobby. EPI itself was established separately by these individuals in 1974 as a tax-deductible research and educational organization, with seed money coming from the entertainer Arthur Godfrey. EPI's first director, Joe Browder, served until 1977; Louise Dunlap, another founding member, served as president until 1986. She was succeeded by the current president, Michael S. Clark.

EPI's history is one of mergers driven by financial and strategic needs. In 1982 EPI merged formally with the Environmental Policy Center (EPC). In 1989 it merged with FOE and the Oceanic Society to create an organization with a primary focus on global ecological issues. Before this merger EPI had a small Washington-based research staff and a foundation grant-driven budget of about $1.5 million. The merger gave EPI/FOE a far-flung staff of over forty, a 1990 budget of over $3 million, and a membership base of about 50,000. In the new organization FOE would be the non-tax deductible advocacy wing, with EPI and the Oceanic Society retaining their more research and educational roles.

The EPI traditionally acted to disseminate information to grass-roots groups, the media, and to policy-makers, with its EPC arm acting as a lobby. It traditionally concerned itself with opposing nuclear power and fighting the proliferation of nuclear weapons, seeking corporate compliance with federal strip-mining regulations and, during the 1980s, promoting greater citizen knowledge about chemical plant production and emissions. Other domestic policy concerns have been water use and pollution, the use of agricultural chemicals, and the potential side-effects from biotechnology. The combined EPI/FOE aims to develop these concerns with a more global focus, while also expanding into such issues as ozone depletion and rainforest depletion.

Christopher J. Bosso (with Chris Pierpan)

Further Readings

Dunlap, Riley E., and Angela G. Mertig, eds. *American Environmentalism: The U.S. Environmental Movement, 1970–1990.* 1992.
Wenner, Lettie M. *U.S. Energy and Environmental Interest Groups.* 1990.

See also ENVIRONMENTALISM; FRIENDS OF THE EARTH; MINING AND SMELTING: HISTORIC IMPACTS; NUCLEAR ELECTRIC POWER; OZONE DEPLETION; TROPICAL RAINFORESTS

Environmental Protection Agency

The Environmental Protection Agency (EPA) is the principal U.S. agency responsible for regulation of pollution hazards, including air emissions and wastewater discharges, solid and hazardous waste disposal, pesticides, and toxic chemicals. It shares with other agencies responsibility for several other environmental hazards, including radiation and loss of wetlands. In addition to its regulatory mandates, the EPA administers two major financial grant programs: construction grants to local governments for public wastewater treatment facilities, and grants under the "Superfund" program for cleanup of abandoned hazardous waste sites.

Despite its name the EPA has no single overall statutory authority for environmental protection. Rather, it administers a series of specific and complex statutes addressed to particular environmental problems: the Clean Air Act, Clean Water Act, Federal Environmental Pesticides Control Act, Toxic Substances Control Act, Safe Drinking Water Act, Resources Conservation and Recovery Act (solid and hazardous wastes), Comprehensive Environmental Response, Compensation, and Liability Act ("Superfund"), major amendments and re-authorizations of these laws, and numerous oth-

ers. These statutes were enacted at different times, established different criteria and often different procedures for setting standards, and each added to the cumulative body of statutes and regulations without synthesizing or simplifying them. Taken as a whole, they represent an unprecedented expansion of federal regulatory authority for protection of the environment and public health. Their nominally vast scope is severely constrained, however, by the proliferation of accountability mechanisms to Congress, to the executive office of the president, to the courts, and to interested political constituencies directly for each proposed regulation. Examples include statutory deadlines, "hammer" clauses (which specify automatic consequences if deadlines are not met), oversight hearings, executive office review and documentation requirements ("regulatory impact assessments"), liberal access to judicial review for interested parties, and judicial precedents enlarging the agency's burden of proof (such as the "hard look" doctrine). Beginning in the 1980s the EPA advocated the use of negotiated rulemaking to reduce the costs and delays inherent in traditional adversarial rulemaking and oversight processes.

The EPA's statutory responsibilities are implemented by nine assistant administrators in Washington and ten regional offices. Four of the nine headquarters units are defined by statutory program domains: air, water, solid wastes and emergency response, and pesticides and toxic substances. Administrative functions define the other five: research and development, enforcement, administration, international activities, and policy, planning and evaluation. Within each assistant administrator's jurisdiction are offices responsible for particular programs, with directors who bear primary responsibility for the substance of regulations. Each office in turn is subdivided into divisions and branches responsible for more specific sub-programs and functions. Each of the EPA's ten regional offices is responsible for working with the states in its region to implement EPA's statutes and regulations. A major element of the EPA's work is in fact intergovernmental relations, since many of its regulatory mandates are delegated to state and local governments for implementation and others require compliance by state and local governments themselves (for instance the operation of public water supply, wastewater treatment, and solid waste disposal facilities).

The EPA's programs have been reasonably successful in helping to reduce major sources of air and water pollution, but far less so in attempting substance-by-substance regulation of pesticides, drinking water contaminants, toxic chemicals generally, and hazards associated with widespread patterns of individual and business activity. Since the mid-1980s and before, therefore, the EPA has promoted policy incentives other than technology-based standards—such as marketable permits for production or emissions of pollutants, reporting requirements for annual emissions of toxic pollutants, and voluntary programs for reduction of the industrial use of toxics and substitution of low-energy lighting—for more cost-effective achievement of its statutory goals. With support from some leading industries, it has also advocated pollution prevention initiatives and life-cycle analysis as both economically and environmentally superior to traditional waste treatment and disposal practices. Most of these initiatives, however, remain voluntary complements rather than substitutes for the EPA's traditional regulatory requirements.

Since the mid-1980s successive EPA administrators have also sought to strengthen the agency's capability for overall management and priority-setting, both within and across its programs, using the concept of risk-based decision making as a common denominator. Quantitative health-risk assessment has been developed into an elaborate analytical procedure for comparison of health hazards, particularly carcinogens, but the use of comparative risk assessment to set priorities across more diverse types of issues remains more qualitative and judgmental; as of 1994 it too remains an administrative initiative rather than a statutory framework.

The EPA was created in 1970 by a Presidential Reorganization Plan that gathered into one independent regulatory agency a number of existing units and their associated statutory authorities. Two principal motivations for creating it were to integrate environmental regulatory functions across the fragmented and disparate programs that existed at the time, and to better anticipate and thereby forestall new pollution problems. In practice, however, the envisioned integration has never occurred. The urgency of demonstrating success in addressing immediate problems, the reality of diverse conceptual and statutory bases for existing programs, and reluctance to disrupt established procedures led to rapid entrenchment of the existing programs. Despite this fragmentation, the EPA established a bipartisan reputation for generally effective management throughout the 1970s, under administrators William

Ruckelshaus, Russell Train, and Douglas Costle; in the early 1980s however its budget was sharply reduced and its reputation and morale severely damaged by the anti-regulatory policies of the Reagan administration under administrator Anne Burford, who was ultimately forced to resign along with virtually all her senior staff. Under subsequent administrators Ruckelshaus, Lee Thomas, William Reilly, and Carol Browner the EPA's reputation and capability have recovered somewhat, though still not in proportion to the continued growth of its statutory responsibilities. Legislation has been proposed to elevate it to Cabinet status as a Department of the Environment, and numerous experts have urged codifying its responsibilities into a single organic statute, but neither of these possibilities has, as yet, transpired.

Richard N.L. Andrews

Further Readings

"Assessing the Environmental Protection Agency after Twenty Years: Law, Politics, and Economics, A Special Symposium Issue." *Law and Contemporary Problems* 54 (1991).

Bryner, Gary. "The Environmental Protection Agency." In *Bureaucratic Discretion: Law and Policy in Federal Regulatory Agencies*. 1987.

Landy, Marc, M. Roberts, and S. Thomas. *The Environmental Protection Agency: Asking the Wrong Questions*. 1990.

See also AIR POLLUTION: REGULATION (U.S.); BURFORD, ANNE MCGILL; NATIONAL ENVIRONMENTAL POLICY ACT (U.S.); POLLUTION PREVENTION; REAGAN, RONALD; RUCKELSHAUS, WILLIAM D.; SUPERFUND

Environmental Protection in Wartime

Environmental disruption is an inevitable and occasionally dramatic concomitant of war. In many instances this combat-associated disruption of the environment is an incidental outcome of hostile military actions; in other instances it may be an intentional component of the strategy of a belligerent. Societal attitudes or cultural norms do exist that tend to limit such disruptions, whether they be incidental or intentional. Moreover those cultural norms have to a considerable extent been translated into legal norms, formal constraints that have thus found their way into one realm or another of international law. Of particular relevance

E

here are: the law of war or armed conflict, international humanitarian law, and international environmental law. The disparate relevant legal restraints from these realms are outlined below, followed by a presentation of the cultural norms that underpin them.

As to legal norms the human environment has in principle been afforded considerable protection from the depredations of war throughout the twentieth century, at least among the greater or lesser numbers of parties to the various relevant multilateral treaties. During combat belligerents are forbidden to destroy enemy property, unless imperatively demanded by the necessities of war; during an occupation belligerents are forbidden to use enemy property in a destructive (non-usufructuary) fashion. These are important limitations in the present context since "property" encompasses agricultural lands, range (grazing) lands, forest lands, and other major components of the environment. Moreover, certain circumscribed natural sites of outstanding universal value constitute a world heritage, the deliberate damage of which is specifically prohibited. Comparable protection is afforded archeological sites of similarly outstanding universal value.

The environment is in principle spared to some further extent because certain environmentally disruptive methods of warfare are prohibited. These include prohibitions against the use of chemical and biological weapons; certain restrictions on the use of incendiary weapons; certain limitations on the use of land mines; a qualified prohibition against the manipulation of the environment itself for hostile purposes; and, more generally, an admonition not to employ methods of warfare likely to cause widespread, long-lasting, and severe environmental damage. The environment is to a further extent spared in principle by prohibitions on attacking certain protected objects indispensable to the survival of the civilian population. These include drinking water installations, agricultural areas, and irrigation works; with certain limitations, dams or nuclear electrical generating stations that would release dangerous forces; and, as already noted, certain specified natural and archeological sites of great value.

Further sources of environmental protection from wartime disruption include commitments to entirely preclude military actions from certain geographic regions; and to exclude nuclear weapons from certain other regions. More general environmental protection is afforded by commitments to conserve birds and other wildlife that migrate across national boundaries; and to protect the high seas from oil pollution.

As to cultural norms, the adoption, interpretation, and observance of the legal norms just summarized depend upon the societal attitudes that they reflect, both as to overall attitudes regarding acceptable forms of interstate conflict resolution and as to specific attitudes regarding acceptable forms of environmental exploitation and disruption. The continued acceptance of warfare as a means of conflict resolution and the widespread refusal to submit to the compulsory and unconditional jurisdiction of the International Court of Justice at The Hague, are the basic causes of wartime damage to the environment. However, the increasingly widespread and ever heightening concern over the state of the human environment provides a welcome counterforce.

The existing legal norms protective of the environment in time of war, even if accepted by a belligerent, are open to a considerable range of interpretation. They, in turn, derive from the laudable—though even more nebulous—fundamental concept of the law of war that the right of belligerents to choose methods of warfare is not unlimited. They also gain further strength from the emerging basic concept of international environmental law that nations do not have the right to cause environmental damage beyond their own borders. Thus it is crucial to recognize that it is societal attitudes that ultimately determine the level of protection afforded the environment, whether in peacetime or wartime. Indeed the importance of cultural norms in determining military actions is fully realized and firmly embedded in the law of war: those military actions not precisely regulated are to be controlled by the principles of humanity and the dictates of the public conscience.

The evolving dictates of the public conscience are to some extent reflected in the hortatory declarations made by the United Nations, often following lengthy debate and detailed roll-call voting. To that end it is instructive to note the strong support that was given to a number of key pronouncements. Thus in 1972 the United Nations Declaration on the Human Environment proclaimed that states have the responsibility to ensure that activities within their control do not cause damage to the environment beyond their own borders; and, moreover, that humans and their environment must be spared the effects of nuclear weapons and all other means of mass destruction. In

1982 the United Nations World Charter for Nature proclaimed that nature shall be secured against degradation caused by warfare, and, moreover, that areas degraded by human activities shall be rehabilitated. And in 1992 the United Nations Declaration on Environment and Development proclaimed that states shall respect international law providing protection for the environment in times of warfare. Not all such resolutions are as widely endorsed as were those just presented. One that did not fare so well in 1980 proclaimed that states have the responsibility to preserve their own environment for present and future generations, at the same time drawing attention to the pernicious effects of military expenditures on the environment. In short, these aspirational statements, although not of a binding nature, do suggest the emergence and strength of cultural norms; and at the same time they contribute to the progressive development of legal norms.

Arthur H. Westing

Further Readings

Bouvier, Antoine. "Protection of the Natural Environment in Time of Armed Conflict." *International Review of the Red Cross* 31 (1991): 567–78.

Falk, Richard A. "Environmental Disruption by Military Means and International Law." In *Environmental Warfare: A Technical, Legal and Policy Analysis.* Ed. Arthur H. Westing. 1984, 33–51.

Goldblat, Jozef. "Legal Protection of the Environment against the Effects of Military Activities." *Bulletin of Peace Proposals* 22 (1991): 399–406.

Westing, Arthur H., ed. *Cultural Norms, War, and the Environment.* 1988.

———. *Environmental Hazards of War: Releasing Dangerous Forces in an Industrialized World.* 1990.

———. "Protected Natural Areas and the Military." *Environmental Conservation* 19 (1992): 343–48.

See also NATIONAL SECURITY, RECONCEPTUALIZING; NUCLEAR WINTER

Environmental Refugees

The number of displaced persons or refugees, both internal and cross-border, already in the many millions, nonetheless keeps increasing by perhaps three million per year. Many of the uprooted continue to flee for reasons of perse-cution, oppression, and war. However, these triggering events appear not to have been worsening in recent years. Others flee from such natural disasters as flooding, drought, and volcanic action, although these triggering events have also not been increasing in frequency or severity. The continuing increase in refugee numbers appears to result primarily from transgressions of the carrying capacity, that is, of unsustainable increases in human (and associated livestock) numbers, often associated with site degradation. Such displaced persons can be referred to as "environmental refugees."

Both human numbers and human aspirations continue to increase in a world of finite dimensions. There is thus no question that the global environment is coming under increasingly severe threat. Since the assaults on the human environment are particularly severe in the Third World (especially throughout much of Africa) and since the developing countries are ill-equipped to deal with these threats to their sustainable development, it is easy to understand why the number of environmental refugees keeps growing.

In addressing the situations that generate environmental refugees, it is useful for analytical and operational purposes to divide them into three categories: 1) those in which the exodus is triggered by an acute event; 2) those in which it is triggered by a gradually worsening situation; and 3) those in which there is a clash of pre-modern and modern cultures. Although each of these three categories is dealt with separately below, it remains clear that there exists a unifying thread: underlying all of them is a transgression of the carrying capacity of the region in question.

Acute natural disasters such as drought and flooding (and of somewhat less widespread significance, also locust outbreaks, hurricanes, earthquakes, volcanoes, and tsunamis or tidal waves) produce environmental refugees that in large measure derive from inappropriate settlement patterns. Acute anthropogenic disasters such as the release of flood waters from breached dams and the release of noxious substances from industrial mishaps (whether poisonous, virulent, or radioactive) can be operationally included in this category. Areas that are subject to disruption from natural or anthropogenic calamities of the sorts just alluded to should be relegated to some combination of extensive uses, for example, perennial-crop agriculture, forestry, horticulture, range management, nature reserve, and recreation. However, a combination of poverty and over-population in Africa and elsewhere in the Third World has forced ever larger numbers of people to settle in such precarious sites.

The slow degradation of rural areas—agricultural or rangeland—through nutrient losses, soil erosion, or salinization to the point where they cannot support their indigenous population is a problem affecting a large number of people—primarily in poverty-stricken and over-populated countries. It is a situation in which the carrying capacity of an area has been exceeded and some or all of its inhabitants are forced to seek a livelihood elsewhere.

The preemption for modern uses (mechanized agriculture, urbanization, industrialization) of large semi-natural areas inhabited by pre-modern indigenous peoples, dependent upon their traditional means of support (subsistence farming, pastoralism, shifting slash-and-burn agriculture, hunting, and gathering) can cause the indigenous people to become displaced. This is a clash of cultures, driven at least in some instances by the needs of the modern component of a country's population for more land and the resources it yields. Although such preemption represents an extraordinarily complex social issue, the issue once again is not so much a "shortage" of land as a "longage" of people.

Thus, as is suggested by all of these categories, it seems clear that the only long-term approach to ameliorating the dilemma of ever-increasing numbers of environmental refugees with any hope for success would be a multi-faceted attempt to achieve environmental security within the broad context of comprehensive human security. The fundamental aim of such comprehensive human security is to bring into balance human numbers with available natural resources in an equitable fashion.

To date, the international community, acting through the United Nations system, formally recognizes and provides succor to two large categories of refugees: 1) persons forced to flee from their own country in fear of racial, religious, or similar persecution (and, less formally, also those fleeing from armed conflict); and 2) Palestinians residing in certain parts of the Middle East in the absence of or, now, displacement from a homeland of their own. The former category is under the aegis of the United Nations High Commissioner for Refugees [UNHCR] (Geneva), the latter under the aegis of the United Nations Relief and Works Agency for Palestine Refugees in the Near East [UNRWA] (Vienna). Environmental refugees, however, whether cross-border or internal, remain as yet formally unrecognized by the international community.

Arthur H. Westing

Further Readings

El-Hinnawi, Essam. *Environmental Refugees.* 1985.

Jacobson, Jodi L. *Environmental Refugees: A Yardstick of Habitability.* 1988.

Westing, Arthur H. "Environmental Refugees: A Growing Category of Displaced Persons." *Environmental Conservation* 19 (1992): 201–07.

———. "Population, Desertification, and Migration." *Environmental Conservation* 21 (1994): 110–14, 109.

See also ENVIRONMENTAL DIPLOMACY; ENVIRONMENTAL PROTECTION IN WARTIME; NATIONAL SECURITY, RECONCEPTUALIZING

Environmental Tobacco Smoke

See TOBACCO SMOKE IN THE ENVIRONMENT

Environmentalism

Environmentalism is a way of looking at the world, the collective view of the environmental movement. As such it is a set of ideas that is complex, constantly evolving, and not without internal contradictions. One way of grasping its meaning is to see environmentalism as a political ideology, in some ways not unlike the classic political ideologies of liberalism, conservatism, and socialism. Ideologies carry and convey a set of social values and seek to alter the societal and political agenda through the expression and interpretation of those values. Ideologies, of course, are not actors; they exist only to the extent that they are or have been held as important by and expressed in some ongoing way by a significant number of people.

There is no doubt that environmentalist ideas have gained momentum and visibility in the latter half of this century. Environmentalism as a perspective has grown and it has altered the very language that we all speak. Everyday discourse now includes such terms as ecology, biodiversity, toxic wastes, trace analysis, recycling, and environmental impact assessment.

Through the advance of environmentalism new values have been added to the mix which individuals take into account regarding their everyday behavior and which governments must reconcile within their decision-making processes. This change is perhaps the best measure of the achievement of environmentalists and the myriad of conservation and environmental organizations over the course of the past century or more.

Most analysts date the rise of environmentalism, if this can be defined in terms of a single event, from the publication of Rachel Carson's *Silent Spring*. This landmark work added several new dimensions to the perspective and focus of the conservation movement and helped to convey a sense of urgency to the wider society. Nature became more than something that existed at a distance from most of human settlement, and nonhuman species were suddenly not the only species at direct risk from human impositions on the natural world. Pollution and human health, shifted to the center of concern, were seen suddenly as inseparable from conservation concerns. Doubts about a wide variety of modern technologies, such as nuclear power and the chemical industry generally, were soon added to this mix. The energy crisis of 1973 (following the wide reading of *The Limits to Growth* in the year or two preceding) added a third dimension to environmental/conservation concerns: sustainability—the sustainability of resources, the sustainability of ecological systems, and the sustainability of both industrial economies and human societies.

This new mix was potent politically in a way that conservation concerns never were before. It made sense to the urban majority and to those who could never afford the time or money necessary to see the beauties of remote wilderness locations. Pollution was suddenly visible— in the air, in the water, and in the existence of a wide variety of diseases. More than that progress itself was doubted by more than a few individuals and so too was the viability and, for some, perhaps even the net desirability of industrial society. Environmentalism imposed a new immediacy on the always real, but long-term, concerns of conservationists.

Environmentalists of the 1960s and 1970s sometimes put traditional conservation concerns aside in favor of pollution, health, and sustainability. But over subsequent decades a reintegration of ideas and values emerged and, in Samuel Hays's words, the environmental movement as a whole seeks beauty, health, and permanence. On reflection, none of these concerns were absent from the history of the conservation movement; the emphases were simply different and evolving, and will continue to evolve in the decades to come.

Environmentalism is multifaceted and the environmental movement seeks to protect beauty as well as wilderness, nature, biodiversity, and ecology. It also seeks to protect human health from the assaults of air and water pollution, toxic chemicals, bioaccumulation, and, in Barry Commoner's phrase, faulty technology. Finally, environmentalism is concerned with waste (and the perils of waste disposal), energy efficiency, and the overexploitation of and human overdependence on both renewable and nonrenewable raw materials. Over time the movement has learned to state matters positively as well as negatively—no longer concentrating on dangers and disasters, but as well on hopeful change. Thus there is a celebration of old-growth forest habitats, wilderness, tropical rainforests, and coral reefs. There is also demand-side management of energy, recycling and reuse of products and materials, compact urban designs, public transportation, bicycles, organic agriculture, dietary change, tree and shrub planting, ecological restoration, solar energy, telecommuting, and pollution prevention through industrial process redesign.

Environmentalism has altered, at least to some extent, almost every aspect of our society, economy, polity, and culture. There has been change within almost every academic discipline, and environmental researchers in every field have been propelled toward an interdisciplinary perspective, at least to some extent. There are strong links between environmentalism and religion, theology, and contemporary spirituality. The arts, literature, music and film have been used to express environmental ideas and have shaped those ideas significantly. The very core values of our many human societies have been altered and will doubtless come to change even more in the future.

Robert Paehlke

Further Readings

Hays, Samuel P. *Beauty, Health, and Permanence: Environmental Politics in the United States, 1955–1985.* 1987.

Paehlke, Robert. *Environmentalism and the Future of Progressive Politics.* 1989.

Shabecoff, Philip. *A Fierce Green Fire: The American Environmental Movement.* 1993.

See also CARSON, RACHEL; CONSERVATION MOVEMENT; EARTH DAY; ECOANARCHISM;

Ecosocialism; Environmental Ethics; Environmental History; Interdisciplinarity; *Limits to Growth*; Religion and Environmental Protection; Whole Earth Image

EPA
See Environmental Protection Agency

Epidemiology

Epidemiology is the study of the distribution of health-related events and disease in human populations. Epidemiological inquiries are directed to either the pattern of occurrence or the cause of disease, or both. Epidemiologists then apply their findings to the prevention and control of health problems. Environmental epidemiology concerns itself specifically with the relationship between environmental agents (pollutants) and ill-health. Environmental agents examined include chemicals, microorganisms, and radiation whose presence, excess, or deficiency can cause the occurrence of adverse health effects.

One important function of environmental epidemiology is to determine whether a specific population or community is experiencing more illness than it should. To determine this, the investigator needs to: 1) define precisely the adverse effect or illness; 2) determine how many people are affected; and 3) identify a standard population with which to compare the community or population under study (i.e., the exposed group). Disease rates in the population exposed to pollutants are then compared with provincial or national disease rates derived from the standard populations. The greater the rates of disease in the exposed population relative to the standard population, the greater the concern about health. Because disease rates can vary considerably with age, gender, race, and other factors, epidemiologists must take these variables into account.

Epidemiologists use a variety of study designs that vary in their rigor and conclusiveness. It is common in environmental epidemiology to undertake ecological studies, which typically use geographic areas as a basis for analysis. In case-control and cohort studies, individuals are units of analysis—in other words, the researcher knows who is exposed to a contaminant and who is not. In ecological studies, the researcher knows only the proportion of the population exposed and the proportion showing the specific outcome under study. An example of an ecological study is the comparison of levels of aluminum in drinking water and rates of Alzheimer's disease. Such studies show an association between aluminum in water and Alzheimer's but cannot prove that aluminum causes Alzheimer's. In ecological studies, researchers cannot make inferences about the individual level of consumption of aluminum in drinking water. Ecological studies are a valuable first step in the investigation of an environmental relationship between exposure and disease. The more definitive study types, however, are the case-control and cohort studies.

Case-control studies, also known as retrospective studies, are studies in which the direction of the research is backward. The investigator starts with the disease and goes back in time to determine its association with possible causes. Typically, a group of disease cases is chosen and compared with a group of persons without that particular disease (the control group). The difference between the two groups regarding exposure and risk factors is determined. An example of a case-control study is the comparison of pesticide exposure history in farmers with and without cancer. A weakness of case-control studies is that exposures are often inferred rather than precisely quantified because they occurred in the past. Case-control studies tend to be more conclusive than ecological studies, but less conclusive than cohort studies.

Cohort studies, also known as prospective studies, are studies in which the direction of the research is forward. The investigator starts with a population free from disease and follows it forward in time to determine the development of disease. The investigator then compares those who developed the disease with those who did not for differences that might explain the possible cause of the disease. An example of a cohort study is the relationship between fat organochlorine levels in breast milk and breast cancer in women who do and do not develop this cancer after the study is initiated.

Although individual epidemiological studies are important in advancing the state of knowledge, the establishment of environmental health policy rests on the interpretation of many individual studies, some of which may conflict with each other. To evaluate the potential for an agent to impair health, epidemiologists apply a framework such as the Bradford Hill criteria of causation to multiple studies. These criteria of causation suggest that some or many of the following conditions should be met before investigators can have confidence that an agent, such as an environmental pollutant, causes a given health effect. These conditions include: 1) a temporal relationship, in which the cause must occur before the effect; 2) a strength of association, in which the greater the relative risk, the more persuasive the association and the less likely that it is due to chance; 3) a dose-response relationship, in which the severity of the response is proportional to the dose; 4) consistency, in which study results carried out in different countries by different investigators are similar; 5) reversibility, in which an agent is more likely to be a cause of a disease if its removal results in decreased risk for that disease; 6) biological plausibility, in which the cause-and-effect relationship is consistent with the current understanding of the disease and its mechanism of causation; and 7) a high degree of specificity in which it can be established that one cause leads to one effect.

Unlike toxicology, which intentionally administers toxic substances to laboratory animals and thereby establishes whether the toxicant causes adverse health effects, epidemiologists study human populations for which the application of toxicants is not possible or ethical. Whereas toxicologists can infer causality between an environmental pollutant and a health effect, epidemiologists can only infer associations between a pollutant and health. Toxicology is limited in its ability to accurately predict that the effects observed in laboratory animals are equivalent to effects experienced in human populations. Epidemiology is limited in accurately assessing the dose and precise toxicants that may have contributed to the observed impaired health. Other factors, known as confounders, may be responsible for the association observed in epidemiological studies. These must be identified and a mathematical correction must be made. Taken together, multiple toxicological and epidemiological studies can effectively link environmental contaminants to health. However, single studies in either discipline are rarely, if ever, conclusive.

Monica Campbell

Further Readings

Goldsmith, J.R. *Environmental Epidemiology: Epidemiological Investigation of Community Environmental Health Problems.* 1986.

Friedman, G.D. *Primer of Epidemiology.* 1974.

Schulte, P.A., and F.P. Perera. *Molecular Epidemiology: Principles and Practices.* 1993.

See also RISK ANALYSIS; STANDARD SETTING; TOXICOLOGY

Erosion

See NEW FORESTRY; SOIL CONSERVATION

Eskimo Curlew

The Eskimo Curlew is a brown shorebird, slightly larger than a robin, with a decurved bill. It is an endangered species, nesting mainly in a small part of northwestern Canada. It migrates east across the Arctic and then south, occurring in large numbers in Labrador in August, before crossing the ocean to winter in southern South America. It returns north through the central United States and Canada, from mid-March through May.

In the 1800s it was abundant, although only thirty-nine nests have been confirmed—the last in 1866. The Eskimo Curlew was regularly shot for sport eleven months of the year. After the disappearance of the Passenger Pigeon in the 1880s, the Eskimo Curlew was hunted for restaurants from the United States to England to Argentina. There is no satisfactory explanation for the curlew's decline while the Lesser Golden Plover—apparently a year-round companion, similarly hunted—still occurs commonly.

Eskimo Curlews were reported in twenty-five of the forty-one years before 1986, the largest number being six until twenty-three were seen in Texas in 1981. There were five reports in 1987 (from the Northwest Territories to Texas) and six in 1990 (Texas, Mexico, Barbados, and three in South America). On July 7, 1992, a geologist flushed a robin-sized curlew off four eggs (one pipping) west of Eskimo Point, Northwest Territories.

The Canadian Wildlife Service plans to ensure a viable population. If surveying migration and wintering areas shows enough Eskimo Curlews to safely take eggs, a hand-rearing project is scheduled, if a similar experiment has proven successful for their close Asian relatives, Little Curlews. There is at present no such plan in the United States.

J. Bernard Gollop

Further Readings

Gollop, J.B., T.W. Barry, and E.H. Iversen. *Eskimo Curlew: A Vanishing Species?*

1986. (Available from Saskatchewan Natural History Society, Box 4348, Regina, SK. S4P 3W6.)

See also HAWK SHOOTING; PASSENGER PIGEON; SHOREBIRDS

European Community: Fifth Environmental Action Programme

Since the establishment in the European Community (EC) of environmental policy as a separate policy field in the early 1970s, all environmental action programs have reviewed trends, recorded events, and pointed the way ahead. The Programme of Policy and Action in relation to the Environment and Sustainable Development with its short title: Fifth EC Environmental Action Programme (Fifth E.A.P.), adopted in 1993, was drawn up at the time of the United Nations Conference on Environment and Development in Rio de Janeiro and constitutes an early example of how the objectives agreed to in Rio might be woven into a political strategy. It is not binding in law and has no budget attached but carries political weight as it is supported by the European Parliament and was agreed on by all Directorates-General (departments or ministries) of the European Commission as well as the governments of the member states of the EC.

The program runs until the year 2000 (with a revision planned for 1996) and follows the novel approach of selecting "target sectors" responsible for a large part of resource consumption and environmental degradation. Recognizing that environmental policy cannot remain an end-of-pipe policy mitigating damage caused as a result of decisions made in other policy fields, a main focus of the program is on the integration of environmental policy requirements into those other policy fields identified below. This integration has since become a legally binding requirement through the entry into force of the Maastricht Treaty establishing the European Union (EU).

Five target sectors have been selected where the consideration of environmental objectives is urgent: industry, energy, transport, agricultural policy, and tourism. Waste management was included in the "themes" of the program together with climate change, air quality and acidification, protection of nature and biodiversity, protection and management of water resources, the urban environment, and coastal zones. Risk reduction is to be attempted in relation to industry (the chemical sector) and nuclear installations, with civil protection services and environmental emergency plans providing support. Specific objectives, targets by the year 2000, actions to be taken (with time frames) are given for each target sector and objective with the actors responsible being identified.

Throughout, the principle of shared responsibility is invoked to underline the need for coordination of all actors and the use of all suitable instruments at their appropriate levels in a combined implementation of measures. The important role local authorities have to play is highlighted. In addition to the legislative instruments traditionally used, the program calls for the increased use of market-based instruments designed to influence producers' and consumers' behavior, and to make prices reflect environmental costs. The lending and provision of grants by EU funds, programs, and financial institutions is to take account of the environmental consequences of projects. The "principle of precautionary action," also legally established through the Maastricht Treaty, is invoked in the program but not explained in detail.

Rather than a program listing specific actions, the EU and its member states have adopted the script for a process by which broad objectives are to be translated into specific targets and action, involving many parties and actors. The direction of this process is identified in the short title of the programme: "Towards Sustainability."

R. Andreas Kraemer

Further Readings

Resolution of the Council and the Representatives of the Governments of the Member States Meeting within the Council of 1 February 1993 on a Community Programme of Policy and Action in Relation to the Environment and Sustainable Development (with the Programme as Annex). *Official Journal of the European Communities*. No C 138, May 17, 1993, 1–98.

Opinion of the European Parliament (*Rapporteur*: Carmen Diez de Rivera-Icaza). *Official Journal of the European Communities*. No C 337, December 21, 1992, 34–50.

Opinion of the Economic and Social Committee (*Rapporteur*: Klaus Boisserée). *Official Journal of the European Communities*. No C 287, November 4, 1992, 27–35.

See also Chemiepolitik (GERMANY); ENVI-
RONMENTAL CASE LAW: EUROPEAN COMMU-
NITY; LEGISLATION: EUROPEAN COMMUNITY;
RIO CONFERENCE (1992); WESTERN EUROPE:
POLLUTION

Eutrophication

Healthy plants—from trees to single-celled algae—grow rapidly when supplied with abundant quantities of the many types of chemical
resources necessary for synthesis and growth.
Equally important for growth to take place is
an environmental setting in which the physical
intensities of light, heat, and environmental disturbances are at desirable moderate levels and/
or a biological setting in which other organisms
do not act to prevent rapid growth. The suffix
"trophic" in "eutrophic" refers to the chemical
resource part of this combined chemical-physi-
cal-biological interaction. Eutrophic (or "well-
fed") connotes an abundance of all necessary
chemical substances for photosynthesis and
plant growth; oligotrophic (or "poorly-fed")
connotes shortage of one or more of such substances. A partial parallel exists with respect to
light intensity among the necessary physical
conditions as related to photosynthesis: here
euphotic refers to a "well-lit" state of surface
waters.

A full explanation of the elements that
determine the trophic state of any particular
aquatic ecosystem is not yet available. Laboratory and small field experiments (for which all
but two or three of the many factors involved
have been kept relatively constant) have provided much insight. To start the discussion here,
all the physical and biological factors will be
assumed to be in a generally beneficial state, or
an "eu-state," with respect to generalized plant
synthesis and growth. The consequences of different levels of chemical resources will be considered first.

In the absence of human intervention,
chemical resources are supplied to plants in an
aquatic ecosystem by: 1) erosive weathering of
rock and transport by air, water, or living things
to the water; 2) chemical "fixing" of some atmospheric gases in the waters; 3) voiding of
wastes which include such chemicals by organisms present in the ecosystem; and 4) by chemical "release" through decomposition and mineralization from some complex organic
substances already in the waters. There are apparently few bodies of water in the world in
which all of these natural activities supply all

chemical resources continuously at the appropriate quantitative levels to permit synthesis and
growth of plants at levels limited only by the
inherent biological capabilities of the plants
themselves. Also, the biological synthesis and
growth processes together with various other
ecological processes tend to remove one or
more types of necessary chemical resources
faster than they are supplied. Thus, on balance,
a process of natural oligotrophication is apparent for most freshwater and marine waters,
with a result that such waters' natural tendencies lean toward a state of oligotrophy in which
plant growth is not profuse. Since all animals
depend ultimately on plant growth, animal
growth is also not profuse in oligotrophic systems.

One of the natural processes of
oligotrophication involves the settling out of
organic particles, produced by living things,
from the euphotic surface waters to poorly lit
deeper waters. Here oxygen that is dissolved in
the water, or obtained from the reduction of
chemical compounds such as nitrates, causes
the oxidation and mineralization of these particles thus releasing chemicals as nutrient resources appropriate again for photosynthesis.
Climatic and atmospheric conditions may force
isolated enriched bottom waters to the euphotic
surface and thus result in increased plant synthesis and growth. Processes such as these may
be termed natural eutrophication. They occur,
usually somewhat unpredictably, as surface upwelling in some parts of the ocean and in large
lakes or as sub-surface flooding over the submerged edges of shallow areas of the continental shelf by deeper oceanic waters. The result is
episodic short-lived natural eutrophication.

Seasonally, both in winter and in summer,
many lakes are stratified horizontally into surface waters and bottom waters due to temperature differences. In spring and fall when temperatures do not vary much from top to
bottom, and when strong equinoctial storms
occur, the whole water mass is "turned over."
Thus nutrients from bottom waters are redis-
tributed. This leads to a seasonal burst of plant
production in spring and fall, even in quite oligotrophic lakes.

In terms of geological time, lakes are temporary features of a landscape because they fill
in gradually due to sedimentation of eroded
minerals and inert organic substances. The
physical processes that determine the availability of plant nutrients in the euphotic zone may
change as a lake becomes more shallow. For

example seasonal stratification because of temperature differences may no longer occur. Depending upon the balance among these physical processes a lake may come to exhibit conditions that resemble an eutrophic state as the lake becomes shallower, but this is not always the case. That it does occur at least sometimes has contributed to much confusion. Thus cultural eutrophication, due to loading of chemicals in the form of plant nutrients into a lake by humans, has been equated erroneously with the natural "aging" process of a lake caused mostly by changes in physical factors related to filling or partial draining of the lake.

Ramon Margalef and others have inferred that in nature oligotrophication is a general continuing process and that eutrophication tends to occur episodically, often seasonally or at intervals of some years. For most waters the balance between natural processes is such that they are usually in a state of oligotrophy or relative infertility. But some waters are naturally eutrophic, for example, where waters drain eroding material rich in phosphates. Cultural eutrophication has generally been a continuing process with an intensity that exceeds the natural oligotrophication process. If the cultural eutrophication becomes extreme, large quantities of offensive gases such as ammonia, hydrogen sulfide and methane may escape to the atmosphere, at levels unprecedented in nature.

Richard A. Vollenweider studied cultural eutrophication comparatively in lakes and then in rivers, estuaries and marine coastal waters. As a process of enrichment with plant nutrients, eutrophication at low levels compensates for shortages of either phosphorus or nitrogen or both. The enhanced growth of algae or leafy plants then is followed by a proliferation of animals that "graze" on them, followed by other animals that prey on the plant-eating animals, etc. The overall result is a cascade of increased biological production. Because eutrophication often involves erratic ecosystemic behavior, small organisms able to reproduce quickly adapt to it better than do large organisms that require longer periods for reproduction.

With greatly increased production in the euphotic surface waters, there follows greatly increased settling out of organic particles into the deeper waters. The ensuing decomposition may demand all the dissolved oxygen in the deeper waters. In highly productive waters of shallow bays photosynthesis during the day may produce enough oxygen for the respiration needs of all organisms during the day but not at night with a result that anoxia may occur occasionally. Bottom and bay waters are each the necessary habitat for a variety of fish species preferred by humans, and these fish cannot survive anoxic conditions. Also shellfish and large insects on the bottom are killed.

With intense cultural eutrophication species of algae that are toxic to animals, including humans, may erupt in abundance. Sensitive humans may suffer disorders of the skin, eyes, and digestive tract. Whether instances of severe toxins in fish (such as ciquatera in tropical fish) are due at least in part to eutrophication has not been resolved.

Small fish, not much prized by humans usually, thrive in the highly productive eutrophic surface waters, apparently not much affected by algal toxins. In a number of ways small fish may act ecologically so as to exacerbate the effects of eutrophication. Unlike the larger fish of bottom waters, the abundance of small fish species tends to vary greatly from year to year. The lower value and greater uncertainty associated with year to year availability of small fish usually offset the value to humans of any increased biological production.

Humans cause harmful effects on aquatic ecosystems of numerous types other than eutrophication. The various cultural influences often occur concurrently in aquatic ecosystems. Some influences of different effects resemble each other, and they may interact within the ecosystem. Thus it is often quite difficult to determine precisely the level of particular effects that can be attributed fairly to cultural eutrophication.

As with other kinds of human abuse of the environment, prevention is generally the least costly and most effective "cure" for cultural eutrophication. In the Laurentian Great Lakes, prevention now relates to human sewage, agricultural practices, and certain mining and manufacturing processes that are most responsible for cultural eutrophication.

Henry A. Regier

Further Readings
De Bernardi, R., G. Giussani, and L. Barbanti, eds. *Scientific Perspectives in Theoretical and Applied Limnology. Memorie Dell' Istituto Italiano di Idrobiologia.* 1990.

Vollenweider, R.A., R. Marchetti, and R. Viviani, eds. "The Response of Marine Transitional Systems to Human Impact:

Problems and Perspectives for Restoration." Proceedings of an International Conference, Bologna, Italy, March 21–24, 1990. In *Science of the Total Environment*. 1992.

Wetzel, R.G. *Limnology*. 2nd ed. 1983.

See also AGRICULTURE: ENVIRONMENTAL IMPACTS; FRESHWATER WETLANDS; GREAT LAKES; PHOSPHATES; WATER POLLUTION ABATEMENT TECHNOLOGIES

Everglades of South Florida

The geography of south Florida is dominated by a "river of grass" called the Everglades. Once stretching 350 miles from Lake Okeechobee to the Gulf of Mexico, the Everglades is a slowly moving shallow river 200 miles wide as it seeps southward among mangrove forests at the shore of Florida Bay. These ecosystems of the land are tied to the marine communities that literally protect both Florida Bay and Everglades by flowing water. At the seaward edge of Florida Bay are thousands of islands referred to as "the Keys." Beneath the ocean skirting the entire 190-mile arc of the keys lies numerous coral reefs.

The Everglades and the adjacent Florida Keys are a marl (mixture of limestone and clay) outcropping ringed by mangrove forests that extend along the south coast from Palm Beach to the Dry Tortugas. This island arc is bounded by an offshore coral reef system—the only such reef in the waters of the continuous United States. The reef affords a rampart against turbulent seas driven north by the Gulf Stream. As the reef and the islands protect the Bay, so the Bay's shallow limestone deposits protect the mangroves and the sloughs that are this "river of grass." The enormity of the water creeping across the virtually flat ledge of the greater Everglades provides shelter and food for numberless fish, birds, reptiles, and mammals.

The entire system of freshwater swamps, lakes, and rivers meshes in these wild estuaries forming a thick tangle of mangrove forests. These saltwater tolerant trees are submerged much of the year. Trees of three different species crowd the tropical waters where the glades meet the sea. The freshwater and saltwater mixing nourishes a native shrimp fishery, sport fishery in bone fish, and rock lobster fishery. The Everglades is home to thousands of wading birds that are attracted by this ecosystem of marl, mud, limestone, and "sawgrass" prairie.

The Everglades is a bird lovers paradise and a modern tragedy with respect to the decline in wildlife—including ibis, wood storks, kites, panthers, crocodiles, and manatees.

Originally preserved as a National Park in 1947, a mere fragment of the greater Everglades ecosystem was set aside protecting the mouth of this "river of grass." But due to the continuing loss of wildlife, conservation groups pushed government agencies to expand preservation to include this larger Everglades ecosystem through purchases of more land areas. Subsequent protection has been granted to Big Cypress Swamp and the three water conservation units of the South Florida Water Management District, and most recently Key Largo. Even with Indian and State Park Lands, the Everglades and Florida Bay ecosystems are in irreparable decay due to declining water quality and quantity, leading to subsequent vegetational changes. The wildlife losses in the past sixty years are dramatic indicators of the demise of the greater Everglades. The ecosystem's productivity has been altered by an interruption of water for urban, agricultural, and recreational purposes. The flows of the lakes and swamps north of U.S. Highway 41 have ceased to replenish, nourish, and cleanse the Everglades.

Beginning in the 1920s flood control, drainage, and channelization projects—most of them federally supported—have destroyed much of the original northern and eastern parts of the larger Everglades, converting them to agricultural and urban land. Between existing farms and Everglades National Park lie some 3,400 square kilometers of water conservation areas, in which water is stored and regulated for discharge to local agricultural, municipal, and park areas. The agency responsible for water discharges is the South Florida Water Management District whose members are appointed by the state. The canals and dikes of these projects have reduced the volume of freshwater flowing southward into the heart of the Everglades. The damage this restricted flow has caused for Florida Bay's seagrass beds has also destroyed dependent fisheries. Water engineering creates an unnatural stabilization of the remaining flow, largely eliminating the flood water that once existed after summer storms. Most of the water that once flowed southward through this swampland wildlife preserve has been diverted for irrigation and urban development around and away from the Everglades National Park.

Water diversions have had major impacts on both breeding and non-breeding water birds.

Large shifts of breeding birds from the park into the water conservation areas occurred when the latter were created in the 1960s. Although breeding populations have fluctuated greatly due to water conditions (including timing and distribution), the overall bird population trend has been downward. The diversity and abundance of plant and animal life in the park and surrounding land have precipitously diminished. Wading bird populations have plummeted by 90 percent since the 1930s when 2.5 million birds fed and roosted in the swamp. The decline is due to the increase of salinity caused by freshwater diversions to surrounding municipal and agricultural developments. In 1975–1976, for example, 23,500 to 26,000 pairs of wading birds nested in Everglades National Park and the water conservation areas; in the late 1980s the highest numbers nesting were 16,500 pairs.

Dams and canals feeding the glades carry agricultural and cattle run-offs or water heavily laden with phosphorus, nitrogen, mercury, and low levels of dissolved oxygen into the Everglades basin. The decline in the water quality there has had a deleterious effect on those bird populations that use the sawgrass. The *jamaicaensis* (sawgrass) is readily replaced by *typha*, or cattails due to these lower quality water discharges by the district into the Everglades National Park. Pollution from agricultural and urban sources is also a problem. Mercury contaminates the Everglades' food webs and is found in toxic quantities in fish and panthers. Excess phosphorus used in agricultural fertilizer has caused eutrophication of extensive wetlands areas, altering the sawgrass vegetation with cattails that are less beneficial to water fowl.

The Everglades is a rain machine in that the watery expanse evaporates in the tropical summer heat to increase the precipitation on which the quality and quantity of urban water supplies depend. These glades, mangroves, and cypress are actually a vast network of waterways and hydric habitats where submerged and emergent vegetation dominate the flat features of the limestone landscape. Here the remaining endangered panthers and salt-water crocodiles and manatees cling to a precarious existence. Everglades National Park and surrounding preserves are all fragments of a larger natural feature that preservationist Marjory Douglas called the "Everglades, a river of grass," that flows from central to south Florida. The National Park proper is at the mouth of this shallow and now contaminated, or often dry, river and does not protect the source of this watershed far to the north. Water control technology has diminished the wildlife of the greater Everglades, but in its proposed restoration the state and preservationists are hoping that technology may bring life back to the glades from which it is vanishing.

Joseph V. Siry

Further Readings

Bancroft, G.T. "Status and Conservation of Wading Birds in the Everglades." *American Birds* 43 (1989): 1258–65.
Cox, George W. *Conservation Ecology*. 1993.
Douglas, Marjory Stoneman. *The Everglades: River of Grass*. 1947.
Hoffmeister, John E. *Land from the Sea: The Geological Story of South Florida*. 1974.

See also CHANNELIZATION; COASTAL MARSHES, CONSERVATION OF; COASTAL ZONE MANAGEMENT; CORAL REEFS; DOUGLAS, MARJORY STONEMAN; EUTROPHICATION; FLORIDA PANTHER; FRESHWATER WETLANDS; MARINE MAMMALS; MERCURY; NATIONAL PARKS: UNITED STATES; SHOREBIRDS; WATERFOWL: CONSERVATION AND HABITAT

Evolution

The concept of evolution is generally equated with that of "development." In the case of biological evolution it is equated with the development of life from nonliving matter and the development of "higher" organisms from these lower and more rudimentary beings. Often considered a modern idea, biological evolution was in fact implied by several early Greek thinkers and explicitly proposed by both Anaximander (611–547 B.C.) and Empedocles (c. 440 B.C.). After its rejection by Aristotle and subsequent Greek philosophers, however, biological evolution was not seriously considered again until the eighteenth century, when it was discussed by Immanuel Kant and the Comte de Buffon. Jean Lamarck and his English contemporary Erasmus Darwin (Charles Darwin's grandfather), at the beginning of the nineteenth century, independently proposed theories of evolution based on the idea of "the inheritance of acquired characteristics."

Though books about evolution continued to be published in the first half of the century, it was not until the publication of Charles Darwin's *The Origin of Species* (1859) that the concept of biological evolution came to be widely discussed and, though sharply attacked, accepted by the majority of scientists. Charles Darwin accepted much that Erasmus Darwin and Lamarck had to say about evolution, but disagreed with them about evolution's mechanism. In defending "the inheritance of acquired characteristics" they had argued that characteristics gained by intentional effort in one generation could be preserved and passed on to the next. (Thus the giraffe's long neck would be the accumulated effect of generations of stretchings by hungry giraffes.) Charles Darwin proposed instead that evolution is driven by two impersonal factors: genetic variation and natural selection.

In Charles Darwin's view (still shared by most biologists) these two principles interact straightforwardly. Genetic variability produces the raw materials of evolution—slight differences in form and structure. Natural selection "weeds out" those variations which tend to hamper the organism in its struggle to survive, and preserves those which help it to adapt successfully to its environment. The neck of the giraffe (or the vertebrate eye, or the bird's feathers) would be not the result of persistent effort by generations of organisms, but of the continual selection of chance mutations.

In the face of scientific, philosophical, and religious criticisms Darwin's theory of evolution has continued to develop and to consolidate its gains. Though Charles Darwin's own qualitative genetic theory proved unacceptable, the rediscovery of Gregor Mendel's work around 1901 provided genetics with a secure scientific foundation. (The marriage of Darwin's theory with Mendelian genetics is commonly called "Neodarwinism.") Subsequent work on population dynamics in the 1920s and 1930s by Sewall Wright, Ronald Fisher, and others further strengthened the Darwinian paradigm, demonstrating that new, useful genetic variations (mutations) are likely to be conserved in relatively small, isolated groups of organisms. (The incorporation of population theory into Neodarwinism is termed "Darwinism, the modern synthesis.") The discovery of the DNA molecule as the carrier of genetic information in 1954 by J.D. Watson and F. Crick and the subsequent explosive development of molecular biology have in the opinion of most biologists strengthened the Darwinian theory still further.

Critics are quick to point out, however, that serious difficulties remain. The origin of prokaryotic (non-nucleated) cells after only 400 million years of conditions suitable for their emergence is a serious puzzle. The successes of molecular biology have revealed that even the simplest cells are far more complex than most biologists would have believed at mid-century; explaining their existence thus becomes in important respects more, not less, difficult. Debates over the nature of biological classification (taxonomy), the units of natural selection, and the relative importance of genetic variation and natural selection continue to divide researchers. The sudden appearance of complex multicellular animal life in the Cambrian period and the equally abrupt appearance of angiosperms in the Cretaceous are hard to explain on Darwinian grounds.

Probably the profoundest theoretical problem facing evolutionary theory is that of specifying what is meant by the term "evolves" over and above the fact than an organism survives and is able to leave descendants. Though it is tempting to say that an organism that evolves is more complex than its predecessors, no generally accepted measure of complexity exists. (It is tempting to state that a more evolved organism contains more *information* than its less-complex relatives; no one is able, however, to specify a noncontroversial numerical scale for biological information.) The result is the impossibility of giving any meaning to the "survival of the fittest" beyond the tautological phrase "survival of the survivors." Problems of this sort lead the philosopher Karl Popper to urge that Darwinism is not a scientific hypothesis but a "metaphysical research project," incapable of being verified or falsified through a direct appeal to experience. He added, however, that such a project is capable of producing factual investigations, which are falsifiable by an appeal to experiences and thus scientific.

It could be argued that current evolutionary thought devalues life by making life appear to be nothing more than the result of the chance combinations of atoms and molecules, themselves devoid of value. But in several respects evolutionary theory provides support for claims of environmentalists that the belief in humanity's separateness from nature must be reassessed. Evolutionary theory shows not only that humanity is related to all other living things through common ancestry; it demonstrates that man and other living creatures, rather than being entirely different in kind, have much in common. (To say nothing of their behavior, humans and chimpanzees share 99 percent of the same

DNA.) The well-known land ethic of Aldo Leopold is based not only on a knowledge of ecological principles but on an assessment of the manner in which new ethical systems have emerged in the course of human social evolution. This in turn was based on his fundamental understanding of humans as an organism among other organisms evolving in an environment.

More recently biologists such as René Dubos, Charles Birch, and C.E. Wilson have argued on the basis of evolution that biocentric viewpoints must replace ancient anthropocentric assumptions. Our best attested biological theories, they would argue, join with our present practical environmental problems to force upon us the realization that we are one organism among many, that all organisms depend on each other to sustain a world in which all can survive, and that if life is to continue on this planet, man will have to change both his notions and his behavior.

Pete A.Y. Gunter

Further Readings

Denton, Michael. *Evolution: A Theory in Crisis*. 1985.

Mayr, Ernest. *The Growth of Biological Thought: Diversity, Evolution, Inheritance*. 1982.

Wilson, Edward O. *Biophilia: The Human Bond with Other Species*. 1984.

See also BIODIVERSITY; DARWIN, CHARLES; GENETIC DIVERSITY; WEB OF LIFE

Exotic Species

Exotic species, also called introduced or alien species, are those organisms not native to a particular ecosystem, that have been introduced by human activity, whether deliberate or accidental. Feral animals are domestic species released or escaped into wild environments that have established self-sustaining populations. Exotics that undergo rapid population and range extension from their point of introduction are referred to as being invasive.

Exotic organisms may be among the most destructive, insidious, and permanent forms of ecological perturbation. Unlike effects from various forms of pollution, poor land-use practices, or overutilization of living resources, which are alleviated when the offending action is halted, exotic organisms, once established, may have negative effects that are permanent in ecological time.

There have always been large-scale movements of organisms into new environments; the fossil record reveals that some of these invasions have had devastating effects on native organisms. After Pangaea separated into the continents and, later, as sea level changes periodically reconnected and re-separated those continents, some mobile organisms invaded lands far from their evolutionary origins and came into contact with organisms having little ability to compete with (or escape from) the invaders. Although catastrophic to less competitive endemic species, such invasions were nevertheless very rare events. Most organisms, past and present, have had little ability or inclination to undergo such major movements.

The background rate of spread of organisms between faunal regions changed dramatically with the rise of the most invasive of all species—humans. Human colonizers have directly usurped resources, altered environments, and caused wholesale extinctions through competition and overkill. Humans have also acted as agents of dispersal, both intentionally and unwittingly, for an unprecedented multitude of organisms.

The effects of exotic species have been evident for as long as humans have traveled with other organisms. European rabbits (*Oryctolagus*), for example, have been destructive agricultural pests for millennia in Great Britain where they were introduced by the Roman conquerors. By the time the British began settling Australia and New Zealand they had established a sentimental attachment to rabbits as British fauna, and so rabbits were brought to these faraway places where they proceeded to wreak a new wave of environmental havoc. Such a failure to learn from previous introductions seems a human failing. Peacock bass (*Cichla*) have had a devastating effect upon the fish and aquatic bird fauna of Lake Gatun, Panama, yet Florida has introduced them in the southern part of the state to control another invasive exotic fish (*Tilapia*). This action is little different than the disastrous introduction of foxes (*Vulpes*) into Australia as a means to control rabbits.

Exotic organisms have figured prominently in human history. Perhaps the most long-lasting and devastating effect of the Crusades was to expose Europeans to the smallpox virus (*Variola*), a disease of Asian origin, and then provide its transport back to Europe. European explorers later introduced smallpox into the New World, where it proceeded to become the leading cause of death for Native Americans. In turn the early explorers returned to Europe with syphilis, a disease formerly restricted to the New World.

Early reference to the effects of exotic organisms are found in Charles Darwin's *The Voyage of the Beagle*. Darwin, writing in the 1830s, was especially struck by how exotic species had so completely transformed the character of the biota of parts of southern South America, and later those on the island of St. Helena. In each area Darwin commented in his journal about the demise of endemic biota caused by exotics.

Only in recent years, however, have most ecologists become aware of the scope of environmental problems posed by exotic organisms. We now know that in addition to threatening endemic species with extinction, some exotic species can additionally cause entire biotic communities to unravel even to the point of altering physical properties of habitat, as for example in the case of feral goats causing reduced vegetative cover and severe erosion on some oceanic islands. Above all else it has become clear that establishment of an invasive exotic species is almost certain to have negative effects on biodiversity; some of these effects can be extreme. For example, the ill-advised introduction of Nile perch (*Lates*) into Lake Victoria (Africa) has resulted in the near-certain extinction of all of the several hundred species of haplochromine cichlid fishes endemic to the lake. Similarly, the accidental introduction of the brown tree snake (*Boiga*) on Guam has resulted in the extinction in the wild of at least ten native passerine birds.

Exotic plants are no less devastating to native biota. The Australian melaleuca tree rapidly invades disturbed areas, and is rapidly spreading in the Florida everglades. This tree typically replaces nearly all natural vegetation, and is virtually unused by wildlife. The result of invasion by melaleuca is that a diverse biotic community is rapidly converted to a monospecific ecological desert. In the northern United States, purple loosestrife (*Lythrum*) has invaded more than 2 million acres of wetlands, replacing native plants and effectively rendering much of this area unsuitable for wildlife.

Most terrestrial exotic species capable of colonizing continental environments prefer disturbed areas. Such organisms have difficulty establishing viable populations in pristine environments, except on islands—where some of the most dramatic effects of exotic species have been documented. In fact, avian extinction since 1600 has been primarily an island phenomenon largely due to the introduction of rats (*Rattus*) and domestic cats (*Felis*). These two species alone have been blamed for reducing global seabird numbers by tens of millions. It is also likely that plant extinction during the same period likewise has occurred primarily on islands, largely due to introduced herbivores of which the goat (*Capra*) has been the most widespread and destructive.

Exotic species generally have a more profound effect on islands because island biota are generally comprised of fewer total species, and island species are less competitive than generalist continental organisms. Island biota are also especially susceptible because of the organisms that predictably do not colonize islands naturally. Medium- and large-sized predatory and herbivorous mammals have no history of long-distance over-water transport. Consequently most island species have had little evolutionary incentive to have defenses against such animals. When animals such as cats or goats are precipitously introduced into an island ecosystem, the island endemics are rapidly eliminated. In a clearly documented instance, rock iguanas (*Cyclura*) were extirpated from Pine Cay in the Turks and Caicos Islands in only six years by feral cats brought in by construction workers building a resort hotel.

Most recently, concern over exotic species has centered around the introduction of zebra mussels (*Dreissena*) to the Great Lakes between Canada and the United States. Zebra mussels were first discovered here in 1988, but within one year had colonized nearly every hard surface in Lake Erie, often at densities exceeding 30,000 individuals per square meter. Only four years later these invasive organisms had spread to all of the Great Lakes and were rapidly moving downstream in the Mississippi River system. Current U.S. Fish and Wildlife Service estimates project a cost of over $4 billion over the decade of the 1990s for maintenance to water intake facilities at water treatment and power plants, loss of endemic fish production, and for cleaning of boats and marine engines. It is likely that zebra mussels will eventually be the major biotic component wherever found in North America, and will have a profound negative effect on most other aquatic species.

The ability of humans to disperse globally, first by sailing ship, and now by jet airplane, has

E

allowed humans to move organisms into new environments at unprecedented rates in ways that never would have occurred naturally. The biota of human-induced landscapes are rapidly becoming homogenized among faunal regions. Most purposeful introductions have been fueled by good intentions, but most have had negative consequences; some have been ecologically disastrous. Most intentional introductions have been carried out on the whim of a limited number of individuals (sometimes only a single person) regardless of what the wishes of the public might have been had they been asked. Knowledge gained in recent years dramatically demonstrates that the ecological price of exotic organisms almost always outweighs any anticipated potential benefits. Even so, new organisms keep appearing in non-native environments, and concerns about the older, more established exotics get pushed further back from the forefront of action. The zebra mussel has alarmed North American aquatic biologists; simultaneously it is rare to hear concern voiced about what has arguably been the most devastating ecological force in North American aquatic environments in the last century—the common carp (*Cyprinnus*). One of the greatest dangers of exotic organisms may be that they can outlast human generations and thus any general perception that they are exotic is lost.

Bruce E. Coblentz

Further Readings

Coblentz, Bruce. "Exotic Organisms: A Dilemma for Conservation Biology." *Conservation Biology* 4 (1990): 261–65.

Elton, Charles. *The Ecology of Invasions by Plants and Animals.* 1958.

See also BIODEPLETION; BIODIVERSITY; BIOREGION; DARWIN, CHARLES; ELTON, CHARLES; EVOLUTION; FRESHWATER WETLANDS; GREAT LAKES

Extinction

See BIODEPLETION

Exxon Valdez

See OIL SPILLS

Federal Insecticide, Fungicide and Rodenticide Act

The Federal Insecticide, Fungicide and Rodenticide Act (FIFRA) is the primary statute by which the U.S. government regulates the manufacture, sale, and use of chemicals designed to control or eradicate unwanted insects, plants, and rodents. The law's origin in 1947 as a simple labeling provision—it did not mandate testing the safety or efficacy of new chemicals—grew out of precedents set by the Federal Insecticide Act (1910) and other early consumer notification laws. FIFRA emerged primarily in response to concerns raised within farming and agricultural chemical industry sectors over the need to prevent unscrupulous competition in the manufacture and sale of a new generation of inorganic pesticides that promised to transform agriculture and other aspects of postwar society. The law was administered by the Department of Agriculture.

FIFRA's status as a labeling law remained intact through the late 1960s, but the emergence of powerful health and environmental concerns eventually led to administrative and legislative changes. In 1970 most regulatory activities regarding pesticides were transferred to the new Environmental Protection Agency (EPA), thereby shifting power over product registration to an agency whose primary focus was to prevent the possibly harmful consequences of pesticide use. The impact on FIFRA enforcement was immediate, as the EPA quickly set out to suspend or cancel the registrations of a number of controversial chemicals.

In 1972 Congress substantially amended FIFRA with the passage of the Federal Environmental Pesticide Control Act (FEPCA). This statute tightened product registration requirements, allowed the EPA to reject the registration for any product or usage that posed "unreasonable adverse effects on the environment," and provided penalties for misuse. But it also mandated that the EPA re-register thousands of existing and new pesticide products within four years, a task for which the agency was supposed to develop comprehensive standards, uniform guidelines, and sophisticated new testing protocols. The law's cumbersome procedural safeguards made implementation problematic; the EPA lacked the resources to carry out ambitious and stringent statutory mandates. Each effort to fix perceived statutory shortcomings met with bitter opposition from one side or another. The remainder of the 1970s was spent in protracted re-authorization battles and disputes over EPA regulatory procedures, all punctuated by occasional "scandals" that reinforced public impressions that FIFRA promised more than the EPA could deliver.

Federal pesticide policy largely languished during the first Reagan administration. Aggressive early use of regulatory loopholes to speed pesticide registration came to a virtual halt in the political turbulence surrounding the EPA in early 1983. Congressional stalemate between defenders of pesticides and their critics in the environmental community persisted through the 1980s, with neither side strong enough to push through statutory change. This was true even in 1986, after industry and environmental group representatives had privately negotiated a major compromise proposal. In 1988, however, Congress passed and President Reagan signed a stripped-down version of the earlier proposal, with legislators focusing particularly on devising specific statutory guidelines for registration and targeting the EPA's efforts toward the relatively few active ingredients from which thousands of discrete products derive. New deadlines were imposed, new fees were levied to finance registration, and a controversial indemnification program that long had inhibited EPA willingness to cancel registrations was dropped. The EPA has since worked to collect and review registration data, and the overall focus of attention has shifted to groundwater contamination and the export of chemicals banned for use in the United States.

Christopher J. Bosso

Further Readings

Bosso, Christopher J. *Pesticides and Politics: The Life Cycle of a Public Issue.* 1987.

Hoberg, George. *Pluralism by Design: Environmental Policy and the American Regulatory State.* 1992.

See also ENVIRONMENTAL PROTECTION AGENCY; INTEGRATED PEST MANAGEMENT; PESTICIDES; REAGAN, RONALD; SUSTAINABLE AGRICULTURE; TOXIC SUBSTANCES CONTROL ACT

Federalism and Environmental Protection: Canada

Since pollution was not a prominent issue when the Canadian constitution was written in 1867 it is not surprising that the constitution does not explicitly allocate responsibility for the environment to either the federal or provincial legislatures. As a result both federal and provincial authority with respect to environmental protection is derivative of other fields of jurisdiction that are mentioned in the constitution. Since almost every aspect of human endeavor has some environmental impact the result is a substantial degree of overlap between federal and provincial powers concerning the environment.

There is little doubt that provincial governments have extensive authority to protect the environment, both in their capacity as owners of public property and their capacity as legislators. The constitution confers upon the provinces ownership of public lands within their borders, thus granting them extensive proprietary authority to conserve and protect natural resources. The provinces' most important source of legislative authority lies in their jurisdiction over "Property and Civil Rights," which has been given a broad interpretation by the courts.

Federal jurisdiction with respect to the environment is less clear. Federal proprietary powers are limited, since federal resource ownership is only extensive offshore and in the Northern territories. Indirect legislative authority to protect the environment is associated with several specific subjects within federal jurisdiction, such as fisheries, navigation, and agriculture. Other federal powers have the potential to support a more comprehensive federal role in environmental protection, including trade and commerce, criminal law, and the residual power to make laws for the "Peace, Order and good Government of Canada," but the limits of such powers remain uncertain.

In the absence of clear constitutional division of powers, federal and provincial governments have established an informal division of roles through intergovernmental negotiations. The Canadian Council of Ministers of the Environment offers a closed forum for such discussions. To date, federal-provincial relations in the environmental field have been closer to discussions among equals than a hierarchical relationship. Unlike the United States the federal government in Canada has not attempted to induce provincial conformance with federal objectives either through the use of grants for environmental administration or through threats to withhold fiscal transfers in other policy areas.

Contemporary federal-provincial relations in the environmental field can be divided into four periods. In the first, from the late 1960s to the early 1970s, both levels of government were eager to exercise their environmental jurisdiction in response to growing public concern for the environment, resulting in jurisdictional tensions. The larger provinces in particular were defensive concerning their natural resources jurisdiction and relatively resistant to increased federal involvement in the environmental field.

During the second period, jurisdictional tensions subsided, reflecting both a decline in public attention to environmental issues, and thus a decline in assertiveness by federal and provincial governments alike, and growing deference to the provinces by the federal government. From the early 1970s to the late 1980s, a practical division of powers emerged, with the federal government conducting research and coordinating joint federal-provincial efforts to establish national standards, and the provinces serving as the front-line enforcers of environmental regulations. Formal bilateral accords were reached between the federal government and seven provinces, in which the provinces agreed to enforce national standards, and the federal government to defer to the provinces so long as they were doing the job. A similar "one window" approach was taken by the federal government in the three provinces that declined to sign formal accords. However, although provincial enforcement of many national standards was uneven at best, the federal government intervened only rarely during this period to enforce national standards.

In the third period, the resurgence of public concern in the late 1980s prompted renewed environmental protection efforts by both federal and provincial governments, and not coincidentally, renewed intergovernmental conflict. The first irritant to provincial jurisdictional sensitivities was the federal government's reassertion of an independent role in the environmental field with the passage of the Canadian Environmental Protection Act in 1988. Intergovernmental tensions were exacerbated when environmental groups won a series of court decisions that forced the federal government to play a more aggressive role in environmental assessment, including performing assessments of the provinces' own projects. The decisions pitted the federal government against the provinces in prominent court cases concerning the Oldman Dam in Alberta, the Rafferty-Alameda dams in Saskatchewan, and the second phase of the James Bay hydro development in Quebec.

As the salience of environmental issues declined in the early 1990s, federal and provincial governments renewed their efforts to accommodate federal and provincial roles in the environmental field. Faced with budgetary constraints, both levels of government are anxious to reestablish "one window" enforcement arrangements.

Kathryn Harrison

Further Readings

Lucas, Alastair. "Harmonization of Federal and Provincial Environmental Policies." In *Managing Natural Resources in a Federal State*. Ed. Owen Saunders. 1986.

Tingley, Donna. "Conflict and Cooperation on the Environment." In *Canada: The State of the Federation 1991*. Ed. Douglas Brown. 1991.

See also ENVIRONMENT CANADA; ENVIRONMENTAL CASE LAW (CANADA): COMMON LAW CAUSES OF ACTION; FEDERALISM AND ENVIRONMENTAL PROTECTION: UNITED STATES; JAMES BAY; LEGISLATION: CANADA; RAFFERTY-ALAMEDA DAMS

Federalism and Environmental Protection: United States

A new federal-state partnership exists in U.S. environmental policy today, a relationship that can best be described as regulatory federalism. Also termed partial preemption, the procedure allows the federal government to return program responsibility to the states while retaining the authority to decide on the acceptability of states' actions. States are given the latitude to design and implement their own laws, but these laws must meet minimum federal standards and objectives. Thus, partial preemption is a delegation of authority but not an abdication of federal control.

Recent environmental statutes enacted by the U.S. Congress and implemented by the U.S. Environmental Protection Agency (EPA) are examples of partial preemption: the Clean Air Act Amendments of 1970, the Safe Drinking Water Act of 1974, and the Resource Conservation and Recovery Act of 1976, among others. These acts and their reauthorization amendments contain a unique partial preemption scheme which environmental enforcement agents refer to as primacy. This technique attempts to encourage states to implement the provisions of the acts by applying for primacy enforcement responsibility. To receive this delegation of authority (or authorization) state laws must be at least as stringent as the applicable federal statutes.

From a national perspective authorization (or primacy) is desirable because it promotes minimal federal standards nationwide as opposed to stringency in some states and laxity in others. From the state perspective primacy allows a state to have some control over its environmental programs. The EPA is responsible for enforcing the federal statutes in states that elect not to seek primacy. Furthermore, if a state is not in compliance with minimum federal standards and procedures, the EPA can revoke its grant of primacy.

At the present time opinions differ widely on the effectiveness of the American states in carrying out their responsibilities so far as environmental protection is concerned. Some argue that because of paltry resources, or a lack of political will, state governments are the principal impediment to effective American government. According to these critics the states lack the fiscal resources and/or technical expertise available to national governments; they suffer from parochialism; they cannot raise revenues to meet service demands; and they are dominated by a conservative, business-oriented elite. Others argue that the institutional reforms of the 1970s and the 1980s changed all this. The supporters of state governments argue that, compared with the federal government, the states are more flexible and innovative and, because they are closer to the problems, are better able to fashion appropriate responses.

At any rate, the states are now implementing key environmental statutes enacted in the 1960s and the 1970s. Nearly all major federal environmental statutes call for shared implementation between the federal and state governments (as described earlier). In addition two dramatic developments affected the states during the 1970s and the 1980s. First, the Nixon, Reagan, and Bush administrations, under their various programs of new federalism, attempted to return power and authority to the states and cities. New federalism, which began with the State and Local Fiscal Assistance Act of 1972, mandated an expanded role for state and local governments. Among other things states would become less subject to fiscal control by the federal government. Initially new federalism involved a number of short-term inducements, such as programmatic flexibility, elimination of de facto dual-planning requirements for categorical grant applications, and increased consultation with state and local decision makers prior to the initiation of direct development activities.

Second, President Reagan's new federalism program had another major objective for environmental policy: to defund federal environmental protection activities. Proponents of the Reagan program argued that the states, with changes in their institutional capacities, were now better able to assume environmental responsibilities. States and cities would make difficult choices about which programs they wanted to retain and which ones they wanted to terminate. Public pressure would force state decision makers to take actions that reflected localized policy preferences. Critics, on the other hand, argued that this devolution was the administration's way to eliminate environmental programs altogether.

During the Reagan and Bush administrations federal grants to the states were subject to substantial budgetary cuts in a number of environmental program areas, including air pollution control, water pollution control, hazardous waste management, pesticide enforcement, wastewater treatment, and safe drinking water. The significance of these cuts can be seen in the level of state dependency on federal funds for these programs. In the early to mid-1980s, federal grants constituted from 33 to 75 percent of the average state budgets for air and water pollution control and hazardous waste management.

Early assessments have revealed that most of the states did not proffer their own funds in the environmental area, at least not in the period from 1981 to 1984. States that did had also demonstrated the political will to assume the administration of federal programs under partial preemption; they also had an ethos conducive to environmental protection. From 1985 to 1994 many of the states replaced lost federal funds by increasing state and local taxes and user fees. Even though we do not have complete information on all the states during the period from 1981 to 1994 we can assume that some of the states did not replace the federal cuts with their own funds. The states faced a national recession during this time and the fiscal climate was not conducive to raising taxes. Indeed, many states were constrained by an anti-taxation ethic regardless of broad public support for environmental protection programs.

Moreover, President Clinton has not yet said what he will do about the devolution of responsibility to the states and cities. Nor has he promised the states more money to fund environmental programs. His appointment of Carol Browner, the former head of Florida's Department of Environmental Regulation, to run the EPA is certain to guarantee attention at the highest levels to the problems faced by the states. Nevertheless, the large federal budget deficit, as well as the president's 1992 campaign pledge not to significantly raise taxes on the middle class, leads one to assume that the states will be left largely to their own resources. Thus, the decentralization of federal environmental programs and reductions of federal grants-in-aid are likely to continue.

The policy implications of new federalism and environmental protection are significant, to say the least. If federal inducements (such as legislation and environmental aid) are necessary conditions for successful environmental management at the state level, then a policy of decentralization will probably not work effectively for all states. If on the other hand, the states are committed to environmental protection and have the necessary fiscal and institutional capabilities to implement federal statutes, then decentralization of environmental programs is a good idea. Or decentralization may work well in some states but poorly in others. In the latter instance, "selective decentralization" (a policy that decentralizes some programs for some states while leaving others alone) may be a more appropriate strategy.

In any case policy makers will need to reconsider the impact of federalism on state environmental policy. The federal government should recognize that the fifty states are not equally able to muster the necessary resources to deal with environmental problems in the 1990s. Novel approaches will thus be required and are particularly appropriate in an era of regulatory federalism, which will likely characterize the 1990s.

James P. Lester

Further Readings

Crotty, Patricia M. "The New Federalism Game: Primacy Implementation of Environmental Policy." *Publius* 17 (1987): 57–63.

Lester, James P. "New Federalism and Environmental Policy." *Publius* 16 (1986): 149–65.

Lowry, William R. *The Dimensions of Federalism.* 1992.

See also BUSH, GEORGE; ENVIRONMENTAL PROTECTION AGENCY; FEDERALISM AND ENVIRONMENTAL PROTECTION: CANADA; REAGAN, RONALD; RESOURCE CONSERVATION AND RECOVERY ACT

Feral Species
See EXOTIC SPECIES

Fernow, Bernhard E.
See FOREST SERVICE (U.S.); FORESTRY, HISTORY OF

Fertilizers
See AGRICULTURE: ENVIRONMENT IMPACTS; EUTROPHICATION

FIFRA
See FEDERAL INSECTICIDE, FUNGICIDE AND RODENTICIDE ACT

Fish Farming
See AQUACULTURE

Fish Tumors

Fish tumors are found in large numbers in many populations of teleosts (bony fishes) throughout the world. It is now recognized that these neoplasms can be caused by exposure to chemical contaminants or by infection with tumor viruses. Other mechanisms for tumor formation may be possible, including the synergistic effects of chemicals and viruses. In general fish that develop tumors as a result of chemical exposure are bottom-dwelling species that are in close contact with contaminated sediments. Examples of this are the English sole flatfish from industrialized regions of Puget Sound, Washington, and the brown bullhead catfish from various contaminated areas of the Great Lakes in North America. Populations of both of these species have been documented with high incidences of tumors.

The types of fish tumors most commonly associated with exposure to chemicals are liver tumors, and various malignancies of the skin, such as squamous cell carcinomas. However, there is little evidence linking chemicals to several other types of fish neoplasms, such as gonadal tumors, leukemias, and some skin papillomas. It is likely that these neoplasms are caused by tumor viruses. There is no evidence that fish tumor viruses are a health hazard to humans that may consume an infected fish. However, fish that have been exposed to chemical contaminants may contain high concentrations of these compounds, and these chemical residues may be a health hazard to humans consuming contaminated fish flesh.

Chris D. Metcalfe

Further Readings

Harshbarger, J.C., and J.B. Clark. "Epizootiology of Neoplasms in Bony Fish from North America." *The Science of the Total Environment* 94 (1990).

Malins, D.C., B.B. McCain, J.T. Landahl, M.S. Myers, M.M. Krahn, D.W. Brown, S.-L. Chan, and W.T. Roubal. "Neoplastic and Other Diseases in Fish in Relation to Toxic Chemicals: An Overview." *Aquatic Toxicology* 11 (1988).

See also GREAT LAKES; PERSISTENT ORGANOCHLORINE COMPOUNDS; PESTICIDES

Fisheries Act (Canada)

Canada's Fisheries Act, first passed in 1868, has contained pollution prevention provisions since its inception. Section 35 makes it an offense to undertake projects that result in the harmful alteration, disruption, or destruction of fish habitats. Section 36 prohibits the deposition of deleterious substances into water frequented by fish. In 1991 amendments to the Act raised fines for violations of either the fish habitat or deleterious deposit provisions to match those outlined in the Canadian Environmental Protection Act. Penalties range from fines of $300,000 for first offenses to $1 million plus up to three years in jail for repeat offenses. The 1991 amendments also require an annual Report to Parliament on the enforcement and administration of the habitat and pollution provisions.

The 1979 separation of the Canadian Department of Fisheries and Oceans (DFO) from Environment Canada resulted in the splitting of federal authority between the two departments and necessitated a Memorandum of Understanding between DFO and Environment Canada regarding the joint administration of the pollution provisions. Environment Canada has retained the lead role in the federal administration of the pollution provisions.

Since early in this century the administration of the Fisheries Act has been delegated or partially delegated to a number of provinces. In the Atlantic provinces and the northern territories the federal government administers the Act. In Alberta, Saskatchewan, Manitoba, and Ontario the provinces administer the Act and in British Columbia and Quebec administration is shared. This results in different relationships of authority among the federal and provincial departments of fisheries and environment in the different provinces.

Pollution prevention regulations under the Fisheries Act apply to the pulp and paper, petroleum refining, metal mining, chlor-alkali mercury, and meat, poultry and potato processing industries. Critics argue that the Canadian tradition of negotiating compliance rather than prosecuting offending firms has made it difficult to enforce regulations.

Glen Toner

Further Readings

Doern, G. Bruce, and Thomas Conway. *The Greening of Canada*. 1994.

Macdonald, Doug. *The Politics of Pollution*. 1991.

See also ENVIRONMENT CANADA; LEGISLATION: CANADA; MERCURY; PULP AND PAPER MILLS

Fisheries Conservation

Conservation of fisheries has for centuries been inhibited by legal problems concerning the legal status of fish, allocation of access to them, and the rights to regulate and enforce any controls necessary to prevent overfishing. Fish are regarded as common property resources, with no distinction drawn between fin fish and marine mammals, as confirmed in the Bering Fur Seal Arbitration (1884). No state or individual has property rights to fish in the sea; rights are acquired by those capturing the fish and reducing them to their possession. For over 300 years this doctrine has been coupled with that of freedom of fishing on the high seas; thus all states, their nationals, and fishing vessels enjoyed rights of unregulated access to high seas living resources. Access could be restricted and regulated only with the consent of the states concerned; there is no means of imposing international regulations, however desirable for conservation purposes.

Historically, conservation has involved development of international law by negotiation of international conventions at global and regional levels through international organizations or *ad hoc*. Where these laws do not exist the result is widespread overfishing: most major stocks of commercial interest are fished above biologically sustainable levels. More fishermen accessed fisheries than the fisheries could efficiently and economically sustain, and conflicts arose concerning access, use of gear, regulation, and so forth. Many species declined dramatically, especially certain stocks of marine mammals, since the few conventions negotiated were based on compromises necessary to secure agreement and were often poorly enforced by the flag states concerned.

A solution adopted by some states was to endeavor to extend national control over fisheries. Traditionally, until the 1970s most states claimed only a narrow belt of territorial sea in which they could exclude foreign vessels from fishing and regarded areas beyond as high seas. Some began to claim wider territorial sea limits; others to assert claims mainly for fisheries purposes to exclusive "maritime zones" of up to 200 nautical miles. However, the International Court of Justice in the Anglo-Norwegian Fisheries Case (1951) held that though special circumstances such as fisheries might justify extension of national limits, such encroachment into the high seas always had "an international aspect"; the validity of new limits depended on the consent or acquiescence of other states fishing in the area.

United Nations Conferences on the Law of the Sea: 1958 and 1960

The 1958 United Nations (UN) Convention on the High Seas codified the freedom of fishing on the high seas, subject to states exercising it with "reasonable regard to the interests of other States" exercising this and other freedoms of the seas. This contributed little to conservation. No specific limit was set on the breadth of the territorial sea; neither was the concept of exclusive fisheries zones accepted by the United Nations Conference on the Law of the Sea (UNCLOS) I in 1958 or II in 1960. Moreover, an accompanying 1958 Convention on the Continental Shelf allocated the sedentary species of the shelf exclusively to coastal states, without any specific requirements for conservation.

A separate 1958 Convention on Fishing and the Conservation of the Living Resources of the High Seas stated that the nature of problems involved in their conservation required that they be solved by international cooperation, but defined "conservation" in terms of the aggregate of measures enabling the "optimum sustainable yield" from fisheries to ensure maximum food and product supplies. It required its state parties to agree upon conservation measures for the high seas and in certain limited circumstances gave coastal states the right unilaterally to adopt conservation measures for areas of high seas adjacent to their territorial seas. Coastal states, however, could not enforce these measures against states that did not accept them (e.g., by participating in relevant conservation treaties).

This Convention has remained largely ineffective, though some coastal and distant water fishing states have adopted conservation measures through *ad hoc* fishery commissions. These have been limited; originally most commissions were concerned with setting an overall total allowable catch (TAC) based on the now discredited concept of maximum sustainable yield (MSY), though later they began to set quotas for individual species, regulate the gear used, declare closed seasons and areas, and require the collection of scientific data. The competence to adopt the measures prescribed was shared among coastal and flag states and the international commissions. Enforcement, notoriously weak, was largely left to flag and coastal states with only a few commissions introducing joint enforcement schemes, which merely allowed participants to mutually inspect each others' vessels and to report any violations of international regulations to the flag state concerned.

Commissions were established to regulate particular species, either globally as in the case of whales, or regionally as for tuna, seals, halibut, and salmon in certain areas, or mixed fisheries in particular regions such as the Northeast and Northwest Atlantic, the North Pacific, the Baltic, the Mediterranean, and elsewhere. All found it difficult to achieve the consensus necessary to fully implement scientific advice on catch levels, or to reduce fishing efforts or the number of entrants to the fishery. To retain members they had to provide "objection procedures" whereby recalcitrant states could opt out of conservatory measures agreed by the majority. The problem of third states fishing the resources and refusing to join the commissions remained intractable. Meanwhile technological developments in fishing vessels, gear used, and means of locating fisheries rapidly intensified the ability to take large quantities of fish, thus further depleting stocks. Few developing states participated in the 1958 Conventions.

Third United Nations Conference on the Law of the Sea: 1973–1982

The larger number of developing coastal states participating in UNCLOS III, concerned by depletion of their coastal fisheries through use by the distant water factory fleets of the industrialized states, supported the introduction of a new jurisdictional approach, based on the concept of a 200-nautical mile Exclusive Economic Zone (EEZ) within which coastal States would exercise sovereign rights over fisheries for purposes of exploitation and conservation. The concept gained ground rapidly, supported also by many concerned developed states such as Canada and Iceland.

The Exclusive Economic Zone

Part V of the 1982 UNCLOS, adopted by UNCLOS III, allows states to claim 200-nautical mile EEZs in areas beyond but adjacent to a twelve-mile territorial sea (Article 55), measured from its baselines (Article 57).

In the EEZ the coastal state exercises sovereign rights, *inter alia*, for purposes of exploring and exploiting, conserving and managing its living resources, and jurisdiction, as provided in relevant parts of the Convention, with regard to marine scientific research and protection and preservation of the marine environment (Article 56). This gives coastal states the opportunity effectively to conserve the resources that are in the EEZ on a more holistic and ecologically sound basis than hitherto. Conservation is fa-

F

cilitated by provisions in Part XIII of the UNCLOS enabling coastal states to control and participate in scientific research and in Part XII requiring and enabling them to regulate pollution from all sources that impact, *inter alia*, on fisheries and their habitats and, in particular, to take measures to protect and preserve rare or fragile ecosystems and the habitats of depleted, threatened, or endangered species and other forms of marine life (Article 194 [5]). They can also impose, in certain specified circumstances—including protection of resources—mandatory measures to prevent pollution in specially vulnerable areas (Article 211 [6]), after discussion of proposed measures in the "competent" international organization (the UN's International Maritime Organization).

Although a coastal state can now determine access to its EEZ, rights are subject to corresponding duties. It must take such conservation measures as will ensure that the fish stocks are not endangered by over exploitation, that stocks are maintained at or restored to "levels which can produce MSY as qualified by relevant environmental and economic factors, including the economic needs of coastal fishing communities and the special requirements of developing States, and taking into account fishing patterns, the interdependence of stocks and any generally recommended subregional, regional or global minimum standards" (Article 61 [3]).

These provisions provide no more than a general framework and general principles within which coastal states are left to develop conservation measures at their discretion. Though they have to determine the allowable catch, promote optimum utilization of the fisheries and determine their own harvesting capacity, they are only required to allow other states (largely at their discretion) access to any surplus based on the state's own requirements (Article 62 [1] and [2]). Various factors could justify suspension of any TACs for a period in the interests of conservation to allow stock recovery.

Since coastal states now also have extensive enforcement powers in the EEZ (Article 62 [4]) conservation stands to be much improved if these new powers are used wisely and effectively. Problems still arise, however, where stocks cross maritime boundaries.

Species Approach

A special cooperative regime is laid down for highly migratory species (Article 64) which are listed in an Annex. States are required to cooperate in the conservation of marine mammals, which can be regulated by a coastal state or international organization more strictly than other fisheries and are not required to be used optimally. In the case of cetaceans states must, in particular, work through the appropriate international organizations for their conservation, management, and study (Article 65). Anadronous species such as salmon (Article 66) and catadronous species such as eels (Article 66) are left to be conserved respectively by their state of origin or the coastal State in whose waters they spend the greater part of their life and can be harvested only within the EEZ. Sedentary species of the continental shelf are, as before, subsumed within the sovereign rights of the coastal state to exploit the resources of the shelf, without specific requirements for conservation. Major revisions of conventions establishing fishery commissions has been necessary as coastal states incorporated areas of high seas within their 200-nautical mile EEZs or exclusive fisheries zones (EFZs) and conventions regulating the taking of Atlantic and Pacific salmon were concluded that reflected the provisions of the UNCLOS regimes.

Shared and Straddling Stocks

A weakness in the UNCLOS regime, currently giving rise to conservation disputes, arises from the ambiguity of its provisions concerning the conservation of shared stocks that traverse the boundaries of EEZs, and straddling stocks which migrate between the high seas and EEZs. Article 63 requires the states concerned (i.e., states fishing such stocks) to agree upon the measures necessary for their conservation, but sets no specific requirements. It is thus left to the states concerned to enter into agreements. Though some states and international entities have done so (e.g., European Economic Community/Norway), difficulties have arisen in other cases—notably in the area of the new North West Atlantic Fisheries Organization (NAFO), whose members include the European Economic Community (EEC) and Canada, where unscrupulous fishing vessel owners from a European Community (EC) member state have reflagged their vessels, registering them in states not party to the Convention, in order to avoid the NAFO conservatory measures. The UNCLOS provisions on conservation of high seas fisheries (articles 116–119) are expressed in general and ambiguous terms.

The United Nations Conference on Environment and Development (UNCED, Agenda

21, Chapter 17, paragraphs 50–53) addressed this problem and called for the convening of a UN Conference on Straddling Stocks and Highly Migratory Species. This opened in 1993 and is continuing. It aims to adopt a Code or agreement on this. A Code of Conduct for Responsible Fishing is being developed through the UN Food and Agriculture Organization (FAO). An Agreement to Promote Compliance with International Conservation and Management Measures by Fishing Vessels on the High Seas, concluded through FAO, opened for signature in 1994.

Over ninety states had claimed EEZs or EFZs even before the entry into force of UNCLOS. It remains to be seen how effective conservation within them will be since many developing states lack the scientific knowledge and enforcement capability to use their new powers fully and effectively. Most of the fishing conventions were renegotiated following widespread adoption of EEZs; as a result, coastal state parties now generally seek advice only from the fishery commissions—which they are not obliged to follow, only to "take into account." Most joint enforcement schemes lapsed with the reduction of most of their area to national jurisdiction.

However, there is evidence that states are beginning to appreciate the advantages for conservation of cooperating in surveillance of fishing vessels; NAFO, the Convention on Conservation of Antarctica Marine Living Resources (CCAMLR) and the EC have all moved in this direction and in 1992 the Niue Treaty on Cooperation in Fisheries Surveillance and Law Enforcement in the South Pacific Region was concluded. The FAO is encouraging such developments, having moved from its early focus on development of coastal fisheries by developing states to a more conservatory approach that also includes awareness of the need to protect fishery habitats and thus to prevent pollution and other disturbances. The United Nations Environment Programme (UNEP) 1986 Noumea Convention for the Protection of Natural Resources and the Environment in the South Pacific Region and the 1992 Convention on the Baltic Sea bring together fisheries conservation and prevention of pollution; others may emulate this trend.

Finally, it should be noted that UNCED and other bodies have drawn attention to the relevance to fishery conservation of the "precautionary principle" developed in relation to pollution control, which requires that action be taken when it seems likely that harm may occur to fish habitats. UNCED has also stressed the concept of "common concern," which entitles other states to place urgent conservatory issues on the agenda of relevant international bodies as, for example, the consideration by the UN of the use of drift nets by the fishing industry (which resulted in the incidental killing of dolphins and small cetacea trapped therein) leading to the adoption by the General Assembly of a resolution condemning their use and to conclusion of the regional 1989 Wellington Convention for the Prohibition of Fishing with Long Drift Nets in the South Pacific.

It should be noted also that some fisheries, especially those on marine mammals, are conserved under wildlife conventions on whose annexes species can be listed if threatened in various ways. Such conventions include those concerning Trade in Endangered Species (CITES 1973); Conservation of Migratory Species of Wild Animals (CCMSWA 1979); and the Conservation of European Wildlife and Natural Habitats (Berne, 1979). UNEP and the International Maritime Organization (IMO) have both developed the conservatory concept of "Special Areas" in relevant conventions, including recent protocols to certain UNEP regional seas conventions, for example, the 1990 Protocol to the 1983 Cartagena Convention concerning Specially Protected Areas and Wildlife in the Wider Caribbean, and the London Convention: Guidelines on Particularly Sensitive Sea Areas were adopted under the auspices of IMO in the context of dumping of wastes in the oceans.

Patricia W. Birnie

Further Readings

Birnie, Patricia W., and Alan E. Boyle. *International Law and the Environment.* 1993.

Burke, William T. *The New International Law of Fisheries: UNCLOS 1982 and Beyond.* 1994.

Hey, Ellen. *The Regime for Exploitation of Transboundary Marine Fishery Resources.* 1989.

Johnston, Douglas M. *The International Law of Fisheries.* 1965.

Koers, Albert W. *International Regulation of Marine Fisheries.* 1973.

Miles, Edward, ed. *Management of World Fisheries: Implications of Extended Fisheries Jurisdiction.* 1989.

Florida Panther

The Florida panther (*Felis concolor coryi*), a
distinct subspecies of the cougar or mountain
lion, is one of the most endangered of all mammals. This rare animal is similar to the western
cougar, but smaller and darker. A few centuries
ago the very name Florida panther would have
been a misnomer since the creature inhabited all
or part of Texas, Louisiana, Mississippi, Alabama, Georgia, Arkansas, Tennessee, South
Carolina, and Florida. Its range is now limited
to portions of the Everglades in Florida, and its
numbers have diminished to perhaps fifty or
fewer individuals in the wild. Historically, the
Florida panther, as most cougars near to human
populations, was shot on sight. Cougar
shootings occurred for two reasons: 1) cougars
attack domesticated animals, not knowing the
difference; and 2) large cats have always been
feared, perhaps justifiably in some circumstances, by humans. By the 1920s the Florida
panther's habitat had pretty well shrunk to territories within the state whose name it bears.

The Florida panther faced thereafter a
wide variety of perils. In the 1930s a deer eradication program to control the fever tick threatened food supplies, but probably most problematic was the access provided to humans by the
1928 construction of the cross-state highway
Route 41 (the Tamiami Trail) and so-called
Alligator Alley in the 1960s. The panther was
given complete protection from hunting in
1958, but the roads themselves were and are as
great a peril. During the 1980s road kills were
the leading source of death. New highways in
the area are being built with wildlife under-
passes and extensive (and expensive) fencing for
the panther and other creatures, even though it
may well be too late for the panther.

In the early 1970s the Florida panther was
thought to be extinct in the wild. This is not the
case but the population is so small that inbreeding is taking place and genetic diversity is continuously declining. Researchers have devised a
plan to save the subspecies that involves leaving some creatures in the wild and, at the same
time, initiating a captive breeding and later re-

lease program. It is hoped that releases will
begin in about two decades when a large captive population has been established. Large
tracts of potential habitat are being established,
but many threats remain including hunters
(even when they do not shoot at panthers, they
may frighten them out of their territory and into
other dangers) and mercury or other toxic substances (large cats are vulnerable because, being at the top of the food chain, they may consume creatures such as raccoons who in turn
feed on fish). A population so small—30 to 50
creatures in the wild— is inevitably a vulnerable
population, but there remains yet some hope for
success.

Robert Paehlke

Further Readings

Hansen, Kevin. *Cougar: The American Lion.*
1992.
Maehr, D.S. "The Florida Panther and Private
Lands." *Conservation Biology* 4 (1990):
167–70.

Fluoride

Fluoride is the most important ionic species of
fluorine, the lightest and most reactive of the
halogen elements. It forms a major component
of minerals such as fluorite (CaF_2) and cryolite
(Na_3AlF_6) and readily substitutes for the hydroxide ion in a wide range of other minerals.
While it is commonly associated with volcanic
rocks and volcanic gases, it occurs ubiquitously
in the environment, occurring to varying extents
in soil, water, biota, and the atmosphere. It is
also being used increasingly in industry, most
notably as an active constituent of dental health
products.

The solubility of most fluoride minerals
is relatively low and levels of fluoride rarely
exceed 1 milligram per liter (mg/l) of water.
Elevated concentrations of fluoride are most
frequently found either in groundwaters obtained from volcanic terranes or, in some
cases, older, cation-exchanged groundwaters
exhibiting extremely low levels of calcium. In
some cases, natural levels of fluoride can exceed 10 mg/l.

Effects of fluoride on plants and animals
are generally well-known. Plants exhibit a
wide range of sensitivities but for the most

part can tolerate all but the most extreme exposure. Animals, including humans, appear to benefit from moderate exposure to fluoride, but can suffer severe toxic effects at higher concentrations. A problem here is that the margin of error between these extremes is relatively small.

Most dental health authorities believe that approximately 1 mg/l fluoride in drinking water will significantly reduce the incidence of tooth decay. The precise "optimal" value will depend on daily fluid intake, which, in turn, depends on climate. In general 1 mg/l is recommended for temperate climates, the value reducing to as low as 0.6 mg/l in hotter regimes. Since the 1940s recognition for the potential benefits of fluoride has inspired many jurisdictions in North America to add fluoride to fluoride-deficient municipal water supplies. Most experts argue that this practice has caused a 50 percent reduction in tooth decay among children during the past twenty years. Many others, however, oppose the fluoridation of water supplies. They argue that tampering with water quality for the purposes of administering medication to the masses is objectionable and sets a bad precedent. They also contend that the benefits of fluoridation are exaggerated and that the observed reduction in tooth decay is primarily the result of improved nutrition and dental hygiene. A further concern is that drinking water represents only one source of exposure to fluoride and that some individuals using fluoride toothpastes and topical fluoride applications in addition to ingesting fluoridated water may risk toxic exposure. In addition there are some industrial sources of fluoride exposure.

The most common toxic effect of fluoride on humans is dental fluorosis, a disturbance affecting the enamel of the teeth during their formation. At its most severe all enamel surfaces are damaged and the teeth are severely corroded and stained. In some cases the condition is developed following long-term ingestion of drinking water containing fluoride in the range 2 to 8 mg/l. Further exposure to fluoride can chemically alter the bone, a potentially crippling condition known as skeletal fluorosis. The problem is endemic in areas with drinking water containing high fluoride concentrations (over 10 mg/l). It is particularly serious in tropical and sub-tropical regions where fluid intake is high and poor nutrition and calcium deficiency exacerbate the problem.

Ken W.F. Howard

Further Readings

Hem, J.D. *Study and Interpretation of the Chemical Characteristics of Natural Water.* U.S. Geological Survey Water-Supply Paper 2254, 1989.

World Health Organization. *Fluorine and Fluorides: Environmental Health Criteria 36.* 1984.

See also FOOD ADDITIVES

F

FOE

See FRIENDS OF THE EARTH

Food Additives

A food additive may be defined broadly as any chemical, natural or synthetic, that is deliberately used in the growth, processing, storage, or distribution of food. There are two basic categories of food additives. Substances intentionally added to food during processing and that serve a specific function are "food-processing additives." These include preservatives, sweeteners, colors, and flavors. Additives intentionally used in the cycle of food production but that unintentionally remain in or on food when we eat it are "unintentional additives." These include chemicals from food packaging, pesticide residues, and hormones and antibiotics from animal products. Approximately 3,000 direct and indirect additives may be used in our foods; almost two-thirds of these are flavorings used to replace natural flavors lost during processing.

In defining "food additive," most government regulations refer exclusively to food-processing additives. Though specific regulations vary among governments, the following substances are often not considered as food additives: salt, sugar, starch, vitamins, mineral nutrients, amino acids, spices, seasonings, flavoring preparations, agricultural chemicals, food-packaging chemicals, and veterinary drugs.

Food-processing additives are used to impart particular qualities to foods and are added after the food has been grown, harvested, and shipped to a food processor. They serve two general functions. First, they are used to prevent food from spoiling by inhibiting the formation of molds, the activity of bacteria, and the development of rancidity. Second, food-processing additives are used to make food more appealing in flavor, color, or texture, more uniform in composition, more suitable to manufacturing procedures, and more extended in shelf-life.

Food-processing additives are used almost exclusively in processed foods and are of the following types:

- *Colors*, which make food look more appealing. Natural pigments and extracts come from plants, animals and minerals. Synthetic dyes are derived from coal tar and petroleum. The majority of colors used in food today are synthetic dyes.
- *Preservatives*, which keep food from going bad. Antimicrobials prevent the growth of microorganisms such as molds, yeasts, and bacteria. Antioxidants protect food from going bad or discoloring when exposed to oxygen. Both types give food and food ingredients a longer shelf-life.
- *Flavors and Flavor Enhancers*, which make food taste better. Natural flavors are derived from natural ingredients processed into concentrated oils and extracts. Artificial flavors are synthetically produced and are used in place of more expensive natural flavors. Flavor enhancers are used to increase the strength of a flavor without adding a different taste to the food. Under some government regulations flavors and flavor enhancers may be considered as food ingredients rather than additives.
- *Sweeteners*, which make food taste sweeter. Artificial sweeteners, generally hundreds of times sweeter than sugar, include aspartame (NutraSweet®), sucralose (Splenda®), saccharin, and acesulfame K (Sunette®; Sweet One®).
- *Texture Agents*, which give food a pleasing texture.
- *Processing Agents*, which make food-processing easier. They may be used to hasten natural processes, to prevent undesired reactions, and to initiate desired reactions.

Governments strictly regulate which foods may contain a certain additive and the level permitted. The safety of an additive is determined by laboratory animal experimentation. A margin of safety is applied (typically of 100) so that no more than 1 percent of a dose causing no effect in test animals may be used in food.

It is generally agreed that most of the food additives in use today are safe. However, there is a small number of additives considered by some scientists to be of questionable safety. These include colors (primarily synthetic), sulfites (preservatives), nitrates and nitrites (preservatives), BHA and BHT (preservatives), flavors, MSG (flavor enhancer), and artificial sweeteners.

Randee Holmes

Further Readings
Holmes, Randee. *Additive Alert! What Have They Done To Our Food?: A Consumer's Action Guide.* 1994.

See also DELANEY CLAUSE; PESTICIDES

Food Chains
The plants, animals, and microorganisms that make up a biological community and their physical surroundings are all interconnected by a complex web of relationships. These relationships are exemplified by the food chain or feeding sequences through which energy flows in the system, and the pathways by which matter (carbon, oxygen, nitrogen, phosphorus, and numerous other chemicals) moves in cycles. Energy and matter are essential to the biological system to maintain its structure and to carry out the various functions of growth, maintenance, and reproduction.

Green plants form the base of the food chain using solar energy that enters the system in the form of radiation. Green plants thus are the first trophic (feeding) level, and are known as "producers" or "autotrophs." Then a wide array of organisms, animals and microbes, eat the plants to obtain their food. These organisms at the second trophic level are known as herbivores (plant eaters), or "primary consumers." Next, at the third trophic level, there are the carnivores or "secondary consumers" that include animals and microbes that feed, parasitize, or prey on the herbivores. Tertiary consumers are animals that eat other carnivores, etc. Finally, when plants, animals, and microbes die, there are other animals and microbes that feed on the dead organisms. These so called detrivores break down the biological material to the basic chemical elements of carbon, oxygen, nitrogen, and other essential chemicals for recycling in the biological system.

The feeding in an ecosystem and the transfer of energy from one level in the food chain to another is not always an isolated sequence as suggested above. A given species population can occupy more than one trophic level according to the source of the food energy consumed. Some carnivores prey on both herbivores and other carnivores that are at different levels in the food chain. Foxes, for example, feed on mice and rabbits, both are herbivores, and they also feed on raccoons and birds, which are both herbivores and carnivores. Actually, when hungry, foxes sometimes will feed on berries and other plant material and thus, in a limited way, are omnivores. This interlocking pattern of feeding is referred to as the food web rather than food chain. Humans feed on both plant and animal material, and therefore are omnivores. Humans are thus both low in the food chain when eating grains and high in the food chain when eating fish and beef.

The number of trophic levels in the food chain is often limited to four or five because of the rapid dissipation of energy in the food chain. For example, when one organism eats another, approximately 90 percent of the chemical energy consumed is dissipated as heat energy, and therefore only 10 percent is passed on in the form of living weight to the next level in the food chain. By this process, the biomass of organisms higher in the food chain is lower than that of organisms lower in the food chain.

The rapid decline in food availability for organisms high in the food chain can be illustrated with a pasture. The forage grasses and forbs in a hectare may produce about three tons of biomass per year. Only 300 kilograms (kg) of this biomass is available to the second level in the food chain after the herbivores have fed on the pasture forage. This declines theoretically to thirty, then three, and finally to only 0.3 kg at the fifth trophic level. If the decline in amount of biomass available to each succeeding level of the food chain is graphed it appears as a pyramid with the plants forming the base of the pyramid.

A complicating factor in investigating food chains is the different rates of metabolism in various organisms. For example, in an aquatic ecosystem the plant community often consists of phytoplankton or microscopic plants. These small plants may have a high rate of metabolism and thus their standing biomass may be relatively small compared with the fishes that are feeding on them. When expressed in biomass, this aquatic system may not show a nice pyramid as was mentioned earlier for the pasture. Instead, the plant biomass for the aquatic sys-

tem may be relatively small compared to the biomass of the fishes. However, in terms of total energy flow this food system is similar to the pasture. The phytoplankton, because of their high rate of metabolism, supply approximately ten times the amount of energy that is present in the fish feeding on them. In fact, energy flow pyramids give the most accurate assessment of the roles of organisms at the various trophic levels.

David Pimentel

Further Readings
Odum, E.P. *Fundamentals of Ecology.* 1971.
Raven, P.H., L.R. Berg, and G.B. Johnson. *Environment.* 1993.

See also Bioaccumulation; Keystone Species; Web of Life

Forest Fires and Conservation

Large and recurrent lightning-caused fires are widespread in conifer forests and pine or oak savannas worldwide. The general rule is that 95 percent of the area burned is due to 5 percent of the fires. In other words a few large fires burn most of the area. These large fires generally recur in any given locality at fifty- to 200-year intervals.

Studies indicate that weather plays a key role in determining the fire regime of different forests. The fire recurrence period is determined by the frequency of an ignition source which has been preceded by a period of warm dry weather. There are generally ample ignition sources as indicated by the large number of fires that occur in most years in forested regions. However, the area burned in a typical fire is usually small because the fuel moisture is not low enough to allow the rapid spread of fire. In occasional years anomalous high pressure weather systems persist over a large area for extended periods, resulting in extreme fuel drying conditions. In such years very large areas are burned. Two recent years with these conditions occurred in Canada, for example, in 1981 when 5.4 million hectares of forest burned and in 1989 when 7.6 million hectares burned. This compares to an average annual area burned in Canada over the past fifty years of approximately 1 million hectares.

Despite the intuitive expectation that fuels are as important as weather the mechanisms that determine forest fire behavior indicate that variation in fuel variables can change fire behavior only 100 times while variation in weather variables can cause a change of 1,000 times. Furthermore forest fires are largely propagated by fine dead fuels; therefore, large tree trunks have little influence on the spread of fires.

In using prescribed fires ecologists and resource managers first define the desired ecological effects and then couple those to the appropriate fire regime. Fire regimes are characterized by fire intensity, duff consumption, fire frequency (interval between fires), and size and pattern of burns, each of which produces particular ecological effects. The prescription in prescribed fires is the explicit statement of both the fire regime and the ecological effects.

Fire Intensity

Fire intensity is the heat output kilowatts per meter (kW/m) from the flaming front. It is related by a simple equation to flame length which is readily measured. The greater the fire intensity (greater flame length), the more likely a tree will be killed, either by scorching the canopy leaves or by killing the cambium around the base of the tree.

Duff Consumption

Duff consumption is the percentage of the duff layer consumed by the fire. The duff layer is the partially decomposed organic horizon above the surface of the mineral soil but not including the litter that lies on top of the duff. The ecological effects of duff consumption include mortality of plants rooted in the duff (a large number of herbaceous plants) and of dormant seeds. Furthermore duff removal exposes mineral soil which is the best germination surface for most forest trees.

Interval between Fires

The interval between fires will determine whether trees have had enough time to reach reproductive maturity. If fires come at too short an interval tree species can be eliminated from the forest because they will not yet be producing seeds.

Size and Pattern of Burns

Sizes and shapes of burns are very important in determining the regeneration pattern of forests. Most seeds effectively disperse to a distance of about four times the height of the parent tree; therefore large burns without surviving seed trees could have regeneration problems. Fortunately most large fires contain numerous patches of surviving trees and therefore the dispersal distances to any part of the burn are not generally great. A few species such as jack pine (*Pinus banksiana*) and lodgepole pine (*Pinus contorta*) have cones which require heat to open and consequently have aerial seed banks that survive the fire.

At one time conservationists thought fires were destructive to natural ecosystems. However, by the 1970s, fire was recognized as a natural part of ecosystems to be used along with other forest management techniques. The scientific knowledge of fires has only developed in the past forty years. Consequently for most ecosystems there is still a limited understanding of the relationship between fire behavior and its ecological effects. In addition incorporation of this scientific understanding of fires has been slow as illustrated by the persisting ideas of the widespread distribution of old-growth forests in North America in presettlement times and of the effectiveness of fire suppression.

It is a common belief that, at the onset of European occupation, North America was covered largely by old-growth primeval forests. However ecologists have found by studying natural disturbances such as fires that forests over 400 years old made up less than 20 percent of the natural landscape, in many cases less than 5 percent.

Another common belief is that fire suppression has been effective in decreasing the frequency and intensity of forest fires. Although fire suppression has been reasonably successful in grassland/savanna vegetation and in isolated blocks of forest it is now clear that there are limitations to fire control in large areas of continuous forest. In such areas fire suppression is only effective in years when fuel moisture conditions are high enough that the area burned by fires would not be large, even in the absence of suppression. The large area burned in the decade of the 1980s has enforced the understanding that weather, and not fuels, determines fire behavior and hence the size of fires. Weather affects large areas (thousands of square kilometers at a time) allowing large numbers of fires to ignite and spread rapidly under very dry conditions. Under such conditions the only economically reasonable approach is for firefighters to focus on public safety and values at risk.

Edward A. Johnson and Kiyoko Miyanishi

Further Readings

Johnson, Edward A. *Fire and Vegetation Dynamics: Studies from the North American Boreal Forest.* 1992.

Van Wagner, C.E. "Fire Behaviour in Northern Conifer Forests and Shrublands." In *The Role of Fire in Northern Circumpolar Ecosystems.* Ed. R.W. Wein and D.A. MacLean. 1983.

———. "The Historical Pattern of Annual Burned Area in Canada." *Forestry Chronicle* 64 (1988): 182–85.

See also FORESTY, HISTORY OF; LANDSCAPE ECOLOGY; OLD GROWTH FORESTS

Forest Fragmentation and Bird Habitats

Fragmentation of forests by human or natural causes decreases forest-interior habitats or "core areas" (i.e., forest areas over 100 meters from an edge) and increases forest edge. The size, shape, and age of a forest fragment, as well as the forest structure all affect the amount of core area available for forest-interior birds. Increasing forest fragmentation on breeding grounds generally leads to reduced population abundance, reduced pairing and nesting success of forest-interior birds, and increased abundance of forest-edge species. Although larger forest fragments may harbor a high abundance of forest-interior birds, nesting success is often significantly lower than that of birds in continuous forests.

Forest-interior species are often absent in small forest patches, despite the presence of forest areas large enough for many territories. The biogeography model of true islands is often invoked to explain the low abundance of such species in isolated forest patches. When species extinctions—through emigration and mortality—are not sufficiently counterbalanced by immigration or reproduction species abundance in isolated forest patches declines. Rates of immigration can be affected by distance from continuous forest and the amount of forest habitat available nearby. In contrast the abundance of forest-edge species appears more closely tied to vegetation complexity than to forest size.

Neotropical migrants appear particularly vulnerable to forest fragmentation on their North American breeding grounds. Many of these species nest on or near the ground and use open-cup rather than cavity nests. Open-cup nests are especially prone to nest predation and brood parasitism. Brood parasitism, the practice of birds laying their eggs in the nests of other birds, is a significant threat in some regions of North America, as cowbird species

expand their ranges. Predator and parasite numbers often are higher near forest edges, resulting in increased nest losses for forest birds near edges. Because they migrate earlier and arrive later than residents and short-distance migrants, neotropical migrants are less apt to renest and, therefore, less able to recover from nest losses. Return rates of territorial adults to smaller forests are often lower than those in contiguous forests. Although minimum forest size for species presence has been estimated for many species little is known about minimum forest size necessary to maintain self-sustaining populations. Moreover minimum size may vary with habitat quality and landscape attributes.

Nearly half of all neotropical migrants breeding in North American forests winter in tropical forests. Fragmentation on the wintering grounds also reduces abundance and survivorship for such forest specialists. Tropical and subtropical forests harbor many forest-specialist species. Forest endemics such as the harpy eagle, resplendent quetzal, woodcreepers, and tropical antbirds are particularly vulnerable to deforestation. Frugivorous species may require an extensive continuous forest to locate ephemeral food. Some species are restricted to forest of a certain altitude, such as the blue bird of paradise of New Guinea. As tropical forests are converted to agriculture, harvested, and developed populations of both wintering migrants and resident tropical forest species decline. Although second-growth forest patches and hedgerows provide habitat for some forest-specialists in many regions forest habitat is scarce.

Fragmentation may diminish the overall habitat quality compared to similar areas in larger forests. Changes in microclimate, sunlight, and vegetation may intensify seasonal and annual weather cycles, reduce insect abundance, and affect the food availability for insectivorous birds. This, in turn, may result in larger forest bird territories in small forests. Edge species are often more aggressive and may compete with interior species for limited resources.

Composition of the surrounding habitat influences the type and extent of fragmentation effects on forest-interior birds. Suburban and agricultural edges, for example, attract different predator communities. The distance of the fragment from a contiguous forest and the degree of isolation from other woodlots is known to affect colonization and impact mating success and abundance. A higher proportion of forested to open area surrounding a fragment can mod-

F

erate the detrimental consequences of reduced forest size. Similarly forest patches interconnected to each other can increase the abundance of forest-interior species and enhance the possibility of successful reproduction. Some forest specialists require specific types or ages of forest (e.g., northern spotted owl).

Resident and short-distance migrants that dwell in forest-interior habitats are also measurably influenced by fragmentation. Some species, particularly raptors and other large birds, are found only in large, contiguous forests. For some species (e.g., northern goshawk, barred owl, pileated woodpecker) even small openings in the contiguous forest allow new competitors or predators to invade and diminish the usable habitat. Other forest species benefit from the increased food supply found in forest openings yet are only found in large extensive forests (e.g., ruffed grouse, sharp-shinned hawk). Little is known about the minimum forest size needed to maintain healthy self-sustaining populations of these species.

Laurie J. Goodrich and Keith L. Bildstein

Further Readings

Askins, R.A., J.F. Lynch, and R. Greenberg. "Population Declines in Migratory Birds in Eastern North America." *Current Ornithology* 7 (1990): 1–57.

Hagan, J.M., III, and D.W. Johnston, eds. *Ecology and Conservation of Neotropical Migrant Landbirds*. 1992.

Terborgh, J. *Where Have All the Birds Gone?* 1989.

See also CLEARCUT; HABITAT FRAGMENTATION, PATCHES, AND CORRIDORS; LANDSCAPE ECOLOGY; NEW FORESTRY; OLD GROWTH FORESTS; TROPICAL DEFORESTATION

Forest Regeneration/Reforestation

Forests are the world's most widespread vegetation type and, with the exception of human food production systems, the most important. They play a major role in regulating atmospheric concentrations of the greenhouse gas CO_2, in the global hydrological cycle, and in the global radiation budget. Forests create critical habitat for the majority of the world's terrestrial animals and microbial species. They regulate soil development and erosion, water quality and stream flow, and provide raw materials, wealth, employment, recreational opportunities, and spiritual values for humans. It is little wonder,

therefore, that people are concerned when natural disturbances or timber harvesting remove forest cover from significant portions of a landscape. The prompt regeneration of the forest—the reforestation of the landscape—after such a disturbance is one of the most fundamental objectives of forest management.

There are five main approaches to the reforestation of a recently denuded area. Three of these involve "natural" regeneration. The other two methods are planting and direct seeding. Natural regeneration has many advantages. It ensures that the local genetic varieties of the local tree species reforest the area, and it is often much cheaper than "artificial" regeneration methods because nature provides the seed and seedlings free. However, successful natural regeneration sometimes requires special harvesting regimes and soil preparation activities, so it is not always "free." It may require more skill than "artificial" regeneration, and is often less predictable. Natural regeneration is normally the method by which partially harvested forests are regenerated. Planting can be the most reliable method of regenerating a particular type of forest quickly, but may be more expensive than natural regeneration. If not done with respect for the seedlings' physiology and ecology, it can result in costly regeneration failures. Planting is most commonly associated with clearcutting. The five main approaches to regeneration are advance regeneration, natural seeding regeneration, vegetative regeneration, planting, and direct seeding.

Advance Regeneration

As a forest matures, the canopy often opens up letting in sufficient light to allow a population of seedlings to become established. These seedlings usually grow slowly. They are suppressed by competition for light, moisture, and nutrients, and may remain less than one or two meters in height for more than a century. Many of these seedlings survive when the overstory is removed by wind, insects, or logging, and, after a period of physiological adjustment to the new microclimate, grow to create a new forest. A drawback of advance regeneration is that it is usually limited to seedlings of shade-tolerant species, whereas the forest that is being replaced may have consisted of more light-demanding species. If the advance regeneration is old, it may be parasitized or diseased, or may not respond to increased availability of light.

Natural Seeding Regeneration

Natural seeding regeneration occurs when seeds are blown by wind or are distributed by animals into an area from which all the trees have been removed, or when seeds buried in the upper soil germinate following the removal of forest cover. However, this regeneration may be unsuccessful if there is a deep organic forest floor which is exposed to hot, dry, microclimatic conditions following forest removal. This combination of surface soil and microclimatic conditions can prevent regeneration. Soil disturbance by fire or mechanical means may be needed to resynchronize the seedbed condition with the new microclimate. Alternatively, shelterwood harvesting may be used. A series of light thinnings a few years before the final clearcut tree harvest stimulates seed production in the remaining trees, allows changes in the forest floor that improve the seedbed, and creates a microclimate in which the established seedlings can survive, but are still sheltered from both hot sun and radiation frosts. However, where the forest floor is thick, such as in many old-growth forests, soil scarification may be necessary even with a shelterwood.

Vegetative Regeneration

Vegetative regeneration can be used with those broad-leaved hardwood species that send up stump sprouts (coppice) or root sprouts (suckers) after the tree is cut or the above-ground portion is killed. A few coniferous species can also do this, such as the redwoods of the Pacific Northwest United States, and the Chinese fir of southeastern China. Coppice regeneration has been used for centuries to reforest harvested broad-leaved forests in Europe, and suckering is the major means by which aspen regenerates after fire or logging. Vegetative reproduction is generally both free and healthy, although it is often so dense that costs are incurred in reducing stem numbers to an appropriate level.

Natural regeneration works only when there is an adequate supply of seedlings, seeds, or sprouts of suitable species. It is appropriate for managed forests but not for reforestation of areas that have remained treeless for many years. It may be unreliable where the supply of seedlings or seeds is insufficient, such as in some northern or high elevation forests where good seed crops are produced only every ten to twenty years, or where seed predation by insects or small mammals is very severe. In such cases reforestation based solely on natural regeneration may be so delayed that the area is "captured" by early seral plants—herbs and shrubs—that can exclude trees for many decades or even centuries. Where these problems occur or where there is a desire to change tree

species, change the genetic make up of a tree population, or increase tree species diversity, artificial regeneration may be used.

Planting

Planting is the most common method of artificial regeneration. Seedlings of various age and size grown in a forest nursery are planted to establish the new forest. Planting can be expensive but, when done carefully using healthy seedlings of the correct species and genotype, with good root systems and an appropriate physiological condition, it is a very reliable regeneration method. The costs are justified by the rapidity, predictability, and regularity of the regeneration. Planting can ensure a healthy new forest of tree species adapted to the site. It can be used to enrich natural regeneration with additional species, or natural regeneration can be used to provide such enrichment in single species plantations.

Direct Seeding

Planted seedlings sometimes have poorly formed root systems because of the way they have been grown in the nursery or the way in which they are planted. Unless care is taken, seedlings may also be in poor physiological condition when planted. These problems can be avoided by "planting" the seed directly in the forest. Direct seeding can be a very effective artificial regeneration method but only if seed is cheap and abundantly available and there is an appropriate seedbed condition. The high cost of seed and frequent limitation on seed supply make this method unpopular, especially if seed predation is a problem.

Conclusion

Each of these five methods of regeneration will be appropriate somewhere but none of them is appropriate everywhere. Different tree species, ecological site types and zones, and differences in silvicultural systems of managing forests require different approaches to regeneration. The key to successful regeneration is to understand the physiology and ecology of the tree species to be regenerated and the site conditions where they are to be established. Many regeneration failures in the past have resulted from lack of respect for the biological and ecological limitations on forest regeneration.

Recent research in old-growth forests has highlighted the importance of large old decayed logs ("nurse logs") as a microsite for seedling establishment in these forests. The suggestion has been made by some researchers that many large, old decayed logs must be retained in harvested forests to mimic this natural process of regeneration. However, studies of the ages of seedlings on old logs and their rates of growth reveal that regeneration by this method would generally be slow and unpredictable, and the supply of suitable logs limited. Further, decayed logs that remain moist in the shade of a forest tend to dry out in harvested areas and become much less suitable as a seed bed and seedling substrate. The ecology of regeneration on nurse logs in an unmanaged old-growth forest is different from that in harvested or naturally disturbed forests.

Hamish Kimmins

Further Readings

Daniels, T.W., J.A. Helm, and F.S. Baker. *Principles of Silviculture*. 1979.

Lavender, D.P., et al., eds. *Regenerating British Columbia's Forests*. 1990.

Smith, D.M. *The Practice of Silviculture*. 1986.

See also CLEARCUT; CLIMAX THEORY; FOREST FIRES AND CONSERVATION; FORESTRY, HISTORY OF; NEW FORESTRY; OLD GROWTH FORESTS; SUSTAINED YIELD FORESTRY

Forest Service (U.S.)

The federal forest service has been centered in the Department of Agriculture since its inception, while most of its sister resource agencies are located in the Department of the Interior. This century-long anomaly stems from a parliamentary maneuver in 1876. Failing to find support in the House Interior Committee, forestry advocates managed to attach a rider to the Agriculture Appropriation bill. The appropriations amendment provided $2,000 to gather forestry statistics and make a report to Congress. Congress was pleased with the 600-page *Report upon Forestry* and continued to fund the fact-finding activity. In 1886 the Division of Forestry was made a permanent part of the Department of Agriculture, itself still lacking Cabinet status, showing an ill-defined concern about the need to do something to protect forested watersheds in the West.

Bernhard E. Fernow, a German-trained forester, was appointed chief of forestry activities. For the next twelve years he collaborated with others on a wide range of research topics, testified on forestry needs to Congress on many occasions, and played a leadership role in the American Forestry Association, a citizens' conservation group. But Fernow did not have any land to manage; federal forests were under the jurisdiction of the General Land Office in the Department of the Interior.

When Fernow left the Division of Forestry in 1898 his successor was Gifford Pinchot, a young aristocrat with some training in forestry. Pinchot was also politically astute, had a good feel for administration, and was willing to vigorously test the status quo. For the time being his small agency's niche would be to work cooperatively with private lumber companies to develop management and reforestation plans. By 1905 more than 11 million private acres would be under review.

During the same period Pinchot worked to have the federal forests transferred from Interior to his jurisdiction in Agriculture. In this and other conservation-related issues, President Theodore Roosevelt was a kindred spirit. In 1905 federal forests were transferred to Agriculture and the agency's name was changed to Forest Service. Within a few years more lands were withdrawn from the western public domain for a total of 150 million acres. Today there are 191 million acres in the national forest system, with most of the addition purchased in the eastern United States or designated in Alaska.

During its first decade the Forest Service developed an administrative structure that still remains. For a federal agency it is decentralized to an unusual degree. The nation is divided into nine regions; regions are comprised of 155 national forests; and forests are made up of 650 ranger districts. To the extent possible decisions are to be made on the ground by persons directly familiar with conditions. Recent environmental regulations have caused a tendency toward centralization, however, as few ranger districts have the mix of expertise to deal fully with modern demands.

The Forest Service's mission also was defined early. Obviously the vast national forest system would demand the lion's share of attention—to survey, inventory, protect, and place under sustained-yield management. These federal resources were seen as part of the nation's resource pool; Congress had authorized their creation in 1897 to assure future supplies of timber and water. Other uses were to be permitted in principle but not uses that might jeopardize timber and water.

Since Fernow's administration the agency has cooperated with other forestry efforts. As more and more state forestry agencies were established in the early years of the twentieth century they found the Forest Service to be a willing partner. The substance of this partnership was bolstered by the 1911 Weeks Act and 1924 Clarke-McNary Act which provided federal matching funds for state activities. Because the states were also active in private forestry affairs federal influence cuts across all lines. These extension activities are under the jurisdiction of State and Private Forestry.

Timely and reliable information is essential to quality management. The Forest Service is unique in that it has its own research arm to undertake both long- and short-term studies germane not only to national forest managers but all other forest jurisdictions. In 1915 the Branch of Research was established to assure shelter from the day-to-day pressures. In 1928 the McSweeney-McNary Act authorized the establishment of experiment stations (some had been in existence since 1908), assuring that research would be responsive to field needs. Today there are eight experiment stations administering seventy-two separate laboratories with a staff of 700 scientists. Also the Forest Products Laboratory was established in 1910 and has provided national leadership in wood and paper technology.

International Forestry was created officially in 1992, adding a fourth division to the Forest Service mission. International activities have been around since the late nineteenth century; these responsibilities had been housed within Research until 1992. International Forestry works cooperatively with United States Agency for International Development, the World Bank, United Nations Food and Agriculture Organization (FAO), and other institutions. Exchange of scientific information is the primary goal.

Harold K. Steen

Further Readings
Robinson, Glen O. *The Forest Service: A Study in Public Land Management.* 1975.
Steen, Harold K. *The U.S. Forest Service: A History.* 1992.

See also PINCHOT, GIFFORD; FOREST REGENERATION/REFORESTATION; FORESTRY, HISTORY OF; NATIONAL FORESTS (U.S.); NEW FORESTRY; SUSTAINED YIELD FORESTRY; WORLD BANK

Forestry, History of
The art of forestry can be traced to developments in China, Japan, Greece, France, and Germany. However, scientific forestry techniques developed in Europe have had the widest influence upon the rest of the world. The word is derived from the French *"foresterie"* and first came into use in English in the decade 1685–1695.

Written records from the Han dynasty in China (206 B.C.E. to C.E. 222) indicate that basic forest management concepts and techniques had been developed as much as 500 years earlier. Furthermore the practice of replanting forests with commercially desirable tree species had already begun.

In Japan, despite the development of basic management techniques during the seventeenth century, increasing population densities, a great expansion of cultivated land, and large-scale building projects by the government resulted in over-exploitation of the resource. The forest and land were so damaged that it was impossible for them to regenerate naturally from seed. Most of Japan's forests are found on mountainous areas of the islands and this failure of regeneration resulted in large-scale land erosion. It took until the first quarter of the nineteenth century for the basic principles of sustained forest management to be worked out and applied. By the middle of the nineteenth century, Japan was replacing logged forests with large quantities of hand-planted seedlings, and detailed management plans for the plantations were being written and applied.

In Europe forestry practices were first developed in Greece during the third to first centuries B.C.E. for the religious use of wood products obtained from sacred groves. Because the groves were neither large nor numerous, care over exploitation had to be taken. Early chroniclers indicate that seedlings were planted in the groves if natural regeneration failed. The necessity for forest management on a commercial scale did not take place in Europe until the "Age of Enlightenment" in the eighteenth century. In the meantime forestry practices were developed for hardwood woodlots in the agricultural areas of Italy, France and southern England. These practices were developed during the seventh to ninth centuries, a period generally termed the "Dark Ages."

Woodlot management involved the coppicing and pollarding of selected hardwood tree species known to sprout easily from stumps. "Coppice with standards" involved the felling of the existing tree and the continuous harvesting of the sprouts as they grew to useful sizes. One sprout, the standard, was allowed to grow to its full size.

While the forests of western and southern Europe have extensive areas of hardwood trees, those of eastern and northern Europe are more boreal in nature and have a high proportion of conifers. The great extent of these forests favored the development of extraction and transportation methods rather than of forest management. Credit for the initial development of forestry practices for European boreal forests is generally given to two groups of landowners. These are cities such as Geneva and Vienna and the aristocratic landowners of the area of what is now central Germany. Geneva, for example, has owned a large forest that was managed since medieval times for the benefit of its citizens: the Sihlwald, which may be the oldest continuously managed forest in Europe.

As the population of Germany expanded and communications links improved, landowners became aware that their forests were being excessively exploited. In the state of Prussia, an official Forest Service was founded by G.L. Hartig (1764–1837) and systematic silvicultural techniques developed. By the middle of the nineteenth century, these techniques had become formalized, extended to the management of natural forests, and the profession of forester founded. At the same time, forestry became a subject of study at several German universities and scientific forestry moved from casual study and intuition to a subject of formal research.

France also developed formal management practices applicable to its hardwood forests and the tropical forests of its African Empire in this period. In 1801 the government founded the Administration of Water and Forests, a government department tasked with the utilization of the forests of France as a national resource. In the same year J.B. Lorentz, who had studied German forestry techniques, published his *Lorentz Manuel du Forestier* and in 1824 became the founding director of the *Ecole nationale forestière* at Nancy in Lorraine, France.

Forestry moved out of its European roots into the wider world in the middle of the nineteenth century with the decision by the British Colonial government to place Dr. Deitrich Brandis in charge of forestry operations in India. Starting in 1865, Dr. Brandis, who had been trained in Germany, founded and established the organization of the Forestry Services of India and Burma. The establishment of a forestry service in these two colonies required the training of numbers of foresters. Until 1885, British colonial foresters were trained at the *Ecole nationale forestière* in France because the *Ecole* also trained foresters for the French Colonial Service and was deliberately oriented toward non-boreal forest management and also the management of tropical forests.

From 1885 to 1906, British foresters were trained at the Royal Indian Engineering College under the tutelage of William Schlich. Schlich, who had also been trained in Germany, continued as director of the Oxford Forestry Institute after it was founded in 1906 with the closure of the Coopers Hill school. Schlich was the author of a *Manual of Forestry* (4 vols.), which remained a leading authority on tropical forestry until the 1930s.

By the closing decades of the nineteenth century forestry could be broadly divided into two schools. Members of the German school advocated plantation-style forestry and monoculture. Management of mixed natural forests had monoculture and the clearcutting of even-aged stands as an objective. Purists in the French community, on the other hand, advocated the maintenance of the natural mix of species in a forest with stands having a wide range of ages and a variety of ecological niches. As early as 1887 the German method of monoculture was noted as creating ecological difficulties and was believed then to probably be unsustainable over many rotations.

Although both Brandis and Schlich had been trained in Germany they were able to adapt the French forestry approach to the forests of the British colonies. Because of this both men had a tremendous influence upon forestry in the British Empire (excluding Canada) and the United States. For example when the Cape Colony (Republic of South Africa) decided to start a forestry department it hired a graduate of the *Ecole nationale forestière*. A forest officer in the French service, the Comte de Vasselot de Regne, hired several new officers. Notable among them were David E. Hutchins and C.E. Lane-Poole, both of whom were graduates of the *Ecole nationale forestière* and had worked in India.

Hutchins left the Cape forest service in 1906, was hired by the British Colonial Office to carry out the first surveys of the forests of Kenya and Cyprus (resulting in the introduction of forestry to these countries), and then wrote landmark reports about the forests of Australia and New Zealand. Settling in New Zealand Hutchins founded a Forestry League that successfully pressured for state intervention in forestry activities. C.E. Lane-Poole also left the Cape in 1906 and, after working in Sierra Leone, transferred his allegiance to Australia. There he founded departments of forestry for the government of Western Australia (1916) and the Australian Federal Government (1927). He was also the founding principal of the School of Forestry at the Australian National University.

In the United States, interest in forestry started with the publication of George Perkins Marsh's *Man and Nature* in 1864 and was followed with the founding of the American Forestry Association in 1875 by the botanist John A. Warder. In 1876 the U.S. Congress directed that the Commissioner of Agriculture found a forestry agency in his department and Dr. Franklin B. Hough (1822–1885), a noted conservation advocate from New England, was nominated to prepare a report on the forests of the nation. Hough's *Report Upon Forestry* (4 vols.) was well received across the continent and in 1881 he was named the head of the new Forestry Division in the Department of Agriculture, retiring in 1884.

The last twenty-five years of the nineteenth century are considered particularly significant in the development of forestry in the United States and Canada. Many people became interested in the subject leading to a "ferment of ideas." One man, however, crossed the border between the two nations, introducing scientific forestry to both countries. This is Bernhard E. Fernow (1851–1923). Trained in Prussia, Fernow emigrated to the United States in 1876, was appointed chief of the Division of Forestry of the Department of Agriculture in 1886 and was the first head of what would later be called the U.S. Forest Service. From 1898 to 1903 Fernow was the founding director of the New York State School of Forestry at Cornell University. In this time he tried the ambitious experiment of introducing German-style forestry to the United States, an effort that initially failed largely because of opposition to the clearcutting of the experimental forest near Saranac Lake, New York.

In 1903 Fernow gave a talk on forestry at the Mining School, Queen's University, Kingston, Ontario, Canada. This lecture led to the founding of a school of forestry at the University of Toronto (1907) with Fernow as its first dean. Subsequently foresters trained at the school took up positions within the newly founded Canadian Forestry Service and in the forestry services of Canada's provinces.

In the United States in 1898 Fernow was succeeded as head of the Division of Forestry (later the U.S. Forest Service) by Gifford Pinchot (1865–1946), a graduate of Yale University who had trained in France. Pinchot, ably assisted by Overton W. Price (1873–1914), who had been the personal secretary of Dr. Deitrich Brandis, reorganized and expanded the service to the national body that it is today. Both Pinchot and Price were dismissed from government service in 1910 by President Taft as the result of a conflict with his Secretary for the Interior, Richard A. Ballinger.

Although this controversy is considered a setback for forestry and conservation in the United States, it was beneficial for forestry in Canada. Freed from the federal service Price was able to assist the government of British Columbia in establishing its Forest Service in 1911 with Harvey R. MacMillan (1885–1976) as its first chief. MacMillan went on to found MacMillan Bloedel Limited, a very large logging company. Several other American foresters, angered by the dismissal of Pinchot, also resigned and secured employment in Canada.

It can be broadly said that while early forestry in the United States was particularly influenced by the French school of forestry, forestry in Canada responded more to German methods and teachings. In very general terms these differences still exist today largely because boreal-type forests are more a feature of Canada than of the United States. By the start of World War I, the relationship between government and industry with regard to forestry was established, particularly in Canada. This relationship is unchanged in many ways to the present time. Finally although the broad outlines of scientific forestry in North America were established by 1914 much research had still to be undertaken. This is particularly true with regard to the natural relationship between wild fires and the many species of coniferous trees found on the continent, the development of accurate and economic technologies for forest mensuration, and the limitations of relying upon natural seedfall for forest regeneration.

Thomas R. Roach

Further Readings

Carron, L.T. *A History of Forestry in Australia.* 1985.

Gillis, R. Peter, and Thomas R. Roach. *Lost Initiatives: Canada's Forest Industries, Forest Policy, and Forest Conservation.* 1986.

Pincetl, Stephanie. "Some Origins of French Environmentalism: An Exploration." *Forest and Conservation History* 37 (1993): 80–89.

Pinchot, Gifford. *Breaking New Ground.* 1972.

Roche, Michael. *Forest Policy in New Zealand: An Historical Geography, 1840–1919.* 1987.

Rodgers, Andrew Denny, III. *Bernhard Eduard Fernow: A Story of North American Forestry.* 1991.

Steen, Harold K., ed. *History of Sustained-Yield Forestry.* 1984.

Tucker, Richard P. "The Forests of the Western Himalayas: The Legacy of British Colonial Administration." *Forest and Conservation History* 26 (1982): 112–23.

See also CLEARCUT; FOREST FRAGMENTATION AND BIRD HABITATS; FOREST REGENERATION/REFORESTATION; HABITAT FRAGMENTATION, PATCHES, AND CORRIDORS; INTERNATIONAL TROPICAL TIMBER ORGANIZATION; NEW FORESTRY; OLD GROWTH FORESTS; TROPICAL DEFORESTATION; TROPICAL RAINFORESTS

Former Soviet Union

A high level of environmental deterioration has been documented in the republics of the former Soviet Union, both by internal reporting and by foreign observers. The cause of this deterioration is generally attributed to the primacy that was accorded industrial output during the Soviet period, combined with a lack of effective incentives to include adequate environmental protection measures as part of this economic expansion. Adding to the problem was the philosophical belief of Communist ideologists that there could be no unwise use of natural resources under socialism. The unfortunate result was a substantial wastage and inefficient use of the USSR's bountiful natural resource base, as well as widespread environmental pollution.

By the 1970s even Soviet sources were acknowledging serious air pollution in industrial cities, water pollution in numerous rivers and lakes, overcutting of commercial forests, widespread poaching of game animals, massive overuse of pesticides, and a variety of other environmental abuses. The extent of these problems, though, was generally understated and incompletely documented. At that time the one issue that highlighted environmental deterioration as an issue of national concern, at least among the intelligentsia, was the threatened pollution of Lake Baikal.

In the late 1980s two events took place that greatly sharpened the interest in environmental problems in the Soviet Union. One was the disastrous explosion at the Chernobyl nuclear reactor; the other was Gorbachev's policy of *glasnost,* which permitted much greater media attention on governmental mismanagement and lack of concern regarding environmental pollution. As a result of the latter a number of official reports were published discussing the environmental situation inside the country in much more detail than had ever occurred previously.

Included among these reports were some that adopted a new way of looking at the severity of the Soviet environmental situation—the preparation of maps of critical ecological zones. In addition to mapping such zones, severity of impacts were qualitatively classified as falling into one of five categories: provisionally favorable, satisfactory, stressed, critical (crisis), and catastrophic.

Initially sixteen critical areas were identified, those being the Aral Sea, the Chernobyl fallout region, the Sea of Azov, the Donbass region, the Black Sea coast, Moldavia (now Moldova), the Caspian Sea, the Fergana Valley, the Semipalatinsk (Semey) region of Kazakhstan, the Kalmyk Republic, the Volga River, the Kola Peninsula, the Ural Mountains industrial region, the Kuzbass coal mining region, the Moscow region, and Lake Baikal. Of these, the latter seven are entirely within the Russian Federation; the Donbass, Black Sea, and Azov Sea problems are shared by Russia and Ukraine; Chernobyl is shared by these two republics and Belarus; the Caspian Sea borders four republics; the Fergana Valley problem is shared by three Central Asia republics and the Aral Sea problem by all five of them. The remaining two problem areas lie within Moldova and Kazakhstan.

Chernobyl is the best-known of these critical regions. The 1986 disaster necessitated the relocation of over 100,000 persons, has involved billions of dollars in cleanup costs to date, and is generally believed to have resulted in several thousand immediate or premature deaths. Sizable areas of Belarus, Ukraine, and Russia will be left uninhabitable and uncultivatable for decades.

The Aral Sea disaster has been produced by the excessive withdrawal of water for irrigation purposes from its two main tributaries, the Amu-Darya and Syr-Darya. This resulted in an Aral Sea greatly diminished in size, salt-dust storms that originate on its newly exposed bottom, damage to crops, and biological harm to local rivers, the Sea, and riparian habitat areas. Pesticide use and water wastage have also been excessive in the region, and public health problems abound.

The Urals industrial region, extending from Perm to Magnitogorsk, may be the next most critical zone. Here the most widespread problem is vast amounts of air pollution that emanate from steel mills, non-ferrous smelters, chemical plants, oil refineries and other industrial operations. Water pollution as a secondary problem is also severe. Adding to the regional problem is another area of deadly radioactive contamination near the city of Kyshtym (near Chelyabinsk), which was the location of at least three major radiation-release accidents in the 1950s and 1960s.

Yet another region of radiation danger is the former nuclear weapons testing site near the city of Semipalatinsk (now Semey) in eastern Kazakhstan. Adding to this problem is a high level of air contamination and heavy-metal pollution from mining and smelters in the Semipalatinsk to Ust-Kamenogorsk (now Oskemen) mining district. The latter set of factors also characterizes the excessive pollution region on the Kola Peninsula, centered around the huge nickel smelter at Monchegorsk.

The Donbass (Donets Basin) and Kuzbass (Kuznets Basin) are both coal-mining and steel-producing regions that suffer from extreme air pollution, and only slightly less water pollution. The mining activities also produce a blighted and contaminated landscape, and inflict severe health problems on the miners.

Moldova and the Kalmyk Republic suffer from the results of poor agricultural land use that has resulted in erosion and chemical contamination, with industrial pollution being a further problem in Moldova. The Fergana Valley, shared by Uzbekistan, Kyrgyzstan, and Tajikistan, likewise has a highly unhealthy mix of agricultural pollutants and industrial contaminants.

The Moscow urban agglomeration, though originally desired by the USSR to be a showplace capital district, nevertheless has evolved into a region with high air pollution, and is one of the few places in the former So-

viet Union where automotive sources are the major contributor. In parts of the city, especially the southeast, industry contaminates both the atmosphere and the rivers. Unmonitored dump sites for low-level radioactive wastes have also been found in many places around the city.

Water pollution, from both municipal and industrial sources, is the primary cause of the Black Sea, Caspian Sea, Azov Sea, Volga River, and Lake Baikal problems. The first four have all realized sharp reductions in their formerly abundant fish stocks, and the Volga and Caspian have been adversely affected by the construction of numerous large hydroelectric dams.

In the USSR at the turn of the 1990s two areas were generally considered to fall into the catastrophic category: the Chernobyl region and the Aral Sea region. Information made available subsequent to the collapse of the USSR might suggest that the area of the Kyshtym disaster should be placed into this category as well. Recent reports on the expedient dumping of nuclear wastes and obsolete reactors, plus a long history of nuclear weapons testing suggest that perhaps Novaya Zemlya and the adjacent Kara Sea should also be accorded this dubious distinction.

In addition to the foregoing regions of severe environmental problems, other specific nodes of intense pollution within the former Soviet Union can be identified. These include what is perhaps the single dirtiest industrial complex on the planet, the giant nickel smelter at Norilsk in the Siberian Arctic. Other specific problem locations are the Irkutsk-Cheremkhovo industrial district along the Angara, the Kansk-Achinsk coal mining and power plant complex in East Siberia, the extensive oil extraction region in the West Siberian lowland, central Armenia, the St. Petersburg region, the Ukrainian steel mill cities of Kryvyy Rih (Krivoy Rog) and Mariupol, the central Kazakhstan mining district, and a host of other specific cities and mining/smelting/refining centers.

Over-hunting, poaching, and pollution have taken a toll on wildlife in the former Soviet Union. Seventy species of wildlife, including twenty-three types of mammals and twenty-one species of birds, are listed as endangered, though many consider this list to be incomplete. To help counter this trend, the various republics have created about 180 nature reserves, some quite large, but these reserves are not always located where the flora and fauna problems are the most acute, and few are adequately funded or staffed.

F

The short-run (and even intermediate-run) prospects for environmental improvement in the former Soviet Union are, unfortunately, not good. The primary problem is the economic crisis which affords no supply of funds that can be devoted to the massive backlog of environmental cleanup tasks at hand. Compounding the problem at the start of the 1990s are a confused administrative organization and a managerial cadre that still largely consists of the same bureaucrats that helped cause the problems in the first place. Extensive changes in national policies, combined with both the will and the funding to implement them, as well as a general economic upturn, must come into being before any significant improvements in the former Soviet Union's environmental situation will be realized.

Philip R. Pryde

Further Readings

Feshbach, M., and A. Friendly. *Ecocide in the USSR.* 1992.

Peterson, D.J. *Troubled Lands: The Legacy of Soviet Environmental Destruction.* 1993.

Pryde, P.R. *Environmental Management in the Soviet Union.* 1991.

See also CHERNOBYL; EASTERN EUROPE: ENVIRONMENTAL PROBLEMS; LAKE BAIKAL

Fragmentation

See FOREST FRAGMENTATION AND BIRD HABITATS; HABITAT FRAGMENTATION, PATCHES, AND CORRIDORS

Franklin Dam

The battle to halt the construction of the Gordon-below-Franklin dam in the Southwest region of the Australian island state of Tasmania is a major milestone in Australian environmental political history and federal-state relations. In July 1983 the High Court of Australia upheld federal legislation designed to block construction of the dam by the Tasmanian government. The decision followed a remarkable sequence of events, including a Tasmanian referendum on the issue, mass environmental protests and arrests, resignations by Tasmanian parliamentarians, and changes of government at both the state and federal levels.

The Tasmanian Hydro-Electric Commission's (HEC) proposal for the Gordon-below-Franklin power scheme was first tabled in the Tasmanian parliament in October 1979. The proposal met with strong opposition from the environment movement, which had strengthened its resolve to stop further dam building in Tasmania's Southwest since its unsuccessful attempt in 1972 to prevent the flooding of the spectacular inland Lake Pedder. The new coalition of environment groups, led by the Tasmanian Wilderness Society under the directorship of Dr. Bob Brown, was determined to save Tasmania's Southwest region—one of the few remaining large temperate wilderness areas in the world.

The Tasmanian Labor government sought to diffuse mounting community conflict by proposing an alternative power scheme on the Gordon-above-Olga river. However, the government was unable to gain the support of the upper house, which sought to revive the HEC's proposal. Faced with a parliamentary deadlock the Labor government held a referendum in an attempt to resolve the issue. The ballot paper, however, presented Tasmanian voters with only two options: the Gordon-below-Franklin scheme or the Gordon-above-Olga scheme. A "no dams" option was not provided. In the ensuing referendum campaign the environment movement urged voters to write "no dams" on their ballot papers. The referendum results revealed a deeply divided community: following a recount of the ballot papers, 47 percent were found to be in favor of the Gordon-below-Franklin proposal; 45 percent voted "no dams"; and the remainder voted in favor of the government's proposed alternative. Despite a change of Labor leadership prior to the referendum, the Labor government failed to maintain the confidence of parliament and a Tasmanian general election was called in 1982. Tasmanian voters elected a new Liberal government under Premier Robin Gray, who resolved to proceed apace with the HEC's original proposal.

Meanwhile opposition to the dam mounted as large public rallies and street marches were held in Tasmania and mainland Australia. Membership of the Tasmanian Wilderness Society grew rapidly as documentary films of the wild Franklin and Gordon rivers reached mass audiences in Australia. A peaceful blockade of the dam site began in December 1982 and the Tasmanian government responded by quickly enacting legislation that made trespass in the World Heritage area a criminal offence. Pro-dam rallies, sponsored by business, unions, and the HEC were also held in Tasmania in support of the Liberal government's action. The environment movement extended its national campaign in several mainland by-elections by asking voters to write "no dams" across their ballot paper—a tactic that met with considerable success.

Prior to the state election in Tasmania, the Southwest region had been nominated by the Liberal federal government (at the request of the former Labor Premier Lowe) for inclusion on the Register of World Heritage Properties under the International Convention for the Protection of the World Cultural and National Heritage 1972 (the World Heritage Convention)—a move that proved to be decisive in determining the final outcome of the dispute. As anti-dam pressure mounted the Liberal federal government offered generous financial compensation in an attempt to persuade the Tasmanian government to halt the dam project. Despite intensive lobbying by the environment movement the federal government declined to take the matter further by enacting overriding federal legislation to stop the dam, maintaining that the decision was ultimately a state matter. In contrast, in July 1982 the federal Labor opposition declared its support for the "Save the Franklin" campaign. When an early federal election was called for March 1983 the new Labor Leader Robert Hawke reaffirmed his party's intention to stop the dam. The environment movement mounted a concerted campaign against the Liberal party in marginal federal seats, a tactic that played a significant part in ensuring the victory of the Hawke Labor government. The new federal government enacted legislation to protect the Southwest world heritage area. However, a defiant Tasmanian government declined to order the removal of construction workers from the dam site, arguing that the federal government lacked the constitutional power to intervene. The federal government responded by bringing proceedings against the state of Tasmania in the High Court of Australia. In July 1983 the High Court, by a narrow majority of 4 to 3, held that the federal legislation was supported by the federal constitutional power to implement international treaties (i.e., the World Heritage Convention), regulate corporations (the HEC), and protect Aboriginal sites.

The Franklin dam campaign ended the dominance of the HEC in Tasmanian politics and demonstrated the growing political potency of environment issues—in this case a concern for threatened wilderness. Although a slender majority of Tasmanians supported the dam, the fate of Tasmania's Southwest wilderness was determined by a national parliament, responding to national pressure and an international treaty. A key figure in the anti-dam campaign, Dr. Bob Brown became the first independent Green member of the Tasmanian Parliament in 1982.

Robyn Eckersley

Further Readings
Lowe, Doug. *The Price of Power: The Politics behind the Tasmanian Dams Case.* 1984.
Sornarajah, M., ed. *The South West Dam Dispute: The Legal and Political Issues.* 1983.
Thompson, Peter. *Power in Tasmania.* 1981.

See also GREEN PARTIES: AUSTRALIA; LAKE PEDDER

F

Freshwater Wetlands

A wetland is a unit of landscape that is characterized by water near or above the soil surface throughout much of the year, unique organic soils, and hydrophytic (water-adapted) vegetation. Included as freshwater or semi-saline wetlands are bogs, marshes, pantanos, muskeg, peatlands, mires, carrs, fens, swamps, estuaries, sloughs, pocosins, some mangroves, ponds, floodplains, and shallow lakes. Wetlands cover approximately 8.56 million square kilometers or 6.4 percent of the earth's surface. It is uncertain how much of this area is freshwater or semi-saline, although the proportion in North America is approximately 95 percent.

Wetland types differ ecologically. Reed swamps such as rice beds are among the most biologically productive ecosystems in the world. Bogs, on the other hand, are characterized by very low productivity. They also tend to have low species diversity in comparison with marshes, for example. Wetlands are often described as ecotones, biologically rich and dynamic zones of transition between two different ecosystems. This is appropriate for many wetlands such as lacustrine marshes, but fens or bogs in the sub-arctic are biologically conservative features that cover vast areas. There is, however, a recognition that within regional landscapes wetlands have key ecological functions, performing often as centers of ecological organization.

Among the ecological functions that have been attributed to wetlands are: water treatment, flood regulation, genetic reserves, high floral and faunal productivity, reproductive and adult habitat for fish and wildlife, climatic control, carbon storage, and substrate stabilization. Wetlands are directly important to humans as sources of wood for building material, biomass (wood, peat, herbaceous) for fuel, food (vegetable and animal), recreational and tourist attractions, raw ingredients of pharmaceutical and other products, fodder, clean water and river base flow. Rice alone is the staple food of over half of the people in the world.

Both the natural and human values of wetlands are under threat worldwide. Some studies have estimated that 50 percent of the world's area of natural wetlands has been converted to other uses. Firm estimates exist for relatively few countries. Some such as those in Europe lost their endowment before inventories were undertaken. By the mid-1970s the United States had lost about 55 percent of its original wetlands; over 85 percent of that was lost to agricultural conversions. Almost 20 percent of the internationally important wetlands in Central and South America are currently threatened by drainage projects. Research in Canada, which contains 24 percent of the world's wetlands, has shown that in the most intensively settled areas 75 percent to 100 percent of wetland area has been converted to other uses.

As a result of their significance and the intensity of the pressures to convert them wetlands are the only landscape unit to be served by a dedicated international convention. The Convention on Wetlands of International Importance Especially as Waterfowl Habitat was signed in 1971 in Ramsar, Iran. The Ramsar Convention, in recognition of the international significance of wetlands, required "wise use" of listed wetlands. The Convention, having no permanent secretariat, has been implemented slowly. Most of the little funding that has been received for this purpose has been obtained from the International Union for Conservation of Nature and Natural Resources (IUCN), Switzerland, and the International Waterfowl and Wetlands Research Bureau, Great Britain. The original signatory countries were mainly developed countries. However, by 1991 more than sixty countries had signed and in excess of 500 wetlands (30 million hectares) had been designated for protection.

"Wise use" was not defined in the Ramsar Convention. A follow-up conference in 1980 in Cagliari, Italy, recommended comprehensive national inventories and policies for wetlands to demonstrate wise use. A 1984 conference in Groningen, Netherlands, recommended that action priorities be established for each country. Finally, in Regina, Canada, in 1987 wise use was defined in terms of sustaining human use and natural properties. In effect, the major means of ensuring wise use has been to designate listed wetlands as specially protected sites such as parks or national wildlife areas.

Thomas H. Whillans

Further Readings

Finlayson, M., and M. Moser. *Wetlands*. 1991.

Maltby, E. *Waterlogged Wealth*. 1986.

Mitsch, W.J., and J.G. Gosselink. *Wetlands*. 1986.

See also BIODEPLETION; BIODIVERSITY; COASTAL MARSHES, CONSERVATION OF; IUCN; WATERFOWL: CONSERVATION AND HABITAT

Friends of the Earth

Friends of the Earth (FOE) was founded in 1968 in the United States when David Brower led a secessionist group out of the Sierra Club. The organization expanded quickly as its combination of strong research, gutsy journalism, and activist politics provided a voice for the growing number of people who were becoming worried about their environmental future and who were not satisfied with the softer politics and naturalist concerns of traditional conservation groups.

From the start Friends of the Earth was conceived as an international coalition. Within a decade affiliates had been formed in most countries of Western Europe, Canada, Australia, and elsewhere. FOE International is the collection of national groups that holds the loose affiliation together. In recent years groups have been organized in Eastern Europe and a number of developing countries. By 1992 there were affiliates in fifty-one countries with a total membership of over 1 million.

The Canadian affiliate of Friends of the Earth was founded in 1978 and, just like the American group, saw its mandate as research-based environmental activism. For the first eleven years of its life, FOE in Canada was a coalition of one or several of the stronger groups in each province, a structure that reflected the regional nature of Canada and gave provincially based groups a voice on national and international issues. As communications became cheaper and groups more sophisticated this structure was no longer needed and in 1990 FOE-Canada became an organization of individual members.

Friends of the Earth affiliates select their own areas of activity. However, they are united in opposing nuclear power and other energy megaprojects, challenging the wider use of toxics, urging protection for habitat and endangered species and for the atmosphere, and promoting citizen participation in environmental decisions. FOE has distinguished itself by recognizing the place of human beings in the environment, emphasizing cultural concerns and international development. It refused to join a coalition to stop the hunting of whales until an exception was granted for the Inuit peoples.

From a research perspective, FOE affiliates are best known for studies of alternative ("soft") energy policies. More recently research has shifted to an emphasis on global climate change and to the impacts of government budgets on the environment.

In 1988, FOE-US moved from San Francisco to Washington, D.C., and in 1990 merged with the Environmental Policy Institute and the Oceanic Society under the name Friends of the Earth. The Canadian affiliate has always been based in Ottawa. In the early 1990s, FOE-US had an annual budget of $3.3 million and a staff of forty; income is derived mainly from foundation grants (50 percent); membership donations (35 percent); and contracts, services, and sales (15 percent). FOE-Canada had a budget of just over $1 million and a staff of seven; income is derived mainly from membership donations (45 percent); contracts, services and sales (35 percent); and foundation and corporate grants (10 percent). Some 20,000 people are members of Friends of the Earth in the United States and about 12,000 in Canada.

David B. Brooks

Further Readings
Friends of the Earth. *Friends of the Earth Newsmagazine.* In earlier years: *Not Man Apart.*
National Wildlife Federation. *Conservation Directory.* Annual.

See also BROWER, DAVID; CLIMATE WARMING; ENVIRONMENTAL POLICY INSTITUTE; ENVIRONMENTALISM; NUCLEAR ELECTRIC POWER; SIERRA CLUB; SOFT ENERGY PATHS

Frogs
See AMPHIBIANS: CONSERVATION AND HABITAT

F

G

Gaia Hypothesis

Originally articulated by James Lovelock in the early 1970s the Gaia Hypothesis puts forward the startling proposition that earth is a coherent entity, approximating in some ways a single living organism. Earth is certainly, in this view, a self-sustaining system. The living planet, the hypothesis asserts, may be unconscious, but yet self-managing. In Lovelock's phrasing the biota, rocks, air, and oceans exist as a tightly coupled entity. For example the clouds, which cool the planet, are taken to have been largely produced by tropical rainforests and the oxygen in the atmosphere to have been produced by living organisms over the many millennia of life. Oxygen, it is noted, comprises 21 percent of the atmosphere. In an atmosphere of 15 percent oxygen fires could not begin; at 25 percent they might not end until most life was destroyed. In many ways then life is seen to adjust in ways that allow life on earth to continue. Recent human interventions do not threaten the existence of life, though they may threaten the existence of large numbers of humans.

Gaia, named after the Greek earth goddess on the suggestion of novelist William Golding, is indifferent to the continuation of any particular species. But in this view there would appear to be a variety of self-regulating mechanisms within the planetary life-system. The long sweep of the carbon cycle has seen plant (and animal) life as a carbon sink slowly removing more carbon dioxide from the atmosphere. This change in turn may have allowed for the escape of more heat from the earth's surface into space—a release that may well have been necessary long prior to recent human interventions into those cycles and adjusted temperatures.

The Gaia Hypothesis is truly an alternative view of the world within or upon which we exist. Many scientists find the proposition that the earth can be seen as a superorganism as preposterous; others see it as essentially teleological and untestable. But is life best seen as existing within or upon earth? For "Gaians" the earth is not, as Bill McKibben has noted, an "environment" within which life develops and exists, so much as a living "system that modifies its surroundings so as to insure its survival." Lovelock himself sees the greatest threats to the diversity of life as combustion, cattle (and modern agriculture generally), and chain saws (in their effect on forests).

Robert Paehlke

Further Readings

Lovelock, James. *Gaia: A New Look at Life on Earth*. 1979.
Margulis, L., and James Lovelock. "Biological Modulation of the Earth's Atmosphere." *Icarus* 21 (1974): 471–89.

See also CLIMATE WARMING; ENVIRONMENT; TROPICAL RAINFORESTS; WHOLE EARTH IMAGE; WILDERNESS

Garrison Diversion

Officially titled the Garrison Diversion Unit of the Missouri River Basin Project, Garrison Diversion is a large public works project that diverts water from the Missouri River in North Dakota. Originally authorized in 1944 (under a different name), it was planned by the U.S. Bureau of Reclamation to irrigate over a million scattered acres of semi-arid land. Return flows would have been discharged to several rivers, including two that flow north into Canada.

Because soil surveys conducted after initial authorization indicated that much of the planned irrigation acreage was unsuitable, the project had to be redesigned and reauthorized. Because of the questionable economic basis of the project, only a more limited plan, for 250,000 acres, was reauthorized in 1965 after years of political maneuvering. Construction began in 1968 with environmental opposition to the project spreading beyond North Dakota soon afterward. In 1970 the Canadian federal government first expressed through diplomatic channels its concern about the potential effects of the project on Canada. In 1971, in order to comply with the new environmental assessment requirements of the National Environmental Policy Act of 1969, the Bureau of Reclamation released the first of what would become a series of environmental impact statements on Garrison Diversion.

In the 1970s and early 1980s the project was the subject or focus of numerous lawsuits, national and international commission inquiries, innumerable scientific studies, legislative and bureaucratic intrigue, diplomatic negotiation, campaign rhetoric, and political protest. The project was repeatedly redesigned to try to reduce or mitigate environmental effects, notably adverse fish and wildlife impacts in North Dakota and Canada. Construction was stopped and delayed several times. A political compromise and a special national commission led in 1986 to reauthorization of Garrison Diversion as an even smaller irrigation project of 130,000 acres with an expanded rural and municipal water supply mandate.

Some environmentally damaging features were deauthorized and others were made conditional on further study. Features that posed theats to Canada, namely transfers of water from the Missouri River basin to the Hudson Bay watershed, were mostly eliminated. Because the 1986 compromise was supported by several U.S. environmental groups, including the National Audubon Society which had led opposition to the project at the national level, and because it alleviated most Canadian concerns, the Garrison Diversion project has since been less controversial. Although the economic rationale of the project continues to be questioned, annual appropriation for further construction of supply features has been forthcoming. The state of North Dakota has continued to work to find a way to build an expanded project, including a key reservoir (Lonetree, renamed Mid-Dakota) that is of continuing concern to environmentalists and Canadians.

Robert V. Bartlett

Further Readings
Bartlett, Robert V. "Adapt or Get Out: The Garrison Diversion Project and Controversy." *Environmental Review* 12 (Fall 1988): 57–74.
Feldman, David L. "The Great Plains Garrison Diversion Unit and the Search for an Environmental Ethic." *Policy Sciences* 24 (1991): 41–64.
Kurian, Priya A., and Robert V. Bartlett. "The Garrison Diversion Dream and the Politics of Landscape Engineering." *North Dakota History* 59 (1992): 40–51.

See also ENVIRONMENTAL DIPLOMACY; INTERNATIONAL JOINT COMMISSION; WATER ALLOCATIONS AND SHORTAGES (U.S. WEST)

Gas Chromatograph

A gas chromatograph (GC) is an analytical instrument commonly used to determine the concentrations of various organic contaminants, such as PCBs, oil hydrocarbons, and pesticides in environmental samples. Modern GCs can detect these compounds in part-per-billion (ppb) quantities in the environment. GC separates a complex mixture of compounds in an environmental sample into its various component compounds. To do this the compounds in the sample are heated in the GC inlet system so that they become gases. The compounds then enter the GC column where they repeatedly adsorb to a "stationary phase" in the column as they are carried along by a "carrier gas." Compounds are separated from each other according to their affinity for the stationary phase. When the compounds leave the column after separation, they are swept by the carrier gas into a detector.

There are different types of detectors for various analytical applications. For instance, PCBs are often analyzed with an "electron capture detector," and most herbicides are analyzed with a "nitrogen-phosphorous detector." Gas chromatographic and mass spectrometric technologies have been combined to form gas chromatograph-mass spectrometers (GC-MS), where the mass spectrometer is used as a mass-selective detector for the GC. These instruments are very powerful analytical tools commonly used to analyze dioxins, and other compounds present in ultratrace (part per trillion) quantities in environmental samples.

Chris D. Metcalfe

Further Readings

Bruno, T.J. *Chromatographic and Electro-phoretic Methods.* 1991.

Harris, D.C. *Quantitative Chemical Analysis.* 3rd ed. 1991.

See also DIOXINS AND FURANS; MASS SPECTROMETRY; PERSISTENT ORGANOCHLORINE COMPOUNDS; TRACE ANALYSIS

Genetic Diversity

Genetic diversity is the amount of genetical variation in or between individuals of the same population or species. It is a component of biodiversity, which includes also species and habitat diversity. Genetic diversity is the basic contributor to the diversity of living forms seen in different species and different habitats.

Genetic diversity is commonly expressed as mean heterozygosity (having inherited different forms [alleles] from parent genes) per locus *(H)* (i.e., the proportion of heterozygous genes in an individual) and frequency of polymorphic loci *(P)* (i.e., the proportion of genes with two or more alleles present, such that the rarer allele(s) is at a frequency greater than can be maintained by recurrent mutation; this frequency is normally taken as either 5 percent or 1 percent). The values of *H* and *P* are obviously affected by the total number of genes screened for variation, and also by the actual genes scored (some genes are more variable than others). Notwithstanding, sufficient data exists to reveal clear differences between variation amounts between species. In general there is greater genetic variety in small, rapidly breeding species than in larger, more mobile ones; and in species that live in variable as opposed to stable environments.

Although animal and plant breeders have always known that virtually any species will respond to selection and must therefore carry a non-negligible amount of variation, the conventional assumption of biologists used to be that most species are invariant (or homozygous) for the great majority of their genes, the only exception being recent mutations in the process of elimination through natural selection and a small number of polymorphic loci (exemplified by the blood groups in mammals). Until the 1920s intraspecific variation was believed to be environmentally determined; experimental breeding was required to show that much intraspecific variation was inherited and that local genetically adapted forms (or ecotypes) undoubtedly existed. In the 1940s this recognition

was formalized with the emergence of the "new systematics," particularly important being the concept of a species as a dynamic genetic entity liable to change in both time and species.

However, the existence of an upper limit to the amount of genetical variation in any particular population seemed to be required by quantitative calculations on "genetic load" (carried out by H.J. Muller in 1950) and "the cost of natural selection" (J.B.S. Haldane in 1957). These calculations were based on the number of deaths resulting from maintaining or substituting inherited variants. Notwithstanding, the assumptions behind the load and cost concepts were shown to be wrong in 1966. In that year two groups (R.C. Lewontin and J.L. Hubby working in Chicago with fruit flies (*Drosophila rseudoobscura*) and H. Harris in London with humans) independently applied the proven biochemical technique of electrophoresis to population samples of a number of enzymes. They showed that both species were carrying far too much variation for survival, yet both were obviously flourishing.

The 1966 reports led to the suggestion that most genetic variation has no effect on its bearers, that it is neutral. During the 1970s an active debate took place between "neutralists" (led by a Japanese theoretician, Motoo Kimura) and "selectionists" (represented by traditional neo-Darwinians). The demonstration that individual enzyme variants almost always have physiologically significant differences, that correlations exist between variation and habitat but not between variation and population size, and that different proteins (and indeed, parts of proteins) evolve at different rates produced a firm consensus in favor of the standard Darwinian interpretation. Adaptation in this view is seen to be the norm (i.e., most variation will sooner or later be advantageous or deleterious, and hence subject to selection), albeit with an improved ecological understanding of selection and the acceptance that many variants are neutral for much of the time (e.g., those produced by mutation in the third member of a codon in the DNA, and probably the majority of DNA variants themselves).

Meanwhile a concern had arisen in the conservation community about the erosion of genetic variation occurring through the agricultural practice of concentrating production on ever fewer varieties, with old, unimproved "land-races" being discarded and lost. One of the major projects in the International Biological Programme was to collect and store what came to be known as "genetic resources"; an International Board for Plant Genetic Resources was established in 1972 and endorsed by the United Nations Conference on the Human Environment. A movement to conserve genetical variety emerged, emphasizing the importance of minimum viable population sizes of populations or species to avoid loss of inherited variants and the risk of extinction through reduction in adaptability. This initiative was advanced by Otto Aide Frankel, an Australian agriculturist, and Michael Soulé, an American geneticist. Its precepts are now widely adopted by conservation bodies including the International Union for the Conservation of Nature and Natural Resources (IUCN) Species Survival Commission.

R.J. Berry

Further Readings
Berry, R.J. *Inheritance and Natural History.* 1977.
Sandlund, O.T., K. Hindar, and A.H.D. Brown, eds. *Conservation of Biodiversity for Sustainable Development.* 1992.
Solbrig, O.T., ed. *Genes to Ecosystems: A Research Agenda for Biodiversity.* 1991.

See also BIODEPLETION; BIODIVERSITY; BIODIVERSITY: PLANTS; CONSERVATION BIOLOGY; DARWIN, CHARLES; HABITAT FRAGMENTATION, PATCHES, AND CORRIDORS; IUCN; RIO CONFERENCE (1992); STOCKHOLM CONFERENCE

Georgescu-Roegen, Nicholas

Nicholas Georgescu-Roegen (1906–) is recognized as a seminal contributor to the theory of steady state economics and, more recently, ecological economics. His most important work, *The Entropy Law and the Economic Process* (*ELEP*), offers a major critique of mainstream (neoclassical) economic theory. Neoclassical economists dismiss Georgescu-Roegen's work on the fallacious notion that it is an energy theory of value. Correctly interpreted *ELEP* elucidates constraints on the market theory of value that are implicit in the second law of thermodynamics. Since neoclassical economic theory is institutionalized in the political-economy of the modern west, the relevance of Georgescu-Roegen's work to environmental issues is apparent. His later work, especially on energy and economics, extends the line of criticism developed in *ELEP* to questions of re-

source allocations and policy and intergenerational equity.

Although Georgescu-Roegen introduces considerations involving the history of science and mathematical theory into his critical work, it fundamentally turns on the entropy law. He argues that conventional economic theory ignores crucial questions about the fundamental means available to sustain processes of economic production as well as questions about the fundamental ends toward which production is directed. On his analysis purely quantitative measures of economic throughput, reflected in the national income accounts, have become the overriding goal of modern economic growth societies. The pursuit of quantitative growth for the sake of growth, he argues, has negative environmental and social consequences (such as so-called externalities and fairness to future generations). Neoclassical economic theory leads toward unrestrained increases in environmental disorder (entropy), as manifested in dwindling stocks of natural resources and increasing levels of pollution. Materialism (consumerism) is the social side of the equation. From Georgescu-Roegen's vantage point the enjoyment or quality of life exceeds in importance any quantity of life.

Max Oelschlaeger

Further Readings
Georgescu-Roegen, Nicholas. *The Entropy Law and the Economic Process.* 1971.
———. *Energy and Economic Myths: Institutional and Analytical Economic Essays.* 1976.

See also GREEN ECONOMICS; SUSTAINABILITY

Giant Panda

The giant panda (*Carnivora*; *Ailuropodidae*; *Ailuropoda melanoleuca*) is a medium-sized (60 to 110 kilogram) mammal and an endangered species. Approximately 1,000 wild pandas remain in the Sichuan, Gansu, and Shaanxi provinces of the People's Republic of China, along with about ninety captives, mostly in Chinese zoos. As the distinctive black and white logo of the Worldlife Fund for Nature (WWF) this species symbolizes wildlife conservation.

Panda habitat is mature forest with a bamboo understory. The pandas' diet consists almost exclusively of bamboo—even though this is poorly digestible food for an animal with a single stomach. They persist in such an odd diet because bamboo, an abundant food resource, fulfills their daily food consumption requirements (12 to 20 kilograms per day). Pandas deal with the die-back of most stems of one bamboo species, following its synchronous flowering, by switching to other bamboo(s). When there are no alternative bamboos, or alternatives flower and die in quick succession, some pandas may starve.

Giant pandas became endangered, with shrinking populations, primarily because of habitat loss and poaching. Forest clearing for agriculture and timber, combined with rapid human population growth in China, has hastened the panda's demise. Pandas are now relegated to high mountain ridges on the edges of their historic range, in twenty-four disjunct populations and habitat totaling 12,250 square kilometers.

Poaching of pandas for sale of pelts in Japan, Taiwan, and Hong Kong increased dramatically in the 1980s with encouragement of free-market economics in China. Despite being illegal, with penalties as severe as the death sentence, poaching continues. It remains the most critical threat since pandas mature slowly (reaching maturity at five or six years), and reproduce slowly (a female can raise at most one young every two years).

China initiated panda conservation in the 1960s by establishing reserves and making hunting illegal. Chinese and foreign scientists have collaborated since 1980 on studies of panda ecology, a survey of range and distribution, training for reserve staff, and management planning. A 1992 Chinese management plan is now the focus of conservation efforts. Its principal goals are an increase in reserves from thirteen to twenty-seven, and the establishment of habitat corridors to link isolated populations and reduce inbreeding.

There are two major hurdles. A culture of conservation is virtually absent in China. Wild places and animals are beyond the experience of most Chinese. Wildlife including pandas and their forest habitats are viewed primarily as commodities, and most rural people are too poor to overlook these resources. Conservation can only proceed with successful reserve protection, and direct economic benefits to local people as a result of reserve establishment.

The panda is also a commodity as the object of lucrative international loans between Chinese and foreign zoos. Pandas are removed from the wild to supply loans, and concerted efforts to breed captives are disrupted. Meanwhile the captive population is not self sustaining. Loans can only be justified when all Chinese and international institutions with pandas cooperate in a managed breeding effort, and when most revenues raised go to conservation of wild pandas.

Donald G. Reid

Further Readings
Catton, Chris. *Pandas*. 1990.
Schaller, George. *The Giant Pandas of Wolong*. 1985.
———. *The Last Panda*. 1993.

See also BEARS: CONSERVATION AND HABITAT; BIOSPHERE RESERVES; WORLD WILDLIFE FUND; ZOOS: INSTITUTIONS IN TRANSITION

Global ReLeaf

Global ReLeaf is an education, action, and policy campaign on community reforestation. The American Forestry Association created the program in 1988 as a means of involving people in the battle against environmental degradation. Friends of the Earth (FOE) launched the Canadian equivalent on Earth Day 1990 to encourage Canadians to expand areas of forests in both urban and rural areas. Through grants from the Global ReLeaf Fund it has been possible for Canadians to plant thousands of trees in communities across Canada.

The Global ReLeaf program also works in conjunction with the Friends of the Earth Atmosphere Campaign which strives to protect the ozone layer and abate climate change. It advocates strong community forestry programs to decrease energy consumption, increase the cooling effect of trees, and cut air pollution. Global ReLeaf is committed to ensuring that forests are maintained in a healthy and productive condition through research and advocacy work. The program maintains an ongoing public education campaign concerning the benefits of trees to the environment.

Global ReLeaf educational materials, such as the *Homeowner's Guide to Planting Energy Conservation Trees*, inspire people to reforest the areas in which they live, work, and play. As a precursor to this guide, the program commissioned a study entitled *The Tree-House Effect*, which discusses the important relationship between trees and energy conservation.

Ellen Hagerman

Further Readings
Global ReLeaf. *Homeowner's Guide to Planting Energy Conservation Trees*. 1992.

———. *The Tree-House Effect.* 1991.

See also Climate Warming; Forest Regeneration; Forestry, History of; Friends of the Earth; Ozone Depletion; Urban Forestry

Global Warming
See Climate Warming

GNP and the Environment
See Economic Growth and the Environment

Gorillas
See Primates: Conservation and Habitat

Grand Canyon

The Grand Canyon, the largest chasm of the Colorado River, is one of the world's most impressive and colorful natural spectacles. It extends from Lees Ferry near the Arizona-Utah border southward and westward to the Grand Wash Cliffs, a distance of 277 miles (445 kilometers). The central section averages one mile (1,600 meters) in depth, but at the deepest point the rim stands more than 6,600 feet (2,000 meters) above the river. The width averages about 10 miles (16 kilometers). Its topography is a series of long, curving cliffs and steep terraces, with erosional features such as towers, buttes, and mesas. Its climate and vegetation vary from Sonoran desert conditions at the bottom to boreal forest along the north rim.

Many ruins and other remains of the desert culture, Anasazi Pueblo, Cohonina, and other early peoples dot the canyon, and in ancient and modern times it has been home to the Havasupai, Hualapai, Navajo, Hopi, and Paiute nations. The first three named have reservations that include portions of the Grand Canyon.

Spanish explorers first saw the Grand Canyon in 1540 when Hopi Indians guided García López de Cárdenas and others in the Coronado expedition to it. More Spanish visitors and American trappers entered the region. The first official American expeditions were those of Joseph Christmas Ives (1857–1858) and John Wesley Powell (1869–1872).

Protected status began in 1893 with President Benjamin Harrison's proclamation of a large Grand Canyon Forest Reserve. President Theodore Roosevelt in 1906 set aside the Grand Canyon Game Reserve in much the same area, and created a much smaller Grand Canyon National Monument in 1908. Arizona's congressional delegation sponsored a bill to establish a national park, which passed and was signed by President Woodrow Wilson on February 26, 1919. The park included only part of the Grand Canyon, but adjacent national monuments were added in 1932 and 1969. Another act of Congress in 1975 almost doubled the size of Grand Canyon National Park to 1,892 square miles (4,901 square kilometers) so as to include the entire canyon with the exception of the Indian reservations.

Water development is an important conservation issue involving the Grand Canyon. After the construction of Hoover Dam in 1936 Lake Mead entered the lower end of the canyon. Glen Canyon Dam, authorized in 1956, controls the flow of the Colorado River through the canyon, and has adversely affected beach erosion and wildlife habitat along the river. In 1963 the Bureau of Reclamation proposed two dams within the Grand Canyon, to be named Marble Canyon Dam and Bridge Canyon (Hualpai) Dam. Environmental groups such as the Sierra Club successfully organized opposition to these dams, and a congressional moratorium on their construction was enacted in 1968.

Other recent issues include the control of low altitude flights over and within the canyon by airplanes and helicopters. Also the National Park Service has attempted to eliminate destructive, non-native species such as the feral burros that were first introduced by prospectors in the 1880s, but has faced opposition from animal rights groups. Predator control programs ended in the 1930s after virtual elimination of mountain lions caused a disastrous population explosion of deer. Tourism has posed a threat to the environment as visitor numbers have risen above 3 million per year. Traffic is now restricted in summer along some rim drives, and more than 80 percent of the national park area is designated as wilderness.

J. Donald Hughes

Further Readings
Crampton, C. Gregory. *Land of Living Rock: The Grand Canyon and the High Plateaus.* 1972.
Hughes, J. Donald. *In the House of Stone and Light: A Human History of the*

Grand Canyon. 1978.

Nash, Roderick, ed. *Grand Canyon of the Living Colorado.* 1970.

See also ANIMAL RIGHTS; COLORADO RIVER; EXOTIC SPECIES; NATIONAL PARK SERVICE (U.S.); NATIONAL PARKS: UNITED STATES; POWELL, JOHN WESLEY; SIERRA CLUB; TOP PREDATORS IN CANADA: AN OVERVIEW

Grasslands

See HABITAT LOSS IN NORTH AMERICA; RANGELANDS (U.S.)

Great Britain: Environmental Problems

In Great Britain, properly the United Kingdom of England, Wales, Scotland, and Northern Ireland, responsibility for environmental matters rests with the Department of the Environment for overall national and international policy. The Ministry of Agriculture, however, deals with such matters as flood protection and coastal defense. Various sector departments have a role to play regarding the environmental aspects of international trade, overseas aid, transport, energy, trade and industry, health, education and agriculture. To complicate matters, all these sectoral policies are dealt with on a country basis in Scotland, Wales, and Northern Ireland, with one Secretary of State in charge of all policy. Finally the local authorities of county councils and district councils cover local public health issues such as noise, dust, and sanitation, and the Employment Department is accountable for health and safety in the workplace.

In the Victorian age Britain was a very polluted place. Air pollution was so severe as to generate regular winter fogs fueled by the smoke of coal burning. Waterways were blocked by untreated sewage and industrial waste. Wild dumping of toxic substances, which leached their contaminated effluent into rivers and groundwaters, was commonplace. Diseases of the lung, the skin, and the eye were often connected to all this pollution, but cause and effect were rarely proved.

As Britain prospered in the late 1800s, so the emergence of regulatory bodies backed by strong legislation, stronger scientific evidence, and growing public concern began to make changes toward reducing pollution and its effects. Air pollution was controlled by the Alkali Inspectorate, which was formed to deal with the chloro-alkali process in 1864. Both its name and its remit were expanded over the years and now the top 5,000 most difficult industries are licensed by a single agency: Her Majesty's Inspectorate of Pollution (HMIP). This operates on the basis of integrated pollution control, utilizing a series of notes of guidance. These in turn operate on the principle of best available techniques not entailing excessive cost (BATNEEC). BATNEEC is not only standardized as to process; it is also geared to limit emissions by applying waste reduction at source. Thus British pollution control policy is continually moving up the pipe to aim at the very management and marketing of products. In this respect, the HMIP is helped by European Community (EC) directives which specify how much of certain substances are permitted in the country as a whole, and particular regions, including complete bans (e.g., PCBs are banned throughout the North Sea basin states from 1994).

Water pollution has shifted from organic waste discharges to toxic chemical effluent, usually of low but potentially hazardous concentrations. To get round the problem the EC has produced an extended list of substances which are strictly controlled in rivers and estuaries. All these substances are subject to BATNEEC, and all are handled by HMIP. In general the extent of water pollution has diminished, though in recent years slight increases have been noted.

It is difficult to ascertain the reasons for this recent shift. In part monitoring has become more sophisticated so there is greater accuracy of information. As well the new water pollution control agency, the National Rivers Authority (NRA), is more independent of industry and sewage treatment works and publishes more comprehensive data. But it has to be said that the application of BATNEEC applies only to certain substances and processes. For the majority a looser approach prevails, namely best practicable means. This allows the NRA to judge strict regulatory rules, especially in cases where industries are going through difficult times, the local employment base is vulnerable to industrial closure, and constituency MPs are anxious that environmental protection is always subservient to growth and prosperity.

Nevertheless, in principle the NRA operates to a policy of creating and enforcing statutory water quality standards. These should take into account the interests of nature conservation, amenity, and recreation. They should form the basis of all future discharge consents. And they should be reviewed in public, with all discharge licenses subject to public inspection.

In practice ministers are slow to promulgate the Statutory Water Quality Objectives (SWQOs). Indeed not all water courses will be subject to designation of SWQOs. Furthermore, the procedures for informing the public are tortuous. The registers of licensed discharges are not readily accessible, and for statistical reasons no given reading has any legal value—only the scientifically minded and the very assiduous will be able to make use of these registers. As the budgets and staff of the NRA get squeezed, so the scope for enforcement is diminished. In time the NRA may be more self-financing by charging for its scanning and monitoring, as well as possibly charging a pollution tax based on the degree to which the assimilative capacity of the water is taken up by a given discharge. But the techniques of determining this effect are still in their infancy, so it will be some years yet before a full environmental charging regime is put in place.

At present, waste management lies in the hands of the county councils. Under the Environmental Protection Act of 1990 the counties had to split their operations into a waste disposal authority and waste regulatory authority. The former may be in public or private hands; the latter is a public executive. The act specifies that any waste producer must pass a legal duty of care when transmitting waste to a contractor. This places the burden of responsibility on the producer to show that the disposer is both competent and reliable.

Similarly changes in the liability rules mean that any landowner is responsible for cleaning up any contaminated land found on properties, irrespective of who contaminated the land. This has led to calls for a contaminated land register so that potentially nasty sites can be avoided. But the legacy of contamination from the Victorian and Edwardian eras is so widespread that the register has not been published by the Department of the Environment. Presumably there is a question of conclusive proof of contamination involved, with the threat from litigation by landowners who may suddenly find their land of no value, and with no insurance to cover the cost of cleanup. As in many other nations, the contaminated land issue remains thoroughly awkward and wholly unresolved.

Habitat protection in the United Kingdom relies on designation of species rich or geologically interesting areas under the titles Sites of Special Scientific Interest (SSSI). At present there are some 5,000 SSSIs in the United Kingdom covering about 7.5 percent of the country. SSSI designation provides no safeguard against damage unless the SSSI is owned by an official conservation agency or by a voluntary nature conservation organization. Only 20 percent of SSSIs are so owned. The rest are notified on a register, and, according to law, any proposal by a landowner to change the land is subject to formal approval by the official country-based nature conservation agency.

In practice about 6 percent of SSSIs are damaged to some extent every year, and about 2 percent are lost altogether. The main trouble comes from road building, urban development and tourism, and agricultural intensification, though willful damage and burning also take a heavy toll. The only means of safeguard is a management agreement, based on terms favorable to the landowner if this person is a farmer. If the conservation agencies do not have the cash to meet these agreements, running at about £7.5 million annually, then the SSSI could well be lost.

In recent years the EC's Common Agricultural Policy has been modified to allow farmers to enter into nationally funded conservation agreements, and to set aside their land for nonagricultural purposes. The two measures are separate. The conservation agreements are specifically geared toward providing nature conservation interest through management policies that are sympathetic to species and habitats. The set-aside policy is still coming to terms with how much of the land can be converted to nature conservation in perpetuity. Meanwhile farmers are encouraged to intensify on the 85 percent of their land which is not set aside.

In general Britain is much better off than its Victorian predecessor, with environmental health now well-established for all people in society. But the rise of toxic substances in all aspects of industrial and transport activity is contaminating both people and nature with new and as yet unquantified environmental health hazards. The scope for control rests increasingly with voluntary regulation by industry rather than the somewhat beleaguered and impoverished regulatory agencies. As the EC and the Rio-based Agenda 21 exercise strengthen sustainable development strategies and as rights-to-know and legal duties expand, so there will be a gradual tightening over environmental misuse and a much greater reliance on self-policing. Meanwhile a plethora of economic incentives in the form of taxes, deposit refund schemes, and tradable permits are seriously being discussed in Europe generally. So far few of these procedures have been put into effect; their time will come.

Timothy O'Riordan

Further Readings

Hughes, David. *Environmental Law*. 1992.
McCormick, John. *Environmental Politics in Britain*. 1992.
Rose, Chris. *The Dirty Man of Europe*. 1991.

See also AIR POLLUTION: IMPACTS; ENVIRONMENTAL CASE LAW: EUROPEAN COMMUNITY; LEGISLATION: GREAT BRITAIN; RIGHT-TO-KNOW (COMMUNITY); RIO CONFERENCE (1992); STANDARD SETTING; TRADEABLE EMISSION PERMITS

Great Lakes

General Features of Laurentian Great Lakes

The North America Great Lakes are sometimes termed the Laurentian Great Lakes because they are located at the edge of the Laurentian Shield. This old geological structure of metamorphic rock extends from northwestern Canada in an arc into central Canada and the northern United States from Minnesota to New York to northeastern Canada and appears also in northern Europe in Scotland and in the northern Baltic Region. Smaller lakes similar to the Great Lakes occur elsewhere along the southerly edge of the Shield in North America and in Europe. They have been deepened by the scouring of continental glaciers. Glacial till is usually found to the south of these lakes overlying sedimentary limestones and shales.

Five large lakes are usually listed as comprising the Laurentian Great Lakes: Superior, Michigan, Huron, Erie, and Ontario in sequence from higher to lower in latitude. Two of these, Michigan and Huron, are not separated by a river and hence are called one lake when the interest focuses primarily on hydrological phenomena. The large rivers that serve as "connecting channels" to these lakes include the St. Mary's, St. Clair-Detroit, and the Niagara. The St. Lawrence River drains the water from this set of lakes into the Gulf of St. Lawrence and the Atlantic Ocean.

For lakes that border on the Shield, in their natural state, inflowing waters are of two types. Waters draining from the Shield are relatively "pure" in that they possess few chemicals such as plant nutrients and thus support only minimal biological production. Waters draining from the sedimentary and glacial till regions south of the Shield contain plant nutrients in sufficient abundance to support moderate levels of biological production. The less fertile the waters the higher their transparency will be except in areas where infertile clays in suspension cause turbidity. Clay turbidity occurs naturally in a few near-shore locales in the Great Lakes but will not be discussed here.

Aside from the concentration of chemical plant nutrients in inflowing waters other major features determine the ecological productivity of lakes. The deeper the water, the faster the flow rate of water through the lake and thus the faster the flushing of accumulated chemicals downstream, the lower the climatic and aquatic temperature, the less productive and the more transparent the particular body of water will be.

The Great Lakes show a general gradient of biological productivity from north to south because all but one of the factors that determine productivity (excepting flow rate) show the relevant gradient from north to south. Generally the less productive a body of water, the less capable it is of assimilating pollutants of human origin without showing major degradation.

In the Great Lakes the less fertile, deeper, colder, more stationary waters were preferred by species of the salmonid family such as lake trout, lake whitefish, and deepwater chubs plus sculpins and freshwater cod. More fertile, shallow, warm, flowing waters were preferred by white bass, smallmouth bass, channel catfish, and minnows of many kinds. Waters intermediate between these extremes were preferred by species of the percid family (such as walleye, blue pike, and yellow perch), the esocid family (such as northern pike and muskellunge), and gizzard shad and freshwater drum. Many kinds of migratory waterfowl, shorebirds, and scavengers such as gulls and eagles thrived along all the shores of the Great Lakes. Extensive wetlands in shallower bays of all the lakes and rivers were particularly productive of food for these birds, as well as for mammals from moose to mink and numerous reptiles such as large turtles.

The salmonid family deserves special note. Two chars—the lake trout and the brook trout—occurred in the form of many distinctive stocks or subspecies that differed anatomically, behaviorally, and ecologically. Grayling appeared as only one stock. Chubs, ciscoes, and lake whitefish each also occurred in numerous stocks. Ecologists note that the various stocks acted as ecologically different "species" so that there may have been 100 such "eco-species" within the Great Lakes salmonid family. The great majority of these "stocks," as well as some entire species that were unique to the Great Lakes, have been rendered extinct. Causes of extinction include human interventions such as eutrophication, toxic pollution, damming of streams, and overfishing, as well as invasion by non-native species such as the sea lamprey, among others.

Some General Features of Pollution

The term "pollution" can have a connotation of a process that causes something to become foul or filthy which may be objectionable for practical, aesthetic, or ethical reasons. The term can also have the religious meaning of destroying the purity and sanctity of something, as in defiling Mother Earth. In the Great Lakes region both of these general connotations, with their varying political implications, may be encountered.

Humans have altered the Great Lakes in many ways. In general terms these alterations can be classified into three primary types: 1) additions or removals of physical features; 2) additions of chemical substances; and 3) additions or removals of biological features. Among all these kinds of changes the term pollution refers only to undesirable additions of chemical substances (no chemical substances as such are removed from these waters for cultural purposes, in part because water is treated as a physical feature). Thus pollution relates to only a fraction—though an important fraction—of undesirable effects caused by humans in the Great Lakes or other locations. Some of the other undesirable effects act indirectly to exacerbate the direct effects of pollution and only few of the others act in ways to moderate or combat the effects of pollution.

Pollution itself comes in various forms:

- Organic wastes such as human sewage or manure from farms decompose in water to use up oxygen required by fish and other organisms; the minerals produced as a result of decomposition then act as nutrients for plants in well-lit waters, causing eutrophication.
- Chemical fertilizers used on land leach into groundwaters and streams, serving as plant nutrients and contributing to eutrophication.

- Pesticides—widely used in urban, rural, and wild forested areas—flow or leach into water courses and cause mortalities unless the pesticides break down naturally and quickly on land.
- Many inorganic poisons are used widely in manufacturing and others are produced as wastes in manufacturing processes; some of each kind inevitably end up in the Great Lakes (e.g., after being transported through the atmosphere from smoky industries upwind).
- Many organic or carbon-based chemicals used or produced in manufacturing have powerful but very insidious effects on living things in the Great Lakes; this is especially the case with some chemicals that include chlorine atoms in their molecules (i.e., organochlorines or chlorinated hydrocarbons).
- Radionuclides (which result from fission of radioactive materials as in nuclear energy utilities), also do insidious harm when released into the environment.

All of the pollutants to which the Great Lakes are subject cause harm to living things within the lakes and on their shores. The harm is also propagated to humans. A particularly bizarre example of such propagation involves some organochlorines such as DDT. Because of its chemical properties DDT is attracted much more to fatty or oily mediums than to watery mediums. Compared to water the surface of living things in water resembles a fatty substance; thus, given an opportunity, an organochlorine molecule will very likely attach itself to a living membrane and be transported though the membrane and into fatty material within the organism. Since the organism usually does not possess enzymes or catalysts that are efficient in breaking down the organochlorine, it is stored there in fatty tissue. When eaten by another organism the organochlorine again becomes sequestered into the fatty substance of the second organism. This process may continue through several steps. The result of these successive steps of bioaccumulation, bioconcentration, and biomagnification may result in high concentrations of organochlorines within terminal predators such as fish, turtles, and gulls. Such concentrations may be sufficient to cause serious developmental abnormalities during the very early stages of life of such creatures, when stored fat has to be used by the embryo. Evidence is accumulating that this is also the case with humans. Disabilities in infants that persist through life may be a greater threat of hazardous contaminants than cancers in adults.

Pollution and Other Stresses
in the Great Lakes

All types of cultural stresses (additions or removals of physical, chemical, or biological materials or entities) have been applied in each of the Great Lakes more or less concurrently since late in the eighteenth century. From the beginning of such unsustainable development the most intense stresses of various types occurred in and near human settlements that became industrial cities and then metropolitan concentrations. The most stressful sites generally were located near relatively fertile, shallow, warm, moving waters in protected bays which were particularly productive of waterfowl, fur-bearing animals, ungulates, large fish, and turtles. Thus the ecologically most valued parts of the near shore and coastal zone were sacrificed first to "progress." Numerous such locales were already offensively degraded by the late nineteenth century.

Canadians and Americans were about equally effective in debasing Great Lakes waters near their most thriving settlements. People of the first nations or native tribes participated in some of the abuses, such as over-harvesting mammals and waterfowl on occasion, but their misdeeds fade to relative insignificance in comparison with those of the European invaders. By the early twentieth century some of the ecological effects of local abuse had already spread to waters that were of interest to those in other locales and even in "the other country." At the time native people were not recognized to have sovereignty of a type that was relevant to a concern about abuses of the Great Lakes. The United States and Great Britain (acting on behalf of Canada at that time) then initiated diplomatic negotiations to bring some order with various kinds of uses and to prevent severe abuses of these waters and of the valued organisms dependent on them.

Over the ensuing decades several formal agreements came into place concerning: 1) the physical use of the quantity of water and structures related to navigation and hydropower; 2) the chemical use of the quality of water for "assimilation" of pollution; 3) the biological use through harvest of organisms such as migratory waterfowl and fish; and eventually 4) the sustainable use of the entire basin ecosystem in which all uses and abuses must be managed.

Initially each of the agreements was formulated as a rather sketchy legal framework. A kind of self-organizing process of governance then emerged with respect to the agreements so that each agreement eventually led to major achievements.

To date no agreement—even the most fully articulated and implemented—has resulted in more than a 50 percent reduction in the relevant set of abuses and their environmental consequences. The growing consensus is that full restoration to a pristine state is not possible, in part because some unique species are now extinct and other non-native species now present in some of these waters cannot be rendered extinct. Badly contaminated sites cannot be remediated fully because some contaminants have leached into geological formations from which it is impossible to retrieve them. Various toxic substances are transmitted backward and forward between the lakes and the atmosphere and thus the lakes are part of biospheric pollution processes. Humans both native and non-native to the basin will likely continue to inhabit the area. Presumably the infrastructure of industrial civilization in the Great Lakes basin will not be destroyed and such locales re-naturalized until the next ice age, which may occur thousands of years from now. In short the Great Lakes as a set can never again resemble closely what they were two centuries ago.

An exception may be Lake Superior—the lake that has been altered least by humans. Multi-jurisdictional efforts are underway to discontinue abuses, to correct or remediate the consequences of pollution, to restore some physical and biological features, and generally to protect the parts that still resemble the primeval state. Full restoration is not possible because many salmonid stocks are extinct, some exotic species will not disappear, new exotic species will enter the lake, toxic substances will enter via atmospheric routes, and all humans—including native people partially assimilated into the ways of European invaders—will continue to be disruptive in many ways. But Lake Superior will become "relatively pristine."

In contrast lakes Erie and Ontario will never again bear much resemblance to their pristine states. A few carefully protected coastal wetlands will exhibit some important features of the pristine but the ecosystem of such "protected locales" will need to be designed in part and husbanded actively by humans committed to this purpose. The remaining areas will need to be "designed with nature" toward a desired

G

outcome based on a shared vision of ecosystemic rehabilitation and subsequent sustainable development.

The other Great Lakes, Michigan and Huron, exhibit strong contrasts between permanently altered parts to the south and less altered parts to the north. Here some semi-pristine areas may be preserved but much of the ecosystems of those lakes will need to be designed with nature, in the same way as lakes Erie and Ontario.

Much of the second half of the twentieth century as it relates to the Great Lakes has involved the discontinuation of the more egregious human abuses and the beginnings of some active rehabilitation to correct the consequences of these abuses. Meanwhile unresolved abuses or potential abuses are being combated, such as the irresponsible behavior of vessel captains that leads to the introduction of non-native species through spilled ballast water, and proposals to control lake levels and river flows through engineered works as a way to protect structures that were built, ill-advisedly, in locations subject to flooding. Gradually the people of the basin are addressing the issue of how to design with nature the ecosystems that have been degraded beyond the possibility of restoration to earlier states.

Some forty-three severely degraded areas around the shores of the Great Lakes and of the great rivers that join them have been submitted to a participatory governance process that will lead to Remedial Action Plans (RAPs) for each of them. Eventually, each lake will have its own Lakewide Management Plan; those for lakes Ontario, Michigan, and Superior are in active development since 1993. Some innovators have initiated a participatory process for creation and broad acceptance of a Great Lakes/St. Lawrence River Ecosystem Charter which may help to inform the general planning process for preserving near pristine areas and for designing areas that are now rehabilitating.

Perhaps this will all come into some degree of operational focus before the twentieth century ends. This would provide an optimistic basis for work in the twenty-first century. Presumably most or all of that century will have run its course before all the Great Lakes and their shared basin will again exhibit a desirable state of ecosystem integrity.

Henry A. Regier

Further Readings

Botts, L., and B. Krushelnicki. *The Great Lakes: An Environmental Atlas and Re-source Book*. Environment Canada and the U.S. Environmental Protection Agency, 1988.

Colborn, T.E., A. Davidson, S.N. Green, R.A. Hodge, C.I. Jackson, and R.A. Liroff. *Great Lakes: Great Legacy?* The Conservation Foundation and The Institute for Research on Public Policy (Ottawa), 1990.

Hartig, J.H., and M.A. Zarull. *Under RAPs: Toward Grassroots Ecological Democracy in the Great Lakes Basin*. 1992.

See also BIOACCUMULATION; EUTROPHICATION; FISHERIES CONSERVATION; INTERNATIONAL JOINT COMMISSION; RESERVE MINING CONTROVERSY; SHOREBIRDS; ST. LAWRENCE RIVER; WATERFOWL: CONSERVATION AND HABITAT

Great Whale Project in Quebec

On September 1, 1993, Hydro-Quebec, the state corporation responsible for the production, distribution, and sale of electricity in Quebec, made public a 5,000-page document justifying a $13.3 billion hydroelectric project on the Great Whale River in the relatively unspoiled northern region of Hudson Bay. This "pre-project report" synthesized and updated two decades of studies conducted for this controversial project.

The Great Whale project consists of constructing a complex of three dams, flooding 1,667 square kilometers of land and 1,724 square kilometers of aquatic territory. Its realization would create some 66,700 jobs between 1996 and 2003. In 2003 the project will begin responding to the yearly 2.2-percent increase in Quebec's anticipated demand for electricity through to the year 2010, with half of this demand assigned to the future needs of business. By way of this project Hydro-Quebec, whose sole shareholder is the government of Quebec, intends to increase its sales, particularly to other Canadian provinces and neighboring American states.

With the publication of the report reaction was swift. Quebec environmental groups have questioned Hydro-Quebec's ability to accurately predict the demand for electricity over the next fifteen to twenty years. Given the economic crisis and the stabilization of American demand, due mainly to energy-saving measures, there is concern about the use of public finances. The province already carries a debt of $31 billion and allocates more than $3 billion of annual revenue to interest on this debt. Since half, and perhaps more, of the increased demand for electricity will come from energy-intensive industries who pay less per kilowatt hour than it costs to produce, one is left with the impression that ordinary citizens will assume the responsibility for this debt. A common assumption also is that a kilowatt saved due to energy-saving programs would cost less and create more jobs than a kilowatt produced by a large dam. Finally, alternative production technologies that are less damaging to the environment must be examined, such as electricity produced by the wind.

The state responds to these arguments in its report by affirming that the project is an indispensable part of Quebec's economic plan. The report suggests that mercury contamination of the water, caused by decomposition of vegetable material in the large reservoirs, will last only one generation. The report also notes that replacement food will be provided (and has already been done) to those who may be poisoned by eating fish caught in the reservoir created by the dam; it also claims that no animal species will be threatened. In this respect, Hydro-Quebec has modified the project so as to not divert a single drop of river water flowing into a lake that provides habitat for freshwater seals. The symbolism of these animals, whose habitat would have been affected by the project, seemed too media-sensitive to state strategists. Another touchy point in popular iconography and for which other nations now feel the right to demand an explanation is the treatment of Amerindians and Inuit, especially the Cree, since 5 percent of their hunting territory will be altered or eliminated by the megaproject.

The Cree believe that this 5 percent loss is significant—the territory to be flooded is vitally important as it contains the most game. The Cree therefore did not accept a $137 million financial compensation offered by Hydro-Quebec. They argued that they have done their part by authorizing a previous Hydro project on the La Grande River, a project in which their hand was forced. For some of the Cree nothing can compensate for the "loss and invasion" of their territory. Charges that the Cree's "radical refusal" may be a bluff to increase the bidding are at the least an oversimplification of their resistence. Many of the arguments made by the Cree are echoed by the government committees charged with supervising the evaluation of the project's impacts.

According to the Cree, on the basis of the state's report, it is false to assert that no animal species will disappear because the sturgeon will be threatened. Their greatest fear though is over-exploitation of fauna by sport hunting and fishing following occupation of the land. A great famine has already resulted from over-exploitation, although the report is silent on the subject of its long-term impact. In the opinion of the Cree Hydro-Quebec would be unable to manage or control what will happen after construction of the dam. At the very least the state will commit itself to barring all whites (except for workers) from hunting and fishing the area during the construction years. The State will take advantage of this decade of construction to discuss means of protecting the region's balance of nature with Native Americans. What should characterize the report and prove to be a first in impact evaluation is the taking into account of the project's cumulative effects, particularly over the long-term.

This analytical point of view is part of the directive from the committees involved in the common evaluation process on which Quebec, Ottawa, and Native American communities have agreed after long debates and numerous public hearings over the past few years. American environmental organizations such as the National Audubon Society that have been following the discussions are not impressed with Hydro-Quebec's reasoning that the cumulative impacts would be too difficult to calculate or too insignificant to be considered. On this subject the Cree have called the report deficient because it does not treat the social impact of the project.

Hydro-Quebec explains these gaps by noting that the Cree and some Inuit refused to collaborate in the study, believing that the questionnaire and its closed questions did not allow expression of indigenous people's perspective. The state declared that it did not have the time to revise the questionnaire. The state then decided to build an airport serving the construction site, ten kilometers from Great Whale. The Cree and Inuit feared that enlarging the local airport would shatter their tiny community under the weight of thousands of workers who would pass through it. No one denies in this debate that Cree culture will be affected. However, when American ecologists, going further than the Cree themselves, speak of the disappearance of Cree culture and blame Hydro-Quebec for the modification of their way of life, Hydro-Quebec counters with the argument that

G

alcohol, drug, and violence problems found among the Cree cannot be blamed on the project since these problems are also found in other Amerindian communities.

The Cree do agree with the U.S. lobbies that support them when they attack Quebec's weak environmental standards for aluminum smelters and magnesium industries, whose production relies heavily on electricity. These industries defend themselves by saying that they are subject to the strictest rules in Quebec. On the other hand Cree opinion differs from that of their American allies on the subject of the relationship between the Great Whale project and Quebec independence. According to the Cree Hydro-Quebec's projects will constitute an obstacle to independence because of the enormous debt they will create. American opponents of Hydro projects suggest that Quebec is counting on its hydroelectric projects to finance independence and that Canada is ready to sacrifice its environmental obligations to keep Quebec in Canada. The Cree—who consider themselves historically linked to federal power—had to drag the Canadian government before the courts to force it to participate in the evaluation of the Great Whale project's environmental impacts.

The publication of Hydro-Quebec's report is the first step in the long process of project evaluation. After numerous hearings, consultations, and debates covering the many aspects of the project, as witnessed in the hundreds of articles published over the past few years in the Canadian press, the protagonists are in agreement on the next step in the evaluation process. This process is as complex and costly as it is grandiose and has consequences as potentially serious as the project itself. The pre-project report is intended for administrators of environmental regulations anticipated by the James Bay and northern Quebecois conventions, which are agreements previously negotiated with Native Americans. These provincial organizations, along with a federal examination commission, are charged with supervising the development of an official impact study. They must first decide if the report made public by Hydro-Quebec satisfactorily addresses the directives issued in 1993.

Within the framework of this exercise, which will take several months, the organizations may ask for further specifications and additional studies by the state. For its part the state believes it has done enough, given that it has spent $256 million over the past two de-cades on many studies, the synthesis of which is its pre-project report. Finally the evaluation process foresees the official report being submitted to a public scrutiny unprecedented in Canada.

In summary the controversy surrounding the Great Whale hydroelectric project offers a real labyrinth of structures, arguments, and power plays. This complexity must be managed and possible bases for discussion should be found in order to finally arrive at a solution that will be satisfactory or at least accepted as inevitable by both groups. Such a solution should foster desire for a common direction or, at the very least, one that is not completely contradictory.

A number of highly specialized competencies have been required in this debate—administrative, judicial, economic, technological, and ecological—but these contributions can be useful only if there is a common ground that facilitates discussion. A possible association between the conflicting parties is found when each becomes aware of its interdependence in the practical realization of the interests it defends and thus distances itself from its radical position. The executive director of the Cree Grand Council, for example, felt obliged to take a public stand in order to distance himself from a pamphlet published in the United States defending certain affirmations that were made and opposing others. He wanted to dismiss the impression conveyed by the media that it was a "new list of lies" concerning the project.

This kind of situation, he said, does not help the Cree, who over the years have spent many millions of dollars coming from previous agreements to provide whites with the information necessary to understand the Cree position. After all, this representative reminded us, it is not "several thousand Cree," but the Quebecois who will have the power to end the Great Whale project. Starting with the acknowledgment that—and this holds true for both sides—in order to realize aspirations the concerns of those who are considered "different" must be taken into account and somehow addressed, communication can begin and the "dialogue of the deaf" will be ended. A solution to conflict becomes possible because something called society begins to form. Such a society comes from the "cooperation of associated men and successive generations," to use the words of sociologist Emile Durkheim.

If this is the path to follow it remains to be seen from a practical perspective just what constitutes this common society within which a solution is possible. We have yet to specify a normative framework within which a solution may be found. Bearing in mind the practical rationality and democratic spirit that animates the possible formation of this new society one can only hope that it will be, in the final analysis, a truly modern society. The Quebec government announced the cancellation of the project on November 18, 1994.

Robert Tessier

Further Readings

Francoeur, L.-G. "Les besoins industriels justifient Grande-Baleine, selon Hydro," *Le Devoir* (September 1, 1993): A1.

Groupe Équipement, avec la collaboration de la vice-présidence Communications et Relations publiques et de la vice-présidence Affaires Amérindiennes et Inuit, Complexe Grande-Baleine: rapport d'avant-Projet, Montréal, Hydro-Québec, août 1993.

Tison, M. "Les Cris se distancient d'un pamphlet publié aux USA contre Grande-Baleine," *Le Devoir* (September 28, 1993): A2.

See also ASWAN HIGH DAM; DEMAND-SIDE MANAGEMENT; ECHO PARK DAM; FEDERALISM AND ENVIRONMENTAL PROTECTION: CANADA; HYDROELECTRICITY; JAMES BAY; MINERAL KING CANYON; RAFFERTY-ALAMEDA DAMS

Green Economics

The conventional way of seeking to take account of environmental issues as they relate to economic activity is through environmental and resource economics, a subset of the mainstream neoclassical school, which essentially seeks to employ the normal tools of neoclassical analysis on environmental issues. Thus the depletion of resources—renewable and nonrenewable—is primarily considered in terms of maximization of the present value of the resource; pollution is dealt with in terms of externality analysis, to be taken into account either through the appropriate definition of property rights, or through imposition of Pigovian taxes.

Such an approach gives no special emphasis to the conservation of natural resources or the environment. Indeed it is sometimes rational to deplete a resource fully, while the attainment of economic efficiency through the internalization of externalities does not imply the achievement of environmental sustainability—the ability of the natural environment to continue to support the human activities that impact on it. It has been perceived that a deeper, more integrated approach to environmental problems—one that transcends any single discipline—is required if these problems are to be resolved. The development of green economics is a response to this perception.

Green economics does not reject the insights and methods of environmental and resource economics; rather it seeks to incorporate them within a wider framework of analysis and ideas. According to Martinez-Alier: "Economics, as the study of the allocation of scarce resources to alternative ends, should be human ecology, and should *also* be the study of the cultural, social and ethical influences on production and consumption" (Martinez-Alier, 1987: 206). There is as yet no consensus on the details of this wider framework, and several different, though similar, formulations of green economics exist.

The most thoroughgoing of these formulations goes under the name "ecological economics," and is promoted by the International Society for Ecological Economics. Its journal, *Ecological Economics*, defines its subject matter thus: "*Ecological Economics* addresses the relationships between ecosystems and economic systems in the broadest sense . . . . It implies a broad, *ecological*, interdisciplinary and holistic view of the problem of studying and managing our world" (Costanza, 1989). A later publication set out the goals, agenda, and policy recommendations for ecological economics (Costanza, et al., 1991). This publication emphasizes the transdisciplinary nature of ecological economics: "(It) goes beyond our normal conceptions of scientific disciplines and tries to integrate and synthesize many different disciplinary perspectives."

Two major differences between ecological and conventional environmental economics are the importance attached by the former to the concept of evolution, and its emphasis on developing a broader *biocentric* perspective. The initial research agenda has five major parts: 1) sustainability: maintaining our life support system; 2) valuation of natural resources and natural capital; 3) ecological economic system accounting; 4) ecological-economic modeling at local, regional, and global scales; and 5) innovative instruments for environmental management (Costanza, et al., 1991).

David Pearce (1992) identifies three factors that are common to all forms of green econom-

G

ics: constraining human greed, sustainability, and decoupling. He perceives that the motivation for the first of these is ethical "concern for others," both for current and future generations of people and other living beings. This ethical emphasis is related to, but is not the same as, the biocentric perspective of ecological economics and implies the notion of "intrinsic value." Sustainability is a common feature with ecological economics. The "decoupling" feature is interesting because it highlights one of the principal disputes in environmental-economic discourse: the compatibility or otherwise of environmental sustainability with economic growth. Clearly there is some scope for "decoupling" the economic growth of production from its environmental impact, but there is no consensus over how much scope. Pearce's broad view is that "growth and environmental quality are compatible, provided the right mix of policy measures is adopted," but this is likely to remain a controversial area in green economics for some time to come. The issues raised by Pearce in this article are further explored in his *Blueprint for a Green Economy.*

In setting out his paths to a green economy Michael Jacobs (1991) does not claim to be articulating a green economics, but rather an "eclectic and rather ad hoc approach." Jacobs regards Pearce's approach as basically neoclassical (i.e., conventional environmental economics) and does not consider this an adequate basis for thinking about the environment. Jacobs stresses the market failures that have led to environmental problems, not just externalities but also the public good, collective nature of much of the environment. He emphasizes the importance of the social and cultural context within which consumer preferences are formed. He is sceptical of techniques of assigning monetary value to complex environmental functions, both on technical grounds, leading to a lack of confidence in the valuations obtained, and because of doubts as to the appropriateness of monetary valuation, especially where potential impacts are considerable, and any or all of uncertain, irreversible, global, or effective over long time periods.

Jacobs feels that such situations should be explicitly recognized as ethical and political issues, which should be addressed through collective discussion and decision-making processes, rather than techniques for evaluating the individualistic preferences of consumers. Thus although both Pearce and Jacobs recommend striking a balance in environmental policy between market-based and regulatory instruments, Pearce emphasizes the need to redress the current situation in favor of the former, whereas Jacobs is more concerned with creating the appropriate public policy framework within which both kinds of instruments can be most effective. The two approaches have much in common; their differences, however, include two distinct perceptions of the nature of a market economy and the best way of acting within it.

So far the discussion of green economics has focused largely on the environment-economy relationship, although all the approaches mentioned have recognized the ethical, cultural, and social issues which this relationship inevitably involves. Paul Ekins's *Gaia Atlas of Green Economics* (1992) develops an approach in which green economics derives from a broader conception of value, and therefore of wealth: "Conventional economics seeks to give value for money . . . . Green economics seeks to subordinate this still important consideration to three greater values: value for nature, leading to sustainability; value for people, based on fulfilment and social justice; and value for human relationships, based on participation . . . . A wider conception of wealth means the progressive bounding of economic activity by tight sustainability constraints, and the explicit direction of that activity by and towards positive human values: personal development and quality of life, participation in society, democracy and justice; and the monitoring of economic performance according to these goals."

In this formulation of green economics, environmental sustainability is still the primary objective, which defines the context within which economic activity takes place. But a range of other objectives are also subscribed to, giving this version of green economics a distinctive orientation across the whole range of social and practical issues.

There is bound to be disagreement as to the extent to which this broader agenda and particular orientation are necessary for the achievement of the environmental goals. A common factor statement for all versions of green economics might be that the environment makes an overall contribution to human life of immense economic value; that this contribution is currently greatly undervalued and is therefore being used unsustainably; that continuing such use will result in considerable disruption to human society, sooner or later; and that moving toward sustainable use of the environment will involve changes in economic techniques and analysis, and broader changes of a social, cultural, and ethical nature.

Such a statement of consensus is of greater importance than the differences in outlook that have been discussed. If the green economists' basic premise of environmental unsustainability is correct it is certain that economics generally will come to give greater importance to their various suggestions as to how this problem should be addressed.

Paul Ekins

Further Readings

Costanza, R. "What Is Ecological Economics?" *Ecological Economics* 1 (1989): 1–7.

———, H.E. Daly, and J. Bartholomew. "Goals, Agenda and Policy Recommendations for Ecological Economics." In *Ecological Economics: The Science and Management of Sustainability*. Ed. R. Costanza. 1991.

Ekins, P. (with M. Hillman and R. Hutchison). *The Gaia Atlas of Green Economics* (UK title: *Wealth Beyond Measure*). 1992

Jacobs, M. *The Green Economy*. 1991

Martinez-Alier, J. *Ecological Economics*. 1987.

Pearce, D., A. Markandya, and E. Barbier. *Blueprint for a Green Economy*. 1989.

———. "Green Economics." *Environmental Values* 1 (1992): 3–13.

See also CONTINGENT VALUATION; ENVIRONMENTAL ETHICS; ENVIRONMENTAL HISTORY; GNP AND ENVIRONMENT; GREEN PRODUCTS; SUSTAINABILITY; TRADEABLE EMISSION PERMITS

Green Parties

Green parties are a feature of the political scene in most of the twenty-four Organisation for Economic Co-operation and Development (OECD) countries. In some countries (e.g., Belgium, Finland, Switzerland) green parties have steadily increased their parliamentary representation. In others (e.g., Germany, Sweden, United Kingdom) green party fortunes—in and out of parliament—have risen and fallen (and in the case of Germany and Sweden risen again) dramatically. Green parties in large federal states such as Australia, Canada, and the United

States are still struggling with the logistics of organizing on a nationwide scale, while in still other countries (e.g., Denmark, Greece, Norway, Turkey) green parties have been unable to make a significant impact. In Iceland a women's party, *Kvennalistinn*, has embraced many green policies. In almost all countries, however, green parties are represented at some level of local government.

There are several reasons for the varying electoral success of green parties worldwide, the electoral system being most significant. Wherever there is proportional representation green parties have generally entered national parliaments quickly. But neither this, nor other factors such as population density, extent of environmental degradation, public awareness of green issues, or political culture provides a uniformly applicable "theory" of green party development. Inspiration did cross national boundaries, particularly during the 1980s, but in each country the green party is most accurately seen as a distinctive product of its national history, political circumstances, local environment, and human personalities.

There are several definitions as to what constitutes a political party but a basic requirement is that a candidate be nominated for election to public office. Therefore, when the United Tasmania Group (UTG) decided in March 1972 to contest the April 1972 state elections in protest against the flooding of Lake Pedder, it became the world's first green party. Although the UTG just missed winning a seat and the dam was built, experience gained enabled the group to halt a similar proposal for the Franklin River and, in June 1983, win one seat in the Tasmanian state parliament—where the Green Independents now hold five seats.

The world's first nationwide green party was initiated in May 1972 with the establishment of the Values Party in New Zealand. In the 1975 national elections Values polled a pioneering 5.2 percent, just short of the 5.6 percent which eight years later gave *Die Grünen* twenty-eight seats in the West German parliament. By 1978 electoral support for Values dropped to 2.4 percent as they were "squeezed" by the non-proportional election system and the voters' desire to remove the controversial Prime Minister, Robert Muldoon.

Thereafter Values dwindled to pockets of local activity, before being reborn as the Green Party of New Zealand (GPNZ) to poll 6.7 percent in the October 1990 national elections. GPNZ is now in an alliance with three other small parties. Some opinion polls suggest that the alliance could win 24 percent of the vote in coming elections.

Inspired by the Tasmanian and New Zealand green parties, the first European green party was founded in the United Kingdom in 1973. Originally called People, then Ecology Party, and finally Green Party, founder members were influenced by the limits to growth debate which had developed largely in the United States during the previous decade. The People party based its program on what "Blueprint for Survival" (*The Ecologist*, 1972) offered as the "principle conditions of a stable society—one that to all intents and purposes can be sustained indefinitely while giving optimum satisfaction to its members . . .

i)   minimum disruption of ecological processes;
ii) maximum conservation of materials and energy;
iii) a population in which recruitment equals loss;
iv) a social system in which individuals can enjoy, rather than feel restricted by, the first three conditions."

Variations on and developments of these principles make up the programs of most green parties today.

Despite its early start, the UK Green Party made no significant electoral impact until 1989 when it polled 15 percent in elections to the European parliament. However, the UK electoral system meant no seats were gained and the party quickly lost political momentum and membership. In common with some of its sister parties (e.g., in Germany and Sweden), the UK Green Party was unprepared and political and organizational mismanagement made it impossible to hold onto, let alone build on, its success.

The early 1980s saw a worldwide increase in public and political awareness concerning environmental degradation and its impact on human societies and their economies. It also saw the main development phase of green political parties, particularly in Europe, but also in the United States and South America.

In Belgium green members of parliament (MPs) were elected for the first time in 1981, two years after a Swiss green party member made history by becoming the first such member to enter a national parliament. Both events went largely unnoticed. It was not until *Die*

Grünen won twenty-eight seats in the German Bundestag (parliament) in 1983, that green parties gained significant attention. In the same year the Finnish green party entered parliament confirming a trend which was to see green MPs elected to fourteen national parliaments within a decade.

Both the Belgian and Finnish green parties offer models of how green parties can handle success. In 1993 the government needed Ecolo and Agalev MPs to support a bill for constitutional reform. In return the green party members negotiated a progressive tax on waste. In Finland a clear message, good organization, and a leadership that inspired confidence was deployed to more than double the number of green parliamentary seats in 1991.

The end of the 1980s saw the end of the Cold War. One after another east European countries embraced democracy. Very often the democratic movements, which pursued a revolution remarkable for its speed and peacefulness, had their roots in an environmental campaigning group (e.g., Polish Ecological Club (PKE), Ecoglasnost in Bulgaria, Danube Circle in Hungary, and the Ecological Library in East Germany).

In early 1989 a Lithuanian green activist was elected to Moscow's Chamber of Deputies and in November and December green parties were founded in Bulgaria, Czechoslovakia, East Germany, Estonia, Georgia, Hungary, Lithuania, Poland, and Romania. A March 1989 opinion poll revealed that 74 percent of Russians wanted to see a green party on future ballot papers. Although around twenty deputies in Moscow are commonly viewed as green and some localities (e.g., Lake Baikal, St. Petersburg) have a strong green presence, a Russian-wide party has yet to evolve.

As elections were held green parties became either part of transitional governments or won seats in parliaments. In the difficult times which followed the euphoria of 1989, not all have held onto their gains. Some (Bulgaria, Czechoslovakia, and Estonia) have lost seats; others split before (Hungary, Poland) or after (Slovenia) elections. In Romania where green parties did win seats and Hungary where they did not, the green party was effectively taken over by deposed Communists anxious to recycle themselves.

Frequently small environmental organizations lost their leading people to government posts—either by election or appointment—which has delayed their development as a vital

TABLE 1:

Green Parties

	Local		National			European		
	Year Party Founded	Seats +/–	Year First Elected	No. of Seats	Date Last Election	Previous No. Seats	No. of Seats	Year first Elected
AUSTRIA								
Die Grüne Alternative*	1986	+	1986	13	1994	(10)	—	
BELGIUM [1]								
Agalev*	1982	+	1981	15†	1991	(11)	1	1984
Ecolo*	1980	+	1981	22†	1991	(6)	1	1984
BULGARIA								
The Bulgarian Greens*	1990	+	1990	0	1991	(14)	—	
DENMARK								
De Grønne*	1983	+	—	0	1990	(0)	0	
EIRE								
Comhaontas Glas*	1981	+	1989	1	1993	(1)	2	1994
ESTONIA								
Eesti Roheline*	1989	+	1990	1	1992	(7)	—	
FINLAND								
Vihreä Liitto*	1987	+	1983	10	1991	(4)	—	
FRANCE[2]								
Les Verts*	1984	+	—	0	1993	(0)	0	
Generation Ecologie	1990	+	—	0	1993	(0)	—	
GEORGIA								
Georgian Greens*	1990	–	1992	11	1992	(0)	—	
GERMANY								
Bündis '90/Die Grünen*	1990	+	1983	49	1994	(8††)	12	1984
GREECE								
Federation d'Organisations	1989	–	1989	0	1992	(1)	0	
Ecologistes-Alternatives	—							
ITALY								
Federation die Verdi*	1987	+	1987	18†	1994	(20)	3	1989
1989								
LUXEMBURG [3]								
Déi Gréng Alternativ*	1983	+	1984	2	1989	(1)	0	
Gréng Lëscht	1986	+	1989	2	1989	(1)	1	1994
Ekologesch Initiativ (GLEI)*								
MALTA								
Alternattiva								
Demokratika* [4]	1989	–	1989	0	1992	(1)	—	
NETHERLANDS [3]								
De Groenen*	1983	+	—	0	1994	(0)	0	
Groen Links*	1989	+	1986	4	1994	(6)	1	1989
NORWAY								
De Gronne*	1988	+	—	0	1989	—	—	
PORTUGAL								
Os Verdes*[5]	1981	+	1987	2	1991	(2)	0	
SLOVENIA								
Zeleni Slovenije	1989	–	1990	8ØØ	1990	—	—	
SPAIN								
Los Verdes*	1985	+	—	0	1993	(0)	0	
SWEDEN								
Miljöpariet de Gröna*	1981	+	1988	18	1994	(0)	—	

TABLE 1 (cont.):

	Year Party Founded	Seats +/–	Year First Elected	No. of Seats	Date Last Election	Previous No. Seats	No. of Seats	Year first Elected
SWITZERLAND								
Die Grüne Partei/								
Le Parti Ecologiste*	1983	+	1979	14	1991	(11)	—	
UNITED KINGDOM								
Green Party*	1973	+	—	0	1992	(0)	0	
AUSTRALIA								
Green Party	1972	+	1984	2†	1993	(1)	—	
NEW ZEALAND								
Values/Green Party	1972	+	—	0	1990	(0)	—	
BRAZIL								
Partido Verde	1988	+	1990	1ØØ	1990	(0)	—	

*   Members of the Coordination of European Greens who created the European Federation of Green Parties in Helsinki on June 19, 1993. Green parties have applied to join from Armenia, Latvia, Lithuania, Scotland (UK), Slovakia, St. Petersburg (Russia), and the Ukraine.

†   Includes members of both lower and upper house. Agalev: 7 in Chamber and 8 in Senate; Ecolo: 10 in Chamber and 11 in Senate; Federation die Verdi: 11 in Chamber and 7 in Senate as part of Progressive Alliance list; and Green Party (Australia): both seats are in the Senate.

††   Die Grünen, the West German green party, was founded in 1980 and entered the federal Parliament in 1983. Prior to the first all-German election in December 1990 Die Grünen held forty-four seats. In the 1990 election Die Grünen won no seats while the East German Green Party won two seats with a coalition of democratic groups, Bündis '90 who obtained six seats. The parties united afterward. All the 49 seats won in 1994 were in the former West Germany.

ØØ   Zeni Slovenije seats obtained in 7-party coalition, United Opposition of Slovenia (DEMOS) which won 53 percent of the vote. Partido Verde seat obtained in coalition with the Partido dos Trabalhadores (Workers Party).

1   Some countries have two green parties. In the case of Belgium this is for legal and linguistic reasons. Agalev is from the Flemish speaking region and Ecolo the French speaking. They cooperate closely in parliament.

2   The French greens have a long history of dividing and uniting which has damaged their electoral chances more than once.

3   In Luxembourg and the Netherlands competing green parties plan to unite soon.

4   Malta will have its first local elections in November 1993.

5   Os Verdes obtained seats in the National and the 1989 European parliament through a Communist Party-led coalition.

feature of any civil society. In most eastern European countries green parties expect their fortunes to improve as it becomes clearer that economic reconstruction cannot be achieved through accelerated exploitation of the environment.

Die Grünen also suffered in the immediate post-Cold War period. Already weakened by internal quarreling it lost all its parliamentary seats in the 1990 all-Germany elections. Paradoxically, but in common with the Swedish green party whose seats were lost a year later, the green vote in Germany was increased in subsequent local elections. A wiser Die Grünen returned to the Bundestag in 1994, fortified by proof that unification is—as they warned—costing hugely more than anticipated. And, as recession deepens over the OECD economies and the motor to recovery is increasingly perceived to lie in a move to the new environmental industries, so green parties, or at least their policies, are likely to be popular in the last decade of the millennium.

Further afield green parties have been active in South and Central America (Argentina, Chile, Costa Rica, Brazil, Mexico, and Uruguay) though the provenance of some of them is suspect. The parties in Argentina and Chile, for example, are thought to be set up by a religious sect. Only Partido Verde in Brazil is well established and has obtained parliamentary representation. In Africa, Egypt has a formally registered Green Party and in Japan, although several attempts to establish a green party have been made, the strongest political impact has been achieved by the Seikatsu Club which, by promoting green consumption, has influenced production of both agricultural and manufactured goods. The Club has a turnover of around $300 million and 80 percent of its board and all of its more than forty locally elected councilors are women.

Women also play a significant role in countries where access to the democratic process is either absent or limited. In the early 1970s Chipko Andolan used the slogan "ecology is permanent economy" in its campaign to prevent the logging which was destroying village economies in the north of India. In Kenya the Green Belt movement (in which women have planted many sets of trees in villages and on farms) passed on information about nutrition, family planning, health, sustainable agricultural techniques, and organizing skills as well as trees. Green Belt's Wangarii Maathai is currently working with the United Nations (UN) to establish similar schemes in eleven other African countries. Although not strictly speaking political parties organizations like these are integral to green party success as they provide practical demonstrations of policies which would otherwise be merely theory.

The evidence of escalating environmental damage during the 1980s prompted reports, manifestos, and action plans from not only green parties, but also governments, industry, and supranational organizations like the European Community (EC) and the UN. The climax of this phase might be seen to be the UN Conference on Environment and Development in Rio de Janeiro in June 1992.

It is clear that green parties have already profoundly affected the environmental performance of governments and the environmental awareness of society; but the next phase matters most. How are all those manifestos to be translated into practical policies which can transform industrial societies to sustainable ones?

European green parties have worked together in a loose coordination since 1979, but in June 1993 twenty-three green parties from east and west Europe formed a European Federation of Green Parties (see table 1). This is evidence they understand the leverage their presence in national and European parliaments gives them, and the importance of learning from each other's experience in policy and strategy if they are going to maintain that leverage into the next century. To succeed from now on Green parties will have to convince electorates in Eu-

rope and elsewhere that their policies are relevant to the economic and political crises that are currently perceived to be barriers to resolving the underlying environmental crisis.

Sara Parkin

Further Readings

Dobson, Andrew. *Green Political Thought: An Introduction.* 1990.
Environmental Politics Quarterly. Spring 1992, et seq.
Parkin, Sara. *Green Parties: An International Guide.* 1989.

See also CHIPKO MOVEMENT; EASTERN EUROPE: ENVIRONMENTAL PROBLEMS; ENVIRONMENTAL MOVEMENT: LESS-AFFLUENT NATIONS; ENVIRONMENTAL GROUPS: WESTERN EUROPE; GREEN PARTIES: AUSTRALIA; LAKE PEDDER

Green Parties: Australia

The existence of a national green party is a relatively new phenomenon in Australia—depending upon how "green" is defined. Two parties now aspire to this status: the Australian Democrats and the Australian Greens.

The Australian Democrats (AD) was founded in 1977 as a party appealing to voters disaffected with the increasingly conservative Liberal Party. The AD has held to social democratic economic and industrial relations policies but, since the early 1980s, developed strong anti-nuclear, environmental, and civil liberties policies. While the party has identified itself as green since the late 1980s, it is regarded as "pale green" by most commentators and has only weak links to both new and old social movements. It occupies an ideological position in the Australian political spectrum comparable to that of the Green Party in Sweden. The party now holds seven seats in the Senate (the seventy-six-seat upper house in the bicameral national parliament) and none in the House of Representatives (the 147-seat lower house).

Formed in August 1992, the Australian Greens (AG) is a federated party incorporating seven of the sixteen green parties—including the strong Tasmanian and Queensland Greens—which had emerged at state and regional levels during the previous decade. It is active in four of the six states and in the Australian Capital Territory. Its formation was initiated by Tasmanian anti-Franklin Dam and wilderness campaigner Bob Brown and other key environmentalists, and strongly influenced by the example of the German Greens. Consequently the AG is strongly based in the environment movement while also looking toward other social movements for its support. Its social, economic, and environmental policies locate the AG to the left of the Democrats and even further so from the National Labor (ALP) government and the Liberal National Party (LNP) coalition in opposition.

While the advent of the Australian Greens has done much to simplify the green political landscape, not all green parties have joined it. The disruption visited on the Nuclear Disarmament Party (NDP) by minor left groups in 1984 led founders of the AG to proscribe members and organizations with other party affiliations, such as the Green Alliance (the reformed Trotskyist Democratic Socialist Party). This has excluded at least five related left-green parties.

On the other hand, the third strong state-based green party—the Greens of Western Australia (GWA)—chose to remain apart from a federation which was perceived to be hierarchical and centralist. With a strong community base, the GWA has outperformed the AD in federal and state elections (the AG does not stand in that State) and, following the 1993 federal elections, is now represented by two senators.

The 1993 Australian federal election results were not as spectacular for green parties as those in 1990, when environmental issues were high on the national political agenda and over 15.9 percent of the electorate voted green—for AD, state-based green parties, and green independents—in the Senate. Nevertheless the final 1993 Senate vote of 8.4 percent displayed a solid core of green support in an election obsessively framed by narrow economic issues. More significantly the AD and the GWA now potentially share the balance of power in the Senate with Labor. As in 1990, green preferences in the House of Representatives (HR) also helped determine government. The AG contested federal elections for the first time in 1993. None of its candidates were elected.

Several interrelated factors suggest reasons for the delayed emergence of a national and identifiably green party in Australia, over a decade after the formation and electoral success of similar parties in Western Europe. First, the two-party preferential electoral system used throughout Australia (except in the Sen-

ate and in Tasmania) places significant hurdles before minor parties seeking election and discourages their formation, especially at the national level. No federal HR seats have been won by green parties or green independents to date. The use of proportional representation has made it possible for greens to win Senate seats. However, Senate seats have statewide electorates for which campaigning is very resource-intensive and expensive, requiring considerable organizational coherence—a deterrent to new social movements and associated new parties competing for votes with the already established AD.

The prominent exception is Tasmania, a small island state with only five electorates and a total population of 435,000. Its Hare-Clark system of proportional representation, which enables election of individuals achieving only 12.5 percent of the total vote in an electorate, has made Tasmania the crucible of green politics in Australia. In 1972 the campaign to save Lake Pedder led to the establishment of one of the world's first green parties, the United Tasmania Group. In 1989 five green independents, led by Bob Brown, captured the balance of power in the Tasmanian parliament with a vote of 17.1 percent, entering into an agreement—the Labor-Green Accord—to support the minority Field Labor Government. This arrangement survived until late 1991.

The second factor related to the delayed emergence of an Australian green party has been the fact that the disenchantment of new social movements with social democratic governments or parties, which fueled the rise of green parties in Western Europe, did not become a powerful force in Australia until the 1990s. Following twenty-three years of federal LNP government, the reformist Whitlam Labor government was elected in 1972, only to be dismissed by a constitutional coup three years later. Not until 1983 was Labor re-elected. In the intervening period, links between Labor in opposition and the old and new social movements remained strong, cooperative, and untested. With Labor in power federally and in most states during much of the 1980s, the relationship soured only slowly—first with the anti-nuclear movement and last with the environment movement.

While significant gains could be had from Labor during the 1980s the opportunity and need for a green party were seen to be insignificant. The effectiveness of the environmental movement during this period—in particular the successes of major national environmental organizations, such as the Australian Conservation Foundation and the Wilderness Society in a series of national battles over wilderness preservation and forest conservation—made conservationists less than keen to invest energy in a multi-issue parliamentary alliance with other social movements, especially ones (such as the disarmament movement) which were fading by the late 1980s. At the 1986 Getting Together Conference, proposals for a national green party were rejected and the fragmentation between social movements persisted throughout that decade.

A third contributing factor was the fate of the Nuclear Disarmament Party (NDP), formed in mid-1984 in protest against the Hawke Labor government's pro-nuclear policies. The NDP made the 1984 federal elections a forum for the anti-nuclear movement's demands to stop uranium mining, close U.S. military bases, ban visits of nuclear-armed planes and ships, and redefine the ANZUS treaty. In the six months to those elections, the NDP gained over 8,000 members but had little structure and few policies beyond its single-issue anti-nuclear focus. So while it polled 7.2 percent nationally in the Senate—and despite the election of the nation's first "new social movement" Senator, Jo Vallentine—the NDP imploded in 1985, partly over conflict caused by Trotskyist involvement in its ranks. The bitter experience of its demise also helped retard the emergence of a national green party.

Peter Christoff

Further Readings

Bean, Clive, Ian McAllister, and John Warhurst. *The Greening of Australian Politics: The 1990 Federal Election.* 1990.

Christoff, P. "Environmental Politics." In *Developments in Australian Politics.* Ed. Judith Brett, Jim Gillespie, and Murray Goot, 1994.

Papadakis, Elim. *Politics and the Environment in Australia.* 1993.

See also FRANKLIN DAM; GREEN PARTIES; LAKE PEDDER

Green Party: Germany

The German green party, whose current official name is *Bündnis '90/Die Grünen* (Alliance '90/ The Greens), emerged out of the ecological and anti-nuclear movement of the 1970s, which in turn had been strongly influenced by the peace and student movements of the 1950s and 1960s. The party was founded in January 1980 as a broad coalition of ecological and new left forces. After making a first impact in local and state elections, the party entered the federal Parliament in 1983. Despite tumultuous internal controversies about its political strategy, the West German greens held their position until 1990 when they narrowly missed the 5 percent mark necessary to gain federal deputies.

The German unification of 1990 required a reorganization of the party. An East German green party had been formed in early 1990 after the breakdown of the Communist regime. Party members fielded a joint list of candidates with the Alliance of East German citizen movements Bündnis '90 (Alliance '90) in the 1990 elections which gained 6 percent of the votes in East Germany and thus entered the federal Parliament. The West and East German greens formally merged in December 1990 and, eventually, the new united green party also merged with the East German Alliance '90 in 1993 to form a new federal party, Alliance '90/The Greens. In the federal elections of October 1994, the Greens polled 7.3 percent reentering the federal parliament.

Formation

The most important catalyst for the formation of green parties was the highly charged debate about the civil nuclear power program in the 1970s. After a series of local protests, the nuclear power issue rose to national prominence with the heavy-handed police action against occupants of a planned nuclear site at Wyhl in Southwestern Germany. The anti-nuclear campaign quickly attracted support from other environmentalists and various left-wing and radical movements which had emerged out of the student movement of the 1960s. After initial successes the anti-nuclear campaign began to run out of options toward the end of the 1970s, and thus the idea of a separate ecological and anti-nuclear party gained currency.

The first environmental party at local level was formed in Lower Saxony in May 1977. The *Umweltschutzpartei* or "Environmental Protection Party" was formed by traditional conservationists who wanted to provide an alternative platform to what they saw as a violent and left-dominated anti-nuclear campaign. Local green parties quickly established themselves elsewhere, and a state party called *Grüne Liste Umweltschutz* or "Green List Environmental Protection" (GLU) was formed in December 1977. Similar green lists were set up in many other states during 1978. Rival organizations known as Colorful or Alternative Lists were formed in Hamburg, Hesse, and Berlin, often dominated by Maoist splinter parties or other, "undogmatic," left groups influenced by anarchist thinking that had become involved in the anti-nuclear campaign.

The resignation of federal deputy Herbert Gruhl (the author of a popular ecological book) from the Christian Democratic Union and his subsequent formation of a national ecological party *Grüne Aktion Zukunft* or "Green Action Future" (GAZ) set the ball rolling for the formation of a national party. A major step forward was made in the spring of 1979 when a range of independent environmental and anti-nuclear campaigners, as well as a variety of other organizations including various splinter parties and representatives of state green parties, got together to form a national list, *Sonstige Politische Vereinigung—Die Grünen* or "Other Political Organization—The Greens" to contest the first direct elections to the European Parliament in June 1979. The new, temporary formation which did not include the predominantly Maoist or anarchist Alternative Lists gained 3.2 percent of votes. It thus failed to reach the 5 percent threshold which is required in all state and federal elections to gain representation, but it qualified for state support under the extremely generous system of public funding of political parties. The major funds flowing to the new organization now provided a major opportunity to build up a new party, and the requirement to reach the 5 percent mark provided another powerful incentive for the hitherto reluctant Alternative Lists to participate in the formation of a new national party.

The federal party *Die Grünen* or "The Greens" was formed in January 1980 in Karlsruhe and initially encompassed all sections that had taken part in the debate about party formation. Soon after its formation, Herbert Gruhl and other more conservative forces left the party in protest against its left-wing character, and in 1981 formed the rival *Ökologisch-Demokratische Partei* or "Ecological Democratic Party" (ÖDP).

Electoral Development
After polling 3.2 percent in the 1979 European elections, the result of 1.5 percent in the 1980

federal elections was a great disappointment to the new party, despite the fact that most potential green voters probably voted Social-Democrat to keep the ultra right-wing Franz Josef Strauss (who had been adopted as chancellor candidate by the conservative parties) out of office. Green party members quickly scored some first successes at state level and by 1983 the Greens were represented in five out of eleven state parliaments.

In the early 1980s the greens benefited mainly from the peace movement which had been mobilizing against the NATO twin-track decision of 1979 to station new intermediate-range nuclear missiles in Germany. Since the Social-Democrats supported this policy, the greens emerged as the only political party representing the peace movement's demands, and prominent green party members, such as Petra Kelly, took a leading role in the actions of the peace movement. While the Social-Democrats changed their policies after losing government office in 1982, this was too late to deny the greens their first major election success in 1983 when they polled 5.6 percent of the vote in the federal elections and gained twenty-seven deputies to the federal Parliament.

The mid-1980s saw other environmental issues come to the fore, in particular acid rain. In 1986 the Chernobyl nuclear accident provided further campaigning opportunities, and the national nuclear debate heated up again with violent protests against the nuclear reprocessing plant at Wackersdorf. Support for the greens kept rising. In 1984 the party polled 8.4 percent in the European elections and sent eight deputies to the European Parliament. The greens reinforced their position at state level with improving poll results and entered two further state parliaments. The federal elections of 1987 saw the greens poll 8.3 percent of the votes and return to the federal Parliament with forty-two deputies.

The fairly steady rise of green support seemed to come to an end in the late 1980s. The 1989 European elections saw only a slight improvement on previous results, with 8.4 percent (nine deputies). While the rise of global environmental issues (e.g., the ozone layer and global warming) led to an international revival of public concern about the environment, the German greens found it difficult to turn these new issues into new public support. The sudden and unexpected collapse of communism in East Germany changed the domestic political agenda completely. Together with the East German civil rights groups, which had played an important role in the end of communism, the greens advocated an independent development of a new democratic East Germany and were against the quick unification of both states. But the unification bandwagon proved unstoppable and the position of the greens was firmly rejected by the voters in the 1990 all-German elections.

To underline their commitment to a separate East German identity the greens had successfully pushed for separate elections in both states so that the 5 percent hurdle applied separately for East and West Germany, and had also resisted a merger of East and West German green parties before the elections. As it turned out this damaged the greens as the party failed to reach 5 percent in the West (4.8 percent) while its eastern counterpart, together with Alliance '90, polled 6 percent. If both western and eastern green voters had counted together, the 5 percent hurdle would have been surpassed.

The 1990 result was not the first step to the ultimate demise of the greens. Instead the specific circumstances of the 1990 election appear to be responsible. In state elections since 1990 the greens have in fact polled very well. In 1991 good results in Hesse (8.8 percent), Rhineland-Palatinate (6.5 percent), and Hamburg (7.2 percent), and in 1993 a record result in Hamburg (13.5 percent), confirmed the greens' position in German politics. In early 1994 opinion polls gave Alliance '90/The Greens 9 percent of the vote nationally, and the party returned to the federal Parliament in October 1994 polling 7.3 percent.

Ideology

Given the heterogeneous nature of the forces that molded the birth of the green party, it is not surprising that the party's programs and policy statements reflect these circumstances. At the beginning of the party's development there was a clear split between those who wanted to form an "ecological" party "beyond left and right," and those that saw the greens firmly embedded within the German left. The party's founding fathers came from radically different backgrounds, and it is a measure of the force of the issues upon which they agreed—in particular rejection of nuclear energy—that enabled these different groups to come together at all. In the end the character of the German greens has from the start been one combining ecological and new left issues. Those who could not agree with that identity, including "survivalists" such as Herbert Gruhl, quickly left the party.

The four basic principles of green politics set out by the greens in 1980 were "ecological, social, grass-roots democratic, and non-violent." The fact that "ecological" comes first and that "social" comes second is significant. Environmental and social concerns have been competing for pole position throughout the party's life. The 1980 foundation program gave relatively little emphasis to environmental issues. From the start the greens presented their positions on a whole range of domestic and foreign policy issues and tried hard to avoid being pigeon-holed as a purely "environmental" party. While all manifestos contained radical environmental demands, such as a complete run-down of the nuclear industry, it was the 1990 federal election manifesto which gave environmental issues most prominence, focusing chiefly on global environmental problems such as global warming.

Through most of the 1980s a number of ideological camps co-existed within the greens. One group, the so-called ecosocialists, based their policies on fairly traditional Marxist thinking and emphasized the left-wing character of the party with policies demanding greater state intervention in the economy and a democratization of industrial relations. The more ecologically inclined camp, on the other hand, sought to stress the environmental threats to the planet and demanded an end to economic growth. A third grouping, the eco-libertarians, stressed free market solutions to environmental problems, but always remained marginal. Most greens, however, did not share either extreme ecosocialist or fundamental ecologist positions. Both groups in fact joined forces against a rising group of pragmatic reformers who accepted the basic agenda of the greens as a left-wing, ecological party but sought to transform the party into a force that could partake in government. It was this strategic question which dominated the internal debate through the mid- to late 1980s, pitching "fundamentalists" (Fundis) against "realists" (Realos). By the early 1990s extreme fundamentalist positions had virtually disappeared, and the basic notion of the greens as a reform party with the need to formulate pragmatic policies was not seriously questioned; however, the degree to which the greens should forego traditional policy positions is still open to debate. In 1993 and 1994 green congresses confirmed the party's pacifist orientation demanding the dissolution of NATO and of the German Armed Forces.

G

Apart from their representation of the demands of the ecological, anti-nuclear, and peace movements which were so important in their early development, the greens have also given voice to a range of other new political issues. Feminism has been an important force within green politics, for example. The greens have also been vociferous in the defense of civil rights and the protection of minorities.

Organization and Strategy

The concept of "grass-roots democracy" has been the guiding principle for the organization of the German green party. Demands for greater political participation had been advanced by the student movement, the citizen initiatives, and new social movements for many years. All shared the analysis that representative democracy as practiced in West Germany had serious deficiencies, and that the established parties lacked internal democracy which blocked the adequate expression of the democratic will of the people. As a consequence, the greens set out to create an organization which embodied the anti-authoritarian principles of the movements that had created it. The party was highly decentralized, with individual members and local parties being invested with most powers. The party ostentatiously tried to avoid creating "leaders," and a detailed system was devised to prevent any individual gaining any dominating influence. This involved, most prominently, the principle of rotation according to which parliamentary deputies had to make way for new party representatives halfway through their elected term.

The internal structure of the party always provided a major debating point. For those who always saw the party as an "anti-party party," the preservation of its decentralized structure was essential to fulfill its function as the political arm of the new social movements. But as the party gained in parliamentary experience the principle of rotation was increasingly contested. Some green deputies refused to abide by it, and a great deal of intraparty friction ensued. In the absence of a hierarchical party organization a number of power centers had in fact been created. Green parliamentarians and green party representatives clashed frequently in public, and with the Realo-Fundi controversy increasing in bitterness, the publicly visible face of the greens was dominated by the image of continuous internal squabbling.

For a variety of reasons the basic aims of a grass-roots democracy were never reached.

The mobilization of the new social movements declined and activism levels dropped throughout the 1980s. Increasingly the greens found it difficult to fill the many positions at local and state government level that their electoral successes had brought them. Thus there were often no active members left to control elected green office holders. At national level it was increasingly obvious that rotation had a damaging effect as valuable experience was lost, prominent and effective political operators were alienated, and the public image suffered. Furthermore the party was arguably unable to formulate and implement any effective electoral strategies.

It was the shock of the December 1990 election defeat, however, which jolted the greens into action. In a special congress in the autumn of 1991, a number of organizational reforms were passed, including the abolition of rotation and the creation of a Land Council giving a platform to state green parties. This was essentially designed to give the realists, who were more dominant in state green politics, a greater opportunity to influence national green politics. The subsequent departure of the last radical fundamentalists combined with the merger of realists with the generally pragmatic and reformist Alliance '90 from East Germany reduced the level of internal party strife substantially. While many of the groups campaigning within the party have dissolved there remains a debate about the degree to which the greens should change their radical programs to appeal to a wider section of the electorate and to ease the negotiations with possible future coalition partners.

Future Prospects

After the green debacle in the first parliamentary elections of the united Germany in December 1990 many observers had written off the greens predicting their terminal decline. But the excellent results in virtually all state elections which they contested in the early 1990s were largely ignored by the foreign press. Despite this revival the greens are still criticized for their lack of cohesion in policy making and little organizational discipline. Frequent demands have been made for the need to professionalize the party and find a way to make it more efficient organizationally without reneging on its alternative identity. Several recent developments appear to go into the right direction. The organizational changes agreed in 1991 seem to pave the way toward such a professionalization. The departure from the party of the last fundamentalists is also seen by many as a positive development, cutting down on the level of internal strife.

Remaining, however, are the problems of the weakness of its organizational base and the volatility of its electoral support. The fusion with Alliance '90 brought only a few thousand new members to the party, and thus the total membership basis is more or less unchanged at around 40,000. The reduction of activity levels provides further problems in having adequate personnel available to fill the many positions at local and state levels which the electoral success of the greens is making available to them.

As to the electorate, green support has consistently remained above the 5 percent mark nationally in the 1990s, and the good 1994 federal election result confirmed the role of the Greens in German politics. But the elections also demonstrated the weakness of green support in the former East Germany. Protest against the way East Germans are suffering from the economic effects of the unification dominated by the West is more likely to be expressed by voting for the former East German Communist Party.

In West Germany, however, green support is quite solid, and all established parties, including the conservative Christian Democrats, have shown their willingness to work with them. With support for the other minor party, the Liberals, dropping, the Greens may thus see themselves increasingly called upon to serve in local and regional government. The prospect of helping to form a government at the federal level also seems closer than at any stage before. Increasingly, the future electoral fortunes of the Greens may depend more on their performance in government than on their ability to mobilize and represent extra-parliamentary protest movements.

Wolfgang Rüdig

Further Readings

Frankland, E. Gene, and Donald Schoonmaker. *Between Protest and Power: The Green Party in Germany.* 1992.

Kitschelt, Herbert. *The Logics of Party Formation: Ecological Politics in Belgium and West Germany.* 1989.

Kleinert, Hubert. *Aufstieg und Fall der Grünen: Analyse einer alternativen Partei.* 1992.

Poguntke, Thomas. *Alternative Politics: The German Green Party.* 1993.

Raschke, Joachim. *Die Grünen: Wie sie wurden, was sie sind.* 1993.

Veen, Hans-Joachim, and Jürgen Hoffmann. *Die Grünen zu Beginn der neunziger Jahre: Profil und Defizite einer fast etablierten Partei.* 1992.

See also ACID PRECIPITATION: EUROPEAN EXPERIENCES; CHERNOBYL; ECOANARCHISM; ECOSOCIALISM; ENVIRONMENTAL GROUPS: WESTERN EUROPE; GREEN PARTIES; GREEN PARTIES: AUSTRALIA; KELLY, PETRA; NUCLEAR ELECTRIC POWER

Green Plan (Canada)

In September 1988 Canada's Prime Minister, Brian Mulroney, announced at a meeting of the United Nations that Canada would develop a sustainable development strategy as called for in *Our Common Future* (1987). In early 1989, he appointed a senior minister to the environment portfolio and created a cabinet committee on the environment. By the time it was launched in December 1990 the Green Plan had experienced a difficult gestation involving two ministers, intense inter-departmental "disputes," and a controversial consultation stage.

Canada's Green Plan, a 174-page document, contains sections on: 1) the cleanup of air, water, and land; 2) renewable resources; 3) endangered spaces and species; 4) the Arctic; 5) global environmental security; 6) environmentally responsible decision making; 7) federal government stewardship; and 8) environmental emergencies. A five-year time frame was established for over 100 policy initiatives and the expenditure of some $3 billion.

Public reaction to the Green Plan was mixed. Environmentalists charged it with being overly cautious and too focused on educational and information initiatives. Industry was relieved that it did not contain a major new regulatory thrust and the provinces were pleased that it did not represent a major federal incursion into provincial jurisdiction. The Green Plan was a government-wide initiative with 60 percent of its budget allocated to departments other than Environment Canada.

The Conservative government, however, began to cut the Green Plan budget almost immediately after its launch. In the February 1991 budget the five-year time frame was extended to six years. Subsequent cuts by the Finance Department reduced the Green Plan budget by

G

$500 million and reallocated much of the spending to the later years. Though these cuts were introduced as part of a larger deficit reduction program, they raised questions about the government's commitment to its own environmental initiatives. Most of the changes proposed in the Green Plan have now been introduced, and the new Liberal government of Jean Chretien has commited itself to retaining and strengthening the Green Plan as part of its sustainable development strategy.

Glen Toner

Further Readings

Toner, Glen. "The Green Plan: From Great Expectations to Eco-Backtracking . . . to Revitalization." In *How Ottawa Spends.* Ed. S.D. Phillips. 1994.

———, and G. Bruce Doern. "Five Political and Policy Imperatives in Green Plan Formation: The Canadian Case." *Environmental Politics* (1994).

See also ENVIRONMENT CANADA; FEDERALISM AND ENVIRONMENTAL PROTECTION: CANADA; *Our Common Future*; SUSTAINABLE DEVELOPMENT

Green Products

According to Leen Stevast, head of consumer affairs at Phillips: "There are no such things as green products." Nielsen Marketing Research adopts a less absolute definitional line, identifying "green" products as those that are marketed on a green image, while "environmentally friendly" products are those for which some environmental claim is made.

Whatever the definition, the greenness of a product is related to its environmental impact: the more negative the impact, the less green the product. Assessing the impact, however, is a major research undertaking, which has led to a new scientific methodology: life-cycle analysis (LCA). As its name suggests LCA is intended to assess the environmental impacts of all processes related to a product from its cradle to its grave, including the extraction of raw materials, processing and production, packaging and distribution, use and disposal. "Every product casts a shadow" claims the forthcoming *LCA Sourcebook.*

Not unexpectedly with a new methodology the early development of LCA has led to a wide variety of problems and inconsistencies, discussed in detail in a report to the European Commission (EC), *Evaluation of Eco-balances.*

Some of the problems relate to divergent criteria and indicators in different LCA analyses. More fundamentally there is also disagreement on whether and how different environmental impacts should be aggregated to come up with a single "score" for a product. The EC report believes that such procedures are controversial and undesirable because they embody, but conceal, subjective valuations.

Even in its early stages LCA has great commercial implications, because it has the potential to be a procedure that provides the scientific basis for the European Community's "eco-label," which after some delays was introduced in 1993. The purpose of an eco-label on a product is to advise consumers that the product has fulfilled certain environmental conditions. Eco-labeling schemes already exist in several countries, including Japan, Canada, the United States, France, and the Netherlands, with the best-known probably being Germany's Blue Angel, which was introduced in 1977. The European eco-label will not necessarily replace existing labels, but it is intended to provide some consistency in this area within the European single market.

As with the Blue Angel the European eco-label classifies products into groups. Different European Community countries have responsibility for different groups. Products are assessed and compared with others in their appropriate groups. The initial groups for the United Kingdom include: washing machines, dishwashers, light bulbs, soil improvers, and hair sprays; for Germany: solar heating systems, laundry and dishwasher detergents, and household cleaning products; for Denmark: insulating materials and various kinds of paper; and for France: batteries, paints, and varnishes.

Predictably there is considerable controversy over the actual implementation of the label. Two points of contention are the stringency of the criteria to be applied and, therefore, the number of eco-labels to be awarded in any product group, and the range of issues to be included in the assessment. Environmental groups have argued for stricter criteria than industry groups and have called for the assessments to include issues such as testing on animals and impacts on biodiversity and indigenous peoples. Such controversy well indicates the range of meanings conveyed by the word "green"—from the narrowly environmental to the inclusion of a variety of other social and ethical issues felt to be related to the environment in a broader sense.

The movement toward eco-labeling is part of a wider impulse called "green consumerism," through which shoppers explicitly seek to weigh environmental considerations when making their purchases. This phenomenon came to prominence in 1988 with the best-selling publication of *The Green Consumer Guide* (Elkington and Hailes, 1988) in the United Kingdom, and its subsequent publication in many other countries. Market analysts were surprised at the extent of green consumerism. While some of the froth has now gone off the market, surveys such as Nielsen's show the products concerned retaining their market share.

Concern to reduce the environmental impact of products is increasingly being focused on the design stage. The U.S. Congress' Office of Technology Assessment defined "green design" as having the dual goal of waste prevention and better materials management. It perceives that designing for green products can not only prevent environmental problems, rather than having to tackle them after the event, but also foster competitiveness and environmental quality in management.

Paul Ekins

Further Readings

Elkington, J., and J. Hailes. *The Green Consumer Guide*. 1988.

Hartwell III, R.V., and L. Bergkamp. "Eco-Labeling in Europe: New Market-Related Environmental Risks?" *International Environment Reporter* (September 23, 1992).

Strategic Analysis in Science and Technology Unit, European Commission. *Evaluation of Eco-balances*. 1993.

SustainAbility. *The LCA Sourcebook*. 1993.

U.S. Congress' Office of Technology Assessment. *Green Products by Design*. 1992.

See also GREEN ECONOMICS; LIFE-CYCLE ANALYSIS; OFFICE OF TECHNOLOGY ASSESSMENT

Green Revolution

The year 1993 marked the twenty-fifth anniversary of the coining of the term "Green Revolution" by Dr. William Gadd of the U.S. Department of Agriculture. The term was coined in 1968 to symbolize the quantum jump in wheat production and productivity achieved during that year in India and Pakistan, as well as to mark the beginning of the advance in rice production triggered by the semi-dwarf, non-lodging varieties of rice bred in Taiwan and at the International Rice Research Institute (IRRI) in the Philippines. This is hence an appropriate time to construct a twenty-five-year balance sheet of the accomplishments and problems generated by green revolution technologies.

It is first important to note two positive gains. In 1893 the population of undivided India (i.e., India, Pakistan, and Bangladesh) was 281 million. Today the population of India alone is over 875 million. In 1893 a massive famine caused over 10 million deaths. In 1993 the grain reserves with the government of India exceeded 25 million metric tons. There has been no famine in India in the past twenty-five years, although there is considerable endemic hunger (or chronic undernutrition) arising from inadequate purchasing power at the household level. Thus, the food security challenge has shifted from one of physical to economic access to food.

The other important gain is the "forest saving" nature of the green revolution. In 1964 India produced 12 million metric tons of wheat from 14 million hectares. In 1993 Indian farmers produced 57 million tons of wheat from about 24 million hectares. To produce 57 million tons at the 1964 yield level, farmers would have required 60 million hectares. The remaining forests would have vanished if India had not taken to a productivity driven pathway for balancing its food budget.

On the negative side of the balance sheet, however, there are five areas of concern:

1. The negative ecological aspects include problems created by the excessive use of chemical pesticides and mineral fertilizers, the damage done to soil health as a result of the use of heavy farm machinery, and the genetic vulnerability to biotic and abiotic stresses caused by genetic homogenity arising from monoculture and the cultivation of some genetic strains over large areas.

2. From the point of view of economics, the cost, risk, and return structure of farming often becomes unfavorable to farm families with small holdings. Although new technologies are scale neutral with reference to their suitability for cultivation in different sizes of farms, they are

not resource neutral. More market-purchased inputs are needed for more output and hence the resource-poor farmers tend to get bypassed by the green revolution.

3. The new technologies often involve greater use of non-renewable forms of energy. This, in turn, contributes and will likely continue to contribute to those factors responsible for global warming.

4. There are problems of equity in terms of both gender and economic status. Frequently the green revolution technologies tend to displace women's labor and cause greater unemployment among them.

5. Indiscriminate mechanization could lead to the displacement of farm labor. We need diversification of labor use and not displacement leading to the phenomenon referred to as "jobless growth."

The global population is growing and land and water resources for agriculture are shrinking. Therefore there is no option except to work for a continuous improvement in the productivity, profitability, stability, and sustainability of major farming systems. This is a major lesson of the green revolution of the last twenty-five years. We need to address urgently the problems relating to ecology, economics, energy, equity, and employment if we are to foster a greener "green revolution." Without productivity improvement, which is the major feature of the green revolution, forests will disappear and small farmers will not be able to increase their income. Thus, the extension of an environmentally sustainable green revolution is both an ecological and economic necessity.

M.S. Swaminathan

Further Readings

Swaminathan, M.S., ed. *Wheat Revolution: A Dialogue.* 1993.

See also AGRICULTURE: ENVIRONMENTAL IMPACTS; AGROFORESTRY; CHIPKO MOVEMENT; SLASH-AND-BURN AGRICULTURE; SUSTAINABLE AGRICULTURE; SUSTAINABLE DEVELOPMENT; TROPICAL DEFORESTATION

Greenhouse Effect
See CLIMATE WARMING

Greenpeace

The international environmental organization known as Greenpeace began in 1970 as the Don't Make a Wave Committee of Vancouver, British Columbia. The Committee was formed to protest a U.S. nuclear weapons test on the Alaskan island of Amchitka. Members of the group chartered an old fishing trawler, which they renamed *Greenpeace,* to reflect a mix of ecological and anti-nuclear weapons sentiments, and announced their plans to stop the test by sailing into the waters near the island. While the group never made it into the test zone, and the weapon was successfully detonated, the wide publicity surrounding the protest was one factor in a later U.S suspension of further tests on Amchitka.

From this single act of highly public protest the group's fame spread, and from its original few activists Greenpeace has grown to become perhaps the world's largest and wealthiest environmental organization. Its main goals (pursued in the form of distinct "campaigns") are the preservation of marine life—most notably whales—and ending all nuclear testing, but it also has branched out into such related areas as the disposal of toxic wastes, protecting Antarctica from development, and preventing energy-related atmospheric deterioration. Greenpeace also opposed the 1990–1991 Persian Gulf War for fear of its effects on the region's aquatic life—a controversial position that further underscored its unique role as an international environmental force.

To promote its goals Greenpeace embraces the American Quaker tradition of "bearing witness"—putting oneself in the path of an objectionable activity—buttressed by the civil rights movement's emphasis on nonviolence. In doing so the organization became the first major environmental group to emphasize dramatic and highly public campaigns of "direct action" over more traditional ways of influencing governments. Such activities, which gained the organization tremendous global renown, included unfurling banners from power plant smokestacks, plugging industrial waste outflow pipes, interposing volunteers between whaling ships and their prey, and sailing into nuclear test zones. Greenpeace's flamboyant but nonviolent direct action also is to be distinguished from the more aggressive, even destructive tactics undertaken by such groups as the Sea Shepherd Society, itself founded by a Greenpeace outcast. To some hard-core environmental activists Greenpeace itself is now bureaucratic and passive, and defections from the organization have spawned direct action groups throughout the world.

Greenpeace's protests have generated their share of government responses, ranging from harassment to outright violence. The navies of more than one nation have used their ships to keep Greenpeace activists away from nuclear tests, while British sailors once tried to sink manned boats being used to halt the ocean dumping of hazardous wastes. In 1980 Spain seized the vessel *Rainbow Warrior* in international waters after it had interfered with whaling. The Spanish government impounded the vessel for five months until, one night, it dramatically escaped. Each incident only enhanced the organization's fame and its reputation for effectiveness. The *Rainbow Warrior* was to figure in the most infamous boost to Greenpeace's global reputation. On July 10, 1985, operatives of the French secret service sabotaged the vessel in the harbor of Auckland, New Zealand, from which the organization had been waging the latest phase in its long campaign against French nuclear weapons testing in the South Pacific. The sinking killed Fernando Pereira, a Greenpeace photographer, aroused worldwide condemnation against France, and seriously strained that nation's relations with New Zealand. The French government, which long had carried out extensive and sometimes violent surveillance and infiltration activities against the organization, eventually apologized to New Zealand, repatriated its imprisoned operatives, and paid Greenpeace $8 million in compensation.

Greenpeace is no longer simply a publicity-seeking direct action group. The organization's deep scientific and legal expertise has been put to wide use in international treaty conferences and conventions, venues where its influence is great. It has branched out into environmental education and mass media efforts and has its own publishing arm based in London. Although Greenpeace USA takes great pains to distinguish itself from the more mainstream national environmental organizations, it is not averse to working with other groups on selected campaigns. In 1988 Greenpeace USA formed a separate lobbying arm to operate within the everyday world of governmental decision making.

Greenpeace is a global organization headquartered in Amsterdam, with offices in over twenty nations. Its far-flung offices and activists in the field are connected together by a satellite-based communications system called Greenlink and it maintains an extensive environmental database. Despite claims from disgruntled activists that Greenpeace's growth has brought centralization and bureaucratization, the international organization remains relatively decentralized, with each national office maintaining a good deal of autonomy. In many ways the real organizational loci remain the campaigns, which traverse national boundaries.

Greenpeace grew phenomenally during the 1980s. It has about five million members worldwide, with over two million in the United States. Greenpeace's worldwide revenues in the early 1990s approached $150 million annually, with its U.S. office alone having a budget of over $50 million in 1990. Greenpeace accepts no corporate donations, and 90 percent of its revenues come from membership dues and other contributions. The organization's global reputation as an uncompromising and effective promoter of environmental values allows it to rely heavily and successfully on direct mail and door-to-door canvassing to attract new members and donations. Such heavy reliance on direct mail and canvassing is expensive, however, and always leaves the organization open to charges that its goals and tactics are calculated precisely to generate greater publicity and revenues. However, controversy can harm fundraising: Greenpeace's opposition to the Persian Gulf War, coming close on the heels of the economic recession of the early 1990s, undoubtedly was a factor in the organization's first drop in revenues in its history. For Greenpeace the 1990s will be a time where uncompromising grassroots activism will run up constantly against the need to effectively manage a massive international organization.

Christopher J. Bosso (with Inez Garcia)

Further Readings

Dunlap, Riley E., and Angela G. Mertig, eds. *American Environmentalism: The U.S. Environmental Movement, 1970–1990.* 1992.

Manes, Christopher. *Green Rage: Radical Environmentalism and the Unmaking of Civilization.* 1990.

See also BALEEN WHALES; ENVIRONMENTALISM; INTERNATIONAL WHALING COMMISSION; RADIOACTIVE FALLOUT

Grinnell, Joseph

See AUDUBON, JOHN JAMES; ECOLOGICAL NICHE

Groundwater Pollution

The World Bank estimates that nearly 1 billion people lack adequate water supplies, while about 1.7 billion people must deal daily with unsanitized water. Meanwhile, irrigated agriculture's seemingly unquenchable thirst for water continues in China, India, the former Soviet Union, and the United States. This occurs as harvesting of forests at record rates continues apace, in the process distorting water cycles, water distribution, and water regulatory regimes. Pressed in this fashion, governments and their citizens worldwide are turning increasingly and substantially to groundwater aquifers to meet their water needs. In the United States, for example, nearly 50 percent of the population relies on groundwater for drinking supplies, with nearly 95 percent of rural dwellers relying on this source. Moreover, 75 percent of major U.S. cities get a majority of their water supply from groundwater aquifers.

While the pollution of surface water has long animated popular concerns about water quality, the worldwide trend toward greater groundwater use has increasingly turned the attention of policy makers toward groundwater pollution. With large-scale rural-to-urban migrations in the developing world straining local water supplies, with irrigated agriculture pumping groundwater at rates drastically exceeding the natural recharge rates of many local aquifers, and with hazardous chemicals entering the water cycle at disturbing rates, many experts project that groundwater pollution will ultimately dwarf surface pollution in scale, scope, and threat to humanity. This said, it must be added that the current assessments of groundwater pollution are essentially "educated guesswork" due to the worldwide lack of reliable data. Moreover, even those who feel that groundwater pollution is not widespread today (e.g., only about 1 to 2 percent of U.S. groundwater is thought to be contaminated) concede that these concentrations vary dramatically by region. They also concede that most groundwater pollution is not being detected and that threats are likely to rise appreciably in the future.

To support these claims experts point to worldwide failures in groundwater testing mechanisms, to the inordinately slow pace of groundwater movement, to the spiraling use and haphazard disposal of synthetic organic chemicals (SOCs) over the past forty years, and to our increasing dependence on groundwater supplies. For example, it typically takes decades after release before toxic chemicals migrate to points where they are detectable. What is more, monitoring of groundwater usually occurs only after a homeowner's complaint or after adverse health effects arise. Likewise, when testing is done its scope is often quite limited. Thus, while 200 different compounds have been found in groundwater in the United States, the water has often been tested only for metals and other inorganics, not for SOCs. Meanwhile, in water-challenged urban areas in developing countries such as Jakarta, Mexico City, and Bangkok, groundwater mining has led to seawater contamination, falling water tables, and land subsidence that has broken water and sewage pipes, increased flooding in low level areas, and wrought severe sanitation problems.

Pollutants in a groundwater aquifer move in plumes, or concentrations of contaminants. They do so at rates and in directions that track the glacial pace of water flow movement (sometimes only inches or feet per year), albeit with variations across different types of pollutants. The universe of pollutants is quite large and includes heavy metals, SOCs, chlorinated volatile organic compounds (VOCs), and radioactive elements. Presently concerns are centered on nitrates and pesticides. Dischargers most culpable for these emissions are as varied and ingenious as the multiplicity of ways wastes can be generated, transported, treated, stored, and disposed. These include leachate from urban landfills, leaking sewers and fuel tanks, nonpoint urban and agricultural runoff, injection wells, surface impoundments, corroding septic tanks, household products containing SOCs, mine tailings, open dump leachate, cracked underground pipelines, and compromised hazardous waste treatment, storage, disposal, and recycling facilities (TSDFs and TSDRs).

Worldwide concerns about the inability of present regulatory regimes to handle this emerging groundwater dilemma have spawned widespread experimentation with market-based incentives. In the United States, for example, implementation of statutes most relevant to groundwater pollution—the Resource Conservation and Recovery Act of 1976, the Hazardous and Solid Waste Amendments of 1984, the Comprehensive Environmental Response, Compensation, and Liability Act of 1980, the Superfund Amendments and Reauthorization Act of 1986, the Toxic Substances Control Act, and the Safe Drinking Water Act—has been plagued by insufficient funding, labyrinthine implementation structures, and inadequate scientific knowledge. In fact, the federal government has actually inhibited aggressive state regulatory action in some instances, including restrictions on pesticide use. Likewise, the World Bank has indicted "institutional failures" as the most significant cause of Third World water shortages generally, shortages that then place additional strains on groundwater supplies and quality. Noting that only Singapore, Korea, Tunisia, and Botswana manage water and sewage treatment adequately, the Bank calls among other things for improving water utilities' performance, decentralization of regulatory regimes, and expansion of the private sector's role in water allocation. Meanwhile, many industrialized countries have recognized the hydrological linkage between surface and groundwater and are emulating France's approach to river basin management. The French eschew command-and-control regulatory regimes in favor of "water parliaments" where resource stakeholders negotiate primarily market-based approaches to mitigating the negative environmental externalities caused by economic development.

Perhaps the most pernicious aspect of government's culpability in abetting groundwater pollution, and the one most responsible for advancing arguments for pricing and other market incentives, is the way many regulatory regimes have subsidized water depletion and pollution. In most countries, irrigated agriculture users seldom pay more than 10 percent of the true cost of water delivery, thus distorting efficient water allocation. Indeed, in many areas of the West and Southwest in the United States, as well as in the industrial heartland of China around Beijing and Tianjin, conflict has ensued over the reallocation of heavily subsidized surface and groundwater rights favoring rural over urban use. At the same time many governments subsidize and encourage the use of pesticides that contribute to agricultural runoff. Meanwhile, competing ministries in both developing and industrialized nations protect existing water rights, and often compete rather than cooperate to transfer surface and groundwater to its highest economic use.

Faced with this situation, many observers have concluded that part of the problem of groundwater allocation and pollution can be eased by relying on price and other market incentives, on increased efficiency measures, and on water re-use. Still, groundwater pollution cannot be addressed by price and market-based reallocation schemes alone. Industry has to internalize the true environmental and natural resource costs of its activities in its price structures. What is more, the institutional capacity of state regulators has to be enhanced, governments must allocate adequate resources for assessing the scope and nature of groundwater contaminants, and institutional barriers to ministerial cooperation must be reduced.

Robert F. Durant

Further Readings
Stein, Edith C. *The Environmental Sourcebook*. 1992.
Stewart, John C. *Drinking Water Hazards*. 1990.
Wilkinson, Charles F. *Crossing the Next Meridian*. 1992.

See also DEEP-WELL INJECTION; LEACHING; OGALLALA AQUIFER; PERSISTENT ORGANOCHLORINE COMPOUNDS; PESTICIDES; RESOURCE CONSERVATION AND RECOVERY ACT; SUPERFUND; VOLATILE ORGANIC COMPOUNDS

Group of Seven

The Group of Seven (1920–1931) is Canada's best-known painting group. Its members actually total eleven; the original seven were Franklin Carmichael, Lawren Harris, A.Y. Jackson, Frank H. (Franz) Johnston, Arthur Lismer, J.E.H. MacDonald, and F.H. Varley. The three additional members include, A.J. Casson (in 1926), Edwin Holgate (in 1931), and L. FitzGerald (in 1932). Although many of its members originally worked in commercial art and on weekend sketching trips, the influence of artists such as Harris who trained abroad prompted them to direct their efforts to painting full-time. Soon they found they were interested in advancing a national cause and developing a program with a specific iconography of Canada's north. Handling was to be bold. ("Don't niggle," Jackson told a student.)

The group dated their own existence from around 1911–1912, although they did not apply the title "Group of Seven" until much later. Tom Thomson was one of the leaders in the development of the group's style but died in 1917 before the group was officially formed. It is Thomson's life and career that provide a key to the early movement. Inspired early in life by Dr. William Brodie, a Canadian naturalist and his great uncle, Thomson painted nature with a keen eye. His depiction of the landscape in Algonquin Park is uniquely sensitive to the contours of the land, time of day, and weather conditions. Other members of the group followed his lead in sensitively depicting the vagaries of Canada's wilderness. In time their work was seen as a contribution to the ecological movement. Canadians recognize the images they created as characteristic of the country. Among other gifts was that of their style; they were among the first "modern" painters in Canadian art.

The Group of Seven's subjects changed in the decade of their search for motifs: from Algonquin Park to Algoma, Lake Superior, and the Arctic. Members felt at home with different parts of the country: MacDonald with Algoma, Harris with Lake Superior, Jackson with the French Canadian countryside, Casson with Ontario villages. Their greatest achievements as painters range in date and color over a wide variety of work but a particularly strong movement occurred around the organization of the institution in 1920.

Members of the group were aware of the conservation cause. Casson lent his name to several environmental endeavors.

Joan Murray

Further Readings

Murray, Joan. *The Best of the Group of Seven.* 1984, rpt. 1993.

———. *The Best of Tom Thomson.* 1986.

———. *Masterpieces of Tom Thomson and The Group of Seven.* 1994.

See also ADAMS, ANSEL; CARR, EMELY; ENVIRONMENTAL AESTHETICS; HUDSON RIVER SCHOOL

Gypsy Moths

Gypsy moth (*Lymantria dispar*; Linnaeus) is a moth of the Lymantriidae family and is considered native to Eurasia, where it sometimes causes damage to forests. It was introduced to Massachusetts for possible use in silk production. The moth became established in New England in about 1869 and has caused sporadic damage since that time. Gypsy moths now occur over much of the northeast and west to Illinois. Small populations also have been found in spots elsewhere in the United States.

As adults gypsy moths are rather inconspicuous. They are protectively colored, some-

what drab, and not very large. Adults do not feed so in this stage they do no damage. Larvae (caterpillars) of the gypsy moth feed on an extensive range of plants, mostly deciduous hardwood trees and especially oak (*Quercus*), which can cause extensive defoliation and sometimes death of the tree. In addition the larvae have hairs that can irritate. During outbreaks larvae occur in such large numbers that they become a nuisance.

Efforts to control the gypsy moth have prompted numerous developments in pest control practices. Scientists with the U.S. Department of Agriculture developed the first preparations of lead arsenate as an insecticide for use against the gypsy moth in the 1890s. Lead arsenate went on to become the most widely used insecticide in agriculture before 1940.

When DDT was introduced for general use in 1945 gypsy moths became an early target with some hoping to eradicate it. Extensive use of DDT did little to stop the spread of the gypsy moth, although it did alleviate some defoliation damage. However, the chemical caused extensive damage to fish and birds. Rachel Carson's *Silent Spring* used eradication efforts against gypsy moth as a prominent example of insecticide use run amok.

Recent efforts to control the spread of the moth have stimulated attempts to find natural enemies of the pest in Europe and Asia. Some were established and they probably helped reduce the intensity of gypsy moth outbreaks. These biological control efforts stimulated other similar research. Development of pathogenic bacteria as insecticides, such as *Bacillus thuringiensis*, was also stimulated by efforts to control the gypsy moth.

Prior to 1991 the gypsy moth population in North America was generally regarded as the European strain. In 1991 the Asian strain was accidentally introduced into the Pacific Northwest. Some entomologists consider the Asian strain to be more dangerous because it feeds readily on at least some conifers and because the female flies, thus increasing the rate of dispersal. An extensive effort to eradicate the Asian strain was launched in 1992.

John H. Perkins

Further Readings

Dreistadt, Steve H., and Donald C. Weber. "Gypsy Moth in the Northeast and Great Lakes States." In *Eradication of Exotic Pests: Analysis with Case Histories.* Ed. D.L. Dahlsten and R. Garcia. 1989.

Dunlap, Thomas R. *DDT: Scientists, Citizens, and Public Policy.* 1981.

Elkinton, J.S., and A.M. Liebhold. "Population Dynamics of Gypsy Moth in North America." *Annual Review of Entomology* 35 (1990).

See also BACILLUS THURINGIENSIS; EXOTIC SPECIES; INTEGRATED PEST MANAGEMENT; PESTICIDES

G

Habitat Fragmentation, Patches, and Corridors

Habitat fragmentation has two components; habitat removal and resultant disconnection of remaining habitat patches which may isolate patch populations of resident organisms. Fragmentation may have specific effects on species which depend on the habitat removed or fragmented. Fragmentation may affect the composition of the landscape (the kinds of resource patches present), the configuration (sizes, shapes, and placements of patches), and the connectivity (the degree to which the landscape impedes or facilitates the movement of species and their access to resources).

The effects of fragmentation may be more widespread but less decisive for particular species if their habitat or resource needs are more flexible. For species with an array of resource needs, however, access to some particular resource patches may be constrained or prevented. For such species the array of resource needs may change seasonally and with life history or reproductive stages. Thus fragmentation requires individuals to solve a dynamical systems problem to ensure survival through their complete seasonal and demographic sequences of resource needs. These dynamics of fragmentation effects can be further complicated if, as in crop rotation, the positioning and timing of resource or habitat patches can be changed by human decisions and thus made unpredictable to wild species.

Because fragmentation of habitat may also divide large populations into patches, numbers of individuals in these patch populations will be smaller depending on: 1) the size of the habitat patch; 2) normal population densities; and 3) whether patch isolation confines individuals to their patch. Patch populations numbering less than about twenty are affected much more by chance events than are larger populations; two or three reproductive female mice can all be eliminated suddenly by one lucky predator. As chance takes more control of population processes, success becomes much less predictable from the general rules for those processes. Both demographic processes (birth, death, age structure) and genetic processes (gene frequency change, adaptation by natural selection) are subject to small population effects. Demographic results can include periodic loss of patch populations which may accumulate into regional and then species extinctions. Genetic results can include loss of genetic variability due to inbreeding because the number of individuals is too small for complete representation of the species genetic diversity. Beneficial effects of small patch populations can also occur. If appropriate genes are already in the patch or if these genes can be introduced to the patch and the patch is a significantly different environment, small populations can become strongly adapted to patch-specific environments.

The degree to which populations are affected by fragmentation, patches, and small population effects depends strongly on the actual degree of isolation of the patches for a particular species. Isolation depends on: 1) the amount and types of habitat removed by fragmentation; 2) the types of habitats inserted in place of those removed; 3) the shape and spatial placement of remaining habitat patches; and 4) the capability of the species for movement. New patch types, such as farm crops, may be inserted and may vary from useful resources to high risk barriers. Perhaps most important of all is the behavioral response of the dispersing individuals to the environments separating residual habitat patches.

Whether or not habitat patches are connected can be demonstrated only by interpatch movement of individuals. Significant isolation can cause loss of genetic diversity or can cause failure to recolonize local extirpations. Although migratory songbirds have excellent movement capabilities their behavioral inability to move between patches of forest nesting habitat isolated by farmland can cause from 15 to 25 percent of farm woods to be without particular bird species for each breeding season. This is essentially the same rate of loss of isolated patch populations as was measured in the same area for woodland mice which might be assumed to have lower mobility. But the behavioral response to intervening alien habitats results in the same proportion of empty patches. Fortunately, recolonizations in each breeding period equal the number of patches where populations are lost; excesses of local extirpations over recolonizations could lead to regional or global species extinctions. These are vital processes which depend on interpatch travelways that are acceptable to the species.

Such travelways often are called movement corridors. These may be seminatural connections left after fragmentation or remedial restorations for management, or they may be novel habitats such as crops, which the species learn to use. Connectivity is an ecological parameter of landscape condition which is a function of the ease of movement of individuals of a species among habitat patches in the landscape. It is an indicator of effects of fragmentation at the population level and at the landscape scale. The historical norm of high connectivity was provided by large interconnecting areas of natural habitat. Addition of artificial corridors is unlikely to substitute for historical, high connectivity and should not be expected to prevent species loss except temporarily and in special cases.

The importance of connectivity to spatially-divided populations can be measured in simulation models. A metapopulation model requires the most assumptions and is the most general. It simulates a set of patch populations interconnected by movements of individuals. Survival of the metapopulation is dependent on interpatch movements and, even when patch populations suffer frequent extirpation or local extinction, the probability of survival of the whole metapopulation is high. Where patch populations are known to differ by having either a net annual production of new individuals or a net loss of individuals a source-sink model can simulate the metapopulation dynamics. Dispersers enter the sinks from the sources and are lost there to mortality. The interconnection of patch populations actually can reduce the survivability of the metapopulation. Another class of models of spatially-divided populations simulates the population dynamics in a spatially explicit way. Time and space designations are attached to population events. This allows interrelationship of landscape characteristics such as composition and configuration to connectivity and population sustainability. Canadian scientists have made major contributions to the landscape ecology of spatially-divided populations.

Some landscapes have depended historically on artificial corridors for connectivity. British and some other European hedges are "laid," or built from living plants and during periodic land ownership restructuring, or "remembrement," in "les bocages" of France, hedges may be installed using "hedge by the meter" kits. Even ancient hedges in Brittany and elsewhere are severely altered at intervals of about nine years by pollarding—a process that allows tenant farmers to take all tree limbs for fuelwood so long as the tree stem stays alive.

Corridors which meet species requirements in terms of dimensions and environmental qualities may also be used for reproduction or other life stages. These are referred to as habitat corridors and they provide conditions more like the historical habitat norm. In Australia elongate habitat patches, such as treed roadside verges, may be called corridors even if they do not connect patches. Similarly riverine corridors may have habitat values unrelated to interconnection of patches. Because riverine strips and other naturally linear landscape elements often follow features of natural landform units they may be part of ecotones—natural edges between ecological zones. Consequently such corridors may have special values in ecotonal processes such as interactions between land and water. Because these linear junctions of environmental zones contain more than one set of resources they often have species from more than one habitat and therefore unusually high biodiversity. If these linear landscape elements follow very large landform units, they may penetrate several climatic and ecological zones and function as corridors at this larger subcontinental and biogeographic scale. Thus southern European species follow valley ecotones into central and northern Europe, and boreal forest species reach all the way to the Arctic Ocean along Canada's Mackenzie River. Corridors can function at many spatial and many temporal scales.

Gray Merriam

Further Readings

Hansen, A.J., and F. DiCastri. *Landscape Boundaries.* 1992.

Saunders, D., and R. Hobbs, eds. *Nature Conservation 2: The Role of Corridors in Nature Conservation.* 1991.

———, R. Hobbs, and P. Ehrlich, eds. *Nature Conservation 3: Reconstruction of Fragmented Ecosystems, Global and Regional Perspectives.* 1993.

See also FOREST FRAGMENTATION AND BIRD HABITATS; LANDSCAPE ECOLOGY

Habitat Loss in North America

When speaking of habitat loss it is necessary to differentiate between actual "loss" and "change" in habitat. An initial loss, such as the effects of clearcutting on a stable-age forest, is usually followed by a seral succession of different habitats. Eventually—sometimes only after hundreds of years—the stable-age condition may be reestablished. In other cases in which the original community was relict an entirely different community becomes established. This is real habitat loss.

It is important to remember that habitat loss or change is not the only factor involved in species loss. In Canada, for example, hunting or trapping was the sole factor leading to the loss in historic times of the four now-extinct species/subspecies of mammals and the three now-extinct species/subspecies of birds. It has been calculated that of the fourteen species of endangered birds in Canada, hunting and/or human persecution are the major causes of endangerment in the case of nine species; of the nineteen species/subspecies of endangered mammals, hunting and/or human persecution can be blamed in the case of eighteen. Factors other than clearcutting or hunting can deny an area to some organisms. Biocides, erosion, or air pollution can make an area uninhabitable by different species for varying periods of time.

Human history represents the story of a long series of cultures that outgrew the carrying capacity of their region, and collapsed or were succeeded by another culture that employed a different set of resources. One also encounters the myth of the "noble savage" who walked lightly upon the land and who inhabited North America for thousands of years but caused no environmental damage. In actual fact, however, pre-contact native North Americans lived in a world they and their ancestors had changed dramatically. Amerindian corn fields, unused for nearly 1,000 years, are still identifiable as such by the reduced tilth and fewer nutrients in the soil. There is fairly clear evidence that early humans in North America were at least partially responsible for the extinction of at least twenty and possibly as many as forty species of medium to large mammals including two or three species of bison, horses, tapirs, camels, llamas, mammoths, giant deer, moose-deer, saiga antelope, ground sloths, giant peccaries, and several species of "shrub oxen." For most of these species we no longer have even common names.

When Europeans invaded North America they encountered not an untouched continent teeming with life to its maximum but one with a depauperate and already-ravaged fauna. Because they came from another continent that had been ravaged by their own ancestors even more, they considered North America absurdly prolific with wildlife. They were, however, just one of the waves of human invaders to hit North America, who in their turn also obeyed the basic rule of virtually all human societies to date: "Cut and get out." Because of more efficient weapons and a social/religious ethic of "Dominion over the beasts of the field" the Europeans have been able to accomplish in 400 years even more destruction than that which had taken the earlier human invasions some 10,000 years to achieve.

It would be helpful then to look at some of North America's most important types of habitat in relation to the impacts of human activities. Some of the habitat types discussed here (including tropical rainforests, rangelands, and old-growth forests) are treated elsewhere in this volume, but several are not.

Eastern and Central Forests

North American forests have been devastated by human activity sweeping from east to west. At the time of the European invasion there were about 6,000 square kilometers cleared by the aboriginal inhabitants of Canada and the United States. Since then, approximately 641,000 square kilometers have been cleared. Most of the early European clearing was done to secure fuelwood. In some regions the trend of increasing annual amounts of forest destruc-

H

tion was reversed between 1920 and 1978 because of farm abandonment and concentration, but since then the destruction has intensified.

The exact amount of habitat loss is impossible to calculate. For example, the area of the Great Lakes "cutover lands" reached 127,000 square kilometers in 1920 but today most of this has regenerated to forest. To be sure, this is not the original pine-beech-hemlock forest, but it is forest nonetheless. Elsewhere in the Eastern Deciduous Forest only a few tiny bits survive. There is much regrowth, some of which now has a species composition approaching that of the original forest, but lacking the size.

North American Grasslands and Savannas

North American grasslands and savannas have been almost completely converted to cropland and pastures, totaling 956,000 square kilometers. Tallgrass prairie has been hit especially hard. In Manitoba, for example, less than 1 percent of the original tallgrass prairie remains, consisting of a few areas each less than 10 hectares in size. This is typical.

Temperate Rainforests

Temperate rainforests have undergone a marked reduction in area because of cutting, especially clearcutting. The effect of clearcutting old-growth rainforest on the survival of the spotted owl is well known. At this writing the struggle to save the old-growth forest around Clayoquot Sound (Vancouver Island) continues. The population of Marbled Murrelet in this region showed a 50 percent drop between 1970 and 1990; at the present rate of decline the species will probably be extirpated from the region within fifty years.

Transcontinental Taiga or Northern Coniferous Forest

From Newfoundland to Alaska, the transcontinental taiga or northern coniferous forest is undergoing more change and habitat loss than any other biome type at present. Fires, pulping, logging, spraying, and clearing for agriculture are the major factors. Alberta has committed about 220,000 square kilometers of its taiga to be cut down over the next sixty years. Manitoba has signed over 20 percent of the total area of the province for cutting by a single company. The area signed away consists of 40 percent of the productive taiga in the province or 198,000 square kilometers. This is the equivalent in size to the U.S. state of North Dakota. The contract is for twenty years, re-newable for another twenty. The company, Repap, is controlled by one person who owns 55 percent of the shares. Thus, 40 percent of the productive taiga in Manitoba is now controlled by one person. Most of the deal was concluded in secret by the government of Manitoba without any public environmental assessment.

One of the characteristic large mammals of the taiga is the woodland caribou. Caribou are few in number, have a low reproductive potential, are secretive, live in small bands and are terribly vulnerable to clearcutting, forest fires, "sports" hunting, poaching, and legal hunting by Treaty Indians. Recent studies in Manitoba have shown that it is not the loss of lichens that first denies a region to woodland caribou but the jackstraw tangle of downed, burned trees that occurs when the roots rot about five years after a fire. The animals show remarkable fidelity to ancestral range until the physical barrier of meter-high tangles stops them. No woodland caribou bands have ever survived a program of even moderately intensive clearcutting in their vicinity. Woodland caribou in Alberta and Manitoba are classified by the Committee on the Status of Endangered Wildlife in Canada (COSEWIC) as "vulnerable," but they should perhaps be classified as "threatened."

Loss of habitat continues in many regions. In one region of Manitoba the percentage of land cleared and cultivated increased from 58 percent to 85 percent between 1948 and 1974, with most of the increase occurring between 1964 and 1970. In the Interlake region of Manitoba, clearing of mature forest for agriculture makes up as much as 7.5 percent of the total area per year. Most of the clearing is subsidized by provincial and federal agricultural agencies.

Labrador is one of the few remaining areas in North America, other than the tundra, where large areas are unexploited for timber. In recent years much of the change/loss has been instigated by governmental initiatives. For example, in Labrador, since near the turn of the century, government financing has supported a series of large-scale logging and pulp operations. Though all have failed they have managed to cut much of the best and easily-accessible timber. Each failed venture has meant reduced chances for real ecologically-sustainable forest operations because less of the commercial-quality easily-accessible forest remains.

Loss of stable-aged ("old-growth") taiga and temperate rainforest is not just incidental to other uses of the forests. In forest succession, maximum productivity of fiber is in "middle-age." "Old-growth" forests parcel energy and materials into increasingly complex numbers of species and microhabitats rather than adding large amounts of fiber. Consequently the aim of market-driven forestry is to eliminate "old-growth" forests and substitute young, preferably monoculture, "tree farms" for maximum production of fiber when they reach "middle-age." Such management is based on the premise that logged areas will never again be permitted to reach an "old-growth" phase. Preservation of biologically-complex, stable-age conditions by selective logging is thus anathema to unregulated profit-oriented forestry.

Tundra

Eleven species of tundra animals (eight mammals and three birds) are listed by the International Union for the Conservation of Nature and Natural Resources (IUCN) as "threatened" throughout their world range and there is concern by IUCN for the survival of twenty-one additional species (eight mammals and thirteen birds). This is a higher percentage than in any other major biome in the world.

Nonetheless tundra is relatively untouched except in certain areas where dramatic changes have occurred. Physical changes such as thermokarst from vehicular traffic are common in restricted lowland or wet areas. Biotic changes are more subtle to detect but do occur. The extensive, misguided wolf poisoning and bounty campaigns in the 1950s and 1960s wreaked havoc not only with wolves, but with colored fox, white fox, wolverine, barren-ground grizzly, and raven occurrences. It has been suggested that the musk ox of eastern Ellesmere Island and northwestern Greenland have never fully recovered from the devastation wreaked on them by the explorers and the expeditions in the Rush for the Pole in the early days of this century. Most of the expeditions fed themselves and their dogs on locally-hunted musk ox and caribou. One expedition, led by the American R.E. Peary, actually partly financed itself through the sale of musk ox and polar bear skins it had taken.

On the basis of the number of species involved there are three important types of tundra breeding range: 1) rocky or cliffy areas with talus; 2) rocky or tussocky uplands, including rolling uplands with birch-heath-cottonsedge tussocks; and 3) sandy eskers. There are two important types of summer range: 1) rocky or tussocky uplands, including rolling uplands with birch-heath-cottonsedge tussocks; and 2) lowlands, stream and lake edges. In addition there is one important type of winter range: well-drained ridges and hillsides. When analyzing these requirements in relation to the relative importance of the species to the tundra ecosystem one must also consider specialized types of caribou winter habitat in tundra, caribou winter range in taiga and forest-tundra, and eskers—winding sandy ridges which function as caribou migration routes and nesting/denning areas for white fox, colored fox, and wolves. This complexity is critical and the preservation of one or two types of habitat will not be sufficient to ensure species well-being. This example should be kept in mind as regards many species in many other types of habitat.

One might also note that only one tundra type is relatively unimportant for animals: lowlands in winter. There is also a marked correlation between those landscape types that exhibit a wide spectrum of snow cover types and their suitability as animal habitats. The more varied the snow cover (patches of exposed ground, varied drift types, complete cover, hard snow, soft snow, etc.) the more species of animals can use the area. Thus, for the tundra, we know which landscape types to protect in order to maintain species.

Coastal Habitats

Coastal habitats are exceedingly important as breeding or overwintering habitats for a wide variety of organisms. In the United States, for example, 70 percent of the commercial fish and 65 percent of the recreational fish come from estuaries. Habitat change may occur through a range of human activities, seemingly unrelated to the coastal habitat concerned: incoming fresh water, damming, poldering, drainage, pollution (dissolved, particulate, thermal), agricultural (haying, grazing), solar salt production, augmenting recreational beaches, and many other forms of imposition. The total loss is thus considerable. For example, in the state of Louisiana, coastal wetlands are lost at a rate of about 100 square kilometers per year, totaling 3,500 square kilometers of the coastal zone. In Florida, about 10 million m^3 of sand have been added to one seventeen-kilometer stretch of recreational beach to increase its width to ninety meters. No information is available on the biological changes caused by the addition or on the source area from which the sand was obtained.

Deserts

The full potential of the human assault on deserts has not been felt in all desert locations. Prior to air conditioning and water transfers the impacts were minimal. Since the widespread use of water transfers has been initiated the loss of desert habitat to agriculture has been extensive throughout the U.S. West and in recent decades the losses to residential development, golf courses, and the like has been severe, especially in California and Arizona. The plants and animals of this specialized habitat in most cases cannot survive elsewhere; their numbers have thus been severely diminished in many cases, especially perhaps in the case of cacti and succulents.

Conclusion

To offset habitat loss and preserve these valuable resources ways must be found to restrain the encroachment of human settlement and resource extraction on the spaces of nonhuman species of all kinds. If limiting human numbers cannot be restrained and even reduced, somehow limiting the average space assumed by each occupant on a daily basis and/or regulating the amount of resources that may be extracted for food production and recreation may be our only options.

William O. Pruitt, Jr.

Further Readings

Colinvaux, P. *The Fates of Nations: A Biological Theory of History.* 1980.

Schaefer, J.A., and W.O. Pruitt, Jr. *Fire and Woodland Caribou in Southeastern Manitoba.* Wildlife Monographs No. 116, 1991.

Turner, B.L., et al., eds. *The Earth as Transformed by Human Actions.* 1990.

See also ARCTIC; BEARS: CONSERVATION AND HABITAT; BISON: CONSERVATION AND HABITAT; CLAYOQUOT SOUND; COASTAL MARSHES, CONSERVATION OF; COUGARS: CONSERVATION AND HABITAT; EVERGLADES OF SOUTH FLORIDA; FLORIDA PANTHER; FOREST FRAGMENTATION AND BIRD HABITATS; FRESHWATER WETLANDS; HABITAT FRAGMENTATION, PATCHES, AND CORRIDORS; IUCN; LANDSCAPE ECOLOGY; OLD GROWTH FORESTS; RANGELANDS (U.S.); SNOW AS HABITAT; TOP PREDATORS IN CANADA: AN OVERVIEW; UNGULATES; WILDERNESS; WILDLIFE PROTECTION: HISTORY; WOLF: A CONSERVATION CHALLENGE

Hardin, Garrett

Born on April 21, 1915, in Dallas, Texas, Garrett Hardin graduated from the University of Chicago in 1936. He obtained his Ph.D. from Stanford University in 1942 studying microbial ecology. Hardin worked for four years at the Carnegie Institution, culturing algae for human food, a position from which he resigned partly because he had been a student of Malthusian population theory under W.C. Allee at Chicago; he knew that the problem of food shortage for an ever-expanding population could not be solved by merely increasing the supply of food.

He joined the biology department at the University of California-Santa Barbara in 1946 and devoted his energies to developing a biology course for the general citizen, honing his skills as educator, public speaker, and iconoclastic thinker. Hardin became an activist in 1963, first in the abortion reform area, then in the environmental movement when his famous 1968 essay, "The Tragedy of the Commons," was published, propelling him to the forefront of environmentalism in the United States. Increasing requests for his services led him to reduce his teaching commitment at the University after 1970; he took early retirement in 1978.

C.J. Bajema has written that Hardin "has forced more people to think about taboo subjects in biology than any other living biologist." He has authored at least a dozen books including *Filters against Folly* (1985), which contains Hardin's recipe for developing critical thinking skills to help "survive despite economists, ecologists and the merely eloquent": a literacy filter (what words best describe the situation?), a numeracy filter (what numbers best describe the situation?) and an ecolacy filter ("and then what?"). Hardin has described himself as an ecoconservative, holding the position that the society that survives is the society that develops and conserves those rules that serve the long-term interests of society.

Fikret Berkes

Further Readings

Bajema, C.J. "Garrett James Hardin: Ecologist, Educator, Ethicist and Environmentalist." *Population and Environment* 12 (1991): 193–212.

Hardin, Garrett. *New Ethics for Survival.* 1972.

———. *Stalking the Wild Taboo.* 1973.

———. *The Limits of Altruism.* 1977.

———. *Promethean Ethics.* 1980.

———. *Naked Emperors.* 1982.

———. *Filters against Folly.* 1985.
———. *Living within Limits.* 1993.

See also COMMON PROPERTY RESOURCE MANAGEMENT; MALTHUS, ROBERT THOMAS; POPULATION CONTROL; TRAGEDY OF THE COMMONS

Hawk Shooting

Like many predatory animals—eagles, falcons, owls, and other raptorial birds—hawks have long been persecuted by humans, chiefly because of alleged or actual injury to game or livestock. Others have been shot simply for sport, or for their trophy value. Systematic efforts to eliminate raptors date from the seventeenth century, when the British aristocracy placed bounties on all predatory birds. Earlier in this century raptors were unprotected in most of North America, and bounties were offered on many species. With a few notable exceptions, turn-of-the-century bird protectionists generally held raptors in low regard, in large part because several species, including the sharp-shinned hawk (*Accipiter striatus*), Cooper's hawk (*Accipiter cooperii*), and northern goshawk (*Accipiter gentilis*) were known to feed principally on wild birds. Hawk shooting was rarely mentioned as a conservation issue at the time and, when it was, raptors were often classified as "good" or "bad" depending upon their diets. As a result, hawk shooting—chiefly for sport but at some sites for bounty profit as well—flourished in North America. This was especially true during fall migration when the large numbers of birds converged in massive flights along established migratory corridors.

In an effort to reverse this trend in 1934 New York conservationist Rosalie Edge purchased a 1,400-acre parcel of land in the central Appalachian mountains of eastern Pennsylvania and converted it from a shooting gallery for hawks into Hawk Mountain Sanctuary, the world's first refuge for predatory birds and a preeminent birding attraction. Persistent lobbying on the part of Edge and others eventually resulted in the passage of the Model Hawk Law in Pennsylvania in 1970, which for the first time afforded hawks year-round protection in that state. Two years later the Migratory Bird Treaty Act between the United States and Canada was amended to protect all migratory hawks in North America.

Hawks continue to be persecuted elsewhere in the world for a number of reasons. In Malta, Italy, and other locations in the Mediterranean, tens of thousands of migrating raptors are shot annually, mainly for recreation, as well as for their value as taxidermy specimens. In the Andes of Colombia, South America, migrating raptors are shot each spring because local villagers believe that fat rendered from the birds' bodies has medicinal benefits, and that shooting the birds hastens the passage of Lent. Although most countries currently have laws protecting raptors enforcement is often lax or nonexistent. The impact of shooting on species populations remains unclear.

Keith L. Bildstein and Laurie J. Goodrich

Further Readings
Broun, M. *Hawks Aloft: The Story of Hawk Mountain.* 1949.
Fenech, N. *Fatal Flight: The Maltese Obsession with Killing Birds.* 1992.
Newton, I., and R.D. Chancellor. *Conservation Studies on Raptors.* 1985.

See also BALD EAGLE; BIRDING; NATIONAL AUDUBON SOCIETY; PEREGRINE FALCON

Hayes, Denis

See EARTH DAY; SOLAR ENERGY RESEARCH INSTITUTE

Hazardous Waste Treatment Facility Siting

The siting of hazardous waste treatment facilities has become one of the most controversial environmental issues to have emerged in recent years. Many nations now face the realization that, whether proposed by governmental agencies or private waste management firms, the selection of a community or communities to host a hazardous waste incinerator, landfill, or treatment facility consistently triggers local public outrage. In most instances the siting proposal is withdrawn or rejected, making it increasingly difficult to open new facilities and introduce new waste treatment technologies.

This phenomenon is most commonly known as the Not-In-My-Back-Yard (or NIMBY) Syndrome. It is also increasingly evident in other areas of facility siting, including those intended for radioactive, biomedical, and solid wastes, as well as controversial facilities such as prisons, drug and alcohol rehabilitation centers, and airports. In all such cases any benefits to be derived from facility siting are likely to be widely distributed. By contrast most costs and risks related to facility operation will be concentrated within a single community (and its neighbors).

This imbalance provides considerable incentives for potential host communities to take aggressive political action intended to thwart siting. Such tactics may include litigation, appeal to administrative bodies, media outreach, or direct political protest. Local, grass-roots organizations often form quickly in such circumstances, galvanizing public opposition in relatively short amounts of time.

National and subnational governments have devised a wide array of siting policies in recent years but most have failed to foster prolonged public dialogue much less attain siting agreements. The most widely employed strategy, at least in North America, has addressed facility siting—and hazardous waste management more generally—as a private, commercial phenomenon. Under such circumstances the role of government is minimized and private firms approach directly those communities they deem promising in facilitating siting agreements, with generous compensation programs expected to dampen any public concerns. Proposed compensation may include employment guarantees to area residents, direct subsidies to local governments, commitments of extensive safety procedures, and assurances against decline in local property values. However, in the vast majority of siting cases that have operated under this "market" approach, compensation has failed to quiet public objections.

North American and European governments have also experimented with more governmentally-dominated siting processes. In these cases designated agencies establish technical siting criteria in search of preferred sites. Upon selecting one or more candidates these agencies attempt to either entice or compel communities to accept them. Governments may pursue fairly aggressive strategies, such as condemning or seizing property they deem most suitable for siting. However, as in the case of privately-dominated siting, these top-down governmental efforts have repeatedly failed to win public support and reach siting agreements.

Numerous alternatives to prevailing siting approaches have been attempted. Perhaps the most promising has been the successful effort in the Canadian provinces of Alberta and Manitoba to transform siting into a larger, voluntary political process. In both provinces governmental officials conducted widespread public information campaigns and agreed to pursue siting only among those communities that volunteered to be actively considered. Through extensive negotiations that placed special emphasis on continuous public involvement, compensation, and the treatment of siting as part of a larger provincial waste management strategy, broadly-accepted agreements were reached in recent years. This voluntary approach has yet to be tested on a wider scale and may prove difficult to introduce given high levels of public alienation with private and public authorities on this issue.

There is considerable debate over the larger policy ramifications of this general inability to site new hazardous waste treatment facilities. On the positive side, the NIMBY phenomenon has effectively ended the historic approach to siting that so often involved the operation of slipshod treatment facilities with little if any public awareness. Indeed the extraordinary pace of NIMBY group formation and passionate commitment of group members suggests increasingly broad public commitment to involvement in environmental governance. Moreover the virtual inability to open new treatment facilities in recent years has put mounting pressure on both private and public concerns to give greater attention than ever before to preventive waste strategies, such as waste minimization and reduction.

On the negative side preventive strategies are not likely to eliminate the need for additional waste treatment capacity. Massive volumes of hazardous waste continue to be generated in all developed nations and the absence of new treatment facilities has generated an increasingly desperate search for treatment options. In many cases promising new treatment technologies are not being widely employed, existing facilities are being kept operational longer than intended, and wastes must be shipped increasingly long distances. Each of these poses an added set of environmental concerns.

In turn the NIMBY phenomenon has contributed to a growing set of intranational and international equity issues concerning the geographic distribution of waste treatment burden in the absence of new facility development. This has served to exacerbate existing race and class tensions, as evidence mounts that nations and regions with high minority populations and the most limited economic and political resources are increasingly becoming magnets for the treatment of wastes that more affluent areas can thwart through political action.

Barry G. Rabe

Further Readings

Gerrard, Michael B. *Whose Backyard, Whose Risk: Fear and Fairness in Toxic and Nuclear Waste Siting* (Cambridge: MIT Press, 1994).

Portney, Kent. *Siting Hazardous Waste Treatment Facilities: The NIMBY Syndrome.* 1991.

Rabe, Barry G. *Beyond Nimby: Hazardous Waste Siting in Canada and the United States* (Washington, D.C.: Brookings Institution, 1994).

Williams, Bruce, and Albert Matheny. *Democracy, Dialogue and Social Regulation: Being Fair Versus Being Right.* 1995.

See also ALTERNATIVE DISPUTE RESOLUTION; CITIZENS' CLEARINGHOUSE FOR HAZARDOUS WASTE; ENVIRONMENTAL JUSTICE MOVEMENT; HAZARDOUS WASTE TREATMENT TECHNOLOGIES; NIMBY SYNDROME; NUCLEAR WASTE

Hazardous Waste Treatment Technologies

The uncontrolled release of hazardous wastes into the environment would not only cause immense harm to human health but would put the environment as a whole at an unacceptable level of risk. It is therefore imperative to manage hazardous waste in such a manner as to protect both human health and the environment. The first step in managing hazardous waste is waste minimization, which includes a group of practices commonly referred to as the 3Rs—Reducing, Reusing, and Recycling. Since even these practices are limited in the extent of their use other methods of storing, treating, and disposing of hazardous waste need to be considered.

Hazardous waste by its very nature contains a complex mixture of contaminants. Treatment of each waste stream or combination of waste streams, therefore, requires a careful selection of applicable treatment technologies to reduce possible risks to health and the environment in accordance with the existing array of acceptable limits. The development of new technologies and the improvement of existing technologies over the years has paved the way for significant reductions in the regulatory limits of allowable concentrations of contaminants in aqueous and gaseous discharges.

Hazardous waste treatment technologies can be classified into three types: 1) conventional technologies (e.g., high temperature incineration, phase separation, chemical oxidation/reduction); 2) developing/demonstration technologies (e.g., Plasma Arc Vitrification); and 3) emerging technologies (e.g., Laser Induced Photochemical Oxidative Destruction). The aim of these technologies is to treat hazardous waste to the extent possible so as to not only meet minimum regulatory requirements but also to minimize any harmful concentration of contaminants in the liquid and gaseous discharges, while still respecting the safety of each process.

Most hazardous wastes are either organic wastes or inorganic wastes—each requiring very different treatment technologies. Waste made up of mainly organic constituents is often treated by high temperature incineration, although other technologies have been developed to treat certain types of waste containing organic constituents (e.g., gas-phase chemical reduction process). Waste containing inorganic constituents is commonly treated by well-known processes using oxidation, reduction, precipitation, and filtration as main treatment steps. *In situ* treatment of hazardous waste requires technologies designed specifically for each particular situation.

Thermal Treatment

Conventional thermal treatment technologies have been used for many years. It is well known that of all the permanent treatment technologies properly designed, incineration systems are capable of the highest overall degree of destruction and control for the broadest range of hazardous waste streams. A wide variety of commercial systems are available with substantial design and operational experience existing for hazardous waste incinerators. The use of incineration and other thermal destruction methods is an important treatment step for most organic hazardous wastes.

Thermal destruction offers many advantages over alternative hazardous waste treatment practices and could help meet in part the anticipated need for increased waste management capacity. However, public opposition to the use of thermal destruction operations has been strong in many locations in recent years. Regulatory agencies in many parts of the industrialized world have responded to public concern by passing regulations and directives placing very low limits on the maximum concentrations of contaminants in the flue gases. The industry in turn has responded with technologies, specifically in the flue gas treatment systems, to meet these very stringent requirements. This coupled with modern computer-based process controls, continuous emission monitoring devices, and data acquisition systems has made incineration systems an environmentally responsible technology for the disposal of many organic hazardous wastes.

Incineration is an engineered process that employs thermal decomposition via thermal oxidation at high temperature, operating in the 1,000-degree Celsius range with temperature requirements in the 1,200-degree Celsius range not uncommon. The organic fraction of the waste is largely destroyed and the total volume is significantly reduced. Generally, combustible wastes or wastes with significant organic content are considered most appropriate for incineration. Technically, however, any waste with a hazardous organic fraction, no matter how small, is at least a functional candidate for incineration. Contaminated soils are also being incinerated with increasing frequency. The most common incineration technologies are: 1) liquid injection; 2) rotary kiln (usually with secondary combustion chamber); 3) fixed hearth (includes multiple hearth); and 4) fluidized bed.

Ample written material in textbooks and/or vendor literature exists to obtain details for each of the four technologies listed including the multitude of air pollution control devices and their arrangement in the flue gas treatment train. A waste heat boiler is often incorporated into the system which recovers the waste heat to produce steam for further use and at the same time cool the combustion gases.

Air Pollution Control Systems

A properly designed air pollution control system (or flue gas cleaning system as it is often called) is an integral part of any good incineration system. Flue gas cleaning system designers and users have many preferences. They also have many components from which to choose. In most cases the control for minimizing contaminant release focuses on acid gases (i.e., hydrogen chloride [HCl], hydrogen fluoride [HF], and sulfur dioxide [SO_2], carbon monoxide [CO], nitrogen oxides [NO_x], hydrocarbons, and particulate matter. The latter includes a great portion of heavy metals that may be present in the waste feed.

Technologies available for flue gas cleaning systems include:

- "knock-out" chambers
- mechanical multi-cyclones
- wet electrostatic precipitators
- wet scrubbers (disposable reagent)
- dry scrubbers
- selective catalytic reduction (NO_x removal)
- ionizing wet scrubbers
- mechanical cyclones
- electrostatic precipitators (dry)
- fabric filters
- wet scrubbers (regenerable reagent)
- semi-dry scrubbers
- electrostatically augmented scrubbers
- irradiation processes

Technologies most commonly used are composed of a system which may include a combination of seven technologies:

- electrostatic precipitator (dry)
- fabric filter (bag house)
- semi-dry scrubber
- ionizing wet scrubber
- electrostatic precipitator (wet)
- wet scrubber (disposable reagent)
- electrostatically augmented scrubber

Each of these seven technologies has been used commercially in full-scale industrial waste incineration systems and has been demonstrated to work effectively. A spray dryer also may be included in the system if a dry discharge of salt and ash is required.

The incineration process in most hazardous waste applications is a continuous high temperature process in which the individual technologies form a complex dynamic system. Hence the emphasis must be on the performance of the system as a whole not just the individual components. Burning of wastes at lower temperatures could result in some release of contaminants; for this reason automatic shutdown devices are a part of modern hazardous waste incinerators.

Physical/Chemical Treatment

Physical/chemical treatment is a process that uses physical and/or chemical means to treat, detoxify, break down, or stabilize waste material to reduce or eliminate completely harmful contaminants in a waste stream. Physical/chemical processes are usually applied to wastes of an inorganic nature although oil/water mixtures and emulsions may be treated first by a physical/chemical process (e.g. emulsion splitting). Many of these technologies are widely used and well proven processes. Others are applied as appropriate.

Although oxidation, reduction, precipitation, and filtration processes are most often associated with physical/chemical treatment processes there are many other technologies that are used for physical/chemical treatment of hazardous waste. See table 1.

TABLE 1

Technologies Used for Physical/Chemical Treatment of Hazardous Waste

calcination	freeze drying
carbon adsorption	high gradient magnetic
catalysis	separation
centrifugation	hydrolysis
chelation	ion exchange
chemical	liquid ion
oxidation	microwave/plasma
chemical	arc discharge
reduction	neutralization/
chlorinolysis	precipitation
coagulation/	oxidation
flocculation	pervaporation
dehalogenation	photolysis
detonation	resin adsorption
dissolution	reverse osmosis
distillation	sedimentation
electroacoustic	solvent extraction
dewatering	stripping
electrodialysis	supercritical fluid
electrolysis	supercritical water oxidation
electrophoresis	suspension freezing
evaporation	ultrafiltration
filtration	vertical tube wet air oxidation
flotation	wet air oxidation
freeze	zone refining
crystallization	

Biological Treatment

Biological treatment relies on living organisms such as bacteria, algae, fungi, and microorganisms to decompose/detoxify contaminants in hazardous waste. Although biological treatment is a well-known technology its application to hazardous waste is sometimes tricky due to the variability of hazardous waste constituents. Given the right conditions, however, biological treatment can handle aqueous/organic waste streams containing biodegradable pollutants. For a list of biological treatment technologies refer to table 2.

TABLE 2

Biological Treatment Technologies

aerated lagoon	landfarming
activated sludge	powdered activated carbon
anaerobic digestion	rotating biological contactor
bioremediation	sequencing batch reactor
composting	trickling filter
enzyme treatment	waste stabilization pond
fluidized bed	
biological contactor	

Solidification

Solidification is better characterized as solidification, stabilization, and fixation. The processes of solidification are intended to immobilize hazardous/toxic constituents within the waste and to greatly reduce the rate at which these constituents are released into the environment. Solidification can also be used as a final treatment step for waste residues resulting from physical/chemical treatment or from an incineration process. Solidification also improves the physical stability of the waste prior to final disposal such as in an appropriately designed landfill.

Most solidification systems involve the addition of stabilizing and hardening agents. These include:

- cement-based agents (e.g., Portland cements, flyash/cement, kiln dust, and soluble silicate-based compounds)
- lime-based pozzolanics
- thermoplastics (including bitumen, paraffin, and polyethylene)
- organic polymers (e.g., urea formaldehyde and unsaturated polyester)

In situ solidification is often applied in landfill remediation work by blending solidification agents into soils with mixing paddles and augers. Several propriety solidification processes are available and can be custom-formulated to meet specific waste streams.

Waste Disposal Methods: Landfilling

Landfilling is a common way to dispose of treated waste residues from hazardous wastes. Properly designed engineered landfills (also known as "secure chemical" or simply "chemical" landfills) provide for the long-term isolation of waste residues from the environment. This is achieved by first limiting the waste residues that are acceptable for landfilling and subsequently controlling all emissions to groundwater, surface water, or air. Three types of landfill are identified: 1) conventional; 2) above-ground; and 3) shallow entombed. In a conventional secure chemical landfill solidified wastes are placed in excavated cells or trenches in such a way that some of the waste is placed below the ground and some above ground eventually forming a mound. In an above-ground landfill the cells are constructed entirely above ground level, eventually forming a mound; in a shallow entombed landfill the cells or trenches are constructed in such a way that all waste residues are placed below ground level and below the fractured zone of the soil thus preventing rapid movement of leachate as would occur within the fractured zone.

In any of these three configurations a secure chemical landfill should be: 1) sited in an appropriate geologic and hydrogeologic setting; 2) isolated from ground, surface, and stormwater contact; 3) secured against public access/exposure; 4) equipped with primary and perhaps secondary liner systems (both flexible membrane and clay liners are used); 5) associated with monitoring wells and related systems; and designed for post-closure maintenance, monitoring, and 6) the collection and treatment of leachate. Daily operation involves strict protocols for laboratory analysis, record keeping, pretreatment, placement, covering, and capping of all wastes accepted.

Developing Innovative Technologies

As in any industry technological changes, development of new processes, and responding to new regulations is an ongoing process. Hence, technologies for hazardous waste treatment are continuously being developed and tried for possible large-scale application. Technologies that fall into this group are too numerous to mention; new technologies are constantly being added while some that showed promise at one time are being discontinued. For example, thermal treatment technologies presently considered to be new or innovative are high- and low-temperature plasmas, molten salt, molten glass, and molten metal baths.

A recent publication by the U.S. Environmental Protection Agency (EPA) reports extensively on technologies being evaluated under the Demonstration Program (ninety-three technologies listed), those under the Emerging Technology Program (sixty-four technologies listed), and those under the Monitoring and Measurement Technologies Program (fifteen technologies listed). In addition EPA assesses international technologies applicable to hazardous waste site remediation.

Conclusion

The proper management of hazardous waste can only be achieved through a dedicated effort whether by operators treating hazardous waste as a business in off-site facilities or by generators who treat that waste in their own on-site facilities. The twenty-first century can hopefully expect to see a continuation of the already great advances in hazardous waste treatment technologies. Most industrialized nations have promulgated stringent regulations and directives for the proper management of hazardous waste so as not to put the environment at risk through emissions of contaminants in liquid discharges, contaminants discharged into the atmosphere, or fugitive releases of contaminants.

Nonetheless, industries that generate hazardous waste must assign first priority to reducing, recycling, and reusing wastes to the maximum extent possible. The maintaining of a clean environment into the twenty-first century and beyond must be given top priority by industry, regulators, and the public alike.

Edgar H. Schmidt

Further Readings

Dempsey, Clyde R., and E. Timothy Oppelt. "Incineration of Hazardous Waste: A Critical Review Update." *Journal of the Air and Waste Management Association* (January 1993): 25–73.

Ontario Waste Management Corporation. *OWMC Guide to Hazardous Waste Terminology.* 1993.

United States Environmental Protection Agency. "Superfund Innovative Technology Evaluation Program." *Technology Profiles.* 6th ed. EPA/540/R-93/526, 1993.

United States Environmental Protection Agency. *Assessment of International Technologies for Superfund Application.* EPA/540/2-88, 1988.

See also CITIZENS' CLEARINGHOUSE FOR HAZARDOUS WASTES; ENVIRONMENTAL JUSTICE MOVEMENT; HAZARDOUS WASTE TREATMENT FACILITY SITING; LOVE CANAL; PERSISTENT ORGANOCHLORINE COMPOUNDS; VOLATILE ORGANIC COMPOUNDS; WATER POLLUTION ABATEMENT TECHNOLOGIES

Heavy Metals

See CADMIUM; LEAD; MERCURY

Herbicides

Herbicides are chemicals used to kill weeds—uncultivated plants that grow in profusion causing undesired effects (i.e., damage to crop, destroying aesthetic landscaping, etc.). Virtually unknown before 1940, herbicides valued at billions of dollars are now manufactured and sold each year. They are extensively used in agriculture, forestry, industry, transportation, recreation, aquatic areas, and the home lawn and garden. Use is most intense in the industrialized countries of North America, Europe, and Japan but herbicides are used in many less industrialized countries as well.

Prior to 1940 a number of chemicals were known for their general ability to kill plants, such as sodium chloride (common salt), smelter wastes, and oil products. However, such compounds were not often used except in highly localized settings such as industrial areas. Farmers were not likely to use such materials because they tended to kill all plants indiscriminately, including crops. Several researchers in the early 1940s, investigating the action of plant growth regulators and hoping to find selective effects on different plants, discovered that 2,4-dichlorophenoxyacetic acid or 2,4-D, possessed the desired differential killing effects. Broad leaved plants were highly susceptible compared to grasses and grains. Moreover, the compound degraded so that after a period it was no longer poisonous to plants.

Thus was born a new industry to find and manufacture synthetic herbicides. Within a few years, 2,4-D was joined by 2,4,5-trichlorophenoxyacetic acid (2,4,5-T; 1944), triazine herbicides such as atrazine (1958), organic phosphorus compounds such as glyphosate (1971), amides such as alachlor (1969), and bipyridylium compounds such as paraquat (1958). These chemicals disrupted plant growth by a variety of different mechanisms. Although compounds can have multiple effects characteristic examples of disruption to plant growth include the following:

1. Hormonal herbicides such as 2,4-D disrupt the normal growth patterns of plants in complex ways.
2. Triazines inhibit photosynthesis.
3. Glyphosate inhibits protein synthesis by interfering with the synthesis of certain amino acids.
4. Amides such as alachlor are general growth inhibitors.
5. The bipyridylium compounds disrupt cell membranes, thus causing the death of cells.

Farmers soon learned that they could partially replace the costly operations of plowing and cultivating with herbicides. Although plowing and cultivating were usually more effective at killing weeds, herbicides were easier, faster, and cheaper to apply. They substantially reduced the amount of labor that had to be invested to produce a crop. Over 10 million kilograms of 2,4-D, for example, were used in the United States in 1951. This compound's use grew to over 30 million kilograms in 1968. After 1960 herbicides became the type of pesticide with the fastest growing sales volumes. By 1985, 755 million pounds of herbicides were produced in the United States compared to 378 million pounds of insecticides and 109 million pounds of fungicides.

Herbicides have become so deeply ingrained in industrial countries that their removal could not be accomplished without substantial disruptions to established patterns and norms. Farming, for example, now occupies only a tiny fraction of the people in the total labor force (e.g., less than 3 percent in the United States). Millions of people who once worked in agriculture now make their livelihoods elsewhere. American cities and suburbs are filled with the retirees or descendants of people who once spent much time killing weeds. Similarly high intensity forestry practices are based on herbicides to control shrubs and hardwoods so as to quickly reestablish a stand of fast-growing conifers. The use of hand labor as an alternative would result in higher overall production and product costs. On the aesthetic side, many people now expect lawns to have only grass in them and will not tolerate dandelions and other broad-leafed plants. Lawns free of these weeds are generally possible only with the selective poisoning action of herbicides.

Proponents of herbicide use have extolled the labor-saving properties of the compounds with their consequent ability to make farm production and other industrial uses more efficient. While these claims unquestionably have merit, extensive herbicide use has also generated much controversy.

Possibly the first major argument over herbicides in the United States occurred in 1959. Cranberry growers had used the compound aminotriazole and residues appeared in the harvested crop. Unfortunately since this compound had tested as a carcinogen in rodent bioassays the U.S. Food and Drug Administration was obliged to seize the contaminated cranberries. Over the Thanksgiving period Americans witnessed an immense debate between the growers and the federal government. Vice-President Nixon, publicly taking the side of the growers, ate four helpings of cranberries in public to demonstrate the herbicide's safety.

In the 1960s herbicides again appeared in a major environmental debate. Military strategists in the United States decided that defoliating vast areas of forest in South Vietnam and destroying strategic crop areas, all with aerially applied herbicides, would help turn the tide of war against North Vietnam and their allies in the South. Thus 3.58 million acres or 8.6 percent of the area of South Vietnam was sprayed at least once between 1965 and 1971. The most popular of several herbicides used was Agent Orange, a 50:50 mixture of 2,4-D and 2,4,5-T. Opponents of the war railed against this ill-considered and devastating strategy. Subsequently American war veterans came to believe they had been poisoned by contamination of Agent Orange with 2,3,7,8-tetrachlorodibenzo-para-dioxin. The combination of the war and the complaints of the veterans created an immensely bad public relations problem for herbicides.

More recently herbicides (in addition to other pesticides) began showing up in groundwater in many locations throughout the United States. Atrazine, for example, is the most commonly detected pesticide in groundwater monitoring in the United States. About 75 to 90 million pounds of the chemical are used each year in the United States alone. Since many citizens including farmers depend upon groundwater for their drinking supplies local, state, and federal governments began to take action to curtail the use of some chemicals and to guard against contamination of aquifer recharge areas.

In addition to the debate over threats posed by residues in crops and groundwater contamination a further argument against the use of herbicides is that of an increased risk of cancer to the people who make and use herbicides. Researchers from the National Cancer Institute studied exposure to 2,4-D among farmers in Kansas and Nebraska. They found an increased risk of contacting non-Hodgkins lymphoma among men who used the chemical intensively over a period of years. Other researchers have argued that the evidence against 2,4-D as a carcinogen, however, is still not strong enough to conclude the case.

Despite the environmental controversy over these ubiquitous chemicals, they also have enjoyed popularity among conservation workers for use in some contexts. No-till farming schemes rely on herbicides almost completely to control weeds and keep a plant cover on the soil all year long. As a result soil erosion in no-till agriculture is vastly reduced compared to practices that involve more plowing. Similarly, wetland biologists who wish to restore or create wetlands have sometimes turned to herbicides to promote the growth of wetland vegetation and keep out invading plants such as reed canary grass.

For the immediate future herbicides will continue to be used. Controversies over their safety or lack thereof will also continue. Alternative technologies for weed control eventually may be encouraged by this argument but no major contenders have appeared to date. At present only a resumption of higher labor inputs could substitute for the current efficiencies gained from using these chemicals. Unless herbicides become politically more unacceptable it is unlikely that industrialized countries will put more labor into weed control under current economic conditions.

John H. Perkins

Further Readings

Belluck, D.A., S.L. Benjamin, and T. Dawson. "Groundwater Contamination by Atrazine and its Metabolites." In *Pesticide Transformation Products*. Ed. L. Somasundaram and J.R. Coats. 1991.

Bovey, Rodney W., and Alvin L. Young. *The Science of 2,4,5-T and Associated Phenoxy Herbicides*. 1980.

Ibrahim, M.A., et al. "Weight of the Evidence on the Human Carcinogenicity of 2,4-D." *Environmental Health Perspectives* 96 (1991).

National Research Council. *The Effects of Herbicides in South Vietnam*. 1974.

See also DIOXINS AND FURANS; INTEGRATED PEST MANAGEMENT; PESTICIDES; SUSTAINABLE AGRICULTURE

Hetch Hetchy Dam

Hetch Hetchy Valley—a spectacular granite canyon at an elevation of 3,700 feet near the edge of the Sierra Nevada range of California—is like the Yosemite Valley: deep, glacially carved, and scenic. John Muir called it the "Tuolumne Yosemite" because it bears the same relation to the Tuolumne River's watershed and glacial history that Yosemite Valley bears to the Merced River. Both complete watersheds were designated as part of Yosemite National Park in 1890. Muir conceived of the Tuolumne's watershed and canyons as the wild and unimproved part of the park.

Following the Reclamation Act of 1902 James D. Phelan, mayor of San Francisco, applied unsuccessfully for the valley to become a reservoir site for culinary water. After the earthquake and fire of 1906 the city reapplied successfully in 1907. So began the Hetch Hetchy controversy, including substantial public and congressional debate. The U.S. Senate approved the reservation of the Hetch Hetchy Reservoir site within Yosemite National Park, and President Wilson signed the bill on December 19, 1913. The dam was completed in 1925.

The controversy was shaped by the direction of the conservation movement at the beginning of the twentieth century, and in turn became a paradigm of the arguments used in subsequent conflicts over the uses of wild lands. During this first national debate over the aesthetic and utilitarian values of natural lands issues of federal land-use policy were debated and ideologies of conservation conflicted; Hetch Hetchy became a symbol of these conflicts. In the absence of a National Park Service (which was not established until 1916) the debate began with the precedent of a dam within a national park. That was only the beginning.

Gifford Pinchot, President Theodore Roosevelt, and progressives siding with San Francisco defended their conservation program, arguing that domestic economic use was more important than sentimental or scenic values. Those who came to be called preservationists—most prominently John Muir of the Sierra Club—spoke for the non-economic uses of natural lands. "Dam Hetch Hetchy!" wrote Muir, "As well dam for water-tanks the people's cathedrals and churches . . . ." Not only did the controversy split the emerging ideology of conservation but it also split conservationist organizations. The Sierra Club of San Francisco dramatized such divided allegiances when many members resigned and Muir and his colleagues campaigned without full Club support.

Partly because the split in the ranks of conservationists became permanent the tone of the arguments between use and preservation and the rhetorical strategies available to these positions were fixed during this controversy. They would be repeated in the controversy over Echo Park Dam (1949–1956) and over the Wilderness Bill of 1964. Yet the legacy of the controversy is itself paradoxical. On the one hand, Hetch Hetchy dramatized the violability of American National Parks and wild areas by economic pressure, which would be repeatedly demonstrated in the century. On the other hand it demonstrated the receptivity of the public to aesthetic and moral arguments about parks and public lands.

Michael P. Cohen

Further Readings

Jones, Holway R. *John Muir and the Sierra Club: The Battle for Yosemite.* 1965.

Nash, Roderick. *Wilderness and the American Mind.* 1967.

See also ECHO PARK DAM; MUIR, JOHN; NATIONAL PARK SERVICE (U.S.); NATIONAL PARKS: UNITED STATES; PINCHOT, GIFFORD; SIERRA CLUB

Heyerdahl, Thor

Thor Heyerdahl (1914–) is a Norwegian anthropologist whose most famous contribution involves his testing of the migratory capabilities of early humans by making voyages in the kinds of crafts that such early peoples might have built. Heyerdahl used his method to dispel the popular notion that the islands of Polynesia must have been settled by Asians. In 1947 Heyerdahl proposed that the tide of migration might have come from the other direction—from the Native American populations of South America. He built a raft of Peruvian balsa, named it Kon-Tiki (after a legendary Peruvian god and the Polynesian sun god Tiki), and successfully sailed to a reef south of the Marquesas. Heyerdahl theorized that Easter Island might have been settled in the same fashion and wrote a book explaining this idea, *Aku-Aku*, in 1958. He also showed that ancient Egyptians could have sailed to the New World in boats made of papyrus reeds. In 1970 his second attempt to achieve this goal was successful in Ra II, a craft named after the Egyptian sun god.

In the course of his widely followed voyages Heyerdahl did a great deal to publicize the fact that the oceans of the world were polluted and filled with litter throughout much of their vast expanse. Although Heyerdahl's theories of migration are disputed his major contribution to environmental and ecological thought—his demonstration that so-called "primitive" peoples without modern technology are nonetheless capable of amazing feats—has helped to temper the judgment of those who encounter such peoples.

Jim Baird

Further Readings
Heyerdahl, Thor. *Aku-Aku*. 1958.
———. *Kon-Tiki*. 1950.
———. *The Ra Expeditions*. 1971.

See also COASTAL DEBRIS AND CLEANUP;
COUSTEAU, JACQUES-YVES

HHW
See HOUSEHOLD HAZARDOUS WASTES

Hopewell, Virginia (Kepone) Spill
The Life Science Products Company of Hopewell, Virginia, produced the pesticide Kepone under an exclusive contract with the Allied Chemical Corporation, for which several Life Sciences executives once worked. In mid-1975, after operating without apparent problems for several years, Life Sciences was shut down suddenly by state health officials following increasing employee complaints concerning apparently work-related respiratory and nervous system disorders. These ailments were attributed eventually to excessive exposure to Kepone, and state officials charged company management with cutting corners on respirators and other safety equipment. Scores of current and former Life Sciences employees were found with high Kepone residues in their blood; several were hospitalized for a range of related illnesses.

State investigators simultaneously uncovered a history of illegal Kepone dumping into the James River, which empties directly into the Chesapeake Bay. These revelations and the discovery of high Kepone levels in local waters led to a temporary ban on seafood sales from affected areas. Life Sciences itself was closed down in 1976. Allied Chemical eventually was found to bear ultimate responsibility for the production of its pesticide and was fined $13 million for health and environmental violations. In 1977 Allied Chemical agreed to cancel all Kepone production. The company also set up a trust fund to contribute toward the medical expenses of the affected employees.

The Life Sciences case highlighted the problems faced by the Environmental Protection Agency in its efforts to implement the 1972 amendments to the Federal Insecticide, Fungicide and Rodenticide Act (FIFRA). In particular the Kepone issue helped to spark renewed debate over flaws in pesticides registration, plus related occupational health and safety regulations.

Christopher J. Bosso (with Inez Garcia)

Further Readings
Bosso, Christopher J. *Pesticides and Politics: The Life Cycle of a Public Issue*. 1987.
Hoberg, George. *Pluralism by Design: Environmental Policy and the American Regulatory State*. 1992.

See also CHESAPEAKE BAY: POLLUTION AND FISHERIES; FEDERAL INSECTICIDE, FUNGICIDE AND RODENTICIDE ACT; PESTICIDES

Household Hazardous Wastes
Every day millions of households use products that are dangerous to human health and environment. Many common cleaning products are poisonous, flammable, corrosive, or irritating to skin, eyes and respiratory systems. Some products contain ingredients which are either known or suspected to aid in the development of heart disease, cancer, lung disease, and damage to the human liver and immune system. Certain household products also contribute to ozone depletion and thereby to increased ultraviolet radiation, which can in turn contribute to the incidence of skin cancer, cataracts, and immunosuppression.

Most hazardous household wastes fall into one of five categories: 1) automobile products, 2) pesticides; 3) cleaning products; 4) paint products; and 5) miscellaneous chemicals such as those found in batteries. Use of many of these substances in poorly ventilated areas may endanger the user's health. Storage of these products in the home can pose a danger, especially if they are accessible to children and pets.

Warning labels list immediate dangers from contact but do not describe the danger to the environment associated with use and disposal. For example, the U.S. Environmental Protection Agency has issued a chemical advisory warning those who handle motor oil to minimize skin contact with oil that has been used by the vehicle (contact with waste oil has been found to cause cancer in laboratory animals). As well one quart of motor oil can contaminate up to 250,000 gallons of water. When these products are used or disposed of, either down the drain or into backyards and landfill sites, the chemicals they contain may contaminate natural resources, such as water supplies, thus posing a long-term risk to humans and wildlife. Phosphates, for example, are a common ingredient in many detergents. When they are released into the environment, they encourage the growth of algae, to the serious detriment of fish and other marine life.

Although the amount of hazardous and ozone-depleting substances that comes from one home may be small, these small amounts from many homes add up to a large problem. For their own protection, as well as that of the environment, householders must become aware of the dangers of these products. People also must take the time to learn how to dispose of them properly. A better alternative would be to minimize the use of toxins in our lives through the use of safer alternatives.

Manufacturers and advertisers encourage people to keep their houses "cleaner than clean." Advertisers also stress the value of a few minutes, by asking the consumer to replace elbow grease with chemical reactions. Oven cleaners alone make use of methylene chloride, petroleum distillates, glycol ethers, and sodium hydroxide—all toxic to human health and the environment. The assumptions in our language might well be examined in order to redefine "clean" to mean toxic free.

Homes and possessions can be clean and environmentally friendly at the same time if the use of commercial chemical cleansers is reduced and safe alternatives are used. For example, clogged drains can be prevented if grease or other food particles are not dumped down the drain. Stains are more easily removed if soiled items are rinsed immediately before the stain sets with water or soda water. Ovens use less elbow grease if a baking sheet is used to catch spills when cooking or baking. In general, people use more detergents and cleaners than is necessary. One-third of the amount recommended by the manufacturer is often sufficient. "Whiter than white" may mean that clothes have been dyed and not cleaned.

Alternatives to commercial chemical cleansers are readily available; many alternatives can be found in the kitchen. A good all-purpose cleaner, for example, is a mixture of equal amounts of white vinegar and water or three tablespoons washing soda in four cups warm water. Vinegar can also be used to replace ammonia, as a deodorizer, fabric softener, window cleaner, freshener, mildew cleaner, and even as a furniture polish if mixed with olive oil and as a drain cleaner if mixed with baking soda. Baking soda can also be used with borax as automatic dishwasher detergent or as an oven, tub, and toilet bowl cleaner.

Caution is required whenever chemical household cleaners are used. These substances should be kept in their original containers with the warning labels intact. They should be used only in well-ventilated areas and should be applied only when the user is wearing protective clothing such as gloves. The containers need to be brought to a municipal hazardous waste depot for disposal.

One's house can also be home to a number of ozone depleting substances. Chloroflourocarbons (CFCs) are found in the refrigerator and in the home or car air conditioner. CFCs are also used as blowing agents in the making of foams which are used as insulation, or furniture stuffing, as carpet underpadding, or in packaging. Electronic equipment—whether a personal computer or a stereo, is sometimes cleaned with solvents containing CFC-113 or methyl chloroform, another ozone-depleting substance (ODS). Methyl chloroform is also used in some paints. Halons too are a powerful ODS. Halons are used in fire extinguishers, including those for the home.

Alternatives are available for most of these products. For products such as air conditioners, which do not have an environmentally-friendly or accessible chemical substitute as of yet, there are at least partial options. It is possible to cool one's home through strategically placed trees, fans, or awnings. Because most of the technology in homes was purchased before the widespread availability of ozone-friendly technologies, consumers must ensure that ozone-depleting substances (ODS) are not released into the atmosphere by ensuring that systems which contain ODS are well maintained.

Susan Tanner (with research assistance from
Andrea Lockwood and Pam Foster)

Further Readings

Environmental Hazards Management Institute. *Household Hazardous Waste Wheel*. 1987.

Friends of the Earth (FOE) Canada. *Clean House, Clean Earth*. 1990.

State of Washington, Department of Ecology. *Turning the Tide on Toxins in the Home*. 1990.

See also HAZARDOUS WASTE TREATMENT TECHNOLOGIES; OZONE DEPLETION

Hudson River School

The Hudson River School, a group of American painters active from 1825 to the 1870s, were so named because of their focus on New York State in and around the Catskill Mountains and the Hudson River valley. The group's best-known member is Thomas Cole (1801–1848), co-founder of the National Academy of Design. Other noted members include Asher B. Durand (1796–1886) and Albert Bierstadt (1830–1902), who explored and painted in the U.S. West prior to joining the School. They associated as well with other noted landscape painters of the day including Thomas Moran. Other members of the School of perhaps less note artistically include: Frederick Edwin Church (1826–1900), a student of Thomas Cole; Martin Johnson Heade (1819–1904); Jaspar F. Cropsey (1823–1900); Thomas Doughty (1783–1856); John F. Kensett (1818–1872); and Worthington Whittredge (1820–1910).

Prior to this time there was little by way of landscape painting or attention to nature within North American art. Several members of the Hudson River School worked abroad; many painted as well in either the U.S. West or New England, but they all paid special attention to the scenery of the east coast, the Catskills, and the Hudson River. Both Cole and Durand, as well as Kensett and Whittredge, worked early on as engravers before switching to painting. An important forerunner is the landscapist Washington Allston. Representative works are found in most American museums, including the Metropolitan and the National Gallery, as well as in the Capitol in Washington, D.C. Thomas Cole associated with and shared the outlook of the poet William Cullen Bryant and in this spirit once himself asserted that " . . . the wilderness is yet a fitting place to speak of God."

The group's chief interest was landscape, usually rendered in most cases in a Romantic style, especially in the work of Cole. Durand, however, is considered more Realist, painting in a crisp style directly from nature, a practice unusual at the time. The group has left considerable theoretical writings, including Durand's "Letters on Landscape Painting" (1855). They were interested in the concept of the "sublime," which conveyed the insignificance of man before the awesome power of nature—this being particularly pronounced in the work of Cole. Various members were concerned with the encroachment of settlement into America's hinterlands, specifically by way of the railroad.

The sensitivity to nature shown by these artists had a significant, if indirect, effect in early conservation efforts. The Western landscapist Moran, however, was active in the national park movement and his work is considered influential in the establishment of Yellowstone National Park. Cole, as well, was active as a conservationist through poetry and public speaking as well as implicitly through his paintings. Roderick Nash has concluded that Cole's art implies that "vitality . . . was sapped in proportion to the distance a society departed from its wild roots." Albert Bierstadt was involved in the very early explorations of the U.S. West and eventually depicted Yellowstone, Yosemite, and the Grand Canyon; Doughty was an avid hunter and fisher. Virtually all members of the School consciously sought to express a love of nature and natural beauty in their paintings.

Jesse Paehlke

Further Readings

Marx, Leo. *The Machine in the Garden: Technology and the Pastoral Ideal in America*. 1964.

McCoubrey, John W. *American Art 1700–1960*. 1965.

Nash, Roderick. *Wilderness and the American Mind*. 1967.

Sweet, Frederick. *The Hudson River School and the Early American Landscape Tradition*. 1945.

See also CARR, EMILY; ENVIRONMENTAL AESTHETICS; GROUP OF SEVEN; WILDERNESS; YELLOWSTONE NATIONAL PARK

HWTF

See HAZARDOUS WASTE TREATMENT FACILITY SITING

Hydrocarbons

See AIR POLLUTION: IMPACTS; SMOG

Hydroelectricity

Water has been used as a source of mechanical power—mainly for milling grain—for well over 2,000 years. Once it was discovered that electricity could be generated by the movement of a conducting wire within a magnetic field people thought of using water as a source of electrical power. Experiments with hydro-turbines began early in the eighteenth century but application was delayed by inadequate metallurgy and mechanics. It was not until the end of the nineteenth century that hydro-turbines were generating electricity commercially.

Hydroelectricity, also called hydropower or water power, is relatively simple. The pressure of falling water can be converted into mechanical energy by allowing it to turn the blades of a hydro-turbine, which in turn spins the magnetic field past coils of wire in the generator.

Any river can produce power, but only a few sites can produce it economically. Good sites combine a large volume of flow dropping over a sizable fall together with geological conditions suitable for dam construction; the best sites are found in hilly or mountainous terrain with abundant rainfall or snow pack. The amount of power that can theoretically be extracted from falling water depends upon both volume and drop (or "head"). The formula is: Power = 9810 x Quantity x Head, where power is measured in watts, quantity in cubic meters per second, and head in meters. Actual power capacity depends upon the efficiency of the plant, typically 70 percent to 90 percent of that calculated by the formula.

Hydroelectric generating systems vary widely in scale. At one end are micro-hydro sites generating up to 15 kilowatts of power; these systems are ideally suited to remote communities or small industries near flowing water. Early systems were all of this scale. Today tens of thousands of small hydro plants (up to 15 megawatts) are operating throughout the world, and many that had been abandoned with the trend to centralization after 1945 are now being rehabilitated.

At the other end of the scale are some of the largest engineering structures in the world, including the James Bay complex in Canada with 5.5 gigawatts (GW) of capacity, Guri in Venezuela with 10 GW, and the biggest of them

all, Itaipu on the Brazil-Paraguay border with 12.6 GW. The proposed Three Gorges project in China if it is ever built (in doubt because of enormous social and environmental costs) would be even bigger. The first truly "large dam" (defined as those over 150 meters in height or one cubic kilometer of storage capacity) was Hoover Dam in the United States, dedicated in 1935. A quarter century later in 1960 there were still only thirteen large dams. Thereafter such projects were completed at a rate of about two per year, and today there are well over 100. Most medium and large dams are designed as multi-purpose structures to serve several purposes, such as irrigation, flood control, and navigation.

Typical hydroelectric installations include a dam, a set of large-diameter pipes ("penstocks"), and a generating station. Smaller systems are "run-of-the-river" as they have no storage capacity and take water flows as they occur. Larger systems include reservoirs behind dams to store water and thus even out seasonal and annual variations of flow. More complex hydro systems can include pumped storage in which unneeded power (generally that produced at night) is used to pump water back up to a higher elevation from which it is allowed to fall during periods of peak demand. In a few places in the world tides are high enough to be used for generating power.

About 2.5 percent of the world's commercial energy production comes from hydropower. The proportion is higher in some countries: around 10 percent in Canada and Norway, 25 percent in Japan, 33 percent in Brazil; and much higher in some smaller countries without fossil fuel resources: 70 percent in Zambia, 85 percent in Portugal, 100 percent in Uruguay, Ghana, Nepal, and Costa Rica. Canada is the world's largest producer of hydroelectricity, followed by the United States, the former USSR, Brazil, Norway, China, Japan, and Sweden.

Hydroelectric capacity has grown rapidly in the past few decades. World capacity grew by 23 percent in the 1980s, but that average obscures growth of 59 percent in Asia and 90 percent in South America. About one-fifth of the world's electricity is generated from hydropower, but in developing countries hydropower's share is more than two-fifths.

Despite rapid growth the potential to develop additional hydroelectricity remains large. According to one set of estimates, whereas Europe had exploited 36 percent of its technically usable hydro capacity and North America close to 60 percent, the developing world has exploited well under 10 percent, even in Latin America. Economically feasible capacity is of course much less than technical potential. Although flowing water is a renewable resource, good hydro sites are not. The best and the most easily accessible sites tend to be used first. Subsequent sites are generally more expensive to develop and further from markets.

Hydroelectricity has many advantages as a source of electricity: 1) power is available on demand with the turn of a switch; 2) it is a relatively predictable and concentrated source of energy; 3) operating costs are low because no fuel is required, labor requirements are low, and generation equipment is highly efficient; 4) emissions to the atmosphere are negligible as are solid and liquid wastes; and 5) both the dams and the generating plants last a long time.

There are also disadvantages: 1) good dam sites are limited; 2) river flows typically vary with season and, more importantly, from one year to the next, so the amount of electricity that can be generated changes; 3) systems are capital intensive and require long construction times; 4) although hydroelectric systems themselves consume none of the water passing through them, evaporation losses can be high in reservoirs; 5) environmental changes occur both upstream and downstream of the dam; and 6) people may be displaced when dams are built and the reservoirs behind them filled.

These disadvantages have not been so widely recognized as they should have been. River flows vary in North America where much of the large dam technology originated, but not to the same extent as in arid regions of developing countries. Reliable flow (defined as the flow that can be expected nine years out of ten) is 60 to 80 percent of average flow in Canada's eastern provinces, and 30 percent in the prairie provinces, but only 5 to 10 percent in much of the Middle East and Africa.

Even though total costs per kilowatt-hour may be lower over time the initial capital requirements mean that hydroelectric systems are expensive to build. Typical figures are now $1,500 to $2,000 per kilowatt of capacity. For most developing countries, at least one-third of that money goes to import equipment and expertise. Construction commonly takes seven to ten years. Fossil fuel-fired generating plants can generally be built for less money and in less time (and they require only about one-tenth as much land per unit of capacity). If the hydro sites are located far from the loads (which is commonly the case) capital costs will increase further because of the need to transport heavy equipment and to build long transmission lines. Smaller hydro systems are less expensive in total expenditures, but typically even more so in unit costs (up to $6,000 per kilowatt).

Since the 1970s evidence has been accumulating to indicate that hydroelectric projects have exacted major environmental and social costs. An incomplete list of environmental impacts includes: 1) losses of productive agricultural land, forests, and wildlife habitat upstream from the dam; 2) losses of silt and fertility and increases in salination downstream; 3) high rates of erosion along streambeds downstream from the dam and along coastal areas where the river meets the sea; 4) increases in some diseases, notably malaria and schistosomiasis (bilharzia); and 5) losses of property and life as a result of dam failure (e.g., Vaiont in Italy in 1963; Koyna in India in 1967). Social effects include: 1) the need to displace people living in the area where the reservoir will be located; 2) loss of sustainable cultures (all too commonly tribal cultures with little political power); and 3) changes in the economic structure from self-reliant subsistence to market-driven economies that favor those with capital. Kariba Dam in Zimbabwe, which was built in the 1960s, forced nearly 60,000 people to move; Akosombo in Ghana, 75,000; and Aswan in Egypt some 110,000 (about half of them in Sudan). Depending on final design and scale, the Narmada project in India (a complex of many dams) would displace between 100,000 and 1 million people, and the proposed Three Gorges Dam in China, between 300,000 and 2 million. There are unfortunately few cases in which local benefits—such as increased fish catches and ease of transportation—have offset local losses. For reasons not fully understood, fish catches tend to rise dramatically for a few years but then drop. As well, impacts on downstream and offshore fisheries have been difficult to predict. Recreation benefits can be important but vary widely by site.

In some cases it appears that just those environmental costs that can be quantified are greater than commercial benefits derived from large dams. Unfortunately, whereas detailed benefit-cost calculations are made in advance to justify construction of hydroelectric projects, very few are made after the fact to determine whether the construction was in fact worthwhile. Those that have been made almost invariably show that the realized benefit-cost ratio was less—in some cases much less—than the predicted ratio. For example, displaced people are commonly forced onto lower quality, sloping land above the reservoir, which increases the rate of erosion and of sediment flowing into the dam, which in turn reduces electricity generation and shortens project life. Costs of hydroelectricity can be understated for other reasons. Estimates generally ignore any charge for the use of the water, which, just as with oil found in the ground, is a resource that should yield a return (in economic terms, a "rent") to its owner, in most cases the state. Estimates of the economic value of water used for hydropower in Canada range from $4.2 to $6.6 billion per year (1984 dollars). Although charges for the use of water have been increasing in Canada and elsewhere few jurisdictions collect the full rent, which means that hydropower appears cheaper than it really is.

Costs can also be understated when rivers cross a boundary from one jurisdiction to another. In some cases, as between the United States and Canada, treaties have come into force to define how benefits and costs will be shared. In other cases construction in one country ignores the effects in another. For example, filling of reservoirs behind dams on the headwaters of the Euphrates River in Turkey reduced power output at downstream dams in Syria, which had earlier built dams that reduced power capacity in Iraq, still further downstream.

Hydroelectricity therefore presents a dilemma. On the one hand it is an attractive source of electricity, demand for which is growing throughout the world, particularly in developing countries. Even with extensive programs for demand management developing countries will need more electricity, and renewable sources such as hydroelectricity are in many cases the "least bad" alternative. On the other hand hydroelectric projects absorb large amounts of capital and have sizable adverse environmental and social effects. The key problem appears to lie with scale. Experience suggests that adverse effects will be larger than

predicted and that they rise sharply with scale. Smaller scale and even micro-hydro projects are not without problems, including environmental problems, but those problems are more easily assessed and, equally important, evaluation, construction, and ultimately management, can more easily be handled at local and regional levels.

Large-scale hydroelectric projects are increasingly controversial, by no means just in developing countries. Controversies dramatic enough to shake governments have occurred in Canada, Australia, and New Zealand, as well as in Thailand and India. More careful environmental and social impact assessments (together with adequate opportunity for public review) prior to final design will help. Most adverse effects are predictable, at least if projects are not too large. However, once hydroelectric projects are large enough to alter whole cultures or ecologies, there may in principle be no way to predict effects. Worse yet the technical and economic scale of the projects may simply exceed the capacity of existing institutions to manage them. With a potential too great to neglect, the most appropriate balance appears to lie in designing hydroelectric systems for smaller scale and for minimum effects, even if such designs reduce somewhat the total power potential.

David B. Brooks

Further Readings

Goldsmith, Edward, and Nicholas Hildyard. *The Social and Environmental Effects of Large Dams.* 1984.

U.S. Congress, Office of Technology Assessment. *Fueling Development: Energy Technologies for Developing Countries.* 1992.

World Bank. *The Future Role of Hydropower in Developing Countries.* 1989.

See also Aswan High Dam; Colorado River; Columbia River Basin; Echo Park Dam; James Bay; Mineral King Canyon; Snail Darter; World Bank

I

IBT

See INDUSTRIAL BIO-TEST LABORATORIES

Ickes, Harold L.

Under the stewardship of Harold Ickes (1874–1952) the conservation impulse begun in the progressive era reached maturity in the New Deal. Ickes was appointed Secretary of Interior by President Franklin Roosevelt in March 1933 and served nearly thirteen years (1933–1947), longer than anyone before or since. In that time Ickes moved from a position supporting maximum natural resource utility to champion regional resource planning, uphold national park integrity based on ecological considerations, advocate wilderness preservation, and oppose lumber, mineral, and grazing intrusions in the nation's public lands. Although Ickes lost two important battles to reorganize the stewardship of the nation's land and resources his legacy reinvigorated the Department of Interior as the premier conservation agency of the federal government. His vision marks him as a key figure in the evolution of the environmental movement.

Ickes began his political career as an independent reform politician in Chicago. Born March 15, 1874, on a farm in Altoona, Pennsylvania, Ickes was sent to live with relatives in Chicago at sixteen after the death of his mother. He graduated from the University of Chicago and supported himself as a political reporter while he learned organizational skills in local reform politics and finished a law degree. Combative and committed, Ickes fought urban special interests with the same ferocity that he later employed against those who would claim privilege to ravage the nation's natural resources. He became an ardent sup-porter of Theodore Roosevelt's bull moose campaigns, found fellowship with Gifford Pinchot, whose abortive campaign for president Ickes managed in 1932. With his wife, Anna Wilmarth, Ickes also supported a variety of reforms for the Native Americans of the Southwest.

When President Roosevelt appointed him to Interior at the age of fifty-nine Ickes believed that "rugged individualism" had been responsible for the rapid deterioration of the land and its resources. As head of the Public Works Administration and as an administrator of the Civilian Conservation Corps Ickes used his political and budgetary power to change the face of the western landscape and to support a variety of soil conservation projects and multiple purpose resource planning efforts such as Tennessee Valley Authority, Central Valley Project, and the Flood Control Act of 1944. Arguing for the federal management of the remaining public domain Ickes supported the Taylor Grazing Act of 1934 and the closure of the public domain to homesteaders.

Ickes was an avid gardener and bred prize dahlias. He took a special interest in the administration of the National Park Service (NPS). Tutored first by Stephen Mather he kept Horace Albright on as NPS director. Albright reinforced Ickes's early appreciation of wilderness and scenic beauty and influenced Ickes's decision to oppose highways in the Blue Ridge Mountains and to support the new idea of wilderness parks. Ickes promoted aesthetic and ecological preservation through the acquisition of such parks as Olympic, Kings Canyon, and the Everglades. He helped persuade President Roosevelt to transfer historic battlefields, cemeteries, and national monuments to the Park Service, including Jackson Hole, Wyoming.

Throughout his tenure Ickes advocated the creation of a true Department of Conservation which would include the transfer of the Forest Service to Interior. Although disappointed that President Roosevelt never supported this idea, the Reorganization Act of 1939 brought Ickes the Bureau of Fisheries and Biological Survey which he merged into the Fish and Wildlife Service. Ickes added important refuges and advanced the cause of wildlife conservation.

When Harry S. Truman became president in 1945 Ickes lost a conservation champion in the White House. He resigned in 1947 over Truman's appointment of oilman Edwin Pauley as undersecretary of the navy fearing the integrity of tideland oil reserves. Harold Ickes's vigilant stewardship of the nation's resources left an important heritage. Fearful of private interests, Ickes showed that federal conservation policies could be used to encourage employment and economic growth and at the same time provide lasting benefits for the environment. A transitional figure between utilitarian conservation and wilderness preservation, Harold Ickes died in Washington, D.C., on February 3, 1952. He was one of the most controversial and effective champions of the integrity of the nation's natural heritage.

Linda J. Lear

Further Readings

Lear, Linda J. *The Aggressive Progressive: The Early Career of Harold L. Ickes, 1874–1952.* 1981.

Strong, Douglas H. *Dreamers and Defenders.* 1988.

Watkins, T.H. *Righteous Pilgrim. The Life and Times of Harold L. Ickes, 1874–1952.* 1990.

See also Conservation Movement; Department of the Interior (U.S.); Everglades of South Florida; National Parks: United States; Pinchot, Gifford; Wilderness

IJC

See International Joint Commission

Incineration

See Municipal Solid Waste: Incineration

Indigenous People and the Environment (New Zealand)

The indigenous Maori settled in New Zealand from Polynesia between 800 A.D. and 1000 A.D. Early hunting practices that used fire and the introduction of mammals such as dogs and rats destroyed both forests and bird species. Environmental awareness and an intimate association between people and land developed. Maori religion was essentially animistic. All natural resources and phenomena were personified and regarded as ancestors in terms of the creation myths. All possessed spirit (*wairua*) or life force (*mauri*). Customary controls included sacredness (*tapu*), specific prohibitions (*rahui*), and the concepts of stewardship and guardianship (*kaitiaki*). Land was regarded as an integral part of personal and group identity, given by the ancestors to be held in trust for future generations.

Since the settlement of New Zealand by Europeans (*pakeha*) in the nineteenth century the main tribes have lost most of their land through sale, purchase, and confiscation (arising from land wars in the 1860s). The Maori relationship with the environment has survived, however, although in a much modified form. Most Maori, like other New Zealanders, are now predominantly urban. Since the 1970s a cultural renaissance has occurred and Maori concerns about the need to retain cultural identity have become increasingly politicized. Judicial redress has also been sought.

Maori concerns have focused on three areas: 1) environmental degradation; 2) affronts to spiritual and cultural beliefs; and 3) breaches of the principles of the Treaty of Waitangi. The work of the Waitangi Tribunal has been a key factor in outlining Maori attitudes and approaches to environmental management. The Resource Management Act of 1991 requires that all resource managers and developers consult Maori people and take into account Maori spiritual and cultural values, including the principle of *kaitiakitanga*—an ethic of stewardship. Tribal groups (*iwi*) can prepare resource management plans, and partnership arrangements between government agencies and *iwi* for the management of resources are being developed under the Conservation Act of 1987 (the management of parts of the public conservation estate) and the Maori Fisheries Act of 1990 (the establishment of *taiapure* or local fisheries). There is potential under the Resource Management Act for the joint management of water and other areas.

Maori are now focusing on ownership and property right issues particularly for unallocated Crown resources. Waitangi Tribunal reports are influential in this area. The desire to develop Maori tribal resources for social and economic development is beginning to conflict with traditional environmental values. This will pose a further challenge for Maori, the environmental movement, and resource managers.

Peter Horsley

Further Readings

Manatu Maori (Ministry of Maori Development) Natural Resources Unit. *Maori Values and Environmental Management.* 1991.

Ministry for the Environment. Working Paper No. 29. *The Natural World and Natural Resources: Maori Value Systems and Perspectives.* 1989.

See also ENVIRONMENTAL JUSTICE MOVEMENT; STEWARDSHIP; TREATY OF WAITANGI (NEW ZEALAND)

Indoor Air Pollution

Worldwide, indoor air pollutants can be divided into four categories based on their derivation:

1. Pollutants from combustion (e.g., carbon monoxide, particulates, volatile organics, and sulfur and nitrogen oxides from cooking stoves, space heaters, and environmental tobacco smoke—ETS).
2. Pollutants from building materials, furnishings, and chemical products (e.g., pesticides, asbestos, and volatile organics including formaldehyde).
3. Pollutants originating from the ground under buildings (e.g., radon).
4. Pollutants from biological processes (e.g., mold, mildew, mites).

Developed Countries

As with outdoor emissions, the impact of indoor emissions on actual air concentrations depends on the amount of air into which the pollution is mixed and ventilation (i.e., the flow of air into and out of this volume). In general most housing in developed countries is situated in temperate latitudes and thus has relatively low air interchange with the outdoors. Under these conditions even rather low emission rates cause indoor concentrations that exceed those out-

doors. Since people spend a great proportion of time indoors—typically 90 percent or more—indoor pollution often dominates total exposure to pollutants such as particulates, nitrogen dioxide, and many volatile organic compounds.

Although evidence links indoor pollutants to infectious and chronic respiratory diseases, allergic reactions and asthma, lung cancer has been of most concern. Household radon and ETS have been linked to lung cancer, both being low-dose examples of well-established carcinogens (radon in uranium mines and active smoking). Most of the lung cancer from household radon appears in smokers, however, because the combination of smoking and radon exposure leads to even greater risks than would be indicated by just a simple addition of the two. Although it would be difficult to significantly reduce average exposures over large populations, reductions for those households with excessive radon exposures are usually possible and practical.

Occasionally a concern in homes, but mostly in commercial office buildings, is the indoor air quality problem known as "the sick building syndrome." Apparently due to volatile chemicals released from furnishings and building materials, the syndrome often takes the form of non-specific complaints such as headaches, dry mouth, and fatigue, in people working in new or recently refurbished office buildings. In recent years more attention has been focused on biological contaminants generated in poorly designed or maintained ventilation systems, carpets, and other potentially moist locations in office buildings and homes.

Developing Countries

Much housing in the developing world is situated in tropical and subtropical regions and typically is relatively well ventilated. In these circumstances it takes fairly high emission rates to produce significant indoor pollutant levels. Unfortunately, there seem to be many situations in which such strong indoor sources exist. In addition, although a minority, hundreds of millions of people in developing countries still use solid fuels for space heating for a significant part of the year and, thus, share with developed countries the difficulty of making trade-offs among space-heating costs, fuel quality and efficiency, ventilation, and indoor air quality.

Sources of Concern

After tobacco the most common indoor combustion source of concern in developed country air pollution studies has been gas cookstoves. In the global context, however, gas stoves are near the upper end of a historic evolution in the quality of household fuels, sometimes called the energy ladder. On the lowest rungs are those households that rely on dried animal dung and scavenged twigs and grass for cooking. The next step up might be crop residues, such as corn stalks, followed by wood, and then charcoal. The first non-biomass fuel on the ladder might be kerosene, as in India, or coal, as in China. Highest on the ladder lie bottled and piped gases and, for some rich communities, electricity. In general, each step involves increases in the cooking system's efficiency, upfront cost, and cleanliness.

When learning to control fire, essentially all of humanity entered this ladder in the middle, with wood fuel. Now, many millennia later, about half have moved up the ladder to the modern fuels. The remainder, however, either still use wood or, for a significant fraction of humanity, have slipped down the ladder to the poorer quality biomass fuels, such as animal dung.

On a global scale then about half of the world's households cook daily with unprocessed solid fuels, either biomass or coal (a more "modern" fuel). An uncertain but significant proportion of this cooking is done under conditions releasing effluents into the living area. Although ventilation rates are often relatively high in the homes of developing countries, the pollutant emission factors for such fuels are so great that indoor concentrations and exposures can be quite substantial. Compared with gas stoves, for example, even stoves using one of the cleaner biofuels—wood—typically release fifty times more pollution when cooking a similar meal.

Tests have shown that unprocessed solid fuels produce hundreds of chemical compounds because of the incomplete combustion that occurs under the operating conditions of simple stoves, which are often just a pit or three rocks. Both coal and biomass stoves pollute under these conditions. Unlike coal, however, biomass generally contains few inorganic contaminants such as sulfur, trace metals, and ash; under proper conditions, therefore, biomass can be burned with no releases other than the products of complete combustion (i.e., carbon dioxide and water). Unfortunately it has turned out to be difficult to reliably create the needed combustion conditions in modestly priced household devices.

As with tobacco smoke, which is also the result of open biomass combustion, the smoke from solid fuel combustion is a complicated and unstable mixture of aerosol droplets, solid particles, and gases. Biomass smoke contains significant amounts of several of the health-relevant pollutants for which most countries have set standards: carbon monoxide, particulates, and volatile organics. In addition the emissions contain many organic compounds that are considered toxic, carcinogenic, or mutagenic, including formaldehyde, benzene, and polyaromatic hydrocarbons. Coal smoke contains all these and other pollutants because of fuel contaminants (e.g., sulfur oxides, inorganic ash particles, and toxic elements such as lead and fluorine).

Although large-scale systematic measurement surveys have not yet been conducted, the results of a number of studies from different parts of the world provide some insight into typical indoor concentrations of the major pollutants produced by solid-fueled household stoves in developing countries. Compared with national standards, World Health Organization recommendations or levels typical in even the dirtiest of cities, these indoor levels are dramatically elevated.

Lacking both internationally recognized standards for household pollution as well as sufficient measurements worldwide, it is difficult to estimate the number of people exposed to excessive indoor levels. Assuming that such standards would be at least as stringent as outdoor standards, the total number of people exposed excessively indoors clearly rivals or exceeds the level exposed to excessive outdoor concentrations in all the world's cities (i.e., 0.5 to 1.5 billion). Given the greater time spent indoors and the known magnitude of concentrations in many situations, however, the contribution to the total global dose (amount actually inhaled) from indoor combustion in developing countries is probably much higher for some pollutants (e.g., particulates) than from any other source.

The toxicologic characteristics of these emissions suggest potential links to four important categories of ill health: acute respiratory infections in children, adverse pregnancy outcomes (such as stillbirth), chronic lung diseases, and lung cancer. A growing number of epidemiological studies have begun to pin down the actual risks.

Studies in Africa, for example, show that young children exposed to wood smoke at home contract serious respiratory infections two to five times more often than other children. This is a significant finding since such infections are now the chief killer of children in developing countries, being responsible for 4.3 million deaths per year, 30 percent more than the next most important category, diarrhea. Studies in China have found elevated lung cancer rates from indoor coal smoke, particularly notable in nonsmoking women cooking with coal for whom the risk can approach that of smokers.

Conclusion

Air pollution is often thought to be a problem mainly of urban outdoor industrial settings, which is thus where most research, control, and monitoring efforts have focused. It is becoming clear, however, that in both developed and developing countries the largest exposures to many pollutants of interest occur indoors, in rural areas as well as cities.

Kirk R. Smith

Further Readings

Samet, Jon M., Spengler, John D., eds. *Indoor Air Pollution: A Health Perspective.* Johns Hopkins Univ. Press, Baltimore. 1991

Smith, Kirk R. "Fuel Combustion, Air Pollution Exposure, and Health: The Situation in Developing Countries." *Annual Review of Energy and Environment 18* (1993): 529–566. Annual Reviews Inc., Palo Alto, CA.

See also AIR POLLUTION: IMPACTS; TOBACCO SMOKE IN THE ENVIRONMENT; TOXICOLOGY; VOLATILE ORGANIC COMPOUNDS

Industrial Bio-Test Laboratories

Industrial Bio-Test Laboratories, Inc. (IBT) was an independent research laboratory, based in Northbrook, Illinois, that performed toxicity studies on hundreds of drugs, pesticides, and other products made by leading North American chemical manufacturers. Between 1953 and 1978, IBT conducted some 22,000 animal studies, about half of which were used to obtain product approvals from authorities in the United States and Canada. Starting in the mid-1970s the U.S. Food and Drug Administration (FDA) and the Environmental Protection Agency (EPA) began investigating alleged flaws in the tests conducted

by IBT. Their inquiries revealed a shocking pattern of data falsification and fabrication: tumors had been wrongly classified or not reported at all, dead animals had been disposed of without autopsy because they were too badly decomposed, new animals had been substituted at random for animals that had died, and new data points had been invented to fill in empty tables. These findings eventually led to the criminal prosecution of several top IBT executives, three of whom were eventually convicted in a federal court on charges of mail and wire fraud.

While both U.S. and Canadian regulatory authorities rejected IBT's test data as unsound, the scandal led to somewhat different actions in the two countries. Canada banned four pesticides and restricted two others in June 1983. By contrast, in July 1983, the U.S. EPA informed the makers of thirty-four pesticides that their products would be suspended unless new data could be generated to establish their safety.

The more significant and longer-term impact of the IBT episode was to tighten up governmental requirements for the conduct of safety testing. Following intense pressure from Congress and the media, both FDA and EPA issued formal "good laboratory practice" (GLP) standards, with EPA closely modeling its approach on that of its more experienced sister agency. FDA's path-breaking program eventually became the basis for an expanded, internationally agreed scheme adopted in 1982 by the member states of the Organisation for Economic Co-operation and Development (OECD). The push for internationalization was fueled by the mutual desire of government and industry to facilitate the cross-national acceptance of test data. Regulations that once were resisted as an infringement on the autonomy of testing laboratories thus provided the basis for less restricted international trade in chemicals.

Sheila Jasanoff

Further Readings

United States v. Keplinger, 776 F.2d 678 (7th Cir. 1985).

See also ALACHLOR CONTROVERSY; PESTICIDES; STANDARD SETTING; TOXICOLOGY

Insecticides

See PESTICIDES

Instrumental Value

Instrumental value is the value that something has in reference to another's ends or purposes. Intrinsically valuable beings—beings that are ends in themselves—may also be instrumentally valuable and vice versa.

When people ask "what good is it?" about an animal or plant, they are usually inquiring about its instrumental value to human beings—is it edible?, does it control garden pests?, will its fur, feathers, or fiber fetch a price on any market? However, one might answer with another question, "Good for whom?," confronting those who pose the original question with two things: first, that other forms of life may also have ends or purposes; and second, that plants and animals that have no value to human beings may be quite valuable to one another. Many environmentalists had rather not provoke such disquieting reflections and prefer instead to make a case for nature conservation on "anthropocentric" (human-centered) instrumental grounds. The anthropocentric instrumental value of nature may be divided into the four basic categories: goods, services, information, and psycho-spiritual resources.

Goods

Many aspects of the environment—air, water, soil, coal, metals, etc.—are consumed directly by people through breathing, drinking, and other sustenance uses. People hunt or gather certain animals and plants and eat them, wear their skins, festoon rooms with their flowers, or hang their antlers on walls. People convert trees to paper, houses, furniture, or fuel. People cure diseases with tinctures and extracts drawn from the bark, leaves, and fruits of plants, and from the fluids, glands, and tissues of animals. The medicinal potential of hitherto undiscovered and/or unassayed plants and animals seems to be the most popular and persuasive instrumental rationale for nature conservation in contemporary culture—a culture, it seems, of hypochondriacs and valetudinarians.

Services

Many natural entities that people do not wish to consume perform free economic and ecologic services. Insects, birds, and bats pollinate human crops; rhizobial bacteria draw natural nitrogen fertilizer into the soil; fungi reduce dead organic matter to simple elements and compounds; forests prevent soil erosion, modulate stream flow, and remove carbon dioxide from the atmosphere.

Information

The DNA of each species is a data-base for genetic engineers who hope to improve human foods and medicines. Pure scientific knowledge of nature is valuable to scientists in the same way that postage stamps are valuable to stamp collectors. And pure scientific knowledge of nature may turn out to have unexpected applications. Electron-photon scattering, for example, was interesting to physicists before anyone thought about using it to create television. Who knows what future use the pure scientific knowledge of, say, bear hibernation may be put to?

Psycho-Spiritual Resources

People like to hike in natural environments, watch birds, view scenic or picturesque vistas, enjoy the grandeur and majesty of mountains or the mystery of swamps and bogs. People value the solitude of wild places where the "otherness" of nonhuman nature can be experienced. People experience religious awe in special, sacred places.

Environmental economists are becoming adept at monetizing all these kinds of instrumental values of nature. When compounded and prorated to future generations they constitute a powerful rationale for nature conservation.

J. Baird Callicott

Further Readings

Myers, Norman. *A Wealth of Wild Species.* 1983.

Norton, Bryan. *Toward Unity among Environmentalists.* 1991.

See also ANIMAL RIGHTS; ANTHROPOCENTRISM; CONTINGENT VALUATION; ENVIRONMENTAL ETHICS; INTRINSIC VALUE

Integrated Pest Management

Integrated pest management (IPM) is a general strategy for controlling pest organisms, usually insects but sometimes weeds, plant pathogens, or other pest organisms. In contrast to specific practices (e.g., pesticides) that suppress a pest population IPM is a methodology and philosophy for combining two or more suppression practices. A detailed understanding of a particular pest, its ecology, and its surroundings are needed before use of an IPM scheme can begin. IPM integrates multiple pest control practices through an understanding of the population ecology of the pest and its natural enemies (usually, parasitic and predatory insects or pathogenic fungi, viruses, and bacteria). In most cases, IPM methods rely first on the natural enemies of pests and on the genetic resistance potential of crop plants. Other methods, such as pesticides, are used as supplements.

IPM was developed in the 1950s to counter serious problems arising from the use of insecticides. Extensive use of insecticides developed after World War II. For example, DDT achieved widespread use in agriculture, forestry, public health, and home and garden use. Success with DDT led to many more chemicals, such as aldrin, dieldrin, chlordane, heptachlor, parathion, carbaryl, and others. Heaviest use of the chemicals occurred in cotton, corn, fruits, and vegetables.

Heavy use of insecticides caused the development of resistance to chemicals in pest insects and the destruction of the natural enemies of the pest species. Resistance made the use of a chemical obsolete because the poison would no longer achieve its objective. Destruction of natural enemies freed the pest from natural suppression, which led in turn to its rapid multiplication. Insecticides thus sometimes created outbreaks of pests, a counter-intuitive result.

In 1959 researchers at the University of California published a theory of "integrated control," in which natural enemies and insecticides were combined in ways that achieved the quick killing power of the insecticide and yet did not destroy the long-term suppressive power of natural enemies. This theory was developed as part of a program to control spotted alfalfa aphid. More recently schemes for IPM began to join theories of broader scope on the ecological management of all farm resources. IPM has also begun to find use in forestry, urban pest control, and other situations.

Currently IPM offers, in theory, the achievement of insect control with a 50 to 90 percent reduction of pesticide use. Some schemes of IPM are in active use in cotton, apple, and other industries. For example, management of boll weevil in the U.S. South and Southeast is now frequently based on IPM strategies. However, reliance on chemicals is still the norm for pest control in agriculture.

IPM is often portrayed in the conservation and environmental literature as an important component of "sustainable" agriculture. Details are seldom provided, however, about what is to be sustained, in which area, over what period of time. Severe problems with resistance, destruction of natural enemies, and pesticide pollution seem to promote the adoption of IPM, which has considerable potential to offer relief from pest damage without itself causing high environmental destruction.

John H. Perkins

Further Readings

Flint, Mary Louise, and Robert van den Bosch. *Introduction to Integrated Pest Management.* 1981.

Perkins, John H. *Insects, Experts, and the Insecticide Crisis: The Quest for New Pest Management Strategies.* 1982.

See also AGRICULTURE: ENVIRONMENTAL IMPACTS; PESTICIDES; SUSTAINABLE AGRICULTURE

Interdisciplinarity

The term "interdisciplinarity" is ambiguous, used to connote cross-disciplinarity, multi-disciplinarity, inter-disciplinarity, and trans-disciplinary approaches to education, problem solving, and inquiry. If traditional disciplines and subdisciplines are conceptualized as "depth" studies that tend toward increasing specialization (more reductive, narrower focus), then interdisciplinary studies may be conceptualized as "breadth" studies that attempt to integrate and even unify depth studies to form a new conceptual system or interdiscipline. The "disciplinary pyramid" metaphor, with intra-disciplinary research at the base (e.g., microbiology), followed in ascending order by cross-disciplinary (e.g., the politics of science), multi-disciplinary (e.g., regional planning), inter-disciplinary (e.g., conservation biology), and transdisciplinary (e.g., systems theory) levels is useful, but imprecise. In practice integrative education and research does not often fall clearly into any one category (or level on the pyramid).

Disagreement over intellectual turf and even open conflict has appeared within research universities, traditionally organized by academic disciplines. Environmental studies and sciences are no exception; they are subject to a constant tension between specialized, disciplinary inquiry and more comprehensive, integrative research. Such stress between traditional (disciplinary) and nontraditional (interdisciplinary) research sometimes encourages innovative responses to environmental issues, such as climate warming, biodiversity, and population.

To advocates of interdisciplinary approaches coordinated research, analysis of problems, and policy recommendations appear to be a more relevant (pragmatic) way to deal with the causes of and solutions for environmental dysfunctions.

Conservation biology is a case in point; a number of disciplines such as wildlife ecology, population biology, forestry, agriculture, and policy analysis have converged on a new focus—biodiversity itself—that eludes any one traditional domain of inquiry. Whether or not conservation biology is a genuinely interdisciplinary approach to biodiversity is not entirely clear. If conservation biology is a new integration, where the whole is greater than the sum of the parts, is it also then a new discipline? Similar questions arise in relation to ethnobotany, although here the issue is less complicated, since two rather than many disciplines have come together to study the interface of plants and particular cultures.

Interdisciplinary studies go beyond the bounds of the natural sciences in integrating the sciences and the humanities, as well as the natural and the social sciences. Ecofeminism combines environmental concern, informed by ecology and other science-based studies, with techniques of feminist analysis; population issues are one area of ecofeminist research, melding discussions of women's rights and reproductive freedom with the perceived need to stabilize and perhaps reduce human populations. Ecological economics goes beyond the bounds of either systems ecology or environmental economics in addressing issues of sustainability, including scientific, philosophical, and economic variables.

Interesting issues also arise in applied contexts. The Environmental Protection Agency (EPA) mandates interdisciplinary approaches to some environmental problems, such as comparative risk assessment, and in determining priorities for action. State governments have discovered that disjointed approaches to solving environmental problems by various state agencies, with turf parceled out along traditional lines, are ineffective. The Sustainable Biosphere Initiative of the Ecological Society of America is predicated on the idea that finding and implementing solutions for complex ecological problems entails stretching traditional disciplinary bounds.

Of all disciplines, perhaps ecology, and especially systems ecology, has been most subject to the tension between depth and breadth studies. Some ecologists believe the discipline studies temporal phenomena that are the consequence of complex, multivariate, typically chaotic processes; others believe that ecology seeks ergodic knowledge that is temporally invariant. The former approach leads ecology in an interdisciplinary direction, where ecological systems and problems are conceptualized as lying at the confluence of biology, geography, climate and other natural factors with cultural influences such as economics and ethics. The latter approach leads ecology toward reductive, quantitative analysis of ecosystems as isolated "objects" for reductive inquiry.

Interdisciplinarity also raises curricular issues. Traditional curricula tend to not meet the needs of students seeking degrees in the environmental studies and sciences. Increasingly such students are required to take breadth studies in areas outside narrow disciplinary bounds. Universities take one of three approaches to these needs, organizing degrees that rely on curriculums that integrate courses taught over a wide variety of departments, reorganizing faculty into multidisciplinary departments that create their own unique courses, or creating separate colleges of environmental science.

At the most philosophical level, interdisciplinarity raises questions of epistemology and ontology. So-called general systems theory, chaos theory, and hierarchy theory have emerged as prominent players in the field. Many questions are raised by such theories. Are systems (wholes) real, that is, entities possessing characteristics that do not exist at the level of parts? Are parts mere abstractions from and simplifications of more complex wholes? Methodologically considered, are interdisciplinary studies something unique? Or are they better characterized as emerging disciplines that address new problems (research foci) in traditional ways?

Max Oelschlaeger

Further Readings

Ehrlich, Paul R., and Edward O. Wilson. "Biodiversity Studies: Science and Policy." *Science* 253 (1991): 758–62.
Laszlo, Ervin. *Evolution: The Grand Synthesis.* 1987.

See also CONSERVATION BIOLOGY; ECOFEMINISM; ENVIRONMENTAL EDUCATION; ENVIRONMENTAL ETHICS; ENVIRONMENTALISM; GREEN ECONOMICS

International Joint Commission

The International Joint Commission (IJC) was created by the Canada-U.S. Boundary Waters Treaty of 1909. The principal purpose of the treaty was to create joint dispute preventative machinery applicable to the use of boundary waters. This machinery took the form of a permanent joint institution—the IJC—and specified rules of procedure. The treaty identifies and the IJC concerns itself with five categories of waters: boundary waters (i.e., those along which the boundary runs), upstream transboundary waters, waters which are tributary to boundary waters, waters which flow from boundary waters, and downstream transboundary waters. The treaty's objectives were to settle all outstanding disputes along the border and to prevent or adjust and settle similar difficulties in the future. In performing this task the IJC has four categories of functions: administrative, quasi-judicial, arbitral, and investigative. In recent decades the IJC's mandate has been broadened to include some transboundary air pollution, but only with the exercise of an investigative function. Much of the IJC's work in practice is constrained in its dependency on references and the precise wording of references, issued by the Department of State (U.S.) and the Department of External Affairs (Canada). Generally references are agreed to and issued simultaneously, but technically issuance from one side is sufficient.

The IJC is composed of three Canadian commissioners and a small permanent professional staff in Ottawa, three U.S. commissioners and a smaller permanent professional staff in Washington, and a permanent professional staff in Windsor, Ontario, whose mandate is limited to Great Lakes matters. A high percentage of all of the IJC's work is oriented to the Great Lakes, both in terms of water quantity (lake levels) and water quality (pollution). The IJC is best known to the public for its investigative functions but its significant ongoing work and real power albeit narrowly constrained is in the administrative and quasi-judicial functions, some of which is beyond appeal.

The key to the accomplishment of the work of the IJC is its ability to "second" on a part-time basis public employees on the budgets of other governmental bureaucracies, which "seconded" employees may then form numerous boards and groups (investigative boards, pollution surveillance boards, boards of control, a formal Water Quality Board, a Science Advisory Board, and specific reference groups).

These boards and groups, generally technical in nature, make recommendations to the six IJC commissioners, who then pass those recommendations through the IJC staffs for further refinement before issuing their own findings or recommendations. This technique blurs the true cost of IJC activity, in that it incorporates it into the budgets of numerous agencies, but it has the advantage of leading to greater governmental acceptance of IJC decisions whence they are issued.

The IJC's duties are regulatory or investigative, or involve the coordination of surveillance and monitoring activities. Historically IJC work has concentrated on approval of hydroelectric, flood control, and reclamation and irrigation structures downstream of the border which involve flood damage upstream across the border; approval of hydroelectric structures and navigation improvements on waters which form the boundary; approval of assorted minor river works; water appropriation questions from both boundary and transboundary waters; and investigations of various types, principally water quantity or quality related, but with a few air quality investigations as well. (In the view of some the IJC has been significantly underutilized as regards air quality and has been thus far nearly absent in the continental acid rain debate.) Its formal authority in all of these matters is judicial and/or investigative.

John E. Carroll

Further Readings

Carroll, John E. *Environmental Diplomacy: An Examination and a Prospective of Canadian-U.S. Transboundary Environmental Relations.* 1986.

Spencer, Robert, John Kirton, and Kim Richard Nossal, eds. *The International Joint Commission Seventy Years On.* 1981.

See also ENVIRONMENTAL DIPLOMACY; GREAT LAKES; TRAIL SMELTER INVESTIGATION

International Tropical Timber Organization

The International Tropical Timber Organization (ITTO) was founded in 1985 to administer the provisions of the 1983 International Tropical Timber Agreement (ITTA) of the United Nations. Adopted after six years of difficult negotiation the agreement was created to provide a framework of cooperation and consultation between producers and consumers of tropical timber. It is the first commodity agreement to deal with a naturally occurring resource, the first to include conservation in its objectives.

ITTO was handed two apparently contradictory tasks: to regulate and promote trade in tropical timber, and to maintain the genetic diversity and ecological balance of tropical forests. Since the twenty-three producer members represent 88 percent (by value, 1991) of global trade in the products covered under the ITTA (saw/veneer logs, sawnwood, veneer, and plywood), and the twenty-four consumer nations account for more than 95 percent of world imports of tropical timber, the potential to influence the future of the resource is obvious.

ITTO is an independent organization, controlled by a council made up of member countries. The secretariat is located in Yokohama, Japan. The Tropical Timber Council meets twice a year and has three permanent committees: reforestation and forest management, economic information and market intelligence, and forest industry. Votes within the council are divided equally between consumers and producers; the voting power of each member depends on the degree of its participation in the trade, although the area of a nation's forests is also given some weight. Thus Japan (the largest importer) has the greatest voice, and major producers also exert considerable influence. This voting structure ensures that ITTO's primary role of promoting the timber trade heavily outweighs its secondary conservation role.

Nevertheless the concept of sustainable use is central to ITTO. In May 1990 ITTO members adopted Target 2000, setting a date by which all tropical timber must be sourced from sustainably managed forests. This is a laudable goal, but highly unrealistic; a 1988 survey, commissioned by the organization itself, revealed that less than one eighth of one percent of logging in tropical forests is carried out sustainably. Although ITTO has developed broad guidelines to assist forest planners and managers in the transition to sustainability, the guidelines are non-binding on members. Action at the national level has been almost nonexistent.

Nongovernmental organizations, some of which were initially very supportive, have become increasingly disillusioned. Many regard ITTO as little more than a lobby group for the industry. Their calls for policy interventions to restrict the trade have been countered by ITTO's argument that such restrictions may actually accelerate the pace of tropical deforestation.

Research and development is an important part of ITTO's work. It coordinates projects funded through the aid agencies of consumer nations; a major emphasis is reforestation and natural forest development. Project funding has risen steadily, but is still relatively small. Funding in general has been a problem for ITTO.

ITTO has published numerous studies; its journal *Tropical Forest Management Update* (1991–) promotes conservation and management of tropical forest resources in the Asia/Pacific region. Other activities include the development of information networks aimed at improving training in forest management.

ITTO's mandate expires in 1994. Renegotiation of the International Tropical Timber Agreement began in 1993 and promises to be difficult. Producers are backing away from Target 2000, seeking the inclusion of temperate and boreal timbers, and a greater emphasis on trade issues. For consumer nations Target 2000 and mandatory reporting of progress toward that goal are primary objectives.

June D. Hall

Further Readings

Hpay, Terence. *The International Tropical Timber Agreement: Its Prospects for Tropical Timber Trade, Development and Forest Management.* 1986.

See also BIODEPLETION; ENVIRONMENTAL DIPLOMACY; FORESTRY, HISTORY OF; JAPAN; RIO CONFERENCE (1992); TROPICAL DEFORESTATION; TROPICAL RAINFORESTS

International Union for the Conservation of Nature and Natural Resources
See WORLD CONSERVATION UNION

International Whaling Commission

Throughout human history whaling has resulted in the extreme depletion of many populations of whales. The rate of depletion accelerated rapidly in the nineteenth and early twentieth centuries. Because of this and also because whales migrate outside the boundaries of national jurisdiction international cooperation became essential to prevent the continued over-exploitation of whales.

The International Convention for the Regulation of Whaling (ICRW) was signed by fifteen countries in 1946, superseding earlier more limited agreements. The Convention's purpose as stated in its preamble begins: "Recognising the interest of the nations of the world in safeguarding for future generations the great natural resources represented by the whale stocks," and concludes: "Having decided to conclude a convention to provide for the proper conservation of whale stocks and thus make possible the orderly development of the whaling industry. . . ." Thus the ICRW had the double aim of protecting whales from over-exploitation, and of maintaining a sustainable whaling industry.

The International Whaling Commission (IWC) was established by the ICRW in 1946. It has the power—by means of a three-fourth majority of members voting—to revise the measures governing whaling laid down in the Schedule to the Whaling Convention. These measures include catch limits, whaling seasons, size limits, inspections, whaling methods, and whale sanctuaries, among others. Members are allowed ninety days to register an objection to schedule changes, in which case they are not legally bound by them. The IWC has a permanent secretariat based in Cambridge, UK.

In 1993 there were forty signatories to the ICRW, thirty-three of whom had paid their full membership dues thereby obtaining voting rights in the IWC (Argentina, Australia, Brazil, Chile, People's Republic of China, Denmark, Dominica, Finland, France, Germany, Grenada, India, Ireland, Japan, Republic of Korea, Mexico, Monaco, Netherlands, New Zealand, Norway, Oman, Russian Federation, St. Kitts and Nevis, St. Lucia, St. Vincent and the Grenadines, Seychelles, Solomon Islands, South Africa, Spain, Sweden, Switzerland, United Kingdom, and United States). The annual IWC meetings are also attended by observers from non-member governments (e.g., Canada), from intergovernmental organizations (e.g., Food and Agriculture Organization [FAO], International Union for the Conservation of Nature and Natural Resources [IUCN]) and from international nongovernmental organizations (e.g., WWF-World Wildlife Fund, Inuit Circumpolar Conference).

The IWC has a Scientific Committee to provide information and advice, including comments on national research whaling programs. Although there is disagreement on whether the ICRW gives the IWC jurisdiction over dolphins, porpoises, and small whales as well as the "great whales," it has been accepted that the

Scientific Committee should examine catches of these small cetaceans and advise on their conservation.

In spite of the objectives of the ICRW to safeguard both whale stocks and the whaling industry, the convention did not define how this could be done. The IWC, composed entirely of whaling or recently ex-whaling countries, was left to act with a free hand during the 1950s and 1960s. It failed completely to prevent the depletion, especially in the Antarctic, of blue, humpback, fin, and sei whales. Vast numbers of whales were still killed each year, reaching a peak of around 64,000 in the 1960–1961 season. Blue and humpback whales were finally protected in 1965 after they had become so rare that to refrain from catching them no longer required an economic sacrifice.

From the late 1960s onward public concern for the plight of the whales made itself felt, leading to the recommendation by the 1972 United Nations (UN) Conference on the Human Environment in Stockholm for a ten-year whaling moratorium. The IWC, however, rejected this call. Instead it adopted a New Management Procedure (NMP) aimed at limiting exploitation to sustainable levels and ensuring that populations already depleted to unproductive levels be protected.

The NMP led quickly to the protection of fin and sei whales in the Antarctic and the North Pacific, but then it ran into difficulties. The Scientific Committee lacked precise enough estimates of whale populations to calculate the maximum sustainable yield level for each stock of whales. Between 1979 and 1981 several countries that had been whaling outside the IWC and others that supported the UN call for a moratorium joined the IWC. With the increased membership and the evident deficiencies of the NMP, a moratorium on all commercial whaling was agreed at the 1982 IWC meeting. It was to start in 1986 and to last indefinitely, with a review in 1990 in the light of its effects on whale stocks. Because three countries maintained objections to the moratorium and continued whaling, the moratorium did not actually come into effect until 1988. Whaling "to satisfy aboriginal subsistence need" was excluded from the moratorium but regulated by a separate management procedure from 1984.

The year 1990 proved far too soon for the Scientific Committee to be able to assess the effects of the moratorium, since estimates of whale populations are not precise enough to show whether they are increasing or decreasing over periods shorter than decades. By 1992 the IWC was considering the adoption of a Revised Management Scheme. This new scheme includes a procedure to monitor population levels and calculate safe catch limits that is far more sophisticated than the 1974 NMP, a comprehensive observation and inspection scheme, and other elements. Meanwhile tension continues between the very few IWC members that still want to go whaling and other members who for several reasons do not consider that it is either necessary or wise for the whaling industry to resume.

Cassandra Phillips

Further Readings
Lyster, Simon. *International Wildlife Law.* 1985.
International Whaling Commission. *Annual Reports.*

See also BALEEN WHALES; DOLPHINS AND PORPOISES; ENVIRONMENTAL DIPLOMACY

Intrinsic Value

Intrinsic value is the value that something has in and of itself—apart from, and in addition to whatever instrumental value it has. An intrinsically valuable entity is an end in (or to) itself, irrespective of its value as a means to another's ends.

That human beings are intrinsically valuable is taken for granted. The intrinsic value of nonhuman natural entities is problematic. When people ask "what good is it?" about an animal or plant, they are usually inquiring about its instrumental value—its usefulness in relation to another's ends or purposes. If one answers that question with another: "what good are you?," the original inquirer at once must confront two things: first, that some value—his/her own and that of other human beings—transcends the instrumental sort; and second, that nonhuman natural entities may also be intrinsically valuable.

The intrinsic value of oneself and other human beings is customarily defended by appeal to a value-conferring property. For example, Jews, Christians, and Muslims believe that human beings are uniquely created in the "image of God" and are intrinsically valuable for that reason. The intrinsic value of nonhuman natural entities and nature as a whole can also be defended biblically in that after each act of creation, God declared his work to be "good," that is, intrinsically valuable. Reason has traditionally been proffered as a more empirical value-conferring property. Some philosophers argue that "sentience," the capacity to experience pleasure and pain, is a more appropriate, as well as a more inclusive, value-conferring property. But since many animals and all plants are neither rational nor sentient, some environmental philosophers suggest that all beings to which having "interests" or having a "good of their own" can be meaningfully attributed be regarded as intrinsically valuable. But science hardly supports the supposition that wholes such as species, ecosystems, and the biosphere have interests or goods of their own. And it is impossible even to imagine that other things about which environmentalists are concerned—the atmosphere and ocean, evolutionary and ecological processes—have interests or goods of their own. Hence this line of argument terminates—unambiguously, at any rate—with the intrinsic value of nonhuman natural beings individually and leaves natural wholes and the nonliving parts of nature out of account.

From a modern scientific point of view all value—intrinsic no less than instrumental—is in the eye of the beholder. "Value" is a verb, in other words, not a noun. Human beings intrinsically value themselves and—hopefully—one another. Other valuing beings also doubtless value themselves and perhaps some of their conspecifics the same way. Though such valuing may be done arbitrarily one usually and naturally intrinsically values fellow-members of one's community and one's community as a whole—family members and family, compatriots and country, human beings and humanity. Since ecology now represents plants, animals, soils, and waters as fellow-members of the "biotic community," we ought intrinsically to value them and the biotic community as a whole.

J. Baird Callicott

Further Readings
Callicott, J. Baird, ed. "The Intrinsic Value of Nature." *The Monist* 75 (1992): 119–278.
Rolston, Holmes. *Environmental Ethics: Duties to and Values in the Natural World.* 1988.

See also ANIMAL RIGHTS; ENVIRONMENTAL ETHICS; INSTRUMENTAL VALUE; RELIGION AND ENVIRONMENTAL PROTECTION

Ionizing Radiation

Radiation is an emanation from matter and is a term usually applied to the electromagnetic spectrum of wave-like photon energy. Unlike sound waves which travel through matter electromagnetic energy waves can travel through a vacuum at the speed of light. Ionizing radiation is radiation which can ionize matter; ionization is always damaging to living cells.

Electromagnetic radiation is normally divided into non-ionizing and ionizing components. This refers to their ability to transfer energy to the electrons orbiting the nucleus of an atom. Non-ionizing radiation can cause the electron to vibrate, resulting in the production of heat; ionizing radiation can provide the electron with sufficient energy to escape from orbit. The liberated electron is called a negative ion because of its negative electrical charge. The remaining part of the atom loses its electrical neutrality and has a net positive charge. It is called a positive ion; the process is called ionization. In living tissue ions are chemically active and can produce free radicals.

Longer waves of the electromagnetic spectrum include radio, television, and microwave radiation. The medium wavelengths include infrared, visible light, and ultraviolet rays. The short wavelengths include X-rays and gamma and cosmic rays. The longer wavelengths are non-ionizing radiation. The same is true for most of the medium wavelengths. However, as the wave length approaches X-ray there is an increasing probability that some will cause ionization; that is, sometimes it displaces an electron. The short wavelengths are all ionizing.

Cosmic rays reach earth from outer space, traveling across the space vacuum. They vary in intensity somewhat from place to place depending on latitude and height above sea level. At higher altitudes and nearer the poles the cosmic rays are more intense. They are also responsible for the ionizing radiation risk associated with high altitude flying.

Gamma and X-rays can be emitted from materials on earth such as radium C and cobalt 60. They are similar in nature but X-rays are emitted by energy changes in the electrons of the atom while gamma rays originate in changes within the nucleus. X-rays used for medical diagnostic purposes are at the "softer" or longer wavelengths of the X-ray section of the electromagnetic spectrum. They are less penetrating than "hard" X-ray or gamma rays, and are used to examine bones or internal organs. Atoms that emit X-rays or gamma rays are called radioactive.

Sometimes the term "ionizing radiation" is also applied to subatomic particles emitted from the nucleus of an atom, which can cause ionization. They are also called ionizing particles and those atoms which emit such particles with statistical regularity are also said to be radioactive.

These radioactive atoms are unstable and periodically undergo a nuclear disintegration, a sub-microscopic explosion, giving off energetic small particles of three types: 1) neutrons; 2) alpha particles; and 3) beta particles. Uranium 235 and plutonium 239 give off neutrons when undergoing nuclear disintegration and if properly configured these emissions cause a nuclear chain reaction releasing large amounts of energy (nuclear reactors or nuclear bombs).

Radium 226 and uranium 238 emit alpha particles. These are nuclei of helium atoms, two protons and two neutrons, having a positive electrical charge. They are large and heavy relative to the other ionizing particles and are quickly stopped by friction in water, air, or tissue. However they are more densely ionizing of particles which they encounter along their short track. Some of the most dangerous radioactive materials, for example plutonium and americium, are alpha emitters.

Strontium 90 and tritium are examples of beta emitters. A beta particle is an electron emitted from the nucleus of an atom. It is more penetrating of living tissue than an alpha particle and less densely ionizing. It is less penetrating than X-rays or gamma rays.

Rosalie Bertell

Further Readings

Bertell, Rosalie. *Handbook for Estimating the Health Effects of Exposure to Ionizing Radiation.* 1986.

See also CHERNOBYL; NUCLEAR ELECTRIC POWER; NUCLEAR WASTES; RADIOACTIVE FALLOUT; RADON, URANIUM MINING: ENVIRONMENTAL IMPACTS; URANIUM MINING: OCCUPATIONAL HEALTH

Irrigation Impacts

Water is an essential requirement for life. In many areas irrigation is a main source of water consumption. Irrigation can improve crop yields and the economic stability of a region by reducing the risk of drought, but demands on the water supply are increasing daily and conflicts are occurring between the various users in areas of limited supply.

Irrigation projects are often massive undertakings developed in conjunction with the development of other water uses. This results in a restructuring of the landscape through the building of dams and canals, the flooding of riparian areas, and the leveling and draining of land. As well residents of the area may be displaced and/or their lifestyles altered. Thus some impacts caused by irrigation can be substantial and essentially irreversible such as the flooding caused by reservoirs. The effect of most other impacts can be reduced, provided that these impacts are considered when designing the project, proper water management is used, only suitable soils are irrigated, and agricultural practices that conserve the soil and water resources are implemented.

Impacts on Water Systems

Riparian Zones
Dams needed for water storage flood upstream terrain and alter downstream flow of water. The flooding destroys wildlife habitat, forest land, or agricultural land. The resultant reservoir is basically a body of deep, stagnant water occupying an area where species that were adapted to daily and seasonally fluctuating water levels and currents once lived. Plant and animal species not adapted to reservoir life are displaced or destroyed. These changes to the water flow may disrupt breeding patterns and destroy spawning, nesting, feeding, and rearing habitats. Dams also block the route of migratory aquatic species. In addition erosion of the reservoir shoreline releases sediments and nutrients downstream which, because of reduced stream flows, results in sedimentation and eutrophication of the downstream channel.

Water Depletion
Water is wasted when irrigation water is inefficiently applied and when evaporation and seepage occur from reservoirs and canals. This reduces the amount of water available for irrigators and other users of the water resource. Waste puts more strain on water systems and creates demand for additional dam construction and aquifer development.

Aquifer depletion occurs when groundwater is removed at a rate greater than the rate at which the aquifer is recharged. Saltwater intrusion into the aquifer may occur in coastal areas if the water table is pumped below sea level. Subsidence of the overlying land surface results when pumping of groundwater removes water and causes a reduction in the aquifer's pore size. As a result of this compaction the aquifer may be unable to contain as much water as it once had.

Water Pollution
Drainage water from irrigated fields can contain dissolved salts, nutrients, pesticides, or suspended sediments—all of which may present disposal problems. Canals and drainage ditches can also spread pathogens. Surface drainage water carries mainly sediment loads, whereas subsurface drainage water carries dissolved salts and nutrients. Leaching of coarse-textured soils can lead to significant losses of plant nutrients (particularly nitrogen) into the subsurface drainage water. As a result groundwater may become contaminated with nutrients or other pollutants that have leached into the aquifer. Disposal of drainage water into water bodies can alter the chemical or sediment characteristics of the water body, and may reduce the suitability of the water for other users or for naturally occurring organisms. Thus further treatment of the water may be needed to make it acceptable for other uses.

Impacts on Land Systems

Leveling and Drainage
Leveling and drainage is often needed in flood irrigation systems. In this process topsoil may be buried, reducing the potential fertility of the field. Drainage of wetlands removes wildlife habitat and reduces the potential for aquifer recharge. Surface water drainage may also result in erosion and off-site flooding.

Soil Erosion
Erosion removes the most productive fraction of the soil. Water erosion occurs in areas with long or steep slopes when the rate of water application exceeds the capacity of the soil to absorb water. Wind erosion in irrigated areas is most likely to occur when crops such as vegetables are grown because they produce very little residue and leave a large part of the soil surface exposed to the wind, especially after the crop has been harvested. The availability of irrigation water to a region may also encourage agricultural production on otherwise marginal agricultural land, thus further subjecting these soils to erosion.

Salinity and Waterlogging of Soil

Many soils unsuitable for irrigation have become saline after they are irrigated. Salinization is especially likely to happen when poor quality irrigation water with a high salt content is applied. Salts dissolved in the water will precipitate on the soil surface unless they are flushed out of the soil with excess water. The salts may accumulate within the rooting zone, developing concentrations at which crops will no longer grow. Furthermore, irrigation water high in sodium causes dispersion of clay particles in the soil, resulting in the formation of undesirable soil structure that is expensive and difficult to correct after the damage is done.

Perching of the water table may be caused by irrigating soils that have a substrate restricting natural soil drainage. This results in water-saturated soils occurring above the restrictive layer, and in the upward or lateral movement of water. Water-saturated soils may affect plant growth as well as the trafficability of the area.

In addition the process of salinization is initiated when evaporation draws salts to the soil surface. Without artificial drainage these soils become increasingly saline and unproductive. Seepage from canals can also result in water-saturated soils adjacent to the canal and the subsequent salinization of this soil.

Richard D. Stushnoff

Further Readings

American Society of Civil Engineers. *Environmental Aspects of Irrigation and Drainage*. 1976.

Hagan, R.M., H.R. Haise, and T.W. Edminster, eds. *Irrigation of Agricultural Lands*. 1967.

Worthington, E.B., ed. *Arid Land Irrigation in Developing Countries: Environmental Problems and Effects*. 1977.

See also AGRICULTURE: ENVIRONMENTAL IMPACTS; EUTROPHICATION; FRESHWATER WETLANDS; GARRISON DIVERSION; GROUNDWATER POLLUTION; HYDROELECTRICITY; LEACHING; OGALLALA AQUIFER; SUBSIDENCE; WATER ALLOCATIONS AND SHORTAGES (U.S. WEST)

IUCN

See WORLD CONSERVATION UNION

Izaak Walton League

The Izaak Walton League of America (IWLA) has been a major force in the U.S. conservation movement for more than seventy years. Founded in 1922 by a group of Chicago sportsmen and named for the seventeenth-century English author of *The Compleat Angler*, the IWLA focused initially on water pollution and the associated threats to sport fishing. In short order, more than 100,000 members joined nearly 3,000 chapters in forty-three states. In 1926 President Calvin Coolidge called upon members to conduct what was to become the first nationwide sampling of water quality. The IWLA has taken a leading role in promoting the enjoyment, wise use, and protection of recreational resources at the local, state, and national levels. Its influence has been felt in the creation of the Upper Mississippi River Wild Life and Fish Refuge (1924), the founding of the Natural Resources Council of America (1946), the establishment of the Outdoor Recreation Resources Review Committee (1958), and the passage of clean water legislation, among many other efforts.

The IWLA has maintained a decentralized structure, currently with 54,546 members and 379 chapters. Diverse initiatives arise at the chapter level. National program areas include air and water quality, stream protection, wetlands, energy efficiency, public lands, outdoor ethics, and farm conservation. The work of the IWLA is supported by a budget of $2 million (1991), derived largely from individual and corporate contributions (59 percent) and memberships (36 percent). Expenditures are directed to programs (76 percent), management (13 percent), and fundraising (11 percent). Publications include *Outdoor America*, the member quarterly, *Outdoor Ethics*, promoting responsible recreation, and *Splash!*, the newsletter of the Save Our Streams program. The affiliated IWLA Endowment, Inc. (founded 1943) funds conservation projects and acquires critical lands for transfer to government or private stewards.

James A. Tober

Further Reading

Fox, Stephen. *John Muir and His Legacy: The American Conservation Movement*. 1981.

Trefethen, James. *An American Crusade for Wildlife*. 1975.

See also CONSERVATION MOVEMENT

J

James Bay

James Bay is a shallow southeastern arm of Hudson Bay in Northeast Central Canada, generally less than sixty meters deep. It is 480 kilometers long from Rupert Bay in the south to Hudson Bay in the north, and 130 kilometers wide between Cape Henrietta Marie in Ontario on its western shore to Pointe-Louis XIV in Quebec on its eastern shore. Its several islands—the largest of which is Akimiski (about 3,000 square kilometers)—are administered by the Northwest Territories. The shores of the bay and some of these islands are now classified as wildlife preserves.

The Cree Indians have lived in the area for thousands of years. The first European to visit the region and see James Bay was Captain Henry Hudson who came in 1610. James Bay was later named for Captain Thomas James who explored the west coast of the bay and wintered on Chartton Island in 1631. James Bay was also explored in the 1660s by the French adventurers Radisson and Desgroseillers who established a fur trading post which was subsequently named Rupert House when the Hudson Bay Company took it over in the late 1660s. Fort George (now called Chisasibi) and Fort Albany also served as Hudson Bay Company posts for the fur trade with the Crees.

Many large, majestic rivers flow into James Bay. This accounts for the low level of salinity of its waters. From west to east, the major rivers that empty into the bay are Attawapiskat, Albany, Moose, Harricana, Nottaway, Broadback, Rupert, Eastmain, and La Grande (formerly called the Fort-George River). The rivers on the Quebec side have recently (between 1971 and 1984) been harnessed for huge hydroelectric projects by the James Bay Energy Society, a totally-owned subsidiary of Hydro-Quebec, one of the most important electric power producers in the world.

The Quebec side of James Bay, sometimes called La Radissonie, is a large region of 341,500 square kilometers (two-thirds the surface of France, twice that of England, and one-fifth of the total area of Quebec) which extends for as much as 700 kilometers in the interior. Its limits are James Bay and the Ontario border on the west, the 49th parallel on the south, the James Bay and St. Lawrence River watersheds on the east and the 55th parallel on the north. With a population of approximately 10,000 inhabitants (7,000 of them Crees and Inuit), it has one of the lowest demographic densities in the world, but much of that territory is utilized since it is the traditional hunting, trapping, and fishing ground of the Crees and, further to the North, of the Inuit.

This Nordic region has been at the center of heated debates since the beginning of the 1970s, when the newly elected Premier Robert Bourassa launched a huge program for developing the rich hydroelectric potential of the region. Electricity generation is a proud part of Quebec's national heritage. It was nationalized in Quebec in 1962 at the height of the quiet revolution by Premier Jean Lesage and the then-Minister of Energy, René Lévesque. After the 1970 October crisis Premier Bourassa decided to outdo his Liberal and Union Nationale predecessors who had built the Churchill Falls complex in Labrador and La Manicouagan in North Eastern Quebec. He launched the multibillion dollar James Bay project, the megaproject of the century as it was then called. Opting for hydroelectricity rather than nuclear or fossil energy-fired plants, the Quebec government decided to build a series of electric power stations on the La Grande River, an operation that necessitated the damming and diverting of several other rivers.

The National Assembly of Québec officially sanctioned the bill for the development of the James Bay region in 1971. Nine Cree villages took the government to court in 1972–1973, but in 1975 a historical agreement was signed between the federal government, the Crees, the Inuit, the Québec government, Hydro-Quebec and two of its subsidiaries. This Convention for James Bay and northern Quebec fixed the rules for the development of the far north, allocating $225 million to the Cree, and giving to the Cree and the Inuit absolute rights on 14,025 square kilometers of communal land, exclusive fishing, trapping and hunting rights on 162,324 square kilometers, and priority fishing, trapping and hunting rights on 880,650 square kilometers. These two groups of native people also obtained a large degree of community self-government, the relocation of the site of one of the dams, and the clearance of trees from reservoir basins before their inundation, with the Cree being given first right to contracts for doing this work. Hydro-Quebec also promised to mitigate the adverse environmental and social effects of the project, and to plant 10 million trees to replace those that were cut or submerged because of the new reservoirs.

The James Bay I project was estimated to cost $1.5 billion but ended up costing nearly $10 billion. James Bay I is now in production with 12,000 megawatts. The new James Bay II project, if and when it is finished, may include not only the much larger Nottaway-Broadback-Rubert (NBR) complex, but also other dams including the controversial Great Whale River project. By itself NBR represents a potential of 8,500 megawatts, while the Great Whale project represents only 3,168 megawatts with an annual energy production of 16.2 trillion watt-hours (TWh). The James Bay II project has provoked a broad debate both within and outside Quebec, especially in New England and New York—potential consumers of some of the electricity.

In any case the issue of hydroelectric power production in the James Bay area is a very complex one, in which numerous conflicting ideas and interests are involved. The present impasse emphasizes the need for a broad public debate which would take into account, among other parameters: 1) the need for energy conservation and environmental impact assessment studies; 2) the need to distinguish between more or less environmentally and socially benign forms of energy production; 3) the existing rights and legitimate interests of all involved parties; 4) the balancing of increased production and exportation of hydroelectricity to the United States against the reduction of acid precipitation originating in U.S. coal and oil-fired power plants; 5) the evaluation of Quebec's real energy needs in the light of environmental and economic considerations; 6) the need to carefully evaluate the views of knowledgeable environmentalists and of others who defend global perspectives rather than particularistic interests; and 7) the overall comparative economic and environmental cost of continuing, transforming, or abandoning various projects.

In sum the James Bay I and James Bay II projects may represent a precious source of renewable energy and economic advantages for Quebec, including the native people involved, but there are also negative repercussions which must be evaluated and eliminated, or at least mitigated as much as possible. The outcome of the present conflict concerning the Great Whale project will certainly point the way to the solution of the problems that will inevitably erupt when Hydro-Quebec seriously proposes to launch the NBR project in the James Bay area.

Jean-Guy Vaillancourt

Further Readings

Chartrand N., and N. Thérien (sous la dir. de). *Les enseignements de la phase I du complexe La Grande.* Montréal: Hydro-Québec, 1992.

Conseil consultatif de l'environnement. *Audiences sur les impacts environnementaux du développement de la Baie James, Tome I: Rapport préparé par le Conseil consultatif de l'environnement, Québec.* 1977.

Environnement Canada. *Le projet hydroélectrique de la Baie James.* Ottawa: Gouvernement du Canada, 1975.

Hydro-Québec (Montréal). *Les milieux naturel et humain au Complexe La Grande.* 1992. (English version available.)

Jay-Rayon, J.C. *Le dossier Baie James.* Ottawa: Collection Dossiers, 1973.

McCutcheon, Sean. *Electric Rivers—The Story of the James Bay Project.* 1991.

Richardson, Boyce. *James Bay: The Plan to Drown the North Woods.* 1972.

Turgeon, Pierre. *La Radissonie—Le pays de la Baie James.* Montréal: Libre Expression.* 1992.

See also DEMAND-SIDE MANAGEMENT; ENERGY EFFICIENCY; GREAT WHALE PROJECT IN QUEBEC; HYDROELECTRICITY; SOFT ENERGY PATHS

Japan

Japan's ecological history must be understood within the context of the nation's geography. The four main islands of Japan (Hokkaido, Honshu, Shikoku and Kyushu) are located at the northeast end of the Asian monsoon belt and are within the temperate weather zone. Approximately two-thirds of Japan's land mass is mountainous and sparsely populated, and a further 20 percent is devoted primarily to agriculture. About two-thirds of Japan is forested—the second highest percentage in the world; however, virtually none of this area can be considered "wild," and indeed the Japanese have no word for "wilderness." The great majority of Japan's 124 million people reside in only 4 percent of the country's area and, as a result, urban population densities are among the world's highest. While the population grew quickly after World War II, the growth rate was below 1 percent by the mid-1950s and is currently 0.4 percent per annum. Japan possesses very few natural resources of its own, a fact which has forced the nation to look outward for raw materials since it opened to the world in the 1850s and 1860s.

Japan has been experiencing the ecological consequences of industrialization for over a century. The problems related to the Ashio copper mine, which began in the late nineteenth century and continue to this day, are the best-known example of pre-World War II industrial pollution in Japan. While limited moves toward pollution control were made in the early twentieth century, the 1931 invasion of China led to their quickly being rolled back. Increased pollution was exacerbated by heavy wartime demand for domestic wood products which led in turn to severe deforestation and erosion. After the war, reforestation became a major national project.

However, in the time since the war Japan's ecological and social systems experienced tremendous change due to economic growth. The 1950s and 1960s were a period of extremely rapid industrialization led by the development of heavy industry and chemical production. Industrial activity was concentrated in very small areas and in the rush to "catch up with the West" little thought was given to emissions controls. Urbanization also proceeded very quickly during these decades, and a combination of household and domestic waste severely taxed ecosystems proximate to urban development. By the late 1950s many communities were suffering the impacts of waste discharge, and diseases previously unknown to medicine began to appear.

While air and water pollution and toxic waste contamination were widespread the series of calamities sweeping Japan came to be symbolized by the "Big Four" cases of *kogai byo* ("environmental disease"). These four were the outbreak of industrial asthma at Yokkaichi, mercury poisoning (Minamata disease) at Minamata and Niigata, and cadmium poisoning at Toyama. In each instance government and business colluded to avoid taking responsibility for (or even admitting the existence of) the problem, and in each case a movement of citizens suffering from the disease slowly came into existence. By the late 1960s the number of people killed or injured by the *kogai byo* was mounting and television images of the suffering victims had earned Japan an international reputation as "the most polluted nation on earth."

By the time the "Big Four" came to trial in 1972–1973 a sense of ecological crisis had developed in Japan. Such specific incidents as the Tokyo photochemical smogs of July 1970 and the 1973 "Great Fish Panic" (concerning PCB levels in fish) underlined the broader picture of a nation choking on pollution. Further the Organization of Petroleum Exporting Countries (OPEC) "shock" of 1973 provided an extremely powerful incentive to increased energy efficiency in Japanese industries. The government responded by implementing some of the world's strictest pollution control legislation. The Basic Law for Environmental Pollution Control introduced in 1967 was strengthened three years later; 1971 saw the creation of a national head office for pollution control (the Japan Environment Agency). The national government passed 149 environmental regulations during the 1970s, and local governments were also very active.

By the late 1970s the levels of most (though not all) pollutants had decreased dramatically. The anti-pollution and energy-efficiency measures established by government and industry acted in conjunction with slower economic growth and the relocation of heavy industry and resource processing overseas. All these changes combined to significantly ameliorate Japan's pollution problems. By the early 1980s the problems of the *kogai byo* days had been largely overcome. Once Japan's environment had been made safe for human habitation interest in pollution problems declined, and the major remaining environmental issue centered around the anti-nuclear movement.

By the late 1980s there were some indications that environmental quality in Japan was beginning to worsen again. Much of this worsening may be traced to the increasingly consumerist orientation of Japanese society. Japan's outstanding recycling programs (the paper recycling utilization rate of 50.3 percent is the world's highest) could not prevent Tokyo's garbage production from increasing from 3.5 to 4.5 million tons between 1985 and 1990. There are also signs that air quality is worsening. Car emission monitoring stations have been showing increased pollution in recent years and in the summer of 1991 Tokyo experienced its first photochemical smog since 1984. Nitrous oxide emissions are actually somewhat worse than they were in the 1970s, primarily because of the rising number of automobiles. Japan has had limited success in cleaning up lakes and marshes since the 1970s, and a substantial part of the underground water supply continues to be badly polluted. Residential sewage, pesticide runoff, and industrial discharges continue to pose water pollution problems.

For decades Japan's steadily growing economy has been having ever greater impacts on the international environment. During the 1950s and 1960s, these impacts were mostly consequences of Japan's need for foreign raw materials (and particularly for wood). Since the 1970s, however, more stringent pollution regulations and economic restructuring have encouraged Japanese businesses to site pollution-intensive industries in other Asian countries. Projects such as aluminum smelters and chemical factories have sparked domestic opposition in many parts of Asia. Japan's demand for timber is also a contentious issue globally. Japan imports more wood products than any other country, and the nation's timber interests have deforested large swaths of the Philippines, Indonesia, Malaysia, the United States, and Canada, and are now expanding into such countries as Chile, Papua New Guinea, Russia, and Australia. Japan's development aid program generally, and such projects as the Narmada Valley dam in India (from which Japan withdrew in 1990) and the Sarawak forestry road in Malaysia especially, have also drawn extensive criticism. Other controversial aspects of Japan's international environmental behavior have included the practice of driftnet fishing, which Japan recently banned; the voyage of the Akatsuki Maru, a Japanese vessel which carried 1.7 tons of plutonium from France to Japan in late 1992; and Japan's role in the Convention on International Trade in Endangered Species of Wild Fauna and Flora (CITES). The nation's reputation in the latter area is improving, as Japan has withdrawn several of its CITES treaty reservations in recent years. Japan, however, is often praised for its low carbon dioxide emissions (the country emits less CO_2 per unit of GNP than any other) and is making rapid strides in chlorofluorocarbon (CFC) reduction.

After a relatively quiet period interest in environmental issues has been increasing among the Japanese government, business community, and citizenry in recent years. The government has been attempting to portray itself as an "environmental superpower" on the world stage and has spent huge sums on environmental research centers and such initiatives as the New Earth 21. Business, perceiving environmental technology as an industry of the future, has been investing heavily, and seldom does a week pass without the announcement of a new pollution-control breakthrough. Japanese citizens' groups concerned with the environment are also growing, though they are still far less established than in most other industrialized countries.

Derek Hall

Further Readings

Barrett, Brendan, and Riki Therivel. *Environmental Policy and Impact Assessment in Japan.* 1991.

Huddle, Norrie, and Reich, Michael. *Island of Dreams: Environmental Crisis in Japan.* 1987.

Ui, Jun. *Industrial Pollution in Japan.* 1992.

See also ASEAN HAZE; AUTOMOBILES: IMPACTS AND POLICIES; CADMIUM; CITES; FISHERIES CONSERVATION; FORESTRY, HISTORY OF; INTERNATIONAL TROPICAL TIMBER ORGANIZATION; MERCURY; RECYCLING; SMOG; TROPICAL DEFORESTATION

Jeffers, Robinson

The poetry of Robinson Jeffers (1887–1962)—a sustained meditation on the human condition, civilization, and nature—has influenced many environmentalists. His reputation reached its nadir after World War II and has paradoxically improved as ecological and social malaise (which he prophesied) has increased. Educated in biblical studies, literature, and medicine, Jeffers spent his adult life in California, living on the Big Sur near Carmel. Natural symbols and the influence of place run throughout the poetry, as in the standard verse line, modeled on the ocean wave—a measured rising that suddenly breaks. Jeffers termed his philosophy "inhumanism," a philosophy that appeals to those who believe the earth has intrinsic value.

Jeffers, however, did not love nature and hate humanity; his concern was to expose human egotism and arrogance while developing a positive alternative to so-called humanism through careful consideration of nature's cycles and patterns. By criticizing the self-love of the human species Jeffers aligned himself with biocentric and ecocentric philosophical views. He believed that the wholesale exploitation of nature was myopic and mean-spirited, and that a more comprehensive philosophy would lead humans to find their appropriate place in the cosmos. Jeffers indicted both Judeo-Christianity and capitalism as culpable for the abuse of nature. He believed that the pursuit of political power and economic wealth were vanities, since the natural rhythms of time and place were the truest guide to the good life. His poetry is deeply religious, best described as pantheistic; he equated natural beauty with the face of God. Jeffers counsels humans to know beauty, and to be like it. However, the poetry is devoid of sentimentalism and unbounded by convention; he found beauty as readily in grassland fires that drove game for gorging raptors as in vistas of the Big Sur.

Max Oelschlaeger

Further Readings

Jeffers, Robinson. *The Selected Poetry of Robinson Jeffers.* 1959.
———. *The Collected Poetry of Robinson Jeffers.* Ed. Tim Hunt. 4 vols. 1988–1993.

See also RELIGION AND ENVIRONMENTAL PROTECTION; SNYDER, GARY

Jensen, Jens

Born in 1860 to a farm family in Dybbøl, Denmark, Jensen studied in the Danish folk high schools and attended Tune Agricultural School

outside Copenhagen. After service in the German military he emigrated to the United States in 1884 and became a laborer in Chicago's West parks. In 1888 he created the "American Garden" in Union Park featuring common native wildflowers and shrubs from the countryside. With this small garden he began his extensive career of creating natural parks and gardens.

As a member of Chicago's Special Park Commission Jensen helped to lay the groundwork for the extensive network of Forest Preserves, first recommended in the Commission's 1904 report and established by the Illinois state legislature in 1911. In 1905 he was made superintendent and landscape architect for all of Chicago's West parks and went to work reshaping Humboldt, Garfield, Douglas, and Columbus parks.

During the same time that he was working on the parks Jensen developed an extensive career as park and garden designer. Borrowing from early concepts of ecology Jensen regarded his designs as idealizations of the native landscape, grouping plants in natural associations and repeating patterns of colors, textures, sunlight and shadow, and outdoor space to evoke deep emotional responses by viewers and build support for broader conservation efforts. He also helped to found two conservation organizations—the Prairie Club and the Friends of Our Native Landscape—both of which fought to preserve the Indiana Dunes area of northern Indiana as well as other scenic, historical, and high quality natural areas throughout Illinois, Michigan, and Wisconsin. From his retirement in 1934 until his death in 1951 Jensen directed his attention to founding "The Clearing" in Ellison Bay, Wisconsin, a school dedicated to the study of nature and the arts.

Robert E. Grese

Further Readings

Eaton, Leonard K. *Landscape Artist in America: The Life and Work of Jens Jensen.* 1960.
Grese, Robert E. *Jens Jensen: Maker of Natural Parks and Gardens.* 1992.
Jensen, Jens. *Siftings.* 1939.

See also CONSERVATION MOVEMENT; ECOLOGICAL RESTORATION; OLMSTED, FREDERICK LAW; URBAN DESIGN

Jevons, W. Stanley

Concern over the sustainability of economic growth is not new. It has been a major theme

J

of economists including Smith, Malthus, and Ricardo who wrote during the early years of the industrial revolution. After a century of continuous economic expansion, however, this concern subsided and most economists believed that economic growth could last forever.

The work of W. Stanley Jevons (1835–1882) reflected both the ideas and concepts of his classical predecessors and the emerging ideas that were to become the foundation of twentieth century neo-classical economics. Indeed Jevons was one of several inventors of "marginal" analysis on which the modern analysis of demand, supply, and markets is based.

Jevons's work, which is rooted in the older traditions of economics, merits attention today for its relevance to conservation and environmentalism. In 1865 he published *The Coal Question* in which he argued that Britain's supremacy in manufacturing and commerce was based on iron made from cheap coal. As production increased mines would have to be deeper and British coal would become more costly. Moreover, with the emergence of oil as a cheaper source of energy in the United States, Jevons believed that Britain's days of economic leadership were numbered.

Jevons's analysis of coal is sometimes cited as evidence of the inherent weakness in the limits-to-growth argument, but this is not a fair assessment of his work. Britain did lose its economic supremacy to the United States, a country much more richly endowed with natural resources. Whether the experience of countries dealing with localized resource scarcities is transferable to the world economy at large remains debatable. Nevertheless, it is to Jevons's lasting credit that his fascination with the more modern tools of economic analysis did not blind him to the fundamental dependence of all economic activity on the natural environment.

Peter A. Victor

Further Readings

Jevons, W.S. *The Coal Question*. 1865.

White, Michael V. "A Biographical Puzzle: Why Did Jevons Write the Coal Question?" *Journal of the History of Economic Thought* 13 (1991).

See also GREEN ECONOMICS; ECONOMIC GROWTH AND THE ENVIRONMENT; NONRENEWABLE RESOURCES; SUSTAINABILITY

Jobs and the Environment

It is deceptively simple to devise a list of the jobs lost and gained as a result of environmental damage and protection. Fishing, hunting, mining, and drilling have employed inestimable millions of people through the centuries. Unrestricted pollution, waste, and resource use create side effects whose costs are borne by society as a whole. Such externalities reduce production costs and in effect subsidize employment. Limitations on logging, exhaust fumes, or pesticide runoff therefore can result in layoffs of workers.

On the other hand, environmental protection has expanded jobs. Limits on resource extraction permit more sustained and sustainable employment over time. Environmental policies have reinvigorated some waning occupations, such as passenger rail service and mass transit, and they have created new occupations in conservation, regulatory enforcement, waste handling (including recycling), wastewater treatment construction, and the manufacture of environmental technology. Other pro-environmental activities are also labor intensive including tree planting, more diversified ("alternative") agriculture, and the hand (as opposed to the chemical) clearing of rights-of-way. Specifically, by one estimate, the industrialized member nations of the Organisation for Economic Co-operation and Development (OECD) spent about $200 billion annually on pollution control in the early 1990s; these outlays had created 5 million jobs in the United States and Western Europe (Renner, 1992; compare OECD, 1978).

But the relationship between jobs and the environment is much more elusive and contentious than is implied by a simple listing of jobs lost and gained. The economic effects of pollution and its control defy easy measurement because the indirect effects of environmental change make it very difficult to specify how many jobs are lost and gained at any given time in any given place. Many things affect the gain and loss of jobs over time. An air pollution regulation may force an inefficient factory to close, with job losses rippling through the community; but closing an unprofitable plant may financially benefit its parent corporation, resulting in more hirings in that corporation in the long term. Conservation and pollution control may not be the decisive factors creating job losses when international competition, technological change, or other factors also contribute to the erosion of certain jobs. Increased use of pollution technology provides little job creation for an economy if the nation must import this technology from abroad. Discerning the degree to which environmental limitations contributed to unemployment *independently* of other market factors is virtually impossible.

Another difficulty in estimating the relationship is the effect of environmental initiatives on job quality. Environmental policies have affected not only the number of jobs, but also their pay, benefits, security, and health and safety. The pioneering environmental laws in industrialized nations included nineteenth-century factory acts that regulated industrial environments. Occupational safety and health laws in the early 1970s corresponded with the rise of the environmental movement. Environmental protection can create well-paid professional jobs but, when it renders some production skills obsolescent, it also can force workers with a lifetime investment in these skills into "under-employment" in jobs with lower skill needs, wages, benefits, and security. Those who argue that environmental policy creates jobs concede that such policy can result in significant dislocation for workers in existing industries.

These complexities and uncertainties contribute to the intense political conflicts that surround jobs and the environment. Individuals, industries, or regions have different, frequently conflicting economic stakes in implementing environmental protection, and so these initiatives may stimulate considerable controversy. Unions will have a stake in protecting existing jobs and pay scales. Local residents will be torn between environmental and economic security; they may be deeply divided over the job creation and the environmental risk entailed in such initiatives as the startup of a toxic waste incinerator in their area. Thus political conflict over jobs and the environment particularly focuses on the displacement of local or sectoral employment. One may expect that as an environmental initiative expands in scope, it will affect a greater number of jobs and localities and thus engender more opposition. Such side payments as job training and unemployment compensation for affected workers can assuage this opposition and address legitimate concerns for equity.

The inherently political nature of the relationship between jobs and the environment invites political adversaries to distort this relationship for political advantage. One may expect that opponents of an environmental proposal will tend to emphasize the threat to existing jobs, while proponents will tend to minimize the independent impact on existing jobs and the potential payoff in job growth in the future.

Public opinion polls offer uncertain guidance for resolving political disputes in which proposed environmental gains conflict with fears of immediate job losses. There is evidence of shifting generational concerns away from economic security and toward "quality of life" concerns, including environmental protection. American public opinion polls in the early 1990s showed majorities willing to sacrifice some local jobs for environmental protection. In this context, the concept of sustainable development—including work sharing and shifts to employment with relatively little environmental impact—constitutes an explicit effort to find a middle ground between the conflicting demands for economic and environmental security.

David Brian Robertson

Further Readings

"Jobs vs. Environment." *The CQ Researcher* 2 (1992): 409–32.

Organisation for Economic Co-Operation and Development. *Employment and Environment.* OECD 1992.

Renner, Michael. "Creating Sustainable Jobs in Industrial Countries." In *State of the World, 1992.* Ed. Lester R. Brown et al. 1992.

See also ENVIRONMENTAL JUSTICE MOVEMENT; ECONOMIC GROWTH AND THE ENVIRONMENT; GREEN ECONOMICS; LABOR AND THE ENVIRONMENT; SUSTAINABLE DEVELOPMENT

Johnson, Lyndon B.

Lyndon B. Johnson (LBJ) (1908–1973) was the 36th president of the United States, ascending into office following the assassination of John F. Kennedy. LBJ's presidency (1963–1969) is characterized by the steady rise of environmental policies on the national agenda. His administration contributed to the shift from the traditional conservation policies of the 1950s to the more active environmentalism of the 1970s. Johnson's broad support of environmental needs and willingness to lend presidential support to various environmental programs provided an impetus to what became known as the environmental movement. But LBJ's preoccupation with Vietnam and the civil unrest it spawned prevented his environmental initia-

J

tives from achieving their promise while he was president.

LBJ presided over many legislative actions in environmental quality and protection. Most began with the goals of his "Great Society," which included a better environment as a necessary way to ensure an improved quality-of-life for all Americans. Along with his dream of a greater America Johnson was catalyzed by his wife, Lady Bird, and her desire for a more beautiful America. He was also influenced by White House science advisers who warned of new environmental problems and the environmental advocacy of Secretary of the Interior Stewart L. Udall.

Johnson brought his considerable presidential personality and federal resources to bear on many environmental issues. Nine LBJ presidential task forces looked into environmental problems ranging from pollution, natural resource preservation, and recreational use of the environment. Congress passed and LBJ signed into law nearly 300 conservation and beautification measures that cost over $12 billion. These dealt with such matters as wilderness areas, endangered species, clean air, solid waste disposal, historic preservation, and many others. They constituted the largest number of environmental actions passed in the nation's history up to this time. Johnson also slowed down development of the Supersonic Transport (SST), so its sonic boom and other environmental problems could be better understood and addressed. In part because of these issues the SST was terminated in 1971.

Given the rapid increase in awareness concerning environmental issues in the 1960s and the activistic legacy of John F. Kennedy, the time was ripe for an increased legislative push in the environmental field. LBJ's legislative success may have been based in part on the luck of timing. However, Johnson, as a consummate politician, sensed the opportunity and pushed a legislative program. He moved the nation forward in the environmental field. Vietnam prevented much that was passed in legislation from being funded adequately and implemented. Also LBJ's Vietnam military policies included the deliberate deployment of toxic chemicals, such as Agent Orange, to defoliate forests. On the domestic front Johnson transmitted to his successors an environmental policy legacy on which they could build.

W. Henry Lambright and Mark J. O'Gorman

Further Readings

Hays, Samuel P. "From Conservation to Environment: Environmental Politics in the United States since World War II." *Environmental Review* 6 (Fall 1982): 24–27.

Lambright, W. Henry. *Presidential Management of Science and Technology: The Johnson Presidency.* 1985.

Melosi, Marvin V. "Lyndon Johnson and Environmental Policy." In *The Johnson Years: Vietnam, the Environment, and Science.* Vol. 2. Ed. Robert A. Divine. 1987.

See also HERBICIDES; KENNEDY, JOHN F.; UDALL, STEWART L.

Johnson, Robert Underwood

Robert Underwood Johnson (1853–1937) was an editor, poet and political activist. Johnson was raised in Indiana and educated at Earlham College, receiving a B.S. in 1871. His long affiliation with Scribner's Publishing Co. began in 1871 and ended with his resignation in 1913 as editor-in-chief of *Century Magazine*, a popular literary journal. In the 1890s, under Johnson's leadership as Associate Editor, *Century* became the leading advocate of a national conservation policy.

Johnson's relationship with John Muir (1838–1914) began with correspondence in the mid-1880s. The two met for the first time in the summer of 1889, when Johnson came west to promote a gold rush series for *Century*. During a camping trip through the high country above Yosemite Valley, they formulated plans that led to the creation of two national parks, Yosemite and Sequoia. With Johnson's encouragement and editorial assistance Muir's literary career blossomed in the 1890s, and his wilderness advocacy was given national exposure in the pages of *Century*.

Johnson himself made invaluable contributions to the cause of national conservation. His connections with the national political leadership were essential for the passage of the Yosemite and Sequoia bills, for recession and incorporation of Yosemite Valley into the National Park, and for development and implementation of the national forest reserve policy. He initiated the idea that led President Theodore Roosevelt in 1908 to call a national governor's conference on forest conservation, and his lobbying in opposition to the damming of Hetch Hetchy Valley helped focus national attention on fundamental policy needs for national parks.

Muir's death in 1914 and the beginning of World War I shifted Johnson's focus to public affairs. He led fund-raising efforts for ambulances on the Italian front and for Italian War Relief and after the war served briefly as Ambassador to Italy (1920–1921). In his later years he directed the literary Hall of Fame in New York for the American Academy of Arts and Letters, and published more than a dozen collections of poetry as well as his memoirs.

Ronald H. Limbaugh

Further Readings

Johnson, Robert U. *Remembered Yesterdays.* 1923.

Limbaugh, R.H., and Kirsten Lewis, eds. *The John Muir Papers, 1838–1957* (Microform ed., 1986).

See also CONSERVATION MOVEMENT; HETCH HETCHY DAM; MUIR, JOHN; REDWOODS; SIERRA CLUB

J

K

Kelly, Petra

Petra Kelly was known worldwide for her passionate and tireless campaigning on behalf of green politics. In 1991 the Sunday Times of London nominated her as one of the 1,000 makers of the twentieth century. Born in post-war Germany, her dedication to non-violence and human rights she learned at university in America during the 1960s, while her work in the European Commission revealed the links between ecology and feminism. Her strength and courage were learned, she said, from her 10-year-old step-sister who died of cancer in 1970.

Kelly was born Petra Karin Lehmann on November 29, 1947, taking the surname of her step-father in 1960. She was educated in Germany, the United States, and the Netherlands and held a B.A. *cum laude* in international politics from American University in Washington, D.C. She was perhaps the best known member of the (West) German Green Party. She served in 1979 as head of list in the European elections and in 1980–1982 was speaker for *Die Grünen*. From 1983 to 1990 she was an elected member of the Bundestag (German Federal parliament), serving on the Foreign Affairs Committee and, in 1983, as speaker for the Green parliamentary group. She won the 1982 Right Livelihood Foundation Award (the "Alternative Nobel Prize").

She has coedited several books including *A Nuclear Ireland?* (1978); *Ökopax—die neue Kraft* (1982); and *Wohin Denn Wir?: Texte aus der Bewegung* (1982). Several collections of her speeches and essays have been published in several languages, the best known being *Fighting for Hope* (1983). She also published *Hiroshima* (1986), *Mit dem herzen denken* (1990), and coedited *The Anguish of Tibet* (1991) and *Guernica und die deutschland* (1992).

Gifted at bringing people together around a particular cause, Petra Kelly helped to organize a "Nürnberg Hearing" to indict the nuclear states in 1983 and, in 1989, she held the First International and Non-Partisan Hearing on Tibet and Human Rights. She condemned breaches of human rights with equal fervor regardless of all other circumstances and was a loyal supporter of the dissident groups in East Germany throughout the 1980s. The tragedy and untimeliness of her death (her partner Gert Bastian shot her before turning the gun on himself) does not detract from the compassion and honesty which Petra Kelly brought to politics. The hope she inspired in all those who heard her speak and her concern to respond to all those who turned to her for help will be her enduring legacy.

Sara Parkin

Further Readings

Kelly, Petra, and John F. Carroll. *A Nuclear Ireland.* 1978.
———, and Jo Leinen. *Ökopax—die neue Kraft.* 1982.
———, and Manfred Coppik. *Wohin Denn Wir?: Texte aus der Bewegung.* 1982.
———. *Hiroshima.* 1986.
———. *Mit dem herzen denken.* 1990.
Parkin, Sara. *The Life and Death of Petra Kelly.* 1994.

See also GREEN PARTIES; GREEN PARTIES: GERMANY

Kennedy, John F.

President John F. Kennedy (1961–1963) supported a modest extension of federal authority over air and water pollution, which the

Eisenhower administration had characterized as "a uniquely local blight." During the 1960 campaign Kennedy vowed to reverse Eisenhower's veto of a $100 million sewage treatment grant bill. This was quickly accomplished in 1961 by passage of legislation which also extended for the first time federal jurisdiction over all interstate and navigable waters. Although he balked at supporting stronger federal enforcement powers proposed by Senator Edmund S. Muskie, Kennedy espoused a new federal air pollution program that was enacted by Congress shortly after his death as the Clean Air Act of 1963. He also gave crucial support to what became the Wilderness Act (1964) and the Land and Water Conservation Fund (1965).

Kennedy responded to publication of Rachel Carson's *Silent Spring* by appointing a special panel of the President's Science Advisory Committee to study the effects of persistent agricultural pesticides. The panel's May 1963 report warned of the potential dangers of DDT and other pesticides, contributing to later bans and restrictions on such chemicals.

Kennedy called for greater protection of natural resources generally in a special message to Congress (February 23, 1961) and convened the first White House Conference on Conservation since 1908. He gave strong support to Stewart L. Udall, who served as Secretary of the Interior through both the Kennedy and Johnson administrations. Udall reactivated interest in public land preservation and launched a "New Conservation" campaign that greatly expanded protection of wild and scenic lands in the national parks, forests, and wildlife refuges during the 1960s.

Norman J. Vig

Further Readings
Kennedy, John F. *To Turn the Tide.* John W. Gardner, ed. 1962.
Sundquist, James L. *Politics and Policy: The Eisenhower, Kennedy, and Johnson Years.* 1968.
Udall, Stewart L. *The Quiet Crisis* (Foreword by John F. Kennedy). 1963 (reissued 1988).

See also AIR POLLUTION: REGULATION (U.S.); CARSON, RACHEL; JOHNSON, LYNDON B.; LEGISLATION: UNITED STATES; MUSKIE, EDMUND S.; PESTICIDES; UDALL, STEWART L.

Kenyan Green Belt Movement
See ENVIRONMENTAL MOVEMENT: LESS-AFFLUENT NATIONS

Kepone Spill
See HOPEWELL, VIRGINIA (KEPONE) SPILL

Keystone Species
In 1969 Robert T. Paine coined the term keystone species to refer to species whose removal would cause a drastic change in community composition. In particular keystone species were originally defined as predators which preferentially ate and controlled the density of a primary consumer species, which in turn was capable of excluding other species from the community.

Although the original connotation of the term implied that removal of a keystone species would cause a decrease in numbers of species in a community, subsequent uses of the term included reference to a wide variety of species with very different effects on their communities. These uses included generalist predators whose removal would increase overall species diversity, and prey species whose removal would either decrease or increase species diversity. In addition species such as pollinators, seed dispersers, and the plants they depend on have been called "keystone" because they appear critical to food webs which support large numbers of species. Finally the "keystone" label has been applied to species which modify the habitat, via foraging (e.g., elephants and sea urchins) or space use (e.g., beaver dams, termite mounds), thereby having critical effects on the species present.

In response to this growing literature that some species have particularly strong effects on the distribution and abundance of other species in their community, many biologists and policy analysts have begun to call for special protection or management for keystone species. However, a recent paper by L. Scott Mills et al. points out several pitfalls of relying on keystone species in conservation contexts. While the term has been useful for showing that all species do not have equal strengths of interaction with each other there has not been an operational definition to reliably classify whether a species is or is not a "keystone." Therefore, subsets of species may be labelled keystone, while other species of similar importance might be ignored. Secondly, a species may play a keystone role in some environmental settings or communities but not in others, making generalization difficult. Finally, giving priority protection to perceived keystone species may obscure other criteria on which species protection decisions should be based. For example loss of combinations of non-keystone species might have greater effects than the loss of a keystone. Also, certain wide-ranging species (e.g., spotted owls or wolverines) may play only a weak role in maintaining species richness in their communities, but their protection may ensure sufficient habitat heterogeneity for other species.

In sum, there are numerous dangers in applying the keystone label, all of which harken back to the risk that applying a keystone/non-keystone dualism to all of nature may overly simplify the complexity of natural systems. However, it is equally clear from experimental work that some species do, in fact, have unusually strong interactions in their communities. Thus, there is certainly an appropriate place in management and policy for incorporating the interaction strengths of particular species. An emerging definition of keystone species spans all trophic groups and community responses, holding that a keystone is one whose impacts on its community are large on an absolute scale, and also much larger than would be expected from its numbers or biomass. Future work to make such a definition operational will advance both basic ecology and application of the concept to conservation issues.

L. Scott Mills

Further Readings

Mills, L.S., M.E. Soulé, and D.F. Doak. "The Keystone-Species Concept in Ecology and Conservation." *Bioscience* 43 (1993): 219–24.

Paine, R.T. "A Note on Trophic Complexity and Community Stability." *American Naturalist* 103 (1969): 91–93.

———. "Food-Web Analysis Through Field Measurement of Per Capita Interaction Strength." *Nature* 355 (1992): 73–75.

See also BIODEPLETION; BIODIVERSITY; FOOD CHAINS; HABITAT FRAGMENTATION, PATCHES, AND CORRIDORS; WEB OF LIFE

Krutch, Joseph Wood

K

A distinguished man of letters, Joseph Wood Krutch (1893–1970) became late in his life a naturalist, a conservationist, and a philosopher of humankind's relation to nature. Born into a bourgeois family in Knoxville, Tennessee, he spent over three decades of his mature life in the New York City area as drama critic for the *Nation* and a literature professor at Columbia University. In that period he was an influential spokesman for modernism, which rejected all the old faiths, including faith in society and nature. But then in the 1930s he began to repudiate that movement for its nihilism. He was likewise unsympathetic with Marxism in politics or art. Instead he turned to the writings of Henry Thoreau, published a biography of him in 1948, and increasingly took an interest in the world of nature.

Moving to Tucson in 1952, he found the deepest happiness of his life exploring the desert flora and fauna. Although an amateur naturalist who eagerly embraced science, he could not agree with the tendency of science to reduce nature, or humanity, to a mechanical formula. Life itself had become for him a wonderful mystery and a source of hope; particularly through sympathetic observation of animals he achieved insight into his humanness, more profound than traditional humanism had revealed. His Tucson-era writings included *The Desert Year* (1952), *The Voice of the Desert* (1955), *The Great Chain of Life* (1958), and *Grand Canyon* (1956). For a rising generation of post-war environmentalists, Krutch expressed an urge to reestablish roots in nature. Like Thoreau he criticized the materialism of his society for its shallowness of purpose and its ecological destructiveness. While others assumed greater political visibility in the environmental movement, he offered a quiet, literate, commonsensical voice, and a deep passion for life.

Donald Worster

Further Readings

Krutch, Joseph Wood. *More Lives Than One.* 1962.

Margolis, John D. *Joseph Wood Krutch: A Writer's Life.* 1980.

See also ENVIRONMENTALISM; GRAND CANYON; THOREAU, HENRY DAVID

L

Labor and the Environment

Throughout the recent history of the environmental movement there has been a public perception—not without foundation—that labor unions and labor union members have been constantly at odds with environmental organizations and environmentalists. There *have* been notable examples of conflict, especially regarding the use of coal and nuclear power (as opposed to alternative energy sources) and regarding the cutting versus the preservation of old-growth forests. However, from the late 1960s to the present, there has also been a less visible history of cooperation and a search for common interests between these two sociopolitical forces.

Labor-environmentalist contacts and conferences date to the 1960s, during the same time that contemporary environmentalism had its origins. There was previously considerable support of conservation movement objectives by some labor organizations. The United Autoworkers Union (UAW), for example, has had an active and effective conservation office since the days of Walter Reuther's presidency (1946–1970). The UAW sponsored labor-environmentalist meetings in the late 1960s and a very large labor-environmentalist-community group conference in 1971.

Over the years there have been several such gatherings at the Walter Reuther Family Education Center in Black Lake, Michigan. This facility—used as the union's main training center for shop stewards and other union officials and activists—has for decades featured solar-heated swimming and shower facilities and had wind-powered electric cars as early as 1971. Barry Commoner addressed the 1971 meeting.

In the early 1970s a series of publications appeared in a cooperative spirit. Leonard Woodcock, then-president of the UAW, published an article entitled "Labor and the Politics of the Environment" in *Sierra Club Bulletin* and Franklin Wallick, another UAW official who was instrumental in the passage of OSHAct, published "Factory Pollution: It Doesn't Go up the Chimney" in *Environmental Action*. Michael McClosky, then-president of the Sierra Club, wrote a 1973 pamphlet entitled *Labor and Environmentalism: Two Movements That Should Work Together*. In the mid-1970s in Australia, with considerable global visibility, unions acted directly in defense of the environment through the use of "green bans"—job actions taken on environmental grounds. About the same time, with both union and environmentalist support, the organization Environmentalists for Full Employment was established in Washington, D.C.

There were generally two issues on which labor-environmentalist cooperation has focused in both the United States and Canada: the relationship between environmental protection and employment and the links between occupational and environmental health. A separate entry on jobs and the environment appears elsewhere in this volume. It is sufficient to note here that considerable attention was given to data showing that there are jobs to be gained from many environmental protection initiatives—in the production, installation, and maintenance of pollution abatement equipment, in recycling, in solar energy and energy efficiency improvements, in public transportation, and so forth. Many in the labor movement and many in the environmental movement have worked hard to defuse or offset the concerns of those whose jobs would appear vulnerable as and when environmental protection initiatives are taken. Those efforts notwithstanding, Ronald Reagan gained considerable support from union members in, for example, the coal mines of Ohio when campaigning on an anti-environmental protection platform.

The relationship between occupational health concerns and environmental health or toxics concerns have provided a more consistent common ground for labor-environment cooperation. Workplace exposures to new toxic chemicals generally come earlier and are at a higher average exposure level than environmental exposures (albeit for fewer hours in some cases). Frequently neither setting can be protected effectively unless both are protected. Even where the solution to occupational exposures is put forward as venting to the air outside the factory gate, workers and their families living in the surrounding community may well be then double victims of exposures to the same chemicals—both occupationally and environmentally. Cooperation on this issue was initiated in several instances by the Oil, Chemical, Atomic Workers' Union (OCAW) and in particular Mr. Anthony Mazzocchi.

In the 1990s union organizations and environmental organizations in both the United States and Canada cooperated in opposition to the North American Free Trade Agreement (NAFTA) effectively enough that two side agreements (on labor and on the environment) became political necessities.

Robert Paehlke

Further Readings

Commoner, Barry. "Workplace Burden." *Environment* 15 (1973): 15–20.

———. "Energy and Labour: Job Implications of Energy Development or Shortage." *Alternatives: Perspectives on Society, Technology, and Environment* 7 (1978): 4–13.

Grossman, Richard, and Gail Daneker. *Energy, Jobs and the Economy.* 1979.

See also ENVIRONMENTAL JUSTICE MOVEMENT; JOBS AND THE ENVIRONMENT; NAFTA AND THE ENVIRONMENT; OSHAct AND OSHA

Lake Baikal

Lake Baikal is located in East Siberia, a short distance north of the Mongolian border. Lying in a deep geological depression called a graben, it contains the world's largest volume of fresh water. The lake extends for about 650 kilometers (400 miles) between the Baikal and Primorskiy ranges to the west, and the Khamar-Daban and Barguzin ranges to the east. Baikal's large size causes it to heat and cool slowly, sometimes taking until January to completely freeze over. Its basin is subject to severe earthquakes.

It is famous as the world's deepest body of fresh water. At its maximum depth, near Olkhon Island, it reaches 1,620 meters. Its surface area is 31,490 square kilometers; this area was increased slightly by a dam at Irkutsk which raised the surface elevation one meter. It is fed by 336 tributaries, of which the largest are the Selenga and Barguzin rivers to the east and the Verkhnyaya Angara at its north end. It is drained by the Angara River which flows into the Yenisey. The Selenga, which originates in the arid steppes of Mongolia, carries considerable sediment and has created a large depositional delta.

Baikal is also one of the world's oldest and most biologically diverse lake habitats. In its waters can be found over 1,000 species of plants and animals, of which a remarkable 73 percent are endemic. Among the endemic species are the world's only freshwater sponge, a freshwater seal (the *nerpa*), and species of transparent gobies (small fish) that can survive the tremendous pressure in the lake's depths. Its biological uniqueness and scientific value make the protection of Lake Baikal a worldwide priority.

Scientific concern about Baikal has intensified over the past thirty years because of significant pollution threats. Timber harvesting and small industries have existed along its shoreline for decades but in the 1960s plans were developed for two very large wood-processing factories. These factories, plus expanded logging operations, would produce vast amounts of water pollutants, and a debate ensued over whether the proposed wastewater treatment plants would adequately preserve the quality of Lake Baikal's waters.

Although Russian conservationists opposed the factories there was little chance they would be canceled. Instead plans and special decrees were adopted that included advanced wastewater treatment plants, limitations on logging, a commission to monitor water quality, and other safeguards to protect the lake. A later regulation mandated that wood pulp produced by the plants be processed elsewhere to preclude further pollution. At this time a number of nature reserves and national parks were established around the Lake Baikal shoreline.

Nevertheless accusations continued that the purification facilities were inadequate and that Baikal was being seriously harmed. In 1987 it was decreed that one pulp mill be converted to furniture manufacturing, a closed-cycle water system be built, and logging be further curtailed. Unfortunately the economic and political crises that followed the 1991 dissolution of the USSR resulted in few of the proposed changes being adopted. Thus the future ecological integrity of this most unique lake is still in considerable doubt.

Philip R. Pryde

Further Readings

Pryde, P.R. *Environmental Management in the Soviet Union*. 1991.
Vorobyev, V., and A. Martynov. "Protected Areas of the Lake Baikal Basin." *Soviet Geography* 30 (1989): 359–70.

See also BIODIVERSITY; EASTERN EUROPE: ENVIRONMENTAL PROBLEMS; FORMER SOVIET UNION

Lake Pedder

During the period 1965–1985 a number of major conservation controversies occurred in Australia, principally concerning wilderness preservation. The initiating issue was a decision by the State Hydro-Electric Commission in 1965 to flood Lake Pedder National Park as part of the Gordon River Power Scheme. Lake Pedder was the "jewel in the crown" of an area of peaks, lakes, and mountains in the rugged and uninhabited "South West" of the island state of Tasmania, an area ultimately to be placed on the World Heritage list in the early 1980s.

Lake Pedder was approximately ten square miles in extent, with a broad sandy beach at its eastern fringe, providing a natural landing strip for light aircraft in the summer months. The only other means of access was on foot, taking at least three days from the nearest roadhead. The peat-stained waters of the lake provided magnificent reflections of the adjacent mountains, making it a mecca for artists and photographers, as much as backpackers and the occasional prospector.

The decision by the Hydro-Electric Commission to flood one of Australia's prime scenic assets caused a public outcry but did not dissuade the Tasmanian government from proceeding with the power scheme, even though the commonwealth of Australia offered compensation to pursue an alternative energy option. Although Lake Pedder was lost the campaign was the catalyst for a powerful conservation lobby to emerge in Australia, saving substantial wilderness tracts in other parts of the nation. The Lake Pedder campaign also put the national and state governments on a collision course about approval procedures in major resource projects. Politically and constitutionally the Commonwealth (the national government) now has the dominant position.

Bruce W. Davis

Further Readings

Davis, Bruce W. "Waterpower and Wilderness: Political and Administrative Aspects of the Lake Pedder Controversy." *Public Administration* 31 (1972): 21–42.
Lowe, D. *The Price of Power: The Politics behind the Tasmanian Dams Case*. 1984.
Sornarajah, M., ed. *The South West Dam Dispute: The Legal and Political Issues*. 1983.
Thompson, P. *Power in Tasmania*. 1981.

See also FRANKLIN DAM; LEGISLATION: AUSTRALIA; TASMANIAN WILDERNESS SOCIETY

Land Ethic

The "Land Ethic" is the capstone essay of Aldo Leopold's conservation classic, *A Sand County Almanac* (1949). There Leopold sketches the prototype of a non-anthropocentric holistic environmental ethic, building upon Charles Darwin's account of the origin and evolution of ethics in *The Descent of Man* (1871).

How could ethics—which Leopold characterizes as "limitations on freedom of action in the struggle for existence"—have been naturally selected? At first glance it would seem that the no-holds-barred competition for scarce resources and mates would have eliminated any tendency toward self-restraint. But because human survival and reproductive success depend upon social organization, and social organization is impossible without limitations on personal freedom of action, human ethics arose and evolved. Ethics therefore are correlative to society. As human society changes, ethics change apace.

Aboriginal human societies included about fifty genetically related persons. Over time these bands merged into tribes, tribes into ethnic confederacies, and ethnic confederacies into nation-states. At each stage in this process of social merger there occurs a correlative expansion of ethics. Darwin explains, "As man advances in civilization, and small tribes are united into larger communities, the simplest reason would tell each individual that he ought to extend his social instincts and sympathies to all the members of the same nation, though personally unknown to him." Today nation-states are merging into a "global village." The proclamation of universal "human rights" is its ethical correlate.

Leopold envisions the next stage. Ecology now represents human society to be a part of an even larger society, the "biotic community." Thus when human beings come to recognize plants and animals, soils and waters as fellow-members of this more comprehensive society, the same "simplest reason" should kick in and a land ethic emerge: "All ethics so far evolved rest upon a single premise: that the individual is a member of a community of interdependent parts . . . . [Ecology] simply enlarges the boundaries of the community to include soils, waters, plants, and animals, or collectively: the land . . . . A [correlative] land ethic implies respect for fellow-members, and also respect for the community as such."

The form or structure of human societies has also changed over time. Therefore just what one's duties and obligations are, as well as to whom one owes them, has changed as well. Since the structure of the biotic community is radically different from the structure of all human communities proper, the duties and obligations one owes non-human fellow-members and the community-as-such are also radically different. For example, Leopold saw nothing wrong with killing and eating some fellow-members of the biotic community—because trophic relations are central to its structure—while doing the same thing to fellow-members of all one's human communities is rigorously proscribed and punished. Because the biotic community is described by ecology, which is concerned with wholes, land ethical duties to the community-as-such eclipse duties to individual fellow-members. Indeed, the summary moral maxim of the land ethic altogether omits mention of fellow-members: "A thing is right when it tends to preserve the integrity, stability, and beauty of the biotic community. It is wrong when it tends otherwise."

J. Baird Callicott

Further Readings
Callicott, J. Baird. *In Defense of the Land Ethic*. 1989.
Flader, Susan L., and J. Baird Callicott, eds. *The River of the Mother of God and Other Essays by Aldo Leopold*. 1991.
Leopold, Aldo. *A Sand County Almanac and Sketches Here and There*. 1949.

See also DARWIN, CHARLES; ENVIRONMENTAL ETHICS; FOOD CHAINS; INSTRUMENTAL VALUE, INTRINSIC VALUE; LEOPOLD, ALDO; WEB OF LIFE

Land-Use Planning
Land-use planning is the process of protecting and improving the living, production, and recreational environment through the proper use and development of land. Its essential justification is the public interest.

The public interest issues that have been more or less sanctioned by law include the core elements of health, safety, and convenience; the ever-present considerations of economic efficiency and social equity; the emerging concerns of environmental quality and energy conservation; the controversial question of visual amenity; and others, from local fiscal well-being to heritage conservation to public transit to affordable housing. Much of what we call urban planning, city planning, or town planning, especially in its early history, is really land-use planning.

The greatest impetus for land-use planning was the physical needs and problems of the industrialized cities of the nineteenth century (beginning around 1800 in Britain, 1840 in the United States, and 1880 in Canada). Almost all the places that have since become major cities and towns acquired their land-use characteristics based first on the railway and then the streetcar.

The railway passenger station anchored the downtown commercial area. The marshaling yards for freight trains consumed large amounts of city space and, in port cities, cut off the harbor from the rest of the city. Industrial firms located near the freight terminals or along rail lines. Housing for the more affluent stayed away while housing for poorer people was left to the land adjacent to industry and railways. Then came the streetcar which dramatically influenced the pattern of residential development. The electrification of streetcars and the extension of the lines were a great stimulus for land development along the routes. The overall pattern of the city took on a finger-like shape.

Two initial challenges commanded the attention of the pioneers of planning: deterioration of living conditions, and deterioration of the appearance of cities. Out of the first came the notion of Garden Cities, entirely new communities designed to facilitate a new pattern of living and working. Out of the second came the notion of the "City Beautiful," the redesign of major thoroughfares and public places in existing cities. A third challenge was speculative suburban development. The protection of land values and the demand for better roads, sewers, and other services made the "City Efficient" a focus of planning.

Since the 1950s downtown railway freight facilities had become obsolete, and redevelopment was the rage. The "exploding metropolis" was an apt term describing the state of affairs of the two decades following World War II. Perhaps the most significant development in terms of land use and city form was the vast expansion in automobile use.

Most of the new housing for the expanding city was provided in the suburbs, mainly in the form of low-density development of one- and two-family houses and the occasional low-rise apartments. Both planners and developers embraced the idea of insulating neighborhoods from through traffic and of providing schools and parks within walking distance. The common gridiron was shunned in preference to loop streets, crescents, and cul-de-sacs.

Most residential development was happening in the suburbs, and industry was also dispersing to suburban locations. A "metropolitan" view emerged and cities were quickly coming to be made up of several constituent communities, each of which was anchored by shopping centers and industrial estates. City regions began to develop, with the two most important public decisions being expressways and regional parks.

Since the 1970s a number of land-use issues have become dominant. Suburban sprawl, characterized by low-density development and segregated land uses, is now considered to be destroying the environment, depleting agricultural land, and squandering energy resources through long commuting. The catch phrases now are jobs-housing balance, intensification, mixed land use, public transit, and sustainable development. Intensification is the key to promoting walking, cycling, and public transit use;

modest increases in density can have a considerable impact in this regard.

The inner city, too, has undergone significant changes. The massive urban renewal projects of the 1950s and 1960s were found to be creating high-rise ghettos and destroying existing neighborhoods. In recent years governments spent billions to revitalize downtowns to prevent further exodus to the suburbs and to attract people and businesses back. Waterfronts and railway properties became upscale shopping and recreational precincts; factory and warehouse districts became luxury condominiums and professional offices; and dilapidated neighborhoods became gentrified residential enclaves.

In a city the common uses occur mostly on privately-owned land. Together, residential, commercial, and industrial uses account for about two-thirds of all urban land. Community control over these is largely negative in the sense that the community can prohibit certain uses and buildings but it cannot actively develop the land for collective or public purposes. In more recent times many communities have used proactive approaches such as negotiated development and transferable development rights to pursue community goals. Land for roads and much of the open space is owned by the public. These are important elements in determining the physical form and quality of the environment.

In any land-use planning exercise there are three related dimensions to think about: physical facilities and features, activities of people that use space, and the purposes for which land is used. The physical environment often accommodates a great variety of activities and purposes. Some have very localized impacts and others might affect an entire region. There are many points of potential conflict. Land-use planning involves trying to foresee and reconcile the conflicts (or "incompatibilities") between land uses.

In Britain, the United States, and Canada the essential form of land development is through private initiatives in the marketplace. In this respect the function of land-use planning is, on the one hand, to provide developers with beneficial conditions for development and, on the other, to safeguard and improve the living, working, and recreational environment, increase local taxes, and coordinate the development of public facilities and services.

Land-use planning, however, is not necessarily a governmental function. Investors often study the pattern of city growth, market conditions, and consumer behavior for their investment decisions and development activity. In fact the earliest professional planners in the United States were working primarily for the private sector.

The land-use planning function in governments today can be divided into the following separate but related areas:

1. Land development policies and plans, which deal with the quality, quantity, intensity, and spatial distribution of land for development and redevelopment.
2. Implementation Strategies, of which there are four general types:
   i. Development control (primarily zoning and subdivision control in Canada and the United States, and the development permit in Britain);
   ii. The construction and coordination of infrastructure and facilities, including the public acquisition and disposal of land;
   iii. Financial instruments such as subsidies, allowance, insurance, guarantees, warranties, and compensation; and
   iv. Fiscal instruments such as taxes, fees, and levies.

Britain has a longer history of modern land-use (town) planning than Canada and the United States. The central government enacts national legislation on "town and country planning." But local authorities have rather wide scopes and powers of planning and implementation, especially through the permit system of development control.

In the United States there is no uniformity in planning administration and organization. Some places have no government land-use planning function at all. In general, local land-use planning is a delegated function by the state government through enabling acts, but there is a great degree of independence of local governments in the United States.

Land-use planning in Canada is generally subsumed under the name "community planning." It is a provincial mandate and where it is delegated to municipalities the province retains a strong supervisory and interventionist role.

There are some unique characteristics about the form and organization of local governments (especially in the United States) which affect the making and implementation of the land-use plan at the local level. These include:

1. The political party in power at the local level may be different from the party in power at the state or national level. This phenomenon is not as prevalent in Canada.
2. In every locality there are different "governmental" organizations and agencies with different mandates (such as education, welfare, health, and utilities). Some are run by elected boards or commissions; some are appointed by the local council; and some are appointed by senior levels of government. This phenomenon is most pronounced in the United States.
3. The pattern of land development (hence tax base and revenue) and local government boundaries do not often coincide, especially in metropolitan areas. Suburbanization has led to imbalanced growth between the inner core and outer perimeter of cities.

All these characteristics have influenced the level of "visionary thinking" and the degree of comprehensiveness in land-use planning. Human behavior is very adaptable and human beings can sustain great environmental stress before breaking down, but the chief aim of good land-use planning is to strain this adaptability as little as possible.

Hok-Lin Leung

Further Readings

Chapin, F.S., and E.J. Kaiser. *Urban Land Use Planning*. 1979.

Leung, Hok Lin. *Land Use Planning Made Plain*. 1989.

See also AUTOMOBILES; BICYCLE TRANSPORTATION; MUMFORD, LEWIS; OLMSTED, FREDERICK LAW; RAILS-TO-TRAILS; URBAN DESIGN

Landfill

See MUNICIPAL SOLID WASTE: LANDFILL

Landscape Ecology

Landscape ecology is a branch of the science of ecology that deals with ecological phenomena at relatively large spatial scales. Whereas most ecological studies focus on small research plots (generally a few acres or less) study areas in landscape ecology range from hundreds to millions of acres. A landscape can be characterized as a mosaic of land forms, vegetation types, and land uses. Landscape pattern often consists of repeated habitat components—for example, patches and corridors of forest in a matrix of prairie or agricultural land—that occur in various shapes, sizes, and spatial configurations. Landscape processes include the flux of materials, energy, disturbances, and organisms between habitats in the landscape. A fire, for instance, may begin in a grassland but penetrate some distance into adjacent forest. The relationship between pattern and process in the landscape is one of the major research topics of landscape ecology.

Landscape ecology began in Europe in the early twentieth century and from the beginning was an applied science closely associated with geography and land-use planning. When landscape ecology began to take hold in North America in the late 1970s and early 1980s its practitioners were largely biologists, later joined by geographers, landscape architects, and others. For obvious reasons landscape ecology in Europe has concentrated mostly on human-dominated landscapes, whereas North American landscape ecologists study wildlands as often as developed areas. The interdisciplinary nature of landscape ecology has contributed to its success in a world where environmental problems are increasingly complex.

Landscape ecology has made notable contributions to conservation. Conventional conservation and resource management consider sites out of context. For example, a collection of woodlots might be analyzed separately in terms of the number of birds they contain or some other indicator of conservation value; the interactions of woodlots with their surrounding landscape is not considered. Similarly plans for timber sales may consider only local areas immediately affected by each sale, not the effect of multiple harvests, road-building, and other perturbations across the landscape. Thanks to landscape ecology, we now know that many ecological phenomena and human activities have effects that extend across the boundaries of individual habitat patches and often encompass huge areas. If a series of timber sales fragments a forest landscape into small patches, those patches may experience a drier microclimate than the original forest, increased susceptibility to windthrow, loss of forest interior

species, reduction of genetic diversity in the remaining populations, and invasion by weedy species. These problems cannot be solved patch by patch, but only across all patches and their matrix. To reduce harmful impacts of timber sales harvests might be spatially aggregated, techniques other than clearcutting could be used so that edge effects are reduced, and corridors of forest could be retained to allow movement of forest-dependent animals from one patch to another.

Another contribution of landscape ecology to conservation was fostering an appreciation of disturbance regimes, patch dynamics, and the consequent heterogeneity of natural landscapes. These patterns and processes are now considered essential components of an area's biodiversity, and management plans are beginning to consider ways of maintaining these phenomena in reserves as well as in multiple-use landscapes.

Finally landscape ecology has helped inform a new paradigm for design of protected areas. No longer are sites considered for protection in isolation from their surroundings. Rather new models emphasize regional networks of reserves, buffer zones, and corridors or other forms of connectivity. These interconnected networks appear to have a higher probability of maintaining biodiversity in the long-term than a system of small or isolated reserves.

Reed F. Noss

Further Readings

Forman, R.T.T., and M. Godron. *Landscape Ecology*. 1986.

Noss, R.F. "A Regional Landscape Approach to Maintain Diversity." *BioScience* 33 (1983): 700–06.

Turner, M.G. "Landscape Ecology: The Effect of Pattern on Process." *Annual Review of Ecology and Systematics* 20 (1989): 171–97.

See also BIODIVERSITY; BIOSPHERE RESERVES; CLEARCUT; FOREST FIRES AND CONSERVATION; FOREST FRAGMENTATION AND BIRD HABITATS; FORESTRY, HISTORY OF; HABITAT FRAGMENTATION, PATCHES, AND CORRIDORS; NEW FORESTRY

Laterization

In some low latitude areas there are extensive sheets of an iron- and/or aluminum-rich duricrust called laterite. The term was first used in South India in the first decade of the nineteenth century to describe a natural building stone. It was described by F. Buchanan at that time thus:

> It is full of cavities and pores, and contains a very large quantity of iron in the form of red and yellow ochres. In the mass, while excluded from the air, it is so soft that any iron instrument readily cuts it, and it is cut into square masses with a pick axe and immediately cut into the shape wanted with a trowel or large knife. It very soon becomes as hard as brick, and resists the air and water much better than any bricks I have seen in India.

Such iron-rich accumulations result naturally, either because of a preferential removal of silica during the course of intense tropical weathering (leading to a *relative* accumulation of the sesquioxides of iron and aluminum), or because of an *absolute* accumulation of these components.

Laterization is the very ability to harden on exposure to air and through desiccation or drying out as noted by Buchanan. Once hardened the laterites are not favorable to root development and plant growth and so tend to produce sterile surfaces. One particular way in which exposure may take place is by accelerated erosion of the surface soil, while forest removal may so modify microclimatic conditions that desiccation of the laterite surface can take place.

It has therefore frequently been maintained that the removal of rainforest in the tropics can cause irreversible laterization to occur, with dire long-term consequences. Indeed, the French geographer, Pierre Gourou, referred to it as "a pedological leprosy," and warned of "lateritic suicide." There are records from many parts of the tropics of accelerated induration brought about by forest removal producing sterile pavements (the bowé or bowals of West Africa). The process can happen rapidly (i.e., within a year) and to a considerable depth.

However, the significance of laterization (which French workers tend to call "bovalisation") should probably not be exaggerated since most tropical soils lack the chemical and mineralogical composition that would make them prone to laterization.

Andrew S. Goudie

Further Readings

Buchanan, F. *A Journey from Madras through the Countries of Mysore, Canara, and Malabar.* 3 vols. 1807.
Goudie, Andrew S. *Duricrusts in Tropical and Subtropical Landscapes.* 1973.
Macfarlane, Marty J. *Laterite and Landscape.* 1976.

See also NONRENEWABLE RESOURCES; TROPICAL DEFORESTATION; TROPICAL RAINFORESTS

Law of the Sea

See UNITED NATIONS CONVENTION ON THE LAW OF THE SEA

Leaching

Leaching is a term used to describe the dissolution, mobilization, and transport of chemicals by a moving body of water. The process occurs widely in the natural environment, and by way of an example, plays a critical role in the transformation of rock, sediment, and organic matter into life-supporting soils. It has also been utilized by industry both in the manufacturing of products and to perform tasks such as the removal of hazardous chemicals from waste. From an environmental perspective the leaching process takes on a more negative connotation. It can result in the flushing of essential chemicals from agricultural soils; it can also bring about the mobilization and release of toxic chemicals from waste disposal sites and mine tailings. In such cases the overall effect is to generate a plume of contaminated water, or "leachate," that can damage vegetation and pollute well water, rivers, and lakes.

In agricultural areas a major concern is the leaching of soil nutrients by infiltrating waters. Typically, these waters move vertically downward at a rate of approximately one meter per year. Leaching can reduce soil fertility; it can also cause widespread degradation of water quality in shallow, underlying aquifers. In some cases widespread damage occurs within five or ten years; where the water table is deep, serious impacts may not be recognized for thirty years or more. The greatest problem usually concerns the leaching of inorganic fertilizers containing nitrogen, phosphorous, potassium, magnesium, and sulfur. The nature and extent of the problem depends on many factors, notably the physical and chemical nature of the soils, the season, rates and timing of fertilizer application, the chemical formulation of the fertilizers, the type of plant and efficiency of plant uptake, and the frequency and intensity of precipitation. Usually it is the more soluble nitrogen compounds that cause the most serious problems, with underlying groundwaters often showing nitrate-nitrogen concentrations in excess of ten milligrams per liter, the recommended drinking water quality guideline. Levels in excess of ten milligrams per liter nitrate-nitrogen are known to cause methaemoglobinaemia in young infants.

Agricultural fertilizers are an example of "distributed" or "non-point source" contaminants that can cause low-level contamination of groundwater over extremely large areas. In contrast the leaching of "point sources" of contamination such as waste products contained in municipal landfills and mine tailing sites can generate highly concentrated leachates that are capable of serious groundwater pollution, though normally on a very localized scale. For example, given that groundwater velocities are typically in the range ten to 100 meters per year, leachate plumes from point sources of contamination will take between ten and 100 years to move just one kilometer from the originating site.

Contamination by landfill leachates is recognized as one of the most serious threats to the potable quality of groundwater supplies. According to Cheremisinoff et al. (1984) the United States generates 33 million tons of household waste and 59 million tons of hazardous waste (not including sewage sludge and agricultural wastes) each day. Of this waste nearly 90 percent is landfilled. They further estimate that North America has upward of 20,000 landfills, of which only 10 percent are properly designed to contain the waste and manage the leachate generated.

The volume of leachate produced in a landfill depends on the amount and distribution of rainfall, the permeability and slope of the soil cover (if any), and evaporative losses. In turn the eventual quality of the leachate produced depends on such factors as the age, composition, thickness, and degree of consolidation of the waste, as well as the way the waste was handled when placed in the landfill. For example, fresh, compacted waste is not yet saturated and must absorb water, perhaps for a period of five to ten years, before leachate production begins. In addition it may take a further twenty years before the leachate approaches its maximum concentration. In modern "engi-neered" landfills, most of these factors can be carefully controlled. Moreover installation of an impermeable landfill liner and leachate collection system can be used to control the volume of leachate present at any one time and treat the leachate if necessary. Unfortunately, while there is little doubt that modern landfills can adequately meet environmental performance standards in the short-term concerns remain for the future when the landfill is still producing leachate, but is closed and no longer generating the revenue necessary to adequately maintain the engineered components and the monitoring systems.

Ken W.F. Howard

Further Readings

Cheremisinoff, P.N., K.A. Gigliello, and T.K. O'Neill. *Groundwater-Leachate: Modelling/Monitoring/Sampling*. 1984.
Howard, K.W.F. "Denitrification in a Limestone Aquifer." *Journal of Hydrology* 76 (1985): 265–80.
Manahan, S.E. *Environmental Chemistry*. 1991.

See also GROUNDWATER POLLUTION; MUNICIPAL SOLID WASTE: LANDFILLS; PESTICIDES

Lead

Lead is a heavy metal found in association with zinc, silver, and other minerals in the earth's crust. When mined, smelted, and released into the environment it is a potent human and environmental poison. Because it is soft, malleable, heavy, resistant to corrosion, and easily melted, lead has been widely used for many diverse applications over the past 3,000 years. Since Roman times lead has been used for plumbing and as a pigment and it has long been recognized as toxic at high doses. More recently lead has been used in solder, pesticides, batteries, ammunition, weights, electrical cable sheathing, and X-ray shields. Since the 1920s, and in spite of the existing information on lead's serious health effects, tetra-ethyl lead has been used as an anti-knock agent in gasoline, and the resulting emissions have spread throughout the globe. There is virtually nowhere, from the Antarctic to the ocean floor, that is uncontaminated by lead pollution, and it is estimated that current levels of lead in human blood and bones are well over 100 times the levels experienced by prehistoric people.

When lead is absorbed into the human body it becomes distributed throughout many organs and is stored in bone. It circulates in the red blood cells and human lead exposure is often measured in terms of micrograms of lead per deciliters of blood (μg/dl). Lead is especially harmful to the human fetus and very young children. At levels as low as 10 μg/dl, lead in maternal or infant blood has been shown to cause developmental delays, reduced intelligence, low birthweights, premature delivery, hearing problems, and reduced stature. At levels over 80 μg/dl, lead causes vomiting, diarrhea, nerve and brain damage, and anemia; and at levels over 100 μg/dl it can be fatal to children. In adults blood lead levels of 40 to 60 μg/dl lead to reproductive problems in men and women and levels of 120 μg/dl can cause death. At 30 μg/dl, lead has been found to result in elevated blood pressure in men, and at levels below 10 μg/dl it causes physiological changes. Lead may also cause cancer. There appears to be no threshold below which lead exposure is benign. Although blood lead levels in North America have declined since the use of unleaded gas became common in the late 1970s, urban levels of 5 to 10 μg/dl in urban North American children are common, and a significant minority of the population has blood lead levels of more than 10 μg/dl.

Tetra-ethyl lead in automotive gasoline was almost entirely phased out in the United States in 1986, and Canada followed suit in 1990, although it is still widely used in the rest of the world, particularly in Africa, Asia, and Latin America. Other important sources of human lead exposure include: drinking water contaminated by lead used in municipal or residential plumbing, peeling leaded paint, dust emitted from smelters, lead in soil from historical automobile emissions or other sources, pottery glazed with lead pigment, leaded foil on wine bottles, and leaded crystal.

Measures to reduce lead exposure include: flushing pipes for several minutes before drinking tap water; washing hands carefully before eating; removing shoes on entry into the house; considering the possible lead content of soil before using it for home or community vegetable gardens; avoiding use of lead crystal or lead-glazed ceramics; wiping possible lead deposits from the neck of wine bottles prior to pouring; considering the possible lead content of old paint, especially if it is flaky or if it is being burned off; and considering all possible

historical as well as current industrial lead emissions before making local land-use decisions.
Beth Savan

Further Readings

Fleming, S., and F. Ursitti. *Scientific Criteria Document for Multi-Media Environmental Standards Development: Lead.* Ontario Ministry of Environment and Energy, 1994.

Mushak, P., J.M. Davis, A.F. Crochetti, and L.D. Grant. "Prenatal and Postnatal Effects of Low Level Lead Exposure: Integrated Summary of a Report to the U.S. Congress on Childhood Lead Poisoning." *Environmental Research* 50 (1989): 11–36.

Wallace, B., and K. Cooper. *A Citizen's Guide to Lead.* 1986.

See also AIR POLLUTION: IMPACTS; ENVIRONMENTAL JUSTICE MOVEMENT; LEAD IN SOILS

Lead in Soils

Lead is ubiquitous in the environment. It has long been recognized as a chronic and acute toxin to wildlife, domestic animals, and humans. It is inhaled and/or ingested by mammals and avian species through air, water, food and inadvertently though dust and soil. Effects of lead poisoning are well documented. The concern over lead in soil stems from its contribution to the overall quantity ingested. The background concentration of lead in soil is approximately 15 milligrams per kilogram. Because of long term mining and smelting activities and extensive use in a wide variety of industrial and consumer products, lead concentrations of surface soil in urban regions and in rural regions near emission sources in excess of 1,000 milligrams per kilogram are not uncommon.

By far, the largest use of lead is in the production of storage batteries, accounting for about two-thirds of current annual production. Until the early 1980s the second largest use of lead was as a gasoline additive. The use of lead in gasoline peaked during the early 1970s. Since the initiation of the phase-down of lead in gasoline in the mid 1970s, its use worldwide has declined substantially.

Children between the ages of six months and six years are considered by most experts to be at the greatest risk to lead contamination in the environment. In addition to the usual sources of lead exposure in food, beverage and air, this population tends to ingest lead from dust and soil through hand-to-mouth play and by sucking on materials containing lead, for example surfaces containing leaded paint. In this population, lead may become a neurotoxin when lead content of blood exceeds about 10 micrograms per deciliter. Neurotoxic effects observed include decreased intelligence, short-term memory loss, impairment of visual-motor functioning, hyperactivity, irritability, reading and spelling under-achievement, and overall behavioral problems.

Both soil and dust contribute to the over-all intake of lead by infants and toddlers and it is difficult to distinguish between the two sources. For our purposes, we consider soil to be that material at the earth's surface in which plants may grow and containing mineral and organic fragments and microorganisms. The main sources of soil contamination by lead are mining and smelting of primary ores, secondary smelting of scrap metal, the past use of leaded gasoline, sloughing off of paint from old painted surfaces, wear of consumer products, and industrial operations involving the production or use of lead-containing material.

Surface soils surrounding existing and abandoned lead, zinc, and copper mining and smelting operations commonly contain lead at concentrations 100 to 1,000 times higher than the background. Contamination is greatest near operations and extends outward from the source at diminishing concentrations for many kilometers. In urban regions past use of leaded gasoline is a major source of lead in surface soils along the major traffic throughways. Despite the fact that lead use as a gasoline additive has diminished substantially, previous deposits of lead, which is essentially immobile in soils, will remain in the soil until removed by erosion or through deliberate mechanical means. Soil in gardens or yards of homes in both urban and rural regions may be contaminated by lead as a result of the sloughing off of old paint from the exterior wall surfaces. Again, although lead is no longer added to household paint, much of what was used in the past remains and will last for a long time unless it is deliberately removed. In older neighborhoods of metropolitan areas concentrations of lead in the surface few centimeters of soils ranging from 1,000 to 5,000 milligrams per kilogram are not uncommon. Likewise, soils close to present and past industrial operations involving the production or use of lead-containing material are observed to contain elevated concentrations of lead.

There are no universally accepted standards for safe levels of lead in soil. Obviously the level depends not only on the concentration in soil but also on the amount of soil ingested, the duration of ingestion, and the extent of exposure from other sources. The threshold for safe levels of lead in soils, in general, vary from about 100 to 1,000 milligrams of lead per kilogram of soil. Regardless of the standard used it is obvious that large acreages of soils will contain lead levels exceeding the standard and decisions regarding the need for remediation will need to be made.

Present methods for the remediation of lead-contaminated soils include washing the soil with a solvent to remove the lead; deep tillage to dilute the high lead surface soil with low lead subsurface soil; chemical fixation to convert soil lead into a biologically inert form; soil covering with uncontaminated soil, concrete or asphalt; and soil removal and replacement with uncontaminated soil. Soil washing and deep tillage presently are not practical on a large scale. Results of chemical fixation are not consistent. Covering with concrete or asphalt may be an unacceptable alternative where the integrity of the site needs to be preserved. The single most widely acceptable permanent solution is probably removal of the contaminated soil followed by replacement with clean soil. Each of the above methods involves considerable expense and remediating all affected areas instantly will probably be well beyond the financial resources available. It would seem, therefore, that once the action levels for remediation of lead contamination are established, priorities should be given to those sites in close proximity to the population at greatest risk or those contaminated areas where toddlers and infants spend most of their active time.

Albert L. Page (with A.C. Chang)

Further Readings

Davies, Brian E., and Bobby G. Wixson, eds. *Lead in Soil: Issues and Guidelines.* Society for Environmental Geochemistry and Health. Science Reviews, Ltd., Northwood, England. 1988.

Florini, Karen L., Krumbhaar, George D., Jr., and Selbergeld, Ellen K. *Legacy of Lead: America's Continuing Epidemic of Childhood Lead Poisoning.* Environmental Defense Fund, Washington, D.C. 1990.

L

Wixson, Bobby G., and Brian E. Davies, eds.
*Lead in Soil: Recommended Guidelines,
Society for Environmental Geochemistry
and Health.* Science Reviews, Ltd.
Northwood, England. 1993.

See also AIR POLLUTION: IMPACTS; AUTOMO-
BILES: IMPACTS AND POLICIES; ENVIRONMEN-
TAL JUSTICE MOVEMENT; LEAD

League of Conservation Voters

The League of Conservation Voters (LCV) was
founded in 1970 by leaders of Friends of the
Earth, among them Marion Edey, who served
as executive director of LCV until 1986. LCV
is a political action committee, formed as a vehicle for environmentalists to become directly
involved in the electoral process. As a non-tax
exempt organization LCV can pursue overtly
political activities, including campaign donations to candidates, that other groups could
not for fear of jeopardizing their tax-exempt
status.

LCV sees its role as keeping score of the
records of candidates and helping those it deems
to be sufficiently pro-environment. It tracks
how members of Congress vote on the environmental issues it defines as most important, publishing the data in an annual *National Environmental Scorecard* which it distributes to
members. LCV also analyzes the environmental records and views of presidential candidates,
and in the 1980s expanded into assessing candidates at the state and local levels. Beyond
public education LCV donates money, technical services, and volunteers to candidates who
support environmental causes. In 1992 it endorsed candidates in 169 congressional races,
claiming a winning percentage of 67 percent,
and in all spent around $600,000 in campaign-
related activities. Although LCV is officially
non-partisan, it tends to support Democrats
because of ideological differences between the
parties, and it endorsed Bill Clinton in the 1992
presidential election.

LCV claims over 50,000 members and has
an annual budget of over $1.5 million. Most of
its revenues come from membership dues and
contributions, and most of its monies are directed at campaign-related activities. The organization is based in Washington, D.C., and has
field offices on the east and west coasts. Its staff
size, never large, tends to fluctuate depending
on the electoral activity at the moment. LCV is
governed by a board of directors, many of

whom are representatives of major environmental groups.

Christopher J. Bosso (with Paul Carney)

Further Readings
Dunlap, Riley E., and Angela G. Mertig, eds.
*American Environmentalism: The U.S.
Environmental Movement, 1970–1990.*
1992.
Wenner, Lettie M. *U.S. Energy and Environ-
mental Interest Groups.* 1990.

See also ENVIRONMENTAL ACTION; ENVIRON-
MENTALISM; FRIENDS OF THE EARTH

Least-Cost Utility Planning

Least-cost energy strategies, rather than looking for ways to produce more and more energy
(more gas wells, more nuclear plants, more
large hydro dams), look just as hard at smarter
ways to use energy. Cogenerating power from
waste steam, for example, should be less environmentally and economically costly than
building a new coal plant.

From the consumer's standpoint choosing
the energy source that is truly cheapest has not
been an easy task because monopoly electric
and gas utilities have kept consumers captive,
foreclosing the ability to choose between different suppliers. Also in many cases energy prices
do not truly reflect all costs: the costs of pollution are more often reflected in tax bills and
health-care costs than in utility bills, artificially
lowering the price of polluting energy and making renewable and conservation technologies
look relatively expensive.

Neither have monopoly utilities achieved
least-cost goals: shielded from competition and
so having reduced incentive to invest on a least-
cost basis, monopolies often make uneconomic
supply decisions. An institutional bias toward
construction rather than conservation, nuclear
power rather than cogeneration, has been evidenced all over the world.

However, lower cost energy alternatives
have become available. Independent power producers can build efficient power plants faster
and cheaper than traditional utilities, and energy conservation technology is being developed and promoted by a growing number of
energy service companies. Such private entrepreneurs feel their options are cheaper than the
plants which monopoly utilities are operating,
contemplating, or building, and they want to
compete for access to energy customers.

Removal of distribution monopolies (giving all energy suppliers equal access to markets), and full-cost pricing (through subsidy removal, taxes on pollution, and tradeable emission permits) would level the playing field between different power sources, and between supply and demand alternatives. Least-cost options would then be visible and available to consumers.

However, monopoly utilities have resisted such fundamental changes and have grudgingly accepted legislated least-cost utility planning exercises instead. "Integrated Resource Planning" (IRP) is one example. In it the utility or regulator attempts to monetize the uncounted pollution costs—at the price of existing abatement technology or at an imputed cost of damage—of each generation technology and adds it, for planning purposes only, to the cost of the generating option, helping the utility to arrive at a deemed cost per technology upon which to base choices for new generation. This may make energy conservation programs that would otherwise appear uneconomic look like the least cost option. Some credit IRP and other least-cost planning approaches with helping Bonneville Power Administration, Seattle City Light, and Wisconsin Electric Power avoid the mistake of building more nuclear plants, and helping British Columbia Hydro cancel a huge dam on the Peace River.

Although IRP can theoretically facilitate better technology choices than traditional utility expansion practices, as a mechanism for giving consumers good price signals about what energy source is truly low-cost, it fails in several ways. No price feedback reaches the consumer, who does not bear the pollution cost in his rates; because no revenues are raised to compensate for the damage presumed to have been done by the pollution, there are no revenues to address the harm presumed done, either to pay for abatement or to distribute to those who might have suffered harm; and because rates don't increase to reflect poor technology choices, energy demand doesn't decline to reflect the cost of pollution.

Competitive bidding, another least-cost planning approach whereby the requirement for new energy supply is met by the cheapest utility or non-utility supplier, shares another flaw of IRP—it doesn't usually look at existing supply in the least-cost plan, thereby forgoing the possibility that old coal or nuclear plants, for example, be closed in favor of more economic new supply or conservation.

More fundamental reform is necessary to allow consumers to optimize society's resources by allowing them to devise their own least-cost energy plans.

Sheila Malcolmson

Further Readings

Ruff, Larry E. *Statement on Integrated Resource Planning for Natural Gas Distribution, before the Ontario Energy Board.* 1992.

Tellus Institute. *Electric IRP in North America: Report to Hydro-Quebec and the Public Interest Groups and Associations.* 1993.

See also BACKCASTING; CARBON TAX; COAL: ENVIRONMENTAL IMPACTS; COGENERATION; DEMAND-SIDE MANAGEMENT; ENERGY EFFICIENCY; HYDROELECTRICITY; NUCLEAR ELECTRIC POWER; TRADEABLE EMISSION PERMITS

Legislation: Australia

The development of legislation to deal with questions of conservation and environmental protection in Australia is as complicated as the colonial history and federation of the Australian states. The legacy of colonization and dispossession of the aboriginal inhabitants, the development of separate states and territories on the basis of arbitrary colonial mapping of the continent and the evolution of a federal system, the drafting and amendment of the constitution and the complex relations between federal, state and local government means that environmental legislation is a growing and complex field. From the initial act of colonization in New South Wales in 1789 aboriginal peoples have been steadily dispossessed and the right to define land use passed to colonial governments and their successors, the federal and state governments. From this flowed a series of acts governing the settlement of the country, the terms for land use, and the scope for environmental degradation. Following from the British colonial heritage, state and federal governments between them have the ability to define and police the use of land, natural resources such as forests and minerals, and the flow of waste products into the environment.

The separate colonies enacted legislation which dealt with various forms of environmental damage. Hence there were orders to restrict tree clearance from streams as this promoted soil erosion, acts to promote soil conservation, acts to regulate the clearance of native vegetation, acts to create "crown" reserves and national parks, and acts to limit the flow of pollutants into rivers, sea, and air.

At the time of federation the constitution left most of the formal rights over the environment in the hands of state governments. Nonetheless the constitution contained clauses that would subsequently be used to justify the federal government taking action and enforcing forms of environmental practices and overriding determinations made by state governments. For example, the Whitlam Labor government passed the Environmental Protection (Impact of Proposals) Act 1974 which meant that all major resource projects required a consideration of the environmental consequences of a project before the federal government would grant either an export license or approval for foreign investment. In the 1980s, during the rule of the Hawke government, the federal government took a greater role, using these constitutional powers and its obligations to fulfill the requirements of international treaties to extend its range of concerns to govern standards of forest management and logging practices (often controlled by state forestry commissions and other bodies) and environmental impact assessment processes (as in the case of the proposed Wesley Vale Pulp Mill in Tasmania when it enforced the use of baseline studies so that the environmental impact of the project could be more accurately assessed). It also used its powers to prevent mining, logging, or road building in environmentally sensitive areas.

The constitution left great powers for environmental legislation, regulation, and management in the hands of the states. Under these powers state governments have set up environmental protection authorities to assess projects, to determine standards, and to implement and police regulations (e.g., the Environmental Protection Act [Victoria] 1970). Some of these state agencies have been quite rigorous in the standards they have applied and the restrictions they have sought to impose have been frequently tested in the courts. As always the final arbiter of what happens has been government, and there are numerous instances of governments using various devices (e.g., indenture bills, specific acts of legislation, or simply directives) and legislation to override or circumvent the operation of environmental agencies and its own legislation (see, for example, the Roxby Downs Indenture Ratification Act [South Australia] 1982 which protected the uranium/copper project from other state environmental regulation).

Local government also has a part, albeit a subservient one, to play in the field of conservation and environmental management. Mostly under state legislation a significant realm is left to local government in the area of planning and on some questions of heritage protection, especially in the state capital cities. Whether buildings are saved or demolished, or parklands maintained or neglected will be the consequence of decisions taken under local government legislation and planning regulations. Various town planning acts and heritage regulations are the main vehicles for the environmental actions of local government.

It is important to note the important role played by international conventions, treaties, United Nations (UN) declarations, and agreements in setting the scene for legislative initiatives in Australia. The federal government, under the terms of its treaty responsibility, has been able to use such declarations as the source of its own interventions on environmental grounds. One of the most significant of these has been its use of the Convention for the Protection of the World Cultural and Natural Heritage and the World Heritage Properties Conservation Act of 1983 to secure protection of wilderness areas in various states, such as Tasmania's South West. Where the federal government has intervened compensation, sometimes of quite generous amounts, has been paid.

Australia was settled under the colonial doctrine of *terra nullius*, incorrectly assuming that the continent was not settled and that no significant order of law governed the use of the land by the aboriginal inhabitants. As colonization and dispossession continued colonial administrators noticed the fallacy of *terra nullius;* however, the doctrine was continually reaffirmed by the courts until 1992. In that year the High Court of Australia handed down a judgment (*Mabo v. Queensland* [1992]) repudiating *terra nullius* and replacing it with a vague concept of native title, which in a restricted number of instances, continues to the present day. The federal government has had legislation passed to recognize this concept of native title and to rework the relationship between native title and other forms of land tenure, though conflict with several of the states and territories (some of which have passed their own legislation) continues. This has an impact on access to land and on the regulation of the environmental management of land. Much legislative effort and difficult negotiations will attend the question of how to achieve a reconciliation between state and federal economic development ambitions, the rights of aboriginal peoples, and the practices necessary to fulfill conservation, heritage, and environmental objectives.

Doug McEachern

Further Readings

Bates, Gerry. *Environmental Law in Australia.* 3rd ed. 1992.

Bonyhady, Tim. *Places Worth Keeping: Conservationists, Politics and Law.* 1993.

———, ed. *Environmental Protection and Legal Change.* 1992.

Fisher, D.E. *Environmental Law: Text and Materials.* 1993.

See also Australia: Resource Use Conflicts; Legislation: Canada; Legislation: European Community; Legislation: Great Britain; Legislation: United States

Legislation: Canada

Canadian federal and provincial governments each have their own laws relating to the environment. To some degree the scope of federal and provincial environmental legislation reflects the constitutional division of powers between the two orders of government. However, since jurisdictional overlap and uncertainty are common in the environmental field, there is substantial overlap between federal and provincial laws. Legislation concerned primarily with the environment is discussed below. However, it should be noted that laws relating to other subjects, such as transportation and energy, also can have implications for conservation and protection of natural resources.

The earliest environmental statute at the federal level, the Fisheries Act, predates Confederation (1867), and remains the centerpiece of the federal role in water pollution control today. At the provincial level public health statutes were passed at the turn of the century and some provinces later added water resource management laws. However, most contemporary federal and provincial environmental laws emerged during two periods of pronounced legislative activity concerning the environment: the first in the late 1960s and early 1970s, and the second in the late 1980s and early 1990s.

In response to growing public awareness during the 1960s of threats to the environment all Canadian federal and provincial governments passed new pollution control laws. At the federal level the most prominent new statutes were the Canada Water Act (1970), the Fisheries Act Amendments (1970), the Clean Air Act (1971), the Ocean Dumping Control Act (1975), and the Environmental Contaminants Act (1976).

In contrast to U.S. environmental legislation Canadian statutes typically grant broad discretionary authority either to individual ministers or to the cabinet as a whole, rather than compelling the executive to take specific actions. For instance, under the Fisheries Act, Cabinet is authorized to issue and enforce national effluent regulations but is not required to do so. The permissive tone of Canadian laws reflects their origins in parliamentary government. Since the legislative and administrative functions are fused there is not the same level of institutionalized distrust as exists between Congress and the executive branch in the American system of government. Thus there is less incentive for legislators to draft very specific legislative language to constrain the executive.

The discretionary tone of the first generation of Canadian environmental laws, combined with a decline in public pressure for environmental protection in the late 1970s and early 1980s, resulted in uneven implementation. For instance a much-noted tension between the Fisheries Act's reliance on sector-specific national effluent standards and the basin-specific, water quality based approach of the Canada Water Act was effectively resolved when the federal government simply declined to implement the water quality provisions of the latter. The discretionary language of environmental statutes also explains the relatively limited reliance on litigation by Canadian interest groups. In the absence of specific statutory directives and deadlines there has been little basis to sue the government.

There are indications in the second generation of environmental laws that the discretionary nature of Canadian environmental laws may be changing. In response to a resurgence of public concern for the environment in the late 1980s, both federal and provincial governments updated their existing environmental legislation and, in several cases, passed new statutes. At the federal level the Canadian Environmental Protection Act which became law in 1988 consolidated several earlier statutes (the Environmental Contaminants Act, the Clean Air Act, the Ocean Dumping Control Act, and parts of the Canada Water Act) and at the same time authorized a broader cradle-to-grave approach to controlling threats to health and the environment posed by toxic substances. It was followed in 1992 by the Canadian Environmental Assessment Act, which for the first time established a legislative framework for federal environmental assessment activities.

Both new statutes contain hints of the action-forcing language common to U.S. environmental laws. Non-discretionary language and deadlines occasionally are used to describe ministerial responsibilities and, for the first time, citizens have been granted a limited form of rights, as in the Canadian Environmental Protection Act's provision for citizens to compel investigation of alleged offenses under the act. However, the new provisions remain weaker than the non-discretionary language and citizen suit provisions prevalent in U.S. environmental laws, and thus are unlikely to provoke a comparable level of litigation. Nonetheless the reforms do offer greater access to information and enhanced opportunities for public participation in the implementation process.

Kathryn Harrison

Further Readings

Franson, Robert, and Alastair Lucas. *Canadian Environmental Law*. 1976 (continuing service).

Lucas, Alastair. "The New Environmental Law." In *Canada: State of the Federation, 1989*. Ed. R. Watts and D. Brown. 1989.

See also ENVIRONMENT CANADA; ENVIRONMENTAL CASE LAW (CANADA): COMMON LAW CAUSES OF ACTION; FEDERALISM AND ENVIRONMENTAL PROTECTION: CANADA; LEGISLATION: AUSTRALIA; LEGISLATION: EUROPEAN COMMUNITY; LEGISLATION: GREAT BRITAIN; LEGISLATION: UNITED STATES

Legislation: European Community

The European Community (EC) is a regional organization based on three treaties binding on its twelve member states (Belgium, Denmark, France, Germany, Greece, Ireland, Luxembourg, the Netherlands, Portugal, Spain and the United Kingdom). Examining the evolution of the legal basis and environmental goals, there are four chronological phases that characterize

EC policy, demarcated by these events: the 1972 Paris Summit, the 1986 signing of the Single European Act, and the development of the Maastricht Treaty and the Fifth Action Program in 1991–1992. As the priorities of the region have evolved during this time span, the EC has established a range of environmental legislation for land management, radioactive substances, wildlife, and worker protection, but this essay concentrates on the areas of air, waste and hazardous substances, and water. The greatest EC effort—and often controversy—has been directed toward these fields.

Prior to the 1972 Paris Summit no explicit community environmental policy existed. The 1957 Treaty of Rome did not make any direct references to the environment. The removal of barriers for, and the actual formation of a common market were the principal goals. An environmental thrust to the treaty had to be extrapolated indirectly: Articles 2 and 36 emphasizing improved quality of life and mandating the protection of community health. With the exceptions of barriers to harmonization, active environmental policy making was left to the discretion of the individual member states.

Nevertheless the EC did establish several directives without a systematic policy approach. The key types of EC legislation are regulations and directives. Regulations impose directly enforceable legal obligations on member states without further national legislation on the subject. Directives lay out goals that individual member states implement by creating national legislation within their own policy process. Because of their flexibility regarding the individual member state context, directives are used more frequently than regulations. The transposition into law and implementation of the directives is the member states' responsibility, leading to a wide variability in the directives' implementation.

Most of the pre-1972 legislation was based on Article 100 of the Treaty, emphasizing the harmonization of the common market. In 1967 the Council of Ministers passed Directive 67/548 on the classification, packaging, and labeling of dangerous substances. Also notable was the Directive 70/157 regulating the noise levels of motor vehicle exhaust systems and Directive 70/220 concerning the motor vehicle air emissions. Regulation 729/70 on countryside protection in less favored areas was closely related to agricultural concerns.

In the EC policy-making process the Commission of the European Community initiates all legislation and supervises the law's implementation, the latter being the prerogative of the individual member states. The Council of Ministers, in this case constituted by the member state environmental ministers, has the responsibility of deciding legislation. The Treaty of Rome provided the European Parliament, indirectly, with a consultative role in environmental affairs. The Court of Justice has the responsibility for interpreting law and deciding when EC actors have failed to act within the legal boundaries of the EC treaty provisions.

The 1972 Paris Summit—a reaction of the member states to the rise of international environmental concern—was also a response to the possibilities of both trade barriers and imbalances in the economic costs being created by individual member states in their different environmental policies. In this context the Council passed the First Action Program in 1973. The action programs have come to serve as the strategic outline for EC environmental policy by defining goals, setting priorities, and establishing principles like "polluter pays."

The Third Action Program, approved in 1983, called for the incorporation of environmental objectives in other policies such as agriculture and energy to sustain the quality of community life. The environmental objectives became an essential ingredient in economic policy, the heart of the common market. However, while these programs presented a strategic scope, they had no constitutional impact. Policy making had to rely mostly on indirect references in the Treaty of Rome Articles 100 and 235 regarding the pursuit of EC objectives.

Much of the EC legislation received its impetus from high profile transnational crises, such as the acid rain damage to Scandinavia and German countryside and the 1976 Seveso disaster. The transnational concern for river and sea pollution made water legislation the most comprehensive body of EC environmental policies. The general thrust of these efforts was to limit the discharge of unwanted substances into the aquatic environment and to define certain water standards for various societal purposes. Accordingly Directive 75/440 set quality objectives for drinking water supplies and standard methods for purification. Directive 80/777 established principles and a system of values for monitoring drinking water. Directive 76/160 established quality objectives for designated bathing waters.

Equally significant for water policy was Directive 76/464. It allowed member states to set quality objectives or emission standards. The directive has acted as the foundation directive for a whole series of application directives that follow the principles set out in 76/464. One application directive is 80/68, which protects groundwater against pollution by dangerous substances and requires the member states to give prior authorization for any discharge of the material.

Air pollution policy developed at a slower rate than water, partially due to member states differing about the merits and methods of air standards and emission restrictions. This situation changed gradually, reflecting pressure and leadership of more active member states like the Federal Republic of Germany. Under the mounting pressure issues raised by the Green Party, Germany placed substantially stricter provisions in its national TA (Technische Anleitungen—"Technical Guidelines") Luft ("Air") regulation in 1983 and 1986 and introduced its Large Combustion Plant Regulation in 1983. After numerous discussions of these issues, the EC passed several important directives including: Directive 80/779 setting air quality standards for sulfur dioxide and smoke particles; Directive 82/884 setting air quality standards for lead; Directive 83/351 amending 70/220 regarding vehicle pollutant limits; Directive 84/360, the framework directive for the industrial pollution control; and Directive 85/203 on air quality standards for nitrogen dioxide emissions.

The 1970s also saw the rise of waste and hazardous materials and noise regulation. Directive 75/442 set up a general framework for the disposal of waste. Directives 78/319 and 78/176 created a definitional framework for disposing of toxic and hazardous waste and for titanium dioxide waste respectively. The release of dioxin in Seveso, Italy, spurred the EC to create Directive 82/501. It placed specific notification duties on operators to prevent major industrial accidents involving hazardous materials. The Seveso aftermath also led to Directive 84/631, regulating the supervision and control of transfrontier hazardous waste shipments. The 1970 directive on motor vehicle noise was amended substantially by new legislation, and directives were extended to tractors (Directive 74/151), motorcycles (Directive 78/1015), construction plant and equipment (Directive 79/113), household appliances (Directive 79/530), and aircraft (Directive 80/51).

While this record constitutes a significant achievement, the Single European Act (SEA) provided environmental policy new momentum. For the first time the EC gave explicit recognition to environmental action, making specific references in Article 100A and Articles 130 R-130T in Title VII of the SEA. This document and the Fourth Environment Program established environmental policy as an independent EC priority. The SEA and the Fourth Program also formulated the environmental dimension as a necessary component of all other EC policies. Article 100A ordains a high level of environmental protection within the framework of single market harmonization while Article 130S make environmental protection a distinct priority and the component of other EC policies.

The SEA alters the environmental decision-making process by introducing qualified majority in the council voting procedure (thus breaking member state deadlocks) and strengthening the Parliament's power on issues concerning the functioning of the single market (100A). The Article VII provisions, however, provide unanimity, yet allow countries greater scope to adopt stricter environmental measures than the EC level. The EC leaders and institutions naturally have differed on deciding which legal base to use for a number of controversial pieces of legislation, such as the titanium waste directive 92/112 and the framework directive on waste 91/156. Called on to set the precedent for these cases the court favored broadening the Parliament's powers in the titanium waste case (C-300/89) but ruled that the main goal of the framework directive was environmental protection (C-155/91) on March 17, 1993. On October 20, 1992, the council signaled its preference for 130S to avoid treating waste as a normal kind of merchandise.

To support this broadening scope of environmental regulation the EC passed several institutional and informational proposals. The council passed a regulation establishing a European Environment Agency although the dispute concerning its location has prevented its operation at present. The agency's designed function is to collect and disseminate information to widen the impact of the EC effort. Another attempt to broaden the impact and to get the society more engaged in the process was Directive 90/313 on the freedom of access to environmental information. This directive stipulates that member states must design programs for citizens to obtain information from environmental authorities. The EC also passed Directive 85/337 creating a framework for imposing impact assessment requirements on specific projects affecting the environment. The economic operator is required to become involved in environmental planning questions.

With several states pressing for stricter air standards air policy continued to be a significant concern. The SEA impact on the decision-making rules is witnessed in the attempt to harmonize policy on car emissions. After receiving the Commission proposal in 1984 the Council finally allowed a compromise—Directive 88/176—in 1987. The Parliament exerted its new powers to help shape Directive 89/458 on small car emissions. The negotiations and compromise on auto emissions were central in smoothing the way for the agreement on specific reductions of large combustion plant emissions, 88/609. However, while 100A has been exercised in some cases, legislation generally has followed the unanimity voting procedure.

The final way the SEA boosted environmental action was indirect. It helped to restore the general enthusiasm for the European integration project. However, the Act did raise some environmental concerns since people questioned the likelihood of environmental impact of a unified single market, in such areas as transport. The agreement to the Maastricht provision and the Fifth Action Program in 1991 and 1992 represented a new EC direction to meet such challenges. The EC in these documents placed a far more constraining definition on economic and social activity, arguing for sustainable development and for environmental protection as a full and separate priority that must be integrated within the other EC issues. Regarding the decision-making process the Maastricht Treaty expands the qualified majority voting to more environmental issues and allows the Parliament co-decision on action program issues. The Fifth Action Program also pushed in new directions by raising the option of utilizing economic incentives to supplement the EC's mainly command and control legislation. The Netherlands in particular has made extensive use of financial and subsidy incentives, such as restructuring the incentives for unleaded gasoline. In considering the carbon tax in 1993 the EC is following the direction of Denmark and other countries that have created their own energy taxes.

The focus on integrating environment and economic development concerns in the Maastricht Treaty and the Fifth Action Program mirrored comprehensive and path-breaking national efforts. Germany is trying to develop a comprehensive packaging waste program centered on a private company, Duales System Deutschland (DSD). Manufacturers and retailers are required to participate in this system by taking their packaging back, thus creating an incentive for recyclable products. In 1993 DSD is facing severe challenges on the questions of logistics, violations of competition and cartel laws, and general bankruptcy. The Netherlands approved a National Environmental Policy Plan in 1989 and 1990, emphasizing sustainable development and environmental protection. The initiative expands the range of possible instruments, including source oriented pollution measures such as altering production processes. The plan includes all ministries in the environmental policy making, and society is organized into target groups that work together to set environmental objectives.

The regional pressures created by such legislation as the German packaging effort and the reusable bottling legislation in Denmark suggested the need for European legislation on packaging waste to prevent irreconcilable economic distortions within the region. The French/German pact on waste trade (August 1992) and the Court of Justice allowance of the Belgian state of Wallonia's "simple" waste ban (Case 2/90; July 9, 1992) raised similar concerns about waste shipments and hazardous waste.

One sees numerous examples in the 1990s of the EC trying a more holistic approach. To help provide citizens with environmental information for consumer choices the EC created the ecolabel (Regulation 880/92) mandating the assessment of the life cycle of products. The Commission has proposed an Integrated Pollution Prevention and Control Directive. This legislation creates a permit system for operating new and old industrial installations. It takes into account land, air, and water effects within an equally weighted framework.

In view of the difficulties raised by the Maastricht Treaty ratification and the European economic downturn of 1992–1993 many do not expect the EC to expand its scope, even in the environmental arena where it has had significant success. Symptomatic are the pressures to remove EC responsibility for areas such as water pollution standards. British officials have called for the application of the subsidiarity principle, requiring the devolution of regulatory authority to more localized levels of government for appropriate issues. A separate issue is the question of harmonizing national regulatory protection and member state implementation.

In 1992 the Commission cited all the member states for failing to adequately and promptly transpose EC legislation into national law.

Anthony R. Zito

Further Readings

DocTer. *European Environmental Yearbook.* 1990.

Haigh, Nigel. *Manual of Environmental Policy: The EC and Britain.* 1992.

See also ACID PRECIPITATION: EUROPEAN EXPERIENCES; *Chemiepolitik* (GERMANY); ENVIRONMENTAL CASE LAW: EUROPEAN COMMUNITY; LEGISLATION: GREAT BRITAIN; RHINE RIVER; SEVESO

Legislation: Great Britain

Environmental legislation in Britain has undergone deep structural changes in the past decade. The country pioneered many areas of environmental law with the early development of public health legislation in the last century, and the implementation of extensive controls concerning land-use planning, nature conservation, and urban smog after World War II. By the early 1970s, however, the very real achievements that had been made had encouraged a degree of complacency. Legislation provided regulators with extensive powers but was riddled with discretion. Few explicit environmental standards or goals of any precision were expressed in the law, and secrecy was the order of the day. Regulators tended to avoid legal confrontation, preferring a policy of negotiation with industry. In the field of pollution control both Labor and Conservative administrations resisted policy initiatives until a scientific case was proved, and the contribution of Britain to transboundary pollution was scarcely acknowledged.

These characteristics of British environmental policy and law no longer hold sway. New legislation introduced in the past few years has radically transformed key areas of regulation. More explicit duties and standards have been introduced, and new administrative bodies established, with a more aggressive approach toward enforcement. The growth of environmental legislation at European Community (EC) level in the past twenty years has been one significant reason for change, forcing Britain to adopt a less insular approach toward environmental problems; other forces have also been at work. The 1989 privatization of the electricity and water industries, which had been major sources of pollution, provided the opportunity to introduce substantial reforms to their regulatory framework, while Parliamentary and influential bodies such as the Royal Commission on Environmental Pollution continually criticized a lack of direction and consistency in United Kingdom (UK) environmental law and policy. The year 1990 saw the publication of the government's environmental White Paper, "This Common Inheritance," a major policy statement which for the first time in many years attempted to give a coherence to Britain's environmental policies. The document was not as far-reaching as many in the environmental movement would like to have seen, but can in retrospect be seen as a significant symbolic marker of a new stage of development in British environmental law and policy.

Some of the most important new UK environmental laws that have been introduced in the past few years will illustrate the nature of the changes taking place. In 1988, to implement EC legislation on the subject, regulators introduced environmental assessment procedures for a wide range of proposed developments. Environmental assessments for major projects such as oil terminals had been carried out in the past but largely on a discretionary basis and in the context of land-use planning procedures. The new requirements are still confined to site-specific proposals, and the possible extension of environmental assessment to various types of plans or policies remains a controversial issue. Empirical research suggests considerable variation in the quality of assessment studies carried out in practice, but the new legislation has at the very least required more systematic evaluations of the environmental implications of new projects than ever existed before.

In the field of pollution control Part I of the Environmental Protection Act of 1990 introduced a new system of integrated licensing for specified classes of industry. A single regulatory agency, Her Majesty's Inspectorate of Pollution, now grants single authorizations dealing with all the emissions from a particular process. In contrast to previous specialized pollution licensing systems, the new statutory provisions introduce an element of public participation into the procedures, and impose more explicit legal duties on the regulatory agency to seek to prevent or minimize emissions wherever practicable. Where emissions are likely to enter more than one physical medium, the agency is obliged to seek the "best practicable environmental option," a wholly new legal concept.

Water pollution legislation was substantially reformed under the Water Act of 1989. The operational arms of former public water authorities were privatized by the creation of new water supply and sewerage service utilities, and a new national public agency—the National Rivers Authority (NRA)—was established in England and Wales with the responsibility to regulate surface and groundwater pollution and to control the abstraction of water. A licensing system remains the main regulatory tool for controlling industrial and sewerage discharges, but is now operated in the context of a more explicit set of policy objectives which are expressed as legal requirements, while at the same time the clear separation of utility and regulatory functions has permitted the NRA to conduct a more aggressive prosecution policy.

Explicit legal controls over waste disposal were first introduced in the early 1970s, with responsibility for site-licensing and enforcement resting with local authorities. But the effectiveness of the system was subject to heavy criticism in subsequent years, and the Environmental Protection Act of 1990 introduced substantial reforms to the legal framework. Producers of waste are now under a new statutory duty of care to ensure that their waste remains in a legitimate stream until final disposal. Licensing procedures for disposal sites have been strengthened, and new provisions have been introduced to ensure that site operators remain legally responsible for the environmental security of their sites after disposal operations have ceased.

Despite the rapid development of new environmental legislation in recent years, common law principles developed by the judiciary remain of importance, especially in the field of civil liability. In the past fifty years British courts have generally rejected strict liability in favor of fault-based principles, but have now been given the opportunity to reevaluate their approach in respect of environmental pollution. A test case concerning groundwater pollution caused by industrial spillages has been working its way up the courts, with the trial judge in 1991 refusing to find liability in the absence of negligence. In a surprise decision the Appeal Court reversed this ruling in 1992 and indicated that in the context of contemporary environmental concerns, strict liability regimes were appropriate. At the end of 1993, however, the highest court, the House of Lords, overturned the Court of Appeal, and held that in the absence of legislation reasonable forseeability rather than causation per se should remain the basis of liability. In doing so, they indicated clearly that the complex policy issues involved in extending strict liability concepts should be the responsibility of Government rather than the courts.

Richard Macrory

Further Readings

McCormick, John. *Environmental Politics in Great Britain.* 1992.

Vogel, David. "Regulation: Lessons from Great Britain." *Public Interest* 72 (1983): 25–50.

See also ENVIRONMENTAL CASE LAW: EUROPEAN COMMUNITY; ENVIRONMENTAL CASE LAW: GREAT BRITAIN; GREAT BRITAIN: ENVIRONMENTAL PROBLEMS; LEGISLATION: EUROPEAN COMMUNITY

Legislation: United States

Over the past twenty-five years, federal and state governments in the United States have adopted and implemented an array of environmental protection and conservation legislation. These range from the Clean Air Act and the National Environmental Policy Act (NEPA) to dozens of other major acts approved from the late 1960s through the early 1990s, including elaborate programs to improve the quality of the nation's lakes and rivers, clean up hazardous waste sites, and protect endangered species and their habitats, among many other ambitious endeavors. This remarkable public policy record may be explained by many factors, including the nation's economic condition and important cultural changes since the late 1940s. Perhaps the most significant variable, however, is public opinion. U.S. policy makers, particularly in Congress and state governments, were highly responsive to a new and persistent public demand for environmental protection. The details of environmental policies have been shaped far more by the intensive lobbying campaigns of environmentalists and the business community, but public support set the process in motion and shaped its basic contours.

Political scientists use an agenda-setting model to explain the development of environmental policies, and to differentiate between fundamental or deeper causes and more proximate or shallow currents of economic, technological, and political change. Environmental problems grew in salience in the 1960s and 1970s as one consequence of the post-war economic boom and its visible impact on environmental quality, particularly the accumulation of toxic chemicals. Changes in societal values in the emerging post-industrial economy made the public more likely to perceive those impacts as unacceptable and to demand governmental intervention. The development of the modern environmental movement and its increasing influence in Washington and in the states, the availability of more and better scientific data on environmental conditions and their effects, and favorable media coverage of environmental accidents all helped to create a political climate in the late 1960s and early 1970s that facilitated a burst of legislative enthusiasm for environmental policy.

At this time, public officials were eager to respond to a concerned public and to take credit for popular actions to protect the environment even when their full costs and impacts were unknown. Between 1970 and 1976 Congress drafted most of the basic framework for U.S. environmental protection policy, which often departed sharply from weak policies that prevailed until 1970. The new legislation emphasized national environmental quality standards and regulatory policies that would be implemented jointly by the federal government and the states. This approach characterized the nation's premier environmental protection statute, the Clean Air Act of 1970, and it extended to the Clean Water Act of 1972, the Safe Drinking Water Act of 1974, the Resource Conservation and Recovery Act (RCRA) of 1976 (the chief policy for control of hazardous waste), and (later) the Comprehensive Environmental Response, Compensation and Liability Act of 1980 (Superfund). All of these programs were assigned to the newly created Environmental Protection Agency (EPA).

Enactment of many natural resource policies had taken place even earlier (for example, the Wilderness Act of 1964 and the Land and Water Conservation Fund Act of 1965) and they too were supplemented and expanded in the 1970s and 1980s. New policies included the Coastal Zone Management Act of 1972, the Endangered Species Act of 1973, the National Forest Management Act of 1976, and the Surface Mining Control and Reclamation Act of 1977, among many others. Jurisdiction over the natural resource programs remained with the traditional land-use agencies in the departments of Interior and Agriculture, with some assigned to the departments of Commerce, Defense (the Corps of Engineers), Transportation, or Energy.

L

Support for these environmental policies was typically bipartisan even if Republicans were less enthusiastic than Democrats about most environmental programs. Legislative roll-call analysis indicates a strong association between partisan affiliation (and political ideology) and support for environmental protection legislation. Even though Republican presidents Richard Nixon and Gerald Ford were often willing to sign environmental bills enacted by Congress, policy leadership fell largely to the Democratic party, which controlled Congress throughout the 1970s.

The decade of the 1970s was also a time of institution building for environmental policy. The EPA was created by executive order under President Nixon in 1970 to consolidate federal regulatory programs previously scattered across the executive branch. The Council on Environmental Quality came into being with the passage of NEPA in 1970. Budgets for environmental programs began to increase as did the staffs of both federal and state agencies dealing with environmental protection and natural resources management. For example, by 1979 the EPA had a staff of over 11,000, making it by far the nation's largest regulatory agency. Following budget and staff cuts in the early 1980s, this pattern of environmental policy institutionalization resumed in the late 1980s and early 1990s. By 1993, EPA's staff had grown to 18,000.

The generally positive political climate for environmental policy was subject to periodic setbacks. The first occurred in the mid- to late 1970s as critics began to complain about the impacts and costs of the new environmental legislation, and to question the capacity of the EPA and other agencies to implement the demanding policies Congress gave them. The greatest challenge to environmental legislation arrived with the election of President Ronald Reagan in 1980. Reagan and his environmental officials, particularly James Watt, Secretary of Interior, and Anne Burford, his first EPA administrator, sharply criticized environmental and resource policies. As part of the president's conservative agenda, they and others sought to reduce the scope of government regulation, shift responsibilities to the states, and rely more on the private sector.

Reagan also urged Congress to slash spending on environmental programs, which it did in the early 1980s. In addition, he instituted an administrative strategy to reduce the burden of environmental programs through careful use of the appointment and oversight powers of the American presidency. However, following initial cooperation with the president, after 1983 Congress was more likely to take issue with his actions in the executive agencies and to reject his budgetary recommendations.

Survey research indicates that the American public's commitment to environmental protection remained strong even when programs were under attack during the Reagan administration, and when they were given lukewarm endorsement during the tenure of President George Bush—1989 to January 1993. Politically, public support translated into congressional criticism of the Reagan and Bush policies, defense of existing environmental programs, and strengthening of the major acts when they were up for renewal, most notably in the cases of RCRA and Superfund in 1984 and 1986, respectively, and for the Clean Air Act in 1990. Divided government and intense interest group pressures in the 1980s also led to legislative gridlock that delayed program renewals and limited new policy development.

As one sign of the public's continuing commitment to environmental protection and the governmental response to it, as of 1993 the federal government was spending at a level of $21 billion a year for all environmental and natural resource programs. Adjusted for inflation, that represented an 85 percent increase since the early 1970s. However, it was also slightly *lower* than federal spending in 1980 as a result of the Reagan era budget cuts.

Another useful indicator of the effects of the cutbacks of the 1980s is the budget of the EPA. As noted, EPA is responsible for implementation of most statutes other than natural resources programs. In constant dollars, the EPA's operating budget in fiscal 1993 was only about 21 percent higher than it was in fiscal 1975, despite the many new responsibilities given to it by Congress in the intervening years. That trend would be far less positive without a 50 percent increase in EPA spending under President Bush. Even with the Bush increases, EPA's operating budget by 1993 was only slightly higher than it had been in the last year of the Carter administration in 1980.

As critics are quick to observe, the aggregate impact on the nation of these statutes, the voluminous and highly detailed regulatory requirements they create, and the expenditures associated with them are far greater than the federal budget numbers alone would indicate. There are high compliance costs for industry and heavy burdens placed on state and local governments, which are often strapped for funds to support mandated state implementation activities. Since virtually all federal environmental protection policies depend on shared federal-state implementation, funding shortages in some states help to explain variable strength in environmental policy across the fifty states. Scholars and environmental activists have noted that some states (such as California, Michigan, Minnesota, New York, Oregon, Washington, and Wisconsin) are invariably more progressive on environmental policies than others, and some are more predictably policy innovators. Among the least progressive states are those with either a limited commitment to environmental quality goals or weak institutional capacities, including insufficient budgets (for example, Alabama, Arkansas, Illinois, Indiana, Louisiana, Mississippi, and Texas).

The most common way to express the nation's continuing commitment to environmental quality goals is to note that federal, state, and private spending on the environment as of 1993 was about $130 billion a year, or about 2 percent of the nation's gross national product (GNP). These expenditures are expected to rise to about 2.5 percent of the GNP by the mid-1990s. Large expenditures and compliance costs are guaranteed for the future for other reasons as well. For example, commitment to environmental restoration at federal facilities such as the Department of Energy's nuclear weapons production plants may well cost the nation nearly $300 billion over the next thirty years if present cleanup standards are maintained.

These substantial expenditures and the burdens associated with environmental regulations lead increasingly to questions about the likely benefits in improved public health and environmental quality these programs will yield. This is particularly the case for clean air, clean water, and toxic and hazardous waste programs, where large additional expenditures often bring marginal gains in improved public health. Critics ask whether these benefits, measured in dollar terms or otherwise, can justify the high costs. Even environmentalists readily acknowledge the need to improve program efficiency and effectiveness. The EPA itself released several reports in the late 1980s and early 1990s that argued strongly for risk-based environmental priority setting as one way to ensure that expenditures are better matched with benefits in risk reduction.

Measuring the success or failure of environmental policies is a difficult undertaking, and there is a high degree of variability from one program to another. Environmental policies take years if not decades to produce the intended results, and some effects are easier to document than others. Unreliable monitoring of environmental conditions over time also makes it difficult to substantiate trends in environmental quality and to associate those changes with public policy actions. Complicating any assessment of U.S. environmental policy is the generally insufficient budgetary resources provided to implementing agencies and frequent opposition and litigation from business and other groups, which can seriously slow implementation.

Despite these limitations, it is evident that some programs have resulted in demonstrable and significant improvements in the nation's environmental quality (the Clean Air Act is an example) or have altered governmental decision-making processes by forcing consideration of environmental impacts (e.g., NEPA). Others may not have improved environmental quality so much as they have prevented further deterioration of the environment that otherwise would have come with economic growth and rising populations over the past two decades; the Clean Water Act is an example. Regrettably, some policies, such as Superfund, have proven to be problematic and largely ineffective thus far. Even here, however, program achievements could be far greater with the adoption of appropriate policy redesigns, with more realistic standards for site cleanup, and with improved implementation by the EPA.

Despite the notable record of U.S. environmental policy over more than two decades, the nation has made little progress in some areas that will require continuing attention. Among these are global (and U.S.) population growth, which is expected to double the world's population by the mid-twenty-first century; policies to promote energy conservation and renewable energy sources, and to decrease reliance on fossil fuels; and a range of concerns that can be subsumed under the heading of sustainable economic development—from changes in agricultural practices to improvements in transportation and the urban environment and ways to integrate international trade and environmental quality.

The recent criticisms of environmental policies and the proposal of new approaches such as comparative risk analysis, pollution

L

prevention, and use of market-based incentives to supplement conventional regulation will also reshape the policy agenda for the 1990s and the early twenty-first century. Perhaps of greatest importance the emergence of new global environmental threats such as climate change and the protection of biological diversity promises to redefine environmental policy ambitions in the decades ahead for the United States and all other nations.

Michael E. Kraft

Further Readings

Portney, Paul R., ed. *Public Policies for Environmental Protection.* 1990.

Rosenbaum, Walter A. *Environmental Politics and Policy.* 3rd ed. 1995.

Switzer, Jacqueline Vaughn. *Environmental Politics: Domestic and Global Dimensions.* 1994.

Vig, Norman J., and Michael E. Kraft, eds. *Environmental Policy in the 1990s: Toward a New Agenda.* 2nd ed. 1994.

See also AIR POLLUTION: REGULATION (U.S.); BUSH, GEORGE; ENDANGERED SPECIES ACT (U.S.); ENVIRONMENTAL PROTECTION AGENCY; NATIONAL ENVIRONMENTAL POLICY ACT (U.S.); REAGAN, RONALD; RESOURCE CONSERVATION AND RECOVERY ACT; SUPERFUND; TOXIC SUBSTANCES CONTROL ACT

Leopold, Aldo

Over a forty-year career Aldo Leopold's contributions as a writer, forester, wildlife ecologist and manager, educator, philosopher, and activist established him as one of the central figures in twentieth-century conservation. Combining the sensibility of a poet, the discipline of a scientist, and the curiosity of a scholar, Leopold both stimulated and exemplified the evolution of conservation from a movement based on narrow utilitarian grounds to one based on a sound understanding of ecological processes and human impacts on ecological systems.

Leopold was born in Burlington, Iowa in 1887 and grew up along the banks of the Mississippi River. Introduced to hunting and fishing as a boy, he absorbed his father's deep-seated commitment to sportsmanship and outdoor ethics. These early lessons fed his decision as a teenager to become a forester. After graduating from Lawrenceville Preparatory School in New Jersey Leopold entered Yale University, where in 1909 he received his Master's degree in forestry. He thus became a member of the first generation of Americans to be formally trained in the field.

After completing his studies Leopold joined the U.S. Forest Service (USFS) as a field officer in the national forests of the American Southwest. Over the next fifteen years he rose through the ranks of the USFS, gaining wide recognition among foresters as an innovative writer, thinker, and administrator, devoting himself in particular to the issues of game protection, soil erosion, rangeland degradation, and wilderness protection in the Southwest. His special concern over the loss of wilderness led him to advocate, beginning in 1921, the establishment of inviolate "wilderness areas" within the national forests. His work led to the designation in 1924 of the Gila Wilderness Area within New Mexico's Gila National Forest, the first such area to be so designated on the public lands of the United States.

In 1924 Leopold moved to Madison, Wisconsin, to assume the assistant directorship of the U.S. Forest Products Laboratory—the primary wood research facility of the USFS. Remaining in this position for four years, Leopold devoted increasing amounts of his time to the cause of wilderness protection and to what had always been his most fundamental interest: the conservation of wildlife (which at the time entailed mainly the protection of game animals). In 1928 Leopold left the USFS to dedicate himself wholly to the task of building wildlife management as a viable field.

Over the next three years Leopold conducted detailed field surveys of game populations and habitats in the north-central United States. This unprecedented effort resulted in a book-length report and, ultimately, the publication in 1933 of *Game Management*, the first text in the field. Combining his extensive field experience with new findings and concepts in animal ecology, Leopold's book contributed significantly to a fundamental shift within game conservation, away from artificial propagation and restrictive legislation and toward the protection and restoration of habitat. In 1933 Leopold accepted an appointment as professor of game management at the University of Wisconsin—the first academic position in the new field.

Up until this point much of Leopold's work in game management consisted of applying the principles of sustained-yield forestry to the management of game animals. But through the

1930s Leopold's thinking gradually evolved to reflect his deepening knowledge of ecology and his growing dissatisfaction with the limits of utilitarian conservation philosophy. This evolution had many stimuli: early experiments in ecological restoration at the University of Wisconsin Arboretum; the disastrous consequences of the Dust Bowl in the high plains; a trip to Germany in 1935 during which he studied the history of European forestry and game management; two trips into Mexico's wild Sierra Madre Occidental; and the expanded interest in wildlife (as opposed to "game") management in the United States in the late 1930s.

As a result of these and other factors Leopold's management philosophy began to stress increasingly the importance of what he termed "land health," or the functional integrity of the biotic community. "The land," he wrote in 1944, "consists of soil, water, plants, and animals, but health is more than a sufficiency of these components. It is a state of vigorous self-renewal in each of them, and in all collectively." In practice this entailed greater emphasis (whether in forestry, agriculture, fisheries management, wildlife management, range management, or other conservation subdisciplines) on ecological function, species diversity, rare and threatened species, and the integration of management efforts. It also gave added importance to wilderness lands, which could provide "a base-datum of normality, a picture of how healthy land maintains itself." In essence Leopold's emerging conservation philosophy superseded both the earlier utilitarian philosophy exemplified by forester Gifford Pinchot and the preservation-oriented school that John Muir represented. Leopold's signal contribution was to synthesize their views within an enlarged context of historical and ecological knowledge.

Another important stimulus to Leopold's thought was his purchase in 1935 of a run-down farm on the floodplain of the Wisconsin River north of Madison. As Leopold and his family worked to restore ecological health to this piece of land it became the focus of his scientific, literary, and philosophical innovations. During World War II Leopold began to write the lyrical essays that would eventually be compiled in his environmental classic, *A Sand County Almanac*. "On this sand farm in Wisconsin," he wrote in its introduction, "first worn out and then abandoned by our bigger-and-better society, we try to rebuild, with shovel and axe, what we are losing elsewhere."

The climax of *A Sand County Almanac* was its philosophical endpiece "The Land Ethic," in which Leopold argued for a broadened definition of community that would "enlarge the boundaries . . . to include soils, waters, plants, and animals, or collectively: the land." Such an expanded definition, it followed, would "[change] the role of *Homo sapiens* from conqueror of the land community to plain member and citizen of it." The Land Ethic would become, in the decades following its publication, an important cornerstone for sustained discussions in environmental ethics, and would establish Leopold as a seminal figure in not only the science and literature, but the philosophy, of conservation.

The manuscript of *A Sand County Almanac* was accepted for publication in April 1947. A week later, on April 21, 1947, Leopold died while fighting a brush fire on a neighbor's farm in Wisconsin.

Curt Meine

Further Readings

Callicott, J. Baird, ed. *Companion to* A Sand County Almanac. 1987.
Flader, Susan. *Thinking Like a Mountain: Aldo Leopold and the Evolution of an Ecological Attitude Toward Deer, Wolves, and Forests*. 1974.
Flader, Susan, and J. Baird Callicott, eds. *The River of the Mother of God and Other Essays by Aldo Leopold*. 1991.
Leopold, Aldo. *A Sand County Almanac and Sketches Here and There*. 1949.
Meine, Curt. *Aldo Leopold: His Life and Work*. 1988.

See also CONSERVATION MOVEMENT; ENVIRONMENTAL ETHICS; FOREST SERVICE (U.S.); LAND ETHIC; MUIR, JOHN; PINCHOT, GIFFORD; WILDERNESS

Life-Cycle Analysis

An assessment of all direct and indirect environmental and other impacts of a given technology—whether a product, a system, or an entire sector in society—is called a life-cycle analysis (LCA). Not only are direct impacts from cradle to grave included, but also indirect effects from materials, energy, and other inputs to the manufacturing process and subsequent handling—from building the production facilities, to the transporting of related goods and services, use of the product, and, finally, disposal, whether in the form of reuse, recycling, or waste deposition (e.g., landfill).

The ideas behind LCA developed during the 1970s under such rubrics as "total assessment," "including externalities," or "least-cost planning." The first applications of LCA were in the energy field, including both individual energy technologies and entire energy supply systems. It was soon realized, however, that the procurement of all required data was a difficult problem. As a result, the emphasis went toward LCA applied to individual products, where the data handling seemed more manageable. Even in this limited arena, however, LCA is still a very open-ended process. For example, the manufacturing of a milk container requires both materials and energy; to assess the impacts associated with the energy input calls in turn for an LCA of the energy supply system. Only as the gathering of relevant data has been ongoing for a considerable duration of time has it become possible to perform credible LCAs.

The impacts to be included in an LCA can be grouped into categories:

1. Economic impacts such as impacts on owners' economy and on national economy, including questions of foreign payments balance and employment.
2. Environmental impacts (e.g., land use, noise, visual impact, local pollution of soil, water, air and biota, regional and global pollution, and other impacts on the earth-atmosphere system, such as climatic change).
3. Social impacts such as those related to satisfaction of needs, health and work environment, risks, and the impact of large accidents, institutions required to cope with new processes or products.
4. Security impacts, including both supply security and safety against misuse or terror actions.
5. Resilience (i.e., sensitivity to system failures, planning uncertainties, and future changes in criteria for impact assessment).
6. Development impacts such as those related to the consistency of a product or a technology as it affects the goals of a given society.
7. Political impacts including impacts of control requirements, and openness to decentralization in both physical and decision-making terms.

It is clear that a list of this kind is open-ended and that some impacts will never become quantifiable. This raises the new issues of how to present and how to use an LCA, which would typically produce a list of impact estimations, some of which are quantified and some which are not, with the quantifiable impacts often given in quite different units (e.g., tons of sulfur dioxide, number of work accidents, capital cost of equipment, etc.).

One approach is to try to convert all impacts into monetary values (i.e., replace the sulfur dioxide amounts with either the cost of reducing the emissions to some low threshold value [avoidance cost] or, alternatively, an estimated cost of the impacts: hospitalization and workday salaries lost, replanting cost of dead forests, restoration of historic buildings damaged by acid rain). Accidental death thus would be replaced by the insurance cost of a human life, and so on (damage costs). Unavailability of numbers has led to the alternative philosophy of interviewing cross sections of affected population on the amount of money they would be willing to pay to avoid a specific impact or to monitor their actual investments (revealed preferences).

All of these methods are deficient: the first by not including a (political) weighing of different issues (e.g., weighing immediate impacts against impacts occurring in the future); the second by doing so on a wrong basis (influenced by people's knowledge of the issues, by their accessible assets, etc.). The best alternative may be to present the entire impact profile to decision makers in the original units and with a time-sequence indicating when each impact is believed to occur, and then to invite a true political debate on the proper weighing of the different issues.

Major product LCAs performed include assessments of aluminum cans and of milk containers, while system LCAs have been mainly the analyses of energy supply systems based on fossil, nuclear, or various renewable energy sources.

The difficulties encountered in using LCA in the political decision-making process have been partly offset by the advantages of bringing the many impacts often disregarded (as "externalities," meaning issues not included in the economic analysis) into the debate. It may be fair to say that LCA will hardly ever become a routine method of computerized assessment, but that it may continue to serve a useful purpose by focusing and sharpening the debate involved in any decision-making process. Hopefully, it will also help to increase the quality of the information upon which final decisions are taken, whether on starting to manufacture a given new product, or to arrange a sector of society (such as the energy sector) in one way or another.

Bent Sørensen

Further Readings

Fava, J., et al., eds. *Society of Environmental Toxicology and Chemistry and SETAC Foundation: A Technical Framework for Life-Cycle Assessments Workshop Report.* 1991.

Lübkert, B., et al., eds. *Life-Cycle Analysis: An International Database for Ecoprofile Analysis.* 1991.

Sørensen, Bent. *Life-Cycle Assessment of Energy Systems*, pp. 21–53, OECD and IEA, Paris, 1993.

See also BENEFIT-COST ANALYSIS; ENVIRONMENTAL IMPACT ASSESSMENT; GREEN PRODUCTS; LEAST COST UTILITY PLANNING; RISK ANALYSIS

Limits to Growth

In 1972 Donella H. Meadows, et al., published *The Limits to Growth: A Report for the Club of Rome's Project on the Predicament of Mankind.* The Club of Rome was an informal group of scholars and business people organized in 1968 by an Italian industrialist, Dr. Aurelio Peccei. The Project on the Predicament of Mankind was an examination of the "world problematique," defined as the interactive dynamic of such problems as poverty, environmental degradation, unemployment, inflation, and loss of faith in institutions. Based on an extrapolation into the future of then existing trends, *Limits to Growth* predicted that in the absence of significant political and economic change environmental stress in the form of resource consumption and pollution, combined with such factors as global population increase, would lead to "growth and then collapse into a dismal, depleted existence." Meadows and her colleagues argued that the objective of economic growth must be replaced by that of a "state of global equilibrium." In support of their argument for sustainability they cited, among others, John Stuart Mill and the 1971 article by Herman Daly, "Toward a Stationary-State Economy."

In contrast to the political dialogue of the 1980s surrounding "sustainable development," *Limits to Growth* divided environmentalists and advocates of the status quo into two sharply divided camps. The validity of the modeling methods used in the project were severely attacked and—it is now widely agreed—were successfully repudiated. The importance of *Limits to Growth*, however, is not the accuracy of its predictions but the fact that it put the contrasting visions of never-ending economic expansion versus a steady-state economy squarely on the table. That debate was first intensified by the OPEC oil embargo in the year following publication, then muted during the remainder of the 1970s and early 1980s as environmentalism declined, for a time, as a political force. The themes then, as noted, re-emerged as reframed by the Bruntland Commission formulation of sustainable development. The inherent political issue, however, is still very much with us. Can we meet the needs of the poor by absolute increases in the wealth of all classes and nations, derived from increasing productivity, while keeping associated resource consumption and environmental degradation to acceptable levels? Or will environmental constraints force us to turn to redistribution of wealth in order to more equitably share the finite pie of a steady-state economy? Depending upon the answers to those questions, environmental politics is seen as either separate from, or central to the traditional distributive politics of the left-right spectrum.

Doug Macdonald

Further Readings

Macdonald, Doug. *The Politics of Pollution.* 1991.

Meadows, Donella H., et al. *The Limits to Growth: A Report for the Club of Rome's Project on the Predicament of Mankind.* 2nd ed. 1974.

Rees, Judith. *Natural Resources: Allocation, Economics and Policy.* 2nd ed. 1990.

See also ENVIRONMENTALISM; ECONOMIC GROWTH AND THE ENVIRONMENT; GREEN ECONOMICS; NONRENEWABLE RESOURCES; SUSTAINABLE DEVELOPMENT

Lizards

See REPTILES: CONSERVATION AND HABITAT

London Smog

Smog is the colloquial term for a mixture of smoke, or particulate matter, and fog, mostly the aerosol of sulfur dioxide (SO_2). The principal components are the emissions of coal burning, vehicle exhausts, and oil-based materials. Smog concentrates under conditions of atmospheric inversion or stability associated with cold anticyclonic conditions. The great London smog of December 4–9, 1952, was unusual in that it lasted for four days and was thicker and more penetrating than any recent fogs, so people were less aware of its killing potential. SO_2 levels reached two micrograms per cubic meter on December 8, and smoke concentrations recorded a high of 1.7 micrograms per cubic meter on December 6–7. Respiratory ailments were seriously worsened by the conditions with deaths peaking at 900 for each of the two days December 5–6 as compared with a normal rate of 260 per day. Even a week after the smog had cleared, deaths were running at 500 per day. In all, some 2,000 people succumbed directly as a result of the conditions.

The incident provided a stimulus for clear air legislation in the United Kingdom (UK) and subsequently in Europe generally. As is often the case, advisory committees had been reporting for decades on the need to reduce smoke pollution, but it took a high profile killer event to goad political and administrative authorities into action. The Clean Air Act of 1956 created smokeless zones and strengthened regulatory standards, as well as extending the remit of the national air pollution control agency. Subsequent declines in SO_2 over UK cities came about as North Sea gas created a spur to inexpensive domestic central heating, and coal burning power-stations elevated their chimneys to widen the spread of sulfurous rain throughout western Europe.

Timothy O'Riordan

Further Readings

Brimblecome, Peter. *The Big Smoke: A History of Air Pollution in London since Medieval Times.* 1987.

See also AIR POLLUTION: IMPACTS; ASEAN HAZE; DONORA, PENNSYLVANIA; SMOG

Long Range Transport

Emission of gases and airborne particulates into the atmosphere results from many industrial and domestic processes including combustion of fossil fuels, smelting and refining of metal from ores or waste materials, waste incineration, and the production of pulp and paper. Concern for the resulting air pollution from all of these processes has led to the development of criteria or standards for many of the common airborne pollutants, and in some instances, regulation of air quality for specific pollutants.

Point sources of air pollution usually threaten the health of humans and ecosystems in the immediate location of the source. The long-term goal for protection of the environment, particularly environments close to point sources of air pollution, is to limit or eliminate the source(s) through some type of improved technology or even through closure of the offending operation. But technological improvements, even if they have been developed, take time to implement. As an interim measure, the chimneys or other devices which convey the gases from the operation into the atmosphere can be extended upward, such that the emissions will be spread over a wider area before they are deposited. This so called "dilution solution" was implemented increasingly in the second half of the twentieth century as industrial operations became larger and awareness of air pollution increased. Tall stacks were even approved of as interim solutions by some environmentalists in the 1960s. Local air quality was definitely improved by the installation of tall stacks.

However, unless the pollutants in the emissions are degradable into harmless forms, the provision of tall stacks simply exports pollution to some other location. By the late 1960s it became apparent that the airborne pollutants from tall stacks were contributing to a serious problem of *Long Range Transport of Atmospheric Pollutants*, which is known by the acronym LRTAP.

Acidic deposition or acid rain was the first major environmental problem to be identified in the context of LRTAP. Acid gases, oxides of sulfur and nitrogen, are produced by many types of combustion as well as from smelting of sulfur-containing ores. When injected into the atmosphere the gases can be conveyed for long distances (up to thousands of kilometers in some instances), are converted into sulfuric and nitric acids, and eventually are deposited in wet and dry deposition (i.e., rain, snow, fog, etc.) onto aquatic and terrestrial systems including structures made by humans. LRTAP does not recognize geographical or political boundaries, with the result that the acid gas emissions from one country regularly fall as acid rain in another country. Recognition of the phenomenon by scientists and environmentalists preceded acceptance of liability and action on the part of the polluting parties, and indeed in many instances the receiving jurisdictions are still the victims of LRTAP.

The attention paid to acid rain and the efforts devoted to cleaning up the emissions of acid gases from coal-fired power plants, metal smelters, and automobile exhaust may have diverted attention from the fact that many other potentially harmful materials also undergo LRTAP. By the mid 1980s, however, it was clear that various metals and radionuclides as well as organic materials were implicated in LRTAP. Mercury, lead, cadmium, arsenic, nuclides characteristic of fallout from specific tests, PCBs, and organochlorine pesticides (including DDT, dieldrin, and toxaphene) were identified in air masses as far north as the Arctic, thousands of kilometers from any known source. Exotic (manufactured) volatile organic compounds were sometimes in as high or higher concentrations in Arctic air than in more southerly, urbanized regions. Improved techniques of sampling and more sensitive and accurate methods of chemical analysis have enabled scientists to investigate over the past decade and a half the patterns of LRTAP. Thus we can track air masses and potential sources of material for LRTAP.

Environmental samples have confirmed the occurrence of LRTAP and subsequent deposition. Cores from lake sediments, ice caps, and long undisturbed snow packs in remote areas of the planet bear traces of inorganic and organic materials that could only have arrived through LRTAP and, furthermore, these cores also provide a historical record of the deposition. The onset of the use of tetraethyl lead in gasoline has provided a signal by increased lead concentration in sediments or snowpacks in remote areas, and following the removal of the compound from gasoline in several large industrialized countries, the decline in lead concentration in LRTAP can be determined as well. Lichens and vascular plants (some of which are decades in age), even in the high Arctic, can similarly tell the story of LRTAP. Food chains in remote areas show accumulation of radionuclides and exotic, manufactured chemicals, and Arctic mammals—both terrestrial and aquatic—have PCBs and organochlorine pesticides in their fat.

Damage to ecosystems or to human health resulting from LRTAP is often difficult to assess with certainty. Concentrations of pollutants resulting from LRTAP are typically much lower than those recorded close to industrial operations. But many of the contaminants are cumulative and persistent; sublethal effects can be expected based on analogies with other, more completely studied systems. Ecosystems in remote areas, especially in Arctic and boreal regions, are slow to develop and slow to recover from insults. The very presence of abnormal materials in remote ecosystems alerts us to the potential damage. Solutions, in terms of controlling the sources of LRTAP—sources which are often multiple and poorly documented—remain problematic.

Pamela Welbourn

Further Readings

Pawlick, T. *A Killing Rain: The Global Threat of Acid Precipitation.* 1984.

Stokes, Pamela. *Airborne Contaminants and Aquatic Systems: An Assessment of Research Needs.* 1988.

See also ACID PRECIPITATION: AQUATIC IMPACTS; ACID PRECIPITATION: TERRESTRIAL IMPACTS; AIR POLLUTION: IMPACTS; AIR POLLUTION: REGULATION (U.S.); ARCTIC; EASTERN EUROPE: ENVIRONMENTAL PROBLEMS; INTERNATIONAL JOINT COMMISSION; LEAD; PESTICIDES; TRAIL SMELTER INVESTIGATION; WESTERN EUROPE: POLLUTION

Love Canal

The Love Canal is a sixteen-acre site located in New York State, near Niagara Falls. It has become a symbol of improper hazardous waste disposal practices, as an estimated 21,800 tons of chemical (liquid and solid) waste were buried there from the early 1940s to 1953. These chemical wastes included wastes from the manufacture of pesticides and other chemicals and about 200 tons of trichlorophenol waste product. The latter in turn contained significant quantities of 2,3,7,8-tetrachlorodibenzo-p-dioxin (TCDD). In addition, the city of Niagara Falls used the site to dump municipal wastes. The Love Canal itself is an incomplete canal dug in the 1890s, to join the upper and lower portions of the Niagara River to produce hydroelectric power and as a means of transportation. By 1938 the Canal was about 3,000 feet long by 100 feet wide, and its southern end was about 1,500 feet from the Niagara River.

The canal was considered to be a good place for a dump because the area was initially sparsely populated, and the canal was surrounded by clay—a substance that retards the movement of chemicals. In 1953 Hooker Chemical (now Occidental Chemical) sold Love Canal to the Niagara Falls Board of Education, and a school was built on the site in 1954. When it sold the property, Hooker specified in the deed of sale that chemical wastes were buried in the ground, and stated that the area was not suitable for construction. In spite of their warning, active residential construction occurred during the period 1966 to 1972 in and around the Love Canal area.

By the mid-1970s problems from the buried waste began to occur, as residents complained of chemical odors. High groundwater levels caused wastes to surface and migrate into the backyards of residents, even though most of the chemical wastes were apparently originally buried in sealed drums. The concerns of residents reached panic levels when chemical analysis showed that TCDD was one component of the chemical contamination and, in April 1978, the Love Canal area was ordered fenced-off by the New York State Commissioner of Health. President Carter declared a federal emergency—the first ever in the United States in the case of a man-made environmental disaster. Eventually 495 of the 564 single-family homes closest to the Love Canal area were purchased from the residents, who were relocated. The Love Canal was sealed by constructing a cap over the contaminated area, which required demolition of 237 of the homes. From 1978 to 1989 the state and federal governments have spent about $250 million on site remediation, relocation, and other measures at Love Canal.

The health effects of humans exposed to toxins at Love Canal are still under investigation. It will still be many years before the full health impact is known. In 1988 it was determined that two-thirds of the most contaminated areas surrounding Love Canal were once again suitable for residential habitation and that the uninhabitable areas could be used for commercial or industrial purposes. The assumption was made that the remedial actions taken will prevent further leakage of contaminants from the Love Canal site. The legacy of Love Canal in the United States is that it expanded the focus of environmental legislation from air and water pollution to include hazardous waste; it signaled the need for citizen participation in environmental policymaking; and it showed industry that public opinion was an important factor in how its operations were conducted.

Ray E. Clement

Further Readings

Levine, Ruth G. *Love Canal: Science, Politics, and People.* 1982.
Silverman, G.B. "Love Canal: A Retrospective." *Environmental Reporter* 20, 20, pt. II. The Bureau of National Affairs, Inc., Washington, D.C. (September 15, 1989): 835–50.
Smith, R.M., et al. "2,3,7,8-Tetrachlorodibenzo-p-dioxin in Sediment Samples from Love Canal Storm Sewers and Creeks." *Environmental Science and Technology* 17 (1983): 6–10.

See also CARTER, JIMMY; CITIZENS' CLEARINGHOUSE FOR HAZARDOUS WASTE; DIOXINS AND FURANS; HAZARDOUS WASTE TREATMENT TECHNOLOGIES; PESTICIDES; RIGHT-TO-KNOW: COMMUNITY (U.S.); SUPERFUND

Lovins, Amory B.

Amory Lovins (1947–) first came to prominence with the publication of an article in 1976 and a book in 1977 advocating a new approach to energy policy called the soft energy path. He advocated a shift away from increasing electricity and fossil fuel production and toward greater reliance on energy efficiency and renewable resources. Lovins's ideas were quickly and sharply attacked and he spent the late 1970s involved in extensive debates—written and oral—over energy policy. His work provides a systematic framework for thinking about alternatives to status quo energy policies, and it was quickly embraced by much of the active solar energy movement in the late 1970s. Even some of his opponents conceded the skill with which he defended his views.

Lovins started college at Harvard at the age of sixteen and, without receiving a degree there, moved on to Oxford University. After a couple of years the University made him a research fellow, at twenty-one the youngest person to hold such a post in 400 years. Throughout this period he had worked as a consultant physicist, getting his first patent at age seventeen. A camper and hiker since high school, his interest in environmental issues led him to work for the London office of Friends of the Earth (FOE), an environmental group started by David Brower. While at FOE he developed and disseminated his ideas for the soft energy path.

In 1982 Lovins, along with his wife L. Hunter Lovins, founded the Rocky Mountain Institute in Snowmass, Colorado, where he is currently research director. The institute employs over thirty people and does policy research on a variety of resource issues, including energy and water. He also works as a consultant to industries and utilities helping them use resources more efficiently, and writes and speaks extensively promoting efficient resource use.

Frank N. Laird

Further Readings

Dumanoski, Dianne. "The Hard and Soft Paths to Energy Future—The Controversial Amory Lovins Rekindles a Crucial Debate." *Boston Phoenix* (September 6, 1977).

Lovins, Amory B. *Soft Energy Paths: Toward a Durable Peace.* 1977.

See also BROWER, DAVID; ENVIRONMENTALISM; FRIENDS OF THE EARTH; SOFT ENERGY PATHS; SOLAR ENERGY

L

LRTAP

See LONG RANGE TRANSPORT [OF ATMOSPHERIC POLLUTANTS]

M

Mackenzie Valley Pipeline
See BERGER INQUIRY

Malthus, Robert Thomas
Robert Thomas Malthus (1766–1834) was a clergyman, an amateur mathematician, and an economist who propounded ten essays on the principle of population between 1798 and 1806. His argument was initially philosophical, a critique of the liberal humanists who believed in the perfectibility of the human race given enlightenment and appropriate welfare policies. Malthus believed that population growth was inevitable primarily as a result of what he regarded as overbreeding among the poor, for whom child labor was a vital source of income. He also produced the "iron law" of resource depletion as population would grow exponentially while resource extraction capabilities would only increase arithmetically. Much of this form of analysis was subsequently adopted by the Club of Rome in the famous essay *Limits to Growth*.

The Malthusian message has been attacked by neo-Marxists, as well as by Marx himself, for justifying the continued impoverishment of the poor, low labor wages because of deliberately constructed unemployment, and the naiveté of moralizing about abstinence and interrupted intercourse as basic measures of birth control. Subsequent studies have suggested that in many, but not all, cases, expectations of real income increases, coupled to improved education and civil rights for women, as well as widely available social welfare provision can encourage a desire for smaller families and a strong incentive to adopt birth control measures. However, the evidence is not universal: birth control is almost universally practiced, and numbers of children are strongly influenced by religious, social class, and economic conditions.

Timothy O'Riordan

Further Readings
Winch, Donald, ed. *Malthus: An Essay on the Principle of Population*. 1992.

See also EHRLICH, PAUL; HARDIN, GARRETT; *Limits to Growth*; POPULATION CONTROL

Man and the Biosphere Program
See BIOSPHERE RESERVES; WILDERNESS

Manatees
See MARINE MAMMALS

Marine Birds
See SEABIRDS

Marine Mammals
There are approximately 122 species of marine mammals from three taxonomic orders: cetaceans (whales, dolphins, and porpoises), sirenians (sea cows—the manatees and dugongs), and carnivores (of which only pinnipeds, or seals, sea lions, and fur seals; sea and marine otters; and polar bears are marine). Although most members of each group share the common trait of feeding in the marine environment, river dolphins and Amazonian manatees feed in fresh water, some seals live in lakes, and polar bears can sometimes be found far from the ocean. Marine mammals are thus a diverse group of animals, representing at least five separate in-

vasions to the sea: cetaceans, sirenians, pinnipeds, otters, and polar bears. Information on cetaceans is given in the entries on Baleen Whales, Dolphins and Porpoises, and International Whaling Commission. This entry deals with the orders Sirenia and the marine representatives of the Carnivora.

Sirenians

The sirenians, or sea cows, comprise a tiny order of only four species: three manatees and the dugong. A giant cold-water dugong named Steller's sea cow inhabited islands off the Kamchatka Peninsula in northeast Siberia until it became extinct at the hands of humans in the latter half of the eighteenth century. It was an up-to-nine-meter-long shallow-water herbivore which fed on kelp. Its meat was tender and said to have tasted like the finest veal. The four extant species are all tropical or subtropical and feed on sea grasses. Sirenians, derived from protoungulates related to early elephants and hyraxes over 65 million years ago, are the only marine mammal herbivores.

The three manatees occur off the coast of West Africa, in the Caribbean (and in Florida), and in the Amazon and Orinoco River systems. While the first two are generally marine, the latter is almost exclusively freshwater. The dugong has the largest geographic distribution, from East Africa around the rim of the Indian Ocean to northern Australia. All four species are in danger from purposeful hunting for food, accidental drowning or suffocation in nearshore set nets, habitat alteration and sea grass destruction, and (to an unknown but probably large degree) coastal pollution near population centers. Caribbean manatees in Florida are often killed by collisions with recreational speed boats; Amazonian and African manatees are eaten by indigenous people, as are dugongs; and all suffer from accidental fisheries-related kills.

Sea and Marine Otters

The sea otter is the largest of any otter. It lives around the north Pacific rim from southern California up through Alaska, the Aleutian chain, and to Japan. Prized for its dense pelage, sea otters used to be hunted intensively, thereby rendering them extinct in much of their range. A small remnant population off central California remained in the United States in the early twentieth century, and has now grown to (and apparently stabilized) at several thousand animals. Sea otters in Alaska are more numerous than in the South; they are also larger, feed mainly on fish rather than the southern diet of sea urchins and crabs, and are believed by many to form a separate subpopulation. They are protected throughout their range, but come into conflict with human shell fisheries due to perceived competition. Such competition is probably real in areas of reduced shellfish; sea otters have high metabolic rates, and a forty kilogram otter may eat up to 30 percent of its body weight, or twelve kilograms, of shellfish per day. Because sea otters are dependent on nearshore bottom-dwelling prey they are thought to be particularly vulnerable to human pollution. Their pelage can easily be fouled by oil, causing loss of thermoregulatory capability (and oil ingestion while grooming); over 1,000 sea otters are believed to have died during the spring 1989 Exxon Valdez tanker oil spill in the Gulf of Alaska.

Marine otters feed in cold nearshore waters of the Humboldt current off Chile and Peru. They are less protected than their northern hemisphere cousins, and are caught for food and pelage throughout their range. Population numbers and species status are unknown. A largely marine mustelid—the sea mink of the northwest Atlantic—became extinct due to hunting in the late nineteenth century.

Polar Bears

Polar bears are the only marine representative of ursids. Although they can survive on diets of terrestrial animals they are excellent predators of fishes and seals and have been seen swimming over 100 kilometers from any ice or land. The Arctic ice is their home, however, and females need it to rear young. Although polar bears are hunted by indigenous people (and often by outsiders brought in by commercial/ sport hunting operations) throughout most of their range around the Arctic circle, they appear to be doing well.

Pinnipeds

The largest group of marine mammals of the order Carnivora is the suborder Pinnipedia, or "feather-footed ones." These include three families: the phocids or true seals (nineteen species), the otariids or eared seals (fur seals and sea lions; fourteen species), and the one species of odobenid, or walrus. All pinnipeds need to come onto land or ice to give birth, and thus have had to compromise between terrestrial and water locomotion. Phocids and otariids/ odobenid are built fundamentally differently:

true seals caterpillar "walk" on their bellies on land and use hind legs modified as flippers for propulsion in water. Otariids and the walrus waddle on all four legs on land and propel themselves with powerful fore-limb strokes in water. While true seals, sea lions, and walruses keep themselves warm mainly by layers of thick blubber, the otariid fur seals have dense and long thermoregulatory pelage.

All species have been subject to human predation. Phocids of the Arctic remain one of the historically important diets of Eskimos and about 2,500 northern fur seals of the Pribilof Islands are hunted for meat and fur in a well-managed yearly take. Their numbers have recently been declining, however, and it is probable that human-reduced fish stocks of the southern Bering Sea and northeast Pacific are in large part responsible for this fur seal decline. It is also possible that entanglement in fishing gear has helped to decimate these animals.

Elephant seals of the northern and southern hemisphere, as well as subantarctic true seals of several species were hunted heavily for meat and oil in the nineteenth and early parts of the twentieth century. All have increased to near pre-exploitation levels since heavy hunting stopped before World War II. Especially crabeater and Weddell seals of the Antarctic have increased, presumably because of decreased competition from human-reduced whale populations.

Several other species are not doing very well, however. Walruses are hunted for their ivory-like tusks, and several populations are severely depressed. Harbor and gray seals of Europe have undergone strong declines due to competition with human fisheries and several apparently pollution-induced massive die-offs. The tropical monk seals have been especially hard hit by habitat degradation. The Caribbean monk seal apparently became extinct about the middle of the twentieth century; the Mediterranean monk seal is following to extinction; and the Hawaiian monk seal is severely taxed by low population numbers. Major contributors to monk seal declines appear to be loss of breeding beaches by human development and by introduction of pigs and dogs. Decline of prey may also be a factor, especially in the Caribbean and Mediterranean.

Summary

Sirenians, mustelids, the polar bear, and pinnipeds have generally not fared well in their contact with humans. All are nearshore or near-ice mammals. However, a combination of twentieth-century developments give some hope for many species: oil is no longer industrially used from marine mammals; insulation for clothes is now generally made from synthetics; and there has been an increasing awareness of need for conservation of these coastal animals. Polar bears and many seals are hunted but not throughout all of their ranges, largely due to high latitude inaccessibility. The major problems are due to increasing competition with human fisheries, and human habitat degradation in its many forms—from easily-seen powerboating to often hidden toxin build-up in marine mammal prey.

Bernd Würsig

Further Readings

Bruemmer, F. *World of the Polar Bear*. 1989.
Chanin, P. *The Natural History of Otters*. 1985.
Reeves, R.R., B.S. Stewart, and S. Leatherwood. *The Sierra Club Handbook of Seals and Sirenians*. 1992.
Reynolds, J.E., III, and D.K. Odell. *Manatees and Dugongs*. 1991.

See also BALEEN WHALES; BEARS: CONSERVATION AND HABITAT; COASTAL DEBRIS AND CLEANUP; COASTAL MARSHES, CONSERVATION OF; DOLPHINS AND PORPOISES; OIL SPILLS; TOP PREDATORS IN CANADA: AN OVERVIEW

Marsh, George Perkins

Although the American conservation movement did not emerge as a national political force until much later, the ideas behind the movement first began to take shape in the 1850s. Along with Henry David Thoreau the critical figure in that period was a New Englander, George Perkins Marsh (1801–1882). Marsh was born in Woodstock, Vermont, and raised in a family of lawyers and political leaders. He attended Dartmouth College, excelled in his academic studies, and followed his elders' model to become a lawyer, a businessman, and a Congressman. That career gave him two advantages: he was free to roam widely through many scholarly fields in his spare time, and he was rewarded for his political activities by appointments as U.S. ambassador to Turkey and Italy, sinecures that allowed him to study first-hand the history and geography of the Mediterranean area. Eventually he taught himself to speak twenty languages and was an internationally-known authority on the development of language. At an advanced age he published his most enduring book, *Man and Nature* (1864), which argued that humans had gained enormous power over the earth and were using it ignorantly to their own detriment.

Marsh drew heavily on his own experience with early Vermont settlement to make his case, but he supplemented it from his extensive readings and travels in Europe. The United States, he warned, might go the way of the ancient Roman Empire, which had left behind it a desolate, impoverished landscape, reduced in both productiveness and population. Marsh was the first to make a systematic account of how the European invasion of North America had changed the original vegetation and animal life. His main theme was rapid, excessive deforestation, which he argued could adversely affect the climate and disturb vital watersheds. Europeans had passed laws to regulate the cutting of forests, but not the Americans, whose restless love of change encouraged them to destroy the forests thoughtlessly and move on to unspoiled lands.

Marsh looked on nature as a world of harmony, stable balance, and order. Humans had become, in his view, a powerful destabilizing force, threatening not only nature itself but also their own well-being. He called for nothing less than a new ethos which, in the interest of self-preservation, would seek to restore the natural equilibrium. Americans must learn from the sorry experience of Old World nations and empires that had neglected their relation with the earth, he argued. They must learn habits of frugality and carefulness, based on scientific evidence, and they must regulate their behavior to protect nature. A small part of Marsh was in tune with his contemporary Transcendentalists such as Thoreau, for whom nature was the deepest source of beauty and morality, but on balance Marsh was more utilitarian than they and a firm believer in progress. Conservation for him was mainly a matter of achieving scientific enlightenment and civilized restraint.

Donald Worster

Further Readings

Lowenthal, David. *George Perkins Marsh: Versatile Vermonter.* 1958.

Marsh, George P. *Man and Nature; or, Physical Geography as Modified by Human Action.* 1864. (A later edition was titled *The Earth as Modified by Human Ac-*

tion. 1885.)

See also CONSERVATION MOVEMENT; THOREAU, HENRY DAVID

Marshall, Bob

Bob Marshall (1901–1939) was an Alaskan explorer, a relentless advocate during the 1930s for preserving samples of the American wilderness, and the primary founder of the Wilderness Society. As a very young child he developed a lifelong infatuation with the exploration of unmapped wilderness. This obsession resulted in his own exploration and initial mapping, on four trips during the late 1920s and 1930s, of the Central Brooks Range of mountains in northern Alaska. While working for the U.S. Forest Service in the 1920s, and eventually earning a doctoral degree in plant physiology from Johns Hopkins University, he came to believe that if something wasn't done soon, no significant samples of American wilderness would remain. Thus in 1935, with several other like-minded individuals (including Aldo Leopold and Benton MacKaye), he founded the Wilderness Society, whose primary mission was to save as much American wilderness as it could. Marshall personally financed much of the society's work from 1935 to 1939.

From 1933 to 1937 Marshall worked as a resource manager for the Bureau of Indian Affairs, and from 1937 to 1939 he was director of recreation and lands for the U.S. Forest Service. Throughout that time he persistently urged Forest Service officials to leave large areas in their jurisdiction roadless and undeveloped. The agency did in fact add some 5 million acres to its "Primitive Area" system (forerunner of the U.S. Wilderness Preservation System) between 1933 and 1939.

Marshall also became famous, at least among fellow outdoor enthusiasts, for marathon mountain hikes, often covering thirty to forty miles in a day. Thus friends and acquaintances were shocked when he died in his sleep on a train on November 11, 1939, just several weeks shy of his thirty-ninth birthday. A police autopsy listed the probable cause of death as leukemia and arteriosclerosis.

James M. Glover

Further Readings

Glover, James M. *A Wilderness Original: The Life of Bob Marshall.* 1986.

Nash, Roderick. *Wilderness and the Ameri-*

can Mind. 1967.

Vickery, Jim Dale. *Wilderness Visionaries.* 1986.

See also ALASKA: PARK, WILDERNESS, AND RESOURCE ISSUES; FOREST SERVICE (U.S.); LEOPOLD, ALDO; WILDERNESS SOCIETY

Mass Spectrometry

Mass spectrometry is applied to a wide range of environmental problems as it permits the detection of trace amounts of pollutants down to 10^{-12} grams and less. One important application of mass spectrometry is the detection and identification of the much publicized toxic compound, 2,3,7,8-tetrachlorodibenzodioxin in the presence of such interferences as polychlorinated biphenyls (PCBs).

Mass spectrometry permits measurement of the mass (m) of an individual charged particle expressed as a ratio, m/z, where z is the number of charges—usually one—borne by the particle. Mass spectrometry entails the ionization of molecules, separation of the ions formed thus according to their m/z ratio, and detection of the separated ions; each stage can be accomplished with high efficiency. Mass spectrometry is an analytical technique in that one can identify a molecule from the mass of the corresponding charged particle.

The most commonly used ionization process involves bombarding gaseous molecules with a beam of electrons. Usually upon electron impact each molecule loses an electron to form a radical cation: a radical in that it has an odd number of electrons, and a cation in that it is positively charged. Fragment ions also can be formed during ionization. Ions are exceedingly tractable such that, in a vacuum, their trajectories can be controlled to a high degree by magnetic and electric fields; ions may be separated in flight through such fields.

The signal intensities of molecular ions (radical cations) and fragment ions detected after separation can be displayed in order of m/z ratio—that is, as a mass spectrum. The mass spectral pattern of intensities, or "fingerprint" are highly specific to the original molecule. Ions are detected with electron multipliers which produce a shower of ions, up to 10^8, for each ion detected; such detectors contribute enormously to the sensitivity of mass spectrometry.

In the most common type of mass spectrometer ions moving rapidly through a magnetic sector are separated by the action of a magnetic field (B). Electrostatic sectors (E) are used to enhance the energy resolution of ions before they traverse the magnetic sector. Of increasing importance are quadrupole mass filters and quadrupole ion traps which employ solely electric fields to control the trajectories of ions moving with relatively low velocities.

Highly precise ion trajectory control combined with high detection sensitivity account for the wide application of mass spectrometry to the identification of molecules, particularly in environmental samples, body fluids, and in the detection of drugs and explosives.

Mass spectrometry when combined with gas chromatography (GC/MS), constitutes a powerful analytical technique. Here, a mixture of compounds can be separated by gas chromatography and analyzed, one by one, as they pass into a mass spectrometer. Within the past decade this technique has been expanded to GC/MS/MS, or tandem mass spectrometry with which the sensitivity and specificity of detection is much improved.

Raymond E. March

See also DIOXINS AND FURANS; EPIDEMIOLOGY; GAS CHROMATOGRAPH; STANDARD SETTING; TOXICOLOGY; TRACE ANALYSIS

Mather, Stephen

See NATIONAL PARKS: UNITED STATES

McCloskey, Michael

Michael McCloskey was born in Eugene, Oregon, on April 26, 1934. An avid Boy Scout in his youth he was drawn to climbing mountains. As an undergraduate at Harvard University, he was active in the Young Democrats and became interested in public policy issues. He received a law degree (J.D.) from the University of Oregon in 1961 and thereafter became a representative of the Sierra Club and Western Outdoor Clubs in the Pacific Northwest from 1961 through 1965. Thereafter he served as assistant to the president of the Sierra Club from 1965 to 1966, as conservation director from 1966 to 1969, as executive director from 1969 to 1985, and as chairman since 1985.

As the second executive director of the Sierra Club McCloskey came to his position with unique credentials. With a degree in law and experience in the politics of public policy he did not, as previous Sierra Club leaders, rise through the outings program, but rather because of his professional expertise and political experience as a conservationist. Drawn to the Sierra Club because he shared its outrage at U.S. Forest Service practices in the Northwest, he represented a new and more sophisticated conservation professional. This became apparent when he wrote the *Prospectus for a North Cascades National Park* in 1962. He campaigned widely for the Wilderness Act in the early 1960s and was a principal legislative advocate for the Redwood National Park. He has written extensively on environmental matters for both professional journals and popular periodicals.

McCloskey brought to the Sierra Club organizational skills which had not previously developed in its largely volunteer structure. Inheriting office during a severe financial crisis he brought order to the club's affairs. Under his administrative care the club was able to consolidate the victories of the 1960s in the North Cascades, Grand Canyon, and Redwoods, and to obtain nearly twenty major additions to the national park system. In addition McCloskey led the Sierra Club toward the more demanding and sophisticated realm of legislation and litigation which the environmental laws of the late 1960s and early 1970s required. He was able to put the club in the lead of this movement with groundbreaking legal action at Mineral King, and with professional lobbying for much of the federal environmental legislation of the 1970s.

As executive director he also advocated and led the Sierra Club from a narrow focus on national parks and wilderness preservation toward a wider environmental agenda, including attention to urban environment, air quality, pollution abatement, and energy policy.

His technical expertise and low-key style of rhetoric, combined with his abilities in analysis and the practical aspects of working through the political process, characterized a new stability and professionalism for the Sierra Club in the post-David Brower era.

Michael P. Cohen

Further Readings

Cohen, Michael P. *The History of the Sierra Club.* 1988.

See also BROWER, DAVID; MINERAL KING CANYON; REDWOODS; SIERRA CLUB; WILDERNESS ACT

Mediterranean Sea, Protection of

As a virtually enclosed body of water, the Mediterranean Sea is particularly fragile when faced with the problem of pollution. With only one outlet to the Atlantic Ocean (through the Strait of Gibraltar) and an eighty-year renewal rate for Mediterranean waters, the sea faces long-term problems with pollution. Since the 1950s ecologists have noted the contamination of the sea, as evidenced by oil slicks and damage to marine life. In the early 1970s one out of every three beaches on the Mediterranean was considered unsafe for swimming. Because eighteen states border the sea, concerted international effort is necessary for its protection to be secured.

Several types of pollution have plagued the Mediterranean Sea over the past fifty years. Land-based sources account for 80 to 85 percent of the pollution problem. Discharges from industries—particularly those located in the Northwest coastal region—have been a continuing problem as more states in the region industrialize. A further problem is agricultural runoff which is increasingly laden with chemical pesticides and fertilizers. In addition discharges of untreated municipal sewage into the sea from coastal cities—worsened by the large numbers of tourists who visit the region every year—ranks as a major pollutant. Sea-based sources of pollution (such as ballast discharge from ships and oil spills) have also been detrimental. The Mediterranean is especially vulnerable to these sea-based sources of pollution since 35 to 40 percent of the world's oil shipments traverse its waters. Airborne pollution, responsible for 50 percent of the sea's heavy metal deposits, is also part of the problem.

While it is generally acknowledged that the pollution of the Mediterranean Sea has disturbed its marine life and its ecosystem, there has been much debate on the precise extent of the damage. Nonetheless, in the early 1970s states in the region recognized that the levels of pollution were serious and agreed that if the situation was left unchecked, improvement was unlikely. The coastal states began in the early 1970s to discuss the possibility of a legal convention for the protection of the Mediterranean. While such a convention could act as a legal framework for protecting the sea, a broader approach to the problem of pollution in the Mediterranean and a coordinating body were seen as essential.

The United Nations Environment Programme (UNEP), invited by the coastal states in 1974 to take a coordinating role, convened the first intergovernmental meeting of Mediterranean states in Barcelona in early 1975. At this meeting UNEP unveiled a Mediterranean Action Plan (MAP) which has since evolved and today is composed of four key components: 1) a legal framework; 2) a pollution monitoring program; 3) an integrated research and planning program; and 4) an institutional base.

The legal component of the MAP is comprised of the Barcelona Convention for the Protection of the Mediterranean Sea against Pollution (1976) and several related protocols. The Barcelona Convention is seen as the framework, while the protocols outline detailed rules of conduct. The first four protocols concern: 1) dumping from ships and aircraft (1976); 2) cooperation in case of emergencies such as oil spills (1976); 3) control of land-based pollution (1980); and 4) the establishment of specially protected areas (1982). A protocol on offshore exploration and exploitation of petroleum, gas, and minerals was put forward for signature in 1992, and a protocol on the transboundary movement of hazardous waste in the region is currently being drafted. The environmental monitoring component assesses the impact of the MAP through a series of data-gathering projects in areas such as marine life, oil, heavy metals, and pesticides found in the sea. The integrated research and planning component carries out numerous studies which are used by states for environmental and economic planning. In the first years of the plan UNEP's Geneva office provided funding and played a coordinating role. In 1979 a trust fund supported by donations from coastal states was initiated, and in 1982 an autonomous secretariat was established in Athens, Greece.

By the 1990s the MAP was widely viewed as a success. Although discharge of pollutants into the sea has not been completely halted, the level of pollution has now stabilized at its 1970s level. This can be seen as an accomplishment since without the measures called for within the MAP, pollution in the sea would likely be much worse. Many states took measures to treat their sewage before discharging it, and to check the flow of industrial and agricultural chemical effluents which were emitted into the sea. Today the coastal beaches are now cleaner than they were in the mid-1970s, with eight out of ten beaches deemed safe for swimming.

The MAP is also viewed as a success because of the high degree of cooperation it has achieved among such a diverse group of coastal states, which range from heavily industrialized to developing countries. Eighteen states (Albania, Algeria, Cyprus, Egypt, France, Greece, Israel, Italy, Lebanon, Libya, Malta, Monaco, Morocco, Spain, Syria, Tunisia, Turkey, and Yugoslavia) and the European Community (EC) now participate in the MAP. Nearly all of the coastal states have ratified or have acceded to the Barcelona Convention and to its protocols. The MAP was the first of UNEP's law-making activities in its regional seas program, and has acted as a model for agreements in other regional seas.

Jennifer Clapp

Further Readings

Haas, Peter M. *Saving the Mediterranean: The Politics of International Environmental Cooperation.* 1990.

Saliba, Louis J. "Protecting the Mediterranean." *Marine Policy* 2 (1978): 171–79.

See also ENVIRONMENTAL DIPLOMACY; LEGISLATION: EUROPEAN COMMUNITY; OIL SPILLS; UNITED NATIONS ENVIRONMENT PROGRAMME; WESTERN EUROPE: POLLUTION

Mercury

Mercury (chemical symbol: Hg), one of the heaviest of metals, has an atomic weight of 200.59. Mercury is unusual among metals in that it can exist in a variety of physical and chemical states under normal environmental conditions. Metallic mercury, sometimes known as "quicksilver," is a silver-colored liquid at normal temperature and pressure. Furthermore it readily vaporizes and thus can exist as a gas as well under normal environmental conditions. Clearly the physical properties of mercury have implications for its environmental distribution.

The chemistry of mercury is also unusual for a metal in that it tends to form covalent bonds, rendering the organic forms of mercury relatively stable. Both inorganic and organic forms of mercury occur in nature. The conversion of inorganic to organic mercury is a particularly important process in the context of environmental impacts and occurs in many aquatic and wetland systems. This bacterial methylation involves the addition of a methyl (CH_3) group to inorganic mercury. The resulting methylmercury is the most dangerous form of the metal.

Mercury has significant biological properties. In contrast to a number of metals (e.g., copper, molybdenum, and zinc) mercury has no known biological function. It does however have a great capacity to combine with molecules that have important biochemical properties; it interferes with the normal functioning of such molecules and thus exerts a *toxic* effect on living things. For vertebrate animals the major toxic effects are manifested through disorders of the brain and nervous system.

In living systems mercury tends to *bioconcentrate* (reach higher concentrations in living tissues than in the surrounding medium), *bioaccumulate* (increase in concentration in living tissues over time), and *biomagnify* (reach higher concentrations in the tissues of organisms at successive links in the food web). Organic forms of mercury are generally speaking more liable to bioaccumulate and biomagnify, and are more toxic than inorganic forms. However, metallic mercury vapor, if inhaled, can be extremely toxic to humans and other animals.

Aside from occupational exposure the major route of mercury to humans is through the consumption of fish. Several incidents which dramatically illustrated the toxicity of mercury occurred between the 1950s and the 1970s. Most notable was Minimata disease, caused by consumption of fish contaminated with methylmercury. Mercury released from a chemical plant contaminated a marine food chain, resulting in very high concentrations of methylmercury in the fish muscle. Humans and domestic animals for whom fish was a major component of their diet acquired a very high dose of methylmercury from contaminated fish. Over 100 Japanese died from methylmercury poisoning. In the 1970s a consignment of mercury-treated grain sent to Iraq to be used as seed was consumed by humans and resulted in more than 1,000 deaths. These and several other mercury-related cases seem to have sensitized governments to the need for strict control of materials containing mercury.

Mercury occurs as metal and as metal salts in the earth's crust. Although the original discoverer of mercury is unknown it is believed that the ancient Chinese, Egyptians, and Romans knew of the metal. Mercury was the name given to the messenger of the gods in Roman mythology. Mercury-related health effects— some leading to death—have probably occurred for centuries particularly through occupational exposure but, either because of absence of clear cause-effect relationships, or because of little attention to occupational health, only recently

has mercury gained widespread attention as an environmental or occupational hazard.

Some of the major uses of mercury by humans relate directly to its toxic or biocidal properties. Mercury was widely used in the past as a biocide (e.g., in the treatment of human bacterial disease such as syphilis) prior to the availability of antibiotics. It is still in limited use in topical antiseptics. Until very recently mercury was a common component of pesticides used to control fungi and insects in crops and stored material as well as to control fouling by algae and invertebrates of ships' hulls. Other applications of this potentially useful metal are in thermometers, barometers, and other manometers. It is still widely used in dental amalgam. Mercury was also in use until recently as a catalyst to produce alkali for pulp and paper processing and as a slimicide (to control the growth of bacteria) in pulp and paper manufacture.

The acceptable level of mercury in fish for consumption varies from 0.5 to 1.0 micrograms per gram (μg/g) (wet weight) depending on the authority. Since the 1970s most European and North American governments, recognizing the risk to human and environmental health through uncontrolled release of mercury, have brought in legislation to control the release of mercury into the environment, and in many instances to prohibit its use. A number of jurisdictions also use an advisory system, warning the public not to eat fish from particular waters. Even in apparently remote areas some lakes are listed with such an advisory. This usually means that the fish exceed the guideline of 0.5 μg/g.

In spite of the regulations now in operation mercury is still a widespread environmental contaminant, being volatilized from many anthropogenic and natural sources, especially through burning fossil fuel. While incidents of acute poisoning are unlikely to occur under present regulations, the need remains for protection of life from mercury contamination, and for vigilance particularly related to the consumption of fish.

Pamela Welbourn

Further Readings

Berkes, Fikret. "The Mercury Problem: An Examination of the Scientific Basis for Policy-Making." In *Resources and the Environment*. Ed. O.P. Dwivedi. 1980.
National Research Council of Canada. *Effects of Mercury in the Canadian Environment*. 1979.
The State of Canada's Environment 1991.

Minister of Supply and Services, Ottawa.

See also ARSENIC; BIOACCUMULATION; CAD-
MIUM; FOOD CHAINS; LEAD; PULP AND PAPER
MILLS; WATER POLLUTION ABATEMENT TECH-
NOLOGIES

Mexico

Mexico—with 89 million people and the second
largest gross domestic product (GDP) in Latin
America—ranks among the upper third of the
world's economies. By most conventional measures Mexico is one of the industrializing
world's success stories, with high rates of urbanization, literacy, and a substantial middle class.
Mexico's rapid development since World War
II, however, has taken a profound toll on its
environment and natural resources, conditions
that Mexico's government has only recently
begun to address.

Mexico is abundant in many natural resources, although certain critical resources—
water, for example—are distributed unevenly
for human utilization and consumption. Southern Mexico's wet tropical forests have earned
Mexico a United Nations (UN) designation as
one of the world's seven centers of biodiversity.
Much of Mexico's northern region is arid, however, requiring extensive irrigation to sustain
agriculture. Mexico also enjoys one of the
world's longest coastlines, with an Exclusive
Economic Zone of 11,000 square miles. Extensive petroleum reserves have made Mexico a
significant exporter of oil.

Mexico's environmental problems are numerous, however. Its population is concentrated
in industrial hubs which suffer from acute air,
water, and land degradation. While population
growth slowed in the 1980s urban centers like
Mexico City, Monterrey, Guadalajara, and various cities along the U.S.-Mexican border grew
at rates exceeding 5 percent annually, stressing
urban capacity. Natural resources are also imperiled. Mexico's forests were depleting at a rate
of 2,347 square miles annually. Critical centers
of biodiversity such as the Lancandon jungle are
presently threatened. Over 60 percent of its
river basins are contaminated by industrial and
agricultural sources.

Policy instruments for coping with these
problems have emerged only recently. Like
many countries Mexico's first general environmental law was promulgated in 1972, inspired
by the Stockholm Conference on the Human
Environment. That law, however, remained
largely symbolic for a decade, lacking enforcement instruments. In 1982 Mexican President
Miguel de la Madrid rewrote the environmental law and elevated environment to cabinet
status, creating the new *Secretaria de
Desarrollo Urban y Ecologia* (SEDUE). These
reforms coincided, unfortunately, with
Mexico's debt crisis. The resulting decade of
diminished growth and austerity severely limited investment in environmental remediation
and conservation efforts. In 1988, at the end
of the de la Madrid *sexenio*, a new environmental law was enacted which set the groundwork for recent administrative reforms. President Carlos Salinas de Gortari, de la Madrid's
successor, subsequently abolished SEDUE,
folding its functions into a new superagency,
the *Secretaria de Desarrollo Social* (SEDESOL)
which presently administers Mexico's environmental policies.

Mexico's current environmental policy regime is comprehensive and improves significantly on previous legislation. It mandates and
lays the legal foundation for the elaboration of
specific technical standards for monitoring
compliance with environmental laws. Its EIS
provisions are among the world's most progressive. The law requires environmental impact
assessments for all federal public works, potentially polluting industries, mining, tourist development, and sanitary works, as well as new
construction in the private sector. The law further provides for the development of state and
local environmental laws and amplifies provisions for citizen participation.

Utilizing these provisions the Salinas administration has embarked on a major campaign to draft regulations and technical standards to give strength to the environmental law.
Since 1988 over eighty such regulatory ordinances and technical norms have been written
covering air, water, and soil pollution, and hazardous waste. Twenty-eight Mexican states
have also adopted environmental laws, supple-
menting national legislation. Salinas has also
undertaken a number of innovative environmental programs. A top priority is Mexico City,
which has launched a major air quality campaign, which includes mandatory testing of vehicular emissions, requires catalytic converters
on all new vehicles, advocates switching to low
lead fuels for vehicles and natural gas for industrial uses, and aims at reducing airborne particulates. Reforestation and urban greenbelt
planning are also major priorities as are inspections and closures of contaminating industries.

In 1991 Salinas shut an aging refinery in Mexico City at a cost of over 5,000 jobs. On other fronts Salinas has banned the harvest of marine turtles, signed the Convention on International Trade in Endangered Species of Wild Fauna and Flora (CITES), entered into a major agreement with the United States to upgrade environmental conditions along the U.S.-Mexican border, curtailed lumbering in critical areas like the Lacandon, and enlisted the military in nationwide reforestation campaigns. Collectively these policy actions have drawn international acclaim, earning the Salinas United Earth's first Green Nobel Prize in 1991.

Mexican environmental policy continues to suffer from a number of serious deficiencies, however. Citizen influence on environmental policy is limited owing to Mexico's one-party system and the governing party's monopoly in Congress. Mexico's fledgling environmental movement lacks resources and remains concentrated in the nation's major urban areas. Policy implementation in Mexico's presidentialist political system tends to be ad hoc and poorly institutionalized, responding to immediate presidential priorities. In the environmental arena an acute lack of technically trained personnel, combined with a patronage-ridden administrative system, effectively diminish administrative efficiency and responsiveness. The resumption of economic growth since 1990 notwithstanding, financial resources for environmental protection remain scarce.

In the long run the Salinas administration's principal impact on the Mexican environment may rest more heavily with its economic reforms than its newly enacted environmental regulations. The Salinas administration has aggressively championed economic liberalization by privatizing national industries and enacting constitutional reforms and legislation that build market incentives into natural resources conservation and pollution control. Some argue that Mexico's participation in the North American Free Trade Agreement (NAFTA), signed in December 1992, promises to reinforce such trends.

Stephen P. Mumme

Further Readings

Barry, Tom, ed. *Mexico: A Country Guide.* 1992.

Darling, Juanita, Larry Stammler, and Judy Pasternak. "Can Mexico Clean up Its Act?" *Los Angeles Times* (November 17, 1991): 1.

Mumme, Stephen P., and Roberto Sanchez. "New Directions in Mexican Environmental Policy." *Environmental Management* 16 (1992): 465–74.

See also AIR POLLUTION: IMPACTS; BIODEPLETION; CITES; NAFTA AND THE ENVIRONMENT; SEA TURTLES; TROPICAL DEFORESTATION

Migratory Birds Convention
See HAWK SHOOTING; SHOREBIRDS

Mineral King Canyon

Mineral King Canyon—a valley and its surrounding lands occupying some 15,000 acres in California—was the locus of an intense land-use controversy in the 1960s and into the 1970s. The resolution of the matter came only in a decision by the U.S. Supreme Court, but along the way many other administrative and legal actors were involved. The lands in question are surrounded on three sides by Sequoia National Park. The U.S. Forest Service opposed inclusion of these lands in the national park (following the creation of the park in 1890) on the grounds that there were incompatible (silver) mining operations within the valley. John Muir, already a prominent citizen conservationist, had called for preservation of the Mineral King lands. In 1926 the lands were established as the Sequoia National Game Refuge.

Mineral King Canyon is within a reasonable drive from both Los Angeles and San Francisco; however, the only possible road access to the area would be through the national park and National Park Service regulations did not permit through roads to pass across park lands. This rule stifled development proposals in the 1950s despite the willingness of the Forest Service (and its overseeing agency the U.S. Department of Agriculture) to entertain such proposals. In 1960 Walt Disney Productions proposed a large ski complex for the canyon area. The proposal called for ski slopes, village complexes, restaurants, and accommodations sufficient for some 1.7 million visitors per year. The development proposal was opposed by conservation organizations including the Sierra Club. Secretary of the Interior Stewart Udall opposed construction of the access road until 1967 when he acceded to heavy political pressure. A 1972 Supreme Court decision held that Sierra Club members would not be affected in their activities by the proposed project. However, in a political/administrative decision at the state level the access road was deleted from the California state highway system. This latter 1972 decision led the Disney corporation to scale down the size of their proposal.

The controversy continued for some years after and eventually the Disney corporation abandoned the project, having suffered too many delays and perhaps too much negative publicity. Shifting public consciousness in the 1970s eventually rendered this particular development impossible. In 1978 Congress added Mineral King Valley to Sequoia National Park. Perhaps even more important in its 1972 decision which rejected standing for the Sierra Club in this case the Supreme Court moved a great distance toward allowing the general notion of legal standing for components of nature. Justice William O. Douglas asked why lakes, rivers, trees, or beaches should not have legal protection and suggested that the court should in general hear those human spokesmen who have an "intimate relation with the inanimate object about to be injured, polluted, or otherwise despoiled." This controversy has been seen since as a major turning point in the history of the U.S. environmental movement.

Robert Paehlke

Further Readings

Caldwell, Lynton K., Lynton R. Hayes, and Isabel M. MacWhirter. *Citizens and the Environment.* 1976.

Hays, Samuel P. *Beauty, Health, and Permanence: Environmental Politics in the United States, 1955–1985.* 1987.

Nash, Roderick Frazier. *The Rights of Nature.* 1989.

See also DEPARTMENT OF THE INTERIOR (U.S.); ENVIRONMENTAL CASE LAW: UNITED STATES; FOREST SERVICE (U.S.); MUIR, JOHN; NATIONAL PARK SERVICE (U.S.); SIERRA CLUB; UDALL, STEWART

Mining and Smelting: Historic Impacts

A dredge superintendent from Breckenridge, Colorado, observed early in the twentieth century that "industry is always to be preferred to scenic beauty." Six decades later Indiana Senator Vance Hartke pictured mining "a runaway technology, whose only law is profit, [that] has for years poisoned our air, ravaged our soil, stripped our forest bare, and corrupted our water sources." Mining and smelting have made an impact on the environment since miners first dug into the ground. The pace increased with industrialization, but for centuries few challenged the industry.

With nineteenth century America preoccupied with the development and utilization of the country's abundant natural resources, the environment was taken for granted. In such circumstances the mining industry flourished. Yet challenges did appear. In 1886 a Pennsylvania family sued a local coal company for polluting a stream running through their property; they lost. But mining had too much economic and political clout and the company successfully claimed that it was making a "natural, proper and lawful use of our own land."

While the industry defeated challenges such as this, in the land of the forty-niner mining suffered major setbacks. Mining had given California statehood and had been its chief industry for several decades. By the 1870s agriculture and urbanization had emerged as powerful economic forces and the three clashed over the state's economic future. The first major conflict occurred in 1872 in Oakland, California, over the proposed building of a smelter. Opposition centered upon the unhealthful, irritating, and offensive fumes. They supplied examples to show the extensive damage that smelting works had imposed upon the atmosphere, vegetation, and land in and near other smelters. Caught off guard the industry presented a weak case about economic and even "health" benefits from smelting. Nonetheless the city council finally decided that Oakland would welcome all smelting works, except those producing gases that would be injurious to the health of "her inhabitants." The battle lines drawn in this controversy would echo down into the next century.

Then came another controversy—this time a concern with hydraulicking, or the use of powerful hoses to wash away tons of earth. In the mountains above Marysville hydraulic mines operated, their tailings washing down into the valley, obstructing the river, and covering the land. Farmers heatedly protested, joined by city dwellers forced to build levees to protect their communities.

No agreement could be reached and litigation followed. In the most famous case, *Woodruff v. North Bloomfield, et al.*, farmer Edward Woodruff filed a complaint accusing the North Bloomfield Company and its co-defendants of raising the riverbed, thus ruining fields, disrupting river commerce, and flooding the valley. This in turn cost "landholders, mechanics, and farmers" money and lost time. The mining industry countered that to grant an injunction against hydraulicking would cripple the industry "to which California owes her rapid rise and wonderful prosperity." Mining drew a rosy picture of its benefits and concluded that California and the United States would suffer direct economic loss should the mines close.

On January 7, 1884, U.S. circuit court judge Lorenzo Sawyer, himself a forty-niner, handed down his decision rejecting the defendants' claims. They were "perpetually enjoined and restrained" from discharging or dumping into the rivers that drained into the valley. Times had changed and the industry had not changed with them. Mining no longer had the economic and political power to easily and consistently impose its will.

The industry in general did not learn a lesson from these setbacks. A few in the industry began to appreciate conservation and environmental ideas, but they were almost "prophets without honor." Sadly it would take even more lawsuits and public outcry to finally bring results.

These two fights were mere preliminaries to the main event: the smelting industry versus the citizens of Butte, Montana. A center of the copper industry, Butte had six "of the most modern" smelters in the world. Unfortunately some smelters still used heap roasting or roasting copper in the open air. The smoke and flumes turned midday into dusk and proved deadly to people suffering from respiratory problems. Here, however, the industry reigned; Butte owed its very existence to mining.

The situation became so bad that in 1891 a suit was filed to stop heap roasting. The industry trotted out the old war horse—the economic argument—claiming that closing the operations would force men out of work and harm the economy. Mine representatives also ardently pushed the smelter's health benefits, arguing that the smoke destroyed the "microbes that constitute the germs of disease." The public outcry proved too great and heap roasting was finally stopped in Butte and the nearby town of Anaconda evolved into the district's smelter center.

The fight was not over. After the turn-of-the-century local ranchers, farmers, and the federal government took the Anaconda company to court over the impact of smelter smoke on the land, crops, trees, and animals. The controversy evolved into a brutal fight. The fight dragged into the 1920s with Anaconda finally reaching an agreement with the concerned parties. By then the government and public was less concerned about such matters. The boom atmosphere of the "roaring twenties" dominated the scene.

Complaints about mine and smelter pollution were not, however, limited to the U.S. West. From such widely scattered states as New York, Georgia, New Jersey, Tennessee, Colorado, and Utah came other protests. The industry's arrogant defense of its "rights" gained it little sympathy. Its refusal to recognize the total industrial impact and to acknowledge its responsibilities showed a callousness that was all too typical of this era.

The issues raised in these early disputes were not resolved. Not until the American public and government became vitally interested in environmental matters in the 1960s and 1970s would the industry finally be brought successfully to the docket on a consistent basis. Regrettably the same lessons need to be relearned as illustrated by the cyanide disaster (1993) at Summitville, Colorado. Poor planning, cutting financial corners, environmental arrogance, weak regulation, and the old rape and run mentality have produced an environmental/financial nightmare. The old ways still live within some segments of the mining industry. The public, industry, and government must therefore remain vigilant.

Duane A. Smith

Further Readings
Smith, Duane A. *Mining America: The Industry and the Environment, 1800–1980.* 1993.

See also COAL: ENVIRONMENTAL IMPACTS; NONRENEWABLE RESOURCES; RESERVE MINING CONTROVERSY; STRIP MINING OF COAL: A HISTORY; URANIUM MINING: OCCUPATIONAL HEALTH

Mishan, E.J.

Most of the debate about economic growth has focused on whether it can be sustained within a planetary environment of limited resources. Edward J. Mishan's important contribution in *The Costs of Economic Growth* (1993) is different. He argued that the continued pursuit of economic growth in Western societies is more likely on balance to reduce rather than increase well-being.

Mishan (1917–) based his argument on the belief that the damages inflicted on other members of society from the production and consumption of certain goods are rising disproportionately. To exemplify his case he discussed the "external diseconomies" or "externalities" related to the defining technology of the age—the private automobile—"one of the great disasters to have befallen the human race."

Unlike some others who see in the past a quality of life made increasingly unavailable by the proliferation of technology, Mishan cannot be dismissed as an economic illiterate. With a Ph.D. in economics from the University of Chicago and a senior faculty position at the London School of Economics his economist's credentials are impeccable. Furthermore he is recognized as one of the leading theorists in "welfare economics." Welfare economics defines for economists the conditions under which individuals and communities can be said to be better or worse off as a result of economic activity. His *Cost Benefit Analysis* (1988) is an authoritative text on the economist's principal tool of analysis for estimating the economic value of proposed projects. It is often used to evaluate adverse effects on the environment.

With respect to economic growth Mishan concludes that the pursuit of human welfare requires the rejection of growth as a prior aim of policy. Instead he favors legislation that recognizes the individual's right to amenity and a substantial reallocation of investment away from industry into the re-planning of towns and cities.

Peter A. Victor

Further Readings

Mishan, E.J. *Cost Benefit Analysis*. 1988.
———. *The Costs of Economic Growth*. 1993.

See also AUTOMOBILES: IMPACTS AND POLICIES; BENEFIT-COST ANALYSIS; ECONOMIC GROWTH AND THE ENVIRONMENT; GREEN ECONOMICS

Monarch Butterfly Migration

The monarch butterfly (*Danaus plexippus*) is not an endangered species, but its monumental North American migrations, the longest in the insect world, have been designated "threatened phenomena" by the International Union for the Conservation of Nature and Natural Resources (IUCN). The butterfly's migrations are threatened primarily by the deforestation of their overwintering sites in Mexico, the destruction of their overwintering sites in California by urban development, and the use of pesticides and herbicides in their northern breeding and feeding grounds across the continent.

Monarchs face the greatest and most immediate risks in ten mountaintop refuges in the Sierra Transvolcanica mountains west of Mexico City. In those high-altitude temperate cloud forests the butterflies gather in the millions to spend the winter clustered in fir trees (*Abies religiosa*). Because the overwintering sites share very specific micro-climatic conditions, and because they are so small (approximately 2.5 hectares) and close together (within a few kilometers of each other), they are very vulnerable to environmental change, whether natural or man-made. With nowhere else to go the monarch butterflies can be killed in large numbers when snowstorms, forest fires, and pest infestations hit the area.

But the monarchs face another threat. With unrelenting population growth in Mexico arable land and wood are in great demand. Local farmers are moving up the mountainsides into monarch habitat, cutting trees for fuel and construction as well as to provide land for their crops and cattle. In the process they are destroying the monarch's overwintering sites.

In 1986 a presidential decree set aside 16,110 hectares at five of the ten sites as "special monarch butterfly biosphere reserves." Despite the decree the destruction of the forests continues with one site completely deforested and another recently destroyed by fire. The site where the butterflies are most numerous also attracts 100,000 tourists every year. This has brought some economic benefits to local people, but has also created new risks to the butterflies and their habitat.

In the winter of 1992 a long period of cold wet weather caused a die-off of tens-of-millions of monarchs. This event focused media and public attention on the dangers facing monarchs in Mexico at the same time as the government was negotiating the North American Free Trade Agreement with Canada and the United States. One of the barriers to acceptance of the trade deal by the United States was Mexico's poor record on environmental protection. Anxious to improve its environmental image the Mexican government during the summer of 1992 arrested illegal loggers and took steps to protect the overwintering sites.

M

In February 1993 an international scientific conference was convened at Avándaro to determine the causes of the high mortality of monarchs the previous winter. As a result of the conference the government acknowledged that additional steps were required to protect the monarch's Mexican habitats. Considerable differences of opinion exist, however, regarding the number of sites that need to be protected, the size needed to provide adequate habitat requirements, and the amount of tree-cutting and other human activity that should be permitted within the protected sites.

The answers to these questions and the dedication to real conservation action before the destruction of the forest is complete will determine the monarch's fate: continued existence or monumental migration collapse before the end of the millennium.

Barry Peers

Further Readings

Brower, Lincoln P., and Stephen B. Malcolm. "Animal Migrations: Endangered Phenomena." *American Zoology* 31 (1991): 265–76.

Malcolm, Stephen B., and Myron P. Zalucki, eds. *Biology and Conservation of the Monarch Butterfly* (No. 38 Science Series, Natural History Museum of Los Angeles County). 1993.

See also BUTTERFLIES: CONSERVATION AND HABITAT; MEXICO; TROPICAL DEFORESTATION

Montreal Protocol

The Montreal Protocol on Substances that Deplete the Ozone Layer, adopted in November 1987, was the first international agreement to establish target dates for reductions on emissions of chemical substances believed to be destroying the stratospheric ozone layer. Negotiated at a conference attended by representatives from sixty states, the protocol supplements the 1985 Vienna Convention for the Protection of the Ozone Layer—a framework treaty calling for international cooperation on assessing the effects of human activities on the ozone layer and the consequences of ozone loss for human health and the environment. The parties revised the protocol in 1990 and 1992 to accelerate the timetable for phasing out substances depleting the ozone layer.

The United Nations Environment Programme (UNEP) has coordinated the international response to the ozone depletion problem since 1977, when it established a Coordinating Committee on the Ozone Layer to assess the growing body of scientific information on the problem of ozone loss. An Ad Hoc Working Group of Legal and Technical Experts was formed in 1982 to prepare an international agreement to protect the ozone layer. Subsequent negotiations leading up to the 1985 Vienna Convention failed to reach a consensus on a timetable for specific targets for reducing emissions of chlorofluorocarbons (CFCs) and other chemicals suspected of destroying stratospheric ozone. A 1986 report of UNEP and the World Meteorological Organization, which projected a 9 percent loss ozone by the mid-twenty-first century, lent a greater sense of urgency that led to the convening of the Montreal Conference and agreement on a protocol.

The original Montreal Protocol obliged developed countries to reduce annual production and consumption of CFCs by 50 percent from 1986 levels by June 30, 1999. Intermediate steps included a stabilization within seven months of the date the protocol came into force and a 20 percent reduction by June 30, 1994. Production and consumption of halons, another family of chemicals linked to ozone depletion, were to be stabilized at 1986 levels by January 1, 1992. Developing countries, which have been responsible for a very small portion of the problem, were permitted to delay compliance with these control measures for up to ten years and in the meantime were to limit increases in their use of the controlled substances. The protocol also restricted trade in the controlled substances with states not party to the protocol.

The adequacy of the Montreal Protocol soon came under question with the release of a report of the International Ozone Trends Panel in March 1988 which concluded that the Antarctic ozone hole discovered several years earlier was caused by anthropogenic pollutants. It noted further that concentrations of stratospheric ozone over populated regions of northern hemisphere were dropping more rapidly than had been forecast previously. The growing sense of alarm prompted a series of international conferences, which in turn led to a meeting in London in June 1990 to revise the protocol, at which more than ninety countries were represented.

The London revisions to the Montreal Protocol provide for the developed countries to completely phase out production and consumption of CFCs, halons, and carbon tetrachloride by the year 2000, and methyl chloroform by the year 2005. Hydrochlorofluorocarbons (HCFCs), which will be used as substitutes for CFCs and which have a less damaging effect on the ozone layer, will be phased out no later than 2040. Developing countries are allowed a ten-year grace period in the phase-out schedule to meet "basic domestic needs." The adjustment is also to be facilitated by financial assistance (from a newly created multilateral fund to be administered by the World Bank) and by offering these countries the best available, environmentally-safe substitute chemicals and related technologies under fair and favorable conditions. Meeting in Copenhagen in November 1992 the parties further revised the protocol to advance the phase-out date for CFCs to January 1, 1996, and halons to January 1, 1994. HCFCs will be gradually phased out by the year 2030. Agreement was not reached, however, on a phase-out schedule for one other ozone-depleting chemical, methyl bromide, which is widely used in fumigation.

The Montreal Protocol and its revisions are arguably the most significant multilateral agreements in the environmental field and are considered a prototype for international responses to other global environmental problems, including climate change. The series of agreements are remarkable for being a timely and comprehensive response to scientific warnings of a problem with consequences that would not have become readily apparent for decades. They demonstrate the advantage of agreements that provide a flexible process through which the parties can modify regulations in response to new scientific evidence on the seriousness and immediacy of the problem and changing political circumstances. The agreements also serve as a model for how the specific needs and interests of developing countries can be accommodated to make them partners in addressing the problem. Substantial reductions already occurring in the production of ozone-depleting substances is reason for guarded optimism that the loss of ozone will be stabilized by the early twenty-first century.

The success of the negotiations on preserving the ozone layer has been attributed to several favorable factors: 1) the relatively small number of chemicals causing the problem; 2) the confidence of leading chemical companies that satisfactory substitutes could be developed in a timely way; 3) the convergence of scientific opinion on the loss of ozone and the potential gravity of the consequences; 4) the shock of the Antarctic ozone hole and evidence that it was caused by anthropogenic pollutants; 5) widespread public concern about the problem in a number of key countries; 6) the strong leadership of the United States at most phases of the negotiations; and 7) the personal diplomacy of UNEP executive director Mostafa Tolba.

Marvin S. Soroos

Further Readings

Benedick, Richard Elliot. *Ozone Diplomacy: New Directions in Safeguarding the Planet.* 1991.

Haas, Peter M. "Banning Chlorofluorocarbons: Epistemic Community Efforts to Protect Stratospheric Ozone." *International Organization* 46 (Winter 1992): 187–224.

Rowlands, Ian. "The Fourth Meeting of the Parties to the Montreal Protocol: Report and Reflection." *Environment* 35 (July/August 1993): 25–34.

See also ENVIRONMENTAL DIPLOMACY; OZONE DEPLETION; TOLBA, MOSTAFA K.; UNITED NATIONS ENVIRONMENT PROGRAMME

Moran, Thomas

See HUDSON RIVER SCHOOL

Mother Earth News

Mother Earth News—established in 1970 by John Shuttleworth and published by Sussex Publications of New York City—is a do-it-yourself magazine emphasizing approaches to the environment that are time-tested, ecologically sound, and profitable. One of the publication's major premises is that domestic and rural solutions to everyday problems were correctly devised long ago and must be remembered and applied to modern circumstances. In 1986 the magazine changed the slogan on its masthead from "More than a magazine—a way of life" to "The original country magazine."

Regular departments featured in each issue include: "Bootstrap Business," "Country Skills," "Backcountry," "Garden and Yard," and "Do It Yourself." As the seasons change so does the monthly emphasis of the magazine: a spring issue may feature a section on planting a garden; one for the fall may concern canning and preserving; and winter numbers may carry articles on woodstoves. Another major topic is natural health, with many articles on homespun remedies and suggestions for the improvement of diet. The magazine's viewpoint combines ecological soundness with recognition of the modern mechanized world and the pervasive influence of the profit motive; *Mother Earth News* has carried an article on "Picking a Pickup" and another on how to make $100 a month recycling old tires. Other sample articles from issues in the 1990s include "Making Root Beer at Home," "How to Make An Old-Fashioned Triangle Shawl," "The Healthy Lawn," "The Art of Making Maple Syrup," and "Getting Your Goat" (how to raise goats). *Mother Earth News* also carries an extensive classified advertising section that offers help for specialized problems and people interested in specific areas of concern.

Jim Baird

See also ENVIRONMENTALISM; FOOD ADDITIVES

Muir, John

John Muir (1838–1914) was born April 21, 1838, the third of eight children, in Dunbar, Scotland. He emigrated with his family in 1849 to central Wisconsin. His father, a severe and rigidly religious man, worked his sons hard clearing land and farming. John left home in 1860 and attended the University of Wisconsin (1861–1863), where he was encouraged by Ezra Carr, a botany professor, and his wife, Jeanne Carr. Leaving school without a degree, he taught school and designed assembly operations at factories in Canada and Indianapolis, where an eye injury temporarily blinded him in 1867.

This critical juncture changed his life. He followed his dream to become a wandering botanist and began an exceptional journal while walking to Florida. The journal, published after his death as *A Thousand Mile Walk to the Gulf* (1916), illustrates his remarkable non-anthropocentric perspective toward nature. Though he planned to continue to South America, after a brief but profound illness he redirected his travels and arrived in San Francisco in the spring of 1868. From there he walked to the Sierra Nevada mountains.

For the next five years he explored the Sierra Nevada from his center in Yosemite Valley, working occasionally as a shepherd, a lumberman, and a tour guide. He began to study the glacial geology of the Sierra and continued to keep a remarkable journal of his experiences, which included several eminent mountaineering feats. Encouraged by Jeanne Carr—who arranged a meeting between Muir and Ralph Waldo Emerson in Yosemite—he began to transform his journals and letters into essays on his adventures and studies.

After 1873 he spent his winters writing in Oakland, California, while continuing to explore at intervals the Sierra, Mount Shasta, the Great Basin, the mountains of Southern California, and—in 1879—Alaska. His writings, published in the *San Francisco Bulletin, Overland Monthly, Harper's,* and *Scribners,* earned him a national reputation. In them he began to decry wasteful lumbering practices, the damages of sheep to the biota of the Sierra, and the lack of appreciation of Americans for their natural environment.

Married on April 14, 1880, to Louisa Strenzel he took responsibility for her father's fruit farm near Martinez, California. With the exception of two trips to Alaska in 1880 and 1881, and one writing project in 1887–1888, he settled into work on the farm, where their two daughters were born.

However, Muir re-emerged at the end of the 1880s as a public figure. At the urging of Robert Underwood Johnson, an editor at *Century Magazine,* Muir wrote several essays proposing a Yosemite National Park which the two men used to lobby Congress. Their efforts were successful in 1890, though a second campaign for a Sequoia Kings Canyon National Park was not immediately successful.

In 1892 Muir helped to found the Sierra Club, as a combination outings club and protective association for the Yosemite Park. He served as president of the Club until his death in 1914. In 1894 he published his major work, *The Mountains of California*—a revision of many of the essays he had written in the 1870s about the Sierra.

Increasingly engaged in conservation activities Muir met with president Theodore Roosevelt in Yosemite in 1893, served as an advisor to the federal Forestry Commission in 1896 (where he conferred with Gifford Pinchot), and continued to write on conservation for eastern magazines. These articles were later collected and published as *Our National Parks* (1903). He also resumed his explorations in Alaska and published a wide range of essays and books in the period 1900–1914, including *Stickeen* (1909), *My First Summer in the Sierra* (1911), and *Story of My Boyhood and Youth* (1913).

Increasingly opposed to the direction of the progressive Roosevelt-Pinchot tradition of conservation in the early twentieth centur y, Muir's writings responded to utilitarian conceptions of resource use, most prominently in the Hetch Hetchy controversy (1907–1913). During this era—which followed his wife's death in 1905—the voice in his writing became more strident.

His legacy is four fold. First, Muir's writings about the Sierra and nature established him as the pre-eminent interpreter of national parks and ideologue of wilderness in the United States. Second, his political activities established him as the father of the national parks movement and the most prominent citizen conservationist in America. Third, his contribution in founding the Sierra Club and the impassioned style of rhetoric he fostered in that institution became a model for citizen conservation activists and organizations. Last is his mythical stature. Muir came to represent nature to Americans so powerfully that nature was represented by himself. Consequently, Earth Day has been celebrated on his birthday since its advent in 1970.

Michael P. Cohen

Further Readings

Cohen, Michael P. *The Pathless Way: John Muir and American Wilderness.* 1984.

Fox, Stephen. *John Muir and His Legacy: The American Conservation Movement* . 1981.

Muir, John. *The Mountains of Califor nia.* 1894.

———. *A Thousand Mile Walk to the Gulf.* 1916.

See also CONSERVATION MOVEMENT; EARTH DAY; EARTH FIRST!; EMERSON, RALPH WALDO; HETCH HETCHY DAM; JOHNSON, ROBERT UNDERWOOD; MINERAL KING CANYON; PINCHOT, GIFFORD; REDWOODS; SIERRA CLUB

Multiple Use Forestry

The world's forests ser ve many dif ferent functions, and forests have been managed to ensure a sustained supply of a wide variety of different values. Forests can provide wildlife habitat, fuel, building and other industrial wood products, employment, watershed values, soil and slope protection, wealth, maintenance of microclimates suitable for agriculture or human habi-

tation, avalanche protection, and recreational, aesthetic, and spiritual values.

Multiple use forestry is the management of a forested landscape to sustain a supply of all desired values somewhere in that landscape all of the time. Not all of these values can be sustained simultaneously on the same hectare of forest. Timber har vesting may be incompatible with maintenance of old-growth spiritual values. Managing for particular wildlife and watershed values may clash with employment of forest workers and some recreational activities. As a result, attempts to achieve multiple uses of particular forests have often led to conflict between forest users, each of whom may desire that the values they are most concerned about are sustained over the entir e landscape. In particular, timber har vesting practices have often conflicted with aesthetic and spiritual values, and sometimes with soil protection, wildlife, and watershed values.

It is the responsibility of a forester to manage a forest landscape for all the values desired from that landscape by the for est owner. In publicly-owned forests this means that all of the many different values desired by the different interest groups in society should be available somewher e. The forester's job is to achieve an acceptable balance of competing forest uses and values across the forest area. The challenge then is how to achieve this.

Forests are constantly changing as they regrow following natural disturbance or timber harvesting. In some forests, or at some times in one particular forest, natural disturbance occurs at a small spatial scale, as when a large old tree dies or is blown over, creating a gap in the forest canopy. In other forests or at other times, forests may be killed over large areas by windstorm, insects, fir e, or disease. In managed for ests, timber harvesting can create a similar range of disturbances, from individual tree selection harvesting to large-scale clearcutting. As the disturbed area regrows toward its original condition, there will be a steady change in the wildlife habitat provided, the hydrological role of the forest, its aesthetic and spiritual values, and the recreational opportunities it provides. In a well-managed forest most desired values will be available somewhere in the forested landscape all of the time because management will produce a mosaic of forest ages and conditions across the landscape. However, the location of a particular value—mature forest, for example—will change over time as mature forests are harvested and younger forests grow

M

to become mature. Thus, while the list of values provided by any one stand of trees at any one time may be limited, the list for that particular stand is constantly changing, and most values should be available somewhere within the forest.

Unfortunately not all forest values can be provided simply by practicing sustainable timber management over the entire forested landscape. For example, the spiritual and aesthetic values of west coast old-growth forest cannot be sustained in stands that are managed for timber extraction, irrespective of the harvest method used. Consequently, multiple-use—a concept that can only be applied at a regional landscape scale—will often require restricted use reserves; some areas will be set aside for wilderness and old-growth values. To balance the lost revenue and timber values some other areas will be managed to maximize sustainable levels of timber production, even if this compromises some of the other values. In the majority of the landscape, however, forests will be managed to ensure a wide variety of social and environmental values area maintained in a mosaic of different forest ages and conditions across the landscape.

Hamish Kimmins

Further Readings
Kimmins, Hamish. *Balancing Act: Environmental Issues in Forestry.* 1992.

See also FOREST FRAGMENTATION AND BIRD HABITATS; FORESTRY, HISTORY OF; HABITAT FRAGMENTATION, PATCHES, AND CORRIDORS; LANDSCAPE ECOLOGY; OLD GROWTH FORESTS; WILDERNESS

Mumford, Lewis
Born at the end of the nineteenth century, Lewis Mumford (1895–1990) witnessed during his own lifetime the enormous impact of the industrial age on the daily surroundings of ordinary people. The Eiffel Tower—built in 1889—presaged the giant skyscrapers served by electric elevators that would change the skylines of cities, while the automobile, patented in 1895, would change their topography. Growing up in Manhattan, Mumford was not only a witness to these changes but a keen observer of their effects on human life.

Labeled a Luddite by some, Mumford in fact was a Renaissance person, eschewing intellectual specialization in order to understand the wholeness of human existence. A largely self-taught scholar (he never completed college) he might well be called the Father of Human Ecology. He gained his vast knowledge not from the study of the writings of others but, as an ecologist should, by walking the streets of cities, carefully noting the impact of architectural scale, physical layout, and aesthetic qualities on the social interactions and psychic lives of people.

Although Mumford was visiting lecturer at several universities in America and abroad, his major contributions were his writings. He wrote an architectural column for *The New Yorker* for several years, as well as essays for other magazines and articles for professional journals; he also wrote some two dozen books. His subject matter, always broadly defined, focused on architecture, on the structure and life of cities, and on the conduct of human social life, especially as it has been affected by technological change. He was highly critical of the role and effects of the automobile on urban life and modern culture.

He is perhaps best known as a historian of cities. His 1961 book, *The City in History: Its Origins, Its Transformations, and Its Prospects,* is still a standard text for urban planners, but these studies provided him a solid grounding for expanding his thinking across the whole realm of human social history, culminating in his monumental two-volume philosophical work, *The Myth of the Machine* (1967–1970). In it, he traces the entire sweep of human social evolution, constantly relating the culturally created environment with the life of the individual human being. He coined the term "megamachine" to describe the stratified, hierarchical systems that characterize "civilized" societies throughout history. Dismissed by some as mere carping at "modernism," these works offer profound insights into the divergence between personal-scaled human "needs" and the environments created by huge techno-bureaucratic societies. For the astute thinker, Mumford points the way to understanding the sources of today's socio-environmental problems.

Mary E. Clark

Further Readings
Mumford, Lewis. *The City in History: Its Origins, Its Transformations, and Its Prospects.* 1961.
———. *The Myth of the Machine, Volume I: Technics and Human Development.* 1967; *Volume II: The Pentagon of Power.* 1970.

See also AUTOMOBILES: IMPACTS AND POLICIES; URBAN DESIGN

Municipal Solid Waste: Incineration

Incineration of municipal solid waste originally served two main purposes: elimination of putrescible materials which might attract vermin, and reduction in the volume of material thrown in a landfill. Within the past twenty years a central aim of almost every incineration project has been to use the heat produced by the combustion of this waste to produce marketable energy such as process steam or electricity generated from steam.

Municipal solid waste can be burned as received from the curb, or it can be processed to produce a finer, more homogeneous fuel with non-combustible materials removed prior to burning. Incinerators which burn waste without processing are often referred to as mass burn systems; processed material fed to incinerators is called refuse-derived fuel (RDF)—a term often also used to describe the incinerator. Pretreatment for refuse-derived fuel normally includes shredding the waste, followed by magnetic separation of ferrous articles; it can also include air classification to remove noncombustibles such as non-ferrous metals and glass as well as some recyclable plastics. The fuel processing thus assists in reclaiming recyclable materials from the waste destined for incineration. However, the added mechanical complexity of the processing equipment means that refuse-derived fuel burning incinerators have a significantly higher initial cost and somewhat lower reliability. This has led to fewer installations of this type.

A third distinction can be made between incinerator types. The mass burn designation is more commonly applied to large systems where the combustion chamber is one relatively large rectangular box designed to supply more than the theoretically required amount of air to support complete combustion; refuse-derived fuel incinerators are similar in this respect. Another design is the modular or two-stage combustion system, in which two cylindrical combustion chambers are used. In the primary chamber, the waste is fed and less than stoichiometric air is introduced leading to a condition similar to pyrolysis. The gases resulting from this process proceed to a secondary chamber where additional air is introduced to permit combustion to proceed to completion. Due to the lower gas flows over the waste this design has lower uncontrolled particulate emissions.

Incinerator emissions contain varying levels of heavy metals, including arsenic, cadmium, chromium, lead, and mercury. Many of these metals are present in the particulate matter suspended in the exhaust, known as fly ash. Good control of the particulate emissions is the most common approach to minimizing emissions of these pollutants. High efficiency particulate control devices such as large electrostatic precipitators or fabric filters are used on state-of-the-art facilities. One metal—mercury—is present in the vapor phase at typical exhaust gas temperatures and is not captured by particulate control devices. Additional control technologies to control mercury emissions include injection of activated carbon into the exhaust gas upstream of a fabric filter used for particulate control, and injection of sodium sulfide upstream of electrostatic precipitators used for particulate control.

Hydrogen chloride is the inorganic gas found in greatest quantities in the exhaust from incinerators. This acid forms from the combustion of chlorinated plastics. Sulfur in the waste also tends to be oxidized to form sulfur dioxide, another acid gas. Both of these gases are typically controlled by injection of either dry lime or a lime slurry into the exhaust upstream of the particulate control device. The reaction products and unreacted lime are gathered in the particulate control device. State-of-the-art systems usually employ a combination known as a spray dry absorber/fabric filter or scrubber/baghouse.

Emissions from municipal solid waste incinerators have been found to contain small but measurable levels of several toxic organic compounds, most notably the polychlorinated dibenzo-p-dioxins (dioxins) and polychlorinated dibenzofurans (furans). While these compounds may be the unburnt residual of dioxins and furans present in the waste studies have indicated that they also form under certain conditions in the combustion and post-combustion regions of incinerators. Their presence in the final exhaust to the atmosphere is thus the result of a series of chemical reactions involving both their formation and destruction. The best method for minimizing emission levels is to ensure good combustion design, so that maximum destruction of both the dioxins and furans, as well as their precursor compounds in the waste is achieved. The scrubber/baghouse control system used in state-of-the-art facilities

M

also has been documented to reduce dioxin and furan emissions, and the injection of activated carbon when used for mercury control reduces such emissions to the atmosphere even more.

The other environmental discharge of significant concern from municipal solid waste incinerators is the ash. Ash is the uncombusted residue left after combustion, and is retrieved from several locations in an incinerator system. Bottom ash is the material left on or discharged from the grate at the bottom of the incinerator combustion chamber. It tends to be of little concern and in some combustion designs may be the largest fraction of the total ash. Particulate captured in the air pollution control system includes fly ash, that material carried out of the combustion chamber in the solid phase. This ash is enriched in heavy metals, and at many facilities when tested using the regulatory leachate tests used to classify a waste has been deemed hazardous (leachate toxic). The metals cadmium and lead have typically been found to be those exceeding the limits set for leachate levels from non-hazardous wastes. Studies have indicated that solidification of these wastes with portland cement and similar pozzolanic compounds eliminates this behavior.

Kenneth E. Smith

Further Readings

DePaul, F. Thomas, and Jerry W. Crowder. *Control of Emissions from Municipal Solid Waste Incinerators*. 1989.

Ontario Ministry of Environment and Energy. *Guidance for Incinerator Design and Operation, Volume I: General*. 1988.

Sawell, S.E., et al. *The National Incinerator Testing and Evaluation Program: Evaluation of Contaminant Leachability from Residues Collected at a Refuse Derived Fuel Municipal Waste Combustion Facility*. Environment Canada Report No. IP-96, July 1989.

———, et al. *The National Incinerator Testing and Evaluation Program: Characterization of Residues from a Modular Municipal Waste Incinerator with Lime-Based Air Pollution Control*. Environment Canada Report No. IP-101, September 1989.

———, et al. *The National Incinerator Testing and Evaluation Program: Evaluation of Solidified Fabric Filter Ash from a Modular Municipal Waste Incinerator with Lime-Based Air Pollution Control*.

Environment Canada Report No. IP-103, November 1989.

See also AIR POLLUTION: IMPACTS; ARSENIC; CADMIUM; DIOXINS AND FURANS; HAZARDOUS WASTE TREATMENT TECHNOLOGIES; LEACHING; LEAD; MERCURY; MUNICIPAL SOLID WASTE: LANDFILL; PACKAGING; RECYCLING

Municipal Solid Waste: Landfill

Over the past twenty years land disposal of municipal solid waste has changed dramatically. The once normal practice of open dumps which are regularly set on fire to reduce volume have become increasingly rare. These have largely been replaced by so-called sanitary landfills, which are covered each day with soil to lessen smells and the attraction of seagulls and rats. Sanitary landfills are now being replaced by engineered landfills, which have clay or plastic liners below and above the landfill and have leachate drainage systems and methane collection systems.

Problems with Landfills

Despite the substantial progress in landfilling citizens still fiercely oppose the siting or expansion of even the best-designed landfills. Opposition to landfills is based on negative groundwater and surface water quality impacts, explosions from methane gas emissions and buildup, toxic releases from organic compound releases, truck traffic problems, noise, odors, litter and dust, nuisance and disease impacts from insects, rodents and birds, and impaired view. Local communities also oppose landfills because of concerns about the social inequity of forcing a few communities to take all the negative impacts and risks associated with landfills. Environmentalists also oppose landfills because they are symbols of our wasteful attitude—a throwing away of valuable resources.

The process for siting landfills is dominated by two major criteria: a site with the best hydrogeological conditions for the landfill (usually deep clay), and a site where the fewest number of people possible are directly affected. This results in garbage being exported from urban areas to farming and rural areas.

A side-effect of the major difficulties encountered in siting landfills is that landfill siting proponents look for one huge mega-dump site instead of stirring up several communities by looking for several small landfills.

Landfills Compared with Other Waste Management Options

Waste management options can be compared on the basis of three factors: 1) resource conservation; 2) environmental impacts; and 3) financial costs.

One option currently preferred to landfills is known as Reduce, Reuse, Recycle or the 3Rs. This approach avoids throwing away used materials, which are recognized to be valuable resources rather than worthless garbage. Since less waste is thrown away the 3Rs cause less environmental damage than landfilling. This lessening of environmental damage becomes even greater with more emphasis placed on the first R—reduction. The costs of 3Rs programs are equivalent to or less than landfill costs, if all siting, closure, long-term monitoring, and cleanup costs of landfilling are taken into account.

Another alternative to landfilling is incineration. In terms of resource conservation the incineration option is not much different from a landfill. Some think that because most incineration of municipal garbage now involves generating energy (either in the form of heat or electricity) that this is a resource conservation option. The experience with energy-from-waste facilities, however, is that the amount of energy generated is minimal and that the energy thus produced is very expensive. From an environmental perspective both landfills and incinerators have major environmental impacts. The major difference between the two in environmental impact is that for landfills the negative impacts are more concentrated on a limited number of people whereas for incinerators the contaminants are widespread over a large area. Incineration is marginally worse than landfills because it is impossible to track the pollution from an incinerator and, therefore, it is even more impossible to clean up the contaminants released by incinerators. From a cost perspective incinerators are more expensive than landfills.

Future of Landfills

The use of landfills is a sign of our failure to properly use and conserve resources. It is a symbol of our wasteful consumer society. The prime objective for landfilling must be to minimize and eventually eliminate the use of landfills. For example, the State of Rhode Island has passed legislation announcing a phase-out of landfills for municipal garbage. Recent studies throughout North America consistently show that at least an 80 percent reduction of garbage generation below present levels would be achievable in a short time, if society would simply become serious about reduction. To be consistent with the objective of minimizing the need for landfill expenditures should be focused on the 3Rs. This contrasts sharply with present expenditure patterns in which most financial resources go into siting, building, and operating landfills.

A secondary objective is to minimize the negative environmental impacts from the landfilling of the materials remaining after the 3Rs. Increasingly governments are looking at above-ground storage facilities as the preferred option for handling the remaining wastes. This is done either through placing materials in a warehouse-like structure made of pre-stressed concrete or in above-ground storage mounds covered with earth. The latter look like the traditional landfill except no wastes are buried below the surface of the ground.

Above-ground storage facilities allow for easier detection of leachate, which allows early action to avoid contamination, elimination of landfill gas problems caused by movement of gases below ground to adjacent properties, and easier remediation, if necessary.

This approach also results in smaller facilities than the traditional mega-landfill and less dependence on soil conditions as an environmental protection measure, because the likelihood of groundwater contamination is greatly reduced. This results in much greater flexibility in siting criteria, which means that impacts on agriculture and on communities can become the dominant deciding factors.

However, regardless of how well such facilities may be designed, the objective should be to minimize, and even eliminate, the need for such disposal and storage facilities. Every time a used material is thrown away, a valuable resource is wasted.

John Jackson

Further Readings

Schall, John. *Does the Solid Waste Management Hierarchy Make Sense?* 1992.

Jackson, John. *Resources—Not Garbage.* 1993.

See also GROUNDWATER POLLUTION; LEACHING; MUNICIPAL SOLID WASTE: INCINERATION; NONRENEWABLE RESOURCES; PACKAGING; RECYCLING

Muskie, Edmund S.

Edmund S. Muskie served in the Maine House of Representatives (1947–1951), as governor of Maine (1955–1959), U.S. senator (1957–1980), and secretary of state (1980–1981). He was unsuccessful as the Democratic candidate for vice president in 1968.

As chair of the Subcommittee on Air and Water Pollution of the Senate Public Works Committee Muskie became the leading congressional proponent of stronger anti-pollution laws. Among his major legislative accomplishments are the Clean Air Act of 1965, which gave the secretary of Health, Education and Welfare authority to set exhaust standards for new cars; the Water Quality Act of 1965, which established a new Federal Water Pollution Control Agency, required the states to set water quality standards based on federal criteria, and gave the federal government limited enforcement powers; the Clean Water Act of 1966, which increased grants for waste treatment; and the National Emission Standards Act of 1967, which gave the federal government preemptive authority to set auto emission standards. California, in this case, was allowed to set stricter standards. Muskie also advanced the Air Quality Act of 1967, which established a federal-state system for control of air pollution similar to that for water pollution; the Clean Air Act of 1970, which established strict federally-enforced air quality and emission standards for both vehicles and industrial sources; and the Federal Water Pollution Control Act Amendments of 1972, which established a federal system of discharge permits to control water pollution.

As the leading Democratic contender for the 1972 Democratic presidential nomination, Muskie spurred President Richard Nixon to support the landmark 1970 Clean Air Act. Muskie is given credit for many of the strict deadlines and "technology forcing" provisions of the law.

Norman J. Vig

Further Readings

Davies, J. Clarence, and Barbara Davies. *The Politics of Pollution.* 2nd ed. 1975.

Jones, Charles O. *Clean Air: The Policies and Politics of Pollution Control.* 1975.

Muskie, Edmund S. *Journeys.* 1972.

See also AIR POLLUTION: REGULATION (U.S.)

Mutation

DNA is the organizing material in all animals and plants, each having a characteristic number of strands and genetic sequence. In humans the cell takes up a volume of about 1.7×10^{-9} cubic centimeters. Of this about 7.3×10^{-12} grams is DNA, organized in forty-six strands called chromosomes. These are paired, with twenty-three strands originating from the mother and twenty-three strands originating from the father of an individual. The chromosomal material is called the human genome and it contains between 60,000 and 100,000 genes together with genetic material having regulatory functions controlling the interaction of these genes. The development and function of every living organism is controlled or mediated by its genes and can be changed, or mutated, by altering these genes.

There are three categories of environmental agents capable of changing genes or genetic material (DNA): 1) ultraviolet and ionizing radiation; 2) viral infections; and 3) chemicals. Human, animal, and plant cells can be classified as somatic (body cells) or reproductive. Mutations, depending on the cell affected, can be somatic or reproductive affecting the organism itself or its offspring.

Damage to DNA may be lethal to the cell, or it may leave the cell alive but unable to reproduce itself. Damage to cellular DNA may also be partially or totally repaired. If the damage leaves the cell reproductively intact this damage may or may not lead to characteristic, functional, or organic changes in the organism. Damage to reproductive cells may leave the organism intact but unable to have normal offspring. The observed change is called a mutation.

If many somatic cells in a human or animal are killed tissue damage occurs and survival of the organism is threatened. If many reproductive cells are killed the person or animal becomes infertile or sterile. These dramatic, lethal changes are not usually called mutations. Partially repaired cells which are still able to reproduce are said to have mutated if they can cause somatic changes such as alteration of enzymes, overproduction or underproduction of hormones, or an ineffective antibody. On the level of the organism this mutation may be observed as chronic illness, autoimmune disease, or cancer. In non-reproducing cells the damage may not be perpetuated and no species effect may be seen.

Partially damaged and partially repaired sperm or ovum may be incapable of fertilization or may precipitate embryonic loss, miscarriage, stillbirth, neonatal or infant death, childhood cancer, or genetic diseases. These are lethal mutations. Somatic cell damage to the embryo or fetus in utero can cause congenital malformations or diseases. These may or may not affect offspring of the affected fetus in later life. Some mutations such as change of eye color or growth pattern are not lethal.

There is a very small possibility that a mutation or change in DNA will result in a beneficial change in the organism. However, in highly evolved dynamically well-balanced organisms—including the human body—the vast number of changes are deleterious and result in eventual death of the cell line. Severe damage such as autosomal dominant mutations terminate with the first offspring, who is either sterile or dies before reaching reproductive maturity. Recessive and partially recessive mutations—that is those not expressed because the matching gene from the other parent is sufficient for the organism—may require several generations before random mating produces a non-viable organism.

Deleterious genes—even when not expressed as a deficit or handicap in the organism—are harmful to the species. The sum of deleterious genes whether expressed or not are said to constitute the genetic burden or genetic load of the population. Efforts to affect genetic composition through deliberate mutational changes is called recombinant DNA when manipulation is direct and eugenics when it is done through breeding.

Rosalie Bertell

Further Readings

Carlson, Elof A. *Genes, Radiation and Society: The Life and Work of H.J. Muller.* Ithaca, New York. 1981.

Gofman, John W. *Radiation and Human Health.* 1981.

Lester, Nina. "Radiation." In *Environment on Trial.* Ed. David Estrin and John Swaigen. 1993.

See also CHERNOBYL; HAZARDOUS WASTE TREATMENT TECHNOLOGIES; IONIZING RADIATION

Nader, Ralph

Ralph Nader is a leading U.S. consumer advocate and public interest lawyer. He was born in Winsted, Connecticut, on February 27, 1934, of Lebanese immigrant parents. He graduated *magna cum laude* from Princeton University's Woodrow Wilson School of Public and International Affairs in 1955. In 1958 he obtained his law degree with distinction from Harvard University, where he was an editor of the *Harvard Law Record*. He was admitted to the Connecticut bar in 1958 and to the Massachusetts bar and the bar of the U.S. Supreme Court in 1959.

During his studies at Harvard and as a young lawyer he testified before state legislative committees on faulty auto design. In 1964 he undertook a consultant study of auto safety for the U.S. Department of Labor. In 1965 he published his best-selling book, *Unsafe at Any Speed: The Designed-In Dangers of the American Automobile*, in which he strongly criticized the construction defects of U.S. cars, especially the General Motors (GM) Corvair. He testified before Senator Abraham Ribicoff's Senate committee and was influential in getting strict new auto safety legislation passed in 1966. He was the target of threats and of spying by the auto industry, which tried to attack his credibility. He counterattacked by suing GM for $26 million for invasion of his private life. GM was forced to admit its unjust conduct and to pay him $425,000, a sum which he used to finance his work for consumer defense.

In 1969 he founded the Center for the Study of Responsive Law, and enlarged his research to investigate safety in coal mines and gas pipelines, water and air pollution, mental health, care of the aged, the food and drug industry, radiation dangers, DDT in agriculture, and cyclamates in diet foods. He attracted young idealistic social science and law students, sometimes called "Nader's raiders." They emphasized corporate irresponsibility toward health and safety and the concomitant government failure to enact and to enforce regulatory legislation.

He and his organization published books on air and water pollution, and reports critical of the Federal Trade Commission and the Interstate Commerce Commission. In 1972 he published *Action for Change* and *Who Runs Congress*; in 1973 he put out *The Consumer and Corporate Accountability Guide* and co-edited *Corporate Power in America*; in 1974 he published *Working on the System: A Comprehensive Manual for Citizen Access to Federal Agencies*; and in 1975 he reissued six volumes of reports under the title *The Ralph Nader Congress Project*. He came out with *The Lemon Book* and *Who's Poisoning America* in 1981. Among his other important books are *The Menace of Atomic Energy* (with J. Abbotts, 1979), *The Big Boys* (1986), and *Winning the Insurance Game* which he co-authored in 1990.

He founded other consumer and environmentalist groups, including Public Citizen Inc. and the Project for Corporate Responsibility; co-founded the Center for Auto Safety; and inspired the creation of the Princeton Project 55 (in 1989) and the Public Interest Research Groups (PIRGs) which now exist in many universities and colleges in the United States and Canada. These PIRGs are involved in various social justice, peace, development, and especially environmental issues that affect the public. Katherine Isaac's book, *Civics for Democracy: A Journey for Teachers and Students*, published by Nader's Center for Responsive Law in 1992, is a manual for young people wishing to get involved in change-oriented action. The consumer revolution which Nader spearheaded in the United States is now spreading not only to Canada where it had an early impact, but also to other countries outside North America.

Jean-Guy Vaillancourt

Further Readings

Buckhorn, R.F. *Nader: The People's Lawyer.* 1972.

Nader, Ralph. *Unsafe at Any Speed.* 1965.

Orton, Jay. *Ralph Nader: A Man and a Movement.* 1972.

See also AIR POLLUTION: IMPACTS; AUTOMOBILES: IMPACTS AND POLICIES; ENVIRONMENTALISM

Naess, Arne

Arne Naess is a Norwegian philosopher known in environmental circles primarily for his work on deep ecology. He is rightly regarded as the founding father of deep ecology, having not only coined the term but also been the primary source of the central ideas associated with it.

Naess was born in 1912 and occupied the chair of philosophy at the University of Oslo for thirty years from 1939 (age twenty-seven) until his voluntary early retirement in 1969. Prior to taking up this chair Naess had already attended meetings of the Vienna Circle, subjected himself to an intense fourteen-month, six-day-a-week psychoanalysis with a colleague of Freud's (also in Vienna), and worked at Berkeley with the noted psychologist and learning theorist E.C. Tolman. During his occupancy of the Oslo chair Naess proceeded to exert an enormous—and enormously beneficial—influence upon the philosophical, social science, and general intellectual milieu of Norway in particular and Scandinavia in general. Indeed he is credited with having almost single-handedly revived Norwegian philosophy and social science after an acknowledged "dead" period. During this thirty year period Naess authored a prodigious volume of work in a variety of languages on a broad range of areas: history of philosophy, philosophy of language and communication, philosophy of science, skepticism, ethics and "normative systems," Spinoza, and Gandhi. In 1958 he founded an innovative and internationally respected journal of philosophy and the social sciences, which he continued to edit until 1975. In addition to these accomplishments Naess established an international repu-

tation as a mountain climber by around mid-century—an activity that expressed his deeply felt and lifelong fascination with and love for the nonhuman world.

Naess's work on deep ecology corresponds roughly to the period since his retirement and so follows upon an already long, rich, and distinguished career. Now in his early eighties Naess remains a vigorous contributor to the development of deep ecological theorizing and an active supporter of the global ecology movement.

Warwick Fox

Further Readings

Fox, Warwick. *Toward a Transpersonal Ecology: Developing New Foundations for Environmentalism.* 1990.

———. "Intellectual Origins of the 'Depth' Theme in the Philosophy of Arne Naess." *The Trumpeter* 9 (1992): 68–73.

See also DEEP ECOLOGY: EMERGENCE; EARTH FIRST!; ENVIRONMENTAL ETHICS; RADICAL ENVIRONMENTALISM

NAFTA and the Environment

The North American Free Trade Agreement (NAFTA) went into effect on January 1, 1994, following approval by the governments of Canada, the United States, and Mexico. While it contains more "green" language than any previous trade pact, NAFTA is also unprecedented in the freedom it allows investors and the extent to which it curtails government policy flexibility—both potential areas of concern for environmentalists. The supplemental North American Agreement on Environmental Cooperation, intended to assuage environmentalists' opposition to NAFTA, establishes a forum for discussing environmental issues among the NAFTA countries but does little more, due to its cumbersome dispute resolution mechanism.

NAFTA's specific environmental impacts stem largely from the trade agreement's provisions regarding standards, investment, intellectual property, subsidies, international environmental agreements, energy, and resolution of trade-related disputes. NAFTA also has more general effects related to national (and subnational) governance and depletion of natural resources.

To facilitate trade in goods NAFTA sets limitations on the types of standards which countries may legitimately use to ban imported goods for health, safety, or other reasons. NAFTA's rules apply to all standards that ". . . may, directly or indirectly, affect trade in goods or services . . . ." between the NAFTA countries. Many environmental regulations fall into this category—both those relating to traded products themselves (such as allowable levels of pesticides on fruit) and to production processes (such as smelter emissions standards), since compliance with these environmental standards affects the producers' costs and the price of the traded goods. Under NAFTA federal governments are required to ". . . seek, through appropriate measures, to ensure . . . ." that provincial and state governments and nongovernmental standards agencies (e.g., Underwriters' Laboratories and the Canadian Standards Association) comply with NAFTA provisions.

Under NAFTA jurisdictions are expected to base their standards on international ones and to work toward harmonizing their standards with those in the other NAFTA countries. In principle this may lead to pressure to accept a lowest common denominator as the acceptable standard, despite the existence of a wide range of environmental regulations and standards in different jurisdictions for a variety of ecological, political, and historical reasons. It is possible that adoption of international standards could set back hard-won environmental and health advances in some countries. Such provisions could also threaten the progressive evolution of environmental policy, since any jurisdiction which takes the lead in a particular regulatory direction might well be more likely to face a trade challenge.

In the event of a standards-related trade dispute the onus falls on the country with higher standards to prove that they are necessary (as determined by scientific and benefit-cost analysis), that they are the least-trade restrictive measure possible to achieve the desired goal, and that they do not discriminate between foreign and domestic firms. A NAFTA panel of trade experts decides any dispute that may arise, and if a standard is deemed to violate NAFTA, it must be rescinded or revised, or else the offending jurisdiction faces trade sanctions approved by the NAFTA panel.

NAFTA states that jurisdictions are also to harmonize their standards enforcement procedures. The agreement sets out detailed rules concerning how standards should be enforced. The North American Agreement on Environmental Cooperation similarly focuses on national enforcement of national laws and regulations, and on procedures for harmonizing rules and their enforcement.

More than previous trade agreements, which deal almost exclusively with trade in goods, NAFTA emphasizes investment, trade in financial and other services, "intellectual property" rights, and access by individual firms to dispute settlement procedures. Investment shifts associated with NAFTA are likely to bring environmental protection measures under increasing pressure in all NAFTA countries.

NAFTA's Investment chapter contains a provision which states that the three NAFTA countries should not waive or weaken their existing environmental measures as a means of attracting investment (Article 1114). This clause is the principal attempt in NAFTA to address the possibility that investment shifts following NAFTA's implementation could lead to the growth of "pollution havens" (jurisdictions with the least-stringent environmental laws, where costs are lower but goods can be freely exported to the other markets). The non-binding language used in this provision gives it little clout. Moreover, it does not address pre-existing differences in the environmental policy framework among the NAFTA countries.

Less attention has been paid to other considerations, such as the likelihood that any increase in trade associated with NAFTA means that more goods are transported farther than before. Any increased transport of goods can place new strains on existing transportation infrastructure resulting in increased energy use, pollution, resource depletion, waste generation, and climate change. Wider demand for raw materials may set back conservation initiatives and/or lead to more rapid depletion of resources.

Like the earlier Canada-U.S. Free Trade Agreement NAFTA bans export subsidies by governments (but specifically permits more general government subsidies only for energy development and military purposes). Since subsidies represent an important tool for governments to use in influencing the economy, these restrictions could hamper efforts to encourage conservation and pollution control, provide incentives for "green industry," and otherwise foster sustainable development.

International environmental agreements often use trade sanctions against non-signatories to encourage compliance. NAFTA permits several such pacts—including the Montreal Protocol on ozone-depleting substances, the Basel

Convention on waste transfers, and the CITES agreement regarding endangered species—to supersede NAFTA if conflicts arise. All NAFTA parties would have to agree before any future international environmental agreements would be allowed to take precedence over NAFTA. This effectively could allow any one NAFTA party to veto its trading partners' flexibility to become active partners in future agreements designed to address global environmental issues (e.g., biodiversity, forestry, climate change, Arctic pollution).

NAFTA's energy chapter, from which Mexico negotiated an exclusion, prohibits nearly all quantitative restrictions on energy exports. The "proportionality clause" of the Canada-U.S. Free Trade Agreement is continued in NAFTA. This clause states that even in an energy supply emergency NAFTA countries must continue to export an amount proportional to the average of exports to total energy production during the three preceding years. All NAFTA parties except Mexico may thus be banned from meeting domestic needs first. Other primary goods, apparently including water, are covered by the same rules.

NAFTA weakens governments' capacity to impose regulations on private investors—taxes, standards, emissions controls, etc.—since firms can play jurisdictions off against each other, producing in and freely exporting from the jurisdiction where production costs are lowest. The argument that trade-induced economic growth will make more financial resources available to devote to environmental protection has been contested by many environmentalists, who argue that tax revenues are unlikely to rise. Government action is required for virtually any efforts to internalize environmental costs of production and implement the widely-accepted "polluter pays" principle, thus making markets work more sustainably; this may be NAFTA's longest-term negative environmental legacy.

Patricia E. Perkins

Further Readings

Canadian Environmental Law Association. *The Environmental Implications of Trade Agreements.* 1993.

Zaelke, Durwood, Paul Orbuch, and Robert F. Housman, eds. *Trade and the Environment: Law, Economics, and Policy.* 1993.

See also CITES; MEXICO; MONTREAL PROTOCOL; REGULATION; TOXIC WASTES IN INTERNATIONAL TRADE

National Audubon Society

In the 1880s George Bird Grinnell, who had grown up in Audubon Park, New York, proposed in the editorial pages of his magazine, *Forest and Stream,* that an Audubon Society, named to honor the noted naturalist and artist John James Audubon, be dedicated to the protection of wild birds and their eggs. By 1898 there were fifteen state Audubon Societies which helped pass the first federal legislation for bird protection—the Lacey Act of 1900 which outlawed interstate sale of birds killed in violation of state laws. In 1905 thirty-six state Audubon groups formed the National Committee of Audubon Societies.

In 1911 the Winchester Repeating Arms Company offered to double Audubon income if they would protect game birds for hunting, and the directors divided on this issue. Grinnell eventually joined the American Game Protection Association which separated from the Audubon Society. In the 1920s Rosalie Edge, a suffragist, sued to obtain the Societies' 7,000-member mailing list to obtain proxies for a board of directors meeting where she revealed that the National Committee had received rents from hunters for trapping muskrats in a bird sanctuary. As membership plummeted due to Edge's revelations the board changed its policy regarding hunting on its property. It changed its name to the National Audubon Society (NAS) in 1940, and in 1941 its official publication *Bird-Lore* changed to *Audubon.*

During the late 1970s and early 1980s Russell Peterson, President Richard Nixon's former chair of the Council on Environmental Quality, was elected president of the NAS and moved the organization into an active political role in influencing government policies. Over the years the NAS has expanded its interests from protecting wild birds from feather hunters to protecting other wildlife, preserving wilderness areas and habitat, and supporting other environmental causes. It has over 500 local chapters located in all fifty states, with membership totaling over 550,000. It maintains education centers, camps, research stations, and bird and wildlife sanctuaries around the country. The main priority of the society continues to be the preservation of wildlife throughout the world.

The NAS now opposes hunting but joins with sportsmen to advocate government preservation of wildlife habitat. It maintains its own wildlife refuges but also urges government to declare more wilderness areas and to restore endangered species such as wolves to national parks and other public lands. In 1986 it launched a campaign to save the Alaskan Wildlife Refuge against the Reagan administration's plan to develop oil rights there. It criticizes the Forest Service's management of national forests and any emphasis on timbering of old-growth trees. It initiated several lawsuits to protect the threatened Northern Spotted Owl against clearcutting in the Pacific Northwest.

While maintaining its active campaigns on behalf of wildlife the society has extended its interest to lobbying for human health issues. It joined an environmental coalition to support reauthorization of the Clean Air Act of 1991. Another coalition which included NAS called for industry to be held responsible for cleaning up toxic waste disposal sites under Superfund. The NAS research staff produced a twenty-year energy plan to use more solar and other renewable forms of energy, conserve the remaining fossil fuels, and rely less on nuclear power.

NAS holds a biennial convention for all members in locations of particular ecological interest. It runs bird-watching expeditions for members and workshops for American and foreign educators on teaching children about nature. It sponsors television specials to bring information about conservation programs into the homes of millions of Americans. Starting in 1900 NAS organized an annual Christmas bird count in order to track as many species as possible and determine whether they are being reduced in numbers. Over 40,000 bird watchers now participate in this annual event. It has substantially increased our scientific knowledge regarding birds' migration patterns.

In addition to *Audubon* the society publishes the bimonthly *Audubon Activist* to inform members about the latest legislative, administrative, and judicial developments in Washington on environmental issues. The Washington office publishes frequent action alerts to members about issues coming to a vote in Congress and urges members to write to their representatives. It maintains a twenty-four-hour hotline in Washington to inform members and the public about current environmental issues.

Lettie McSpadden

Further Readings

Fox, Steven. *John Muir and His Legacy: The American Conservation Movement.* 1981.

National Audubon Society. *Audubon* and *Annual Reports.*

See also AUDUBON, JOHN JAMES; BIRDING; HAWK SHOOTING; SEABIRDS; SHOREBIRDS; WATERFOWL: CONSERVATION AND HABITAT

National Environmental Policy Act (U.S.)

On January 1, 1970, President Richard Nixon signed into law a statute then unique in the history of legislation. The National Environmental Policy Act of 1969 (NEPA) was to become one of the most widely emulated pieces of American legislation and one of the most widely misinterpreted and widely misunderstood. The purpose of NEPA was not—as some critics have asserted—the control of pollution, the writing of impact statements, or the indiscriminate listing of all environmental impacts. Its fundamental objective was to establish for the government of the United States basic principles regarding action affecting the environment, and to reinforce this mandate with action-forcing procedures and a statutory council to oversee implementation.

NEPA as enacted was divided into three sections and a preamble which declared it to be "An Act to establish a national policy for the environment, to provide for the establishment of a Council on Environmental Quality, and for other purposes." This statement was followed by a Statement of Purpose; Title I, Declaration of National Environmental Policy; and Title II, Council on Environmental Quality. Drafting of the Act occurred over the two-year period 1968–1969. There was widespread and strong public pressure on Congress to adopt a national policy to correct what were perceived to be environmentally destructive practices of federal agencies in pursuit of their statutory mandates. In the 90th and 91st Congresses as many as thirty-five bills were introduced to enact a broad national environmental policy and to establish a non-partisan council of ecological advisers.

Aside from establishing a Council on Environmental Quality (CEQ) and its specifying functions, set out in Title II, the principal provisions of NEPA were stated in Title I Section 101b detailing the substantive provisions of NEPA as follows:

In order to carry out the policy set forth in this Act, it is the continuing responsibility of the Federal Government to use all practicable means, consistent with other essential considerations of national policy, to improve and coordinate Federal plans, functions, programs, and resources to the end that the Nation may—

1. Fulfill the responsibilities of each generation as trustee of the environment for succeeding generations;
2. Assure for all Americans safe, healthful, productive, and aesthetically and culturally pleasing surroundings;
3. Attain the widest range of beneficial uses of the environment without degradation, risk to health or safety, or other undesirable and unintended consequences;
4. Preserve important historic, cultural, and natural aspects of our national heritage, and maintain, wherever possible, an environment which supports diversity, and variety of individual choice;
5. Achieve a balance between population and resource use which will permit high standards of living and a wide sharing of life's amenities; and
6. Enhance the quality of renewable resources and approach the maximum attainable recycling of depletable resources.

The action-forcing provisions, detailed in Section 102(2)c were, in effect, instructions to the federal agencies on how the substantive provisions of NEPA should be implemented. Although logically apparent in the text of the act, the connection was rarely observed by either the agencies or the courts. The environmental impact requirement was generally treated as a free-standing provision administered and often adjudicated without reference to other provisions of the act. Following are the operative provisions of Section 101(2)(c):

> The Congress authorizes and directs that, to the fullest extent possible: 1) the policies, regulations, and public laws of the United States shall be interpreted and administered in accordance with the policies set forth in this Act, and 2) all agencies of the Federal Government shall:
>
> c. Include in every recommendation or report on proposals for legislation and other major Federal actions significantly affecting the quality of the human environment, a detailed statement by the responsible official on—

> i. The environmental impact of the proposed action,
> ii. Any adverse environmental effects which cannot be avoided should the proposal be implemented,
> iii. Alternatives to the proposed action,
> iv. The relationship between local short-term uses of man's environment and the maintenance and enhancement of long-term productivity, and
> v. Any irreversible and irretrievable commitments of resources which would be involved in the proposed action should it be implemented.

The provisions of NEPA were largely the work of congressional committee staff, the Congressional Research Bureau, and individual Senate and House members. Unlike most legislation NEPA originated in Congress instead of the White House or the major nongovernmental conservation and environmental organizations. President Nixon initially opposed the bill and established a cabinet-level environmental council to make NEPA unnecessary. But once enacted NEPA received more presidential support than it was to receive under subsequent presidential administrations. At no time, however, was NEPA or the environment a high White House priority, and many of its provisions under Title II were never put into effect.

Although NEPA had public acceptance it had little public understanding and did not elicit the focused attention given to specific issues such as clean air and water, endangered species, and wilderness protection. The environmental organizations had relatively little interest in it until they discovered that the impact statement provision enabled them to block or to force revision of the federal actions which they opposed.

NEPA was unique or certainly exceptional in the broad sweep of its mandate. In effect it amended the mission statutes of all federal agencies having impacts upon the environment. Its substantive objectives enumerated in Section 101(b) differentiated it from all other statutes. NEPA principles articulate basic goals of environmental policy rather than addressing specific contentious issues and environmental hazards. A political weakness of NEPA was that it dealt with general principles, not with particular issues that aroused popular apprehension and protest. Unlike Not in My Back Yard (NIMBY) issues, siting of incinerators, clearcutting of ancient forests, and additions to or subtractions from the endangered species list, NEPA did not arouse passionate advocacy and intense lobbying. Elections may turn on NIMBY issues but environmental principles per se, although widely favored, may fail to obtain popular support sufficient to overcome public apathy, inertia, and political expediency. It was therefore possible for successive presidents with little commitment to NEPA principles to largely ignore the CEQ, to prevent implementation of most of Title II of the act, to severely restrict the CEQ budget, and to leave commissioner positions unfilled.

During the gestation and drafting of NEPA a persisting question was whether the legislation could be written in such a way that federal agency personnel would be compelled to pay attention to the principles declared by the act. Would NEPA become no more than a high-sounding rhetorical statement which would have little if any effect upon agency policy and performance? Many members of Congress wanted to satisfy an unmistakable public demand for action of some kind without imposing any new responsibility upon government or antagonizing influential congressional committees. However, on April 16, 1969, the concept of an environmental impact statement (EIS) was introduced in a hearing before the Senate Committee on Interior and Insular Affairs. Paradoxically the EIS, intended to force action on the substantive provisions of the act, became, in the minds of many people and in the opinion of many in the judiciary, the essence of the act itself.

Whatever its effect in the United States—other than the necessity of impact assessments—NEPA has been one of the most widely emulated of U.S. laws in other countries. At least eighty-three governments have been reported as having adopted the impact assessment concept. Many states and many nations have now written NEPA-like environmental protection provisions into their constitutions. At the time that NEPA was being drafted a number of constitutional amendments for the environment were being proposed. But the congressional advocates of environmental protection believed that a statute with an action-forcing provision (i.e., the environmental impact statement requirement) would achieve their objectives whereas a constitutional amendment would arouse latent opposition. The amending process would be unavoidably attenuated and the outcome uncertain.

At the time of its enactment no one—including federal agencies, the private business sector, and the academic community—took the act seriously. Among the news media only the newsweekly *Time* adequately assessed the potential of the act. NEPA had no militant advocates comparable to groups importuning Congress for legislation on behalf of clean air and water, control of toxic materials, protection of endangered species, or preservation of natural areas. The substantive provisions of Section 101(b) have never been actual presidential priorities. Provisions declared in principle could: 1) become politically controversial if applied in practice; 2) complicate presidential agendas, and provide little political reward.

Even so NEPA had advocates that regarded it as environmental Magna Carta. Its twentieth anniversary in 1990 was the occasion for numerous symposia and a declaration by President George Bush. Yet three years later the future of NEPA was uncertain. In February 1993 the Clinton administration proposed legislation to abolish the CEQ and transfer oversight of the EIS process to a cabinet level Department of Environmental Protection. Opposition in the House of Representatives to the placing oversight of NEPA in a single cabinet-level department led to compromise wherein an Office of NEPA Compliance with a single director subject to Senate confirmation replaced the CEQ. Whether this new arrangement would result in more effective implementation of NEPA or merely in monitoring implementation of environmental impact assessments was not clear. President Clinton then established an Office of Environmental Quality within the White House Staff, but was unable to legally abolish the CEQ without amending NEPA. A skeleton CEQ continued under a director and three full time staff members.

In July 1994 the leadership in the Senate Committee on Environment and Public Works reversed its earlier support of the President's proposal and called upon him to restore the CEQ to its full statutory status as the principal overseer of NEPA. The CEQ has been an integral part of NEPA and central to its administration.

As of mid-1994 restoration and continuation of its statutory role seemed probable. The full implementation of NEPA however, remains to be achieved and requires a more positive reinforcement by the President.

Lynton K. Caldwell

Further Readings

Caldwell, Lynton K. *Science and the National Environmental Policy Act: Redirecting Policy Through Procedural Reform.* 1982.

———. *Man and His Environment: Policy and Administration.* 1975.

Rosenbaum, Walter A. *Environmental Politics and Policy.* 1991.

Smith, Zachary A. *The Environmental Policy Paradox.* 1992.

See also COUNCIL ON ENVIRONMENTAL QUALITY; ENVIRONMENTAL IMPACT ASSESSMENT; ENVIRONMENTAL PROTECTION AGENCY

National Forests (U.S.)

The National Forest System today consists of 191 million acres in forty-four states, Puerto Rico, and the Virgin Islands. These public lands comprise 8.5 percent of the total land area. There are 185 administrative units: 155 national forests, twenty national grasslands, and ten land utilization projects. Since 1905 they have been managed by the U.S. Forest Service—the largest agency in the Department of Agriculture.

On March 3, 1891, President Benjamin Harrison signed into law authorization for himself and future presidents to reserve certain forested lands from the public domain. Promptly on March 30 he proclaimed the nation's first federal forest, the Yellowstone Park Timberland Reserve in Wyoming, which in 1908 was renamed the Shoshone National Forest. The Yellowstone reserve consisted of 1.2 million acres, and in the next few years, 16.3 million acres were added. President Grover Cleveland set aside another 21 million acres in 1897 without consulting Congress and set off a furor that nearly caused the whole effort to be abolished.

For the six years following 1891 Congress debated the purposes for which the forests could be established. Parliamentary pragmatism had caused all such language to be deleted from the original law, leaving only the authority for presidential proclamation. Amid the ruckus prompted by President Cleveland's actions, Congress ended its debate and on June 6, 1897, a rider to the appropriations bill for the Geological Survey became law and described the purposes for the forests. No reservation was to be made except to protect future supplies of water and timber; the tone of the statute is clear, the reserves were to enhance commercial activities in the West.

President William McKinley declined to proclaim any reserves, and it would not be until after 1901 that President Theodore Roosevelt would resume the reservation process. In the meantime the forest reserves were managed by the General Land Office (GLO) of the Department of the Interior. In 1901 GLO established its Division R to handle management responsibility, but widespread and essentially chronic corruption in Interior coupled with an inadequately staffed Division R prompted the Roosevelt administration to transfer the forests to the Bureau of Forestry in the Department of Agriculture. The transfer took place on February 1, 1905, and shortly thereafter the agency's name was changed to Forest Service. In 1907 the reserves were renamed as national forests.

President Roosevelt and his chief forester, Gifford Pinchot, made full use of the authority to create and expand national forests. As part

---

TABLE 1

Selected FY 1991 Statistics

National Forest System	191 Million Acres
National Forest System Lands Burned	98 Thousand Acres
Insect and Disease Suppression	1.5 Million Acres
Wilderness	33.6 Million Acres
Watershed Improvements	35,091 Acres
Wildlife and Fish Habitat Improvements	486,538 Acres
Reforestation	503 Thousand Acres
Recreation Use	279 Million Visitor Days
Trail System	116,585 Miles
National Scenic Byways	4,900 Miles
National Wild and Scenic River System	3,417 Miles
Livestock Grazing	9.5 Million Animal Unit Months
Grazing Allotments Administered	10 Thousand Permits
Mineral Cases Processed	25,349
Timber Sold	6.4 Billion Board Feet
Timber Harvested	8.5 Billion Board Feet
Road System	368 Thousand Miles
Woodland Owners Assisted	153,090
Research Publications	2,404
Permanent Full-Time Employees	34,861
Human Resource Programs	134,620 Persons Served
Expenditures	$3.42 Billion
Receipts	$1.44 Billion

The Forest Service

United States Department of Agriculture

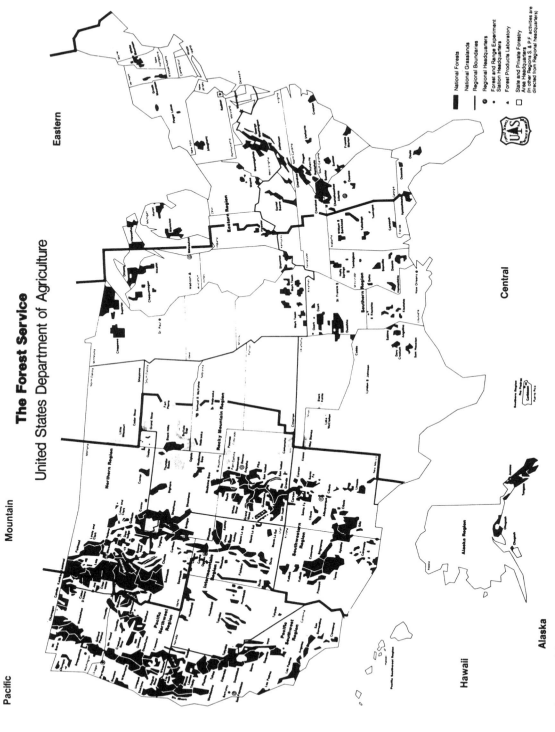

Courtesy of the Forest History Society, Durham, N.C.

453

of the broader conservation movement Roosevelt proclaimed over 100 million new acres as national forests, but in 1907 Congress asserted its authority and essentially eliminated the president's ability to set aside more. From then on it would be Congress and not the president that would establish national forests.

For a decade Congress had debated the wisdom of authorizing the purchase of lands east of the Mississippi River for national forest purposes. On March 1, 1911, the Weeks Act was signed into law. Thereafter it was possible to purchase and add land to the national forests to protect the headwaters of navigable rivers. Until then all forests had been reserved from the public domain. The distinction is more than academic; purchased forests tended to not have federal mineral and other rights, greatly confounding their future management. Perhaps not so significant, Interior committees in Congress claimed jurisdiction over reserved forests, while Agriculture committees handled those that were purchased. Today, more than 24 million acres, essentially all of the eastern national forests, have been purchased under the Weeks Law and subsequent authorizations.

The National Forest Management Act (NFMA) of 1976 is another turning point. For the first time, Congress prescribed how the national forests were to be managed, instead of delegating broad authority to the executive branch agency. This law and others also mandated a planning process that included the general public. Finally NFMA gave statutory permanence to all national forests. Most had existed on the basis of an executive proclamation, and technically, any president could have rescinded the order. The national forests are now here to stay.

Harold K. Steen

Further Readings

Robinson, Glen O. *The Forest Service: A Study in Public Land Management*. 1975.
Steen, Harold K. *The Origins of the Natural Forests*. 1992.
———. *The U.S. Forest Service: A History*. 1992.

See also BIOSPHERE RESERVES; FOREST SERVICE (U.S.); FORESTRY, HISTORY OF; NATIONAL PARKS: UNITED STATES; PINCHOT, GIFFORD; SUSTAINED YIELD FORESTRY

National Park Service (U.S.)

The National Park Service was formed within the Department of Interior in 1916 to "conserve the scenery and the natural and historic objects and the wildlife therein and to provide . . . for the enjoyment of future generations" and "the preservation of nature as it exists" (1916 Park Organic Act, U.S. Congress: 1, 3). An inherent juggling act was foisted on the service by asking it to offer public access while preserving nature undisturbed.

The service is headed by a national director, who oversees ten regional offices and 366 areas covering more than 80 million acres. The 51 national parks and numerous national rivers, seashores, preserves, monuments, battlefields, historic sites, and so forth receive more than 270 million annual visitors.

Guidance for management comes from the Organic Act and successive congressional mandates, the enabling legislation for each area, and the regulations for specific activities within all or part of the system. During the first decades, manipulations such as predator control, animal feeding, and fire suppression were the norm. However, a vigorous push to extract park timber and mineral resources during World War II, combined with an Interior Department campaign to build dams even within national parks, eventually led to a public cry for park policy revisions. The current era of management largely began with the Leopold Report of 1963, which called for greater use of science and a shift toward nature-based management.

The Leopold Report and national legislation of the 1960s and 1970s brought a new emphasis on the preservation of entire native communities and the natural disturbance regimes (e.g., fires and flooding) that maintain them. The Park Service was also reoriented so that areas were managed for either recreational, historic, or natural values, which helped dissipate some of the contradictions of the Organic Act mandate.

Most research is conducted at the park level, though this has never been a major emphasis of the Park Service and it has been severely criticized for research inadequacies in recent years. Less than 2 percent of the annual budget is devoted to research and fewer than 25 percent of the parks have basic biological inventories, despite the fact that these lands contain 30 to 50 percent of the rare and endangered species in the United States and are vital to national biodiversity conservation. The newly resurrected National Biological Survey, with its mission to inventory and coordinate knowledge of biological resources on public lands, will undoubtedly improve this situation.

However, baseline information alone will not solve the many problems that come from the joint pressures of internal use and external development. Shenandoah and Great Smoky Mountains National Parks are blanketed by industrial smog. Yosemite valley resembles an urban freeway. In the Everglades historic water diversions have decimated wetlands and reduced wading bird numbers by 90 percent since 1900.

Even if we could protect our parks from external threats, these "islands" are neither large enough, nor sufficiently connected to other protected areas to support many native animals and communities. This has led people in and out of the Park Service to advocate a new ecosystem approach to management, in which essential linkages such as animal migrations and watershed flows are preserved and planning is large-scale and long-term. Ecosystem management requires cooperation and integration between all regional land managers. Private and public groups are currently trying to put ecosystem ideas to work in areas from the Pacific Northwest to the Great Lakes. Legislation and economic incentives are a few tools that can encourage this transformation, but ultimately its success will rest on wide public recognition that the preservation of natural areas is good for our air, water, and economies, as well as our minds and spirits.

Anne Peyton Curlee

Further Readings

DiSilvestro, R.L. *Reclaiming the Last Wild Places: A New Agenda for Biodiversity.* 1993.

Freemuth, J.C. *Islands under Siege: National Parks and the Politics of External Threats.* 1991.

National Research Council. *Science and the National Parks.* 1992.

Sax, J.L. *Mountains Without Handrails: Reflections on the National Parks.* 1980.

Simon, D.J., ed. *Our Common Lands: Defending the National Parks.* 1988.

See also CONSERVATION MOVEMENT; DEPARTMENT OF THE INTERIOR (U.S.); EVERGLADES OF SOUTH FLORIDA; NATIONAL FORESTS (U.S.); YELLOWSTONE NATIONAL PARK

National Parks: Australia

The nation of Australia is a federation of states which agreed (as independent colonies) to form a commonwealth under the Australian constitution in 1901. The Australian constitution specifies the areas of responsibilities granted by the states to the commonwealth which includes such matters as foreign affairs and defense. Environmental planning and management, and more specifically national park management, is not mentioned in the constitution. Hence these areas remain under the control of state governments.

By 1901 four of the states (then colonies) had declared "national" parks; since then all states, and later territories, have continued to declare and manage national parks. Conse-

TABLE 1

National Parks in Australia by State

State or Territory		1989	1990	1991
Australia Capital Territory	No. of Parks	1	1	1
	Area	94,000	94,000	94,000
	% reserved	39.1	39.1	39.1
Northern Territory	No. of Parks	6	5	12
	Area	542,213	179,000	1,775,618
	% reserved	1.8	0.13	1.3
New S. Wales	No. of Parks	63	68	69
	Area	3,100,513	3,145,000	3,188,180
	% reserved	3.9	3.92	3.9
Queensland	No. of Parks	94	336	339
	Area	2,978,544	3,627,000	4,019,484
	% reserved	3.9	2.1	3.9
South Australia	No. of Parks	12	12	14
	Area	2,648,453	3,021,000	3,035,293
	% reserved	2.7	3.1	3.1
Tasmania	No. of Parks	14	14	14
	Area	863,925	881,000	1,359,548
	% reserved	12.7	12.8	20.0
Victoria	No. of Parks	30	31	32
	Area	1,201,555	2,283,000	2,390,651
	% reserved	5.3	10.0	10.5
Western Australia	No. of Parks	51	59	59
	Area	4,724,830	4,835,000	4,849,395
	% reserved	1.9	1.9	1.9
Federal Parks	No. of Parks	3	4	4
	Area	1,890,108	2,117,000	2,122,145
	% reserved	—	—	—
Total for Australia	No. of Parks	274	530	544
	Area	18,044,141	20,180,000	22,834,314
	% reserved	2.3	2.6	2.9

*Kakadu N.P., Uluru N.P.: the area and number is listed under Federal Parks (commonwealth managed) but included in the percentage figures for the Northern Territory.

Source: Wescott, 1991; Hooy and Shaughnessy, 1992.

TABLE 2

Growth in National Parks in Australia, 1968 to 1990

State or Territory		1968	1978	1990	1991*	Proportionate Increase in Total Area 1968 to 1990
Australian	No. of Parks	0	0	1	1	
Capital	Area	0	0	0.094	0.094	—
Territory	% reserved	0	0	39.1	39.1	
Northern	No. of Parks	4	12	5	12	
Territory	Area	0.19	0.25	3.14	1.77	—
	% reserved	0.14	0.19	0.13	1.3	
New	No. of Parks	19	46	68	69	
South	Area	0.80	1.70	3.14	3.19	3.9
Wales	% reserved	1.0	2.1	3.92	3.9	
Queensland	No. of Parks	254	323	336	339	
	Area	0.90	2.18	3.63	4.02	4.0
	% reserved	0.54	1.26	2.1	3.1	
South	No. of Parks	6	8	12	14	
Australia	Area	0.21	0.23	3.02	3.04	14.4
	% reserved	0.2	0.23	3.1	3.1	
Tasmania	No. of Parks	—	12	14	14	
	Area	0.29	0.65	0.88	1.36	3.0
	% reserved	4.2	9.6	12.8	20.0	
Victoria	No. of Parks	20	26	31	32	
	Area	0.15	0.26	2.28	2.39	15.2
	% reserved	0.7	1.14	10.0	10.5	
Western	No. of Parks	35	42	59	59	
Australia	Area	0.33	4.56	4.83	4.85	14.6
	% reserved	0.13	1.8	1.9	1.9	
Federal	No. of Parks	—	—	4	4	—
Parks	Area	—	—	2.117	2.12	—
	% reserved	—	—	—	—	—
Total for	No. of Parks	338	469	530	544	
Australia	Area	2.9	9.8	20.1	22.8	7.0
	% reserved	0.38	1.27	2.6	2.9	

Notes: Areas × 10⁶ hectares.

Source: Wescott, 1991; *Hooy and Shughnessy, 1992.

quently the vast majority of national parks in Australia are declared and managed by state governments.

In an attempt to set some guidelines for state governments the then Council of Nature Conservation Ministers (CONCOM, now Australia and New Zealand Environment and Conservation Council, ANZECC), made up of state and federal conservation ministers, adopted the following definition of a national park: "A relatively large area set aside for its features of predominantly unspoiled natural landscape, flora and fauna, permanently dedicated for public enjoyment, education and inspiration and protected from all interference other than essential management practices, so that its natural attributes are preserved" (McMichael, 1980). This definition does not attempt to explain the meaning of the word "national" in the context of "national park" but since it cannot refer to the level of government managing the park most observers presume it refers to the parks being of national significance. This definition is not binding on state and territory governments.

National parks in Australia developed sporadically from the first declared—the (Royal) National Park in 1879 outside Sydney—through to the late 1960s. The late 1960s marked a watershed for conservation in Australia and since 1968 the increase in national park area and size has been very substantial (see Table 2).

The figures for 1990 in Table 2 account for any area a state government labeled a "national park" by June 30 of that year. The number of parks is very high because of the Queensland government's policy of naming separate islands as separate parks.

The Australian national park system covered approximately 2.9 percent of the Australian land mass and contained approximately 22 million hectares in 1991 (the most recent figures available; Hooy and Shaughnessy, 1992). There are also a series of other reserves and protected areas, bringing this figure up to approximately 6.4 percent of the continent.

In the marine environment there are 158 protected areas covering over 39.5 million hectares in Australia with over 34.3 million of these hectares in the Great Barrier Reef Marine Park. This marine park is managed by the Great Barrier Reef Marine Park Authority under the commonwealth government auspices.

In conclusion the Australian national park system is very extensive in both area and percentage reservation, which has shown a massive increase in the past twenty-five years. The vast majority of these parks are managed by state governments and the individual parks vary from extremely large (e.g., Rudall River National Park at 1,569,459 hectares) to small islands in the Great Barrier Reef of only a few hectares.

Geoff Wescott

Further Readings

Hooy, T., and G. Shaughnessy, eds. *Terrestrial and Marine Protected Areas in Australia (1991)*. Australia National Parks and Wildlife Service, 1992.

McMichael, D.F. "An International Perspective." In *The Value of National Parks to the Community*. Ed. J. Messer and G. Mosley. Australian Conservation Foundation, 1980: 34–43.

Wescott, G. "Australia's Distinctive National Parks System." *Environmental Conservation* 18 (1991): 331–40.

See also CORAL REEFS; NATIONAL PARKS: CANADA; NATIONAL PARKS: UNITED STATES; YELLOWSTONE NATIONAL PARK

National Parks: Canada

In 1885 the first national park in Canada was established incorporating Banff Hot Springs in the Rocky Mountains. Modeled on Yellowstone National Park and Arkansas Hot Springs in the United States it was intended to preserve the scenery and encourage tourism on the new Canadian Pacific Railway. Thereafter additional parks were established for a succession of reasons including: scenic protection (e.g., Glacier National Park, 1886); preserving endangered species (e.g., Wood Buffalo National Park, 1922); providing a park in each province (e.g., Riding Mountain National Park, 1929); contributing to regional economic development (e.g., Kejimkujik National Park, 1967); and extending the system into the north (e.g., Auyuittuq National Park, 1976). Key initiatives in the development and management of the park system were: The Rocky Mountain Park Act of 1887, the creation of the Dominion (of Canada) Parks Branch in 1911, The National Parks Act of 1930, the first Parks Canada Policy in 1964, a National Parks System Plan in 1971, and a revised policy in 1979. Today the national parks are administered by Parks Canada in the Department of Canadian Heritage, with headquarters in Ottawa, and a new policy is being considered.

There are at present thirty-four national parks located in all the provinces and territories of Canada. The largest park in the system—and one of the largest in the world—is Wood Buffalo National Park (44,670 square kilometers) and the smallest is St. Lawrence Islands National Park (6 square kilometers). The most southerly park is Point Pelee National Park (16 square kilometers) and the most northerly is Ellesmere Island National Park (37,775 square kilometers).

National parks attract many visitors—mainly in summer—largely from Canada and the United States. Banff National Park, one of the most popular, attracts 4 million visitors annually, while some parks in the north receive fewer than 1,000 visitors per year. Visitation is increasing in most parks and the economic impacts of park use can be considerable.

Today the objective of Parks Canada is "to provide for all time representative natural areas of Canadian significance in a system of national parks, and to encourage public understanding, appreciation and enjoyment of this natural heritage so as to leave it unimpaired for future generations." More specifically the aim is to provide at least one park in each of the thirty-nine biophysical regions of the country. In 1990 the federal government, concerned that only twenty-one regions were represented in the system, and stimulated by the Endangered Spaces Campaign, proclaimed in the Green Plan its intention to establish five new national parks by 1996, and reach agreements to establish a further thirteen parks to complete the system by the year 2000. This proposal will require the support of the general public, local residents, the provinces, native governments, and other land users. The government also intends to establish marine national parks to represent the twenty-nine marine regions around Canada's three coasts and the Great Lakes. Fathom five in Ontario was the first of these.

Some Canadian national parks have now been recognized by the United Nations Educational, Scientific, and Cultural Organization (UNESCO) as World Heritage Sites (e.g., Nahanni National Park) and biosphere reserves (e.g., Waterton Lakes National Park); others also are being considered for such status. Several national parks, such as Waterton Lake and Kluane, that are adjacent to protected areas in the United states are recognized as international parks.

National parks face a variety of problems. These include the environmental impact of increased recreational use and tourism development, the need to ensure public safety, pollution such as acid precipitation caused by activities outside parks, ecological imbalances due to past management of fires and predators, and threats to the ecological integrity of parks as a consequence of their limited size and isolation. A balance must be found between preservation and use, parks must be zoned to reflect carrying capacity and appropriate use of various habitats, more parks must be created, a regional approach to their management adopted, and public education increased.

Public interest groups particularly concerned with national parks include: the Canadian Parks and Wilderness Society, the World Wildlife Fund (Canada), and the Canadian Nature Federation.

John Marsh

Further Readings

Dearden, P., and R. Rollins. *Parks and Protected Areas in Canada.* 1993.
Hummel, Monte. *Endangered Spaces: The Future for Canada's Wilderness.* 1989.
Stephenson, Mary-Lee. *Canada's National Parks: A Visitor's Guide.* 1983.

See also BIOREGION; BIOSPHERE RESERVES; CANADIAN NATURE FEDERATION; CARRYING CAPACITY; CONSERVATION MOVEMENT; GREEN PLAN (CANADA); HABITAT FRAGMENTATION, PATCHES, AND CORRIDORS; NATIONAL PARKS: AUSTRALIA; NATIONAL PARKS: UNITED STATES; WOOD BUFFALO NATIONAL PARK; WORLD WILDLIFE FUND

National Parks: United States

The United States national park system comprises over 350 units which together cover more than 80 million acres. These units are found in forty-nine states, the District of Columbia, and areas outside the continental United States. The park system is a diverse and sometimes confusing set of land designations. Besides the familiar national park designation there are also national monuments, national preserves, national lakeshores, national rivers, wild and scenic rivers, national scenic trails, national military parks, national battlefield parks, national battlefield sites, national battlefields, national historic parks, national memorials, national recreation areas, and national parkways.

Early Park History and Policy

It has been said that the national park idea is one of America's contributions to world civilization and culture. Yellowstone National Park—located primarily in Wyoming—is the world's first national park. The setting aside of Yellowstone is usually considered a break from past American public land policies since its 2 million plus acres were reserved from various forms of entry and instead set aside for public enjoyment. Other parks such as Yosemite and Crater Lake followed Yellowstone, prior to the establishment of the National Park Service in 1916.

Much has been written about the national park idea as it developed in the United States. Historian Roderick Nash, in *Wilderness and the American Mind* (1982), has suggested that several key factors influenced the development of the national park idea: affluence, belief in democracy, American's experience with nature, and the extent of the public land base. Another historian, Alfred Runte, has offered a more controversial thesis to explain the public acceptance of national parks in America. Dubbed the "worthless lands" thesis Runte's argument is that the early national parks were economically valueless and thus more easily set aside as national parks. Runte added that a view of these natural areas as natural "wonders" comparable to Europe's monuments of civilization also contributed to their reservation.

Some of the early national parks were administered by the U.S. army, which, by most accounts, did a credible job in park administration, perhaps also leaving a model for both the style and uniform of the early park rangers. After the discovery of cliff dwellings and other Native American sites Congress passed the Antiquities Act of 1906, which gave the president the authority to declare national monuments. These early monuments were administered by a variety of agencies such as the army and United States Forest Service, and were often located in southwestern states. Later presidents would use the 1906 Act to set aside areas (such as the Grand Canyon) until Congress either chose to make them national parks, or to protect the areas in the absence of congressional initiative.

Calls for the creation of a national agency to manage the national parks began as early as 1900, but it was the controversy over the damming of spectacular Hetch Hetchy Valley in Yosemite National Park which led to the establishment of the National Park Service (NPS) in 1916. The "Organic Act" which created NPS charged the bureau with a mission that has often been in tension with itself. The key section of the 1916 Act calls on NPS, in areas under its administration, to "conserve the scenery and the wild life therein, and to provide for the enjoyment of the same in such manner and by such means as will leave them unimpaired for the enjoyment of future generations" (16 *United States Code* 1–1a). Many park policy observers have dubbed this section the source of the "use versus preservation" dilemma facing NPS.

The early policy of the NPS was clearly tilted toward the promotion of park visitation and enjoyment. From an agency survival perspective this policy seems essential. The NPS faced both a hostile Forest Service and a not always sympathetic Congress. Early directors Stephen Mather and Horace Albright needed to build support for the bureau and did so by combining public enjoyment, local economic benefits, and a popular belief that the parks were a wonderful public good into a successful coalition-building strategy. Mather and Albright were also successful in getting new units added to the system.

The Park System Widens

There are two pivotal changes which occurred to the park system. The first added historic preservation to the bureau's mission. In 1933 Horace Albright was able to convince President Franklin Roosevelt that the great Civil War battlefields belonged under NPS care, thus finally distancing the mission and purpose of the NPS from the mission of the Forest Service. Debate continues to this day as to whether historic preservation remains secondary to the preservation of natural areas in the eyes of many in the NPS.

The Forest Service was also successful, however, in fending off new national park proposals by setting aside primitive areas inside the more utilitarian-based national forests. These areas would later form the core of the U.S. wilderness preservation system. The Forest Service did lose its national monuments to NPS in the 1933 presidential order.

The second change had to do with a redefinition of the "purity" of the national parks, with the inclusion of national recreation areas in the park system. President Roosevelt's Secretary of Interior, Harold Ickes, saw the national recreation area concept as a way to increase the park system at the expense of the Forest Service. These areas would be less "pure" than national parks, but would still have recreation as the dominant land use. The first national recreation area was Lake Mead in Nevada. Today the concept has evolved into a catch-all which includes areas around water impoundments such as Lake Mead, urban areas such as Golden Gate, and quasi-natural areas such as Hells Canyon which is under the administration of the Forest Service. It seems very possible that the national recreation area concept opened the door to the bewildering set of areas now in the U.S. park system.

The Environmental Era

The post-World War II era saw a tremendous explosion of public use of parks. NPS director Conrad Wirth developed the noted multi-year "Mission 66" development plan to deal with this growth. This plan, however, began to drive the NPS and the environmental movement apart, as environmentalists came to view the bureau as too development oriented. NPS opposition to the movement to pass a Wilderness Act also fueled environmentalist criticism.

Concern for the other "half" of the NPS mission began to grow in the 1960s. In the 1930s NPS had begun taking a closer look at the management and research needs of the "preservation" side of the bureau's mission. In 1933 NPS issued the report *Fauna of the National Parks of the United States*, written by George Wright, Ben Thompson, and Joseph Dixon. This report was the first attempt to bring biological expertise into park resource preservation concerns. Wright's untimely death dealt a blow to the effort, however. The 1960s saw the effort resurface, with continued calls for a focused research and resource management component to the NPS mission. By the early 1990s many of the large national parks had resource managers added to park staff. A 1992 National Academy of Science Report *Science and the National Parks* called for an accelerated and focused science program in the parks. President Bill Clinton's secretary of the Interior, Bruce Babbitt, devised a plan to create a National Biological Survey (NBS) that may have rendered this call more problematic, since that research effort will likely become in part an NBS function.

Concern for park resources and values has been reflected in another way as well. During the 1970s and 1980s repeated attention was drawn to the so-called "external threats" issue. That issue concerned activities outside national parks that impaired the resources and values within the parks. Some examples include air pollution, nearby mineral extraction, and adjacent land development. Progress on addressing the threats problem has been slow, because of the complexity of jurisdictional and political issues.

However, one of the proposed solutions to the threats problem—ecosystem management—has gained currency throughout the federal land policy environment. Ecosystem management is based on the assumption that current park and other federal, state, and private land boundaries are inadequate to protect many of the biological resources which often intermingle between them. Ecosystem management envisions a more "holistic" approach to natural resource management, in which the entire ecosystem of which a park is only a part would be managed to maximize the protection of ecosystem processes. The concept is in its infancy, and remains fraught with conceptual difficulties, as the controversial attempt to pioneer ecosystem management in Greater Yellowstone in the late 1980s would attest. The effort to further refine and implement ecosystem management is likely to continue; it appears to have the full support of both the current administration and each of the land management agencies.

The National Park Policy Environment

The policy environment surrounding the National Park Service can be viewed in terms of who sets national park policy, and whether that policy should usually err on the side of "use" or on the side of "preservation." It seems clear that the past twenty or so years have seen an increased politicization of the NPS, with more and more agency decisions often made outside the career levels of the agency. The actors include both higher level appointees in administrations of both political parties, and members of Congress who have developed both an interest and an expertise in national park policy. These actors are supported by a variety of interest groups who fall on both sides of the use versus preservation question. The Reagan administration policies often received support from concessionaires operating within parks, local "gateway" communities, and local members of Congress in whose districts or states lie various national parks. Conversely, a more pro-preservation administration such as President Carter's or President Clinton's would find support from environmentalists and members of Congress favoring the preservation side of the NPS mission. It is fair to say that there is often not much deference to NPS expertise on how to manage national parks, by either pro-use, or pro-preservation forces unless a management decision is non-controversial.

The NPS, like any other large organization, has a variety of actors who hold different opinions about proper national park policy. Dominant among them are the park superintendents, still drawn primarily from the "park ranger" job series. Superintendents must often walk a tight line between use and preservation policies, due to the influence of other non-agency actors in the policy arena. Park resource managers and scientists are strong advocates for the preservation side of the NPS mission, and have occasionally criticized park management for what they perceived as overly pro-use policies. In addition there are several factions within NPS made up of groups of members with particular formative agency experiences and career networks, which have been useful as the members entered management ranks. Two of the most important have been anecdotally reported as the "Yosemite Mafia" and the "Alaska Mafia." The first group is influential in bureau law enforcement and park ranger policies, with its formative experience in Yosemite National Park. The second group had formative experiences during NPS development of the Alaska national park units in the late 1970s and early 1980s, and has carried that experience with it into management positions throughout the NPS.

New National Parks?

There continue to be calls for new U.S. national parks. Such calls appear increasingly difficult to bring to fruition for a number of reasons. First, there is often intense local opposition to park units which curtail traditional resource extraction, or multiple-use activities, as well as hunting. This opposition at times has led to political compromises which create units of the park system to allow hunting, grazing, and sometimes mineral activity. There is debate over whether such units have, or have not compromised the park system. Second, some people argue that the current park system is so underfunded that new units would put an excessive strain on NPS budgets. Such arguments at times may be disingenuous strategies designed in opposition to the proposed new units.

The national park idea and the national park system are on balance a success. The idea has spread, and there are park systems all over the world. While not all aspects of the American system can or should be copied (the issue of the treatment of indigenous people perhaps being one example) it nevertheless remains a magnet for tourists, scientists, and environmentalists from around the world.

John C. Freemuth

Further Readings

Foresta, Ronald. *America's National Parks and Their Keepers.* 1984.

Freemuth, John. "The National Parks: Political Versus Professional Determinants of Policy." *Public Administration Review* 49 (1988): 278–86.

Runte, Alfred. *National Parks: The American Experience.* 1987.

See also ALASKA: PARK, WILDERNESS, AND RESOURCE ISSUES; BUREAU OF LAND MANAGEMENT; CONSERVATION MOVEMENT; DEPARTMENT OF THE INTERIOR (U.S.); FOREST SERVICE (U.S.); HETCH HETCHY DAM; ICKES, HAROLD L.; MINERAL KING CANYON; NATIONAL PARK SERVICE (U.S.); REAGAN, RONALD; WILDERNESS ACT; YELLOWSTONE NATIONAL PARK

National Security, Reconceptualizing

A nation has the legitimate function of providing security to its citizenry. Traditionally this

solemn governmental obligation has been considered to refer only to the security of the nation from potential enemy attacks, thus falling entirely within the aegis of the nation's military sector.

The concept of national security, however, needs to be expanded to one in which protection from external military aggression represents only one part of an array of securities for which a nation must assume responsibility. Such a reconceptualization of national security is an amalgam of interlocking social and environmental securities, none of which can have a favorable long-term prognosis unless all of them are at least reasonably well satisfied. Additionally involved is the notion that most of the threats to national security can be handled only at an international level—sometimes globally, but more often regionally, that is, jointly by a group of contiguous nations.

Social security—the first of the two major linked components of comprehensive human security—is comprised of four interconnected parts: 1) political security, based on participatory democracy by an informed public, a free press, and a robust legal system; 2) military security, based on a purely defensive and thus non-provocative posture and on the rejection of nuclear or other weapons of mass destruction; 3) economic security, based on a guaranteed minimum income and on access to housing, medical care, old-age care, child care, and education; and 4) personal security, based on justice, equity, gender equality, and respect for others.

Environmental security—the second of the two major linked components of comprehensive human security—is comprised of two interconnected parts: 1) environmental protection, based on protection from wartime and similar vandalism, protection from medically unacceptable environmental pollution, and—for special areas—protection from all permanent human intrusions; and 2) sane resource utilization, based on use or harvesting at levels and with procedures that either maintain or restore optimal resource services or stocks. In further reference to environmental protection, the protection of special areas from all permanent human intrusions—which in the aggregate should amount to perhaps 10 to 12 percent of each nation—is the sine qua non for conserving the world's biodiversity. Regarding sane resource utilization the exploitation of renewable resources must be carried out strictly on the principle of sustained use or sustained discard; and the exploitation of non-renewable resources strictly on the principles of efficiency and frugality.

The interconnectedness and reciprocal dependence of environmental security issues and social security issues can be readily illustrated. Natural biogeochemical cycles and ecosystems have national political boundaries superimposed upon them; they are also affected by national development activities as well as by international economic and other ties. The former natural phenomena are thus often disrupted by the latter social ones. Many of the major crops in developed countries now have a limited genetic base and depend for their future improvement and even survival on plant varieties from developing countries. Furthermore international tension arises in part from such environmental problems as acid rain, pollution of international rivers and regional seas, famine owing to soil erosion, major industrial accidents, and exploitation of regional international commons. Thus it is clear that common threats force nations to seek ways in which to foster international environmental security, thereby contributing to both national and global security. Moreover environmental stress may be applied locally or regionally, but the effects might be felt regionally or globally. Among such possible effects are the movement of environmental refugees from areas of stress to other areas, creating a new stress there.

Those environmental abuses deriving from immediate survival needs could, and should be substantially reduced through the establishment of more nearly equitable global systems of natural resource distribution on the one hand and through the global sharing of expertise in environmental conservation and rehabilitation on the other. However, equitable distribution and sharing of this sort must, in the long term, be coupled with an essentially stable global population, indeed, a global population that becomes stabilized at some level significantly lower than the one of today.

In the meantime it is vital that we begin eliminating unnecessary environmental abuses. For example, a retrenchment of the military sector of society will provide not only a direct boon to the environment through a reduction in wartime disruption, but also an indirect one—by making available material, financial, and intellectual resources for the pursuit of socially and environmentally valuable improvements.

Arthur H. Westing

Further Readings

Brown, Lester R. *Redefining National Security*. 1977.

Ullman, Richard H. "Redefining Security." *International Security* 8 (1) (1983–1984): 129–53.

Westing, Arthur H. "An Expanded Concept of International Security." In *Global Resources and International Conflict: Environmental Factors in Strategic Policy and Action*. Ed. Arthur H. Westing. 1986: 183–200.

———. "Environmental Dimensions of Maritime Security." *Maritime Security: The Building of Confidence*. Ed. Josef Goldblat. 1992: 91–102.

———. "Human Rights and the Environment." *Environmental Conservation* 20 (1993): 99–100.

See also ENVIRONMENTAL PROTECTION IN WARTIME; ENVIRONMENTAL REFUGEES; NUCLEAR WEAPONS PRODUCTION; NUCLEAR WINTER

National Wildlife Federation

The National Wildlife Federation (NWF) of the United States, perhaps the largest conservation organization in the world, is a coalition of state wildlife federations. Founded in 1936 NWF is comprised of individual members within the state federations who are predominantly hunters and fishers. In 1993 total membership in the organization stood at 5,300,000. NWF has one president and chief executive officer, Jay D. Hair, as well as thirteen regional directors and ten NWF Natural Resource Centers spread throughout the country. NWF has an organization in every state as well as the Virgin Islands, with periodical publications including *International Wildlife*, *National Wildlife*, and *Ranger Rick*, a children's magazine.

The organization is politically complex, with a long history of skillful leadership. The state-based organizations—which are primarily hunting and fishing oriented—are not the principle source of funds for the national organization (based in Washington, D.C.). Following World War II the national organization took on direct "associate" members, a good proportion of which are oriented to wildlife appreciation, more than to a consumption-oriented wildlife protection perspective. Many join simply to obtain the high-quality publications. For example, by the 1970s *Ranger Rick* had achieved a circulation of over 2 million. The organization is generally unified on questions of habitat protection, the protection of endangered species, and wildlife conservation. However, all of its several types of members do not share the same view of hunting in particular. Some see it as desirable and appropriate and others do not.

The organization has, however, taken strong preservationist stances in solidarity with a wide variety of conservation and environmental organizations. It has in recent years considerably broadened the range of issues in which it involves itself. The NWF has taken strong positions on air and water pollution and on toxic wastes. The organization's self-stated mission is to " . . . educate, inspire and assist individuals and organizations to conserve wildlife and other natural resources and to protect the Earth's environment." It sponsors programs for school educators, youth hiking and backpacking camps, and a wide variety of educational programs concerning predators, soil, air pollution, water, forests, eagles, and many other topics.

Robert Paehlke

Further Readings

Hays, Samuel P. *Beauty, Health and Permanence: Environmental Politics in the United States, 1955–1985.* 1987.

National Wildlife Federation. *1993 Conservation Directory.* 1993.

See also CONSERVATION MOVEMENT; DEEP ECOLOGY: EMERGENCE; WILDERNESS; WILDLIFE PROTECTION: HISTORY

Natural Resources Defense Council

The Natural Resources Defense Council (NRDC) was founded with a Ford Foundation grant in 1970 by six lawyers concerned with environmental issues. In its early years it generated many landmark environmental law cases designed to force the U.S. Environmental Protection Agency (EPA) to enforce environmental statutes such as the Clean Air and Clean Water acts. It challenged many nuclear reactors, arguing that the environmental impact statements (EIS) written for them were inadequate and did not take into consideration many real threats to human health from radiation.

While maintaining an active litigation schedule, in later years NRDC expanded its tactics to include testimony to Congress on many legislative issues, including re-authorizing the Clean Air and Clean Water acts. NRDC started a citizens' legal action program in 1982 in which its attorneys sue industrial polluters directly when they believe that government is unable or unwilling to enforce the laws effectively. It also expanded its staff to include scientists and economists and often negotiates directly with industry when its board of directors feels that this would be productive.

NRDC conducts educational workshops in many law schools for students interested in public interest litigation. It provides scientific and legal internships to graduate students. Its quarterly publication, *The Amicus Journal,* was established in 1979 and features articles on timely issues concerning pollution, public health, and resource conservation. It also publishes a monthly NRDC *Newsline* for its membership giving details about court cases in which it is involved, as well as reporting on relevant congressional and agency hearings.

NRDC maintains offices in New York, Washington, San Francisco, Los Angeles, and Honolulu; its national headquarters is in New York where it purchased a building in 1988 and refurbished it for energy efficiency. It depends for revenues on contributions, foundation grants, and dues from its 125,000 members.

Because of its public health concerns, NRDC's primary focus initially was pollution control. In 1986 a staff NRDC attorney participated in the Campaign for Pesticide Reform through which forty-one organizations negotiated with the agricultural chemical industry to reach an agreement about the Federal Insecticide, Fungicide and Rodenticide Act. Some of this was incorporated in amendments to the law Congress passed in 1988. In 1988 NRDC published *Pesticide Alert: A Guide to Pesticides in Fruits and Vegetables* and drew attention to the danger from eating apples sprayed with Alar.

In recent years NRDC has focused on natural resource conservation, arguing in coalition with other environmental groups that government agencies should manage public lands with greater sensitivity to ecological concerns. In the 1980s NRDC developed economic cost-benefit arguments showing that the Forest Service spends more taxpayers' money administering the timber harvesting program than the lumber generates in revenues. NRDC works through the Public Lands Institute to protect wildlife and publicly owned wilderness areas managed by the Bureau of Land Management. It argues for increasing grazing fees to reflect the true costs of the program and for reducing the number of steers permitted on public lands to halt the degradation and erosion of public lands. Like other conservation groups NRDC believes many water projects in the U.S. West subsidize industrial farming at the expense of the taxpayer. It considers the Department of Interior's offshore oil and gas leasing program one of the greatest threats to the ocean environment.

Lettie McSpadden

Further Readings

Natural Resources Defense Council. *Annual Reports.* 1970– .
———. *The Amicus Journal.* 1979– .
———. *Twenty Years Defending the Environment: NRDC 1970–1990.* 1991.

See also AIR POLLUTION: REGULATION (U.S.); BUREAU OF LAND MANAGEMENT; DEPARTMENT OF THE INTERIOR (U.S.); ENVIRONMENTAL CASE LAW: UNITED STATES; FEDERAL INSECTICIDE, FUNGICIDE AND RODENTICIDE ACT; GREEN ECONOMICS; PESTICIDES; REGULATION; RESOURCE MANAGEMENT

Nature

Despite its most obvious usage to indicate the nonhuman matter of which the planet is composed, nature is a term of such dangerous ambiguity as to make it one of the more abstruse terms in the English language. Although the word "nature" is commonly used to refer to the nonhuman it is by no means uncommon for someone to assert that humans are also a part of nature, thus effectively redefining the term to mean virtually everything in material existence. To add to the confusion the word is also used in a normative fashion to indicate that which is as it ought to be, therefore opening the possibility of asserting that certain things or behaviors may be "unnatural," which is inevitably a term of derision and one that is commonly employed to implore those accused to behave "naturally," that is, as we would wish them to behave. And because of this second level of meaning it is a common ploy to infer that if something is ordinarily done (i.e., is "natural") then it has an existence and an authority independent of human social activities. Once so isolated and deprived of any semblance of human authorship such behavior seems beyond reproach or alteration, and therefore takes on a kind of protected existence, free from critical examination.

In this usage nature can be regarded as a dangerous term since it can potentially facilitate the concealment of social norms and injustices beneath the facade of the natural. Hence the concern of some—such as Barthes—that nature be revealed as historical (that is, as a social compendium of norms rather than as an external collection of givens). The subtle blending of the normative and the objective—of moral directives and of material entities—greatly enhances the potential for abuse, since the assurance with which we speak of physical nature, through science, lends an aura of certainty to the normative aspect of nature as well. But what is perhaps most important in this critique of the ambiguity and volatility of "nature" is the realization that nature is not a thing but a concept—a term of convenience that permits the speaker to imply and to name the whole of nonhuman being as a single "other," as an external entity available to human inspection and manipulation. The conceit of regarding all nonhuman existence as being resident in the category "nature," and thus subject to whatever characteristics have been designated for that category, enables the speaker to reduce the domain of heterogeneous otherness to the sameness of the category "nature." Nature is, then, a linguistic and conceptual device which facilitates our approach to, interaction with, and manipulation of the diversity of otherness which confronts us in consciousness.

Yet in the vernacular, and particularly in the discourse of the environmental movement, nature is also used to point to the domain of being that is threatened by technological excess and which it is imperative that societies move to defend. In that sense nature may refer not only to the material other but to the quality of wildness which confronts and frustrates the societal goal of prediction and control. Nature as wildness, as the self-willed other, seems to be an emerging connotation which may, if it persists, substantially alter the concept of nature.

Neil Evernden

Further Readings

Evernden, Neil. *The Social Creation of Nature.* 1992.
Leiss, William. *The Domination of Nature.* 1972.
Lewis, C.S. *Studies in Words.* 1967.

See also DEEP ECOLOGY: MEANINGS; ENVIRONMENT; RESOURCISM; WHOLE EARTH IMAGE; WILDERNESS

Nature Conservancies

To date twenty-two national organizations have been created directly by the "nature conservancy movement": one in each of the United Kingdom, the United States, Canada, and nineteen Central and South American countries. They are all generally dedicated to the preservation of biological and ecological diversity, endangered species and habitats, and unique natural features, although the priorities and methods have varied from country to country. The original conservancy was the British Nature Conservancy Council (NCC), a statutory body formed at the insistence of the Royal Society for Nature Conservation. Based in Peterborough, England, the NCC existed from 1949 to 1991, when it was replaced by Nature Conservancy councils in Scotland and Wales and English Nature (EN) in England.

Inspired by the British initiative but privately funded, The Nature Conservancy (TNC) of the United States was established in 1951 from the Ecologist's Union, an independent group that between 1917 and 1946 had been the committee on "Preservation of Natural Conditions in the United States" (its name after 1932) of the Ecological Society of America. The British and U.S. experiences stimulated the emergence in 1962 of the nongovernmental Nature Conservancy Canada from the Nature Reserves Committee of the Federation of Ontario Naturalists. Development of the Central and South American organizations was fostered through the "Latin American Division" (formerly the "International Program") of TNC. Given that these private groups require strong local bases the connection with TNC has been downplayed.

The main products of the NCC are "National Nature Reserves" and "Sites of Special Scientific Interest." By 1991 Britain contained 128 of the former and 3,536 of the latter, comprising 43,000 hectares and 782,000 hectares, respectively. Both purchase and management were the responsibility of the NCC. The majority of these preserves were created after the late 1960s when attention was redirected from large agriculturally valuable estates to smaller marginal farms. The 1991 transformation to three organizations was undertaken in order to be more responsive to regional needs, particularly those in Wales and Scotland. Moreover change was motivated politically by a number of prominent conflicts that had occurred in the late 1980s between the interests of the NCC and those of economic development. EN and its Welsh and Scottish counterparts have continued to acquire protected areas and with collective budgets that are consistent in magnitude with the past practices of the NCC. A comparative evaluation of performance would be premature.

In the United States TNC, based in Arlington, Virginia, stirred the conservation establishment by soliciting and obtaining the cooperation of corporate bodies for the purchase of land that contained ecologically important natural areas. In contrast to confrontational environmental groups TNC cultivated working relationships with members of the business community. The resultant criticism was mollified somewhat by the fact that by 1993 TNC represented over 750,000 members and had "secured" 3.06 million hectares of land, more than 400,000 hectares of which was being maintained in over 1,300 preserves. The other 2.66 million hectares were secured using a variety of legal devices such as easements and trusts.

One of the most important achievements of TNC has been the "Natural Heritage Programs." Proposed by Dr. Robert Jenkins in 1974, the heritage concept is a systematic method of assembling information in order to set priorities for protecting natural areas. Spatial data on biological and ecological diversity, endangeredness, and land tenure are stored and managed in central computers. Natural Heritage Programs exist in all fifty U.S. states, four Canadian provinces and nineteen Central and South American nations. The trend has been for governments in these jurisdictions to gradually assume fiscal responsibility for their respective programs while TNC provides technical assistance.

In Canada the Toronto-based Nature Conservancy Canada has secured over 44,500 hectares of land since 1962. Securement has occurred mainly through the creation of nature preserves. Preserves have been purchased directly, donated, or obtained by another conservation group with Nature Conservancy Canada aid. Support has been provided in four provinces by "Conservation Data Centres," the Canadian organization's label for Natural Heritage Programs. A membership organization in 1993 for only three years, Nature Conservancy Canada has been joined by more than 15,000 individuals.

The Central and South American organizations that administer conservancy interests have constituted new opportunities for international conservation efforts. For example, during the 1980s in Costa Rica, after negotiating a discounted exchange with one bank, TNC purchased part of the national debt through the *Fundación de Parques Nacional* (FPN) that it helped to found. The government of Costa Rica then reimbursed FPN in local tender and conservation allocations. Another U.S. bank simply donated its Costa Rican loan to TNC in return for recognition of charitable action. These were very influential pioneering initiatives that helped to stimulate similar actions by bodies such as the World Bank. In other Central and South American countries TNC assisted natural area protection more conventionally via technical assistance in parks planning and land-use management and through its Natural Heritage Programs. It would be difficult and perhaps misleading to credit the conservancies with preservation of a given amount of natural area in Central and South America where their roles are less clearly defined than in the institutional ecology of Britain, the United States, and Canada.

Thomas H. Whillans

Further Readings

Dair, I. "Building a New Organization for Nature Conservation." *Long Range Planning* 26 (1993): 54–63

Grove, N. "Quietly Conserving Nature." *National Geographic* 174 (1988): 818–44.

See also BIOSPHERE RESERVES; DEBT-FOR-NATURE SWAPS; IUCN; WORLD BANK

Nature Fakers

The nature fakers controversy began in 1903 with the publication of John Burroughs's essay, "Real and Sham Natural History," in the *Atlantic Monthly*. Burroughs attacked a number of prominent nature writers, including Ernest Thompson Seton, Charles G.D. Roberts, and William J. Long, accusing them of fabricating their natural history facts. This stimulated four years of debate waged in magazine articles and letters to editors. President Theodore Roosevelt quickly sided with Burroughs, but at first avoided public involvement. He did, however, write private letters scolding the errant authors' publishers.

William J. Long, a Congregationalist minister with a Ph.D. from the University of Heidelberg, heatedly defended himself and became the focus of the controversy. Science, he argued, is interested only in general truths about animals, whereas he studied individual animals that dis-

played individual talents. His later report of a woodcock setting its own broken leg and applying a mud cast to it did not win over his critics. Burroughs continued the assault with a series of magazine articles and *Ways of Nature* (1905). The controversy came to a head in 1907, when President Roosevelt launched his own attack against Long, Jack London, and others accused of being nature fakers. He placed the major blame on their publishers. Long began writing very successful textbooks on English and American literature. He did not publish another nature book until after Roosevelt's death in 1919.

This debate concerning authors' responsibility for accuracy in nature writing helped to establish standards for the field. It was a literary reflection of a tension within the nature study movement between scientific and emotional approaches to understanding our relationship with the natural world. Burroughs resolved this conflict by arguing that literary naturalists have a dual responsibility to faithfully describe the objective facts of nature and communicate their significance in terms of one's subjective response to nature. The debate also encompassed the argument over whether animals are instinct-driven machines or capable of reason. Many of the so-called fakers' tales were unbelievable, but some were not that far off the mark. For example, Long's view of wolves as social animals that are not blood-thirsty killers was similar to present views.

The term "nature fakers" (sometimes spelled "fakirs") eventually acquired new uses. Supporters of the Hetch Hetchy dam applied it to their opponents and park rangers involved in law enforcement use it to demean interpretive naturalists.

Ralph H. Lutts

Further Readings

Burroughs, John. "Real and Sham Natural History." *Atlantic Monthly* 91 (1903): 298–309.

Long, William J. "The Modern School of Nature-Study and Its Critics." *North American Review* 176 (1903): 688–98.

Lutts, Ralph H. *The Nature Fakers: Wildlife, Science and Sentiment.* 1990.

See also BURROUGHS, JOHN; NATURE STUDY MOVEMENT; SETON, ERNEST THOMPSON

Nature Study Movement

The rise of popular interest in natural history in the late nineteenth and early twentieth centuries along with the progressive educational movement of the same period has come to be known as the Nature Study Movement. The popularity of both originated in part from demographic changes associated with increasing urbanization, the desire to escape urban stress to a romanticized rural life, and growing concern about the loss of wildlife. The explosion of public interest in nature led some turn-of-the-century social critics to decry the growing "cult of nature."

Following the Civil War people—especially urban dwellers—increasingly valued outdoor recreation and parks as sources of physical and emotional health. Railroads (later, automobile companies) encouraged vacation travel to national parks and resorts. Organized summer camps for children began in the 1870s and grew in popularity. In 1887 newspapers and magazines began raising funds to send poor urban children to Fresh Air Camps. Youth groups also promoted the virtues of nature and life in the out-of-doors. Collecting specimens—from bird eggs to butterflies to wildflowers—became popular hobbies. Opera glasses made bird watching acceptable to those who, influenced by the growing animal welfare movement, preferred not to study birds with a shotgun.

Publishers found a ready market for field identification guidebooks. By the turn-of-the-century some authors even felt it necessary to explain to their readers why they had produced still another wildflower guide. Nature literature was also very popular. Books by Henry Thoreau, John Burroughs, Olive Thorne Miller, Bradford Torrey, John Muir, Ernest Thompson Seton, Charles G.D. Roberts, William J. Long, Jack London, and many other authors were read by an eager public. Some of these authors were befriended by President Theodore Roosevelt, who encouraged outdoor pursuits, nature study, and conservation during his presidency. Nature essays and stories were printed in school editions for a growing classroom market.

As an educational movement nature study began with object teaching, which came to the United States in the 1860s. This method, which was influenced by the theories of the Swiss educator Johann Heinrich Pestalozzi, was based on the study of actual objects and emphasized the biological and physical sciences. Louis Agassiz and Wilbur Jackman influenced the early development of the movement. Nature study focused on the child's own experiences of nature, exercised students' full range of senses and reason, and provided themes that promised to integrate all school subjects. Liberty Hyde Bailey and others at Cornell University also hoped that farm children who grew to love nature might be more willing to remain on the farm as adults. By the early twentieth century it was endorsed by the educational establishment and accepted as an innovative and sometimes mandated part of the curriculum in many states. The movement was championed by the American Nature Study Society and the *Nature-Study Review.*

The movement declined in the 1920s after giving birth to the elementary science education and progressive education movements. It is still practiced as an important strand in contemporary environmental education, of which it was a progenitor.

Ralph H. Lutts

Further Readings

Lutts, Ralph H. *The Nature Fakers: Wildlife, Science and Sentiment.* 1990.

Olmsted, Richard R. *The Nature-Study Movement in American Education.* Ed.D. diss., Indiana University, 1967.

Schmitt, Peter J. *Back to Nature: The Arcadian Myth in Urban America.* 1969.

See also BAILEY, LIBERTY HYDE; BURROUGHS, JOHN; ENVIRONMENTAL EDUCATION; MUIR, JOHN; NATURE FAKERS; SETON, ERNEST THOMPSON; THOREAU, HENRY DAVID

Nelson, Gaylord A.

Former U.S. Senator Gaylord A. Nelson was born on June 5, 1916, in Clearlake, Wisconsin. A lawyer and veteran of World War II, Nelson served in the Wisconsin state senate from 1948 to 1956 and was elected governor in 1958. Nelson is often regarded as the "father of Earth Day"; his environmental record has its roots in his fights against pollution during his days as governor.

Nelson was elected to the U.S. Senate in 1962 and emerged as one of the earliest Democratic critics of the war in Vietnam. Nelson's activism continued a tradition of midwestern progressivism with respect to consumer protection and opposition to what he regarded as wasteful subsidies for big business. More important was the fact that during his Senate tenure Nelson kept seats on the committees on the Interior and Insular Affairs (where he focused on natural resource issues) and on Public Works (where he stressed fights against air and water pollution).

Earth Day, the story goes, grew out of Nelson's idea to hold environmental "teach-ins" like those used to protest the war in Vietnam. Nelson enlisted the support of Pete McCloskey, a Republican Representative from California, got office space with the public interest group Common Cause, hired law school student Denis Hayes as an organizer, and set about raising funds for a day of environmental education and activism. Interest in Earth Day spread quickly, and the magnitude and impact of the event, held on April 22, 1970, surpassed its planners' wildest dreams.

Nelson's Senate career ended when he was defeated for reelection in the Reagan landslide of 1980. Since 1981 he has served as legal counsel and associate executive chairman of the Wilderness Society, which in 1990 presented Nelson with its Ansel Adams award and established a scholarship fund in his name to finance awards for excellence in environmental law and public policy, natural resource studies, and environmental journalism.

Christopher J. Bosso (with Steven Sharobem)

Further Readings

Milbrath, Lester. *Environmentalists: Vanguard for a New Society.* 1984.
Shabecoff, Philip. *A Fierce Green Fire: The American Environmental Movement.* 1993.

See also ADAMS, ANSEL; EARTH DAY; WILDERNESS SOCIETY

NEPA

See NATIONAL ENVIRONMENTAL POLICY ACT (U.S.)

New Forestry

New Forestry (NF) is a term coined in the late 1980s by scientists and U.S. Forest Service (USFS) managers working at the H.J. Andrews Experimental Forest in Oregon. In a 1989 paper discussing the origins of NF, Jerry Franklin wrote, "Is there an alternative to the stark choice between tree farms and total preservation? . . . My associates and I in the Andrews Ecosystem Research Group believe that an alternative does exist, and we call it the 'New Forestry.' We view the new approach as a kinder and gentler forestry that better accom-

modates ecological values, while allowing for the extraction of commodities."

NF differs from tree farming in at least three ways. One is its focus on complex ecosystems rather than just commercially valuable trees, including maintaining: a) the proper balance of habitats, hence viable populations of indigenous species; b) the full range of natural processes; and c) the capacity of ecosystems and individuals for defense and self-repair. In NF harvest of wood and other marketable commodities is a secondary objective that must be consistent with conserving indigenous species and overall ecosystem health in perpetuity.

The fact that many of the processes important to species and ecosystem health play out over large areas leads to a second distinguishing characteristic of NF: its focus on managing landscapes and whole regions rather than just individual forest stands. A third distinguishing characteristic is the explicit recognition that different forest types may require different management approaches, from which it follows that NF, rather than being a single technique, becomes a process of understanding the natural structures and rhythms that characterize a given forest type, and designing management practices that protect or, where necessary, restore those.

To better understand NF it is necessary to understand "old forestry," and to do this it is useful to briefly review the history of forestry over the past 150 years. At least some of the approaches utilized in NF are not new at all, but rather date to earlier practices that were largely supplanted by what, for lack of a better term, is best described as "industrial" forestry (though it has been widely utilized by government agencies as well as forest industries). Industrial forestry, which originated in Germany during the mid-1800s, essentially views the forest as a factory for producing wood, much as the modern farm is a factory for producing food. At the time of its inception the forests of central Europe were greatly degraded from centuries of uncontrolled cutting. German foresters adopted industrial forestry as a means of rejuvenating their forests while at the same time putting the practice of forestry on a solid business basis. Only the fastest growing and most commercially valuable trees were grown, and these were managed according to economic criteria that maximized income. Plochman describes the resulting management: "The deciduous high forests were converted by seeding and planting into softwood monocultures. Rotations were shortened, natural regeneration was replaced by plantations, and old forms of silviculture, like single-tree selection, replaced by clearcutting."

Industrial forestry was not widely adopted on public lands in the United States until the late 1940s. It was opposed by Gifford Pinchot, the first chief of the USFS, who in 1898 wrote: "A serious check to the progress of forestry was the general praise given to the European methods of forest management and the frequent, strenuous, and utterly impractical advice to apply them to the forests of North America." This does not mean, however, that forests of the United States were managed ecologically. Much of the logging done in the nineteenth and early twentieth centuries was accompanied by no management whatsoever: to use the old but apt phrase, it was cut and run. By the end of the nineteenth century few of the original forests remained in the United States east of the Mississippi and north of the Ohio rivers; cutover land had converted largely to scrubby trees and brush. Roughly one-half of the original old-growth Douglas-fir in western Oregon and Washington had been cut by the mid-1930s, and more than one-half of cutover lands was either non-stocked or poorly stocked with trees.

The end of World War II triggered an explosion in economic activity and domestic building, and consequently a large increase in the demand for wood in industrialized countries. The USFS responded by embracing the techniques of European forestry, as did the forestry colleges that were the training grounds for future generations of foresters (at the time, industrial techniques were called the "new forestry"). In the decades that followed, technology added some new twists, such as fertilizers, herbicides, and genetic selection for fast growing trees. Many countries, particularly in the tropics and southern temperate zones, cleared native forests and planted plantations of fast growing non-native trees.

At the same time that foresters in the United States and elsewhere were embracing the techniques of industrial forestry the changing social landscape within industrialized countries was making these techniques less acceptable to the public. Increasing urbanization was producing a populace for whom wildlands were less important as a source of commodities than they were for other values, such as recreation and spirituality. One of the first places that the social backlash against industrial forestry appeared was Germany, the country that gave it

birth. There, social concerns were accompanied by the realization on the part of foresters that industrial forestry as they were practicing it was neither economically nor ecologically sound: fully one-third of the total harvest in Germany was unplanned (i.e., harvested before rotation age) because plantations were being killed by winds, ice, or insects. By the early 1960s, Germans were abandoning industrial forestry for their own brand of NF, which included restoring the full complement of native trees, partial cutting, long rotations, and concentration on high value wood products rather than high quantity.

During the late 1960s controversy erupted in the United States over clearcutting of national forests leading Congress to pass in 1976 the National Forest Management Act (NFMA), which required the USFS to develop plans in consultation with the public. NFMA, however, did little to alter the basic orientation of the USFS toward the primacy of timber production on public lands.

Opposition to industrial forestry continued to build in the United States and other timber-producing countries through the 1970s and 1980s, including not only urban people, but rural as well: peasants in India were hugging trees to keep them from being cut; indigenous people in Canada were barricading logging roads. As in Germany, scientific evidence was also accumulating that industrial forestry, widely applied, had created significant ecological problems in the United States Pacific Northwest. The most dramatic of the scientific issues related to species that required old-growth forests or other habitats that were not maintained in industrial forests.

During the late 1980s and early 1990s two old-growth dependent birds—the northern spotted owl and the marbled murrelet—were granted protection under the Endangered Species Act (ESA), as were several breeding populations (stocks) of salmon, whose numbers had diminished due to a combination of dams on the Columbia river system and degradation of stream habitat due to logging and grazing. Numerous other species of mammals, fish, and amphibians, as of 1995, are considered by biologists to be at risk because of habitat degradation. Other scientific issues emerged during this same period. The standard practice of dispersing clearcuts throughout a matrix of older forests, once thought to benefit wildlife, had led to excessive roading and fragmentation of remaining older forest into isolated blocks that were at risk to fire and wind. Moreover, growing evidence indicated that large dead wood and noncommercial plant species—things that had no place in industrial forestry—performed important functions within forest ecosystems.

It is from this cauldron of social and scientific issues that NF emerged as an approach to restoring balance between commodity production, protection of long-term forest health, and maintenance of the full range of values provided by forests. As of 1995 NF was still evolving, along with its share of skeptics and critics, as well as proponents. The chief of the USFS announced in 1992 that the agency would institute "ecosystem management" and the Bureau of Land Management issued a similar declaration in 1994; however, it remains to be seen how these policy changes will be translated into practice. After years of fighting the USFS, many environmentalists and biologists view NF as just another attempt by the agency to disguise a continued focus on timber production. At the same time, however, there is a growing grass roots movement within the USFS and the U.S. Bureau of Land Management away from timber primacy, toward ecosystem and landscape management. Where this will lead is uncertain, but at this point it seems likely that, as in Germany, industrial forestry on public lands in the United States will eventually become a thing of the past.

David A. Perry

Further Readings

Franklin, J.F. "Towards a New Forestry." *American Forests* (December 1989): 37–44.

Hopwood, D. "Principles and Practices of New Forestry." British Columbia Ministry of Forests, Land Management Report 71. Victoria, B.C., 1991.

Perry, D.A., and J. Maghembe. "Ecosystem Concepts and Current Trends in Forest Management: Time for Reappraisal." *Forest Ecology and Management* 26 (1989): 123–40.

———. "Ecosystem Management: Basic Principles and Thoughts on Socioeconomic Implications." Proceedings, 1993 Silviculture Conference. Forestry Canada, Ottawa, 1993.

See also Bureau of Land Management; Clearcut; Forest Service (U.S.); Forestry, History of; Old Growth Forests

New Zealand: Anti-Nuclear Foreign Policy

The origins of New Zealand's nuclear free policies are threefold: growing public support that first emerged in the 1960s, clear political commitments from the 1972–1975 and 1984–1987 Labour governments, and the strong personal convictions of their respective leaders—prime ministers Norman Kirk and David Lange. The genesis of the policies occurred in 1962 with an Australian Labour party suggestion that the Antarctica nuclear weapon free (NWF) zone be extended to the Southern Hemisphere. Church-based peace groups in New Zealand influenced by the British Ban the Bomb movement, supported this with a large petition. Trade Union pickets also began to oppose U.S. warship visits.

The first genuinely popular peace movement, however, emerged only with U.S. intervention in Vietnam. Large-scale public mobilization against the war eventually resulted in the small contingent of New Zealand troops being withdrawn by the 1972 Labour government. Kirk built on this sentiment and stated that no nuclear powered warships would enter New Zealand's waters.

Opposition was also growing to French atmospheric nuclear tests in the South Pacific. The Labour governments of Australia and New Zealand jointly petitioned the International Court of Justice at the Hague seeking an interim injunction against the tests. This was followed in 1973 by a New Zealand navy frigate being sent into the test zone with a cabinet minister on board. In 1974 France moved its tests underground. A NWF zone for the South Pacific was proposed by Kirk in 1975 and endorsed by the United Nations (UN) General Assembly.

The resumption of U.S. ship visits by the 1976 national government saw growing public opposition. Peace squadrons—flotillas of small boats—were formed to hinder the entry of warships into ports. The environmental movement also opposed ship visits and organized a huge petition against nuclear power in 1976. The technology became politically unacceptable.

During the early 1980s peace groups flourished (300 existed) and targeted local authorities requesting that they become NWF zones. By 1983 half the population was living in such zones and Labour pledged to make New Zealand nuclear free. All major political parties except the ruling national party supported this stance. Labour became government in 1984. Polls indicated that 56 percent of New

Zealanders opposed visits by nuclear armed ships. Lange thus had a mandate to articulate the policy. Opposition from the United States, Australian, and British governments served to stiffen Lange's and the government's resolve even when the United States suspended New Zealand from the ANZUS military alliance. Lange became an eloquent and powerful advocate for the policy nationally and internationally. Public support continued. The New Zealand Nuclear Free Zone, Disarmament and Arms Control Act became law in 1987. Nuclear weapons and nuclear powered ships were banned from New Zealand and its territorial waters.

By 1989 public support for the policy reached 80 percent. The national party was forced to change its position and when it became government in 1990 the nuclear ban remained. While there is still active debate about New Zealand's involvement in military alliances, the NWF policy is now part of New Zealand's national identity.

Peter Horsley

Further Readings

Lange, David. *Nuclear Free—The New Zealand Way.* 1990.

Locke, Elsie. *Peace People—A History of Peace Activities in New Zealand.* 1992.

See also ENVIRONMENTAL PROTECTION IN WARTIME; NATIONAL SECURITY, RECONCEPTUALIZING; NUCLEAR WEAPONS PRODUCTION; RADIOACTIVE FALLOUT; URANIUM MINING: ENVIRONMENTAL IMPACTS

NIMBY Syndrome

The Not-in-My-Back-Yard or NIMBY syndrome refers to intense, sometimes emotional, and often adamant local opposition to facilities that residents believe will adversely affect their health and well-being, property values, or environmental quality. The negative response by the community is usually explained by the distribution of costs, risks, and benefits associated with the facility. The costs and risks are geographically concentrated while the benefits accrue to a larger, more dispersed population. Thus, despite the benefits the facility might offer for the state or nation, community residents often object. Highly vocal and persistent opposition carries a low cost to residents and it has a high rate of success. The short-term effect of such opposition is often political gridlock, which forces project proponents to look elsewhere for a more receptive community or to reformulate their proposal until it meets with community acceptance.

This common characterization of citizen behavior is incomplete and in some ways inaccurate. There have been few rigorous efforts to conceptualize the NIMBY response or to assess its policy implications, and only a handful of empirical studies have tried to clarify its behavioral and political dynamics. Given what appear to be significant differences in the actual risks faced by host communities and in the contexts in which projects are proposed, social scientists need to ask whether the NIMBY characterization holds across different issue areas, various kinds of facilities, and differences in community socioeconomic structures.

The frequency of NIMBY responses in the 1980s and early 1990s suggests to some observers that a single phenomenon is at work in all cases of locational controversy. Citizen opposition is said to be "rational" in the sense that local residents may well be worse off if a facility is sited no matter what the benefits to the community, state, or nation. Moreover, the public's response may be unaffected by provision of scientific studies of risk, assurances of safety offered by proponents, various pledges to uphold environmental and other laws, and offers of monetary compensation.

Such descriptions fail to do justice to the intricacy of policy history, personal experience, attitudes, perceptions, and motivations that spur citizens to adopt such a stance. Generally absent from such accounts is any recognition that contextual variables matter in shaping the way in which the public perceives a project and hence its response to it, or that those variables affect the feasibility of policy responses that might be taken to break a political stalemate. We need a more comprehensive description to understand the NIMBY phenomenon, its effects, and ways of dealing with it.

Other conditions would appear to affect the form and intensity of community opposition. Among these are: 1) the magnitude of environmental and health risks posed by the facility, including the reliability of risk estimates and the degree of consensus among technical experts; 2) public perception of environmental and health risks and other facility impacts on the community; 3) the record of performance and reputation of government agencies or other project proponents, particularly their perceived credibility and competence; 4) the extent and nature of media coverage and the salience of the issues; 5) the political skills and leadership abilities of community activists and project proponents; and 6) the extent, form, and timing of opportunities for public involvement in decision-making. Assessments of NIMBYism and its effects, and the pursuit of conflict-resolution strategies would benefit from refinement of our conceptualization of this political phenomenon as well as by empirical testing of such propositions, whether through analytic case studies, survey data, or other methods.

The same can be said for broadening our understanding of both the proximate and underlying causes of NIMBY behavior. The conventional view of NIMBYism offers an implicit model of public behavior. Individuals living near a proposed facility perceive it as risky and threatening, which leads to varied forms of oppositional behavior recognized as NIMBY. This behavior is said to be a function of distrust of the project sponsors, attitudes toward the project that are local and parochial (and which do not consider broader ramifications), limited or incorrect information about the siting issues, a high level of concern about the project's risks, and an emotional response (e.g., outrage) to the conflict. In this model, the local community is seen as behaving selfishly and acting out of technical ignorance and fear in rejecting facilities thought both necessary and safe by experts and governmental and corporate decision-makers.

A second view incorporates a more positive assessment of citizen behavior. Project proponents may seek to impose significant risks on a local populace without its free, informed consent. While local citizens may or may not be knowledgeable about technical details, their evaluation of what constitutes an acceptable level of risk—based on a "cultural" rather than "technical" definition—may be politically legitimate, as may be their strategic use of protest. Equity issues are often prominent in local opposition. Citizens ask who benefits from the project and why their community or neighborhood should be saddled (unfairly) with the burden. By forcing consideration of such concerns, opposition to construction of risky industrial facilities may be seen as a moral triumph for citizens and evidence of a healthy democratic politics at the local level.

Whichever conception best fits the circumstances of a case, these contrasting views suggest that the NIMBY response is a more complex and multidimensional political phenomenon than generally acknowledged. The direct causes are fairly well understood and are represented in both models, even if little is known about how contextual variables shape the form and outcome of controversies. This overview of conditions promoting NIMBYism suggests that any search for solutions must deal with fundamental characteristics of contemporary society and decision-making processes in government and industry. Both empirical and theoretical studies suggest the promise of approaches that emphasize building agency credibility through genuine commitment by policymakers to public participation, design of methods for meaningful information exchange and public dialogue on the issues, promotion of equity in risk distribution, sharing in project benefits (in part through compensation to communities bearing the risks), and the adoption of mitigation and control procedures that include strict safety standards and significant citizen roles in facility oversight and operating decisions. Extensive citizen involvement and adherence to principles of voluntary acceptance of facilities lie at the heart of such processes.

Michael E. Kraft

Further Readings

Kraft, Michael E., and Bruce B. Clary. "Citizen Participation and the NIMBY Syndrome: Public Response to Radioactive Waste Disposal." *Western Political Quarterly* 44 (1991).

Mazmanian, Daniel, and David Morell. "The 'NIMBY' Syndrome: Facility Siting and the Failure of Democratic Discourse." In *Environmental Policy in the 1990s: Toward a New Agenda*. Ed. Norman J. Vig and Michael E. Kraft. 2nd ed. 1994.

Portney, Kent. *Siting Hazardous Waste Treatment Facilities: The NIMBY Syndrome*. 1991.

See also ECOANARCHISM; HAZARDOUS WASTE TREATMENT FACILITY SITING; MUNICIPAL SOLID WASTE: INCINERATION; MUNICIPAL SOLID WASTE LANDFILL; NUCLEAR WASTE; RIGHT-TO-KNOW: COMMUNITY (U.S.)

No-Till Agriculture

Early systems of producing crop plants did not include tilling the soil. Seed was broadcast into most fertile areas and existing green plants were cut and allowed to dry as a mulch to protect the new seeds and conserve moisture. A similar system is still in use in parts of Central America, where the *tapado* system includes chopping existing vegetation and allowing it to dry, then broadcasting maize, bean, grain sorghum, and other crop seeds into the mulch. Such systems depend on hand labor for land preparation, seeding, weeding, and harvest. Productivity per unit of land area or labor is relatively low.

Tillage, the mechanical stirring or inverting of the topsoil in preparation for planting crops, is used to prepare a seedbed that is relatively free from weeds and allows mechanized planting at uniform depth into moist soil. Coupled with selective chemical herbicide application either in the planted row or across the field this system allows rapid germination of the desired crop and suppression of undesirable plants or weeds. The conventional wisdom about tillage is that we need a "clean seedbed" to start the crop right.

No-till agriculture in the modern sense is an improvement on the pre-history systems that did not disturb the soil prior to planting. New mechanical planters with sharp leading disks or coulters can move through the residue left by a previous crop and deposit seed, fertilizer, and insecticide if needed in a uniform and appropriate place beneath the soil surface. Planting is especially easy into stubble or residue of a crop such as soybean, since very little dry material is left on the surface by the time of planting the next crop. If there is heavy residue from a previous crop of maize, wheat, or grain sorghum it may be necessary to chop the residue to create a more uniform planting environment. Today's planters move through most residues to allow direct planting without any previous land preparation.

Such a system of no-till planting has the advantage of conservation of moisture in the area of the seed since there is no stirring and minimal drying of the immediate area around the seed. In addition, there is little disturbance of the topsoil and weed seeds are not brought to the surface, therefore making them less likely to germinate. Chemicals are often used at planting or immediately after to kill or suppress those weeds that do germinate. Some perennial weeds may become a problem in this system. There is energy and time savings because primary land preparation is eliminated. One disadvantage is that soils do not warm up as quickly in a no-till planting system—especially in northern latitudes—and this can delay planting or inhibit early crop growth. No-till planting may be followed by cultivation to control weeds that are not suppressed by chemical herbicide.

The ridge planting system is one that combines the advantages of eliminating primary land preparation, creating permanent wheel traffic patterns to minimize compacted soil areas, and saving moisture in the seed zone. This system also opens the door to weed management without chemical herbicides, if a rotary hoe and cultivator are used to clean out weeds as they germinate and then re-form the beds or ridges for the next season.

No-till agriculture is generally considered an environmentally friendly system, since it eliminates most mechanical disturbance of the soil and leaves crop residues on the surface. This prevents the majority of soil erosion. The negative dimension is a need for chemical herbicide when there is no mechanical cultivation for weed control. The move toward reduced tillage or conservation tillage systems is a rapid one in the major crop areas of the central regions of North America.

Charles A. Francis

Further Readings

Pesek, J., et al. *Alternative Agriculture*. National Research Council, 1989.

Phillips, R.E., et al. "No-Tillage Agriculture." *Science* 208 (1980): 1108–13.

See also AGRICULTURE: ENVIRONMENTAL IMPACTS; ENERGY EFFICIENCY IN AGRICULTURE; HERBICIDES; SOIL CONSERVATION; SUSTAINABLE AGRICULTURE

Noise Pollution

The term "noise pollution" is a relatively recent one; however, the concept that noise, or sound, can have adverse effects on people and other organisms has been around for centuries. Prior to the introduction of the concept of noise pollution, noise-related problems had been recognized in two major areas of concern for social or physical well-being. The first relates to the workplace. Many occupations have the potential to result in undesirable exposure to noise, and, in the past, impairment to or even loss of hearing resulted from certain occupational exposures. Most jurisdictions now address this and noise exposure in the workplace is frequently regulated by law. The second area relates to generally lower levels of sound which, although not impairing hearing, may intrude upon the well-being of individuals or groups in various situations, for example in a person's private home. These types of noise problems have been considered a nuisance rather than as health-related and indeed the concept of nuisance in the common law has been used to deal with such disturbances. Local bylaws also frequently address noise, again in terms of nuisance or annoyance.

Noise pollution is considered to be a particular problem in urban areas, where automobiles, airplanes, trains, and construction projects cumulatively affect the environment. The impact of noise is a function of two things: the level of sound and the effect of that sound on people or other living things. While it is highly likely that organisms other than human beings are adversely affected by noise, this article deals only with humans in the context of noise pollution. The main reason for this limitation is the lack of consistent and reliable data for the effect(s) of noise on other organisms.

The noise or sound environment for any individual is complex and variable. Individual people experience noise in highly subjective and variable ways. Involuntary noise exposure may evoke a very different response from exposure experienced voluntarily. For example, noise related to airports may be highly disruptive for residents who are unwilling recipients of the noise; the same level of noise may go apparently unnoticed by individuals who derive benefits from the airport.

People can accommodate or habituate to noise, or tolerate it because they know that it offers some compensating advantage. For example, the level of noise in a discotheque is far greater than traffic noise, yet the former is accepted voluntarily while the latter can cause great distress. Intermittent noise can be more disturbing than steady continuous noise. Although the responses are in part subjective, they are nevertheless real and have to be incorporated into decisions concerning standards for acceptable levels of environmental noise.

Scientific and medical studies are available and have to be used in establishing criteria for noise pollution. Noise can have clinical health effects or behavioral effects on people. Most scientific data on the subject originates in studies of: occupational health, airport and other heavy traffic noise, and modern amplified musical instruments, such as that experienced in discotheques or through earphones. Experimental studies of human responses to noise have emphasized sleep and speech disturbances at measured noise levels.

Best understood are the effects of noise on hearing loss, for which there are clear dose-response relationships. However, aside from occupational exposure and exposure to amplified music, the type of environmental noise that is of concern under the subject of noise pollution is rarely sufficiently severe as to permanently damage human hearing.

At noise levels too low to have clinical effects on hearing a number of health conditions including hypertension and conditions generally related to "stress" have been attributed in part to noise; there is still controversy about these so called "non-auditory" health effects. However, dose-response relationships have not been unequivocally established for noise with any clinical conditions other than hearing loss.

Noise has clear effects on certain behavior, notably through interference with speech, sleep, and the performance of certain tasks, although for the latter there is some ambiguity about the extent to which task performance is affected by noise. The response known as "annoyance" summarizes most of the behavioral effects listed above. Annoyance—although apparently a subjective measure—nevertheless has been shown repeatedly to be related to given levels of noise. This can be expressed as "percentage of highly annoyed" for a given noise metric. The range of noise covered by the annoyance reaction includes the range to which "non-auditory health effects" and behavioral effects have been attributed. Therefore the use of the noise-annoyance relationship provides a conservative means of assessing the effects of noise pollution on people.

Without question certain individuals are extremely sensitive to noise, and further complications arise from the fact that certain special groups of the population, such as young children and the elderly, are more severely adversely affected than the average adult in the population. These types of variation raise the same kind of philosophical questions as do extreme sensitivities to other environmental factors such as air pollutants. Is it feasible/possible to protect the most sensitive, or are the criteria more appropriately based on a (hypothetical) average person? For noise exposure the practical questions are perhaps more problematical because of the variability of the noise environment and the subjective nature of the human response.

Quantification of noise intensity and magnitude uses measures known as noise metrics. These metrics measure the instantaneous sound level, the cumulative sound energy of a single noise, and the cumulative sound energy measured over a given period of time.

The most widely-used noise metric is the A-weighted decibel, symbol (dBA). The human ear is sensitive to a wide range of sound intensities, and the decibel scale is a logarithmic scale of sound intensity, accommodating this wide range in a manageable manner. The best analogy is to the Richter scale of earthquake intensity. The decibel is a unit of sound pressure and can be measured with an instrument called the sound level meter. The A-weighted scale most accurately mimics the characteristic response of the human ear to sound intensities.

On the dBA scale everyday sounds range from 30 (very quiet) to 100 (very loud). Normal speech between two people about 2 meters apart creates a level of 65 dBA. Other noise metrics include the maximum sound level (Lmax), which is the instantaneous maximum sound level in dBA (note that this measures intensity only) and the Sound Exposure Level (SEL) which measures both intensity and duration. Another metric, the Day-Night Noise Level (Ldn), is a parameter that integrates noise over a twenty-four-hour period, with a weighting factor in the calculation that penalizes nighttime noise. This is due to the fact that noise during the night is recognized to be more disruptive than noise during the day.

Most occupational health agencies identify a noise exposure limit to protect hearing as 90 dBA for eight hours per day. Such a concise definition is clearly not possible to protect the average person from damage related to noise pollution, bearing in mind the subjectivity of the response to noise, and the variation in voluntary versus involuntary exposure.

Generally accepted criteria for residential or farm areas where outdoor activities require relatively quiet background are Ldn not above 55 dBA or (less stringent, e.g., for limited use such as playgrounds) Leq (the average or "equivalent" sound level) not above 55 dBA. Where noise appears to be inevitable restrictions on land use are often indicated.

To protect individuals from noise interference with indoor activities in normal residences the criteria are generally Ldn not above 45 dBA, with somewhat more stringent criteria for schools. In instances in which it appears impossible to reduce outside noise mitigating measures such as sound insulation of buildings and specially constructed windows may be required to make the noise environment acceptable for educational activities, listening to radio or television, and normal social interactions.

Pamela Welbourn

Further Readings

Federal Environmental Assessment and Review Process, Environment Canada. Vancouver International Airport Parallel Runway Project: Report of the Environmental Assessment Panel. 1991.

U.S. Environmental Protection Agency. *Information on Levels of Environmental Noise Requisite to Protect Public Health and Welfare with an Adequate Margin of Safety.* 1974.

See also AUTOMOBILES: IMPACTS AND POLICIES; LAND-USE PLANNING; SUPERSONIC TRANSPORT (SST); URBAN DESIGN

Non-Utility Generation

Non-Utility Generation (NUG) can be defined as electric power generated by a person or company other than the local utility. A "utility" is the company that holds the exclusive or near-exclusive legal right to distribute and retail electricity in a given geographic area. Also known as parallel generation or independent power, non-utility generation has enjoyed explosive growth in North America and around the world since about 1978, moving from almost non-existence to rivaling utility construction in many jurisdictions.

NUG tends to be associated with "alternative energy," renewable energy, appropriate technology, high-efficiency cogeneration, and other systems collectively described as "soft energy technology" by Amory Lovins in *Soft Energy Paths*. Lovins ascribes the following characteristics to soft energy technology: sustainability, diversity, flexibility, and being matched in scale and energy quality to the end-use. Although there is no absolute reason why non-utility generators could not adopt the centralized systems known collectively as "hard technology," economic, business risk, legal, and environmental factors tend to force the centralized technologies into the hands of centralized utilities.

The predominant sources used by today's non-utility generators are natural gas cogeneration, small hydro, wood, wind, solar, and municipal and agricultural waste. The advent of NUG in any one jurisdiction has usually been preceded by legislation requiring that monopolistic utilities purchase power from NUGs at negotiated rates.

The primary effect of non-utility generation has been to introduce competition into the power generation business, which had previously been the exclusive domain of the local power distribution utility. This has had the benefits of dampening power rate increases, and opening a market for more sustainable energy technologies that utilities have been slow to develop on their own.

Jake Brooks

Further Readings

Lovins, Amory B. *Soft Energy Paths: Toward a Durable Peace.* 1977.

See also COGENERATION; LOVINS, AMORY B; SOFT ENERGY PATHS; SOLAR ENERGY; WIND ENERGY

Nonrenewable Resources

Nonrenewable resources are natural materials whose availability reflects the composition of the earth's crust, its oceans, and its atmosphere. Key commodity groups are minerals, metals, and fossil fuels. Changes in quantity can occur but only on geological time scales—hence, the alternative term of "stock resources."

In principle any rate of use of nonrenewable resources will diminish future rates of use and this characteristic distinguishes nonrenewable from renewable (or "flow") resources, which are replenished regularly. However, the distinction between the two is not sharp. Conservation of matter means that nonrenewable stocks do not disappear, but are dispersed from relatively concentrated sources in the earth (and highly concentrated materials after processing) to dilute waste streams—witness the growing markets for scrap metals and the reuse of glass. Moreover, forests and wildlife can be depleted as thoroughly as minerals (perhaps even more so if species becomes extinct). If there are some flow resources (e.g., sunlight) not subject to depletion, so too are there some stock resources, such as those extracted from the ocean (e.g., bromine, magnesium) or from the atmosphere (e.g., argon, oxygen), so large as to make exhaustion meaningless.

Despite these similarities there is one important sense in which the concept of nonrenewable resources does have special meaning. Unlike manufacturing or farming, and regardless of whether the product is gemstones or gravel, nonrenewable resources require a prior stage of production to "create" reserves and resources. At any given time there is a stock of deposits known to be present in the ground and judged exploitable under certain price-cost conditions. That stock is limited in two dimensions: knowledge of additional sources of supply (the geological dimension) and ability to exploit lower grade and unconventional sources (the technological dimension). Geological exploration works to increase the discovered stock of deposits and, if successful, extends the intensive margin because it permits a higher rate of exploitation. Technological research works to increase the exploitable stock of deposits and, if successful, extends the extensive margin because it permits deposits that were formerly inferior in quality to be exploited. For example, the traditional sulfide ores of Sudbury, Canada, once almost the only source of nickel, must today compete with lower grade laterite ores found in many countries. Technology will also find more efficient ways to use (or recycle) resources and substitutes to replace them. For example, as tin prices rose because of limited deposits and unstable political conditions in Southeast Asia, "thin tin" cans were developed as were durable plastic and ceramic containers.

The important point, and the one missed by those who fear near-term exhaustion of mineral resources is that, in industrial societies, both margins are defined mainly in economic, not geological, terms. According to economic theory, increasing scarcity of some nonrenewable resource should be reflected by a secular rise in its real (inflation-free) price. With some exceptions (e.g., oil, mercury) just the reverse has occurred; mineral prices have declined over time. Indeed for the more common metals as well as for key minerals, including those used in fertilizers, the amounts available tend to increase geometrically with arithmetic increases in technical abilities to exploit.

"Reserves" are defined as that amount of material known to be present with a high degree of certainty and exploitable at current costs and prices. They are "shelf inventories" measured to permit corporate and regional planning for the next few time periods. "Resources" include materials that are only known to a lower degree of certainty or that are not exploitable under current conditions. Because resources can be converted to reserves with exploration and research it is inappropriate to divide reserves by current consumption rates to derive a so-called "life index." The sustainability rule for nonrenewable resources is not to restrict use but to ensure that the rate of consumption minus recycling does not exceed the sum of the rates at which resources are being converted to reserves plus that at which substitutes are being developed.

Nonrenewable resources do require special treatment in economic theory. The ability to capture rents even at the margin and the rule that the present value of rents should be constant over time imply adjustments in the rate of exploitation for individual mine owners and for society as a whole. Both must balance expectations of future prices and current interest rates (as well as other variables such as political conditions, taxes, and environmental standards) to determine the optimum rate of production (the intensive margin) and the lowest grade that is worth mining (the extensive margin). Of course private mine owners and public resource managers may use different interest rates, and they are likely to differ about the importance of other variables. Nevertheless mineral deposits are not completely different from other capital assets. With some exceptions, more commonly related to human events such as wars than to geological scarcity, supplies available have grown to meet human demands.

A seemingly cornucopian approach to nonrenewable resources does have limitations. Three deserve mention. First, a few nonrenewable resources do not fit the pattern described above. Notably, commercial accumulations of petroleum are for the most part limited to sedimentary beds that can maintain open pores and cavities only above about 20,000 meters of depth in the earth's crust. Moreover, after use as fuel, petroleum products are exhausted to the atmosphere and not recoverable. For both reasons, petroleum resources are more limited than other nonrenewables. However, existing supplies remain substantial, and imperfect substitutes exist for both supply (e.g., oil sands) and demand (e.g., ethanol). Thus the impact of the limitation is greatly attenuated.

Helium offers a more dramatic example. It occurs concentrated in a few natural gas deposits subject to exhaustion. However, helium is also found in essentially unlimited but dilute quantities in the atmosphere. Therefore, the problem is not one of absolute exhaustion but of a sharp discontinuity in the cost curves as exploitation shifts from one source to another. In such cases, prices will rise to cover the higher costs of exploitation from new sources, and those uses that cannot afford the higher prices will be forced to turn to substitutes. By the nature of their geological occurrence, cost

discontinuities are more likely to occur with rarer elements, which may follow a bimodal distribution of quantity versus grade rather than the unimodal distribution typical of more abundant elements.

Second, exhaustion is definitely a problem for specific mining districts. Changes in consumption patterns, technological change favoring alternative sources of supply, or depletion of local ore bodies can result in the abandonment of mining towns and the decline of entire regions. In this situation the term "nonrenewable" applies in an apparently literal sense. (Only apparently: mineral deposits typically cease being exploitable long before physical exhaustion because added costs of extraction are greater than the returns that can be realized.) Research to reduce costs and regional planning to diversify the economy are recommended to prolong the life of communities dependent upon mining.

The third and most important problem lies in the fact that extraction and use of nonrenewable resources invariably degrades renewable resources—in a word, the environment. Problems such as acid mine drainage, waste piles, land subsidence, and vegetation burned off by smelters have troubled mining districts for decades. Ironically the very forces that extend the intensive and extensive margins of exploitation to preclude depletion of nonrenewable resources simultaneously increase the threats to renewables. Larger-scale mining implies more land degradation, or the ability to operate in remote or wilderness areas. More complex and lower grade ore bodies imply the use of greater quantities of energy and of biological and chemical extraction techniques. Few of these problems are insurmountable but they nevertheless present significant dangers to the natural environment.

In summary although in a geological sense nonrenewable resources are absolutely limited in quantity, this does not, in practice, appear to be a serious human problem. What does appear to be a problem is degradation of the supposedly renewable resources during the extraction and use of nonrenewables.

David B. Brooks

Further Readings

Barnett, Harold J., and Chandler Morse. *Scarcity and Growth: The Economics of Natural Resource Availability.* 1963.
Hartwick, John M., and Nancy D. Olewiler. *The Economics of Natural Resource*

Use. 1986.

Vogely, William A., ed. *Economics of the Mineral Industries.* 1976.

See also COAL: ENVIRONMENTAL IMPACTS; MINING AND SMELTING: HISTORICAL IMPACTS; OIL SHALE; RESOURCISM; URANIUM MINING: ENVIRONMENTAL IMPACTS

Not-in-My-Back-Yard
See NIMBY SYNDROME

Nitrous Oxides
See ACID PRECIPITATION: TERRESTRIAL IMPACTS; AIR POLLUTION: IMPACTS; SMOG

Nuclear Electric Power

Commercial nuclear power was born in the United States as a stepchild of the nuclear arms race when President Dwight D. Eisenhower proposed "Atoms for Peace" in a dramatic speech before the United Nations in 1953. The first "peaceful" plant, with a rating of 72 MegaWatts electric (MWe), was an adapted submarine reactor. It was brought on line in Shippingport, Pennsylvania, on December 2, 1957, exactly fifteen years after Enrico Fermi and collaborators produced the first sustained nuclear reaction at the University of Chicago as part of the wartime Manhattan Project. The Shippingport plant was considered a demonstration unit, too small to be economically competitive.

The Growth of Nuclear Electric Power

After five years of government subsidy a 170 MWe plant was opened at Indian Point, twenty-six miles north of New York City. At this point private industry entered with the firm belief that nuclear power would be an economically competitive source for electric generation. The future seemed assured since electric power was expanding at a remarkable 7 percent per annum (doubling time of ten years). By 1971 nuclear enthusiasts in the United States projected the construction of 500 plants—1000 MWe each—by the year 2000 (Starr, 1971). Many of the industrial countries made similar projections.

By 1992 this fantastic "dream" had in effect been reduced to less than one fifth its projected size, owing to over-estimation of the market for electricity, under-estimation of the potential for energy efficiency, and misjudgment

of the environmental costs and risks of nuclear electric plants. In 1992 the United States had 109 plants with a total capacity of 98,729 MWe, about 600 times the capacity of the 1962 Indian Point plant. The 109 plants accounted for 19 percent of electric energy produced in the United States. Worldwide there was a total of 424 plants in thirty-two countries and a total capacity of 330,651 MWe.

In the first decade after 1962 nuclear electricity grew with a doubling time of approximately two years. By 1992 this extremely rapid growth had slowed, but worldwide the numbers still showed near doubling during 1982–1992. Worldwide nuclear electricity was the second most important source of electric energy. Measured in billions of kilowatt-hours per annum, the amount was 1,500 for coal, 600 for nuclear, 300 each for natural gas and hydroelectricity, and less than 100 for petroleum.

Aside from the United States, major current producers of nuclear electricity are (with their installed capacity in thousands of MWe): France (57), Japan (34), Germany (22), Russian Federation (18), Canada (14), Ukraine (13), United Kingdom (12), Sweden (10), Spain (7), South Korea (7), and Belgium (5). In all these countries nuclear power contributes a significant fraction of electric generation, but only in France (and Lithuania) is this fraction as high as 75 percent.

The initially very rapid growth of nuclear power, including the up-sizing of nuclear plants from 170 to 1,200 MWe in ten years, was unprecedented in the history of technology development. Some argue it may underlie much of nuclear power's current troubles.

Despite these worries it is noted by a proponent of nuclear power (Taylor, 1989) that nuclear electric energy has been delivered, on the average, with greater safety, less environmental impact, and at less cost than most prevailing methods of generating base-load electricity. Whereas this claim is strongly challenged by environmentalists, it remains true that any reasonable assessment of nuclear power would assign risks which are, on the average, different but not more severe than competing technologies such as coal. Two specific worries remain: 1) the potential for catastrophic accidents; and 2) the unresolved problem of high level waste disposal.

The Risk of Catastrophic Accidents

The risk of catastrophic accidents has been extensively studied via probabilistic risk analysis

(PRA) with the conclusion that large accidents are highly unlikely and, in some sense, "can't happen." Unfortunately the 1986 accident at Chernobyl in the Ukraine proved this conclusion wrong. Chernobyl was the largest environmental release of radioisotopes in a single event ever, and is surpassed only by the total release by atmospheric nuclear testing in the years 1945–1980. Other near catastrophic nuclear accidents (the 1979 accident at Three Mile Island in the United States, and the 1957 accident at Windscale in the United Kingdom) were smaller than Chernobyl by at least four orders of magnitude, but nonetheless led to extensive environmental contamination, contributing to the public's distrust of nuclear electric power.

Because different models of reactors have different designs and engineered safety, it has been argued by nuclear proponents that one should not generalize on the basis of Three Mile Island or Chernobyl. This argument has not been widely accepted by publics and around the world, who in many cases have based their opposition to nuclear power first on Three Mile Island and later on Chernobyl.

A corollary of the argument that Chernobyl is special is the conclusion by many nuclear specialists that all reactors of the Chernobyl design (fourteen in the former Soviet Union, more in Eastern and central Europe) should be closed and decommissioned. That conclusion has not been accepted, in large part because of the heavy dependence of the respective nations on the flawed reactors.

In this situation increasing numbers of nuclear engineers have advocated a program to design a new generation of "intrinsically safe" reactors. This effort notwithstanding we have arrived in a situation in which few new nuclear plants are under construction or on order. In the United States no new plants have been ordered since 1978.

The Problem of High Level Nuclear Wastes

As nuclear fuel is consumed the fuel elements must be removed and replaced. The spent fuel contains a large quantity of radioactive fission products, some of which continue to emit hazardous ionizing radiation for thousands of years. This requires the permanent storage of spent fuel, and raises the issue of how this may be safely done. Society has struggled for more than twenty years with this problem and has not found an acceptable solution for it.

Whereas nuclear engineers have argued that there are a number of feasible solutions to the problem, so far none have been accepted by most governments and publics. This picture applies particularly to the United States, Sweden, and Germany, less so in France. Instead of the desired "permanent solution" spent fuel is kept in "temporary" swimming pools on the reactor site. The breakdown of long-term waste disposal has been driven by the public's antipathy to hazardous waste and undesirable facilities of all kinds known as the Not-in-My-Back-Yard or NIMBY Syndrome. Only in France have nuclear wastes been handled by reprocessing spent fuel, and encasing the reprocessed material into glass.

Waste disposal has been poorly handled in formerly centrally planned countries as well, where instead of citizen participation delaying any decision, the problem has been the lack of public participation and technically incompetent ways of waste burial.

The Future

In 1993 after thirty-one years of commercial nuclear electric power, characterized by rapid growth at the beginning and slow growth in the middle, we are currently entering, at least for an interim, a period of decline. Chernobyl-type plants will or should close; many U.S. plants will reach their useful life and will continue to close in ever larger numbers as licenses run out and no new plants are on order. This leaves new nuclear construction to a handful of countries such as France, Japan, South Korea, Taiwan, and China.

How and where will nuclear power make a recovery? In democracies with vocal publics and many alternatives, such as the United States, Sweden, and Germany, the near future of nuclear looks unpromising. In technically strong countries such as France and Japan, with relatively uninvolved publics and no real alternatives, the future for nuclear electricity is promising. Other nations, such as the fragments of the former Soviet Union, with political instability, defective existing plants, many choices, and an environmental crisis of extreme proportions, the future of nuclear power is anybody's guess. Thus, overall the question of the future of nuclear power has no simple answer, but depends on a complex web of technology, resources, social systems, and public perceptions.

Christoph Hohenemser

Further Readings

Hohenemser, C., R.L. Goble, and P. Slovic. "Institutional Aspects of the Future Development of Nuclear Power." *Annual Review of Energy* 15 (1990): 173–200.

Starr, C. "Energy and Power." *Scientific American* 225 (1971): 37–49.

Taylor, John J. "Improved and Safer Nuclear Power." *Science* 244 (1989): 318–24.

"World List of Nuclear Power Plants Operable, Under Construction." *Nuclear News* 36 (1993): 43–62.

See also CHERNOBYL; FORMER SOVIET UNION; IONIZING RADIATION; LOVINS, AMORY B.; NIMBY SYNDROME; NUCLEAR WASTE; RISK ANALYSIS; URANIUM MINING: ENVIRONMENTAL IMPACTS

Nuclear Power

See NUCLEAR ELECTRIC POWER

Nuclear Testing

See RADIOACTIVE FALLOUT; NUCLEAR WEAPONS TESTING

Nuclear Waste

High Level

High-level radioactive waste is an inevitable by-product of the generation of electricity from nuclear fission. It constitutes the "back end" of the nuclear fuel cycle that begins with exploration and mining of uranium ore and proceeds through conversion, enrichment, and fabrication of fuel for nuclear power plants; its use in reactors; interim storage of the used or "spent" fuel; and finally reprocessing and/or disposal.

The fuel rods in commercial nuclear power plants are used for three to five years and are then insufficient for optimal power production. The buildup of the fission products from the nuclear reaction eventually makes the continued use of the fuel rods uneconomical because they interfere with the fission reaction by absorbing neutrons. These irradiated fuel rods and fuel assemblies, which contain substantial quantities of unused uranium (94 percent of the spent fuel) and plutonium (1 percent) are much more radioactive than the new fuel because of the accumulated fission products (5 percent). Hence the designation high-level waste. The fuel rods remain highly dangerous for thousands of years due to their emission of alpha and beta particles and gamma rays (which harm living tissue) and because of the long half-life of some of the constituent parts. Most of the radioactivity decays quickly, but enough remains that the U.S. Environmental Protection Agency (EPA) standards for disposal of high-level waste specify 10,000 years of isolation from the biosphere to protect public and environmental health.

Since the 1950s (the beginning of commercial nuclear plants) this so-called spent fuel has been stored in water-filled basins at each reactor site. Initially it was assumed that such storage would be for only a short period to allow heat to dissipate, after which the waste would be reprocessed to separate the usable plutonium and uranium from the unusable fission byproducts. The former would be reused and the latter disposed of permanently. For all practical purposes, fuel reprocessing in the United States was ended in the late 1970s under President Jimmy Carter. Some nations such as France and Great Britain reprocess spent fuel from their own reactors, and do so under contract for other nations as well. But reprocessing greatly increases the volume of radioactive wastes that require disposal while lowering their radioactivity only slightly. In the United States all spent fuel is considered to be high-level nuclear waste and is slated for eventual disposal in geologic repositories, the method of disposal chosen by the United States and all other nations as preferable to the alternatives. The choice of reprocessing is of critical importance for the ultimate quantity of nuclear waste and thus the need for sites at which repositories can be constructed.

Although continued water storage on site presents no unsurmountable technical or safety problems that have not already been dealt with, it is far more expensive than other forms of storage and is not a practical option for the future. As power plants run out of storage space (which is increasingly occurring in the 1990s) they will need to rely on either another form of temporary storage (i.e., dry storage in steel and concrete casks) or on approved permanent disposal sites. Some utilities already use dry cask storage, and others anticipate use of this method in light of the expected delay in opening of permanent repositories. Ultimately protection of public health and the biosphere, as well as security of the waste itself and its plutonium content, leads most analysts to favor permanent disposal in geologic repositories.

Estimates of the total amount of high-level nuclear waste vary, but the stock of commercial spent fuel rods (the major component of civilian high-level waste) in the United States in

1993 totaled about 25,000 metric tons; about 2,000 metric tons are added each year. For the world as a whole the annual production of high-level waste is about 8,000 tons a year. The U.S. Department of Energy (DOE), charged with regulation of military nuclear facilities and assigned managerial authority for radioactive waste from civilian nuclear plants, estimates that the total quantity will reach some 40,000 metric tons by the year 2000, and 80,000 metric tons by the year 2025. The quantities would be greater should additional nuclear power plants be constructed. Comparable amounts are accumulating in other nations equally or more reliant on nuclear energy than is the United States. One recent estimate is that the world would require one waste repository (holding 70,000 tons per site) every nine years to meet the anticipated production of nuclear waste if present and planned power plants continue to operate.

On the basis of volume the accumulated military wastes in the United States greatly exceed wastes from commercial nuclear reactors, constituting some 90 percent of the total. However, the former are primarily in liquid form and the latter compacted into fuel rods. Spent fuel rods constitute less than 1 percent of the volume of radioactive wastes in the United States, but they account for 95 percent of the radioactivity from all sources, both civilian and military. In addition commercially-generated wastes are increasing much faster than military-related wastes. Thus the long-term nuclear waste problem can be said to be primarily one of spent fuel rods from commercial power plants.

The amounts and sources of high-level waste make it clear that issues regarding its disposal are inseparable from the larger question of energy policy, especially government actions affecting the components of a nation's mix of energy sources. Nuclear utilities are especially anxious to find a solution to the problem of high-level waste, and opponents of nuclear power are as eager to raise questions about the safety of waste disposal proposals, particularly those associated with permanent repositories. If the utilities and government cannot find acceptable solutions for the disposal of nuclear waste, there is little prospect for commercial nuclear power after existing reactors have completed their expected useful lives. This is now about forty to sixty years on average, depending on the standards applied.

High-level nuclear waste has become politically controversial because both technical and social problems have arisen in the siting of the engineered, multiple-barrier, geological repositories that are the preferred solution for long-term and safe disposal of the waste. The United States specified this approach in the 1982 Nuclear Waste Policy Act, which it modified in 1987 with the Nuclear Waste Policy Amendments Act to focus on a single site (Yucca Mountain, Nevada). Construction and operation of high-level waste repositories are highly complex undertakings though not especially technically complicated. Potentially suitable sites must be identified and thoroughly evaluated—in a process called site characterization, and then, if acceptable, contractors must excavate and construct the repository, and fuel must be transported to the site for disposal. Each stage of this process presents difficult managerial and political challenges.

Characterization alone is an expensive and time-consuming process, made especially difficult by the exacting EPA technical standards for minimizing long-term environmental and health risks. In the United States, for example, characterization of the proposed site at Yucca Mountain is expected to involve over 2,000 scientists and engineers, take over six years, and cost in excess of $6 billion. Some 100 miles of tunnels must be excavated in volcanic rock about 300 meters (1,000 feet) below the surface of the mountain—but above the water table. Waste will be transported to the repository and placed in the tunnels over a fifty-year period, after which time the repository would be sealed permanently and marked to warn future populations.

Engineers assume that the storage canisters themselves will last no more than a few hundred years. After that time, containment would depend on the stability of the volcanic rock at the site. Once stored in the repository, fuel will stay at temperatures above that of boiling water for 300 to 1,000 years, and then gradually fall. Thus, should water come into contact with the waste, it would vaporize and might well escape, carrying radioactivity with it.

The rest of the process of repository construction may be more straightforward than the site assessment, but it is just as subject to management problems and political controversies. DOE's effort to site a repository has been afflicted by a wide range of obstacles, including managerial incapacities of DOE and its contractors, scientific uncertainties surrounding site assessment, and especially social and political battles with the state of Nevada, which has adamantly refused to accept the site. The high cost of the facility is also at issue. In 1990 DOE estimated the total cost at $26 billion (in 1988 dollars) for a single repository and $34 billion if two were constructed. Even if costs run no higher than these estimates, critics suggest that such geologic repositories are far more costly than available alternatives such as above-ground, permanent facilities.

Nevada's continuing opposition, and that of other states in earlier years, stems from intense public opposition to nuclear repositories, which is rooted in public fear of nuclear power and nuclear waste. The antagonism between DOE and the state is exacerbated by public distrust of the capabilities of the implementing agency (DOE) to ensure safe construction and operation of the repository. Similar difficulties have affected the repository siting process since its inception, although it is not clear how much of the public opposition can be attributed to poor implementation decisions by DOE and how much to inherent public resistance to location of nearby repositories that are believed to impose a risk on the local population (see the entry on the NIMBY syndrome elsewhere in the volume). Much the same picture of public opposition is found in other nations. In 1993 no long-term geologic repository existed anywhere in the world.

Failure to solve these technical, management, and political problems will likely mean the eventual abandonment of nuclear power as a leading source of energy worldwide. As of the early 1990s, nuclear power in the United States provided about 6 percent of energy consumption and about 22 percent of electricity used. Most other nations are less dependent on nuclear power for electricity, although some (France, Belgium, Hungary, Korea, Sweden, Switzerland, Spain, and Japan, among others) are more dependent.

At present nuclear power provides only about 5 percent of the world's total energy production and about 16 percent of its electricity, nearly all of which (95 percent) is produced by the industrialized nations. However, concern over global climate change attributable to the use of fossil fuels (by far the largest source of energy at some 88 percent) has resurrected interest in nuclear power despite continuing problems with the waste issue. Public concern about the safety of nuclear power both in the United States and in other nations—sharply higher after the 1979 Three Mile Island and 1986 Chernobyl accidents—has significantly constrained its further development to date, as have economic and regulatory hurdles. So far utilities have been reluctant to reboard the nuclear ship. The choice facing developing nations, where an enormous growth in energy production is expected over the next several decades, is even more problematic. Whether a new generation of safer and cheaper nuclear reactors can play a significant role in a sustainable energy economy of the future remains to be seen.

Low Level

In addition to producing high-level radioactive waste, commercial nuclear power plants, among other sources, generate a variety of low-level wastes. Low-level waste (LLW) is any material contaminated by radiation and emitting low levels of radioactivity. The radioisotopes found in LLW are far less potent than those in high-level waste and have relatively short half-lives, but they are nevertheless potentially injurious to living organisms. They need to be contained for anywhere from several days to 500 years—far less than necessary for high-level waste.

LLW includes irradiated tools and other equipment, clothing, ion exchanger resins, animal carcasses, medical and pharmaceutical waste, and assorted residues from nuclear research and defense activities. An estimated 1.1 million cubic feet of LLW was shipped to commercial facilities in the United States in 1990—a far smaller volume than in earlier years due to compacting and other methods used to reduce volume. As the cost of disposal rises, incentives exist to reduce the quantity of waste. Disposal costs rose from about $1 per cubic foot in 1975 to about $50 in 1990. The total annual volume of commercial LLW produced over the next twenty to thirty years is expected to remain at approximately 1 million cubic feet per year in the United States, although much depends on the rate of decommissioning of nuclear power plants, which will produce large quantities of waste. Recent estimates indicated that about 56 percent of the total volume of LLW in the nation is generated by utilities using nuclear power plants (constituting 75 percent of the total radioactivity), 31 percent by industry, 2 percent by hospitals, 6 percent by government, and 4 percent by universities.

In addition to the 1 million cubic feet per year of commercial wastes, the DOE generates more than 4 million cubic feet of LLW annually from its defense and research activities. This waste is handled separately from commercial waste and is disposed of at DOE sites.

For commercial nuclear power plants the source of most LLW is the reactor's core and cooling system. High-temperature water circulating in the reactors causes corrosion of exposed metal surfaces, particularly in the miles of piping, which must be removed. The purification of the cooling water results in very radioactive LLW waste, which must be disposed of in heavy, lead-lined casks. Other waste products are created in the process of cleaning the plants after the inevitable leaks, and in routine maintenance of the plants. One expert has estimated that a single large, water-cooled, nuclear reactor may generate 600 to 1,400 cubic meters of LLW each year—a level that increases as a plant ages and suffers more leaks and deterioration of equipment. By the year 2000 commercial reactor waste is expected to total some 4 million cubic meters. Such waste historically has been buried in shallow trenches into which drums and other waste containers are placed and covered with earth.

Defense related high-level and transuranic wastes (with isotopes heavier than uranium) as well as some defense-related LLW in the United States are stored at federal facilities in South Carolina, Idaho, and Washington, with a major new facility for such wastes in New Mexico (the Waste Isolation Pilot Project or WIPP) still struggling for approval after years of technical and political controversy. Other defense-related LLW are stored at commercial sites.

Since the late 1950s the states have been permitted to regulate small amounts of LLW generated from commercial, medical, and research activities, and most of these wastes were deposited in landfills in six locations in Nevada, Washington, South Carolina, Illinois, Kentucky, and New York, only three of which were operating by the late 1980s. Two of the closed sites had difficulties containing the waste, and the use of shallow land burial of LLW has lost favor. Surface containment in engineered facilities has been preferred in recent years. Some nations (e.g., Germany and Sweden) prefer deep geologic disposal, similar to the way they handle high-level waste.

Concerns over the inequitable burden on the states accepting LLW led the U.S. Congress to adopt the Low-Level Radioactive Waste Policy Act in 1980. The law made each state responsible for the LLW generated within its borders and established a process for the formation of interstate compacts to develop regional

LLW repositories to be placed in a host state. The three states accepting LLW were given the right to refuse waste from outside their own regions. The hope was that this process would result in a small number of more carefully engineered and secure facilities, and thus minimize health and environmental risks associated with a more dispersed and less well regulated collection of LLW sites. It would also promote some degree of equity by creating new sites and by forcing states to deal with the waste produced within their borders.

Unfortunately the act has proven to be difficult to implement, and the goals remained elusive through 1993. A 1986 deadline for establishing the compacts was extended in amendments to the act adopted by Congress in 1985. As of 1993 nine compacts representing forty-two states had been formed. The existing Hanford site will serve the Northwest and Rocky Mountain compacts, and Barnwell, South Carolina, will serve the eight-state Southeast compact temporarily until a new site is completed in North Carolina. In other locations the process has been highly controversial. As has been the case with high-level radioactive waste, public fear of LLW and the NIMBY reaction have made siting difficult. The result is that generators of LLW will be forced to store their wastes on site at nuclear power plants and at other facilities until the impasse is resolved or to pay high fees to have it shipped out of the region to an approved site. Economics will continue to be an important factor. For example, the Barnwell site in South Carolina anticipated imposing an access fee of $220 per cubic foot for waste from outside the Southeast. Adding the transportation cost disposal of LLW at Barnwell will raise the total disposal cost three- to five-fold for some generators in New York and California. Barnwell is expected to close after 1996, adding to the pressure to develop new sites. Some estimates for new, smaller facilities run as high as $500 per cubic foot for Class A nuclear waste (the least dangerous kind), and higher for Class B and C wastes, which require more expensive packaging and more secure disposal.

These developments create a deepening crisis for the disposal of LLW that resembles that surrounding high-level wastes. In this case as well, social scientists and policy analysts will need to focus on identification of suitable decision-making processes for waste siting that might restore some degree of responsibility and cooperation among the states and their citizens.

A great irony of these program failures is that well-intentioned federal policies to create a few safe facilities may have the effect of creating thousands of scattered, poorly controlled, and potentially unsafe sites around the nation. Devising solutions to this problem will severely test the capacity of governmental institutions in the United States and elsewhere.

Michael E. Kraft

Further Readings

Carter, Luther J. *Nuclear Imperatives and Public Trust: Dealing with Radioactive Waste*. 1987.

U.S. Office of Technology Assessment. *Managing the Nation's Commercial High-Level Radioactive Waste*. 1985.

Dunlap, Riley E., Michael E. Kraft, and Eugene A. Rosa, eds. *Public Reactions to Nuclear Waste: Citizens' Views of Repository Siting*. 1993.

See also IONIZING RADIATION; NIMBY SYNDROME; NUCLEAR ELECTRIC POWER; NUCLEAR WEAPONS PRODUCTION; NUCLEAR WEAPONS TESTING; RADIOACTIVE FALLOUT

Nuclear Weapons Production

The end of the cold war between the United States and the former Soviet Union in the early 1990s has led to a major reduction in the production of nuclear weapons which had continued unabated from World War II onward. Throughout the forty-five years of major production, the nuclear weapons complexes manufactured and assembled weapons and components, conducted atomic weapons research, development, and testing, and primarily processed four nuclear materials: highly enriched uranium, plutonium, lithium, and tritium. In the United States by 1990 the federal nuclear complexes employed over 90,000 at seventeen sites in thirteen states.

The forty-five year production of nuclear weapons left a legacy of environmental problems which, in the United States alone, may take anywhere from an estimated $155 to $300 billion and at least fifty years to remedy. Many U.S. production sites are so contaminated they have been referred to by some experts as possible "national sacrifice zones." The United States and many of the republics of the former Soviet Union have made agreements to share resources and information in the cleanup of contaminated areas.

There are six major environmental problems identified as consequences of nuclear weapons production:

1. Contamination of Ground and Surface Water
2. Contamination of Soil and Sediments
3. Contamination of Air
4. Potential of Accident
5. Inadequate Storage
6. Decommissioning of Nuclear Power Plants

Contamination of Ground and Surface Water by Reactive and/or Toxic Wastes

At the Fernald, Ohio, Feed Materials Production Center (now closed) more than 300,000 pounds of uranium oxide has filtered into the surrounding water supplies. In Richland, Washington, at the Hanford Reservation, billions of gallons of radioactive waste contaminate more than 100 square miles of groundwater. Wastes from the Idaho National Engineering Laboratory in Arco, Idaho, have polluted the Snake River Aquifer. Plutonium waste is moving toward the reservoir. The Savannah River Plant in Aiken, South Carolina, has released toxic poisons into the Tuscaloosa aquifer and Strontium 90 into surface waters.

Contamination of Soil and Sediments by Reactive or Toxic Waste or Both

It was a regular practice at former Soviet nuclear production facilities to dump barrels of toxic and hazardous waste on or near the sites. In the United States high level waste was often deposited in liquid storage tanks until the 1970s. Low level and transuranic waste was placed in metal containers in the ground or deposited in the ocean until the early 1960s.

At Rocky Flats, in Golden, Colorado, a former assembly site for nuclear triggers, soil around the site is contaminated with high levels of plutonium. At the Portsmouth Uranium Enrichment Plant in Piketown, Ohio, from 1974 to 1984 radioactive waste was rototilled into the soil.

Contamination of the Air by Reactive or Toxic Waste or Both

In Fernald, Ohio, at the Feed Materials Production Center, filters in vent stacks remained unrepaired for years, permitting unknown quantities of uranium dust to escape. Billion of cubic meters of gas with radioactive fission and activation products were discharged into the air at the Hanford Reservation in Richland, Washington from 1944–1988 as policy or by accident. Over 1,300 residents of Washington and Oregon received dangerously high doses of radioactive iodine without any warning.

Potential of Accident Due to Human Error, Aging Equipment, or Poor Maintenance
A U.S. Department of Energy technical team in a 1992 report found that 177 underground storage tanks at Hanford Reservation were potentially dangerous. In September, 1957, at the Chelyabrinsk plutonium production plant in the southern Ural mountains, a tank full of radioactive waste exploded, poisoning 8,900 square miles, forcing the evacuation of 250,000, and causing a number of fatalities. In October, 1957, a water-cooled graphite moderated reactor at a nuclear weapons complex near Liverpool, England caught fire and spread fallout over most of Western Europe. Thirty-nine cancer deaths have been traced to this accident. In April, 1993, an explosion at the Tomsk plant in Siberia, used to separate plutonium and uranium, spread traces of plutonium over forty-six square miles.

Inadequate Storage of Low Level, Transuranic, and High Level Wastes
In the former Soviet Union low level and transuranic wastes were routinely dumped on the ground without adequate safeguards. The environmental group Greenpeace reported in 1993 that 13,000 containers of waste were dumped in the Kara and Barents Seas from the former Soviet Union nuclear program. Other than storage at nuclear production facilities such as Rocky Flats, Colorado; Hanford, Washington; and Idaho Falls, Idaho, the United States has no sites currently accepting low level and transuranic military waste.

The Waste Isolation Pilot Project in Carlsbad, New Mexico, designed to permanently store low level and transuranic military wastes, will not be ready until the late-1990s because of technical difficulties and political challenges. The Nuclear Waste Policy Act of 1982, as amended, led to the selection of the Yucca Mountains high level waste facility—the first U.S. permanent underground repository— 100 miles northwest of Las Vegas, Nevada. After $15 billion in development costs questions have been raised about earthquake faults and young volcanic activity in the area and possible calcium deposits found at the site. The scheduled date of operation is tentatively established at 2010.

Decommissioning of Nuclear Power Plants at the Weapons Facilities
After thirty years of bombardment by neutrons the metallic walls of a reactor pressure vessel become brittle which can result in cracks that might expose the highly radioactive materials. Tubes in the reactors' steam generators can crack releasing radioactive water. Although reactors' lives can be extended for up to forty-five years, most are ready for decommissioning after that. Decommissioning costs an estimated $1 billion per reactor and, in the United States alone, it will cost $200 billion to decommission the reactors used in weapons production.

Roger Anderson

Further Readings
Anderson, Roger. "Environmental, Safety and Health Issues at Nuclear Weapons Production Facilities, 1946–1988." *Environmental Review* 13 (1989): 69–92.

Funke, Odelia. "National Security and the Environment." In *Environmental Policy in the 1990s: Toward a New Agenda.* Ed. Norman J. Vig and Michael E. Kraft. 2nd ed. 1994, 323–45.

Idelson, Holly. "Nuclear Weapons Complex Braces for Overhaul." *Congressional Quarterly Weekly Report* 50 (1992): 1066–72.

United States Congress, Office of Technology Assessment. *Complex Cleanup: The Environmental Legacy of Nuclear Weapons Production.* 1991.

See also Environmental Protection in Wartime; Nuclear Electric Power; Nuclear Waste; Radioactive Fallout

Nuclear Weapons Testing
Wide controversy surrounds the environmental impact of nuclear weapons tests. Since the first American test (named Trinity) in New Mexico desert in 1945, weapons tests continued sporadically by nations developing nuclear and thermo-nuclear bombs. Tests occurred in the atmosphere, in underground chambers, beneath the surface of the sea, and in the stratosphere on the borders of space. All spurred debates on the

short-run and long-term impacts of radioactivity upon populations and environments as it became clear that the tests portended consequences for each.

Following the New Mexico test in July, 1945, the U.S. bombed the Japanese cities of Hiroshima and Nagasaki with similar devices, not only to hasten the end of the war in the Pacific, but to test the effects of nuclear explosions upon people and their environment. High rates of birth defects, leukemia, and lymphatic cancers among Japanese survivors demonstrated the lingering effects of radioactive fallout from the bombs. The U.S. continued its testing in the immediate post-war period in the Marshall islands of the South Pacific where islanders had little power to object and at the Nevada Test Site on the U.S. mainland beginning in 1951. Larger thermo nuclear (H-bomb) tests occurred in the South Pacific by 1952 with much publicity surrounding the subsequent irradiation of the crew on a Japanese fishing boat, the Lucky Dragon, from a test in 1954. Meanwhile the Soviet Union developed its atomic and thermo-nuclear weapons with accompanying tests. Heavy testing by both powers including Great Britain in the Australian desert by the late 1950s led to a world-wide fallout alert. Concerns mounted about the consumption through the food chain of Iodine 131 and Strontium 90. The iodine lodged in thyroids and Strontium 90 in bone marrow. Thyroid damage causes developmental problems in the unborn and young children. Bone marrow damage was associated with leukemia and problems with the immune system. Also military personnel experienced direct exposure to fallout in various tactical experiments conducted with the weapons dating back to the American tests in the South Pacific at Bikini in 1946. The Atmospheric Test Ban Treaty of 1963 was a direct outgrowth of the detection of the dispersal of radioactive fallout that occurred not evenly throughout the world but in "hot spots" where it suddenly rained from the sky. Two latecomers to the nuclear club, France and China, continued to test in the atmosphere: France until 1974 and China until 1980.

In the U.S., those populations directly downwind from the tests in Nevada were the most at risk, although this was not revealed at the time. In 1953 over 4,000 sheep in Utah died after a test in Nevada. The placing of the mainland test site in Nevada made most of the continental U.S. subject to fallout from the prevailing winds that moved radioactive debris from west to east across the nation. Fallout was particularly heavy in southern Utah after the "Dirty Harry Test" in Nevada in 1953. Later, residents unsuccessfully sued the government contending that high incidents of cancer in the area were a direct result of the testing program. Some sources, which many regard as hysterical, claim a significant drop in Scholastic Aptitude Tests (SAT scores) among the populations born in the U.S. and especially in Utah in the late 1950s who were exposed to fallout in early infancy; that test fallout weakened the immune systems paving the way for the AIDS epidemic later in the century. Finally the dying of forests in the northern hemisphere often associated with acid rain has been attributed to nuclear fallout beginning in the 1950s as well as to the installation of nuclear power plants.

Underground testing also has environmental consequences. When gases escape or "vent" as they often do they are heavy with radioactive material. In the explosion chamber itself entrapment of contaminated materials occurs that will remain for thousands of years and be a potential source of pollution to underground water supplies. The stratosphere or space has experienced nuclear testing with the resulting injection of nitrogen oxides into the stratosphere, where they "catalyze ozone destruction." A U.S. test 400 kilometers above Johnson Atoll on July 9, 1962 caused severe electromagnetic disturbances in the ionosphere, disrupted the Van Allen belts, and spread radioactive pollution in the stratosphere. Tests carried out in the Pacific, especially those detonated underwater or close to coral reefs, damage their structure. When this occurs, toxins from the coral often appear, which fish consume harmlessly, but when humans consume the fish, ciguatyera poisoning follows. Severe symptoms of nausea, lack of muscle control and even temporary blindness presents problems to populations depending on fish as a main source of protein.

Generally nations have chosen to test their weapons in areas where populations have little political power and are outside of the national decision making process. Often these are poorer areas and contain minority populations who suffer major environmental and health damages. As of 1990 world-wide testing has totaled 1,892 explosions both in the atmosphere, stratosphere, and underground. Some estimates assert that the number of cancer cases resulting from atmospheric testing in the Twentieth Century will cause two and one half million cancer cases for the present generations and those of the future. In the northern hemisphere estimates suggest that 430,000 cancer deaths will occur by the year 2000 caused by atmospheric explosions.

William D. Rowley

Further Readings

Bethe, Hans Albrecht, and Edward Teller. *The Future of Nuclear Tests.* 1961.

Jonathan M. Weisgall. *Operations Cross-roads: The Atomic Tests at Bikini Atoll.* 1994.

Philip L. Fradkin. *Fallout: An American Tragedy.* 1989.

Ralph Graeub. *The Petkau Effect: Nuclear Radiation, People, and Trees.* 1992.

Richard L. Miller. *Under the Cloud: The Decades of Nuclear Testing.* 1986.

See also ENVIRONMENTAL JUSTICE; FOOD CHAIN; NUCLEAR WEAPONS PRODUCTION; NUCLEAR WASTE; RADIOACTIVE FALLOUT

Nuclear Winter

It was suggested in 1982 that a large-scale nuclear war might inject smoke into the atmosphere sufficient to prevent a high proportion of the sunlight from reaching the ground. That contamination would in turn reduce the ambient temperatures to well below the freezing point on a hemispheric—if not global—scale for a period of up to several years. This predicted weather anomaly soon became known as "nuclear winter." That original suggestion, as well as some subsequent support for it, was based on conjectured large-scale nuclear-war scenarios, on very rough estimates of dust and soot generation, and on computer simulations using highly simplified models of atmospheric circulation. Subsequent refinements of those analyses have suggested a substantially less severe and considerably shorter-term impact on the weather.

Thus, in the terrible event that very large numbers of nuclear weapons were to be detonated during a brief period to destroy combustible urban and industrial targets, sufficient aerosols could be generated—especially soot, but also ash, dust, and oily droplets—to partially obscure sunlight over and beyond the target areas in large moving patches over a period of perhaps several weeks throughout the interior portions of the major landmasses in the northern hemisphere, and perhaps beyond. If this were to occur in summer, the resulting temporary reductions in ambient ground-level temperatures (of perhaps 10 degrees Celsius to 20 degrees Celsius) would be likely to cause considerable agricultural and other habitat damage during that season. The ecological impact of the suggested transitory temperature reductions would be considerably less pronounced if the war occurred during the dormant winter season. Severity of ecological impact would also decrease with increase in latitude. Further speculation has been made that injections of soot into the atmosphere might stabilize the upper atmosphere for some months. This could disrupt monsoonal patterns for one or even two growing seasons, leading to rainfall deprivation in regions where the agriculture depends upon that precipitation.

Extended low-temperature anomalies aside, the foreseeable long-term, widespread, and severe environmental disruptions and their ecological ramifications would be tragic, both for the effect they would have upon the immediate survivors of a nuclear holocaust and in their own right. The blast (shock) wave from a ground burst causes huge amounts of direct damage to everything in its path over a considerable area; the intense pulse of thermal radiation is not only lethal over a large area, but might lead to devastating wildfires; the pulse of nuclear radiation is deadly to both flora and fauna over an immense area; and radioactive fallout can be medically, agriculturally, and ecologically damaging on a grand scale.

Beyond the hideous immediate and relatively close-in effects on the biotas of blast, heat, and ionizing radiation from each of the many thousands of nuclear bombs that would be expended in a large-scale nuclear war, surviving plants and humans and other animals would be exposed to radioactive fallout throughout huge geographical areas, exacerbated to the extent that existing nuclear facilities were targeted. Moreover, the stratospheric ozone might be depleted for a period of several months or more owing to heat-generated oxides of nitrogen. There is thus the further possibility of widespread ultraviolet (UV-B) radiation reaching the earth's surface during that time at levels injurious to the biotas, both terrestrial and marine.

Arthur H. Westing

Further Readings

Pittock, A. Barrie, et al. *Environmental Consequences of Nuclear War, Volume I: Physical and Atmospheric Effects: Volume II: Ecological and Agricultural Effects.* 1985–1986.

Solomon, F., and R.Q. Marston, eds. *The Medical Implications of Nuclear War.* 1986.

Turco, R.P., et al. "Climate and Smoke: An Appraisal of Nuclear Winter." *Science* 247 (1990): 166–76.

Westing, Arthur H. "The Ecological Dimension of Nuclear War." *Environmental Conservation* 14 (1987): 295–306.

See also IONIZING RADIATION; NATIONAL SECURITY, RECONCEPTUALIZING; NUCLEAR WEAPONS PRODUCTION; RADIOACTIVE FALLOUT

O

Occupational Health
See LABOR AND THE ENVIRONMENT; OSHACT
AND OSHA

Occupational Safety and Health Act
See OSHACT AND OSHA

Odor Pollution
The human sense of smell is a very sensitive, real, and physical response to the presence of odor molecules in the air. Some odor compounds are able to be detected by the human nose in concentrations of parts per trillion, well below the levels of detection of analytical instruments.

Until recently nuisance odor was seen as a relatively insignificant member of the wider family of air pollution problems—a concept evidenced by the relative lack of treatment of the subject in the scientific air pollution literature. This is despite the fact that the World Health Organization defines health in terms of complete physical, social, and mental well-being, effectively meaning that both health and amenity must be taken into account when considering air pollution problems. It is also despite the fact that the legal concept of "odor nuisance" and general urban zoning laws concerning odorous industries have long been established. Scientific neglect of odor appears to have arisen because odor, as an air pollutant, has not been perceived by the relevant authorities to be a critical health issue and because it is generally acknowledged as being extremely difficult to quantify and control. However, community concern for environment, particularly a more recent concern for amenity and "sanitization" of environment (approximately half of all air pollution complaints to regulatory agencies in developed countries involve odor) has provided a strong impetus for odor research and control.

The major problems in developing an odor control strategy involve defining acceptable levels of odor and identifying odor sources. The physical ability of an individual to detect odor in the environment varies, with factors such as age, sex, pregnancy and desensitivity of smell receptors contributing to individual variation in odor perception. Individual reactions to odor also vary; state of health, culture, lifestyle, and degree of familiarity with the odor and the odor-forming process all contribute to the subjective assessment of odor as a nuisance. Many industries, including feedlots, fellmongers, abattoirs, sewage and chemical plants are inherently odorous, and the odorous pollutants emitted can include compounds of sulfur, nitrogen, selenium and halogen, as well as hydrocarbons, alcohols and oxygenates. Interactions of odors may be quite complex, and frequently masking will occur where one odorous compound dominates, even though a suite of odors is present.

Although odor cannot be easily measured by instrument, odor concentrations can be assessed by panels of observers in a technique known as dynamic dilution testing. With this reproducible sensory analysis technique a dilution device is used to present odor to the panel. The odor threshold is that concentration of a compound or mixture of compounds which is distinguished from odor free air by half of the panel of observers. By definition, such a threshold has an odor concentration of one odor dilution unit per meter cubed (1 ODU/m^3).

Nigel J. Tapper

Further Readings
Douglas Porteous, J. "Smellscape." *Progress in Human Geography* 9 (1985): 356–62.

Tapper, N.J., and A.W. Sudbury. "Mapping Odor Sources from Complaint Statistics, Volume I: Identifying the Major Source." *Journal of the Air and Waste Management Association* 41 (1991): 433–41.

See also AIR POLLUTION: IMPACTS

Odum, Eugene

Eugene Odum, a pioneer in ecosystem ecology, was born in 1913 and received an A.B. in zoology from the University of North Carolina at Chapel Hill in 1934. In 1939 he completed a Ph.D. at the University of Illinois, where he studied in the V.E. Shelford/S.G. Kendeigh "school" of community ecology. Joining the University of Georgia faculty in 1940 he remained to retire as Calloway Professor Emeritus of Ecology in 1984.

Odum emerged as a leader in "systems" ecology—a branch that emphasizes calculating ecological energy budgets, computing primary and higher-order production, and determining the efficiency of energy and nutrient transfer among ecosystem components and between ecosystems. A contributor to the rise of "bioeconomics," Odum has written several influential textbooks organized around the ecosystem concept. *Fundamentals of Ecology* (1953) taught students that, instead of beginning with discrete natural phenomena or individual species, they should start with the large scale or whole ecosystem, and proceed with consideration of its components, not as isolated units, but as interacting parts that function together to produce a unique whole. *Ecology and Our Endangered Life-Support Systems* (1989) stresses ecosystem theory as a common denominator that can be used to conceptually couple the "goods and services" needed by humans and those needed by nature.

An early investigator in the fields of radiation ecology and human impact on natural ecosystems, Odum was a key figure in the establishment of the Savannah River Ecology Laboratory at the Savannah River (atomic) Plant in Aiken, South Carolina, the Marine Institute at Sapelo Island, Georgia, and the Institute of Ecology at the University of Georgia, Athens. For his contributions to ecological theory Odum has been awarded La Institute de la Vie by the French government, the Crafoord Prize by the Royal Swedish Academy of Science, and the Tyler Ecology Award by the Tyler Foundation.

Susan P. Bratton

Further Readings
Odum, Eugene. *Fundamentals of Ecology.* 1953.
Worster, Donald. *Nature's Economy.* 1977.

See also CARRYING CAPACITY; ECOSYSTEMS; ELTON, CHARLES

Office of Technology Assessment

The Office of Technology Assessment (OTA) is an agency of the U.S. Congress set up by the Technology Assessment Act in 1972 to advise Congress on issues involving technology. The Office was originally established as a source of advice regarding technological choices and their impact(s), for use in conjunction with legislative and appropriating functions of Congress. Today OTA sees its role more broadly as providing objective analyses of major public policy issues related to scientific and technological change. Studies—known as technology assessments—are undertaken at the request of committees of Congress.

OTA's supreme body is the Technology Assessment Board (TAB) of six senators and six representatives nominated in equal number by the party leadership in the two houses. The OTA director sits on TAB as a non-voting member. TAB meets approximately every six weeks; it formulates policies for OTA, appoints the director, and approves studies.

TAB is in turn advised by the Technology Assessment Advisory Council (TAAC), comprising the members of the public (usually scientists and academics) and the Comptroller General and the Director of the Congressional Research Service ex officio. TAAC meets twice a year to review the activities and reports of OTA and undertake any other related tasks the board may direct.

The day-to-day running of the office falls to the director who in turn appoints the staff. In March 1994 OTA had 143 permanent employees and fifty-three temporary employees. Of these about 130 are researchers. The pay and conditions of staff are linked to federal scales. Over 50 percent of the permanent and temporary analytical staff have doctorates and a further 30 percent hold Master's degrees. About 35 percent hold science degrees. Outside experts can be contracted for particular tasks. In addition a very large number of specialists—some 1,300 in any one year—may be involved in meetings of advisory panels or workshops relating to individual studies.

OTA's current budget (fiscal year 1994) is $21.3 million and is subject to annual appropriations procedures.

OTA's analytical staff are distributed between two operating divisions: the Industrial, Commercial, and International Security Division; and the Health, Education, and Environmental Division—each supervised by an assistant director. The divisions are further divided into four and three "programs" respectively—each managed by a program director. Issues related to environment and conservation are in the main, though not exclusively, handled through the Oceans and Environment Program and the Energy Program.

The procedures for conducting technology assessments involve a number of steps. First requests may be made by the chairman of any standing, special, select or joint committee of Congress. (TAB members and the director of OTA may also request studies but these are rare.) Requests must be approved by TAB and issues so selected will normally be: 1) important to Congress; 2) of significant social impact; 3) appropriate for study by OTA; and 4) practicable in terms of the resources available. Requests have emanated from many committees but particularly from the House Committee on Energy and Commerce; the House Committee on Space, Science, and Technology; and the Senate Committee on Commerce, Science, and Transportation.

Following TAB approval a request is assigned to the relevant program. Staff will be assigned to a study by the program manager and will number from three to five for a major assessment, one of whom will be project director. A program may have three major assessments in progress at any one time. Auxiliary help may be sought by engaging in-house contractors for specific tasks.

Early in an investigation, the project director assembles an advisory panel representing the whole spectrum of opinion on the policies under study to advise on the direction of the study and to review the drafts produced by the staff, including the final report. The panel normally meets three times.

Most of the work is carried out by the staff, with the assistance of specialist work commissioned from outside contractors. A large project can expend up to $500,000 in contractor expenses. Workshops of invited experts are also widely used.

The final report is written up by the staff and subjected to rigorous internal and external review. A report on a controversial subject might be sent to as many as 200 external reviewers, in addition to the advisory panel. Finally, after satisfying itself that the usual processes have been observed, TAB authorizes publication.

OTA's reports can be long and run to several hundred pages of A4 printing. Thus they are usually accompanied by an executive summary and a one-page report brief.

OTA reports are highly regarded and widely used in Congressional hearings, as the basis for legislation and as part of the budgetary process. Their chief strength is that they define policy options in a comprehensive and impartial way which enables the body politic as a whole to address difficult major issues.

OTA has also been given powers by the Technology Assessment Act to nominate members to a number of statutory advisory commissions concerned with Medicare payments—the Prospective Payment Assessment Commission, the Physician Payment Review Commission, and the Prescription Drug Payment Review Commission. OTA is required to report annually on the activities of these Commissions. It is perhaps a tribute to OTA's reputation for impartiality that such functions have been ascribed to it by Congress.

Rhodri H. Walters

Further Readings

Office of Technology Assessment. *Annual Reports.*

Report of the Carnegie Commission on Science, Technology and Government. *Science, Technology and Congress: Analysis and Advice from the Congressional Support Agencies.* 1991.

Walters, Rhodri. "The Office of Technology Assessment of the US Congress." *Government and Opposition* 27 (1992): 89–108.

See also ENVIRONMENTAL ASSESSMENT (CANADA); ENVIRONMENTAL IMPACT ASSESSMENT; RISK ANALYSIS

Offshore Drilling

See OIL SPILLS

Ogallala Aquifer

The Ogallala Aquifer sprawls across 174,000 square miles of the American Great Plains from southwest Texas to South Dakota. Its sands and gravels, weathered from the Rocky Mountains, lie atop Triassic "red beds," an impervious layer of clay which allows rainwater to be trapped and stored indefinitely. Easily North America's largest source of underground water, its reserves are sufficient to completely fill Lake Huron.

Largely untouched until the 1950s, the Ogallala then began to be utilized by a new, increasingly powerful irrigation technology. The transformation was striking. Vast areas that had parched and blown in the Dust Bowl of the 1930s now blossomed with abundant crops of wheat, corn, alfalfa, grain sorghum, and soybeans. New feedlots based on area grain crops increased ranch productivity. Today the Ogallala supports an annual $20 billion agricultural economy.

This new abundance was based originally on the all-out exploitation of a seemingly inexhaustible resource. But by the early 1980s the costs of unrestrained development had begun to become apparent. With nearly 150,000 water wells pumping on the high plains, Kansas had already exhausted 38 percent of its reserves. A Department of Commerce study concluded that by 2020 the general level of the Ogallala would have dropped 23 percent. In the same year Texas would have used up two-thirds of its total supply. In many places 95 percent of reserves were being removed per year, with only 5 percent being replaced.

Growing realization that the Ogallala aquifer's waters are not only a limited resource, but might in two or three generations become imperiled, has led to increasing conservation efforts. Most of these have been private actions: crops that require less water, reduced or carefully timed irrigation, water recycling, reduced tillage, new irrigation technologies, and even cloud-seeding and hail-reduction programs. Some public programs are also being employed. In parts of Texas, Kansas, and Nebraska limits have been placed on the spacing of new wells. In parts of Nebraska a five-year program of limited water allocation and well metering has been imposed. Serious reconsideration of the nature and scope of water law is occurring throughout the region.

While improved management practices have eased fears that the aquifer will be depleted in a few generations the present situation is still untenable. In some areas lowered water levels have made irrigated agriculture uneconomical. In most regions pumping still removes more water per year than rain can replace.

Pete A.Y. Gunter

Further Readings

Green, Donald E. *Land of the Underground Rain: Irrigation on the Texas High Plains.* 1973.

Zwingle, Erla. "Ogallala Aquifer: Wellspring of the High Plains." *National Geographic* 183 (1993): 80–109.

See also SUSTAINABLE AGRICULTURE; WATER ALLOCATIONS AND SHORTAGES (U.S. WEST)

Oil Shale

Prehistoric layers of sedimentary rock containing oil in the form of a solid, powdery organic substance known as "kerogen" are called oil shale. Low grade deposits underlie portions of Central and Eastern United States and Alaska. The richest U.S. deposits, containing an estimated 80 percent of all recoverable oil shale, are found in the Green River Formation—a sedimentary layer underlying more than 16,500 square miles of Colorado, Utah, and Wyoming. Most of this resource is found on public land. Colorado's Piceance Basin contains most of the highest grade kerogen found in the United States. The oil can be recovered by heating the kerogen to approximately 900 degrees Fahrenheit underground ("in situ") or above ground. The U.S. Department of the Interior has estimated that 80 billion barrels of oil could be recovered from the Western oil shale deposits with existing technologies and perhaps 600 billion from all U.S. deposits—approximately fifteen times the amount of proven U.S. conventional petroleum reserves.

Repeated efforts to commercialize the production of petroleum from the high-quality Western kerogen have failed for more than a century. Major obstacles have been the high cost and technical complexity in developing a commercial facility, the environmental damage associated with refining, and the more competitive price of alternative fuels. "Scaling up" existing technologies to commercial size (50,000 to 100,000 barrels per day oil production) is estimated to cost between $1 and $5 billion. Refining produces high volumes of air pollutants including dust, large particulates, sulfur oxides, and nitrogen oxides. Large draughts of surface or groundwater are also required: each barrel of oil from shale requires two to six barrels of production water. The most severe environmental problem is solid waste. A barrel of oil produced from shale yields one to two tons of shale waste. A small (50,000 barrel per day) production facility would produce 50 million tons annually of largely unusable shale waste containing mineral salts and trace minerals. No environmentally satisfactory method has been developed for the disposal of wastes in such huge volume.

Public and private sector interest in oil shale stirred briefly as a result of national energy problems during the 1970s. Presidents Nixon and Ford both advocated greater public and private expenditures for research and development of synthetic fuels, including oil shale, as a substitute for imported petroleum. Energy corporations were attracted by the prospect of federal subsidies and other incentives for oil shale research. The federal government's most significant initiative was the Synthetic Fuels Corporation, an organization created in 1980, which was authorized to spend part of its initial $20 billion appropriation on oil shale projects. However, the oil shale boomlet quickly dissipated. Environmental organizations and many local interests in the affected states vigorously opposed the projects. Rapidly falling world petroleum prices soon made all synthetic fuels commercially uncompetitive. Several federally subsidized pilot projects involving oil shale failed badly. Energy interests lost any remaining enthusiasm when the Exxon Corporation withdrew from the high-profile Colony, Colorado, oil shale project in 1982 after investing $500 million. In 1985 Congress terminated the Synthetic Fuels Corporation, abruptly ending any significant U.S. oil shale research and development.

The future of commercial oil shale refining is unattractive so long as the economic and environmental problems remain unsolved. In recent years federal governmental support for energy research and development has moved decisively away from all synthetic fuels and will not revive unless a severe domestic shortage of petroleum should occur again.

Walter A. Rosenbaum

Further Readings

Darmstadter, Joel, Hans H. Landsberg, and Herbert C. Morton. *Energy Today and Tomorrow: Living with Uncertainty.* 1983.

U.S. Environmental Protection Agency. *Oil Shale and the Environment.* EPA Document No. 600/9-77-033. 1977.

See also AIR POLLUTION: IMPACTS; DEPARTMENT OF ENERGY (U.S.); DEPARTMENT OF THE INTERIOR (U.S.); ENERGY CRISIS

O

Oil Spills

A large oil spill such as the one that occurred from the Torrey Canyon in the English Channel in 1967 or from the Exxon Valdez in Prince William Sound, Alaska, in 1989 is a particularly striking example of human contamination and disruption of the environment. It generates considerable public reaction, particularly in response to news media images of oiled beaches, seabirds, and marine mammals. Oil spills represent one of the most intense and localized examples of environmental degradation. Since the Torrey Canyon there have been extensive studies of oil spill occurrence, including the sources, fate, and effects of oil in marine, freshwater, and terrestrial environments; considerable effort has been devoted also to the development of cleanup or countermeasures. There has also been ongoing assessment of legal and regulatory aspects and economic impact. The objective of this entry is to provide a general introductory perspective to oil spills.

Sources and Nature of Oil

According to the listing provided in the National Research Council's 1985 publication *Oil in The Sea: Inputs, Fates, and Effects* the principal sources of oil inputs to the marine environment are:

1. Municipal and industrial runoff (31 percent)
2. Tanker operations such as ballast water discharge (22 percent)
3. Tanker Accidents (12 percent)
4. Other transportation sources (12 percent)
5. Atmospheric deposition (10 percent)
6. Natural sources, i.e. seeps (8 percent)
7. Refineries (3 percent)
8. Offshore production (2 percent)

The total quantity of oil entering the oceans is estimated to be 3.2 million tons per year but could be as large as 8.8 million tons. This quantity corresponds to about 0.1 percent of total annual oil production. Tanker accidents and offshore blowouts and spills—although generating only a fraction of the total input—

are regarded as most serious because of the intensity of the contamination. Chronic releases of oil are viewed as more tolerable because continuing dilution and steady degradation usually prevent the occurrence of visible oil slicks.

Of recent concern has been the widespread contamination in the Middle East resulting first from the Iran-Iraq war and later from the invasion of Kuwait. The quantities of oil released during these military conflicts are not known accurately, but they are much larger than any tanker accidents. Table 1 gives the location, date, and an estimated volume of oil spilled for some of the more significant oil spills.

Most spills are of crude oil and occur during exploratory drilling, production from offshore wells (e.g., Ixtoc I in 1979), tanker accidents (mainly as a result of grounding, collision, or fire), leakage from storage facilities (e.g., Mizushima Refinery in 1974), and pipeline ruptures. There are also spills of petroleum products such as gasoline and diesel fuels, heating oils, heavy oils, and bunker fuels which are generally smaller in volume. Crude oil is a complex mixture of (mainly) hydrocarbons including alkanes, cyclocalkanes, aromatics, polycyclic aromatics, waxes, asphaltenes, and a variety of oxygen, sulfur, and nitrogen compounds as well as metals, notably vanadium. Oils differ greatly in their chemical and physical character, properties, and toxicity, thus it is difficult to generalize about the behavior and effects of an oil spill. Each spill tends to have its own character as influenced by the type and quantity of the oil, weather conditions, and the nature of the impacted ecosystem.

A feature of oil spill statistics is that during any year much of the oil (perhaps 90 percent) is spilled in a very few incidents (perhaps 5 percent). There is a large number of minor spills which contribute relatively little to the total quantity of oil spilled and result in only local impacts. Often the volume spilled is uncertain. It is thus difficult to compile reliable oil spill statistics and determine trends because of different reporting practices in different jurisdictions. The number of significant spills (those exceeding 100 tons) averages about 30 per year. A 1989 Exxon report lists sixty-five spills exceeding about 8,900 tons over the twenty-two-year period from 1967 to 1989 (i.e., about 3 spills per year which are newsworthy on a worldwide basis and which result in extensive contamination). No obvious trend of increase or decrease in spill frequency is evident.

TABLE 1

A Selection of Significant Oil Spills with Approximate Volumes

Date	Spill and Location	Estimated Volume (m^3)
1991–1992	Kuwait Invasion	1 million
1979–1980	Ixtoc I Blowout, Mexico	1 million
1978	Amoco Cadiz, France	270,000
1967	Torrey Canyon, England	140,000
1975	Jacob Maersk, Portugal	95,000
1993	Braer, Shetland Islands, United Kingdom	93,000
1974	Metula, Chile	60,000
1974	Mizushima Refinery, Japan	43,000
1989	Exxon Valdez, Alaska	40,000
1977	Ekofisk Blowout, North Sea	30,000
1976	Argo Merchant, United States	30,000
1969	Santa Barbara Blowout, United States	8,000
1970	Arrow, Canada	7,000

Principal Source: Exxon (1989). In many cases the volume spilled is subject to considerable error.

Behavior of Oil Spills

Most oil is spilled on the open ocean where it becomes subject to a number of processes collectively termed "weathering." Some oil may reach shorelines and become stranded on rocks or sandy beaches. There may be interaction with floating or shore-locked ice. A small quantity of oil may sink and reach bottom sediments. Figure 1 depicts the processes to which oil is subject.

Most oils float on water, their densities lying in the range 0.8 to 0.9 g/cm^3 compared with a typical ocean water density of 1.024 g/m^3. Sinking is therefore unlikely unless: 1) the oil is inherently dense; 2) it becomes subject to strong downward currents; or 3) it becomes attached to dense mineral matter such as sand or diatomaceous material.

Oils spread over the water surface as a result of interfacial tension forces giving a characteristic sheen of thickness 0.5 to 10 micrometers (μm), but most of the oil tends to remain as relatively thick patches of 0.1 to 2 millimeters (mm). Often the area of the thick patches is only 10 percent of the total but they may contain 90 percent of the oil. The action of wind causes the slick to move or drift usually at 2 to 3 percent of the windspeed and in the direction of the wind. The oil slick is also subject to tidal and residual ocean currents and to the Coriolis drift which is to the right in the Northern Hemisphere. Considerable efforts have been devoted to compiling and testing mathematical models of oil trajectories in various marine environments with a view to being able to predict where oil will drift in the days following a spill, and especially which shorelines may be impacted. Unfortunately the mechanics of oil slicks subject to varying winds and currents become quite complex and the predictive capability varies greatly in accuracy.

Crude oils are usually quite volatile, containing a substantial fraction of low boiling gasoline-range hydrocarbons. These hydrocarbons evaporate from the slick and in some cases may cause a fire hazard. Typically 20 to 30 percent of a crude oil will evaporate in the days following spillage but the rate and extent of evaporation depends on the nature of the oil, the temperature, the oil thickness, and factors such as prevailing wind speeds and solar radiation. As the oil evaporates it becomes denser and more viscous, and ultimately it may form asphalt-like pancakes or tar balls which drift eventually to a shoreline.

Some of the more soluble hydrocarbons dissolve in the water, but the amount dissolved is usually small, probably less than 1 percent. This dissolved oil is significant, however, in that it can cause toxicity to marine organisms.

The oil is also subject to emulsification of two types. First is oil-in-water emulsion or dispersion in which small (1 to 100 μm) droplets of oil become conveyed into the water. The droplets' rising velocity is so slow that they may remain permanently in the water. This process of natural dispersion is particularly rapid in stormy conditions when the sea surface is subject to breaking waves. It may result in a significant fraction (e.g., 50 percent) of the surface oil being conveyed into the water column. Dispersed oil may also cause toxic effects.

The second emulsification process is water-in-oil emulsion formation in which small (1 to 10 μm) drops of water become incorporated into the oil. This oil is lighter in color than the usually black crude oil and is colloquially termed "chocolate mousse." These "mousses" may contain up to 80 percent water and can be very viscous and even semi-solid in properties. Some oils are particularly susceptible to the formation of stable mousses while others are not. The reasons for this are not fully understood but it appears that stability is enhanced by the presence of certain high molecular weight waxes and asphaltenes in the oil.

The oil on the surface and in the water column is subject to biodegradation and to chemical reaction—principally by photolytic processes. These processes are generally slow, extending over periods of weeks and months, whereas the physical weathering processes occur in a time frame of days. Figure 2 attempts to convey an approximate impression of the relative importance of these processes at various times.

When oil is spilled under ice it tends to collect at the ice-water interface in the form of pools or sessile drops about five to ten mm thick. The behavior of the oil is strongly influenced by the topography of the oil interface and by under-ice currents. When the ice melts the oil migrates to the surface—in the case of saline conditions, through the brine channels in the ice. There has been concern that a large oil spill in the Arctic would effectively reduce the albedo and thus induce substantial melting of the polar ice cap, but the effect would be local and of the order of 100 square kilometers at most which is much less than the natural year-to-year variation in ice cover.

On shorelines, the oil tends to adhere to rocky surfaces, drying-out and thickening during low tide. It may penetrate deeply (i.e., tens of cm into cobble and sandy beaches) resulting in long-term contamination problems. Oiled shorelines represent one of the most lasting environmental impacts of an oil spill. Generally under continued wave action a shoreline will recover from oil contamination in a period of a few years, however, under more quiescent conditions (such as in salt marshes) the impact may be more severe and more prolonged.

Oil spills also occur on land as a result of pipeline or transportation accidents. The oil flows and spreads following the local topography penetrating into the soil where it has a strong and prolonged phytotoxic effect. Particular concerns exist about the effect of such spills in tundra or taiga underlain by permafrost. Contaminated soils may be removed, landfilled or burned, and in some cases natural biodegradation processes can be enhanced by application of fertilizer.

The persistence, and thus the long-term impact of an oil spill is highly variable, but in most cases the major impact occurs in the months or year following the spill. Little impact is usually observed after three years.

Countermeasures

A considerable inventive effort has been devoted to developing methods of oil spill recovery and treatment. Most reviews of this topic note that the primary effort should be devoted to prevention rather than response. When a vessel is in danger of spilling its oil cargo, the obvious first priority is to stop spillage and remove oil from the threatened vessel by lightering.

Spilled oil is usually contained by oil booms which float on the water surface and have a skirt or barrier extending some fifty cm deep to prevent further spreading. Booms are routinely stored at marine response facilities and can be deployed rapidly and effectively provided that sea conditions are reasonably calm. In some cases a boom is routinely deployed around a tanker in port. In high waves few booms can successfully contain oil because they are overwashed by oil and water. They also fail in high currents.

A variety of oil recovery devices have been devised which remove the oil from the water surface and pump it to storage, usually in a barge or flexible bladder tank. These skimmers or "slick lickers" usually operate on the principle of a belt or disk which moves through the oil, collecting it and then passing the oily surface through some scraping device which removes the oil, allowing it to fall into a well from which it is pumped. Most operate satisfactorily under calm conditions but fail under stormy conditions.

Oil sorbents are widely used to remove oil in relatively small quantities from water and shoreline surfaces. These are usually hydrophobic solid fibrous materials such as polypropylene which attract oil but repel water. In most cases the oiled sorbent must be disposed of after use although some recovery and reuse is possible. This countermeasure is thus quite expensive and is best applied to relatively small quantities of oil during final cleanup.

Since oils are flammable burning is a feasible countermeasure in some instances. The disadvantages include the spread of fire to structures and vessels in the vicinity, the difficulty of igniting cold weathered oil, and the dense clouds of black smoke which form as a result. Burning is most feasible and desirable in remote, cold climate regions.

Chemical dispersants represent one of the most effective means of intervening to change the behavior of the oil. These are surface active or detergent chemicals similar to the familiar domestic dishwashing liquids which can be applied to the oil slick from boat, aircraft, or by hand. They reduce the oil-water interfacial tension and promote the formation of oil-in-water emulsion or dispersion. A ratio of one volume of dispersant to twenty to fifty volumes of oil is usually recommended but under turbulent conditions ratios of one to 100 can be effective. Some controversy surrounds the use of dispersants because they do not remove the oil, they merely relocate it. The net effect of chemical dispersion is usually to reduce the impact of oil on shorelines, birds, and sea mammals, but to increase the impact on pelagic organisms such as fish. Decisions regarding the use of dispersants thus involve trading one set of impacts for another. It is possible, however, as part of contingency plans to identify in advance those conditions in which the application of dispersants will have a net benefit, and thus allow preparation for their rapid use without the delay and uncertainties surrounding decision-making during stressful emergency conditions.

Regrettably in most large spills the extent to which human intervention has been able to mitigate the behavior or effects of the oil has been restricted to less than 10 percent of the oil. The large volumes spilled and areas affected, the often adverse weather conditions, and the inability to deploy personnel and equipment safely in sufficient quantities in the hours and days immediately after the spill all severely reduce the effectiveness of countermeasures. The most attractive option is aerial application of chemical dispersants with an acknowledgment that it may cause severe but short-term and local impacts on the marine environment.

Effects

Spilled oil generally affects organisms by: 1) directly coating body or respiring surfaces with oil, usually leading to death in the case of birds and mammals by destroying the insulating properties of feathers and fur; 2) causing toxicity by the absorption of hydrocarbon from water and air usually during respiration, and by ingestion of contaminated food, water, or oil directly during preening; and 3) affecting the ecosystem by destroying food organisms, interfering with reproduction processes or habitat, interfering with predator-prey relationships, and causing failure of normal chemoreception systems.

There is substantial literature, including extensive reviews of the effects of oil on microorganisms, invertebrates, fish, birds, mammals, and plants. The concentrations at which specific hydrocarbons cause specified toxic responses in test organisms have been fairly well documented. Oil is usually at its most toxic when it is fresh. Weathered oil is relatively innocuous.

There is no doubt that in the immediate vicinity of a large oil spill a region or volume of the marine environment becomes subject to lethally toxic conditions. A larger surrounding region experiences conditions in which sensitive organisms such as birds and larvae may be severely impacted, but many organisms will survive. A further region will experience elevated oil concentrations but at levels which cause little or no effects. Some tainting may occur to fish and shellfish. It may take many years for conditions to recover sufficiently to allow recolonization and reestablishment of the original ecosystem.

Each oil spill is unique in the nature of the oil, the volume spilled, the oil behavior, the success of countermeasures, and nature of the oil's impacts. It is often difficult to assess the total impact of the oil because of uncertainties about the "base-line" conditions, and the presence of large year-to-year variations in ecosystem characteristics induced by factors such as weather. Viewed in the context of environmental disruption over a period of days and weeks an oil spill is a severe and distressing example of environmental damage. Viewed in the longer term context of a decade most oil spills are unlikely to have lasting environmental effects.

Donald Mackay

Further Readings

Cormack, D. *Response to Oil and Chemical Marine Pollution.* 1983.

Engelhardt, F.R., ed. *Petroleum Effects in the Arctic Environment.* 1985.

Exxon Production Research Co. *Review of Oil Spill Occurrences and Impacts.* 1989.

National Research Council (U.S.). *Oil in the Sea: Inputs, Fates, and Effects.* 1985.

————. *Using Oil Spill Dispersants on the Sea.* 1989.

See also COASTAL DEBRIS AND CLEANUP; COASTAL MARSHES, CONSERVATION OF; CORAL REEFS; MARINE MAMMALS; SEABIRDS; SHOREBIRDS

Old Growth Forests

The magnificent forests that clothe some landscapes in the humid tropics and in the Pacific Northwest of the United States have become a center of controversy. How much old-growth forest can we afford to (or indeed, *not* to) preserve from the chainsaw? To begin it is important to distinguish between two highly valued, and sometimes coincident types of forest: virgin and old growth. Virgin forests are usually recognized on the basis of having been free of disturbance by modern society, whereas old growth can be defined as forest ecosystems dominated by old trees. Because many forests are naturally subjected to recurring large-scale disturbances (e.g., fire, windstorms) some virgin forests are not old growth, and because modern society has not always destroyed old trees during its use of forests many managed stands may qualify as old growth.

The expansive tropical forest biome is characterized by extensive tracts of virgin, old-growth forest because until recently human disturbance to much of this region was minimal, and natural, large-scale disturbance is very uncommon. Extensive areas of the northern boreal forest in North America and Eurasia also have escaped human influence, but large catastrophic fires are sufficiently frequent so as to make stands composed of old trees uncommon. Throughout Europe there are few—if any—tracts of forest that have escaped human intervention and truly virgin forest probably no longer exists, but stands composed of old trees (even planted ones) can be found. In Great Britain the term "ancient woodland" is applied to stands that occur on tracts never subjected to intensive agricultural uses. These forests often support a unique flora which is lacking in forests that have grown back on pasture or plowed lands. These ancient forests are valued not only for their biological composition but also as a cultural heritage, representative of the intensive silvicultural practices, known as coppice and standards, that persisted for centuries in the old world. They may be neither virgin nor old growth, but they are worthy of protection just the same.

In western North America extensive tracts of virgin coniferous forest still exist. Many of these are old-growth forests but disturbance by large-scale fires has been widespread and throughout the region virgin forests in three developmental stages—young or immature, mature, and old or overmature—are interspersed in a complex mosaic. The overmature, virgin forests are the classic example of "old growth," valued for their beauty, structural complexity and unique habitat features. From the standpoint of preserving representative examples of virgin forest, however, the young and mature stages also require careful consideration. Many of these forests may not be entirely free from human influence, as fire suppression activities during this century probably have prevented the normal fire regime from operating in many stands. The dilemma of wedding natural fire regimes with preservation of old-growth forests will challenge policy makers in coming years.

In the Pacific Northwest, where the political controversy over preservation of old-growth forests has been intense, objective definitions of old growth have been proposed and the extent of remaining old growth has been estimated. A variety of forest stand characteristics form the basis for defining old growth in this region: 1) two or more species of trees representing a wide range of ages and sizes and meeting some minimum of age for the oldest trees, typically greater than 200 years; 2) a deep, multilayered forest canopy; and 3) an abundance of coarse woody debris, including downed logs, standing dead trees and snags that remain propped up by neighboring trees. These criteria were chosen to help distinguish old-growth forests from other natural or managed stands partly on the basis of their distinctive ecological functions, but authors of such definitions always stress that caution must be exercised in the use of such definitions because they place somewhat arbitrary limits on a continuous, highly variable system.

Based upon this sort of definition estimates have been made of the extent of old-growth forests in the Pacific Northwest both prior to non-native settlement and at present. In the Douglas-fir region of Oregon and Washington about 60 to 70 percent of commercial forest land was covered by old growth around 1800. In the late 1980s approximately 10 percent of federal lands (National Park Service, Bureau of Land Management, U.S. Forest Service) in western Oregon and Washington still supported old-growth forests. The rate of cutting of these forests has been greatly reduced in the 1990s, partly as a result of the Endangered Species Act and its protection of habitats for the northern spotted owl.

In much of eastern North America large-scale disturbance probably was sufficiently infrequent that extensive areas of old-growth forest were common, but human disturbance has been very widespread and virgin stands are few. Moreover, the disruptive influence of introduced pathogens (e.g., chestnut blight, Dutch

elm disease) has greatly altered the dynamics of most stands, so that the value of virgin tracts for examining natural ecological processes is limited. In this region old growth must be defined on the basis of forest structure as well as tree age and size, with less rigid restrictions regarding human activities. In particular, three critical observations and conclusions should be stressed in considerations of old growth preservation in eastern North America: 1) old growth requires a non-restrictive definition that may vary across the complex landscape within the region; 2) existing old-growth forests in the region usually are not replicas of the presettlement forest; and 3) most of the existing old growth may require some form of management, rather than preservation, to optimize its social and ecological value.

Old-growth forests are valued for their ecological diversity, especially such classes as structural and species diversity. High structural diversity—the variety of shapes, sizes, and composition of objects in an ecosystem—both enhances the aesthetic value of old growth and the diversity of organisms living in these forests (i.e., species diversity). For example, the multilayered nature of old-growth canopies can support many different bird species with parallel life histories at different heights. Broken tops or unusual crown shapes may be favored nest sites for certain species, and cavity-nesting birds depend upon the heart-rot associated with old trees.

It is the prevention of local or global extinction of species that drives much of the effort to preserve old-growth forests. In this regard, a fundamental distinction must be drawn between species diversity in temperate and tropical forests. Grave concerns have arisen over the possibility that deforestation in the tropics will result in the global extinction of a multitude of species. Yet extensive deforestation of Europe and eastern North America apparently resulted in the extinction of only a few species. This paradox is explained by the enormously higher species diversity of tropical versus temperate forest regions. Many tropical species are exceedingly rare and, most importantly, are highly restricted in their geographical distributions (i.e., endemics) so that their elimination from relatively small areas (local extinction) also results in their total extirpation worldwide (global extinction). In contrast, few temperate zone species are endemics and local extinction only rarely results in global extinction. Thus, cutting of temperate zone old-growth forests, within limits, is unlikely to result in widespread species extinction, although some notable and politically-charged examples will probably continue to surface.

In the end, the decision to preserve old-growth forests often means foregoing very high immediate income from sale of commodities and epitomizes the differences between value systems based upon the market economy and upon non-economic human interests. Almost everyone who visits the cathedral of the old-growth forest is struck by some presence greater than the big trees and diversity of species. Modern cultures are now expressing this quasi-religious awe by distributing the significantly large costs of ecosystem preservation across the society, but the choice of the optimum area to be preserved will be a subjective and often emotional decision rather than one that translates to objective, economic terms.

Timothy J. Fahey

Further Readings

Barnes, B.V. "Old-Growth Forests of the Northern Lakes States: A Landscape Ecosystem Perspective." *Natural Area Journal* 9 (1989): 45–57.

Natural Areas Journal (Quarterly Publication of the Natural Areas Association). Vol. 8, No. 1 and No. 3 (1988) and Vol. 9, No. 1 (1989).

Peterken, G.F. "Conservation of Old-Growth: A European Perspective." *Natural Areas Journal* 12 (1992): 10–19.

Spies, T.A., and J.F. Franklin. "Old Growth and Forest Dynamics in the Douglas-fir Region of Western Oregon and Washington." *Natural Areas Journal* 8 (1988): 190–201.

See also BIODEPLETION; BIODIVERSITY; CARMANAH VALLEY; FOREST FRAGMENTATION AND BIRD HABITATS; FOREST SERVICE (U.S.); FORESTRY, HISTORY OF; HABITAT FRAGMENTATION, PATCHES, AND CORRIDORS; LANDSCAPE ECOLOGY; NEW FORESTRY; SUSTAINED YIELD FORESTRY; TROPICAL DEFORESTATION; TROPICAL RAINFORESTS

Oldman River

The Oldman River in southern Alberta has been at the center of long-standing controversy over the construction of a dam. The headwaters of the Oldman River are to the west in the Rocky Mountains. The idea for damming the Oldman was first conceived in 1966 by the Prairie Farm Rehabilitation Administration. The purpose is to impound river waters within a reservoir for later use by farmers, ranchers, municipalities and industry.

After numerous studies the Premier of Alberta announced in August 1984 the decision to proceed with the construction of a dam at the Three Rivers site along the Oldman River. Design of the dam was completed in 1985 and construction on a diversion tunnel commenced in 1986. One report concluded that there could be negative environmental impacts affecting the Peigan Indian Reserve, located about twelve kilometers downstream from the dam site.

The Friends of the Oldman River was incorporated in September 1987 for the sole purpose of opposing the construction of the Oldman River dam. The Society was formed after the license to construct the dam was issued by the Alberta government. In November 1987 it was successful in getting the provincial court to quash an interim license issued by the Alberta government to construct the dam. However, a second license was reissued and construction proceeded.

The society also appealed to the federal and Supreme courts on several occasions to get the federal government to revoke the license and to conduct a proper environmental assessment. In January 1992 the Supreme Court of Canada made a landmark ruling in which it concluded that the government of Canada must conduct an environmental review of provincial projects where there is a federal regulatory role or funding. It also ordered the federal government to conduct an environmental assessment of the Oldman dam.

In May 1992 a federally appointed environmental assessment panel recommended the dam be decommissioned by opening flood gates until appropriate mitigating measures were developed and approved. The federal government rejected this recommendation, and the dam was finished in the summer of 1993. The history of the Oldman dam is one of federal and provincial governments consistently refusing to fully apply their own environmental legislation, and of the determination of citizens to ensure that these are invoked.

Kevin McNamee (with Cliff Wallis)

Further Reading

Estrin, David, and John Swaigen. *Environment on Trial.* 1993.

See also FEDERALISM AND ENVIRONMENTAL PROTECTION: CANADA; HYDROELECTRICITY

Olmsted, Frederick Law

Frederick Law Olmsted (1822–1903) is widely regarded as the father of landscape architecture in the United States. During his lifetime he contributed to over 600 important commissions, but his best-known work is New York City's Central Park (1858–1878), which he designed with his original partner Calvert Vaux. This remarkable urban park predated state and national parks in America, and was the first large recreational space ever designed for an urban area.

Beyond a rural one-room schoolhouse Olmsted never received any formal education. Prior to his work on Central Park he traveled extensively throughout England and the southern United States, alternately pursuing careers in farming and journalism. During this time he became an outspoken opponent of slavery and was a noted social critic of the plantation society in the South.

It was during these travels that he developed his strongly-held belief that people needed exposure to nature, and that urban life would be made more tolerable by the presence of natural scenery. In addition, he firmly believed that his parks, along with other public institutions, should be accessible to all. Olmsted's designs envisioned more than just parklands. With admirable foresight into the future needs and development of urban areas, Olmsted sought to create suburban paradises that combined the best of city and rural life, including natural beauty and ease of access. His insights in these regards led to the development not only of the discipline of urban landscape architecture, but was the forerunner of the concept of the planned community. He designed such a community, combining practical living spaces with rural trappings, in Riverside, Illinois.

In addition to the famous Central Park, Olmsted's best-known designs include Boston's Emerald Necklace, Buffalo's park system, Prospect Park in Brooklyn, Montreal's Mount Royal Park, the grounds of Stanford University, the World Columbian Exposition in Chicago, the Vanderbilt's Biltmore Estate in North Carolina, and U.S. Capitol grounds in Washington, D.C.

He broke off his partnership with Vaux in 1872 and took on other partners, including his son. After his death his firm's eminence in its field was continued by his son Frederick Law Olmsted, Jr., and his stepson John Charles Olmsted. His offices in Brookline, Massachusetts, are now operated by the National Park Service as the Olmsted National Historic Site.

Larry Olmsted

Further Readings
Nash, Roderick. *Wilderness and the American Mind.* 1967.
Olmsted, F.L. *A Consideration of the Justifying Value of a Public Park.* 1881.

See also JENSEN, JENS; LAND-USE PLANNING; NATIONAL PARK SERVICE (U.S.); URBAN DESIGN; URBAN FORESTRY

Olson, Sigurd F.

Sigurd F. Olson (1899–1982) was a writer, wilderness visionary, and conservation activist from the 1920s until the day he died at the age of 83. His enduring outdoor monument is the Boundary Waters Canoe Area in Minnesota and Ontario. This wilderness region, also known as Quetico-Superior, contains the land, lakes, and rivers that were central to Olson for the whole of his adult life. Along with many others he struggled for and achieved its preservation one step at a time over many decades from the 1920s through to 1978 and beyond. In 1930 the Shipstead-Nolan Act withdrew some public lands in northern Minnesota from appropriation (and logging) and disallowed logging within 400 feet of the banks of waterways. The Minnesota lands, known as the Superior National Forest, became a focal point for fly-in hunting and fishing. But in 1949, after a long struggle, President Harry S. Truman signed Executive Order 10092 establishing an "air reservation" over the forest.

Ontario's Quetico Provincial Park was also the site of preservationist struggles. In 1958 the Superior National Forest was renamed the Boundary Waters Canoe Area and in 1960 Ontario Premier Leslie M. Frost exchanged letters with U.S. officials establishing a protected area on both sides of the border. But it was not until 1978, when the Boundary Waters Canoe Area Bill was passed in Washington, that logging was banned and the level of wilderness character was more clearly established (restricting motorboats and snowmobiles, for example). This bill also expanded the area on the Minnesota side and, in general, these lands were matched on the Canadian side.

Olson was active within numerous conservation organizations over the years, especially the Isaak Walton League, the National Parks Association, and the Wilderness Society. He was president of the National Parks Association for five years and became president of the Wilderness Society in 1968. He campaigned for the Indiana Dunes National Lakeshore, Olympic National Park in northwestern Washington, the Everglades, the redwoods, and the Grand Canyon waters.

Olson's other lasting monument is his writing. He began in the 1920s with newspaper articles on wilderness tripping and moved on to magazines, perhaps most notably with "Why Wilderness?" published in 1938 in *American Forests*. His magazine articles were central to the campaign for Quetico-Superior, particularly in the 1940s and 1950s. It took many years and many rejections before Knopf took a chance on publishing Olson's first book, *The Singing Wilderness*, which the American Library Association named the Notable Book of 1956. Olson then wrote nine books over the decades during which most people are planning or living retirement. In all his writing he conveyed the view that "Wilderness to the people of America is a spiritual necessity, an antidote to the high pressure of modern life, a means of regaining serenity and equilibrium."

Robert Paehlke

Further Readings

Olson, Sigurd F. *The Singing Wilderness.* 1956.

Searle, R. Newell. *Saving Quetico-Superior: A Land Set Apart.* 1977.

Vickery, Jim dale. *Wilderness Visionaries.* 1986.

See also ISAAK WALTON LEAGUE; WILDERNESS; WILDERNESS SOCIETY

One-Child Family (China)

Population control as a national goal has so far found its most dedicated adherent in the People's Republic of China. During the early decades of the Maoist regime, the warnings of Liu Zheng, Ma Yinchu, and other Chinese demographers were not only ignored, but suppressed. By 1980, however, with China's population approaching one billion (having doubled in less than forty years), the government recognized its error and officially reversed its policy. It introduced coordinated efforts to reduce the rate of population growth and bring it to zero by the year 2000; the announced goal was "no more than two children per family by 1985."

This goal was further extended with the promotion of the "one-child family." Posters and signboards everywhere urged families that "Just one will do." This goal was to be achieved in several ways: by postponing the legal age of marriage until mid- or late-twenties (premarital sex has not been widespread in China); by employing widespread educational and propaganda methods (more than one child is "anti-patriotic"); and by providing ready access to free contraceptives.

In addition, the central government instituted a more socially coercive program in Sichuan Province, where the ratio of population to arable land greatly exceeded the national average. The one-child family was to be stringently enforced through social stigmatism. Women wishing a child were given permits "to try" in a ranked order. Women without permits or who already had one child and became pregnant, faced unrelenting social pressure from neighbors to undergo an abortion. (This pressure was orchestrated by government-sponsored neighborhood "grannies," who checked on the reproductive lives of all local women.)

Toward the end of the 1980s this one-child program was relaxed due to strong resistance to it, especially among rural peoples, who were clearly killing female babies in order to have one *male* child. Although the one-child program had ample support not only through government propaganda, but also through local social coercion and significant government financial subsidies to parents who had only one child, it has not been as successful as hoped, especially in rural areas.

Mary E. Clark

Further Readings

Beijing Review. *Population and Other Problems. China Today, Beijing Review* Special Feature Series. 1981.

China's Only Child. Documentary film. Time/ Life NOVA (WGBH Boston, 1984).

See also ECOFEMINISM; POPULATION CONTROL; SUSTAINABLE DEVELOPMENT

OPEC

See ENERGY CRISIS

Orangutans
See PRIMATES: CONSERVATION AND HABITAT

Organic Agriculture
See SUSTAINABLE AGRICULTURE

Organochlorines
See PERSISTENT ORGANOCHLORINE COMPOUNDS; PESTICIDES

Osborn, Fairfield
After retiring from investment banking in 1935 Fairfield Osborn (1887–1968) dedicated himself to conservation and the natural sciences. He was appointed president of the New York Zoological Society in 1940. In 1947, with the support and encouragement of the Zoological Society, he helped establish and became president of the Conservation Foundation, which worked to advance knowledge and understanding of the earth's "life-supporting resources." He received support from the Conservation Foundation to write his best-selling book, *Our Plundered Planet* (1948). Drawing on developments in biology, ecology, and anthropology in the 1930s and 1940s Osborn argued for a biological approach to human history.

Although near the end of his life he told an interviewer, "I'm not a scientist—and I don't pretend to be one," he worked within and promoted the biological and natural sciences. He spent the last forty years of his life trying to repair what he saw as the disastrous "eclipse of the biologists under the terrific impact of the physical scientists and industry." From the 1940s to the 1960s Osborn worked with scientists and conservationists in the Conservation Foundation to educate Americans about their interdependence with nature. He believed that an alliance between biological and natural scientists, conservationists, educators, private enterprise, and government could create a sustained-yield economy that could end American's war against nature. But in the 1950s, like many other conservationists, he shifted his emphasis from science and resource conservation to controlling the "population bomb." Sponsored by the Conservation Foundation, Osborn's books, *The Limits of the Earth* (1953) and *Our Crowded Planet* (1962), examine the growing threats to the global environment caused by the exploding human population.

Under his leadership, the Conservation Foundation in the 1950s and 1960s helped fund studies on pesticide use, ecology and land use, and on population and conservation. In the 1960s he became more pessimistic about the human future, fearing that human impact on the environment was accelerating at such a rate that there was little time left to prevent a catastrophe. He was encouraged, however, by the growth of the "environmental movement" in the 1960s.

Osborn's writings, speeches, and activities as the president of the Conservation Foundation since the 1940s helped lay the institutional and political foundation for the environmental movement of the late 1960s and 1970s. His belief that science should mediate between competing social and political interests encouraged a generation of scientists to do environmental research and advise the public about the social consequences of science and new technologies. Modern environmentalism grew out of the work of scientists and conservationists such as Osborn, Paul Sears, Barry Commoner, and Paul Ehrlich, who were committed to both environmental protection and public education.

Chris H. Lewis

Further Readings
Osborn, Fairfield. *Our Plundered Planet.* 1948.
———. *The Limits of the Earth*. 1953.
———, ed. *Our Crowded Planet*. 1962.

See also CONSERVATION FOUNDATION; CONSERVATION MOVEMENT; ENVIRONMENTALISM; POPULATION CONTROL; SEARS, PAUL

OSHAct and OSHA
The goal of the Occupational Safety and Health Act (OSHAct) of 1970 is "to assure so far as possible every working man and woman in the Nation safe and healthful working conditions" and directs each employer in the United States to provide a workplace "free from recognized hazard" that could kill or seriously injure any of the workers in it.

Toward this end the OSHAct created the Occupational Safety and Health Administration (OSHA) within the U.S. Department of Labor and gave to OSHA discretionary power to set and enforce health and safety standards. The OSHAct also empowers OSHA to enforce its standards by inspecting workplaces and imposing civil and criminal penalties on employers who fail to comply with the general provision of the OSHAct or agency standards promulgated under its authority. Individual states, with approval from OSHA, can operate their own state plans so long as these plans provide employees with rights and protections equal to those created by the OSHAct and by federal OSHA. By statute all standards and enforcement decisions are subject to review by the U.S. federal courts. The OSHAct also created an independent Occupational Safety and Health Review Commission (OSHRC) to review agency enforcement decisions, and the National Institute for Occupational Safety and Health (NIOSH) in the Department of Health, Education, and Welfare (later renamed Health and Human Services) to provide OSHA with scientific advice.

In what was for that time a radical departure from standard regulatory practice the OSHAct gave employees specific rights to participate in OSHA rule-making and enforcement activities. These worker rights include the right to participate in standard setting, workplace inspections, and the monitoring of hazards; to have access to information about hazards and agency findings; to appeal agency rulings to the federal courts; and to be protected from employer discrimination for exercising these rights.

OSHA has not lived up to the expectations of workplace safety and health advocates. There are problems with the statute itself. The "substantial evidence" test that it applies to agency rules invites overly broad judicial review. Because it is an independent agency OSHRC affords employers a second chance to challenge OSHA enforcement decisions. It is difficult to assess the degree to which state-plan states comply with federal policy. The provisions for citizen participation in enforcement rely too heavily on the initiative of individual workers and unions and create too few in-plant mechanisms to facilitate worker input. The OSHAct does not guarantee compensation for workers who participate in inspections or protect workers' right to refuse hazardous work.

OSHA has also been frustrated by intense business opposition to strict regulation. Affected employers have lobbied the president, Congress, and the Department of Labor to slow the standard-setting process, to take costs into account when setting standards, and to limit enforcement. Corporate interests also routinely challenge agency decisions in court. While the courts have by and large upheld OSHA's authority, for most of the agency's history the White House and the Department of Labor administrators who oversee OSHA have been receptive to the business point of view, whether out of sympathy for the affected firms or for the wider impact of OSHA standard setting on inflation and employment. Only one OSHA administrator—Dr. Eula Bingham—who served during the Carter years, aggressively pursued workplace protection.

As a result OSHA's standard setting and enforcement activities have been disappointing. While there are over 700 standards on the books, including thirty comprehensive health standards, many of the safety standards are outdated, many known safety hazards are not covered, and the existing health standards cover only a small percentage of the toxic substances that threaten workers. According to the most reliable estimates between one-half and two-thirds of the known workplace carcinogens remain unregulated by OSHA standards.

OSHA's enforcement activities are even more limited. OSHA's budgets have declined while the number of employees covered by the OSHAct has increased. Many of the OSHA-approved state-plans are underfunded. As a result there are too few inspectors—approximately 2,150 to cover 5.9 million employers. To compensate OSHA tries to target high-hazard industries and the most dangerous establishments in the manufacturing sector. But the total inspectorate is so small and the number of potential targets so large that most employers in high-hazard industries are rarely inspected.

OSHA's civil penalty structure is too weak to be effective. Until Congress revised it in 1991 the OSHAct prescribed a maximum fine of only $1,000 for serious violations likely to result in physical harm, and $10,000 for willful or repeated violations. But in practice the penalties were much lower. In 1988 the average penalty for a serious violation was $261. In the late 1980s the agency adopted a "megafine" policy for "egregious cases," but megafines remain the exception, not the rule, and they have been substantially reduced in negotiations with employers. While the average fine for serious penalties has risen (to $365 in 1990) fines in general still remain far below statutory ceilings. Even after Congress increased most maximum penalties sevenfold in 1990 and established a $5,000 minimum for willful violations the agency remained reluctant to use these new powers.

Limited enforcement means that the potential to deter health and safety violations is diluted. Consequently there are major gaps in industry compliance with OSHA standards. For example, from one-third to one-half of the companies inspected had exceeded OSHA standards for lead and silica, both commonly recognized hazards for which companies routinely test. The record is likely worse for the hundreds of substances which OSHA regulates but does not effectively monitor.

Reform proposals vary widely. Conservatives want the existing "command-and-control" approach jettisoned, and government to adopt market-based methods of regulation, including greater reliance on worker compensation to create economic incentives for firms to protect workers. Others argue that firms should be given wide discretion to adopt the most cost-effective compliance techniques. Until recently organized labor and the public interest movement opposed efforts to change the OSHAct, but widespread dissatisfaction with OSHA's performance has recently led health and safety advocates to propose their own reforms. A wide variety of worker-oriented changes are being discussed, including legislation to force the agency to set priorities and develop relatively binding timetables for rule-making; legislative limits on the application of cost-benefit tests to OSHA standards; substantially increased penalties for violations of the act; increased criminal penalties for endangering workers; and "right-to-act" provisions that would require firms to establish employee-run workplace safety and health committees that would become an integral part of shop floor decision-making about occupational safety and health.

Charles Noble

Further Readings

Mintz, Benjamin W. *OSHA: History, Law, and Policy.* 1984.

Noble, Charles. *Liberalism at Work: The Rise and Fall of OSHA.* 1986.

U.S. Congress. Office of Technology Assessment. *Preventing Illness and Injury in the Workplace.* 1985.

See also ENVIRONMENTAL JUSTICE MOVEMENT; LABOR AND THE ENVIRONMENT; RIGHT-TO-KNOW: WORKPLACE (U.S.); STANDARD SETTING; TOXICOLOGY

OTA

See OFFICE OF TECHNOLOGY ASSESSMENT

Our Common Future

The General Assembly of the United Nations established in 1983 a special independent body—the World Commission on Environment and Development—to review the urgent environmental problems confronting the world community and to formulate long-term strategies for addressing them. The twenty-one-member commission, chaired by Prime Minister Gro Harlem Brundtland (q.v.) of Norway, worked from May 1984 through February 1987 to design, in Brundtland's words, "a global agenda for change." Published in 1987 under the title *Our Common Future*, the commission's report was quickly accepted as a definitive statement of global environmental thinking at the end of the twentieth century.

One accomplishment of the wide-ranging report was to elevate the discussion of major environmental issues to the supra-national, or global level by calling attention to the interconnectedness of the planet's living and nonliving systems. This view tended to dissolve well-entrenched conceptual boundaries among previously discrete policy sectors such as energy, environment, and development. Political boundaries also were challenged by the report's assumption that the protection of the global commons and of shared planetary ecosystems called for action transcending the powers of sovereign nation states.

The report's most frequently cited, as well as most vigorously debated proposal was that environmental action around the world should henceforth be focused on the achievement of "sustainable development," which the Commission defined as "development that meets the needs of the present without compromising the ability of future generations to meet their own needs." This definition incorporated the optimistic belief that environmental quality and economic growth were not contrary goals but could be brought into a harmonious relationship through cooperative public and private sector activities. The definition also assumed that present and future human needs warranted equal respect, a position that was deeply at odds with accepted patterns of resource use around the world.

Criticism of *Our Common Future* centered on the ambiguities of the term "sustainable development," which many felt detracted from its capacity to mobilize action. The point most often noted was the commission's failure to specify the level of consumption that future development should seek to sustain in different regions of the world. In the absence of specification it appeared that the rich could continue to secure a high standard of living for their successors whereas the descendants of the poor would be entitled only to levels adequate for survival. Yet, this implication sat most uneasily with the report's overall plea for a more equitable distribution of the earth's resources.

The report proved to be a potent action-forcing document in spite of its conceptual weaknesses and lack of specificity on important policy issues. Its publication triggered reinvigorated academic and political debate on the environment, as well as a spate of international meetings and conferences culminating in the United Nations Conference on Environment and Development (UNCED) held in Rio de Janeiro, Brazil in 1992. Through its upbeat message, as well as its call for concerted global action, *Our Common Future* provided the impetus for a new era of comprehensive, worldwide environmental cooperation.

Sheila Jasanoff

Further Readings

World Commission on Environment and Development. *Our Common Future*. 1987.

See also BRUNDTLAND, GRO HARLEM; RIO CONFERENCE (1992); SUSTAINABLE DEVELOPMENT

Ozone Depletion

Ozone is a colorless, pungent gas which can sometimes be smelled as the distinctly "fresh" smell after a thundershower or the "electric" smell of a subway train. Ozone represents only a tiny fraction of the earth's atmosphere; of every million molecules of air, only ten are ozone. The ozone layer is located between ten and forty kilometers above the earth's atmosphere. However, if it was compressed to ground-level, the ozone layer would form a band only the height of three dimes.

The stratospheric ozone layer acts as our planet's sunscreen, providing an invisible filter to protect all life forms from overexposure to the sun's ultraviolet (UV) rays. UV rays are classified according to their wavelengths. UV-A is the least damaging form of UV radiation and reaches the earth in greatest quantity. Most UV-A rays pass right through the ozone layer. UV-B radiation is potentially very harmful. Fortunately, most of the sun's UV-B radiation is absorbed by ozone in the stratosphere. UV-C radiation is potentially the most damaging because it is very energetic. All UV-C is absorbed by oxygen and ozone in the stratosphere; it never reaches the earth's surface. Thus, the danger from ultraviolet radiation comes mainly from the UV-B range of the spectrum, although UV-A poses some risk if exposure is long enough.

Ozone depletion occurs when the natural balance between the production and destruction of stratospheric ozone is tipped in favor of destruction. Although natural phenomena can cause temporary ozone loss, chlorine and bromine released from synthetic compounds have been confirmed as the main cause of a net loss of stratospheric ozone in many parts of the world since 1980.

Emissions of chlorofluorocarbons (CFCs) alone account for more than 80 percent of total stratospheric ozone depletion. Other synthetic compounds including halons, carbon-tetrachloride, methyl chloroform, hydrochloro-fluorocarbons (HCFCs), and methyl bromide also contribute to ozone depletion.

All of these chemicals are members of a large class of chlorine and bromine-containing compounds known as industrial halocarbons. They are used widely in goods such as refrigerators, air conditioners, furniture and carpet foam, solvents for electronic equipment and metal parts, sterilizers for hospital equipment, pesticides, and fire extinguishers. Ozone-destroying halocarbons can be found in almost every home and work space in the Northern hemisphere.

Increased UV-B exposure will affect human, plant, and animal life. UV-B radiation causes skin cancer, hastens skin aging and can cause eye cataracts. The immune systems are also weakened by over-exposure to UV-B radiation. Increased exposure to UV-B radiation leads to decreased growth, decreased photosynthesis, and decreased flowering in many plant species. As a result, global food production could be reduced by 1 percent for every 1 percent increase in UV-B radiation reaching the earth.

Ozone depletion significantly affects the productivity of phytoplankton, the single-celled organisms at the base of the freshwater and marine food web. The long-term ecological consequences of phytoplankton loss in fresh and salt waters are unknown. Any sustained loss of phytoplankton quantity and quality will, however, directly and adversely, affect the global marine food supply. These are only a few of the possible impacts of an increase in UV-B radiation due to stratospheric ozone loss.

It will take cooperation on a global scale to solve this environmental problem but action can be taken at all levels of society. National and local governments, industry, individuals, and community groups can all play a role in preventing further damage to the ozone layer.

World governments have responded to the ozone crisis with action to control, limit, and to phase out the manufacture of certain ozone-depleting substances. In response to the warnings of scientists, the United Nations Environment Programme (UNEP) began assessing the science of ozone depletion and its implications for public policy in 1977. By 1981 the possibility of developing a global convention to protect the ozone layer was being explored. In 1985 the Vienna Convention for the Protection of the Ozone Layer was enacted and then amended in 1987 under the title of the Montreal Protocol on Substances that Deplete the Ozone Layer.

Alternatives for ozone-depleting substances exist. All levels of government and individuals share the responsibility for seeking out and using these technologies. State or provincial and municipal governments can also establish rules requiring the use of control and alternative technologies as a complement to national laws and international agreements. This is especially important regarding the implementation of recovery and recycling legislation; enforcement, in this case, can only be effective with the whole-hearted support of all levels of government.

Individuals can help to protect the ozone layer through lifestyle choices. Through consumer choice people can and must influence industry to develop environmentally-sustainable technologies. Through their voice and their vote people can indicate to government a desire for ozone-friendly legislation.

Lifestyles must also change to protect life from increased ultraviolet radiation, for the ozone layer, even under ideal conditions, will be unable to rejuvenate itself until well into the second millennium. People must protect themselves from UV-B rays by creating a barrier between the sun and their skin. The barrier may be in the form of sunscreen, sunglasses, a long-sleeved shirt and pants, a hat, or a roof! Clouds are not an effective barrier for UV-B rays. People must also try to minimize exposure, especially during the hours between 11:00 A.M. and 1:00 P.M. when the sun's rays are the strongest and most damaging. Some schools in Australia have already changed their recess time to reduce the children's exposure.

It is only through cooperative individual, industry, and government action that we will be able to meet the needs of the present without compromising the quality of life of future generations.

Pamela Foster

Further Readings
Atmospheric Environment Service, Environment Canada. *Ozone Depletion: An Environmental Citizenship Primer.* 1993.

See also MONTREAL PROTOCOL; OZONE POLLUTION

Ozone Pollution

Ozone, a gas composed of three atoms of oxygen, is today best known for its role in the stratosphere, where it screens the earth's surface from most of the life-damaging ultraviolet light from the sun. Ozone remains beneficial, however, so long as it never comes into direct contact with humans or other life, since ozone, like chlorine, is a strong oxidant capable of harming living tissues. (It is this property that makes both chlorine and ozone useful in purifying drinking water and for other uses.)

The amount of ozone in the troposphere (the lower atmosphere, which we breathe) is normally minuscule but increases slightly after an electric storm, imparting a familiar odor to the air. But in areas where photochemical smog forms, primarily in urban areas where thermal inversions trap a layer of cool air below a warmer layer, the catalytic action of sunlight on the accumulating gases emitted by automobiles and industries creates a relatively high concentration of ozone.

The smog-forming gases, primarily released during combustion of fossil fuels at high pressures and temperatures (as in internal combustion engines and electricity generating plants) are mainly nitrogen oxides and incompletely burned hydrocarbons. Nitrogen oxide (NO) can be further oxidized to the brownish gas, nitrogen dioxide (NO_2), by reacting with oxygen (or ozone when it is present). During daylight ultraviolet light (the sort that is less dangerous to life) is absorbed by NO_2, releasing a free oxygen atom that quickly reacts with molecular oxygen (O_2) to form ozone (O_3). The ultraviolet light also converts unburned hydrocarbons to highly active free radicals; together, these gases undergo chain reactions that cause ozone and peroxyacylnitrates (PANs, which are eye and throat irritants) to build up rapidly, causing damage to humans, animals, and plants.

When ozone is breathed it oxidizes the lining of the air sacs in the lungs, causing them to leak fluids. This edema makes gas exchange (release of carbon dioxide and uptake of oxygen by the blood) more difficult. Warm weather, youthfulness, and exercise all exacerbate the effect, generating the school "smog alerts" called in some cities. Prolonged exposure to ozone can cause the irreversible damage to lungs known as emphysema.

Plants are also sensitive to ozone damage, including a number of leafy crops (spinach, beans, tobacco), and some trees (the West Coast's ponderosa pines). The ozone enters via the leaves' stomata, attacking the chloroplasts; widespread yellow mottling and, with pines, premature leaf drop, are symptoms of ozone toxicity. In the mountains surrounding Los Angeles, severe damage to the forests is evident, the weakened trees succumbing to insects and disease.

In addition, ozone, like chlorine and other oxidants, affects rubber objects and painted surfaces and hastens corrosion of metals. By shortening useful lifetimes of these items, ozone adds to the costs of upkeep and replacement.

Laws in some states requiring catalytic converters to remove unburned hydrocarbons from car exhausts and other regulations on more efficient combustion processes have reduced the emissions per vehicle, but the continued growth in numbers of vehicles has largely offset these gains. Most urban areas globally now experience moderate to severe air pollution, including ozone and other products of photochemical smog formation.

Mary E. Clark

Further Readings

Stern, A.C., ed. *Air Pollution*. 3 vols. 2nd ed. 1968. (See especially articles in Vol. 1 by Haagen-Smit and Wayne, Stockinger and Coffin, and Goldsmith.)

See also AIR POLLUTION: IMPACTS; ASEAN HAZE; OZONE DEPLETION; SMOG

O

P

Packaging

Packaging is defined as a set of enclosures used to protect, store, contain, transport, display, and sell products. The packaging industry has classified packaging into three basic groups: 1) primary packaging, which comes into direct contact with the product; 2) secondary packaging, which unites several primary packages; and 3) tertiary packaging, which serves to transport products from manufacturers to retailers. In the United States approximately 4 percent of the value of all finished goods is spent on packaging.

Functions

Packaging is used to perform a variety of functions, including:

- Protection during shipping, storage, and shelf-life from damage or theft
- Ease and efficiency of shipping, storage, and display
- Prevention of malicious product tampering
- Prevention of food spoilage or contamination
- Consumer protection (or child protection) against exposure to hazardous contents
- Compliance with government regulation
- Provision of information
- Attractiveness and merchandisability
- Consumer convenience

Another function of packaging that has become more prominent in recent years in response to consumer concerns is that of avoiding or minimizing the adverse environmental consequences resulting from the manufacture, use, or post-use fate of the package.

Which of these functions are most important and which type of packaging can best achieve them depend on the characteristics and purpose of the product and the tastes and preferences of the consumer. The following examples serve as illustration:

1. If the product itself is non-rigid or fragile, then its packaging must provide protection from both dynamic forces (such as the shock and vibration of transit) and static forces (such as top-to-bottom compression or other damage from stacking).

2. The massive shift in consumer preferences for single-serving foods and microwavable products has tended to require increased and more complex packaging.

3. The retail merchandising trend toward self-service shopping has been accompanied by reduced sales staff to provide product information and protect against pilferage; the "blister pack" (packaging made of semi-rigid clear plastic to encase small products and offering space for product information) addresses both of these problems, even though such packaging is commonly perceived by the public to be wasteful or excessive.

Material Composition

The major material components of packaging (based on all packaging sales in the United States) are paper, 48 percent; glass, 25 percent; plastics, 15 percent; steel, 6 percent; and aluminum, 2 percent.

Paper is valued as a packaging material because it provides acceptable levels of protection, strength, and durability for the lowest cost in many applications. The primary uses of paper in packaging are for corrugated boxes, folding and setup boxes and cartons, and paper bags and sacks.

Glass offers many desirable properties as a packaging material: it is rigid, inert, transparent, impermeable, odorless, and microwavable. The major packaging applications of glass are beer and soft drink bottles, food and other bottles/jars, and wine and liquor bottles.

Plastics have several desirable characteristics that help explain why they have been by far the fastest growing of the packaging materials. These include the fact that plastics are relatively unbreakable, moisture-resistant, lightweight, and durable. Another crucial attribute is the diversity of forms and features that plastics can assume in terms of shape, color, texture, and opacity. The diversity of plastics results from the complexity and variety of polymers available. These include low-density polyethylene (LDPE), a flexible material used in films, wraps, trash bags, and some lids; high-density polyethylene (HDPE), a translucent or colored material used in milk jugs, water bottles, motor oil containers, detergent bottles, and other bottles; polypropylene (PP), a stiff material used in battery cases and other containers, as well as in films for food packaging; polystyrene (PS), a foam material used in carry-out food containers, as well as in food trays and lids (in nonfoam form); polyethylene terephthalate (PET), a tough material used in soft drink bottles and other food and medical containers; and polyvinyl chloride (PVC), a clear, stiff material used in shampoo bottles, water bottles, and other bottles, as well as in films and blister packs.

Steel has numerous appealing packaging properties; among them are high specific strength and stiffness, durability, formability, and imperviousness to air and water. Prominent uses of steel in packaging are for food cans; beer and soft drink cans; other non-food cans; and barrels, drums, and pails.

The major packaging applications of aluminum are beer and soft drink cans, other cans, aluminum foil, and closures. Attractive properties of aluminum, in general, as a packaging material include its light weight, thermal conductivity, resistance to oxidation, and superior barrier qualities. Aluminum cans are also lighter and less expensive to produce than steel cans and, relative to bottles, their cylindrical shape holds more volume and is more efficient in terms of stacking. Specific desirable features of aluminum foil include the fact that it is impermeable, nonabsorptive, greaseproof, inert, and highly formable.

Environmental Issues

Packaging raises a number of environmental concerns, the most prominent of which is due to the fact that packaging is the largest component of the solid waste stream, comprising about 30 percent of municipal solid waste in the United States. Packaging contributes to the toxicity as well as to the volume of municipal solid waste. For example, lead and cadmium, both toxic metals, serve as pigments in some colored printing inks which are used in packaging. Chlorinated substances—such as PVC, which is used in some packaging—when incinerated as solid waste produce dioxins, highly toxic organic compounds, and hydrochloric acid, a corrosive that contributes to acid precipitation.

In addition to its contribution to solid waste disposal problems packaging may also adversely affect the environment in other ways such as:

1. Inhibiting resource conservation, an environmental issue often linked with reducing the amount of solid waste
2. Causing environmental damage during the manufacture of packaging or during the extraction or the processing of the materials used in packaging
3. Causing environmental harm during the use of the product (an example of this would be the damage to the ozone layer caused by the use of CFCs as a propellant in aerosol spray containers)
4. Endangering wildlife from certain types of discarded packaging (such as threats to waterfowl from plastic ring carriers for six-pack cans)
5. Contributing to litter (when packaging is improperly discarded)

Opportunities to Reduce Adverse Environmental Consequences

Retailers, distributors, product manufacturers, packaging manufacturers, and raw materials suppliers can all take steps to improve the environmental performance of packaging. Consumers can make a contribution as well by using less packaging, purchasing products with environmentally "friendly" packaging, and separating discarded packaging for reuse or recycling. Some of the principal methods available to reduce the adverse environmental consequences of packaging include:

1. Use more environmentally-benign methods for extracting and processing raw materials used in packaging and for manufacturing the packaging itself. Some pulp mills, for example, have been able to reduce the environmental discharge of chlorinated organic compounds by eliminating the use of elemental chlorine in their paper bleaching process.
2. Remove toxic or hazardous constituents of the packaging. For instance, eliminating CFCs in aerosol spray containers has reduced the environmental threat to the stratospheric ozone layer. Eliminating the use of heavy metals—such as lead, cadmium, and chromium—in packaging would reduce the adverse environmental effects of the packaging's ultimate incineration or landfilling.
3. Reduce the amount of packaging per product. One method of accomplishing this, termed "lightweighting," is to minimize the material to perform a specific packaging function. For example, glassmakers have learned how to maintain the strength of glass containers while making them thinner. Between 1984 and 1987 the weight of the average sixteen-ounce non-refillable glass bottle was reduced from just over nine ounces to just over seven ounces. Aluminum manufacturers have achieved similar success, reducing the amount of aluminum in a standard-size aluminum can by over 20 percent between 1980 and 1988.
4. Design packaging to promote its reuse. This alternative often requires the product distributor to design and operate a reuse infrastructure. An example is bottled water delivery services that use refillable bottles.
5. Design packaging to promote its recycling. One way to accomplish this is to make packaging out of a single material, since such packaging is much easier to recycle. For example, manufacturers of plastic containers are beginning to replace the conventional paper labels with labels made of the same plastic material as the container itself. A related option is to use a single type of plastic resin to make any specific item of packaging,

since homogeneous plastic waste is relatively easy to recycle.

6. Use recycled material to make packaging. Virtually all materials, including plastics, can be recycled in packaging applications. For instance, some detergent bottles now come in three layers, the central layer of which contains recycled plastics. In addition, some single-layer motor oil containers and soft drink bottles now use a blend of virgin and recycled polymers.
7. Among the packaging materials that satisfy functional requirements, use the one that minimizes the environmental damage produced over the life cycle of the package. This alternative involves consideration of the "cradle to grave" environmental consequences of alternative packaging materials, not simply the environmental consequences associated with their final disposition.

One environmental approach that has been almost universally discredited is increasing the biodegradability of packaging (in order to reduce the volume of solid waste in landfills). Because modern landfill conditions prevent solid waste exposure to air, water, or sunlight, almost nothing—including so-called "biodegradable" materials, such as paper—degrades in them. Furthermore, attempts to make a packaging material more biodegradable—such as by adding starch to plastic resins that can be attacked and degraded by microorganisms in the natural environment—tend to reduce the structural integrity and performance of the material. As a result, more packaging material will generally be required to achieve the same function, and efforts to recycle the packaging material are likely to be impeded, or fully undermined. (One successful application of degradable materials, however, is in plastic carriers for six-pack cans; because the plastic rings break down when exposed to the elements, the threat to wildlife is reduced.)

Policy Options
Industry may voluntarily embrace some of the aforementioned methods of reducing the adverse environmental effects of packaging because: 1) production costs may be correspondingly reduced in a few cases, such as lightweighting; and 2) it provides a marketing opportunity to attract environmentally-conscious consumers who favor "green" products.

Because environmental effects are not fully reflected in market transactions, however, some form of government involvement is typically needed to remedy this market defect. Government might consider introducing some or all of the following types of policies to reduce the environmental harm from packaging:

1. Ban toxic or hazardous components of packaging. Banning the use of CFCs in aerosol spray containers is an example of this type of government action. Another example would be to ban the use of toxic heavy metals in packaging. Because bans are an extreme form of government intervention they should be invoked only when the environmental objective is unambiguous and the ban is necessary to achieve (and capable of achieving) that objective. Bans of questionable merit include the attempts of some communities to eliminate the use of particular types of plastic packaging because of what is thought to be their egregious contribution to the solid waste stream. Banning such plastic packaging, however, will tend to cause more solid waste both because of the increased amount of packaging required by the substitute material and because the substitute material may result in more food spoilage. A superior alternative would be to institute policies to increase the recycling of plastic packaging.

2. Promulgate and enforce environmental standards. Examples include emissions standards for the extraction and processing of materials used in packaging and for the manufacture of the packaging itself; environmental controls limiting the toxicity of the packaging or the environmental hazard resulting from the use or disposal of the packaging; and recycling standards for packaging, which would require that the packaging either consist of a specified percentage of recycled material or be made of recyclable material (meaning that the packaging material has achieved a specified recycling rate).

3. Provide information to promote environmentally responsible packaging. Government policies of this type include educating consumers and businesses about the importance of environmentally-responsible packaging; serving as a clearinghouse of information to industry about methods of reducing the adverse environmental effects of packaging; informing consumers about lifestyle and purchasing opportunities to eliminate, reuse, or recycle packaging; and identifying for consumers which types of packaging and packaging materials are most desirable from an environmental standpoint. One type of consumer information could take the form of "negative labeling," such as a statement that specific packaging is in violation of achievable recycling guidelines or fails to satisfy some other environmental objective.

4. Help develop a recycling infrastructure. Examples include requiring households to separate recyclables, including discarded packaging; providing curbside collection of recyclables; and constructing and operating materials recovery facilities.

5. Introduce economic charges or fees. Examples of economic charges for environmental purposes include emissions fees involving the extraction and processing of materials used in packaging or the manufacture of the packaging itself; taxes on virgin materials; deposit-refund systems for bottles or other packaging; and solid waste disposal or pre-disposal charges levied either at the manufacturing level, at the point of sale, or at the pick-up site. Economic charges have several desirable features: 1) unlike other government fees or taxes, environmental charges do not create a market distortion, but remedy an existing market distortion; 2) environmental charges are fair, in the sense that the parties bearing them are the ones whose production and purchasing decisions lead to the environmental damage; and 3) economic charges allow companies and consumers to trade off packaging's functional properties versus its environmental consequences within a traditional market framework.

Obviously, specific environmental programs may overlap the preceding policy categories. For instance, environmental labeling requirements for packaging may be considered to be both an informational policy and a type of government standard. Similarly, a government-mandated bottle deposit fee may be considered to be both an economic charge and a mechanism to help promote a recycling infrastructure.

Robert F. Stone

Further Readings

Stilwell, E. Joseph, R. Claire Canty, Peter W. Kopf, and Anthony M. Montrose. *Packaging for the Environment: A Partnership for Progress.* 1991.

Stone, Robert F., Ambuj D. Sagar, and Nicholas A. Ashford. "Recycling the Plastic Package." *Technology Review* 95 (July 1992): 48–56.

United States Congress, Office of Technology Assessment. *Facing America's Trash: What Next for Municipal Solid Waste?* October 1989.

See also CADMIUM; LEAD; MUNICIPAL SOLID WASTE: INCINERATION; MUNICIPAL SOLID WASTE: LANDFILL; OZONE DEPLETION; PULP AND PAPER MILLS; RECYCLING

Paley Commission

On January 22, 1951, President Harry S. Truman established the Paley Commission—also called the President's Materials Policy Commission—a group of citizens assisted by a staff of White House officials and consultants and named after its chair, William Paley, head of the Columbia Broadcasting System. Truman charged them with analyzing the long-term prospects for national supplies of various material resources, including coal, oil, metals, lumber, and agricultural fibers. The nation had experienced wartime shortages, rationing of many of these resources, and rapid post-war increases in demand, so the president was concerned that shortages would slow economic growth and threaten national security in the event of another major war.

The final report, released in 1952 just six months before the end of Truman's administration, advocated a strong role for government in encouraging conservation of resources along with increased production. The commission expressed great concern that shortages could sharply increase prices for a variety of materials and thereby stifle economic growth. The report stated clearly that materials policy should seek to encourage and direct the private sector, not replace it, but it still argued for an agency within government that could centralize and coordinate materials policy, then scattered among numerous agencies. The commission

also argued that Americans needed to change their values to place greater emphasis on conservation, which they interpreted as efficient use, not hoarding or doing without. They sought to ensure adequate supplies through the year 1975 with prices no more than doubling after inflation. Such goals required both a strong ethos of efficient use and greater emphasis on research and development to increase supplies at reasonable prices. The report was ignored by the Eisenhower administration, but championed by some conservation groups.

Frank N. Laird

Further Readings

The President's Materials Policy Commission. *Resources for Freedom.* 1952.

See also CONSERVATION MOVEMENT; *Limits to Growth*; NONRENEWABLE RESOURCES; RESOURCE MANAGEMENT; RESOURCISM

Panda

See BEARS: CONSERVATION AND HABITAT; GIANT PANDA

Paper Mills

See PULP AND PAPER MILLS

Parks and Park Policy

See NATIONAL PARK SERVICE (U.S.); NATIONAL PARKS: AUSTRALIA; NATIONAL PARKS: CANADA; NATIONAL PARKS: UNITED STATES

Parrots

See WILD BIRD TRADE

Particulates

See AIR POLLUTION: IMPACTS

Passenger Pigeon

The passenger pigeon (*Ectopistes migratorius*) offers probably the most famous example of avian extinction in modern times. Less than two centuries ago billions of these birds inhabited eastern North America, breeding in Canada and the northeastern states and partly migrating southward to the southeastern Atlantic and Gulf states for the winter. Probably no other American bird was ever so numerous. The passenger pigeon resembled the mourning dove (*Zenaida macroura*) but was larger (about sixteen inches or 40 centimeters) with a longer pointed tail and a blue-gray head. The underparts were pinkish in the male and gray in the female. The pigeon's diet consisted of various invertebrates, seeds, berries, and nuts, especially beechnuts. The flocks sometimes devastated newly planted grain fields but otherwise did little damage to crops.

Flocks of pigeons in search for food roamed in almost incredible numbers and could literally darken the skies for hours. Mark Catesby, Pehr Kalm, Alexander Wilson, and John James Audubon observed flocks that possibly contained over a billion birds. The pigeons bred in equally impressive colonies, and a typical nesting site could cover thousands of acres. The pigeons laid their single egg in a flimsy nest of twigs, and often more than 100 pairs occupied the same tree. From the 1870s on the species' decline was dramatic: the last great nestings took place during that decade, and the last wild birds were encountered at the turn of the century. A few individuals still survived in captivity, and the last passenger pigeon, the famous Martha, died on September 1, 1914, at the Cincinnati zoo.

A variety of explanations have been offered for the species' rapid decline, such as imported avian disease, destruction of the bird's food supply by forest clearance, and ruthless slaughter for human consumption. Year after year hundreds of thousands of birds were killed and shipped by railway carloads for sale in the markets of eastern cities, the hunting pressure easing up only after the great nesting colonies were gone and the commercial attraction lost.

Mikko Saikku

Further Readings

Schorger, A.W. *The Passenger Pigeon: Its Natural History and Extinction.* 1955.

See also AUDUBON, JOHN JAMES; BIODIVERSITY; CAROLINA PARAKEET; HAWK SHOOTING; NATIONAL AUDUBON SOCIETY

PCBs

See PERSISTENT ORGANOCHLORINE COMPOUNDS

Peregrine Falcon

The peregrine falcon (*Falco peregrinus*), formerly known as the duck hawk in North America, is by common consent the quintessential falcon. Indeed, the species has long been used in falconry. The practically cosmopolitan, 600- to 1,000-gram (approximately crow-sized) raptor feeds chiefly on birds, including waterfowl and shorebirds among others, aerially pursuing its prey at high speeds in a variety of expansive landscapes on six continents and numerous oceanic islands. Peregrine falcons are open-habitat raptors at all times of the year. The species is both territorial and traditional in nest-site use, with records of continual occupation at several specific breeding locations dating from the thirteenth century through the present. Restricted in breeding-sites by its limited ability to construct a nest, the species tends to breed on natural (cliff) and artificial (building and bridge) ledges, frequently at great heights, and often overlooking water. If the cliff is a small one and nestlings are crowded one or more young may fall from it. Peregrine is Latin for "wanderer" or "migrant," and many northern-latitude populations are highly migratory; many others, however, are mainly resident.

Rarely common, even in the centers of its range (the world population in 1982 was estimated at less than 20,000 breeding pairs) North American and European populations of peregrine falcons greatly declined in the 1950s and 1960s as a result of organochlorine contamination. DDT and its metabolites induced eggshell thinning by inhibiting calcium movements within female peregrines, which, in turn, decreased reproductive success when thin-shelled eggs were crushed by incubating adults. At the same time, cyclodiene insecticides (aldrin, dieldrin, etc.) and their metabolites increased adult mortality. As a result, the species was extirpated from several portions of its historic European and North American range.

Over the past twenty years many depleted peregrine falcon populations have increased substantially, both because of more limited use of organochlorine pesticides, and because of successful captive-rearing and release programs. In North America many captive-reared birds were released into urban environments, where the species is now breeding in large numbers. Populations in Great Britain have increased to the point that many pigeon fanciers have called for the removal of some birds from the British population. As of late 1993 the species remains on the U.S. Endangered Species List.

Keith L. Bildstein and Laurie J. Goodrich

Further Readings

Cade, T.J. *The Falcons of the World.* 1982.
———, J.H. Enderson, C.G. Thelander, and C.M. White. *Peregrine Falcon Populations: Their Management and Recovery.* 1988.
Ratcliffe, D.A. *The Peregrine Falcon.* 1980.

See also PESTICIDES

Permaculture

See AGROFORESTRY; SUSTAINABLE AGRICULTURE

Permafrost

Permafrost is soil, sub-soil, or bedrock that is frozen continuously for more than two consecutive years in alpine or Arctic areas. While the concept appears rather static the reality is a complex and dynamic phenomenon with very clear environmental implications. On the surface there may be an active layer of soil six to thirty inches deep which melts each summer and freezes again each fall. This active zone includes an organic mat on the surface which is critical for all vegetative growth and the ponding so frequent in tundra areas. The active layer also acts as insulation preserving the stability of the permafrost below. In some areas the permafrost may contain a significant percentage of ice crystals or even large chunks of ice. Stability of land forms requires that the ice remain permanently frozen. In North America permafrost may vary from a few feet at 60 degrees north latitude to several thousand feet thick in the high Arctic islands. It is a product of the interaction between the cooling effect of the surface weather and the heat emanating from the earth's core. As a result there may be scattered patches of permafrost in the southern Arctic (due to vegetation or north facing slopes); then discontinuous permafrost (unfrozen areas under lakes and rivers); and finally continuous permafrost as one proceeds north.

From a geophysical and an environmental point of view it is essential to keep permafrost areas permanently frozen since these areas provide the foundation for all that occurs above. Permafrost was once described as ice cream composed of soil and water. If the active layer is disturbed by human activity then settlement begins to erode the permafrost below and, where ice content is high, there can be collapsing land forms and demolished buildings. When the Alaska Highway was constructed during World War II, engineers did not fully comprehend the problems of permafrost and sections of the highway disappeared. In the decades following World War II extensive scientific and technical research led to the development of mitigative construction techniques for roads, airstrips, buildings, and pipelines. For instance, in the construction of the Trans-Alaskan Oil Pipeline (Alyeska), long stretches of pipeline had to be elevated at great expense to keep the hot oil from melting the surrounding permafrost. Gravel pads with refrigeration coils were also used where caribou had to cross the right of way. These innovative designs helped to escalate the capital cost of the pipeline from $900 million to $8.5 billion. Permafrost has added a whole new dimension to the challenges of engineering and construction. Also the future stability of permafrost may be seriously eroded if global climate change impacts the Arctic as some predict. Thus this phenomenon presents a series of environmental challenges for the future.

Robert J.D. Page

Further Readings

Livingston, John. *Arctic Oil: The Destruction of the North.* 1981.
Page, Robert. *Northern Development: The Canadian Dilemma.* 1986.

See also ALASKA: PARK, WILDERNESS, AND RESOURCE ISSUES; ARCTIC; BERGER INQUIRY; CLIMATE WARMING; SNOW AS HABITAT

Persistent Organochlorine Compounds

Organochlorine (halogenated aromatic) compounds have been used in the open environment as pesticides (DDT) and in industry in many applications such as heat transfer fluids, dielectric fluids, plasticizers, flame retardants and diluents (PCBs). They are produced as byproducts of industrial processes (polychlorinated dibenzo-p-dioxins [PCDD], and polychlorinated dibenzofurans [PCDF]). They can be found throughout the environment in all compartments. They persist because they resist degradation by acids, bases, heat, or hydrolysis, and they are incorporated into and are concentrated in the food chain. The frequently identified and studied compounds include DDT and its degradation products and congeners (DDE), PCB and its congeners, as well as the PCDDs and PCDFs. Others in the group used in many applications include the polychlorinated benzenes, terphenyls, and naphthalenes, and the polybrominated biphenyls (PBBs).

As a group these compounds are lipophilic—a characteristic which allows them to be incorporated in fat and flesh of animals: fish, fish-eating birds, and in marine mammals and humans where they can be found concentrated in fat, milk, and blood.

The profile of congeners found in environmental media depends on the composition of the PCB mixture released. However, the PCB composition of human milk is different from that found in the environment in that the lower chlorinated congeners predominate. Different metabolic degradation and therefore, different half-lives for the various congeners, explain the patterns of persistence and possibly patterns of toxicity.

Toxicity

PCB toxicity has been studied extensively in laboratory animals and in humans accidentally and occupationally exposed. Health effects include biochemical enzyme changes in the liver, blood lipid alterations, respiratory problems, liver damage, and a skin condition called chloracne. Long term studies of workers exposed to PCB do not demonstrate unusual mortality or cancer incidence patterns.

Offspring of women exposed to PCB in capacitor plants show slightly decreased birth weight. A study of women who consumed large amounts of Great Lakes fish also demonstrated a pattern consistent with this, including lower birth weight and smaller head circumference. Follow-up of children through age four showed a variety of cognitive developmental alterations which correlated with prenatal exposure (cord blood PCB level).

Large-scale poisonings of humans occurred in 1968 in Japan though contaminated rice oil (*Yusho*) and in Taiwan in a similar epidemic eleven years later in 1979 (*Yu-cheng*). Together, about 4,000 people were poisoned. Many of the findings in these episodes, which at first were believed to be directly related to PCB, were actually related to furans in the PCB mixture. Prominent features of the poisoning were a variety of skin lesions (chloracne, hyperpigmentation, skin plaques, and mucous membrane swelling), as well as systemic symptoms (jaundice, neuropathies, and gastrointestinal disorders). Occupationally-exposed workers with blood PCB levels similar to those poisoned in Japan and Taiwan did not show

the same degree of symptoms and signs of toxicity.

Although more than half the people affected in these outbreaks recovered from the skin lesions and most continue to improve, some of their systemic symptoms persist. Affected children exposed in utero were small for gestational age at birth and had premature closure of the skull bones, erupted teeth, and retarded growth. Many of these children were also exposed in early infancy though breast milk but the contibution of this to the delayed developmental milestones observed may not be as important as the prenatal exposure.

Some congeners of PCB (e.g., those with coplanar structure) behave as tetrachloro dibenzo-p-dioxins (TCDD) in that they bind to the same cellular receptors as TCDD (e.g., the aryl hydrocarbon receptor: Ah). They are considered to have similar toxicity.

Toxic Equivalency Factors

The ability to predict from its molecular structure the binding of a particular congener of PCDD, PCDF, or PCB to the cellular Ah receptor (the common pathway for the mechanism of action) allows the development of a system whereby the toxicity of each congener can be measured against a reference, the most toxic. This system, called the TEF system, has been widely accepted. It provides a framework to examine the varied results of human exposure experience, to assess the risk from the contaminants in the environment, and to legislate their control in food and environmental media.

Organochlorines in Food

The Canadian Food and Drugs Act and Regulations (1986) does not allow PCDD in food with the exception of fish which may contain up to twenty picograms per gram (pg/g) of 2,3,7,8-TCDD, the most toxic congener of the dioxin and furan family. Major surveys of foods carried out in Canada have focused on the Ontario food basket. These surveys show that some plant products have low concentrations (eight parts per trillion [ppt] or less) of O_8CDD in some peaches, wheat, and potatoes while nine other congeners were not detectable. Such was not the case with animal products in which low levels (five to twelve pg/g) were detected (chicken, prime beef, U.S. eggs and hamburger). PCB and mirex were not detected but a variety of other organochlorines (hexachlorobenzene and DDT breakdown products: DDE, and pentachlorophenol) were present in many animal and plant products. Fruits and vegetables tend to be relatively free of the lipophilic residues in contrast to animal products. U.S. plant and animal products tended to have higher residues than Ontario products. Current Canadian guidelines for PCB in foods are .2 parts per million (ppm) in meat and fish, .5 ppm in poultry fat, and .1 ppm in eggs. Although there is a maximum acceptable concentration of .003 ppm for PCB in water, these compounds are rarely present due to their lipophilic nature.

Overall, residues of the persistent organochlorines in food are declining despite their presence in animal products in small amounts and their large proportional lifetime contribution to total exposure from this source. Great Lakes fish have higher concentrations of organochlorine residues and some areas continue to be closed to commercial fishing. Concentrations in fish are monitored according to species and lake throughout Ontario, with guidelines in effect setting limits on consumption.

Organochlorine presence in human milk has implications for children's total exposure. Infants receive a large proportion of their lifetime exposure from breast milk in the first year of life. Recent Canadian surveys show that organochlorine residue levels in human milk are declining. There are no recommendations against breast feeding infants as a result of current organochlorine concentrations in breast milk, however, since the effects demonstrated are related to prenatal exposure.

Although humans have been the focus of investigation as targets of the environmental contamination by the persistent organochlorine compounds, effects on the larger ecosystem have the possibility of greater impact overall. The widespread use and the large amounts of PCB which are estimated in landfill sites and disposed of at sea continues to be a potential threat to the environment. The concentration of these compounds in environmental media has been declining but will remain for generations. The destruction of PCB by high temperature incineration provides one possible solution but this in turn produces PCDD and PCDF which are themselves problematic.

Adverse effects on the reproduction of fish-eating birds and toxicity in marine mammals whose unique food supply continues to be contaminated may have greater implications for species survival than for humans whose food supply is broader and whose exposure can be controlled through a variety of legislative and other control methods.

Lesbia F. Smith

Further Readings

James, R.C., H. Busch, C.H. Tamburro, S.M. Roberts, J.D. Schell, and R.D. Harbison. "Polychlorinated Biphenyl Exposure and Human Disease." *Journal of Occupational Medicine* 35 (1993): 136–48.

Ontario Ministry of Agriculture and Food, and Ministry of the Environment. *Polychlorinated dibenzo-p-dioxins and polychlorinated dibenzofurans, and other organochlorine contaminants in food.* August 1988.

Safe, S. "Toxicology, Structure-Function Relationships, and Human and Environmental Health Impacts of Polychlorinated Biphenyls: Progress and Problems." *Environmental Health Perspectives* 100 (1992): 259–68.

See also BIOACCUMULATION; DIOXINS AND FURANS; FOOD CHAINS; GREAT LAKES; MARINE MAMMALS; PESTICIDES; TRACE ANALYSIS

Pesticides

Definition and Classification of Pesticides

Pesticides are chemicals, naturally occurring or synthesized, that are used to control pests. Pesticides are subdivided into several classes based on the type of pest that is its chief target and for which it is sold. The most common classes include insecticides (to control insect pests), fungicides (to control plant pathogens), herbicides (to control weeds), nematicides (to control nematodes), viricides (to control virus), and rodenticides (to kill rodents). However, the effect of most pesticides is not exclusively limited to one class of pests alone.

Pesticides are also classified into compound groups, depending on their chemical properties. The chemical characteristics of a compound provide information about the mechanism of toxicity and the short- and long-term effects on the target organism. The major compound groups include: organochlorines (chlorinated hydrocarbons, such as DDT, dieldrin, and chlordane); organophosphates (such as parathion and malathion); carbamates (such as aldicarb); and pyrethroids (such as permethrin).

Extent of Pesticide Use

In the United States about 434 million kilograms of pesticides are used annually, of which 68 percent are herbicides, 23 percent insecticides, and 10 percent fungicides (Table 1). Since 1945 the use of synthetic pesticides in the United States has grown thirty-three-fold. However, the increase in pesticide use is even larger than this figure suggests, since new pesticides have been introduced that have at least ten-fold greater toxicity and effectiveness than some of the older pesticides. For example in 1945 DDT was applied at a dosage of approximately two kilograms per hectare (kg/ha). Today, similarly effective insect control is achieved with pyrethroids and aldicarb applied at 0.1 kg/ha and 0.05 kg/ha, respectively.

An estimated 320 million kg of pesticide is applied for control of pests in U.S. agriculture. Pesticides are applied to about 62 percent of the total agricultural land in the United States, including pastures, at an average rate of about 3 kg/ha. The application of pesticides for pest control is not evenly distributed among crops. For instance, in the United States 93 percent of the hectarage of row crops (e.g., corn, soybeans, and cotton) is treated with some type of pesticide, whereas less than 10 percent of the forage crop hectarage is treated.

Herbicides are currently being used on approximately 90 million ha in the United States—greater than half of the nation's cropland. Field corn alone accounts for 53 percent of agricultural herbicide use, and almost three-quarters of the herbicide is applied to corn and soybeans combined.

The unequal distribution is similar for insecticide use. Of the approximately 62 million kg of insecticides applied to 5 percent of the total agricultural land (Table 1), approximately 25 percent is used on cotton and corn. Some crops are treated as many as twenty times per season (e.g., apples and cotton), whereas other crops may be treated only once (e.g., corn and wheat).

Insecticide use also varies considerably among geographic regions. Warm regions of the United States often suffer intense pest problems. For example, although only 13 percent of the alfalfa hectarage in the United States is treated with insecticides, 89 percent of the alfalfa area in the Southern Plains states is treated to control insect pests. In the Mountain region, where large quantities of potatoes are grown, 65 percent of the potato cropland receives insecticide treatment, but in the Southeast, where only early potatoes are grown, 100 percent of the potato cropland receives treatment. Cotton insect pests, such as the boll weevil, are also more of a problem in the Southeast than in other regions. In the Southeast and Delta states 84 percent of the cotton cropland receives treatment, whereas in the Southern Plains region less than half of the crop (40 percent) is treated.

Fungicides are primarily used on fruit and vegetable crops. For example, approximately 95 percent of grapes and 97 percent of potato hectarage are treated with fungicides, whereas neither corn nor wheat hectarage is treated.

TABLE 1

U.S. Hectarage Treated with Pesticides and Amounts Applied

Hectare Quantity Treated (Numbers are in millions of hectares and kilograms)

Land-Use Category	Total hectares	All Pesticides ha quantity treated		Herbicides ha quantity treated		Insecticides ha quantity treated		Fungicides ha quantity treated	
Agricultural	472	114	320	86	220	22	62	4	38
Government and Industrial	150	28	55	30	44	NA	11	NA	NA
Forestry	290	2	4	2	3	<1	1	NA	NA
Household	4	4	55	3	26	3	25	1	4
Total	916	148	434	121	293	26	99	5	42

Total for hectarage treated with herbicides, insecticides, and fungicides exceeds the total treated hectares because the same land area can be treated several times with several classes of chemicals.

NA=not available.

Crop Losses and Agricultural Technologies

Currently an estimated 37 percent of all crop production in the United States is lost each year to pests (13 percent to insects, 12 percent to plant pathogens, and 12 percent to weeds) in spite of the use of pesticides and nonchemical controls. Although pesticide use has increased during the past five decades, crop losses have not shown a concurrent decline, largely due to changes in agricultural practices and cosmetic standards. According to survey data collected from 1942 to the present, losses from weeds have fluctuated with an overall slight decline, due to improved chemical, mechanical, and cultural weed-control practices, from 14 percent to 12 percent. During that same period U.S. crop losses from plant pathogens, including nematodes, increased slightly, from 10.5 percent to approximately 12.0 percent. This increase results in part from reduced sanitation (because fungicides can substitute for sanitation), higher cosmetic standards, and abandonment of crop-rotation practices.

The share of crop yields lost to insects has nearly doubled during the past fifty years, despite a more than ten-fold increase in both the amount and toxicity of synthetic insecticides used. The increase in crop losses per hectare due to insects has been offset by increased crop yields obtained with higher-yielding varieties, and greater use of fertilizers and irrigation.

The increase in crop losses despite intensified insecticide use is due to several major changes that have taken place in agricultural practices. These changes include: 1) the planting of some crop varieties that are more susceptible to insect pests; 2) the destruction of natural enemies of certain pests, which creates the need for additional pesticide treatments; 3) the increase in the number of pests resistant to pesticides; 4) the reduction in crop-rotation practices; and 5) the increase in monocultures and resultant reduced crop diversity.

Techniques to Reduce Pesticides

The increase in crop losses associated with recent changes in agricultural practices suggests that some alternative strategies exist that might reduce pesticide use. Two important practices that apply to all agricultural crops include widespread use of monitoring and improved application equipment. Currently a significant number of pesticide treatments are applied unnecessarily and at improper times due to a lack of treat-when-necessary programs. Furthermore, pesticide is unnecessarily lost during application. For example, only 25 to 50 percent of the pesticide applied by aircraft actually reaches the target area when applied under ideal conditions. Considering that on average less than 0.01 percent of applied pesticide actually reaches the target pests, it is obvious that enormous quantities of pesticides are not only being wasted, but dispersed into the environment. By increasing monitoring and improving application equipment, more efficient pest control can be achieved.

There are numerous nonchemical alternatives for pest control. None of these technologies is the "silver bullet." The prime success of alternative controls is that they can be employed in various combinations depending on the crop, the environment, and the specific insect pests, weeds, or pathogens attacking the crop. The most important nonchemical controls include biological control with natural enemies (predators and parasites) of pests, breeding crops for resistance to pests, and increasing the practice of crop rotations and crop polycultures.

By substituting nonchemical alternatives for some pesticides used on forty major crops, it is estimated that total agricultural pesticide use can be reduced by approximately 50 percent in the United States. The added costs for implementing these alternatives are estimated to be approximately $1 billion. These alternatives would thereby increase total food production costs about 0.6 percent for the consumer.

Several studies confirm that it would be technologically feasible to reduce pesticide use in the United States by 35 to 50 percent without reducing crop yields. Several countries (e.g., Denmark, Sweden, the Netherlands) and the province of Ontario in Canada have already implemented programs aimed at reducing agricultural pesticide use while maintaining viable levels of crop protection and without decreasing crop yields. For example, Sweden adopted a pesticide reduction program in 1986 and achieved a 50 percent reduction in agricultural pesticide use (compared to the average pesticide consumption of the period 1981–1985) in 1990. Yields of crops slightly increased over this period. A further 50 percent reduction in Swedish pesticide use is targeted for 1997. Also, the Netherlands, where agricultural pesticide use is probably the most intensive in the world, implemented a program in 1991 to reduce pesticide use by at least 50 percent by the year 2000.

P

Environmental and Economic Impacts of Pesticide Use

Pesticides have contributed to the impressive productivity of U.S. agriculture, with an estimated $16 billion in crops saved each year by the $4 billion U.S. investment in pesticidal controls. This cost/benefit assessment, however, does not include the human health costs or the costs of the environmental problems associated with pesticide use. Although efforts are made to contain pesticide sprays within the target crop-area, pesticides—especially those applied using airplanes and large mechanical sprayers—often reach adjacent vegetation, wildlife, soil, and water. In this way the impact of pesticides is felt far beyond the designated target area.

Pesticides adversely affect the health of humans exposed to them. Based on survey data a recent World Health Organization report estimated there are 1 million human pesticide poisonings each year in the world with about 20,000 deaths worldwide. In the United States pesticide poisonings are reported to total a minimum of 67,000, with the number of accidental fatalities estimated at twenty-seven each year. Also, there are between 6,000 and 10,000 cases of cancer in the United States associated with pesticide use.

In addition, several thousand domestic animals are poisoned by pesticides each year. Dogs and cats are the most commonly poisoned animals because they usually wander freely about the home and farm and therefore have greater opportunity to come into contact with pesticides than other domesticated animals. Central records on domestic animal poisonings are not kept, making an overall economic assessment extremely difficult.

In cultivated and wild areas naturally present predators and parasites help keep pest species in check. When pesticides destroy both pest and beneficial natural enemies, frequently other pests present reach outbreak levels. For example, in cotton and apple crops, pesticide destruction of natural enemies results in the outbreak of numerous pests, including cotton bollworm, tobacco budworm, cotton aphid, and cotton loopers in cotton crops; and European red mite, red-banded leafroller, San Jose scale, rosy apple aphid in apple crops. The additional pesticide applications required to control these pests, plus the increased crop losses they cause, are estimated to cost the United States about $520 million per year.

Another vital group of insects that pesticides frequently kill are honeybees and wild bees, essential for the annual pollination of about $30 billion in fruits and vegetables in the United States. The losses incurred with the destruction of honeybees and loss of pollination each year are conservatively estimated to be $320 million.

Another serious and costly side-effect of heavy pesticide use has been the development of pesticide resistance in pest populations of insects, plant pathogens, and weeds. At present some 900 species exhibit resistance to commonly applied pesticides. When resistance occurs farmers must increase pesticide applications to save their crops. Even so, crop losses frequently are higher than normal. This resistance problem is estimated to cost the United States $1.4 billion each year in increased costs of pesticides and reduced crop yields.

Basically, pesticides are applied to protect crops from pests and to increase yields, yet at times the crops themselves are damaged by pesticide treatments. This occurs when: 1) the recommended dosages suppress crop growth, development and yield; 2) pesticides drift from the targeted crop to damage adjacent valuable crops; and 3) residual herbicides either prevent chemical-sensitive crops from being planted in rotation or inhibit the growth of crops that are planted. In addition, excessive pesticide residues may accumulate on crops, necessitating the destruction of the harvest. When crop seizures and insurance costs are added to the direct costs of crop losses caused by pesticides, the total yearly loss in the United States is conservatively estimated to be nearly $1 billion.

Ground and surface waters frequently are contaminated by applied pesticides. Estimates are that nearly one-half of the ground and well water in the United States is or has the potential to become contaminated with pesticides. To adequately monitor this contamination an estimated $1.3 billion would need to be spent each year. Not only are pesticides not monitored, but also no steps have been taken to prevent the widespread contamination of U.S. water resources.

Pesticides wash into streams and lakes where they cause substantial fishery losses. Thus, high pesticide concentrations in water directly kill fish; low dosages primarily kill small fish fry. Also, pesticides eliminate aquatic insects and other small invertebrates which are food for fish.

Birds, mammals, and other wildlife also are killed by pesticides. The full extent of wildlife destruction is difficult to determine because these animals are often hidden from view, camouflaged, highly mobile, and live in protected habitats. Based on the available data, U.S. bird losses associated with pesticide use represent an estimated loss of about $2.1 billion per year. No estimate can be made of mammal losses because of a lack of data.

The known costs of human health hazards and the diverse environmental impacts associated with U.S. pesticide use total approximately $8 billion each year. Thus, based on a strictly cost-benefit basis, pesticide use remains beneficial. No estimate exists for the total environmental and health costs of using pesticides worldwide, but it may be as high as $100 billion each year. Decisions about future pesticide use need to be based not only on the benefits, but on a careful consideration of the risks they create. Perhaps in this way an equitable balance can be achieved.

David N. Pimentel

Further Readings

Briggs, S.A. *Basic Guide to Pesticides: Their Characteristics and Hazards.* 1992.

Pimentel, D., and H. Lehman, eds. *The Pesticide Question: Environment, Economics and Ethics.* 1993.

See also BIOACCUMULATION; FOOD CHAINS; HERBICIDES; INTEGRATED PEST MANAGEMENT; SUSTAINABLE AGRICULTURE

Peterson, Roger Tory

See BIRDING

Peterson, Russell W.

Russell Peterson claims that it was his son's childhood interest in birds that turned him into an "environmentalist." Born in Wisconsin in 1916 Peterson studied at the University of Wisconsin, obtaining a doctorate in chemistry in 1942. He spent twenty-six years with E.I. DuPont de Nemours & Co., Inc., moving up through management to become director of a division responsible for launching new business ventures. Upon retiring he served from 1969–1973 as governor of Delaware, where he was instrumental in changing a commission form of government to a cabinet form and in saving Delaware's unspoiled coastal zone from then-planned heavy industrialization.

Since 1973 his efforts have been focused in the public arena, across a broad spectrum of areas, including renewable energy, environmen-

tal management and conservation, nuclear issues, criminal justice, and public policy. His varied roles with environmental organizations include: chair of the U.S. Council on Environmental Quality, president of the National Audubon Society, director of the Office of Technology Assessment, U.S. Congress, board of directors for World Wildlife Fund, chair of Global Tomorrow Coalition, vice chair and president of Better World Society, vice president of World Conservation Fund, goodwill ambassador for United Nations Environment Programme, and executive committee member for Population Crisis Committee, among others. In the area of energy he has served as chairman of the advisory board for the Solar Energy Research Institute, founding chairman of the Bio-Energy Council, and as a member of the board of directors of Alliance to Save Energy. And in regard to nuclear issues, he served as a member of the President's Commission on the Accident at Three-Mile Island, and as chair of the Center on the Consequences of Nuclear War.

Peterson has been visiting professor at three universities, has been awarded honorary degrees by fourteen universities and colleges, and has received many awards from environmental and scientific organizations. In addition, he takes a great interest in higher education, arguing strongly for broadly educated "professional generalists"—new age Renaissance scholars—to augment the efforts of specialists in preserving the planet.

Mary E. Clark

Further Readings

Peterson, Russell W. "Integrated Studies: Education for the Professional Generalist." *L & S Magazine* (Spring 1988).

———. "Why Not a Separate College of Integrated Studies?" In *Rethinking the Curriculum: Toward an Integrated, Interdisciplinary College Education.* Ed. Mary E. Clark and Sandra A. Wawrytko. 1990.

See also COUNCIL ON ENVIRONMENTAL QUALITY; ENVIRONMENTAL EDUCATION; INTERDISCIPLINARITY; NATIONAL AUDUBON SOCIETY; OFFICE OF TECHNOLOGY ASSESSMENT; SOLAR ENERGY RESEARCH INSTITUTE; WORLD WILDLIFE FUND

Phosphates

From the late 1940s synthetic detergents rapidly replaced traditional soaps in many of their uses, especially household laundering. A synthetic laundry detergent is a mixture of chemicals, including the principal ingredient—the surface active agent or surfactant—and so-called builders that enhance the action of the surfactant, primarily by softening the wash water. In the early detergents the principal surfactant was alkyl benzene sulfonate (ABS) and the chief builder phosphates. A detergent might contain as much as 30 percent ABS and from 20 to 50 percent phosphates. Both ABS and phosphates were to cause environmental problems.

ABS did not biodegrade readily and consequently continued its excellent foaming action in municipal sewage treatment plants and in receiving waters, producing large amounts of unsightly foam. This problem was solved from the mid 1960s with the substitution of the readily biodegradable LAS (linear alkyl sulfonate).

About that time many communities in North America and Western Europe began to report adverse effects on lakes from excessive algal growths. Scientists soon established that in most instances the cause was increased amounts of phosphorus entering lakes from various sources: municipal sewage treatment plants (the largest contributor), certain industries, and agricultural lands. The phosphorus in sewage effluent had two main sources, human wastes and detergent phosphates. Two courses of action were obvious: reduce, even eliminate, phosphates in detergents and remove phosphorus from sewage plant effluent. In America and Europe the construction of municipal sewage treatment plants was intensified from the late 1960s. Old and new plants now provided not only traditional primary and secondary treatment but also the new tertiary treatment, rapidly developed to remove phosphorus from sewage effluent.

Meanwhile, detergent companies (aware as early as anyone about the role of phosphorus in algal growths) had privately been seeking a substitute for phosphates in detergents. However, for a time they publicly denied that phosphorus was the element responsible for excessive algal growths, and in the early 1970s exploited a minority (and short-lived) scientific view that carbon was chiefly responsible. By the late 1960s the detergent industry had found only one satisfactory substitute for phosphates, namely the sodium salt of nitrilotriacetic acid, commonly referred to as NTA. Aware of this substitute, the Canadian federal government regulated the amount of phosphates in deter-

gents under the 1970 Canada Water Act. From August 1, 1970, phosphates were limited to 20 percent, and from January 1, 1973, to 5 percent, by weight. In the United States on the other hand, the government, although initially in the late 1960s supportive of the idea of reducing phosphates in detergents, requested the detergent industry in late 1970 voluntarily not to use NTA until allegations that it was carcinogenic could be checked. Canadian authorities were not convinced of the soundness of the allegations against NTA and never regulated it. Eventually, in 1980 the U.S. Environmental Protection Agency declared that it could find no reason to restrict the use of NTA.

Meanwhile, in September 1971 the U.S. government created a furor when it reversed itself and recommended the use of phosphate detergents in place of recently formulated nonphosphate detergents, many of which it had concluded contained builders that were hazardous to human health. Before that in the United States some municipalities, the first being Chicago which followed Canada's lead, and soon thereafter some states bordering the Great Lakes (including New York, Indiana, Michigan, and Wisconsin) passed laws reducing the percentage of phosphates in laundry detergents. In several instances the U.S. detergent industry went to court in attempts to block or overturn a city or state regulation. Meanwhile, the industry's ongoing research led to the discovery of other substitutes for phosphates, including citrates, carbonates, silicates, and aluminosilicates.

In America and Europe by the 1980s, greatly expanded and enhanced sewage treatment facilities, the great reduction of phosphates in detergents, and modified agricultural practices had together combined to reduce appreciably the quantities of phosphorus entering the aquatic environment. Consequently, the algal pollution problem in lakes was brought under control in most locations.

William McGucken

Further Readings

Kehoe, Terence. "Merchants of Pollution? The Soap and Detergent Industry and the Fight to Restore Great Lakes Water Quality, 1965–1972." *Environmental History Review* 16 (1992): 21–46.

McGucken, William. "The Canadian Federal Government, Cultural Eutrophication, and the Regulation of Detergent Phosphates." *Environmental Review* 13

(1989): 155–66.

———. *Biodegradable: Detergents and the Environment.* 1991.

See also EUTROPHICATION; GREAT LAKES; WATER POLLUTION ABATEMENT TECHNOLOGIES

Pinchot, Gifford

Gifford Pinchot was one of a scientific elite that came into the federal government at the end of the nineteenth century dedicated to managing natural resources for the maximum good for the greatest number. A graduate of Yale University, Pinchot studied forestry in France and Germany and became convinced of the need to apply scientific management techniques to American forests. Galvanized by the disastrous Pestigo, Wisconsin, fire of 1871 the American Association for the Advancement of Science opposed the disastrous deforestation of midwestern forests designed to provide farmland for settlers. They convinced Congress to pass the Organic Act of 1897 to preserve American forests, maintain watershed flows, and provide for a continuous lumber supply for a growing nation. In the 1890s several million acres of forested land were set aside in forest reserves under the control of the Department of Interior whose General Land Office (later Bureau of Land Management) saw as its primary mission the privatization and exploitation of all natural resources.

President William McKinley convinced Congress to transfer authority over the forest reserves of the United States from Interior to Agriculture and appointed Pinchot chief of the forestry bureau in the Department of Agriculture in 1898. This was accomplished in 1905, at the same time that President Theodore Roosevelt (whose confidant Pinchot had become) appointed Pinchot first chief of the USDA's reconstituted Forest Service. Pinchot created a decentralized system of forest rangers and supervisors whose independent judgment determined the uses to which various forests were put. He believed that forest development was crucial to the economic health of western ranching, mining, and agricultural interests. But he insisted that ranchers pay for the privilege of grazing their cattle on the public lands, and this earned him the hostility of the western ranching community. Congress, at the behest of the Western delegations, passed legislation to prevent more forest reserves in 1907, but President Roosevelt added

16 million acres to the reserve at Pinchot's urging before signing the legislation.

Despite Pinchot's continuing conflict with developmental interests, he was also opposed by some in the conservation movement. His was a philosophy of "wise use" of American natural resources by which he meant for all resources to be developed to the maximum extent possible for sustainability. Despite his policy of reseeding and planting areas that had been clearcut and burned over, he opposed the philosophy of preservation advocated by John Muir, who advocated keeping some natural resources in their original state for their own sake. Muir competed with Pinchot for the attention of President Roosevelt, but failed to save the Hetch Hetchy Valley which was turned into a reservoir for San Francisco despite Muir's arguments that it was the "twin" of the Yosemite valley and should be preserved as another national park.

Pinchot founded the Society of American Foresters (SAF) in 1900 to represent the interests of the new profession of foresters in the United States. Today SAF is the official accreditation agency for schools of forestry around the nation. He also chaired the National Conservation Commission in 1908 which studied forest resources and argued that nonrenewable resources (e.g., petroleum, natural gas, and coal) would become exhausted without careful management. The commission advocated use of hydroelectric power because it was renewable. In 1909 Pinchot convinced President Roosevelt to host a North American Conservation conference, but President Taft vetoed the idea of a World Conservation conference at the Hague.

In 1910 President Taft dismissed Pinchot from the Forest Service after he had feuded with then Secretary of the Interior Ballinger about the exploitation of Alaskan land by mining companies. Even after his departure Congress gave to the Forest Service authority to buy up abandoned exploited land, and national forests were created in the southeast and midwest during the 1920s and 1930s when poor agricultural practices on private lands made them economically inviable.

Pinchot later became head of forestry in Pennsylvania and was elected governor for two terms. He advocated mine-mouth generation of electric power to be transmitted in interstate commerce. Until his death in 1946 he remained the primary symbol of the progressive conservation movement in the United States.

Lettie McSpadden

Further Readings

Culhane, Paul. *Public Lands Policy.* 1981.
Pinkett, Harold. *Gifford Pinchot: Public and Private Forester.* 1970.
Udall, Stewart. *The Quiet Crisis.* 1963.

See also CONSERVATION MOVEMENT; DE-PARTMENT OF THE INTERIOR (U.S.); FOREST SERVICE (U.S.); FORESTRY, HISTORY OF; HETCH HETCHY DAM; MUIR, JOHN

Piping Plover

The piping plover (*Charadrius melodus*) is a small North American shorebird that uses a variety of open beach habitat throughout its range and annual cycle. The piping plover is North America's only endangered shorebird. The bird stands about ten centimeters high, with a sand-colored back and white belly that provide camouflage from predators in an exposed habitat. There are approximately 5,482 adults distributed among three geographic areas. Northern Great Plains birds breed from eastern Alberta to Lake of the Woods, Minnesota-Ontario and south to Nebraska. Great Lakes birds have seriously declined so that only seventeen pairs remain in northern Michigan. Atlantic birds breed from Newfoundland to North Carolina. Piping plovers winter primarily on the Gulf Coast. Habitats used in their western range include alkali flats, large prairie lakes, and scoured river sandflats. Great Lakes and Atlantic birds use traditional sand beaches. During the winter, piping plovers occupy beaches and algal salt flats.

In the spring, breeding males arrive at breeding sites and defend areas often in territories they used the year before. Females are drawn to these territories via elaborate aerial displays and courtship calls. Many nests, consisting of shallow pits in the sand lined with pebbles or shells, are constructed by both male and female until the female chooses a nest. Both members of the pair incubate their four eggs and care for young. Often females desert broods after the precocial chicks hatch, leaving males to care for fledglings.

The vulnerable nature of the piping plover's beach habitat renders adults, eggs, and chicks susceptible to natural and man-induced factors. Flooding of nests and predation have always contributed to piping plover mortality. With man's encroachment these factors have intensified and taken a greater toll. Human garbage brings unnatural num-bers of predators to nest sites; water control schedules on rivers can result in flooding nests and chicks.

Recognizing that piping plovers had de-clined and threats were increasing, the species was declared endangered in Canada (1983) and the U.S. Great Lakes (1984), while the U.S. Atlantic and Northern Great Plains birds are listed as threatened (1984). A cooperative international effort was launched as a result of these actions. In both Canada and the United States, there is a national coordinator for piping plover recovery, as well as a Great Lakes-Northern Great Plains recovery team and an Atlantic recovery team. The four teams have written and worked to implement their respective recovery plans. The first species-wide census was carried out in 1991 as a result of collaboration among the teams and with the cooperation of over 1,000 biologists from ten nations.

Conservation strategies focus on protecting habitat at breeding and winter sites. A successful effort has been launched on Atlantic and Great Lakes sites to protect nests from predators by placing fences around and above nests. These predator exclosures are the prime reason for continued existence of the bird on the Great Lakes. More difficult to resolve are water control policies. Successful mediation of this problem has occurred for birds nesting on the Missouri River. Less successful has been the effort to resolve water management on Lake Diefenbaker in Saskatchewan where each year most nests are flooded due to dam-released water. This is the largest piping plover breeding site in the world, yet it has little reproductive success. Future efforts focus on conservation of winter habitat. Plans to deepen and extend the Gulf Intracoastal Waterway severely threaten habitat for 90 percent of the piping plovers seen in the winter. Since little other suitable winter habitat has been found, loss of this habitat would imperil the species further existence.

Susan M. Haig

Further Readings

Haig, S.M. "The Piping Plover." In *Birds of North America No. 2.* Ed. A. Poole, P. Stettenheim, and F. Gill. 1992.
———, and J.H. Plissner. "Distribution and Abundance of the Piping Plover: Results and Implications of the 1991 International Breeding and Winter Census." *Condor* 95 (1993): 146–56.

See also COASTAL MARSHES, CONSERVATION OF; ESKIMO CURLEW; FRESHWATER WETLANDS; SHOREBIRDS

PIRGs
See NADER, RALPH

Pollution

To a society specifically attuned to the material aspects of existence it is inevitable that pollution should be taken to refer to the physical contamination of the surrounding environment. Yet pollution is far from unique to modern industrial societies, and indeed has been regarded by some anthropologists as a ubiquitous phenomenon. In the broader sense employed by other societies pollution refers to the defilement of the purity or sanctity of something—but not necessarily only to the physical world. It is equally possible to speak of a moral pollution—some act that contaminates the non-material aspects of social life. In either case it constitutes a means of persuasion, for to accuse someone of pollution is to accuse him or her of an act that places the whole of society in jeopardy. It is therefore used when purely moral persuasion fails, as a kind of threat of impending disaster which can persuade the offending individual to repent.

In the current environmental debate both aspects of pollution are clearly present, for although the argument may focus on an act of material desecration, there is almost always an implication of moral pollution as well. That is, in pointing to some unsanitary act, the environmental advocate is simultaneously impugning the moral qualities of the polluter, and in defending that act the polluter may in turn be decrying the conceptual pollution of the marketplace which is implicit in the environmentalist's accusation. Thus the intermingling of the two aspects of pollution tends to conceal the social significance of the debate. And, since the term is taken to signify a material misdemeanor, the simple act of correcting that behavior may prematurely interrupt a debate which is more profoundly about moral pollution—that is, about the underlying assumptions of the opposing sides as to what constitutes appropriate behavior. Pollution is simultaneously then an act of defilement, a means of moral coercion, and an indicator of underlying disagreements about societal goals.

Neil Evernden

Further Readings
Cotgrove, Stephen. *Catastrophe or Cornucopia.* 1982.
Douglas, Mary. *Purity and Danger.* 1966.
Evernden, Neil. *The Social Creation of Nature.* 1992.

See also ENVIRONMENTAL ETHICS; ENVIRONMENTALISM; EPIDEMIOLOGY; POLLUTION PREVENTION; THROWAWAY MENTALITY SOCIETY; TOXICOLOGY

Pollution Prevention

In the late 1980s pollution prevention emerged as a new emphasis in environmental policy. Its central concept is that it is far preferable to prevent pollution than to manage it or find ways to remedy it through cleanup.

A pollution prevention approach looks for ways to minimize pollution, through methods such as reducing the use of toxics, increasing the efficiency of systems or methods, or substituting less toxic materials in production and products. A hierarchy of choices is established: the highest priority is to minimize the volume or toxicity of pollution created; the next best approach is to reuse or recycle materials; treatment of materials to render them less harmful to the environment is lower on the hierarchy; and the final choice is safe disposal of that which cannot be avoided or recycled.

This hierarchy is based upon the realization that traditional methods of control are inadequate for addressing many pollution problems. Controlling pollutants at the point where they enter the environment is inefficient at best, and sometimes ineffective. At the same time, population and consumption continue to grow. Where pollution controls fail or prove inadequate, society pays for this failure in environmental degradation and in expensive cleanup operations, and many contaminated areas simply cannot be restored at all. Policies to improve or protect the environment must be fashioned in a context of increasingly difficult challenges. Costs for treatment, cleanup, and disposal have risen rapidly, and continue to grow. Rather than solving the problem, traditional control methods often shift problems from one medium to another, requiring multiple, expensive techniques for handling the same pollutants across media. Furthermore, experts are redefining the focus of environmental concerns. Research is showing that some of the most severe problems arise from many dispersed sources rather than limited numbers of large polluters; dispersed sources do not lend themselves to traditional control methods. Pollution prevention focuses on opportunities earlier in the process, highlighting the need to look for ways to design products, materials, and production to protect the environment. It encourages polluters to find the most cost-effective means to reduce or eliminate pollution sources. This approach has the benefit of encouraging cross-media analysis rather than taking the single-medium approach embodied in most environmental statutes.

The Environmental Protection Agency (EPA) quickly embraced this idea and began to promote it, largely by sponsoring voluntary programs. Existing statutes have made it difficult for EPA to write regulations based on cross-media analysis and tradeoffs. One of the most powerful tools for pollution prevention is information. Better information helps polluters identify the problem and analyze alternative solutions. The EPA has conducted research to develop techniques, established pilots for pollution prevention, and initiated programs to educate the public—especially industry—about the benefits of this approach. The EPA also began to provide more information to the public about emission sources and about the effects of various chemicals on human health and the environment.

In 1990 Congress passed the Pollution Prevention Act, which established pollution prevention as national environmental policy. The 1990 Clean Air Act contained provisions for promoting prevention over control. Pollution prevention remains primarily a voluntary approach, though the EPA is working to integrate this concept into its policy and regulatory efforts wherever feasible. As Congress reauthorizes existing environmental statutes, it will undoubtedly put greater emphasis on source reduction.

Under the existing legal framework, there are several reasons why polluters adopt pollution prevention programs. Publicly available information has provided a powerful incentive to reduce toxic emissions, as demonstrated by the Toxics Release Inventory (TRI). TRI was the first major environmental database created on the principle that the public has a right-to-know about the release of highly toxic chemicals from industry. Since TRI was first published (1987) many companies have reduced emissions; some others have made public commitments to do so. Some organizations may reduce pollutants as a matter of principle, others for the good public-

ity or competitive advantage it brings; some see pollution prevention as a strategy to forestall or prevent regulation; still others pursue pollution prevention approaches to minimize future liabilities from improper (though not necessarily illegal) use or disposal of toxic materials. Perhaps most importantly polluters often save money by finding ways to reduce the materials used during production processes or those remaining as waste products. Further, insofar as an organization can reduce the volume of materials it disposes, it reduces disposal costs. For a number of reasons, costs for disposal have increased dramatically over the past decade; costs for handling toxic materials are particularly high.

One important tool for pollution prevention is market incentives. If market incentives can provide sufficient motivation for prevention, then fewer regulatory controls would be necessary. In theory market incentives can provide the most efficient means for encouraging appropriate choices. That is, relying on market forces leaves greater choice to individuals and companies to find the best solutions. Government can affect market forces in a variety of ways. It can encourage prevention by the products it purchases. For example, federal agencies are very large paper consumers; they now purchase recycled paper and could purchase chlorine-free paper to promote this new technology. Government can impose taxes or fees, underwrite research, provide tax breaks for innovation, and stop subsidies and other protective measures for environmentally undesirable activities. By educating consumers the government (and the business sector) has created new markets for less polluting products. "Green" labeling, for example, is designed to attract consumers to products that are produced with less toxic materials or cleaner (less polluting) techniques. Such labels have stimulated a whole new arena for competition.

Pollution prevention represents a new environmental and managerial ethic. The flexible, cross-media strategies that characterize pollution prevention will call for flexible enforcement policies and techniques. Success in pollution prevention should result in correspondingly less reliance on specific regulatory requirements for each media, focusing instead on environmental results. Some fear that lack of specific requirements will only make it easier to pollute. Although regulations are expensive to develop and often result in suboptimal standards, it is possible to require pollution prevention techniques rather than pollution controls. The success of the preventive approach ultimately requires attention to all aspects of production and consumption patterns. It requires government, business, and consumers to make choices—policy and regulatory, production and marketing, purchasing and use—based upon the principle of minimizing environmental impacts.

Odelia Funke

Further Readings

Environmental Law Institute. *The Tools of Prevention: Opportunities for Promoting Pollution Prevention under Federal Legislation.* April 1993.

Environmental Protection Agency. *The United States Experience with Economic Incentives to Control Environmental Pollution.* Document 230-R-92 001, 1992.

Wirth, Senator Timothy, and Senator John Heinz, sponsors. *Project 88-Round 2. Incentives for Action: Designing Market-Based Environmental Strategies.* Washington, D.C., May 1991.

See also AIR POLLUTION: REGULATION (U.S.); ENVIRONMENTAL PROTECTION AGENCY; GREEN PRODUCTS; HAZARDOUS WASTE TREATMENT TECHNOLOGIES; POLLUTION; PULP AND PAPER MILLS; REGULATION; WATER POLLUTION ABATEMENT TECHNOLOGIES

Pollution Probe

Pollution Probe, a Toronto, Ontario-based environmental public interest organization founded in 1969, has in recent years been one of the leaders in the establishment of environmental rights in Canada. Pollution Probe was instrumental in convincing the Ontario government of the necessity of an Environmental Bill of Rights (EBR), which it then helped to develop and draft. Pollution Probe has also promoted the inclusion of citizen's environmental rights into the Canadian Environmental Protection Act.

Pollution Probe is also presently working to ensure that international trade does not result in increased environmental degradation by incorporating environmental safeguards in Canada's trade policies and international agreements. Pollution Probe published *The Environmental Dimension of Free Trade* and *Minimal Environmental Safeguards to be included in NAFTA.* Pollution Probe has advocated the inclusion of environmental provisions in the North American Free Trade Agreement (NAFTA), the establishment of a North American Commission on the Environment to increase the level of environmental protection continent-wide, and the development of strong environmental principles to guide international trade through the Organisation of Economic Co-operation and Development (OECD).

Pollution Probe produces extensive educational materials on environmental issues and their solutions. Each year the organization answers 20,000 requests for information packages, pamphlets, and special reports from students, teachers, homeowners, corporations, media, government, and other environmental groups. Pollution Probe has recently succeeded in explaining environmental problems and solutions to millions of Canadians by: 1) launching the "Enviro-Challenge Tour," a busload of exhibits, which visited forty-three communities showing Canadians how they can conserve; 2) producing *The Canadian Green Consumer Guide, The Kitchen Handbook—An Environmental Guide,* and *The Canadian Junior Green Guide*; and 3) distributing a series of environmental guides for small- to medium-sized businesses. Pollution Probe sees change coming from an empowered and environmentally literate public.

Pollution Probe emphasizes reductions in the production of toxic contaminants at their source, phasing out the most dangerous chemicals used in industry and commerce, and reducing the public's exposure to toxics. Pollution Probe continues to seek permanent solutions to the persistent toxic chemicals that are discharged into the Great Lakes, such as through the Sunset Project. The "Sunset Protocol" is set to identify and evaluate toxic substances as candidates for phase-out, and then implement legislation, economic and other policy tools to eliminate them from commerce in Canada.

Pollution Probe is working with other organizations to ensure that a 20 percent reduction in carbon dioxide (CO_2) emissions is achieved at the municipal, provincial and national levels and energy efficiency in Ontario is improved by 25 percent by the year 2005. Pollution Probe's publications produced for presentation to the Ontario Environmental Assessment Board Hearing include *If the Answer is Incineration, Someone Asked the Wrong Question, Incineration Compared to Energy and Waste Management Alternatives: A Full Environmental Costs Analysis,* and *The Potential for Regulations and Standards to Contribute to Electricity Savings in Ontario.* Pollution Probe's objective through its interventions at regulatory hearings is to ultimately change gas and electricity pricing structures so that the incentive for utilities is to conserve energy, not sell energy.

Janine Ferretti

Further Readings
Chant, Donald A. *Pollution Probe.* 1970.
Degler, Teri. *The Canadian Junior Green Guide.* 1990.

See also ENERGY PROBE; ENVIRONMENTAL CASE LAW (CANADA): COMMON LAW CAUSES OF ACTION; MUNICIPAL SOLID WASTE: INCINERATION; NAFTA AND THE ENVIRONMENT

Population Control
As Darwin pointed out, all organisms have an "excess" ability to reproduce: parents produce more offspring than is required to replace themselves. Without checks all populations would grow exponentially. For most species, population growth is kept under control by failure to find a suitable place to live, or to obtain enough food, or by predators or parasites. Less often, it is due to failure of some to mate successfully.

The maximum population sustained by an ecosystem for a given species is called its "carrying capacity." When a population exceeds this limit, either some members migrate away or it suffers a massive die-off. Human populations differ from other species in this respect only in having: 1) the ability to increase carrying capacity through technological inventions, such as agriculture and fossil fuel-based industrialization; and 2) the ability to consciously regulate births.

During the long period of human foraging societies, local populations grew extremely slowly, with birth rates barely exceeding death rates. Although these low growth rates were largely due to biological factors—lactational suppression of ovulation, leading to spacings of five years between births, plus deaths from childhood diseases of about half the children born—it appears that taboos on intercourse, use of abortifacients (abortion-inducing herbs), and even infanticide were also employed in conscious efforts to control population size. Evidence for conscious control lies in the ability of hunting-gathering populations to rebound after abnormally high losses from famine or other catastrophes. Even these peoples, however, are known to have increased the local carrying capacity by range management and "tending" wild plants.

It is believed that the adoption of horticulture and animal husbandry came about not through sudden "discovery" of new techniques with higher yields that then permitted populations to expand, but as the result of growing population pressure on limited foraging resources. Indeed, the agricultural revolution has been an ongoing one, permitting: 1) an increasing yield of food, fiber, and fodder per hectare of land; and 2) the expansion of agriculture into previously unfruitful areas, through terracing, irrigation, deforestation, soil-building (as in high farming in Europe in the Middle Ages), and, most recently, liberal use of fertilizers and pesticides.

The effects on population growth were two-fold. Clearly, more food permitted larger populations, and the advent of cooked grains meant earlier weaning of infants, hence closer birth spacing. Yet more dense, settled populations increased the rates of infant mortality, especially from contagious diseases. Both factors tended to push up the number of births per female from five for foragers to eleven or twelve in settled agricultural communities. Yet high death rates, exacerbated by not infrequent famines and wars, prevented too rapid population growth, and in many societies, large numbers of children became culturally desirable. Major religions promoted fertility and proscribed birth control; the status of both men and women became linked to reproductive ability. For the past several thousand years, high birth rates and high death rates have been the accepted norm among agricultural societies. Population growth continued slowly, but steadily, with little conscious attempt at control.

In Europe, during the Renaissance and into the nineteenth century industrial era, living conditions for the masses steadily declined, especially in cities where there was an absence of clean drinking water and adequate municipal sanitation. Dwellings lacked sunlight or adequate ventilation. As a consequence death rates remained high. Only toward the end of that century did sanitary engineering, with its provision of safe water supplies and urban sewer systems and treatment plants generate a significant fall in death rates, further assisted by the widespread introduction of vaccination for common childhood diseases. In the industrializing nations of the world, a widening gap between still high birth rates and falling death rates caused a rise in populations, that gradually plateaued when birth rates declined.

The recent spread of similar public health improvements into the less industrialized countries of the world has caused a similar divergence between births and deaths there. However, in the less developed countries the rates of change have been greatly accelerated, steepening the rate of population growth and making the transition to a steady population size more difficult. Not until birth rates equal death rates globally will zero population growth (ZPG) be attained. Today the global population is growing at approximately 1.8 percent per year, or doubling each forty years.

The control of population as a social or national goal is a recent idea, which is linked with family-planning clinics worldwide, which help women (and their husbands) to restrict unwanted births. The clinics provide education regarding ways to avoid pregnancy, including contraception, and make contraceptives, abortion, and sterilization available to all. Yet cultural or religious factors may limit the range of services offered in a particular locale. For example, Japan has outlawed oral contraceptives (the Pill) but permits abortions, while in Catholic Ireland, vasectomies are obtainable but abortion is illegal, even after incest.

Beyond voluntary services, some governments have sought more forceful means of population control. To combat teenage pregnancies and the spread of venereal diseases, as well as to limit population, the Mexican government has mounted a massive media campaign and distributed free condoms in supermarkets. In India the government of Indira Gandhi offered a payment to men who agreed to be sterilized, but although the amount was significant for the poor peasants being targeted, the policies largely failed. In the 1980s China, suddenly waking up to its population problem, instituted a one-child-per-family program, but this, too, reportedly is less strongly enforced than when it was first introduced.

Neither threats nor rewards seem to alter reproductive behavior. Japanese women today are having fewer than two children each, and a worried government is trying to encourage them to have more children, without success. Most of the industrialized nations have decreased their birth rates and are near zero population growth (discounting immigrants). But their birth rates did not all decline at the same time. They began to fall in France about the time of the French revolution, but in England

not until a century later. The fall in Russia coincided with its revolution. In the United States birth rates fell first in the liberal Protestant areas, where men and women experienced high levels of personal autonomy. In none of these cases was there availability of modern contraceptives, nor any direct social policy encouraging fewer births.

Studies of falling birth rates in non-industrial countries suggest several primary factors. One is the level of literacy (though not of wealth), especially as it empowers women; another is the ability of women to choose the number of children they will bear, rather than being controlled by their husbands; a third is a sense of political control over their lives by both men and women; a fourth, following from the last, is a sense of equity and security in one's society. As the state of Kerala in India demonstrates, high income is not necessary for ZPG, but literacy, equality, and personal autonomy all are. Contrary to some arguments, a high GNP per capita may not be nearly so important to attaining a stable population as are democracy and social justice.

Mary E. Clark

Further Readings

Clark, Mary E. *Ariadne's Thread: The Search for New Modes of Thinking.* 1989. (See especially chapters 3 and 13.)
Ehrlich, Paul R., and Anne H. Ehrlich. *The Population Explosion.* 1990.

See also CARRYING CAPACITY; EHRLICH, PAUL; HARDIN, GARRETT; ONE-CHILD FAMILY (CHINA); SUSTAINABLE DEVELOPMENT; ZERO POPULATION GROWTH

Porpoises

See DOLPHINS AND PORPOISES

Postmaterialism

Postmaterialism is a set of political values held by individuals who were socialized primarily in the "postindustrial" period beginning in the 1960s. Postmaterial values are central to a "new politics," which focuses on gender and racial equality, broader participation in policy processes, freedom of expression, minimum standards of living, and environmental protection.

The theory of postmaterialism was the product of a series of books and articles by Ronald Inglehart. Inglehart argued that the relative affluence and security of the post World War II decades profoundly changed the context in which citizens of western democracies were socialized. Based on Maslow's hierarchy of needs, Inglehart argued that the postindustrial age freed many people from worry about material goods, because they no longer were in short supply, and allowed them to focus on "higher" order needs, such as quality of life, influencing decisions, and environmental aesthetics. These postmaterial values produced generations more concerned with environmental quality because more fundamental needs were not threatened.

This theory articulates how postmaterial values lead to pro-environmental orientations. The argument is that environmentalists are more likely to be postmaterialists because it is precisely the individual without the perceived threat to safety, security, and physical nourishment who can be concerned about the aesthetic use of natural resources. This also is one explanation for the environmental policy arena experiencing constant pressures for expanded involvement of publics in policy formation. The same relative security that frees people to value the environment also leads them to focus on *how* decisions are made. The "higher level" postmaterial values that form environmental preferences also heighten the demand for open participatory processes. Both environmentalism *and* participation, in this view, are the joint product of postmaterial values.

The impact of postmaterialism on environmentalism depends on the national context in which it operates. Countries have their own distinctive political cultures which structure the character of postmaterial value change, fundamental perceptions of the relationship of humans and the environment, and the degree to which both are inter-related. Political scientist Scott Flanagan believes that Japan's political culture responded differently to postindustrial change than did the North American and European democracies. Japan also has its unique political and social structures, and a distinct culturally-based orientation to the environment and natural resources. Thus others have shown that two distinct kinds of environmentalists can be found in Japan: those who are responding to the Western style influence of postmaterialism and those whose attitudes are rooted in traditional Japanese culture and who are mobilized to action through traditional political and social structures.

Postmaterialism also may account for what many believe to be a class basis to the environmental movement. In particular environmentalism has been labeled middle-class and upper-middle class elitism, with those classes, of course, also being more likely to have the physical and economic security associated with postmaterialism.

Likewise the rise of the modern environmental movement seemed to have a distinct generational flavor to it. The youthful "new politics" generation that provided the energy for Earth Day and the great growth in environmental activism was precisely the age cohort first hypothesized to develop postmaterial values on a mass basis.

Postmaterial values seem to lead to environmentalism, and postmaterialism itself grows out of personal economic and physical security. The question then remains as to the fate of environmentalism in tough times. Would significant economic problems lead to material, rather than postmaterial values and hence to a lower place on the political agenda for environmental issues? The answer—at least for the short-to-middle run—is probably "no" because political values are rather stable for any individual, and as the pro-environmental, postmaterial cohorts continue to mature they will not only retain those postmaterial values but they also will continue to move into positions of enhanced political and social influence. With that enhanced influence, and the commitment to participation and to environmentalism, the postmaterialists will sustain the environmental agenda long into the coming decades.

John C. Pierce

Further Readings

Inglehart, Ronald. *Culture Shift in Advanced Industrial Society*. 1990.

Milbrath, Lester W. *Environmentalists: Vanguard for a New Society*. 1984.

Pierce, John C., Nicholas P. Lovrich, Taketsugu Tsurutani, and Takematsu Abe. *Political Knowledge and Environmental Politics in Japan and the United States*. 1989.

See also EARTH DAY; ENVIRONMENTALISM; PUBLIC OPINION AND THE ENVIRONMENT (U.S.); SUSTAINABILITY

Postmodernism and the Environment

The term "postmodernism" has different meanings within the natural and social sciences, architecture, literature, art, and the humanities. Postmodern currents run through disciplines as disparate as environmental history, restoration ecology, ecotheology, and ecophilosophy. Postmodernists employ a variety of techniques, such as critical rhetoric, hermeneutics, post-structural analysis, and discourse theory. While some themes run across postmodern thought, such as the opposition to essentialism (the idea that there are timeless, universal truths), it cannot be claimed that a postmodern paradigm exists. At least four aspects of postmodernism are relevant to environmentalism and conservation. These include: deconstruction, reconstruction, sustainability, and postmodern environmental studies.

Deconstruction

Deconstructive postmodernists believe that the modern age is based on inherently flawed Enlightenment, capitalistic, and scientific narratives that must be repudiated before culture can be constructed anew. In contrast, the dominant stream of environmentalism, called by a variety of names including "resourcism" and "reform environmentalism," attempts to solve environmental problems by fine-tuning the present post-industrial paradigm. Thus, so-called modernists contend that ecological dysfunctions can be eliminated through sustainable development; deconstructionists dismiss this contention, and argue that ecocrisis reveals the contradictions structurally (and therefore permanently) inherent in the growth dynamic of capitalistic, industrial society. Deconstructive analysis, literally the close reading of a text that exposes its underlying ideology and assumptions (subtexts), has been brought to bear on the reality of history, truth, democracy, the human soul, objectivity, and even science itself. These ideas are framed as contingencies, textual artifacts and human inventions maintained through intellectual dogmatism and political and economic enfranchisement. Deconstructionists decry virtually all foundational claims; thus they open themselves to charges that they are self-defeating, since the possibility of human existence requires an assumptive framework—cultural leaps of faith.

Reconstruction

Reconstructive postmodernists believe the present is a late-modern period, where culture is caught between the anomalies of modernism (e.g., global ecocrisis) and a postmodern age of sustainability. The reconstructive (also called

affirmative) tendencies of postmodern thought are advocated by some environmentalists as strategies for ameliorating ecocrisis. Affirmative postmodernists share with deconstructionists the idea that culture can be read as a text, but move beyond the analysis of social anomalies to pragmatic issues involved in societal transformation, placing particular emphasis on the transformative role of discourse. Reconstructive postmodernists argue that change requires reinterpretation of the meaning of foundational texts. Textual analysis discloses that civilization is at the center and nature is at the margin of the dominant cultural narrative; accordingly, the earth is exploited without limit. But affirmative postmodernists do not repudiate textual tradition in toto; the text of history, for example, backgrounds any discussion of the environmental movement itself. Thus, transformation to a postmodern age of sustainability entails giving a voice to concerns (as in Aldo Leopold's "thinking like a mountain") which the dominant narrative marginalizes. Rather than deconstruction, affirmative postmodernists naturalize the category of "history," so that human beings are recontextualized as members of the land community.

Sustainability

If reconstructive postmodernism has a constant theme it is the importance of sustainability (a term distinct from "sustainable development"). Postmodernists argue that all discourse is subject to the formal requirement of sustainability, since any cultural narrative that leads humans to degrade either natural ecology or social ecology is not a viable strategy for life. Postmodernists generally revel in diversity and ambiguity, believing that Cartesian certitude and definitive analysis, and thus closure of the processes of discussion and further inquiry, are more illusion than reality. Postmodernist environmentalists seek to reopen questions—economic theory being one example—that are generally believed closed. As a deconstructive prelude to such a reopening of economic discourse postmodernists argue that mainstream economic theory is a rhetorical construction modeled on classical physics and maintained by a discourse of power that places socially dominant groups at the center of society while marginalizing others. Alternative forms of economic discourse, such as steady-state economics or ecological economics are introduced as conceptual strategies for building a sustainable society. So construed, ecological economics is postmodern, that is, a challenge to the prevailing, modern neoclassical paradigm. However, no postmodern economic theory has achieved either the political support or moral authority to displace mainstream economics.

Postmodern Environmental Studies

Postmodern environmental studies cover a wide subject matter, including gender issues, environmental history, environmental ethics, and postmodern science and social science. The use of ecological science (information, metaphors, and presuppositions) is a theme running through postmodern environmental studies and movement. Environmental historians attempt to incorporate ecological threads into historical narratives. Ecological economics recontextualizes neoclassical economic theory within the frame of systems ecology. Ecofeminists weave post-structural feminist analysis together with ecological narrative in a way that goes beyond masculinist objectivity to embrace the more than human as kindred spirits. Postmodern poets weave the ecological narratives of primal oral peoples into their work. Bioregionalists emphasize local knowledge and people living in affiliation with the land, thus inverting the modern paradigm that puts the city at the center and the rural on the margin.

Max Oelschlaeger

Further Readings

Cheney, Jim. "Postmodern Environmental Ethics: Ethics as Bioregional Narrative." *Environmental Ethics* 11 (1989): 117–34.
Evernden, Neil. *The Social Construction of Nature.* 1992.

See also ECOFEMINISM; ENVIRONMENTAL EDUCATION; ENVIRONMENTAL ETHICS; SUSTAINABLE DEVELOPMENT; SUSTAINABILITY

Powell, John Wesley

John Wesley Powell was an explorer of the American West who also played a leading role in reclamation and rational land-use planning. His acute ideas on the importance of water, irrigation, and a federal policy for agricultural development in the West were a half century ahead of his time, and met strong opposition from others who thought that rain would follow the plow. Born in Mount Morris, New York, on March 24, 1834, he was the second son of Joseph Powell, a Methodist lay preacher.

During his childhood and youth in Ohio and Illinois he developed strong interest in geology and biology. He taught school and served as secretary of the Illinois State Natural History Society. A year after volunteering for service in the U.S. army at the start of the Civil War he led an artillery battery at the battle of Shiloh, where he lost his right arm on April 6, 1862. Although he rose to the rank of brevet lieutenant-colonel he preferred to be called "Major Powell."

After the war Powell was appointed professor of geology at Illinois Wesleyan University and Illinois Normal University, where he found sponsorship for his explorations in Colorado and Wyoming in 1867 and 1868. His noted Colorado River expeditions began in the following year, when he set out from Green River, Wyoming, with nine other men in four heavy wooden rowboats, intending to explore the river through unknown canyons that lay ahead. After almost three harrowing months, six men and two boats emerged from the lower end of the Grand Canyon. Since most of the records of this journey were lost Powell led a second river trip in 1871 and 1872. He also studied the customs, language, and literatures of the American Indians, particularly those of the Paiutes north of the Grand Canyon. He was founder and first director of the Bureau of American Ethnology, which preserved and published Indian traditional materials.

During his most active years Powell worked for federal land management and conservation. He helped bring the United States Geological Survey into being, and served as its first director (1881–1894). He published reports recognizing the crucial role of water development in the West, arguing that the Homestead Law could not be extended beyond the Hundredth Meridian without major changes to adapt settlement and land-use patterns to the arid conditions there. For two years (1888–1890), before his political enemies killed the appropriations, he headed an Irrigation Survey to select sites for reservoirs and irrigation projects. He died on September 23, 1902, after receiving many honors and awards. Many ideas he had pioneered became the basis for the creation of the Bureau of Reclamation in the year of his death.

J. Donald Hughes

Further Readings

Powell, John Wesley. *Exploration of the Colorado River of the West and Its Tributaries.* 1875.

Stegner, Wallace. *Beyond the Hundredth Meridian: John Wesley Powell and the Second Opening of the West*. 1953.

Terrell, John U. *The Man Who Rediscovered America: A Biography of John Wesley Powell*. 1969.

See also BUREAU OF LAND MANAGEMENT; COLORADO RIVER; GRAND CANYON; WATER ALLOCATIONS AND SHORTAGES (U.S. WEST)

Predators

See BEARS: CONSERVATION AND HABITAT; COUGARS: CONSERVATION AND HABITAT; TIGERS: CONSERVATION AND HABITAT; TOP PREDATORS IN CANADA: AN OVERVIEW; WOLF: A CONSERVATION CHALLENGE

Primates: Conservation and Habitats

The mammalian order primates is one of the most important and interesting in the animal kingdom, including some 250 living species of apes, monkeys, lemurs, lorises, galagos, and tarsiers and, of course, our own species: *Homo sapiens*. Our nonhuman primate relatives are valuable to us in many ways, and the rapid growth of the science of primatology over the past thirty years has reflected this. Studies of these animals have taught us a great deal about the intricacies of our own behavior; they have clarified questions about our evolution and our origins; and they have played a significant role in biomedical research. Nonhuman primates are also one of the most conspicuous groups of animals in the world's tropical forests and are often the best symbols for tropical forest conservation.

Unfortunately wild populations of most nonhuman primates are decreasing all over the world, with many spectacular species—such as the mountain gorilla, the golden lion tamarin, the muriqui, the indri, and the aye-aye—already on the verge of extinction, and numerous others headed in the same direction. The major reason for the decline of primates is destruction of their tropical forest habitat. More than 90 percent of all primates are found in the tropical forests of Asia, Africa, and South and Central America, and these forests are being destroyed at an alarming rate. Rates of forest destruction vary greatly from region to region. In some areas, such as Amazonia and the Zaire basin, it is only beginning. In others, such as the island of Madagascar and the Atlantic forest

region of eastern Brazil, much of the forest has already been lost and the conservation task ahead is to save those remnants that have managed to persist.

Another significant threat to primate populations worldwide is hunting, mainly as a source of food but also for their supposed medicinal value, to obtain skins or other body parts for ornamentation, to use them as bait for other animals, or even to eliminate them from agricultural areas where they have become crop-raiders. The effects of hunting also vary greatly from region to region and from species to species, but hunting of primates as food is known to be a very significant threat in at least three parts of the world: the Amazon region of South America, West Africa, and Central Africa. Many thousands of primates are killed every year in these regions for culinary purposes, and certain species (e.g., woolly monkeys and spider monkeys in Amazonia) have already been eliminated from large areas of otherwise suitable forest habitat by overhunting.

Live trapping of primates—either for export or for local use—is also a threat. Live primates are used in biomedical research and testing or they may be sold as pets or for exhibition, both internationally and within the countries in which they occur. For the most part this is a less significant factor than habitat destruction or hunting, but for certain endangered and vulnerable species that happen to be in heavy demand, it could be quite serious. Species that have been hurt by the trade in live primates include the chimpanzee and the cotton-top tamarin, both of which were important biomedical research models, and the woolly monkeys, which are popular pets for local people in Amazonia.

All of these factors have combined to bring about a worldwide decline in primate populations. According to the International Union for Conservation of Nature and Natural Resources (IUCN) one out of every two of the world's 250 primate species is already in some danger and one in five is highly endangered and could be extinct by the turn of the century or even sooner if something isn't done quickly. It is important to note that these are minimum estimates. Almost every time specialists go into the field to investigate the status of poorly known species they find it necessary to add to the endangered list.

To prevent the extinction of the world's nonhuman primate species the Primate Specialist Group (PSG) of IUCN's Species Survival Commission (SSC) put together a Global Action

Plan for Primate Conservation in 1978. The purpose of this plan was to make the PSG's goal of maintaining the current diversity of the order primates a reality. The original Global Action Plan for Primate Conservation has now been updated by a series of new regional plans for Africa, Madagascar, Asia, and South and Central America, which will guide primate conservation activities for the remainder of this decade. In addition the PSG publishes *Primate Conservation: The Journal of the IUCN/SSC Primate Specialist Group*, and a series of newsletters including *Asian Primates*, *Neotropical Primates*, and *Lemur News*.

Four countries discussed below are of particular concern in terms of primate conservation, either due to high numbers of species, high levels of endemism, high levels of threat, or a combination of these criteria. These include Madagascar, Brazil, Zaire, and Indonesia.

Madagascar

Home to fourteen genera and fifty species and subspecies of lemurs, all of which are endemic, the island of Madagascar must be considered the country of highest primate conservation concern in the world. Many lemurs are already endangered and several are on the verge of extinction. The highest priority species include the hairy-eared dwarf lemur (*Allocebus trichotis*), Sclater's lemur (*Eulemur macaco flavifrons*), the golden bamboo lemur (*Hapalemur aureus*), the greater bamboo lemur (*Hapalemur simus*), the Lac Alaotra lesser bamboo lemur (*Hapalemur griseus aloatrensis*), the silky sifaka (*Propithecus diadema candidus*), Perrier's sifaka (*Propithecus diadema perrieri*), Tattersall's sifaka (*Propithecus tattersalli*), and the crowned sifaka (*Propithecus verreauxi coronatus*).

Brazil

By far the richest country in the world for primates Brazil also has much more tropical forest than any other country. More than 35 percent of Brazil's sixty-nine primate species are endemic, and many of these are already endangered. Most of the endangered species are found in the Atlantic forest region of eastern Brazil, where habitat destruction has reduced a once rich forest ecosystem to only about 1 to 5 percent of its original extent. The most endangered species in the Atlantic forest are the muriqui (*Brachyteles arachnoides*) and the four lion tamarins (*Leontopithecus spp.*), all of which are endemic to the region. In Brazilian Amazonia,

species of special concern are the spider monkeys (*Ateles spp.*), and the woolly monkeys (*Lagothrix spp.*), both of which have been reduced to precariously low levels in some areas by heavy hunting.

Zaire

The richest country on the African mainland for primates, Zaire's primate fauna is very poorly known. Special conservation attention should be placed on the pygmy chimpanzee (*Pan paniscus*) and the eastern lowland gorilla (*Gorilla gorilla graueri*)—both of which occur only in Zaire—and on the highly endangered mountain gorilla (*Gorilla gorilla beringei*).

Indonesia

The country with the richest primate fauna in Asia and the second largest area of tropical forest in the world, Indonesia is essential to maintaining the diversity of the world's primate fauna. Of particular importance there are the orangutan (*Pongo pygmaeus*), the four primate species endemic to the Mentawai Islands off the coast of Sumatra, and the six Indonesian species of gibbons (*Hylobates spp.*).

Roderic B. Mast and Russell A. Mittermeier

Further Readings

Eudey, A.A. *Action Plan for Asian Primate Conservation: 1987–91.* WWF Primate Program and IUCN/SSC Primate Specialist Group. Washington, D.C., 1987.

Marsh, C.W., and R.A. Mittermeier, eds. *Primate Conservation in the Tropical Rain Forest.* 1987.

Mittermeier, R.A. "Primate Diversity and the Tropical Forest: Case Studies from Brazil and Madagascar and the Importance of Megadiversity Countries." In *Biodiversity.* Ed. E.O. Wilson. 1988.

———, Warren G. Kinzey, and Roderic B. Mast. "Neotropical Primate Conservation." *Journal of Human Evolution* 18 (1989): 597–610.

———, William R. Konstant, Martin E. Nicoll, and Olivier Langrand, compilers. *Lemurs of Madagascar—An Action Plan for their Conservation, 1993–1999.* IUCN/SSC Primate Specialist Group Publication. Washington, D.C., 1992.

Oates, J.F. *Action Plan for African Primate Conservation: 1986–89.* WWF Primate Program and IUCN/SSC Primate Specialist Group. Washington, D.C., 1985.

See also BIODIVERSITY; IUCN; TROPICAL DE-FORESTATION; TROPICAL RAINFORESTS

Prigogine, Ilya

Winner of the Nobel Prize for chemistry (1977) and founder of generalized thermodynamics, Ilya Prigogine was born in Moscow on January 25, 1917. His family moved to Germany and then to Belgium, where he received his secondary and university education. Today he divides his time between the Ilya Prigogine Center for Studies in Statistical Mechanics at the University of Texas at Austin and the Instituts Internationaux de Physique et de Chimie at the Université Libre de Bruxelles.

From his early days as a university student Prigogine was fascinated by the difference between the way time was treated by natural scientists and by humanists. The strong tendency among scientists was to treat time as predetermined, repetitive, and reversible. Among humanists (as, for example, in the philosophy of Henri Bergson, a source of Prigogine's reflections) time was treated as irreversible, contingent, and in part unpredictable. This difference in approach not only divides the "humanities" and the "sciences": it suggests a dualism of "man" and "nature," with man vital, purposive, creative; and nature, by contrast, mechanical, "purposeless," inert. One implication of Prigogine's new thermodynamics and chemical kinetics, however, is that this dualism is no longer necessary. Man can reaffirm his ancient covenant with nature.

"Far from equilibrium" (i.e., with sufficient input of energy and matter), Prigogine argues, intrinsically irreversible chemical reactions arise. In classical thermodynamics the expenditure of energy and consequent production of entropy result in either static crystallization or the destruction of order. Far from equilibrium processes, however, produce dynamic form: chemical clocks and chemical waves, ultimately living cells and multicellular organisms. The emergence of these "dissipative structures" involves not only mutual communication between the parts of the system (hence an element of holism), but a strong element of contingency. Professor Prigogine argues that his viewpoint contains profound implications not only for our understanding of the origin of life, the nature of evolution, and the character of the organism, but for our entire philosophy of nature.

Pete A.Y. Gunter

Further Readings

Coveney, Peter, and Roger Highfield. *The Arrow of Time: A Voyage through Science to Solve Time's Greatest Mystery.* 1990.

Prigogine, Ilya, and Isabel Stengers. *Order out of Chaos: Man's New Dialogue with Nature.* 1984.

See also EVOLUTION; GEORGESCU-ROEGEN, NICHOLAS

Public Opinion and the Environment (U.S.)

Public opinion pollsters in the United States began to pay attention to environmental problems in the mid-1960s, mirroring the emerging societal salience of these problems. Trend data indicate that public awareness and concern about pollution increased dramatically through 1970, when it "peaked" (temporarily) with the celebration of the first Earth Day (April 22). Shortly thereafter public concern about environmental quality began to decline, leading some commentators to predict that environmental problems would fade from the public agenda, but such concern did not disappear. In 1980, for example, a National Opinion Research Center (NORC) survey found 48 percent saying that the country was spending "too little" on environmental protection and only 15 percent saying "too much"—with the rest saying "about right" or expressing no opinion (the comparable figures for 1973—the first year the item was used—were 61 and 7 percent, respectively).

Ironically the 1980s saw a rejuvenation of environmental concern, as the Reagan administration's controversial anti-environmental agenda (led by Interior Secretary James Watt) stimulated an increase in environmental activism and public support for environmental protection. The increase in public concern about environmental problems and support for environmental protection continued into the Bush administration, and reached unprecedented levels by 1990 when the twentieth anniversary of Earth Day was celebrated. For example, NORC found the percentages saying government was spending "too little" versus "too much" on the environment to reach 71 percent versus only 4 percent in 1990. Similarly, Gallup found 79 percent saying they would be willing to pay higher prices for pollution control, up from the 63 percent giving that response

P

in 1970. While the U.S. public's level of environmental awareness and concern has dipped a bit following 1990, it remains extremely high, to the point that support for environmental protection can be regarded as a "consensual" issue which generates little open opposition.

Why has public concern about environmental quality in the United States become so strong? A number of reasons seem plausible. First, despite past efforts at environmental protection, new problems have continually emerged. Concerns about generic air and water pollution, for example, have given way to concerns about toxic wastes, acid rain, and ozone depletion. Second, whereas earlier problems such as litter and loss of natural areas, and even air and water pollution, were often seen as aesthetic or quality-of-life concerns, new problems are recognized as direct threats to human health and well-being. Third, earlier problems often appeared delimited in scope, whereas the continual emergence of problems at all geographical levels—from toxic wastes at the local level to ozone depletion at the global level—creates a sense of overall ecological deterioration. Fourth, virtually everyone is vulnerable to omnipresent and growing environmental threats, and future generations are seen as especially threatened.

These arguments are given plausibility by poll results. For instance, a 1991 Gallup poll found only 18 percent saying that the United States had made a "great deal of progress" in dealing with environmental problems since 1970, 62 percent saying "only some," 19 percent saying "hardly any," and 1 percent unsure. Likewise, only 19 percent expressed a "great deal of optimism" that we would "have our environmental problems well under control in twenty years," 60 percent "only some optimism," and 18 percent "hardly any optimism at all," with 3 percent unsure. In view of these results it is not surprising that Gallup found 57 percent of the public indicating that "life on earth will continue without major environmental disruptions" *only* if "immediate and drastic action" is taken, 31 percent if "some additional actions" are taken, only 8 percent if "about the same actions" as currently in place are taken, and 4 percent unsure.

In addition to contributing to strong support for environmental protection by government (and industry), increased public concern about environmental deterioration has in recent years contributed to a growth in individual behaviors on behalf of environmental protection.

For example, Cambridge Reports/Research International found the percentage of Americans saying that they had made "changes in [their] day-to-day behavior because of [their] concerns about the environment" to increase from 48 percent in 1987 to 80 percent in 1992. However, whereas behaviors such as recycling and green consumerism (choosing products on the basis of their environmental impacts) have become fairly popular, more personally costly actions such as giving up automobiles for public transportation have not been widely accepted. In the political arena increasing minorities report having voted on the basis of candidates' environmental records, working on behalf of pro-environmental candidates, and contacting officials regarding environmental issues.

Supportive public opinion is a valuable resource for a social movement, and the U.S. environmental movement has been very successful in achieving and maintaining public support. Not only do majorities of Americans see environmental problems as serious and favor increased efforts at environmental protection, but they also hold highly positive views of environmentalism. Recent Gallup polls, for example, have found that approximately three fourths of American adults consider themselves to be "an environmentalist." Even more striking are results from a 1991 survey by Environment Opinion Study that asked respondents, "Do you think of yourself as closer to being an environmentalist or an anti-environmentalist?" An overwhelming 89 percent identified themselves as environmentalists, and only 5 percent as anti-environmentalists, with the rest being either neutral or unsure. Results such as these suggest why politicians and corporate officials increasingly fear being labelled as anti-environmentalists.

Although the American public is strongly pro-environmental in the abstract, there is little doubt that most Americans have not yet translated this concern into major changes in their lifestyles or in their political behavior (as witnessed by Reagan's election to a second term). However, the linkage between attitudes and actions is often weak, and it is unrealistic to expect the public to translate its environmental concern into concrete behaviors—especially when the behaviors are personally costly (often inequitably so), their necessity is not fully understood, and they are not required of everyone and therefore viewed as of questionable efficacy. Modifying these variables should result in a more effective translation of Americans' pro-environmental opinions into appropriate actions.

Riley E. Dunlap

Further Readings

Dunlap, Riley E., and Rik Scarce. "The Polls—Poll Trends: Environmental Problems and Protection." *Public Opinion Quarterly* 55 (1991): 651–72.

———. "Trends in Public Opinion Toward Environmental Issues: 1965–1990." In *American Environmentalism: The U.S. Environmental Movement, 1970–1990.* Ed. Riley E. Dunlap and Angela G. Mertig. 1992.

See also BUSH, GEORGE; EARTH DAY; ENVIRONMENTALISM; POSTMATERIALISM; REAGAN, RONALD; WATT, JAMES G.

Pulp and Paper Mills

Paper and related products are made from wood as a raw material or from recycled wood and paper products. In the course of converting the initial ingredients into finished paper a number of processes are involved. At each stage of each process there is potential for pollutants to be released into the environment. Some of these are gaseous, contributing to air pollution, while others are liquids or solids, contributing to water pollution. Occasionally pollution of land may also occur. The present account takes a "cradle to grave" approach and identifies the major types of pollutants for all stages of the process.

Pulp and paper production often represents a highly significant economic activity for a country or a region, as is the case for Canada. Pulp and paper mills have tended to develop as single-industry towns relatively distant from large urban areas, in part because of the relationship between the mills and the forests and also because of the need to limit the distance for transportation of wood to the mills. Furthermore the nature of the processes involved in making paper requires large volumes of water and, therefore, mills are typically sited on or near large water bodies such as lakes, rivers, or oceans. All of these factors have relevance to the impacts, real and perceived, of pollution and the control of pollution from the pulp and paper industries.

In the past, the various types of undesirable by-products from the pulp and paper industries tended to be accepted as inevitable consequences of the activity. In this respect the pulp and paper industry is no different from many other environmentally damaging activities. Such attitudes are no longer acceptable, although the degree of non-acceptance still varies among different sectors of society and in different parts of the world. Addressing and controlling the problems of pollution from the pulp and paper industry involves a number of scientific disciplines including ecology, epidemiology, toxicology, and engineering. Also involved are economic and social considerations.

The initial stages of preparation of pulp involve sawing logs from felled trees. Sawmills in the past were often powered by water and the sawdust often found its way into rivers, either accidentally or through dumping. This process can cause natural toxins from wood to enter the aquatic ecosystem. Even disregarding potential toxins the wood dust can deplete the water of oxygen through its biochemical oxygen demand (BOD).

Sawed logs have traditionally been transported by water. These floating masses of logs on river surfaces deprive normal plant activity of light for photosynthesis. In addition BOD is exerted. Modern operations are often less dependent on water at this stage, rather using rail and road transportation for logs. To address all potential pollution from pulp and paper industries, or for any "cradle to grave" comparisons among industries, air pollution related to this transportation should be taken into account.

The necessary removal of bark from logs, by physical means, releases tannins (potentially toxic, natural components of bark) into water and exerts BOD. Then the wood is made into chips which are used directly for pulping.

Essentially the pulping consists of digesting the wood chips to remove the natural cementing materials which hold the fibers together in the tree, washing the pulp and treating it chemically through several stages, including heating in strong alkalis. Water pollutants that are released through these stages include chips and fibers of wood, dark-colored liquor containing many organic compounds, dominated by lignin, a natural component of wood, terpenes, and phenols (generally toxic) which are natural components of trees, and various particulates including inorganic and organic materials which are washed from the wood. The process uses large volumes of water, from 10,000 to 400,000 gallons per ton of paper. Some of this water is returned unaltered, but adverse effects on aquatic life are exerted through high BOD, through toxins, and through interference with light penetration for photosynthesis.

Gaseous emissions in the course of the pulping process include oxides of sulfur, other sulfur compounds with pungent and unpleasant odors (causing the smell which in many people's experience is characteristic of pulp mills), ammonia and various other flue gases. These gases are potentially damaging to plant and animal life, as well as human health. Beyond direct health effects the air pollutants represent aesthetic problems and elements of nuisance which interfere with human use and enjoyment of property and the natural environment.

Space does not permit detailed descriptions of available pulping processes, but the so-called kraft process is the most commonly used. A relatively large amount of recycling of chemicals is built into the kraft system. This improves the economics of the process as well as limiting emissions to the environment.

The final stage of treatment involves bleaching. At present, chlorine bleaching is the usual way to produce pure white pulp and paper products. Newsprint and other types of paper do not use chlorine to the same extent. Of the 145 pulp mills currently operating in Canada, for example, forty-six use chlorine. Technology is being developed to replace chlorine with chlorine dioxide; this will decrease the amount of chlorine released to the environment.

In the latter part of the 1980s the use of chlorine has been the greatest source of public pressure on the pulp and paper industry. Major concerns have arisen because chlorine combines with organic materials, resulting in the formation of a variety of chlorinated organic compounds, collectively known as AOXs. Dioxins and furans, some of which are exquisitely toxic, are included in the AOX category. Furans and dioxins are already addressed in many jurisdictions, and pulp mill effluent is regulated in terms of these compounds. Other AOXs have not been systematically tested, nor are they currently regulated, but certainly many such compounds have been detected in water downstream from mills that use chlorine. Furthermore, field and laboratory tests have shown that fish suffer harmful effects from pulp mill effluent. However, the causal link is unproven. Recent (1992) scientific studies carried out for Canada's federal Department of the Environment have indicated that while pulp mill efflu-

ent can be damaging to aquatic life, the effects are not related to organochlorines, but to some other factors, as yet unidentified. Possibly these are natural products, or other secondary pollutants.

Environmentalists have argued that the risk of continuing to contaminate receiving water with organochlorines is not justified and that chlorine bleach should not be used at all. Some scientists agree that it is prudent to try to eliminate the entire family of organochlorine compounds. Other scientists, as well as advocates for the pulp and paper industry argue that if organochlorines are not the causal compounds in the toxicity of pulp mill effluent, then zero discharge regulations make neither economic nor scientific sense. The argument continues that large sums of money would have to be invested to meet the zero discharge of chlorine forcing some companies to close; the money, therefore, would be better spent on research to identify the unknown factors.

In Canada the government of British Columbia plans to introduce regulations that call for the elimination of all chlorine-compound pollution within a short (specified) time period. To date (1993), no other jurisdiction in the world has imposed such a zero discharge regulation for chlorine although Ontario is currently attempting a similar elimination, under its Municipal and Industrial Strategy for Abatement (MISA) program.

The complexity of the chlorine issue exemplifies many environmental issues. Technical, scientific, economic, political and philosophical components are entangled in the discussion and the decisions made by regulatory agencies will be at best some kind of compromise to address the multi-stakeholder problem.

Pamela Welbourn

Further Readings

The State of Canada's Environment 1992. Minister of Supply and Services, Ottawa.

Sang, Susan, and Burkhardt Mausberg. *Developing Options for Technology Based Standards for the Pulp and Paper Sector in the Great Lakes Basin.* Canadian Institute for Environmental Law and Policy, 1992.

See also Dioxins and Furans; Eutrophication; Mercury; Water Pollution Abatement Technologies

R

Race and Environmental Protection

See ENVIRONMENTAL JUSTICE MOVEMENT

Radiation

See IONIZING RADIATION; NUCLEAR WASTE; RADON; URANIUM MINING: OCCUPATIONAL HEALTH

Radical Environmentalism

Radical environmentalism is best understood as a cluster of eco-political philosophies which purport to explain the roots of the environmental crisis while prescribing the attitudinal "paradigm shifts," social changes, and political strategies needed to reverse environmental decline. Deep ecology blames environmental destruction primarily on anthropocentric attitudes, which view the natural world as a means to human satisfaction rather than as an intrinsically valuable end in itself, tracing such attitudes to Western religion and mechanistic science. Social ecology (sometimes called ecological anarchism) locates the human urge to dominate and destroy nature in hierarchical human social structures (where one group dominates another). Ecofeminism roots the destruction of nature foremost in patriarchy, asserting that since women and nature have become closely associated, their oppression and liberation are necessarily linked. Eco-Marxism (and eco-socialism) argues, contra many environmental radicals, that capitalist systems, rather than industrialism per se, is the central culprit in environmental decline. The lines between these four major types of radical environmentalism is often blurred, as individuals blend these diagnoses, and strategies based upon them, in many ways, both consistently and inconsistently.

The differing diagnoses of radical environmentalism produce different strategic priorities. Deep ecologists tend to promote ecocentric values through grass-roots activism defending wilderness and biodiversity; those most cynical about U.S. politics often participate in Earth First!, the militant vanguard of deep ecology. Earth First! is radical in a way the other environmental radicals usually are not, employing extra-legal tactics including civil disobedience and sabotage (labeled "ecotage" or "monkey-wrenching") in efforts to thwart human activities threatening to sensitive habitats. But the central goal of deep ecology is to overturn anthropocentrism, fostering a paradigm shift whereby people would value nature for its own sake. Consequently deep ecologists place a high priority on education to foster consciousness change. Such efforts often include the promotion of pagan spiritual sentiments (which many believe provide an important tributary to deep ecological consciousness), through diverse forms of art and ritual (see Taylor, 1993).

Social ecology believes that basic structures of the economy and the state must be challenged, especially market capitalism which precludes an ecological orientation by rewarding with survival those market competitors who seek growth without ecological concern. In the absence of structural changes, whatever change in consciousness occurs will not prevent the destruction of nature, or create an authentic human species aware of its embeddedness in nature. Less suspicious of technology and industrialism than most deep ecologists social ecologists envision decentralized societies of municipalities, governed through participatory self-rule, linked together in confederations, and characterized by mutual aid, ecologically benign technologies, goods produced to last for generations, and the regional, democratic control of land. Since "second nature" (human culture), is embedded in "first" nature (the natural world), and likewise results from an evolutionary process, social ecology is relatively optimistic; it is possible for humans to recognize that hierarchical systems destroy both nature and authentic human nature, and thus do not promote survival. It is also possible to develop lifeways that would harmonize human culture with the natural world. Unlike deep ecology, social ecology has not spawned large numbers of grass-roots environmental groups, remaining instead primarily an intellectual enterprise (although some social ecologists participate in a variety of social justice and environmental organizations).

Although a diverse movement, ecofeminists target patriarchy (and like social ecologists, often hierarchy itself) as a prerequisite to transforming those human cultures which are destructive to nature and women. Ecofeminists devote a great deal of attention to criticizing the conceptual bases underlying the exploitation of women and nature; they often argue that the logic which subjugates women is the same logic which supports anthropocentric and dualistic premises dividing people from nature. (In this respect ecofeminism has affinity with deep ecology.) A high priority for ecofeminists is creating communities of resistance by developing women's ethics of care and reciprocity. Thus ecofeminists have been involved in a host of peace, social justice, and environmental movements. They also often participate in other radical environmental groups, insisting that the role of patriarchy not be overlooked. This helps explain how ecofeminist perspectives have become influential within all radical environmental branches.

Deep and social ecologists, and ecofeminists, all tend to view political decentralization as an essential path toward constructing sustainable human communities. This explains the affinity of many environmental radicals with bioregionalism, which asserts that political boundaries should follow the contours of distinct regional ecosystem types, and commerce between these regions should be limited, because local self-rule and self-sufficiency makes it possible for people to know and responsibly care for their own unique habitats.

Eco-Marxism and ecosocialism share social ecology's skepticism that changes in thinking will lead to ecologically sustainable societies. Unlike social ecology and the other forms of environmental radicalism that favor political

decentralization, eco-Marxism is suspicious of bioregional political models. Eco-Marxists argue that decentralization is incompatible with planning, the redistribution of resources, and the widespread distribution of environmentally appropriate technologies, that ecologically sustainable societies would require. Eco-Marxism has remained largely an intellectual radicalism. Although Eco-Marxists have participated in green politics in many ways, like social ecologists, they have not inspired many grass-roots environmental movements.

Uniting these often competing environmental radicalisms is the fervent belief that the axial organizing principles of modern societies must be overturned. Although some look for ecologically sustainable models in the lifeways of foraging peoples and in the planet's remnant indigenous peoples, and others seek to borrow selectively from the human technological legacy in mapping sustainable pathways, all ecological radicals agree that modern societies must be fundamentally altered, that resource limits to growth must be acknowledged, and that societies adaptive to such ecological realities must evolve, if human culture and a healthy biosphere are to continue their evolutionary unfolding.

Bron R. Taylor

Further Readings
Dobson, Andrew. *Green Political Thought.* 1990.

Eckersley, Robyn. *Environmentalism and Political Theory.* 1992.

Taylor, Bron R. "Earth First's Religious Radicalism." In *Ecological Prospects: Scientific, Religious, and Aesthetic Perspectives.* Ed. Christopher Chapple. 1993.

Zimmerman, Michael E., et. al. *Environmental Philosophy: From Animal Rights to Radical Ecology.* 1993.

See also ANTHROPOCENTRISM; BIOREGION; DEEP ECOLOGY: MEANINGS; EARTH FIRST!; ECOANARCHISM; ECOFEMINISM; ECOSOCIALISM; ECO-SPIRITUALITY

Radioactive Fallout

Radioactive fallout is produced when radioactive material injected into the atmosphere by nuclear and thermonuclear explosions falls back to the earth. Most nuclear weapons were tested above ground until the 1963 Limited Test Ban Treaty. Fallout became a source of great public concern during the 1950s and early 1960s.

The United States Atomic Energy Commission tried to downplay the hazards of fallout. However, the widely publicized 1954 *Lucky Dragon* incident alerted the public to the danger. The Japanese fishing vessel's crew became sick and one person died after it was dusted with fallout from a test in the Pacific Bikini Islands. Fallout-contaminated fish entered the market. The incident also brought the dangers of the radioactive isotope Strontium-90 (Sr-90) to public attention. Iodine-131, which accumulates in thyroid tissue, and other isotopes are also dangerous. Sr-90 though warranted special concern because of its ability to pass through the food chain into milk and accumulate in the growing bones of children.

Public information programs conducted by Consumer's Union, Greater St. Louis Citizens' Committee for Nuclear Information, and other organizations alerted the public to the hazard and mobilized opposition to atmospheric testing. These campaigns and the resulting media coverage became one of the largest public education efforts to focus on an ecological concept—the food chain or web. Reports that fallout from bomb tests in Nevada killed sheep and harmed ranchers also raised concern.

Fear of World War III and global contamination raised the prospect that humans might destroy themselves. Motion pictures exploring this Doom's Day theme and others about fanciful monsters created by radiation added to this fear. *On the Beach* (1959), which premiered in eighteen cities around the world and in eight languages, was the most prestigious of the end-of-the-world films. National campaigns to promote the contruction of fallout shelters added to this fear.

Throughout her book *Silent Spring* (1962) Rachel Carson used the public's existing knowledge of fallout to teach how pesticides similarly spread through the food web, accumulate in plant, animal, and human tissues, and produce cancer, birth defects, and mutations. The first pollutant named in her book was Sr-90. She gave a definitive voice to the fear that by destroying our environment, humans may destroy their own species. This anxiety, born in the fear of radioactive fallout, is distinctive of the late twentieth century environmental movement.

Atmospheric testing and the resulting fallout left a legacy of contamination and health problems in the American West and elsewhere around the world.

Ralph H. Lutts

Further Readings

Fradkin, Philip L. *Fallout: An American Nuclear Tragedy.* 1989.

Lutts, Ralph H. "Chemical Fallout: Rachel Carson's *Silent Spring*, Radioactive Fallout, and the American Environmental Movement." *Environmental Review* 9 (1985): 210–25.

Weart, Spencer R. *Nuclear Fear: A History of Images.* 1988.

See also ENVIRONMENTAL PROTECTION IN WARTIME; FOOD CHAINS; NUCLEAR WEAPONS PRODUCTION; NUCLEAR WEAPONS TESTING; NUCLEAR WINTER; WEB OF LIFE

Radon

The earth's mantle contains radioactive elements: elements with unstable nuclei which undergo nuclear disintegration spontaneously with statistical regularity. One such natural element is uranium. When uranium decays it produces alpha particles (a form of ionizing radiation) and radium, which is also a radioactive chemical. When radium undergoes nuclear disintegration it produces alpha particles and radon, a radioactive gas. Radon in turn undergoes nuclear disintegration producing alpha particles and radioactive decay products (sometimes referred to as "daughter" products) namely radioactive forms of lead, bismuth, and polonium. Ultimately this chain of decay products and ionizing radiation ends in a stable (non-radioactive) isotope of lead.

All of the decay products produced in this chain are solids except for radon which is a gas. In natural rock formations the radium produces the gas in pockets within the rock where it reaches an equilibrium situation, decaying into its solid decay products at a rate in equilibrium with its production by radium. These solid radioactive products are in general trapped within the rock as they decay to lead.

Radon gas can escape from the rock formation when there is an out-cropping of the ore body or when natural gas or water flows through the ore bed. The gas is highly soluble in water and can also escape from the water to air when underground streams surface, enter caves, or discharge into rivers or lakes.

Disturbance of uranium ore beds makes all of the radioactive particles which naturally occur with the uranium more bioavailable. This occurs in several ways. The pulverizing of the rock and uranium extraction process produces many surfaces from which the radon gas can escape into air or water. Radon is a heavy gas, about seven times heavier than air, so it stays near the surface of the earth and pollutes the air layer which humans and animals breathe.

Uranium mine tailings are highly radioactive because of all of the radioactive decay products left after the uranium is extracted. As much as 98 percent of the radioactive chemicals in the ore can be left at the mine and mill site after extraction.

When the tailings are stored in a lake, for example Quirke Lake near the Elliot Lake, Ontario mines, they can leach into the watershed. In the early 1980s a significant concentration of radium was found in the Serpent River. Efforts to control the leaching were introduced, which now must be maintained long into the foreseeable future. Radon dispersion from tailings is more difficult to prevent than radium dispersion.

Dry tailings blow in the wind and wash into the lakes and rivers with the rain. As the radium spreads, so does the radon gas and its decay products. Although half of the radon decays into its solid decay products each 3.8-day period, with a ten-kilometer per hour wind it can travel 240 kilometers in a day and 960 kilometers before half of it has decayed to solid radionuclides. The solid radioactive daughter products are deposited on the ground along its path.

Radon gas is further spread when contaminated water or gas is drawn into a home through pipe lines or water seeps into cellars. The digging of a cellar can also directly disturb small orebeds locally deposited. Homes which are well sealed and insulated tend to build up the radon gas entering the home through basements, water, or gas lines. Also, natural building materials (e.g., rocks or fill) which contain radium, can release radon into a home, office building, or plant.

Phosphate usually occurs near uranium deposits in nature, and phosphate fertilizers can sometimes carry radium and radon into otherwise relatively uncontaminated areas including farms or vegetable gardens.

The health problems related to radon gas have to do with its being drawn into the respiratory tract and lungs with air. The radon itself is a readily inhaled gas and the real damage to lung tissue is thought to be due to all of the radioactive lead, bismuth, and polonium it produces and deposits in the lungs. These radioactive chemicals release alpha particles, ionizing radiation, in very close proximity to lung tissue. They can kill cells, cause fibrosis (damaged tissue), or initiate lung cancer.

Body water washes the radioactive decay products through the lung tissue and into the blood stream. The radionuclides travel to all parts of the body including reproductive organs and are capable of causing damage to them or to arteries, the liver, kidney, or tubules on their way to being excreted in urine. Some of the radionuclides are mistaken by the body to be nutrients and are stored in bone. They can affect blood cells which are produced in bone marrow resulting in anemia or reduced ability to fight infections or tumors. The degree of damage is roughly related to the degree of exposure and the body's ability to heal itself. It can be most serious for children, the elderly, and the chronically ill. Damage to sperm or ovum can later be expressed as a genetic disease in offspring.

Some exposure to radon gas is inevitable but some can easily be avoided. For example, good ventilation of indoor air, meaning a change of air every hour, can prevent radon build-up. Stabilizing uranium tailings and securing them away from the air, water, and food chain is necessary remedial work in North America. As well, whether or not to become the leading or dominant uranium producer in the world is an important health and political question for Canada, for example.

Either stopping the use of phosphate fertilizer for growing tobacco or stopping cigarette smoking would reduce lung and circulatory problems in the population. The radon decay products, especially polonium 210, have been found in the lung tissue of smokers. It is apparently trapped in the tars of the growing tobacco leaf.

Your local department of health can provide information on ways to test your home for radon gas. If possible, get a type of monitor which you leave in place for three months and then have read by the firm which provided the monitor. This gives a better idea of average level since there are wide differences with lifestyle, showering, use of gas ovens or heaters, local humidity, and ventilation. There are also seasonal changes. Radon is measured by one of three different standards:

1. pico Curies per liter of air (pCi/liter). A Curie is the measure of radioactivity (i.e., the rate of nuclear disintegrations) in one

gram of radium. A pico Curie is one Curie x 10^{-12}.

2. Bequerels per liter of air (Bq/liter). One Bequerel represents one nuclear disintegration per second (sixty per minute).

    One Curie (Ci) = 3.7 x 10^{10} Bq
    One pico Curie (pCi) = 0.037 Bq

3. Working Level Month (WLM). One "working level" is defined as any combination of short-lived radon daughter products (through polonium 214) leading to a total emission of 1.3 x 10^5 million electron volts (MeV) of alpha energy per liter of air. A WLM is exposure to one working level for 170 hours (eight hours per day, for five days per week, for 4.25 weeks). One WLM is about 0.6 rad (12 rem or 120 mSv) dose to lung tissue, with a range of 8 rem to 16 rem (80 to 160 mSv). (Note: 1 Sievert (1 Sv) = 100 rem; 1 milli Sievert (1 mSv) = 100 millirem (mrem); 1 micro Sievert (1 µSv) = 100 microrem (µ rem).)

In the United States remediation is recommended if radon levels are above 4 pCi/l (150 Bq/m³) or if the whole body dose to the public exceeds 0.5 rem (5 mSv) a year. In Canada remediation is recommended if radon levels exceed 20 pCi/l (rounded up to 800 Bq/m³ averaged over a year) or whole body dose to the public exceeds 0.5 rem (5 mSv) per year. In 1990 the International Commission on Radiological Protection, the standard recommending body which the United States and Canada follow, lowered the maximum dose recommended for the public from 0.5 rem (5 mSv) to 0.1 rem (1 mSv) per year. The new recommendations are not yet established as legal limits in North America. Two U.S. States—Minnesota and Massachusetts—are attempting to set maximum dose to the public even lower, namely at 0.00005 rem (0.05 mrem or 0.5 µSv) per year. This would bring nuclear and radiation industries in line with standards used for the chemical industries, namely to initiate no more than one cancer per 100,000 persons over a lifetime (seventy years). (Note: the standard for chemical industries uses cancer incidence not cancer fatality.)

Radiation dose to lung tissue is converted to an equivalent dose (for inducing fatal cancer) to the whole body by multiplying by 0.12. A lung dose of 12 rem would be considered equivalent to a 1.44 rem dose to whole body (weighting factors are recommended by the In-

ternational Commission on Radiological Protection).

The annual absorbed radiation dose resulting (on average) to the public from radon 222 and its decay products through polonium 214 is: 630 micro Gray to tracheo-bronchial tissue, 80 micro Gray to lung tissue and 850 micro Sievert effective whole body dose equivalent.

Rosalie Bertell

Further Readings

Nero, A.V., et al. "Radon Concentrations and Infiltration Rates Measured in Conventional and Energy Efficient Homes." *Health Physics* 45 (1983): 401-05.

Office of Air and Radiation, Environmental Protection Agency. *The Inside Story: A Guide to Indoor Air Quality.* 1988.

See also INDOOR AIR POLLUTION; IONIZING RADIATION; URANIUM MINING: OCCUPATIONAL HEALTH

Rafferty-Alameda Dams

As part of a provincial development project a Saskatchewan crown (public) corporation built two dams on the Souris River in southeastern Saskatchewan in 1988–1990. The Souris flows from Saskatchewan into North Dakota and then northward into Manitoba. These dam projects rose to prominence because of the important court cases and intense federal-provincial conflicts they generated.

The federal Environmental Assessment Review Process (EARP) was established by Cabinet Decision in 1974 and reinforced by Order-in-Council in 1984. In June 1988 the federal minister of the environment accepted a Saskatchewan environmental impact assessment of the Rafferty-Alameda project and issued a license pursuant to the International River Improvements Act allowing the project to proceed. At two separate points the Canadian Wildlife Federation (CWF) challenged the federal actions in the courts.

The CWF sought the quashing of the federal license, arguing that the federal government had not complied with its own EARP guidelines order. The federal court agreed, ruling in April 1989 that the project must be subject to a federal assessment because it impacted on a number of areas of federal responsibility including international relations, transboundary water flows, migratory birds, interprovincial affairs, fisheries, and federal lands. The court also held that the guidelines order was a law of general application and legally binding on federal agencies.

The federal court's two decisions in Rafferty-Alameda, as well as the Supreme Court of Canada January 1992 ruling in the Oldman Dam case in Alberta, had the effect of broadening and strengthening the guidelines order and forcing new federal legislation. While various federal governments had considered legislating environmental assessment since the 1970s, the Conservative government finally tabled legislation in June 1990. After a difficult and lengthy legislative process the Canadian Environmental Assessment Act (CEAA) received Royal Assent in June 1992. CEAA had still not been proclaimed when the Conservatives were defeated in the October 1993 general election. The new Liberal government has committed to proclaiming CEAA early in its mandate.

Glen Toner

Further Readings

Vanderzwagg, David, and Linda Duncan. "Canada and Environmental Protection: Confident Faces, Uncertain Legal Hands." In *Canadian Environmental Policy*. Ed. Robert Boardman. 1992.

See also CANADIAN NATURE FEDERATION; ENVIRONMENTAL ASSESSMENT (CANADA); ENVIRONMENTAL CASE LAW (CANADA): COMMON LAW CAUSES OF ACTION; HYDROELECTRICITY; JAMES BAY

Rails-to-Trails

The gradual contraction of massive railroad networks in the United States, Britain, Canada, and other nations in the second half of the twentieth century has spawned a grass-roots movement to convert abandoned railroad corridors to trails for bicycling, walking, running, and other uses. By the end of 1993 the United States had over 550 rail-trails with a total combined length of 6,800 miles.

Rail-trails range in length from less than a mile to 200 miles; the average is 12.2 miles. Width of the greenway corridor varies from forty feet to 200 feet; width of the trailway itself is generally eight feet in rural areas and ten to twelve feet in urban settings. The trails are created by removing the steel rails and wooden ties, decking, and railing bridges and trestles, and providing warning signs or signals at road crossings. The most common surfacing materials for U.S. rail-trails are crushed stone (26 percent of trails), asphalt (27 percent), or simply leaving the original ballast or cinders (33 percent).

Although isolated forest rail-trails were established for hiking and equestrian use as early as the 1920s, the movement's genesis in the United States is traced to 1965 when volunteers near Chicago began to develop the Illinois Prairie Path on an abandoned electric interurban corridor. Two years later the state of Wisconsin purchased for $13,200 an abandoned Chicago and North Western Railroad corridor near Lacrosse and opened the nation's "skinniest state park," the Elroy-Sparta Trail: thirty-two miles long and 100 feet wide.

Other noteworthy rail-trails include the Burke-Gilman Trail in Seattle (which opened in 1976), the Washington and Old Dominion Railroad Regional Park outside Washington, D.C. (1981), the 200-mile Katy State Trail in Missouri (1990), the Pinellas Trail in St. Petersburg, Florida (1990), and the Minuteman Trail near Boston (1992). The premier rail-trail in England is the Bristol-Bath Railway Path (1979).

The practicality of converting unused rails to trails was given a boost by Congress in 1983 with the passage of the so-called "railbanking" amendment to the National Trails System Act, under which corridors can be banked for possible future rail use and interim trail use instead of being irrevocably abandoned. Under railbanking the federal government's Interstate Commerce Commission maintains regulatory authority, and no portions of reversionary property revert to non-compatible uses.

Rail-trails received more help in 1985 when the private Rails-to-Trails Conservancy was established to inventory the scope of rail-trail activities throughout the United States, publicize the benefits of rail-trails, advocate for trails within the government and the court system, and provide assistance to communities in effecting corridor conversions.

An additional boost came in 1991 with the passage of the Intermodal Surface Transportation Efficiency Act (ISTEA) which allocated, over six years, $3.3 billion of previously unavailable federal transportation dollars for nonautomobile projects such as rail-trails. By late 1993 more than $90 million had been spent on 140 rail-trail projects.

By 1993 Canada had approximately two dozen rail-trails open or under development and the national Canadian Rails-to-Greenways Network was in formation. Fledgling rail-trail movements were also reported in Australia and Spain.

Peter Harnik

Further Readings

Little, Charles E. *Greenways for America.* 1990.

Royal Commission on the Future of the Toronto Waterfront. *Regeneration.* 1991.

See also BICYCLE TRANSPORTATION; HABITAT FRAGMENTATION, PATCHES, AND CORRIDORS; URBAN DESIGN

Rainforest Action Network

See ENVIRONMENTAL MOVEMENTS IN LESS-AFFLUENT NATIONS

Rainforests

See TROPICAL RAINFORESTS

Rangelands (U.S.)

Rangelands of the United States are most commonly associated with the arid regions of the Great Plains and the intermountain and far West. Rangelands are also associated with western coniferous forests, southern pine forests, and eastern deciduous forests. In all, fifteen major rangeland types exist within the continental United States.

California Annual Grassland

The California Annual Grassland is the westernmost U.S. rangeland type. Wedged between the Sierra Nevada Mountains and the Pacific coast, it features a Mediterranean climate of mild, wet winters and long, hot, dry summers. Severe livestock grazing depleted its native perennial grass cover, replacing it with exotic annual oat and brome grasses. At higher elevations, evergreen shrubs mix with annual grasses to form a distinctive chaparral component.

Palouse Prairie

The Palouse Prairie is an extensive rangeland type that once occupied eastern Washington, northern Oregon, and western Idaho. Today, much of its historic range is farmed in wheat. Remnants can be found in the Blue Mountains of Oregon and Washington where thin soils and a short growing season prevent cultivation. Palouse-like prairie is also found in western Montana. There, as elsewhere, Idaho fescue and bluebunch wheatgrass are the principal grasses.

Hot Desert

The Hot Desert is one of the largest but least productive U.S. rangeland types for livestock. It is divided into the drier Mojave desert of southeastern California; the frost-free and moister Sonoran desert of southern Arizona; and the cooler Chihuahuan desert of southern New Mexico and west Texas. Heavy livestock grazing has reduced the grass component of the Sonoran and Chihuahuan deserts and increased the presence of shrubs such as mesquite and creosotebush.

Cold Desert

The Cold Desert is the largest U.S. rangeland type. In the intermountain steppe of western Wyoming, southern Idaho, eastern Oregon, and eastern Nevada, sagebrush grassland (big sagebrush and cool-season bunchgrasses) is the dominant cover. Below 1,235 meters in the arid, saline bottom lands of Utah and western Nevada, salt desert replaces sagebrush grassland. Heavily impacted by livestock grazing, salt desert supports halophytic grasses and shrubs.

Piñon-Juniper Woodland

A distinct class of rangeland types are those dominated by tall shrubs and low trees. The Piñon-Juniper Woodland is ubiquitous, occurring at elevations from 1,400 to 2,400 meters from Washington to New Mexico. Heavy livestock grazing and fire control have caused woodlands to increase in density and to encroach on grasslands.

Mountain Browse

Mountain Browse is a minor rangeland type of the Sierra Nevada, Cascade, and Rocky Mountain ranges occurring between low elevation grasslands and high elevation coniferous forests. Shrubs, such as chokecherry, buckbrush and mountain mahogany, are common.

Oak Woodland

The Oak Woodland, dominated by shinnery oak in southeastern New Mexico, Gambel oak in the southern Rocky Mountains, and oak savannahs in California, Oregon, Arizona, and central Texas, is a more extensive rangeland type.

Western Coniferous Forest

The Western Coniferous Forest is an important but often ephemeral rangeland type of the mountain West associated with seral stages of ponderosa pine, Douglas fir-aspen, lodgepole pine, and spruce-fir. Of these forests, ponderosa pine rangelands are the most persistent and the most important for livestock.

Alpine Tundra

The Alpine Tundra rangeland type lies above spruce-fir in the high Sierra Nevada, Cascade, and Rocky Mountain ranges. Receiving up to 1,500 millimeters of rain and snow, it is valued most for water yield, aesthetics, and recreation.

Great Plains: Shortgrass Prairie, Northern Mixed Prairie, Southern Mixed Prairie

In contrast, rangeland types of the Great Plains are valued principally for livestock production. The Shortgrass Prairie extends from northern New Mexico into northern Wyoming and supports a shortgrass cover of blue grama and buffalograss. The Northern Mixed Prairie lies to the north in eastern Montana and the western Dakotas and supports the highest diversity of short, mid, and tall grasses of all U.S. rangeland types. The Southern Mixed Prairie, the most important of the three for livestock production, reaches from eastern New Mexico to southern Oklahoma and eastern Texas and is divided into true mixed prairie, desert prairie, high plains bluestem, and oak savannah. Like its mixed and shortgrass prairie neighbors, it co-evolved with heavy grazing by American bison.

Tallgrass Prairie

The Tallgrass Prairie lies east of the mixed and shortgrass prairies and west of the deciduous forests of the midwest and Atlantic states. Although most of it has been cultivated, remnants of indiangrass, switchgrass, and bluestem rangeland persist in the Flint Hills of Kansas, the Osage Hills of Oklahoma, the Nebraska sandhills, and the Texas Coastal Prairie. Like the other prairies, it also co-evolved with heavy grazing by American bison.

Southern Pine Forest and Eastern Deciduous Forest

The final major U.S. rangeland types occur adjacent to and east of the Mississippi River. The Southern Pine Forest is the preeminent live-stock-producing rangeland in the United States. Encompassing much of the deep South, it provides a large share of the nation's timber, beef, and fee-hunted wildlife. The Eastern Deciduous Forest, lying to the north and east of the Southern Pine Forest, in Missouri, Indiana, Ohio, Kentucky, Virginia, and Wisconsin, is a rangeland type heavily modified by farming and industrialization but nonetheless increasingly important for livestock production.

Karl Hess

Further Readings

Barbour, M.G., J.H. Burk, and W.D. Pitts. *Terrestrial Plant Ecology*. 1987.
Holechek, J.L., R.D. Piper, and C.H. Herbel. *Range Management: Principles and Practices*. 1989.
Kuchler, A.W. *Potential Natural Vegetation of the Conterminous United States*. 1964.

See also BISON: CONSERVATION AND HABITAT; EXOTIC SPECIES; HABITAT FRAGMENTATION, PATCHES, AND CORRIDORS; LANDSCAPE ECOLOGY; UNGULATES

Raptors

See BALD EAGLE; HAWK SHOOTING; PEREGRINE FALCON

Reagan, Ronald

Ronald Reagan's presidency (1981–1989) was characterized by an effort to roll back environmental regulations and to open public lands and coastal areas to greater resource exploitation. During the 1980 campaign Reagan attacked the Clean Air Act as excessive and advocated deregulation of the economy to stimulate growth.

Reagan thus broke sharply with the Republican tradition of conservationism dating back to the presidency of Theodore Roosevelt. Reflecting the views of the "sagebrush rebels" and other Western development interests, Reagan appointed James G. Watt of the antigovernment Mountain States Legal Foundation as secretary of the interior. His choice of Colorado lawyer Anne M. Gorsuch (later Burford) to head the Environmental Protection Agency (EPA) signaled a desire to reduce the regulatory burden on industry. Much of her agenda was drawn from the recommendations of the conservative Heritage Foundation.

Faced with a Congress that remained generally supportive of environmental legislation—despite a new Republican majority in the Senate—Reagan attempted to carry out his policies by executive and administrative means. He appointed ideologically conservative officials to most high environmental and resource management positions—many of them drawn from large corporations and user groups that were subject to regulation. The budgets and personnel of EPA and other environmental programs were cut substantially in the early years of the administration. In constant dollars federal spending for pollution control and abatement declined 36 percent between 1980 and 1983. The EPA's total staff was cut about 20 percent, while that of the Council of Environmental Quality was slashed over 70 percent.

Vice President George Bush was appointed chair of a Task Force on Regulatory Relief, which rescinded and revised hundreds of previous executive orders and environmental regulations to reduce their impact on industry. The regulatory review process was further centralized by Executive Order 12291 (1981), which required "regulatory impact analyses," assessing the costs and benefits of all new regulations. The Office of Information and Regulatory Affairs in the Office of Management and Budget (OMB) delayed and revised numerous environmental regulations under the order. Executive Order 12498 (1985) tightened the review process further by requiring agencies to submit their regulatory calendars to OMB a year in advance.

These executive measures, together with other administrative actions taken by Reagan appointees, aroused strong opposition in the environmental community and in Congress. Environmentalists challenged many EPA and Interior Department decisions through lawsuits in the courts, while congressional committees conducted numerous oversight hearings and investigations of administrative procedures. Among Watt's most controversial actions were efforts to allow mineral exploration in wilderness areas and to open nearly all of the Outer Continental Shelf to oil and gas leasing. Burford's close relations with regulated industries and refusal to disclose information on alleged political influence in the distribution of Superfund cleanup funds led to a citation for contempt of Congress in late 1982 and to her resignation along with more than twenty other top EPA officials in March 1983. Watt was forced to resign later that year over some tactless remarks concerning the ethnic composition of a commission established to investigate his coal-leasing policies.

Reagan eased his confrontational approach to environmental policy after 1983 by appointing more moderate and respected officials such as William Ruckleshaus and Lee Thomas to head the EPA. The EPA gradually regained funding, stability, and credibility in Reagan's second term, though its operating budget remained well below pre-1981 levels. The Interior Department under Secretary Donald P. Hodel continued most of Watt's policies, more than doubling of the allowable timber cut on public lands in the latter half of the 1980s. Laws such as the Surface Mining Control and Reclamation Act were largely unenforced.

Reagan's huge defense buildup contributed to massive chemical and radioactive contamination of military bases and weapons production facilities. (Cleanup costs are now estimated at several hundred billion dollars.) His hands-off energy policy also encouraged rising fuel consumption and oil imports after 1986 as energy prices fell. Reagan eliminated most energy conservation and renewable energy programs and opposed higher fuel efficiency standards for automobiles.

Another area in which Reagan reversed policies was in support of global population control efforts. All aid to United Nations (UN) and other international family planning programs was cut off in 1984 due to ideological opposition to abortion.

While the Reagan administration proposed little new legislation, Congress revised and strengthened several of the major environmental statutes, including the Resource Conservation and Recovery Act (1984), Safe Drinking Water Act (1986), the Comprehensive Environmental Response, Compensation, and Liability ("Superfund") Act (1986), and the Clean Water Act (1987)—the latter over Reagan's veto. The president did, however, succeed in blocking revision of the Clean Air Act throughout the 1980s, despite mounting evidence of damage to northeastern lakes and streams from acid precipitation and strong diplomatic protests from Canada. Reagan continued to argue that more research was needed on acid rain before control of power plant emissions could be justified, a position later abandoned by President George Bush.

One of the few environmental accomplishments of the Reagan administration was nego-

R

tiation of the 1987 Montreal Protocol to the Vienna Convention on protection of the earth's ozone layer. The Montreal agreement originally called for a 50 percent reduction in the production of CFCs and related ozone-depleting chemicals by 1998—a goal later raised to complete phaseout by the mid-1990s.

Reagan's efforts to achieve regulatory reform through the "administrative presidency" largely backfired. The overt ideological biases and confrontational styles of many of his environmental appointees alienated members of both parties and large segments of the public. But the weakening of morale and institutional capacity at the EPA and other regulatory agencies may have adverse long-term consequences. (In constant dollars the EPA's operating budget remained lower in 1990 than in 1980, despite many added mandates.) Public opinion surveys indicated rapidly rising concerns over the environment in the late 1980s, and environmental organizations grew rapidly. Consequently President Bush adopted a more pro-environmental stance in the 1988 election.

Norman J. Vig

Further Readings

Shabecoff, Philip. *A Fierce Green Fire: The American Environmental Movement.* 1993.

Shanley, Robert A. *Presidential Influence and Environmental Policy.* 1992.

Vig, Norman J., and Michael E. Kraft, eds. *Environmental Policy in the 1980s: Reagan's New Agenda.* 1984.

See also BURFORD, ANNE MCGILL; BUSH, GEORGE; ENVIRONMENTAL PROTECTION AGENCY; LEGISLATION: UNITED STATES; RUCKELSHAUS, WILLIAM D.; SAGEBRUSH REBELLION; SUPERFUND; WATT, JAMES G.

Recycling

Recycling is the use of a discarded material in some new form, a process by which society's wastes are given a second life. One of the most familiar and traditional examples is the recovery of yesterday's newspaper for use as a raw material in the production of a new paper product such as a shoe box, a napkin, or even a sheet of newsprint in tomorrow's newspaper.

While the word "recycling" is recent, the concept and practice are not. Recycling processes of one type or another have existed for thousands of years. As long as people have been making things from raw materials they have found reasons to make use of waste materials. These wastes, or "secondary resources," are derived from one of two sources: 1) production processes, which often generate waste (i.e., "scrap" materials); and 2) the discard of something after it has been used (i.e., "consumed").

The roots of the recycling industry in North America and Europe were the rag pickers who appeared around the turn of the century. This early form of "curbside collection" involved carts which were wheeled up and down city streets by a collector who called out for rags, bones, and other discards that had some commercial value. Over the next several decades these recyclers slowly evolved into the "scrap dealers and brokers" who became the core of recycling, particularly with respect to industrial scrap. Many of the large recycling businesses now in operation are family firms that were built over the past seventy-five years from humble beginnings.

Recycling first moved more into public view during World War II. With many people occupied in the war effort there were staff shortages in primary resource industries such as mining. As well, many countries were cut off from their traditional (import) sources of raw materials. The increased requirement for waste materials in various manufacturing processes led, in North America, to "victory drives" where citizens brought their old tires or scrap metal to central collection points as their contribution to "winning the war."

Through the 1950s and 1960s the most visible signs of recycling were the "newspaper drives" which were traditionally operated by local Scout troops. These programs were driven very directly by market forces. When the recycling industry of the day—the scrap dealers and brokers—needed waste paper to meet the demands of the pulp and paper industry they would raise prices, and local community groups would respond by running a paper drive. There was still a great deal of other recycling activity, but it mainly involved scrap materials recovered from industrial sources, with little public visibility.

The current era of recycling programs began in the late 1960s and early 1970s as an outgrowth of the new "ecology movement." Neighborhood depots for newspapers, cans, and glass bottles and jars were established—not in response to economic factors, but to promote the conservation of raw materials and energy. For the first time there was a significant educational component to such programs. This was logical since the people operating the recycling programs were not raising funds for other activities (as were most Scout paper drives) but were using recycling to advance the cause of conservation and environmental protection.

There was a strong worldwide growth in support for energy conservation in the 1970s, triggered in part by the energy shortages and rising prices resulting from the emergence in 1973 of the Organization of Petroleum Exporting Countries (OPEC). As the wave of awareness and concern regarding the "energy crisis" grew, it served to support greater growth in new recycling policies and programs. Recycling was viewed as a practical way to conserve energy.

In both Canada and the United States government funding in the 1970s designed to foster energy conservation was used, directly and indirectly, to finance the expansion of community-based and municipal recycling programs. In the United States, for example, the federal pool of "oil overcharge" funds which had been collected from oil companies and directed toward energy conservation was used to finance multimillion dollar recycling initiatives in states such as Connecticut and Massachusetts. In Canada federal job creation programs which were designed to promote energy conservation—such as the $19 million EnerAction Program—became the primary source of startup and research and development (R & D) funding for dozens of recycling programs.

There was a second major factor which helped spur the growth of recycling in the 1970s—local opposition to the siting of new landfills (or "dumps," as they were more commonly known). In the 1990s this force continues to be a significant factor in public support for recycling.

The industrial scrap recycling sector and the municipal (community) recycling sector have followed substantially different evolutionary paths over the past twenty years. The former, led by the traditional scrap dealers, involves recovery and recycling of scrap from industrial sources, mainly in manufacturing facilities. It has remained relatively unchanged from the 1950s onward. Municipal recycling programs, which include local community efforts, involve recovery of materials from residences, but also from businesses located in a municipality (e.g., offices and stores). The status of this latter sector (i.e., municipal recycling) has both expanded and changed very rapidly since the

first neighborhood depots were launched by environmental activists.

The first multi-material curbside collection program was launched in Canada in 1974 in the east end of the City of Toronto. It marked the beginning of a trend toward more convenient, more professional recycling operators for the residential sector. In 1977 the first primitive test of the "Blue Box recycling system" was carried out near Barrie, Ontario, at Canadian Forces Base Borden. A special recycling container was provided to all houses on the base—to make participation more convenient, but also to make it more "real." From a societal standpoint it was important for people to have recycling "hardware" in the same way that their garbage cans and bags added to the reality of waste disposal.

From 1981 to 1983 the blue box was tested more fully in a 1,600-home pilot project in Kitchener, Ontario. Following the clear success of this effort the program was expanded citywide in September 1983. Over the next ten years city after city adopted the model developed in Kitchener. There are now more than 50 million people in Canada and the United States who participate each week in a blue box recycling program. Different forces contributed to this growth in various provinces and states. In some cases economic factors have been instrumental; in others the establishment of policy goals or even statewide or provincewide mandates have been the driving force.

While this growth in residential (curbside) recycling was occurring throughout the 1980s there was a parallel expansion taking place in commercial recycling in North America. People who were becoming accustomed to recycling in their homes began to look for ways to recycle at work. Office paper recycling programs started to spread rapidly, and blue boxes began to appear in company cafeterias and lunchrooms so that cans and bottles could be recovered for recycling. Cardboard recycling had existed for years in large generators, such as grocery stores. Smaller stores, offices, and factories began to collect their cardboard for recycling, often less because of economic factors and more because people wanted it to happen.

From the mid- to late 1980s there were many new policies and programs being developed by municipal and senior (i.e., provincial, state, and federal) governments to support and encourage the growth of recycling in both the residential and industrial-commercial-institutional (IC&I) sectors. Some examples include:

- Landfill "bans" have been adopted by municipalities as a means of forcing recycling of a material such as cardboard. If you can't send a material to landfill you have little choice but to adopt a recycling program.
- Mandatory recycling ordinances have been adopted by a number of U.S. states. Cities of a certain size are required to establish curbside recycling for specified materials such as newspapers, cans, and bottles.
- Payment of "diversion credits" have been adopted by both municipal and senior governments. Designed to provide a financial incentive to those operating a recycling program, through the payment of a specific number of dollars for each ton diverted from landfill.

Such initial supporting mechanisms were relatively blunt and simple in their design and application. Over the past five years the analysis of recycling and its place in society has become more sophisticated, as have the programs that governments have developed to encourage and support recycling development. Recycling was first viewed by many people as just another waste management option. However, there is now a growing public belief that a recycling program is in fact fundamentally different from landfill and incineration. The "3Rs"—reduction, reuse, and recycling—are increasingly viewed as representing a departure from the traditional cycle of consumption, waste generation, collection, and disposal. The following examples indicate aspects of the trend that has begun to develop in this regard.

The 3Rs Hierarchy
The "hierarchy" represents a belief that waste reduction, reuse, and recycling should be pursued very explicitly in that order. Recycling has even been called "the 3rd rate 'R'" by those promoting the benefits of reduction, or waste prevention. There is evidence that greater environmental and economic benefits can be achieved by not producing waste in the first place, rather than continuing to generate waste, unabated, as long as recycling programs are in place.

Consumer versus Conserver Society
Similar to the "hierarchy" consideration above, the movement away from a consumer society toward a conserver society does not necessarily fully support recycling as a high priority. Those who promote increased conservation will see recycling as a better alternative to traditional consumption and disposal practices, but they also recognize that perhaps the best option is simply not to consume as many resources in the first place.*

Product Stewardship
Since the late 1980s, when Germany passed its "Green Dot" (*Der Grüne Punkt*) packaging legislation, there has been a growing worldwide trend toward greater environmental and economic responsibility being held by those who manufacture and sell various products. In a typical "product stewardship" scenario a producer is held responsible, to some extent, for the cost of operating a recycling program so that the product (or the package it was sold in) does not end up in a landfill or incinerator. In the case of Germany's law 100 percent of the financial burden, as well as all of the responsibility for securing markets for recovered packaging, is assigned to producers. Since all manufacturers, as well as all importers, are subject to this requirement, a "level playing field" is maintained among competing businesses.

Market Development Efforts
There are now regulations in certain jurisdictions, such as Canada, which require labeling to indicate whether recycled content of a product has been derived from a production process or from a "post-consumer" source. The use of post-consumer waste is viewed as being more beneficial than the use of manufacturing scrap because it helps to create a market demand for materials that have been recovered through more visible means such as neighborhood depots or municipal curbside collection programs.

The more in-depth analysis indicated by these trends has developed at least partly in relation to needs that have arisen as society has worked to institutionalize recycling. The key barriers to these efforts over the past decade have included economics on a macro and micro level as well as more specific issues such as the need for market development to accommodate increased volumes of recovered materials.

In recent years there has been a growing concern about the cost of recycling programs, particularly on the part of municipal governments who operate residential curbside collection systems. In a simplified view it is possible to state that it is more expensive to run a recycling program than to simply send resources to the local landfill. The more significant economic benefits of recycling often occur more at the macro level (e.g., through a reduction in the economic and environmental costs paid by society generally for primary resource extraction such as mining and forestry). It is likely that recycling will continue to be subject to a more comprehensive analysis over the coming decade, as society considers how recycling and other conservation measures fit into our future.

Jack McGinnis

Further Readings

Platt, Brenda, et al. *Beyond 40 Percent: Record-Setting Recycling and Composting Programs.* Washington, D.C.: Institute for Local Self-Reliance, 1990.

U.S. Congress Office of Technology Assessment. *Facing America's Trash: What's Next for America's Municipal Solid Waste?* 1989.

Young, John E. "Reducing Waste, Saving Materials." In *State of the World 1991.* Ed. Lester R. Brown, et al. 1991.

See also CONSERVER SOCIETY; GREEN PRODUCTS; LIFE-CYCLE ANALYSIS; MUNICIPAL SOLID WASTE: INCINERATION; MUNICIPAL SOLID WASTE: LANDFILL; NONRENEWABLE RESOURCES; PACKAGING; STEWARDSHIP; THROWAWAY MENTALITY SOCIETY

Redwoods

By their age, size, stature, and breathtaking beauty the giant sequoias and coastal redwoods of California stand as a testament to nature's supreme achievement in the evolution of trees. Both species—the coastal redwood (*sequoia sempervirens*) and the giant sequoia (*sequoiadendron giganteum*)—are in the sequoia family. The coastal redwood of California has historical roots that seem as ancient as antiquity itself. Fossil records show that 125 million years ago these trees spread across the United States, Canada, Greenland, Europe, China, and the former Soviet Union. Dinosaurs roamed the groves, and hugeness was status quo. A cooling and drying of the earth's climate pushed the dinosaurs into oblivion and left the trees in just 1 percent of their former range. Rather than adapt to the changing conditions the redwoods retreated to areas where the growing conditions were more to their liking. Today the redwoods grow mostly in a band 450 miles long and twenty miles wide along the northern California coast. The seventy-five remaining groves of giant sequoias are on the slopes of the southern Sierra Nevada.

The coastal redwood requires a temperate climate, rich soil, and abundant moisture. And along the coast, where westerly winds come in moisture-laden from the Pacific to meet the heated air of the interior valleys, heavy fogs provide a large measure of the water they require. The trees are found within this fog belt from south of Monterey Bay to the Oregon border, reaching inland no more than thirty miles at points where the fog penetrates. A few scattered groves extend south as far as the northern part of San Luis Obispo County, while Oregon lays claim to those that reach north to the Chetco River.

Redwoods are unique in that the secret of their size is simple: the trees grow rapidly as long as they are alive, and they live a long time. Redwoods live at least 1,500 years on average, and sequoias survive twice that long. Sprouted from seeds so small that 123,000 weigh just a pound, the big trees are vulnerable as saplings, but once grown are almost impenetrable. Tannin makes their wood impervious to most insects, and the foot-thick bark acts like armor against the threat of fire. A mature tree lives on what seems an almost geologic time scale, shedding the centuries like fallen needles. Although raw number dimensions fall far short in describing the incredible stature of the redwoods it helps to realize their unparalleled natural essence by pointing out that the tallest redwood, the Tall Tree in Redwood National Park, is 367.8 feet high, forty-four feet in circumference, and fourteen feet in diameter. In addition, the largest sequoia, the General Sherman Tree in Sequoia National Park, measures 272 feet with a circumference of 102 feet, a 36.5-foot diameter, and a volume of 52,508 cubic feet.

Despite their sheer beauty, size, and limited range, as compared to their prehistoric status, the redwoods have been ruthlessly exploited (in the name of human progress) to near eradication. It was the onslaught generated by the modern machine/industrial age, with its insatiable appetite for natural resources, that took a devastating toll on the remaining stands of redwoods. As early as 1930 Walter Fry and John R. White observed and reflected upon the wanton destruction of the redwoods by the persistent devices of humanity. They feared that the California giants would eventually join the extinct realm of the passenger pigeon, dodo, and the great auk due to reckless human folly and greed. They succinctly pointed out that the patient work of nature over thousands of years was simply disappearing in a single day by the force of the axe, the saw, and dynamite. Their warnings were heeded but were short-lived.

Prized for durable, decorative wood, redwoods were cut at an alarming rate—more than a billion board-feet a year for nearly twenty-five years. By the 1930s one-third of the forests had been leveled. By the early 1960s only about 5 percent of the original stands remained, and the redwoods that had not become houses, boats, or bridges were in private hands only too willing to shake those of the western timber barons.

Protection for the groves developed slowly during the twentieth century. Ironically, it is easier to destroy a forest than protect one. In an instrumental sense the wasting of the sequoias have played a large role in arousing general sentiment against the depletion of all our trees. In 1902 Big Basin became the first redwood park. Today there are more than forty state and national parks and forests that contain big tree groves. Given the decline in redwoods the Sierra Club recognized that federal protection of the surviving trees was an ecological necessity. The threat of annihilation persists against the redwoods simply because important stands remain vulnerable, and questions abound about the meaning of "protection."

Due to the persevering efforts of the Sierra Club and after years of political battling, Congress in 1968 approved a fragmented park that meandered down the coast for forty miles. Despite passage of the Redwood National Park Act in 1968 the chainsaws of Georgia-Pacific, Simpson, and Arcata Redwood hit the virgin trees on the steep, fragile slopes bordering the newly designated National Park. Knowing that Congress would not act to expand the park's boundary in order to save additional trees, the Sierra Club took legal action through the newly founded Sierra Club Legal Defense Fund and subsequently filed suit against the National Park Service to force the agency to protect the park from encroaching logging activity on its boundaries.

Perhaps the greatest move toward preservation came with the 1978 expansion of Redwood National Park. Although the acquired land included park-quality trees the bulk of the addition was marred by sixty square miles of clearcuts, skid roads, and haul trails which cumulatively threatened downstream parklands. In response to this tragic environmental phenomenon a $33 million restoration project, the largest in National Park Service history, is now half complete and nearly all the logging roads in the park have been obliterated and 750,000 redwoods and Douglas firs have been planted on the cutover lands.

This action clearly represents the hope that the redwood forest will be able to survive and thrive. It is also important to keep in mind that the old-growth virgin forests remain vulnerable to extinction and it is here that we as a society must decide whether to destroy the primordial past or preserve the future of these truly beautiful natural and very "big" creations.

Joseph Michael Pace

Further Readings

Carranco, Lynwood, and John T. Labbe. *Logging the Redwoods.* 1975.

Fry, Walter, and John R. White. *Big Trees.* 1930.

Leydet, Francois. *The Last Redwoods and the Parkland of Redwood Creek.* 1969.

Turner, Tom. "Redwood Visions." *Sierra* 77 (March-April 1992): 26–28.

See also MINERAL KING CANYON; NATIONAL PARK SERVICE (U.S.); NATIONAL PARKS: UNITED STATES; SIERRA CLUB

Reforestation
See FOREST REGENERATION/REFORESTATION

Regulation
Environmental regulation establishes maximum acceptable levels of pollutants in air, water, soil, and other environmental media; specifies how emissions of hazardous pollutants are to be controlled; and how substances or activities hazardous to human health or the environment shall be managed to prevent unacceptable health or environmental risks from exposure. Until 1970 few environmental regulations existed in the United States, except for legislation concerned with public health or safety. The several federal pollution laws enacted in the 1960s did not encourage active federal or state pollution control. Essentially, pollution control was considered a state and local responsibility, but not a compelling one.

A dramatic change occurred with the outpouring of federal environmental legislation between 1970 and 1990. During this period twenty-seven of the thirty-six federal environmental pollution laws were written. Among the most important legislative enactments are the Clean Air Act (1970), the Federal Water Pollution Control Act Amendments (1972), the Toxic Substances Control Act (1976), the Resource Conservation and Recovery Act (1976), the Comprehensive Environmental Response, Compensation, and Liability Act or "Superfund" (1980), together with major amendments later. Additionally, President Richard Nixon in 1970 created by executive order the Environmental Protection Agency (EPA) to be the principal federal agency for implementing and enforcing federal environmental legislation. EPA is the largest federal environmental regulator, but responsibility for enforcing environmental regulations is divided among more than twenty agencies. Many state and local governments responded to these federal initiatives with additional laws. The new legislation fundamentally altered the nation's approach to governmental regulation by creating new regulatory federalism in which Washington assumed the primary authority to set pollution control standards which the states were expected to implement. And, unlike previous federal regulations, the new environmental regulation significantly affected almost all important economic sectors.

The new legislation was partially a response to growing evidence of environmental pollution and highly publicized environmental crisis. Equally important to its creation were vigorous bipartisan congressional support, skillful promotion by increasingly influential environmental organizations, growing political activism among scientists and increased middle-class concern about quality-of-life issues.

These environmental laws exemplify a "command-and-control" style of regulation involving: 1) a statement of regulatory goals, such as the elimination of all pollution discharges into navigable bodies of water, declared in the Federal Water Pollution Control Act Amendments (1972); 2) the acquisition by regulatory agencies of scientific data concerning the health and environmental impacts of suspected pollutants; 3) the creation by regulatory agencies of quality standards that specify the maximum acceptable concentration of regulated pollutants—in effect, what will legally be considered "pollution"; 4) the determination by regulatory agencies of emission standards that specify the maximum permissible pollution emissions from all important sources and, often, the acceptable control practices; and 5) the creation of enforcement procedures for emission controls, usually involving a permit system for polluters associated and sanctions for noncompliance.

These laws often set emission standards unachievable with technologies existing at the time. This "technology forcing," which frequently failed, assumed that required control technologies would be developed if compelled by legislation. Congress, impatient at the pace of regulation and distrustful of EPA, also packed environmental laws with progressively more numerous and stringent deadlines for program accomplishment. Between 1970 and 1990 the EPA was legislatively ordered to meet about 800 such statutory deadlines and failed about 80 percent of the time. While Congress has attempted to micro-manage the EPA in many other ways through regulatory laws, legislators have still been compelled to allow the EPA, and other regulatory agencies, great discretion in determining how to implement the laws due to the technical complexity, the lack of scientific information and the inexperience associated with environmental programs.

Federal environmental laws are highly controversial. They inevitably draw the EPA and other federal regulatory agencies into the political and scientific disputes common to risk analysis. Moreover, traditional economists are outspoken critics of command-and-control regulation which they believe is economically inefficient and administratively underproductive. They assert that existing regulatory policies lack the financial incentives to encourage better compliance by regulated interests, and that more efficient emission controls can be achieved if decisions about appropriate technologies are left to regulated interests as well. Additionally, regulated interests commonly complain of regulation's excessive costs and advocate, with most economists, that benefit-cost analysis should be routinely required for any environmental regulation.

Scientists have also criticized federal regulatory laws for focusing upon a single environmental medium such as air or water, for specifying different risk criteria for each program, and for dividing regulation among many different agencies. Many experts also believe that the EPA's priorities should be altered in two important respects: 1) regulatory emphasis should shift from end-of-pipe controls to preventing the creation of pollutants; and 2) the agency should have a clear set of pollution control priorities based on scientific evidence about the relative risks from various pollutants. These problems also illustrate the congressional habit of reacting to pollution problems by creating new regulatory laws without concern for consistency or clear program priorities and, often, without convincing scientific evidence of the problem's seriousness. In recent years, minority leaders have also argued that regulatory programs have discriminated against the underprivileged by exposing them inequitably to risks from hazardous facilities such as toxic waste sites.

Compelling evidence of disappointing program accomplishments has gradually persuaded many environmentalists that radical reform of existing regulatory programs may be essential. With relatively few exceptions, such as the impressive urban air pollution reductions achieved by the Clean Air Act, most regulatory programs do not appear very successful. The most conspicuous difficulties involve the regulation of toxic substances, the "Superfund" Act, and control of many major surface and groundwater contaminants, such as nonpoint runoff. Environmental leaders and organizations have been more willing to recognize that these failures betray many of the problems noted by regulatory critics.

A number of significant regulatory reforms have already been implemented. These include provisions in the 1990 Clean Air Act Amendments permitting limited "emissions trading" and other kinds of marketplace strategies endorsed by economists to provide economic incentives for regulated interests to control their emission of acid precipitation precursors. Another measure is the Pollution Prevention Act, passed by Congress in 1991, requiring EPA and its regulated polluters to give increasing attention to pollution prevention strategies. Amendments to the Resource Conservation and Recovery Act, the Safe Drinking Water Act and "Superfund" passed in the 1980s have given the states greater latitude for innovation in implementing these major programs. In the early 1990s the EPA initiated administrative procedures to encourage more coordinated pollution management across environmental media and to utilize scientific risk assessment more aggressively in determining its regulatory priorities. EPA has initiated administrative procedures to identify and to eliminate discriminatory regulatory practices.

Additional reforms are very likely in the 1990s. Among the most frequently advocated of these reforms are increasing use of "marketplace" alternatives to command-and-control regulation, more encouragement for innovative state and local regulation, and greater concern for the protection of whole ecosystems. The 1990s will be crucial in determining the fate of existing regulatory programs. If the array of legislative programs enacted in the 1970s and 1980s cannot be invigorated by reform in the 1990s, powerful economic and political pressures will mount for a radical restructuring of the national regulatory regime.

Walter A. Rosenbaum

Further Readings

Bryner, Gary C. *Blue Skies, Green Politics: The Clean Air Act of 1990.* 1993.

Portney, Kent E. *Controversial Issues in Environmental Policy: Science vs. Economics vs. Politics.* 1992.

Portney, Paul, ed. *Public Policies for Environmental Protection.* 1990.

See also AIR POLLUTION: REGULATION (U.S.); ENVIRONMENTAL PROTECTION AGENCY; POLLUTION PREVENTION; STANDARD SETTING; SUPERFUND

Reilly, William

See BUSH, GEORGE; ENVIRONMENTAL PROTECTION AGENCY

Religion and Environmental Protection

The religions of humanity involve diverse worldviews and ways of living organized around what different peoples experience and value as sacred. Depending on its vision of the sacred and ethical standpoint, the religious faith and practice of a community or individual may deepen respect for nature and promote environmental protection, or it may encourage neglect and abuse of the environment.

Religion as Part of the Problem

The environmental problems that human beings have created are in part a reflection of the fundamental beliefs and values that guide human behavior, as well as other factors, such as ignorance and poverty. In recent decades a number of scholars have endeavored to show that the values and attitudes that have led Western industrialized societies to exploit nature ruthlessly have roots in the worldviews and moral thinking of Christianity and Judaism as well as other Western intellectual traditions.

For example, some claim that these religions are dualistic, separating God and the world, spirit and the earth, humanity and the larger community of life, and that thereby humanity is thought to have divine authorization to subdue and dominate nature. The result is an anthropocentric, patriarchal worldview in which nature apart from humans has only instrumental value and no intrinsic worth or sacred value. Consequently nature is denied respect, excluded from moral consideration, and exploited. Even though these harsh criticisms do not accurately describe the variety and complexity of Christian and Jewish teaching, there is some truth in them with respect to certain parts of these traditions. They also suggest how the myths, symbols, and rituals of a religion may influence the way people understand and interact with their environments.

Religion as Part of the Solution
Recognizing the relevance of religion to conservation, a small but growing number of historians, philosophers, and theologians have scrutinized the variety of religious traditions for ideas that encourage the abuse of nature. But more than this they have also worked: 1) to retrieve those aspects of religious traditions that have positive ecological value; and 2) to reconstruct the major living religious traditions so that they unambiguously teach respect for the whole community of life. The religious thinkers who undertake these tasks are keenly aware that whatever a people value as sacred commands deep respect and is likely to be cherished and protected.

Regarding the work of retrieval Christian and Jewish scholars have endeavored to show that despite criticisms leveled against it their sacred scripture actually contains elements of a land ethic grounded in a theocentric worldview that forbids a destructive anthropocentric attitude toward nature. Some Islamic philosophers have focused attention on the sacramental nature of the entire creation in classical Islamic thought. Reacting against the patriarchal image of God in Western culture, some ecofeminists have tried to revive the ancient worship of the Goddess, the great earth mother, as providing a non-dualistic understanding of spirit and nature and a religious basis for a biocentric ethics.

Others turn to Eastern religions. Buddhist philosophy, for example, conceives the universe as an evolving organic whole and emphasizes the interdependence of the individual and nature, teaching a reverence for all life and the practice of *ahimsa* or non-injury. The recent surge of interest in the spiritual teachings and practices of North American Indians and other indigenous peoples has been prompted in part by a sense that these traditions contain an ecological wisdom, including a sense of the sacredness of nature and the interdependence of all life, that has been lost by industrialized societies.

The ecological reconstruction of a faith requires the recovery of forgotten environmental values and also new visions and practices adequate to the challenges of the contemporary global situation. Christian and Jewish thinkers have attempted to recover and develop pantheistic visions of God that emphasize the immanence of the divine in nature as well as transcendence. Some theologians imagine the universe as God's body. In general ecological reconstructions seek to integrate religious and moral vision with contemporary biology, ecology, and physics and the new scientific understanding of cosmogenesis. Equally important is the endeavor of each faith to find its own unique pathway to a shared global ethic of peace, justice, and sustainable living. The concept of environmental justice is increasingly used to connect environment and issues of social equity.

Religious traditions commonly nurture faith and moral action with methods of spiritual growth, some of which may be of benefit to environmental conservation. All of the major world religions emphasize that one primary objective of spiritual practice is the overcoming of self-centeredness and the expansion of an individual's sense of community with and caring for others. Methods of spiritual transformation that extend care and compassion to future generations and to animals and other living beings can inspire environmental protection.

Throughout the world there are an increasing number of organizations and movements that link religion and environmental activism. For example, the Hindu faith is a major force in the Chipko movement in India, which has fought successfully to protect Himalayan forests. The World Wide Fund for Nature has formed an international Network on Conservation and Religion. A program on "Justice, Peace and the Integrity of Creation" has been instituted by the World Council of Churches. Shomrei Adamah (Keepers of the Earth) seeks to promote environmental stewardship through traditional Jewish wisdom and spirituality. The National Religious Partnership for the Environment in the United States has brought together leaders from the Roman Catholic, Orthodox, mainline Protestant, historic Black, and evangelical churches, as well as from the major Jewish religious communities to cooperate in establishing programs of environmental education and protection that will involve millions of citizens.

A mature religious faith involves a wholehearted trust in and commitment to a liberating vision of the moral and spiritual ideal. If the environmental movement is to effect a lasting transformation of the way people live and do business it will need support from the vision and inspiration of a new shared social faith that is religious in quality, nurtured by artists, poets, educators, and religious leaders, as well as scientists and political leaders.

Steven C. Rockefeller

Further Readings

Adams, Carol, ed. *Ecofeminism and the Sacred.* 1993.

Birch, Charles, William Eakin, and Jay B. McDaniel. *Liberating Life: Contemporary Approaches to Ecological Theology.* 1990.

Brown, Joseph Epes. *The Spiritual Legacy of the American Indian.* 1990.

Nash, James A. *Loving Nature: Ecological Integrity and Christian Responsibility.* 1991.

Nash, Roderick Frazier. *The Rights of Nature: A History of Environmental Ethics.* 1989.

Prime, Ranchor. *Hinduism and Ecology: Seeds of Truth.* 1992.

Rockefeller, Steven C., and John C. Elder, eds. *Spirit and Nature: Why the Environment is a Religious Issue.* 1992.

Spretnak, Charlene. *States of Grace: The Recovery of Meaning in the Postmodern Age.* 1991.

Swimme, Brian, and Thomas Berry. *The Universe Story: From the Primordial Flaring Forth to the Ecozoic Era—A Celebration of the Unfolding of the Cosmos.* 1992.

See also ANTHROPOCENTRISM; ASIAN ENVIRONMENTAL THOUGHT; CHIPKO MOVEMENT; ECO-SPIRITUALITY; INTRINSIC VALUE; LAND ETHIC

Reptiles: Conservation and Habitat

The conservation of reptiles is gaining momentum and organizations and agencies that once overlooked these taxa are now evaluating them in their decisions to designate protected areas and preserve habitat.

The status of crocodilians, snakes, lizards, turtles, and the tuatara, and their conservation is being dealt with on a number of international fronts. The International Union for the Conservation of Nature and Natural Resources (IUCN) Species Survival Commission, through its specialist groups is currently establishing lists of species that are in need of conservation or habitat protection. In addition, various countries are assessing the plight of endemic reptiles, and the general public, on the whole, appears to be more accepting of these creatures. Although the fate of the spotted owl, killer whale, Florida panther, and other such "high-profile" species garner more press coverage and debate about the preservation of habitats, a variety of reptile taxa are now being afforded that consideration in many political arenas and public forums.

Historically it was only those reptile species that had human appeal that were considered worthy of protection and concern—such as the sea turtles. However, in these relatively enlightened times, even species frequently considered repulsive, such as the San Francisco garter snake and the American crocodile, now have their supporters, and their habitats are being preserved in an effort to maintain the remaining populations of these endangered species.

Sea turtles, having greater appeal to humans and of greater economic importance than other species of reptiles, have received more attention and conservation effort over the years. The collection of turtle eggs from nesting beaches, the slaughter of turtles for meat, oil, and shell, and the incidental drowning of turtles in trawler's nets has received international press coverage and public reaction. This has resulted in the protection of nesting beaches, consortia to collect eggs for artificial incubation and hatchling release, and lobbyists to press for legislation mandating the use of turtle extruder devices (TEDs) in trawler's nets.

In North America unique species such as the San Francisco garter snake (*Thamnophis sirtalis tetrataenia*) and the Coachella Valley fringe-toed lizard (*Uma inornata*) have actually been at the forefront of major controversies regarding construction projects and economic concerns in efforts to preserve their remaining habitat. For the first time in years governments and nongovernmental organizations are looking at endangered reptiles and the threatened habitats of these animals when considering the classification of wetlands and areas of environmental significance for protection.

Commercial exploitation of crocodilians for their hides, iguanas and turtles for the pet trade, and sea turtles for the soup pot has been slowed by the Convention on International Trade in Endangered Species of Wild Fauna and Flora (CITES) legislation, concerns of local government, and public protest. Commercial farming and ranching operations for the captive propagation of crocodilians have been established in many countries, including Colombia, Venezuela, Guyana, Brazil, Zimbabwe, New Guinea, and the United States. The South American countries mentioned plus Panama and Costa Rica have also been instrumental in spearheading captive breeding efforts for the green iguana (*Iguana iguana*). This has already proven to dramatically decrease the number of wild caught specimens taken from these countries. The effort is also creating tremendous interest among local residents and, in many areas, is the first real environmental conservation ethic practiced.

Ecotourism also has had an effect by publishing the plight of some reptiles such as the Galapagos tortoises, Komodo monitor, and the sea turtles. In some cases the revenues derived from these tours is directed toward the conservation of the species involved, or in saving a part of their habitat. This industry, as it continues to grow in the future, will need to take precautions so that it does not become so commercial as to be a threat to the very species it is publicizing.

In many parts of the world the situation is no better, and, in fact is even worse than it was ten years ago. Many species and habitats continue to be destroyed or go unprotected. Madagascar is a case in point. Not only are areas of habitat in Madagascar disappearing at an alarming rate, but large numbers of rare and endangered reptiles are being exported "quasi-legally" to the pet trade from that country. Although the Madagascar officials appear to have recognized the unique status of their mammal and bird populations, the reptiles and amphibians are still regarded as second-class citizens when it comes to protection, and when the financial temptation is great.

The concerns of reptile conservation have been addressed at numerous meetings over the past decade or two. Two world congresses on herpetology, a wide variety of symposia, and special task forces in many countries around the globe have examined the plight of endangered reptile species. Although the answers to many concerns may not yet be known, the process is in place, and this class of animals is being given serious consideration as never before.

Although the complete picture is very discouraging there is optimism for some species and some habitats and it is encouraging to record the success that has been achieved in the past few years. It is hoped that more will be done—more expediently in the future.

Thomas A. Huff

Further Readings

Wilson, E.O. *The Diversity of Life*. 1992.
Tortoise and Freshwater Turtle Specialist Group. *Tortoises and Freshwater Turtles: An Action Plan for their Conservation.* IUCN, 2nd ed., 1991.

See also CITES; ECOTOURISM; EVERGLADES OF SOUTH FLORIDA; IUCN; SEA TURTLES; WILDLIFE PROTECTION: HISTORY

Reserve Mining Controversy

The Reserve Mining Company of Silver Bay, Minnesota, during the 1970s was at the center of what was then the most expensive and most complex environmental dispute in history (the costs of litigation for all parties totaled many tens of millions of dollars).

Reserve had pioneered the processing of taconite (low-grade iron ore) in the 1950s. Under permits issued by the state of Minnesota and the U.S. Army Corps of Engineers, Reserve commenced full operations in 1955. Taconite ore was mined inland, shipped forty-seven miles on a company-owned rail line, and processed at a plant on the shore of Lake Superior. Ore pellets were then shipped to steel mills from a company harbor. Huge volumes of ground waste rock were deposited directly into the lake; after the last expansion of the plant this amounted to approximately 67,000 tons per day.

Complaints that Reserve was harming Lake Superior ecologically and aesthetically began to be widely heard in the late 1960s. Studies of the impact of Reserve's operations on Lake Superior were undertaken by the U.S. government in advance of permit revalidation proceedings. The resulting critical report, although never officially released, was leaked to the press. Most of the attention of a subsequent Lake Superior enforcement conference was directed at the issue of Reserve's lake disposal. The conference met several times from 1969–1971 without producing any resolution to the controversy.

In 1972 the U.S. Environmental Protection Agency (EPA) sued Reserve for water pollution violations. In 1973, during final preparations for the trial, EPA and the Minnesota Pollution Control Agency announced discovery that Reserve's tailings, present in the municipal water supply of Duluth and other communities drawing from the lake, were very similar to asbestos. The focus of the trial shifted from pollution to public health. Developments in the controversy were widely reported.

The presiding judge concluded the nine-month trial in April 1974 by finding against Reserve and ordering it to end immediately all discharges to air or Lake Superior. The court of appeals also found against Reserve, but ordered that the company be given time to develop an acceptable on-land disposal site. Following involved and protracted political, administrative, and legal proceedings which lasted until April 1978 Reserve was issued permits for an on-land disposal facility. The $370 million project, which included expenditures for air pollution control, was completed by early 1980, whereupon Reserve ceased disposing its wastes directly into Lake Superior.

In addition to being a fascinating story and an important episode in environmental history, the way the Reserve Mining case was handled by the courts has continuing relevance to the regulation of hazardous substances on the basis of risk. *Reserve Mining v. EPA* is still one of the most significant decisions in environmental law and has been cited in dozens of cases.

Robert V. Bartlett

Further Readings

Bartlett, Robert V. *The Reserve Mining Controversy: Science, Technology, and Environmental Quality.* 1980.

Farber, Daniel A. "Risk Regulation in Perspective: *Reserve Mining* Revisited." *Environmental Law* 21 (1991): 1321-57.

See also GREAT LAKES; MINING AND SMELTING: HISTORIC IMPACTS; STRIP MINING OF COAL: A HISTORY; ARMY CORPS OF ENGINEERS (U.S.)

Resource Accounting

Macroeconomic management makes extensive use of the national economic accounts which record monetary flows and transactions within the economy. The primary purpose of the accounts is to record economic activity, not to measure aggregate well-being in the nation. Nonetheless national accounts are widely used to indicate well-being and rates of change in national aggregates such as gross national product (GNP) are widely construed as measures of "development." Whether the accounts are designed to record economic activity or measure well-being or both they are deficient in respect of their treatment of natural resources. Economic activity involves the use of materials and energy and, once transformed into products, those same resources become, sooner or later, waste products. Any measure of economic activity which ignores these materials and energy flows will fail to record important activities which affect the sustainability of the economic activity. In the same way any measure of well-being which ignores the resource and energy flows will fail to measure sustainable well-being. For these reasons there is now widespread consensus that the national accounts need to be modified at least with respect to the way in which environmental "stocks" and "flows" are recorded.

Material and energy flows begin at the point of extraction, harvest, or use of natural resources. They end by being waste products, such as emissions to ambient environments, discharges to water, and solid waste to land or sea. Logically then GNP needs to be modified to account for:

- Any depreciation of natural capital stocks, in the same way that net national income equals gross national income less estimated depreciation on man-made capital. This is a measure of the "draw down" of natural capital;
- Any damage losses accruing to human well-being from the extraction, processing and disposal of materials and energy to receiving environments.

Both adjustments involve economic valuation. The first adjustment involves a valuation of the natural capital stock; the second involves valuation of such things as health impairment; pollution damage to buildings, crops, and trees; and aesthetic and recreational losses and other forms of "psychic" damage. National accountants do not agree on how best to make the appropriate adjustments. At the very least one form of adjustment to gross measures of national income would be:

Modified GNP = Conventional GNP
+ Value of Environmental Services
− Value of Environmental Damage.

For example, additions to national parks or improvements in pollution levels would be reflected in positive entries for modified GNP, and damage done would enter negatively. The way in which damage done should be measured is disputed. Some experts measure it by the expenditures necessary to offset the damage—the so-called defensive expenditures. Others wish to measure it using the kinds of valuation techniques which attempt to elicit willingness-to-pay (WTP) to avoid damage or to improve environmental quality. Under certain circumstances it happens that defensive expenditures are perfect measures of WTP, but the use of defensive expenditures generally to measure damage done is strongly disputed in the national accounting literature. Moreover, defensive expenditures include both final and intermediate expenditures, breaking the equivalence between factor incomes and expenditures which is fundamental to conventional national accounting. Defensive expenditures by firms tend to be intermediate expenditures, while those by households are final expenditures. It is significant that the literature showing how expenditures can be perfect measures of WTP relates only to the household context.

Depreciation on stocks of natural capital also requires valuation and is relevant if the interest is in some measure of sustainable income—the income that a nation can receive without running down its capital base. In the conventional accounts this is partly accounted for by estimating net national product (NNP) which is defined as:

$$NNP = GNP - D_k$$

where D_k is the depreciation on man-made capital (machines, roads, buildings). The further adjustment that is required is:

$$NNP = GNP - D_k - D_n$$

where D_n is the depreciation of environmental assets.

Thus far there is no formalized structure for compiling resource accounts although some countries do compile satellite accounts for sectors such as water and forestry. Most other direct adjustments attempt to deduct environmental costs from GNP and estimate the depreciation on natural capital stocks. The de-

bate on which are the appropriate modifications is ongoing.

Dominic Moran

Further Readings

Pearce, D.W., and J. Warford. *World without End: Economic Environment and Sustainable Development.* 1993.

Peskin, H.M. *Accounting for Natural Resource Depletion and Degradation in Developing Countries.* 1989.

See also CONTINGENT VALUATION; ECONOMIC GROWTH AND THE ENVIRONMENT; GREEN ECONOMICS; SUSTAINABLE DEVELOPMENT

Resource Conservation and Recovery Act

The Resource Conservation and Recovery Act (RCRA) was passed in 1976 with the dual goals of: 1) protecting health and the environment; and 2) conserving valuable energy resources. These goals were to be accomplished by controlling the disposal of solid and hazardous waste and by encouraging resource recovery and conversion. It replaced the Solid Waste Disposal Act, which had been passed in 1965 and amended in 1970. RCRA was itself amended in 1984 and its reauthorization is presently being considered by the U.S. Congress.

Content of RCRA

RCRA deals with the responsibilities of federal and state solid waste management programs. It creates a regulatory framework to provide for acceptable solid waste disposal and encourages recycling, energy recovery, and conservation. It also provides significant guidance for the regulation and management of hazardous materials. This includes setting safety standards for the production, transportation, use, and disposal of hazardous materials.

Part of RCRA involves a tracking system which requires the U.S. Environmental Protection Agency (EPA) and the states to monitor and control hazardous waste at every point in the waste cycle. Hazardous wastes are defined in both generic terms (as ignitable, corrosive, reactive, or toxic) and by listing specific wastes and industrial waste streams. Generators (including businesses, universities, and hospitals) must determine whether their wastes are hazardous and oversee the ultimate fate of the waste. Firms handling hazardous wastes at any stage of the process are also required to obtain a permit from the EPA or an authorized state agency.

Reauthorization

RCRA was reauthorized in 1984 with the passage of the Hazardous and Solid Waste Amendments (HSWA). Regulations are now in place which forbid land disposal of certain hazardous wastes unless EPA rules that such disposal will not endanger human health or the environment. Landfilling of bulk or non-containerized liquids is now prohibited. There is also a ban on disposal of bulk liquids in salt domes, using oil contaminated with hazardous wastes as a suppressant, and injection of hazardous waste into or above any underground source of drinking water. At the same time industry is encouraged to pursue methods of hazardous waste disposal other than land-based containment.

The 1984 amendments also reduced the amount of waste exempted from regulatory coverage from 1,000 kilograms (2,200 pounds) to 100 kilograms (220 pounds) per month. In addition the EPA is empowered to regulate companies producing less than 100 kilograms of waste per month if it is deemed necessary to protect public health. Furthermore owners of underground storage tanks containing petroleum or other hazardous substances are required to meet new regulatory guidelines for continuous monitoring to ensure the early detection and correction of leaks.

Present and Future Considerations

RCRA and its 1984 amendments expired in 1988. While Congress has continued to appropriate funding it has not been able to reach consensus on reauthorization. One issue blocking RCRA is a dispute over the interstate transportation of garbage. The increasing tide of garbage the nation generates, combined with the dwindling number of landfills in which to place it, has generated bitter conflicts between states and regions which import and export solid waste, mostly in the form of municipal trash.

A second issue centers around environmentalists' attempts to have incinerator ash classified as hazardous waste. (Incineration is one of the three major options for waste disposal, along with recycling and using landfills.)

A third issue blocking reauthorization is the effort by several congressional leaders to put in place a national bottle-deposit system that mandates the recycling of glass, plastic, and metal beverage containers. Finally, there exists an array of concerns involving the disposal of hazardous industrial waste (estimated to be about 7.6 billion tons nationwide), which essentially remains unregulated.

Leslie R. Alm

Further Readings

Collins, John P., and Walter P. Saukin. *The Hazardous Waste Dilemma: Issues and Solutions.* 1981.
Davis, Charles E. *The Politics of Hazardous Waste.* 1993.
Schumacher, Aileen. *A Guide to Hazardous Materials Management.* 1988.

See also DEEP-WELL INJECTION; ENVIRONMENTAL PROTECTION AGENCY; HAZARDOUS WASTE TREATMENT TECHNOLOGIES; MUNICIPAL SOLID WASTE: INCINERATION; RECYCLING

Resource Management

Resource management is the attempt to maximize present net benefits derived from the utilization of resources. The decision concerning the best time to use resources is called intertemporal assignment. Resources will be consumed earlier if the expected return in the present is greater than it is in the future. The value of future resource utilization depreciates by a certain rate over time. This rate—the discount rate—represents the common wisdom that money today is worth more than money tomorrow.

Resource management involves balancing intertemporal assignments so the total capital stock (the source of income) is not reduced. The total capital stock consists of natural capital (K_n), human capital (K_h), manufactured capital (K_m), and cultural/moral capital (K_c). The rate of resource exploitation is based upon the discount rate, with higher rates implying that the resource will be consumed in earlier periods.

Various resources may be managed under this conceptualization: depletable (e.g., oil, natural gas), renewable (e.g., trees, migratory birds, fish), or environmental (e.g., air, water). No specification is made on how value is to be assigned to resources, what discount rate is appropriate, or how intertemporal assignments should be judged. Firms or governments may use this approach for managing resources. Private actors may use a higher discount rate than governments, raising the problem that private actors might exploit resources faster than society would prefer. Private actors are more likely to exploit resources which can be captured by private property regimes. This makes private management of public goods such as migratory birds or air unlikely.

Management models differ in how values are assumed to be represented and by substitutability among resource types. A neoclassical-economic model assumes that the future is at least as well-off as the present so long as the total capital stock $(K_n + K_h + K_c + K_m)$ does not decrease. For example, the use of natural capital (wood) to build a house transforms it into manufactured capital, but the total capital stock remains at least constant. Furthermore there is no preference for any given resource; individuals value the services derived from their use. For instance it does not matter if a pot is copper or aluminum since the goal is to obtain a device in which to heat water. This lack of preference is termed perfect substitutability of resources. The valuation of resources, in this model, is that which rational individuals assign to resources (an "egocentric" perspective). This valuation reflects both preferences and scarcity, and is seen in prices for many resources where markets are viable.

A second model of resource management insists that not all resources are perfectly substitutable. The so-called "London School" advocates protection of certain critical natural resources, such as air and water. Adherents argue that natural resources should be protected unless the societal opportunity costs associated with not exploiting the resource are sufficiently great. Current use of resources must be offset by an increase in the total capital stock to account for the loss of the resource to future generations. Value should be assigned not by individuals but by reference to humanity as a whole (an anthropocentric view). While accepting maintenance of the total capital stock, this school dictates *a priori* certain resources are critical and should be protected for humanity.

A third approach emphasizes the immorality of conceiving of the environment as a bundle of goods and services for human use. Most resources have an intrinsic value which must be respected (an ecocentric view); the valuation of resources from either an individual or a societal perspective is wrong. In this school of thought K_n is critical and should be maintained even at the cost of foregoing economic development. Since the scale of resource consumption necessarily increases with population this school also advocates a steady-state population and economic activity.

Advocates of the neoclassical economic position are coming to accept the need for an ecosystems approach to managing the resources. It is impossible to protect a resource if the surrounding ecosystem is undermined. For example, the preservation of a species of bird is meaningless if its habitat is destroyed by farmers applying DDT. Many benefits are derived from ecosystems and these benefits are often not priced: trees are not only a resource for human use, but a habitat for animals as well. Many economists, therefore, believe it is important to consider the resource not in isolation, but rather the full range of benefits a resource provides within an ecosystem.

The rate of resource extraction may be slowed with reductions in original resource input. In the short-term recycling can assist in forestalling resource depletion. By decreasing the need for inputs which have not previously been used (virgin inputs), one can extend resources. Recycling can be especially critical for nonrenewable resources, since it is not possible to regenerate these resources once depleted. Recycling has limits, however: there will always be need for some virgin material input, and recycling requires inputs of its own. The second law of thermodynamics dictates that the amount of recovery from recycling will be less than 100 percent—some of the resource is always lost. Some materials change their properties under recycling; paper is recyclable, but its fiber length and tensile strength decrease with each cycle. The Environmental Protection Agency recommends the best way to conserve resources is through a reduction in the amount of virgin materials used. In the long run it is necessary to move from nonrenewable to renewable resources.

Kevin H. Olson

Further Readings
Turner, R. Kerry, ed. *Sustainable Environmental Economics and Management.* 1993.

See also DISCOUNTING THE FUTURE; GREEN ECONOMICS; INTRINSIC VALUE; NONRENEWABLE RESOURCES; RECYCLING; RESOURCISM

Resource Management Act (New Zealand)

Until 1991 environmental law in New Zealand was as fragmented as in any other jurisdiction. The Resource Management Act 1991 provides for integrated management of all natural and physical resources except minerals. Access to minerals is governed by the Crown Minerals Act 1991 while the environmental aspects of mineral development are regulated by the Resource Management Act. The system is directed toward the sustainable management of natural and physical resources.

The act contains nine structural elements: 1) the purpose of the act; 2) the principles declared by the act; 3) national environmental standards; 4) national policy statements; 5) New Zealand coastal policy statements; 6) regional policy statements; 7) regional plans; 8) district plans; and 9) resource consents. The relationship between these elements is set out in the legislation. Sustainable management as the purpose of the act in section 5 sits at the apex of the system. This is complemented by the duty in section 6 to recognize and provide for stated matters of national importance; the duty in section 7 to have particular regard to prescribed other matters; and the duty in section 8 to take into account the principles of the Treaty of Waitangi. Each of the management instruments provided by the legislation is linked in discrete ways to the purpose of the act and hence to the other principles stated by the legislation. Consistency is the test which governs the relationship among plans and policy statements. National environmental standards are directly enforceable regulations. The terms and conditions of a resource consent constitute legally enforceable rights and obligations.

The definition of "sustainable management" in section 5(2) is critical to the philosophy driving the legislation. It may be paraphrased to refer on the one hand to the use, development, and protection of resources from the human perspective and, on the other hand, to their sustainability in human, ecological, and environmental terms. Although the protection of the environment is not the purpose of the act, the environment and the values of the environment play a critical role. Thus:

- In section 5(2)(c) the avoidance of adverse effects of activities on the environment is part of sustainable management.
- In section 6 the preservation and protection of particular aspects of the natural environment are matters of national importance.
- In section 7 amenity values, ecological values, heritage values, and the maintenance and enhancement of the quality of the environment are other matters to which there must be particular regard.
- In section 12 a general duty is placed on every person to avoid any adverse effect on the environment.
- In section 104(4)(g) a requirement is made that a determination of an application for a resource consent shall have regard among others to sections 5, 6, and 7.
- In section 105(2) the grant of a resource consent for a non-complying activity is prevented, unless the determining authority is satisfied, having considered the matters in section 104, that any effect on the environment will be minor.

Does the act (section 5 in particular) specify priorities that will be afforded clear and unequivocal judicial recognition? Four decisions—three of the Planning Tribunal and one of the High Court—have commented on this. In two the issue turned upon amenity values, included in the definition of "environment." Although section 5(2) contemplates the avoidance of adverse effects of activities on the environment there is no specific reference in section 5 to amenity values. The maintenance and enhancement of amenity values are a matter for particular consideration under section 7(c) and the maintenance and enhancement of the quality of the environment under section 7(f). Thus in seeking to protect amenity the Planning Tribunal relied upon section 7 and not upon section 5.

In *Marlborough* the Tribunal commented at 280 "we must pay particular regard to the s[ection] 5 *principle*, and in doing so bear in mind that the Act places *strong emphasis* upon sustainable management." However, the act does not refer to section 5 as a principle nor does it express itself in terms of emphases. In *Shell Oil* the Tribunal said at 85 and 86 "we are not required to have regard to s. 5, it being the only section in Part II without such directions, but we nevertheless consider that great weight must be afforded a section which sets forth the *base philosophy* of the whole Act." But section 5 is the purpose of the act and not a matter for consideration, however important it might be.

Different reasons prompted a similar conclusion in *Kennett*. The obligation in section 104(2) was to have regard to the provisions in Part II and no account was taken of their nature. However, at 31 "the matters in Part II of the Act, which are referred to in s[ection]

104(4)(g) are not necessarily to be given the primacy that one might otherwise expect having regard to the way in which they are expressed in Part II." The High Court has endorsed this approach by pointing out that the act neither expressly nor by inference specified the weight to be attached to the general purpose of the act in the application of section 104. This is so since a statement of purpose is intrinsically different from the question of weight to be attached to competing considerations. Section 104 was thus applied within its own context and without reference to section 5.

The critical question of the status and effect of section 5 has so far been avoided. Until this point is answered judicially, it is not possible to assert that the statement of purpose in section 5 creates by its very nature either priority or overriding legal effect. Once this is determined, then the legal direction of resource management will become clear.

Douglas E. Fisher

Further Readings

Fisher, Douglas. "The Resource Management Legislation of 1991: A Juridical Analysis of Its Objectives." In *Resource Management*. Brooker & Friend Ltd. 1991, 1–30.
High Court. *Batchelor v. Tauranga District Council*. (1992) 2 N.Z.R.M.A. 137.
Planning Tribunal. *Marlborough Hockey Assoc. Inc. v. Marlborough District Council*. (1992) 1 N.Z.R.M.A. 274.
———. *Shell Oil New Zealand Ltd v. Wellington City Council*. (1992) 2 N.Z.R.M.A. 80.
———. *Kennett v. Dunedin City Council*. (1992) 2 N.Z.R.M.A. 22.

See also ENVIRONMENTAL CASE LAW: NEW ZEALAND; NONRENEWABLE RESOURCES; RESOURCE MANAGEMENT; TREATY OF WAITANGI (NEW ZEALAND)

Resourcism

Resourcism is a term of relatively recent origin used to depict that manner of viewing the world which reduces virtually everything to two entities: people and resources. Since by "resources" we generally mean anything which can be bent to human use or consumption, then virtually anything is potentially a resource. All that is required to achieve that designation is the discovery of a use (as when we speak of the Amazon rainforest as a resource from which science may someday extract important medical benefits). But while it is commonplace to speak of resources (and nowadays even of "human resources"), the striking feature of resourcism is its tacit expectation that we exist solely in a domain of resources, whether of present use or potential use. In Heidegger's earlier terminology it is the view of the world as a "standing reserve" awaiting exploitation by human societies.

To its critics the disturbing feature of resourcism is the single, homogenizing system of value that it brings to its worldview. The flattening of the world to the single category of resource conceals or denies the diversity of existence and the plethora of value which humans, and other organisms, have typically encountered in their experience of the world. Resourcism constitutes a kind of "lowest common denominator" of material existence and makes it difficult or impossible to speak of a heterogeneity of values or to deal in anything except economic evaluation. Hence, the ubiquity of resourcist assumptions has a tendency to constrain debate to terms consistent with those assumptions, and to inhibit nonconformist considerations. Moreover, in reducing the categories of existence to two—humans and resources—resourcist assumptions reinforce the idea that all nonhuman beings are definable in terms of their utility to human societies. Such anthropocentric assumptions inevitably impede the possibility of altering the human-nonhuman interaction and reinforce the drive to global management, control, and exploitation.

Neil Evernden

Further Readings

Ehrenfeld, David. *The Arrogance of Humanism*. 1978.
Evernden, Neil. *The Natural Alien: Humankind and the Environment*. 2nd ed. 1993.
Livingston, John. *The Fallacy of Wildlife Conservation*. 1981.

See also ANIMAL RIGHTS; BIODEPLETION; DEEP ECOLOGY: MEANINGS; ECOPHILOSOPHY AND ECOPSYCHOLOGY; ENVIRONMENTAL ETHICS; ENVIRONMENTALISM; GAIA HYPOTHESIS; NATURE; NONRENEWABLE RESOURCES; RADICAL ENVIRONMENTALISM; RESOURCE MANAGEMENT; WHOLE EARTH IMAGE; WILDLIFE PROTECTION: HISTORY

Restoration Ecology

See ECOLOGICAL RESTORATION

Rhine River

The Rhine (Rhein, Rhin, Rijn) is the major river of Western Europe with a catchment basin covering ten countries, the main ones being Switzerland, Germany, France, and the Netherlands. It is an important shipping lane for a heavily industrialized area which also has a strong agricultural structure: economic production in its basin is second in the world. About 20 million people depend on the Rhine for their drinking water, out of a population of some 55 million in the basin.

River management began with the construction of dikes and levees as flood protection in the Middle Ages, which gradually increased erosion upstream and flood hazards downstream. A conflict over shipping rights between France and the Netherlands lead to the establishment of an international commission on navigation in 1815 and the conclusion of a treaty in 1831. The commission today addresses issues such as the safe transport of dangerous substances on board ships. Since the nineteenth century navigation on the Rhine was facilitated through the construction of weirs and locks which also harnessed the river for hydro-power generation and hindered the passage of fish. The meandering and shifting river with ecologically rich, natural flood plains was converted to a straight, fast-flowing and erosive shipping canal supporting little life.

In the late nineteenth century overfishing was the greatest threat to fish life—salmon stocks in particular—and an international commission was established to coordinate fishing regulations. Its function was soon redundant as fish stocks diminished with the onset of large-scale water pollution. The commission was eventually overtaken by the International Commission for the Protection of the Rhine against Pollution which today coordinates joint monitoring of water quality and incident alarm systems, provides for exchanges of information about pollution abatement techniques, and helps coordinate research.

Through these efforts and action taken by riparian countries, particularly the construction of sewage treatment plants, water pollution with "traditional" oxygen-demanding pollutants has decreased markedly since the 1960s. Progress, though insufficient, has been made concerning heavy metals and some micropollutants. A memory of past pollution remains in riverbed sediments which in some downstream stretches must be treated as hazardous waste. Significant pollution with "modern" substances, such as nitrilotriacetic acid (NTA) and ethylenediaminetetraacetic acid (EDTA), or chlorinated organic compounds, occurs from time to time and has to be met with specific reduction programs. The concentration of eutrophication-inducing nutrients in the river has increased in recent years as a result of the use of fertilizer and food concentrates in the agro-industry, and the reduction of these is now a protection priority.

Improving the quality of the Rhine became a priority after the fire on the Schweizerhalle site of Sandoz, the chemicals company in Basle, Switzerland. On November 1, 1986, nearly thirty tons of chemicals (mainly biocides) were flushed into the river with fire-fighting run-off killing aquatic life along its length. Although the pollution was an environmental disaster it provided the impetus to launch a program for ecological restoration—the Rhine Action Programme. This program is aimed at improving water quality so that migratory fish like salmon and sea trout return to the Rhine and its tributaries, guaranteeing drinking water production from the river, reducing sediment pollution so that it can safely be applied to agricultural land, and protecting the North Sea from Rhine pollution, including nutrients.

Measures now planned include the lowering or opening of dikes to restore flood plains and the construction of slow-flowing parallel backwaters as refuges for fish, plant, and bird life. Increasingly, river management on the Rhine takes account of the river's and associated ecosystems' ecological functions and shifts from yesterday's civil engineering approach to quantitative water management and today's environmental technology approach to pollution control toward ecological revival.

Consider finally the words of Samuel Taylor Coleridge, written in 1828 under the title *Cologne*:

> In Köhln, a town of monks and bones,
> And pavements fang'd with murderous stones,
> And rags, and hags, and hideous wenches;
> I counted two and seventy stenches,
> All well defined, and several stinks!
> Ye Nymphs that reign o'er sewers and sinks,

The river Rhine, it is well known,
Doth wash your city of Cologne;
But tell me Nymphs, what power
devine,
Shall henceforth wash the river
Rhine?

R. Andreas Kraemer

Further Readings

Kleij, W. van der, R.H. Dekker, H. Kersten, and J.A.W. de Wit. "Water Management of the River Rhine: Past, Present and Future." *European Water Pollution Control* 1 (1991): 9–18.

Schulte-Wülwer-Leidig, A. "International Commission for the Protection of the Rhine Against Pollution—The Integrated Ecosystem Approach for the Rhine." *European Water Pollution Control* 2 (1992): 37–41.

Pearce, F. "Greenprint for Rescuing the Rhine." *New Scientist* (June, 26 1993): 25–29.

See also Army Corps of Engineers (U.S.); Colorado River; Columbia River Basin; Eutrophication; Hydroelectricity; St. Lawrence River

Rhinoceros: Conservation and Habitat

The five rhinoceros species (*Perissodactyla: Rhinocerotidae*) are among the most severely threatened animals on earth. With the exception of the white rhinoceros population in South Africa and, to a lesser extent, the black rhinoceros populations in Kenya and Namibia, rhinos are in decline or at extremely low levels throughout their range. Poaching for horn has wiped out over 90 percent of the world's black rhinoceros—once the most abundant species in the family by far, with a population of 65,000 to 70,000 in the late 1960s—in less than twenty years. The most recent catastrophic decline has been the loss of most of the Zimbabwe population, once the healthiest in Africa with some 2,000 to 3,000 animals. The 1992 censuses revealed that the population had been reduced to only a few hundred despite concerted anti-poaching efforts by Zimbabwe's Operation Stronghold. Although poaching of the Asian species has been less severe, largely because the Javan and Sumatran species are shy and hard to find, their numbers are also very low.

The 1993 figures for rhinoceros populations are:

- Black rhinoceros (*Diceros bicornis*, Africa): 2,500
- White rhinoceros (*Ceratotherium simum*, Africa): 5,730+
- Indian rhinoceros (*Rhinoceros unicornis*, northern India, Nepal, and Bangladesh): 2,000
- Javan rhinoceros (*Rhinoceros sondaicus*, western Java and central Vietnam): under 100
- Sumatran rhinoceros (*Dicerorhinus sumatranus*, Southeast Asia): 800.

The chief threat to all rhinoceros species is the illegal trade in their horn, though habitat loss is also a factor for the Javan and Sumatran rhinos. The trade feeds two main markets. In Yemen rhino horn is used to make handles for traditional daggers, or jambias, worn by men as a symbol of their manhood and dedication to Islam. Despite efforts to control the trade over 750 kilos of horn were smuggled into Yemen between August 1990 and March 1992. In May 1992 the Grand Mufti of Yemen issued a religious edict banning the killing of rhinos. Since then the government has confirmed its intention to implement its decree prohibiting trade in and use of raw horn.

The other major market is in the far east, where rhino horn is used as a medicine, primarily to reduce fever. Contrary to popular opinion it is not used as an aphrodisiac except to a very small degree in a few localized areas.

The demand for horn has made it one of the most valuable wildlife products in the world. African rhinoceros horn prices in Taipei in 1993 averaged $4,718 per kilogram. Horn from the far rarer Asian species averaged $41,026 per kilogram. Some of the greatest demand today may come from speculators in Taiwan and elsewhere who are building up private stockpiles of horn, in the hope that the value of their hoards will increase sharply should rhinos become extinct.

Efforts to protect rhinos against poachers in Africa have proven to be costly and largely ineffective in the long run. Even shoot-to-kill policies, as practiced in Kenya and Zimbabwe, have not stopped poaching. Kenya, however, has had some success in placing its rhinos in guarded sanctuaries, and the small population there is slowly increasing. Zimbabwe is now following a similar policy. In South Africa, where poaching has not been a serious problem, the white rhinoceros population has grown steadily over the past thirty years.

Recently Namibia and Zimbabwe began cutting the horns off their remaining rhinos in the hope of eliminating their value to poachers. Unfortunately this measure has not worked. The horns grow back at the rate of 0.54 and 0.33 kilograms per year for adult and juvenile black rhinos. Poachers appear willing to kill even dehorned animals for the small amounts that remain. Only five of eighty white rhinos dehorned in Zimbabwe were still alive eighteen months later. Further, studies have shown that in areas of Namibia where hyenas and lions occur, dehorned cows are unable to protect their calves from these predators, leading to 100 percent calf mortality within the first year.

All rhinoceros species are listed on Appendix I of the Convention on International Trade in Endangered Species of Wild Fauna and Flora (CITES). However, the CITES ban has had only a limited effect on the market, in contrast to the Appendix I listing of the African elephant that closed down much of the world's ivory trade within a few months of its passage in 1989. The probable reason for this lies in the difference between the markets for ivory and rhino horn. Unlike ivory, rhino horn is not valued as a luxury item or a status symbol (except in Yemen), but as medicine. The chief market for ivory was in Japan and the West, whereas rhino horn is most valued by traditional users in China and neighboring countries. This meant that worldwide publicity of the sort that convinced most users to observe the ivory ban has been of little effect in lowering the demand for rhino horn. Nonetheless the CITES ban has assisted in closing much of the market for horn in Japan and a few other countries.

Despite this, some southern African countries, notably South Africa and Zimbabwe, argue that the ban has failed so signally that limited trade in horn should be legalized to provide funds for rhinoceros conservation efforts. Proposals to do so were, however, rejected at the 1992 meeting of the CITES parties in Kyoto, Japan.

In March 1993 the CITES standing committee passed a resolution calling on the chief marketing countries to consolidate and destroy their stocks of rhino horn. This was followed by measures calling for possible sanctions against China and Taiwan, in conjunction with similar measures taken to protect the tiger (q.v.).

In 1994 South Africa again proposed that its white rhino population be downlisted from Appendix I to Appendix II of CITES, despite the concerns of many conservationists that any re-laxation of the ban will only make laundering of smuggled horn easier and dilute efforts to bring pressure to bear on the market countries—thus making a desperately bad situation even worse.

Ronald Orenstein

Further Readings

Berger, Joel et al. "'Costs' and Short-Term Survivorship of Hornless Black Rhinos." *Conservation Biology* 7 (1993): 920–24.
Penny, Malcolm. *Rhinos: Endangered Species*. 1988.
Redmond, Ian. "Sir Peter's Paradox." *BBC Wildlife* 11 (1993): 42–44.

See also AFRICA: ENVIRONMENTAL PROBLEMS; CITES; ELEPHANTS: CONSERVATION AND HABITAT; TIGERS: CONSERVATION AND HABITAT; WORLD WILDLIFE FUND

Right-to-Know: Community (U.S.)

Community right-to-know is a term that usually refers to access to information about environmental hazards to human health, especially those posed by toxic or hazardous chemicals. The Emergency Response and Community Right-to-Know Act of 1986 (EPCRA, formerly called SARA Title III since it constitutes the third title of the Superfund Amendments and Reauthorization Act of 1986) gives community residents access to information about chemicals in the community by requiring facilities to file reports with government agencies.

Provisions of EPCRA fall into three categories: emergency response, community right-to-know, and the toxics release inventory. Because EPCRA was passed in part as a response to the accidental release of a very toxic chemical, methyl isocyanate (MIS), at the Union Carbide plant in Bhopal, India, in December 1984, it focuses strongly on emergency response. States and localities are required to establish emergency planning committees composed of representatives from the community, industry, and emergency response and health groups. These committees develop emergency response plans for chemical spills. Their planning is based on information reported under the community right-to-know provisions of EPCRA, which require facilities that store, manufacture, or use any hazardous chemical in quantities over a specified threshold to submit an annual inventory to the emergency planning bodies and the fire department. One of these entities must arrange to make the information accessible to community residents as well.

A separate provision of EPCRA requires only manufacturing facilities to submit to the federal Environmental Protection Agency (EPA) annual reports of their releases of a list of about 350 toxic chemicals. Congress requires this so-called Toxic Chemical Release Inventory (also known as the Toxics Release Inventory or TRI) to be available to the public in several forms, including an electronic database. This electronic format has allowed people to manipulate the complex data with relative ease to conduct research on companies with plants in several different states or localities, to consider the chemical burden of a community or water body, or to identify the fate of a particular toxic chemical (such as an ozone-depleting substance) throughout the United States. Facilities must also report their efforts to reduce pollution, providing monitors with some measure of progress in reducing toxic chemical exposure in a community.

Although the TRI is only one of several provisions of EPCRA, it is often considered to be the primary element of community right-to-know. Community right-to-know (RTK) originated in 1979, when the Philadelphia occupational safety coalition PHILAPOSH and the Environmental Cancer Prevention Center sponsored a conference on toxic substances in the workplace. Attendees asked why only workers should know about hazardous substances (see Right-to-Know: Workplace [U.S.] entry) when all members of the community are exposed to the same substances, albeit at lower levels. Opponents of the demand for community RTK argued that citizens already could obtain the necessary information, that an RTK program would entail considerable paperwork, and that local RTK laws would encourage industries to relocate to areas without RTK. In 1981 Philadelphia passed that nation's first RTK law that covered both workers and the community. Other local areas, especially in California, soon followed; New Jersey and a very few other states passed state laws. These local and state laws differed in the substances, threshold amounts, and industries covered. After the spill in Bhopal several RTK bills were introduced in Congress. Portions of these bills, most of which affected either emergency response or community RTK, were combined into EPCRA.

Implementation of EPCRA differs widely across jurisdictions. The Local Emergency Planning Committees (LEPCs) were to create an emergency response plan by October 14, 1987, one year after EPCRA was signed into law. By that date many LEPCs had not even been formed. However, by now virtually all committees have been formed and most have developed some kind of emergency response plan. Some LEPCs have been very successful at encouraging broad community participation and have even extended their activities beyond emergency response planning to provide a forum where citizens and industry can work together to reduce the risk of community exposure to toxic substances in the environment. Other LEPCs are dominated by industry or emergency response personnel.

Information available through the Toxic Chemical Release Inventory has stimulated other kinds of community activity. The Working Group on Community Right to Know, a loose consortium of environmental and public interest groups based in Washington, D.C., keeps track of many of these activities. They include: 1) state toxics use reduction laws; 2) agreements between a neighborhood group and a company to reduce toxic emissions; 3) voluntary undertakings by a company or a facility to reduce emissions; and 4) lawsuits to enforce permitted emission limits. In addition, the Chemical Manufacturers Association (CMA) has developed a voluntary industry program called "Responsible CARE," in which members agree to limit toxic emissions, work with the public, and provide technical assistance to smaller companies to achieve these goals. The EPA and state regulators use TRI data to enhance regulatory programs.

Although the TRI is closely associated with the term "community right-to-know," it has limitations as a public information source. First, access to the electronic form of the information is somewhat difficult. The EPA makes the data available on computer disks and on-line through the National Library of Medicine, where citizens must establish an account and learn to work with a relatively difficult user interface. To overcome these difficulties, many states have established their own electronic TRI databases, providing access to the public in various ways. In addition, RTK-NET, a project of two Washington, D.C.-based nonprofit groups, places the TRI data along with other resources and assistance in using the data online and offers low-cost access to other nonprofits.

A second barrier to right-to-know is implicit in the data. EPCRA and the TRI make information about chemicals available to the public, while people are often more interested in the risks posed by those chemicals and the levels of exposure they are likely to experience. Provision of this information is not required under the law. For this reason most communities must rely upon intermediaries—public interest groups, manufacturers, or, less often, regulators—to acquire supplementary information and interpret it in a way that may allow the lay public to understand and act upon it.

A related barrier in right-to-know is the difficulty of promoting public participation in reducing risks of exposure to toxics in the environment. Because the data are so difficult to acquire and understand, and because of the lack of scientific understanding of the health effects of low levels of exposure, many people remain uninterested in the issue. Public interest groups thus often play a role not only in interpreting the information but in promoting public activity. Many chemical manufacturers have established community advisory panels as a forum for public participation concerning this issue.

A new movement has arisen in response to some of these limitations. The "right to know more" focuses on the need for supplementary information, especially adding nonmanufacturers to the list of reporting facilities and expanding the kinds of data provided. Bills have been introduced in Congress to implement these expansions of the current right-to-know.

Susan G. Hadden

Further Readings

Hadden, Susan G. *A Citizen's Right to Know: Risk Communication and Public Policy.* 1989.

Lynn, Frances, and Jack Kartez. "Environmental Democracy in Action: The Toxics Release Inventory." *Environmental Management* 18 (1994), 511–521.

See also BHOPAL; ENVIRONMENTAL JUSTICE MOVEMENT; ENVIRONMENTAL PROTECTION AGENCY; RIGHT-TO-KNOW: WORKPLACE (U.S.); SUPERFUND

Right-to-Know: Workplace (U.S.)

Worker right-to-know (RTK) refers to employees' access to information about the substances to which they might be exposed in the workplace, especially information concerning long-term health effects such as cancer or injuries to reproductive cells. Because workplace exposures often occur at relatively high concentrations and over the worker's entire time on the job, workers are often at higher risk of experiencing undesirable side-effects than the population at large.

Occupational disease, such as that affecting chimney sweeps and coal miners, has been recognized from early times. Especially following World War II many new chemicals and petrochemicals were introduced into the marketplace. To help workers prevent accidents with these new substances the Manufacturing Chemists Association (MCA) (now the Chemical Manufacturers Association [CMA]) developed voluntary industry standards for labeling. The labels—principles of which are incorporated into federal law and regulations under the Federal Hazardous Substances Labeling Act—emphasized consistency and ease of use across substances; they provided the name of the substance, a signal word indicating the level of hazard, a statement of the hazard (e.g., flammable; strong irritant), precautionary measures, and instructions for safe handling and use, and for accidental exposure.

After twenty or so years of experience with these substances, people began to realize that some of them posed long-term health risks, such as cancer or damage to reproductive cells, in addition to the short-term hazards covered by the MCA labels. The workplace RTK movement represents employees' efforts to be sure that they are aware of the identity and possible risks posed by substances with which they work.

The Occupational Safety and Health Act of 1970 (OSHAct) provides the regulatory framework for worker safety in the United States. It requires employers to provide jobs and places of employment that are free from recognized hazards to workers and establishes the Occupational Safety and Health Administration (OSHA) in the Department of Labor. In response to the special problems posed by long-term hazards in the workplace, the law also established the National Institute for Occupational Safety and Health (NIOSH), a research body in the Department of Health and Human Services, to develop and recommend exposure standards based on its research. OSHA's attempts during the 1970s to promulgate exposure standards for some substances posing long-term hazards were slowed by the difficulty in obtaining adequate scientific evidence and by court challenges to almost every standard.

In the absence of exposure standards workers sought information remedies. In 1977 OSHA began to consider a generic regulation that would require employers to inform workers about risks in the workplace, especially long-term health risks from handling chemicals. In November 1983 OSHA promulgated the "hazard communication rule." As amended in August 1987 it requires virtually all employers to place labels on containers of substances in the workplace and to maintain a file of Material Safety Data Sheets (MSDSs) that provide more detailed information about each hazardous chemical found in the workplace. Employers must also provide appropriate training programs.

The success of any RTK program rests in part on the availability of information about hazards. One of the most difficult problems inherent in the workplace RTK program was the extent to which employers were themselves aware of risks posed by products used in the workplace. The Material Safety Data Sheet answers this difficulty since original manufacturers of chemicals must supply an MSDS every time a chemical is shipped. Downstream users must also supply MSDSs as they ship their products to end-users. MSDSs must contain the identity of the chemical, its physical and chemical characteristics, its physical and health hazards, primary routes of entry, permissible exposure limits as established by authorities, precautions for safe handling and use, control measures for reducing exposure (such as personal protective equipment or engineering controls), emergency and first aid procedures, name and address of the chemical manufacturer, and the date of preparation and last change to the MSDS. Thus the obligation to provide an MSDS ensures that manufacturers will collect all available information about a substance into a concise form and disseminate it widely. Gaps in available information are also highlighted by this requirement, although no manufacturer is required to conduct additional research to create new information about health hazards.

A second condition of a RTK program is access to the available information. Employers must keep files of MSDSs and make them readily available to employees and to their union representatives. Since MSDSs are not always present at the time of chemical use, however, employers must also label containers with brief descriptions of the hazard and, often, means for avoiding it or post signs in the workplace to indicate containers of hazardous substances. In addition, MSDSs are not always easy to understand and act upon; therefore, employers must provide training programs in which they explain the hazards and how to avoid them. The regulation specifies the minimum content of the training program, including ensuring that workers know they have the right to know.

A third condition of the RTK is utility of information. If workers cannot understand information provided they cannot take action to limit their exposures or otherwise reduce their risks. Many people believe that workplace RTK (like community RTK) does not fully meet this goal. Multiple names for the same chemical may inhibit access to the correct information. MSDSs are often many pages long, so that finding a particular bit of desired information may be difficult. MSDSs are also often difficult to understand, focusing on emergency response rather than on long-term, low-level exposures. Scientific information about such exposures is often lacking, and many MSDSs provide the available information by reference to specific laboratory tests, rather than providing a summary of the data in lay language. However, employers are not required to help workers understand what animal tests or the absence of human data may imply for their own health. In response to these concerns the State of New Jersey developed some information forms that are consistent in format and much easier to understand. These forms have been adopted by some employers and states.

A different kind of problem arises in workplaces such as auto repair shops where many different chemicals and mixtures are used in small quantities. The regulation does not encourage employers to develop training programs that focus on categories of substances (such as paint strippers or degreasers)—a format that many people believe would enhance worker understanding. Instead, the regulation focuses on training about specific substances. Some alternative training programs have been developed.

A final factor that makes the RTK powerful is the ability to act upon the information received. The regulation requires that employees' physicians and unions, where present, be able to see information about their exposures. However, it does not provide any remedies to workers who feel that they are inappropriately exposed to hazardous substances in the workplace. This concern has led to the growth of the "right to act" movement. Workers have also begun to band together with citizens, using the information available both under community as well as worker RTK, to get employers to reduce their use of toxics within the workplace, which results in reducing toxic emissions to the environment as well.

Susan G. Hadden

Further Readings

Hazard Communication Standard. 52 Fed. Reg. 31,877 et seq., 1987. Codified at 21 C.F.R. 1910.1200 (e) (1).

Nelkin, Dorothy, ed. *The Language of Risk: Conflicting Perspectives on Occupational Health*. 1985.

Schroeder, Elinor P., and Sidney A. Shapiro. "Responses to Occupational Disease: The Role of Markets, Regulation, and Information." *Georgetown Law Journal* 72 (1984): 1231–1309.

See also ENVIRONMENTAL JUSTICE MOVEMENT; EPIDEMIOLOGY; LABOR AND THE ENVIRONMENT; LEGISLATION: UNITED STATES; OSHACT AND OSHA; RIGHT-TO-KNOW: COMMUNITY (U.S.); TOXICOLOGY

Rio Conference (1992)

The United Nations Conference on Environment and Development, also known as the Rio Conference or Earth Summit or by its acronym UNCED, was held in Rio de Janeiro, June 3–14, 1992. These dates mark the twentieth anniversary of the landmark United Nations Conference on the Human Environment held in Stockholm. The largest gathering of world leaders in UN history, the Rio Conference tackled a large and complex agenda of environmental and economic issues with the objective of reaching broad international agreement on a long-range strategy that would reverse disturbing global environmental trends, while mitigating the conditions of poverty and underdevelopment that afflict much of the world's population. Among the principal issues on the conference agenda were threats to the atmosphere, including climate change, ozone depletion, and transboundary pollution; deterioration of terrestrial resources, including deforestation, soil erosion, desertification, and contamination of freshwater; loss of biological diversity and the functioning of the biotechnology industry; threats to marine ecosystems and depletion of the living resources of the oceans; illegal traffic in toxic products and wastes; and the prevalence of poverty in poorer countries and impediments to their economic development.

As with other major UN theme conferences two large gatherings took place simultaneously in Rio which addressed a common theme, but with very different formats. The official conference, held at the RioCentro convention facility in the outskirts of the city, was attended by delegates from 178 nations, including heads of state from 118 countries, who came for the summit phase during the last two days of the conference. Also represented were numerous UN agencies and other intergovernmental organizations concerned with specific environmental problems, as well as 1,400 accredited NGOs.

The other gathering, known as the '92 Global Forum, was an informal melange of events in the form of street fair that was held in Flamingo Park in downtown Rio. The 18,000 participants from 166 countries, having affiliations with as many as 7,000 NGOs, exchanged ideas and publicized their viewpoints and projects through displays, lectures, seminars, demonstrations, and press conferences, as well as by an exercise in drafting treaties calling for stronger international action than those adopted at the official conference. The colorful forum received much of the press coverage from the 8,000 journalists assigned to the conference.

The stimulus for the Rio conference was the influential report of the UN Commission on Environment and Development (Brundtland Commission), entitled *Our Common Future* (1987), which concluded that poverty and underdevelopment were major causes of environmental degradation in much of the world. The UN General Assembly officially authorized the conference by Resolution 44/228 (December 22, 1989) and urged the attendance of heads of state. A preparatory committee, known as PrepCom, coordinated preparations that included four negotiating sessions held between August 1990 and April 1992, which were notable for the extensive participation of nongovernmental organizations.

The official conference adopted several major documents after negotiations which at times were quite contentious. The Rio Declaration on Environment and Development sets forth twenty-seven general principles that are to guide international policy in the coming decades. They are oriented toward protecting the global environment while meeting the needs of human beings through sustainable and environmentally sound development in all countries. The document reaffirms the often quoted Article 21 of the 1972 Stockholm Declaration, which asserts the fundamental right of sovereign states to exploit their natural resources, but to do so in a way that does not damage the environment beyond their borders.

Agenda 21 is a lengthy, nonbinding document which presents a comprehensive action plan for addressing the problems of environment and development at the local, national, regional, and global levels well into the next century. It emphasizes that a fundamental reform in economic behavior is needed to prevent further environmental degradation while improving the quality of life of the world's poor. It also spells out the institutional and financial means that will be necessary to carry out the proposed programs, including a substantial transfer of economic and technical resources from the industrialized countries that goes well beyond existing levels of foreign assistance. It envisions the active involvement of diverse types of people in the pursuit of sustainable development, including women, the young, indigenous groups, farmers, industrial workers, business interests, scientists, and engineers.

Two treaties that are binding on ratifying states were finalized at the conference, and each was signed by 153 states. The Framework Convention on Climate Change seeks to stabilize concentrations of atmospheric greenhouse gases within a time frame that will prevent "dangerous anthropogenic interference with the climate system." It also obliges industrialized countries to develop and report on plans to bring their emissions of these gases to "earlier levels" by the year 2000. Future negotiations will be held on a timetable for specific limits on emissions of carbon dioxide. The Convention on Biodiversity requires states to develop plans for protecting species and habitats. It is also designed to ensure that biotechnology companies will have access to genestocks from throughout the world and that developing countries will share in the benefits of the products developed from the genetic raw materials they provide.

The sessions at the Rio Conference were characterized by an intense and often contentious dialogue between the industrialized countries, which emphasized the need for decisive international action on ecological problems, and the developed countries, which were not willing to sacrifice what they viewed as their right to economic development and a better quality of life for their people. The industrial-ized countries were reluctant to acknowledge special responsibility for addressing global problems such as ozone depletion and climate change; less developed countries resisted accepting an international obligation to restrain population growth. Much of the discussion at Rio centered on the commitments the highly developed countries should make to provide "new and additional" funds to help developing countries implement *Agenda 21* and more generally to reform the international economic system.

The United States was criticized for being out of step with most of the world on several key issues being discussed at the conference. All other industrialized countries favored including a specific timetable for freezing and eventually reducing emissions of carbon dioxide in the Framework Convention on Climate Change, but in the end deferred to the United States, which was not yet willing to make such a commitment. The United States also stood alone among the developed countries in its refusal to sign the Biodiversity Treaty, contending that the property rights of the biotechnology industry were not adequately protected. The United States advocated a treaty that would slow the destruction of tropical forests, but encountered strong resistance from nations that export tropical timber, led by Malaysia, and attacks on its own forestry practices. Thus, the United States had to settle for a weaker Declaration of Forestry Principles. In the year following the conference, however, the United States' positions converged considerably with those of the other leading industrialized countries.

One of the most significant outcomes of the Rio Conference may prove to be the UN Commission on Sustainable Development, which was subsequently established by the General Assembly to facilitate activities that would both implement and strengthen the myriad of proposals contained in *Agenda 21*. The Commission, a high level body that will report to the Economic and Social Council (ECOSOC) of the UN, will monitor the progress states are making toward fulfilling commitments made at Rio, coordinate the activities of numerous international and nongovernmental organizations, and review progress on funding projects in the field of sustainable development.

Marvin S. Soroos

Further Readings

Haas, Peter M., Marc A. Levy, and Edward A. Parson. "The Earth Summit: How Should We Judge UNCED's Success?"

Environment 34 (October 1992): 7–11, 26–33.

Johnson, Stanley P., ed. *The Earth Summit: The United Nations Conference on Environment and Development*. 1993.

Parson, Edward A., Peter M. Haas, and Marc A. Levy. "A Summary of the Major Documents Signed at the Earth Summit and the Global Forum." *Environment* 34 (October 1992): 13–15, 34–35.

See also BRUNDTLAND, GRO HARLEM; ENVIRONMENTAL DIPLOMACY; *Our Common Future*; STOCKHOLM CONFERENCE; UNITED NATIONS ENVIRONMENT PROGRAMME

Risk Analysis

Risk analysis is the process of identifying the health and environmental hazards associated with exposure to a variety of substances or activities and then determining the best strategies for preventing unacceptable risks. A typical hazardous substance might be chemical waste from manufacturing; monitored activities often include the handling of hazardous substances in the workplace or home. Risk analysis is sometimes used synonymously with "risk assessment" but risk assessment customarily implies only the identification and characterization of health and environmental hazards. Federal agencies responsible for enforcing health and environmental regulations since the 1970s almost always conduct risk analysis as part of this process.

Federal environmental legislation has been concerned primarily with hazards to human health and safety although a few laws, such as the Clean Air Act (1970), mandate the evaluation of hazards to vegetation, property, or other aspects of the environment. Environmentalists have increasingly advocated that environmental hazards be included in risk analysis required by federal health and safety legislation. The risk analysis required by federal law also gives greatest priority to cancer-related (carcinogenic) hazards, an emphasis reinforced by the public's deep fear and preoccupation with carcinogenic risks.

Risk analysis associated with environmental health and safety was mandated in federal law as early as the Food, Drug and Cosmetic Act of 1938, but the vast majority of such legislation has been passed since environmentalism became a potent political movement in the early 1970s. The risk analysis now required by federal law is conducted primarily by four agencies: the Environmental Protection Agency (EPA), the Food and Drug Administration (FDA), the Occupational Health and Safety Administration (OSHA) and the Consumer Product Safety Commission (CPSC). Seven of the nine major federal laws mandating risk analysis for environmental hazards are implemented primarily by the EPA. In addition to the Food, Drug, and Cosmetic Act (1938), these laws include the Federal Insecticide, Fungicide, and Rodenticide Act (1947), the Clean Air Act (1970), the Clean Water Act (1965), the Safe Drinking Water Act (1976), the Resource Conservation and Recovery Act (1976), the Toxic Substances Control Act (1976), and the Comprehensive Environmental Response, Compensation, and Liability Act or "Superfund" (1980). The Occupational Health and Safety Act (1970) is enforced by OSHA and the Consumer Product Safety Act by the Consumer Product Safety Commission.

Institutional arrangements for risk analysis vary between the responsible agencies but involve five common procedures:

1. Hazard Identification: determination of whether exposure to a substance or activity increases the incidence of adverse health, safety, or environmental impacts such as cancer.
2. Risk Assessment: estimation of the magnitude and probability of adverse impacts from exposure to a substance or activity—for instance, the kind of cancers that may be caused and their likelihood within a human population.
3. Risk Estimate: estimation of the actual adverse impacts of an identified hazard in light of its known distribution, amount of exposure to humans or the environment, and probability of creating adverse impacts.
4. Risk Communication: transmission of information about the estimated risk from a hazard to relevant audiences including public officials, regulatory agencies, scientists, the media, and the public.
5. Risk Management: the development of strategies, such as regulatory laws or marketplace interventions, for the management of unacceptable hazards according to criteria such as technological feasibility, health risks, cost-benefit analysis, or other standards.

Federal environmental laws mandating risk assessment differ greatly in the standards they require of regulatory agencies when determining acceptable risks. Every major law has its distinctive mix of criteria, often vague and frequently inconsistent with other laws, but several broad types are commonly found. A few laws permit no health risks, such as the "Delaney Clause" in the Food, Drug and Cosmetic Act (1938) stating that no food additive may be considered safe if it is found to induce cancer in man or animals. Other laws, such as the Clean Air Act (1970), require regulatory agencies to use a margin-of-safety criterion providing an additional margin of safety beyond acceptable risk limits for normal populations to protect those unusually sensitive to a hazard. Many laws require regulators to protect against unreasonable risk or substantial danger to public health or safety. Other laws, such as the Safe Drinking Water Act, require regulation of any adverse health impacts from a hazard.

Risk analysis has proven to be scientifically difficult and contentious, as well as politically controversial and problematic, in its conclusions. The criteria written into environmental laws to guide regulatory officials in defining acceptable risk are often numerous and vague, encouraging controversy over the law's proper interpretation. Such disputes frequently become matters of political debate and litigation.

Many risk assessment problems also arise directly from the uncertain science supporting the process. Relatively few chemicals, such as asbestos, have been proven beyond scientific dispute to be highly toxic. More often little or no scientific information exists on the distribution or severity of possible environmental pollutants and the acquisition of experimental data may take decades. No reliable data exist, for instance, on the toxic effects of an estimated 79 percent of commercial chemicals. Without this data, scientists must estimate toxicity and associated exposure risks by extrapolation from fragmentary information and plausible disagreements among experts is common. Estimates of human health risks are often extrapolations from animal studies or epidemiological data whose reliability is disputed. Sometimes congressional decisions to regulate specific substances or activities, such as abandoned hazardous waste sites, have been inspired more by public fears and presumptions about health risks than by expert agreement on the actual environmental risks.

One common controversy in risk assessment concerns "de minimis" risk or the level of risk that can be safely ignored by regulatory agencies. Scientific studies suggest that many toxic substances pose human health risks, albeit very small, even at very low exposure levels. Thus, there is no absolutely "safe" exposure level for such substances. Critics assert that Congress and regulatory agencies should be more willing to declare risk levels below which no effort will be made to regulate substances in light of the huge costs and small health benefits likely to be involved. Environmentalists often disagree in the belief that the scientific evidence supporting de minimus standards is still unreliable and that, in any case, any level of health risk is unacceptable if it can be reasonably avoided.

Another common controversy concerns the "inference guidelines" used by experts in animal studies. Experts must often choose among several different guidelines for inferring human risks from such experiments. Different guidelines, or decision rules, will yield different estimates of human risk and experts must often decide whether to follow a guideline that increases, or decreases, the likelihood that a substance will be declared an unacceptable risk. Experts often cannot agree upon the appropriate guideline to follow. Generally, environmentalists and other proponents of environmental regulation favor guidelines that increase the likelihood a suspected substance will be declared a significant human health risk. Critics assert that the environmentalist position creates excessive regulation and imposes huge, unnecessary costs upon the nation by overestimating the dangers of many commercial and industrial substances.

Whenever it occurs, regulation imposes large costs upon the producers and users of substances or activities deemed to create environmental or health hazards. Those bearing these regulatory costs have been quick to challenge in court the reliability of risk analyses affecting them, thereby adding considerable time, expense, and unpredictability to the environmental regulatory process. The litigation common to risk analysis has invested federal judges with great authority in determining the scientific, as well as legal issues in risk assessments and provoked considerable controversy about the appropriateness of judges acting as science referees.

The increasing proliferation of federal environmental regulations, the continuing creation of more than 1,500 new industrial and commercial chemicals annually, and the accumulation of scientific research are likely to encourage further growth and complexity to risk analysis in both the public and private sectors. Risk analysis will also continue to be among the most politically contentious of all issues inherent to environmental regulation well into the next century.

Walter A. Rosenbaum

Further Readings

Cohrssen, John J., and Vincent T. Covello. *Risk Analysis: A Guide To Principles and Methods for Analysing Health and Environmental Risks.* 1989.

Formaini, Robert. *The Myth of Scientific Public Policy.* 1990.

Glickman, Theodore S., and Michael Gough, eds. *Readings in Risk.* 1990.

See also BENEFIT-COST ANALYSIS; DELANEY CLAUSE; ENVIRONMENTAL IMPACT ASSESSMENT; OSHACT AND OSHA: STANDARD SETTING

Risk Assessment

See ENVIRONMENTAL IMPACT ASSESSMENT; RISK ANALYSIS

Road Salt

Throughout snowbelt regions of Canada, Europe, and the United States, winter maintenance of urban roads and highways involves the annual application of many millions of tons of road de-icing chemicals. These chemicals are readily mobilized in airborne spray, snow melt, and surface water runoff, and can cause serious environmental damage.

Road de-icing chemicals take several different forms, but common salt (NaCl) is the cheapest and most commonly used. It is particularly cost-effective at temperatures above −12 degrees Celsius. In practice NaCl is normally applied in pure mineral form, but it is also used in conjunction with abrasives such as sand. While the preferred practice is to apply pure NaCl to all major roads and highways, mixtures of sand and between 5 percent and 95 percent NaCl can be highly effective on many routes. Mixtures of sand and 5% NaCl are invariably used on gravel roads since pure NaCl tends to damage the road surface during a thaw. Calcium chloride ($CaCl_2$) is more effective than NaCl at temperatures in the range −12 degrees Celsius to −34 degrees Celsius but is less frequently used because it is two to four times more expensive and can make the road surface slippery when wet.

Environmental damage resulting from NaCl road de-icing chemicals is well documented. Most accounts concern visible impacts such as damage to vegetation, weakened concrete engineering structures, and corrosion of vehicles. However, a less obvious concern is the impact of NaCl on ground and surface water quality with the risk that salinity can increase to levels that would make the water unsuitable for consumption and some industrial applications. In Metropolitan Toronto, for example, a region that receives well over 100,000 tons of NaCl annually at a rate approximating 200 grams for every square meter of land, calculations have shown that concentrations of sodium and chloride in underlying groundwaters will exceed acceptable standards for drinking water within a few years. While standards for chloride are usually set for aesthetic purposes of taste, sodium is more contentious since the ion has been linked with the development of hypertension, a condition affecting perhaps 20 percent of the U.S. population.

Alternatives to NaCl and $CaCl_2$ are numerous, but all are considerably more expensive and none can be considered environmentally "safe." Calcium Magnesium Acetate (CMA), for example, is less corrosive and readily biodegrades, but it is also less effective than NaCl, is difficult to store due to its hygroscopicity, and removes excessive amounts of oxygen from the soil during decomposition. It can also develop skin and bronchial problems among road maintenance crews. Oxygen consumption is also a problem with alcohols and glycols which due to their non-corrosive properties are commonly used at airports. These chemicals are difficult to handle, and consume so much oxygen during chemical decomposition that even diluted solutions must be prevented from entering streams and rivers. Streams and rivers also need to be protected from technical urea and ammonium compounds. While these alternatives to NaCl are used in specific situations, their widespread use would cause excessive fertilization of roadside soils and cause serious impacts on ground and surface water quality.

Ken W.F. Howard

Further Readings

Howard, K.W.F., and P.J. Beck. "Hydrogeochemical Implications of Groundwater Contamination by Road De-Icing Chemicals." *Journal of Con-*

taminant *Hydrology* 12 (1993): 245–68.

Scott, W.S., and N.P. Wylie. "The Environmental Effects of Snow Dumping: A Literature Review." *Journal of Environmental Management* 10 (1980): 219–40.

See also AUTOMOBILES: IMPACTS AND POLICIES; GROUNDWATER POLLUTION

Rodale, J.I.

See SUSTAINABLE AGRICULTURE

Roethke, Theodore

Theodore Roethke (1908–1963) is one of America's best poets of nature, not just of the beauties and wonders of the physical world but of humankind's relationship with that world and its ability to redeem and to heal the mind and soul. As a boy in Saginaw, Michigan, Roethke grew up absorbed in the natural but human-directed processes he observed in a huge greenhouse which was the family business. Roethke was also familiar with the ways of wild nature through his play in a field the family also owned and trips to the wilderness of Michigan's peninsulas. Although he received praise for his first volume of poetry, *Open House* (1941), he did not find his own voice as a poet until he began writing of the greenhouse and other experiences of nature in *The Lost Son and Other Poems* (1948). The height of recognition came with the granting of the Pulitzer Prize for *The Waking* in 1953, but Roethke's reputation as a poet of skillful technique and great emotional power has continued to grow since his death.

While Roethke made his living as a teacher and poet in residence (primarily at the University of Washington), he was bedeviled by manic depressive mental illness. From this condition came some of Roethke's best confessional poetry and his most unique use of nature in his work, for Roethke does not wallow in the misery of his condition but instead explains through his poetry how his relationship with nature helps to make him whole again. Specifically, it is the little creatures of nature that inspire and aid him, the mouse, the slug, the minnow—even the bacteria which caress and cleanse a wound. Roethke is the poet of those small and humble beings whose acceptance of their tiny roles make us understand that our own troubles can be borne as well.

Jim Baird

Further Readings

Roethke, Theodore. *Roethke: Collected Poems.* 1966.

———. *Straw for the Fire: From the Notebooks of Theodore Roethke.* Ed. David Wagoner. 1974.

Seager, Allan. *The Glass House: The Life of Theodore Roethke.* 1968.

See also SNYDER, GARY

Ruckelshaus, William D.

William D. Ruckelshaus, an Indiana attorney, graduate of Princeton and Harvard Law School, was the first administrator of the U.S. Environmental Protection Agency (EPA) from 1970 to 1973. He was appointed to this post by President Richard Nixon from a briefly held position within the U.S. Justice Department in Washington, D.C. The initial administrative task was daunting—an integrated entity had to be created out of fifteen different agencies and parts of agencies. That task had to be conducted simultaneously with the development of rules for the reduction of air pollution within 120 days of passage of the 1970 Clean Air Act. Not everything that EPA did in its early days pleased environmentalists (or Congress or industry), but on balance the effort was sincere, if sometimes cautious and overly deliberate and bureaucratic. The prompt administrative ban on the use of DDT, for example, enhanced the new agency's credibility considerably.

During EPA's early years there was much new environmental legislation: the Federal Water Pollution Control Act of 1972, the Federal Insecticide, Fungicide, and Rodenticide Act (FIFRA) of 1972, the Ocean Dumping Act, the Noise Control Act, the Coastal Zone Management Act, the Marine Mammals Protection Act, and, perhaps most important of those initiated in the initial Ruckelshaus years, the Endangered Species Act of 1973. After his stint at EPA Ruckelshaus was pressed to take on other, to say the least, daunting tasks as head of the FBI and as Deputy Attorney General, resigning from the latter post in 1974 rather than firing Watergate special prosecutor Archibald Cox.

Since 1974 Ruckelshaus has spent most of his time in the private sector serving most notably as senior vice president for Law and Public Affairs with the Pacific Northwest forest industry giant Weyerhauser Corporation (1975–1983) and as chairman and CEO of Browning Ferris Industries (BFI) of Houston, Texas, from 1988 to the present. BFI is one of the largest waste disposal companies in the world. But perhaps Ruckelshaus's greatest challenge came when he was called on to at least partially restore the political credibility of the Reagan administration and the professional credibility of the EPA following the disastrous tenure of Anne Burford (and that of James Watt in the U.S. Department of the Interior). Environment was probably President Reagan's most important liability heading into reelection. Reagan and his administration upon entering office in 1980 had pointedly ignored the moderate advice on environmental matters of Ruckelshaus and others. But Ruckelshaus was one of the few environmentally and administratively experienced Republicans whose credibility could help to retrieve the political mess on this front. Why he was willing to see this through is not entirely clear; perhaps he will reveal his reasons some day in an interview or an autobiography.

Ruckelshaus' second EPA service lasted from 1983 into 1985. Reagan's second term (1984–1988) witnessed a much less dramatically limited U.S. environmental policy than it had during the early (pre-Ruckelshaus) days of the first Reagan term. (Two positive initiatives that developed just after Ruckelshaus's second EPA leave-taking were the 1986 amendments to the Safe Drinking Water Act and the 1986 passage of Right-to-Know legislation.) Ruckelshaus has also served for some time as a trustee with both the Conservation Foundation and the World Wildlife Fund.

Robert Paehlke

Further Readings

Hays, Samuel P. *Beauty, Health, and Permanence: Environmental Politics in the United States, 1955–1985.* 1987.

Shabecoff, Philip. *A Fierce Green Fire: The American Environmental Movement.* 1993.

See also BURFORD, ANNE McGILL; ENDANGERED SPECIES ACT (U.S.); ENVIRONMENTAL PROTECTION AGENCY; FEDERAL INSECTICIDE, FUNGICIDE AND RODENTICIDE ACT; LEGISLATION: UNITED STATES; REAGAN, RONALD; SAGEBRUSH REBELLION; WATT, JAMES G.

Russia

See FORMER SOVIET UNION

S

Safe Drinking Water Act

See FEDERALISM AND ENVIRONMENTAL PRO-
TECTION: UNITED STATES; LEGISLATION:
UNITED STATES

Sagebrush Rebellion

During the late 1970s the federal government,
responding to the growing influence of environmentalism, proposed comprehensive changes in
its traditional Western public land policies that
provoked the "Sagebrush Rebellion." Public
land issues assume enormous political and economic importance in the West where the federal
government owns more than half the land area
of the thirteen Western states. The abundant
natural resources on this land include an estimated 30 percent of the nation's remaining oil
and gas reserves, 40 percent of its coal reserves,
and wilderness areas containing about a third
of the nation's remaining virgin forests. Conflict
between the states, the federal government, and
various private resource developers over use of
these resources have continued for over a century.

The rebellion exemplified a profound
transformation underway in public land politics. Before World War II interests using the
public domain largely fought among themselves
for access and advantage in resource exploitation. By the latter 1970s resource users found
this access increasingly challenged, and often
limited by the growing force of environmentalist policies and organizations. Leading the rebellion were Western governors and legislators,
vigorously supported by stockraisers, hardrock
miners, timber companies, energy corporations,
and other resource users. The coalition was
dedicated to protecting or enlarging their existing access to the public lands and to preventing

major restrictions on that access imposed by
newly proposed environmental regulations. The
Westerners, fighting specific reform proposals
in state legislatures, Congress, administrative
agencies, and the courts, professed their ultimate goal to be the transfer of all federal lands
to state ownership.

The rebellion's immediate provocation was
the Carter administration's many initiatives to
restrict the access to environmentally sensitive
public lands and to control the environmental
damage from resource development. These actions included Forest Service and Bureau of
Land Management proposals to increase substantially the designated wilderness areas on
which all development was prohibited, the enactment of the Surface Mining Control and
Reclamation Act (1977) to regulate coal surface
mining, proposals by the Bureau of Land Management to restrain stockraiser access to federal
grazing lands, and rigorous new environmental
controls on energy exploration and hardrock
mining on public domain. The rebellion also fed
upon historic Western resentment of the federal
government's alleged neglect of regional economic interests and its obtrusive management
style.

The rebellion seemed destined to be a formidable political force when President Ronald
Reagan publicly endorsed it during his election
campaign and appointed another Westerner
and outspoken Sagebrush Rebel, James G.
Watt, to be his Secretary of the Interior. But the
rebellion quickly lost momentum. Neither Congress nor the courts proved hospitable to reversing the major environmental policies opposed
by the Sagebrush rebels. The White House saw
little political advantage in promoting the
movement and Watt's forced resignation tainted
its image. Western interests lost enthusiasm

when they discovered that state ownership of the public lands would create even greater legal restraints on resource use. Many resource interests concluded, additionally, that more could be achieved through negotiation and compromise with resource agencies and their environmental constituencies. Watt and his successors temporarily achieved a few of the movement's goals, such as increased energy exploration on public land, by administrative methods. By 1990, however, the rebellion's policy objectives were largely unrealized and its political force was exhausted.

Walter A. Rosenbaum

Further Readings

Lacey, Michael J., ed. *Government and Environmental Politics: Essays on Historical Developments since World War Two.* 1989.

Meiners, Roger E., and Bruce Yandle, eds. *Regulation and the Reagan Era: Politics, Bureaucracy and the Public Interest.* 1989.

See also BUREAU OF LAND MANAGEMENT; BURFORD, ANNE MCGILL; FOREST SERVICE (U.S.); RANGELANDS (U.S.); REAGAN, RONALD; WATT, JAMES G.

Sahabat Alam Malaysia

See ENVIRONMENTAL MOVEMENTS: LESS-AFFLUENT NATIONS

Saint-Basile-Le-Grand

Saint-Basile-le-Grand is a quiet and relatively prosperous agricultural and commuter community of approximately 9,000 people, situated 35 kilometers southeast of Montréal. On the evening of August 23, 1988, a fire broke out in a barn serving as a depot for the storage of PCBs and other toxic wastes. PCBs are non-biodegradable substances used by many industries in transformers and condensers and in certain chemical compounds requiring products resistant to heat or friction. There is an ongoing controversy concerning methods for disposing of PCBs, especially since they liberate very toxic gases such as furans and dioxins when burned at temperatures below 1800 degrees Celsius. These gases cause allergies, nausea, and severe headaches, as well as other serious skin and respiratory problems, and are even capable of altering the genetic codes of animals and humans.

Firemen succeeded in putting out the fire in about five hours, but a column of heavy smoke had already touched three municipalities (Saint-Basile, Saint-Bruno, and Sainte-Julie) and required the evacuation and relocation of over 6,000 people. Fortunately the prevailing winds did not carry the toxic cloud over the Montreal area. As for human health, stress seems to have been more prevalent than actual physical damage. Because of scientific uncertainty concerning the toxicity levels of PCBs and the nature and the quantity of toxic wastes stored on the site, and because of a lack of experience with such accidents, a state of confusion developed among the citizens and the officials involved, forcing the government to create improvised programs for mental health, for medical checkups, and for financial compensation for affected citizens.

PCBs have been in wide use since the early 1960s, but their production has been banned throughout North America since 1978. However, many PCBs still exist in older condensers and transformers, and in storage depots awaiting a final disposal solution. PCBs were stored on the Saint-Basile site since the late 1970s. In 1979 the site owner, Marc Levy, obtained a permit from the Quebec Ministry of the Environment to operate the storage facility. In 1981, when the presence of PCBs was discovered and made public by the media, the municipality asked the government to revoke the permit. The request was refused and in 1983 a municipal inspector again warned the owner, reporting that the site was dangerous, because of rusting barrels and a lack of conformity to new security standards. However, the PCBs remained in place, with no corrective steps taken except cosmetic ones, in spite of the fact that no new permit was issued or forthcoming. Levy fled to Florida just after the fire erupted, and has remained there in hiding to this day, refusing to give interviews or to return.

The acute crisis in Saint-Basile lasted eighteen days, after which the government, on the advice of a team of international experts, allowed the people to return to their homes. Ten days later government officials withdrew from the area, leaving behind much acrimony and dissatisfaction, despite the generous compensation provided. The government promised to rapidly remove the remaining PCBs, but found the task insurmountable, transporting the chemicals to England, and back when dockers refused to unload them. Some barrels are now stored at the Manic 2 power station and the rest remain in Saint-Basile.

The Saint-Basile PCB fire has raised many issues concerning environmental disasters, not the least of which involves the ability of individuals to work together in times of crisis. Because of the involvement of concerned citizens and journalists, and thanks to the post-mortem evaluation of the crisis by officials and by experts such as the sociologist Hélène Denis, we may be in a better position to cope with such events in the future. However, given that toxic wastes are still with us in many forms, we are virtually certain to witness similar catastrophes elsewhere.

Jean-Guy Vaillancourt

Further Readings

André, Pierre. "*Que faire des déchets dangereux?*" *Le Devoir* (April 1992): B14.

Denis, Hélène. *La gestion de catastrophe: le cas d'un incendie dans un entrepot de BPC à Saint-Basile-le-Grand.* *Québec: Les publications du Québec,* 1990.

———. *Gérer les catastrophes, L'incertitude à apprivoiser.* Montréal: Les Presses de l'Université de Montréal, 1993.

See also DIOXINS AND FURANS; HAZARDOUS WASTE TREATMENT TECHNOLOGIES; PERSISTENT ORGANOCHLORINE COMPOUNDS; TOXICOLOGY

Schumacher, E.F.

E.F. Schumacher (1911–1977) is best known for his influential book, *Small is Beautiful,* in which he critiqued conventional economics and, specifically, the goal of economic growth. According to Schumacher economic growth is inadequate for meeting real human needs because it places too much emphasis on increasing output rather than on the value of work for its own sake. Moreover, he argued that economic growth is unsustainable because of the limitations of basic resources and the capacity of the environment to absorb the impacts of growth.

Underlying Schumacher's analysis was the belief that economics is derived from a view of the meaning of life. He observed that the only fully developed system of economic thought is derived from materialism. Though he did not present a thoroughly worked out alternative system of economics he laid much of the groundwork for an "economics as if people

mattered" within the context of a physically limited planet, with technology as the linchpin.

As well as a deep thinker Schumacher was a man of action. In 1965 he founded the Intermediate Technology Development Group and advised governments worldwide on applying "intermediate technology" to solve the problem of poverty.

Schumacher's credibility was based partly on his training in economics in Germany, the United Kingdom, and the United States and his career as a professional economist. He was highly regarded by J.M. Keynes for his work on international finance and he contributed to the famous Beveridge report on full employment that laid the foundations for much of post-World War II macro economic policy.

What distinguished Schumacher from his economic peers was his determined effort to remember that economics is simply a means to an end and that the end itself—the purpose of living—merits far more attention than it usually receives in public discourse.

Peter A. Victor

Further Readings

Hession, Charles H. "E.F. Schumacher as Heir to Keynes' Mantle." *Review of Social Economy* XLIV (1986): 1–12.

Schumacher, E.F. *Small is Beautiful.* 1973.

See also APPROPRIATE TECHNOLOGY; ASIAN ENVIRONMENTAL THOUGHT; ECONOMIC GROWTH AND THE ENVIRONMENT; GREEN ECONOMICS; NONRENEWABLE RESOURCES; SUSTAINABLE DEVELOPMENT

Sea Otters

See MARINE MAMMALS

Sea Turtles

Turtles first arose during the Permian Period more than 200 million years ago. By the time the dinosaurs ruled the earth during the "Age of Reptiles," turtles were well established in freshwater, terrestrial, and marine environments. Whatever forces led to the demise of the dinosaurs at the end of the Cretaceous Period did not drive sea turtles to extinction, and two families still inhabit the world's oceans today. The *Cheloniidae,* or hard shelled sea turtles, include at least six living species, the most numerous of which are: greens (*Chelonia mydas*), ridleys (*Lepidochelys olivacea*); loggerheads

S

(*Caretta caretta*). Some authorities list a dark variety of the green turtle as a separate species. The *Dermocheliidae* are represented by only one extant species: the leatherbacks (*Dermochelys coriacea*).

All sea turtle species lay eggs and must come ashore to nest. The females dig holes on tropical and subtropical beaches into which they deposit from fifty to 200 round, white, leathery eggs. After covering the eggs, they return to the sea. A female may deposit from one to ten or more nests in a year. However, most individuals skip one or more years between reproductive migrations to their nesting beaches. The eggs incubate in the sand for forty-five to sixty-five days. Upon emerging from the nest cavity, the hatchlings enter the sea.

Indigenous coastal peoples have harvested sea turtles for millennia. The eggs of all species are edible. Depending upon the species the turtles are prized for their meat, leather, tortoise shell, oil, and calipee (a cartilaginous fatty tissue from which turtle soup is made). In the late nineteenth century a European taste for turtle soup contributed to the decimation of many turtle populations in the New World tropics. A growing human population, improved access to remote nesting beaches, and mechanized fishing gear further reduced sea turtle populations as they were exploited far beyond their capacity for sustainability in the twentieth century. For example, millions of eggs were collected each year from green turtle nesting beaches in Malaysia in the 1930s, but the harvest declined throughout the remaining years of the century as the turtle population collapsed under the heavy exploitation. After a long and successful evolutionary history, all species of sea turtles are now listed as threatened or endangered with extinction worldwide due to overexploitation and habitat destruction.

Exploitation of sea turtles continues even today. The turtles are particularly vulnerable on nesting beaches and in shallow, near-shore feeding areas such as sea grass beds and coral reefs. Nesting females are cumbersome and easily slaughtered on land, and eggs are easily gathered even as they are being laid. Thousands of young hawksbill (*Eretmochelys imbricata*) and green turtles are killed and stuffed for sale in tourist markets as souvenirs each year. The shells of hawksbills are still highly prized as a source of tortoise shell for jewelry, and turtle oil is still used for waterproofing boats, as a local remedy for respiratory illness, and in cosmetics. Intentional harvesting of sea turtles and their eggs is now illegal or strictly regulated in most countries. However, tens of thousands of adult and larger juvenile sea turtles are drowned each year in trawl nets or other gear intended for finfish or shellfish. Because sea turtle eggs are believed by many indigenous peoples to have aphrodisiac qualities, lucrative black markets exist even in countries where nests are protected by law.

It is not surprising that destruction of the nearshore marine and coastal habitats continues to contribute to the decline of sea turtle populations as human populations grow. More than 50 percent of the human population lives in the coastal zone. Prime feeding habitats for sea turtles such as coral reefs and sea grass beds are damaged by dredging, offshore mining, and pleasure boat anchorage. Sand mining for construction materials destroys nesting beaches. Beach nourishing projects, in which sand is pumped from the ocean bottom to restore eroded resort beaches, may bury sea turtle eggs under an additional meter or more of sand. In such cases it is impossible for hatchlings to escape from the nests. Oil spills at sea can encase hatchling sea turtles in petroleum residue, resulting in blindness or drowning. Some turtles may eat floating tar balls resulting from spills of heavy crude oil. They also frequently eat floating plastic bags discarded from boats, mistaking them for jellyfish. The tar or plastic easily becomes impacted in a turtle's esophagus or intestines and causes death by starvation. Electric lighting on or near beaches disorients female turtles emerging from the sea, causing many to return to the water before completing their nests. Even if nesting is successful, the lights can disorient the hatchlings. Instead of entering the surf under cover of darkness, they wander on the beach until sunrise. At dawn, they become easy prey for shorebirds or die of desiccation.

Conservation measures have been instituted in an attempt to rebuild sea turtle populations to their former levels of abundance. Eggs are protected in natural nests or removed to hatcheries for artificial incubation. Artificial incubation is not without its risks, however, because the sex of hatchlings depends upon the temperature at which the eggs are incubated. In one project in the United States researchers discovered that they had been rearing male turtles almost exclusively for the first several years of their conservation project. In some projects turtles are released into the wild shortly after the eggs hatch. In others they are reared in captivity for nine months to a year in a process called headstarting. Before their release into the wild the headstarted turtles are grown to a size at which they are no longer susceptible to predation by sea birds and most fish. Unfortunately, headstarting has never been demonstrated to result in an increase in any sea turtle population.

Although most conservation efforts have concentrated on nesting beaches, eggs, and hatchlings, recent computer models of sea turtle population dynamics indicate that it may be more important to protect larger juvenile and adult sea turtles. These life stages are most severely affected by fishing gear. The National Academy of Sciences in the United States has determined that the shrimp fishery is the greatest source of human-induced mortality for sea turtles in U.S. waters. Fortunately, turtle excluder devices (TEDs) can be inserted into commercial trawl nets to ensure that sea turtles escape before they drown.

While some conservation programs protect the eggs or turtles themselves, other efforts center on setting aside refuges by protecting nesting beaches or feeding habitats. Laws regulating the placement, usage, and color of electric lights provide protection near some nesting areas. However, sea turtles may travel thousands of kilometers between their nesting beaches and their feeding grounds. One government's laws protecting adults, eggs, and hatchlings on a nesting beach cannot ensure the survival of a species if juveniles and adults are killed in feeding habitats under the jurisdiction of another country.

The heavy exploitation of the late nineteenth and early twentieth centuries has already caused a dramatic decline of all marine turtle species. In spite of the many conservation efforts presently underway around the world most marine turtle populations continue to decline. Attempts to reintroduce sea turtles into areas from which they have been extirpated have not been successful. It remains to be seen whether sea turtles have the flexibility to survive the effects of human alteration of the coastal environment, their most recent evolutionary challenge.

Nat B. Frazer

Further Readings

Carr, Archie F. *The Sea Turtle: So Excellent a Fishe.* 1986.
Mrosovsky, Nicholas. *Conserving Sea Turtles.* 1983.
National Academy of Sciences (U.S.). *Decline of the Sea Turtles: Causes and Prevention.* 1990.

See also BALEEN WHALES; COASTAL DEBRIS AND CLEANUP; COASTAL MARSHES, CONSERVATION OF; COASTAL ZONE MANAGEMENT; CORAL REEFS; DOLPHINS AND PORPOISES; FISHERIES CONSERVATION; MARINE MAMMALS; OIL SPILLS; SEABIRDS; SHOREBIRDS

Seabirds

Seabirds are those species that spend long periods away from land and obtain all or most of their food from the sea while flying, swimming, or diving. Seabirds occupy all of the world's oceans. Some are inshore feeders, while others feed offshore foraging over deep water in pelagic regions out of sight of land and independent of it for both feeding and resting. The group comprises four taxonomic orders within the vertebrate Class *Aves* (Birds)—*Sphenisciformes* (penguins), *Procellariiformes* (albatrosses, fulmars, prions, petrels, and shearwaters), *Pelecaniformes* (tropicbirds, pelicans, cormorants, and frigatebirds), and *Charadriiformes* (gulls, terns, noddies, skimmers, and auks)—totalling thirteen families and about 280 species, all of whose evolutionary histories have been principally marine. All share certain life history characteristics that endanger them as a group: they are long-lived, reach sexual maturity slowly, and have low reproductive rates with correspondingly slow recovery rates. Some marine-associated birds such as loons, grebes, seaducks, and phalaropes are also sometimes referred to as "seabirds," but these have been shaped largely by terrestrial and freshwater systems and have become only secondarily adapted to the sea.

Seabirds display a marked non-random pattern of distribution in their marine environment. They return to land to reproduce, often forming immense single-species or mixed-species colonies. These breeding places represent compromises between the oceanographic conditions that provide an adequate and predictable food supply and land sites within range of this food source with available nesting sites and few ground predators. Locations meeting these requirements are few. During the non-breeding season the birds are usually restricted to nutrient-rich waters and/or upwellings and "fronts" or other oceanographic mechanisms that bring food to the surface and concentrate it there.

One obvious consequence of this clumped distribution throughout the year is a high risk of exposure of seabird populations to pollution and other hazardous human activities.

Many seabird populations have become endangered due to the rapid acceleration of certain activities by man in marine areas. Assaults range from egging and hunting to offshore oil drilling, oil spills, contamination with persistent pollutants, competition with commercial fisheries, and increased human disturbance. Precisely how these disturbances and environmental stresses affect marine life and ecosystems is by no means clear. But some seabirds are now showing marked changes in population size and status, changes known to be associated with the widespread industrial expansion and marine resource development occurring in all oceanic zones. Some species have undergone serious declines in numbers and require immediate action to reduce the chances that they will become extinct. Others have exploded in numbers and come into conflict with man by becoming pests through fouling of urban and rural habitats, or by competition for food and transmission of diseases.

Two contrasting patterns of life-history have evolved among seabirds. "Generalist" species are opportunistic and adaptable, often able to take advantage of human-induced changes in the marine environment; "specialists" are tied to a particular set of conditions, cannot adapt easily to change, are highly vulnerable to man's disturbance of coastal waters and habitats, and have shown steady decreases in population size. Analysis of trends of Atlantic seabirds over the past seventy-five years indicate dramatic growth of generalists such as northern fulmar (*Fulmarus glacialis*), black-legged kittiwake (*Rissa tridactyla*), and large *Larus* gulls (e.g., herring gull, *Larus argentatus*; great black-backed gull, *Larus marinus*). Increases appear to be caused by the explosion in quantity of the artificial food supply made available by expanding fisheries and human populations. Specialist species including storm-petrels, terns, and the auks have decreased in numbers. Overall, the future of the "specialist" seabird species must be considered precarious, particularly as human disturbance is likely to be even more extensive in the future.

Direct exploitation of seabirds for food, oil, fish bait, fertilizer (from guano), and clothing is now small, with subsistence hunting restricted largely to developing countries. However, unregulated hunting of seabirds continues in certain developed nations such as the unsustainable kill of thick-billed murres (*Uria lomvia*) in eastern Canada from September 1 to March 31 and Greenland through most of the year. Habitat disturbance and reduced annual productivity occurs even where regulation is attempted such as the annual harvest of shearwater chicks in Australia and New Zealand and the collection of eggs of the African penguin (*Spheniscus demersus*) in South Africa. But the most serious current threats to seabirds come from the indirect effects of other human activity: pollution or predation that affect the birds directly at sea (oiling, drowning in fish nets) or when they come ashore to breed (introduced alien animals, artificial increases in natural predators, human disturbance, tourism), or indirectly by altering the quality and quantity of their food (fishery developments and overharvesting, contamination by persistent chemicals). Additional problems associated with increasing human populations and their demand for food and with global warming pose an ominous threat.

The present conservation needs for the world's seabirds, particularly the more specialized colonially-breeding species, require the total protection of the most important breeding colonies (land and adjacent waters) and key feeding areas both inside and outside the breeding season. Sites used for reproduction require protection from the many sources of human disturbance, both direct and indirect. An international system of enforcement must be developed to ensure that regulations are respected and effective in the attainment of management and conservation objectives.

The nature of the management task is formidable. Since close to 70 percent of the planet is covered with ocean, and since seabirds can be found almost everywhere there is open water, managing seabirds and assessing threats that endanger them is a global exercise requiring coordination of effort on a regional, national, and international basis. Seabird biologists must therefore not limit thoughts to a single colony or species, or even a small area of ocean, but must collectively agree to standardize protocols and coordinate activities, and to sample entire ranges of species and whole oceans, similar to the approach adopted by oceanographers to ask "large-scale" questions. Only in this way can we expect to succeed in the formulation of a meaningful conservation policy and the identification of processes and actions by which seabird diversity and abundance can be protected and maintained.

David N. Nettleship

Further Readings

Bartonek, J.C., and D.N. Nettleship, eds. *Conservation of Marine Birds of Northern North America*. 1979. United States Fish and Wildlife Service, Wildlife Research Report No. 11, Washington, D.C. 1979.

Croxall, J.P., ed. *Seabirds: Feeding Ecology and Role in Marine Ecosystems*. Cambridge University Press, Cambridge, U.K. 1987.

Nettleship, D.N., and D.C. Duffy. "Seabird Populations." In *Wildlife 2001: Populations*. Ed. D.R. McCullough and R.H. Barrett. Elsevier, London, U.K. 1992.

———, J. Burger, and M. Gochfeld, eds. *Seabirds on Islands: Threats, Case Studies, and Action Plans*. Birdlife International, Cambridge, U.K. 1994.

See also BIRDING; COASTAL DEBRIS AND CLEANUP; COASTAL MARSHES, CONSERVATION OF; SHOREBIRDS; WATERFOWL: CONSERVATION AND HABITAT

Seals

See MARINE MAMMALS

Sears, Paul

In his influential book, *Deserts on the March*, ecologist Paul Sears (1891–1990) argued that the 1930s Dust Bowl and the dust storms that swept across the American Great Plains were caused by ignorance and misuse of the land. He advocated the appointment of a resident ecologist to supervise land use in each county and to teach farmers that the land and all renewable resources needed to be protected and preserved. Although resident ecologists were not appointed, Sears's advocacy of the need for ecologists to advise government, industry, and society about land use and conservation influenced generations of ecologists.

In the 1940s and 1950s, Sears worked to develop and promote ecology as "an instrument for the long-run welfare of humankind." Like Aldo Leopold, William Vogt, Fairfield Osborn, and Harrison Brown, Sears warned that failure to understand the biological consequences of accelerating population and economic growth threatened the human future. Joining with other prominent scientists he participated in the 1955 Princeton conference, *Man's Role in Changing the Face of the Earth*, where he continued to argue that scientists must advise society about the social and biological implications of economic and technological development. As president of the American Association for the Advancement of Science in 1956 he encouraged scientists to examine the social implications of accelerating human population and standard of living, warning that such growth was creating "a problem without precedent in all geological history."

The work of scientific activists such as Sears, Barry Commoner, Rachel Carson, Linus Pauling, and George Woodwell in the 1950s helped make ecology a "subversive science" by the 1960s. Sears believed that ecology was subversive because it "mounted a powerful threat to established assumptions in society." Indeed, leaders of the growing environmental movement in the 1960s looked to ecology to support their demands for conservation. With the growth of the environmental movement Sears and other scientific activists helped make ecology an ongoing critique of humanity's relationship to the global environment. From the 1930s to the 1980s he influenced generations of conservationists and environmentalists who worked to increase public understanding of the natural world.

Chris H. Lewis

Further Readings

Sears, Paul. *Deserts on the March*. 1935.

———. "Ecology—A Subversive Subject." *BioScience* 14 (1964): 11–13.

———. *The Living Landscape*. 1966.

See also DESERTIFICATION; LEOPOLD, ALDO; OSBORN, FAIRFIELD; POPULATION CONTROL

Sedimentation

Accelerated soil erosion is a major and serious impact of human interventions that result in environmental change. Although construction, urbanization, war, mining, and other such activities are often significant in accelerating the problem, the prime causes of accelerated erosion are deforestation and agricultural activities. Forests protect the underlying soil from the direct effects of rainfall, generating an environment in which erosion rates tend to be low. The forest canopy protects the underlying soils, and these soils themselves have a less erodible structure under forest. Roots also protect and stabilize the soil, reducing the risk of debris flows.

An inevitable consequence of the accelerated erosion produced by human activities has been accelerated sedimentation. This leads to the accretion of material on floodplains, lower colluvial toe-slopes, and in lake basins. Accelerated erosion and sedimentation are therefore an important cause of landscape change. However, one serious consequence for humans is the sedimentation that may take place in reservoirs, shortening their lives and reducing their capacity.

Agriculture is not the sole cause of accelerated sedimentation. Also important in particular localities is the addition of sediments to stream channels as a result of the need to dispose of mining and other wastes. A classic example of this is provided by the effects of nineteenth-century hydraulic mining in the Sierra Nevada mountains of California. This mining led to the addition of vast quantities of sediments to the river valleys draining the range which in turn raised their beds, changed their channel configuration, and caused flooding of lands that had previously been immune. Of even greater significance was the fact that the rivers conveyed burgeoning amounts of sediment into the estuarine bays of the San Francisco area, causing extensive shoaling.

Accelerating sedimentation is by no means a new environmental problem. There is increasing evidence to suggest that silty valley fills in Germany, France, and Britain, many of them dating back to the Bronze and Iron Ages, are the consequence of accelerated slope erosion produced by the activities of early farmers. Indeed, in recent years, certain formative events have been identified to account for spasms of sedimentation at different times in Britain over the past 9,000 years. These include initial land clearance by Mesolithic and Neolithic peoples; agricultural intensification and sedentarization in the late Bronze Age; the widespread adoption of the iron plough in the early Iron Age; settlement by the Vikings and the introduction of sheep farming.

It is not always possible, however, to pinpoint land cover changes as the cause of valley bottom alluviation. Even under natural conditions these landforms are unstable features subject to alternations of cut and fill, and so, for example, climatic changes can also cause accelerating rates of sedimentation (or incision). There has been considerable discussion in the literature about the causes of phases of alternating erosion and aggradation in the Mediterranean basin.

The prime solution to accelerated sedimentation is to restore a good land cover. In some parts of eastern America and the Midwest sedimentation rates on floodplains have declined substantially in the last five or so decades either as a result of the abandonment of cultivation or because of effective soil conservation measures.

Andrew S. Goudie

Further Readings

Goudie, Andrew S. *The Human Impact on the Natural Environment.* 4th ed. 1993.

Vita-Finzi, Claudio. *The Mediterranean Valleys.* 1967.

See also COASTAL MARSHES, CONSERVATION OF; NO-TILL AGRICULTURE; SOIL CONSERVATION; SUSTAINABLE AGRICULTURE

Seton, Ernest Thompson

Ernest Thompson Seton (1860–1946) was born in England, immigrating with his family to Canada in 1866. Trained in the best art academies of Toronto, London, New York, and Paris, Seton exhibited animal and bird paintings at the Art Association of Montreal, the Ontario Society of Artists, the Royal Canadian Academy, the World's Columbian Exposition, and the Paris Grand Salon. After homesteading in Manitoba and Saskatchewan in the 1880s he travelled extensively in Canada, Britain, and Europe, but resided primarily in New York, Connecticut, and, after 1930, in New Mexico where he eventually died. Guided by scholars such as Elliot Coues, Spencer Baird, J.A. Allen, C. Hart Merriam, Frank Chapman, Robert Bell, John Macoun, and William Hornaday, he used money from commissioned scientific illustrations for the American Museum of Natural History, Smithsonian Institution, and U.S. Biological Survey to subsidize extensive field work and writing. As a biologist and naturalist he was wholly self-taught.

Seton's *Studies in the Art Anatomy of Animals* (1896), the product of painstaking dissections undertaken over several years, was applauded by artists and scientists alike. His career as the father and most respected raconteur of the realistic animal story was launched with the publication of *Wild Animals I Have Known* (1898). This book was followed by many other animal "biographies" embellishing field observations on animal behavior drawn from the author's thirty-six volumes of handwritten journals. After being lumped by John

Burroughs with the Nature Fakers in 1903, Seton responded by producing *The Life Histories of Northern Animals* (1909). This was expanded and republished as *The Lives of Game Animals* (1925–1928) and was awarded both the Daniel Giraud Elliott and John Burroughs medals. *The Arctic Prairies* (1911) describes a scientific expedition to the Northwest Territories undertaken in association with E.A. Preble in 1907 during which Seton mapped Aylmer and Clinton-Colden Lakes for the Royal Geographical Society. He wrote *Two Little Savages* (1902–1903), a combination of fiction, autobiography, natural history, and ethnology, which provided the pedagogical framework for his youth organization, the Woodcraft Indians (later Woodcraft League), precursor of the Boy Scouts of America of which he was a founder and the Chief Scout (1910–1915). After 1915 he continued his scientific and popular writing and lecturing, but devoted increasingly more time to the defense of North American Indians. In Santa Fe he established the Seton Institute, with a faculty including several Native people, to pursue the ideals of the indigenous peoples to which he ultimately married both his art and his science in an ecological worldview stressing human dependency on nature and demanding respect for biodiversity.

In his lifetime Seton wrote over 400 articles and short stories examining mammalogy, ornithology, natural history, and Native traditions of North America. He published more than forty books in hundreds of editions, many of which have been translated into several languages.

John Henry Wadland

Further Readings

Anderson, H. Allen. *The Chief: Ernest Thompson Seton and the Changing West.* 1986.

Keller, Betty. *Black Wolf: The Life of Ernest Thompson Seton.* 1984.

Wadland, John Henry. *Ernest Thompson Seton: Man in Nature and the Progressive Era.* 1978.

See also BURROUGHS, JOHN; NATURE FAKERS; NATURE STUDY MOVEMENT

Seveso

Seveso is a town in northern Italy which gained notoriety in the environmental literature as the site of an explosion of the biocide hexachlorophane in 1976. The heat of the explosion created the contaminant product dioxin (trichlorodibenzo-paradioxin-TCDD) which is allegedly one of the most poisonous artificial substances created by humans. It could be as much as 70,000 times more poisonous than cyanide, and also carcinogenic for both humans and other mammals. About eighteen square kilometers of surrounding land were contaminated by the dioxin. Despite expensive topsoil removal the area is still largely sealed from human habitation. Even a year after the event, and following evacuation of some 1,000 people, birth defects were up by over 40 percent. About 250 abortions were completed among a deeply Catholic population. Two years later the offending plant was dismantled. The total cost of cleanup was estimated to be $150 million. The Seveso nightmare led to the passage of the Seveso Directive by the European Community (EC). This directive requires all hazardous chemical companies to publish their waste emissions, to inform the community of possible risk involved, and to establish a reliable evacuation program in the event of accident. This directive has proved difficult to implement, and has triggered much research in risk communication research.

Timothy O'Riordan

Further Readings

Haigh, Nigel. *EC Environmental Policy and Britain.* 1991.

See also BHOPAL; DIOXINS AND FURANS; HAZARDOUS WASTE TREATMENT TECHNOLOGIES; LEGISLATION: EUROPEAN COMMUNITY; SAINT-BASILE-LE-GRAND; TOXICOLOGY

Shorebirds

Shorebirds (suborder *Charadrii*, order *Charadriiformes*) are primarily small to medium-sized wading birds. There are 216 species of shorebirds in the world. Members of four families breed in Canada and the United States: *Haematopodidae* (oystercatchers), *Recurvirostridae* (stilts, avocets), *Charadriidae* (plovers), and *Scolopacidae* (sandpipers, snipe, woodcock, phalaropes, godwits, curlews, dowitchers, turnstones).

Most species frequent marshes, beaches, and mudflats of oceans, lakes, ponds, or streams. Others are found only in arid habitats, and a few in woodlands. Most shorebirds feed on terrestrial or aquatic invertebrates, often insects; some eat seeds or plant material. All species breeding in Canada and the United States are migratory. Some travel enormous distances between northern breeding areas and southern "wintering" sites, often via long non-stop flights over oceans after acquiring fat reserves at staging areas where food is abundant. During the breeding season shorebirds are normally dispersed, but they often congregate at staging sites during migration, sometimes in flocks of hundreds of thousands.

Historically, shorebird populations were threatened by hunting. As recently as the early 1900s market hunters in Canada and the United States shot hundreds of thousands of shorebirds. This was thought to have contributed to the decline of a number of species, including the Eskimo curlew, which is now nearly extinct. Numbers of other species increased after implementation of the Migratory Birds Convention, signed in 1916 by Great Britain (for Canada) and the United States. All shorebirds were described as migratory game birds, with only two species given an open hunting season. Only common snipe and American woodcock can be legally hunted in Canada and the United States; all other shorebirds are treated as "nongame." Protection of shorebirds is a national responsibility: in Canada by the Canadian Wildlife Service (Environment Canada), and in the United States by the U.S. Fish and Wildlife Service (Department of Interior). Shorebirds are now protected from hunting in most of the northern hemisphere, but are taken for food in some southern countries. Present hunting pressures are not thought to significantly affect most species of shorebirds.

The International Council for Bird Preservation World Check-list of Threatened Birds: *Birds to Watch* (1988) lists twenty-three species of shorebirds, including the piping plover, Eskimo curlew, and bristle-thighed curlew in North America. In Canada the piping plover, mountain plover, and Eskimo curlew are designated as "Endangered" by the Committee on the Status of Endangered Wildlife in Canada (COSEWIC).

Although populations of most shorebirds breeding in the northern hemisphere are not considered in imminent danger of extinction, concern centers around their habit of gathering in large flocks at specific locations during migration, and their dependence on wetland habitats. This behavior exposes a large number of shorebird species to environment modification, pollution, and human disturbance.

Habitat modification from industrial development, agriculture, and urbanization is thought to be the greatest problem now facing shorebirds. Large proportions of wetlands worldwide are being lost or degraded by dredging, soil disposal, landfills, impoundments, reservoirs, drainage ("reclamation"), and hydrologic diversions. Grassland species can be detrimentally affected by cultivation of their habitat and lowering of the water table due to irrigation.

Environmental contaminants, particularly organochlorine insecticides and oil spills, are also a major concern in some areas. DDT is still used in rice fields in Latin America, which harbor wintering shorebirds. High levels of cadmium and mercury have been found in birds wintering in Great Britain, and selenium in shorebirds breeding in certain areas of Texas.

Human or human-related disturbance can also be a problem for migrating, wintering, or breeding shorebirds. People, pets, or vehicles may destroy eggs or young, or may affect them indirectly by exposure to predation or temperature extremes. Continual disturbance of flocks at staging areas may prevent them from acquiring sufficient fat reserves to complete migratory flights. Shorebirds have rarely been considered pests (with the exception of localized areas where they may be involved in aircraft strikes, or competition with harvesters for mollusks), and are much admired for their aesthetics. They are also good indicators of wetland "health." Shorebird populations are difficult to monitor, but there are indications that numbers of some North American species are declining (International and Maritime Shorebird Surveys). Recent conservation efforts have emphasized protection of staging and wintering sites supporting large concentrations of shorebirds. In the Americas the Western Hemisphere Shorebird Reserve Network (WHSRN) was initiated in 1985 for this purpose. "Hemispheric" sites have been designated in Canada, the United States, and a number of South American countries. In 1993 WHSRN expanded to become "Wetlands for the Americas" and established a cooperative alliance with two other international agencies concerned with wetland conservation, the International Waterfowl and Wetland Research Bureau, and the Asian Wetland Bureau. These organizations effectively cover all continents containing shorebirds, except Antarctica.

Cheri L. Gratto-Trevor

Further Readings

Collar, N.J., and P. Andrew. *Birds to Watch.* ICBP Technical Publication No. 8, Smithsonian Institution Press, 1988.

Hayman, P., J. Marchant, and T. Prater. *Shorebirds: An Identification Guide to the Waders of the World.* 1986.

Senner, S.E., and M.A. Howe. "Conservation of Nearctic Shorebirds." In *Behavior of Marine Animals.* Ed. J. Burger and B.L. Olla. 1984.

See also COASTAL MARSHES, CONSERVATION OF; ESKIMO CURLEW; FRESHWATER WETLANDS; PESTICIDES; PIPING PLOVER; SEABIRDS

Sierra

Originally named the *Sierra Club Bulletin,* the Sierra Club's official journal began publishing in 1893 as an annual number and its changes reflect the changing roles of the club.

Administered by an editorial board, composed at first of professors from the University of California and Stanford, and produced by volunteers, the journal achieved a high standard of quality; the contents through its first fifty years were largely in support of the club's purposes: "To explore, enjoy, and render accessible the mountain regions of the Pacific Coast; to publish authentic information concerning them; . . . ." Early issues contained essays about explorations, history, and recreation, as well as philosophical, literary, and scientific studies of mountains, first of the Sierra Nevada, and then in a wider arena. Also included were notes of club activities, photographs of the mountains, and book reviews.

The *Bulletin,* as it was informally called, became under Francis P. Farquhar (editor, 1926–1946) a somewhat more specialized outdoor periodical, a magazine oriented to mountaineering. In the era after World War II, and especially under David Brower (editor 1946–1952) conservation became the magazine's dominant theme, and it became a monthly, edited by a paid staff, though the larger and more formal annual number continued to be published as a volunteer effort. A *Fifty-Seven-Year Index* (1893–1949) was published in 1952.

By the 1960s the annual was published only on a sporadic basis; the monthly became more professional and political in content. Though it still included articles on outings and mountaineering its lead pieces focused in a highly detailed analytical and polemical manner on the club's campaigns about wilderness, National Parks, and national conservation policies. During this era and the early 1970s the *Bulletin* became a sophisticated political journal of conservation.

In the late 1970s, in an attempt to bolster the club's membership, the magazine was directed toward a wider audience and began to accept advertisements. In 1977 the name was changed to *Sierra,* signaling its increasingly commercial and glossy format. *Sierra,* publishing a distinctively more popular and less professional content since then, continues to comprise a combination of materials about recreation and conservation matters.

Michael P. Cohen

Further Readings

Cohen, Michael P. *The History of the Sierra Club: 1892–1970.* 1988.

Gilliam, Ann, ed. *Voices for the Earth: A Treasury of the Sierra Club Bulletin.* 1979.

See also BROWER, DAVID; SIERRA CLUB

Sierra Club

The Sierra Club is a nongovernmental organization based in the United States and dedicated to environmental preservation worldwide.

History

The club had its origins in the Sierra Nevada of California from which its name derives. John Muir and Joseph LeConte, founders of the club, discussed their vision for the future of the Sierras as early as 1870. In the 1880s Muir and Robert Underwood Johnson battled successfully for the designation of Yosemite National Park and unsuccessfully for a park in Kings Canyon. Johnson encouraged Muir to "start an association," and by the end of 1889 meetings were taking place in San Francisco. Those participating included individuals committed to the establishment and defense of a Yosemite National Park as well as others who were eager to form a club to promote mountain recreation. In the end the Sierra Club served both purposes. Its articles of incorporation established the following goals: "To explore, enjoy, and render accessible the mountain regions of the Pacific Coast; to publish authentic information concerning them; to enlist the support and coöperation of the people and the government in preserving the forests and other natural features of the Sierra Nevada Mountains." The Sierra Club was incorporated on June 4, 1892, with John Muir as its first president and an elite membership from the San Francisco Bay area.

In 1901 Muir and William Colby, club secretary from 1900 to 1949, organized the first Sierra Club outing. The outings have proliferated to the present, and are now conducted by chapters and groups as well as by the national organization. The outings have been the initial attraction for many who have become leaders of the club and have helped to propel the modern Sierra Club into a mass membership organization of significance.

In the early years of the twentieth century the Sierra Club faced its first major political test. The city of San Francisco proposed to dam the Tuolumne River in Yosemite's Hetch Hetchy Valley as a water supply. Most of the membership lived in or near San Francisco, and so the club was badly divided. Muir, Colby, and a majority of club members worked tirelessly—but ultimately unsuccessfully—to defeat the dam. Colby emerged as the club's most effective politician, and the Sierra Club emerged as an organization of national stature. The movement for a National Park Service to better protect the parks was furthered, but the division between the utilitarian conservation embodied by Gifford Pinchot and the preservationist ideals of John Muir was solidified.

Prior to World War II club leaders pioneered in technical rock climbing, ski mountaineering, and other wilderness recreational specialties. Many were on close terms with the heads of federal land management agencies and influential in the establishment of several new national parks. Thus, the club continued to provide leadership in both recreation and preservation politics.

As the National Park Service itself has discovered, recreation and preservation are often on a collision course. The Sierra Club discovered it too. After World War II it became increasingly sensitive to the possibility that its encouragement of mountain access was undermining its commitment to parks preservation. The club became increasingly identified with the movement to preserve wilderness areas for recreational use, and a wilderness conference was convened in Berkeley in 1949. Thereafter wilderness conferences were held biannually for more than twenty years. The club's new sensibilities were reflected in 1951 in a broadened set of purposes. "Explore, enjoy, and render acces-

sible the mountain regions of the Pacific Coast" was replaced by "explore, enjoy, and preserve the Sierra Nevada and other scenic resources of the United States."

The Sierra Club's increasingly preservationist and ecological perspective strained relationships with more utilitarian-minded managers in the Interior and Agriculture departments. Successful battles were fought in the 1950s to defeat dams proposed to be built in Colorado's Dinosaur National Monument and in the 1960s to defeat dams proposed for the Grand Canyon. Aggressive lobbying against the Grand Canyon dams cost the club its federal tax exemption but enhanced its reputation as a champion of parks preservation. The club was active in creating national systems of wilderness areas, wild rivers, and recreational trails. It was particularly influential in establishing North Cascades and Redwoods national parks. In the 1970s it joined forces with a host of other conservation organizations to assure passage of the Alaska National Interest Lands Conservation Act (1980), which made unprecedented additions to the national park, national wildlife refuge, and national wilderness preservation systems.

Organization

Between 1892 and 1952 membership grew from 283 to about 7,000. It no longer seemed plausible for all the club's activities to be managed by volunteers, and David Brower was appointed executive director. The Brower Era (1952–1969) was marked by creation of a publishing empire that brought the club's message to millions, expansion of the club's vision to include the global environment, aggressiveness in pursuing a preservationist political agenda, and a tenfold increase in membership. During the same period, the club lost its tax-exempt status and witnessed increasing conflict between the volunteer board and the professional staff headed by Brower. In 1969 Brower was forced to resign and was replaced by Michael McCloskey in a position described as chief of staff.

Organizationally the club has continued to prosper. In 1994 the Sierra Club is an influential, main-stream environmental organization numbering more than half a million members and budgeting $38 million annually. It is organized into thirteen regions and sixty-three chapters, which are subdivided into 400 local groups. It publishes Sierra Club books and calendars in various formats and *Sierra* magazine. It engages in education, sponsors outings, and promotes political action at international, national, chapter, and group levels. The Sierra Club Foundation, a tax-exempt entity established in 1960, emphasizes fundraising in support of non-political, non-legislative conservation programs. The Sierra Club Legal Defense Fund, a tax-exempt entity established in 1971, litigates natural resource issues for the Sierra Club and other public interest organizations. The Sierra Club Political Committee, established in 1976, promotes candidates for public office who share the club's environmental concerns. Sierra Club Canada became a separate corporation in 1992.

The club's prominent status and global concerns are reflected in its current mission statement: "To explore, enjoy, and protect the wild places of the earth; to practice and promote the responsible use of the earth's ecosystems and resources; to educate and enlist humanity to protect and restore the quality of the natural and human environment; and to use all lawful means to carry out these objectives."

Craig W. Allin

Further Readings

Allin, Craig W. *The Politics of Wilderness Preservation.* 1982.

Cohen, Michael P. *The History of the Sierra Club: 1892–1970.* 1988.

Turner, Tom. *Sierra Club: 100 Years of Protecting Nature.* 1991.

See also BROWER, DAVID; ECHO PARK DAM; HETCH HETCHY DAM; JOHNSON, ROBERT UNDERWOOD; McCLOSKY, MICHAEL; MINERAL KING CANYON; MUIR, JOHN; *Sierra*

Silkwood, Karen G.

Karen G. Silkwood (1946–1974), a health and safety officer for the Oil, Chemical and Atomic Workers' International Union (OCAW), died mysteriously on November 13, 1974 on her way to a meeting with David Burnham, a reporter for the *New York Times*. At that meeting she was to deliver the results of her six-week special investigation of violations of Atomic Energy Commission regulations regarding the handling of plutonium at Kerr-McGee's plutonium plant in Cimarron, Oklahoma.

Silkwood was born in Corpus Christi, Texas, on February 19, 1946. She completed primary, secondary, and two years of college education in preparation for a medical technology career. Karen left school and married, giving birth to three children. In 1972, after the dissolution of her marriage, Karen moved to Oklahoma City and took a job as a laboratory technician at the Kerr-McGee plutonium facility in Cimarron, about twenty miles outside the city.

The Cimarron facility was built in 1970 primarily to make plutonium-filled fuel rods for the Atomic Energy Commission's fast-breeder program in Hanford, Washington. By the autumn of 1974 Kerr-McGee had been obliged to report seventy-three contamination incidents. Silkwood and other workers claimed that many other incidents went unreported including one in which a fire erupted in a plutonium waste container shooting radioactive dust into the air. Seven workers breathed in the dust, but it was alleged that Kerr-McGee managers waited a day before calling the plant physician and delayed lung tests of the exposed workers for at least a week. Silkwood, elected to the union's governing board, received many such worker complaints and on September 26, 1974 she, together with two other union officials, explained the situation at OCAW headquarters in Washington, D.C. The OCAW could do little because the workers lacked proof, hence Silkwood undertook the task of gathering evidence after her return to Oklahoma.

Silkwood's manila envelope containing the evidence she had gathered was in her hand when she left the Union meeting to go to meet David Burnham on the night of November 13, 1974. Her car—a Honda Civic Hatchback—swerved off the road, travelling on the left shoulder until it hit a concrete abutment, became airborne, and landed in a culvert. She was killed instantly.

The time between the Washington meeting on September 26, and the crash, as well as circumstances of the event, led many to believe that there was a concerted effort to silence Silkwood. At 6:30 P.M. on November 5, after Silkwood had been grinding and polishing plutonium pellets in a glove box, she was found to be contaminated. Her decontamination by company radiation safety officers took an hour. The company took urine and fecal samples for analysis but assumed she had no internal contamination because one nasal passage was blocked. Silkwood registered contaminated again on November 6. Company officials said her contamination was coming from off-site and proceeded to examine her apartment. The examiners claimed to find plutonium throughout the apartment and even on the cheese and bologna in the refrigerator. On November 7 Kerr-McGee personnel spent the day decontaminating Silkwood's apartment.

Silkwood was panic stricken and refused to go to work or to see the company doctor. She abandoned her apartment while company workers went through all of her possessions. They reported finding most were contaminated. Silkwood was admitted to the Baptist Memorial Hospital the evening of November 9, was sent by the company doctor to Los Alamos (the nuclear weapon laboratory) on November 10 for more tests, and then released. The company decontaminating crew was still working in Silkwood's apartment when the word came of her accident on November 13. She was dead on arrival at the Logan County Memorial Hospital.

Silkwood's car was pulled out of the culvert and sent to a garage by order of an Oklahoma Highway patrolman. The rear bumper dent would seem to suggest that she had been bumped by another car. Tire skid marks on the road were covered with new macadam and the side of the road regraded; indeed, all traces of the crash were obliterated within a month after her death. Police had gathered no evidence.

Kitty Tucker and Sara Nelson, members of the National Organization for Women, with permission from Silkwood's parents, filed a lawsuit against Kerr-McGee in 1976 charging the company with willful, wanton, and reckless negligence by its failure to protect workers and the public from the harmful effects of plutonium. A jury trial in the U.S. District Court for the Western District of Oklahoma ruled in favor of Karen Silkwood on May 18, 1979, assigning $10 million in punitive damages and $505,000 in compensatory damages against Kerr-McGee. In 1981 the 10th Circuit judges denied that punitive damages could be applied by a state against a nuclear corporation operating under the Atomic Energy Act. However, this ruling was overturned by the Supreme Court on January 11, 1984. The dispute was settled out of court in 1985 and the $10.5 million was reinstated to cover court costs and provide a fund for Silkwood's three children.

Silkwood has become a hero to the antinuclear movement and a symbol of concern for human survival.

Rosalie Bertell

Further Readings
Rashke, Richard. *The Killing of Karen Silkwood: The Story Behind the Kerr-*

McGee Plutonium Case. 1981.

See also BREEDER REACTORS: ENVIRONMENTAL PROBLEMS; ENVIRONMENTAL JUSTICE MOVEMENT; IONIZING RADIATION; LABOR AND THE ENVIRONMENT; NUCLEAR ELECTRIC POWER; NUCLEAR WASTE; URANIUM MINING: OCCUPATIONAL HEALTH

Slash-and-Burn Agriculture

Slash-and-burn agriculture (shifting cultivation or swidden cultivation) is a traditional farming system found in many parts of the humid tropics. It has been in use for centuries and still remains the dominant land-use practice on about 30 percent of the arable soils of the world. It provides sustenance for an estimated 300 million of the world's poorest people. Shifting cultivation is strictly a subsistence level form of agriculture guaranteed to maintain practitioners in perpetual poverty.

Shifting cultivation, however, provides a basis for the maintenance of cultural values and social stability. It is sustainable for people living at low population densities. It is found in a variety of forms that rely on nutrient cycling and crop diversity for their success.

In this system small areas of forest are cleared during the local dry season. Whenever possible logs are cut from the most valuable tree species and sold to provide a cash income. The debris is burned just before the next rainy season starts. Burning helps to control pests and diseases and enables the cultivators to clear land quickly and efficiently with the least amount of labor. The higher soil temperatures that follow clearing and burning also accelerate the decomposition of organic matter in the top layers of the soil.

About half of the nitrogen and phosphorus in the burnt material and nearly all the remaining nutrients are released into the soil from the ash after burning. These nutrients are flushed from the ash by the rain and have the effect of raising the pH of the upper layers of the soil. Nutrients in concentrated form are thus available for one to four cropping cycles after clearing although the fields are often abandoned after only two cropping cycles. Crops such as corn, rice, beans, cassava, yams, and plantains are planted in holes dug with a planting stick (South America), in mounds for root crops (Africa), or by using handtools to till the soil (Southeast Asia). Intercropping is common and weeds are removed manually.

The harvesting of crops and leaching by rain lowers the fertility of the soil. Simultaneously, the replacement of relatively easily removed broad-leaved weeds by harder-to-manage grasses quickly impedes further cropping. The fields are then abandoned for a period of fallow ideally lasting for up to fifteen to twenty years.

The secondary forest grows rapidly during the fallow, using the nutrients remaining in the soil. Essential minerals (including phosphorus, potassium, and calcium) are extracted from lower soil layers and are stored in the biomass of the trees. Unlike nitrogen fixation this is a slow process that concentrates nutrients where they can be used to grow a crop after another cycle of clearing and burning. This means that the fallow period does not directly improve soil fertility. The success of shifting cultivation is thus based on nutrient cycling and the suppression of weeds and pests during the fallow period.

Shifting cultivation is rapidly being replaced by an unbalanced, unsustainable form. Two circumstances, often acting in concert, cause this situation. The population of farmers expands so that traditional practices can no longer support the number of existing humans and competing land-use practices reduce the available area. Under these circumstances the farmers reduce the length of the fallow. A similar, but much more damaging form of slash-and-burn is practiced by migrants to the humid forest. Migrant farmers clear low-fertility soils and are then under great pressure to expand the length and intensity of the cropping period. This is accomplished by decreasing the length of the fallow, breaking the cycle of weed control, and replenishing nutrients.

As the time available for the fallow period decreases the fertility and productivity of the soils decline. This contributes to the economic hardship and impoverishment of the farmers who lack access to other economic opportunities and are often isolated from development programs. Commercial activities such as the expansion of plantations, farms, ranching, logging, and mining also push migrants into areas where shifting cultivation is practiced sustainably. To make the land support more people ever larger areas of forest are cleared and fallow periods are shortened still further.

Recent estimates show that about 25 percent of the total global warming effect is attributable to the clearing of tropical rainforests and the single largest cause of clearing is shifting cultivation. The clearing of tropical forests (deforestation) is proceeding at a rate of 17 million hectares per year. Most of the deforestation is taking place in tropical America and Asia. These regions accounted for 40 percent and 37 percent respectively of the estimated net carbon emissions from deforestation in 1989. Tropical Africa ranks third, with 23 percent of the emissions.

The deforestation of upper watersheds is also having major negative effects upon downstream water systems. Tropical forests are the world's greatest depositories of plant and animal genetic diversity and their destruction means considerable losses to all life on this planet.

Dale E. Bandy, Dennis P. Garrity, and Thomas R. Roach

Further Readings

Lal, R., P.A. Sanchez, and R.W. Cummings, eds. *Land Clearing and Development in the Tropics.* 1986.

Sanchez, P.A. *Properties and Management of Soils in the Tropics.* 1976.

See also AGROFORESTRY; BIODEPLETION; CLIMATE WARMING; ENVIRONMENTAL MOVEMENTS: LESS-AFFLUENT NATIONS; POPULATION CONTROL; SUSTAINABLE DEVELOPMENT; SUSTAINED YIELD FORESTRY; TROPICAL DEFORESTATION

Smog

The term "smog" was originally coined in 1905 by Dr. H.A. Des Voeux of the London-based Coal Smoke Abatement Society. It was used to describe the mixture of smoke and fog that often settled over that city. Since that time the term has been applied with ever-increasing frequency to a wider range of air pollution types that involve neither smoke nor fog, for example the photochemical (or Los Angeles-type) smog.

Smoke particulate and sulfur dioxide (SO_2) are the primary constituents of sulfurous (or London-type) smog, and are mainly generated in the combustion of fossil fuels. A feature of this type of smog is the atmospheric transformation of SO_2 by oxidation to sulfur trioxide (SO_3), which then reacts with water vapor (H_2O) in the presence of catalysts to form a weak sulfuric acid mist (H_2SO_4). This acid may subsequently react with other atmospheric substances to form sulfate particles which settle out. Sulfurous smog is especially well developed in urban/industrial areas that have large emissions of high sulfur content fuels and poor dispersion conditions associated with high levels of humidity. Such was the case in London during the nineteenth and first half of the twentieth century, culminating in "The Great Smog" of 1952, which was a catalyst for action on Britain's appalling air pollution problems. During the period December 5–8, 1952, a particularly dense smog was at least partially responsible for the deaths of approximately 4,000 people. The highest mean daily smoke concentration in ambient air during the episode was 4,460 micrograms per meter cubed ($\mu g/m^3$), but levels were believed to have been as high as 14,000 $\mu g/m^3$ over shorter periods. The event resulted in the formation of the Beaver Committee in 1953 whose investigation of the air pollution and report ultimately led to the British Clean Air Act of 1956.

Another type of smog frequently referred to is the photochemical smog which has at its root the atmospheric transformation of oxides of nitrogen and hydrocarbons, primary pollutants whose major source in urban areas is usually the motor vehicle. This type of smog is initiated by the action of ultraviolet (0.37–0.42 micrometer waveband) solar radiation upon the nitrogen oxides in the presence of hydrocarbons. The photochemical smog sequence is centered around the naturally occurring nitrogen dioxide (NO_2) photolytic cycle (see Table 1, chemical reactions 1 through 3), where solar irradiation of NO_2 causes photodissociation into nitric oxide (NO) and atomic oxygen (O). Ambient molecular oxygen (O_2) then combines with O to form ozone (O_3), which then reacts with the NO to produce NO_2 and O_2. In the NO_2 cycle, which is strongly controlled by the diurnal radiation cycle, there is no net production of any pollutants, because O_3, NO, and NO_2 are formed and destroyed in a continuous process. In photochemical smog formation the cycle is unbalanced by the conversion of NO to NO_2 without an equivalent consumption of O_3. This is enabled by the presence of reactive hydrocarbons (H_C) which are oxidized to form organic radicals (reaction 4), with subsequent reactions producing net NO_2, O_3, and various other secondary pollutants including aldehydes, ketones, and peroxyacetyl nitrates (PAN) (reactions 5 through 9). The complex mix of air pollution that results has a characteristic odor (mainly due to the aldehydes present), hazy brownish color (due to particulate scattering and NO_2), and the oxidants present (especially O_3, aldehydes and PAN) can cause health problems, including irritation of the breathing passages, in the general urban population.

TABLE 1

Simplified Set of Reactions Involved in Photochemical Smog Formation

NO_2 Photolytic Cycle

1. NO_2 + u.v. radiation – NO + O
2. $O + O_2 – O_3$
3. $O_3 + NO – NO_2 + O_2$

Additional Reactions Forming Photochemical Smog

4. $O + H_C – H_C O^*$
5. $H_C O^* + O_2 – H_C O_3{}^*$
6. $H_C O_3{}^* + NO – H_C O_2{}^* + NO_2$
7. $H_C O_3{}^* + H_C$ – aldehydes, ketones, etc.
8. $H_C O_3{}^* + O_2 – O_3 + H_3 O_2{}^*$
9. $H_C O_X{}^* + NO_2$ – peroxyacetyl nitrate

* indicates that the compound formed is a chemical radical

Source: Modified from Oke, 1987.

Although most widely associated with air pollution of the Los Angeles Basin, photochemical smog is found quite widely around the world, and is especially evident in locations subject to large vehicular emissions, air stagnation, and strong solar radiation. For these reasons Mexico City has a severe photochemical smog problem. Because of the important role of solar radiation, outside of the tropics photochemical smog formation tends to be restricted to the summer/autumn season.

Nigel J. Tapper

Further Readings

Bridgeman, Howard. *Global Air Pollution: Problems for the 1990s.* 1990.

Brimblecombe, P. *The Big Smoke: A History of Air Pollution in London since Medieval Times.* 1987.

Oke, T.R. *Boundary Layer Climates.* 1987.

See also AIR POLLUTION: IMPACTS; ASEAN HAZE; DONORA, PENNSYLVANIA; LONDON SMOG

Smoking and the Environment

See TOBACCO SMOKE IN THE ENVIRONMENT

Snail Darter

The snail darter (*Percina tanasi*)—a fish less than seventy-five millimeters long—attracted much attention when on January 31, 1977, the Sixth U.S. District Court of Appeals accepted the argument of the Tennessee Endangered Species Committee that in order to protect the species the Tennessee Valley Authority's (TVA) almost completed Tellico Dam should not be permitted to proceed. This reversed the April 23, 1976, decision of the District Court of Knoxville and was upheld on June 15, 1978, by the Supreme Court. Over $100 million had been spent on the dam. The Supreme Court allowed that only Congress could advance the dam.

The case was significant as an early test of the U.S. Endangered Species Act of 1973 which empowered the Departments of Interior and Commerce for protection of both populations and habitat of endangered and threatened biota. The antecedent act (1969) only protected species threatened directly with global extinction.

The snail darter was discovered in 1973 accidentally by University of Tennessee biologists David Etnier and Bob Stiles. It appeared to live only in clean running water over gravel bars of the Little Tennessee River. The dam would have flooded that habitat and eliminated the species. Based on a 1974 report by Dr. Etnier, the U.S. Fish and Wildlife Service in 1975 placed the darter on the Endangered Species List and identified its critical habitat area upstream of the dam. The later court actions were paralleled by attempts by the TVA to transplant the darter into the nearby, but more polluted Hiwassee River. In 1975 and 1976 over 700 darters were translocated and in the mid-1980s a new breeding population was verified. The darter was also discovered in northwest Georgia and northeast Alabama so that by 1989 at least nine independent populations were known. The species' status was thus changed from "endangered" to the less serious "threatened."

This change was moot in terms of the Tellico Dam because, much earlier, Congress had passed without debate an amendment to some energy legislation that exempted the dam from federal laws. President Jimmy Carter signed the legislation. On January 1, 1980, the dam began operation and its elimination of the snail darter from the Little Tennessee River.

Thomas H. Whillans

Further Readings

Ono, R.D., J.D. Williams, and A. Wagner. *Vanishing Fishes of North America*. 1983.

Williams, J.D., and D.K. Finnley. "Our Vanishing Fishes: Can They Be Saved?" *Academy of Natural Sciences of Philadelphia Frontiers* 41 (1977): 21–32.

Williams, J.E., et al. "Fishes of North America Endangered, Threatened, or of Special Concern: 1989." *Fisheries* 14 (1989): 2–20.

See also CARTER, JIMMY; ENDANGERED SPECIES ACT (U.S.); ENVIRONMENTAL CASE LAW: UNITED STATES; HYDROELECTRICITY; TENNESSEE VALLEY AUTHORITY

Snakes

See REPTILES: CONSERVATION AND HABITAT

Snow as Habitat

Snow covers about 53 percent of the land area of the Northern Hemisphere at some time during the year. Duration varies greatly, but the major distinction is between snow covers which are permanent (lasting all winter) and those which are intermittent.

Snow affects all life forms in boreal regions. The characteristics of a snow cover that are important to living things are duration, thickness, hardness, and density. All snow on the ground is subject to metamorphosis that affects its internal properties and modifies the crystals. Heat, moving from the soil below, may have been stored from the previous summer or it may be heat rising from the core of the earth. Water molecules sublime from the attenuated tips of the arms of the warmer flakes closest to the soil and attach themselves to the colder flakes above. In time the basal layer of the cover is eroded and modified into a series of fragile columns made up of scroll-like or pyramidal cups up to 10mm diam. This layer is properly termed *pukak*.

The metamorphosis occurs both in the forest and in the tundra, governed mainly by: 1) the amount of heat flowing from the earth; and 2) the lack of heat and moisture in the supranivean air.

In the taiga or northern coniferous forest the snow season is characterized by little wind, a marked reduction in incoming solar energy, and few incursions of maritime or tropical air masses. The result is a snow cover that arrives early in the autumn and lasts all winter, unaffected by thaws or wind. Taiga snow occurs in two phases: *api,* the snow on the ground, and *qali,* the snow on the trees.

In the tundra there are also two phases but these are controlled by wind. Wind may move the particles, breaking apart the fragile flakes and jumbling them about. When the particles settle again they fit together more snugly, so the cover becomes denser and harder. Hard, dense, wind-compacted tundra snow is termed *upsik.* Above the *upsik* is another phase, the wind-moved, blowing snow or *siqoq,* which is either consolidated into a succession of drift forms or moves along and above the *upsik* surface. *Upsik* occurs in two facies which have ecological importance. Convex ground surfaces, blown clear of snow winter after winter, are called *vyduvi* and are subject to extreme cryopedological processes. Concave ground surfaces collect snow winter after winter, are called *zaboi,* and are protected from temperature extremes. *Zaboi* may be regulators of mesic habitats in an expanse of otherwise rather xeric conditions.

All snow covers act to reduce the extremes of fluctuations of soil temperature and moisture. Thus plants, invertebrates and small mammals are protected. Some birds, from tiny tits to large capercaillie, burrow into the snow cover for protection not only from low temperatures but also from predation. On the other hand, the snow cover may act to retard diffusion of subnivean carbon dioxide, with resulting effects on small mammals. Snow cover governs the winter feeding and traveling activities of caribou, other ungulates and other supranivean mammals such as wolves, foxes, marten, and fisher. Snow cover has influenced the evolution of winter-white coloration of hares and weasels, "snowshoe" foot feathers of grouse, and claw extensions of collared lemmings.

Qali has been a factor in the evolution of the shape of spruce trees; it is a powerful influence on vegetation type because it governs some aspects of forest succession. *Qali* governs arboreal activity of many birds and arboreal mammals. It affects man-made structures such as powerlines and radio towers by breaking them. It also affects measurement of total snowfall, runoff, and evaporation.

William O. Pruitt, Jr.

Further Readings

Formozov, A.N. *Snow Cover as an Environmental Factor and its Importance in the Life of Mammals and Birds.* Original Russian publication: 1946. Trans. W. Prychodko and W.O. Pruitt, Jr. as Occasional Paper No. 1, Boreal Institute, University of Alberta.

Osburn, W.S. "The Dynamics of Fallout Distribution in a Colorado Alpine Tundra Snow-Accumulation Ecosystem." In *Radioecology.* Ed. V. Schultz and A.W. Klement. 1963.

Pruitt, W.O., Jr. "Snow and Living Things." In *Northern Ecology and Resource Management.* Ed. R. Olson, et al. 1984.

See also ARCTIC; FORESTRY, HISTORY OF; PERMAFROST; TOP PREDATORS IN CANADA: AN OVERVIEW; UNGULATES

Snyder, Gary

Gary Snyder (1930–) is a skillful poet whose concern for the environment and attempt to find an alternate way to approach the natural world other than as a resource to feed humankind's greed has made him an important figure in ecological circles as well. Born in San Francisco and raised in the Pacific Northwest, Snyder came into contact with the natural world early through jobs as a fire lookout, sailor, and logger. He also became a mountain climber and trail guide. These activities made him aware of the damage done to nature by the excesses of industrial society. Snyder graduated from Reed College and attended the University of Indiana and the University of California at Berkeley but gathered many experiences from his travels, like his fellow founding members of the Beat Generation, Jack Kerouac, Allan Ginsberg, and Neal Cassady. In 1957 Snyder moved to Japan where he lived for several years, residing in a monastery and not only studying but converting to Mahayana-Vajrayana Buddhism, a religious and philosophical viewpoint that greatly influenced his later thought about how to live in harmony in nature. While living in Japan for over a decade Snyder also traveled extensively throughout Asia.

Snyder published his first volume of poetry, *Riprap,* in 1959, and has produced over two dozen books of poetry and prose since. He has won the Bollingen Prize, a Guggenheim Fellowship, and the Pulitzer Prize for the volume of poetry, *Turtle Island* (1974). Snyder was a member of the United Nations Conference on the Human Environment in 1972 and has amplified his role as a literary figure to become a leading figure in the fight to save the environment, making many speeches and appearances annually at ecological conferences and meetings. He has published a book of such ecological speeches, *The Real Work: Interviews & Talks, 1964–1979* (1980).

Snyder's poetry is influenced by his travels and studies, with Native American myths, legends, and chants, Buddhist thought, and legends and stories from other world cultures mixed into a poetic form which often leans in the direction of the Japanese haiku, although most of Snyder's poems are not as clipped and enigmatic as poems of that form. (In fact, Snyder's ecological bias is so clear in most of his work that some literary critics regard his poetry as didactic, weakening its artistic effect.) Just as the haiku offers a snapshot, a frozen moment designed to show the beauty of nature at any time independent of thought or abstract theory, Snyder's poetry attempts to present to the reader a world which needs no justification for its existence and no purpose other than to be in all of its complexity and to be respected for that being. Snyder sees humanity's place as a part of nature, a partner with the natural world rather than its master.

Jim Baird

Further Readings
Snyder, Gary. *Earth House Hold: Technical Notes & Queries to Fellow Dharma Revolutionaries.* 1969.
———. *Turtle Island.* 1974.
———. *Left Out in the Rain: New Poems 1947–1986.* 1988.

See also ASIAN ENVIRONMENTAL THOUGHT; ROETHKE, THEODORE

Social Ecology

See ECHOANARCHISM; RADICAL ENVIRONMENTALISM

Soft Energy Paths

Amory Lovins introduced the concept of soft energy paths in a famous article in the October 1976 issue of *Foreign Affairs*, and in his 1977 book, *Soft Energy Paths: Toward a Durable Peace. Foreign Affairs* is a prestigious, high-visibility journal, widely read by government officials and policy analysts. Energy policy was an important topic three years after the oil embargo and dramatic increases in fossil fuel prices, and hence these writings were very timely.

The soft energy path presented an analytical breakthrough—a new way of thinking about society's energy needs, namely that energy policy should be based on the end-use demand for goods and services that require energy, and that energy supply should be tailored to supply those goods and services in the most frugal and environmentally benign way possible. In particular, supply should be matched to demand in quality, meaning that expensive, high-quality forms of energy, such as electricity, should not be used to perform tasks that require only low-temperature heat, such as heating hot water for a house. Electricity should be used only for applications that require its unique properties, such as telecommunications. Energy use should be frugal in getting the most goods or services out of every unit of energy; energy policy, therefore, should encourage maximum energy efficiency (e.g., by insulating houses instead of burning more fuel oil).

This analytical perspective led to radically different policy conclusions than did the thinking that had been dominating government and industry officials up to that time. Conventional analysis assumed that continued economic growth required continued growth in energy consumption, measured as the number of barrels of oil or tons of coal that are consumed (primary energy consumption) instead of number of rooms heated or miles driven (end-use functions). Conventional analysis concluded that energy policy should encourage the building of ever more power plants, coal mines, offshore oil wells, and so on, assuming energy demand would increase indefinitely. A soft path analysis, on the other hand, showed that a growing economy could still function while actually reducing the consumption of primary fossil and nuclear fuels.

The soft path analysis also argued that fuels should be (but were not) priced to reflect their long-term replacement (marginal) cost. If so priced, consumers would be encouraged to purchase very different energy sources than under existing prices. In particular they would purchase much more energy efficient and renewable energy sources, less fossil fuels, and no nuclear power. This conclusion gave the solar energy and environmental movements the analytical tools they needed to make their cases more convincingly. It also caused defenders of conventional thinking to attack furiously both Lovins and soft energy paths.

Soft energy path analysis helped to redefine key terms in the field, such as thinking about energy conservation as increased efficiency instead of as freezing in the dark. In doing so it has changed the way many analysts have thought about energy policy, receiving increasing recognition in mainstream policy and industrial circles.

Frank N. Laird

Further Readings
Lovins, Amory B. *Soft Energy Paths: Toward a Durable Peace.* 1977.
Newsletter of the Rocky Mountain Institute, 1739 Snowmass Creek Road, Snowmass, CO 81654-9199.

See also BACKCASTING; ENERGY EFFICIENCY; LOVINS, AMORY B.; SOLAR ENERGY; WIND ENERGY

Soil Conservation

The soil is a dynamic, life-sustaining system, composed of inorganic and organic substances. A high level of biological activity (including plants, macro- and microorganisms) is the sign of a healthy soil; a principal measure of this is the capacity of soil to sustain abundant plant growth, termed soil productivity. This term does not necessarily refer to agricultural production. Some soils are suited to annual cropping, while others are best suited for pasture or forest cover. The soil resources of this planet are essentially finite because soil formation processes occur over thousands of years. As a result, in the face of declining soil productivity, increasing pollution, and increasing world population, the importance of conserving this vital resource is clear.

Soil conservation is the preservation and improvement of soil productivity and requires erosion control, avoidance of pollution, and the maintenance and enhancement of soil organic matter content, soil structure, and nutrients. In the past soil conservation focused on control of wind and water erosion, but it is now recognized that the main adverse effect of erosion is the lowering of productivity by removal of the organic matter and nutrients in the lost materials. Soil conservation also addresses the general decline in soil quality, recognizing that various physical, chemical, and biological degradation can lower productivity, and can occur in areas where erosion is not a problem.

Soil Conservation Techniques

Land-Use Planning
Matching the use of the land to its capability is done to minimize inputs and to ensure continued production. Land use is broadly classified into cropland, pastureland, woodland, wildlife land, recreational land, and miscellaneous uses. When preparing a land-use plan, consideration is given to soil properties such as depth, permeability, texture, structure, and fertility, as well as to landscape properties such as steepness of slope. Soil maps, the basis of conservation planning, classify soil areas on the basis of many of these soil characteristics, thereby identifying the intensity of land use for which the soil areas are suited.

Management
Good management will reduce the impact of a particular land use. Choosing one technique over another, along with economic factors and personal preference, will determine the effectiveness of a conservation plan. Management techniques can be divided into two groups: vegetative and mechanical.

1. Vegetative Methods—A series of different crops, some providing more income and some providing more soil protection, is known as a crop rotation. Crops grown for the sole purpose of soil protection are called cover crops. Management techniques to improve crop growth, such as using viable and vigorous seed, ideal seed placement, adequate fertilization, and narrow row spacing will provide earlier, better soil cover.

   Grasses, trees, and other perennial plants are the natural way to control erosion. These methods provide denser vegetation for a longer period of time, helping to minimize a number of problems. Waterways can be grassed; shelterbelts can slow the wind; and strip cropping can reduce wind and water erosion. Steep slopes, saline areas, and chronically wet areas can be revegetated to reduce soil degradation while providing food and cover for wildlife.

2. Mechanical Methods—These widen the choice of vegetation, allowing a higher-income crop to be grown even though it may provide less soil protection. Terraces and contour tillage help reduce water erosion and prevent eroded soil from leaving the field to pollute a stream. Minimum tillage or zero-till methods leave more crop residue on the soil surface to protect against erosion, while reducing fuel, time, and money inputs.

Tillage changes, which are short-lived, require little monetary investment unless new equipment must be purchased. Building structures such as terraces is expensive, but increased land-use flexibility and the long-term use of such structures may justify the cost.

Obstacles to Soil Conservation
The importance of soil conservation is easily acknowledged in theory, but too often it becomes overlooked or ignored in practice. Several reasons for this include economic factors, uncertainties concerning management practices, political and cultural factors, as well as ignorance and apathy.

Economic Factors
A soil conservation dilemma is that the practices necessary to achieve it are often not privately profitable. Product price instability and increasingly inflexible costs for inputs, labor, and land cause producers to have short-term planning horizons. As a result they will heavily undervalue the long-term benefits of soil conservation. Immediate economic survival will always take precedence over soil conservation for the future. This is particularly evident in many developing countries where individual poverty and short-term, national economic goals place great demands upon the land resource, thereby increasing the degree of land degradation. The general public must assume some responsibility for this situation. By demanding abundant, perfect, low-cost food and fiber products, while simultaneously expecting producers to be responsible land stewards, the public forces the producer's decision; achieving both of these goals is difficult under the existing socioeconomic conditions.

Insecurity and Uncertainty
A traditional management practice may barely produce profits, but there is often no margin of error to gamble on a new method, even if there may be benefits from higher yield or reduced soil loss. New practices may require outside investment and some source of guarantee that the people will not lose everything in the short term.

Farm land leasing is an integral part of the agricultural industry, but the insecurity of short-term leases reduces the incentive to practice conservation. Even a five-year contract does not give a renter adequate time to benefit from many long-term conservation practices. Lease provisions that properly allocate conservation costs and benefits to landlord and tenant would add incentive to conserve.

Political Factors
Government policies often send contradictory messages to producers. Producers are encouraged to maximize production, but at the same time to undertake conservation methods that remove erodible land from production. Governments must ensure that all programs and policies, within and between departments and between levels of government, are compatible with desired objectives.

Cultural Factors
There is pride in certain agricultural traditions. Straight rows, a dark, residue-free surface, or a weed-free field are highly regarded, but the impact of water and wind is increased. Solutions to soil problems must overcome tradition before they will be given fair consideration.

Ignorance and Apathy
Soil degradation is often a slow and subtle thing. People may not be aware of the amount of degradation that is occurring, or the impact it will have in the long term. Also, a damaged area is easily overlooked if the rest of the field remains productive. Short-term outlooks are apathetic about future needs. Land that is ruined now is lost to future generations. Conservation practices may be postponed or never implemented because of indifference or due to reluctance to spend money to assist unknown beneficiaries, whether they live downstream, or will live in a future time.

On-site costs of soil degradation are significant, whether it be eroded fields, overgrazed pastures, or lost potential of a cut-over forest. However, the off-site costs to the public are even greater, including: sedimentation and subsequent dredging of lakes, rivers, reservoirs, and ditches; water pollution and purification; loss of fish and wildlife habitat; overall loss of national productivity; and decreased aesthetic value. Soil degradation affects everyone; therefore, it is in everyone's best interest to encourage soil conservation on both agricultural and non-agricultural land.

Colette T. Stushnoff

Further Readings
Barrow, Christopher J. *Land Degradation: Development and Breakdown of Terres-*

trial Environments. 1991.

Lovejoy, Stephen B., and Ted L. Napier. *Conserving Soil: Insights from Socioeconomic Research*. 1986.

Troeh, Frederick R., J. Arthur Hobbs, and Roy L. Donahue. *Soil and Water Conservation*. 1991.

See also AGRICULTURAL LAND PROTECTION; AGROFORESTRY; CARRYING CAPACITY; ECOLOGICAL RESTORATION; NO-TILL AGRICULTURE; SEDIMENTATION; SUSTAINABLE AGRICULTURE

Solar Energy

The flow of solar energy reaching the earth, even in recent years, is about 8,000 times greater than all the fossil fuel energy used from coal, oil, and natural gas. Contrary to common perception fossil fuels provide only a small addition to the natural processes driven by solar energy, including light, warmth, food, wood, and clean water. It is therefore reasonable to hope that we could use just a little more solar energy to reduce or replace our current dependence on fossil fuels.

About a third of the solar energy reaching the earth is reflected back into space by the atmosphere. A quarter goes to evaporation of sea water, powering the wind and waves, and growth of plants through photosynthesis. These all provide possible indirect methods of using solar energy which are the subject of much research. The residual 40 percent is absorbed by the earth and is the subject of this article.

There are three main ways to use solar energy directly. One is to light and heat buildings through sun-facing windows using the structure of the building as a heatstore over sunless periods. This is passive solar building design. A second way is by a specially designed solar collector using a fluid medium (usually water) to transfer heat into a remote store. The heat may be used directly or to drive a heat engine to make electricity. This is active solar heating. The third way is direct conversion of solar radiation into electricity by photovoltaic cells.

Passive Solar Building Design

Passive solar design attempts to satisfy the building occupants' need for heat, light, and cooling as far as possible by natural means, using the building itself to collect and store solar heat when needed, to exclude it when not needed and to encourage natural cooling. The design involves the local environment as well as the building. Some call this "design with nature." Without modern methods for heating, cooling, and lighting, our ancestors had to design with nature, but appropriate technology can also play a role. We will discuss passive design mainly for middle latitudes where there is need for both winter heating and summer cooling, but the principles are valid at all latitudes.

Ideally, a passive solar building has unimpeded access to sunshine during the winter heating season when the sun is low in the equatorial sky (south in the northern hemisphere). It is protected from cold winds by the natural contours of the ground or evergreen vegetation, and from unneeded summer sun by deciduous vegetation or screens. A site sloping to the equator helps. Careful layout of subdivisions is necessary with mainly east-west streets, properly placed trees, and minimum tarmac.

While passive solar design goes back at least as far as the Ancient Greeks the modern era began in the 1970s, stimulated by the oil price hikes of 1973 and 1979. One early modern direct-gain design used large windows on the equatorial side to admit solar heat and a massive masonry building to store it. Some houses had windows covering the entire south wall. Another early design used a "Trombe wall," a masonry south wall covered with glazing. Some designs worked well but were rarely cost-effective, especially when oil prices began to drop in the 1980s. The direct gain design often overheated, since in most climates it is difficult to balance glass and mass to ensure comfortable temperatures.

In the 1980s designers began to put more emphasis on reducing the heat loss of buildings by improved insulation and sealing. With smaller heat loss internal heat gains from people and appliances can provide a major part of the heat load, and moderately sized windows allow solar gain to provide much of the residual heat load. While a 150-square-meter direct-gain house might have fifty square meters of sun-facing windows, a superinsulated solar design has only ten square meters, with an auxiliary seasonal heat load of five gigajoules (GJ) in Boston compared with forty GJ for the direct-gain house. And the overheating problem is solved.

Recently, attention is being given to large commercial buildings which have energy needs largely governed by internal factors rather than heat loss through the walls and roof. New technologies are influencing building design. These include compact fluorescent lights, light pipes (which allow daylight to be piped to interiors of large buildings, superglazings (with very low heat loss and control of solar transmission), high efficiency appliances and furnaces, and heat-recovery ventilators.

Active Solar Heating

Solar radiation can be absorbed directly by glazed flat plate collectors to produce temperatures up to about 90 degrees Celsius. Water flow through the collector may be either by natural convection (thermo-syphon) or driven by a pump. In cold climates the water must be protected from freezing. Recent research and certified standards have much improved collector performance. Israel has nearly a million installations serving 70 percent of the population with solar hot water (in 1993).

Solar radiation can be focused by mirrors to produce high temperatures. Focusing collectors are of three main types: the parabolic trough, the parabolic dish, and the solar power tower. The parabolic trough concentrates up to 100 times on a pipe running along the focal axis of the trough. This gives temperatures of 300 degrees Celsius suitable for process steam or electricity generation. During the 1980s the LUZ company built nine power plants in California with a total capacity of 350 megawatts. LUZ has since gone out of business, but the plants are working well and research continues in the United States. Parabolic troughs are also being developed in Australia and Southern Europe.

The parabolic dish, with concentration ratios up to 1,000 giving temperatures up to 1500 degrees Celsius, is under development in several places mainly for remote applications. The solar power tower has a field of heliostats (sun-tracking mirrors) focusing sunlight on a fixed receiver on top of a tower, and generating temperatures as high as 1300 degrees Celsius. Demonstration projects have been built and more are planned in California and Southern Europe.

Photovoltaics

Becquerel discovered the photovoltaic (PV) effect in 1839—that light falling on certain materials can produce electricity. This remained a scientific curiosity until the 1950s when silicon solar cells were made with a conversion efficiency of 11 percent. In 1958 solar cells were used on the Vanguard satellite, at a cost of $600 per watt. The cost was down to $200 per watt by 1970 and to $6 per watt by 1992. Production and use of solar cells has grown with the lower costs and higher efficiencies. In 1992 annual output was fourteen megawatts (MW) in Japan, ten MW in North America, and five MW in Europe. Production is rising and may soon reach 100 MW per year worldwide. Most solar cells are now used in calculators, but there is large potential for other uses as costs drop.

The most common solar cells are made from silicon crystal, with average efficiencies of 15 percent, which may soon rise to 20 percent. The cell is a wafer of two adjacent thin slices of silicon crystal, each doped with different trace elements. This creates an internal voltage across the junction and enables light to drive an electric current of about one watt. Several cells are wired together to form a PV module.

Development of more uses for solar cells will stimulate production of cheaper and more efficient cells. Some uses, such as remote radio stations, are already cost effective. More will become so as prices drop. One demonstration solar car with 1.2 kilowatt (kW) solar cells on the roof and lead batteries has a range of 140 kilometers, and maximum speed of eighty kilometers per hour.

Single crystal silicon can be replaced by other materials which may be deposited in thin films over large areas. The thin film cell has a lower efficiency but is cheaper to produce. Research proceeds in several directions using various materials and new production methods to reduce costs and increase efficiency. One interesting possibility is to use different cells in series utilizing different parts of the solar spectrum to give an overall efficiency as high as 40 percent.

Toward a Solar Economy

In the 1970s interest in solar energy was stimulated mainly by fear of oil shortages. Renewed interest in the 1990s is mainly due to growing awareness that the 6 billion tons of carbon emitted each year by burning fossil fuels is environmentally intolerable and may undermine the world economy itself. Many studies have concluded that we can make a gradual transition from fossil fuels toward a new age of energy efficiency and solar energy. No new technologies are needed, only modest realistic advances in those already in use or under development.

The key to the transition is a shift of focus from energy supply to a detailed analysis of the end-use services provided by energy. This has already revealed many opportunities to provide better services with less energy. The main barriers to a transition are political and institutional. Present energy rules are biased against solar energy as governments stimulate the development of nuclear and fossil fuels.

As poor countries try to catch up with the richer nations, they need to utilize their abundant solar energy resources to leap-frog the energy mistakes of the rich nations. A typical poor country could thus raise its economic prosperity significantly with no additional use of fossil fuels. A solar transition will help to solve major global problems, especially north-south disparities and environmental degradation.

Cyril Carter

Further Readings

Carter, C., and J. DeVilliers. *Passive Solar Building Design*. 1987.

Duffie, J., and W. Beckman. *Solar Engineering of Thermal Processes*. 1992.

Flavin, C., and N. Lenssen. *Beyond the Petroleum Age: Designing a Solar Economy*. 1990.

Goldenburg, J., T. Johansson, A. Reddy, and R. Williams. *Energy for a Sustainable World*. 1988.

See also BACKCASTING; DANIELS, FARRINGTON; LOVINS, AMORY B.; SOFT ENERGY PATHS; SOLAR ENERGY RESEARCH INSTITUTE; WIND ENERGY

Solar Energy Research Institute

The U.S. Congress mandated the creation of the Solar Energy Research Institute (SERI) in 1974 in its first major piece of solar legislation—the Solar Energy Research, Development, and Demonstration Act of 1974—part of a wave of energy-related legislation passed in the wake of the 1973 oil embargo and price increases. SERI would centralize and coordinate solar energy research and development, which had previously been scattered among a number of federal agencies, mainly the National Science Foundation and the National Aeronautics and Space Administration, and would promote solar research within the government.

SERI was not in operation until 1977, in part due to protracted conflict over where the facility would be established. Representatives and senators vied to have it located in their home states, suggesting that many saw a big future in solar energy. Under the Carter administration SERI was sited in Golden, Colorado, and administered for the government by the Midwest Research Institute in Kansas City, Missouri. Its first director was Paul Rappaport, a scientist drawn from RCA and an expert in photovoltaic technology, which converts light directly into electricity. The second director was Denis Hayes, a well-known environmental and solar energy advocate and the organizer of Earth Day in 1970 and Sun Day in 1978.

The SERI budget grew rapidly in the late 1970s, but was cut sharply when President Ronald Reagan took office in 1981. The new administration tried to suppress a recently finished SERI study which argued that solar energy and energy efficiency could have a major role in the U.S. economy, but staffers managed to get the study out and published by a commercial publisher. Many of the staff were laid off and the budget remained flat for ten years. After the Gulf War in 1991 President George Bush upgraded SERI to a national lab, renamed it the National Renewable Energy Laboratory, and increased its budget.

Frank N. Laird

See also BUSH, GEORGE; EARTH DAY; REAGAN, RONALD; SOLAR ENERGY

Soviet Union

See FORMER SOVIET UNION

Spotted Owl

See NEW FORESTRY; OLD GROWTH FORESTS

St. Lawrence River

The St. Lawrence River flows in a weak slope north-eastward from Lake Ontario (seventy-six meters above sea level) to the Gulf of St. Lawrence, linking the Great Lakes to the Atlantic and draining one of the largest freshwater masses in the world. It runs for 182 kilometers between the province of Ontario and the United States, then briefly between Ontario and Quebec, and finally for most of its length inside Quebec, at the southern end of the Canadian Shield. Past Quebec City its waters gradually become saltier. It is one of the twenty great rivers of the world, the thirteenth largest as far as its flow is concerned (7,300 cubic meters per second at its starting point), fifteenth for the surface of its drainage basin (1.3 million square kilometers), and nineteenth for its length (1,500 kilometers with 4,200 kilometers of shoreline).

Native people used to call the St. Lawrence "the road that walks." Jacques Cartier, who reached it in 1535, mentions it as "the most abundant in all sorts of fish than any man has ever seen or heard of." Its main tributaries are the Ottawa, Assumption, Richelieu, Yamaska, Saint-François, Saint-Maurice, Chaudière, Saguenay, and Manicouagan rivers. It comprises numerous and diversified ecosystems including wetlands (roughly 55,000 hectares on which 220 species of animals depend), rapids (International Rapids, Soulange Rapids, and Lachine Rapids near Ville Lasalle), lakes (Saint-François, Saint-Pierre, Saint-Louis), and islands (Wolfe Island, Thousand-Islands, Île de Montréal, Île Jésus, Îles de Sorel, Île d'Orléans, Île-aux-Coudres, Île-aux-Grues), and ports (Montreal, Sorel, Trois-Rivières, Quebec, Baie-Comeau, Port-Cartier, Sept-Îles). Various canals and locks and an eight-meter-deep waterway have been built to bypass its rapids and to make the whole length of the river seasonally accessible to all but the largest ocean-going cargo ships.

The St. Lawrence is the vital artery of Canada. It lies at the heart of one of the richest agricultural, industrial, and commercial areas of North America, creating thousands of jobs in the transport, fishing, and recreation sectors of the economy. At first the St. Lawrence was used for the fur trade, then for transporting wood, and more recently for transporting iron ore and cereals. It is an important, but relatively untapped, source of hydroelectricity with a potential of 6,000 kilowatts. The power dam at Beauharnois has a capacity of 1,653 megawatts and is one of the largest single hydro power dams in the world. Three-quarters of the industries of Quebec and much of its agriculture are situated in the St. Lawrence valley. Nearly four million Quebecois (70 percent of the population) live on the shores of the St. Lawrence, and half of them draw their drinking water, of dubitable quality, from it at forty-eight points serving 104 municipalities. Agricultural, industrial, and municipal wastes, coming from as far as the Great Lakes, through the heavily polluted Niagara River, make the St. Lawrence's water, especially past Montreal, quite unsuitable for human use, including swimming, and render the fish dangerous for human consumption. The Société pour Vaincre la Pollution (S.V.P., distinct from S.T.O.P.—the Society to Overcome Pollution—which focuses on air pollution) a

Montreal-based, French-speaking environmental group estimates that 90 percent of the fish from Lake Saint-Louis, which is situated upstream from Montreal, are polluted with mercury, as well as with mirex and other chemical substances. Salmon, which used to migrate to the Great Lakes, have virtually disappeared from the St. Lawrence. It is estimated that 265,000 tons of dangerous products, mainly acids, sulfates, and chlorine, are illegally dumped into the river each year.

The St. Lawrence Action Plan—a joint five-year operation of the federal and Quebec governments launched in 1988—was designed to produce a complete evaluation of the state of the St. Lawrence and to obtain a reduction of 90 percent of the toxic liquid discharges of the fifty worst polluting factories (including fifteen in the pulp and paper sector) along the St. Lawrence and Saguenay rivers from Valleyfield to Baie-Comeau, by the year 1993. According to recent reports, it might actually reach that goal by 1995. A multidisciplinary federal-provincial task force of twenty-five experts works to achieve that objective, and to protect 5,000 hectares of habitats, to create a marine park, to clean up contaminated federal aquatic sites, to preserve certain threatened species, and to restore wetlands along the St. Lawrence.

As of 1993 some of the factories had noticeably reduced their discharges and their biological demands in oxygen, but not quite enough to let the aquatic fauna survive in the vicinity of those industries. The government, which uses sophisticated measures to study both toxicity level of discharged chemical substances and their effect on the ecosystem, evaluates the impact of each industry on the river and has taken legal action against ten of them. In early 1993 the worst offender—Tioxide—decided to close its doors and move to Louisiana rather than to clean up its operations.

Phase I of the St. Lawrence Action Plan is making positive progress but is insufficient to resolve the majestic river's multifaceted pollution problems since, for example, only 50 percent of Montreal's domestic effluents are presently being treated before reaching the river. A coalition of fourteen Quebec environmental groups called *Stratégies Saint-Laurent* is now pressing for the Quebec government's involvement in the implementation of Phase II of the St. Lawrence Action Plan, which is much more impressive than Phase I and also entails many economic advantages for the regions involved. It would further depollute the St. Lawrence, so that in the year 2000 or so, people will at least be able to swim once again at certain points along the river. If the Environmental Protection Agency (EPA) in the United States succeeds, as promised, in eliminating most sources of contamination from its side of the Niagara River, of Lake Ontario, and the other Great Lakes where the St. Lawrence originates, and if Phase II of the Action Plan is completely implemented, then we might again someday be able to contemplate all of the St. Lawrence's beauty, to monitor its evolution, to swim in it, and to safely drink and draw water and fish from it, in other words, to tread lightly on the magnificent "road that walks."

Jean-Guy Vaillancourt

Further Readings

Creighton, Donald G. *The Empire of the St. Lawrence.* 1956.

Ensemble des fiches d'information sur les 50 industries visées par le Plan d'action Saint-Laurent. Montréal: Équipe d'intervention du Plan d'action Saint-Laurent, 3rd ed. 1992.

Noël, André. "Quand les gens se baignaient dans le Saint-Laurent . . . ." *L'eau, l'obsession du XXIe siècle, Cahier spécial de La Presse* (May 30, 1992): 4.

See also GREAT LAKES; INTERNATIONAL JOINT COMMISSION; MERCURY; PULP AND PAPER MILLS

Standard Setting

Standards are simply points of reference governing industrial activity. Some standards deal with environmental protection, health, and safety, but standards also exist for most products, equipment, technologies, and industrial production. In the latter cases environmental or health effects are often not considered.

Standards can take the form of numbers, for example when a number is used to reflect acceptable levels of pollutants or contaminants in the air or water. They can take the form of lengthy engineering documents indicating the performance characteristics expected for particular technologies, equipment, or products. Standards can specify the manner in which an activity is to be carried out, for example standards governing an industrial process in a factory. Standards can also provide a framework for qualitative or quantitative evaluation, for

example the standards for good laboratory practice.

The term "standard" is often used in different ways. For example, in many countries standards are viewed as a voluntary alternative to government regulations, while in the United States standards are synonymous with government regulations or rules. In everyday language standards are equated with excellence, but in industrial contexts, and where standards are associated with environmental protection, standards normally reflect minimum levels of acceptable performance.

Any standard can be voluntary or mandatory. Mandatory standards are rules, normally accompanied by sanctions for noncompliance, while voluntary standards operate as guidelines. In fact the distinction between voluntary and mandatory standards is often blurred in practice, because some mandatory standards are seldom enforced or are only used as reference points in negotiating compliance with legislated objectives. As well some voluntary standards are later "referenced," or adopted by government. They are used or modified as if they had been developed by government initially.

Standards can be developed by governments but more often they originate with industry organizations or with independent organizations in which both government and industry officials participate. Many standards-developing organizations exist within each country, only some of which are formally accredited. Often their interests and work programs overlap. In virtually every case industry plays an important role in providing the necessary data to support standards development, in setting the priorities and time frame, and in the actual development of standards. Even in the case of government-developed mandatory standards, industry data is used as the basis for assessment, and industry will be consulted with respect to the feasibility and acceptability of the proposed standards.

For any standard to constitute a point of reference it must be accepted. To determine acceptability, those engaged in standards development bring a combination of technical and/or scientific expertise, economic and trade considerations, practicality, and market strategies into the discussion. Even when mandatory standards are developed by government in the fields of environmental protection and occupational health and safety a variety of factors will influence the assessment and the eventual standard. In many standards organizations efforts are made to distinguish technical and scientific assessments from other considerations by creating special panels, hearings, or committees to review scientific issues, but in no case is the eventual decision regarding a standard simply a product of such committees. In a few instances efforts are also made to examine the social, community, or ethical implications of particular standards, but such qualitative assessments are always combined with other considerations as well.

A distinction is often made between prescription and performance standards, particularly in conjunction with environmental and health protection. Prescription standards are set rules (or guidelines) in advance of an activity or a product that will be marketed. They are generally applicable. Standards governing the height of a smokestack or the acceptable level of pesticide residues on fruit are examples of prescriptive standards because they affect how the pollution or fruit will be produced. Prescription standards apply to all instances where smokestacks are built or fruit is marketed, regardless of whether harm is caused in any specific case. By contrast performance standards refer to the degree of damage, harm, nuisance, or other negative effects that will be permitted. Recently, emphasis has been placed upon using performance standards, which are said to deal most directly with the harm or negative effects. Harm is difficult to measure accurately, however, and the burden of record-keeping necessary to ensure environmental protection using performance standards is great. Moreover, ethical problems exist with using performance standards when health-related risks are involved because testing "after the fact" provides insufficient protection for human populations. In such cases prescription standards are used.

Members of the public normally encounter environmental standards in the form of government regulations and often focus their attention on issues of compliance and enforcement. Less evident, but equally important, is the origination of particular standards, which often are developed initially by voluntary nongovernmental organizations and later adapted or simply adopted by governments. Public review of standards, mandated by some environmental legislation, normally concerns only whether the original standard will be made more or less stringent.

Arguments for greater stringency are made both by members of the public and/or environmental advocate groups and occasionally by firms which sometimes use stringent standards as anti-competitive measures or as non-tariff barriers to trade. Arguments for less-stringent standards are often made by those who feel themselves (and not their competitors) unfairly burdened by the cost of meeting the standards, which can be expensive and only sometimes deliver the intended result in terms of environmental protection.

Historically, standards have been developed nationally, and subsequently perhaps adapted and approved as international guidelines—often, but not always, through organizations operating under the auspices of the United Nations. International standards are usually voluntary, but significant pressure is placed upon signatories to international conventions and on participants in international standards development to adopt international standards as national standards. It is in the international context that arguments about the use of particularly stringent national standards being used as non-tariff barriers to trade can be most persuasive. This has the unfortunate side effect of promoting acceptance of the less-stringent standards, which are often also sought by many Third World countries, which find it difficult to meet the costs and administrative burden imposed by stringent standards.

Today more standards activity is taking place at the international level initially, although national delegations comprised of industry and sometimes government officials, still play the predominant role. General Agreement of Tariffs and Trade (GATT) has adopted a standards code promoting international harmonization of standards. International standards activities are now complemented by standards initiatives taken in conjunction with regional trade agreements. For example both the European Economic Community (EEC) and the North American Free Trade Agreements call for harmonization of standards. In the European case significant efforts have been made to develop EEC-wide standards, but EEC standards often constitute only framework agreements or "essential requirements" which must be complemented by and are often mainly enforced as national standards.

Liora Salter

Further Readings
Andrews, Richard N.L. "Risk-Based Decisionmaking." In *Environmental Policy in the 1990s.* Ed. Norman J. Vig and Michael E. Kraft. 1994.

Wilson, G.K. "Legislating on Occupational Health and Safety: A Comparison of the British and American Experience." *European Journal of Political Research* 14 (1986): 289–303.

See also AMERICAN CONFERENCE OF GOVERNMENT INDUSTRIAL HYGIENISTS; LEGISLATION: EUROPEAN COMMUNITY; NAFTA AND THE ENVIRONMENT; OSHACT AND OSHA; POLLUTION PREVENTION; RIGHT-TO-KNOW: COMMUNITY; TOXICOLOGY

Stein Valley

The Stein River rises in the Coast Mountains east of Pemberton, British Columbia, and runs into the Fraser River near Lytton, about 160 kilometers north of Vancouver. The 1,060-square-kilometer watershed covers several ecological zones, linking the cool, wet coast climatic zone with the hot, dry interior zone. The valley is part of the traditional territory of the Nlaka'pamux (or Thompson) people, who are one of the four linguistic groups encompassed by the interior Salish people. First proposed for preservation in 1973 the valley was the object of logging versus wilderness conflict throughout the 1970s and 1980s. The conflict pitted forest companies with mills in Lytton and Boston Bar against wilderness preservation groups. After a number of studies and mediation processes the provincial government approved plans for a logging road into the valley in early 1985. This announcement galvanized the environmental opposition and brought a declaration from the Lytton Indian band that it would oppose development until the Nlaka'pamux land claim on the area was settled.

Faced with a strong Native-environmentalist alliance the government reconsidered. In October 1985 it referred the issue to the Wilderness Advisory Committee (WAC), a panel struck to offer advice on several contentious wilderness issues. After examining scores of submissions on the Stein the WAC issued a rather ambiguous report. It suggested that the lower Stein should be designated as a recreation area (a category providing less protection of natural values than the provincial park designation). It recommended that the middle part of the valley should be logged, but advised that no logging road up the valley should be constructed without the formal consent of the Lytton Indian band. The uncertainty that followed began to dissipate in 1989 when the area's major forest company, Fletcher Challenge Canada Ltd., imposed a moratorium on all activities in the valley, including road surveying. With the Native band resolved to block a road and the company apparently willing to admit that it had sufficient alternate timber supplies many observers concluded that the valley would not be logged. While this seems a reasonable hypothesis, the government has not removed the valley's timber volumes from the totals used in the calculation of the allowable annual cut. And there has been no move to designate the area a park. Instead the government has given the lower and upper Stein sections an inferior form of protection, designating both as wilderness areas under the terms of a section of the Forest Act which leaves them under the jurisdiction of the Ministry of Forests.

Jeremy Wilson

See also CARMANAH VALLEY; CLAYOQUOT SOUND; OLD GROWTH FORESTS

Stewardship

Stewardship is broadly defined as an individual's responsibility to manage his or her life and property with proper regard to the rights of others. Applied to nature, stewardship is the moral obligation of an individual to use the land and its soil, water, plants, and wildlife in such a manner as to protect and enhance their integrity and fruitfulness for future generations.

The meaning of stewardship has evolved over time. The Christian Bible's Genesis states that God placed Adam in the Garden of Eden "to dress it and keep it." In *The Dominion of Man* (1970), John Black argues that man is made in God's image and should act "in a responsible way in relation to the lower order of creation, in the same way as God acts upon man." Plato's *Phaedrus* declares in a similar vein that: "It is everywhere the responsibility of the animate to look after the inanimate," and that man is sent to earth by God "to administer earthly things" in God's name.

Stewardship as understood today is the product of two intellectual traditions: enlightenment and romantic. The enlightenment saw harmony between nature and reason. Nature was the source of wealth, and reason was the tool to extract wealth and sustain nature's fertility. Thomas Jefferson wrote to James Madison (1789) that "the earth belongs in usufruct to the living." The living could harvest the earth's bounty so long as their use of it did not impair its plentitude for future generations. Such use meant utilitarian and sustainable stewardship, such as crop rotation and the use of fertilizing legumes to maintain soil productivity.

European and American romanticism broadened the meaning of stewardship. Wolfgang von Goethe, William Wordsworth, and Henry David Thoreau saw the intrinsic and intuitive value of nature, and the importance of a contemplative relationship between individuals and their immediate environments. For Thoreau nature was more than an object to be dominated and exploited by humans; it was a living community, valuable in itself and co-equal with people. Caring for nature meant more than a utilitarian obligation. Moral considerations, gleaned from nature itself, best informed people in their dealings with the earth. Forest management, Thoreau noted in "The Succession of Forest Trees" (1860), begins with consulting nature, "for she is the most extensive and experienced planter of us all."

Industrialization and rapid population growth in Europe and North America in the late 1800s gave greater urgency to an ethic of stewardship. George Marsh wrote in *The Earth as Modified by Human Action* (1874) that: "Man has too long forgotten that the earth was given to him for usufruct alone, not for consumption, still less for profligate waste." Later, an emerging conservation movement gave poignancy to Marsh's warning as it focused on the depletion of natural resources. Individual greed, it seemed, had supplanted the virtue of personal stewardship.

The meaning of stewardship changed dramatically in the early 1900s. Conservationists like Gifford Pinchot recast stewardship from the moral duty of individuals to the perfunctory duty of professionals dedicated to the wise use of the earth and its resources for the benefit of society in general. In contrast, preservationists such as John Muir rebelled against the idea that nature's sole purpose was to serve humankind, and sought instead the virtual exclusion of people from remaining wildlands.

Preservation as envisioned by Muir left little room for individual stewardship beyond building fences. Yet Muir's bio-centric views did influence Aldo Leopold and his evocation of a land ethic in *A Sand County Almanac* (1949). Leopold called for a new standard of stewardship to change "the role of *Homo sapiens* from conqueror of the land-community to plain member and citizen of it" and to expand con-

servation from "economic self-interest" to "a conviction of individual responsibility for the health of the land." Husbandry, what Leopold called the heart of conservation, was a virtue that could not be practiced by government on behalf of the individual. Husbandry of somebody else's land, he insisted, was a contradiction in terms.

Leopold's land ethic profoundly influences environmental thinking today. Eugene Odum, in *Ecology and Our Endangered Life-Support Systems* (1989), sees strong scientific and technical support for the proposition that ethics are essential to human survival and the human life-support environment. Arne Naess, in "The Shallow and the Deep, Long-Range Ecology Movements" (1973), argues that human use of nature should be tempered with ecological humility and understanding. And naturalist writers in the vein of Wendell Berry focus on how people can and should make a living from the land. They blend into the meaning of stewardship the religious root of man's responsibility for nature, the contemplative and ethical view that the value of nature transcends human needs, and the enlightenment-based regard for sustainable land use. Stewardship is a caring and personal bond between people and land, or what Berry terms the mutual dependence of mind and place. It is a bond that sustains the richness and diversity of nature while providing a sustainable and healthy living for people.

Karl Hess

Further Readings

Jackson, Wes, Wendell Berry, and Bruce Coleman. *Meeting the Expectations of the Land: Essays in Sustainable Agriculture and Stewardship.* 1984.

Leopold, Aldo. *A Sand County Almanac.* 1949.

Passmore, John. *Man's Responsibility for Nature.* 1974.

Worster, Donald. *Nature's Economy: The Roots of Ecology.* 1979.

See also ECO-SPIRITUALITY; ENVIRONMENTAL ETHICS; INTRINSIC VALUE; LEOPOLD, ALDO; MUIR, JOHN; ODUM, EUGENE; PINCHOT, GIFFORD; RELIGION AND ENVIRONMENTAL PROTECTION

Stockholm Conference

The United Nations (UN) Conference on the Human Environment, held in Stockholm, Sweden, from June 5 to 16, 1972, was the most important event in the early history of international environmentalism. It grew out of the increasing concern for the global environment which developed in the late 1960s and early 1970s and marked the first time the world's governments came together to discuss the environment as an issue in its own right. The conference brought together representatives from 113 countries (with Romania being the only Eastern European country in attendance) and over 400 intergovernmental and nongovernmental organizations. A primary purpose of the conference was the creation of a framework for UN attempts to address environmental problems.

The road to Stockholm began with a May 1968 proposal to the UN from the Swedish government regarding the possibility of holding an international conference on "the problems of the human environment." Once the idea had been approved a preparatory committee (PREPCOM) of twenty-seven nations was struck, and it was during the PREPCOM meetings held between 1970 and 1972 that the agenda and the substantive agreements of the conference were worked out. A special staff, headed by Conference secretary-general designate Maurice Strong, was established to organize the event. Many writers acknowledge Strong's crucial role in the success of the conference.

The first few days of Stockholm were marked by confrontation over such issues as whaling, the Vietnam War, apartheid, colonialism, and nuclear testing. At a deeper level the conference was characterized by confrontation between "developing" and industrialized countries. Stockholm was organized primarily on the initiative of northern nations, and developing countries were adamant that concern for the environment should not be used by the north as a barrier to southern economic growth. Most developing countries took the position that industrial pollution was not their problem and would not be in the near future, and were much more concerned with poverty-related issues. The issue of sovereignty over development paths was also contentious, with the Chinese delegation in particular being an outspoken defendant of the rights of less-developed countries to use their resources as they see fit. These conflicts were not, however, fatal to the conference, and in fact led to a more realistic and broader concern for the human dimension of environmental change and for such issues as desertification. Developing countries were able

to exercise a good deal of influence at Stockholm.

The conference also marked a watershed in nongovernmental organization (NGO) participation in international environmental politics. The Swedish government organized a simultaneous Environment Forum for NGOs, an event which set the pattern for NGO involvement in UN environmental affairs. While many NGOs were disappointed at the amount of influence they were able to exercise at Stockholm, their presence was indirectly important in many ways and the international links formed were crucial to the development of international environmentalism.

There is a wide range of opinion on the success (or lack thereof) of the Stockholm Conference. Given the record of many other international conferences, however, Stockholm's legacy is impressive. Barbara Ward (co-author, with René Dubos, of Only One Earth [1972], a document that attempted to outline a philosophical foundation for Stockholm) has commented that the conference "recorded a fundamental shift in the emphasis of our environmental thinking." Perhaps most importantly Stockholm brought a great deal of legitimacy to the environment as a valid issue for government concern and focused particular attention on the social, political, and economic dimensions of ecological change. Other crucial legacies were the Declaration on the Human Environment, the List of (twenty-six) Principles, and the Action Plan. The Action Plan led to the formation of the United Nations Environment Programme (UNEP) as a focus for environmental action within the UN system.

Stockholm initiated a set of international activities aimed at increasing human knowledge of the environment and at protecting and improving the environment worldwide. The principles enunciated in these documents were to form the basis for international environmental law during the 1970s and 1980s. Four major treaties were negotiated at or after Stockholm: the Convention on the Protection of the World Cultural and Natural Heritage, the Convention on the Prevention of Marine Pollution by Dumping of Wastes and Other Matter, the Convention on International Trade in Endangered Species of Wild Fauna and Flora (CITES), and the Convention on the Prevention of Pollution from Ships (MARPOL). Many local and regional initiatives, such as the European Environmental Bureau, may be traced to the impact of the conference, as may the International

Referral System for Sources of Environmental Information (INFOTERRA). Finally, Stockholm saw the beginning of a new role for NGOs in influencing governmental and popular opinion on environmental matters. The practical initiatives and philosophical interest in environmental problems established by the Stockholm Conference continue to play an important part in global environmentalism.

Derek Hall

Further Readings

Caldwell, Lynton. *International Environmental Policy: Emergence and Dimensions.* 2nd ed. 1991.

McCormick, John. *Reclaiming Paradise: The Global Environmental Movement.* 1989.

See also ENVIRONMENTAL DIPLOMACY; RIO CONFERENCE (1992); UNITED NATIONS ENVIRONMENT PROGRAMME

Strip Mining of Coal: A History

Strip mining, to remove the earth, rock, and other material above a coal seam, and then to remove the coal using steam shovels, was hailed as one of the technological and economic miracles of the late nineteenth and early twentieth centuries. J.B. Warriner, an industry spokesperson, emphatically stated the benefits in 1918. Stripping offered an economical solution to the problem of producing the largest quantity of coal for the least expenditure. It increased total output, provided a cleaner product, prevented losses in cutting and handling, and recovered coal that was unobtainable by other methods. The industry would even argue that such methods offered conservation of this precious natural resource: "any reduction secured in any of these losses is true conservation."

There remains some question as to when and where miners first tried strip mining. In the 1820s miners used mule-drawn scrapers and shovels to remove overburden in a primitive form of strip mining. Certainly it was used in Kentucky and Illinois by the 1870s. Large scale commercial, mechanized strip mining appeared in the twentieth century. It soon emerged in both eastern and western coal regions of the United States and moved ahead full throttle, until critics raised environmental and social issues and serious questions about all those claimed benefits.

Malcolm Ross in his 1933 book, *Machine Age in the Hills*, examined the impact coal mining had on the people of West Virginia and Kentucky. In poignant and bittersweet chapters he examined coal-district poverty, boom-and-bust economic cycles, and the other side effects of strip mining. Unfortunately the industry did not pay heed and the long run result was, in several ways, disastrous. The time, however, was not yet ripe for a general outcry, although several states, including West Virginia, Kentucky and Illinois, passed laws regulating surface mining. Enforcement then, as always, was the key.

The American public learned more about the social and environmental horrors of strip mining when the Appalachia region (Pennsylvania to Alabama) emerged as an issue during the presidential campaign of 1960. The strip miner became a rascal of no mean proportions; "raper," "polluter," and "exploiter" were some of the more polite terms used to describe this fiend. Strip mining, which had gained increased popularity in the 1940s and 1950s as an economic alternative to underground mining, stood focused in the glare of public opinion.

Articles in national magazines and books, such as Harry Caudill's *Night Comes to the Cumberlands*, further aroused attention. Strip miners resorted to their tried-and-true defense as the best, cheapest, and safest method of mining. The unreconstructed displayed those popular bumper stickers: "Ban Mining. Let the Bastards Freeze to Death in the Dark." But such efforts won few converts. Locally they sometimes carried the day, nationally they lost. The industry's defense collapsed under a barrage of criticism.

Opponents marshaled testimony such as this observation about strip-mined devastation near Hazard, Kentucky: "Huge gashes have been ripped out of the mountainsides and lie raw and exposed, with no green cover . . . . It is as though the entire landscape, as far as the eye can see, had gone through a hideous convulsion or been ravaged by some crazed monster."

They fought not only about Appalachia, but about mining's impact on the plains of Wyoming and Montana. The result was congressional hearings and finally federal legislation. A variety of bills followed aimed at strip mining and the whole industry. Among those were the Mineral Policy Act (1970), the Threatened and Endangered Species Act (1973), and the Federal Land Policy and Management Act

(1976). The government's new involvement with strip mining was shown in Wyoming. Before turning a shovelful of coal the Spring Creek Coal Company was required to draft an environmental statement to cover the entire projected twenty-five-year period of operation. State and local governments also responded with their own regulations. The free-wheeling days of strip mining disappeared.

After nearly a century of having their own way strip-miners had difficulty in readjusting, but—surprisingly—did adjust. However, even changed attitudes and methods did not resolve all of the basic issues. The final decision regarding the ultimate role of strip mining is yet to be made. Are the changes—the new emphasis on reclamation—enough? Regulation can go only so far; ultimately, the public needs to balance lower priced coal against environmental considerations. Answers may be found in public, government, and industry cooperation. Planning for the future, however, does not resolve the pre-1970s environmental horrors left behind by an unregulated and profit-motivated industry. Found from east to west, this legacy will take determination, motivation, and millions of dollars to clean up and reclaim. Strip mining will not go away, either yesterday's remains or tomorrow's demands.

Duane A. Smith

Further Readings
Caudill, Harry M. *Night Comes to the Cumberlands.* 1963.
Smith, Duane A. *Mining America: The Industry and the Environment, 1800–1980.* 1993.

See also ALTERNATIVE DISPUTE RESOLUTION; COAL: ENVIRONMENTAL IMPACTS; MINING AND SMELTING: HISTORIC IMPACTS; RESERVE MINING CONTROVERSY; URANIUM MINING

Strong, Maurice
See RIO CONFERENCE (1992); STOCKHOLM CONFERENCE

Subsidence
While not all ground subsidence is caused by humans (it is, for example, a common feature in areas of soluble rocks such as salt, gypsum, or limestone), it can be caused or accelerated by humans in a variety of ways: 1) by the withdrawal of subterranean fluids (e.g., oil, brine,

gas, and water); 2) by the removal of solids (e.g., coal) through underground mining; 3) by the disruption of permafrost; and 4) by the compaction or reduction of sediments (e.g., by oxidation) because of drainage and irrigation.

The withdrawal of subterranean fluids can cause catastrophic ground collapse, particularly in limestone areas, where sinkholes may open up (e.g., in the Witwatersrand of South Africa, and in Florida and Alabama in the United States). In such cases sudden loss of life and property damage may occur. More often the subsidence process is gradual, but the results can still be massive. Subsidence produced by oil abstraction has been especially serious in California, where no less than 9.3 meters of subsidence occurred in the Wilmington oilfield between 1928 and 1971. Broadly comparable declines in the level of the ground surface have taken place as a result of groundwater abstraction for industrial, agricultural, and domestic purposes. Subsidence in excess of 7.5 meters has occurred in Mexico City and 8.5 meters in the Central Valley of California. Some great cities (e.g., Venice, Bangkok, and Tokyo) are suffering from increased marine flood risk because of this process.

The subsidence produced by mining is perhaps more familiar, especially in coal and salt mining areas, though its importance varies according to local factors; seam thickness, seam depth, the width of working, the degree of filling with solid waste after extraction, geological structure, and the method of working adopted. In general, however, the degree of vertical displacement that occurs is less than the thickness of seam being worked, because a mass of collapsed rock occupies a greater space than when naturally compacted. As a general rule the surface expression of deep seated collapse may be equal to little more than one third of the material removed.

Other forms of subsidence can result from land drainage in areas of organic soils. The lowering of the water table makes peat prone to rapid oxidation and wind deflation so that its volume decreases. In the English Fenlands some 3.8 meters of subsidence was measured between 1848 and 1957.

In areas underlain by permanently frozen subsoil—permafrost—disruption of its thermal equilibrium can cause melting and subsidence to produce subsidence depressions—thermokarst. When, for example, surface vegetation is cleared for agricultural and engineering reasons the depth of thaw will tend to increase as the insulating effects of the vegetation are removed. The movement of tracked vehicles, the siting of pipelines, and the construction of warm houses, can also cause permafrost degradation.

Related to ground subsidence is building subsidence. In areas of expansive soils, the wetting and drying out of certain clay minerals can cause ground heaving and sinking to occur, damaging building foundations.

Thus subsidence is a very diverse environmental problem. The damage caused on a worldwide basis can be measured in billions of dollars each year. Among the effects are broken dams, cracked foundations, offset roads and railways, fractured well casings, broken pipelines, deformed canals and ditches, bridges that need releveling, saline encroachment, and increased flood damage.

Andrew S. Goudie

Further Reading

Coates, Donald R. "Large-Scale Land Subsidence." In *Mega-Geomorphology*. Ed. Rita Gardner and Helen Scoging. 1983, 212–34.

Johnson, A. Ivan, ed. *Land Subsidence*. IASH Publication No. 200. 1991.

See also COAL: ENVIRONMENTAL IMPACTS; MINING AND SMELTING: HISTORIC IMPACTS

Superfund

The Superfund program in the United States is the world's oldest and largest program to clean up hazardous waste sites. The program has been underway for well over a decade and involves a commitment of over $15 billion in public funds with the hope of many times that amount in private sector expenditures to clean up an expected 2,000 or more sites. It began with the passage of the Comprehensive Environmental Response, Compensation, and Liability Act of 1980 (CERCLA), it was reauthorized and modified in the Superfund Amendments and Reauthorization Act of 1986 (SARA), and was subsequently reauthorized in 1991 without significant changes. New reauthorization hearings are currently underway in the U.S. Congress and major program changes will be considered.

Public sensitivity to the problems posed by hazardous waste sites increased dramatically during the 1970s and 1980s as people living on or near such sites became aware of them

through a series of incidents and discoveries. In the United States the discovery of hazardous waste depositories from past industrial activity at Love Canal and the Valley of the Drums and other such sites increased public demand for cleanup actions. Similar events sparked programs in other nations including Denmark, the Netherlands, and Germany. Superfund is the largest and perhaps most controversial of these efforts.

The U.S. government responded to public demands by dividing the problem of dealing with hazardous waste into two broad programs. First, the Resource Conservation and Recovery Act (RCRA) of 1976 is aimed at preventing new hazardous waste sites from being created by a program that regulates the production, transportation, and disposal of currently produced waste. Second, the Superfund program—as CERCLA and SARA are popularly known—deals with the cleanup of old and abandoned sites found to have past contamination. While both are federal programs RCRA is primarily administered by the states under guidelines from the U.S. Environmental Protection Agency (EPA) and Superfund is primarily administered directly by EPA with state participation.

RCRA, for the most part, is financed by the regulated public—primarily operating businesses—through activities to meet the program's regulatory requirements. Compliance with RCRA then becomes another cost of doing business. Superfund, on the other hand, deals primarily with past problems and, therefore, the benefits of cleanup do not, for the most part, accrue to the private businesses which pay its costs. Superfund is financed by two main sources: a special fund created by taxes on industries which produce specific wastes and some broader tax sources, and a most unusual device: an extremely broad liability doctrine aimed at those responsible for the pollution.

The Superfund program consists of numerous components but the basic stages involved in cleanup can be simply described. First, there is a process for identifying, investigating, and ranking sites so that the most serious can be put onto a National Priority List (or NPL). Second, there are a series of actions to investigate the nature of the problems posed and lay out alternative actions (called a Remedial Investigation and Feasibility Study or RI/FS). Third, there is a phase in which EPA makes a formal decision (called the Record of Decision or ROD) choosing the alternative to be followed, and fourth, those in charge of the cleanup formulate and carry out a cleanup plan (the Remedial Design and Remedial Action or RDRA). Finally, when the work is finished and the cleanup standards are met, a formal decision is required to de-list the site, to take it off the National Priority List. These processes are often time-consuming and expensive. Conservative estimates hold that the average length of time from listing to completion and de-listing consumes over ten years. The average cost of remediation exceeds $30 million per site.

In practice the most controversial aspects of the Superfund program center on two issues: 1) who pays; and 2) how clean is clean enough. Initially policy makers expected the number of sites to be few enough so that public funds would be adequate to pay most of the cost and cleanups could be thorough. But the number of sites proved to be far higher than expected and remediation a far more costly process than anticipated. Controversy has come as EPA works to use the "polluter pays" principle to shift costs from public to private funds producing resistance, and as pressures increase on the EPA to contain costs by lowering cleanup standards.

Simply stated the EPA's goal has been to make private businesses pay the bulk of cleanup costs under a "polluter pays" principle. The set of potentially liable parties (capped PRPs or Potentially Responsible Parties) includes: the generators, transporters, and disposers of waste, and the owners of the polluted land. The U.S. courts have supported the EPA's efforts by defining what polluters can be held liable for quite broadly. Liability is retroactive, strict, joint, and several. This means that parties can be found liable for past activities (regardless of the state of the law and practices at the time), without findings as to guilt or negligence, and single parties can be held liable for the whole problem regardless of the size of their contribution to it. This means that the EPA has the ability to go after a few parties—usually big businesses with sufficient resources—for the bulk of cleanup costs.

In addition the EPA has strong administrative powers it can use to force PRPs to undertake cleanups using their own resources. The most important of these is the power to issue unilateral administrative orders which direct parties to undertake a cleanup. If the parties do not comply and the EPA pays for the work itself, then the non-complying parties can be charged the amount expended multiplied by three. Not surprisingly the prospect of treble

damages is sufficient to make parties issued such orders comply in nearly all such cases.

Given the size of the public funds available and the powerful administrative and legal tools at its disposal the EPA has been more successful than its European counterparts in two respects: it has achieved more remediation at a larger number of difficult sites, and it has succeeded in getting more private funds committed and expended toward this public purpose. Also not surprisingly these successes have been achieved at the expense of considerable legal transaction costs and acrimony.

Robert T. Nakamura

Further Readings
Acton, Jan Paul. *Understanding Superfund: A Progress Report.* 1989.
Church, Thomas W., and Robert T. Nakamura. *Cleaning Up the Mess: Implementation Strategies in the Superfund Program.* 1993.
Mazmanian, Daniel J., and David Morrell. *Beyond Superfailure: America's Toxics Policies for the 1990s.* 1992.

See also ENVIRONMENTAL PROTECTION AGENCY; HAZARDOUS WASTE TREATMENT TECHNOLOGIES; LEGISLATION: UNITED STATES; RESOURCE CONSERVATION AND RECOVERY ACT; TOXIC SUBSTANCES CONTROL ACT

Superinsulated Houses

The purpose of a house is to provide shelter for people. This involves avoiding cold and draft in winter, and heat in summer, ideally maintaining indoor temperatures in the range of 20 to 25 degrees Celsius. The means to do this include building architecture and materials, including some that are specifically aimed at energy management. In most climates it is possible by such "passive" measures to fulfill the requirements of a suitable shelter, with active heating and cooling becoming necessary only in extreme cases. In most present buildings this optimum has not been reached, as active heating and cooling are still in use. The problem is that houses have long life expectancies, and therefore the era of cheap fossil fuels still determines building style in most parts of the world.

The proper passive features of a house depend on climate. With sunny days and cold nights heavy building materials can be used to average out the temperature differences because of the delay in temperature change caused by the heat capacity of the materials. In situations of cold days and nights insulation materials placed in walls and windows can reduce heat losses from the buildings. Together with tightness and controlled air exchange this can reduce the heat requirements to what is produced by the body heat of people occupying the house, plus heat from operating appliances in the building. The amount of mineral wool or glass wool insulation materials, which have to be placed in the wall structures to achieve this, ranges from twenty centimeters to nearly one meter, depending on outside climatic parameters. Care has to be exercised to avoid "cool bridges" (i.e., heat transmission leeways through support frames, window frames, and the like).

Windows require transparent insulation material to fulfill their purpose as daylight transmitters. "Smart" windows have been designed, which change their reflection and transmission properties when outside solar radiation levels change, and increase their insulating properties when needed. The technology controls passage of both solar and thermal radiation, independently.

In climates where cooling is required and no nighttime lowering of temperature can be utilized, a suitable scheme involves cooling by evaporation. When moisture is evaporated a considerable amount of energy is removed from the air and its temperature drops. Naturally circulating air between a moist basement and a ("Persian") chimney (to get rid of the water vapor) may be sufficient, but in some cases forced circulation involving, for example, an underground reservoir with added moisture may become necessary. If the climate is windy the wind may drive the circulation. For techniques such as natural evaporative cooling to work the building again must be well insulated to minimize the heat influx. Both heating and cooling, therefore, should be combined with superinsulation. The constant soil temperature some ten meters below the surface also can be used in both heating and cooling systems.

Experimental houses utilizing the techniques described are abundant all over the world. Energy efficient building styles and insulation requirements are increasingly becoming part of national building codes.

Bent Sørensen

Further Readings

Shurcliff, W. *Superinsulated Houses and Double Envelope Houses*. 1981.

See also DEMAND-SIDE MANAGEMENT; ENERGY EFFICIENCY; LEAST-COST UTILITY PLANNING; SOLAR ENERGY

Supersonic Transport

The decision against the development and construction of a supersonic commercial passenger aircraft in the United States was one of the first self-conscious collective decisions against the assumption that bigger and faster was always better. It was not a decision easily taken. The aerospace industry had been a mainstay of U.S. economic growth for several decades leading up to the 1960 plan to develop an 1,800-mile-per-hour commercial airliner. Air travel had been predominantly an American innovation from the outset; it was a central source of technological pride. Major developments in the aircraft industry usually began in the United States. Moreover technological prowess in the air was crucial to any nation's military and strategic position. Nonetheless a decision was taken against proceeding with progress in the form of supersonic transport (SST).

Opposition to the SST came from several sources on several grounds. Throughout the 1960s there had been growing concern with air traffic noise in most large U.S. cities. Early commercial jet aircrafts were louder than propeller-driven planes and considerably louder than comparable planes today. The SST was likely to increase this problem and spread it from being predominantly a problem for those who lived and/or worked near to an airport. Sonic booms, it was expected, would affect a wide corridor across the continent. William Shurcliff of the Citizens' League against Sonic Boom edited a widely-read book entitled *SST and Sonic Boom Handbook*. Environmental groups, including the Sierra Club, the Environmental Defense Fund, the National Audubon Society, and Friends of the Earth were concerned about air pollution, especially upper atmosphere pollution and about the effects of air traffic noise on wildlife. They entered the public debate in 1967. Also of concern, though of less concern than it would have been after 1973, was the fact that fuel efficiency per passenger mile was considerably lower on the larger, faster SST.

The decision was from the outset a public decision because the predominant share of development funds were public funds. Senator William Proxmire of Wisconsin led the opposing forces. The press urged the debate forward on both environmental and economic grounds.

The consummation of the debate took place in the days leading up to and following the first Earth Day (April 22, 1970). In December of that year the U.S. Senate voted to discontinue funding; in March of 1971 the House followed suit in a very close vote (215 to 204). The SST could not fly on its own.

Robert Paehlke

Further Readings

Caldwell, Lynton K., Lynton R. Hayes, and Isabel MacWhirter. *Citizens and the Environment: Case Studies in Popular Action.* 1976.

Huard, Leo A. "The Roar, the Whine, the Boom and the Law: Some Legal Concerns about the SST." *Environmental Law Reporter* 1 (1970): 68–107.

See also EARTH DAY; ENVIRONMENTALISM; NOISE POLLUTION

Sustainability

When sustainability became a by-word of the environmental movement it culminated several decades of social learning. A century ago those concerned with the preservation of beautiful natural places called themselves conservationists. Concern about increasing industrial pollution in the 1950s and 1960s lead to a sister movement of persons who called themselves environmentalists. Both movements, in those early days, accepted the premise that modern society was basically sound and that destruction of nature could be averted or restored by better technology as well as by better and vigorously enforced laws. Most current public discourse about environmental problems continues to accept that premise.

Most ordinary people do not pay close attention to environmental problems, but those inclined to look would observe, in many cases by the early 1970s, that: 1) world population was increasing swiftly; 2) stocks of many resources were declining sharply; 3) deforestation was epidemic; 4) species extinction was accelerating; 5) deserts were expanding; 6) soils were depleting swiftly; 7) fish stocks were diminishing; 8) wildlife habitat was disappearing; 9) toxic poisons circulated from air to water to food to soil and bioaccumulated up the food chain; 10) the protective ozone shield was thinning rapidly; and 11) the buildup of greenhouse gases threatened to alter climatic systems—perhaps sending them into chaos. Without intend-

ing to, just by doing better and better that which people had always done, humans were changing the way the planet's life systems worked.

Better laws and better technology alone were unlikely to reverse those accelerating trends. It became clear to many in the 1970s and 1980s that continued environmental damage was rooted in the fundamental beliefs and values of modern society and that society itself must be transformed. But how should society be transformed? A book entitled *Limits to Growth* (Meadows, et al., 1972) ignited a furious debate about a "no-growth" society. The phrase failed to catch on as it became obvious that "no growth" did not fit the dynamics of living systems. Other writers began discussing an "equilibrium" society but further thought disclosed that a dynamic, learning, society would frequently be far from equilibrium.

In the later half of the 1970s the phrase "sustainable society" began to be used and soon became widely accepted. The phrase implied that our present trajectory was not sustainable but it did not pre-judge how a sustainable society would be structured. It allowed for dynamic learning and personal growth and development. No one argued against the desirability of sustainability, but there was considerable disagreement about what it would require in everyday practice. Even so, people of many persuasions felt comfortable under this umbrella. The perceived need to urgently address global environmental problems drew the conservation and environmental movements together so that they are now close partners and nearly indistinguishable.

The United Nations General Assembly established in 1983 a World Commission on Environment and Development (WCED). In its report, *Our Common Future* (1987), it called for "sustainable development." The phrase caught on, becoming the topic of hundreds of books, thousands of conferences, and billions of discussions. It became the central focus of the United Nations Conference on Environment and Development held in Rio de Janeiro in June 1992. This first planetwide summit of national leaders was soon dubbed the "Earth Summit" and firmly established environmental concerns and the sustainability of society and its ecosystems at the top of the world's agenda.

A much quoted definition of sustainable development in *Our Common Future* reads: "Sustainable development is development that meets the needs of the present without compromising the ability of future generations to meet their own needs." Many people have interpreted that statement as endorsing the view that economic growth is both desirable and sustainable. Many environmentalists caution, however, that indefinite growth is an oxymoron and that we must distinguish growth from development. Development has no inherent limits but continued growth is physically impossible.

For example, the world's human population is currently doubling every thirty-five to forty years. If that growth were to continue the present world population of 6 billion would double to 12 billion by 2035 and would double again to 24 billion by 2070. Continuing at that rate until 2200 the world's population would double four more times to 384 billion. The human population will never reach that size because nature would intervene long before to limit runaway population growth. Economic throughput (the speed with which we take things from the earth, process them, use them, and discard them as waste) increases even faster than population growth. That growth also must stop at some point since the planet's life systems cannot tolerate indefinitely an increasing depletion of stocks and increasing dumping of wastes. At the very time when increasing numbers of people would need sustenance we would be crippling the ability of life systems to provide it.

Tragically, population growth is such a sensitive issue that the WCED did not forthrightly confront it; the topic was excluded from discussion at the Earth Summit. Meanwhile, economic growth is urgently being encouraged by nearly every nation. Even though humankind shrinks from confronting this contradiction in its thinking it will not change the physical reality that growth in population and physical throughputs must cease. The question is will we make that change foresightedly and thoughtfully? Or, will we require nature to teach us through the elimination of life-supporting systems.

Foresighted change must begin by changing the way we think, value, and behave. Space limitations permit only the sketchiest portrayal of the way a sustainable society might work (see Milbrath, 1989, for a book-length elaboration). Life in a viable ecosystem would be its core value—not consumption or wealth. It would emphasize love, not only for those near and dear but also for future generations of humans and other creatures. It would emphasize partnership rather than domination; cooperation more than competition; justice more than power. Quality in living would be sought

through self-realization rather than striving for wealth. Work would be separated from employment; everyone would work but only some would be employed thus obviating the need for economic growth to provide jobs. Self esteem would derive more from skill, artistry, effort, and integrity than from employment and wealth.

We face a huge relearning task that is being forced on us by the present absence of long-term sustainability. The continued good functioning of life systems depends on how thoughtful and foresighted our learning will be.

Lester W. Milbrath

Further Readings

Meadows, Donella, Dennis Meadows, Jorgen Randers, and William W. Behrens III. *Limits to Growth*. 1972.
Milbrath, Lester W. *Envisioning a Sustainable Society: Learning Our Way Out*. 1989.
World Commission on Environment and Development. *Our Common Future*. 1987.

See also ENVIRONMENTALISM; GNP AND THE ENVIRONMENT; *Limits to Growth*; NONRENEWABLE RESOURCES; POPULATION CONTROL; RIO CONFERENCE (1992); SUSTAINABLE DEVELOPMENT; THROWAWAY MENTALITY SOCIETY

Sustainable Agriculture

Until the late 1980s "sustainable agriculture" was a term primarily used by individuals seeking alternatives to conventional industrial agriculture. Those individuals included a diverse group of farmers, researchers, and agricultural and rural critics. In spite of their somewhat different agronomic and conceptual approaches members of this group gradually came to use the term because they all agreed that conventional agriculture was not sustainable over the longer term. In the late 1980s, under a variety of pressures, agricultural establishments around the world also started using the term "sustainable agriculture," albeit in a very narrow sense.

The two oldest and most widespread schools of alternative agriculture are organic farming (or sometimes "ecological" or "biological" farming) and biodynamic agriculture. Both are practice-based alternatives, but derive from larger worldviews. The concept of organic farming originated in the turn-of-the-century works of F.H. King and 1940s updates by Sir Albert Howard. Both authors examined the traditional agricultural practices of Asia and stressed their durability—a feature they attributed to a series of rotational and composting approaches which maintained the health of the soil. These approaches were championed in the United Kingdom by the Henry Doubleday Research Institute and in the United States by J.I. Rodale, the founding editor of *Organic Gardening*, and then later by his son, Robert Rodale. Internationally, organic farming is promoted by the International Federation of Organic Agriculture Movements (IFOAM).

Biodynamic agriculture is based on lectures given in the 1920s by Rudolf Steiner, a philosopher and reformer in a number of fields. Biodynamic agriculture also stresses the health of the soil and uses many of the same rotational and composting techniques of organic farming. In addition various natural "amendments" are prepared and added to the soil, and crops are planted according to lunar cycles. There is an international network of biodynamic agriculture organizations.

From the 1950s to the early 1980s practitioners of these two alternative approaches were dismissed with contempt by agricultural establishments in the United States and Europe as being unscientific and/or retrograde. Organic and biodynamic farmers and their supporters were often equally contemptuous of the promoters of modern industrial agriculture because of the environmental and social disruptions it appeared to be causing. In the 1970s the Rodale Research Farm was established to conduct long-term research on organic farming—both to better understand the processes underlying it and to give it scientific legitimacy.

At the same time the challenges of environmental degradation, fossil fuel dependence, and concerns over the impacts of the green revolution in the Third World led to the emergence of three new alternative approaches: agroecology, permaculture, and regenerative agriculture. While each draws heavily upon ecological and systems theories, all three have broader social and environmental agendas than either organic farming or biodynamic agriculture.

Agroecology seeks to understand the ways in which the demonstrated sustainability of many traditional and indigenous Third World agricultural systems has been achieved through social, economic, and technological adaptations to the local environment and culture. It focuses primarily on farm and village level systems, but includes a strong concern for land tenure and social justice issues.

Permaculture employs an ecological landscape design approach which stresses the inclusion of multi-story cropping and aquacultural systems as well as the integration of household systems into the total design. Rather than seeking to understand and extract the ecological and social wisdom of long-existing systems as agroecology does, permaculture seeks to design and create new ecosystems-based models. It was developed by Bill Mollison, an Australian landscape architect.

Regenerative agriculture was first championed by Robert Rodale, who stressed the importance of regenerating not only farms, but farm families and communities. More recent elaborations have sought to ground regenerative agriculture in an expanded ecological hierarchy theory that includes social and technological systems at each level. In addition the conceptual scope has been broadened to encompass the total *food system*—which includes not only production-related matters, but food processing, distribution, preparation, use, recycling, and disposal.

Agroecology and regenerative agriculture each include an examination of the broader setting of agriculture and how it interacts with larger trade, aid, and technology transfer patterns. The disparities between the rich and poor regions and countries and the role that corporate influence and power play in creating and maintaining these disparities are of concern, particularly in terms of how they affect the prospects for genuine rural development and sustainable agricultural development.

The different alternative approaches all agree on one point: that industrial agriculture is unsustainable over the longer term. In the United States the farm crises of the 1980s persuaded many farmers and finally the agricultural establishment of the need for changes in agriculture. "Sustainability" became the most widely accepted label acknowledging this need. In response the U.S. Department of Agriculture set up a small "low-input sustainable agriculture" program (which is now named the "Sustainable Agriculture, Research, and Education" program. The international agricultural research centers organized under the Consultative Group on International Agricultural Research (CGIAR) group of the World Bank also adopted the term and set up some research programs.

Sustainable agriculture is a not very descriptive term, and it raises its own basic questions: What or who is to be sustained? How? For how long? And at what cost? The various alternative schools approach these questions with a multi-decade (or multi-century) time horizon and a concern for intergenerational equity. Their specific answers range from sustaining farm fields, soils, aquifers, and habitats to peasant and farm families and their rural villages and communities to crop germplasm and rural cultural and biodiversity.

In contrast, the basic concepts and approaches of conventional agriculture are much narrower and typically focus only on making agricultural production more environmentally sound, while maintaining its economic viability. Rarely are issues of social justice, land reform, or rural development included. In addition, the powerful economic interests and imbedded professional specialties associated with conventional agriculture are deeply resistant to many of the concepts and changes suggested by alternative agriculturalists.

Thus, between the two broad approaches, one sees not only different visions of the future direction of agriculture, but a clash between different paradigms. The conventional "production paradigm" is being challenged by a new "healthy food systems" paradigm based upon the long-term health of the relevant natural, social, and technological systems. Alternative agriculturalists are also challenging the policies, institutions, research models, and methodologies that have facilitated the gradual incorporation of agriculture into larger industrial systems. The systems-based, interdisciplinary, and localized approaches they call for will require a fundamental administrative and political restructuring away from the functional specialization of modern bureaucracies and away from top-down research and extension models.

How successful alternative agriculturalists will be remains unclear. However, as a field in which particular issues of sustainability have been explored in depth over a long period of time alternative agriculture offers a rich reservoir of concepts and experience which ought to be more widely accessed to enrich the larger debates on sustainable development.

Kenneth A. Dahlberg

Further Readings

Dahlberg, Kenneth A. "Sustainable Agriculture—Fad or Harbinger?" *BioScience* 41 (1991): 337–40.
Douglass, Gordon A. *Agricultural Sustainability in a Changing World Order.* 1984.
Harwood, Richard R. "A History of Sustainable Agriculture." In *Sustainable Agricultural Systems.* Ed. Clive A. Edwards, et al. 1990.

See also AGRICULTURE: ENVIRONMENTAL IMPACTS; AGROFORESTRY; FOOD ADDITIVES; GREEN REVOLUTION; NO-TILL AGRICULTURE; PESTICIDES

Sustainable Development

Some have called the concept of sustainable development an oxymoron—a contradiction in terms. As a concept that has arisen from an extended process of international diplomacy (the World Commission on Environment and Development) the concept is clearly a conscious attempt to blend what appear to be opposites. Doing so on a global scale does not make the intellectual challenge any easier. The roots of this challenge nonetheless run deep reaching back at least to the UN-sponsored Stockholm Conference of 1972 at which many less-affluent nations challenged the view of some within the wealthy nations that environmental protection might require restraints on global economic growth. It is simply too glib, it was argued at Stockholm, for those in already rich nations to tell others that the time had suddenly come for global restraints on population growth and economic expansion.

The same arguments appeared among the most telling criticisms of the book *Limits to Growth* published in 1972. This important work had all but ignored the distinctive needs of the poor nations; it argued that in the future growth would likely be limited for all by pollution and resource shortages. The sponsors of *Limits* were led by these criticisms to commission a new work (*Mankind at the Turning Point*) to rectify the omissions of the initial effort. Sustainable development, then, is a concept which has grown out of a history of rich nation-poor nation dialogues. The concept is first and foremost a conceptual recognition that environmental protection will not be embraced by those in poor nations (or those in poor circumstances within rich nations) if such protection is perceived to be in conflict with enhanced economic opportunities. The concept also has roots in and links to the IUCN's 1980 publication *World Conservation Strategy.*

One of the crucial insights underlying the sustainable development concept is the realization that there are severe environmental costs associated with the absence of economic development. Desperate, hungry people will till any soil regardless of the long-term consequences; they will be tempted to cut any tree for fuel if they have no other option but cold; and many of them will poach any wild animals for which anyone will pay. This insight is at the core of the concept of sustainable development; the concept implicitly asserts that *both* development *and* environmental protection are essential. In the view of sustainable development advocates these are not contradictory objectives.

Too little attention has been given, however, to another dimension of sustainable development as it was set out in *Our Common Future*. The less-affluent nations will require significant increases in total energy production and consumption in the coming decades, the report asserts, but the rich nations as well will need to achieve whatever economic output they can on declining total energy consumption. Given the existing technical possibilities for enhanced energy efficiency, it is argued, declining consumption is plausible within the technically advanced and energy profligate wealthy nations. Unfortunately, the mechanisms for increasing global energy (and economic) equity are not obvious. As well, military budgets could be reduced and some of those funds could be transferred to aid, but this is hardly a certain outcome even with the demise of the cold war which could hardly have been anticipated when the concept was initially advanced.

However, the primary problem with the concept of sustainable development is that it has been used by some within rich nations as an argument for continued economic growth, albeit growth somewhat more mindful of environmental protection and/or resource use conservation. The problem lies not so much with initiatives of that sort, but with the failure to appreciate that additional increments of economic growth are far more urgent elsewhere. Many advocates of deep ecology and sustainability have had severe doubts about sustainable development as a notion. The promising side of the visibility of this concept is that it is a conceptualization that can bring to the table those (both rich and poor) who otherwise might simply reject environmental protection out of hand. It is a conceptual means of beginning the political process of integrating environment and economy. Sustainable development then is also a recognition that no one can ignore any longer the concerns advanced by environmentalists.

Robert Paehlke

Further Readings
MacNeill, Jim, Pieter Winsemius, and Taizo Yakushiji. *Beyond Interdependence: The Meshing of the World's Economy and the Earth's Ecology.* 1991.
World Commission on Environment and Development. *Our Common Future.* 1987.

See also AFRICA: ENVIRONMENTAL PROBLEMS; BRUNDTLAND, GRO HARLEM; ENVIRONMENTAL JUSTICE MOVEMENT; ENVIRONMENTAL MOVEMENTS: LESS-AFFLUENT NATIONS; ENVIRONMENTALISM; ECONOMIC GROWTH AND THE ENVIRONMENT; IUCN; *Limits to Growth*; *Our Common Future*; WORLD BANK

Sustained Yield Forestry

"Sustained yield" to most people is a biological concept. The soil has a specific capacity to produce wood, and this capacity should be sustained through prudent management. Fires should be prevented or quickly suppressed; the site should be fully reforested following logging; and every effort should be made to protect the basic resource—the soil.

Today there is substantial advocacy for sustaining biological diversity, not just the trees but all of the forest's flora and fauna in a yet-to-be defined "natural" system. The difference between sustaining trees and sustaining forests has developed into a full-fledged controversy, with biology being overlayed by ethical debates on the "proper" place of humankind in the broad scheme of things.

Initially the concern was pragmatic. In the latter nineteenth century, scientists and those in government saw that local shortages of wood and water slowed—even threatened—westward expansion. The process was seen as simple. Protect the forests from devastating fire, especially those caused by expanding agriculture and industry. The threat of fire encouraged landowners to liquidate the resource before it was lost. New state laws assigned liability to farmers whose escaped land-clearing fires destroyed surrounding forests. State forest agencies were established to provide suppression.

Protection was a good, first step, but more was required. Landowners needed to be shown how to manage their forests for the long term, and there were few foresters available for the task. National forests and certain privately owned forests became "demonstration forests." Those interested could see for themselves just how to "practice" forestry, that is, sustained yield.

Agriculture runs on annual cycles, but forestry cycles are often longer than human life spans. Even if the forest was protected from fire, and even if the landowner had adequate knowledge to manage, the long term carried risks and the biggest risk was uncertainty. Suppose the owner decided to reforest following logging: during what was believed to be a 100-year wait, property taxes could be increased and markets could shift. Some owners argued that the prudent thing to do would be to abandon land after logging, instead of passing on risks to subsequent generations. Thus a major thrust of public forestry during the early years of the twentieth century was to improve reforestation technology and to address issues raised by property taxes, both real and imagined. The public forests themselves were held in reserve for that future date when they would be needed as a full partner in sustained yield.

During the Great Depression of the 1930s advocates of a new sort of sustained yield came onto the forestry scene. As local timber supplies disappeared communities were devastated by job loss. It was jobs and sawmills that needed sustaining; this could be done by husbanding remaining supplies and earmarking them for community stability.

In 1944 Congress agreed (58 Stat. 132), and a half-dozen sustained-yield units were established in the West. One of these pooled federal and private supplies and the others used only federal. Outside competition was eliminated; the timber was to be used only for support of the local community.

This socioeconomic version of sustained yield proved unpopular outside of the selected communities, and no units have been established since 1952. The private sector did not like them because they tended to reduce competition and played favorites, one company over another. The public sector, for different reasons, agreed that such subsidies were not a proper use of public forests.

The broader context of postwar America was significant. A robust economy and pent up demand joined forces to build homes in unprecedented numbers—homes built largely of wood. At the same time the long-predicted decline in private timber supplies shifted demand to the public sector. Before World War II the vast federal holding supplied just 2 percent of the national cut; by the 1950s the national forest share was passing 25 percent on its way to a full third.

No surprises for the specialist; it was all part of the long-term forestry plan, but the general public began to express its concern.

Most of this concern initially focused on private forestland, which historically has been regulated under state jurisdiction. Throughout the 1940s state after state enacted forest practice acts to begin the legal imposition of sustained yield on private land. Most of the original acts made modest demands: provide for reforestation following logging and some degree of fire protection. These laws received wide support from environmental groups as well as industry as the preferred option to federal regulation. By the 1950s the majority of commercial forestland—public and private—was under sustained yield management, at least in principle.

Competition for resources paralleled population growth, and the U.S. Department of Agriculture's Forest Service—the agency with management responsibility for the national forests—sought legislative shelter from competing interests. Congress complied with the Multiple Use-Sustained Yield Act of 1960 (74 Stat. 215). Now sustained yield was more than a technical policy document; it was the law governing national forests. The act listed the resources to be sustained: "outdoor recreation, range, timber, watershed, and wildlife and fish." Wilderness and minerals were defined as compatible. "'Sustained yield of the several products and services' means the achievement and maintenance in perpetuity of a high-level annual or regular periodic output of the various renewable resources of the national forests without impairment of the productivity of the land." The brief text also stated, "and not necessarily the combination of uses that will give the greatest dollar return or the greatest unit output." Some old thoughts, and some new.

Sustained yield at the state level, that is for private land, evolved similarly. Often instead of providing for reforestation in many states the private operator now had to achieve reforestation with the proper mix of species, spaced just so across the land. Erosion control and watershed protection, and sometimes aesthetic considerations, might be included. States generally lagged the federal lead, but they have tended to follow along.

The next decades saw Congress involving itself with sustained yield, sometimes directly and sometimes not. The Rare and Endangered Species Act of 1973 (87 Stat. 884) expanded from earlier laws to include flora as well as fauna and also looked specifically at habitat protection. Those who had been growing forests for their trees found themselves at serious odds with the sweep of history. Other components of the forested ecosystem would at times be given priority over trees.

Three years later the National Forest Management Act of 1976 (90 Stat. 2949) included a section to "provide for diversity of plant and animal communities based on the suitability and capability of the specific land area in order to meet overall multiple-use objectives. . . ." This requirement goes beyond in still-debated ways the Endangered Species Act to "protect" existing ecosystems from "change." The courts are far from through in sorting all this out, but it seems clear that sustained yield today is much more than providing for continuous economic productivity.

Harold K. Steen

Further Readings
Parry, Thomas B., et al. "Changing Conceptions of Sustained-Yield Policy in the National Forests." *Journal of Forestry* (1983): 150–54.
Steen, Harold K., ed. *History of Sustained-Yield Forestry: A Symposium*. 1984.

See also CLAYOQUOT SOUND; CLEARCUT; FOREST REGENERATION/REFORESTATION; FOREST SERVICE (U.S.); FORESTRY, HISTORY OF; MULTIPLE USE FORESTRY; NATIONAL FORESTS (U.S.); NEW FORESTRY; OLD GROWTH FORESTS

Synthetic Fuels
Synthetic fuels are combustible gases and liquids derived from coal, oil shale, tar sands, or biomass. The most common synthetic fuels (often called "synfuels") are liquids resembling petroleum created by "liquefaction" from pulverized coal and a combustible gas produced by "gasification." Between 1880 and 1930 coal gas was widely used for lighting, heating, and industrial production in the United States. Although petroleum and electricity have replaced coal gasification in the United States, synthetic fuels are still important elsewhere. During World War II Germany obtained 90 percent of its peak wartime aviation and motor fuel needs from coal liquefaction. The Republic of South Africa, with the world's largest coal liquefaction facility, produces 30,000 barrels of crude oil equivalent daily.

Synthetic fuels production in the United States has been constrained by severe technical, economic, and environmental problems despite the enormous coal and oil shale feedstocks available. "Scaling up" existing synfuels technologies to commercial production capacity has been costly and unsuccessful, discouraging energy corporations from further research and development programs. Especially damaging to private investment was the Exxon Corporation's withdrawal in 1982 from the Colony, Colorado, experimental oil shale project. The company, having invested $500 million, estimated the project would require $5 billion to complete. Commercial synfuels facilities, if technologically feasible, also require heavy investment. A small commercial synfuels facility producing 50,000 barrels of liquid fuel or 250 million cubic feet of natural gas would cost from $1 to $2 billion. Additional risks are created because synthetic fuels cannot compete in energy markets at current world energy prices.

Environmentalists have frequently been joined by residents of potential production sites in vigorously opposing synthetic fuel development because of the large resource demands and environmental hazards created by the technologies. Water consumption is a major concern, especially in the semi-arid western states where many plants would inevitably be located. A coal gasification facility utilizes approximately 2 million gallons of water daily for each 250 million cubic feet of high-energy gas; some commercial technologies may require 1.2 billion gallons of water hourly. The large volume of solid, liquid, and gaseous waste produced by synfuels facilities includes trace elements of many toxic substances, such as hydrides of arsenic, antimony, and chlorine, and other residues known to be carcinogenic and mutagenic as well as such air pollutants as carbon dioxide, sulfur oxides, and particulates. Little is known about the long-term environmental consequences of these pollutants, such as possible groundwater contamination near facility sites.

American interest in synthetic fuels was briefly aroused following the severe economic and political shocks created by domestic petroleum shortages after the 1973 Arab oil embargo and the 1976 Iranian Revolution. Synfuels seemed to many political leaders an attractive strategy for reducing continuing U.S. dependence on imported petroleum because national coal reserves contained enough energy to meet all national requirements for several centuries while providing a readily available, secure synthetic fuel feedstock. Rising world petroleum prices also implied that synfuels might become economically competitive. In 1975, President Gerald Ford proposed governmental incentives to achieve synthetic fuel production equal to 1 million barrels of oil daily by 1985. Congress was initially indifferent to synfuels and President Jimmy Carter's National Energy Plan of 1977 proposed only a few small-scale experimental synfuels projects. Congressional enthusiasm soon awakened, stimulated by the new Department of Energy and the prospect of large federal spending for experimental projects in many legislative constituencies. In response, the Carter administration decided in 1979 to include in its proposed National Security Act a provision creating a U.S. Synthetic Fuels Corporation. The new corporation, intended to encourage with federal subsidies the private development of commercial synthetic fuels facilities, was granted initial funds of $20 billion and authorized to spend as much as $80 billion.

By the mid-1980s the synthetic fuels boomlet had collapsed. Experimental projects, proving technologically and economically unsuccessful, became political liabilities. Falling world petroleum prices, growing concern about environmental problems, flagging private sector interest, and the Reagan administration's distaste for non-nuclear federal research subsidies assured an end to the Synthetic Fuels Corporation which Congress terminated in 1985. Without an energy crisis to reawaken national interest in synthetic fuels, the United States since the mid-1980s continued its historic dependence on petroleum, natural gas, and direct coal combustion as primary energy sources. Synthetic fuels, having become a stagnant technology, appear to face unpromising domestic prospects in the next several decades.

Walter A. Rosenbaum

Further Readings
Rosenbaum, Walter A. *Energy, Politics, and Public Policy.* 1987.
United States General Accounting Office. *Federal Efforts to Control the Environmental and Health Effects of Synthetic Fuels Development.* 1984.

See also Energy Crisis; Oil Shale

T

Tasmanian Wilderness Society

The Tasmanian Wilderness Society (TWS) was established in 1974, following the defeat of conservation groups attempting to prevent flooding of the Lake Pedder National Park by the Hydro-Electric Commission of Tasmania, in Australia's island state. The TWS expanded rapidly from 1980 onward, after the appointment of the charismatic and visionary Dr. Bob Brown as Director. Espousing principles of nonviolent action volunteers blockaded the Lower Gordon river from December 1982 onward, in an effort to prevent hydroelectric development in this World Heritage area. A judgment of the High Court of Australia in July 1983 granted power to the commonwealth government to halt construction of Lower Gordon dam, thus retaining the region's wilderness qualities. Having achieved victory the TWS dropped the word "Tasmanian" from its title, took on a national orientation and made forest conservation its principal objective. Thus far, it has been only partially successful, but continues to play a significant role in Tasmanian environmentalism on a variety of issues.

Bruce W. Davis

Further Readings

Hay, Peter, Robyn Eckersley, and Geoff Holloway, eds. *Environmental Politics in Australia and New Zealand*. 1989.
Rainbow, Stephen. *Green Politics*. 1993.

See also AUSTRALIA: RESOURCE USE CONFLICTS; FRANKLIN DAM; LAKE PEDDER

Tellico Dam

See SNAIL DARTER

Tennessee Valley Authority

Founded in 1933 as a multi-purpose, regional development agency for the Tennessee River Basin, the Tennessee Valley Authority (TVA) was a gemstone of President Franklin D. Roosevelt's New Deal. Roosevelt charged the quasi-governmental agency with planning for the proper use, conservation, and development of the natural resources of the seven-state, poverty-racked, and electricity-deficient region. Central to that mission was providing cheap electricity from its high-dam flood control network to meet the valley's needs and to power its economic development. Nonetheless, during its first three decades, TVA's three-member boards of directors viewed the agency as more than just another power company. TVA's responsibilities to its 80,000-square-mile service area also included fertilizer research and agricultural development, river development for navigation enhancement, natural resource conservation, and forestry management. By the 1960s most observers attributed a great portion of the economic, social, and resource revival of the region to TVA's leadership in economic development, air and water pollution monitoring and modeling, and husbanding of natural resources.

By the end of the 1970s, however, electric power generation began to dwarf all other TVA programs. In addition, hydroelectric power supplies from its 29 dams were overshadowed drastically by electricity produced from 11 coal-fired plants, with plans for nuclear power to supply nearly 50 percent of the valley's power needs by the year 2000. In the process the agency not only became the nation's largest generator of electricity, but also attracted the ire of environmentalists, anti-nuclear activists, its 160 municipal and cooperative power distributors, and Tennessee Valley consumers.

Most responsible for these circumstances were TVA's notoriety as the nation's largest sulfur dioxide polluter, its early association with strip-mined coal, its repeated nuclear plant safety violations, and its spiraling electricity rates. Most disturbing to valley residents, these rate increases were necessary to pay capital costs for meeting power demands that TVA had vastly overestimated in the previous decade. As such, TVA began to sustain a level of regulatory scrutiny unseen since the attacks on its very existence by private utilities in the 1930s. The agency jousted routinely with the Environmental Protection Agency, the Nuclear Regulatory Commission, state government agencies, citizens groups, and the U.S. Congress.

By the late 1980s, Roosevelt's vision of TVA as a "moral force," as a "yardstick" against which all private power companies would be judged, as a natural resource management exemplar, and as a social agency with a social purpose seemed naive. In the aftermath of the Reagan administration's assault on TVA budgets, what was left was an agency raked by daunting debt ($18 billion in 1992); a moribund, over-built, and scandal-ridden nuclear power program; and mounting congressional distrust. Concomitantly, its coal-fired power plants were in disrepair, its federal appropriations were diminishing, its thirteen-tier organizational structure housed 37,000 employees in a bloated bureaucracy, and its plan to become a "nuclear oasis" in the United States were on hold. So dire was the situation that one major business publication pronounced TVA "a bankruptcy waiting to happen."

Between 1988 and 1992, however, TVA board chairman Marvin Runyon led a pronounced down-sizing, restructuring, refinancing, and retooling of the agency that reduced the TVA work force by almost half—to 19,235 employees. Structurally, Runyon eliminated eight tiers of management and adopted a corporate management structure reflecting TVA's strategic goals (a power group, a resources group, and a customer group). Meanwhile, he saved $27 billion by renegotiating TVA's coal-procurement contracts, invoked budget cuts of 25 percent in TVA's non-power programs, reduced overall annual interest costs on its $18 billion debt of $202 million a year, and privatized many TVA activities. Some praised Runyon's efforts as long overdue belt-tightening. Others reviled them as too severe, too restrictive of TVA's New Deal multi-purpose legacy, too pro-nuclear in orientation, and too

starkly diminishing of TVA's recent emphases on energy conservation, resource protection, and social equity. Assessments aside, however, Runyon's efforts enshrined a "new deal" for the agency that will affect its environmental and natural resource directions well into the twenty-first century.

With coal and nuclear power units today generating 59 percent and 13 percent respectively of TVA's power capacity, and with a strategic goal of becoming North America's premiere electric utility, TVA confronts major financial, natural resource, and environmental protection challenges over the next decade. Mounting debt has already forced TVA to cancel completion of its last three nuclear units, despite the billions of dollars already invested in them. Most indicative of its regulatory plight is the agency's reaction in 1992 to the Clean Air Act of 1990. Environmentalists attacked TVA's plans to purchase emission allowances for SO_2 pollution from the Wisconsin Power and Light Company. These represented little more than one percent of its total projected use or sale. As well, TVA's announced plan to meet the act's acid rain requirements by buying low-sulfur coal from the West to fire two of its power plants was thwarted. It was forced instead to install scrubbers to protect jobs in Kentucky's high-sulfur coal mines.

Robert F. Durant

Further Readings

Durant, Robert F. *When Government Regulates Itself: EPA, TVA, and Pollution Control in the 1970s.* 1985.

Hargrove, Erwin C. *Prisoners of Myth: The Leadership of the Tennessee Valley Authority, 1933–1990.* 1994.

Hargrove, Erwin C., and Paul K. Conkin, eds. *TVA: Fifty Years of Grassroots Bureaucracy.* 1983.

McDonald, Michael J., and John Muldowny. *TVA and the Dispossessed: The Resettlement of Population in the Norris Dam Area.* 1985.

Wheeler, William B., and Michael J. McDonald. *TVA and the Tellico Dam, 1936–1979.* 1986.

See also ACID PRECIPITATION: LEGISLATIVE INITIATIVES; COAL: ENVIRONMENTAL IMPACTS; ENVIRONMENTAL PROTECTION AGENCY; HYDROELECTRICITY; NUCLEAR ELECTRIC POWER; STRIP MINING OF COAL: A HISTORY

Thoreau, Henry David

Henry David Thoreau (1817–1862) is recognized both as a writer and naturalist, as well as a seminal contributor to North American environmental thought, inspiring not only such nineteenth-century luminaries as Frederick Law Olmsted and John Muir, but many twentieth-century figures as well, including Aldo Leopold and Joseph Wood Krutch. His international reputation is considerable, as exemplified by his influence on Mohandas K. Gandhi and the philosophy of nonviolent civil disobedience. Even here, however, Thoreau's affect on environmentalism is evident, since nonviolent civil disobedience has been the guiding credo for environmental protest. While earlier readers of Thoreau categorized him as a transcendentalist following the lead of Ralph Waldo Emerson, more recent interpretations rank Thoreau as the more consequential thinker who transformed if not abandoned Emersonian transcendentalism. Although Thoreau had mentors, his work does not so much follow that of others as set a style that countless others have followed. Contemporary readings recognize his work as pursuing research relevant to environmental studies and sciences, including such areas as anthropology, ecology, botany, meteorology, linguistics, and ecophilosophy, especially deep ecology.

Thoreau's Nature Philosophy

More so than any other American nature writer Thoreau asks ecologists, natural historians, nature lovers, and environmental activists to find their sense of meaning, their direction and purpose through immediate contact with the living creatures, the vicissitudes of the seasons, and the varied textures of the earth. Most of the secondary literature does his philosophy an injustice, in part because it is dreary and pedantic while his own writings are bright and lively.

Nothing (including the present essay) can substitute for an encounter with Thoreau's writings, preferably a reading set in the woods or along the seashore or a mountainside. In such places, where the built-up environment has receded, and with it everyday cares and concerns, spontaneous encounter with a more than human life-world is possible. Thoreau places great emphasis on the importance of lived experience as such, for it leads to a sympathy with intelligence lying outside the bounds of positive science and traditional philosophy. Although the writing is leavened throughout by Thoreau's erudition there is no attempt to communicate book knowledge as an end in itself. Rather he calls the reader's attention to the book of nature, the structures and patterns of existence obscured by the curtain of culture. Thoreau counsels his readers to walk in the wild on a daily basis, for immediate experience reminds the walker that neither the scientist nor the philosopher, merchant, or minister has a privileged claim on truth. So-called knowledge, according to Thoreau, is too often "positive ignorance"—that is, shibboleth and dogma masquerading as eternal verity. Lived experience enables the walker to engage culture critically rather than succumb to conventional wisdom. The often quoted Thoreauvian aphorism—in wildness is the preservation of the world—is not then so much a preservationist credo (although often interpreted as such) as the heart of his nature philosophy.

Thoreau's Science

The reinterpretation of Thoreau's work has also extended into its implications for the social and natural sciences. In a postmodern context in which science is viewed as writing, thus erasing any absolute line of distinction between science and literature, Thoreau's scientific reputation can only grow. Even in his own time, however, Thoreau's scientific contributions were recognized; he worked on occasion for such notables as Louis Agassiz and was extended an invitation (which he declined) to join the (now American) Association for the Advancement of Science. Today Thoreau is recognized as making observations that either predate the emergence of a later, named scientific discipline or were substantive contributions to already established disciplines.

His "Succession of the Forest Trees" is an ecological work that remained for four decades as a definitive work on forest succession. And while his *Journal* is many things, it is also a compendium of irreplaceable botanical, sociological, and anthropological information on mid-nineteenth-century New England. For ecologists, and especially for those concerned with anthropogenic impacts on the native flora of New England, the botanical record that Thoreau compiled is invaluable. Thoreau may even be read as doing a kind of proto-linguistics, since his work manifests a keen attention to language, including words and their meanings, and distinctions between the languages of oral, so-called primitive, and literate, so-called civilized, people. Finally, to an extent still not fully appreciated, Thoreau was among the first thinkers to consider the broad implications of the emerging evolutionary paradigm. Beginning with his studies at Harvard University he became an evolutionary thinker in the broadest sense of the term, and came to believe that any adequate grasp of our own humanity had to reconcile itself with evolutionary process. Such an intuition perhaps explains why Thoreau remains an inspiration to many environmental thinkers.

Max Oelschlaeger

Further Readings
Harding, Walter, and Michael Meyer. *The New Thoreau Handbook*. 1980.
Thoreau, Henry David. *The Complete Works*. 1906.

See also Conservation Movement; Deep Ecology: Meanings; Emerson, Ralph Waldo; Environmentalism; Krutch, Joseph Wood; Leopold, Aldo; Muir, John; Olmsted, Frederick Law; Postmodernism and the Environment; Wilderness

Three Mile Island
See Nuclear Electric Power

Throwaway Mentality/Society
Throughout human history people have husbanded their resources to avoid future shortages. Only in the past fifty years have we developed the inclination to readily throw away things that our ancestors would have husbanded. Why?

Our capitalist economy is driven most powerfully by the desire for wealth and jobs. The faster we make and sell things, the more jobs are available and the greater the available wealth for entrepreneurs. A huge advertising industry has been developed to encourage people to consume faster and faster. Television in the United States alone broadcasts approximately 20,000 commercial messages each day.

As our homes filled up with what we have come to perceive as junk, the market system came to our rescue by developing items designed to be thrown away after one use: beverage containers, tableware, cameras, books, clothing, writing materials, sporting goods, and on and on. Throwaways did not just go to the dump; they also littered public places.

By succumbing to the allure of throwaway, we forgot (or never learned) that there is no "away." The first law of thermodynam-

ics tells us that matter and energy can neither be created nor destroyed; they can only be transformed: everything has to go somewhere. As our landfills overflowed our throwaway mentality came back to haunt us: we now were confronted with a huge waste disposal problem. Ironically, we did not see our folly as a waste of resources, or even as a detriment to ecosystems, but rather as a pileup of litter, for which there was no more room at the dump. What then?

Solid waste specialists urge acceptance of the following hierarchy of priorities for reducing wastes: 1) reduce potential waste at the source by making more durable products, easily repairable products, and simple packaging; 2) reuse products, such as beverage containers, again and again; 3) recycle those products that cannot be reused to recover the basic materials; 4) incinerate burnables to recover their energy and reduce volume; and 5) landfill the wastes that remain.

Industrial and commercial interests that gain wealth by making and selling as much as possible resist the first two priorities. Most of them enthusiastically endorse recycling, however, and mount vigorous media campaigns in support. Skeptics that asserted that people would never recycle have been proven wrong as North Americans strongly rallied to the cry for recycling. Even so, less than half of household wastes are recycled—in some localities, hardly any. Municipal officials happily report how much recycling saves in "tipping fees" but ignore savings of resources or reduced injury to ecosystems. Meanwhile, industrial and commercial interests still busily dream up new products to be discarded after little use while landfill space becomes scarcer and scarcer.

So long as we give priority to having a job and getting as rich as possible we will be prey to the special interest groups that foster a throwaway mentality. Obscenely rich people who have never known privation are particularly susceptible. Unhappily for the earth that is the reality of the lifestyle of most North Americans.

Lester W. Milbrath

Further Readings
Kharbanda, O.P., and E.A. Stallworthy. *Waste Management: Towards a Sustainable Society*. 1990.
Milbrath, Lester B. *Envisioning a Sustainable Society: Learning Our Way Out*. 1989.

See also ENVIRONMENTALISM; NONRENEW-
ABLE RESOURCES; PACKAGING; RECYCLING;
SUSTAINABILITY

Tigers: Conservation and Habitat

The tiger (*Panthera tigris*), the largest member
of the cat family (*Carnivora: Felidae*), once
ranged across much of southern and eastern
Asia from the Caucasus to Bali and eastern
Russia (Ussuriland). Today, three of the eight
races are extinct: the Bali tiger (*Panthera tigris
balica*) since the 1940s, the Caspian tiger
(*Panthera tigris virgata*) in the early 1970s, and
the Javan tiger (*Panthera tigris sondaica*) since
about 1980. Of the surviving subspecies, as of
1993 the South China tiger (*Panthera tigris
amoyensis*) is nearly extinct, with less than fifty
animals thought to remain. There are some 250
to 400 Siberian tigers (*Panthera tigris altaica*)
left in the wild, 400 to 500 Sumatran tigers
(*Panthera tigris sumatrae*), possibly 900 to
1,500 Indo-Chinese tigers (*Panthera tigris
corbetti*) and 3,100 to 5,300 Bengal tigers
(*Panthera tigris tigris*). In total there are between 4,600 and 7,700 wild tigers remaining
(1993 figures)—a number that continues to fall
under pressure from poaching and loss of habitat.

The tiger is thus one of the most endangered of the world's large mammal species. Its
prospects for survival in the wild anywhere
outside India are growing increasingly dim. In
March 1994, in recognition of the threat to the
species, India and nine other Asian countries
(Bangladesh, Bhutan, Burma, Cambodia, Indonesia, Malaysia, Nepal, Thailand and Vietnam),
in association with the United Nations Environment Programme (UNEP), agreed to establish
a Global Tiger Forum to embark on a worldwide campaign to save the tiger.

Through most of this century the decline of
the tiger has been caused largely by extensive
deforestation as the human population in Asia
increased. In India the Bengal tiger also suffered
from big game hunting and the demands of the
fur trade. In 1973, in response to growing concern about the tiger's survival, the government
of India established Project Tiger. This was a
comprehensive program involving total protection for tigers and the establishment of a number of special tiger reserves. Official census figures from Project Tiger suggested that it was a
considerable success, boosting tiger numbers in
India from 1,800 in 1971 to 4,334 in 1989.
Unfortunately, despite Project Tiger's undoubted successes, there appears to be evidence
that these figures were far too optimistic and
that the actual figures may be only slightly more
than half of the official total.

Project Tiger has also been unable to stem
the worst problem currently facing tigers—
poaching and illegal trade, primarily for the sale
of bones to the oriental medicine market. Tiger
bone is used to treat a wide range of conditions,
ranging from rat bites to typhoid fever and
chronic dysentery. In 1991 China exported
31,000 bottles of "tiger wine" containing (or
said to contain) tiger bone. Prices for tiger bone
now outstrip those for skins. In South Korea
import prices have averaged $127 per kilogram
between 1975 and 1992, but selling prices have
been far higher—up to $1,874 per kilogram in
1992.

Researchers have found carcasses in which
only the bones have been removed, with the rest
of the animal, including its pelt, left to rot.
Poaching levels are difficult to determine exactly, but an estimated 400 tigers fell prey to
poachers in India alone between 1988 and
1992. The Siberian tiger, which is relatively easy
for poachers to track in the snow, has been
particularly hard hit, with more than sixty being lost to poachers in 1992. Several conservation organizations have now pledged funds to
assist anti-poaching operations in Russia.

Protective measures in the range countries
vary but enforcement is inadequate throughout
the tiger's range. Tigers have been listed on
Appendix I of the Convention on International
Trade in Endangered Species of Wild Fauna and
Flora (CITES) since 1975 (except for the Siberian tiger, which was added in 1987), but five
of the fourteen range countries are not parties
to that treaty. Investigations by conservationists
have shown that tiger bone has been openly
available for sale in China, Taiwan, and other
countries despite CITES protection.

In September 1993, under pressure from
international conservation organizations, the
CITES Standing Committee passed a resolution
calling on the consumer countries to impound
stocks of tiger bone and to provide and implement adequate legislation to control the market,
or face possible sanctions. In the same month
the United States certified China and Taiwan
under the Pelly Amendment over trade in tiger
and rhinoceros—a move that permits the president to impose trade sanctions against countries
violating international wildlife agreements. In
anticipation of these decisions China banned
the use of tiger bone in May 1993, including the

sale of bone from its single tiger breeding center at Hengdaohezi in Heilungjiang Province. In early 1994 China reported burning 1,100 pounds of confiscated tiger bone.

A CITES delegation visiting China and Taiwan in early 1994 was informed that both countries had made some progress in controlling the market for tiger and rhino parts. Others have suggested, however, that the trade has merely been driven underground and will reappear.

Even if poaching can be controlled tigers still face severe threats as the human population of Asia continues to grow. In the twenty years of Project Tiger's operation India's population has grown by 300 million, and pressure on tiger reserves has increased. Few areas can now support tiger populations large enough to be self-sustaining in the long term, and those areas that remain are under threat. Some voices are even questioning the human cost of preserving such large and dangerous animals, though in the worst area for man-eaters, the Sunderbans of India, the use of face masks worn on the back of the head has shown great promise as a way to reduce tiger attacks.

There is a large, healthy, and carefully-managed captive population of Siberian tigers, and some believe the best chance for its survival lies in high-tech zoo techniques like in-vitro fertilization. Other races are not as well represented in captivity. Captive breeding, however, though important, should in no way replace efforts to conserve wild tigers in their Asian habitats.

Ronald Orenstein

Further Readings

Jackson, Peter. "The Status of the Tiger in 1993 and Threats to Its Future." *Cat News* 19 (1993): 5–11.

Mills, Stephen. "The Tiger, the Dragon and a Plan for the Rescue." *BBC Wildlife* 12 1 (1994): 50–53.

Seidensticker, J., and S. Lumpkin, eds. *Great Cats: Majestic Creatures of the Wild*. 1991.

See also CITES; COUGARS: CONSERVATION AND HABITAT; RHINOCEROS: CONSERVATION AND HABITAT; TOP PREDATORS IN CANADA: AN OVERVIEW; TROPICAL DEFORESTATION; UNITED NATIONS ENVIRONMENT PROGRAMME

Tobacco Smoke in the Environment

Environmental tobacco smoke (ETS) is a major source of indoor air pollution. ETS or "second-hand smoke" is composed of biomass combustion products caused by the incomplete burning of tobacco from cigarettes, cigars, and pipes. ETS gases and particles contain many of the same toxic carcinogenic agents as are found in fossil fuel combustion products, such as carbon monoxide, benzene, formaldehyde, and cadmium.

Sidestream smoke makes up about one half of the smoke generated during smoking and is the major component of ETS, contributing nearly all of the vapor phase constituents and over half of the particulate matter. In total the gases and particulate matter of ETS contain more than 4,000 compounds, including over forty known or suspected human carcinogens. The inhalation of ETS is also known as "passive" or "involuntary" smoking.

Most North Americans spend the majority of their time indoors in a confined environment. There are many potential sources of indoor air pollution, including chemicals emanating from building materials, furnishings, consumer products, gases from combustion appliances like space heaters and furnaces, and biological contaminants from a variety of sources. However, higher levels of mutagenic particles are found in homes with ETS than in homes with wood stoves or in outdoor urban environments with numerous diesel trucks and buses.

The risks of tobacco consumption have been well documented since the 1962 report of the Royal College of Physicians and the 1964 U.S. Surgeon General's report both of which established a causal relationship between smoking and lung cancer. The morbidity and mortality rates associated with tobacco use establish it as nothing less than the number one preventable cause of death. An estimated 430,000 tobacco-related deaths occurred in the United States and 40,000 in Canada in 1992.

Overall, the population risk of ETS is more pervasive than that posed by any other indoor man made pollutant released into the general environment. The body of evidence on the harmful effects of ETS exposure is compelling:

- In 1986 the U.S. Surgeon General and the U.S. National Research Council confirmed that ETS causes lung cancer in nonsmoking adults and poses a significant health risk to children.
- In Canada a report of the Working Group on Passive Smoking headed by Dr. W.O. Spitzer of McGill University, Montréal, Québec, concluded that there

was "strong evidence of an association between residential exposure to environmental tobacco smoke and both respiratory illness and reduction of lung function" and "evidence [was] consistent with a relationship between exposure to environmental tobacco smoke in the workplace and respiratory symptoms."

- In 1991 a report of the U.S. National Institute for Occupational Safety and Health (NIOSH), in conformance with the Occupational Safety and Health Administration (OSHA) carcinogen policy (*Identification, Classification, and Regulation of Potential Occupational Carcinogens*) identified ETS as a "potential occupational carcinogen," legal terminology for a substance causing cancer or reducing its latency period.
- In December 1992 the U.S. Environmental Protection Agency (EPA) classified ETS as a Group A (known human) carcinogen. This designation assigns ETS to the same classification as the most deadly carcinogens such as arsenic, asbestos, benzene, vinyl chloride, coke oven emissions, and radon.

The major conclusions from the EPA study indicate that ETS presents a serious and substantial public health concern. In the United States for example, among adults ETS is a human lung carcinogen responsible for approximately 3,000 lung cancer deaths. The American Heart Foundation has also linked ETS to as many as 53,000 heart disease deaths annually among non-smokers.

Among American children the EPA report also concludes that ETS exposure is causally associated with an increased risk of lower respiratory tract infections, such as bronchitis and pneumonia. The report estimates that between 150,000 to 300,000 of these cases annually in infants and young children up to eighteen months of age are attributable to ETS. The EPA report also concludes that ETS exposure "is causally associated with increased prevalence of fluid in the middle ear, symptoms of upper respiratory tract irritation and a small but significant reduction in lung function." ETS exposure is also cited as being "causally associated with additional episodes and increased severity of symptoms among children with asthma." The EPA report estimates that 200,000 to 1 million U.S. children with asthma are negatively affected by exposure to ETS. As well, "ETS expo-

sure is a risk factor for new cases of asthma in children who had not previously displayed symptoms."

Field studies, controlled experiments, and mathematical models show that under typical conditions of smoking and ventilation ETS diffuses rapidly throughout homes and workplaces and persists for long periods after the smoking ends. It represents one of the major sources of indoor-air particulate pollution in buildings where smoking is permitted. Studies of indoor air quality in commercial and public buildings shows that particulate levels in areas where smoking is permitted are considerably higher than in nonsmoking areas. Studies using personal air monitors have shown that a single smoker in a home can double the amount of particulate air pollution inhaled by nonsmoking members of the household.

Environmental tobacco smoke can be completely removed from the indoor air only by removing the source—various forms of smoking. Restricting smoking to a separate room but on the same ventilation system may reduce some of the nonsmokers' exposure to ETS. However, this approach does not reduce ETS loading of the building and hence will not eliminate risk. ETS pollutants readily disperse through a common air space and, in public or commercial buildings, most ventilation systems recirculate much of the contaminated indoor air. Unless there is a reduction of the total amount of ETS circulating within the total air system there will be little reduction in the health risk created by ETS. Research indicates that total removal of tobacco smoke through air cleaning or ventilation is both technically and economically impractical.

There is no established, health-based threshold for exposure to environmental tobacco smoke below which ETS exposure is considered safe. This position is supported by the U.S. EPA which generally does not recognize a "no-effect" or "safe level" for cancer-causing agents. Therefore, the EPA recommends that exposure to environmental tobacco smoke be minimized wherever possible. In fact, the EPA and other authorities including NIOSH recommend only two solutions with respect to ETS exposure: the prohibition of smoking indoors or, if this is not possible, smoking confined to an enclosed area, under negative pressure, separately ventilated, and exhausted directly to the out-of-doors.

Christine Pryde

Further Readings

National Institute for Occupational Safety and Health (NIOSH). "Environmental Tobacco Smoke in the Workplace: Lung Cancer and Other Health Effects." *Current Intelligence Bulletin* 54 (June 1991).

U.S Department of Health and Human Services (DHHS). *The Health Consequences of Involuntary Smoking: A Report of the Surgeon General.* DHHS Pub. No. (PHS) 87-8398, 1986.

U.S. Environmental Protection Agency, Office of Research and Development, Office of Air and Radiation. *Respiratory Health Effects of Passive Smoking: Lung Cancer and Other Disorders.* 1992.

See also AIR POLLUTION: IMPACTS; CADMIUM; INDOOR AIR POLLUTION; VOLATILE ORGANIC COMPOUNDS

Tolba, Mostafa K.

A distinguished scientist, diplomat, and inspiring leader, Mostafa K. Tolba was born in the town of Zifta, Egypt, on December 8, 1922, the only son of a school teacher. Tolba graduated from the University of Cairo (Hon. B.Sc. in Botany) in 1943 and obtained his Ph.D. in plant pathology from the Imperial College, London, in 1949. Between 1949 and 1959 he was on the academic staff of the University of Cairo, where he created an active research school in microbiology. In 1957–58 he was on the staff of the University of Baghdad (Iraq), and between 1960 and 1970 he held senior offices in higher education and national science policy and planning in Cairo. In 1970 he was appointed minister of youth, and in 1971 he became the first president of the Egyptian Academy of Scientific Research and Technology. In 1972 he headed the Egyptian delegation to the United Nations (UN) Stockholm Conference on Human Environment and played a distinguished role in its deliberations. In 1973 he became the deputy executive director of the newly established UN Environment Programme (UNEP), and in 1976 he became the executive director, a post that he held until his retirement at the end of 1992.

Between 1950 and 1973 he published some ninety-five research papers in fields of microbiology, and between 1974 and 1992 he published and edited several volumes addressing world environmental issues, including his latest, *The World Environment 1972–1992.*

He received several academic recognitions including Honorary Doctor of Science, from Moscow University (1978), State Faculty of Agriculture, Gembloux, Belgium (1985), Hanyang University, Seoul, Republic of Korea (1987), Kenyatta University, Kenya (1989), Fellowship of the Imperial College, London (1988), Honorary Professorship, Bejing University, China (1987), among others.

During his twenty years with UNEP he had a considerable impact on international policies in fields of environment and development. His most notable contributions include his role in negotiating regional conventions to protect the Mediterranean, the Red Sea and the Gulf of Aden, the Gulf and several other regional seas; conventions for environmental management of the Zambezi River Basin and the Chad Lake Basin; world conventions, including the Vienna Convention and its Montreal Protocol (ozone), the Basel Convention (hazardous wastes), as well as conventions on biodiversity and climate; and his driving role in outreach programs that involved industry, parliaments, youth, nongovernmental organizations, and women in the world environment movement. During those twenty years he remained the principal manager and the principal scientist of UNEP.

Mohammed Kassas

Further Readings

Tolba, M.K., et al., eds. *The World Environment 1972–1992.* 1992.

See also MONTREAL PROTOCOL; UNITED NATIONS ENVIRONMENT PROGRAMME

Top Predators in Canada: An Overview

The polar bear, grizzly, black bear, wolf, wolverine, and cougar are Canada's six top predators. These slow-reproducing and, for the most part, large-bodied mammals require immense home ranges and diverse prey-rich habitats. Globally, Canada may represent the last refuge of these top predators. Besides this sobering fact, there are other reasons to conserve these top predators.

Top predators play vital roles in natural systems and, as such, are indicators of ecosystem integrity. Although it may be possible for an ecosystem to function without top predators, the ecosystem will necessarily change because of the elimination of these summit species. The system, not being what it used to be, or could be, then becomes "impoverished." Conserving top predators, therefore, is key to maintaining biodiversity. This is easier said than done, however, since many of these large carnivores in North America are already officially listed as endangered species.

Top predators are of value to humans for several reasons: 1) in terms of traditional aboriginal cultures; 2) in terms of their economic significance where tourism and wildlife viewing can occur; and 3) in terms of their very charismatic nature—these species should be conserved for their own sake.

Finally, there is an urgency to conserving top predators in Canada since their conservation status in this country ranges from abundant—but in peril—to rare or vulnerable, threatened, endangered, through to those on the brink of extinction, such as the Eastern cougar (*Felis concolor couguar*).

Polar Bear

The polar bear (*Ursus maritimus*), an Arctic marine mammal, is very slow reproducing, becoming sexually mature only after reaching four to six years of age. Breeding on average every third year, some females may not even replace themselves during their lifetimes. Of the more than fifteen polar bear subpopulations worldwide, Canada is home to twelve—approximately 12,500 to 20,000 animals. Although the polar bear is the one top predator that still occupies almost all its historic range this large-bodied mammal is now absent from the eastern and western edges of its range.

Grizzly Bear

Grizzly bears (*Ursus horribilus*) are the slowest reproducing top predator, with females becoming sexually mature after five to eight years of age. Reproducing at three to eight year intervals they may give birth to only one or two young. Grizzlies require immense home ranges, from alpine habitats through to mountainous and coastal ranges. Extirpated from 99 percent of their range in the lower forty-eight United States, many of these remnant populations are entirely confined to protected areas. In Canada approximately 25,000 grizzlies occupy just over half their historic range. Canada's grizzly population, where not already designated as threatened or extirpated, is listed as vulnerable.

Black Bear

The North American black bear (*Ursus americanus*) is a creature of forested habitats, so its future depends on whether sufficient for-

ests remain intact. Black bears reproduce more quickly than polar or grizzly bears, but their age of reproduction depends on quality and quantity of habitat. In some areas of Canada females will not have their first litters until they reach five to seven years of age. Throughout North America black bears have lost at least 50 percent of their range. Currently considered Canada's most abundant top predator with an estimated population of about 285,000, over less than 1/2 their former range, black bears, like the grizzly, wolf, and cougar, have been extirpated from the prairies. Canada's Black bears are listed on the Convention on International Trade in Endangered Species of Wild Fauna and Flora (CITES) Appendix II as concern over trade of bear parts increases.

Wolf

The wolf (*Canis lupus*), once the most widely distributed mammal in the world, is considered the fastest reproducing of these six top predators. Wild wolf packs are family units dominated by an alpha pair. The high social structure in wild packs precludes breeding by any but the alpha pair, and that only once a year, unlike many domestic dogs. Wolves have been removed from 95 percent of their range in the lower forty-eight United States and are now protected as an endangered species. Extirpated from the Canadian prairies and from the Atlantic provinces wolves are still relatively abundant in Canada with approximately 50,000 to 60,000 animals occupying about 80 percent of their historic range. Wolves are still subject to liberal hunting seasons and, in some areas, ongoing predator control programs.

Cougar

Cougar (*Felis concolor*) favor remote wilderness habitats. Unlike these other top predators cougar can breed in any season, giving birth to one to six kits per litter. On average, only one or two kits survive to adulthood. Canada's eastern cougar (*Felis concolor couguar*) is endangered and thought by many to be extinct. Therefore, British Columbia and Alberta share the national responsibility for the future of Canada's cougar population, which numbers approximately 2,800 to 4,400.

Wolverine

The largest member of the weasel family, and the most mysterious top predator of them all, the wolverine (*Gulo gulo*) is a solitary creature, found only in remote wilderness habitats. Scavengers by nature, wolverine rely on carcasses left over from, for instance, predator kills. Reproduction depends largely on food conditions; when food conditions are good, females may give birth to two or three kits, but even then not every year.

Almost eliminated from the eastern part of North America, wolverine populations are fragmented throughout the western United States, with the exception of Idaho. Canada's eastern wolverine (east of Hudson Bay) is listed as "endangered" and the western population is "vulnerable." A rare species by virtue of its natural biology—found in very low numbers over large areas—wolverine are taking their last stand, like the others, in northwest North America, largely in British Columbia, the Northwest Territories, Yukon, and Alaska.

Sherry L. Pettigrew

Further Readings
Hummel, M., and S.L. Pettigrew. *Wild Hunters: Predators in Peril.* 1991.
———. *A Conservation Strategy for Large Carnivores in Canada.* 1990.
Novak, M., et al. *Wild Furbearer Management and Conservation in North America.* 1987.

See also Bears: Conservation and Habitat; Cougars: Conservation and Habitat; Florida Panther; Habitat Fragmentation, Patches, and Corridors; Landscape Ecology; Marine Mammals; Wolf: A Conservation Challenge

Toxic Pollutants, Transport and Fate
When the effects of individual pollutants on the environment are assessed it is important to discover the routes by which they are spread, and whether any changes to the pollutants occur while in the environment. Routes of transport include movement through the air, wet deposition from the air (rain or snowfall), dry deposition (dustfall), transport through water systems (rivers, ocean currents, groundwater), and sedimentation (particulate deposition) from water bodies. Pollutants may be present as vapors in the air, dissolved in water, or can be attached to suspended particulate matter in the air or water. Pollutants can also be spread by water runoff, erosion, or windblown dust. To determine the exposure of humans to pollutants it is vital to know how the pollutants are transported. This knowledge will allow experts to allocate the total pollutant exposure between the major exposure pathways: dermal contact, breathing, and ingestion of food and water.

The fate of pollutants in the environment is as important as their routes of transport. Some pollutants undergo transformations in the environment resulting in new substances that may have different effects (the hazard of the new substance can be greater or lesser). The various factors that may affect pollutants in the environment include exposure to sunlight (photochemical transformation), reactions with other chemicals including chemical oxidation and reduction (chemical transformation), and bacterial degradation (biological transformation). Organic molecules are generally affected to a much greater extent than metals, but chemical transformations of metals are also important (i.e., the effects of metallic lead and lead oxide are different). Chemicals that remain in the environment for long time-periods (i.e., several years) without being changed or degraded are called "persistent." Chemicals that are very toxic but which are quickly degraded into harmless forms when exposed to environmental conditions are generally not of great concern. Chemicals of greatest concern are those that are both highly toxic and very stable in the environment.

Which routes of exposure are most important for a specific pollutant, and whether the pollutant will undergo transformations in the environment depend on the physical and chemical properties of the pollutant. Two of the key physical properties of molecules that affect their behavior in the environment are their vapor pressure and solubility in water. Another important factor for some compounds is their solubility in the fatty (lipid) tissues of humans and other organisms. Pollutants that are highly soluble in lipids are "lipophilic," and will bioaccumulate in the fatty tissues of organisms exposed to the pollutant. The chemical properties of pollutants depend on the specific structure of molecules, and as over seven million different compounds have been registered, it is a complex task to determine the transport and fate of pollutants in the environment.

Ray E. Clement

Further Readings
Schwarzenback, R.P., P.M. Gschwend, and D.M. Imboden. *Environmental Organic Chemistry.* 1993.

See also BIOACCUMULATION; EPIDEMIOLOGY; GROUNDWATER POLLUTION; LEACHING; LONG RANGE TRANSPORT; PERSISTENT ORGANOCHLORINE COMPOUNDS; TOXICOLOGY; TRACE ANALYSIS

Toxic Substances Control Act

The Toxic Substances Control Act (TSCA), Pub. L. No. 94-469, was enacted in 1976. Title I of TSCA provides the U.S. Environmental Protection Agency (EPA) with authority to regulate or prohibit the manufacture, distribution, or use of chemical substances that pose unreasonable risks to human health or the environment. Although not the focus of this discussion, subsequent amendments have added three titles to TSCA: Title II, the Asbestos Hazard Emergency Response Act (1986); Title III, the Indoor Radon Abatement Act (1988); and Title IV, the Lead-Based Paint Exposure Reduction Act (1992).

Unlike other federal environmental laws that regulate chemical risks after a substance is used, the major objective of TSCA is to characterize and understand the risks associated with chemical substances before they are introduced into commerce. However, the EPA does not have absolute authority to require testing of new and existing chemicals or to regulate the production of chemicals. The EPA is required to balance the economic and social benefits of a chemical against any identified health risks and to regulate only those chemicals that pose an "unreasonable" risk of harm to human health or the environment.

TSCA's statutory framework contains several key components. First, TSCA requires the EPA to compile and maintain the TSCA Inventory—a list of chemical substances manufactured or processed for commercial purposes in the United States. The original inventory was released in 1979 and contained some 55,000 chemicals; the list is updated periodically to add chemicals that have successfully undergone a ninety-day EPA review process described below.

Second, manufacturers wanting to introduce or import a chemical not listed on the TSCA Inventory or propose a significant new use for a listed chemical are required under Section 5 to submit a premanufacture notice (PMN) to the EPA administrator. The PMN must contain information about anticipated categories of use, production amounts, and employee exposure to the chemical. The PMN must also contain any testing data that examines adverse health or environmental effects of the chemical, either conducted by the manufacturer or by other parties. The EPA has ninety days to review the PMN, at which time either the chemical substance is listed, the manufacturer is required to submit additional information, or the EPA initiates administrative action to regulate, limit, or ban the substance.

Although manufacturers must submit testing data in their possession they are not required to perform long-term toxicity or other tests as part of the PMN review unless the EPA has issued a testing rule for the chemical under Section 4. Testing rules are required when chemicals are designated by the Interagency Testing Committee (a multi-agency committee established under Section 4) for priority consideration. Once chemicals are identified by the Interagency Testing Committee as potentially harmful, the EPA has one year to develop the testing rule for the chemical or chemical group, or to publish reasons for not doing so.

Third, if the results of testing, PMN review, or screening of the inventory of existing chemicals provides evidence that the chemical presents an unreasonable risk to human health or the environment the EPA may impose a variety of restraints on the marketing of the chemical under Section 6, including absolute bans, production limits, and restrictions on the use or concentration of the chemical. The agency conducts a risk assessment to determine if the risk is unreasonable. As of 1992, only six chemical substances including asbestos, chlorofluorocarbon, dioxins, and polychlorinated biphenyls (PCBs) had been regulated under this section. PCBs were the only chemicals targeted for regulation specifically in TSCA.

Certain chemicals are exempted from TSCA requirements. Most notable are pesticides, which are regulated under the Federal Insecticide, Fungicide and Rodenticide Act (FIFRA) and food additives, drugs, and cosmetics, which are subject to the federal Food, Drug and Cosmetic Act and are thus excluded from TSCA jurisdiction.

Denise Scheberle

Further Readings

Conner, John D., et al. *TSCA Handbook.* 2nd ed. Rockville, Maryland: Government Institutes, 1989.

Plater, Zygmunt J.B., Robert H. Abrams, and William Goldfarb. *Environmental Law and Policy: Nature, Law and Society.* 1992.

See also ASBESTOS; FEDERAL INSECTICIDE, FUNGICIDE AND RODENTICIDE ACT; FOOD ADDITIVES; RADON; RESOURCE CONSERVATION AND RECOVERY ACT; SUPERFUND; TOXICOLOGY

Toxic Wastes in International Trade

The export of toxic wastes by industrial countries has grown markedly in recent years, and the effects have become a serious problem for many waste importing countries. Within industrialized countries, which produce 90 percent of all hazardous waste, environmental regulations grew more stringent and disposal costs soared in the 1980s. At that time there were few barriers to the export of toxic wastes to countries with less strict environmental laws. As a result, many Western firms began to seek opportunities to dispose of their hazardous wastes abroad. Numerous countries in need of foreign exchange, including those in the developing world, agreed to import the waste and to store it in landfills. The price that they received, although much less than disposal costs in the producing countries, was in many cases significant for the waste recipients.

The bulk of toxic waste exports goes to other industrialized countries, with the United Kingdom and Canada receiving much of the hazardous waste exported by the European Community (EC) countries, and the United States, respectively. Industrialized countries importing toxic waste claim to have the ability to dispose of it safely, and see the waste importing business as both important and lucrative. Less industrialized countries which import toxic waste, however, often lack the facilities to dispose of it in an environmentally sound way. The hazardous wastes—including heavy metal scrap, outdated pesticides, PCBs, and incinerator ash—have frequently been delivered to less industrialized countries in leaking containers or in no containers at all, and have been dumped in the open air on beaches, in fields, or in poorly constructed landfills. The result has been leakage of the hazardous materials into the environment, including contamination of soils and water supplies, posing a serious threat to human, animal, and plant life.

Public awareness of the international toxic waste trade grew considerably in the 1980s when large-scale dumping of hazardous wastes in less industrialized countries was reported in the media. One of the most notorious examples of intended toxic waste export was the voyage of the ship, the *Khian Sea*. This ship set sail from the United States in 1986 with its cargo of 14,000 tonnes of toxic ash from Philadelphia's municipal incinerator. After the ash was dumped on a beach in Haiti, the Haitian government ordered it removed. Only 10,000 tonnes of ash were reloaded on the ship, which then set sail to find another location to dump the remainder of its cargo. The ship tried to unload the toxic ash in Africa, Europe, the Middle East, and the Far East, but the wide publicity of the voyage ensured that no government would accept it. After twenty-seven months of trying to find a dump-site, the ash mysteriously disappeared from the ship in Southeast Asia, believed by many to have been dumped at sea. While in the case of the *Khian Sea* there was ample warning to governments to not accept the ship's cargo, there have been hundreds of other incidents of actual toxic waste dumping by Western firms in many countries in Africa, Asia, Eastern Europe, Latin America, and the Caribbean.

By the late 1980s there were several initiatives to ban or regulate the international trade in toxic wastes. The increasing incidence of cross-border toxic waste trading with less industrialized countries prompted the environmental group Greenpeace to launch an international campaign to halt the practice. By the early 1990s a growing number of developing countries had also advocated a complete ban on the trade. Most industrial country governments have rejected the idea of a ban on the toxic waste trade, and have sought instead to regulate it. The United States and the EC countries implemented legislation in the mid-1980s which required that importing country governments be notified of intended exports of hazardous wastes and give their consent to accept it before shipments were made. This system of notification, known as prior informed consent (PIC), proved to be unenforceable, and there continued to be incidents of U.S. and EC waste dumping in less industrialized countries without prior consent.

The United Nations Environment Programme (UNEP) began to draft an international treaty to regulate the trade in toxic wastes in 1988. This initiative led to the Basel Convention on the Transboundary Movement of Hazardous Wastes and their Disposal, which was signed by delegates from thirty-three countries in 1989. The treaty came into force in mid-1992, when the required twenty government ratifications had taken place. The Basel Convention is designed to regulate the transborder shipments of hazardous wastes by installing a mandatory system of notification to importers of hazardous materials, similar to the U.S./EC PIC notification system, while it strictly forbids the export of waste to Antarctica. The convention encourages countries to dispose of their own toxic wastes within their own borders, rather than to export them to other countries. However, signatories of the convention are free to enter into bilateral waste trade deals, such as those which the United States has negotiated with both Mexico and Canada. These bilateral deals are permitted provided that wastes under these agreements are disposed of in a manner which is no less environmentally sound than that outlined in the Basel Convention. Radioactive wastes and wastes intended for reuse or recycling are not regulated by the Basel Convention.

Many less industrialized countries have expressed concern that the Basel Convention does not provide adequate protection from the dumping of toxic waste in their territories, and have implemented additional safeguards. For example, the sixty-eight African, Caribbean, and Pacific (ACP) states agreed with the European Economic Community (EEC) in the LomÇ IV Convention (signed in 1989) to prohibit exports of hazardous and radioactive wastes from the EEC to the ACP states. The ACP states also agreed not to import such wastes from non-EEC countries. In addition, the Organization of African Unity acted to ban waste imports altogether through the signing in 1991 of the Bamako Convention on the Ban of the Import into Africa and the Control of Transboundary Movement and Management of Hazardous Wastes within Africa. Similarly, several Central American countries agreed to ban imports of toxic waste by signing the Agreement on Transboundary Movement of Hazardous Wastes in the Central American Region in 1992. Large areas of the world, such as Eastern Europe, the Middle East, and Asia, however, do not have regional agreements banning the import of hazardous wastes, and these areas have been increasingly popular targets for toxic waste exporters in recent years.

While there are a number of international agreements designed to regulate or ban the cross-border shipments of toxic wastes, the trade continues to take place in the 1990s and thus still poses a serious threat to human health and the environment. There are two major reasons why toxic waste trade may continue to

grow in the 1990s: 1) it is very difficult to monitor this trade, since much of it takes place outside of the law, and such exports will undoubtedly continue to go unregulated; and 2) not all hazardous wastes are regulated by all of the international waste trade agreements (for example, the Basel Convention's requirement of importing government notification and consent is easily by-passed by waste exporters who label their wastes as commodities to be recycled, which are not regulated by the agreement).

Over 90 percent of the toxic wastes exported to less industrialized countries in 1992 were claimed to be for purposes other than disposal, such as recycling, reuse, and, in some cases, humanitarian aid. Wastes that are recycled in less industrialized countries are typically incinerated under poor health and safety conditions, with toxins often released into the environment. In addition, only a small percentage of such wastes are actually recoverable, and large amounts of the imported product end up as hazardous waste material which must then be disposed of, usually in poorly constructed landfills. The result is that the international toxic waste trade continues under the misleading pretense of recycling.

As of early 1993 ninety-four countries had legislated a ban on toxic waste trade. These countries were not satisfied with the Basel Convention which only regulates the trade, but does not stop it. Only two of the countries banning the trade—Norway and Italy—are themselves producers of hazardous wastes.

Jennifer Clapp

Further Readings

Center for Investigative Reporting. *Global Dumping Ground.* 1991.
Greenpeace. *The International Trade in Wastes: A Greenpeace Inventory.* 1990.
Hilz, Christoph. *The International Toxic Waste Trade.* 1992.

See also ENVIRONMENTAL DIPLOMACY; HAZARDOUS WASTE TREATMENT TECHNOLOGIES; UNITED NATIONS ENVIRONMENT PROGRAMME

Toxicology

Toxicology is a relatively young, multidisciplinary science that examines the adverse effects of chemicals on living organisms. Toxicologists study the nature of adverse effects and assess the probability of their occurrence in humans and other living organisms under specified exposure situations. An emerging, related field of study concerns ecotoxicology which focuses on the systematic diagnosis and treatment of stressed ecosystems.

The most fundamental concept in toxicology is that of the dose-response relationship. Typically, experimentation on laboratory animals such as mice and rats is used to generate a dose-response relationship. A chemical is administered in varying doses to small groups of animals which are then sacrificed and examined for adverse toxicological endpoints. Toxicological endpoints may range from death, malignant or benign tumors, and cell necrosis (death) to subtle biochemical alterations such as changes in enzyme activity or behavioral effects. The resulting mathematical relationship of the dose-response curve is used by scientists and regulators to predict what exposures to chemicals in the environment might impair human or ecological health. Health impacts are dependent on the inherent toxicity of each chemical, its dose, and also on host factors such as genetic susceptibility, age, gender, and nutritional status.

The primary routes of exposure to toxicants are through ingestion, inhalation, and dermal absorption. Exposure may be acute or chronic. Acute exposure occurs over a relatively short period of time and at high levels, as may occur with accidental chemical releases. Chronic exposure occurs over a much longer time period at doses which may not have immediately discernible health effects. For example a community may experience chronic, low-level exposure to pollutants in air, drinking water, or food.

Once an environmental contaminant is absorbed into the human body and enters the blood circulatory system, it can be transported to other organs and tissues to exert its toxic effect. The body is designed to detoxify and eliminate most toxicants. For example, water-soluble substances are readily excreted by the kidney. Fat-soluble compounds such as organochlorines (examples are PCBs, DDT, and dioxins) are more difficult to eliminate. They may first undergo biotransformation in the liver to make them more excretable and less toxic. However, for several environmental contaminants, such as benzo[a]pyrene, biotransformation in the liver leads to the formation of metabolites that are more toxic than the parent compound.

Toxicants are capable of exerting damage on single or multiple tissue sites and organs. Arsine gas, for example, acts primarily in the bloodstream and causes the rupture of blood cells. Carbon tetrachloride damages primarily the liver. Mercury and lead can damage the central nervous system, the kidney, and the blood production system. Other compounds such as chlorinated hydrocarbon insecticides may reach relatively high concentrations in the body's fat deposits without any apparent toxic effects there. The increased mobilization of fat by the body, as may occur during starvation or pregnancy, can release elevated levels of chemical to the circulatory system for transport to target organs where it may cause damage.

Toxicology is a broad field with many subspecialties including genetic, reproductive, behavioral, biochemical, and regulatory toxicology. Although a major focus continues to be the study of cancer as manifest by clinical evidence of disease, increasing attention is devoted to understanding more subtle toxicological endpoints such as reproductive or neurobehavioral effects. Furthermore, increasing effort is being directed to the development and application of more sensitive toxicological tests known as biomarkers (also known as biologic markers). Biomarkers are technologically powerful indicators of biological events occurring at the physiologic, cellular, subcellular, and molecular levels. Advances in the development and utilization of biomarkers permit researchers to detect smaller amounts of toxicants in the body as well as to monitor smaller biological responses to these toxicants. The use of biomarkers in toxicological and epidemiological studies is anticipated to greatly accelerate the identification, prevention, and control of health risks from environmental contaminants faced by human populations, particularly as they relate to chronic, low dose exposures.

Monica Campbell

Further Readings

Doull, J., C.D. Klassen, and M.O. Amdur. *Casarett and Doull's Toxicology: The Basic Science of Poisons.* 1980.

Loomis, T.A. *Essentials of Toxicology.* 1978.

Timbrell, J.A. *Introduction to Toxicology.* 1989.

See also EPIDEMIOLOGY; LEAD; MERCURY; PERSISTENT ORGANOCHLORINE COMPOUNDS; REGULATION; STANDARD SETTING; TOXIC SUBSTANCES CONTROL ACT

Trace Analysis

Current understanding of chemicals and their effects on the environment is largely due to the ability of modern analytical chemistry to detect very low concentrations of these chemicals. When Rachel Carson published her classic book, *Silent Spring*, in 1961 trace analysis was thought to be that which was done at parts-per-million (ppm) concentrations. At that time few scientists believed that industrial pollution at such levels could have a significant impact on environmental systems. As scientists studied these effects they needed better tools to identify the many chemicals present in air, water, soil, and biological samples, and to determine how much was present at lower and lower concentrations. In the thirty years since *Silent Spring* "trace" analysis has meant parts-per-billion, parts-per-trillion, and now parts-per-quadrillion. These terms are defined in table 1.

At first glance, the concentration units ppt and ppq may seem to be so small as to be almost unimaginable. For example, the compound 2,3,7,8-tetrachlorodibenzo-p-dioxin (TCDD) has been detected in soil at concentrations as low as 1 ppt, and analytical methods are sensitive enough to detect TCDD in water samples at concentrations lower than 1 ppq. One ppq of TCDD in water is the equivalent of one second of time in almost 32,000 millennia! However, these quantities do not seem so unreal if the number of atoms or molecules of a pollutant are considered. Instruments that are detecting 1 ppq of TCDD in one liter of water are really sensing almost two billion TCDD molecules. Therefore, there is a lot of room for detection limits to be reduced even further, and the definition of "trace" in ten years may be much lower than indicated in Table 1.

Trace analysis at such low concentrations as ppt and ppq is not easy. Sophisticated instruments and specially trained analysts are required for this work. In the environment samples are always complex mixtures of hundreds or even thousands of different compounds and elements, and the key to trace analysis is to separate specific substances from all of the other sample components. It is also important to keep in mind that all measurements possess an inherent level of error, and measurements of substances present at trace concentrations can be expected to possess a much greater level of error than those present at much greater concentrations. At concentrations in the ppb range or lower, analytical measurements of substances in environmental samples can be expected to differ from the real concentration by 25 percent or more. At ppq concentrations, measurements could easily differ from the real values by 100 percent or more. These errors are not serious if unbiased methods are used and if several replicate measurements are made.

Ray E. Clement

Further Readings

Clement, R.E. "Ultratrace Dioxin and Dibenzofuran Analysis: 30 Years of Advances." *Analytical Chemistry* 63 (1991): 1130A–1139A.
———. "Environmental Sampling for Trace Analysis." *Analytical Chemistry* 64 (1992): 1076A–1081A.

See also BIOACCUMULATION; CARSON, RACHEL; DIOXINS AND FURANS; EPIDEMIOLOGY; GAS CHROMATOGRAPH; MASS SPECTROMETRY; STANDARD SETTING; TOXICOLOGY

Trade and the Environment
See NAFTA AND THE ENVIRONMENT; TOXIC WASTES IN INTERNATIONAL TRADE

TABLE 1

Meaning of Trace Analysis Concentration Units

Concentration Unit	Short Form	Meaning of Term	Number of Grams of Pollutant in 1.0 Gram Soil or 1.0 Liter Water	
			Soil	Water
1 part-per-million	ppm	1 part in 10^6	1 microgram (0.000001 g)	1 milligram (0.001 g)
1 part-per-billion	ppb	1 part in 10^9	1 nanogram (0.000000001 g)	1 microgram (0.000001 g)
1 part-per-trillion	ppt	1 part in 10^{12}	1 picogram (0.000000000001 g)	1 nanogram (0.000000001 g)
1 part-per-quadrillion	ppq	1 part in 10^{15}	1 femtogram (0.000000000000001 g)	1 picogram (0.000000000001 g)

Tradeable Emission Permits

The most common policy for dealing with pollution is to set regulations on emissions and impose fines for non-compliance. For many years economists have observed that this can be an unnecessarily costly approach for achieving environmental objectives. They have also noted that even the most stringent regulation on emissions from each source will fail to limit total emissions if the number of sources increases as an economy grows.

Tradeable emission permits have been developed to reduce the overall costs of environmental protection, and to limit total emissions in the face of continued economic growth. In principle the idea is very simple. Under a scheme of tradeable emission permits sources that emit less than the amount permitted can bank the difference for future use or trade it with another source. Trade in emissions affects the allocation of the total permitted emissions but does not affect the total itself.

The main argument in favor of such a scheme is that, by introducing flexibility into a rigid program of command and control, considerable savings can result in achieving environmental protection objectives. This is accomplished by allowing trade to assign the responsibility for abatement to those sources for which control is the cheapest. Furthermore, tradeable emission permits encourage the development of new methods and technologies for reducing discharges and, by reducing costs, the pace of abatement may be increased as well.

Tradeable emission permits are in use or are being considered for: chlorofluorocarbons (CFCs), to protect the ozone layer; carbon dioxide (CO_2), to prevent climate change; acid gases, to prevent acid rain; lead in gasoline, to protect human health; nitrogen oxides and volatile organic compounds, to limit ground level ozone; and persistent toxics, to protect the Great Lakes. Most experience to date with tradeable emission permits comes from the United States, although the idea originated with Canadian economist John Dales in the 1960s.

The development of tradeable emissions in the United States began in the mid-1970s when the U.S. Environmental Protection Agency (EPA) introduced an emission trading program to reduce the cost of attaining air pollution standards under the Clean Air Act. This Act allows for four kinds of trades: 1) netting, in which plants making modifications or additions can avoid various technological and administrative requirements by reducing emissions from other points within the same plant; 2) offset trading, in which new sources entering a "non-attainment area" must arrange for an even greater reduction from existing sources in the same area; 3) bubbles, in which an imaginary bubble is placed over multiple emission points in one or many plants or firms in an air quality district: the total emissions for the bubble is fixed and the controls at each source can be adjusted to meet the total emissions in the most cost-effective way; and 4) banking, in which an existing firm earning emission reduction credits can save them for later use or sale.

The system just outlined is sometimes referred to as emission reduction credit trading because it allows trades based on reductions in emissions from regulated levels. It has been used primarily to offset the impact of new and modified sources in areas where local pollution exceeds national ambient air standards. Another approach known as emission allowance trading is used to redistribute emission quotas so that firms can meet national emission reduction targets in the most cost-effective way.

One example of how emission allowance trading can be an effective tool of environmental policy is its use in eliminating lead in gasoline in the United States. Before 1982 U.S. refineries were limited in the amount of lead they could put in gasoline. Some small refineries had difficulties meeting the limits. In 1982 trades were allowed among refineries who could buy credits from the larger refineries. Subsequently the lead allowed in gasoline was reduced in stages. Refineries that cut back more quickly than required could bank the difference for later use or sale. As a result of the program lead emissions were reduced faster than otherwise and substantial cost savings were achieved.

In November 1990 the U.S. Clean Air Act was amended to implement emission allowance trading among major sources of sulfur and nitrogen oxides, the precursors of acid rain. The number of permits will be reduced in two steps during the years 1995 and 2000. Trade among plants and across pollutants is allowed, though new plants still have to meet new source performance standards and existing plants have to satisfy standards set under state implementation plans.

Early signs indicate that, in practice, tradeable emission permits can achieve environmental objectives more cheaply and flexibly than the traditional regulatory approach. There are, however, several reasons why they are likely to remain of limited practical use. First, whereas economic considerations call for a large, uncontrolled market to maximize the economic gains from trade, environmental considerations for most pollutants favor a small, regulated market to avoid unacceptable local impacts.

Second, there can be problems arising from using historical emission rates to establish initial allowances. It can penalize those sources that have already taken steps to reduce their emissions to the advantage of those that have lagged behind. Also, by the time a trading system is introduced, some sources may have reduced their loadings below the historic level on which their allowance was based. This means they could trade reductions already achieved to other sources who are then able to increase their emissions without any real reductions to offset the increase.

These types of problems can be addressed through the careful design of the trading system. To do so, however, can add a level of complexity and administrative cost that must be set against the expected savings from trading. What is more difficult to overcome is the concern of some that any use of tradeable emission permits implies that the environment is up for sale to the highest bidder, rather than being something of inestimable value that should remain beyond the influence of market forces.

Nevertheless, faced with an emerging consensus that the use of some materials should be phased out entirely from use, and that the total emission of some contaminants should be limited to protect human health and the environment, tradeable emission permits offer an economically attractive way to achieve these goals.

Peter A. Victor

Further Readings

Dales, John. *Pollution, Property and Prices.* 1968.

Foley, Dermot, Moira Knott, and Robert Seeliger. *Economic Instruments in Action.* 1993.

Government of Canada. *Economic Instruments for Environmental Protection.* 1992.

Tietenberg, T.H. *Emissions Trading: An Exercise in Reformulating Pollution Policy.* 1985.

See also ACID PRECIPITATION: LEGISLATIVE INITIATIVES; AIR POLLUTION: REGULATION (U.S.); CARBON TAX; GREEN ECONOMICS; LEAD; POLLUTION PREVENTION; REGULATION; STANDARD SETTING

Tragedy of the Commons

The expression "tragedy of the commons" has come to symbolize environmental degradation to be expected whenever many individuals use a scarce resource held in common. As originally formulated by the human ecologist Garrett Hardin, the "tragedy" is the outcome of economically rational, individualistic decision-making. "Picture a pasture open to all," said Hardin. Each cattle owner will want to maximize gains by keeping as many cattle as possible. But sooner or later, the carrying capacity of the land will be reached.

Explicitly or implicitly, each herder will ask, "What is the utility to *me* of adding one more animal to my herd?" Each new animal will bring the herder a positive utility of nearly +1. But the effects of overgrazing will be shared by all, and the herder's loss will only be a fraction of –1. Thus, the herder's rational decision, according to Hardin, "is to add another animal to his herd. And another; and another . . . But this is the conclusion reached by each and every rational herdsman sharing the commons. Therein is the tragedy."

If the only commons of importance were a few grazing areas, the "tragedy" would be of little general interest. But almost all resources, and the environment in general, can be considered a commons jointly used by many, in which potential users are difficult to exclude, and the activity of any one user may affect the welfare of all others. Hardin himself used the grazing commons as a metaphor for the problem of overpopulation. The dominant legacy of his famous essay, however, has been in the area of natural resource management.

The best known formulation of the commons dilemma is Hardin's, but the history of the concept probably goes at least as far back in time as Aristotle who observed that "what is common to the greatest number has the least care bestowed upon it. Everyone thinks chiefly of his own, hardly at all of the common interest." Two modern resource economists, Anthony Scott and Scott Gordon, writing in 1954 and 1955, respectively, are usually credited with the first statement of the conventional theory of the commons. The "tragedy" has also been formalized as a Prisoner's Dilemma game in the mathematical theory of games.

The most significant contribution of the "tragedy of the commons" metaphor has been to highlight an age-old fundamental problem—the divergence between individual and collective rationality, together with the ecological idea of interdependence—and to bring these under close scrutiny in the fields of environmental studies and resource management. The metaphor brought home the basic idea that resources once abundant and freely available to all tend to become ecologically scarce; unless their use is somehow regulated in the common interest, the outcome will be mutual ecological ruin.

Hence, much of the technical literature on commons since Hardin's seminal idea has concentrated on exploring the potential solutions to the commons dilemma, and narrowed it down to basically three approaches: government property and centralized regulatory controls; privatization or the establishment of private property rights in the commons; and communal property rights or the application of the same kind of social rules and local political controls that have traditionally governed the use of commons.

Findings from a large number of cases, many of them interdisciplinary and covering a diversity of resource types, geographical areas, and cultures, are consistent with the conclusion that sustainability of resource use is not intrinsically associated with any one particular type of property-rights regime. Government property, private property, and communal property have all been associated with both success and failure. Avoiding the "tragedy" is possible with an appropriate mix of well-defined property rights in the commons (private or communal, depending on the case) in which users have responsibilities as well as rights, and participate in decision-making.

The original "tragedy of the commons" model did not distinguish between common-property and open-access, and deterministically predicted the demise of all such resources. A more comprehensive theory of common-property takes into account property rights arrangements, information needs, communication and cooperation among users, and rule-making and institutions that may provide for exclusion and for regulation of use. These considerations have been found to apply not only to local commons but also to regional and global commons.

Fikret Berkes

Further Readings

Berkes, F., ed. *Common Property Resources: Ecology and Community-Based Sustainable Development.* 1989.

Bromley, D.W., ed. *Making the Commons Work.* 1992.

Feeny, D., F. Berkes, B.J. McCay, and J.M. Acheson. "The Tragedy of the Commons: Twenty-Two Years Later." *Human Ecology* 18 (1990): 1–19.

Hardin, G. "The Tragedy of the Commons." *Science* 162 (1968): 1243–48.

Ostrom, E. *Governing the Commons.* 1990.

See also COMMON PROPERTY RESOURCE MANAGEMENT; HARDIN, GARRETT; RESOURCE MANAGEMENT

Trail Smelter Investigation

In 1935, after almost a decade of bitter, often acrimonious negotiations, the government of Canada agreed to pay the United States $350,000 in compensation for damages caused by smoke emitted from the Consolidated Mining and Smelting Company of Trail, British Columbia. Since at least 1926 residents across the border from Trail in Steven's County, Washington, had complained that the emissions were the source of considerable damage to their crops, orchards, timber lots, and general farm property, resulting in extensive economic dislocation. Faced with a loan embargo by the local banking community and unable to sell their seemingly worthless property, the farmers, through state politicians, demanded that the State Department take the matter up with the government of Canada.

After several years of protracted discussions between the two governments the issue was eventually referred to the International Joint Commission for resolution. Despite three years of intensive study and investigation the United States, on behalf of the Washington farmers, refused to accept the unanimous recommendations of the commission. Finally, in 1935, the two governments formally approved a convention under which it was agreed that Canada would pay financial compensation for damages incurred before January 1932, while any damages thereafter would be sent to a joint tribunal for final resolution. The investigation came to a close when in 1938 the Trail Smelter Arbitral Tribunal issued an interim report awarding another $78,000 to the Washington farmers. In rendering its final decision in 1941 the tribunal concluded that no further monetary compensation was required, but imposed a strict smoke control regime to avoid further damages.

What appears to be another in a long line of cross-border diplomatic disputes between Canada and the United States is, on closer inspection, a significant moment in the history of international environmental politics. Indeed, the Trail Smelter Investigation not only stands as one of the earliest and most comprehensive environmental assessments undertaken in North America prior to the 1970s, but is also regarded among legal scholars to be the foundation of international law on transnational air pollution. The dispute demonstrates that environmental politics has long been a crucial form of resistance to the impact of industrialization and not merely a contemporary phenomenon. The final resolution of the Trail Smelter Investigation also underlines the extent to which environmental law has been fundamental to the consolidation of industrial capitalism in North America.

James Allum

Further Readings

Dinwoodie, D.H. "The Politics of International Pollution Control: The Trail Smelter Case." *International Journal* 72 (1972): 219–35.

Rubin, Arthur P. "Pollution by Analogy: The Trail Smelter Arbitration." *Oregon Law Review* 50 (1971): 259–92.

See also ENVIRONMENTAL CASE LAW (CANADA): COMMON LAW CAUSES OF ACTION; ENVIRONMENTAL CASE LAW: UNITED STATES; ENVIRONMENTAL DIPLOMACY; INTERNATIONAL JOINT COMMISSION

Train, Russell

In the mid-1960s Russell Train had an interest in wildlife conservation which had developed during his travels in Africa, but he earned his living as a judge in the U.S. tax courts. He had founded the African Wildlife Foundation and had already been active in the U.S. branch of the World Wildlife Fund (WWF). But it was Fairfield Osborn who persuaded Train to turn a citizen's interest into a profession by leaving the bench to become president of the Conservation Foundation. Train then moved from that post into a succession of important governmental posts including undersecretary of the U.S. Department of the Interior and then first chairman of the Council of Environmental Quality (under President Richard Nixon). Thereafter, President Gerald Ford appointed him administrator of the Environmental Protection Agency (EPA). (It was appointees like Train that allowed 1960s and 1970s Republican administra-

tions to avoid the negative historical judgments regarding environmental matters that will likely befall the Reagan and Bush regimes.)

Despite his links to the Republican party (albeit the moderate wing) Train later openly criticized some of the Reagan administration's environmental policies. He also warned President George Bush that "the (environmental) problems hitting us now are hellishly more complex and difficult." Since leaving formal public office Train has served in a number of important posts both temporary and permanent, including the position of chairman of the board of the WWF.

Robert Paehlke

Further Readings

Rathlesburger, James, ed. *Nixon and the Environment*. 1972.

Whitaker, John C. *Striking a Balance: Environment and Natural Resources Policy in the Nixon-Ford Years*. 1976.

See also BUSH, GEORGE; CONSERVATION FOUNDATION; COUNCIL ON ENVIRONMENTAL QUALITY; ENVIRONMENTAL PROTECTION AGENCY; OSBORN, FAIRFIELD; REAGAN, RONALD; WORLD WILDLIFE FUND

Transmission Lines

Transmission lines—the large high voltage power lines often built on steel towers—transport electric power from generator stations to the locations where it is consumed. Transmission lines are frequently interconnected into a transmission grid to reduce costs and assure reliable supply. The operation of such grids is typically directed from a dispatch center which provides both routine system dispatch and emergency control.

The history of transmission lines has been a history of constantly increasing voltages. The highest voltage in general operation in 1900 was about 50,000 volts (50 kilovolts [kV]). By 1940 it had climbed to 300 kV and by the early 1970s it had reached 765 kV where it now remains. A simple physical reason explains this history. The power carried in a line is the product of the voltage and current (VI). However, resistive loss is the current squared times the resistance (I^2R). Thus, there is a strong economic incentive to increase the voltage so as to keep the current, and losses, low. As operating voltages have climbed power companies have typically kept their older lower voltage systems in operation. Today transmission grids consist of several voltage levels interconnected through transformer substations.

Electric power systems use alternating current (AC) because, in contrast to direct current (DC), with AC it is relatively easy to increase and decrease voltage using transformers. Typical transmission lines involve three main current carrying wires or "phases" in order to achieve the most efficient transfer of power and operation of large machinery. In recent years decreasing costs for solid state power converters have allowed greater use of DC transmission lines. These lines, which involve only two current carrying wires, are typically cost-effective only for point-to-point transfer of bulk power over fairly long distances. They are sometimes also used to provide dynamic isolation between power systems.

The width of the "right-of-way" over which a transmission line passes varies with voltage and with regulatory regimen. Some rights-of-way are owned by the utility; some are leased or operated under easement. In the United States, building is not allowed on high voltage transmission line rights-of-way, but it is allowed in some other countries. For ease of access and safety trees have traditionally been cleared from the land over which high voltage lines pass, and sometimes herbicides have been used to control plant growth. Recently a number of utilities have developed procedures to reduce the amount of clearing that is required for transmission lines. Progress has also been made in designing transmission towers which present a reduced "visual profile." Empirical evidence on the question of whether transmission lines have an effect on adjacent property values is limited and contradictory.

All electric power produces electric fields (whose strength is determined by the voltage) and magnetic fields (whose strength is determined by current). Electric fields are easily shielded; magnetic fields are not. The strength of fields decreases rapidly with distance from the source. The fields associated with high voltage lines can induce voltages on nearby conducting objects such as metal fences or large vehicles. If such objects are not properly grounded these voltages can result in shocks. Modern construction rules are designed to minimize such problems. Induced voltages can also lead to difficulties in the operation of farms. For example, cows may get weak shocks from milking machines. Such "stray voltage" problems are more commonly associated with lower voltage distribution lines rather than transmission lines and can generally be controlled with proper grounding.

Particularly in foggy weather the strong electric fields associated with very high voltage lines can result in an electrical breakdown of the air leading to corona discharge. Corona can cause noise, trace amounts of ozone, and radio interference. Procedures for preventing corona are well understood and now routinely applied in the design of new lines.

Some research has suggested that exposure to fields may pose health risks, but the evidence at this point remains both incomplete and contradictory. If field exposure does pose a health risk, stronger fields may not pose greater hazards, and fields from distribution lines and building wiring may be as or more important than fields from transmission lines.

M. Granger Morgan

Further Readings

Electric Power Research Institute. *Transmission Line Reference Book: 345 kV and above.* 1982.

Elgerd, Olle I. *Electric Energy Systems Theory: An Introduction.* 1971.

Nair, Indira, M. Granger Morgan, and H. Keith Florig. *Biological Effects of Power Frequency Electric and Magnetic Fields.* U.S. Office of Technology Assessment, OTA-BP-E-53, 1989.

See also HERBICIDES; HYDROELECTRICITY; LAND-USE PLANNING; OZONE POLLUTION

Transport and Fate of Pollutants

See TOXIC POLLUTANTS, TRANSPORT AND FATE

Treaty of Waitangi (New Zealand)

The Treaty of Waitangi—the basis of constitutional government in New Zealand—was signed by representatives of the English Crown and chiefs of the indigenous Maori tribes on February 6, 1840. English sovereignty was imposed in exchange for the protection of Maori lands, fisheries, and treasures (taonga). An English and a Maori version were signed. Initially recognized as a treaty of cession under international law, it was soon disregarded by settler governments intent on English settlement. Within Maori society, however, the Treaty has always been recognized as an affirmation of rights and highly valued as a sacred pact.

The Treaty has recently been brought to the forefront of debate on race relations and resource management and allocation issues. Rising Maori protest resulted in the enactment of the 1975 Treaty of Waitangi Act. A Waitangi Tribunal was established to hear claims by aggrieved Maori over government actions that were contrary to the principles of the treaty.

Early tribunal reports (1983–1985) dealt with resource depletion and pollution concerns and were a key factor in the recognition of the principles of the Treaty, and Maori spiritual and cultural values in resource management legislation (Environment Act [1986], State Owned Enterprises Act [1986], Conservation Act [1987], Maori Fisheries Act [1989], Resource Management Act [1991]). A bicultural jurisprudence is gradually beginning to evolve.

The landmark 1987 Court of Appeals case, *New Zealand Maori Council v. the Crown*, saw the special relationship between the Maori people and the Crown as one of an ongoing partnership, requiring the partners to act reasonably and with the utmost good faith toward each other. In excess of 200 claims have been lodged with the tribunal. Given the complexity of the claims and the tribunal's limited resources governments are encouraging direct negotiation to settle outstanding grievances. A multimillion dollar fishing settlement has recently been finalized.

Peter Horsley

Further Readings

Ministry for the Environment. *Taking into Account the Principles of the Treaty of Waitangi.* 1993.

Orange, Claudia. *The Treaty of Waitangi.* 1987.

Stokes, Evelyn. "The Treaty of Waitangi and the Waitangi Tribunal: Maori Claims in New Zealand." *Applied Geography* 12 (1992): 176–91.

See also ENVIRONMENTAL CASE LAW: NEW ZEALAND; ENVIRONMENTAL JUSTICE MOVEMENT; INDIGENOUS PEOPLE AND THE ENVIRONMENT (NEW ZEALAND); RESOURCE MANAGEMENT

Tritium

Tritium (T or ^{3}H) is the heaviest isotope of hydrogen, the most abundant element in the solar system. It is produced naturally in the atmosphere by the bombardment of nitrogen with cosmic neutrons, according to reaction:*

$$^{14}N + n \text{ fi } T + {}^{12}C$$

Tritium atoms are readily incorporated into water molecules as T_2O which then reside in the lower stratosphere for up to twenty years before falling to the earth's surface in the form of meteoric precipitation.

Tritium is radioactive and emits low-energy negatively charged beta particles. It decays with a half-life of 12.26 years to form helium ^{3}He—its stable and chemically inert daughter product. Concentrations of tritium are normally expressed in tritium units (T.U.), where 1 T.U. represents 1 atom of T for every 10^{18} atoms of hydrogen. In turn, 1 T.U. is equivalent to 7.1 disintegrations of T per minute per liter of water. Since natural rates of tritium production are low ($5\pm3 \times 10^{-5}$ atoms s^{-1} m^{-2}), natural levels of tritium in meteoric precipitation are usually considerably less than 20 T.U.

In the early 1950s, however, levels of naturally-produced tritium were swamped when atmospheric testing of thermonuclear devices released large quantities of tritium into the atmosphere. This practice continued at an increasing rate until 1963 when a moratorium on atmospheric testing of thermonuclear devices was agreed between the United States and the Soviet Union. By this time tritium in precipitation had increased by several orders of magnitude and exceeded 1,000 T.U. throughout much of the northern hemisphere. In the extreme north values as high as 10,000 T.U. were recorded. Since 1963 tritium levels have reduced significantly and, in most parts of the northern hemisphere, present concentrations of tritium in precipitation rarely exceed 100 T.U. While the effects of atmospheric testing on tritium in precipitation were less severe in the southern hemisphere, rates of recovery have also tended to be more gradual.

Although levels of tritium recorded in precipitation during the 1950s and 1960s may seem excessive, any mild environmental concerns have been far outweighed by the research benefits gained from its use as an "environmental tracer." These benefits arise from the fact that elevated tritium provides a "signature" or "fingerprint" for water that fell as precipitation since thermonuclear testing began in 1952. Tritium analyses therefore allow post-1952 water to be tracked as it passes through the various compartments of the hydrologic cycle, in surface water bodies and below ground. For example, elevated tritium has been used to study mixing in the upper layers of the ocean and circulation rates in lakes. It has also been used extensively in groundwater studies, to investigate vertical flow through low permeability sediments, to estimate groundwater flow velocities and to identify mechanisms and determine rates of groundwater recharge. The latter is particularly of interest in remote parts of the world where good quality meteorological data is difficult to obtain.

Ken W.F. Howard

Further Readings

Gat, J.R. "The Isotopes of Hydrogen and Oxygen in Precipitation." In *Handbook of Environmental Geochemistry, Vol. 1A.* Ed. P. Fritz and J. Ch. Fontes. 1980, 21–47.

Faure, G. *Principles of Isotope Geology.* 1986.

See also GROUNDWATER POLLUTION; NUCLEAR ELECTRIC POWER; NUCLEAR WEAPONS PRODUCTION; RADIOACTIVE FALLOUT; RADON

Tropical Deforestation

Tropical forests of the moist sort—by far the most important forests—can be defined as evergreen or partly evergreen forests, in areas receiving not less than 100 millimeters of precipitation in any month for two out of three years, with a mean annual temperature at least of 24 degrees Celsius and essentially frost-free. They usually occur at altitudes below 1,300 meters, though often in Amazonia up to 1,800 meters and generally in Southeast Asia up to only 750 meters. In mature examples of these forests, there are several more or less distinctive strata. In certain instances, many trees are deciduous.

These forests are exceptionally important by virtue of both their carbon stocks and their enormous biodiversity. They are important for many other reasons too, notably their specialist hardwoods and their watershed functions. But their carbon stocks in plants and soil comprise around half of all such stocks contained in the world's forests. Deforestation leads to large emissions of carbon dioxide, the greenhouse gas that contributes around half of global-warming processes. As for their biodiversity, they certainly harbor more species than the rest of the world. It has recently been estimated that just their canopies supply habitat to 30 million

insect species, possibly twice as many or even more. This is to be contrasted with total species, animal and plants combined, in the rest of the tropics and the rest of the world, estimated at 4 million. Due to deforestation these moist forests are by far the main locus of the mass extinction of species that is overtaking the biosphere, a mass extinction that if unchecked will be the largest such episode since the demise of the dinosaurs and associated species 65 million years ago.

Deforestation refers to the complete destruction of forest cover through forest clearing for agriculture of whatever sort (cattle ranching, smallholder agriculture whether planned or spontaneous, and commodity-crop production through, for example, rubber and oil palm plantations); as well as clearing for mining and dams. Thus deforestation means that not a tree remains, and the land is given over to non-forest purposes. There are certain instances too where the forest biomass is so severely depleted—notably through the very heavy and unduly negligent logging of dipterocarp forests in Southeast Asia, resulting in the removal of, or unsurvivable injury to, the great majority of trees—that the remnant ecosystem is a travesty of natural forest as properly understood. Decline of biomass and depletion of ecosystem services are so severe that the residual forest can no longer qualify as forest in any practical sense of the word. So this particular kind of over-logging is included under the term "deforestation."

Note that the forests are also often subject to much disruption as a consequence of such interventions as light to moderate logging or shifting cultivation of a traditional (sustainable) style. These latter activities often lead to significant degradation of primary forests, though without eliminating the forest cover outright. While this aspect of forest conversion is important with respect to tropical-forest values such as biodiversity and watershed mechanisms, it is not considered here as a form of deforestation—even though the aggregate expanse of forest degradation per year is roughly reckoned to be at least as large as the area deforested.

So far as we can discern from bio-climatic data, tropical forests formerly covered around 14.5 million square kilometers. The amount remaining today is approximately 7.5 million square kilometers, meaning that almost half has already been eliminated. Deforestation in 1989 has been estimated at 142,200 square kilometers, for an annual deforestation rate of 1.8 percent. Using this latter data we can calculate that in 1992 the expanse deforested has amounted to approximately 150,000 square kilometers, and the rate has risen to 2.0 percent.

A deforestation rate of 2.0 percent in 1992 does not mean that all remaining forests will therefore disappear in another half century (actually less due to the compounding effect). Patterns and trends of deforestation are far from even throughout the biome. In Southeast Asia it is likely—supposing recent land-use trends and patterns persist unvaried—that virtually all forest will be eliminated by the end of the century in Thailand and Vietnam, and virtually all primary forest in Philippines and Myanmar. Little forest of whatever sort is likely to remain in another twenty years' time in most of Malaysia, and in Indonesia outside of Kalimantan and Irian Jaya. But in Papua New Guinea with its low population pressures (fewer than four million people in an area of 461,700 square kilometers, almost half the size of British Columbia), there could well be sizable tracts of forest remaining for several decades into the next century.

A similarly differentiated picture emerges in Africa. One hypothetical scenario is that if recent land-use patterns and trends persist unchanged, we can realistically anticipate that hardly any forest will remain in Madagascar, East Africa, and West Africa beyond the end of the century, due to the combined pressures of population growth and peasant poverty. But in the Zaire basin, comprising Gabon, Congo, and Zaire, only 45 million people occupy an area of 3 million square kilometers. Moreover, these countries are so well endowed with mineral resources that their governments sense little urgent need to exploit their forest stocks to fund development, although the situation may change rapidly with the opening of the Trans-Gabon Railway, a large African Development Bank investment in sawmilling in Congo, and increased foreign investment for commercial logging in Zaire. Note, moreover, that the population total is projected to reach 112 million, for a 149-percent increase, as early as the year 2025.

In Latin America, subject to the same qualifications, it is difficult to foresee much forest persisting long into the next century in Mexico, Central America, the Atlantic-coast sector of Brazil and Amazonian Ecuador. The Colombian Choco may survive a while longer. Amazonia presents a mixed picture. The sectors in Peru and Bolivia may join that in Ecuador within another few decades, by being largely

eliminated. By contrast, the Venezuelan sector is hardly affected thus far, and much of it may well remain intact for a good time to come; while the Colombian government has recently assigned a large proportion of its Amazonian forest to the care of its tribal peoples, who do not generally engage in destructive forms of forest exploitation.

The Latin American situation is dominated by Brazil, with well over half of the region's forests (and well over one quarter of all tropical forests). There has been creeping attrition of Brazil's Amazonian forest throughout the past two decades, with a sharp acceleration in the deforestation rate during 1987 and 1988, albeit followed by a marked decline in the rate during 1989–1992. The 1987–1988 rate appeared to average around 50,000 square kilometers of forest burned, but by 1991 it had declined to 11,130 square kilometers. The recent decline in the deforestation rate, however, appears to have been due more to Brazil's economic recession than to enhanced legislation and better law enforcement. Many observers anticipate that as Brazil's economy recovers, there will be a resumption of progressively increasing deforestation. But so vast is Brazil's expanse of forest that even the outburst of burning during the late 1980s leaves the proportionate amount of deforestation behind a good number of other countries with higher percentage rates. Fortunately we can hope that while the peripheral states along the southern, eastern, and even northern borders of Brazilian Amazonia may well continue to experience extensive deforestation, the west-central bloc could conceivably survive with scant depletion for several more decades.

There is even better prospect for the Guyanas, with more than 400,000 square kilometers of forest and only 2 million people. Until the road linking Guyana south to Brazil is built, little deforestation appears likely.

To consider the overall analysis from a different standpoint, we can note that ten countries are losing forest at a rate of 4,000 square kilometers or more of forest each year. These are: Brazil, Colombia, India, Indonesia, Malaysia, Mexico, Myanmar, Nigeria, Thailand, and Zaire. Their collective total in 1989 was 87,300 square kilometers, or 69 percent of all deforestation.

Note also that ten countries—or, in the case of the Guyanas, a group of countries—each possess 200,000 square kilometers or more of remaining forest. These are: Brazil, Colombia,

Gabon, the Guyanas, Indonesia, Myanmar, Papua New Guinea, Peru, Venezuela, and Zaire. Their collective total in 1989 was 6,418,500 square kilometers, or 80 percent of remaining forests. Just three countries, Brazil, Indonesia and Zaire, still possessed rather more than 4 million square kilometers altogether, or over half of the entire biome.

As for the percent rate of annual deforestation, ten countries (or groups of countries) feature rates that are more than twice the average rate for the biome, namely 1.6 percent. These are: Central America, Ecuador, Ivory Coast, Madagascar, Mexico, Myanmar, Nigeria, Philippines, Thailand, and Vietnam. Of these, all except Central America, Ecuador, Mexico and Myanmar are three times or more above the biome-wide average; four countries are 4.5 times or more above the average, namely Thailand 8.1 percent, Madagascar 8.3 percent, Nigeria 14.3 percent and Ivory Coast 15.6 percent. Six countries (or groups of countries) feature a rate that is less than half the average biome-wide rate. These are: Gabon, the Guyanas, Kampuchea, Peru, Venezuela, and Zaire.

In 1979 tropical forests lost 75,000 square kilometers of their expanse. So the 1989 figure of 142,200 square kilometers represented an 89-percent increase in the deforestation rate during the 1980s. There is strong reason to believe that this acceleration in the deforestation rate will itself accelerate during the foreseeable future unless vigorous measures are undertaken with due urgency to tackle the main causes of deforestation, namely the commercial logger, the cattle rancher, and the slash-and-burn farmer.

In 1989 the commercial logger was affecting some 45,000 square kilometers of new forest each year, much the same as ten years ago. Of this, roughly two-thirds, or 30,000 square kilometers, was in Southeast Asia, where it was so heavy and negligent that it amounted to forest destruction. Cattle ranching, almost entirely confined to Central America and Amazonia, caused 15,000 square kilometers of forest to be cleared in 1989—rather less than ten years earlier. Forest conversion to cash-crop plantations (e.g., oil palm, rubber), plus forest destruction for roads, mining, and other activities of similar relatively smallscale sort, amounted to perhaps 10,000 square kilometers. So in 1989 these three categories totaled 55,000 square kilometers. The rest, a little over 87,000 square kilometers, was ostensibly due to slash-and-burn farmers, mainly shifted cultivators—though this was, and remains, a very rough-and-ready estimate, advanced with the sole aim of gaining an insight into the proportionate share of forest destruction attributable to this agent. To the extent that this latter estimate was broadly correct, shifted cultivators accounted for 61 percent of all forest destruction—a proportion that since 1989 appears to have been increasing steadily.

Shifted cultivators are subject to a host of forces—population pressures, pervasive poverty, maldistribution of traditional farmlands, inequitable land-tenure systems, inadequate attention to subsistence agriculture, adverse trade and aid patterns, and international debt—that they are little able to comprehend, let alone to control. Thus they reflect a failure of development strategies overall, and their problem can be confronted only by a major restructuring of policies on the part of governments and international agencies concerned. Without an integrated effort of sufficient scope—which appears to lie beyond the planning capacities and political commitment of governments and agencies in question to date—there is every prospect that we shall witness the continuing demise of most tropical forests during the coming decades. Indeed, and supposing the 1980s' increase in the deforestation rate increases further during the 1990s, the amount deforested in the year 2000 could well be as much as 3.5 percent of remaining forests. This would herald the onset of probably the largest and fastest land-use change in the whole of human history.

Moreover several other sources of deforestation could emerge within the foreseeable future. First is acid rain, already manifest in the forests of southern China, and expected to appear shortly in central and western Indonesia, Peninsular Malaysia, southern Thailand, southwestern India, West Africa, southeastern Brazil and northern Colombia, and Venezuela. Eventually acid rain could affect as much as one million square kilometers of forest, though how much would suffer enough injury to be effectively eliminated is not known.

The second potential new source of deforestation is the phenomenon of moisture-cycling feedbacks within Amazonia. Disruption of moisture cycling through partial deforestation may eventually result in the steady desiccation of remaining forests (however well safeguarded through conventional protection methods), causing moist forests to give way to drier forests, even to woodlands. Unlike the first new source of deforestation, however, this is not expected to have much impact on tropical forests for some time to come.

Third is the prospect of greenhouse-effect feedbacks leading to significant changes in temperature and rainfall regimes. While these feedbacks would possibly entrain more favorable forest conditions in the equatorial belt, they could generate disruptive and depletive impacts on seasonal forests in the outer tropics. Fortunately this new source of deforestation is not likely to become apparent for several decades yet.

Norman Myers

Further Readings

Myers, Norman. *The Primary Source: Tropical Forests and Our Future.* 1992 (expanded edition).

United Nations Food and Agriculture Organization. *Tropical Forest Resources Assessment.* 1993.

See also AFRICA: ENVIRONMENTAL PROBLEMS; BIODEPLETION; BIODIVERSITY; CHIPKO MOVEMENT; CLIMATE WARMING; ENVIRONMENTAL REFUGEES; INTERNATIONAL TROPICAL TIMBER ORGANIZATION; SLASH-AND-BURN AGRICULTURE; TROPICAL RAINFORESTS

Tropical Rainforests

Tropical rainforests are among the best-known ecosystems on earth. The advent of television has enabled us to probe the splendors and complexities of these forests; we can visit Amazonia from our armchair. Yet despite their obvious public appeal and their marked attraction to biologists we know all too little about the forests. We know more about certain sectors of the moon's surface than about the deepest heartlands of Borneo. The final unexplored frontier of life on the planet is not in the deep ocean but in the tropical rainforest canopy, where we don't even know whether there are 2 million or 30 million insects.

In fact we don't really know what to call these forests. Strictly speaking rainforests are forests with year-round rainfall and hence evergreen vegetation. But many forests with lots of rainfall experience a dry season of several months, meaning their trees are semi-deciduous at least. According to strict scientific standards rainforests make up only about one-third of tropical moist forests. But no matter, "rainforest" conjures up images of hothouse

atmosphere, luxuriant plant growth, and teeming animal life—all we associate with tropical rainforests. According to this designation remaining forests cover about 7.5 million square kilometers, or 6 percent of earth's land surface—and they are home to at least half, perhaps three-quarters and conceivably a still greater proportion, of earth's species. A single hectare of Borneo forest can feature at least 100 woody plant species (trees, bushes, and shrubs) and occasionally, in the wettest lowland areas, more than 200 species. By comparison, in the Appalachian forests of the United States, among the richest in tree species of any temperate forest, you will find no more than twenty-five species; and in Ontario, Canada, probably no more than a dozen or so. In the Sarawak sector of northern Borneo, with its 126,000 square kilometers, there are at least 2,500 tree species, whereas in Great Britain, with 244,000 square kilometers, there are only about thirty-five species. As for plant species other than woody sorts, we can expect to encounter 1,000 species within just a few hectares of tropical rainforests—vines, orchids, and other epiphytes, bamboos, milkworts, violets and the like—whereas in Great Britain there are only about 1,400 such species altogether.

This remarkable divergence between tropical and non-tropical forests alerts us to the fact that what makes one tick is very different from what makes the other tick. If we are to keep tropical forests ticking at all we shall have to recognize that the strategies we have developed in temperate zones, whether for exploitation or management or preservation, do not work nearly so well, if at all, in tropical forests. Our scientific surveys must be different, our logging practices too, our planning of parks the same again. In fact, we must operate differently from start to finish. Using the same term "forests" for a bunch of trees in the tropics and a bunch of trees elsewhere is highly misleading. The two categories may reveal a few immediate similarities, but from there on they go their separate ways. How much better we might understand tropical forests if we gave them a new name, indicating that they are a fundamentally different state of affairs from the forests with which we are more familiar in the temperate zones, let alone the boreal zones.

Remote as they may seem tropical forests contribute to our daily lives in ways few people are aware of, let alone understand. Through myriad raw materials apart from specialist hardwood timber, tropical forests support the well-being of each and every one of us. Our wake-up cup of coffee may come to us courtesy of a bush in Ethiopia's forests, which, being the ancestral source of all coffee plantations around the tropics, continues to supply germplasm materials to boost productivity and to resist diseases. Without these genetic contributions from Ethiopia's forests—which are 90 percent gone—we could soon be facing the $3 cup of coffee.

By the time we have finished breakfast we are likely to have enjoyed a wide range of foods, notably fruits, that owe their existence, in one way or another, to tropical forests. And so it goes on, through to the late-night cup of drinking chocolate, which originally derived from the native home of the cocoa tree in western Amazonia and the Pacific Coast zone of Ecuador. In the latter country a particular variety of cocoa with better taste and other virtues than almost all other gene pools of wild cocoa has been reduced to just a few surviving individuals in the one-square kilometer biological reserve at Rio Palenque.

Tropical forests also supply many new foods. As agriculturalists investigate more of the abundant stocks of foods to be found in the forest we can look forward to an ever-greater selection for our meal tables. In New Guinea alone over 250 kinds of trees bear edible fruits, only 100 or so of which are consumed by local communities. No more than a couple of dozen reach the marketplaces of Southeast Asia, and a mere two or three arrive in the supermarkets of the wider world beyond. There is much scope for agronomists and others to develop entirely new, and nutritious and tasty, forms of food.

When we visit our neighborhood pharmacy for a medication or pharmaceutical product there is roughly one chance in four that our purchase owes its manufacture, either directly or indirectly, to raw materials from tropical forest plants. The product may be an analgesic, an antibiotic, a tranquilizer, a steroidal compound, or a cough drop. The commercial value of these end products now amounts worldwide to some $20 billion a year. According to the National Cancer Institute of the United States, there could well be at least five plants in Amazonia alone, plus another five in other parts of tropical forests, with the potential to generate superstar drugs against cancer. Still other plants could supply an assortment of birth-control materials that are more effective and safer than the famous "pill"—and could meet the contraceptive needs of men as well as women.

Tropical forests bestow still further benefits, this time of environmental form. Consider the climate connection. Deforestation often results in reduced rainfall, which can be unusually significant for agriculture, and the prospect of feeding two billion people in the humid tropics. A number of tropical crops are more susceptible to climatic changes than temperate-zone crops usually are, and a marginal decline in rainfall can sometimes cause a substantial decline in staple crops. In Peninsular Malaysia two northern states have experienced disruption of rainfall regimes to the extent that 20,000 hectares of paddy rice fields have been abandoned and another 72,000 hectares have registered a marked production drop-off in this "rice bowl" of the Peninsula, leading to an overall shortfall of well over one quarter of the Peninsula's rice harvest.

A far bigger climate dislocation will ensue from deforestation's contribution to the greenhouse effect. Most deforestation is caused by burning rather than by activities such as logging that leave wood intact. A tree is half carbon and when it burns it releases its carbon into the atmosphere where it combines to form carbon dioxide. This gas accounts for almost half of global warming—the phenomenon that threatens to cause massive disruption of climates far and wide, notably in North America and Europe. True, most of the additional carbon dioxide in the global atmosphere comes from combustion of fossil fuels on the part of developed nations. But forest burning in the tropical developing world contributes roughly 30 percent of the problem. Moreover, forest burning is expanding so rapidly that its proportion may well rise to a level that almost catches up with fossil-fuel combustion by early next century. It will not stay at that level for long, however, since there will soon be hardly any more forests left to burn—unless of course we get on with a far more vigorous job of safeguarding the forests.

Through this climate connection, then, the future of the Canadian wheat grower is tied in with the future of Amazonia, and the welfare of corn consumers everywhere is intimately related to the welfare of forests in Borneo. We might bear this in mind the next time we sit down to a breakfast bowl of cornflakes or enjoy a packet of popcorn with the evening television show.

During the past several years the deforestation problem has been becoming worse, and faster than ever. At the same time the outlook has improved immeasurably through a regular sunburst of interest in tropical rainforests on the part of both citizens and politicians in developing countries and developed countries alike. At long last it appears as if people want to get on top of the problem before it gets on top of us.

First of all there has been one series after another of citizen activities by on-the-ground groups in tropical-forest countries. In India the Chipko people or "tree huggers" have beaten back the loggers who planned to fell local forests in disregard of local needs. The community in question valued the forests for their fruits, fodder, medicinal materials, and fuelwood—all of which could be harvested sustainably. They saw little benefit for themselves in watching the trees being converted into board feet of timber for remote commercial interests. Their tree-hugging efforts took several years to persuade the loggers to look elsewhere, but finally the Chipko people—mostly semi-literate peasants—won the day. Their success was subsequently replicated by another grass-roots initiative at Silent Valley in southern India, when local people halted a dam that would have flooded a large part of "their" forest. As it turned out the beleaguered forest contained a wild variety of rice with genetic resistance to a disease that was threatening to ravage much of Asia's rice crop.

In many other countries too there have been grass-roots initiatives to counter deforestation. In Kenya the Greenbelt Movement, run entirely by women, planted more trees in its first year of operation than the government achieved during the previous ten years. This exercise relieves excessive exploitation pressure on remaining forests. There is a similar greenbelt movement achieving similar success in Colombia. In Indonesia there are 400 local conservation groups, with sufficient collective clout at national level that they regularly gain the ear of government ministers. In Costa Rica, Ecuador and a lengthy list of other countries there is a similar burgeoning of local-level activism. Even in Brazil there is a flourishing community of nongovernmental bodies that the government feels it must heed—and that have played a part in Brazil's reducing its deforestation rate by two-thirds in recent years.

Similarly, citizen supporters of tropical forests are on the march in developed countries. In 1985 the Rainforest Action Network in the United States was almost alone in its campaign. Today there are more than 200 Rainforest Action Groups around the United States, mainly on college campuses, and another one springs up every ten days. A parallel story can be told in Canada, Britain, Germany, Holland, Sweden, and a number of other countries way outside the tropics, all recognizing their common responsibility for the common heritage in far-off rainforests.

The grandeur and diversity of a tropical forest stretches us, may even make our faculties operate with a sharpness we do not generally sense. A tropical forest is a luxuriant community where growing, ever-more growing, is the essence of it all. Its diversity, its interactions, its sense of wholeness are all so advanced that it is far beyond the scope of our imaginations—let alone our intellects—to grasp how advanced they are. We feel cut down to size, even as we stand taller than before.

Norman Myers

Further Readings

Myers, Norman. *The Primary Source: Tropical Forests and Our Future.* 1992 (expanded edition).

See also BIODEPLETION; BIODIVERSITY; CHIPKO MOVEMENT; ENVIRONMENTALISM; FORESTRY, HISTORY OF; RIO CONFERENCE (1992); TROPICAL DEFORESTATION

Turtles

See REPTILES: CONSERVATION AND HABITAT; SEA TURTLES

U

Udall, Stewart L.

Stewart Udall (1920–) was U.S. secretary of the Interior from 1961 through 1968—a most critical time in the evolution of the environmental movement in North America. His position was then the most important environmentally-related post in the U.S. government from the time of publication of Rachel Carson's *Silent Spring* through to the passage of the National Environmental Policy Act (NEPA) and the creation of the Environmental Protection Agency (EPA). Regardless of the conservation and environmental protection achievements of the administrations of John F. Kennedy and Lyndon B. Johnson, Udall had a role to fulfill and, it has been said, his grasp of the responsibilities of that office was unlike anyone's in the history of the office, aside from Gifford Pinchot.

During this period there were several notable pieces of conservation legislation, by far the most important of which was the Wilderness Act of 1964. This act permanently set aside some tens of millions of acres of land out of the reach of logging, mining, and road-building. During the years in which Udall served in the Interior four new national parks were established, as well as fifty-six wildlife refuges, nine national recreation areas, twenty-two national historic sites, and eight national seashores and lakeshores. All of this and a very visible role as a champion of conservation causes from a person, a lawyer and three-term congressman from Arizona, who later admitted he was not fully versed in or sympathetic to conservation and environmentalism on taking office. As Udall himself put it, speaking to Philip Shabecoff: ". . . people would say, 'Udall, what are you going to do about ecology?' And I would answer, 'What's ecology?'"

But it was after his time in Washington, as a private attorney in New Mexico, that Udall may have made his greatest contribution to the human side of environmental protection. From 1978 until very recently Udall has litigated and lobbied on behalf of the victims of the nuclear weapons industry in the U.S. Southwest—uranium miners and their families, victims of radioactive fallout from atmospheric testing of nuclear weapons, and workers at the nuclear test sites. A compensation bill was finally passed, with the help of western republicans in the Senate, and signed by President George Bush on October 15, 1990. Udall spent his own money on this effort and received no compensation until after fourteen years of work had been completed. The settlement was an acknowledgment by the U.S. government of some of the most significant domestic environmental and health impacts associated with the Cold War.

Robert Paehlke

Further Readings
Udall, Stewart L. *The Quiet Crisis*. 1988.

See also Carson, Rachel; Department of the Interior (U.S.); Environmental Protection in Wartime; Johnson, Lyndon B.; Kennedy, John F.; Nuclear Weapons Production; Radioactive Fallout; Wilderness Act

UNEP

See United Nations Environment Programme

Ungulates

The ungulates comprise the large herbivorous mammals, including among living taxa the even-toed *artiodactyls* (cattle, deer, camels, pigs: 187 species), the odd-toed *perissodactyls* (horses, rhinos, tapirs: sixteen species), and the *probscidians* (elephants: two species). Ungulates are native to all continents except Australia and Antarctica. With the aid of bacteria in their gut, ungulates digest the major structural component of plants—cellulose—and are thus able to exploit for energy the large biomass stored in ground vegetation and shrubs—the biggest part of the biosphere's terrestrial photosynthetic layer. Trees are beyond the reach of most ungulates with the exception of giraffes and elephants, since no living ungulate is a true tree-climber, though there were a few such species in the distant past of the Tertiary Period.

Three principle feeding strategies have evolved in ungulates to digest plant tissue. The least specialized system is found in pigs. It relies on selective feeding on easily digestible plant parts rich in nutrients and energy (such as roots, fruits, nuts, and shoots) and is supplemented by assorted animal foods (such as insects, carrion, small mammals, bird eggs, and fledglings). The food is digested with little processing or fermentation in a generalized digestive system little different from our own. In the pig-like American peccaries some fermentation takes place within pouches in the stomach and in the large intestines.

The advanced systems feature large fore or hind gut pouches for the fermentation of the ingested plant matter, with *artiodactyls* featuring fore-gut and *perissodactyls*, hind-gut fermentation. Thus cows ferment ingested grass in a complex enlargement of the foregut called the rumen. During fermentation about 60 percent of the digested energy is liberated as volatile fatty acids and absorbed into the body directly from the rumen by a dense network of blood vessels. The fermenting plant mass in the rumen is repeatedly regurgitated, re-chewed, saturated with saliva, and swallowed for further fermentation. From the rumen the ferment passes into the true stomach where the bacteria and protozoa are subjected to acid digestion. The dissolved bodies of the unicellular organisms supply the ruminant with protein and vitamins. The partially digested matter undergoes further digestion and extraction in the small intestines and is subjected once more to bacterial fermentation in the caecum—a pouch formed at the beginning of the large intestines. Consequently, before passing out, the food mass has been fermented twice in the ruminant and is well digested. However, passage is slow. Moreover, the

lower the protein content and thus the digestibility of the forage, the slower the passage and the lower the food intake. Ungulates that are subject to low-quality forage may die of starvation due to plugged rumens in which fermentation has ceased.

Horses' fodder is first subjected to fine shredding by a battery of enormous teeth. It then passes into the true stomach where only the most digestible fraction of the forage is liberated. The poorly digested food mass, after some absorption by the small intestines, is subjected to fermentation in the very large caecum. Although less thoroughly digested the food passes through the gut much more rapidly in horses than in ruminants. Furthermore, the poorer the food, the faster its passage. This allows horses to extract per unit time a lot of nutrients and energy from coarse, hard-to-digest plants. Consequently horses and their relatives can live on poorer forage than ruminants, but ruminants require much less food than horses.

Ungulates are prey to large predators. The majority of them escape predation by running and hiding if they live in forests, and by crowding into large herds and by swift, enduring flight if they live on open plains. Large-bodied species may also stand and defend themselves against predators, humans included. This, however, can be exploited by hunters, and many large ungulates became extinct during human colonization of continents and islands. Alive today are but a fraction of the species which existed during the Ice Ages, before the spread and growth of human populations.

Our most important domestic animals are ungulates, including cattle, sheep, goats, pigs, horses, donkeys, camels, llamas, and reindeer. Ice Age people lived primarily off herding ungulates, mainly reindeer. The demise of ungulates continues where habitat for wild species is lost to agriculture, urbanization, and deforestation, while populations are also depleted by illegal killing for luxury markets. In North America, however, wild ungulates have prospered since effective conservation measures were introduced about seventy-five years ago. Over 30 million wild ungulates live currently in the United States and Canada, the majority being white-tailed deer and mule deer. Northern and central Europe also have good conservation practices and the comparable figure for Europe is 12 million. Wild ungulates, where abundant, are creators of wealth. They contribute significantly to the approximately $70 billion dollars of annual expenditures spent on wildlife-based activities in North America. The hunting and viewing of ungulates generates a high level of employment in the many industries that support these subsistence and recreational activities.

Valerius Geist

Further Readings

Banfield, A.W.F. *The Mammals of Canada.* 1974.

Geist, V. "How Markets in Wildlife Meats and Parts, and the Sale of Hunting Privileges, Jeopardize Wildlife Conservation." *Conservation Biology* 2 (1988): 1–12.

Halls, L.K., ed. *White-Tailed Deer: Ecology and Management.* 1984.

See also BISON: CONSERVATION AND HABITAT; ELEPHANTS: CONSERVATION AND HABITAT; HABITAT FRAGMENTATION, PATCHES, AND CORRIDORS; LANDSCAPE ECOLOGY; RANGELANDS (U.S.); RHINOCEROS: CONSERVATION AND HABITAT

Union of Concerned Scientists

The Union of Concerned Scientists (UCS) is a public interest group founded in 1969 by a group of Massachusetts Institute of Technology (MIT) faculty and students opposed to nuclear power. It has a contributing membership of about 100,000 scientists and a thirty-two-person staff in Cambridge and Washington, D.C. A Scientists' Action Network of about 8,000 scientists stands ready to educate the public and media regarding the hazardous nature of the nuclear arms race and nuclear power generation.

Originally the UCS was dedicated entirely to the principle of nuclear arms reduction and stabilization of national security policy. It devotes approximately 75 percent of its resources to promoting nuclear arms control. It also criticized the Strategic Defense Initiative advocated by the Reagan administration. The other 25 percent of its resources are devoted to criticism of the nuclear power industry. UCS argues that the United States should phase out its current generation of nuclear plants which it does not consider safe. Acceptable use of nuclear power will require new reactor and safety system designs and vastly improved management and regulatory supervision.

Scientists from UCS have become the chief alternative source of information on nuclear power issues to the government. They have appeared on numerous news and discussion shows such as ABC's Nightline to argue that the Nuclear Regulatory Commission (NRC) is not an effective regulatory force over the nuclear industry. UCS legislative counsel testified to the Senate Committee on Energy in 1986 against the idea of standardizing U.S. nuclear plants to achieve speedier licensing. It is UCS's policy position that all plants should be considered separately for safety. UCS also argued, unsuccessfully, before the NRC that the regulator should shut down eight reactors similar in design to the reactor involved in the 1979 accident at Three Mile Island. The Union also initiated a law suit against NRC's ruling that safety benefits must be balanced against costs of any safety improvements.

UCS publishes a quarterly report to its members, entitled *Nucleus*, informing them about the major public policy debates in Washington about nuclear arms control and nuclear power safety. It also provides briefing papers for its members' use in their public education activities.

Lettie McSpadden

Further Readings

Ford, Daniel. *Three Mile Island: Three Minutes to Meltdown.* 1981.

Kendall, Henry, and Steven Nadis. *Energy Strategies: Toward a Solar Future.* 1980.

Union of Concerned Scientists. *Annual Reports* and *Nucleus.* 1988.

See also ENVIRONMENTAL PROTECTION IN WARTIME; NUCLEAR ELECTRIC POWER; NUCLEAR WEAPONS PRODUCTION; RADIOACTIVE FALLOUT

United Nations Convention on the Law of the Sea

Origins of UNCLOS

The unique United Nations Convention on the Law of the Sea (UNCLOS), consisting of 320 articles and five annexes, was adopted in 1982 by a vote of 130 to four, with seventeen abstentions. This vote came after ten years of negotiation in the United Nations Conference on the Law of the Sea (LOSC), which took place from 1973–1982, following four years of preliminary discussions in preparatory committees instituted by the UN General Assembly (UNGA). The UNGA charged the LOSC in a resolution adopted in 1970 (GAR 2570) with the task of developing a single convention "dealing with all matters relating to the law of the sea . . . bearing in mind that the problems of ocean space are closely interrelated and need to be considered as a whole."

The convention originated from the growth of concern among developing countries in the 1960s that the newly highlighted mineral wealth of the deep seabeds (consisting mainly of manganese nodules lying on the seafloor) because of technical and economic difficulties might be exploitable only by the Western industrial countries under the prevailing doctrine of the freedom of the seas without any international supervision or controls. It was soon realized that questions raised in establishing an international regime were inextricably related to almost all other aspects of the law of the sea. These included definition of the areas falling under national and international jurisdiction, regimes for exploitation and conservation of living and nonliving resources, in and on the seabed and in the waters above, protection and preservation of the marine environment from pollution and other threats and regulation of scientific research to mention but a few of the over 100 items on the LOSC's agenda.

Common Heritage Concept

The UNGA also adopted unanimously in 1970 a Declaration of Principles Governing the Sea-Bed and Ocean Floor (GAR 2749) and the Subsoil Thereof, beyond the Limit of National Jurisdiction (the Area). This proclaimed the area and its resources to be "the common heritage of mankind," unappropriable by states, in which no states or persons could acquire rights incompatible with the international regime to be established and the principles of the declaration. All activities regarding exploration and exploitation of the resources and other related activities must be governed by the international regime.

Neither the declaration, nor the UNCLOS itself, which gives content to the "common heritage concept," applies to resources other than mineral resources of the deep seabed. Living resources in general and mineral resources found in the continental shelves and territorial sea are not so regarded. The different status and jurisdictional regimes governing exploitation and conservation of these resources, especially in areas bordering national and international jurisdictional areas, gives rise to ambiguities and underlies current disputes.

Entry into Force of UNCLOS

Although the UNCLOS was signed by 159 states and other entities its entry into force required sixty ratifications plus the elapse of a further year following the deposit of the sixtieth ratification. Since the sixtieth ratification was deposited by Guyana on November 16, 1993, the convention entered into force on November 16, 1994.

Entry into force, however, does not make the UNCLOS binding on all states; only on those ratifying it, apart from such provisions as can now be regarded as codifying customary law or which have entered sufficiently widely into state practice to be now regarded as part of customary international law. Among other things, it is generally considered that its provision on fisheries (Part V and Part VII, Section 2) and on protection and preservation of the marine environment (Part XII) can be so regarded, as can the jurisdictional and navigational provisions (Parts I–IV) and those relating to the continental shelf (Part VI).

This is not, however, the case in relation to the international regime for exploitation of the area. Major industrialized states, such as the Federal Republic of Germany, the United Kingdom and the United States, which were among those abstaining on adoption of the UNCLOS, did so because of their objections to the nature of the "common heritage" regime established in Part XI of UNCLOS. The status of the area and its resources as common heritage, the rejection of state sovereignty and other claims to its *in situ* resources, and the vesting of all rights therein in mankind as a whole, on whose behalf the authority established by UNCLOS was required to act and the subjection of several activities to its supervision are not disputed. The extensive powers and role of the authority and other aspects of its control, which are set out in great detail, remain, however, controversial. Without the participation of major industrialized states UNCLOS will not be fully effective since their financial, technical, economic, and scientific support is indispensable to the establishment and operation of the authority and its committees, as well as the new International Tribunal for the Law of the Sea and other dispute settlement processes instituted by the UNCLOS.

The Secretary-General's Consultations on UNCLOS

The UN Secretary-General thus held informal consultations with representatives of developed and developing states on outstanding UNCLOS issues to seek agreement on amendments to the controversial provisions and on the means of achieving this. An agreement relating to the implementation of Part XI of the UNCLOS of 10 December 1982 was concluded before the UNCLOS entered into force and included therein were approved modifications in a GAR (General Assembly Resolution) of 28 July 1994, adopting it and opening it for accession. Its parties will regard it and Part XI as a single instrument, and states that have already ratified UNCLOS will be regarded as party also to the agreement, unless they expressly indicate to the contrary.

As reservations to UNCLOS are not allowed and it is thus not possible for states to "pick and choose" which parts of the UNCLOS they will ratify, it is essentially a "package deal." The interrelatedness of the provisions on environmental protection and conservation with the jurisdictional provisions allocating access to resources and laying down terms and conditions for such access are an essential element in achieving UNCLOS' preambular aim of establishing "a legal order for the Seas and Oceans which will promote the conservation of their living resources, and the study, protection and preservation of the marine environment."

Patricia W. Birnie

Further Readings

Birnie, Patricia W., and Alan E. Boyle. *International Law and the Environment*. 1993.

Churchill, Robin R., and A. Vaughan Lowe. *The Law of the Sea*. 2nd ed. 1988.

See also COASTAL DEBRIS AND CLEANUP; COUSTEAU, JACQUES-YVES; ENVIRONMENTAL DIPLOMACY; FISHERIES CONSERVATION; NONRENEWABLE RESOURCES

United Nations Environment Programme

The United Nations Environment Programme (UNEP) was created by the UN General Assembly in December 1972, following a decision at the United Nations Conference on the Human Environment (UNCHE) calling for a new UN environmental body. UNEP was designed to be the "environmental conscience of the UN system" and to be "catalytic": to coordinate the activities of other UN agencies and to spur them to integrate environmental considerations into their ongoing activities. Headquartered in Nairobi, Kenya, UNEP was the first UN agency to be located in a developing country. This helped to overcome some of the developing countries' early suspicions regarding environmental issues.

UNEP deals with problems of global and regional commons, transboundary pollution, and national problems. From its beginnings the organization has been a strong proponent of environmentally sustainable development. It has supported research, training, and projects in comprehensive styles of environmental protection and economic development, ("environment and development" and "eco-development"), seeking to impart ecological rules for resource management and economic development to national officials. UNEP has also been active in establishing scientific consensus about environmental problems, and in mobilizing scientific pressure on national governments, as well as seeking to mobilize grass-roots support worldwide for its activities. Mostafa Tolba, UNEP's second executive director, regards the elevation ". . . of the issue of the environment to the top of the political agenda, particularly in the developing countries" as one of the major accomplishments of the organization. [See "Living History Interview with Dr. Mostafa Kamal Tolba" *Transnational Law & Contemporary Problems* 2 (Spring 1992)].

UNEP is controlled by a fifty-eight-member governing council, which met annually until 1987 and now meets every other year. Members serve staggered four-year terms, and are elected by the UN General Assembly on the basis of geographic representation. Its major constituency is environmental ministries. UNEP's annual budget grew from $20 million in 1973 to $100 million by 1993. The 1993 governing council approved a budget for 1994–1995 of $120 to $130 million, subject to the availability of funds.

UNEP's first executive director, Maurice Strong, coined the phrase "the process is the policy," which captures much of UNEP's strategy of bolstering international environmental concern and building national capacity for managing environmental problems. Until recently UNEP focused on environmental assessment and environmental management, seeking to create a broader concern and sense of urgency about environmental problems through its assessment activities, while concurrently supporting national and international efforts at environmental management. Its executive directors (Maurice Strong [Canada, 1973–1975],

Mostafa Tolba [Egypt, 1976–1992], Elizabeth Dowdeswell [Canada, 1993–]) have acted as ambassadors for the environment. They have raised environmental issues with other agencies and heads of state, while also seeking to publicize them among populations at large. UNEP also seeks to encourage other UN agencies to integrate environmental considerations into their own activities, largely through shared projects. Between 1972 and 1985 UNEP supported 995 projects, 55 percent of which were funded by co-operating agencies or supporting organizations. Since 1990 UNEP has been responsible for assessing the environmental impact of projects submitted to the Global Environmental Fund.

UNEP also seeks to involve the public and nonstate actors in its activities. UNEP makes use of close contacts with the international scientific community, using scientific advisory groups to assess environmental quality in coordination with many ongoing management efforts. UNEP maintains close contact with nongovernmental organizations (NGOs) through the Environmental Liaison Centre (ELC) in Nairobi, as well as inviting NGOs to participate in many UNEP-sponsored activities. UNEP engages in public education by sponsoring television programs and other educational activities aimed at the general population worldwide. More than 10,000 educators in over 140 countries have been involved in UNEP's educational activities.

Training national officials in techniques for environmental management and assessment has also been a principal activity. From 1973 to the present 20 percent of UNEP's resources have been devoted to training. By 1985 27,000 people had participated in UNEP training programs including sessions on, for example, environmental monitoring; conservation; and managing forests, land usage, fresh water, oceans, pests, and chemical and industrial risks.

The secretariat has grown from some 180 professionals worldwide in the mid-1980s to 252 in 1991. Many members of the Secretariat are part of a broader transnational group of experts—an ecological epistemic community—who share common causal understandings of the multiple interactive factors that cause environmental degradation, a belief that comprehensive (or "holistic") policies should be adopted collectively to ameliorate and avert further environmental decay, a commitment to the scientific method, and a common set of principled beliefs or values concerning the need to preserve the physical environment. This cognitive orientation underlies the organization's efforts to promote more comprehensive environment and development policies; as well it attracts support from many scientists worldwide.

UNEP's environmental management activities encompass treaties and guidelines for environmental protection. UNEP has been active in the area of international environmental law. Over forty of the nearly 100 multilateral environmental treaties adopted outside the European Community (EC) since 1973 were concluded under UNEP's auspices. These include treaties for conservation (the 1973 Convention on International Trade in Endangered Species of Wild Fauna and Flora [CITES]; as well as administrative support for the 1979 Bonn Convention on the Conservation of Migratory Species of Wild Animals), preserving biodiversity (1992 Convention on Biodiversity), stratospheric ozone protection (1985 Vienna Convention for the Protection of the Ozone Layer; 1987 Montreal Protocol; 1990 London amendments; and 1992 Copenhagen amendments), regulating trade in hazardous wastes (1989 Basel Convention on the Control of Transboundary Movements of Hazardous Wastes and Their Disposal), controlling climate change (1992 Framework Convention on Climate Change), and over twenty-three treaties between 1975 and 1983 covering ten regional seas and nearly 140 countries, largely modeled on the 1975 Mediterranean Action Plan. The Oceans and Coastal Areas and Regional Seas Programme, covering these regional seas, is widely regarded as one of UNEP's major successes.

The UNEP secretariat operates as an important partner in negotiations: as executive director, Tolba often exercised intellectual and entrepreneurial leadership during negotiations, and the staff actively sought to assure the inclusion of the scientific community's current ecological understanding in the political management of environmental risks.

UNEP has also helped develop non-binding "soft law" for environmental management. Guidelines were drawn up for managed shared natural resources (1978), weather modification (1980), offshore mining and drilling (1982), a World Charter for Nature (1982), banned and severely restricted chemicals (1984), marine pollution from land-based sources (1985), environmentally sound management of hazardous wastes (1987), environmental impact assessment (1987), and for the exchange of information about chemicals in international trade (1987). A 1977 Global Plan of Action for Marine Mammals provides guidelines for the management of coastal zones to protect marine mammals. Further guidelines were developed for workplace environmental quality and health, pesticide handling, and handling and disposing of toxic chemicals and hazardous wastes. A program for the Environmentally Sound Management of Inland Waters was launched in 1986, a program for river basin management for the Zambezi (Zambezi Action Plan) was adopted in 1987, and similar programs are being developed for the Lake Chad basin, the Aral Sea, the Nile river basin, the Danube, the Orinoco, and Lake Titicaca. UNEP also maintains an Industry and Environment Office in Paris.

Environmental assessment has been a keystone of UNEP's activities. The Earthwatch program, composed of the Global Environmental Monitoring System (GEMS); the Global Resource Information Database (GRID); INFOTERRA (a referral system for identifying worldwide sources of environmental information); the International Registry of Potentially Toxic Chemicals (IRPTC); and the annual state of the environment reports, has accounted for 16 percent of UNEP's total budget since 1973, and 23 percent in 1988–1989. UNEP administers GEMS, which coordinates networks of national monitoring stations, with other UN agencies. UNEP administers the Background Air Pollution Monitoring Network (BAPMoN) with the World Meteorological Organization (WMO), which monitors atmospheric concentrations of stratospheric ozone, methane, sulfur dioxide, and nitrogen oxides. Health-related networks are maintained primarily by the World Health Organization (WHO). One network, covering fifty countries, monitors urban air quality; a second, consisting of 448 stations in fifty-nine countries or territories, monitors water quality; and a third, run by WHO and the Food and Agriculture Organization (FAO), monitors food contamination. The Human Exposure Assessment Locations program assesses total exposure of specific population groups to pollutants from all sources. The World Glacier Inventory helps measure ice depth and movement related to possible climate change. In 1982 UNEP along with FAO used satellite reconnaissance to produce a comprehensive assessment of the world's tropical forest resources. Since 1985 UNEP has been seeking to integrate environmental and social data within GRID to provide an early warning system of social threats from environmental degradation as well as providing useful resources for urban and regional planners. IRPTC in Geneva administers a data bank of profiles on the heath and environmental effects of over 600 widely used and traded chemicals.

Several notable failures stand out. The 1977 United Nations Plan of Action to Combat Desertification, which UNEP implements, has failed to muster significant funds and has not had a noticeable impact on halting desertification. UNEP's success at coordination efforts with other agencies has been spotty. While UNEP attempted to ensure that "environment" became a cross-cutting element in the various development-related activities of the UN system, UNEP lacked sufficient leverage within the UN system to effectively influence programmatic efforts by other agencies.

UNEP's future role was reaffirmed by the governing council at its seventeenth session in May 1993 and at the first substantive session of the Commission on Sustainable Development in June 1993. In the aftermath of the 1992 United Nations Conference on Environment and Development in Rio de Janeiro, a clear-cut division of labor is being defined between UNEP and the newly created Commission for Sustainable Development. The Brundtland Commission suggested that UNEP should be "the principal source on environmental data, assessment, reporting, and related support for environmental management as well as be the principal advocate and agent for change and co-operation on critical environmental and natural resource protection issues." Elizabeth Dowdeswell, UNEP's new executive director, indicates that she hopes that UNEP will concentrate on building up widespread social and political consensus for sustainable development, while continuing to focus on the development and application of scientific consensus to international environmental management. The seventeenth session also authorized a change in priorities from sensing and monitoring to enhancing capacity building, particularly in developing countries.

Peter M. Haas

Further Readings

Gosovic, Branislav. *The Quest for World Environmental Cooperation.* 1992.

Haas, Peter M. *Saving the Mediterranean: The Politics of International Environmental Protection.* 1990.

U

Haas, Peter M. "Save the Seas." In *Ocean Yearbook 9*. Ed. Elizabeth Mann Borgese, et al. 1991.

Tolba, Mostafa K. et al. *The World Environment 1972–1992: Two Decades of Challenge*. 1992.

See also BRUNDTLAND, GRO HARLEM; CITES; DESERTIFICATION; MEDITERRANEAN SEA, PROTECTION OF; MONTREAL PROTOCOL; *Our Common Future*; RIO CONFERENCE (1992); STOCKHOLM CONFERENCE; SUSTAINABLE DEVELOPMENT; TOLBA, MOSTAFA K.; TOXIC WASTES IN INTERNATIONAL TRADE

Uranium Mining: Environmental Impacts

As of 1995, the mining and milling of uranium occurs mostly in Canada, Australia, and the Union of South Africa. This activity is called "the front end" of the somewhat over-optimistically labeled "nuclear fuel cycle"—a process which policymakers envisioned as the efficient, interconnected, sustainable production and refinement of radioactive ores, fuel preparation for nuclear reactors and atomic weaponry, production and release of nuclear energy, and the disposal of nuclear waste. Each step of this procedure involves risks to the public and the natural world. This entry emphasizes the environmental effects of uranium mining and milling in the United States—a former leader in uranium production—and pays heed to how the U.S. federal government regulates this industrial activity.

Following World War II the U.S. government created the Atomic Energy Commission (AEC) to both promote and regulate the domestic development of atomic energy. Congress empowered the AEC with many legal and bureaucratic prerogatives, including complete authority over the production of uranium, which officials recognized as a critical step in the control of nuclear weapons. The AEC's raw material division continued the nation's wartime uranium procurement policy by purchasing foreign ores; but also was directed by the Atomic Energy Acts to strengthen the nation's security by creating a domestic uranium mining and milling industry capable of producing sufficient quantities of "yellowcake"—enriched uranium oxides needed for nuclear weapons and fuel.

During the 1950s and 1960s the commission worked in a number of channels to develop the nation's uranium resources. The AEC enlisted the cooperation of the Bureau of Mines, U.S. Geological Survey, and the Bureau of Indian Affairs to determine the extent of the nation's uranium reserves. The AEC also lobbied in Congress to clear legal title for uranium claims on lands previously reserved by miners under the terms of the Mining Act of 1872, and the Mineral Act of 1920. Perhaps the AEC's most significant achievement was a generous program of subsidies for uranium exploration, development, freight, and production costs that was unprecedented within the mining industry. For example, the AEC paid out close to $2,500,000 for discovery bonuses from 1948–1953, established minimum uranium prices for a period of ten years, and built over 300 miles of roads as part of its access roads program. The AEC then publicized its incentives, and showed how successful prospectors took advantage of these subsidies. This campaign struck a mother lode in the consciousness of tens of thousands of Americans who caught "uranium fever." They hiked, drove, and flew over public and private lands on the Colorado Plateau and Wyoming to search for the mines that could make them overnight millionaires in the uranium boom.

The environmental effects of this feverish activity were many and varied. Each of the stages of mine development—prospecting, road-building, mining, and milling—had significant effects upon wildlife habitat and wilderness; and frequently led to substantial radiation, air, and water pollution. Prospecting for any mineral, including uranium, creates deleterious environmental effects since mine operators and workers drill many thousands of bore holes and explode thousands of tons of dynamite to determine both the size of the ore body, and the percentage of uranium in the deposit. While most claims did not contain ore in commercial quantities, and therefore were not heavily exploited, prospecting in the West degraded habitats in ways that make restoration highly problematic.

The major environmental impacts of uranium mining occur when access roads, mines, and mills are developed. In the first instance, AEC roads opened thousands of acres of land previously classified as wilderness for commercial and recreational use. Trucking ore from mine to mill also produced contaminated trucks and extensive spillage along the way. More importantly, once underground and strip-mines were exploited, miners were often exposed to high concentrations of radioactivity. In the first years of this industry, miners were unprotected from the deadly effects of uranium daughters (the by-products of the decay of uranium or other radioactive elements) and radon gas.

However, not only miners were at risk. In the years following the initial boom, radioactive mill tailings were used as building materials in Grand Junction, CO, which led to the radioactive poisoning of families in the area. Families were also at risk, as adults, children, and livestock wandered into abandoned mines and were hurt by mine falls or by exposure to radiation. The Abandoned Mine Lands Program caps mine openings to keep people and animals from these hazards.

Another significant effect of uranium mining is air pollution. Radon gas escapes from mines, mill tailings and dumps into the environment; often, these emanations are comparatively minor, because they are not contained. However, radon is a carcinogen, and exposure in contained settings such as mines and basements is so dangerous that its measurement and regulation is one of the principal concerns of the Environmental Protection Agency's air and radiation office.

Uranium mines also can have severe impacts on the availability and quality of water resources. In the early days, mine operators in Grants, New Mexico purchased water rights from local Mormon carrot farmers and thus displaced a well-established local industry. Evidently the "carrots" extended by the AEC were more valued than those produced by New Mexican farmers! Uranium mining also pollutes water supplies through mineral "dewatering," in which (operating or abandoned) mines draw water from the surrounding rock and sub-surface reservoirs, and by pumping or gravity send this water contaminated with suspended radioactive particles into rivers.

Uranium mills also produce considerable water pollution. The milling process entails five basic stages in which the ore transported from the mine-head is sorted, crushed to a uniform consistency, leached, and precipitated in heavy metal and acidic solutions, while wastes are delivered into a tailings pond. The mill ponds were not impervious to the seepage of radioactivity and heavy metals into the groundwater; and were also subject to accidental discharges. In July 1979 the mill tailings pond at Church Rock, New Mexico, burst, spilling 93 million gallons of radioactive water and eleven tons of mill tailings into the Rio Puerco. The ensuing

investigation into the causes and effects of the spill revealed a high rate of groundwater pollution and radioactive mineral dewatering from the surrounding mines.

Even after mining and milling was discontinued in the United States as a result of low uranium prices and cheaper foreign uranium oxides, the mines and mills of the West produced adverse environmental impacts. Piles of mill tailings, dumped beside the mills from which they were processed, are a source of air and water pollution. Many of these piles are not stabilized adequately, and when the weather is windy, tailings disperse to the four corners of the nation. The U.S. federal government has recently attempted to deal with the radioactive legacies of the Cold War. The Uranium Mill Tailings Control Act of 1979 provided federal funds to clean up mill tailings from the 1950s booms. Nevertheless wide areas of the "Atomic West" are scarred by abandoned mines and mills. By some counts there are over 100,000 acres of land contaminated by uranium mine wastes. The environmental impacts of historical uranium mining continue to be discovered.

Peter D. Shemitz

Further Readings

Miller, E. Willard, and R.M. Miller. *Environmental Hazards: Radioactive Materials and Wastes: A Reference Handbook,* 1990.

Ringholz, Raye. *Uranium Frenzy: Boom and Bust on the Colorado Plateau.* 1989.

Shuey, C., P. Robinson, and L. Taylor. "The 'Costs' of Uranium: Who's Paying with Lives, Lands, and Dollars." *The Workbook* 10 (3) (1985).

See also IONIZING RADIATION; MINING AND SMELTING: HISTORIC IMPACTS; NUCLEAR ELECTRIC POWER; NUCLEAR WEAPONS PRODUCTION; RADIOACTIVE FALLOUT; RADON; STRIP MINING OF COAL: A HISTORY; URANIUM MINING: OCCUPATIONAL HEALTH

Uranium Mining: Occupational Health

U.S. state and federal officials became involved in the regulation of the safety and health of uranium mining and milling workers as early as 1950, when the Public Health Service (PHS) began environmental surveys that studied the occupational health programs at most of the nations' uranium mills.

Researchers who sought to determine how workers were protected against uranium ores' radiation, as well as the acids and heavy metals used in the milling process, found inadequate precautions for male employees. First of all, miners were unprotected from the normal hazards of the job, which included roof cave-ins, falling into pits, mine fires, accidents with heavy equipment, breathing diesel fumes, handling explosives, high noise levels, and breathing silica dust. They also included the more insidious dangers of inadequately ventilated mines whose high concentrations of decaying radon daughters (the by-products of uranium decay) caused many miners to eventually contract a variety of cancers. Another hazard in the early mines was the common practice of eating lunch and drinking contaminated water in the mines.

The health dangers did not, however, remain in the workplace. Workers often wore their contaminated clothes home, placing their families at risk. Management must have been at least partially cognizant of the dangers of working with uranium, for women mill workers were restricted to mill laboratories and they were neither permitted to be in direct contact with ores, nor allowed to collect samples in the mill. There was a clear double standard, but workers in the mines and mills themselves also ignored safe mining practices such as wearing the uncomfortable paper face masks mandated by management.

Mill workers were protected more effectively than were mine workers. As early as 1957 the Atomic Energy Commission (AEC) Licensing Division created health and safety rules, and required uranium mills to demonstrate that they were qualified to determine the maximum dosage of radiation, monitor personnel for this dosage, and comply with the technical standards and regulations to protect worker health and safety. The AEC licensing regulations did not, however, protect mine workers, who were exposed to many more occupational hazards. Harold Price, the director of the Licensing Division, disavowed responsibility, stating: "I think it is our position that we do not have authority to regulate the mines, and we certainly don't have any licensing authority over the mines."

However, people began to recognize society's responsibility to the mine workers, and in 1955 administrators from the U.S. Bureau of Land Management, PHS, industry, and officials from the AEC and major producer states attended the Seven States Uranium Mining Conference on Health Hazards, and adopted the first standard for exposure to mine radiation, setting a maximum of 100 micromicrocuries for each of the three radon daughters.

In contrast to uranium procurement, the uranium mining and milling health policy was determined by a broad coalition of special interests. In 1959 the Federal Radiation Council (FRC), primarily an advisory body consisting of the secretaries of the departments of Health, Education and Welfare, Agriculture, Commerce, Defense and Labor, as well as the chairman of the AEC, and the special assistant to the president for science and technology, turned its attention to radiation in uranium mines. FRC was ineffective, which was not surprising considering the contradictory agendas of these executive departments. These high-level policymakers studied the criteria for mine level radiation standards throughout the early 1960s, but could not resolve effectively the strong differences of opinion and varying value judgments of their witnesses. Eventually they established a unit for measuring radiation, the working level which measured the radioactive energy in one liter of air. The working level provided the standard by which uranium mines would be measured in the future. The debate about the objective worth of epidemiological studies and the connection between health and industrial pollution would continue to divide the nation's leadership through the 1980s.

Many people tried to break the FRC stalemate. Congress passed the Federal Metal and Nonmetallic Mine Safety Act of 1966, which authorized the secretary of the interior to establish and enforce health and safety standards, and inspection schedules for uranium mines. Finally in 1967 W. Willard Wirtz, the secretary of labor, unilaterally issued an order establishing a .3 working level for all mines supplying contracts to the federal government on the authority granted by the Public Contract Act of 1936. Since all U.S. uranium mines fell in that category, this order required mine operators to provide ventilation for mine shafts and facings.

The mine operators uniformly protested this order as technically and economically unfeasible. In the late 1960s it was difficult to measure the radiation levels of miners at a .3 working level, as the dosimeter used to calibrate this level was not invented until the 1970s. Wirtz bowed to pressure from the AEC and uranium mining industry, and revised his directive.

During the 1970s the uranium industry enjoyed a robust decade of growth, as the major oil companies invested heavily in uranium reserves, mines, and mills to provide fuel for the nuclear power plants ordered by utilities. Even the workers benefited from this boom in the uranium business in health terms. Doctors, government officials, and mining unions pressured the prosperous mine operators to address the concerns of earlier reformers: to ventilate underground mines, provide changing rooms and laundry facilities, and forbid workers to drink water collected from the walls of mines or fail to wear respirators. However, these reforms came late to an industry which collapsed economically in the United States during the 1980s. Today officials recognize the failure of the government to protect the health of uranium workers, and this belated understanding led to the passage of the Radiation Exposure Compensation Act of 1990. The passage of this bill does not necessarily end the struggle for worker health compensation and protection. Many miners failed to obtain or retain proof of their employment and face an unsympathetic Justice Department. The workers of the Cold War era continue to pay the price for the U.S. national security.

Peter Shemitz

Further Readings

National Research Council. *Health Risks of Radon and Other Internally Deposited Alpha-Emitters: BEIR 4*. 1988.

Taylor, L. "The Health Effects of Radiation: The Controversy Continues." *The Workbook* 10 (1985): 10–11.

Wagoner, Joseph K., and S.D. Hyg. "Uranium: The United States Experience, A Lesson in History." Unpublished paper, Environmental Defense Fund (1/1980).

See also NATIONAL SECURITY, RECONCEPTUALIZING; NUCLEAR ELECTRIC POWER; NUCLEAR WEAPONS PRODUCTION; OSHACT AND OSHA; RADON; URANIUM MINING: ENVIRONMENTAL IMPACTS

Urban Design

Urban design has to do with the physical shaping of the city and is consequently closely linked with urban planning, architecture, landscape design, and site planning. Its primary purpose is to enhance the quality of the city's spatial environment and, by so doing, to improve the quality of human life. It is concerned with the aesthetics and function of public space, the sensory environment of public streets, squares, parks, and groupings of buildings. In this sense urban design goes further than the consideration of individual buildings, or specific projects, since its underlying aim is to establish context—the relationships and connections between the city's individual parts that create spatial order, continuity, and coherence. The urban designer, therefore, deals with external and internal spaces; with their location, scale, and form, and the linkages between them. The designer is concerned with making places for social interaction and recreation; with spatial sequence along traveled routes; with communicating meaning through intentional symbols; and with the urban landscape—the texture of urban surfaces, rock, earth and water, and plants.

While urban design has traditionally been concerned with these essentially social, aesthetic, experiential functions, the need to understand cities in relation to their environmental, rural, and economic context was first recognized in the nineteenth century by the Scottish biologist and planner Patrick Geddes. In the United States the concept of the interconnected greenway and river corridor was introduced by the landscape architect Frederick Law Olmsted. The "Emerald Necklace" in Boston and the parkway system for Niagara Falls are two early examples of linked natural corridors and urban land conservation that are extant today. Philip H. Lewis's environmental corridors for the states of Wisconsin and Illinois, and Ian L. McHarg's book, *Design with Nature*, were among the eloquent statements in the 1960s and 1970s of the fundamental role that the natural science disciplines must play in the planning and protection of the larger landscape.

These developments notwithstanding, the role of natural systems in the *internal* shaping of cities has been virtually ignored, both by established urban design and planning doctrine, and by the biological sciences until the early 1980s. Various recent writers have commented that the acknowledgment and harnessing of the forces of nature represent a powerful resource for shaping a beneficial urban habitat. Ignored or subverted, they magnify problems that have plagued cities for centuries, such as floods and landslides, poisoned air and water. It is also being recognized that the design doctrines that have provided the inspiration for the built environment since the Bauhaus movement of the

1920s can no longer be seen as a valid basis for urban form. In a world increasingly concerned with vanishing plants, animals, and natural or productive landscapes there has been a marked propensity to bypass the environment most people live in—the city itself.

Urban planning and design has traditionally operated on the premise that ecological processes are either nonexistent in cities, or have little relevance to design process and form. Their underlying disciplines are to be found in engineering, architecture, and horticulture, not ecological determinism. With the rise of the environmental movement, and an increasing awareness that urban issues must be addressed as a part of the overall environmental agenda, an ecological view of the city itself is now emerging as an essential component of urban design, one that is in tune with contemporary issues and imperatives of energy conservation and the protection of nature in cities worldwide.

Thus, a number of important ideas are emerging in the field of urban design as this affects conservation and environmentalism. First, the notion that natural processes are central to the protection and integrity of the larger landscape must also become part of the design of the city itself. Society, for instance, needs to: 1) rethink the role of the city's parks and open spaces, from purely recreational and aesthetic uses to those that contribute to the city's ecological health and productivity; 2) recognize that the byproducts of urban processes—such as waste water, used materials, and nutrients—should maintain or enhance rather than degrade the larger landscape that ultimately receives them; 3) understand the central role of plants in the creation of felicitous urban micro-climate, the enhancement of air quality and carbon balance, and wildlife diversity; 4) restore the health of rivers, woodlands, and wetlands that have been destroyed or impaired by urbanization; and 5) to nurture the social diversity and quality of life of urban people and neighborhoods.

Second, a number of citizen movements and initiatives have emerged that are addressing these and related environmental issues. They include the Green Cities Movement, Urban Wildlife groups, societies for ecological restoration and many others. And at a grass-roots level citizen groups are taking the initiative in restoring the city's natural heritage in local neighborhoods and within watersheds. This larger bioregional perspective provides the opportunity to bring together ecological, community,

cultural, and economic concerns, that provide a holistic and environmentally relevant basis for urban design, and for the protection and conservation of the city's natural areas and processes.

Michael Hough

Further Readings

Baines, Chris. *The Wild Side of Town: How You Can Help the Wildlife around You.* Elm Tree Books and BBC Publications, 1986.

Banerjee, Tridib, and Michael Southworth. *City Sense and City Design: Writings and Projects of Kevin Lynch.* 1990.

Hough, Michael. *City Form and Natural Process.* 1984.

Spirn, Anne Whiston. *The Granite Garden.* 1984.

See also AUTOMOBILES: IMPACTS AND POLICIES; BICYCLE TRANSPORTATION; BIOREGION; ECOLOGICAL RESTORATION; JENSEN, JENS; LAND-USE PLANNING; OLMSTED, FREDERICK LAW; RAILS-TO-TRAILS; URBAN FORESTRY; URBAN FORM

Urban Forestry

An "urban forest" is the sum of all woody and associated vegetation in and around dense human settlements. Extending from the downtown core to rural areas being considered for development, urban forests comprise street trees, residential trees, and park trees, as well as trees in unused public and private land, in transportation and utility corridors, and on watershed land.

The definition of an urban forest incorporates human beings as an integral part of the urban forest ecosystem. Gary Moll of the American Forestry Association defines urban forests as those areas in and around populated regions that either have or have the potential for tree growth. Therefore, people should consider trees and associated vegetation and animals when designing and developing their communities.

The tendency, however, has been to build cities to accommodate motor vehicles, sidewalks, and huge concrete buildings. A 1991 survey by the American Forestry Association revealed that, of the twenty cities considered, the average life span of a downtown street was only thirteen years. In many cities more trees are dying and being removed than are being planted. In downtown areas trees may be relegated to the status of "outdoor furniture" in concrete planters, to be replaced at two-to-five-year intervals. This is largely due to a lack of effective urban forestry management.

Ideally urban forestry entails allocating sufficient soil area for roots to spread, selecting appropriate tree species for soil type and location, planting in areas that will not obstruct human activities, and implementing a comprehensive maintenance program which includes regular watering, pruning, and removal of dying trees. As well human beings must be discouraged from causing undue harm to trees. Herbicides, rock salts for deicing, lime from concrete, cleaning solvents, oil, and even dog urine can all contribute to the early demise of the root system. Also walking on the soil that surrounds the trees or using heavy machinery in construction results in compacted soil, which denys the roots adequate oxygen for growth.

In some cases the urban tree cover may approach a closed canopy, offering significant amounts of shade, wind protection, and noise reduction. Compared to rural areas, however, the survival rate of trees and other greenery in urban regions is significantly lower. The fragmented nature of urban forests also offers less protection from sun and wind exposure and makes it difficult to sustain a large variety of plant and animal life. Owing to fragmentation, the natural purifying function and water flow cannot be sustained.

Because forests have traditionally been assessed for their commercial harvest value, the importance of urban forests to human beings has been greatly undervalued. The urban forest plays a key role in cooling cities and reducing energy costs. Within a city trees break up "heat islands"—exposed areas such as those covered in asphalt, that absorb the sun's energy and radiate it back as excessive heat. These portions of cities are three-to-five degrees hotter than heavily shaded areas. For every degree of increased temperature, 4 percent more energy is used by additional air conditioning requirements. Trees also cool areas through the process of transpiration, in which water is drawn through conducting tissues in the stem and escapes from openings in the leaves, thereby cooling the air.

Trees act as windbreaks and sources of shade. This in turn helps conserve energy. A recent study commissioned by Global ReLeaf Canada, entitled *The Tree-House Effect*, shows that three trees properly planted around a home can reduce air-conditioning use by 10 to 50 percent. Trees planted as windbreaks can also considerably reduce heating costs in the winter. Other economic benefits of maintaining greenery around buildings include an increase in property values. Neighborhoods with ample tree cover have far higher real estate values. The U.S. Forest Service estimates that market values for homes with trees increase at rates ranging from 7 to 20 percent.

Trees planted and cared for inspire not only a sense of pride and confidence, but also a sense of responsibility in communities. Aesthetically, a neighborhood or backyard made up of the flashing colors and sounds of wildlife set amid greenery and flowers is far more welcoming than block after block of concrete or asphalt. Trees are essential to offsetting the negative effects of environmental degradation. They absorb carbon dioxide from the atmosphere and turn it into life-giving oxygen. In a typical semi-mature forest the annual net storage of carbon dioxide could be the equivalent of four tonnes. The total absorption of carbon dioxide during photosynthesis, however, would be closer to forty tonnes. Indirectly, urban trees also reduce carbon dioxide in the air by decreasing the amount of energy needed to cool and warm a building. Because of their ability to reduce energy consumption urban trees are fifteen times more effective in reducing carbon dioxide buildup than rural trees.

Urban deforestation is a significant contributor to global warming. Millions of trees are lost as cities expand and become more densely populated. With fewer trees to absorb the carbon dioxide emissions in cities, the percentage of locally emitted carbon that can be captured is greatly reduced. As well, cutting down trees begins a process of releasing carbon back into the atmosphere. Even if the wood from these trees is utilized in relatively permanent ways, the loss of branches, roots, and bark will result in carbon release.

While trees reduce the effects of many pollutants, they also suffer from the negative effects of pollutants, just as people do. Continual exposure of trees to pollutants can lead to reduced growth, reduced reproduction, and susceptibility to insect damage, disease, or environmental stresses that can ultimately kill them.

Scientists are aware of the benefits of trees to decreasing both particulate and gaseous pollutants. However, the data necessary to measure the overall public health benefits is still inadequate. A campaign in Los Angeles to plant 1

U

million trees prior to the 1984 Olympics was based on a claim by the City of Los Angeles' Planning Department that these trees could filter up to 200 tonnes of particulate smog from the air every day, but this estimate was known to be both imprecise and incomplete.

Trees also reduce water pollution by absorbing compounds such as nitrates which can cause excessive algal growth in lakes and waterways. By breaking the fall of rain water trees also reduce the amount of surface runoff, reducing siltation and soil erosion.

One of the most underrated values of trees is their ability to reduce noise pollution. This quality is especially valuable during warm parts of the year because warmer air is a better conductor of sound. Deciduous trees, which dominate most urban forests, have sound-reducing foliage during the spring and summer seasons when it is needed most.

Today, the benefits of trees are being widely heralded as more and more cities become involved in community forestry programs. Programs such as Global ReLeaf combine education with the action of planting trees to help people understand and appreciate how trees can improve their environment and save them money too. By understanding the ecological benefits of trees to urban areas, it is also more likely that communities will lobby municipalities to integrate trees and vegetation into the design and planning of their cities. Given that there are more than 150 million tree planting sites available in North America's towns and cities, the potential for expanding the benefits of trees is significant.

Ellen Hagerman

Further Readings

Gordon, David, ed. *Green Cities: Ecologically Sound Approaches to Urban Space.* 1990.

Hough, Michael. *City Form and Natural Process.* 1984.

Smyth, Bob. "Britain's 'Green Revolution': Bringing Nature Back to the City" in *UNESCO Sources* (July/August 1990).

See also CLIMATE WARMING; FORESTRY, HISTORY OF; LAND-USE PLANNING; SUSTAINED YIELD FORESTRY; TROPICAL DEFORESTATION; URBAN DESIGN

Urban Form

The most important green products may well not be recycled paper or environmentally benign cleaning materials. The most important "products" are probably our transportation systems and the urban configurations which virtually determine the character of those systems. Intra-urban transportation patterns and decisions go a long way in determining air quality, levels of acid precipitation, levels of climate warming, water quality, availability of habitat especially in near-urban settings, energy and materials use levels, and many other components of environmental quality. These matters are widely understood.

What is less widely appreciated is the strength of the relationship between decisions regarding transportation mode and urban form. Urban form—the shape, spread, and patterning of our cities—is the single greatest determinant of how we will choose to convey ourselves. The higher the density of population on a per hectare basis, the more likely we are to elect to walk or cycle to work or to any other daily activity. As well, the higher the population density, the higher the proportion of trips that will be made by some means of public transportation (streetcars, buses, subways, or trains). Obviously, the causal arrows flow in both directions here—good public transportation systems can lead to a reconfiguration of work and residential patterns and densities. But on a worldwide basis the correlation is almost perfect: sprawling cities are almost totally automobile dependent; compact cities have much more diverse transportation systems. They offer more options for intra-urban travel.

In Los Angeles, Phoenix, or Houston—sprawling western U.S. cities of very low levels of residential density—perhaps 5 percent of the population travel to work on foot or by bicycle and less than 10 percent use public transportation. In New York, Chicago, Boston, and Toronto, and other more densely populated cities, nearer to 10 percent walk or cycle and 18 percent (Chicago) to 33 percent (Toronto) use public transportation. Typical European cities are, again on average, even more compactly arrayed. There 20 percent to 25 percent walk or cycle to work and about an additional 40 percent use public transportation. The differences, overall, are startling. European cities, such as Paris, Amsterdam, and London are three to four times as densely populated as the most sprawling of U.S. cities, yet are not widely seen as undesirable places to live by those who live there, or those who live in North America. The total auto miles traveled per person and total gasoline consumption per person is dramatically different—less than half and, in some cases, less by two-thirds.

These patterns by and large are less a function of wealth than a function of history. Prosperous cities and prosperous individuals choose to avoid driving when the distances are small, the parking is expensive, and the public transportation is convenient. The ease and convenience of public transportation is determined by the frequency of bus or streetcar schedules and the distance from home or work to the nearest stop. Each of these factors is a result of population and user density. (It is critical to realize, however, that very high densities—extended arrays of high-rise apartment blocks—are not by any means necessary. Other options such as single-family homes on narrower lots, low-rise apartments, "row" housing, duplexes and triplexes, and luxury townhouses, even mixed with single-family housing in any number of ways would achieve the desired objective.) Urban form, then, provides both the need and opportunity for a variety of viable and affordable public transportation options, including the opportunity for reasonable walking and cycling possibilities for more than a few people.

The environmental advantages of relatively compact cities are numerous. Air quality and energy efficiency are both obvious and important. But other advantages include reduced per capita infrastructure needs: less concrete, wire, pipe per capita for connections, streets, sidewalks, sewers, and so forth. There would also be less imposition of human settlement on near-urban recreational space, wetlands, habitat, agricultural land, and relatively "natural" spaces. (Individuals would not have to travel so far to "get away from it all.") There is also a possibility that there would be a reduction in heating energy if a higher proportion of residences were structured with at least some walls and ceilings/floors in common.

Another dimension of urban form that carries important environmental implications is mixed-function, mixed-use planning. Historically we have tried to separate work and residence in urban settings. In the era of smokestack industries this may have made sense (if one lived upwind and upstream). But it makes less sense today. Living relatively near to work could help to make for a more pleasant urban life. So could living near to a neighborhood pub, commerce, restaurants, entertainment, and educational institutions. Some city cores are experiencing something of a renaissance in recent years. It has been too little appreciated that this trend and possibility has profound environmental advantages as well as the obvious social and cultural advantages. It is here that social justice, environmental justice, and environmental protection will intersect in North America's future.

Robert Paehlke

Further Readings

Lowe, Marcia D. "Rethinking Urban Transportation." *State of the World 1991.* Ed. Lester R. Brown, et al. 1991.

Newman, Peter, and Jeffrey Kenworthy. *Cities and Automobile Dependence: An International Sourcebook.* 1989.

See also AUTOMOBILES: IMPACTS AND POLICIES; BICYCLE TRANSPORTATION; ENERGY EFFICIENCY; ENVIRONMENTAL JUSTICE MOVEMENT; LAND-USE PLANNING; RAILS-TO-TRAILS; URBAN DESIGN

U

Values Party (New Zealand)
See Green Parties

Volatile Organic Compounds

Volatile organic compounds (VOCs) are chemicals with a carbon-based skeleton whose vapor pressures are greater than 10^{-2} kiloPascals (KPa) and which are generally present in the atmosphere only in the gaseous state. VOCs are widely used in both commercial/industrial applications and common household products.

Sources and Uses

Commercial and industrial source categories include vehicles, fugitive gasoline vapors, petroleum refineries, architectural coatings and building materials, graphic arts (printing), wastewater treatment, vapor degreasing, dry-cleaning, chemical manufacturing (e.g., pharmaceuticals, plastics, rubber, and resins), and automobile assembly (including auto body painting).

Household products containing VOCs include cosmetics, hair sprays, personal deodorants, carpet and room deodorizers, furniture polishes and waxes, paint and paint thinners/strippers, and pesticides. One other major source of volatile organic compounds in households with smokers is environmental tobacco smoke (ETS).

Natural sources of VOCs include both coniferous and deciduous trees, crops, and grassland. VOC emissions from conifers seem to be independent of light but increase exponentially with temperature indicating both a diurnal and a seasonal variation with emissions lower at night and in the winter months. Emissions from deciduous trees are both light and temperature dependent and only occur from about April to September inclusive and during daylight hours. Crops and grasses are larger sources of VOC emissions than deciduous trees but are much smaller sources than conifers.

It has been estimated that total hydrocarbon emissions from biogenic sources equal or exceed those from anthropogenic sources on a total-mass basis. Anthropogenic VOCs are emitted to the atmosphere from both area sources and point sources. For the province of Ontario area sources account for about 90 percent of the total anthropogenic VOC emissions and point sources account for the remaining 10 percent. The approximate apportionment of area sources is as follows: vehicles (35 percent); off-highway engines, railroad, aircraft, and marine sources (7 percent); and miscellaneous area sources including residential, commercial, industrial, and incineration emissions (6 percent) and fire and VOC evaporative processes (43 percent). Point source emissions include petroleum refineries (2 percent); chemical manufacturing (2.5 percent); pulp and paper sources (1.5 percent); primary metals (1.5 percent); and other manufacturing (3 percent). The distribution of anthropogenic VOC emissions is unlikely to be markedly different in other jurisdictions of similar size although on a local scale some sectors may be more heavily weighted than others.

Reasons for Concern

Many volatile organic compounds may be classified according to one of the following U.S. Environmental Protection Agency (EPA) categories: HS—hazardous substance (defined by EPA primarily on the basis of toxicity to aquatic life); HW—hazardous waste; or PTP—priority toxic pollutant. Some examples are benzene, toluene, trichloroethene, carbon tetrachloride and ortho-, meta-, and para-dichlorobenzene.

A smaller group of VOCs is arguably of much more interest; those that are known human carcinogens, probable human carcinogens, or animal carcinogens as defined by the International Agency for Research on Cancer (IARC); the National Toxicology Program (NTP); or the National Cancer Institute (NCI). Benzene, methylene chloride, vinyl chloride, carbon tetrachloride, and chloroform are VOCs known or thought to be carcinogenic by at least one of the above agencies.

Volatile organic compounds are also important in the formation of ground-level (tropospheric) ozone. Ozone is a known respiratory irritant, elevated levels of which may cause coughing, shortness of breath, nose and throat irritation, and short-term, non-permanent changes in lung function. Although a great deal is known about the effects of exposures to single doses of ozone there is much controversy about the health significance of these effects. Much less is known about chronic exposure to ozone; however, changes in the lung are thought to result from either cumulative damage or side effects from adaptive responses to repetitive daily or intermittent exposures.

Elevated ozone concentrations are also damaging to agricultural crops and other vegetation including sod grass, and ornamental plants such as Christmas trees and nursery-grown coniferous and deciduous plants.

Ozone is formed in the troposphere by photochemical (sunlight-driven) reactions between VOCs and oxides of nitrogen (NO_x). Some VOCs important in ground-level ozone formation include aromatics (such as 1,2,4-trimethylbenzene and m-xylene), alkenes (such as isoprene, a-pinene, and ethylene), alkanes (for example butane and n-hexane), and aldehydes (such as formaldehyde and acetaldehyde). The atmospheric chemistry is complex and all the interrelationships are not yet fully explained; however, the role of VOCs may be briefly summarized as follows.

Nitrogen dioxide molecules interact with sunlight (indicated by $h\nu$), being dissociated into nitric oxide and an oxygen atom.

$$NO_2 + h\nu \rightarrow NO + O \ (1)$$

The oxygen atom produced in this way reacts rapidly with an oxygen molecule to form a molecule of ozone.

$$O + O_2 \rightarrow O_3 \ (2)$$

Ozone, however, can then react with the nitric oxide, reforming nitrogen dioxide and oxygen molecules.

$$NO + O_3 \rightarrow NO_2 + O_2 \ (3)$$

In the absence of any other chemical reactions these three steps come to a steady state, in which the relative proportions of NO, NO_2, and O_3 are determined by the intensity of the sunlight. However, if reactive VOCs are present, they are capable of reacting with trace levels of highly reactive components in the atmosphere (including ozone, oxygen atoms, and particularly the hydroxyl radical, OH) to form oxygen containing free radicals (denoted by RO_2). These react very rapidly with NO to reform NO_2,

$$RO_2 + NO \rightarrow NO_2 + RO \ (4)$$

This perturbs the steady state described above, making more NO_2 available to participate in reaction (1), leading to enhanced production of ozone via reaction (2). The overall effect is that the VOCs are consumed, while the oxides of nitrogen are cycled around reactions (1) and (3). For this reason, the reactive VOCs have been described as the fuel required for the formation of ground-level ozone.

Lastly, a very small number of VOCs are of concern due to their potential to deplete stratospheric ozone. The important compounds are the chlorofluorocarbons (CFCs), more commonly known as Freons, which are widely used as refrigerants and for cleaning printed circuit boards; halons, used in fire control equipment; methyl chloroform, used as a solvent for metal cleaning and as an aerosol propellant and in pesticides; and carbon tetrachloride which has been used in the production of CFCs as well as in rubber cement, shoe and furniture polish, paints, lacquers, and stains, printing ink, and floor waxes. The long atmospheric lifetime of these chemicals (greater than seventy-five years in some cases) and their efficiency in destroying ozone in the stratosphere has lead to a large-scale phase-out of their production and use as detailed in the Montreal Protocol (1987) and subsequent amendments (London and Copenhagen). Hydrochlorofluorocarbons (HCFCs), compounds containing less chlorine than the traditional CFCs, are being substituted until more suitable replacements are developed. HCFCs are less stable than their CFC counterparts and so have a much shorter lifetime in the atmosphere and reach the stratosphere in much smaller quantities yet they, too, are being phased out. The phase-out schedule is as follows: halons by January 1, 1994; CFCs, methyl

TABLE 1

Daily Median Concentrations (μg/m³) by Site Type for Selected VOC

Median Concentration (number of samples)

Chemical	Rural	Urban	Indoor
Benzene	1.5 (246)	5.8 (3,812)	5.6 (1)
Carbon Tetrachloride	0.0 (86)	0.7 (2,754)	N/A
Chloroform	0.0 (82)	0.3 (2,696)	N/A
Formaldehyde	3.3 (12)	8.7 (332)	54.0 (273)
Methylene Chloride	0.2 (1)	2.9 (590)	N/A
Toluene	1.3 (248)	10.9 (2,519)	31.7 (101)
Trichloroethene	0.1 (84)	1.1 (2,056)	N/A

Source: Adapted from Shah and Singh, *Environmental Science and Technology* (1988).

chloroform, and carbon tetrachloride by January 1, 1996; and HCFCs by January 1, 2030.

Concentration Levels of Volatile Organic Compounds

Concentrations of VOCs in urban outdoor air are generally between 0.1 and 10 micrograms per cubic meter (μg/m³). Levels in indoor air may be as much as one order of magnitude higher. The EPA has published a National Volatile Organic Compounds Data Base containing almost 200,000 records of ambient and indoor air concentrations of 320 VOCs. A summary of that data base appears in *Environmental Science and Technology* (1988). Table 1 is adapted from that summary. Note: the median concentration is that concentration at which half of the observations show higher concentrations and half of the observations show lower concentrations.

Peter Steer and Neville Reid

Further Readings

Edgerton, Sylvia A., et al. "Inter-Urban Comparison of Ambient Volatile Organic Compound Concentrations in U.S. Cities." *Journal of the Air Pollution Control Association* 39 (1989): 729–32.

Finlayson-Pitts, B.J., and J.N. Pitts. *Atmospheric Chemistry: Fundamentals and Experimental Techniques.* 1986.

Seinfeld, John H. "Urban Air Pollution: State of the Science." *Science* 243 (1989): 745–52.

Shah, Jitendra J., and Hanwant B. Singh. "Distribution of Volatile Organic Chemicals in Outdoor and Indoor Air." *Environmental Science and Technology* 22 (1988): 1381–1388.

See also AIR POLLUTION: IMPACTS; INDOOR AIR POLLUTION; MONTREAL PROTOCOL; OZONE DEPLETION; OZONE POLLUTION; SMOG; TOBACCO SMOKE IN THE ENVIRONMENT

Water Allocations and Shortages (U.S. West)

Americans living on the short grass plains, in the Southwestern deserts, and the high and dry expanses of great basins and valleys throughout the Rocky Mountains have always been greatly concerned with the allocation of water. Since the 1870s and into the early 1990s westerners have routed most of the region's water to agriculture. In this period nearly 85 percent of diverted stream flows have gone to irrigation. With inadequate precipitation for normal crop production westerners realized the need to divert stream flows and to pump aquifers to realize the great farming potential of western soils. Their legal and social institutions advanced irrigation and assigned subordinate priorities to industries, recreation, and, lately, instream flow protection. This system worked well so long as water sources carried enough flow to supply all of the rights assigned to them, and so long as enough viable rights existed for growing or changing economies.

However, throughout much of the West, allocation procedures failed to stem growing shortages arising from two general problems. First, over-development in irrigation meant many projects lacked sufficient water. Westerners used the powers of the state and the federal government in a variety of ways to overcome the social and economic problems associated with the over-construction of ditch systems. Next, after World War II water "shortages" and allocation problems arose where the Western society and economy has centered in its metroplexes rather than its rural areas. Not only have urbanites demanded more water for city growth, but out of the metroplexes grew environmental movements with a focus on stream preservation for both recreation and ecological preservation.

Most Western states have allocated water through some form of the prior appropriation doctrine. In the 1850s and 1860s Californians regulated stream diversions for mining in remote sites thereby establishing the precedents for the prior appropriation doctrine. The first person to use water in "beneficial" pursuits—nearly always some form of economic production—had priority to divert stream flow before any one else who developed a beneficial use of the same stream at a later date—"first in time, first in right."

Westerners quickly realized the great potential of this practice in rapidly allocating water resources to stimulate economic development. Anyone who dallied in developing water rights for irrigation, city systems, or industries took the chance of someone else developing the reliable flow of a stream first.

Two institutionalized patterns of prior appropriation have governed in the West: the Colorado and Wyoming systems. The courts assigned water rights regulated by a state engineers office in the Colorado system. Within the Wyoming system the state engineer decided and administered water rights directly.

Those Western states not fully arid have allocated water under a combination of prior appropriation doctrine and common law riparian doctrine. Common law normally guaranteed owners of stream banks the use of flowing water undiminished in quantity and quality by upstream uses. The California system combined aspects of both riparian and prior appropriation doctrines. Other states, such as Oregon, Washington, the Dakotas, Nebraska, Texas, and Kansas, all followed the California system. Each of these states shared a common characteristic—nearly half of the state received ample precipitation for crops while a semi-arid or arid clime characterized the other half. After World War II some states, such as Texas and Kansas, switched to a prior appropriation system for a more efficient economic exploitation of water resources.

The allocation of water between states has taken several forms. The federal government has contributed through Supreme Court decisions and by facilitating interstate water compacts. In *Kansas v. Colorado* (1907) the Supreme Court established the doctrine of equity, which weighs one state's use of water against the other's. Ever since equity has guided the court's decisions in interstate water conflicts. To help states avoid expensive litigation Congress has sanctioned the use of interstate compacts. Delph Carpenter, a Colorado water attorney, first promoted the idea and the Colorado River Compact of 1922, presided over by Herbert Hoover, then Secretary of Commerce, guided the seven states of the Colorado River basin in allotting stream flow among themselves. Since 1922 every Western state has entered compacts dividing interstate river flows.

These steps toward achieving a fair allocation of water have not prevented chronic water shortage problems in the West. Initially shortages arose due to over-proliferation of irrigation companies or poor engineering. By 1890 Colorado irrigation companies had rights to seven times the annual flow of the Arkansas River. The Highline Canal Company near Denver, the Imperial Valley Company in California, and the Truckee Company in Nevada all suffered severe water shortages and canal mishaps resulting from poor engineering.

Beginning in the late nineteenth century the "Irrigation Crusade" arose to address Western water shortages and to encourage further economic growth through irrigation. William Smythe, the originator of the movement, published the influential *Irrigation Age* from 1891 to 1895. Yearly irrigation congresses resulted in westerners lobbying for greater federal support for irrigation enterprises. John Wesley Powell, while disavowing some notions of the crusade, lent a powerful voice for government support and planning in Western water development, especially in his *Report on the Lands of the Arid Regions of the United States* (1878) and through his work in the U.S. Geological Survey.

By 1902 growing problems in Western irrigation and strong lobbying of the crusade led to the passage of the Reclamation Act of 1902.

This began the federal government's role in building massive irrigation projects throughout the West. The Reclamation Service, renamed the Bureau of Reclamation in 1923, completed Roosevelt Dam on the Salt River in Arizona—its first major project—in 1914. Since then the Bureau has built world-renowned structures such as Hoover Dam and Grand Coulee Dam, thereby plugging all of the major rivers in the West.

Besides the Bureau, the Army Corps of Engineers worked to supplement agricultural and urban water supplies. After the costly Mississippi flood of 1927 Congress charged the Corps with flood protection throughout the entire drainage, eventually opening the entire trans-Mississippi West to the Corps' efforts. In the 1960s, under the provisions of the Pick-Sloan Plan, the Corps and Bureau shared dam building throughout the Missouri River basin. By the 1990s their combined efforts raised dams on nearly every conceivable site; despite these efforts water shortages, spurred largely through urban growth, loomed throughout the West.

As early as 1900 some large Western cities faced water shortages and with well-funded war chests built elaborate systems, often with considerable conflict, to overcome limitations to growth. Los Angeles tapped the Owens Valley through an elaborate conveyance system over 230 miles long; San Francisco battled the Sierra Club and John Muir for a hold on the Hetch Hetchy Valley in Yosemite Park; Denver began buying troubled irrigation systems and reached deep into the Rocky Mountain watersheds for additional supplies.

World War II boosted Western urban growth, which has continued apace. Many Western cities faced water shortages with most stream flows previously allocated to agricultural uses. Urban water strategies differed considerably. Cities along the front range of Colorado turned to buying agricultural rights throughout the Arkansas and Platte River valleys. Las Vegas developed plans to supplement its Colorado River rights with water from the northern, and better watered, part of Nevada. Phoenix received massive federal aid through the construction of the Central Arizona Project, which carries Colorado River water. The Metropolitan Water District, a combine of southern California cities, has worked to effect regional planning and system building.

Besides becoming the centers of rising water demands cities have become the hub of environmental movements demanding new approaches to water allocation and solutions to water shortages. Environmentalists' apprehensions have focused on two problems: recreation and ecological preservation. Fishers want trout streams; for different reasons, both wildlife preservationists and hunters demand riparian ecosystems capable of sustaining wildlife populations; river rafters, kayakers, and canoeists all want rapids foaming and full; and preservationists want rivers wild for the sake of having them left "natural."

Traditional allocations of water pay little heed to environmental concerns. Today, the 600-mile-long Columbia River has a mere fifty miles of free-flowing stream, and 450 "major" dams stand in the basin. By 1986 over 700 miles of streambeds in western Kansas, one state agency estimated, had become dry. Barren stretches mark the Snake River all along its route and placid reservoirs now cover some of its former raging rapids. The mouth of the Colorado River now gives only a trickle of saline water to the Gulf of California. The spread of pump irrigation has depleted massive groundwater aquifers like the Ogallala, which stretches from the Panhandle of Texas throughout the High Plains to South Dakota. This withdrawal threatens large wetlands such as Cheyenne Bottoms in Kansas, as well as the farmers themselves, with destruction.

In the last twenty years mounting criticism of traditional allocations have demanded new measures for dividing and preserving water. Throughout the West many economists have advocated water-marketing and transfers, which would allow a market in water rights to determine the use of water. Some states, such as Colorado and New Mexico, have added instream flow rights to their prior appropriation systems, but the water rights to streams have dates allowing the needs of cities and irrigation systems, with earlier dated rights to most of the flow anyway, to come first. Some states, such as Texas and Kansas, have experimented with self-governing districts to conserve groundwater supplies. Environmentalists have taken to the courts to defeat new projects such as Two-Forks on the South Platte River in Colorado. In general westerners are shifting water resources away from agricultural uses to urban, and are devising new ways of moving water to uses with greater economic efficiencies and fewer environmental drawbacks.

James E. Sherow

Further Readings

Lee, Lawrence B. *Reclaiming the American West: An Historiography and Guide.* 1980.

Pisani, Donald J. "Deep and Troubled Waters: A New Field of Western History?" *New Mexico Historical Review* 63 (1988): 311–331.

See also ARMY CORPS OF ENGINEERS (U.S.); COLORADO RIVER; COLUMBIA RIVER BASIN; HETCH HETCHY DAM; OGALLALA AQUIFER; POWELL, JOHN WESLEY; RANGELANDS (U.S.)

Water Pollution Abatement Technologies

Water pollution abatement technologies fall into two broad categories: 1) end-of-pipe pollution control technologies, which take the generation of pollutants as a given and then attempt to limit their environmental release; and 2) pollution prevention technologies, which attempt to reduce or eliminate the generation of pollutants in industrial processes at their source.

End-of-Pipe Pollution Abatement Technologies

Conventional end-of-pipe pollution abatement technologies are divided into three broad categories or levels: 1) primary treatment technologies; 2) secondary treatment technologies; and 3) tertiary treatment technologies.

Primary Treatment Technologies

Primary treatment systems are used to remove suspended organic and inorganic materials from waste waters. Primary treatment is usually achieved through gravity separation using mechanical clarifiers, or sedimentation lagoons. Mechanical clarifiers are large circular tanks equipped with sludge removal rakes. Settled solids deposited on the clarifier floor are drawn to the center of the tank by rotating mechanical raking systems. They are then drawn off and de-watered prior to disposal. Chemicals, such as lime or certain polymers, are sometimes added to improve the settlement of solids. Sedimentation lagoons are simple shallow basins which allow suspended solids to settle to the bottom of the basin. When full, the basins are drained and then cleaned using earth moving equipment. The sludge produced by primary treatment systems of these types is usually de-watered and then incinerated, landfilled or, sometimes, spread on agricultural land.

Secondary Treatment Technologies

Secondary treatment technologies include aerated lagoons, activated sludge, trickling filters, and oxidation ponds. Used to remove dissolved organics through oxidative decomposition by microorganisms, this type of system reduces the biological oxygen demand (BOD) associated with the effluent.

Aerated lagoons are medium-depth basins designed for the biological treatment of wastewater on a continuous basis. Oxygen is supplied to the lagoon by mechanical devices such as surface aerators or submerged turbine aerators. Aerated lagoons are often used as a polishing step following the removal of organics from the waste water.

Activated sludge is an aerobic biological treatment system consisting of an aeration tank followed by a sedimentation tank. In this process high concentrations of microorganisms are suspended uniformly throughout the aeration tank to which the waste water is added. The organic materials in the waste water are metabolized by the microorganisms and the metabolic products are removed as the waste water moves through the sedimentation tank.

Trickling filters consist of a large open vessel containing a packed medium that provides a growth site for microorganisms. Waste water is applied to the medium by a rotary distributor. The treated waste water is then collected through a drain system. Soluble organics are consumed by the microorganisms and converted into carbon dioxide, water, and protoplasm.

Oxidation ponds consist of shallow basins. These assure an adequate supply of oxygen without mechanical mixing. Aeration is achieved through oxygen transfer at the surface and by the photosynthetic action of algae present in the ponds. Microorganisms then cause aerobic degradation of the organic contaminants in the water.

Tertiary Treatment Technologies

To further improve the quality of waste water effluent, tertiary processes are sometimes used to remove some additional organic pollutants, taste and odor producing substances, and dissolved organic substances. The most commonly used tertiary treatment systems include granular activated carbon absorption, powder activated carbon, or granular media filters.

Granular activated carbon filtration removes large organic molecules from the waste water, while a companion sand filter removes solids. The water flows through a bank of parallel carbon columns where the pollutants are absorbed by the carbon, gradually filling its pores. From time to time the carbon is removed, regenerated, and the absorbed substances incinerated.

In powder activated carbon treatment powdered carbon is added to biological treatment systems. The absorbent quality of the carbon aids in the removal of organic materials. Powder activated carbon treatment also enhances color removal, clarification, and reduces biological and chemical oxygen demand.

There are several types of granular media filters, such as sand dual media, and multimedia, filters. Such filters essentially consist of a coarse layer of coal above a fine layer of sand, and a third layer of heavy fine material (usually garnet) beneath the coal to keep the fine particles on the bottom. As waste water passes through such filters, the suspended matter is caught in the pores of the coal.

Pollution Prevention Technologies

The traditional end-of-pipe pollution control technologies just outlined suffer from a number of limitations. First, pollutants cannot be completely captured. Therefore some pollutants inevitably escape into the environment. Second, those pollutants that are captured by end-of-pipe pollution control systems must be disposed of somehow. As a result pollutants are often moved between media, but still ultimately released into the environment. This is a particularly serious problem where persistent toxic substances are concerned.

The pollution prevention approach does not suffer from these limitations. Pollution prevention technologies seek to avoid the creation of pollutants in industrial processes in the first place. This greatly reduces, or eliminates, the problems of inter-media transfer and disposal associated with the traditional pollution control model.

The pollution prevention approach has a number of other significant advantages including: reduced energy and resource use; minimized waste disposal costs; reduced environmental liability; and improved competitiveness through increased efficiency. Pollution prevention methods and technologies include: input substitution, product reformulation, production process redesign, improved operating and maintenance practices, and in-process recycling.

Input substitution involves the replacement of toxic substances used in production processes with less toxic or non-toxic alternatives, or the use of raw materials whose use does not lead to the production of hazardous wastes. Product reformulation entails changing the formulation of the final product to reduce or eliminate the amount of waste formed during the process. This approach involves modifying or redesigning the production process to reduce or eliminate the use and release of harmful substances and other wastes. Improved housekeeping methods, system adjustments, and product and process inspections can often result in reductions in the use and generation of harmful substances and other wastes. In-process recycling is the reuse of wastes within closed-loop production processes.

Many governments and businesses are beginning to incorporate the pollution prevention model into their approach to water pollution abatement. This is an important step toward ensuring the environmental sustainability of our economic activities.

Mark S. Winfield

Further Readings

Mausberg, B. *The Pollution Prevention Resource Bibliography: A Reference Manual to Support Pollution Prevention Activities in the Great Lakes Basin.* Canadian Institute for Environmental Law and Policy, 1993.

Sang, S. *Developing Technology-Based Standards under the Municipal-Industrial Strategy for Abatement in Ontario: A Case Study of the Petroleum Refining Industry.* Canadian Institute for Environmental Law and Policy, 1991.

———, and B. Mausberg. *Developing Options for Technology-Based Standards for the Pulp and Paper Sector in the Great Lakes Basin.* Canadian Institute for Environmental Law and Policy, 1992.

See also AIR POLLUTION ABATEMENT; EUTROPHICATION; HAZARDOUS WASTE TREATMENT TECHNOLOGIES; POLLUTION PREVENTION

Waterfowl: Conservation and Habitat

All of the major ecological habitat regions in North America except severe deserts support one or more of the many species of native waterfowl including swan, goose, and duck species. Whether in the Arctic tundra, the boreal forest, mixed or eastern hardwood forests, the prairie grasslands and parklands, the montane, or the coastal and marine environments—the common habitat element permitting waterfowl to exist is water. The most important and critical waterfowl habitats are natural wetlands, of a wide variety, including lakes, ponds, marshes, swamps, flowing streams and rivers, estuaries, tidal marshes, and coastal waters. High quality wetland habitats may also be artificial or temporary and their water may be fresh, brackish, or salt. Terrestrial areas adjacent to these wetlands are used by waterfowl to differing degrees but are essential for nesting, feeding, or loafing. Wetlands and their surrounding semi-terrestrial habitats which frequently undergo temporary flooding are among the most productive life-support systems in the world.

Waterfowl habitat must provide all of the birds' nutritional, physiological, and behavioral requirements throughout the year. The fluctuating demands of the birds' annual cycle—from breeding to molting, migrating, and wintering—see many waterfowl populations using a variety of habitats in different ecological regions from one season to the next. The lesser snow goose breeds and molts in the Arctic tundra; migrates across the boreal forest and prairies, where it stops to rest and feed (often for several weeks) around large wetlands; and winters along the coastal marshes of the Gulf of Mexico. The harlequin duck nests along turbulent mountain streams; and molts and winters along rocky, surf beaten, coastal shores. More sedentary populations of ducks and geese which winter farther north may avoid the risks of a long migration but in return face the stress of seeking adequate food over the coldest period of the year when the habitat is least productive.

Through adaptations the various waterfowl species are able to exploit their habitats differently and more efficiently. This ecological partitioning of the habitat into many separate niches by waterfowl is very successful and allows several different species to occupy similar habitats at the same time. For example, one prairie pothole may provide high quality wetland habitat for ten or more species of duck during the breeding season. Certain species reduce their dependence upon wetland food resources by foraging and grazing on the nearby upland (e.g., Canada and snow geese, mallards, northern pintails, and American wigeon). They are largely herbivorous at these times. Diving ducks on the other hand are most committed to the wetlands because of their carnivorous diet of animal matter which is found in or below the water. Other ducks such as northern shoveler and teal exploit plant and animal food resources nearer the water surface.

Waterfowl exhibit various strategies to reduce predation and disturbance while nesting hence partitioning their breeding habitats in other ways. Many species of ducks (e.g., mallards, northern pintail, teal, gadwall) and some geese (e.g., Canada and white-fronted) scatter over the available upland habitat taking advantage of vegetation to conceal their nests. Even if one nest is found predators have difficulty finding the next. Lesser snow geese nest in large colonies on the open tundra where there are too few predators to destroy all the nests. Other waterfowl nest in vegetation surrounded by water (canvasback, redhead, and ruddy ducks) or on islands (Ross' geese, eiders) or on cliffs (Canada geese). Wood ducks, goldeneye, bufflehead, and mergansers nest in trees using natural cavities or ones abandoned by woodpeckers. During periods of drought some populations of waterfowl (e.g., northern pintails, blue-winged teal, canvasback, redheads) leave the prairie pothole nesting areas and fly north to large wetland complexes in the boreal forest and Arctic regions (e.g., Athabasca Delta, Mackenzie Delta, Old Crow Flats). There, the more stable water levels support the birds through their molt and even give some an opportunity to breed. Much of the management and conservation of waterfowl habitat in the United States and Canada is devoted to providing adequate feeding and nesting areas.

Canada contains some of the richest and most extensive wetland—waterfowl habitat—areas in the world: the longest coastline of any country (243,000 kilometers) and numerous estuaries; 15 percent of the world's fresh water; 14 percent of Canada's total area of 997.6 million hectares is wetlands. The majority of North American waterfowl breed in Canada. Concern about wetland protection in Canada dates back more than a century. In 1887 the lieutenant governor of the North-West Territory foresaw the loss of waterfowl habitat to European-style settlement and recommended that the north end of Last Mountain Lake in present-day Saskatchewan be set aside to preserve breeding grounds for a wide variety of "wild fowl." North America's first sanctuary for waterfowl was established there on June 8, 1887. Since then Canada has protected over 11.3 million hectares (1.1 percent of Canada's area) as federal Migratory Bird Sanctuaries and 300,000 hectares as National Wildlife Areas, much of them, wetlands for waterfowl resting, wintering, and migration staging.

Unfortunately many people still treat wetlands as wastelands; draining marshes, diking flood plains, and filling low lands contribute to the loss of waterfowl habitat. In the United States (excluding Alaska and Hawaii) only 385,000 of an original 870,000 square kilometers of wetlands remain—a 56 percent overall loss. Because wetlands are imperiled around the world and because migratory waterfowl are an international resource dependent upon international habitats the "Convention on Wetlands of International Importance, Especially as Waterfowl Habitat" was developed. Under this agreement Canada, for example, has designated thirty waterfowl habitat sites totaling 12.9 million hectares under this convention, more than any other member state. By 1991 sixty countries had signed and 488 sites were listed in total. By drawing attention to the serious threats to wetlands it is hoped the protection of waterfowl habitat can be furthered globally.

Philip S. Taylor

Further Readings

Bellrose, F.C. *Ducks, Geese and Swans of North America.* The Wildlife Management Institute. 2nd ed. 1976.

Gillespie, D.I., H. Boyd, and P. Logan. *Wetlands for the World: Canada's Ramsar Sites.* Canadian Wildlife Service, Environment Canada, 1991.

Palmer, R.S., ed. *Handbook of North American Birds: Waterfowl.* 1976.

Ratti, J.T., L. Flake, and W. Wentz. *Waterfowl Ecology and Management: Selected Readings.* 1982.

See also COASTAL MARSHES, CONSERVATION OF; FRESHWATER WETLANDS; SEABIRDS; SHOREBIRDS

Watt, James G.

James Gaius Watt, appointed by President Ronald Reagan as secretary of the interior and chairman of the cabinet council on natural resources and the environment, served from January 1981 until his resignation in October 1982. Watt, a westerner, came to the cabinet with a history of opposition to major environmental and conservation measures enacted during the 1970s, having served the previous eleven years as president of the Mountain States Legal Foundation, a conservative public interest law firm that initiated many legal challenges to federal environmental and conservation laws.

Watt was extremely popular among Republican conservatives and Western proponents of the Sagebrush Rebellion but aroused intense opposition among environmental and conservation interests for his outspoken and unapologetic advocacy of aggressive natural resource development on the public lands under his department's jurisdiction. His confrontational style, partisan approach to resource management, and harsh attacks on environmentalists seemed to epitomize a hostility toward environmental regulation and resource conservation that environmentalists believed was pervasive in the Reagan administration. Watt also clashed frequently with Congressional Democrats angered by his efforts to obstruct the implementation of conservation and regulatory programs they strongly supported.

Much of the controversy associated with Watt's cabinet tenure was incited by an ambitious program he proposed, shortly after assuming office, to rapidly increase the pace and scope of resource development on the public domain and to relax existing restrictions on resource development. The most controversial of these initiatives included a five-year program to lease one billion acres of federal offshore lands for energy production; a program to accelerate fossil fuel production, mining, grazing, and lumbering on federal lands; a measure to curtail protection of endangered species; and a proposed reclassification of wilderness areas to permit energy exploration and other previously prohibited activities. Most of these proposals, requiring legislative approval, were severely modified or rejected by Congress. However, Watt had an enduring impact on federal environmental policies throughout the 1980s. He successfully used his administrative authority to substantially diminish enforcement activities in his department's Office of Surface Mining charged with controlling environmental damage from coal mining. He also weakened many conservation regulations implemented by his department through administrative revision.

By mid-1982 Watt's highly publicized, rancorous controversies with environmentalists, Congress, and other critics and his often intemperate public pronouncements had become a political embarrassment to the Reagan administration. Under pressure from the White House, Watt was compelled to resign from the cabinet in late 1981, thus ending one of the most embittered periods in the history of relations between the Department of the Interior and conservationists.

Walter A. Rosenbaum

Further Readings
Hays, Samuel P. *Beauty, Health, and Permanence: Environmental Politics in the United States, 1955–1985.* 1987.
Rosenbaum, Walter A. *Environmental Politics and Policy.* 2nd ed. 1991.

See also BUREAU OF LAND MANAGEMENT; BURFORD, ANNE MCGILL; DEPARTMENT OF THE INTERIOR (U.S.); REAGAN, RONALD; SAGEBRUSH REBELLION

Web of Life
The web of life is a concept that organisms and processes within and among ecosystems are tied to each other through numerous relationships including pathways of energy and nutrient transfer. Early ecologists thought of relationships within ecosystems as hierarchical. In 1881 Karl Gottfried Semper provided a basic description of food chains and noted that animals at the top of food chains were fewer in number than those at the bottom. Charles Elton, in *Animal Ecology* (1927), showed that food chains were linked to each other to form a food web. Each food web includes plants and microorganisms as producers, animals as first and higher-order consumers, and decomposers or reducers which break down dead organisms, returning nutrients and energy to the ecosystem. The food web recognizes that some species may capture energy at more than one trophic level, or step in a food chain. Omnivorous bears, for example, may consume leaves, berries, bulbs, honey, insect larvae, carrion, and fish. Bears are thus part of several different food chains, including those originating in streams or in the oceans. As the study of food webs advanced, ecologists found, due to the second law of thermodynamics, energy flows within an ecosystem with some loss at each transfer, while nutrients are often conserved and recycled. The overall efficiency of energy transfer in food-webs is generally low, with tropical rainforest capturing 3.5 percent of available solar radiation via photosynthesis, and most other ecosystems capturing less than 2 percent of the available energy. Energy transfer between consumed and consumer in a food web is usually less than 10 percent efficient.

In the past three decades the web of life has been increasingly utilized to refer to life on earth as a whole. Ecologists have demonstrated that ecosystems are critically linked to each other. Salt marshes, for example, serve as nurseries for juvenile fish that eventually inhabit open ocean ecosystems. Marshes also export energy and nutrients that support marine fisheries. The earth's vegetation is an important sink, or depository, for carbon dioxide. James Lovelock and Lynn Margulis have proposed, in the Gaia hypothesis, that life on earth may help to regulate its own physical environment, by greater or lesser productive and consumptive activity, which in turn, modifies the balances of gases in the earth's atmosphere

The concept of the web of life has thus replaced the older notion of the "Great Chain of Being," in which the most noble animals, including humans, were at the top. The web of life distinguishes the organisms capable of capturing energy, such as green plants and bacteria, as the most important, and recognizes the critical role played by decomposers. As the application of the web of life has become more global environmentalists have argued for greater human recognition of the interdependence of our fate and the quality of our life with that of other species. In the web of life "everything is connected to everything else."

Susan P. Bratton

Further Readings
Elton, Charles. *Animal Ecology.* 1927.
Odum, Eugene. *Fundamentals of Ecology* 3rd edition. 1971.

See also BIOACCUMULATION; BIODIVERSITY; COASTAL MARSHES, CONSERVATION OF; ECOSYSTEMS; ELTON, CHARLES; FOOD CHAINS; GAIA HYPOTHESIS; ODUM, EUGENE

Weinberg, Alvin Martin

Alvin Martin Weinberg was born in 1915 and began his distinguished career as a physicist and nuclear engineer at the University of Chicago during World War II. In 1945 he joined Oak Ridge National Laboratory, where he served as director from 1955 to 1974, a post from which he exerted seminal influence not only on the development of nuclear power in America, but also on the post-war relationship of science and technology with the state. Weinberg introduced the phrase "big science" into policy discourse in the 1960s while reflecting on the criteria by which government should spend money on expensive research projects. He compared the accelerators used by high energy physicists to the pyramids of ancient Egypt and the cathedrals of medieval Europe and warned that cultures that had devoted too much of their resources to such non-utilitarian monuments had usually fallen on hard times. Stressing that publicly funded basic research should both connect with human affairs and have an impact on neighboring disciplines, Weinberg directed research programs at Oak Ridge toward such applied ends as energy production and environmental protection.

In the early 1970s Weinberg, a prescient political operator, recognized that federal funding for research on nuclear power was dwindling while new sources of support were materializing for environmental research. His policy initiatives in this period were therefore aimed at securing the laboratory's future by forming new political alliances. These decisions helped to establish Oak Ridge as an important presence in the emerging field of environmental impact assessment. Weinberg's influential 1972 article on science and "trans-science" alerted policy makers and analysts to the fact that policy-relevant questions formulated in scientific terms could not always be answered by science.

Weinberg received many awards and honors for his services to science and public policy, among them the Atoms for Peace Award and the E.O. Lawrence Award (1960), the Enrico Fermi award (1980), and the Harvey Prize (1982).

Sheila Jasanoff

Further Readings
Weinberg, Alvin M. *Reflections on Big Science.* 1967.
———. "Science and Trans-Science." *Minerva* 10 (1972): 209–22.

See also NUCLEAR ELECTRIC POWER; NUCLEAR WASTE

Western Canada Wilderness Committee

Formed in 1980 the Western Canada Wilderness Committee (WCWC or WC²) has been British Columbia's major wilderness preservation group for more than a decade. Its membership reached a peak of about 30,000 in 1991. The group has played a leading role in campaigns to preserve South Moresby, Clayoquot Sound, the Carmanah valley, the Kitlope valley, the Chilcotin wilderness, and many other areas. In the late 1980s it also began to address international wilderness issues, devoting considerable effort to a global wilderness mapping project (the "Wilderness is the Last Dream" [WILD] project), and to campaigns to save areas such as the Penan (Borneo).

The WCWC disavows civil disobedience tactics, seeking to achieve its goals through research and education. Rather than concentrating on direct lobbying of politicians and bureaucrats it has premised its tactics on the belief that governments are most effectively moved by shifts in public opinion. The WCWC has used a wide array of approaches to mobilize public support. It has produced books on areas such as Meares Island; conducted research on threatened species (for example, the marbled murrelet); sponsored national and international tours; distributed its very successful endangered wilderness calendars as well as posters and other merchandise; produced videos; constructed hiking trails into the Carmanah and other areas to allow wider public access; and engaged in a number of court battles.

The group's trademark, though, has been the tabloid-style report. Focused on specific wilderness preservation candidate areas and distributed free of charge, WCWC reports typically combine hard information on the area with photographs juxtaposing the splendors of old-growth forests against the ugliness of the massive clearcut. Several areas and issues have been showcased in this way, with print runs of specific editions running as high as 200,000. In addition to serving to increase awareness of threatened areas these papers are an important fundraising instrument. Most of the organization's work has been done by dedicated volunteers. (It was estimated, for example, that construction of the trail into the Carmanah absorbed over 8,000 hours of volunteer labor.) The group has survived a couple of periods of membership decline and heavy indebtedness.

Jeremy Wilson

Further Readings

Henley, Thom. *Rediscovery: Ancient Pathways, New Directions.* 1989.

Western Canada Wilderness Committee. *Carmanah: Artistic Visions of an Ancient Rainforest.* 1989.

———. *Meaves Island: Protecting a Natural Paradise.* 1985.

See also CARMANAH VALLEY; CLAYOQUOT SOUND; OLD GROWTH FORESTS; WILDERNESS

Western Europe: Pollution

Western Europe consists of a total population of over 350 million people who enjoy one of the most wealthy and industrialized lifestyles in the world. In general environmental pollution is found more in areas of poverty than in areas of affluence. This is because the rich countries have been pushed by public opinion and technological change into adopting stringent pollution control measures and innovating in cleanup technology, while the poorer countries are still developing their economies against a backdrop of inefficient factories, poor regulation, and inadequate economic penalties.

For Western Europe the prime mover in pollution control is the European Community (EC). This is because, under the 1985 Single European Act, environmental protection and sustainable growth became prime objectives of the twelve EC nations. Since 1972 the European Commission, the EC's executive arm, has published five action plans for the environment each spawning a series of binding directives on member states. Of significance for European environmental protection policy is the fact that waste emissions cross national borders. Norway and Switzerland, for example, emit hardly any sulfur dioxide (SO_2) because of their large hydropower schemes and clean industry. Yet sulfur deposition in both countries is very high. Similarly much of the water pollution in the Rhine flows through the Netherlands, but emanates in Switzerland, France, and Germany. The Dutch have to dredge contaminated sludge from the river mouths, and expensively incinerate it or consign it to landfills, when most of the materials are from other countries. Presently the Dutch are experimenting with a novel idea of establishing environmental covenants whereby the German, French, Swiss, and Luxembourg polluters pay for dredging and environmental remediation instead of being taken to the courts.

In general European pollution is passing from the early smog and organic discharges, most of which are now controlled by a combination of tough cross-border regulation and economic charges. The newer sources of pollution include chemicals associated with cleaning solvents and the paint industry; hazardous waste from chemical, hospital, and nuclear installations; nutrients from municipal sewage works and agricultural intensification; and automobile exhausts, notably NO_x and hydrocarbons. This is the result of a shift in the economy toward service industries that increasingly rely on the microchip; the vast increase of car production and ownership (vehicle numbers have increased sevenfold since 1950 while population has not yet doubled); and the widespread use of chemicals in agriculture. As well the construction of municipal sewage treatment plants has concentrated phosphates and nitrates in rivers and groundwater sources, while the proliferation of the chemical industry into pharmaceutical, fertilizer and pesticides, solvent manufacture, and specialized plastic products has considerably increased the range and distribution of organic materials.

The net result of all this is the reduction in conventional biological oxygen element losses in many western European rivers, as well as the lowering of heavy metal contamination as the most obvious emissions are controlled by EC directives and subsequent national legislation. Similarly, local SO_2 deposition has been curtailed, though SO_2 in general remains high due to greater dispersion. Nevertheless the conversion of coal to oil and subsequently to gas, the introduction of CO_2 removal technology, and the greater efficiency of industry have all contributed to the lowering of SO_2 in Western Europe. In Eastern Europe SO_2 levels remain dangerously high due to large, and very inefficient coal burning plants, and the continuation of industry that has never been in a strong competitive position.

The "new" pollutants involve Volatile Organic Compounds (VOCs), NO_x and hazardous emissions from incinerators, and poorly regulated solid waste dumps. There are several hundred types of VOCs, many of which leak from valves, vents, and loading/ unloading, and are almost undetectable by regular monitoring. Solvents account for some 40 percent of non-traffic VOC pollution followed by the petroleum industry. Europe accounts for about 6 percent of global VOC emissions, mostly from Germany, the United Kingdom, and France. VOCs contribute significantly to lowland ozone and photochemical smog. Along with NO_x these emissions are the most health-affecting pollutants in urban air. They can cause respiratory problems as well as skin disease, liver and kidney failure, and microtoxicity. There is also evidence of plant growth damage arising from tropospheric ozone concentrations that are common in sunny European summers.

Nutrient additions to rivers and groundwater are sufficiently ubiquitous to give rise to concern over the health of European watercourses, including the northern North Sea. In the late 1980s plankton concentration increased to affect the coastal tourist industry, while eutrophic conditions in the species rich Waddensee in the northeast Netherlands, is causing great concern for the future of healthy commercial fish populations and bird numbers. In 1990 the North Sea states agreed to limit phosphate and nitrogen additions to the North Sea by 50 percent by 1998. This is a highly ambitious target given that the sources are not fully monitored or even documented, and the means of limitation are restricted in view of limitations on the growth and effectiveness of the regulatory agencies. In any case the scientific justification for both the cause and consequence of national increases in the southern North Sea is not yet fully provided.

So this policy is essentially the application of the precautionary principle whereby fail-safe measures are put into effect in advance of formal cost-benefit justification on scientific grounds. The application of precaution is particularly pertinent when common access sources are affected and where all contributing countries are expected to share the same level of burden for environmental restoration. Polluter pays, precaution, control at source, burden sharing, and waste minimization are the five centerpieces of current European environmental protection strategy.

Timothy O'Riordan

Further Readings

The Economist. *Atlas of the New Europe.* 1992, 193–222.
Johnston, Stanley, and Guy Corcelle. *The Environmental Policy of the European Communities.* 1992.

See also ENVIRONMENTAL CASE LAW: EUROPEAN COMMUNITY; ENVIRONMENTAL JUSTICE MOVEMENT; LEGISLATION: EUROPEAN COMMUNITY; POLLUTION PREVENTION; RHINE RIVER; SEVESO; VOLATILE ORGANIC COMPOUNDS

Wetlands

See COASTAL MARSHES, CONSERVATION OF; FRESHWATER WETLANDS; WATERFOWL: CONSERVATION AND HABITAT

Whales

See BALEEN WHALES; INTERNATIONAL WHAL-
ING COMMISSION

White, Gilbert

Gilbert White of Selbourne, England (1720–
1793), was perhaps the master naturalist in the
history of a nation highly mindful of such matters. White was a writer empathetically oriented
toward nature, paying special attention to the
complex associations among the many creatures and elements of the natural world. In this
it could be said that he was a forerunner of the
modern science of ecology. A village parson
who had studied at Oxford (during an impoverished moment in its long history), White spent
the better part of his life observing the wonders
of nature within his parish. He observed and
recorded the thousands of ways that all God's
creatures had a significant role to play in nature.
White sought a renewed harmony between humanity and nature. He explicitly rejected notions of a human mastery of nature through
science—a view so predominant in his time and
until recently.

White's master work was *The Natural
History of Selbourne,* published in 1789, but
receiving little attention until the 1830s. Virginia Woolf described this book as "one of
those ambiguous books that seem to tell a plain
story . . . and yet by some apparently unconscious device of the author's has left a door
open, through which we hear distant sounds."
The description is even more apt today. The
hindsight afforded by contemporary environmentalism as a new perspective on history allows an even fuller appreciation of White's contribution. The parts of nature we now know are
not separate, interchangeable, or expendable.
Nature is not a machine; it is an interdependent
whole. White understood that and hoped for a
better appreciation of that reality in his time
and since.

White's observations of the countryside
and nature in Selbourne were recorded in journals beginning in 1751. He also carried on an
extensive correspondence regarding these same
subjects and published a volume called *The
Garden Kalendar.*

Robert Paehlke

Further Readings

Holt-White, Rashleigh, ed. *The Life and Letters of Gilbert White.* 2 vols. 1901.
Mabey, Richard. *Gilbert White.* 1986.

White, Gilbert. *The Natural History of
Selbourne.* 1789.

See also NATURE STUDY MOVEMENT

Whole Earth Image

An imaginative experiment with extra-terres-
trial perspectives on the earth is already evident
in some of the earliest works of Western culture.
Two thousand years ago, for example, the
Greek author Lucian imagined the viewpoint of
his hero borne to the moon straddling the left
wing of a vulture and the right wing of an eagle,
and drew humbling lessons from a vista in
which all of Greece was reduced to some four
inches. With the rise of technologies associated
with ventures of navigation and global exploration, such imaginings took an increasingly
literal and visual form. Thus in 1492, as
Carolyn Merchant has noted, Nurenburg
mapmaker Martin Behaim and artist
Glokenthon used strips of parchment on a
spherical shell to create the first extant globe,
an *Erdapfel* (earth apple). During World War II,
under the influence of new technical capabilities and ideological imperatives, the American
image of the earth and its cartographic representation were strikingly transformed. As A.K.
Hendrikson observed, in addition to a fixation
on the Arctic that emphasized the proximity of
Russia and the United States, depictions in the
popular media increasingly presented the earth
from an airborne perspective in which the
earth's sphericity and unity were emphasized.

Satellite and missile technology during the
Cold War years increasingly allowed the actual
achievement of this viewpoint, and in 1969 a
photographic image of the entire planet from
the outside was produced by the National Aeronautics and Space Administration (NASA)
Apollo 8 mission. An analysis of the reception
and proliferation of the NASA "whole earth
image" tells us a great deal about the challenges
and dilemmas of contemporary Western environmentalism, and perhaps some of its blind
spots.

Shortly after its appearance the image was
heralded by poets and commentators as usher-
ing in a new age of global unity and humility.
Presenting a single borderless oasis of blue and
green surrounded by cold black space the image seemed to highlight the need for all humans
to rally around the preservation of their shared
and fragile home. It was seen to quin-
tessentialize the "worldview" of the environ-

mental and peace movements, and rapidly became their icon, appearing ubiquitously in their publications, and promotional products, and informing their thinking. Notions of the global ecosystem, of "spaceship earth," and the Gaia hypothesis, for example, implicitly derived their cogency from the visual gestalt of the whole earth image. At the same time the image was widely used in futuristic symbology that depicted technological mastery and control of people and resources on a planetary scale, and was harnessed to lend a variety of connotations to commercial products by advertising.

This bimodal distribution of the image in popular culture is curious. That groups with such ostensibly divergent goals and values should share this image is not simply the result of a reactionary appropriation of a potentially liberatory icon, on the one hand, nor of the counter-cultural poaching of the symbolic product of the industrial-military complex's multi-billion dollar space program on the other. Rather, it may point to deep contradictions at the heart of Western environmentalism. For in embracing this image so readily Western environmentalism seems to reveal an internalization of some of the currents of modernity it claims to protest, and to entrench its North-centered and technocratic orientation to environmental problems.

As can be seen by comparing it to premodern earth imagery the whole earth image is quintessentially modern (i.e., emerging from the Enlightenment project) in a variety of ways. It relies on a hugely sophisticated technology, to which very few have access, to provide an unambiguous realist image of the earth from the outside. It relies on vision alone—the most distancing of senses—and on a pan optic viewpoint, to reduce the entire planet to manageable proportions ("The earth was eventually so small I could blot it out of the universe simply by holding up my thumb," said U.S. astronaut Buzz Aldrin), and to render the entire planet visually available. These inherent features of the photographic image lend themselves to the kind of representations prevalent in advertising, which portray the earth as trivialized (an egg to be eaten, a tennis ball, a yo-yo); as embedded in rectilinear grids; as an artifact for use (a burning candle, an integrated circuit board, a peripheral device hooked up to a computer); and as subject to human mastery (a lemon being squeezed, a ball underfoot).

These inherent features of the image also make it an appropriate icon for a Western environmentalism that has tended to see environmental questions worldwide in increasingly global, technocratic, and North-centered perspective. These tendencies within Western environmentalism can be traced at key points over the movement's history: in the export of a nineteenth century German model of rational scientific management of forests for sustainable yield to the British colonies; in the ideals of Progressive era conservation; in the classics of the "global environmental revolution," such as Paul Ehrlich's *Population Bomb* (1968), the declarations of the Stockholm Conference on the Human Environment (1972), the *Ecologist's* "Blueprint for Survival" (1972), the Club of Rome's *Limits to Growth* (1972) and the debates on global carrying capacity it initiated, and in the Brundtland Report's (1987) wedding of growth to environment under the banner of sustainable development.

The distance, globality, and holism of the whole earth image tends to blur the role of difference and conflict in environmental destruction, and instead frames environmental problems through a single threatened global ecosystem as a unit of analysis. Such a framing, when placed in the context of contemporary North-South relations, can all too easily justify technocratic intervention in the lives of people around the globe, by those with most technical expertise and power in the international arena, on behalf of "everyone." The whole earth image, like the possessive form environmentalists often use in referring to "our earth," embodies doubled meanings of connected belonging and hubristic ownership. These troubling aspects of environmental thought have been increasingly challenged, and especially by voices from the South or those very familiar with a Southern perspective. (See especially here the writings of Wolfgang Sachs, as well as Ramachandra Guha, Johan Galtung, Sharad Lee, Frederick Buttel, Robyn Eckersley, and Michael Redclift.)

Thus the whole earth image, which inspires and evokes in us impulses of concern, humility, and wonder, also emerges from and embodies a worldview with troubling environmental implications. We cannot hope for pristine tools and images in our work toward livable environments; but critically evaluating and rebuilding these is part of that work.

Yaakov J. Garb

Further Readings

Garb, Y.J. "The Use and Misuse of the Whole Earth Image." *Whole Earth Review* 45

(1985): 18–25.

———. "Attitudes Toward Nature: An Analysis of Visual Imagery." In *Essays on Perceiving Nature*. Ed. D. DeLuca. University of Hawaii Perceiving Nature Conference Committee, 1988.

———. "Perspective of Escape? Ecofeminist Musings on Contemporary Earth Imagery." In *Reweaving the World: The Emergence of Ecofeminism*. Ed. I. Diamond and G. Orenstein. 1990.

Hendrikson, A.K. "The Map as an 'Idea': The Role of Cartographic Imagery during the Second World War." *The American Cartographer* 2 (1975): 19–53.

Merchant, Carolyn. *Ecological Revolutions: Nature, Gender, and Science in New England*. 1989.

Sachs, Wolfgang. *Global Ecology: A New Arena of Political Conflict*. 1993.

———. *The Development Dictionary: A Guide to Knowledge as Power*. 1992.

See also CONSERVATION MOVEMENT; *Ecologist*; ECOSYSTEMS; EHRLICH, PAUL; ENVIRONMENTALISM; FORESTRY, HISTORY OF; GAIA HYPOTHESIS; *Limits to Growth*; NATIONAL SECURITY, RECONCEPTUALIZING; NATURE; *Our Common Future*; RESOURCISM; STOCKHOLM CONFERENCE; SUSTAINABLE DEVELOPMENT

Wild Bird Trade

Trade in live wild birds is a huge international business. An estimated 9 percent of all bird species are affected by the trade, and for some—particularly a number of parrots and finches—it is the chief threat to their survival. One species, Spix's macaw (*Cyanopsitta spixii*), has been reduced by illegal trapping to a single wild individual, though a few dozen birds survive in captivity. Chicks from the last known nest of this species were offered on the international market for $40,000.

In recent years there has been an intensive effort on the part of many conservationists to end the international wild bird trade altogether. Others argue that the trade should be retained but put on a sustainable basis; and projects intended to do so have been set up in Senegal, Suriname, and Indonesia. This disagreement has caused an intense and often bitter debate within the conservation community. In 1994 the nineteenth General Assembly of the World Conservation Union (IUCN) passed a resolu-

tion calling for a moratorium on imports and exports of wild birds by January 1996 if the requirements of the Convention on International Trade in Endangered Species of Wild Fauna and Flora (CITES) and of sustainability are not being met; however, the United Kingdom, speaking for the European Community (EC), stated that they would not comply with this recommendation.

Wild birds in trade are almost always intended to be sold as pets. There are exceptions, such as birds of prey traded for falconry and bustards (*Otididae*) valued in Arab countries as prey for falconers. Aviculturists and bird fanciers have therefore been responsible for much of the demand, particularly for parrots and African estrildid finches. Some breeders, however, are now coming to see the wild bird trade as a threat to their own efforts as wild-caught birds normally sell for far less than captive-bred or, particularly, hand-reared ones. For example, African finches fetch higher prices in Australia, where their import is banned, than they do in Europe, with the result that Australian aviculturists have made far greater efforts to breed them.

The volume of birds trapped for the trade can be staggering. Some 20 million birds, mostly small estrildine finches, are trapped annually by birdcatchers in Senegal, the major outport for birds in West Africa. Between 1981 and 1985 the United States imported over 703,000 neotropical parrots of at least ninety-six different species.

Mortality of birds in international trade varies, though it can be extremely high; it has been estimated that only 10 percent of the birds imported into the United Kingdom survive past their first year in captivity. Half of the birds trapped in Senegal may die before they are exported.

The most severe aspect of the problem of the wild bird trade is the effect of illegal—and therefore unregulated—trapping and smuggling. Many countries have passed laws severely restricting or banning the export of wild birds. However, these laws are often weakly enforced, and are avoided by smugglers who move birds across poorly-guarded borders into neighboring countries that do permit export. Many of the birds exported from Senegal almost certainly originate from other countries in West Africa. In South America between 10,000 and 40,000 parrots per month have been smuggled out of the Orinoco delta of Venezuela through Guyana and other countries. The density of macaw populations in the delta has declined drastically. Endangered hyacinth macaws (*Anodorhynchus hyacinthus*) from Brazil have been exported in large numbers through Argentina. Illegal trapping has reduced the population of hyacinths from an estimated 100,000 to a current level of no more than 3,000 birds.

Some countries, such as Indonesia, have established quotas for parrot exports. Quotas that have been set, however, are often too high and are frequently exceeded. A study of trade in parrots from the North Moluccas found both that there was insufficient biological information to identify sustainable levels of offtake and that quotas failed to take into account the substantial number of birds taken by trappers without permits. For at least some parrots setting a sustainable quota may be impossible; a model of effects of trade in red-fronted macaws (*Ara rubrogenys*) suggested that capture of as few as 3 percent of the population annually would result in a decline from which recovery would not be certain, even if harvesting were stopped.

Many birds popular in aviculture are listed on CITES Appendix I (most endangered) and Appendix II (potentially endangered). For example, forty-four species and subspecies of parrots were listed on Appendix I as of 1993, and are therefore barred from international commercial trade. All other parrots except the budgerigar (*Melopsittacus undulatus*), cockatiel (*Nymphicus hollandicus*) and ring-necked parakeet (*Psittacula krameri*) are listed on Appendix II.

Pressure from conservation and animal welfare organizations has led to restrictions on the trade in a number of countries. The EC bars some species from import. In 1992 the United States passed the Wild Bird Conservation Act, which banned the import of any bird species listed on the CITES appendices as of October 1993. In addition a growing number of international airlines are now refusing to carry shipments of wild birds.

The attention given to the international bird trade has largely ignored another serious component of traffic in wild birds. This is the very large internal trade in birds in countries like Brazil, Argentina, and Indonesia. Heavy trapping of seedeaters (*Sporophila spp.*) in the first two countries has led to serious declines in several species, despite the fact that they rarely show up in international trade. From 25 to 35 percent of chattering lories trapped in the North Moluccas are sold domestically within Indonesia. Because few statistics on domestic trade are kept, and it does not come under the purview of CITES, the scope of its effect on bird populations remains poorly understood.

Ronald Orenstein

Further Readings

Beissinger, Steven, and Noel Snyder, eds. *New World Parrots in Crisis*. 1992.

Carter, N., and D. Currey. *The Trade in Live Wildlife: Mortality and Transport Conditions*. Environmental Investigation Agency, London 1987.

Lambert, Frank. *The Status of Trade in North Moluccan Parrots with Particular Emphasis on* Cacatua alba, Lorius garrulus and Eos squamata. IUCN, 1993.

See also BIODEPLETION; CITES; TROPICAL RAINFORESTS; WORLD WILDLIFE FUND

Wilderness

Wilderness has been of interest to North Americans in part because so much wild land has been developed so quickly that a sense of loss has occurred within a single lifetime. In recent years the vestigial remains of natural ecosystems have become a focal point of the environmental movement. Underlying this interest is the reality that Western history itself has been partly defined by the tension between civilization and the idea of wilderness. Wilderness played a significant if unappreciated role in shaping first European and then North American culture.

The idea of wilderness, as articulated by historians and philosophers and as celebrated by poets, nature writers, and painters has had a major influence on the environmental movement. More recently, conservation biology and other disciplines have stressed that ecological problems either directly or indirectly affect the wilderness ecosystems that sustain most of the diversity of life on earth; in consequence, many environmental policy issues involve wilderness preservation (or "conservation"—a term sometimes used synonymously). An adequate treatment of wilderness, therefore, must incorporate its ecological, historical, political, and philosophical aspects.

Historical Considerations

Environmentalists emphasize the dramatic change in the relative balance between wilderness and civilization. Human population and settlement was historically sparse and scattered, and technologies and ideologies that determined interactions between culture and nature were relatively benign. The earth, its associated biological systems, and the flora and fauna seemed limitless and infinitely resilient to human assault. It has been argued that a fateful turn, from a condition of relative harmony and balance with nature to one of increasing dysfunctionality, occurred with the domestication of animals and the cultivation of cereal grasses. Others contend that agriculture itself is blameless, and that the relentless humanization of wild lands and destruction of native species is more a consequence of the increasing global dominance of European culture, the industrial revolution, and the rise of capitalism.

The North American continent, known to many of its native peoples as Turtle Island, is a case in point. When Europeans first came to the Americas they saw a vast, untamed wilderness inhabited only by "savages." By colonizing the so-called "new world" Europeans believed that they brought civilization and order, including a proper religion, to a chaotic and barbaric wilderness. The Columbian quincentenary offered opportunity for reinterpretation of the colonization of Turtle Island. Native Americans, joined by environmentalists, argued that the consequences of European colonization were unmitigated disasters for both natural ecosystems (ecological imperialism) and indigenous cultures (colonialism).

Whatever the interpretive frame used to judge the past recent events indicate that the earth's biophysical processes and natural ecosystems constitute a finite system. Wilderness is sometimes metaphorically conceptualized as an "endangered species," implying a change in the interpretive frame by which natural ecosystems are conceptualized. Whereas the wilderness was once perceived as without limit and as an obstacle to be overcome, natural ecosystems are now perceived as susceptible to not only injury but irreversible degradation. Anthropogenic factors increasingly appear to exceed in scope and consequence the natural limits of variability.

Rainforests are a case in point, as they are home to as yet unmeasured, even to the nearest order of magnitude, biodiversity. Since around 15,000 B.C.E. rainforests have covered 12 percent of the earth's surface; they now cover approximately half of that range—a consequence of exponential growth rates in human population and economic development. Conservation biologists estimate that the last of the world's rainforests may be eradicated by the year 2050, and with them the majority of the earth's flora and fauna. Wilderness preservation, under any name, thus figures prominently in efforts to prevent a mass extinction of species.

Ecological Considerations

Determining what is natural seems difficult if not impossible apart from wilderness ecosystems to which humanized ecosystems can be compared. International concern for wilderness preservation increased after creation of the United Nations (UN) Man and the Biosphere (MAB) program (1970). Under the MAB program more than 280 areas have been protected as "biosphere reserves" in over seventy countries; these biosphere reserves are designed primarily to protect biodiversity. With 110 participating countries the goal is "to develop a scientific basis linking the natural and social sciences for the rational use of the biosphere—that portion of the Earth which contains living organisms—and for the improvement of the relationship between humans and the environment." Considerable areas of the North American land mass have also been protected, including more than 90 million acres in the U.S. Wilderness Preservation System.

However, existing reserves around the world are in many ways failing, primarily because the loss of biodiversity and the degradation of natural ecosystems continues; accordingly, the rationale upon which such reserves are based has been subject to criticism and modification. Theory now appears to converge on the ideas that: 1) restoration as well as protection of wilderness ecosystems are necessary; 2) reserves should be large enough to stand alone whenever practical; 3) smaller reserves should be connected by corridors; 4) buffer zones should surround all reserves; and 5) human activities in buffer zones should be regulated through bioeconomic analysis, predicated on a respect for local culture, rather than conventional analysis that assumes the Western economic model as normative.

Scientific and philosophical debate, sometimes contentious, swirls around even such basic issues as defining wilderness ecosystems. Although the U.S. Wilderness Act (1964) defines wilderness as "an area where the earth and its community of life are untrammeled by man, where man himself is a visitor who does not remain," others argue that it is fallacy to think of wilderness as uninhabited by humans. Such issues are of increasing consequence, given the encroachment of human populations on histori-cally wild ecosystems, such as Amazonia.

Development of Amazonia proceeds largely on a Western economic model, guided by criteria that are indifferent to the implica-tions of economic development for either social or natural ecology. Critics of "development" believe that it is more accurately termed "maldevelopment," since it serves the interests of multinational corporations and Third World elites rather than indigenous peoples living in close relation to the land. Studies of native peoples by ethnobotanists and cultural anthro-pologists confirm that humans have occupied and modified natural ecosystems since prehis-tory. However, successful groups evolve ways of living in a condition of dynamic equilibrium with the ecosystem. In comparison to modern culture the influence of prehistoric aborigines on natural ecosystems was negligible, due to low population densities, appropriate technolo-gies, and belief systems (such as totemism) that encouraged reverence for nature.

Since World War II bioregionalism has emerged as the most fully developed alternative to the economic development model. Rather than profit and efficiency as guiding criteria bioregionalists emphasize local cultures living in close relation to the native flora and fauna in ways that preserve nature's economy. That is, human societies would function within the con-straints of natural limits to economic growth and human population. Bioregionalists argue that moving toward sustainability involves reinhabiting the land, since local residents are likely to have the intimate knowledge and ethi-cal concern necessary to preserve the land com-munity.

Political Considerations

Wilderness preservation involves national and international politics. The UN Conference on the Human Environment in Stockholm (1972) marks the dawning awareness that ecological problems, including the protection of endan-gered species as well as wilderness ecosystems, necessarily involves coordinated international approaches. Progress has been slow, notwith-standing modest successes such as the MAB program (1970) and the Montreal Protocol on Substances that Deplete the Ozone Layer (1987; 1990). More recently, the UN Conference on Environment and Development, known as the Earth Summit (1992), made some strides to-ward protection of biodiversity, and also ad-dressed questions of stabilizing population and greenhouse gases. To date the difficult equity issues raised by global ecocrisis and wilderness preservation have not been addressed; the con-sensus of expert opinion is that developed na-tions have a moral obligation to assume eco-nomic responsibilities that help Third World countries meet human needs consistent with wilderness preservation.

Wilderness politics in North America per-haps began with the creation of the Sierra Club (1892), although statutes regulating wildlife and lands were created as early as 1694, when Mas-sachusetts established a closed season on deer. Recent statutes which have helped preserve wild-life and lands in the United States include the Wilderness Act (1964), the National Environ-mental Policy Act (1969), the Endangered Spe-cies Act (1973), and the Alaska National Inter-est Lands Conservation Act (1980). Some environmental organizations argue that these statutes do not go far enough, since wilderness *ecosystems themselves* remain unprotected.

Notwithstanding what is termed "second wave" environmentalism, that addresses issues such as global ecology, equity, and biodiversity, so-called resourcism (reform environmentalism, progressive conservation movement) has been politically dominant throughout the twentieth century. The movement was given form by Gifford Pinchot and Theodore Roosevelt (c. 1907) as an anthropocentric, utilitarian phi-losophy. Resource conservationists view unhumanized ecosystems, such as old-growth forests, as a source of raw materials to fuel the advance of civilization. The guiding maxims are optimal exploitation and development of natu-ral resources for social utility, measured eco-nomically. While systems ecology, chaos theory, and conservation biology have made resourcism for the most part scientifically untenable, it still prevails politically. Resourcism has emerged in new guise as the so-called wise-use movement, interpreted by some as an "environmental back-lash." The environmental movement (called by a variety of names) has constituted the oppos-ing force in wilderness politics.

Beyond issues of public policy commenta-tors arrayed across a wide political spectrum have argued that wild lands offer some measure of security from totalitarian states and the threat of a global dictatorship. Recent history confirms that unhumanized ecosystems such as mountains, jungles, and forests provide cover for rebels and guerrillas that even military su-perpowers have been unable to penetrate suc-cessfully.

Psychological, Philosophical, and Ethical Considerations

Wilderness is not so much a thing as informed perception of natural relations among various parts of the world in which humankind lives. The knowledge provided by contemporary natural sciences, such as conservation biology and ethnobotany, arguably influence our changing perception of wild ecosystems. Just as the explorers who came to the Americas 500 years ago took back to Europe an image of a new world, a world of wild lands, people, and great wealth, and helped set in motion the modern age, so too the contemporary explorers of wild lands bring back information that might set in motion a new age, sometimes called the age of ecology.

It has been argued that the opportunity to explore and interact with wild nature during early childhood and adolescence is important to the normal growth and maturation of the psyche. Psychological research indicates that humankind has domesticated itself, which implies that wilderness recreation is important not only to adolescent development but to the nurture of the adult psyche. However, pursuit of outdoor recreation creates many unanticipated problems, including destructive human impacts on wildlife and natural ecosystems. Some wonder whether humans are not loving wild nature to death.

The idea of wilderness varies across time and place, reflecting its social construction, much like the boundaries that demarcate wilderness areas on maps. The distinctive modern idea of wilderness evolved over several thousands of years. Following the Neolithic revolution ancient peoples became increasingly aggressive in endeavors to humanize the land. They became aware of themselves as beings partially dependent upon but distinct from nature, and accordingly devised increasingly abstract and complicated explanatory schemes to account for their relation to, domination of, and separation from the natural world. These schemes recognized a limited mastery over the land through technology, while preserving the idea that some forces were beyond control; they also conceived of the landscape as divinely designed for human habitation, cultivation, and modification.

Ultimately the earth came to be conceived as valueless until humanized—no more than a standing reserve for the purposes of human appropriation. The first scientific revolution gave Western culture the idea that *man* was the master and possessor of nature. Everything that followed in the wake of modernism, such as the market economy, represented an unparalleled amplification of the exploitation of the wilderness for utilitarian ends. Accordingly some environmentalists (such as E.O. Wilson) argue that no "greening of society" will occur apart from an environmental ethic that embraces a wilderness concept. Perhaps a postmodern idea of wilderness indicates a path toward a deep ecological ethic that is also an ecological practice—a sustainable way of life in which humankind again lives in dynamic equilibrium with nature.

Max Oelschlaeger

Further Readings

Nash, Roderick. *Wilderness and the American Mind*. 2nd ed. 1973.

Oelschlaeger, Max. *The Idea of Wilderness: From Prehistory to the Age of Ecology*. 1991.

Snyder, Gary. *The Practice of the Wild*. 1990.

See also BIODIVERSITY; BIODEPLETION; CONSERVATION BIOLOGY; LANDSCAPE ECOLOGY; STOCKHOLM CONFERENCE; TROPICAL RAINFORESTS; WILDERNESS ACT

Wilderness Act

The Wilderness Act of 1964 (Public Law 88-577) provides the basic mechanisms by which Congress can legally set aside undeveloped federal land as wilderness. In seven sections it defines wilderness, outlines the extent of a National Wilderness Preservation system, and prescribes permitted uses, prohibited activities, and special provisions within wilderness.

The act defines wilderness generally as "an area where earth and its community of life are untrammeled by man"; such land, therefore, retaining a primeval character, without permanent human improvement, shall be protected and managed. In addition to this ideal language, the act includes more specific terms, that such land, "affected primarily by nature" is defined as providing outstanding opportunities for solitude and primitive recreation, of a minimum size to allow management, and may contain features of scientific, educational, scenic, or historical value. Consequently, the definition contains both ideal and practical aspects, but emphasizes naturalness and solitude.

A substantial portion of the act speaks to the extent of the system and the procedures for admitting areas. Fifty-four areas comprising 9.1 million acres were immediately admitted. In addition the act instructed the Secretary of Agriculture to review all U.S. Forest Service primitive areas, and the secretary of the interior to inventory all roadless areas in the National Park System, national wildlife refuges, and game ranges. In the absence of an enabling act for the Bureau of Land Management at that time, no provisions were made for designating wilderness for that agency. It also provided for open public hearings.

The most highly contested portion of the act provides for accepted and prohibited uses of wilderness areas. Roads, permanent or temporary, motor vehicles, motorized equipment, and mechanical transport are prohibited, except for emergency use or administration of the areas. However, substantial exceptions are outlined, including established uses of aircraft and motorboats, actions to control fire, insects, and disease, prospecting for minerals, continued applicability of mining and mineral leasing laws until 1983, water resource development, and livestock grazing, where already established.

The ideal expressed in the Wilderness Act is a product of the thinking of an American literary tradition characterized by John Muir, Robert Marshall, Aldo Leopold, Sigurd Olson, and Wallace Stegner. The practical aspects of designation and exclusions represent political compromises.

In practical terms the first proposal for a national Wilderness System was put forward in 1951 by Howard Zahniser, executive director of the Wilderness Society. With support from David Brower, executive director of the Sierra Club, Zahniser lobbied Congress for an act that would replace the loose administrative categories under the discretion of federal administrators. His goal was a congressionally established system, responsive to public consensus, which would permanently protect wild areas. The bill Zahniser drafted, in conjunction with a number of citizen conservation groups, was first introduced in 1956, was hotly contested, went through sixty-five different versions, and was the occasion for eighteen hearings across the country.

In this process many features of Zahniser's proposal were lost, including lands administered by the Bureau of Indian Affairs and Forest Service primitive areas. A National Wilderness Advisory Council was eliminated, and prohibitions on non-wilderness uses were less restrictive.

The importance of the Wilderness Act of 1964 extends beyond its specific aims. Marking growing dissatisfaction with the degrading natural environment and with the discretionary rights of federal agencies—especially the Forest Service—it was the first of a set of environmental laws which, responding to broad public perceptions, would enable the U.S. Government to assess the quality and regulate the degradation of resources of land, biota, air, and water.

Michael P. Cohen

Further Readings

Hendee, John, et. al., eds. *Wilderness Management.* 1978.

Nash, Roderick. *Wilderness and the American Mind.* 1967.

See also BIOSPHERE RESERVES; BROWER, DAVID; FOREST SERVICE (U.S.); NATIONAL PARKS: UNITED STATES; WILDERNESS; ZAHNISER, HOWARD

Wilderness Society

The Wilderness Society is one of the "big ten" environmental advocacy organizations in the United States. Its overriding mission, as its name implies, is to work for the preservation of roadless, undeveloped land in North America. The society was founded in 1935 by Robert Marshall, Aldo Leopold, Benton MacKaye, Harvey Broome, Bernard Frank, Harold C. Anderson, Ernest Oberholtzer, and Robert Sterling Yard. It was chiefly financed by Marshall until his death in 1939; and through the Robert Marshall Wilderness Fund, until that fund was depleted by efforts to preserve wilderness in Alaska in the mid-1970s.

In its early years the society focused on lands managed by the U.S. Forest Service and National Park Service. It was an active participant, for example, in preventing the San Gorgonio Primitive Area in the San Bernardino National Forest from being developed as a ski resort. Also, along with the Sierra Club and Izaac Walton League, the society was heavily engaged for five years (roughly 1950–1955) in defeating a proposed federal project to construct a major dam in Echo Park Canyon in Dinosaur National Monument, along the Utah-Colorado border.

In 1955, following the long-awaited resolution of the Echo Park controversy, the Society's co-director, Howard Zahniser, drafted the first "wilderness bill." The purpose of this proposed legislation was to establish a nation-wide system of wilderness lands. In 1964, nearly ten years and many debates later, such a bill—though much weaker than the original one—was finally passed into law. Major projects from 1964 to 1976 included active support of the Alaska Native Claims Settlement Act, passed in 1971; active support for the Eastern Wilderness Act, passed in 1973; and active support for the Federal Land Policy and Management Act and National Forest Management Act, both passed in 1976.

In the 1980s, several environmentalists with important Washington connections were hired in critical positions. For example, Gaylord Nelson—recognized as the "founder" of Earth Day in 1970 and a respected senator from Wisconsin for several terms—became the organization's chairman, a full-time paid position. Cecil Andrus, formerly President Jimmy Carter's Secretary of Interior, became the society's corporate consultant. The organization continued to work on particular wilderness preservation projects, and was instrumental in writing and helping to get passed new wilderness legislation exemplified by the addition in 1984 of 8.6 million acres to the National Wilderness Preservation System.

Today the Wilderness Society is among the more financially-stable environmental groups in the United States. Recent major projects include helping to protect ancient forests of the Pacific Northwest and California; prevent oil drilling in the Arctic National Wildlife Refuge; implement comprehensive planning for the Greater Yellowstone Ecosystem; expand the National Wilderness System; promote policies to preserve biological diversity; and expand the United States' system of officially designated wild and scenic rivers.

James M. Glover

Further Readings

Fox, Stephen. *John Muir and His Legacy: The American Conservation Movement.* 1981.
———. "We Want No Stragglers." *Wilderness* (Winter 1984): 5–19.
Glover, James M. *A Wilderness Original: The Life of Bob Marshall.* 1986.

See also ALASKA: PARK, WILDERNESS, AND RESOURCE ISSUES; ECHO PARK DAM; IZAAK WALTON LEAGUE; MARSHALL, BOB; SIERRA CLUB; WILDERNESS; WILDERNESS ACT; YELLOWSTONE NATIONAL PARK

Wildlands Project

The Wildlands Project promotes the restoration and protection of all intact ecosystems and native biological diversity in North America. Officially incorporated as North American Wilderness Recovery, the ambitious effort was officially launched in 1992 with the publication of a special issue of *Wild Earth*, a journal begun by Dave Foreman, cofounder of Earth First! The emerging discipline of conservation biology guides the strategy. (The project's science director is Reed Noss, who in 1992 also became the editor of the journal, *Conservation Biology.*) Conservation biologists stress the importance of integrating diverse types of ecological research to determine the habitat requirements for species. This data can be entered into Geographic Information Systems databases, making it possible to map the habitat requirements for species and the status of ecosystems, thereby providing models that ecologists and biodiversity activists can use to articulate conservation priorities.

The project intends to support scientific research and mapping of North America, collate various mapping efforts, and evaluate the mapping conducted by government agencies. Thus it hopes to determine "wilderness core reserves," "buffer zones," and "connecting corridors" that would ensure ecosystem viability. The core reserves would permit little human presence; the surrounding buffer zones would allow only those human activities that have been proven as compatible with the flourishing of the core reserves; and inter-regional corridors (themselves surrounded by buffers) would link the reserves. These corridors would allow species to migrate between reserves, thereby reducing the danger that disruptions in one reserve would produce extinctions; corridors would also ensure a wider interchange of genetic material—another key element of biological diversity. Project proponents assert that systems of connected and buffered reserves represent the best prescription for preserving intact, diverse ecosystems.

The project's political strategy is to draw together scientists, grass-roots biodiversity activists, private landholders, and environmental groups such as the Nature Conservancy to secure critical habitat while simultaneously lobbying North American governments to support research and policies congruent with managing ecosystems for long-term biological diversity.

Bron R. Taylor

Further Readings

Grumbine, R. Edward. *Ghost Bears: Exploring the Biodiversity Crisis.* 1992.

Hudson, Wendy, ed. *Landscape Linkages and Biodiversity.* 1991.

Noss, Reed F., and Allen Y. Cooperrider. *Saving Nature's Legacy: Protecting and Restoring Biodiversity.* 1994.

Soule, Michael. *Conservation Biology: The Science of Scarcity and Diversity.* 1986.

See also BIODEPLETION; BIODIVERSITY; CONSERVATION BIOLOGY; EARTH FIRST!; HABITAT FRAGMENTATION, PATCHES, AND CORRIDORS; LANDSCAPE ECOLOGY; RADICAL ENVIRONMENTALISM

Wildlife Conservation Society

See ZOOS: INSTITUTIONS IN TRANSITION

Wildlife Protection: History

Wildlife protection is a fairly recent concept in the United States. Although Euroamericans have appreciated animals for hundreds of years, the late nineteenth century marked the first period of organized, systematic attempts to legislate treatment of wild creatures.

At that time an increasingly urban population, removed from the processes of the natural world, looked to the wilderness and its inhabitants with increasing interest. City dwellers turned to the outdoors, sparking the first "back to nature" movement. John Muir, a mountaineer and founder of the Sierra Club, observed this trend in his book, *Our National Parks* (1901). "Thousands of tired, nerve-shaken, over-civilized people," he wrote, "are beginning to find out that . . . wildness is a necessity." For many urban Americans, contact with animals— the embodiment of wilderness—became a way to regain their lost vitality.

As interest in wild animals increased, so did the desire to protect them. Sport hunters were among the first to advocate wildlife legislation. Their call for conservation was conveyed through a variety of journals, including *American Sportsman, Forest and Stream, Field and Stream,* and *American Angler*—all of which emerged during the 1870s and 1880s.

In part, what pushed sport hunters toward conservation in the late nineteenth century was an alarming decline in wildlife populations. Especially poignant was the destruction of the passenger pigeon and the buffalo—two species with large populations that were decimated in an unusually rapid period. Many Euroamericans had viewed the supply of game in the New World as being limitless. The extinction of the passenger pigeon and near-extinction of the buffalo, however, signaled to some that comprehensive restrictions on hunting had become essential. The problem was not killing for sport, but killing for profit. Market hunters supplied eastern markets with a staggering variety and number of wild animals.

Many sport hunters, on the other hand, wished to dissociate themselves from the destructive habits of poachers and market hunters. A well-born Englishman, William Henry Herbert—also known as "Frank Forester"— outlined good field etiquette and the proper methods of gunning and angling in his two-volume *Field Sports* (1848). In addition to promoting English hunting values to American sportsmen, Herbert urged that they band together to protest the mercenary destruction of game. Organizations such as the Boone and Crockett Club, formed in 1888, attracted gentleman hunters who lobbied for protection of wildlife. Accordingly, Congress passed the Lacey Act of 1894, which permitted jail sentences and fines for the wanton destruction of wildlife in Yellowstone National Park, and the Lacey Act of 1900, which prohibited the smuggling of protected game into states without restrictions.

In the late nineteenth and early twentieth centuries, sport hunters also sought to protect birds. Toward this end they joined numerous bird lovers, many of whom were women, who hoped to protect these animals from destruction. During this time, market hunters killed large numbers of birds to supply the markets for food and fashion. Decorative plumes for women's hats had become especially profitable. The National Association of Audubon Societies, established in 1905, worked to inform the public about the destruction of birds and lobbied for stronger federal involvement in the conservation of wildlife. Using the Forest Reserve Act, President Theodore Roosevelt in 1903 set aside Pelican Island in Florida as a refuge for egrets, pelicans, and terns. Although appreciative, the Audubon Society recommended that additional federal lands important to bird populations be protected. By 1904, President Roosevelt had created more than fifty sanctuaries. Wardens—some of whom were hired by the Audubon Society—patrolled these lands to ensure the enforcement of game laws.

In 1913, Congress passed the Weeks-McLean Act, which accorded federal protection to migratory game birds.

Humanitarians joined sport hunters and bird lovers in advocating wildlife protection in the late nineteenth and early twentieth centuries. However, humanitarians differed from the other two groups in their emphasis on individual animals rather than species and in their concern for animal suffering. Sport hunters desired to protect wildlife to ensure that humans could continue hunting, and bird lovers wanted to protect attractive creatures that humans could admire and observe. In contrast, humanitarians worried about cruelty to animals. To them, capacity for feeling became the basis for protection of animals.

Largely influenced by English thinkers, American humanitarians established animal welfare societies concerned not only with domestic creatures but also with wildlife. The Society for the Prevention of Cruelty to Animals, formed in the United States in 1866, advocated protecting buffalo and wild birds. Humanitarians, however, were far from single-minded. Some focused on the duty of humans to be merciful to inferior animals; others assumed the more radical position that sentient creatures have rights. The various factions of the humane movement became increasingly specialized, as they organized to oppose hunting, meat-eating, and the confinement of wild animals in zoos and circuses.

Few advocates for wildlife protection extended their sympathy to include predators during the late nineteenth and early twentieth centuries. Sport hunters, bird lovers, and humanitarians denounced these carnivorous animals, often depicting them as greedy and rapacious as well as inconvenient to humans. Wolves were especially hated and feared during this period, and conservationists joined ranchers in arguing for their extermination in the late nineteenth and early twentieth centuries. As the federal government increasingly assumed responsibility for predator control throughout the West, populations of rodents and ungulates exploded, at times resulting in destruction of vegetation and starvation of animals.

As scientists revealed the necessity of predation in the 1920s and 1930s, advocates for wildlife protection gradually came to appreciate the role of wolves and other carnivores in natural systems. The environmental movement of the 1960s and 1970s produced a new ethic regarding wild animals—one based on

ecological precepts. Aldo Leopold, author of *A Sand County Almanac, with Essays on Conservation from Round River* (1949), became its leading spokesman. Before his death in 1948, Leopold suggested that "A thing is right when it tends to preserve the integrity, stability, and beauty of the biotic community. It is wrong when it tends otherwise." Environmentalists developed a strong interest in saving grizzlies and wolves—animals that had been despised for centuries. These predators, protected under the Endangered Species Act of 1973, became important symbols of the wilderness.

In the late twentieth century, motivations for protecting wildlife remained diverse and complex. Like early humanitarians, animal rights advocates continued to emphasize individual creatures and the need to protect them from suffering. Environmentalists focused on the need for species diversity. These two groups, which sometimes overlapped, remained controversial. Many Americans resisted the idea that animals should be valued apart from their usefulness to humans—and wolves and grizzlies continued to be killed in the West in the early 1990s. Still, that this issue sparked a debate at all indicated how much attitudes toward wildlife had changed.

Lisa Mighetto (Historical Research Associates, Seattle)

Further Readings

Dunlap, Thomas R. *Saving America's Wildlife.* 1988.

Mighetto, Lisa. *Wild Animals and American Environmental Ethics.* 1991.

Nash, Roderick Frazier. *The Rights of Nature: A History of Environmental Ethics.* 1989.

Reiger, John F. *American Sportsmen and the Origins of Conservation.* 1986.

See also Animal Rights; Bambi; Bears: Conservation and Habitat; Bison: Conservation and Habitat; Endangered Species Act (U.S.); Hawk Shooting; Leopold, Aldo; Muir, John; National Audubon Society; Passenger Pigeon; Top Predators in Canada: An Overview; Ungulates; Wilderness; Wolf: A Conservation Challenge; Yellowstone National Park

Willingness-to-Pay
See Contingent Valuation

Wind Energy

Wind energy has been used by sailing ships since about 5,500 years ago, probably first in the Mediterranean region. Evidence for the use of wind energy through turbines is present from about 2,500 years ago in India and later China and Persia. The most commonly used technique was a vertical axis turbine, often with blades made of cloth or wood. The European Renaissance about 500 years ago saw the development of horizontal axis turbines, which were perfected to the Dutch-type windmills during the following centuries. Around 1900 modern aerodynamical blade construction was introduced by Paul la Cour in Denmark, and wind turbines based upon this concept were abundant for a number of decades. These devices produced mechanical energy and direct current (DC) electricity, in competition with steam turbines based on fossil-fuel burning. Wind energy lost this competition, but remained a source of energy on many islands and isolated regions (e.g., in the form of multiblade wind turbines used for pumping water).

Following incidents of disrupted fossil-fuel supply (Suez crisis 1956–1957, Arab supply refusal 1973–1974), several countries adopted programs for rapid development of alternative energy sources. Among these, grid-connected alternating current (AC) power producing windmills were developed by J. Juul in Denmark, and several such concepts were put into production during the 1970s. Presently Denmark is the lead country with 3 to 4 percent of total electric power produced by wind turbines, followed by California, Holland, and Germany. Current energy planning in several European countries calls for 10 percent of electricity produced by wind before the year 2000.

One advantage of the present generation of wind turbines is the modular concept that allows for either decentralized siting or concentration in wind turbine farms. Each turbine unit is currently 400–1000 kilowatts (kW), the result of a continuous increase in size since the new interest in wind energy started in 1975 when average turbine size was about 30 kW. In densely populated areas, environmental protection of landscapes sets limits to the installation of turbines, which has led to a new development of offshore wind farms, the first of which has been operating in Denmark for a few years. Wind conditions are typically better over sea, thereby partly offsetting the higher cost of maritime foundation work.

More closely viewed a modern wind turbine consists of a tower (metal and concrete construction is preferred over steel-truss construction, for environmental reasons) and a nacelle with two or three long, slender blades. The blades are made of fiberglass, advanced coal fibers, or laminated wood. The nacelle usually houses a transmission shaft with a gear exchange and an electric generator, plus yawing and control mechanisms. In some constructions the blade pitch may be altered, and some form of automatic brake prevents excessive speed. In case an induction generator is used, the attachment of the electric generator itself to a large grid provides a firm speed control, whereas for synchronous generators, an electronic speed controller has to be added. Several other wind turbine concepts have been researched, but the one just described has gained universal approval by manufacturers.

Wind energy is presently seen as very attractive, because of its low level of environmental impacts, as compared with fossil or nuclear power plants. However, it is important to realize that two considerations fold into the assessment of wind-based power: first is the availability of wind; and second are the impacts caused by the balance of the system, including energy storage if the entire utility network contains only renewable energy converters with varying output.

Wind energy is created as a result of the interplay between the earth's rotation and the input of solar radiation. The day-night cycle produces differential warming of the atmosphere, and the varying friction offered by different land profiles and surface textures combine to produce quite complex patterns of wind. The total fraction of the solar radiation input, which is converted to wind, is small (just under 1 percent) but the amount of wind energy intercepted by a well-placed wind turbine is often higher than the amount of solar radiation falling on an area of the same size. In broad terms mid-latitudes are the most favorable for wind energy, and smooth surfaces such as oceans or plains have higher average winds than rugged surfaces.

For the interconnected electric utility grids prevailing in industrialized countries, the current structure can accommodate up to about 25 percent wind energy without serious problems due to the variability of wind inputs. For higher penetrations of wind energy, it becomes necessary to install either energy storage or back-up units with rapid startup times. The energy stores may be furnished by reservoir-based hydro power, in regions where this renewable energy source is available, or it could be supplied by battery storage, compressed air storage, or a fuel such as hydrogen or methane, produced by surplus wind power or other renewable energy sources.

Environmental impacts associated with wind turbines are land use, visual impact, noise, telecommunication interference, and microclimate alterations. None of these impacts are large-scale and most can be controlled through proper technology. Furthermore, they are reversible in the sense that they disappear if the turbines are removed. A few are not controllable, such as the aerodynamic noise similar to that of the natural wind hitting trees and buildings, and the possible effects of locally slowing down the speed of winds, as one would do if a significant amount of energy is extracted in a given location (large wind parks).

Other impacts, such as social and economic impacts, are well-studied. Social impacts arise from manufacture and maintenance work, while the direct economic impacts are currently close to that of conventional energy systems.

Bent Sørensen

Further Readings

Sørensen, Bent. *Renewable Energy*. 1979.
———. "A History of Renewable Energy Technology." *Energy Policy* 19 (1991): 8–12.

See also HYDROELECTRICITY; NONRENEWABLE RESOURCES; SOFT ENERGY PATHS; SOLAR ENERGY

Wolf: A Conservation Challenge

The wolf is among the world's most persecuted species. Almost since settlement days in North America it has appeared atop the lists of the most feared and the most hated. Still today, wherever it lives, it is the most controversial species of wildlife. Concurrently the wolf, seen as a symbol of vanishing wilderness, has many supporters who recognize its worth, both to humans and as part of ecological communities. Television specials about the wolf break viewer records, and sales are brisk for books, magazines, calendars, audio and video tapes—anything featuring wolves.

There is a mystique about the wolf, expressed in childhood stories about Russian troikas racing from danger, and Jack London fic-

tional accounts of glinting eyes just beyond the light of the campfire and death in the snow. Along with "The Three Little Pigs," and "Peter and the Wolf," such stories plant, in generations of children as well as adults, the totally mythical danger wolves present to human life. And yet the howl of a wolf floating across a northern lake in the evening shadows enriches many backpacking and canoe trips. It is the highlight; the crowning experience; and the event most talked about back home.

How can one species represent such a paradox? What has that paradox meant to its welfare? And how will it influence its future? How we treat the wolf and its habitat represents one of the most significant challenges in conservation, both practically and ethically. It is litmus to no less than the depth of our environmental conscience.

Once the wolf was the largest ranging terrestrial mammal in the world, living in all environments except the hottest desert regions of the Northern Hemisphere, found across Europe, Asia, North and Central America, and northern Africa. However, the wolf's inherent adaptability and behavioral plasticity, reflected by such an enormous range and diversity of habitats and prey species, has failed to protect it over much of that area. It has been killed, or has vanished as a result of habitat loss, from urban and most agricultural regions. Even sparsely settled lands in western United States and in south-central and south-western Canada have lost the wolf through deliberate "control" programs and unregulated human shooting, snaring, and trapping.

As a consequence the wolf is listed as "vulnerable" in the Red Book of Endangered Species—the master list compiled by the International Union for the Conservation of Nature and Natural Resources (IUCN). The entry under gray wolf reads: "exterminated over large areas of its range and seriously depleted in much of the remainder. It must be considered as highly vulnerable until human attitudes towards the species change." Most recent population estimates suggest that approximately 88,000 wolves live in the former Soviet Republics; 58,500 in Canada; approximately 10,000 in China, mostly in Inner Mongolia; 7,500 in the United States, mostly in Alaska (6,000); between 5,000 and 2,000 in former Yugoslavia; 2,000 or less in each of Iran, Afghanistan, India, Rumania; and 1,000 in each of Poland, Spain, and Portugal. Even smaller remnants hang on in Finland, Sweden, and Saudi Arabia.

"Gray wolf," "timber wolf," "Arctic wolf," and "tundra wolf" are all subspecies of the same species, *Canis lupus*. The red wolf of eastern United States, *Canis rufus*, is a different species, extirpated in the wild by the mid-1900s. It has been the subject of apparently successful recovery programs in the late 1980s in North Carolina and Tennessee. Different, too, is the coyote, *Canis latrans*, sometimes called by the confusing misnomer "brush wolf." Coyotes, in comparison with wolves, have advanced their range with human settlement. They do well in agricultural and even urban lands provided ravines or scattered woodlots are present.

The most contentious aspect of gray wolf behavior is its predatory activities on ungulates (hoofed mammals). Because predators kill, prey populations superficially might appear to decline. At the moment of predation that may be the case. But if prey numbers are just as great in subsequent breeding seasons, and just as many females breed, then the effects of predation have been only temporary. Such situations occur if a prey population offsets its losses with increased breeding, known as "compensatory reproduction." This form of compensation occurs if range conditions, and therefore nutrition, improves for remaining prey animals. For example, moose (*Alces alces*) and white-tailed deer (*Odocoelius virginianus*) under good nutrition tend to twin more commonly and to breed at an earlier age.

Similarly, losses from predation may be irrelevant if the prey population approaches the maximum size the range can hold based on available nutrition, known as the "nutrient-climate ceiling." In a prey population of that size, either predators would claim lives or starvation would ensue, or both. In this situation, wolf predation is considered to represent "compensatory mortality."

Because of the possible compensations in prey populations, and other factors such as the presence of buffer prey species to absorb some effects of predation, wolf predation has been shown to influence a prey population in a variety of ways. In slightly more than half the studies in which conclusions can be drawn, wolves appear to have limited the size of the prey population. In other situations their predation is irrelevant. Under good conditions of range and climate ungulate populations even have been shown to erupt in numbers despite the presence of a wolf population.

Painstaking research, and not just casual observation, is required to interpret the relationship between wolves and their prey—one of nature's truly complex relationships. The desire to hold an opinion about wolves (even when based upon little evidence), often bolstered by the similarly superficial evidence of others (especially after an unsuccessful hunt) characterizes much hostility against wolves. Such casual observations have been, and on occasion still are translated into political pressure for wolf control. Sometimes, a veneer of science is thrown over such control operations by setting them up "experimentally," with a non-kill area for comparison. Without control of environmental variables, such as weather or abundance of other large mammal species that may influence predatory relationships, results of such experiments are difficult to evaluate. By then, of course, the killing of wolves has taken place; the people who called for such action have been appeased; and so the political objective has been reached. Increasingly, however, people question the morality of such heavy-handed science, which adds yet even more controversy.

Such political demand for wolf control has occurred in western Canadian provinces and in Alaska repeatedly in recent years. Sometimes, even when biological data have been adequate to suggest that wolves were limiting their prey, enormous public protests against the killings have taken place. Clearly, now, there are considerable political costs to government wolf killing that may tip the balance away from such actions in the future.

Wolves are contentious, too, because at times they kill livestock. Such killing occurs almost exclusively in fringe agricultural areas, because good agricultural land normally is cleared and not adequate for wolves. Governments have countered with wolf control, wolf bounties, or with subsidies for livestock losses. Researchers have experimented with the use of various aversion techniques such as emetics placed in meat, or the employment of guard dogs.

Despite persecution the wolf has survived in much of the northern half of North America, where habitat is still suitable and extensive, and human populations are low. Its survival rests on several factors. Some provinces list the wolf as both a game and a furbearing animal and so regulate its kill in game management zones as is done for other species. Gone are the days of indiscriminate, widespread bounties. Provincial and territorial wildlife policies increasingly have recognized that old procedures of outright persecution, practiced until the 1950s and 1960s, are no longer valid with today's greater public interest and concern over wildlife and wild lands. Both British Columbia and Alaska have considered zoning plans for wolves under a policy that wise management must cater to a spectrum from complete protection, to managed exploitation, to more intensive provision of human hunting success. What may be an ecologically, and publicly, responsible balance among such zones, is, however, difficult to decide.

Research on wolves is curtailed by its expense, requiring the use of radio telemetry and aerial monitoring. Most research is conducted for short periods of time only, by governments anticipating or already practicing wolf control. Some independent, long-term university-based research occurs, notably on Isle Royale in Lake Superior and in Algonquin Provincial Park in Ontario. And federal governments have sponsored long-term studies in Lake Superior National Forest in Minnesota, and in Wood Buffalo and Riding Mountain national parks in Northwest Territories and Manitoba respectively. Objectives of such research often encompass assessments of the impacts of predation, and the spacing behavior of wolf packs. Other interesting new research focuses on wolf genetics, using techniques such as DNA fingerprinting to identify family relationship within and among packs. Additionally, there is interest today in the adequacy of parks in protecting large carnivores around the world, and the wolf is an example of the problem presented by such large-ranging space-demanding animals.

In 1968 famous pioneer wolf researcher, the late Douglas Pimlott, wrote: "The fate of the wolf will be determined in the latter decades of this century, when wolf kills approach the levels of recruitment in ungulate herds. What will our attitude be then? Will we be willing to share deer, moose, caribou with them?"

The broad societal answer is clearly "yes." On a percentage of population basis, less people hunt, and more people visit parks to enjoy and not kill wildlife than ever before. But native people increasingly want a historic subsistence component to their lifestyle. As well, for many residents living in depressed economic conditions in northern areas, "getting your moose" is of more than recreational interest.

Society may never reach consensus about wolves. But the extremely limited amount of formal protection for the species set against a possibly expanding environmental ethic gives one hope that our collective wisdom will neither allow us to further diminish the species' range, nor blot out its howls from our parks and remaining wild lands, because without the howl of the wolf to quicken the pulse of nature, true wilderness cannot exist.

John B. Theberge

Further Readings

Carbyn, L.N. *Wolves in Canada and Alaska.* Canadian Wildlife Service, 1983.

Hummel, Monte, and Sherry Pettigrew. *Wild Hunters: Predators in Peril.* 1991.

Pimlott, D.H. "Wolf Control in Canada." *Canadian Audubon Magazine* (November–December 1961).

See also ALGONQUIN PROVINCIAL PARK; BEARS: CONSERVATION AND HABITAT; COUGARS: CONSERVATION AND HABITAT; HABITAT FRAGMENTATION, PATCHES, AND CORRIDORS; IUCN; TOP PREDATORS IN CANADA: AN OVERVIEW; WILDLIFE PROTECTION: HISTORY

Wolverine

See TOP PREDATORS IN CANADA: AN OVERVIEW

Wolves

See WOLF: A CONSERVATION CHALLENGE

Women and the Environment

See ECOFEMINISM

Wood Buffalo National Park

Wood Buffalo National Park (44,807 square kilometers), Canada's largest and the world's second largest national park, straddles the border between Alberta and the Northwest Territories. Despite its remoteness and rather difficult access the park, which attracts approximately 6,000 visitors each year, is one of Canada's most threatened. Originally established in 1922 to protect the last rapidly declining herd of wood bison, it is an excellent example of the northwestern boreal plain. Large tracts of various boreal ecosystems remain in a wilderness state, including North America's largest undisturbed grass and sedge meadows—prime habitat for bison.

The mighty Peace and Athabasca rivers merge within the park and empty into Lake Athabasca. At the confluence lies one of the world's largest and finest inland deltas. It attracts waterfowl by the millions. The park contains extensive salt plains, unique in Canada, where salt springs emerge from the base of a low escarpment. Salt deposited on the surface forms mounds which can be up to two meters high and nine meters long.

A portion of the park consists of dense boreal forest interspersed with muskeg, countless bogs, swamps, and meandering streams. These features are the product of a vast underground water system which dissolves the underlying gypsum bedrock, causing surface collapse. The resulting largest single karstland area in the world provides the only natural nesting habitat for the whooping crane, an endangered species whose population has been brought from the brink of extinction to approximately 140 birds in 1992.

The park also harbors bald eagles and the southernmost breeding population of the rare peregrine falcon. It is home to approximately 3,500 bison, the largest free-roaming and self-sustaining bison herd in existence; as well it supports the highest density of wolves on the continent. In 1983 Wood Buffalo National Park was named a UNESCO World Heritage Site, "one of the world's most priceless and irreplaceable natural treasures."

However, the continued existence of the park's exceptional features and wildlife depends on the maintenance of a delicate ecological balance. The construction in 1968–1970 of the W.C. Bennett Dam on the Peace River in British Columbia altered the water regime in the park. Because dramatic seasonal floods no longer occur dependent habitats and wildlife have suffered. The delta is slowly drying up, and the diversity of its flora and fauna will continue to decrease as long as the drying continues. In addition pollution from upstream paper mills and agriculture further affects the park's ecosystem and wildlife. Logging, a non-conforming park use, had been permitted. Some unusually old spruce forests were being lost until environmental groups challenged the matter in court and succeeded in ending the logging in 1992.

Although the park was established to protect wood bison the introduction of plains bison to the park in the 1920s resulted in an epidemic of bovine tuberculosis and brucellosis. Subsequent attempts to eliminate the diseases failed and, in a 1989 proposal, Agriculture Canada threatened to slaughter the entire herd. A solution to the presence of the two bovine diseases in the herd has not yet been found.

B. Theresa Aniskowicz

Further Readings
Aniskowicz, B.T. "Life or Death?" *Nature Canada* 19 (1990): 35–38.

See also BISON: CONSERVATION AND HABITAT; ENVIRONMENTAL CASE LAW (CANADA): COMMON LAW CAUSES OF ACTION; HYDROELECTRICITY; NATIONAL PARKS: CANADA; PEREGRINE FALCON; WOLF: A CONSERVATION CHALLENGE

World Bank

The International Bank for Reconstruction and Development, more commonly known as the World Bank, is an agency of the United Nations established in 1945 to make loans to member nations. As the largest single external source of funds for development projects the World Bank starting in 1982 was repeatedly accused of failing to integrate environmental values into its lending policies. Yet it has been a leader among international organizations; industrialized countries rely on it to play a major role in the formation of a policy consensus and in the management of environmental issues in the developing world; and, through the Global Environment Fund, it plays a major role in shaping the international agenda on environmental issues. The bank now agrees that environmental protection is an integral part of the development process and has adopted important initiatives to meet both objectives.

The World Bank was the first multilateral development agency to recognize the importance of environmental parameters in development lending and to create a unit in 1971 responsible for reviewing projects, suggesting ways to mitigate harmful environmental impacts, and sensitizing the rest of the organization and developing countries to these issues. Yet, quantification difficulties, the suspicions of developing countries, and internal resistance complicated the adoption of a progressive and sustained policy. A skeleton staff only reviewed projects after appraisal. The bank failed to follow its own guidelines; underestimated the capacity and willingness of local bureaucracies to follow agreed-upon provisions and schedules; and did not enforce negotiated agreements. Ignorance of the sociological, political, or natural context of projects led to many project failures, several of which became *causes célèbres*.

In 1987 the World Bank admitted that it had "stumbled" and vowed to increase lending, expand the staff, and strengthen project evaluation. Five priorities were identified: 1) destruction of natural habitats; 2) soil degradation; 3) depletion of freshwater resources; 4) pollution; and 5) global environmental issues. The bank's environment department is responsible for internal coordination, research and planning, staff support and training, data base development, and external relations, while environmental units in each regional division supervise environmental assessments and help develop national policies.

This reform was implemented slowly. Of the roughly $20 billion in total lending for fiscal year (FY) 1992, $1 billion—twice the 1991 amount—was allocated to free-standing environmental projects, many of which were disaster relief. The number of strict environmental projects did not increase spectacularly: two were funded in 1989; eleven in 1990; and thirteen in 1991, as against three in 1975 and 1980. Half the loans approved since 1990 contained environmental components, mostly in the agricultural sector, compared to 38 percent in 1989 and 7 percent in 1980 (the loose definition of what constitutes an environmental component makes comparisons difficult, however).

The bank requires an environmental assessment (EA) for every project likely to have a significant impact on the environment. Task managers classify projects according to their potential environmental impact into three categories (A, B, C), with full-fledged assessments to be conducted for category A projects, and limited ones for category B. Members of the environment department join the feasibility study team and draft a separate report made available before financial evaluation. Negotiations with the borrower cannot proceed without the green light from the regional environmental divisions (RED). EAs are the borrower's responsibility and vary in breadth, depth, and type of analysis. About 8 percent of all projects funded by the end of FY 1992 required a full assessment (most concerning the power and agriculture sectors); 39 percent more limited studies; and 42 percent none. In contrast the bank had estimated in the 1970s that two-thirds of its projects required no particular precaution. EAs are required for all sectoral projects but not for structural adjustment projects. Because in many countries EAs face problems linked to the weakness of environmental institutions, the lack of national policies, and the prevalence of lending for policy and small-scale projects, the bank has promoted national environmental action

plans (NEAP) and called for their urgent implementation. The Dublin Club of African countries, created in 1990, is intended to support the NEAP process through training, information sharing, network building, evaluation and monitoring. Thirty plans were expected to be completed by 1993.

The EA directives reinforced the organization's ability to stop or modify projects early, thus avoiding a subsequent whirlwind of political controversies. Only in 1985 did it suspend disbursements and only in 1989 did it cancel a loan for the first time for environmental reasons. In 1993, only after years of controversy, pressures from donors and nongovernmental organizations (NGOs), and the release of a critical report, did the bank withdraw its financial support for a controversial series of dams in India. In other cases outright bans rather than complex environmental assessments were preferred. The bank decided to stop lending for projects in fragile ecosystems in June 1986, declared an end to support for commercial logging in tropical forests in July 1991, and in June 1992 vowed never to finance the building of roads through virgin rain forests in Latin America.

The World Bank also insists that EAs and NEAPs take the needs of local peoples into account. It has agreed that indigenous groups should participate in the design and execution of bank-assisted projects that affect their welfare, but has encouraged them to develop a direct dialogue with their respective governments. The borrower must allow public participation as soon as a project is assigned to the A category. If it does not, or will not distribute information on the project, the bank may refuse to lend money. A 1991 U.S. congressional amendment also mandates the U.S. executive director to share information about all proposed projects likely to have significant environmental impacts. NGOs are increasingly involved in project design, and the bank officially supports their role in strengthening local participation in development planning.

Despite significant progress and the adoption of numerous environmental directives designed to guide project appraisal, obstacles remain. First, the blind transfer of foreign scientific models, techniques, and criteria has led to project designs unsuited to local conditions. Second, lending volume, the speed of project preparation, and the number of loans still matter to task managers and to member governments, whereas environmental guidelines complicate their task. Third, in response to various political pressures, the bank has accumulated different concerns that are often conflictual, ranging from economic growth, debt, and poverty reduction to sustainable development, public participation, and global environmental problems.

Fourth, environmental protection legitimizes orthodox political and economic conditions imposed on the borrowers. The bank argues that removing state subsidies and price controls, remedying inequitable fiscal policies, promoting the role of women, and controlling population growth all benefit the environment. These various links can trigger new oppositions since environmental concerns appear to cloak other interests and threaten political stability. Finally, few governments are ready to adopt drastic conservation measures unless the impact of environmental destruction compromises their political survival or the country's short-range development prospects. Borrowers will favor environmental projects that increase employment, that have visible and immediate benefits within the national boundaries, and that reinforce the authority of the state. Many developing countries also question the new global environmental agenda. They would prefer more people-oriented projects with visible political and human impacts. Indeed, the bank has acted chiefly when it could make an economic, social, or political link between environmental degradation and human welfare.

The bank hopes to improve performance by limiting its involvement in controversial projects, by creating the conditions for effective national implementation of agreed upon procedures, by internalizing environmental concerns through institutional and policy frameworks, by creating local constituencies, and by relying on NGOs for supervision. The emphasis is on gaining local support and commitment as well as increasing local capacities. At the same time its policy also reduces the control that it has over its own performance. EA procedures, intended to protect the bank from economic and political project failures, create new vulnerabilities as they throw the organization into the thicket of national politics. Environmental progress has thus reduced the autonomy of the organization by forcing it to assume a larger political role.

Philippe Le Prestre

Further Readings

Le Prestre, Philippe. *The World Bank and the Environmental Challenge.* 1989.
World Bank. *The World Bank and the Environment: A Progress Report, Fiscal 1991.* Environment Department. 1991.
————. *World Development Report 1992: Development and the Environment.* 1992.

See also ENVIRONMENTAL IMPACT ASSESSMENT; HYDROELECTRICITY; RIO CONFERENCE (1992); SUSTAINABLE DEVELOPMENT

World Commission on Environment and Development

See BRUNDTLAND, GRO HARLEM; *Our Common Future*; SUSTAINABLE DEVELOPMENT

World Conservation Union

Established in 1948 as the International Union for the Protection of Nature (IUPN), this forward-looking concern gradually assumed world leadership in its vital field and renamed itself in 1957 the International Union for Conservation of Nature and Natural Resources—hence the most familiar and widely-used acronym of IUCN, despite its further name-change latterly to The World Conservation Union. Under the presidency of Professor Jean Baer of Switzerland, IUCN had given rise (originally as its "fund-raising arm") to the World Wildlife Fund (WWF, now widely styled the World Wide Fund for Nature). The presidency of WWF was soon assumed by Prince Bernhard of the Netherlands, founder of the Order of the Golden Ark, and subsequently by the Duke of Edinburgh. With headquarters in Brussels for its first decade, IUCN later moved to a location near Lake Geneva before settling closer to the town of Geneva, Switzerland, in Gland, Canton of Vand.

The World Conservation Union is now a globally-operating and highly-influential union of sovereign states, government agencies, national and international nongovernmental organizations, and loyal friends and supporters who are dedicated to its most noble though basically very practical cause. According to its own 1993 pamphlet entitled *What is IUCN?* the organization is concerned with the initiation and promotion of scientifically based action "that will establish links between development and the environment, to provide a lasting improvement in the quality of life for people all over the world." This concern is rooted in a profound belief in the basic importance of the main themes indicated in its longer title of which the above acronym is probably by far the most-used globally in the entire field of conservation.

The stated mission of IUCN (as repeated in its 1993 pamphlet) is "[t]o provide leadership and promote a common approach to the world conservation movement in order to safeguard the integrity and diversity of the natural world, and to assure that human use of natural resources is appropriate, sustainable, and equitable." Accordingly, its main objectives are:

1. To ensure the conservation of nature, and especially of biological diversity, as an essential foundation for the future.
2. To ensure that wherever the earth's natural resources are used by humans this is done in a wise, equitable, and [so far as possible] sustainable way.
3. To guide the development of human communities toward ways of life that are both of good quality and in enduring harmony with other components of The Biosphere.

IUCN has fostered numerous allied or cognate activities through the voluntary networks provided by its system of commissions (currently six), an expanding number of regional and country offices, and its central secretariat at world headquarters provided in 1992 largely from far-sighted Swiss governmental sources. IUCN's address is Rue Mauverney 28, 1196 Gland, Switzerland (phone: (4122) 999-0001; fax: (4122) 999-0002). The Director-General until recently was Sir Martin W. Holdgate and is now H.E. David K. McDowell, formerly New Zealand ambassador to Japan.

Through these structures IUCN works to:

1. Monitor and evaluate the status of nature and natural resources, trends in their use, and policies and practices concerning their management;
2. Analyse the obstacles to more-effective protection of nature and management of natural resources;
3. Harness intellectual and operational resources in order to solve the problems revealed by the above analysis;
4. Catalyse action . . . in order to achieve more effective conservation of nature and natural resources in keeping with the principles set out in its *Caring for the*

Earth, the 1991 follow-up of its 1987 *World Conservation Strategy*;
5. Contribute to an increased global awareness of the interrelationships between conservation, long-term survival, and human well-being through publications, information, dissemination, and education;
6. Provide scientific advisory services to organizations;
7. Link the conservation constituency together as an effectively-operating entity for achieving conservation, building a dialogue with the corporate sector;
8. Cooperate with all agencies advocating reduced pressure on the "carrying capacity" of the world and reduction in the aggregate consumption of world resources; and
9. Develop national and regional strategies for sustainability, capacity-building, and institutional support—a process often led by IUCN regional and country offices in collaboration with governments and non-governmental organizations.

The elements of IUCN's structure include: 1) the General Assembly, which is convened every three years to determine policies and the broad elements of IUCN's programs; 2) the Council, which is elected by the General Assembly, and meets at least annually to review the execution of the program; and 3) the Commissions, consisting of "bodies of volunteer experts" who make a major contribution to the development and execution of the IUCN program. The six current commissions, in chronological order of establishment, are: Ecology, Education and Communication, Environmental Law, Environmental Strategy and Planning, National Parks and Protected Areas, and Species Survival. The IUCN Commissions constitute a global network of more than 6,000 scientific and other specialists

The chief executive of IUCN is its director-general, whose period of office is normally limited to a maximum of two three-year terms between general assemblies. The role of the director-general is to plan and coordinate the execution of the program with the support of the secretariat currently employing some 200 persons in its headquarters and another 500 elsewhere in the IUCN network outlined above.

Leading publications of IUCN include the already-mentioned *World Conservation Strategy* and *Caring for the Earth*, plus the *Global Biodiversity Strategy* which is "a systematic and comprehensive plan to protect the world's genes, species, and ecosystems," the *Red List of Threatened Animals* which is published periodically, *Red Data Books* and species *Action Plans* assessing international conservation priorities of various groups of plants and animals following the celebrated *Red Data Books*, the *United Nations List of National Parks and Protected Areas*, "which lists national parks, nature reserves, World Heritage sites, and biosphere reserves worldwide," and the *IUCN Bulletin* (the quarterly journal of the Union) and *Interact* (a forum for exchanging views among the membership). In addition there are many other newsletters produced by programs, specialist groups, and commissions of or connected with IUCN, while the library at headquarters is growing rapidly and, with an estimated potential of two kilometers of shelf-space, has the potential to become preeminent.

Regarding finance, IUCN membership constitutes a basic source of discretionary funds. Specific financing of programs and projects is also provided by multilateral organizations (including United Nations agencies such as UNESCO and UNEP), the Commission of European Communities, individual governments and aid-agencies, international nongovernmental organizations (such as WWF), foundations, the corporate sector, and individual donors. In 1993, the total expenditure of IUCN amounted to about 57 million Swiss francs.

As it grows in scope and size, one can only hope that IUCN will never become too large and self-satisfied to be effectively functional in serving its basic ends which become more and more crucial with the ever-increasing numbers and profligacy of humankind.

Nicholas Polunin

Further Readings

IUCN. *World Conservation Strategy: Living Resource Conservation for Sustainable Development.* 1980.

McNeely, Jeffrey A. *Economics and Biological Diversity: Developing and Using Economic Incentives to Conserve Biological Resources.* 1988.

See also CITES; SIERRA CLUB; UNITED NATIONS ENVIRONMENT PROGRAMME; WORLD WILDLIFE FUND

World Resources Institute

Founded in 1982 the Washington, D.C.-based World Resources Institute (WRI) is a not-for-profit corporation formed to provide research and technical assistance to governments (particularly in the developing world), to the private sector, and to environmentally-related nongovernmental organizations. WRI has a full-time staff of approximately 105 researchers, policy experts, and assorted technical personnel, complemented by a network of advisors and policy fellows in more than fifty nations. Its current budget is around $10 million, most of which is financed by private foundations, governmental and international agencies, and corporations.

WRI is headed by Jonathan Lash, former Vermont secretary of natural resources. His predecessor, James Gustave Speth, helped to found the Natural Resources Defense Council and was chair of the U.S. Council of Environmental Quality under President Jimmy Carter. Speth in 1993 moved on to become director of the United Nations Development Programme (UNEP).

In many ways WRI sees itself as an ecologically-oriented think tank that seeks above all to promote economic health without promoting environmental degradation. Its stated aim is to generate and disseminate accurate information about global resource and environmental conditions, assess current problems and forecast possible new ones, and to assist decisionmakers in both the private and public sectors in developing creative and technically-sophisticated responses to pressing needs. It does so primarily through a broad array of publications, conferences, and seminars, and by supplying mass media throughout the world with background materials and ecologically-focussed analyses.

WRI's current policy research programs focus particularly on biological resources and institutions (e.g., global biodiversity); economics and population (e.g, tax policies to promote environmental ends); climate, energy, and pollution (e.g., greenhouse gases); technology and the environment (e.g., technology diffusion); and resource and environmental information (e.g., world resource databases).

Christopher J. Bosso (with Chris Pierpan)

Further Readings

Foundation for Public Affairs. *Public Interest Profiles, 1992–1993.* 1992.

World Resources Institute. *World Resources Institute at a Glance.* 1993.

See also ENVIRONMENTALISM; NATURAL RESOURCES DEFENSE COUNCIL

World Wildlife Fund

The World Wildlife Fund (WWF) is one of the largest and most important conservation organizations in the world. In the United States it is based in Washington, D.C., and has a membership in excess of 1.25 million. It is the largest private organization in the United States working to protect endangered wildlife and wildlands; its emphasis is on the species and spaces within the tropical forests of Latin America, Asia, and Africa. WWF emphasizes ending the international trade in endangered wildlife, and establishing and protecting national parks and wildlife reserves throughout the world. Its U.S. president is Kathryn S. Fuller and the current chairman of the board is Russell E. Train. The annual budget of WWF (U.S.) grew from some $14 million in 1984 to nearly $60 million by 1992.

Internationally WWF is the World Wide Fund for Nature International and is based in Gland, Switzerland. By 1993 its affiliate and associate national organizations numbered twenty-eight (on five continents). The WWF logo, a giant panda over the letters WWF, is used in the activities of these organizations on a global basis; it is perhaps the most widely recognized symbol of conservation in the world. Since it was founded in 1961 WWF has invested in excess of $330 million in over 10,000 different projects in 130 different countries. WWF International funds scientific research on wildlife and supports everyday, on-the ground, conservation programs and initiatives on four continents (Europe, Asia, Africa, and Latin America); similar efforts are sponsored in the United States, Canada, and Australia by WWF national organizations in those countries. There is a considerable sponsorship of training programs for park and wildlife managers and the training and equipping of anti-poaching teams. Every effort is made to support existing local groups and governments in the efforts which they have undertaken themselves.

WWF has broadened its focus to include issues of sustainable development; it seeks to link wildlife conservation with the meeting of human needs in ways that do not threaten fragile habitats. In Nepal WWF has funded planting for fuelwood use so that the Annapurna Conservation Area can be protected from such harvests. As WWF (U.S.) has recently put it: "Land abuse, population growth, and pollution threaten some of the world's most critical ecosystems. WWF has long recognized that we cannot simply defend isolated species and habitat. To conserve the world's natural resources for future generations, we must also help alleviate the human crises and development pressures that put wildlands and wildlife in danger." WWF has thus entered campaigns and efforts regarding sustainable forestry practices, toxic emissions, climate warming, and more equitable trade between industrial and developing countries.

WWF efforts in Africa began in 1962 and in recent years have emphasized the protection of elephants, primates, hippos, and many other species. WWF's efforts in Africa have been carried out in cooperation with the Nature Conservancy, World Resources Institute, Wildlife Conservation International, and the African Wildlife Foundation. In Asia WWF's efforts are especially intensive in Indonesia, Bhutan, Philippines, Thailand, Papua New Guinea, and Nepal. Trade Record Analysis of Flora and Fauna in Commerce (TRAFFIC), WWF's large wildlife trade monitoring arm, is very active in Asia, seeking to halt trade in bear parts, and other endangered species in Taiwan, China, and elsewhere. TRAFFIC operates fifteen offices worldwide and has been responsible for shutting down smuggling operations involving rhinos, elephants, spotted cats, parrots, sea turtles, and tropical timber. In Latin America and the Caribbean WWF's conservation efforts are particularly notable throughout the tropical rainforests of South America, in Mexico and Central America, and with regard to endangered coral reefs. Internationally WWF works cooperatively with the World Conservation Union (IUCN), the International Council for Bird Protection, the International Waterfowl Research Bureau, and the Charles Darwin Foundation.

In the United States WWF is actively employed in the effort to halt trade in endangered species such as parrots; other activities include work with Native American conservation efforts, and conservation innovation grants. WWF is critical as a conservation lobbying organization within both the United States and Canada. In the United States it works to defend and foster the Endangered Species Act. WWF Canada, headed by Monte Hummel and based in Toronto, seeks to implement similar legislation, which does not yet exist in Canada. As well WWF Canada has sought an expansion of protected habitats and spaces, ultimately seeking protection for 12 percent of Canada's land area. An eloquent case for this latter goal was made in Hummel's *Endangered Spaces: The Future for Canada's Wilderness.*

Robert Paehlke

Further Readings

Dudley, Nigel. *Forests in Trouble: A Review of the Status of Temperate Forests Worldwide.* WWF International, 1992.

Hummel, Monte, ed. *Endangered Spaces: The Future for Canada's Wilderness.* 1989.

World Wildlife Fund (U.S.). *Annual Reports.*

See also BIODEPLETION; BIODIVERSITY; CITES; CONSERVATION MOVEMENT; CORAL REEFS; ELEPHANTS: CONSERVATION AND HABITAT; ENDANGERED SPECIES ACT (U.S.); IUCN; TROPICAL RAINFORESTS

Worldwatch Institute

The Worldwatch Institute (W.I.) may be the most frequently cited and influential environmental research institute in the world. It was founded in 1974 by agricultural economist Lester R. Brown with a startup grant from the Rockefeller Brothers' Fund. Based in Washington, D.C., W.I. seeks to inform a worldwide audience of decision makers, journalists, scholars, students, and the general public regarding the links between the world economy and its environmental support system. With more than thirty employees, many of whom are high-level experts on the environment and on public policies, it has become an important, independent, and nonprofit environmental think tank and research organization, and a global environmental early warning system. In fact W.I. gives the earth an annual physical check-up, examining its various vital signs and presenting blueprints for sustainability. The W.I. works toward raising the public's awareness of global environmental problems and of the ongoing deterioration of the earth's natural systems, and to influence policymakers to be responsive to demands for sustainable development and environmental protection.

Using a global, integrative, interdisciplinary, and policy-oriented approach the W.I. was among the first research institutes to focus attention on acid precipitation, ozone depletion, global climatic change, sustainable development, soil erosion, deforestation, ecological disasters in Eastern Europe, and wood, food, and water shortages in the Third World. Compiling documented evidence from around the world it publishes the famous annual report *State of the World: A Worldwatch Institute Report on Progress Toward a Sustainable Society,* which is nearly simultaneously translated in twenty-seven languages, a feat which even *Reader's Digest* does not surpass. This moderately priced paperback is read by hundreds of thousands of people all over the world. More than 100,000 English copies are now sold each year. An international survey by Pennsylvania State University researchers of 235 environmental leaders ranked *State of the World* third, behind Aldo Leopold's *Sand County Almanac* and Rachel Carson's *Silent Spring,* as the world's most influential book on the environment. In 1993 it was required reading for over 1,300 courses at over 600 colleges and universities in the United States alone. It has spawned a ten-part series on public television entitled "Race to Save the Planet."

Worldwatch groups have been established in Norway, Belgium, India, and Japan to help translate and distribute W.I. publications. In 1992 W.I. launched a second annual report called *Vital Signs: The Trends that Shape our Future* to help readers identify future trends concerning the environment. W.I. also publishes *Worldwatch,* a bi-monthly magazine launched in 1988, from which articles are then syndicated weekly in 100 newspapers, and the celebrated *Worldwatch Paper* series which now consists of more than 110 timely reports on environmental topics. Book-length reports are also published in a new Environmental Alert book series created in 1991. W.I. research and publications are especially concerned with overconsumption, transportation, international aid and trade, population increase, water resources, recycling, urban planning, food production, air pollution, soil erosion, biodiversity, industrial wastes, military spending, unemployment, illiteracy, women in Third World development, health, grass-roots movements, and poverty in the South. These publications are not only readable and useful, but also marketable. In 1989 sales of W.I. publications paid for over half of its operating expenses. The rest of the funding comes from private foundations, United Nations (UN) organizations, and other nongovernmental supporters.

The president and director of research of W.I. is Lester R. Brown, who received a MacArthur Foundation "genius" award and the UN 1989 Environmental Prize for his work. Christopher Flavin and Sandra Postel are vice-presidents for research and equally frequent contributors to W.I. publications. Former secretary of agriculture Orville Freeman chairs W.I.'s board of directors. Brown and his associates have also worked closely in recent years with senator, now vice-president, Al Gore Jr. W.I. estimates that it generates or contributes fourteen articles per day, seven days a week, to major periodicals around the world. Its experts are also rapidly becoming important electronic media figures.

W.I. was present and active at the Rio Summit in June 1992. Brown, in a speech that was one of the highlights of the Speakers' Forum, called for an " . . . environmental revolution [that] will succeed only if it stabilizes population size, reestablishing a balance between people and the natural systems on which they depend . . . This new transformation will be based on a shift away from fossil fuels."

W.I. is sometimes criticized for its apocalyptic tone, and for neglecting the fact that imperialism, multinational corporations, rich landowners, and cash crops for exportation are also factors that create poverty. Some Third World critics of Western neo-Malthusianism are wary of W.I.'s repeated emphasis on population control in poor countries rather than on overconsumption in rich countries. However, a closer reading of its publications shows that W.I. also calls for more aid, fairer trade, conversion of military budgets, equality of women,

changing dietary habits away from meat, and wider access to education and health services, as well as birth control. It also insists on the fight against poverty, famine, racism, nuclear and fossil energy, Western consumerism, industrial pollution, and the automobile.

Jean-Guy Vaillancourt

Further Readings
Brown, Lester R. *Building a Sustainable Society.* 1981.
———, et al., eds. *State of the World.* Published yearly since 1984.
———, Christopher Flavin, and Sandra Postel. *Saving the Planet: How to Shape an Environmentally Sustainable Global Economy.* 1992.

See also Agriculture: Environmental Impacts; Automobiles: Impacts and Policies; Climate Warming; Environmentalism; Rio Conference (1992); Sustainability

WWF
See World Wildlife Fund

Xerces Society
See Butterflies: Conservation and Habitat

Yellowstone National Park

Yellowstone, the world's first national park, was formed in 1872 to preserve the area's magnificent vistas and vast system of geysers and steam pools. Yellowstone's first superintendent, Nathaniel P. Langford, described the park as "probably the most remarkable region of natural wonders in the world."

Today Yellowstone Park is treasured not only for the hundreds of geysers and thousands of hot springs that make up the largest functional geothermal system in the world, but also for the faunal abundance that has earned it the name "America's Serengeti" and the great plant diversity resulting from the convergence of seven floral zones. Grazing bison and elk, abundant wildflower meadows, lava formations, and spectacular waterfalls and vapor plumes are just a few common sights for visitors. More than 1,700 plant species and 300 bird, 70 mammal, 12 fish, 128 butterfly, and 24 amphibian and reptile species inhabit the region.

Yellowstone's forests, grasslands, and lakes cover a broad volcanic plateau, with a 600,000-year-old caldera at the center and high peaks of the Northern Rocky Mountains on three sides. Straddling the Continental Divide and the Wyoming, Idaho, and Montana borders, Yellowstone's 2.2 million acres lie at the heart of a vast expanse of contiguous public land that includes seven national forests, three national wildlife refuges, and Grand Teton National Park, and contains the headwaters of three major North American rivers.

The military was responsible for early park management, which had a lasting impact even after the U.S. National Park Service was formed and took over Yellowstone in 1918. For many years the park was managed with a strong utilitarian philosophy. Hunting was allowed until harvests became so large that game animals were feared to be headed for extinction. Even after hunting was outlawed in 1883 weak enforcement meant the continuation of widespread poaching. Bison numbers were of special concern since Yellowstone contained the only remaining wild North American herd after the slaughter of the 1800s. Early regulations limited timbering, mining, fishing, and grazing and called for fire control, predator eradication, and the feeding of "beneficial" wildlife. Wildlife viewing was also promoted, and Yellowstone hotels had platforms where tourists could watch grizzly bears eat garbage.

Concern about these and other manipulations of park processes spurred a review of Park Service management, culminating in the Leopold Report of 1963. The report advised that parks be managed in a natural manner to preserve intact portions of the pre-Columbian American landscape. National legislation of the 1960s and 1970s and acceptance of new ecological models also furthered a shift in management toward the maintenance of natural processes and native biological diversity. In the 1970s the United Nations recognized the internationally-unique thermal and biological features of the park, by designating it a World Heritage Site and International Biosphere Reserve.

The focus on maintaining ecological processes and components eventually forced recognition of the large-scale ecological connections between Yellowstone Park and its environs. Grizzly bear researchers Frank and John Craighead were the first biologists to note that preserving grizzlies in Yellowstone required complementary management throughout the entire grizzly habitat use area, or "ecosystem," which encompasses far more land than just the park. This was the first application of ecosystem concepts to park management, though earlier supporters and staff were concerned that many Yellowstone game species required winter range outside the park.

The challenge for current managers is to fulfill their preservationist mandate although Yellowstone was formed before there was any understanding of the complex, large-scale web of biotic and abiotic processes that supports the park's natural wealth. The park cannot by itself support viable populations of many of its species, nor even protect its geothermal features. Threats to the park's integrity come from inside and outside its borders.

Annual visitation to the park recently passed 3 million and surrounding communities are growing at rates that are among the fastest in the United States. There are concerns that park tourism and external development are threatening wildlife habitat, and development on neighboring lands could drain enough pressure from aquifers that park geysers would cease to erupt. The widespread fires of 1988 and recent controversial attempts to return wolves to Yellowstone have pointedly shown the challenge of maintaining natural processes and native communities in an area with so much commercial activity.

Congress and public and private organizations have called for coordinated natural resource management across the Greater Yellowstone Ecosystem and better science for managers. Attempts have been made in these directions with the regional interagency "Vision" exercise and a new regional biological inventory, but the success of such efforts depends on greater public recognition that the traditional adherence to departmentalized planning, management, and knowledge will result in the loss of the magnificent creatures and natural wonders of Yellowstone. Because the Yellowstone region holds the most nearly intact complex of wildlife and wildland in the lower forty-eight states, and because it is an international flagship for conservation management, success or failure in preserving its resources has profound implications.

Anne Peyton Curlee

Further Readings

Bartlett, R.A. *Yellowstone: A Wilderness Besieged*. 1985.
Clark, T.W., and S.C. Minta. *Greater Yellowstone's Future*. 1993.
Fishbein, S.L. *Yellowstone Country: The Enduring Wonder*. 1989.

See also BEARS: CONSERVATION AND HABITAT; BIOSPHERE RESERVES; NATIONAL PARK SERVICE (U.S.)

Yosemite National Park

See HETCH HETCHY DAM; JOHNSON, ROBERT UNDERWOOD; MUIR, JOHN; NATIONAL PARK SERVICE (U.S.)

Yucca Mountain

See NUCLEAR WASTE

Z

Zahniser, Howard

Howard Zahniser (1906–1964) is widely regarded as the architect of the U.S. Wilderness Act, a landmark piece of environmental legislation signed by President Lyndon Johnson on September 3, 1964. After becoming executive secretary of the Wilderness Society in 1945, following fifteen years working for the Bureau of Biological Survey, U.S. Department of Agriculture, Zahniser worked tirelessly to ensure a permanent place for wilderness in America's land-use policy. He believed that legislation was the only way in which wilderness areas would be fully protected.

Zahniser's first public call for a wilderness act was made in 1951 to the Sierra Club's Wilderness Conference. He called for a concerted effort to establish an enduring system of wilderness areas that are legally protected from development. In the winter of 1955 Zahniser produced the first draft of a wilderness bill, in which he defined wilderness as ". . . an area where the earth and its community of life are untrammeled by man . . . ." This definition withstood nine years of debate and Congress adopted it when it passed the Wilderness Act in 1964.

Zahniser also drove the national campaign to ensure that Congress would pass the Wilderness Act, and inspired many to think it possible. Senator Hubert Humphrey (D-Minnesota) was one convert; he was the first to table a wilderness bill in Congress on June 7, 1956. Eighteen hearings on the proposed bill followed from 1957 to 1964. Two days after testifying at the last hearing Zahniser died on May 5, 1964. Four months later his vision was realized with the designation of fifty-four areas totaling over 9 million acres as legally protected wilderness.

Kevin McNamee

Further Readings

Fox, Stephen. *The American Conservation Movement: John Muir and His Legacy.* 1985.

Nash, Roderick. "Path to Preservation." *Wilderness* 48 (165): 5–11.

See also ECHO PARK DAM; JOHNSON, LYNDON B.; SIERRA CLUB; WILDERNESS; WILDERNESS ACT; WILDERNESS SOCIETY

Zero Population Growth

Zero Population Growth (ZPG) is a public interest group started in 1968 by demographers, biologists, and others concerned about the density of the human species on the planet earth. Its membership includes eminent demographers, other scientists, environmentalists, and politicians. It has 300 active local chapters dedicated to educating the public regarding global population problems.

ZPG campaigns to inform all citizens of the need to restrict their numbers to zero, one, or at most two children per couple. It urges that all forms of birth control be made available to all members of society and that government fund birth control research to improve available technology. It opposes pro-natalist public policy such as taxes that favor large families and urges career opportunities for women. Its members believe that parenthood should be a voluntary choice made by the individual, not the government. ZPG also urges that abortion facilities be available to all women regardless of income.

ZPG argued against U.S. policy in the 1980s that withheld support from the United Nations Population Fund to assist other nations in their efforts to control worldwide population increases. ZPG demographers argue that the planet can sustain a population of about 4 billion people on healthful diets. At present rates of growth it estimates the world population may level off at about 14 billion people in the middle of the twenty-first century, up from the early 1990s level of about 5.3 billion, many of whom subsist on inadequate diets.

ZPG publishes a monthly *ZPG National Reporter* and seeks media coverage of the population problem by distributing television and radio public service announcements, literature, buttons, bumper stickers, and posters. ZPG seeks to stabilize the population of the United States, which it considers the key to ultimately controlling the associated social, environmental, and resource problems on a global scale. It uses litigation, education, and lobbying to advance its cause.

Lettie McSpadden

Further Readings
Ehrlich, Paul R. *The Population Bomb.* 1968.
ZPG National Reporter. Monthly publication of Zero Population Growth.

See also EHRLICH, PAUL; ENVIRONMENTALISM; HARDIN, GARRETT; ONE-CHILD FAMILY (CHINA); POPULATION CONTROL

Zoos: Institutions in Transition
Throughout the world there are at least 1,100 collections of living animals annually serving over 800 million visitors. Lumped together as "zoos," they include oceanariums and aquariums, insectariums, "living museums" and institutions specializing in waterfowl, cranes, and crocodiles, as well as general expositions of world fauna or the animals of particular regions. Whatever the nature of their collections most zoos are in transition for wild animals are disappearing in nature.

While settling earth's most productive habitats and converting them to agriculture and other human uses humanity has dramatically reduced the numbers of wild creatures, and this process is accelerating. Most people are becoming urban, with the result that the vast majority will never again see a significant diversity of wildlife, except in zoos. Inevitably zoos are evolving from living museums of natural history to environmental resource and education centers; from zoological displays to wildlife conservation parks.

Zoo Animals Must Be Bred in Zoos
The efforts of "conservation park" biologists to teach environmentalism are powerfully focused by wildlife extinction. Already "zoo" animals have become largely unavailable from nature. They must be propagated in captivity. Yet, no single collection has the space or resources to sustain any meaningful number of species by itself. Thus, in an extraordinarily collaborative effort, many zoos have banded together in national, regional and international programs aimed at long-term propagation of species vanishing in nature.

Collaborative Species Survival Plans
The first and largest of three cooperative efforts, a model for all that have followed, is the Species Survival Plan (SSP) of the American Zoo and Aquarium Association (AZA) founded in 1981. Selecting species one by one, the SSP develops cooperative breeding programs jointly managed by specific groups of zoo experts, for example for Bali mynas, lowland gorillas, Siberian tigers, and snow leopards.

Every SSP animal is considered physically and behaviorally. Its social and parental or genetic profile within its population is developed. Species-specific expertise on its propagation and significance to the future of its kind is painstakingly considered, and each is placed within a studbook that acts as a register for future matings. The SSP animal is managed first to assure the survival of its species, not for the individual interests of the zoo that may own it. Animals originally acquired at great cost are moved from collection to collection in their own best interest—in an altruistic way, not necessarily in response to zoo desires for display.

Not only do participating zoos and aquariums create far-flung partnerships in the service of propagation, but also they use these efforts as tools to call public attention to the plight of vanishing species and the need for conservation. But the growing zoo stewardship of more and more vanishing species losing their homes in nature is an increasingly difficult role.

Sustaining Vanishing Species
Some conservationists look to zoos to sustain disappearing animals in hopes of future reclamation of their now vanishing homelands and subsequent reintroduction, or to provide "Flagship" animals to act as the core of local conservation programs. Actual instances of animals returned to nature from zoos are still few, but dramatic. Arabian oryx and golden-lion tama-

rins are recent examples while red wolves and California condors are current experiments.

Intrinsically long-term zoo care of small wildlife populations must deal with biological constraints, such as genetics and demography, and equally unforgiving logistic problems, such as available space and support. To deal with biological requirements, zoos must sustain large numbers of each species they would preserve and monitor the lives of each individual. Behavioral challenges and those of disease must be met and each propagation program arranged so as to avoid inbreeding of closely related animals.

One result of intensified zoo propagation and conservation efforts has been greatly heightened interest in zoo research. In 1992, AZA reports, North American zoos conducted more than 1,000 conservation and research projects and produced over 500 publications.

Extrinsically zoo conservationists face the unresolved and overwhelming issues of choice. With limited space and resources (all the zoo animal spaces in the world could fit within New York's Borough of Brooklyn) and current technology zoo capacity worldwide could not sustain as many as 1,000 species of sizable land vertebrates and very little attention has been given to invertebrates. For this reason zoos are experimenting with the long-term cold storage of sperm and ova. Success with significant numbers of species is elusive, even doubtful, but the possibility of increasing zoo capacity, by keeping large portions of SSP populations in a "frozen zoo," spurs continuing research.

For many species losing their homes in nature some sort of habitat restoration may eventually occur. For many more, it will not. But zoo propagation can probably aid the survival of 15 percent or more of all the terrestrial vertebrates likely to become extinct in the next century—perhaps 40 percent of larger species.

For the present poignant questions haunt zoo conservationists: Which species losing their homes should be cared for? Which must be rejected? How long must the chosen species be cared for?

Zoo Education

Among the most serious threats to wild creatures is that they will be ignored; condemned by humanity to the same closets of irrelevance and curiosity as silent movies and corset stays. In our increasingly unnatural world live zoo animals and their simulated habitats provide profound and moving experiences. They live with

us near our homes, daily creating news and arousing interest. They do not permit us to ignore the fact that their kind exists. They constitute the unique impetus of zoo education programs.

Utilizing this impetus are growing numbers of zoo-school partnerships working "to teach," as one zoo educator puts it, "how nature works." The Wildlife Conservation Society (WCS; founded as the New York Zoological Society in 1895) has developed school programs using zoos to teach conservation and ecology that are now used in forty-three U.S. states and several foreign countries. Many zoos now offer special courses and special zoo-school class programs.

It is suggestive that virtually every major population center in the world has a zoo. Together, they constitute an enormous international educational resource for conservation and environmentalism. They are already in place, already with public interest, and already with some level of support. And, most compellingly, they have living representatives from environments we seek to conserve. Nevertheless, most are under-used by environmentalists.

Zoos Saving Wildlife in Nature

Some zoos are focusing programs directly upon the survival of their collection's creatures in their native habitats, whether those be local or overseas. Zoos in Frankfurt, London, Jersey Island, Chicago, Minneapolis, Washington, D.C., and elsewhere all have significant overseas conservation programs. The largest is that of the WCS based in its Bronx Zoo/Wildlife Conservation Park in New York City. In 1994 WCS operated 226 conservation programs in forty-six nations. More than 100 major parks and refuges have been one result of its efforts and that of scores of trained indigenous conservationists. As a whole, AZA reported, 390 projects in sixty-three countries were sponsored in 1991 by North American institutions alone.

Thus, the zoo's role in conservation has evolved beyond its traditional roles in local public education and recreation. It is now beginning to address the long-term maintenance of vanishing species, basic research in conservation biology, and even local and overseas programs to save nature directly.

William Conway

Further Readings
Olney, P. *International Zoo Yearbook* 32, Zoological Society of London, Regent's

Park, 1992.

Tudge, C. *Last Animals at the Zoo.* 1992.

Wiese, R., K. Willis, J. Bowdoin, and M. Hutchins. *AAZPA Annual Report on Conservation and Science.* American Association of Zoological Parks and Aquariums, Bethesda, Maryland, 1992–1993.

See also ANIMAL RIGHTS; BIODEPLETION; BIOSPHERE RESERVES; CALIFORNIA CONDOR; CITES; ENVIRONMENTAL EDUCATION; IUCN

Index

The main entry for each topic is listed in **boldface**.

captive breeding 102, 514, 706–708
carbamates 517
carbaryl 365
carbon 33, 134, 284, 298, 301
carbon dioxide
    acid precipitation, aquatic impacts of 2
    carbon tax 107
    climate warming 129
    desertification 176
    ecological restoration 198
    forest regeneration/reforestation 288
    Gaia Hypothesis 301
    indoor air pollution 362
    instrumental value 364
    Pollution Probe 527
    Rio Conference, 1992 571
    snow as habitat 594
    synthetic fuels 618
    tradeable emission permits 636
    tropical deforestation 642
    tropical rainforests 646
    urban forestry 661
    web of life 676
carbon filtration 672
carbon monoxide **106–107**
    air pollution, impacts of 17, 18
    air pollution, regulation, United States 19
    automobiles, impacts and policies of 51, 52, 54
    coal, environmental impacts of 134
    hazardous waste treatment technologies 346
    indoor air pollution 361, 362
    in tobacco smoke 626
carbon tax **107–108**
carbon tetrachloride 434, 505, 634, 666
carcinogens 17, 21, 29, 42
Caribbean 154, 422
caribou 23, 39, 40, 515
Carmanah Pacific Park 109
Carmanah Valley **108–109**, 676
Carmichael, Franklin 333
Carnegie Institution 342
Carolina parakeet **109**
carp 37, 272
Carpenter, Delph 670
Carr, Emily **109–110**
Carr, Ezra 436
Carr, Jeanne 436
carrying capacity **110–111**, 259, 528, 637–638
Carson, Rachel **111–112**, 149, 150, 209, 261, 334, 386, 541, 583, 635, 649, 700
Cartagena 281
Carter, Jimmy 5, 22, **113–114**, 156, 213, 418, 460, 480, 577, 593, 600, 619, 687, 698
Cartier, Jacques 601
Cascade Mountains 545, 546
case-control studies 262
Caspian Sea 294, 295
Cassady, Neal 594
Casson, A.J. 333
catalytic 4

Catesby, Mark 514
catfish 309
Catlin, George 149
cats 271, 699
Catskill Mountains 354
cattle 650
Caudill, Harry 607
CCAMLR. *See* Convention on Conservation of Antarctica Marine Living Resources
CCMSWA. *See* Conservation of Migratory Species of Wild Animals
CEAA. *See* Canadian Environmental Assessment Act
Center for Analysis of Environmental Change 31
Center for Auto Safety 445
Center for Constitutional Rights 251
Center for Environmental Philosophy 244
Center for Marine Conservation 135
Center for the Study of Responsive Law 445
Center on the Consequences of Nuclear War 521
Central African Republic 10
Central America 31, 206, 320, 465, 472, 533, 534, 643, 644, 691
Central Arizona Project 670
Central Brooks Range of mountains 424
Central Park 500
Central Valley 608
Central Valley Project 359
Century Magazine 382
CERCLA. *See* Superfund
cetaceans 62–64, 179–181, 280, 369, 422
CFC. *See* chlorofluorocarbon
CGIAR. *See* Consultative Group on International Agricultural Research
Chad Lake 628
Chamber, Whittaker 64
channelization 46, **114–115**
Chapman, Frank 584
Chapman, Oscar L. 192
Charles Darwin Foundation 699
Chatham College 111
Chaudière River 601
Chavis, Benjamin F., Jr. 251
Chelyabrinsk plutonium production plant 485
Chemical Manufacturers Association 567, 568
Chemiepolitik, Germany **115–116**
Cheney, Jim 243
Chernobyl 4, **116–118**, 190, 191, 245, 324, 479, 482, 294, 295
Chernousenko, V.M. 116–117
Chesapeake Bay 103–104, **118–121**, 352
Chesapeake Bay Critical Areas Act 121
chestnut blight 498
Cheyenne Bottoms 671
Chicago 19, 70, 238, 252, 303, 359, 379, 500, 522, 544, 662, 707
Chihuahuan desert 545
Chilcotin 677
Chile 181, 320, 369, 378, 422
chimpanzees 269, 533, 534
China

Council of Nature Conservation Ministers 456
Council on Competitiveness 96
Council on Environmental Quality 95, 150, **155–157**, 249, 410, 448, 449–452, 521
Council v. Commission 229
Cousteau almanac of the Environment 157
Cousteau, Jacques-Yves **157–158**
Cousteau Society 157
cowbirds 287
Cox, Archibald 575
coyotes 155, 692
crabs 422
Crafoord Prize 490
Craighead, Frank and John 703
cranes 706
Crater Lake National Park 458
Cree 252, 313–314, 375–376
creosote 120
Cretaceous Period 579
Croatia 187, 189
crocodiles 267, 268, 706
Cropland Reserve Program 12
cropping systems, environmental implications **158–160**
Cropsey, Jaspar F. 354
Crosby, Alfred W. 248
Crown Minerals Act 562
crown-of-thorns starfish 154
Crude Oil Equalization Tax 213
Cruise Missiles 69
crustaceans 2, 37, 76, 78, 267
cryolite 27, 282
Cuba 16
curlews 585
Cutler, Rupert 113
cyanide 585
cyclamates 445
cycling 54, 55, 57, 393, 662
cyclocalkanes 494
cypress 268
Cyprus 427
Czech Republic 187, 190, 191, 318

D
Dales, John 636
Dallas, Texas 252, 342
Daly, Herman E. 244, 415
dams
    agriculture, environmental impacts of 15
    Army Corps of Engineers, United States 41
    Aswan High Dam 45, 46
    Colorado River 140
    environmental case law, United States 233
    environmental protection in wartime 258
    Franklin Dam 296
    Garrison Diversion 301
    Great Whale project in Quebec 312
    hydroelectricity 36, 123, 355
    irrigation impacts 372
    James Bay 375
    least-cost utility planning 400

    Oldman River 499
    Rafferty-Alameda Dams 543
    Tennessee Valley Authority 621
    Wilderness Society 686
    World Bank 695
Daniel Giraud Elliott medal 585
Daniels, Farrington **161**
Danish Society for the Conservation of Nature 246
Danube Circle 318
Danube River 190, 655
Darling, Jay Norwood "Ding" **161–162**
Darman, Richard 95
Dartmouth College 423
Darwin, Charles 80, 97, 153, **162–163**, 268–270, 271, 303, 391–392
Darwin, Erasmus 268–269
Dasmann, Raymond F. 84, 110
Davis, John 187
Day-Night Noise Level 475
dBA 475
DDE 516
DDT
    bioaccumulation in food chain 76
    butterflies, conservation and habitat of 98
    eagle, bald 61
    Eastern Europe, environmental problems of 189
    Environmental Defense Fund 236
    Great Lakes 310
    gypsy moths 334
    integrated pest management 365
    long range transport 417
    organochlorine compounds, persistent 515
    peregrine falcon 514
    pesticides 517
    resource management 561
    shorebirds 586
    toxicology 634
debt formature swap 466
debt-for-nature swaps **163–164**, 466
Declaration of Forestry Principles 571
Declaration of Principles Governing the Sea-Bed and Ocean Floor 652
Declaration on the Human Environment 606
deconstruction 531
deep ecology 44, 45, 164–167, 186, 195, 200, 202, 204, 243, 244, 446, 539–540, 616, 623
deep-well injection **167–168**
deer 24, 64, 90, 650, 684, 692
Defenders 168
Defenders of Furbearers 168
Defenders of Wildlife **168–169**
deforestation 9, 10, 14, 153, 186, 377, 424, 498, 570, 591, 612, 642–647, 661, 700
Delaney Clause **169**, 573
Delaware 118, 521
Delhi University 122
demand-side management **169–170**, 215
Dene 71

gas chromatograph **302–303**
gas chromatography 425
gasification 618
GATT. *See* General Agreement of Tariffs and Trade
Gause, G.F. 197
GC/MS. *See* gas chromatography
Geddes, Patrick 659
geese 673–674
Geist, Valerius 89
GEMS. *See* Global Environmental Monitoring
    System
General Accounting Office 156
General Agreement of Tariffs and Trade 603
General Land Office 93, 172, 173, 290, 452, 523
General Motors 445
General Sherman Tree 551
Genesis 604
genetic diversity **303–304**
    aquaculture 37
    biodiversity 80
    biodiversity 82
    Florida panther 282
    forest fragmentation and bird habitats 287
    forest regeneration/reforestation 289
    forestry, history of 292
    freshwater wetlands 297
    Green Revolution 329
    habitat fragmentation, patches, and corridors
        337
    mutation 442
    pesticides 519
genetics 269
Geneva 292, 655, 696
Geneva Convention 5
Geographic Information Systems 687
Geological Survey 452
George, John 149
George Washington University 206
Georgescu-Roegen, Nicholas **304**
Georgia 113, 251, 282, 318, 432, 490
Georgian Bay 24
Germany
    acid precipitation, aquatic impacts of 2
    acid precipitation, European experiences 3, 4,
        5
    acid precipitation, terrestrial impacts 7
    aluminum 28
    Black Forest 89
    breeder reactors 91
    Chemiepolitik 115
    Chernobyl, fallout 116, 117, 118
    deep ecology, meanings 165
    Eastern Europe, environmental problems 187
    environmental groups, Western Europe 246
    foresters 468
    forestry, history of 291
    green parties 317, 323
    International Whaling Commission 369
    Kelly, Petra and green politics 385
    legislation, European Community 404, 405,
        406

    New Forestry 469
    nuclear electric power 478, 479
    nuclear waste 483
    recycling 550
    Rhine River 564
    sedimentation 584
    Superfund 609
    synthetic fuels 618
    tropical rainforests 647
    United Nations Convention on the Law of the
        Sea 652
    Western Europe, pollution 677, 678
    wind energy 690
Ghana 355
giant panda 66, 67, **304–305**, 699
gibbons 534
Gibbs, Lois Marie 125
Gila National Forest 412
Gila Wilderness Area 412
Ginsberg, Allan 594
giraffes 269, 650
Glacier National Park 23, 61, 457
Glacken, Clarence J. 248
glass 510, 511
Glen Canyon Dam 141, 306
Global Action Plan for Primate Conservation 533
Global Environment Fund 694
Global Environmental Facility 79
Global Environmental Fund 654
Global Environmental Monitoring System 655
Global Forum 570
Global Plan of Action for Marine Mammals 655
Global ReLeaf **305–386**, 661, 662
Global Resource Information Database 655
Global Tiger Forum 625
Global Tomorrow Coalition 521
Global 2000 Report 156
Global 2000 Report to the President 113
global warming. *See* climate warming
Glokenthon 679
glycols 574
glyphosate 349
GM. *See* General Motors
GNP 10, 200, 411, 529, 558, 559
goats 271
gobies 390
God 370, 379
Godfrey, Arthur 255
godwits 585
Golden Gate 459
Golding, William 301
Goldsmith, Edward 199
Gordon River 296
Gordon River Power Scheme 391
Gordon, Scott 637
Gore, Al(bert) Jr. 251, 701
gorillas 533, 534
Gortari, President Carlos Salinas de 429
Gorz, André 203
goshawk 288
Gourou, Pierre 396

National Assembly of Québec 376
National Association of Audubon Societies 688
National Audubon Society **448–449**
    Audubon, John James 47
    birding 87
    butterflies, conservation and habitat 99
    California condor 102
    Canadian Nature Federation 106
    conservation movement 150
    environmental justice movement 251
    Garrison Diversion 302
    Peterson, Russell W. 521
    supersonic transport 611
    wildlife protection, history 688
national battlefield parks 458
National Biological Survey 173, 454, 460
National Cancer Institute 350, 646, 666
National Committee of Audubon Societies 448
National Conservation Commission 523
National Emission Standards Act 442
National Energy Board 71
National Energy Plan 619
National Energy Policy Plan 214
national environmental action plans 695
National Environmental Policy Act
    Calvert Cliffs 104
    Council on Environmental Quality 155
    environmental assessment, Canada 224
    environmental case law, United States 234
    environmental impact assessment 248
    environmental justice movement 251
    Garrison Diversion 302
    legislation, United States 409, 410, 411
    wilderness 684
    Udall, Stewart L. 649
    United States **449–452**
National Environmental Policy Plan 407
National Environmental Scorecard 400
National Forest Management Act 409, 454, 469, 618, 687
National Forest Service 92
national forests 23, 449, **452–454**, 616, 617
National Geographic Magazine 157
national historic parks 458
National Institute for Environmental Health Sciences 251
National Institute for Occupational Safety and Health 503, 568, 627
national lakeshores 458
National Library of Medicine 567
National Marine Fisheries Service 211
national memorials 458
national military parks 458
national monuments 458
National Opinion Research Center 535
National Organization for Women 590
National Park (Royal) 457
National Park Service, United States **454–455**
    Alaska, park, wilderness, and resource issues 23
    Bureau of Land Management 94

    conservation movement 150
    Department of the Interior, United States 172, 173
    Grand Canyon 306
    Mineral King Canyon 430
    national parks, United States 458
    old growth forests 498
    recycling 552
    Sierra Club 588
    Wilderness Society 686
    Yellowstone National Park 703
National Park System 686
national parks
    Alaska, park, wilderness, and resource issues 22
    Australia **455–457**
    bears, conservation and habitat 68
    biosphere reserves 85
    bison, conservation and habitat 88
    Canada **457–459**
    Canadian Nature Federation 106
    Hetch Hetchy Dam 351
    Lake Baikal 390
    Mineral King Canyon 430
    National Park Service, United States 454
    resource accounting 559
    Sierra 587
    United States **458–461**
    Wood Buffalo National Park 693
    World Conservation Union 697
    World Wildlife Fund 699
    Yellowstone National Park 703
National Parks Act 457
National Parks Association 501
national parkways 458
National Pollutant Discharge Elimination System 121
national preserves 458
National Priority List 609–610
national recreation areas 458
National Religious Partnership for the Environment 556
National Renewable Energy Laboratory 600
National Research Council 142, 493, 626
National Rifle Association 150
national rivers 458
National Rivers Authority 307–308, 408
national scenic trails 458
National Science Foundation 600
National Security Act 619
national security, reconceptualizing **461–462**, 659
National Toxicology Program 666
National Trails System Act 544
National Trust 246
National Volatile Organic Compounds Data Base 667
National Wilderness Advisory Council 686
National Wilderness Preservation System 23, 687, 685
National Wildlife 462
National Wildlife Areas 674

Organisation for Economic Co-operation and Development 3, 249, 317, 363, 380, 527
Organization of African Unity 633
Organization of Petroleum Exporting Countries 113, 212, 377, 415, 549
organochlorine compounds 310, 514, **515–517**, 538, 634
organochlorine pesticides 75, 76, 180, 417, 586
organophosphates 517
Orinoco River 422, 655
oryx 706
Osage Hills 546
Osborn, Fairfield 148–149, 209, **502**, 583, 639
OSHA. *See* Occupational Safety and Health Administration
OSHAct and OSHA **502–504**. *See also* Occupational Safety and Health Act
Oslo University 92
Ottawa 106, 142, 238, 367, 457
Ottawa River 24, 601
otters 24, 89, 127, 421–423
Our Common Future 93, 327, **504–505**, 570, 612, 616
Outdoor America 373
Outdoor Ethics 373
Outdoor Recreation Resources Review Committee 373
overfishing 153, 154, 181, 278, 310, 564, 651–653
overgrazing 9, 10, 597
Overland Monthly 436
owls 32, 38, 288, 343. *See also* spotted owl
Oxford Forestry Institute 292
Oxford University 418, 679
oxidation 345
oxidation ponds 672
oxygen 476, 494, 505, 506, 661, 672, 678
oystercatchers 585
oysters 76, 104, 119, 139
ozone
    air pollution, impacts 17, 18
    air pollution, regulation, United States 21
    automobiles, impacts and policies 54
    climate warming 130
    layer. *See* ozone depletion
    pollution 51, 52, **506–507**, 636, 636, 640, 666, 678
    smog 592
ozone depletion **505–506**
    acid precipitation, legislative initiatives 6
    air pollution, impacts 17
    air pollution, regulation, United States 21
    amphibians, conservation and habitat 31
    Arctic 38
    biodepletion 79
    biodiversity 81
    Canadian Environmental Protection Act 105
    conserver society 151
    Earth Day 186
    Environmental Defense Fund 237
    environmental diplomacy 238

    environmental groups, Western Europe 245
    Environmental Policy Institute 256
    green party, Germany 324
    household hazardous wastes 353
    Montreal Protocol 434
    NAFTA and the environment 447
    nuclear winter 487
    packaging 510
    public opinion and the environment 536
    right-to-know, community, United States 567
    Rio Conference, 1992 570
    sustainability 612
    tradeable emission permits 636
    United Nations Environment Programme 654, 655
    Worldwatch Institute 700

P

Pacific Conservation Biology 147
Pacific Ocean 235, 279, 280, 486
Pacific Railroad Act 172
Pacific Rim National Park 108
packaging 27, 406, **509–513**, 624
Packard, Vance 151
Paehlke, Robert 26
Paine, Robert T. 386
Paiutes 306, 532
Pakistan 51, 329
Paley Commission **513**
Paley, William 513
Palm Beach 267
Palme, Olaf 93
Palouse Prairie 545
Panama 270
PANs. *See* peroxyacylnitrates
panthers 267, 268
paper. *See* pulp and paper; pulp and paper mills
Papua New Guinea 97, 99, 378, 643, 644, 699
Paraguay 355
parakeets 682
parathion 365, 517
Paris 584, 655, 662
Paris Grand Salon 584
Paris Summit 404–405
Park Organic Act. *See* Organic Act
parks
    Algonquin Provincial Park 25
    biodepletion 79
    Canada 457
    Environment Canada 218
    rails-to-trails 544
    See also national parks
parrots 81, 109, 681–682, 699
particulates
    air pollution, impacts 17, 18
    air pollution, regulation, United States 19
    aluminum 28
    ASEAN haze 44
    automobiles, impacts and policies 51, 52, 54
    carbon monoxide 107
    desertification 176

wilderness 684
wildlife protection, history 688
Ross, Malcolm 607
rosy periwinkle 79
Roszak, Theodore 204
Routley, Richard 242
Roxby Downs Indenture Ratification Act 402
Royal National Parks, Australia 457
Royal Canadian Academy 584
Royal Commission on Environmental Pollution 408
Royal Indian Engineering College 292
Royal Society for Nature Conservation 465
Royal Society for the Preservation of Birds 87
Royal Society for the Protection of Birds 246
Royal Swedish Academy of Science 490
Ruckelshaus, William D. 257, 547, **575–576**
Ruckleshaus, William 547
Rudall River National Park 457
Rudd, Robert 149
ruminants 650
Runte, Alfred 248, 458
Runyon, Marvin 622
Rupert Bay 375
Rupert River 375
Russia
    Eastern Europe, environmental problems 187
    green parties 318
    International Whaling Commission 369
    Japan 378
    nuclear electric power 478
    population control 529
    Soviet Union, former 294, 390
    tigers, conservation and habitat 625
    whole earth image 679
    See also Soviet Union
Rutgers University 78
Rylands v. Fletcher 225, 227

S

S.T.O.P. *See* Society to Overcome Pollution
S.V.P. *See* Société pour Vaincre la Pollution
sablefish 24
Sachs, Wolfgang 680
SAF. *See* Society of American Foresters
Safe Drinking Water Act 256, 275, 332, 409, 547,
    554, 572, 573, 576
Sagebrush Rebellion **577–578**, 675
Sagoff, Mark 241–244
Saguenay River 157, 601
Sahabat Alam Malaysia 255
Sahara Desert 84, 208
Sahelian drought 9, 10
Saint Francis of Assisi 204
Saint-Basile-Le-Grand **578–579**
Saint-François River 601
Saint-Maurice River 601
salamanders 30, 31, 32, 33
salinization 175, 373
Salish people 604
salmon 24, 36, 37, 61, 139, 279, 280, 309, 469,
    564, 601

Salmonid Enhancement Program 36
salt 574, 608
Salt Lake City, Utah 141
salt marshes 495. *See also* wetlands
Salt River 670
Salten, Felix 64
San Bernardino National Forest 686
San Diego Wild Animal Park 102, 103
San Francisco 8, 97, 99, 137, 185, 299, 351, 430,
    436, 463, 523, 587, 594
San Gorgonio Primitive Area 686
Sand County Almanac, A 391, 413, 605, 689, 700
Sandoz 115, 564
sandpipers 585
Santa Barbara County 103
Sapelo Island 490
Sapontzis, S.F. 34
SARA. *See* Superfund Amendments and Reauthori-
    zation Act
Sarawak 378
Saskatchewan 224, 278, 524, 543, 584, 674
Saudi Arabia 691
Sauer, Carl 148
Sava River 189
savannah 12, 546
Savannah River Ecology Laboratory 490
Savannah River Plant 484, 490
savannas 286
Save Our Streams 373
Sawyer, Lorenzo 432
Scandinavia 6, 28, 405, 446
Schlesinger, James 104
Schlich, William 292
Schrepfer, Susan 248
Schumacher, E.F. **579**
Science 143
Science Council of Canada 151
Scientists' Action Network 651
Scott, Anthony 637
Scribners 436
Scribner's Publishing Co. 382
scrubber/baghouse control system 439
scrubbers 346
sea cows 421
sea lions 421–423
Sea of Azov 294
Sea Shepherd Society 330
sea trout 564
sea turtles 557, **579–581**, 699
sea urchins 154, 386, 422
seabirds 24, 38, 127, 135, 493, **581–583**
seaducks 581
seals 38, 139, 279, 390, 421–423
Sears, Paul 148, 209, 502, **583**
seas 189
Seattle, Washington 145, 544
Seattle City Light 401
Second Conference on Conservation Biology 147
second-hand smoke 626–628
secondary resources 548
sedimentation 138, 153, 372, **583–584**, 597

swans 673, 673–674
Sweden
    acid precipitation, aquatic impacts 2
    acid precipitation, European experiences 3
    acid precipitation, terrestrial impacts 7
    Eastern Europe, environmental problems 191
    green parties 317
    green parties, Australia 321
    hydroelectricity 355
    International Whaling Commission 369
    nuclear electric power 478, 479
    nuclear waste 482, 483
    pesticides 519
    Stockholm Conference 606
    tropical rainforests 647
    wolf, a conservation challenge 691
Switzerland 236, 298, 317, 369, 482, 564, 677,
    696, 697, 699
SWQOs. See Statutory Water Quality Objectives
    (SWQOs)
Sydney 48, 457
Sydney River 127
synthetic fuels **618–619**
Synthetic Fuels Corporation 493, 619
Syria 208, 357, 427

T

taconite 557
Taft, William Howard 523
taiga 133, 495, 593
tailings 657, 657–659
Taiwan 305, 329, 479, 516, 565, 566, 625–626
Tajikistan 295
takings 13, 234
*Talking Leaves: A Bioregional Journal of Deep
    Ecology and Spiritual Activism* 205
Tall Tree 551
tamarins 533, 534, 706
tannins 537
Tansley, A.G. 205
Tanzania 153
Taoism 44, 45, 204
tapirs 650
tar sands 214, 618. *See also* oil sands
tarsiers 533
Task Force on Regulatory Relief 547
Tasmania 165, 296, 317, 391
Tasmanian Hydro-Electric Commission 296–297,
    391, 621
Tasmanian Wilderness Society 296, **621**
Tatshenshini River 106
taxes
    agricultural land protection 13
    carbon tax 107
    climate warming 133
    federalism and environmental protection,
        United States 276
    Great Britain, environmental problems 308,
        309
    green parties 318
    land-use planning 393

NAFTA and the environment 448
    packaging 512
    pollution prevention 526
    Superfund 609
    sustained yield forestry 617
taxonomy 269
Taylor Grazing Act 93, 173, 359
Taylor, Loralei 31
Taylor, Paul W. 34, 241–243
Technology Assessment Act 490, 490–491
Technology Assessment Advisory Council 490
Technology Assessment Board 490, 490–491
technology forcing 442, 553
TEDs. *See* turtle excluder devices
Tellico Dam 593
Tennessee 65, 251, 282, 387, 432, 593, 692
Tennessee Endangered Species Committee 593
Tennessee River 621
Tennessee Valley Authority 233, 359, 593, **621–
    622**
Terborgh, John 197
terns 581, 688
terpenes 537
Texas
    bats, conservation and habitat 65
    birding 87
    coastal debris and cleanup 135
    comparative risk 145
    cougars, conservation and habitat 154
    Environmental Defense Fund 237
    environmental justice movement 252
    Eskimo Curlew 263
    Florida panther 282
    legislation 411
    Ogallala Aquifer 491, 492
    rangelands 545
    shorebirds 586
    Texas Coastal Prairie 546
    water allocations and shortages, United States
        West 669, 670
Thailand 43, 51, 154, 625, 643, 644, 699
thermal treatment technologies 345
thermodynamics 535, 561
Third Action Program 405
Third World Peace Prize 93
Thirty Percent Club 5
Thomas, Lee 257, 547
Thompson, Ben 460
Thomson, Tom 24
Thoreau, Henry David 149, 210, 242, 387, 423–
    424, 467, 605, **623–624**
Three Gorges Dam 355, 356
Three Mile Island 252, 479, 482, 651
throwaway mentality/society **624–625**
Tibet 385
tigers, conservation and habitat 566, **625–626**
Tilapia 270
tilapia 37
Times Beach 177, 252
titanium 405, 406
Tlingit 22